A Student's Dictionary of Classical and Me[...]

A Student's Dictionary of Classical and Medieval Chinese

THIRD EDITION
NEWLY REVISED AND EXPANDED

By

Paul W. Kroll

With the assistance of

William Baxter, William G. Boltz, David R. Knechtges, Y. Edmund Lien,
Antje Richter, Matthias L. Richter, Ding Xiang Warner

BRILL

LEIDEN | BOSTON

Typeface for the Latin, Greek, and Cyrillic scripts: "Brill". See and download: brill.com/brill-typeface.

ISBN 978-90-04-49939-3

PRINTED BY DRUKKERIJ WILCO B.V. - AMERSFOORT, THE NETHERLANDS

Contents

Preface to the Third Edition

Most people know the wry definition of "lexicographer" that Samuel Johnson (1709–1784) included in his *Dictionary of the English Language*, viz., "a harmless drudge that busies himself in tracing the original, and detailing the figurification of words." Fewer perhaps are familiar with the words of the great classicist, Joseph Scaliger (1540–1609), which likely worked to influence Johnson's definition, that "the worst criminals should be neither executed nor sentenced to forced labor, but should be condemned to compile dictionaries, because all tortures are included in the work." Drudgery and torture, not an appealing combination.

There is, however, an apt quotation from Thomas Hobbes (1588–1679) that provides fairer purpose than either Scaliger or Johnson. Hobbes said, "Seeing that *truth* consisteth in the right ordering of names (i.e., words) in our affirmations, a man that seeketh precise *truth* had need to remember what every name he uses stands for, and to place it accordingly—or else he will find himself entangled in words, as a bird in lime-twigs—the more he struggles, the more belimed." The vivid image of Hobbes's word-entangled belimed bird may also call to mind the book title *Caught in the Web of Words,* the admirable biography of James Murray (1837–1915), founding author of the *Oxford English Dictionary*. It seems that the snares of dictionary-making are usually referred to more often than the joys. But there *are* delights as well as miseries, and I have felt oddly privileged and content, first to have composed this dictionary and then to continue adding to, and I hope improving, it in the years that have followed its first appearance.

The sentiment behind Hobbes's adjuration "to remember what every name stands for, and to place it accordingly" is rather similar to Confucius's urging to *zhengming* 正名, or "get the names/words right." Which itself inevitably reminds one of the classic saying from the *Xici zhuan* 繫辭傳, that "words do not get to the end of meaning" 言不盡義. Though that realization be ultimately incontrovertible, words are what we have, and we must take care to employ them as keenly as possible. Absent language well and properly used, we struggle to make lucid sense of how we interpret both the external and internal worlds in which we live and to communicate our thoughts with others.

When overhearing in these latter days the words of authors from premodern China, our attention must be even more closely focused than in our native tongue, whatever that may be. And aid can come in many forms. Some people have told me they consult this dictionary not only to discover meanings but also as a thesaurus. This indeed satisfies one of its chief goals—to give help and guidance about how to understand and translate a word in various local environments. Since no language's semantics coincide equally with another's, an etymological dictionary (which has its own specific and valuable importance) can provide but minimal assistance when attempting to make sense of a connected text. For the etymon is only where a single word's meaning starts. To think it is always an exact or sufficient description is to think that the overflowing goblet 濫觴, traditionally illustrating the source of the Yellow River, fully defines the waterway's whole course as it swells, veers, and advances through a thousand miles of diverse landscapes.

I have known individuals who, when discussing interpretations of texts, will declare with unbending conviction that "word X *always* means Y." That is not, however, how languages work in actual usage on the page—much less in an author's mind. A particular spelled word, or in Chinese a discrete graph, may always look the same orthographically, but it *means* differently as it turns a different aspect of itself to the fore in different contexts. When translating from one language to another, these different meanings can only be expressed by different words in the target language. Being alert to semantic range and to varying possibilities of contextual meaning is crucial in attaining a more mature understanding of a language. This is why memorizing vocabulary lists is an exercise of benefit for beginners only.

This third edition of the dictionary you have in hand contains over a thousand revisions and additions to the second edition's definitions, as well as dozens of wholly new entries. Whereas for the second edition the *léger de main* of the typesetters managed, despite many changes, to retain the same pagination as the first edition, in this new version the changes are of such a number and extent that a complete repagination and resetting of the text has been done. This of course includes an updating of the index.

Of the good people at Brill, two must specially be acknowledged. I most happily reiterate and renew my continuing thanks to Albert Hoffstädt, advocate for excellence in scholarship and for the *bonae litterae* in life, without whom this third edition would have remained simply the scribblings defacing my desk-copy of the second edition. For necessary assistance in effecting the production of this volume, I also wish to thank Eleonora Capaccioni, who handled all manner of technical computer issues and frustrations with supreme competence and good grace, even when the darkness seemed impenetrable.

And as ever, in the end my deepest and daily gratitude is to my wife, Amy Strickland, indispensable partner and dear companion.

PAUL W. KROLL
August 2021

Acknowledgments

Many persons—too many to list individually here—have helped me while working on the dictionary, in different ways and at different times, and I thank all of them collectively and profoundly. There are, however, two people who must be mentioned by name.

That this dictionary is a reality is largely owing to Albert Hoffstädt, senior editor for Asian Studies at Brill, who can rightly be called the prime mover of it. Albert is a cultivated gentleman at home in several languages, and it was good fortune of the highest order to have him as editor and advocate. Working with him throughout the process has been a great pleasure.

To my wife, Amy Strickland, I am more than grateful. What I owe her extends far beyond the limits of this project. Her presence and support, from first to last, means everything.

September 2014

Introduction

For the nearly fifty years that I have been studying Classical Chinese the one constant but unsatisfied desideratum of English-speaking students and scholars has been for a Chinese-English dictionary that focuses specifically on premodern texts. In the absence of such a reference work, those seeking such help have usually had to resort *faute de mieux* to the 1931 *Mathews' Chinese-English Dictionary*, prepared originally for the China Inland Mission and heavily indebted to Herbert Giles' 1892 *Chinese-English Dictionary*. The inadequacies of Mathews' (and Giles') dictionary for this purpose are well known and do not need detailed rehearsal. Probably the most troubling fact is that, although mostly focusing on late imperial and modern usage, it indiscriminately mixes together vocabulary of all periods, from the early layers of the *Shang shu* to early twentieth-century merchant and missionary vocabulary, and snatches of much else in between, with the unhappy result that students infer all terms and meanings to be equally applicable throughout three thousand years of Chinese history. The seemingly random arrangement of various meanings for any particular word is likewise unfortunate, leading to the pick-and-choose approach so maddeningly familiar to any instructor who hears students explain that after all they "got" this or that definition from *Mathews'*, so how could it not be correct?

The magnitude of compiling a dictionary that might rectify or at least improve the situation has been a ready deterrent for a long time. The abandonment in 1955 of the Harvard-Yenching Institute project for a comprehensive *Chinese-English Dictionary* served to depress hopes substantially.[1] Yet the scope of our wishes did not shrink, as what was usually spoken of as most desirable was an English equivalent of massive, encyclopedic dictionaries such as Morohashi Tetsuji's 諸橋轍次 *Dai Kan-Wa jiten* 大漢和辭典 (1955-60) or the *Zhongwen dacidian* 中文大辭典 (1962-68, rev. ed. 1973)[2] or the *Hanyu dacidian* 漢語大詞典 (1986-94). Such a dictionary would be ideal, of course. But its completion would call for the dedicated work of dozens of scholars for more years than any of them would be willing to sacrifice, given the lack of funding for such a large and lengthy project and the realities of professional imperatives in American higher education currently.

---

1 Especially with realization of what would ultimately be required, seeing that the "preliminary print" of a fascicle giving the entry on the single graph *zi* 子 ran to sixty-eight double-column pages.

2 Despite what is often said, this is not just a "Chinese version" of Morohashi.

Nevertheless, something better than *Mathews'* and the other available options is needed, especially for students in their first years of studying Classical Chinese. It is no use if we allow the perfect to be forever the enemy of the good. Hence, the present work which, imperfect as it is, hopes to make a start toward the ultimate dictionary we all desire.

A Student's Dictionary of Classical and Medieval Chinese is meant for practical use in reading and translating. It is not an etymological dictionary, nor is it a phrase dictionary (*cidian* 辭典). As a lexicon of some 8,300 individual graphs (thus, a *zidian* 字典), it aims to provide immediate assistance for the interpretation and translation of words in certain contexts. In this regard perhaps it is worth stressing that a Chinese graph, or character, is not itself a word. It is the representation of a word. Moreover, one and the same graph may represent different words, words that may either be related in meaning or that may be totally unrelated. Where possible, I have tried to arrange the contents of individual entries in a manner that may suggest a certain development of meanings or understandable progression from a basic sense to various derived meanings. But when a single graph is used to represent fundamentally different words, this is not possible and should not be expected.

The term "Classical Chinese" itself as normally used by scholars has two different references. The first is as a general, inclusive term for what might otherwise be called premodern Chinese, as when we speak of teaching a course in (that is, with texts written in) Classical Chinese. The second, as used in the title of this book, is as a narrower term for a specific stage of premodern Chinese, covering roughly the language used in texts dating from the Warring States period (481-221 BCE) through the Qin (221-206) and Han (206 BCE-220 CE) dynasties. Complementing this usage, "Medieval Chinese" refers to the language used in texts dating roughly from the third century to the tenth century, that is, from the Wei-Jin-Nanbeichao period (220-589) through the Sui (589-618) and Tang (618-907) dynasties.

Specialists in Chinese historical linguistics make finer distinctions and divide the language of this millennium and a half into several more stages. But the twofold division into "classical" and "medieval" Chinese, with its transition during the third century CE, is widely used by scholars in Chinese history, literature, and religion, and is adopted here. From the third century on, many new meanings came into play for existing graphs (or to put it more accurately, many new words came to be represented by existing graphs) and many new graphs were developed. Although we cannot be strictly precise in these matters, because such a large percentage of texts known by name (and doubtless even more that are unidentified) have been lost to us, it is helpful for readers of texts to have a sense of this general periodization and to recognize, for example, that a meaning attested for a particular graph only from medieval times is not applicable to the graph when it appears in, say, a text from the Warring States or Western Han eras. Where such distinctions can be made with reasonable reliability, they are marked parenthetically in the dictionary as "(med.)." New characters and meanings of existing characters that came into general use after the tenth century are not included in this dictionary. I hope that someone soon might take up the task of compiling a successor dictionary for the late imperial period, from the Song dynasty through the Qing, with its multitude of new coinages deriving from popular culture and vernacular speech.

The three determining factors in making sense of any text are grammar, context, and vocabulary. That order reflects the relative importance of these factors in reading classical and medieval Chinese. This dictionary will provide substantial help with vocabulary. Context of course is text-specific and cannot be prescribed. However, there is a certain amount of general cultural knowledge that hovers around particular words, which one learns from long experience but which may also be learned in advance. Many entries in the dictionary therefore include comments of a discursive nature, in addition to definitions. This is the kind of information I impart orally to students in my courses, and I hope some of it will be of use here in written form.

Grammar is the most important of the three elements mentioned above. The grammar of classical and medieval Chinese depends crucially on the so-called "empty words" (*xuzi* 虛字) that indicate grammatical relationships and aid in the proper construal of syntax. For these words, it does not suffice to learn a translation. One must learn for each the grammatical *function* it serves and be prepared to translate as needed, within the bounds of that function. These words are marked in the dictionary as "(GP)," that is, grammatical particles, and the entries for them center on explanation of their function. Unlike other entries, these usually include sample quotations which give a more extended illustration of their usage. All of the detailed GP entries, or GP segments of entries, were drafted by William G. Boltz, for whose contributions I am most grateful.

Every reader of texts needs assistance in identifying technical terms, starting with plants and animals. There are discrete dictionaries available for all manner of specialized fields, and a seasoned sinologist will eventually accumulate dozens of them. But it is useful to have much of this information accessible in a single place. Hence this dictionary includes hundreds of entries giving accurate identifications of plants and animals, as well as items in various other areas of common experience, such as astronomy, the bureaucracy, foreign names, etc., that a reader of historical and literary texts is likely to encounter. Certain important terms drawn from Buddhist texts and from religious Daoism, both fields exercising major cultural influence in medieval times, also find a place here.

Another frequent difficulty, especially in poetry, is the binome (*lianmianci* 連綿詞) or two-syllable word, usually alliterative or rhyming in structure, and marked as "(bn.)" in the dictionary. The graphs representing such words are often variable, the most important feature of the word being its phonetic shape. Sometimes a binome includes a graph that is a bound form, appearing only as an element of that binome. Often the "normal" meaning associated with a particular graph included in a binome (that is, its meaning as an independent word) has no relationship with the meaning of the binome. Binomes have been appropriately characterized as *Gestalt* constructions, comprising more than the sum of their parts, or as *impressifs* gesturing toward a certain imagistic effect but without a rigidly fixed semantic core. Like some other scholars, I typically render binomes by a pair of (usually) alliterative or assonantal synonyms, in order to suggest something of their original phonetic effect. However, this does not mean that a binome is at root a "synonym compound," nor is a Chinese phrase that is in fact a synonym compound rightly called a binome. Because binomes often present particularly challenging problems in translation, the dictionary includes several hundred of them, with suggested renderings for various contexts.

A special feature of the dictionary is the inclusion of the Middle Chinese reconstructed pronunciation, marked as "MC," of every word. Too often we read premodern Chinese texts as though just decoding a semantic puzzle. But the sound of a word is important as well as its sense,[3] and having even a rough idea of the actual sound of a word in earlier times, not just its pronunciation in Modern Standard Chinese, is always worthwhile. This is especially, though not only, the case when reading literary texts that are most keenly attuned to the conscious blending of sound and sense. Of course we know that the sound of words in Classical Chinese (understood inclusively) changed through time. Here again, although finer distinctions can be made, there are two primary divisions applicable to the 1,500-year period with which we are concerned, usually called Old Chinese and Middle Chinese. "Old Chinese" normally refers to the linguistic reconstruction of the language of texts from the Warring States period through the Han dynasty, in other words the language of what we earlier defined (in its more narrow sense) as "classical Chinese." On the other hand, "Middle Chinese" is a linguistic reconstruction largely based on the language represented in the *Qieyun* 切韻 rhyming dictionary of 601 CE, dating from approximately the midpoint of the period we have defined as that of "medieval Chinese."

Why, one may ask, are only the Middle Chinese readings supplied in the dictionary, and not the Old Chinese readings too? The simple answer is that there is a relatively stable consensus about Middle Chinese readings (though specialists argue about certain points of detail), whereas the linguistic reconstruction of Old Chinese continues to generate broad dispute and widely divergent representa-

---

3   Consider how naturally, in composing a written text, we decide on one among several alternative phrasings because to our inner ear it "just sounds better."

tional models. Moreover, Old Chinese itself is in large part a back-projection from the established phonological values of Middle Chinese and is thus largely an abstract outgrowth (or perhaps we might say pre-growth) of it. Given the relative certainty of Middle Chinese reconstruction and the relative uncertainty of Old Chinese, it has therefore seemed the safest course in a dictionary meant for general use to provide only the Middle Chinese readings for words. Of the several systems for Middle Chinese reconstructions that have been proposed over the years, that of William Baxter and Laurent Sagart enjoys the widest acceptance among scholars. William Baxter has checked the MC readings in the dictionary and corrected an abundance of errors that appeared in the first printing. His generosity in doing so is much appreciated.

In addition to forty-plus years of my own notes about various words and their usage, I have incorporated in the dictionary definitions and interpretations gleaned from numerous other sources. It is a pleasure to acknowledge how much I have learned—and continue to learn—from scores of other sinologists, past and present, who have commented in useful and convincing ways about one or another word or term in books and articles. I have freely made use of their insights here. Thus, much of what will be found in the dictionary is a gathering of the wisdom published in various forms and outlets during the past hundred years of sinological study. Three scholars whose works I have most benefited from are Richard B. Mather, David R. Knechtges, and Edward H. Schafer. Countless other colleagues will also find their own suggestions regarding particular words or terms echoed here. In this sense the dictionary is far more of a collective production than it appears from the title page.

Six friends and colleagues (besides Prof. Baxter), whose names appear with mine on the title page, have assisted materially in the compilation of the dictionary. Each of these individuals supplied drafts of up to a hundred entries, and their commitment to the project has been integral to its success. Without their contributions and constant encouragement, my burden would have been much heavier. Each of them deserves significant credit for the dictionary's merits. I am responsible for the final form of all entries, and all mistakes should be laid at my door. In the second edition of this book, I have made revisions and additions to some two hundred entries, in order to sharpen and improve the treatment of certain words. But thanks to the magic of the typesetters, the overall pagination of the first printing has been maintained in the revised edition, as have nearly all of the original page-breaks.

No one is more aware than I of the inadequacies and deficiencies of the present work. But a start must be made, if we are ever to have the ideal dictionary we eventually wish to see. I hope this dictionary will be a first step toward that goal and might ease to some degree the labors of those engaged in the teaching and studying of premodern texts. We are all partners together in the great enterprise of sinology.

It is only through the common and accumulated research of all scholars—past, present, and future—that our understanding of classical and medieval Chinese can advance.

PAUL W. KROLL
September 2014; February 2017

Symbols and Abbreviations Used in the Dictionary

⊙	used for or graphically interchangeable with the following (may be followed by more than one other graph)
→	see entry for character that follows; usually indicating same graph but listed under different main pronunciation, sometimes indicates synonymy or near-synonymy of different graph
>	leads logically to, meaning extends or expands to
<	derived from (usu. to indicate derivation from a foreign word)
abb.	abbreviation, abbreviated
ADV	adverb(ial)
alt.	alternative(ly)
ant.	antonym
approx.	approximately
Arab.	Arabic
bn.	binome, 2-syllable word
Budd.	Buddhist
c.	century
ca.	circa, about
cf.	compare with
cmpd.	compound
cog.	cognate
Dao.	Daoist, primarily medieval religious Daoist
e.g.	*exempli gratia*, for example
equiv.	equivalent to
esp.	especially
euph.	euphemism
gen.	in general, general(ly)
Gk.	Greek
GP	grammatical particle
i.e.	*id est*, that is
incl.	including
interr.	interrogative
Iran.	Iranian
Jpns.	Japanese
lit.	literature
MC	Middle Chinese
med.	medieval
mod.	modern

N.B.	*nota bene*, take special note of
OBJ	object
OC	Old Chinese
onom.	onomatopoeic
opp.	opposite, opposed to
Pers.	Persian
prob.	probably
rdup.	reduplicated
ref.	reference, refers to
sgl.	singly or singular
Skt.	Sanskrit
Sog.	Sogdian
SUBJ	subject
syn.	synonym(ous)
Tib.	Tibetan
trns.	translation
trsc.	transcription
Turk.	Turkic
usu.	usually
VB	verb, verbal
Viet.	Vietnamese

Organization

Entries are arranged in alphabetical sequence, according to each graph's Pinyin romanization. Graphs with identical pronunciation are placed in order of their signific's (*bushou* 部首, or "radical") sequence in the standard list of 214 significs established in the *Kangxi Dictionary* 康熙字典.

Graphs with two or more pronunciations are listed under each of them but are given their main entry under one designated pronunciation, cross-referenced to by all of the others.

Within the body of an entry, if reference is made to a different graph which is followed by one pronunciation and then a second in parenthesis, this means the particular meaning in question carries the first pronunciation but this is a secondary pronunciation to be found under the main entry whose pronunciation is the one in parenthesis.

Tone Marking in MC Reconstructions

Pingsheng 平聲 words are unmarked; *shangsheng* 上聲 words are marked with final (unpronounced)-X; *qusheng* 去聲 words are marked with final (unpronounced)-H; *rusheng* 入聲 words are marked with final (pronounced)-p, -t, or -k.

A

ā

阿　ā　MC 'a　→ 阿 ē.

āi

哀　āi　MC 'oj
1. to have suffered the loss of a loved one, be in mourning, bereave(ment).
    a. be grieved, sorrowful, mournful, lamenting; lugubrious, poignant, flebile (stronger than 悲 bēi).
    b. to pity, sympathize with, express sympathy for, feel compassion.
2. (as sentence initial) but alas!

埃　āi　MC 'oj
1. dust, dirt, grime.
    a. the impure, mundane world.

欸　āi　MC 'oj
1. onom. sigh of sadness.
    ǎi　MC 'ojX
1. onom. sigh of affirmation or agreement.
2. (med.) (bn.) ～乃 ǎinǎi (MC 'ojX-nojX), onom. of rhythmic sweep of a boat's oars, or of oarsman's song.

ái

皚　ái　MC ngoj
1. sgl. or rdup., snow-white, niveous; candent, albescent; glistening whiteness, as white as can be; unstained, spotless, chaste.

磑　ái　MC ngwoj
1. rdup., lofty and tall, peaked and piled; also, thick and hard, dense and solid; also, glistening whiteness, ⊙ 皚皚 áiái.
    wèi　MC ngwojH
1. whetstone.
    a. hone, sharpen.
2. (med.) rolling mill, used to pulverize grain into flour.
    a. (med.) pulverize, grind.
    b. (med.) ～傘 wèisǎn, sieve.

騃　ái　MC ngeajX
1. fool(ish), senseless; blockhead, dunce; fatuous, asinine.

ǎi

矮　ǎi　MC 'eaX
1. short in stature.
    a. diminutive, dwarf(ish).

藹　ǎi　MC 'ajH
1. sgl. or rdup., lush, rife, clumped, dense, luxuriant; abundant; thick, dim, shadowed.
2. full and rich, mellow, as of scents, character, or speech.
3. plump, ample, chubby.
4. ⊙ 靄 ǎi, mass of thin clouds.

靄　ǎi　MC 'ajH
1. sgl. or rdup., thin mists, mass of thin wind-driven clouds, cloud-wisps; rack, wrack.
    a. built-up clouds, cumulus, cloudy puffs.

ài

優　ài　MC 'ojH
1. catch one's breath, have difficulty breathing; breathless; breathe spasmodically, pant.
2. indistinct, faint.
    a. as if, somewhat like, seemingly.

愛　ài　MC 'ojH
1. be partial to.
    a. be fond of, care for; be attached to, cherish, love (ant. 惡 wù, abhor; 憎 zēng, detest).
    b. affection, kindness.
    c. dear to one; admirable, treasured.
2. to pity, sympathize with.
3. be overly partial, jealous of.
    a. to stint, begrudge, be loath to part with.
4. (med.) frequently, regularly.
    a. (med.) easily; prone to; with pleasure.

曖　ài　MC 'ojH
1. overcast, overshadowed, beclouded; sunless; heavy, lowering; hidden from view, bedimmed.

a. rdup., unseen in haze, masked in darkness.

2. ⊙ 靉 *ài*.

礙   ài   MC ngwojH

1. impede, hamper, hinder; obstruct, block off.
2. resist(ance); stricture; friction.

艾   ài   MC ngajH

1. wormwood, mugwort, artemisia (*Artemisia argyi*), an herbaeous perennial that grows on mountain slopes and riverbanks, used as a medicinal herb and as moxa in moxibustion > to cauterize in moxibustion.
2. the color of artemisia leaves, grayish-green.
   a. an aged person, with hair gray as artemisia leaves.
3. to end, to stop.
4. nurture, care for, protect.
5. pretty, beautiful.
6. rdup., onom. for stuttering.

yì   MC ngjojH

1. ⊙ 刈 *yì*, to cut, mow, reap; 乂 *yì*, to govern.

薆   ài   MC ʻojH

1. screen, conceal, cover, hide, esp. with dense vegetative growth.
   a. (med.) brood over, wrapped in thought.
2. sgl., rdup., or (bn.) ～蔚 *àiduì* (MC ʻojH-twojH), richly overgrown, rife and rank.
3. full-scented, odoriferous, aromatic.

隘   ài   MC ʻeaH

1. narrow, strait(ened); closed in, constricted.
   a. constriction, exiguity.
2. narrow pass, defile.
   a. strategic point.

è   MC ʻeak

1. ⊙ 阨 *è* 1, to stop, cease; close off, delimit; 2, in dire straits, poverty-stricken.

靉   ài   MC ʻojH

1. (bn.) ～靆 *àidài* (MC ʻojH-dojH), heavy with clouds, bedimmed and beclouded; ～靅 *àipèi* (MC ʻojH-phjojH), lowering and layered with clouds.

yǐ   MC ʼj+jX

1. (bn.) ～靆 *yǐxì* (MC ʼj+jX-xj+jH), overclouded in murk, darksome and dim.

餲   ài   MC ʻaejH

1. putrid smell of spoiled food; carious; mouldy, fusty.

ān

噞   ān   MC ngom

1. (bn.) ～囈 *ānyì* (MC ngom-ngjiejH), mutter and mumble while dreaming, babble in one's sleep.
2. (med.) (bn.) ～哢 *ānlòng* (MC ngom-luwngH), chiffer-chaffer of birds.
3. (med.) (bn.) ～默 *ānmò* (MC ngom-mok), tight-lipped and taciturn, still and speechless; keep mum, mump and mumble.

安   ān   MC ʻan

1. firmly in place; cog. 鞍 *ān* saddle, 按 *àn* press on.
   a. stable, secure; safe (ant. 危 *wéi*, dangerous).
   b. tranquil, calm, eirenic (ant. 動 *dòng*, in movement).
   c. contented, at ease, comfortable, unworried, settled.
2. settle down in a place; install, arrange.
3. settle a question or situation, take care of, deal with, dispose of; be even-handed (toward).
   a. placate, pacify, comfort, console.
4. interr. GP: whereby? whence? > either "how?" or "where?" e.g. ～能治人 *ān néng zhì rén*, How can one govern others?; ～知魚之樂 *ān zhī yúzhi lè*, Whence do you know the happiness of the fish?
5. an element in various foreign place-names, e.g. ～息 *ānxī* (MC ʻan-sik), Aršak, Parthia(n), Arsacid; ～都 *āndū* (MC ʻan-tu) and ～石 *ānshí* (MC ʻan-dzyek), Antioch, also equiv. preceding; ～國 *ānguó*, Bukhāra.
   a. ～息香 *ānxīxiāng*, "Parthian aromatic," bdellium, gum guggul; (med.) also, benzoin resin (from Sumatra).
   b. (Budd.) sgl., when used as surname for monks, ethnonym indicating Parthian ancestry.
6. (med.) surname, usu. of Sogdians hailing originally from Bukhāra.

庵   ān   MC ʻom

1. thatched hut, cottage.
   a. (Budd.) hermitage, sanctuary, retreat, usu. for one or but a few religious.

盦　ān　MC ʼom

1. lid, cover; cap.
   a. by synecdoche, container, vessel, basin.

菴　ān　MC ʼom

1. ～藺 *ānlǘ*, cottage-thatch artemisia (*Artemisia keiskeana*), seeds used medicinally, stalks used in thatching.
2. (med.) ～摩勒 *ānmólè* (MC ʼom-ma-lok), emblic myrobalan (*Emblica officinalis*), the tree and astringent fruit (Skt. *āmalaka*, Pers. *amīla*), originally an import from Central and Southeast Asia, one of 3 ingredients of *sanle* 三勒 (→ 勒 *lè*).
3. ⊙ 庵 *ān*, thatched hut, cottage.

yǎn　MC ʼjemX

1. (med.) (bn.) ～藹 *yǎnʼǎi* (MC ʼjemX-ʼajH), lush and abundant, of vegetation; thick and clumped, of vegetation or clouds.

諳　ān　MC ʼom

1. know by heart, understand completely; know fully, from experience.
   a. experienced in; versed in, expert at.

鞍　ān　MC ʼan

1. saddle, where one sits on horseback securely; cog. 安 *ān*, securely in place, 按 *àn*, press down.
2. saddle-like depression between two higher areas of land.

鎄　ān　MC ʼom

1. (of sound) muffled, muted, deadened; inaudible, faint, feeble; low.

鵪　ān　MC ʼom

1. (med.) ⊙ 鶉 *yàn*, turnix; buttonquail; bustardquail.

ǎn

唵　ǎn　MC ʼomX

1. darkened sky, overcast; cloudy, gloomy; somber.
   a. lightless, unlit, unilluminated; unenlightened, ignorant, in the dark.

yǎn　MC ʼjemX

1. rdup., cloud-covered, dull and dim.

àn

岸　àn　MC nganH

1. riverbank; shore.
   a. flank of a mountain.
2. lofty, imposing; haughty.
3. exposed aloft, be revealed to view.
   a. push back on one's brow.
4. high goal or objective.

按　àn　MC ʼanH

1. press firmly down or on, put firmly in place, place before one (less forceful than 抑 *yì*); cog. 安 *ān*, secure, 鞍 *ān*, saddle.
   a. pat, rub, stroke; place one's hand on; strike, as a musical instrument; ply, as a writing-brush; wield, as the reins of a horse.
   b. repress, restrain; curb; discipline, train.
   c. indicative of author's or editor's personal comment: "let me make a point of . . .; take special note of . . .", like N.B., *nota bene*.
   d. to inspect, examine; try out, test.
2. lean on, rely on; comply with; according to.
   a. in accord with or following on what has happened previously, thereupon.

暗　àn　MC ʼomH

1. occluded, obscure, sun-dark (ant. 明 *míng*); opaque (ant. 亮 *liàng*)
2. hidden, secret, covert, unnoticed, out of sight.
   a. inwardly, privately, to oneself.
3. be in the dark, unwitting, unawares, ignorant.
4. ～藹 *ànʼǎi* (MC ʼomH-ʼajH), clumped and massed together; also, long-off and faraway.

案　àn　MC ʼanH

1. small rectangular table for dining or writing.
   a. files, records, documents, placed on such a table, esp. of official or legal matters.
2. lean on, rest on, rest against.
   a. rely on, according to.
3. (bn.) ～衍 *ànyǎn* (MC ʼanH-yenX), low-lying, shallow and sunken; also, uneven, rough and ragged.

犴　àn　MC nganH

1. ferocious animal from the northland, perhaps a leopard or tapir.

a. sgl. or 狴~ *bìàn*, fearsome guardian of prison doors > by metonymy, prison.

豻   **àn   MC nganH**   ⊙ 犴 *àn*.

闇   **àn   MC 'omH**

1. to close the door behind oneself; retire alone.
   a. behind closed doors; covert(ly), private(ly); inwardly, to oneself; ⊙ 暗 *àn* 2, 2a.
   b. be in   the dark, unwitting, ignorant of; confused about; ⊙ 暗 *àn* 3.
2. darkness, tenebrity; hidden, obscure, occluded; ⊙ 暗 *àn* 1.
3. evening, nighttime.
   a. eclipse, of sun or moon.
4. downcast, dispirited.
   ān   MC 'om
1. 諒~ *liàng'ān*, ritual mourning dwelling for ruler.
   yǎn   MC 'jemX
1. quick(ly), sudden(ly), ⊙ 奄 *yǎn*.

黯   **àn   MC 'eamX**

1. black; darkened hues; lightless, dull, gloomy; crepuscular.
   a. (bn.) ~黮 *àntǎn* (MC 'eamX-thomX), ~慘 *àncǎn* (MC 'eamX-tshomX), dim and dreary, somber and sullen, grim and gloomy.

áng

卬   **áng   MC ngang**

1. 1st-person pronoun: I (early usage; later for archaic effect).
2. ⊙ 昂 *áng*, rise, raise high, lift up; high-rising; also, under-rafter, lever-arm.
   yǎng   MC ngjangX
1. ⊙ 仰 *yǎng* 1, look up, raise the head; upward; 2, look up to, regard with respect; 3, (med.) anticipate, hope for, look forward to.

昂   **áng   MC ngang**

1. raise up, rise, lift up, lift high.
   a. high, high-rising.
   b. hold up one's head.
   c. (med.) (bn.) ~藏 *ángzàng* (MC ngang-dzangH), proud and redoubtable, high above the norm.
2. rdup., an aspiring spirit, lofty aims, shooting for the stars.
3. under-rafter, lever-arm.

àng

枊   **àng   MC ngangH**

1. hitching-post, for horse.
2. long eave-bracing architectural arm, lever.

盎   **àng   MC 'angH**

1. earthenware jug, pitcher, porringer, with wide body and small mouth.
2. appear, show, be seen, manifest.
3. rdup., complete and in control.

āo

凹   **āo   MC 'eaw**

1. concave; cavity, depression relative to surrounding area; indentation, dent; recess; pit, sink; hollow.

áo

嗷   **áo   MC ngaw**

1. rdup., hue and cry, raucous racket, brawling clamor, din and commotion, bickering babble; also, plaintive cry, cry of distress, "oh no!"
2. the cronking of geese, crunkling of cranes.

嶅   **áo   MC ngaw**

1. (bn.) 碉~ *diào'áo*, → 碉 *diào* (*chóu*).
2. (med.) ⊙ 磝 *áo* 1, stony rock-strewn hill.

嶅   **áo   MC ngaw**   ⊙ 嶅 *áo*.

廒   **áo   MC ngaw**

1. (med.) granary, storehouse.

敖   **áo   MC ngaw**

1. to stray, range easily, ramble at will; stroll, saunter.
2. squabble, bicker, wrangle.
3. ⊙ 熬 *áo*, dry-fry; stew, boil.
   ào   MC ngawH
1. ⊙ 傲 *ào*, haughty, complacent; high-borne.

熬   **áo   MC ngaw**

1. dry-fry, roast.
   a. (med.) simmer, stew; decoct.
   b. do a "slow burn" temperamentally, stew about something, simmer with anger.
2. rdup., calling out in complaint, voicing lament; also (med.) burning brilliantly, flushed with fire.

獒　áo　MC ngaw
1. large hound, variously described as 4 *chi* 尺 in height, fierce, and trainable to know its master's desires.

璈　áo　MC ngaw
1. (Dao.) musical instrument esp. associated with Dao. goddesses, sometimes described as 雲 ～ *yún'áo*, "cloud ao," exact shape unknown but reputedly consisting of a group of small chime-stones suspended from a wooden bar attached to a long grip held by the left hand, with a small mallet in right hand to strike the lithophones.

磝　áo　MC ngaew
1. stony rock-strewn hill, ⊙ 嶅 *áo*.
   a. rdup., hill or slope of stones and scree.
   qiāo　MC khaew
1. rdup., rocky and barren, unyielding and infertile (of soil).

翱　áo　MC ngaw
1. soar; hover.
   a. ～翔 *áoxiáng* (MC ngaw-zjang), wheel on wing, sweep round and hover; wander at whim.

聱　áo　MC ngaw
1. turn a deaf ear to others' opinions, be deaf to; heedless.
2. (med.) ～牙 *áoyá*, harsh and dissonant, jarring rigmarole (of literary style).

螯　áo　MC ngaw
1. chela, pincer-like claw of crustacean (e.g. crab) or arachnid (e.g. scorpion).

謷　áo　MC ngaw
1. slander; vilify, defame; heap abuse on.
2. rdup., ⊙ 嗷嗷 *áo'áo*, clamorous tumult, raucous and rackety; also, plaintively crying.
   ào　MC ngawH
1. imposingly high.
2. ⊙ 傲 *ào* 1, haughty, high-held; arrogant.

遨　áo　MC ngaw
1. (med.) ⊙ 敖 *áo* 1, to stray; range easily, ramble at will; stroll; saunter.

鏖　áo　MC 'aw
1. kettle, cooking-pot.

2. heated conflict, "heat of battle," frenzied attack.

鰲　áo　MC ngaw　⊙ 鼇 *áo*.

鼇　áo　MC ngaw
1. fabulous omophoric giant sea-turtle; usu. imaged as 3, bearing on their backs the paradise isles of Penglai 蓬萊, Yingzhou 瀛洲, and Fangzhang 方丈, or as 4, upholding the pillars of the world at the 4 cardinal points of the world-surrounding ocean.

ǎo

媼　ǎo　MC 'awX
1. respectful term for an elderly woman: granny, old dame, milady.
2. term ref. to any woman: woman, lady.
3. ～神 *ǎoshén*, female spirit of Earth, "Goddess Knobby."

拗　ǎo　MC 'aewX
1. break, break off; snap; fracture.
   ào　MC 'aewH
1. (med.) disagreeable, disputative, quarrelsome; contrary; disobedient, disobliging.
   yù　MC 'juwk
1. quell, suppress; restrain.

ào

傲　ào　MC ngawH
1. high-borne, high-held.
   a. haughty, proud, arrogant.
   b. self-content, complacent.
   c. scornful, overweening; strutting; disdain(ful).
2. irritable, irascible; impatient.

坳　ào　MC 'aew
1. depressed surface area, recess, indentation, dent; concavity; pit, sink, hole.
   a. ravine, hollow; pass; undulating hills.

奡　ào　MC ngawH
1. ⊙ 傲 *ào*, high-borne, high-held; haughty, proud.
2. (bn.) 熹～ *dào'ào*, → 熹 *dào*.

奧   ào   MC 'awH
1. southwest corner of a house, traditionally reserved for the most honored resident and where sacrifices to spirits and household gods were held.
   a. inner recesses
2. the kitchen god, stove god.
   a. lord, master; (med.) patron, backer.
3. deep and hard to get to or through, impenetrable, of plant growth or of concepts.
4. enigma(tic), inexplicable, obscure, profound, difficult to understand.
5. pigpen, piggery, where slops and remnants of meals are thrown.

   yù   MC 'juwk
1. ⊙ 燠 yù, humid, sultry; 隩 or 澳 yù, back-bay, cove in a riverbank.

懊   ào   MC 'awH
1. sgl. or in bns. ～惱 àonǎo (MC 'awH-nawX), ～憦 àolào (MC 'awH-lawH), regret deeply, heartsick; vexed, worried, fretful.

澳   ào   MC 'awH   → 澳 yù.

隩   ào   MC 'awH   → 隩 yù.

驁   ào   MC ngawH
1. thoroughbred horse of the highest quality.
   a. gallop unrestrained.
2. untamed, unbroken.
3. (med.) of rare ability, a ne plus ultra.
4. ⊙ 傲 ào, high-lifted, high-held; haughty, proud.

B

bā

八   bā   MC peat
1. numeral eight; eighth.
2. numbering the four cardinal directions plus intermediate points.

巴   bā   MC pae
1. sgl. or cmpd. ～蛇 bāshé, giant snake.
2. feudal state in Zhou times and of area thereafter, comprising the eastern part of present-day Sichuan; often paired with Shu 蜀, covering the western part of present-day Sichuan.
3. ～豆 bādòu, croton seeds (Croton tiglium), used as a strong purgative.

笆   bā   MC pae
1. (med.) ～籬 bālí or 籬～ líbā, bamboo fence or railing.
2. (med.) ～茅 bāmáo, maiden-grass (Miscanthus sinensis), with purplish flowers.

芭   bā   MC pae
1. unidentified fragrant plant, in Chuci.
2. ～蕉 bājiāo, banana (Musa basjoo), stalk used medicinally and, when retted, for making cloth; also planted for decorative purposes.

   pā   MC phae
1. ⊙ 葩 pā, corolla, outer envelope of flower.

豝   bā   MC pae
1. sow, female pig.

bá

拔   bá   MC beat
1. root out, uproot, extirpate; pull out.
   a. pick up, pull back; e.g. ～楗 bájiàn, pick the lock, pull back the bar.
   b. draw out (from obscurity), raise up, promote.
2. drawn out, upthrust(ing); surpass, excel; outstanding.
3. seize, grasp.
4. capture, overcome.
5. change, molt; make turn; come around to.
6. ～汗那 báhànnà (MC beat-hanH-naH), Ferghana (syn. 大宛 dàyuān); (med.) ～悉密, báxīmì (MC beat-sit-mit), Basmïl, Türkic tribe and dynastic family; (med.) ～拽古 báyègǔ (MC beat-yet-kuX), Bayïrqu, Türkic tribe.

   bèi   MC bajH
1. thinned out (vegetation).

胈   bá   MC bat
1. fine hair on the shins or thighs.
2. roots of grass.

茇　bá　MC bat

1. root of a plant.
2. spend the night in the fields, camp out, bivouac, bushwhack.
3. (bn.) 蓽～ *bìbá*, → 蓽 *bì*.

bèi　MC pajH

1. rdup., wheel and turn in flight, soar aloft, wing one's way.

跋　bá　MC bat

1. trample underfoot, tread on; encroach on.
   a. advance while tramping on grass, or while traversing hills; traipse over.
   b. ～扈 *báhù*, traipse-tail, thrash-tail, display a swaggering air of insolence.
2. trip over, stumble.
3. (med.) colophon, writing appended to the end of a text evaluating it or commenting on the circumstances of its composition.
4. (med.) ⊙ 撥 *bō* 3, vibrate, shake; pluck (zither strings), flick, flap.

軷　bá　MC bat

1. sacrifice offered to the god of the road before traveling by carriage.

魃　bá　MC bat

1. drought-demon.

鲅　bá　MC bat

1. (med.) (bn.) 鼥～ *tuóbá*, → 鼥 *tuó*.

bǎ

把　bǎ　MC paeX

1. take in the hand, grasp, hold, clutch, grip; pick up.
   a. control, manage, handle.
2. measure-word for held things, handful, fistful.
3. (med.) pretext, ostensible reason or excuse.

bà　MC paeH

1. a handle, hilt, haft.

pá　MC bae

1. ⊙ 爬 *pá*, scratch, claw; rake over.

bà

弝　bà　MC paeH

1. the grip, of a bow.
   a. handle, hilt.

罷　bà　MC beaX

1. stop, cease, put an end to, conclude; be done with, finish, give up.
   a. give up or lay down one's official duties; retire.

pí　MC bje

1. ⊙ 疲 *pí*, fatigued, wearied, exhausted; played out; feeble, on the wane; incompetent.

霸　bà　MC paeH

1. exercise hegemony over, hold in thrall, control by might; hegemon, overlord.
   a. (med.) stand out from, overtop; surpass, prevail.

pò　MC phaek

1. ⊙ 魄 *pò* 2, faint sliver of moon during first 3 days of the month; gen. term for moonlight.

靶　bà　MC paeH

1. halter, for horse.
2. hilt, hasp, handle; grip, of bow.

bái

白　bái　MC baek

1. the color white; associated in *wuxing* correspondences with the phase or agent of metal, the season of autumn, direction west, etc.; e.g. ～虎 *báihǔ*, white tiger, emblematic animal of autumn; also, ref. the western quadrant of the sky; ～日 *báirì*, white light of day, broad daylight.
   a. symbolic of decline, decay, aging.
2. plain; ordinary, common, simple; undistinguished; ～丁 *báidīng*, ～身 *báishēn*, ～衣 *báiyī*, plain folk, ordinary people, commoners, plainly-clothed, (Budd.) laymen.
3. clear to see or understand, plain; make clear.
   a. say plainly, declare, report, inform; reveal, make evident; esp. communication from inferior to superior; (med.) often a simple indication of statement: to address.
   b. candid, frank; undisguised, unadorned.
4. blank, bare; stark; empty; e.g. ～足 *báizú*, barefooted, (Budd.) monk, mendicant.
   a. with no purpose; in vain, idle; idly.
5. (med.) ～地 *báidì*, all of a sudden, unexpectedly, abruptly.
6. euph. for silver; e.g. ～魚 *báiyú*, silver carp (*Hypophthalmichthys molitrix*).

7. ～石英 *báishíyīng*, "bloom of white stone," quartz; ～芳香 *báifāngxiāng*, ～茅香 *báimáoxiāng*, vanilla grass, sweetgrass (*Hierochloe odorata*), aromatic herb resembling citronella.
8. (Budd.) when used as surname for monk, ethnonym indicating Khotanese ancestry.

bǎi

佰   **bǎi**   MC paek
1. a company of 100 soldiers.
   a. leader of such a company, centurion, kentarch.
2. ⊙ 陌 *mò*, cross-path between fields, balk, terry.

捭   **bǎi**   MC peaX
1. use both hands to beat the sides of something; to pound, clap; strike from the side.
2. ⊙ 擘 *bò*, pry open, force open; separate; e.g. ～闔 *bòhè*, open and close, ref. persuasive argumentation by which alliances are secured or broken.

擺   **bǎi**   MC beaX
1. break apart, separate, pry open.
2. shake off, cast off.
   a. shake, wave, swing, brandish.
   b. smack, smash.
3. arrange, put in order.

百   **bǎi**   MC paek
1. one hundred; one-hundredth.
   a. multiple of hundreds.
2. a full complement of, all types or kinds; e.g. ～官 *bǎiguān*, the hundredfold officials, the bureaucracy; ～年 *bǎinián*, ～齡 *bǎilíng*, 100 years, a full lifespan ending naturally; ～家 *bǎijiā*, 100 schools of thought, all the different lineages of interpretation.
3. ～舌 *bǎishé*, various species of bush-warbler, esp. *Horornis cantans* (all reclassified as *Cetiidae*); sometimes confused with the small myna.
4. ～濟 *bǎijì* (MC paek-tsejH), Paekche, name of kingdom founded in southwestern part of Korean peninsula in 1st c. BCE and occupying most of western portion of peninsula in med. times until defeated by rival kingdom of Silla (Xinluo 新羅) in 660.

bài

唄   **bài**   MC baejH
1. (Budd.) chanting in Sanskrit, usu. of *mantra* or *dhāraṇī*; or sutra-chanting in Chinese with purportedly Indic intonation; psalmody.

拜   **bài**   MC peajH
1. pay respects to, offer a formal salutation; throughout most of early and medieval times, to bow from the waist with clasped hands, bow with respect; also, prostrate oneself from a kneeling position in which torso was held upright.
   a. perform a ceremony.
2. pay a formal visit to; greet formally.
3. designate formally, as in being appointed to office.
4. to make bent, bowed, broken.

敗   **bài**   MC baejH
1. overthrown, pulled down; quashed; defeated, conquered, vanquished; destroyed.
   a. fall behind, lose out; blunder.
   b. decline; wither, decay, deteriorate.
2. food gone bad, spoiled, turned, stale.
      MC paejH
1. transitive VB forms of 1 above.

稗   **bài**   MC beaH
1. tare, a grainfield weed; esp. cockspur, barnyard millet (*Echinochloa crus-galli*), aggressive weed that removes nutrients from the soil.
   a. fodder, hay, barnyard feed.
2. euph. for something of inferior importance, trifling, trivial, nugatory; e.g. ～官 *bàiguān*, officials supposedly charged with reporting the gossip of the streets; (lit.) ～史 *bàishǐ*, bibliographic category incl. anecdotes, gossip, hearsay, fiction.

粺   **bài**   MC beaH
1. polished rice.
2. ⊙ 稗 *bài* 1, tare, cockspur.

bān

扳   **bān**   MC paen   → 扳 *pān*.

斑   **bān**   MC paen
1. mottled, mixed in color, dappled; flecked, spotted, maculated.

a. sgl. or ～白 *bānbái*, hair flecked with white.

b. (bn.) ～剝 *bānbō* (MC paen-paewk), degged and dappled.

2. (bn.) ～蝥 *bānmáo* (MC paen-maew), cantharis, blister-beetle (various species of *Mylabris*), destructive borer of gourds and beans; also 螌蝥 *bānmáo*.

扁　bān　MC pean

1. (med.) (bn.) ～斕 *bānlán* (MC pean-lean), vividly various, diversely dazzling, esp. of literary style.

班　bān　MC paen

1. divide, separate.

2. distribute, give out; spread widely, broadcast.

   a. make pervasive; promulgate, proclaim; disseminate, propagate; diffuse, circulate.

   b. spread out, smooth out; e.g. ～荊 *bānjīng*, spread out thornwood mats; euph. for meet by chance.

3. class(ify), organize, assort(ment); group, rank(ing).

   a. classification, company, category, bracket.

   b. impose order on; manage; exercise control of or leadership over.

4. return, come back, esp. an army from campaign.

5. ⊙ 斑 *bān* 1, mottled, mixed in color, dappled.

6. a surname.

瘢　bān　MC ban

1. scar; pock; blotch; blemish.

   a. gen. term for defect, flaw; drawback, shortcoming.

肦　bān　MC paen

1. ⊙ 頒 *bān* 1, issue, promulgate.

fēn　MC bjun

1. (med.) large-headed.

般　bān　MC pan

1. (med.) transfer, transport, move to.

2. (med.) category, class, kind.

   a. (med.) similar to, resembling, like.

3. ⊙ 頒 *bān* 1, distribute; issue; promulgate; proclaim; 斑 *bān* 1, mottled, mixed in color, dappled.

pán　MC ban

1. used as first element in several binomes meaning: whirled round, swing back and forth, to and fro, round and about, turning and twirling, etc., e.g. ～桓 *pánhuán* (MC ban-hwan), ～旋 *pánxuán* (MC ban-zjwen), ～還 *pánhuán* (MC ban-hwan).

2. (ADV) in turmoil, confusedly, as if one's head is spinning.

bō　MC pa, pat

1. (Budd.) ～若 *bōrě* (MC pa-nyae), trsc. Skt. *prajñā*, wisdom, gnosis; ～若波羅蜜 *bōrěbōlúomì* (MC pa-nyae-pwa-la-mit), trsc. Skt. *prajñāpāramitā*, perfection of wisdom; ～泥洹 *bōníhuán* (MC pa-nej-hwan), trsc. Skt. *parinirvāṇa*, to enter complete extinction.

螌　bān　MC paen

1. (bn.) ～蝥 *bānmáo* (MC paen-maew), cantharis, blister-beetle (various species of *Mylabris*), destructive borer of gourds and beans; also 班蝥 *bānmáo*.

頒　bān　MC paen

1. issue, promulgate, proclaim; distribute, disseminate; diffuse.

   a. give out, give away.

   b. give as reward or boon.

2. ⊙ 斑 *bān*, mottled, dappled; esp. ～白 *bānbái*, white-flecked hair.

fēn　MC bjun

1. (med.) large-headed.

bǎn

坂　bǎn　MC pjonX　⊙ 阪 *bǎn*.

板　bǎn　MC paenX

1. board of wood, plank.

   a. placard, plaque.

2. placard or bulletin bearing an imperial or governmental order.

3. tablet, esp. official's tablet held upright in the hands while attending court.

   a. (med.) be appointed to an official position.

   b. (med.) suffix appended to official title signifying the office is honorific and without stipend or responsibilities, title by courtesy.

4. rdup., go against the norm, reverse the usual course; anomalous and unwonted.

版   bǎn   MC paenX
1. wooden planks used in framing of rammed-earth walls.
    a. measure of length, equiv. 8 "feet" (*chi* 尺).
2. placard on which to inscribe characters, e.g. the name of a hall, garden, etc.
3. household register, census roll.
4. ⊙ 板 *bǎn* 3, official's tablet held in both hands while attending court; be appointed to an official position.

蝂   bǎn   MC paenX
1. (med.) (bn.) 蝜～ *fùbǎn*, → 蝜 *fù*.

阪   bǎn   MC pjonX
1. slope of a hill; talus; declivity; embankment.

bàn

伴   bàn   MC banX
1. companion, associate; comrade.
    a. accompany, keep company with, associate with.
2. entail, involve.

半   bàn   MC panH
1. half, one-half, half of.
    a. in the middle of; midpoint.
2. (med.) mostly, partly, for the most part; more or less, in the (same) way of; sometimes.
3. (med.) the whole, all of; esp. when used in parallel collocations to 全 *quán* or 俱 *jù* in poetry.

拌   bàn   MC banX   → 拌 *pàn*.

瓣   bàn   MC beanH
1. melon-seed.
    a. gen. term for seed-bearing part of plants; ovule.
2. section of a fruit.

絆   bàn   MC panH
1. the rope or langle used to hobble a horse.
    a. to hobble, langle, tie with a cord or thong.
    b. cording or rope used to snare birds or small animals.
    c. tether; leash.

2. (med.) tie off loose ends, wind up; bring to a close, conclude.

辦   bàn   MC beanH
1. to manage, deal with, occupy oneself with, handle, take care of.
    a. succeed in doing; complete.
2. (med.) deal with by inflicting punishment, discipline, correct with force.
3. possess; (be) provide(d) with; prepare, take care of in advance, get ready.
    a. procure; purchase, buy.

靽   bàn   MC panH
1. crupper, leather strap around horse's rump and attached to saddle to keep the latter from slipping.

bāng

邦   bāng   MC paewng
1. state, a certain territory under the authority of a certain group of people.
    a. feudal state, feudal territory.
    b. enfeoff, bestow as a fiefdom.
2. gen. term for state, country.

bǎng

榜   bǎng   MC pangX   → 榜 *péng*.

牓   bǎng   MC pangX
1. (med.) placard, name-plaque, esp. showing the name of a building or gate, usu. horizontal.
2. (med.) announce(ment), give notice of; put up a sign.

bàng

棒   bàng   MC baewngX
1. ⊙ 棓 *bàng* 1, cudgel, club.

棓   bàng   MC baewngX
1. cudgel, club; thick stick.
2. flail, implement for threshing grain.

蚌   bàng   MC baewngX
1. freshwater clam or mussel (*Unionidae*), some with pearls, esp. *Anodonta chinensis*.

蜯 bàng　MC baewngX　⊙ 蚌 *bàng*.

謗 bàng　MC pangH
1. speak ill of, slander, calumniate, defame, vilify (publicly).

bāo

包 bāo　MC paew
1. (en)wrap; bundle, wrapping.
    a. surround, encircle.
    b. to cloak; invest.
2. include, comprise; contain.
    a. tolerate; accommodate.
3. measure-word for round items, e.g. fruit.
4. a surname.
5. ⊙ 苞 *bāo* 4, densely growing, rife; 庖 *páo* 1, kitchen.

胞 bāo　MC paew
1. womb; amnion, placenta.
    a. caul, afterbirth.
2. born of the same parents.
3. ⊙ 脬 *pāo*, bladder; 庖 *páo*, cook, butcher.

苞 bāo　MC paew
1. snoutbean (*Rhynchosia volubilis*).
2. club-rush, bulrush, sedge (*Scirpus*), esp. type used for weaving mats and sandals.
3. pomelo, shaddock (*Citrus grandis*).
4. bract of a plant, leafy or leaflike part usu. found at the base of the flower, sometimes quite colorful.
    a. sepals, flower bud.
    b. rind, "wrapping," esp. of fruit.
5. dense growth of plants, flourishing, rampant.
6. ⊙ 包 *bāo* 1, enwrap, pack(age).

襃 bāo　MC paw　⊙ 襃 *bāo*.

襃 bāo　MC paw
1. long, flowing robe.
    a. ample, capacious; generous.
2. invest with dignity.
3. speak generously of, praise, endorse; e.g. 〜貶 *bāobiǎn*, praise and blame, esp. the practice of registering subtle judgments by means of careful choice of words.

báo

雹 báo　MC baewk
1. hail(stone); sleet.

bǎo

保 bǎo　MC pawX
1. protect(or), guard(ian); e.g. 太〜 *tàibǎo*, grand guardian, one of the 3 highest-ranking court titles (along with *taifu* 太傅 and *taishi* 太師), given to individual of great prestige who may be called on by emperor for advice.
2. sustain, cause to persist; conserve, keep safe, protect.
    a. nourish, foster; comfort.
    b. keep hold of, hold fast to.
3. mutual security group.
4. guarantee, pledge.
5. ⊙ 堡 *bǎo*, bastion, small fort.

堡 bǎo　MC pawX
1. bastion; small fort.

寶 bǎo　MC pawX
1. treasure; precious item; jewel; costly.
    a. to treasure, regard as precious; prize, treasured because of value or importance (cf. 珍 *zhēn*, because of rarity)
    b. often an epithet of things pertaining to the emperor, also to Budd.
2. (med.) imperial seal, substituted by Empress Wu (r. 685-705) for 璽 *xǐ* because of latter's unlucky phonetic similarity with 死 *sǐ*.

葆 bǎo　MC pawX
1. lush, thickly growing; shaggy; bushy; clumped.
2. conceal, cover over, screen; keep hidden.
3. tassels, fringe, esp. made of plumes and hanging from a carriage's canopy as ornamentation.
4. ⊙ 保 *bǎo*, protect; 寶 *bǎo*, treasure; 褓 *bǎo*, swaddling.

褓 bǎo　MC pawX
1. sgl. or cmpd. 襁〜 *qiǎngbǎo*, swaddling clothes; wrap an infant in swaddling.

飽 bǎo　MC paewX
1. eat one's fill, eat to satiety.
    a. sufficiency, fullness.

犤   **bǎo**   MC pawX
1. black and white brindled horse.

犦   **bǎo**   MC pawX
1. bustard (*Otis tarda*).
2. ⊙ 犤 *bǎo*, black and white brindled horse.

bào

報   **bào**   MC pawH
1. repay, requite; recompense, reward.
  a. (Budd.) retribution or effects of karma.
2. revanche, reprisal, vengeance; retribution.
  a. decide on proper punishment for a crime; retributive justice.
3. report back to, inform.
4. reply, respond to, answer.
5. sacrificial ritual of thanksgiving to the spirits, in early times.

抱   **bào**   MC bawX
1. embrace, surround with both arms; hug to one's chest; clasp.
  a. enfold, enwrap; wrapped (up) in.
  b. hold close, hold tight; carry close to one's heart; cherish.
  c. (med.) nest, brood on, of birds.
2. encircle, surround.
3. the space enclosed in an embrace.

暴   **bào**   MC bawH
1. violent, turbulent; like a raging fire.
  a. combustible; inflamed; tempestuous, vehement; feverish, sudden, all at once.
2. brutal, savage; unchecked, untamed.
3. mistreat, bully, harass; dismay; terrorize, terrify; lay waste.
4. to fight barehanded.
  pù   MC buwk
1. ⊙ 曝 *pù*, expose to the sun, apricate; dry out, dessicate(d); adure, adust; reveal, bring into the open.

瀑   **bào**   MC bawH   → 瀑 *pù*.

爆   **bào**   MC paewH
1. crepitate, crackling of fire.
  a. explode, burst; pop.
2. swell, push out; distend; protrude.
3. quick-fry on a high fire.

  a. burn(ed) out, burn(ed) up; e.g. (med.) ～炭 *bàotàn*, "burned to soot," Tang coll. for "mother" of a geisha (妓 *jì*)—because most madams were retired (burned out) geishas.

虣   **bào**   MC bawH
1. (med.) ⊙ 暴 *bào*.

豹   **bào**   MC paewH
1. leopard (*Felis leopardus; F. irbis*).

鉋   **bào**   MC baewH
1. (med.) plane, scraper.
  a. (med.) to plane, remove parings till smooth.

皰   **bào**   MC baewH
1. pimples, on the face.

鮑   **bào**   MC baewX
1. dried fish.
  a. salted fish.
2. a surname.

bēi

卑   **bēi**   MC pjie
1. low, physically (ant. 高 *gāo*, high), low-lying.
2. low, in social status, morals, or culture (ant. 尊 *zūn*, honored, respected); lowly, humble; mean, vulgar; inferior.
  a. disparage, disdain, slight.
3. decline, wane; drop in circumstances, situation, or prestige.

悲   **bēi**   MC pij
1. sad(ness), grief; saddened, grieved; disheartened, heavy of heart, dismay(ed).
2. take to heart, feel deeply in one's heart; sentiments, emotions, feelings.
3. be deeply concerned about, pity, commiserate with; yearn for, keep in mind; anxious(ly).
  a. (Budd.) trns. Skt. *karuṇā*, compassion.

杯   **bēi**   MC pwoj
1. cup.
  a. give a cup to drink from.

桮   **bēi**   MC pwoj   ⊙ 杯 *bēi*.

椑   **bēi**   MC pjie   → 椑 *pí*.

盃 bēi MC pwoj ⊙ 杯 *bēi*.

碑 bēi MC pje
1. stele, upright stone slab bearing a carved text, usu. square-topped (cf. 碣 *jié*, round-headed stele).
   a. the inscription on such a stone; e.g. 墓～ *mùbēi*, tomb inscription, commemorating the deceased.
2. in early times a stone pillar by the palace gate used to mark the sun's shadow (primitive sundial) or by the gate of the ancestral temple for tethering animals to be sacrificed.

陂 bēi MC pje
1. slope, incline, grade.
2. dike, embankment.
   a. to dike, bank up; block.
   b. riverbank; riverside.
   c. embanked pond or pool; reservoir.
   bì MC pjeH
1. slope, slant, incline; lean, tilt.
   pō MC pha
1. (bn.) ～陀, ～陁 *pōtuó* (MC pha-da), cragged and ragged, canted and angled, rough and rugged.

鵯 bēi MC pjie
1. (bn.) ～鶋 *bēijū* (MC pjie-kjo), jungle crow (*Corvus macrorynchus*), often mistaken for raven, syn. 雅烏 *yǎwū*.

běi

北 běi MC pok
1. north, northern, northward, northerly; in *wuxing* correspondences associated with the agent water, season of winter, color black, etc.
2. undergo a defeat; cause one to turn tail and retreat.

bèi

倍 bèi MC bwojX
1. double; to double.
   a. augment, add to.
2. multiple; (after a numeral n) n times, n-fold.
3. turn from; be contrary to; defy; ignore

備 bèi MC bijH
1. procure, provide for, prepare.
   a. make ready, take precautions; have at one's disposal.
   b. prudent; careful; forward-looking.
2. complete(ly), thorough(ly); comprehensive(ly).
   a. full, replete with.
3. (med.) compensate (legal).

奰 bèi MC bijH
1. indignation, resentment; anger.
2. (bn.) 屓～ *xìbèi*, → 屓 *xì*.

孛 bèi MC bwojH
1. burst out, explode; distend, puff up.
   a. bud, pop; bubble, bulge.
2. sgl. or ～星 *bèixīng*, aphelial (tailless) comet, "bursting star; exploder"; cf. 彗 *huì*, perihelial (tailed) comet.

悖 bèi MC bwojH
1. contrary, counter; willful, recalcitrant.
   a. disobey, oppose, rebel against; go counter to; refractory.
2. erroneous, inexact, wide of the mark; absurd, perverse.
3. confuse(d), delude(d); mislead(ing); irregular.
4. to obscure, obstruct.
5. ⊙ 勃 *bó*, burgeon, flourish; burst out.

憊 bèi MC beajH
1. tired, fatigued; exhausted, weary, worn-out.

梖 bèi MC pajH
1. (med.) ⊙ 貝 *bèi* 4, sgl. or ～多 *bèiduō* (MC pajH-ta), abb. or trsc. of Skt. *pattra*, leaves of the palmyra palm (*Borassus flabellifer*) used as writing material, esp. for Budd. texts.

狽 bèi MC pajH
1. cmpd. 狼～ *lángbèi*, → 狼 *láng*.

琲 bèi MC bwojH
1. (med.) pearls placed or strung in a row.

糒 bèi MC bijH
1. dried food; provisions.

背 bèi MC pwojH
1. the back, of a vertebrate.
2. reverse side or back of an object.
3. north side of a building (because usu. opening to the south).
4. behind (the back of), private(ly), in secret.

MC bwojH

1. turn one's back on; turn against, tergiversate; go counter to.
   a. repudiate, reject; disobey, oppose.
   b. separate oneself from; leave, depart, move away from.
2. (med.) recite aloud from memory (with one's back to the text).

bēi   MC pwoj

1. (med.) carry on one's back.

被   **bèi   MC bjeX**

1. blanket, quilt, cover(let).
2. cape, cloak, cope, mantle.
   a. cover (oneself), put on clothes, wear as clothes, don; clad; cloak.
   b. overlay, put on top of, add above.
3. reach, extend to.
4. receive, incur; be subjected to, undergo, suffer.
   a. (GP) preceding VB or VB-phrase as passive marker, indicating object of an action; e.g. 忠而〜謗 *zhòng ér bèi bàng*, loyal but vilified.

pī   MC phje

1. ⊙ 披 *pī* 3, drape over one's shoulders, cloak oneself in; a cloak, cape, shawl, mantle; 4, fling away, scatter.

誖   **bèi   MC bwojH**

1. ⊙ 悖 *bèi* 1-3.

貝   **bèi   MC pajH**

1. cowry, sea-snail, gastropod mollusc (*Cypraeidae*).
   a. cowry-shell, used in early times as medium of exchange; by metonymy, gen. term for property, esp. valuables.
2. conch, musical wind instrument made from a seashell; Budd. trumpet sounded to call the assembly together (Skt. *śaṅkha*).
3. 〜母 *bèimǔ*, fritillary, various species of *Fritillariae*, bulbous herbs with drooping bell-shaped flowers.
4. (med.) ⊙ 梖 *bèi*, sgl. or 〜多 *bèiduō* (MC pajH-ta), abb. or trsc. of Skt. *pattra*, leaves of the palmyra palm (*Borassus flabellifer*) used as writing material, esp. for Budd. texts; e.g. 〜書 *bèishū*, Budd. writings.
5. a surname.

輩   **bèi   MC pwojH**

1. a row, series, or class of people or things.
   a. in the same category as preceding noun; similar, comparable to; a group(ing) of, cohort of.
2. hierarchy or position in a family, clan, or generation.
3. plural marker, when suffixed to a countable noun.

鞁   **bèi   MC bjeH**

1. outfittings of a carriage or chariot, incl. harness for horse or ox; equipage, accoutrements.
   a. to harness a horse or ox.
2. to tack a horse, provide with saddle, bridle, bit, etc.

韛   **bèi   MC bijH   ⊙ 鞁 *bèi*.**

bēn

奔   **bēn   MC pwon**

1. to dart, run; hurry; go headlong, race toward.
   a. urge, quicken; hasten.
2. flee, run from, bolt; abscond, get away from.
3. cast aside or ignore normal social restraints; unconstrained, unobservant, unfettered, unbound.
   a. elope, join a man without proper rituals of engagement and marriage.

賁   **bēn   MC pwon   → 賁 *bì*.**

běn

本   **běn   MC pwonX**

1. tree-trunk.
2. root, of plant; rootstock; e.g. 〜末 *běnmò*, root and branch, first to last; also, means to an end.
   a. get to the root of, study intently.
3. base, basic; foundation; origin(al) principal; innate; e.g. 〜心 *běnxīn*, deepest heart, true feelings.
   a. basically, originally; actually, in fact; primary consideration.
   b. former, previous; e.g. (Budd.) 〜德 *běndé*, merits planted previously (or in former existence); 〜誓 *běnshì*, a former vow; 〜志 *běnzhì*, long-held wish.
4. possessed by or pertaining to oneself; e.g. 〜朝 *běncháo*, the present dynasty; 〜土 *běntǔ*, homeland, home country.

5. edition of a book, version.
6. (med.) main body of a financial holding, principal, capital.

畚　běn　MC pwonX
1. round basket woven of plant fibers for carrying earth; hod.

苯　běn　MC pwonX
1. (bn.) ～尊 běnzǔn (MC pwonX-tswonX), clumped and clustered, raggedly overgrown.

bèn

坌　bèn　MC bwonH
1. dust.
    a. be dusted with, powdered with.
2. join together; collect, amass.
    a. altogether, uniform(ly), en masse.

笨　bèn　MC bwonX
1. (med.) ungainly; lumpish, hulking; unwieldy.
    a. (med.) clumsy, maladroit, inept, awkward.

bēng

崩　bēng　MC pong
1. collapse of a mountain.
2. crumble down, cave in; slip down, slide down; collapse; founder, disintegrate; e.g. ～波 bēngbō, "collapsing waves," residual or fading influence.
    a. (med.) (bn.) ～騰 bēngténg (MC pong-dong), go to wrack and ruin; also, pulsing and pounding.
3. euph. for death of a ruler or ruler's chief wife.
4. (med.) sudden onset; e.g. ～波 bēngbō, swelling surge; pell-mell; ～迫 bēngpò, swift and sudden, abruptly, hurriedly, in no time.

祊　bēng　MC paeng
1. place of sacrifice to ancestors in the courtyard of ancestral temple.
    a. 2-part sacrifice to ancestors on successive days, first in the temple courtyard, then at the side of the gates.

絣　bēng　MC peang
1. braid or cord of different colors of twisted silk or of bast fibers.
2. cord for stringing shells.
3. connect, link up, join.

跰　bīng　MC pjieng
1. crisscross; interlock.

běng

嗙　běng　MC buwngX
1. rdup., lusciously lush, of fruit; profusely plenteous.

琫　běng　MC puwngX
1. ornamentation on the pommel or scabbard of a sword worn at the waist.

菶　běng　MC puwngX
1. rdup. or (bn.) ～茸 běngróng (MC puwngX-nyowng), lush and luxuriant, rank and rampant; rdup. (med.) also, mixed and messed, strewn and scattered, in deep disarray.

鞛　běng　MC puwngX　⊙ 琫 běng.

韸　běng　MC puwngX　⊙ 琫 běng.

bèng

塴　bèng　MC pongH
1. lower a coffin into the ground.

迸　bèng　MC peangH
1. run off in all directions; disperse, disband.
    a. dispel, repel, drive off.
2. burst open or out, surge out.
    a. break open, split open; shatter, fragment.

屏　bǐng　MC pjiengX
1. ⊙ 屏 bǐng 2 (→ píng), set aside; remove; withdraw from.

bī

偪　bī　MC pik　⊙ 逼 bī.

柀　bī　MC pjeX
1. China fir (Cunninghamia lanceolata); syn. 柀 shān (→ qián).
2. disintegrate, collapse, fall apart; smash, destroy.

福　bī　MC pik
1. sgl. or ～衡 bīhéng, horizontal length of wood attached to an ox's horns, by which it can be led or driven.

2. rack for holding arrows.
3. door-brace.

皀   bī   MC pik
1. old dialect word for a kernel, grain.

逼   bī   MC pik
1. press hard against; compel, urge, force.
   a. oppress; constrain.
   b. (bn.) 〜迸 *bībèng* (MC pik-peangX), coursing current, plunging rush; also, helter-skelter.
2. be hard by, crowd against; encroach on.
3. confined, crowded in; hemmed in; straitened; narrow.

鎞   bī   MC pej
1. (med.) long hairpin.
2. (med.) a medical probe, lancet, esp. for treating eye afflictions.
3. ⊙ 篦 *bì*, double-edged fine-toothed comb.

bí

鼻   bí   MC bjijH
1. nose; naric, narial, nasal; nostrils.
   a. to smell, sniff.
2. eyelet, grommet, esp. for threading.
   a. pierce the nose of an animal, to attach a ring for leading.
3. a distinctly protuberant part of an object, like the handle of a seal or boss of a mirror.
4. beginning, opening; inaugural, premier; e.g. 〜祖 *bízǔ*, earliest ancestors.
5. trsc. of Skt. *v*, e.g. (Budd.) 阿〜 *ābí* (MC 'a-bjijH), trsc. Skt *avī*[*ci*], "the interminable," lowest and most baleful of Budd. hells, syn. 無間 *wújiān*.

bǐ

俾   bǐ   MC pjieX
1. enable, cause, bring about; lead to, culminate in.
   pì   MC bjijH
1. (bn.) 〜倪 *pìnì* (MC bjijH-ngejH), ⊙ 埤堄 *pìnì*, → 埤 *pì*; also, look at askance.

匕   bǐ   MC pjijX
1. spoon; ladle.
   a. cmpd. 〜首 *bǐshǒu*, "spoon-head," dagger with a spoon-shaped handle.
2. arrowhead.

妣   bǐ   MC pjijX
1. mother, esp. deceased mother (cf. 考 *kǎo*, deceased father).
2. female ancestors of grandmother's generation and earlier.

彼   bǐ   MC pjeX
1. demonstrative pronoun indicating the one implied, understood, or singled out, also the one further removed or less obvious: that, those, the other, there; e.g. 〜一時此一時也 *bǐ yīshí cǐ yīshí yě*, That was one time, this is another time; 〜長而我長之 *bǐ zhǎng ér wǒ zhǎng zhī*, that one being elderly, I treat him as elderly; 所敬在此所長在〜 *suǒjìng zài cǐ suǒzhǎng zài bǐ*, the one shown respect lies here, the one shown honor as an elder lies there.
2. other(s), other than oneself or than subject; e.g. (Budd.) 〜岸 *bǐ'àn*, the other shore (of the stream of transmigration).
   a. 3rd-person pronoun: (s)he, they; e.g. 〜奪其民時 *bǐ duó qí mín shí*, they deprive their people of the proper (growing) season; 吾何畏〜哉 *wú hé wèi bǐ zāi*, why should I be in awe of them?

比   bǐ   MC pjijX
1. (put) side-by-side, parallel; bring together, juxtapose; compare.
   a. (lit.) analogy, parallel situation or description; esp. traditional poetic trope in *Shijing* that makes explicit comparison, simile.
   b. imitate; repeat, duplicate.
   c. comparable to; alike, similar.
   d. 〜目 *bǐmù*, by legend 2 one-eyed fish swimming as pair; also, flounder, various flatfish incl. sole and dab; (lit.) euph. for seemingly inseparable man and woman.
2. align with, associate with, collaborate.
   a. accord with, agree with; comply, accommodate.
3. sgl. or rdup., repeatedly; successively, consecutively.

a. all, each one of; e.g. ～家 *bǐjiā*, every household.

4. by the time that . . .; reaching the time that . . .; when . . .

    a. (med.) previously, formerly, past; e.g. ～日 *bǐrì*, former days.

5. near to, close to.

    a. (med.) near in time: recent(ly); ～者 *bǐzhe*, recently; ～來 *bǐlái*, recently; also, formerly; also, originally.

6. "closeness," name of 8th hexagram of the *Yijing*.

7. (Budd.) ～丘(尼) *bǐqiū(ní)* (MC bjijH-khjuw [-nrij]), trsc. Skt. *bhikṣu(ṇī)*, ordained male (or female) monastic.

秕　bǐ　MC pjijX

1. atrophied or stunted grain; grain that does not ear; kernel-less.

    a. worthless, purposeless, no-account, useless.

筆　bǐ　MC pit

1. writing-brush.

    a. write with a brush.

2. (med.) traces of the writing-brush; written text; paintings; calligraphy.

3. (med.) unrhymed or utilitarian writings, as distinguished from 文 *wén*, rhymed or refined writings.

鄙　bǐ　MC pijX

1. low, mean; vulgar, uncouth; rude, coarse; menial, uncultured, rough; plain.

    a. humilific self-reference: "My boorish self."

2. regard as of little or no account; vilipend.

3. administrative unit in Zhou times, comprising 500 households.

4. borderland settlement, border town.

    a. far-off locale; beyond the outskirts; the outback.

bì

必　bì　MC bjit

1. suffuse; cover everywhere.

2. rdup., stately and impressive, awe-inspiring.

坒　bì　MC bjijH

1. arrange by degrees, step-wise; terrace one above the other, as a stair.

    a. juxtapose; compare; correlate.

壁　bì　MC pek

1. wall.

2. sheer rockface; cliff.

3. protective embankment; rampart.

    a. fortification; stockade.

    b. to wall off; protect, barricade.

4. "Wall," one of the 28 lunar lodgings, comprised of α Andromedae and γ Pegasi, in the northern quadrant (*xuanwu* 玄武) of the sky; also called 天街 *tiānjiē* (Heaven's Street), 天梁 *tiānliáng* (Heaven's Bridge).

婢　bì　MC bjieX

1. female slave or servant.

    a. concubine.

嬖　bì　MC pejH

1. favor with affection or attention, treat with special fondness, be partial to.

    a. one treated in preceding way: a favorite, a minion; paramour.

幣　bì　MC bjiejH

1. offering of silk used in sacrifice or as a gift.

    a. an object of value used as a gift.

2. property, belongings; goods.

    a. an object of value used as currency.

    b. currency; money.

3. (med.) fine decor, trimmings.

庇　bì　MC pjijH

1. to cover, screen.

    a. protect, shelter.

庳　bì　MC bjieX

1. low, in size or stature.

    a. short; squat.

2. sunken; concave.

弊　bì　MC bjiejH

1. destroy(ed), tear down; ruin(ed), demolish(ed), wreck(ed); ravage(d).

    a. wasted, use(d) up; abuse(d); batter(ed); ill-treat(ed), mistreat(ed).

2. recreant; pernicious.

    a. malady; detriment; handicap, weakness, defect; drawback, disadvantage.

3. fall down; tumble forward.

4. rdup., exceedingly fastidious, officiously concerned, fussy and finicky, painstakingly meticulous, falling all over oneself with care.

5. ⊙ 敝 *bì* 4, self-depreciatory reference: "my humble (worthless) . . .."; 蔽 *bì*, cover over, conceal; protect, shelter.

弻   bì   MC bit

1. frame used for maintaining a bow's shape when it is unstrung.
   a. to correct; keep right, maintain.
2. assist(ant), aid(e).
   a. sustain; uphold.
3. "Straightener," name of one of the 2 supplementary or "hidden" stars of the Northern Dipper (the other is → 輔 *fǔ*), being an invisible star located amidst the Dipper's bowl.

彋   bì   MC pjit

1. shoot, let fly (an arrow).

必   bì   MC pjit

1. (ADV) necessarily, certainly; inevitably, invariably; is certain to VB (cf. 須 *xū*, need to), is sure to VB, will VB without fail, obliged to VB; make sure of.
2. (med.) sgl. or 〜其 *bìqí*, 〜若 *bìruò*, marker of conditional or hypothetical phrase: if (it is the case that . . .), supposing, let it be (as follows) . . .

怭   bì   MC bjit

1. rdup., nonchalant and unconcerned, rude and blasé.

愎   bì   MC bik

1. headstrong; obstinate, stubborn; willful; resistant to suggestion; intransigent, intractable.

擗   bì   MC bjiek

1. beat the breast.
2. open out; unfold.
   a. break open, rend.
3. (med.) slash at, swipe.

敝   bì   MC bjiejH

1. badly used, dilapidated; deteriorated; spoiled; ruined.
   a. worn out, used up; wasted; in poor shape.
2. destroy; bring down.
3. throw aside, throw out; discard.
4. self-depreciatory reference: "my humble (self) . . .; my worthless . . ."
5. ⊙ 蔽 *bì*, cover over, conceal, hide; protect.

斃   bì   MC bjiejH

1. fall forward, fall prone; slump down, esp. from illness or harm.
   a. drop dead; lay down one's body, die, perish.

柲   bì   MC pijH

1. handle, hilt, esp. of weapon.
2. bow-frame, for maintaining bow's shape when unstrung, ⊙ 弻 *bì* 1.

毖   bì   MC pijH

1. careful, attentive; cautious.
2. warn, caution against; admonish; exhort.
3. work hard at, take pains with; wear oneself out with effort.
4. ⊙ 泌 *bì*, bubble up; plash.

泌   bì   MC bjit

1. bubble up, as water from a spring; plash; spill out.

狴   bì   MC bejH

1. sgl. or 〜犴 *bì'àn*, animal of legendary ferocity, reputedly like a tiger or leopard; suitable guardian of prison doors > by metonymy, prison.

玜   bì   MC pjit

1. chape, ornamental jewel on the end of a scabbard.

璧   bì   MC pjiek

1. jade-disc, circlet, with round hole in middle; often used ceremonially and as symbolic of a covenant or guarantee, as between persons, states, heaven and a dynastic house, etc.

畁   bì   MC pjijH

1. give to, present to, bestow on; favor with.

畢   bì   MC pjit

1. long-handled net for catching birds or other small game; fork-net.
   a. to net game.
   b. 2-pronged pitchfork.
2. finish, bring to an end.
   a. (ADV) finally, at last; to the end.
   b. (med.) VB suffix indicating action is already finished.

3. all of, to the last one; completely.
4. (med.) be ready with, prepared for.
5. "Net," one of the 28 lunar lodgings, comprised of 8 stars in the shape of a game-net, equiv. Hyades, in the western quadrant (*baihu* 白虎) of the sky; cmpd. ～昴 *bìmǎo*, "Net and Mane," Hyades and Pleiades, constellations that appear in autumn and signal the decline of the year.

痹　bì　MC pjijH
1. pain or stiffness caused by cold or damp; rheumatism.
   a. numbness; paralysis.

皕　bì　MC pik
1. two hundred.

眒　bì　MC pijH
1. (med.) stare intently, glare; glower, scowl.

碧　bì　MC pjaek
1. semi-precious stone of blue-green color.
2. color midway between blue and green; can shade in either direction, depending on context; cyan-blue, bright light-blue, deeply saturated blue (esp. of sky or water, e.g. ～空 *bikōng*, "the cyan void," ～溪 *bìxī*, deep- or bright-blue stream); leek-green, prasine, pea-green, smaragd, emerald (esp. of vegetation, e.g. ～樹 *bìshù*, prase-green trees).

祕　bì　MC pijH　→ 祕 *mì*.

箅　bì　MC pejH
1. perforated plate, usu. of bamboo, placed between the 2 halves of a double boiler, upon which food is steamed, or wicker basket lowered into a kettle for steaming rice.

篦　bì　MC pej
1. double-edged fine-toothed comb.

筆　bì　MC pjit
1. wicker gate, usu. of brushwood or bamboo.
   a. anything made of wickerwork.
2. (med.) (bn.) ～篥 *bìlì* (MC pjit-lit), Central Asian reed-pipe, reed-whistle, a double-reed cylindrical pipe with 7 fingerholes, 2 thumbholes, and an elliptical restraining hoop surrounding the reeds, somewhat resembling an oboe; ⊙ 觱篥 *bìlì*.

罼　bì　MC pjit
1. ⊙ 畢 *bì* 1, long-handled net for catching birds and other small game; fork-net.

臂　bì　MC pjieH
1. arm; esp. forearm, below the elbow.
2. grip of a bow; handle of a crossbow.

胜　bì　MC bejH　⊙ 髀 *bì*.

苾　bì　MC bjit
1. fragrant, aromatic, odoriferous; rdup., heavily redolent, deeply fragrant.

萆　bì　MC pjiejH
1. ～麻 *bìmá*, "tick-hemp," castor-oil plant (*Ricinus communis*).
2. ⊙ 蔽 *bì* 1, 2, cover over, conceal, hide; protect.

蓽　bì　MC pjit
1. (bn.) ～茇 *bibá* (MC pjit-bat), ～撥 *bibō* (MC pjit-pat), long pepper, pipal (*Piper longum*).
   a. ～澄茄 *bìchéngqié*, cubeb, Java pepper (*Piper cubeba*).
   b. (med.) sgl. or cmpd. ～豆 *bìdòu*, garden pea.
2. ⊙ 篳 *bì*, wicker door; wickerwork.

蔽　bì　MC pjiejH
1. cover over; conceal, hide, camouflage (more abstract than 掩 *yǎn*).
   a. mask, veil; keep from sight; blinker(ed).
   b. occlude; shade, put in the shade; darken.
   c. block out; impede, obstruct(ion).
2. protect; shelter; close around, close up.
3. extend over, cover all parts of; include, contain; sum up.
4. (bn.) ～芾 *bifèi* (MC pjiejH-pj+jH), runty, stunted; half-grown, immature, undeveloped.
5. decide; judge, adjudicate.
6. game-piece, draughtsman.

薜　bì　MC bejH
1. (bn.) ～荔 *bìlì* (MC bejH-lejH) creeping fig (*Ficus pumila*); also used metaphorically to describe garb of recluse.
bò　MC peak
1. Chinese angelica (*Angelica sinensis*), "female ginseng," an herb commonly used in traditional Chinese medicine.
2. wild or uncultivated hemp.

bó   MC baewk

1. to split, to break in two.

pì   MC phek

1. ⊙ 僻 *pì* isolated, remote.

裨   bì   MC pjie   → 裨 *pí.*

襞   bì   MC pjiek

1. pleat, fold, crease; plicate, ruck, shirr; a gathering of fabric.

    a. (bn.) ～襀 *bìjī* (MC pjiek-tsjek), pleated and plicate, crease and crimp.

觱   bì   MC pjit

1. (bn.) ～沸 *bìfèi* (MC pjit-pj+jH), spurt and bubble, as of springwater.

2. (bn.) ～發 *bìbō* (MC pjit-pat), bitter and biting, chill and frigid, of cold winter wind.

3. (med.) (bn.) ～篥 *bìlì* (MC pjit-lit), Central Asian reed-pipe, reed-whistle, a double-reed cylindrical pipe with 7 fingerholes, 2 thumbholes, and an elliptical restraining hoop surrounding the reeds, somewhat resembling an oboe; ⊙ 篳篥 *bìlì.*

詖   bì   MC pjeH

1. one-sided, tendentious; prejudiced.

    a. biased, slanted, skewed.

賁   bì   MC pjeH

1. decorate(d), embellish(ed), adorn(ed), ornate; highly-wrought; refine(d).

2. "refinement," name of 22nd hexagram of the *Yijing.*

bēn   MC pwon

1. ⊙ 奔 *bēn*, run, hasten; flee.

2. fleet-footed; agile, rapid; e.g. 虎～ *hǔbēn*, "agile as tigers," epithet for soldiers.

fén   MC bjun

1. large in size.

2. protuberant; uplifted.

歕   bì   MC bijH

1. tremendous; overpowering; forceful, formidable; mighty, powerful.

    a. ～屓 *bìxì* (MC bijH-xijH), exerting enormous power, fearsomely forceful.

蹕   bì   MC pjit

1. clear the road and prohibit other traffic when the ruler goes out.

2. (med.) imperial retinue, cortege.

躃   bì   MC pjiek   ⊙ 躃 *bì.*

躄   bì   MC pjiek

1. lame; hamstrung; limping; halt of foot.

辟   bì   MC pjiek

1. law, statute; set right by law, apply the law.

    a. judicial punishment; penal sentence; chastise(ment).

2. crime, criminal act; miscreant; malfeasance.

3. gen. term for sovereign and nobility; orbi-principian; baronial; e.g. ～公 *bìgōng*, 百～ *bǎibì*, the host of high lords.

4. summon to official service; appoint to office; ordain to a post.

5. expel, get rid of; eliminate; e.g. ～穀 *bìgǔ*, eliminate grains from the diet.

6. (bn.) ～易 *bìyì* (MC pjiek-yek), flee in fear, turn tail terrified.

7. (Budd.) ～支伽 *bìzhīqié* (MC pjiek-tsye-gia), trsc. Skt. *pratyeka*, one who lives in an age without a buddha and attains enlightenment on his own.

8. ⊙ 避 *bì*, avoid, get free of; renounce; 躄 *bì*, lame, limping; 嬖 *bì*, treat with special fondness; a favorite.

pì   MC bjiek

1. ⊙ 闢 *pì*, break open; open for use, reclaim (land); clear away; develop; 僻 *pì*, far to one side, off-center; distorted, perverted; 譬 *pì*, compare, draw a parallel with; 睥 *pì*, (bn.) ～睨 *pìnì*, → 睥 *pì.*

避   bì   MC bjieH

1. avoid, evade, elude; shun, keep away from, get out of the way of; turn away from.

    a. put distance between, move away; give way; get free of.

    b. renounce; abandon; let alone.

2. not come up to the level of, be inferior to.

閉   bì   MC pejH

1. bar a gate.

    a. to bar; lock; doorbar, doorbrand; barricade.

2. obstruct, block off; close off.

    a. shut away, hide.

3. stop, put an end to.

4. old term ref. 2 fortnightly periods called 立秋 *lìqiū* (advent of autumn) and 立冬 *lìdōng* (advent of winter).

5. ⊙ 祕 *bì* 2, bow-frame, for keeping bow's shape when unstrung.

閟 bì MC pijH
1. close a gate; close in, shut in.
2. close up, shut away; hide, cover up; block out, block up.
3. bring to a close, conclude; complete; finish; shut the door on.
4. quiet, still; closed off from outside disturbances; private, secret.

陛 bì MC bejX
1. steps, stairs, esp. those leading to the throne.
  a. cmpd. 〜下 bìxià, "you below the throne-steps," indirect form of address to ruler as if speaking to (and through) those close to him owing to his unapproachability: "Your exalted majesty"; also, deferential address from one gentleman to another: "my good sir."
2. lower platform of a 2-tier hall (cf. 階 jiē 2, upper platform).

韠 bì MC pjit
1. untreated leather knee-covers, worn outside garments, used in sacrificial ceremonies.

馝 bì MC bjit
1. savory-smelling food; deliciously aromatic.

柲 bì MC bjit
1. (med.) ⊙ 苾 bì, aromatic, odoriferous.

駜 bì MC bjit
1. stout and strong, well-fed, of horses.

髀 bì MC bejX
1. femur; thigh.
  a. by extension, buttocks; haunch(es); gluteal.
2. gnomon of a sun-dial.

髲 bì MC bjeH
1. a switch of hair; false hair, wig.

biān

甂 biān MC pen
1. earthenware plate or platter.

砭 biān MC pjem
1. needle or lance(t) made of highly sharpened stone, for medical use
  a. to lance, pierce; probe; puncture; prick.
2. (med.) to cure; remedy, correct.

籩 biān MC pen
1. bamboo tazza, to contain dry food-offerings in ritual sacrifice.

編 biān MC pjien
1. string together bamboo writing-slips.
  a. a bundle of such strips, constituting a book or section of a book.
  b. compile; edit.
2. plait, weave.
  a. bind together, connect different parts together to make one whole.
3. arrange in order; put in sequence; in a row, sequential.
4. 〜草 biāncǎo, knotgrass, knotweed (Polygonum aviculare), ⊙ 萹 biān.

萹 biān MC pen
1. sgl. or 〜蓄 biānxù, 〜筑 biānzhú, knotgrass, knotweed, doorweed (Polygonum aviculare).

蝙 biān MC pen
1. (bn.) 〜蝠 biānfú (MC pen-pjuwk), the bat (Chiropterae).

邊 biān MC pen
1. border, edge; margin; flank.
  a. border region, frontier; boundary.
2. side, by the side of; adjacent.
3. (med.) a part of something; aspect; facet.
4. 〜雁齒 biānyànchǐ, dryopteris, male-fern (Dryopteris crassirhizoma, Dryopteris filix-mas).

鞭 biān MC pjien
1. horsewhip, made of leather; lash, thong; goad.
  a. to whip, lash, flog; flagellate.
  b. incite to action, whip up, flog on; goad.

鯿 biān MC pjien
1. "flat-fish," bream, esp. white bream (Parabramis pekinensis); syn. 魴 fáng.

biǎn

惼 biǎn MC penX
1. ⊙ 褊 biǎn 2, constricted in view or temper; tense, high-strung, edgy; strained; fretful.

扁 biǎn MC penX
1. horizontally inscribed board, plaque, or placard, usu. with name of a place or structure.

2. flat; thin and evenly spread.
3. ～豆 *biǎndòu*, "flatbean," lablab bean, hyacinth bean (*Dolichos lablab, Lablab purpureus*).

    piān   MC phjien
1. ～舟 *piānzhōu*, flatboat, skiff.

窆   biǎn   MC pjiemX
1. lower a coffin into the grave; lay to rest.
    a. bury; inter, inhume.
2. grave, tomb-pit.

褊   biǎn   MC pjienX
1. narrowly cut clothing.
    a. narrow; close; tight, taut.
    b. small; skimpy, scanty.
2. constricted in view or temper, narrow-minded; strait-laced, tense, high-strung, edgy; uptight; strained; mean-spirited.

貶   biǎn   MC pjemX
1. reduce; diminish.
2. reduce in rank or responsibility; demote; degrade.
3. devalue; criticize; blame, cast aspersions (ant. 襃 *bāo* 2a, praise, speak generously of).

鶣   biǎn   MC pjenX
1. sore-hawk, immature hawk (2 yrs. old or less), in 2nd stage (of 3) of plumage change.

biàn

便   biàn   MC bjienH
1. ease(ful), comfortable; convenient; expedient.
    a. read(il)y; at hand, handy, at one's disposal.
    b. (med.) place at one's disposal, lend, esp. goods or money (usu. at interest).
2. advantageous, beneficial; e.g. ～宜 *biànyí*, beneficial, fit the circumstances; also, get the better of, find an opportunity's advantage.
3. skilled, practiced; proficient.
4. relieve oneself, ease nature; e.g. 小～ *xiǎobiàn*, urinate; 大～ *dàbiàn*, defecate.
5. normal, ordinary; everyday; casual.
6. (med.) then, thereupon.
    a. (med.) right then, immediately.
    b. (med.) already.
7. (med.) on the contrary, to the contrary.
    a. (med.) even if, granting that.

    pián   MC bjien
1. shrewd in speaking, slick, glib; guileful; e.g. rdup. or (bn.) ～辟 *piánbì* (MC bjien-bjiek), glib and guileful, smooth-talking; also, fawning and flattering.
2. rdup., full-bellied, roundbellied, well-fed, fat and full.

卞   biàn   MC bjenH
1. law; rule.
2. impatient, nervous; impetuous; irascible.

弁   biàn   MC bjenH
1. men's conical cap made of animal skin or hide, worn in Zhou times for everyday observances.
    a. cap made of maroon cloth or silk, worn for sacrificial rituals.
    b. cap made of white deerskin, worn during hunts or in military service.
    c. cap bestowed at age of manhood (20 *sui*).
2. (med.) place in front, at the head of, at the beginning, such as preface of a text.
3. fight barehanded.

徧   biàn   MC penH   ⊙ 遍 *biàn*.

忭   biàn   MC bjenH
1. happy, glad; gay; elated.

抃   biàn   MC bjenH
1. clap one's hands, in delight or rhythmically to music.
    a. to hail, applaud.
2. slap; tap, rap.

拚   biàn   MC bjenH
1. ⊙ 抃 *biàn*, clap the hands; slap.
    pān   MC phaen
1. throw aside, cast away; set aside.
    fān   MC phjon
1. ⊙ 翻 *fān*, flutter; fly up.

艑   biàn   MC benX
1. large shipping vessel, transport boat.

變   biàn   MC pjenX
1. change, alter(ation), variation, permute, permutation; change into, transform(ation).
    a. external, momentary or apparent change, e.g. change of animal's coat or plumage; molt; shed.

b. deviation, when change becomes too great.

2. sudden change from the expected order of things; catastrophe; mischance, miscarriage; reversal.

    a. factious incident, insurrection; revolt, rebellion.

3. adapt(ation); versatile, variable; flexible.

    a. capricious, changeable.

4. unusual, unordinary; unfamiliar.

5. (Budd.) trsc. of Skt. *puṇya*, merit[orious deed] < Turk. *buyan* (with metathesis).

辨　**biàn**　MC bjenX

1. differentiate, tell apart, distinguish; single out; divide into constituent parts.

    a. discern, make out, ascertain; decipher; explain the reason why.

    b. distinct, discrete; clear-cut.

2. ⊙ 辯 *biàn*, dispute, argue; eloquent; 遍 *biàn*, everywhere, pervasive.

    bàn　MC beanH

1. manage, deal with; succeed in doing, complete; prepare, provide with.

辮　**biàn**　MC benX

1. sew together, tie together; weave; join.

2. hair-braid, plait.

辯　**biàn**　MC bjenH

1. argue out alternatives, dispute; debate, controvert.

    a. quibble, cavil; quarrel over; querulous, captious.

2. eloquent; well-spoken, articulate; persuasive.

3. ⊙ 辨 *biàn*, differentiate, distinguish; define; 變 *biàn* 1, change, transform.

遍　**biàn**　MC penH

1. everywhere, all around; widely, extensively; far and wide; pervasive; spread everywhere.

    a. (Budd.) ～香 *biànxiāng*, "everywhere fragrant," trns. of Skt. *paricitra*, mythical paradise tree whose fragrance is pervasive.

2. (med.) measure-word for actions that are complete from beginning to end, e.g. recitings or readings of a text, performances of a multipart musical piece.

biāo

彪　**biāo**　MC pjiw

1. tiger stripes.

    a. by synecdoche, tiger.

2. richly figured, distinctively patterned, brightly trimmed; striated.

杓　**biāo**　MC pjiew

1. handle of a spoon or ladle.

    a. the 5th, 6th, and 7th stars of the Big Dipper (ε, ζ, η Ursae Majoris) which make up the constellation's handle.

2. pull out or away, draw out or from.

3. strike, smite; batter, beat.

    sháo　MC dzyak

1. ⊙ 勺 *sháo* 1, ladle, spoon.

標　**biāo**　MC pjiew

1. crown of a tree, highest branches.

2. tip or end of a branch; nib.

    a. end-point; extremity; acme, zenith.

3. most visible exterior manifestation; conspicuous, salient.

4. guidepost; sign, emblem; ensign.

    a. signal; flag.

    b. indicate, betoken; mark, signify; make known; show forth.

5. standard; criterion; norm.

瀌　**biāo**　MC pjew

1. rdup., squalling and pelting, falling thick and fast, of rain or snow.

熛　**biāo**　MC pjiew

1. flash; spark(le), flicker; twinkle; gleam; flame, blaze.

2. ⊙ 飆 *biāo*, tempest; whirlwind; shimmer(ing).

猋　**biāo**　MC pjiew

1. run quickly, dash, hightail; speed, race, rush.

2. ⊙ 飆 *biāo*, tempest, gale; whirlwind; shimmering light.

穮　**biāo**　MC pjew

1. to weed a field.

臕　**biāo**　MC pjew

1. (med.) fat(ty), fleshy; pinguid; suety.

鑣   biāo   MC pjew
1. horse's cheek-bar, bit; e.g. 揚～ *yángbiāo*, jerk the bit, take control.
   a. by synecdoche, horse.
2. rdup., gorgeously trimmed, lavishly decked (esp. of a horse).

颮   biāo   MC pjiew   ⊙ 飆 *biāo*.

飆   biāo   MC pjiew
1. tempest, flaw; sudden violent onset of wind; squall, gale, bluster; whirlwind; gust(y).
2. shimmering, rapidly and violently shaking light.

颷   biāo   MC pjiew   ⊙ 飆 *biāo*.

驫   biāo   MC pjiew
1. running apace, galloping rapidly.

髟   biāo   MC pjiew
1. long (human) hair; fringe; shag(gy).
2. (bn.) ～鼬 *biāoyòu* (MC pjiew-yuwH), drifting and floating; rippling and waving.
   piào   MC phjiewH
1. (animal) mane, esp. long.

麃   biāo   MC pjew
1. to weed a field, ⊙ 穮 *biāo*.
2. rdup., bold and brave, martial and mighty; also, ⊙ 瀌瀌 *biāobiāo*, falling (or coming) thick and fast.
   páo   MC baew
1. a kind of roe-deer, variously equated with 麅 *páo* or 麞 *zhāng*

biǎo

表   biǎo   MC pjewX
1. outer clothing, outerwear; outer layer of clothing.
   a. adorn, deck out, trim.
2. exterior, outer side of; far side of, beyond (ant. 裏 *lǐ*, inside, within).
   a. border, line-marker.
3. show outwardly; manifest, exhibit; express, announce; publish; inform.
   a. (lit.) manifesto, memorial, exposition; genre of prose writing, usu. presented to the throne and expressing one's opinions regarding governmental matters; to memorialize.

4. indicate, signify, mark; standard, norm, criterion; ⊙ 標 *biāo* 4-5.
5. gnomon of a sundial.
   a. gauge; measure; judge.
6. chart, table; schematic layout of information.
7. prefix ref. to collateral cousins from father's sisters or mother's siblings (cf. 從 *cóng*).

裱   biǎo   MC pjiewX
1. woman's headwrap.
2. protective end of scroll.

褾   biǎo   MC pjiewX
1. (med.) sleeve-cuff; wrist-band.
2. (med.) decorative edging of a cap.

biào

摽   biào   MC bjiewX
1. strike, hit; beat.
   a. strike one's breast.
2. fall, drop, plop down; shed.
   biāo   MC pjiew
1. wave away, wave aside; throw off, throw aside.
   a. lift away, rise up; stream out.
2. ⊙ 標 *biāo* 4, sign, emblem, ensign; show forth, indicate, betoken.

biē

鱉   biē   MC pjiet
1. lesser soft-shelled turtle, trionyx (*Amyda sinensis*) (cf. 黿 *yuán*, greater soft-shelled turtle).
2. bracken (*Pteridium excelsum*), syn. 蕨 *jué*.

bié

別   bié   MC pjet
1. to separate, part (from); set apart; detach; divide.
   a. (med.) discern, distinguish, see or consider separately.
2. additional(ly); (an)other; adjunct.
   a. (med.) distinctive(ly); special(ly); extraordinary, particular(ly); separately, each itself...
   MC bjet
1. be separated, parted; set apart; detached; divided; e.g. ～宮 *biégōng*, detached palace; ～業 *biéyè*, villa, country residence.

襒　bié　MC bet
1. wipe; wipe off or away; wipe down, brush off (as in cleaning).

蹩　bié　MC bet
1. (bn.) ～躠 biéxiè (MC bet-sjet), limp lamely, drag one foot after the other, trudge and plod, shuffle and stagger.

biè

鷩　biè　MC pjiet
1. the golden pheasant (*Chrysolophus pictus*).

bīn

彬　bīn　MC pin
1. rdup., half-and-half, in equal parts, evenly distributed; proportioned conformity, poised in proportion; esp. ref. to equally balanced substance and ornament, base and polish, matter and manner.

斌　bīn　MC pin　⊙ 彬 *bīn*.

檳　bīn　MC pjin
1. (med.) (bn.) ～榔 bīnláng (MC pjin-lang; cf. Malay *pinang*), areca palm, betel palm (*Areca catechu*), also the betel-nut, areca-nut.

濱　bīn　MC pjin
1. waterfront, riverbank, seashore.
    a. edge, margin; border, boundary.
2. adjoin, be adjacent to.
3. approach, close to; at the point of, at the brink of.

瀕　bīn　MC pjin　⊙ 濱 *bīn*.

玢　bīn　MC pin
1. (bn.) ～豳 bīnbīn (MC pin-pin), striped and streaked, barred and banded.

繽　bīn　MC phjin
1. sgl. or in bn. ～紛 bīnfēn (MC phjin-phjun), profuse, copious, plentiful; diverse and varied, mixed and multifarious, jumbled and muddled, mixed and mingled, full and flurrying.
2. variegated, mixed in color.

豳　bīn　MC pin
1. area in central Shaanxi where Gong Liu 公劉, reputed distant ancestor of the Zhou 周 people and great-grandson of the mythical Hou Ji 后稷, founded his state.
2. (bn.) 玢～ bīnbīn, → 玢 *bīn*.

賓　bīn　MC pjin
1. guest, usu. invited or honored; cf. 客 *kè*, guest, stranger; disciple, retainer (often uninvited).
    a. be a guest, behave as a guest > recognize or submit to someone's authority.
    b. treat as a guest, receive as a guest.
    c. treat with decorum.
    d. (med.) ～客 bīnkè, "honored retainer," monitor, in Tang times one of 4 individuals supervising the everyday conduct of the heir-apparent.
        　bìn　MC pjinH
1. ⊙ 擯 *bìn*, expel, reject, shun; 儐 *bìn*, person doing the honors at a ceremony.

邠　bīn　MC pin
1. ⊙ 豳 *bīn*, first-founded city of Zhou ancestor Gong Liu; 彬 *bīn*, perfectly proportioned between substance and refinement.

鑌　bīn　MC pjin
1. (med.) finely fused iron, wrought iron.

bìn

儐　bìn　MC pjinH
1. receive or entertain as a guest.
    a. person doing the honors at a ceremony.
2. arrange, set up, dispose properly.
3. ⊙ 擯 *bìn*, expel, reject, shun.
        　bīn　MC pjin
1. treat with respect, esp. ancestors or spirits in sacrifice.

擯　bìn　MC pjinH
1. throw out, expel; reject; shun.
    a. reprehend, censure.
2. ⊙ 儐 *bìn* 1, receive guests.

殯　bìn　MC pjinH
1. encoffin a corpse in preparation for burial.
    a. lay out a corpse in coffin.
    b. place where the encoffined corpse is kept before burial.

2. final preparations for burial, esp. conveying coffin to tombsite.

臏   bìn   MC bjinX
1. kneecap, patella; shinbone, tibia.
2. punishment of cutting off kneecap or the lower legs.

髕   bìn   MC binX   ⊙ 臏 *bìn*.

鬢   bìn   MC pjinH
1. temple-hair; earlocks, sidelocks.
   a. tresses; dangling curls, freaks.

bīng

兵   bīng   MC pjaeng
1. armaments, weapons.
   a. man-at-arms, soldier; army, troops.
   b. warfare.

冰   bīng   MC ping
1. ice; icy; frozen.
   a. frigid, cold, gelid.

捀   bīng   MC ping
1. cover of an arrow-quiver.

bǐng

丙   bǐng   MC pjaengX
1. 3rd of the 10 heavenly stems; used for "C" in a sequential order.
   a. ～夜 *bǐngyè*, 3rd of the 5 night-watches, approx. 11 p.m.-1 a.m.

柄   bǐng   MC pjaengH
1. axe-handle.
   a. gen. term for handle, haft, hilt.
   b. basis, basic, fundamental.
2. grasp by hand, control, wield; govern; authority; power.
3. object of discussion, topic taken up.
4. tenon, often with 鑿 *zuò* (*záo*) mortise.

棅   bǐng   MC pjaengH   ⊙ 柄 *bǐng*.

炳   bǐng   MC pjaengX
1. bright, brilliant; splendid.
   a. illumine, shine on, light.
2. set alight, set fire to, kindle.

稟   bǐng   MC pimX   ⊙ 稟 *bǐng*.

秉   bǐng   MC pjaengX
1. hold in hand, take up by hand, grasp.
   a. hold onto; maintain, preserve; conserve; persist in.
2. sheaf or bundle of grain-stalks.
3. measure of capacity, equiv. 16 *hu* 斛 ("bushels"), 160 *dou* 斗 ("pecks").
4. ⊙ 柄 *bǐng* 2, control, wield; authority, power.

秉   bǐng   MC pimX
1. receive from above, accept in bestowal.
   a. bestow on, grant to.
2. endowment received from Heaven; one's constitution, natural qualities.
   a. unique characteristics, quiddity.
3. (med.) report to a superior.
   lǐn   MC limX
1. ⊙ 廩 *lǐn*, granary; grain rations.

邴   bǐng   MC pjaengX
1. rdup., glad and gleeful, overjoyed.

鞞   bǐng   MC pengX
1. scabbard or sheath for sword.
   a. scabbard's ornamentation.
   pí   MC bej
1. ⊙ 鼙 *pí*, small war-drum used on horseback.

餅   bǐng   MC pjiengX
1. various doughy concoctions, ranging from noodles to buns and balls; wheat foods; pasta.

麨   bǐng   MC pjiengX   ⊙ 餅 *bǐng*.

bìng

並   bìng   MC bengX
1. side by side, coordinate(d); equally; both; in parallel.
   a. (al)together, uniformly.
   b. (med.) completely, entirely.
2. moreover, what's more; and also.
3. by the side of, alongside; trace along the edge.
4. at the same time, simultaneous(ly).

併   bìng   MC pjiengH
1. conjoin, combine; bring two things together; attach; annex.

2. together; both; equally, on a par with; uniformly.
3. (med.) entirely, completely.
######　bǐng　MC pjeng
1. ⊙ 屏 bǐng (píng) 2, set aside; remove, withdraw from.

幷　bìng　MC pjiengH
1. combine two things, conjoin (with), join together; match; attach to, annex; e.g. ～夾 bìngjiā, "double pincer," pliers, to pull arrows from target; ～線 bìngxiàn, combine 2 or more single yarns by twisting them together, "doubling."
2. (med.) be like, resemble; coordinate with; juxtapose.
3. (med.) preceding negative phrase, adds emphasis: absolutely (not), definitely (not).
4. ⊙ 並 bìng 1, together, in parallel, on a par with; equally, both; uniformly. N.B. This usage of the graph ～ relatively rare until after the Tang.

病　bìng　MC bjaengH
1. ill(ness), sick(ness); disease; descriptive of wide range of symptoms, from fatigue to critical conditions.
　　a. malady, ail(ment); indisposition, infirmity.
2. fault, defect, imperfection, failing.
3. troubled about or by, disturbed by, uneasy about.
　　a. solicitous about, concerned over.
　　b. deplore, find objectionable.

竝　bìng　MC bengX　⊙ 並 bìng.

bō

剝　bō　MC paewk
1. strip off or peel the outer layer; to bark, skin, hull, husk.
　　a. flay, excoriate (literal and figurative).
　　b. shave off or away, shear.
2. exploit, use selfishly, peel away another's benefits.
3. fall off, drop away.
4. "peeling away," name of 23rd hexagram of the Yijing.

撥　bō　MC pat
1. scatter, disperse; spread out, spread far.
　　a. sweep open, spread open, spread wide.
2. throw out, sweep away; get rid of; dismiss; eliminate, remove.
　　a. refuse, reject; e.g. (Budd.) ～無 bōwú, deny belief in.
3. vibrate, shake.
　　a. pluck the strings (of a chordophone); by metonymy, a plectrum.
　　b. (med.) (bn.) ～剌 bōlà (MC pat-lat), onom. of flick and pluck of zither strings, or flap and flick of fish-fins.
4. put in order, arrange.
5. break apart, break off.
　　a. crooked, bent.

播　bō　MC paH
1. sow, disseminate; broadcast.
　　a. disperse; spread.
2. change location freely, stray, ramble, drift.
　　a. flee from, run away.
3. fling off, cast away, throw out; reject.
######　bǒ　MC paX
1. ⊙ 簸 bǒ, winnow; stir; shake, joggle.

波　bō　MC pa
1. wave (of water); breaker, whitecap; surf.
　　a. undulate, ripple; wrinkle; wind round.
2. well up, surge; flow; rush, gush.
3. sweep or slide a glance over; turn one's gaze on.
4. (Budd.) ～羅密 bōluómì (MC pa-la-mit), trsc. Skt. pāramitā, perfection; (med.) also, jackfruit tree (Artocarpus heterophyllus) and fruit, imported from Southeast Asia; (Budd.) ～羅竭諦 bōluójiédì (MC ba-la-gjot-tejH), "gone to the farther shore."
5. (med.) ～律 bōlǜ (MC pa-lwit), Balūr, kingdom in the Gilgit valley; syn. 勃律 bólǜ.
######　bēi　MC pje
1. ⊙ 陂 bēi 2, embankment; embanked pond or pool.

玻　bō　MC pha
1. (med.) (bn.) ～璃 bōlí (MC pha-lje), transparent or lightly tinted glass, brought from the Western Regions in Tang times usu. in the form of blown cups, pots, dishes, etc.; sometimes, quartz crystal.

磻　bō　MC pa
1. sharp stone, perhaps flint, from which arrowtips were made.

鉢　bō　MC pat　⊙ 鉢 bō.

襏　bō　MC pat

1. 〜襫 *bōshì*, straw- or rush-woven raincloak.

鉢　bō　MC pat

1. small bowl.
   a. (Budd.) abb. trsc. of Skt. *pātra*, alms-bowl of a monk.

餑　bō　MC bwot

1. froth or bubbles on the surface of a cup of tea.

餺　bō　MC pak

1. (med.) (bn.) 〜飥 *bōtuō* (MC pak-thak), short noodles.

bó

伯　bó　MC paek

1. 1st in seniority of a sequence of 3 or 4 brothers (2=仲 *zhòng*, 3=叔 *shū*, 4=季 *jì*).
2. sgl. or 〜父 *bófù*, father's elder brother; 〜母 *bómǔ*, wife of father's elder brother.
3. 3rd of the 5 ranks of nobility, usu. translated "count" or "earl."
4. in pre-imperial times, source of authority in a particular region, "the Sire of X."
5. in pre-imperial times, chief of an alliance of feudal lords; ⊙ 霸 *bà*.
6. (med.) 〜勞 *bóláo*, various species of shrike (*Laniidae*).
7. (med.) 〜濟 *bójì* (MC paek-tsejH), Paekche, name of med. kingdom occupying most of western portion of Korean peninsula; syn. 百濟 *bǎijì*.
8. ⊙ 佰 *bǎi*, a company of 100 soldiers; leader of such a company: centurion, kentarch; 陌 *mò*, cross-path between fields, balk, terry.

勃　bó　MC bwot

1. burgeon, flourish.
2. burst out, surge up; insurgent; pop, puff; explode.
   a. sgl. or 〜然 *bórán*, 〜如 *bórú*, sudden(ly), all of a sudden, abrupt(ly), forthwith; quickly changing, volatile > seething, short-tempered.
3. (med.) (bn.) 〜窣 *bósū* (MC bwot-swot), short and squat; also, cramped and confined; also, walk with mincing steps.

4. (med.) 〜律 *bólü* (MC bwot-lwit), Balūr, kingdom in the Gilgit valley; syn. 波律 *bōlü*.
5. ⊙ 渤 *bó*, bubbling; breaking, surging (of waves); 孛 *bèi*, perihelial (tailed) comet; 悖 *bèi*, contrary, counter, recalcitrant; erroneous, absurd; misleading.

博　bó　MC pak

1. to the broadest degree possible; broad, wide-ranging, extensive, vast.
   a. universal, catholic, all-inclusive; encyclopedic.
   b. extensively, amply; wholly, completely; utterly.
2. barter, exchange; purchase.
3. casting sticks or rods, such as those used in the game *liubo* 六〜 ("six rods"); also ref. various board-games using draughtsmen or tokens.
   a. to game, gamble; e.g. 〜徒 *bótú*, gamester; also (med.), of a gambler's character, inferior, lowly, mean.

帛　bó　MC baek

1. gen. term for silk or anything made of silk, esp. tabby or plain-weave silk.
2. (Budd.) when used as surname for monk, ethnonym indicating Khotanese ancestry.

搏　bó　MC pak

1. set one's hand to.
   a. clutch at, claw at; fight hand-to-hand; wrestle with.
   b. grab, seize; clutch; hold onto.
   c. set upon, assault.
   d. strike, beat.
   e. clap, smack.

柏　bó　MC paek

1. cypress; esp. thuja or arborvitae; symbolic of long life and endurance in adversity; often planted with pines around gravesites.
   a. 扁〜 *piānbó*, "flat cypress," or 偏〜 *piānbó*, "sideways cypress," both *Thuja orientalis*; 刺〜 *cìbó*, "prickly cypress," i.e. juniper.
   b. 黃〜 *huángbó*, cork-tree; syn. 黃蘗 *huángbò*, → 蘗 *bò*.

欂　bó　MC pak

1. (bn.) 〜櫨 *bólú*, term for bracket construction, ref. bracket-arm and cap-block of column that supports roofbeams.

泊 **bó** **MC bak**
1. moor a boat; come to anchor.
 a. pause; come to rest.
2. sedate, tranquil.
3. ripple, riffle.
4. ⊙ 薄 *bó* 1, thin; meager, paltry.
 pō **MC bak**
1. (med.) small lake, usu. manmade.

浡 **bó** **MC bwot**
1. burst forth.
 a. bubble up; froth.

渤 **bó** **MC bwot**
1. bubble, boil.
 a. breaker, surging wave; esp. cmpd. ～海 *bóhǎi* or ～澥 *bóxiè*, the Surging Sea, i.e. East China Sea.
 b. (med.) froth on boiled tea.

礴 **bó** **MC bak**
1. (bn.) 磅～ *pángbó*, → 磅 *páng*; (bn.) 磐～ *pánbó*, → 磐 *pán*.
2. (bn.) 槃～ *pánbó*, → 槃 *pán*.

箔 **bó** **MC bak**
1. (med.) screen made of bamboo or reeds.
2. (med.) bamboo tray for raising silkworms.
3. (med.) thinly beaten leaf or sheet of metal.

簙 **bó** **MC pak**
1. board-game, ⊙ 博 *bó* 3.

膊 **bó** **MC pak** → 膊 *pò*.

舶 **bó** **MC baek**
1. (med.) ocean-going vessel, esp. merchant ship, argosy.

艴 **bó** **MC bwot**
1. enraged, furious < face suddenly contorted with anger.
 a. flushed.

葍 **bó** **MC bok**
1. (bn.) 蘿～ *luóbó*, → 蘿 *luó*; (bn.) 薝～ *zhánbó*, → 薝 *zhán*.

薄 **bó** **MC bak**
1. dense undergrowth, underbrush, tangle; bosk, copse, thicket; swath, mead.
2. crowd, crush; press against, force; push near to, close to; e.g. ～暮 *bómù*, pressing on toward evening, advesperate, tenuous sundown.
3. thin (ant. 厚 *hòu*, thick); slight, weak, tenuous, diffuse; shabby; meager, paltry, negligible, inconsiderable; inferior; e.g. ～怒 *bónù*, a trace of anger; ～革 *bógé*, thin (i.e. soft) leather; ～命 *bómìng*, slighted by fate, unfortunate destiny; ～倖 *bóxìng*, thin (i.e. bad) luck; ～田 *bótián*, "thin fields," infertile, fallow land; ～相 *bóxiàng*, ill-starred.
 a. disapprove of; consider worthless; scorn.
4. thin out; deplete, weaken; diminish; impoverish.

襮 **bó** **MC powk**
1. embroidered collar.
2. outer clothing, outerwear.
 a. exterior, outer; exposed.
3. expose, reveal; show outwardly.

踣 **bó** **MC bok**
1. fall forward.
 a. head-over-heels, upside-down; overturn, topple.
 b. fall dead.
2. collapse, ruin; bring down.

鎛 **bó** **MC pak**
1. dibble, small pointed hoe for weeding or making holes for planting.
2. mallet-struck large bell with flat rims and sculpturally elaborate suspension device.
3. ornamented with gold; gilt, gilded.

鑮 **bó** **MC pak** ⊙ 鎛 *bó*.

馞 **bó** **MC bwot**
1. (med.) rdup., bursting with scent, richly redolent, pungently perfumed.

駁 **bó** **MC paewk**
1. bay horse with white spots.
 a. dappled, spattled.
2. (med.) denounce, decry, condemn; refute, deprecate, negate; retort, rebut.
3. fabulous one-horned beast with white body, black tail, tiger's teeth and claws, and drum-like voice.

髆 **bó** **MC pak**
1. shoulder-blade.

bǒ

簸 bǒ MC paX
1. winnow, free grain from chaff by tossing in the air and passing through fine-mesh basket or by forcing a current of air through it.
2. to wave, swing back and forth; brandish.
  bò MC paH
1. (med.) winnowing-basket.

跛 bǒ MC paX
1. lame; limping.
  a. impaired; crippled.
  bì MC pjeH
1. stand with weight on one leg; lean, list.

bò

擘 bò MC peak
1. pry open, force open; split open, slice open.
  a. separate, move apart.
  b. draw a bow.
2. the thumb.

檗 bò MC peak ⊙ 蘗 *bò.*

蘗 bò MC peak
1. sgl. or 黃～ *huángbò,* (yellow) cork-tree, Amur cork-tree (*Phellodendron amurense*), pith of which is yellow and bitter, used in dyeing, and the outer bark of which is used medicinally.

bū

哺 bū MC pu
1. late afternoon, equiv. *shen* 申 double-hour, approx. 3-5 p.m.
  a. (med.) early evening, dusk, twilight.

逋 bū MC pu
1. flee, flee from, run away; steal away; escape; evade, elude; fugitive.
  a. put something off, avoid an obligation; delay.
2. be in debt, in arrears; to owe.

餔 bū MC pu
1. meal taken at end of afternoon, around the time of *shen* 申 double-hour (approx. 3-5 p.m.).
  a. eat, dine.
2. ⊙ 哺 *bū,* late afternoon; (med.) early evening.

bǔ MC buH
1. to feed, provide food for.

bǔ

卜 bǔ MC puwk
1. predict outcome of particular event by interpreting the cracks made ritually on carefully prepared and dried turtle shells or deer scapulae when heated with a poker; also, the cracks themselves.
  a. to divine, foretell; prognosticate.
2. burst, pop.

哺 bǔ MC puH
1. food chewed in the mouth.
2. to feed, esp. the young or helpless; nurture, nurse.
  a. a bird's feeding of its chick.

捕 bǔ MC puX
1. catch; seize, apprehend; have custody of; capture, arrest.
2. constabulary, police.

補 bǔ MC puX
1. mend or patch clothing.
2. repair, restore; remedy, redress; improve, ameliorate.
3. add to, supplement; supplete, supply (a deficiency); replenish; e.g. (med.) ～遺 *bǔyí,* Suppletor of Omissions, an anaplerotic post in Tang bureaucracy.
4. fill a vacant official position.
5. benefit, help, provide needed assistance.

bù

不 bù MC pjuw
1. generic pre-verbal negative: not; e.g. 王～悅 *wáng bù yuè,* The king was not pleased; 二者 ～可得兼 *èrzhě bùkě dé jiān,* Those two things cannot be combined together.
  fǒu MC pjuwX
1. ⊙ 否 *fǒu.*

布 bù MC puH
1. tabby woven from bast fibers (hemp, flax, kudzu, etc.); linen, cloth; usu. simple fabrics; e.g. ～衣 *bùyī,* plain garb, plain-garbed persons, i.e.

commoners, also (med.) one without an official position.

    a. (med.) also ref. silk fabric; lawn (if thin or sheer); sendal, sindon (if very fine).

2. in early times, also used as medium of exchange, hence euph. for currency.

3. spread out, lay out; distribute; e.g. ～散 *bùsàn*, scatter, bestrew.

    a. (bn.) ～濩 *bùhù* (MC puH-huH), spread and scatter afar, disperse and disseminate.

4. bestow, dispense; e.g. (Budd.) ～施 *bùshī*, dispense charity, bestow largesse, give alms, trns. of Skt. *dāna*.

5. set out for view, display; publish.

    a. proclaim, announce; declare; state.

6. ～穀 *bùgǔ*, the cuckoo (*Cuculus canorus*), syn. 鳲鳩 *shījiū*.

怖　bù　MC phuH

1. fear(ful); dread, feel terror.

    a. terrify, unnerve, panic.

步　bù　MC buH

1. a pace, usu. equiv. 2 steps, a double-step; from Qin up to early Tang (624 CE) equiv. 6 "feet" (*chi* 尺), approx. 60 inches, then equiv. 5 "feet," also approx. 60 inches (because *chi* recalibrated); 300 pre-Tang *bu* equiv. 1 *li* 里, 360 Tang *bu* equiv. 1 *li* 里.

    a. to pace, march, step, advance; e.g. (Dao.) ～虛 *bùxū*, "pacing the void," esoteric practice most fully developed in Shangqing context, involving ritualized visualization and procession along the network of stars making up the Northern Dipper.

    b. course (of action).

2. (med.) riverside mooring-spot for boats.

簿　bù　MC buX

1. register, registry, in which accounts or inventories are kept.

    a. ledger, logbook; notebook; file, dossier; roster.

    b. registrar; accountant, actuary; e.g. (med.) 主～ *zhǔbù*, chief registrar, 3rd-ranking (of 4) centrally appointed officials in a district (*xian* 縣), intendant of official records and seals.

蔀　bù　MC buwX

1. drape or awning, to deflect light.

    a. to drape, veil, screen.

2. Callippic cycle, period of time equiv. 4 Metonic cycles (1 Metonic cycle, → 章 *zhāng*, equiv. 235 synodic months, i.e. 19 years incl. 7 intercalary months), 76 years.

部　bù　MC buwX

1. portion, section, (de)part(ment), division; category, class; e.g. (med.) 四～ *sìbù*, 4 bibliographic groupings of "classics" (*jing* 經), "histories" (*shi* 史), "masters" (*zi* 子), "literary collections" (*ji* 集); also (Budd.), 4 classes of disciples, i.e. *bhikṣu* (monks), *bhikṣunī* (nuns), *upāsaka* (male devotees), *upāsikā* (female devotees); (med.) 六～ *liùbù*, Six Departments under the Bureau of State Affairs (*shangshu sheng* 尚書省) in Sui-Tang times, i.e. departments of personnel (*libu* 吏～), revenue (*hubu* 戶～), rites (*libu* 禮～), war (*bingbu* 兵～), punishments (*xingbu* 刑～), public works (*gongbu* 工～).

    a. apportion, divide; classify, categorize.

2. staff, company, contingent, troop; personnel under one's command.

3. to lead, govern; manage.

C

cāi

猜　cāi　MC tshoj

1. have doubts or questions about, suspicious, wary. N.B. The meaning "guess, conjecture" for this graph does not occur till post-Tang times.

    a. envy, begrudge; resent.

2. (med.) be surprised at, astonished.

3. (med.) peer at, espy; keep an eye on.

cái

才　cái　MC dzoj

1. heaven-given talent, genius, gift(ed), innate capacity, implanted quality.

    a. talent, ability, skill.

2. ⊙ 纔 *cái* 1, just now; 2, barely, merely, just; 裁 *cái*, cut to form, tailor, style, pattern.

材   cái   MC dzoj
1. wood in natural state, timber, lumber.
2. basic resource, heaven-given capacity, genius, gift, talent; ⊙ 才 *cái* 1.
3. (med.) coffin.
4. ⊙ 裁 *cái*, cut to form, tailor, style, pattern; 財 *cái*, material resources, property, goods, wealth.

纔   cái   MC dzoj
1. just now; only now; e.g. ～至 *cáizhì*, only just arrived.
2. just, barely, merely; e.g. ～分 *cáifēn*, just discernible, barely distinguishable.

裁   cái   MC dzoj
1. cut to form, tailor; style, fashion; conform to pattern, fit.
    a. trim, pare, cut out (from larger sheet), snip out or off; reduce, diminish.
2. pattern, form, model; outline.
3. regulate, discipline, make hew to principle.
4. judge, adjudicate, apply established rule to; sentence, condemn.
5. implant, a cutting grafted onto a parent stalk.
6. ⊙ 纔 *cái* 1, just now; 2, barely, merely.

財   cái   MC dzoj
1. material resources; property, belongings, goods.
    a. wealth, material worth.
2. ⊙ 才 *cái*, genius, gift, talent, skill; 纔 *cái* 1, just now; 2, barely, merely; 裁 *cái*, cut to form, tailor, style, pattern.

cǎi

寀   cǎi   MC tshojX
1. ⊙ 埰 *cài*, appanage, designated land and its revenues granted by feudal lord to high dignitary.
2. (med.) 僚～ *liáocǎi*, official colleague, associate.

彩   cǎi   MC tshojX
1. ⊙ 采 *cǎi* 2, variegated in color, colorful, bright-hued, gaudy, prismatic.
    a. striated, streaked.
    b. multi-colored silk item.
    c. embellished, elaborately trimmed, lavish, ornate; esp. of lit. style.
2. (med.) ⊙ 采 5, have good luck in gambling, glowing with success, carry the day.

採   cǎi   MC tshojX
1. ⊙ 采 *cǎi* 1, pick, pluck, gather.
    a. cull, select, choose, adopt; extract, exploit.
    b. collect, cluster; bunch up, assemble.

睬   cǎi   MC tshojX
1. ⊙ 采 *cǎi* 4, take notice of, pay attention to, heed.

綵   cǎi   MC tshojX
1. multi-colored silk item.
2. ⊙ 彩 *cǎi* 1, variegated in color, colorful, bright-hued, gaudy, prismatic.
    a. striated, streaked.
    b. embellished, elaborately trimmed, lavish, ornate; esp. of lit. style.

采   cǎi   MC tshojX
1. pick, pluck, gather.
    a. cull, select, choose, adopt; extract, exploit.
    b. collect, cluster; bunch up, assemble.
2. variegated in color, colorful, bright-hued, gaudy, prismatic.
    a. striated, streaked.
    b. multi-colored silk item.
    c. embellished, elaborately trimmed, lavish, ornate.
    d. (lit.) coloration, gloss, fine rhetorical polish.
3. rdup., lavish luxuriance, esp. of vegetation.
4. take notice of, pay attention to, heed.
5. (med.) have good luck in gambling, glowing with success, carry the day.
6. ～橡 *cǎichuán*, sawtooth oak (*Quercus acutissima*), syn. 柞 *zuò*.

cài   MC tshojH
1. appanage, designated land and its revenues granted by feudal lord to high dignitary; ⊙ 埰 *cài*.

cài

埰   cài   MC tshojH
1. appanage, designated land and its revenues granted by feudal lord to high dignitary.

cǎi   MC tshojX
1. burial plot, gravesite.

縩   cài   MC tshojH
1. seam, stitch (clothing).
2. (bn.) 綷～ *cuìcài*, → 綷 *cuì*.

菜　cài　MC tshojH

1. leaf-vegetables, edible greens.
   a. culled herbs.
2. ⊙ 採 *cǎi* 1, pick, pluck, gather; cull, select.

蔡　cài　MC tshajH

1. large turtle, the carapace or plastron of which was used in divination.
2. wild plants, greenery, grasses, shrubs.
3. old feudal state during the Zhou dynasty, located in present-day southeastern Henan.
4. a surname.
   sà　MC sat
1. banish(ment).
2. ⊙ 殺 *shài* (*shā*), diminish, reduce, lessen.

cān

參　cān　MC tshom

1. participate in, take part, partake in or of; join in; e.g. ～事 *cānshì*, join in the work of; ～朝 *cāncháo*, take part in court ceremonies.
   a. assist, cooperate; enhance; e.g. ～軍 *cānjūn*, military coadjutant, official title of military aide, also of bureaucratic aide.
2. juxtapose, place side-by-side; arrange, put together; e.g. ～列 *cānliè*, lay out in order, array.
   a. even out, put on same footing, comparable to; e.g. ～壽 *cānshòu*, of equal longevity.
   b. reach to the same level as; e.g. ～天 *cāntiān*, reach the heavens, touch the sky.
   c. (bn.) ～潭 *cāntán* (MC tshom-dom), ～驔 *cāndiàn* (MC tshom-demX), in regular ranks, following after one another.
3. refer, consult, confer; deliberate; take (an issue) up with; e.g. ～干 *cān'gān*, concern oneself with, take an interest in; (Budd.) ～禪 *cānchán*, take (dharma) instruction under.
   a. bear witness to, validate, verify.
4. pay one's respects to (inferior to superior).
   sān　MC sam
1. ternion, triad, group of three; e.g. ～夷 *sānyí*, exterminate (as punishment) 3 generations of family; ～伍 *sānwǔ*, by 3s and 5s, intersperse, shuffle together; also, place together for sake of comparison.
   a. form a triad with (2 others).
   shēn　MC srim
1. Triaster, one of the 28 lunar lodgings, comprised of the 7 stars of Orion in the western quadrant (*baihu* 白虎) of the sky; seen by the

Chinese as the image of a faithful vassal, with the 3 stars of Orion's belt (in Western terminology) regarded as the man's heart, perhaps giving rise to the constellation's name; but name might instead derive from man-shaped ginseng root (see 2, next), in which case the rendering "Triaster" would be a misnomer.
   a. ～商 *shēnshāng*, ～心 *shēnxīn*, ～辰 *shēnchén*, Shen and Xin, Triaster and Heart (alt. names for latter, Shang and Chen), basically Orion and Scorpio, which are on opposite sides of sky and so never seen at night at the same time, hence euph. of far-distant persons with no hope of meeting.
2. sgl. or 人～ *rénshēn*, ginseng (*Panax ginseng*), fleshy root of which was used importantly in medicine and cooking.
   a. 丹～ *dānshēn*, red sage (*Salvia miltiorrhiza*), root used medicinally; 苦～ *kǔshēn*, bitter-root; shrubby sophora (*Sophora flavescens*), root used medicinally; 沙～ *shāshēn*, whorled bluebell, ladybell (*Adenophora tetraphylla*), root used medicinally.
3. rdup., long and lanky; long-drawn, extended.
   cēn　MC tsrhim
1. (bn.) ～差 *cēncī* (MC tsrhim-tsrhje), used in many contexts descriptive of irregular appearance: unevenly unequal, erratically arrayed, disparately displayed, diversely disposed, randomly ranged, zig-zag, jagged and jogged, riffled and ruffled; also, one way or another, somehow or other, something like, resembling in some points; also, ref. reed-organ, mouth-organ (→ 笙 *shēng*) because of pipes' unequal length; also, ref. swallows' flutter, because of chevron-shaped tailfeathers.

滄　cān　MC tshan　⊙ 餐 *cān*.

餐　cān　MC tshan

1. meal, repast, e.g. 素～ *sùcān*, "bread of idleness," consume what you have not labored for.
   a. eat, sup, e.g. ～霞 *cānxiá*, sup on auroral clouds (fare of Dao. transcendents).

驂　cān　MC tshom

1. 3-horse team, troika.
2. trace-horses of a team-of-four.
   a. synecdoche for the horse that one rides.
3. in a war-chariot carrying 3 men, the man on the right side.
4. (bn.) ～驔 *cāndiàn* (MC tshom-demX), careering and cavorting.

cán

慙 cán   MC dzam
1. abashed, ashamed; e.g. ～德 *cándé*, abashed at one's conduct.
2. discomfited, nonplussed.
3. (med.) recall with emotion, be moved by; grateful for.

慚 cán   MC dzam   ⊙ 慙 *cán*.

殘 cán   MC dzan
1. injure, harm, damage; destroy; kill, wipe out.
2. cruel, ruthless, merciless; brutal, vicious.
3. fade away, welk, shrink, wither, erode; crumble, decompose, deteriorate, decay; dim (light), gutter (candle); sully.
  a. incomplete, fragmentary; remnant, vestige, trace; e.g. ～雪 *cánxuě*, leftover (unmelted) snow; 賣～牡丹 *màicán mǔdān*, unsold peonies.

蠶 cán   MC dzom
1. cocoon, of silkworm.
  a. to tend silkworms.
  b. whorled, cocoon-shaped.

cǎn

嶜 cǎn   MC tshomX
1. bite, sting, esp. of mosquitoes.
     zā   MC tsop
1. hold in the mouth; savor.

憯 cǎn   MC tshomX
1. heartache, pang, heartsore; pain, throe; anguish (-causing), agonizing, miserable.
  a. gloomy, grim; e.g. ～憺 *cǎndàn*, gloomy and glum.
  b. (bn.) ～悴 *cǎncuì* (MC tshomX-tshwijH), haggard and careworn, wan and wasted.
2. heartless; torturous; brutal, cruel.
3. ⊙ 黲 *cǎn*, dimmed, pallid; smudged; e.g. ～綠 *cǎnlù*, pale green.
4. rdup., heartsore and saddened, hapless and heavy-hearted; also, pale and pallid, dim and faded.

憯 cǎn   MC tshomX
1. ⊙ 憯 *cǎn* 1, heartache, heartsore, pang, throe, anguish; gloomy, grim; 2, heartless, torturous; brutal, cruel.

2. pre-VB modifier indicating past tense (syn. 曾 *céng*), esp. as intensifier of negative phrases: e.g. 胡～莫懲 *hú cǎn mòchéng*, why has he never reproved them?

黲 cǎn   MC tshomX
1. dimmed color; pallor, pallid.
  a. smudged, bleared.

càn

燦 càn   MC tshanH
1. ⊙ 粲 *càn* 2, resplendent, brilliantly shining, sparkling, scintillating, glittering, glistening; 3, highly visible, clearly manifest.

璨 càn   MC tshanH
1. reflective glitter of gems; sparkle; spangle, flash, coruscate.

粲 càn   MC tshanH
1. highly polished rice of best quality.
2. shining, scintillant, glistening, glittering, sparkling.
  a. (bn.) ～爛 *cànlàn* (MC tshanH-lanH), aglitter and aglow, brilliant and bedazzling, of bright view and also of lit. style.
3. clearly visible, manifest, open to view.
  a. brightly wreathed laughter, showing white teeth.

cāng

倉 cāng   MC tshang
1. granary; storehouse.
2. (bn.) ～卒, ～猝 *cāngcù* (MC tshang-tshwot), ～皇, ～煌 *cānghuáng* (MC tshang-hwang), hustle and bustle, hurried and flurried, in a rush, harum-scarum, pothered and pressed; also, throw into turmoil, ruffle and fluster, hurly-burly.
3. (bn.) ～庚 *cānggēng* (MC tshang-kaeng), oriole, esp. black-naped oriole (*Oriolus chinensis*), esp. associated with summer; syn. 鶯 *yīng*, 黃鳥 *huángniǎo*, 黃鸝 *huánglí*.
4. ⊙ 滄 *cāng*, iron gray-blue, watchet, cold-blue; 蒼 *cāng* 1, glaucous, gray-green, blue-green; 2, grizzled gray-black, 3, silvery gray.

傖 cāng   MC dzraeng
1. (med.) sgl. or ～父 *cāngfù*, oafish lout, country churl; insulting term used by Jiangnan-area people for northerners in Nanbeichao period.

a. (med.) (bn.) 〜嚀 *cāngníng* (MC dzraeng-nraeng), oafish, coarse and uncouth, rude and rubish, uncivilized.

滄　**cāng　MC tshang**
1. cold, shivering; cool(ing).

滄　**cāng　MC tshang**
1. iron gray-blue of deep water, watchet.
   a. pallid blue; slate-gray; gray.
   b. cold, chilly; cold-blue.
   c. (bn.) 〜浪 *cānglàng* (MC tshang-lang), watchet whitecap, blue-gray billows, name of a portion of the Han 漢 river, also of a Dao. paradise isle in the Eastern Sea.
2. ⊙ 蒼 *cāng*, glaucous, grizzled.

蒼　**cāng　MC tshang**
1. glaucous, gen. term for blue-green hues of low saturation; cf. 滄 *cāng*, iron gray-blue.
   a. gray-green, grizzled, as of dense mountain forests, or of distant undergrowth; e.g. (bn.) 〜茫 (MC tshang-mang), shade-spreading verdure; see also *cǎng* 1 below.
   b. bluish-green, e.g. sgl. or rdup., elegant variation for the blue of the sky, cerulean.
   c. verdigris; patinated.
2. grizzled gray-black, color of hair > the common folk, e.g. 〜甿 *cāngméng*, "grizzled farmers," the populace.
3. silvery-gray, shadowy and faint, soft and silvery, as of moonlight, e.g. rdup., wanly white, ashen white; (med.) 〜涼 *cāngliáng*, coolly silver.
4. (med.) (bn.) 〜黃 *cānghuáng* (MC tshang-hwang), turn upside-down, inside-out, change to the contrary; also, shocked and startled, fazed and flustered, pressed and pothered.
5. 〜耳 *cāngér*, cocklebur (*Xanthium sibiricum*).
   cǎng　MC tshangX
1. (bn.) 〜莽 *cǎngmǎng* (MC tshangX-mangX), distantly indistinct, faint and far-off, blurred and boundless, dimmed by distance; also (med.), in a haze, dazed and perplexed, fuddled and baffled, withdrawn and listless.

鶬　**cāng　MC tshang**
1. sgl. or 〜鴰 *cāngguā*, 〜雞 *cāngjī*, gray crane (*Grus lilfordi*).
2. (bn.) 〜鶊 *cānggēng* (MC tshang-kaeng), ⊙ 倉庚 *cānggēng*, → 倉 *cāng*.

cáng

藏　**cáng　MC dzang**
1. store up grain.
   a. store up, reserve, hoard; keep safe.
2. hide away, secrete; e.g. 〜拙 *cángzhuó*, cover up one's faults.
3. (bn.) 〜摧 *cángcuī* (MC dzang-dzwoj) or 摧〜 *cuīcáng*, onom. for sad sounds, sound of fulling-block, sad animal cries, etc.
   zàng　MC dzangH
1. storehouse, depository, treasury.
2. bury, inter.
   a. burial-ground.
3. internal organs, viscera, ⊙ 臟 *zàng*.
   zāng　MC tsang
1. ⊙ 臧 *zāng* 1, prized; advantageous, favorable; 贓 *zāng*, plunder, spoils.

cāo

操　**cāo　MC tshaw**
1. grasp, hold onto, have in hand.
   a. manipulate, operate, work with; control, keep hold of, manage, have the upper hand.
2. tenacity; commitment, commit to; fidelity.
3. (med.) stroke, caress.
4. designation for tune to be played on zither (*qin* 琴).
5. in the style, manner, or fashion of; e.g. 凌雲之〜 *língyún zhi cāo*, in the manner of skimming over the clouds.

糙　**cāo　MC tshawH**
1. (med.) coarse unhulled rice.
   a. (med.) rough, coarse, (c)rude.

cáo

嘈　**cáo　MC dzaw**
1. make a din, racket; strepent, strepidation.
   a. rdup., dinned and deafened.
   b. (bn.) 〜啐 *cáocuì* (MC dzaw-tshwojH), 〜雜 *cáozá* (MC dzaw-dzop), 〜囐 *cáozá* (MC dzaw-dzat), clamor and racket, clamorous wrangle, deafening din, raucous uproar, chaotic commotion, brouhaha, hubbub, blathering babble; (bn.) 啾〜 *jiūcáo*, → 啾 *jiū*.

cáo

曹 cáo MC dzaw
1. paired, counterpart(s); complement(ary).
2. group, class, kind, category.
   a. service, administration; designation of clerical or administrative unit of larger agency.
3. (med.) suffix for 2nd-person plural, esp. when addressing inferiors.
   a. (med.) suffix for 3rd-person plural, esp. in early Budd. translations.
4. a surname, notably that of ruling family of the Wei 魏 (220-265) dynasty.

槽 cáo MC dzaw
1. horse trough.
   a. by synecdoche, stall.
   b. anything trough-shaped or with similar use: vat, cask, tun.
2. (med.) waterway; canal.

漕 cáo MC dzaw
1. transport by water; river transport.

艚 cáo MC dzaw
1. (med.) transport boat, packet.
   a. (med.) gen. term for boat, vessel, craft.

蟛 cáo MC dzaw
1. sgl. or bn. 蟛 ~ qícáo, → 蠐 qí.

cǎo

屮 cǎo MC tshawX ⊙ 草 cǎo.

懆 cǎo MC tshawX
1. rdup., sorry and disheartened, plaintively piteous, heavy-hearted.

草 cǎo MC tshawX
1. plants, herbaceous plants; esp. when paired with 木 mù, trees, woody plants.
   a. depending on context: grasses, herbs, forbs, straw, weeds.
2. grassland, weedland; uncultivated countryside.
   a. euph. for those who live in the countryside; e.g. ~萊 cǎolái, grasses and weeds, i.e. country folk, plain folk.
   b. rude, crude, coarse; uncultivated, unrefined, rustic; e.g. ~具 cǎojù, coarse viands, inferior fare; ~昧 cǎomèi, raw material out

of which phenomena were formed; also, the time of unformed chaos.
3. draft, unpolished preliminary composition; sketch, rough outline; e.g. ~立 cǎolì, ~創 cǎochuàng, create, work up; (med.) ~麻 cǎomá, "draft on hemp," i.e. imperial proclamation, because in Tang times imperial orders (zhao 詔) were written on paper made of yellow hemp fiber.
   a. early, initial, beginning stage; e.g. ~駒 cǎojū, very young colt; (med.) ~濫 cǎolàn, "first overflowing," i.e. the start of something.
4. (med.) draft script, the most free calligraphic style with characters often abbreviated and connected with each other by brush-strokes, offering largest possibility of individual expression.
5. rdup., struggling in disorder, troubled and disturbed; also (med.), rash and sloppy, hasty and hurried, slapdash, rushed and urgent, precipitately; (bn.) ~次 cǎocì (MC tshawX-tshijH), same as preceding; also (med.), out in the open, in the fields.

騲 cǎo MC tshawX
1. (med.) dam, a mare that has foaled.
   a. (med.) gen. term for any mother-animal.

cè

側 cè MC tsrik
1. to one side, side(ways).
   a. used humilifically as ADV: to VB "off to the side," inconspicuously, unworthily.
2. incline(d), slant(ed), oblique, pitch(ed), cant(ed), cock(ed).
   a. partial (to), prejudiced (toward); unjust.
3. place oneself at or in, ensconce oneself.
4. ⊙ 惻 cè, sorrow(ful), commiserate; 仄 zè 1, slanting, oblique, awry, irregular; 2, oblique or "deflected" tones of the spoken language, i.e., 上 shǎng, 去 qù, and 入 rù (as opp. to "level" tone 平 píng).

冊 cè MC tsrheak
1. writing tablet, tabulature.
   a. record, written document.
2. brevet of investiture, imperial patent of nobility or appointment to high office.
3. ⊙ 策 cè 6, plan for action, stratagem.

厠 cè MC tsrhiH
1. latrine, privy, toilet.

2. pigsty, piggery.

3. apply oneself to, take part in or as.

　　cè　MC tsrhik

1. ⊙ 側 *cè* 1, to one side, sideways; 2, inclined, slanted.

惻　cè　MC tsrhik

1. sorrow(ful), suffer(ing); grieve for, commiserate, condole.

　　a. (bn.) ～愴 *cèchuàng* (MC tsrhik-tsrjangH), anguished and aggrieved, sorrowing in sympathy.

2. rdup., fervently earnest, single-hearted, sincere.

測　cè　MC tsrhik

1. measure of depth of water, fathom.

2. to fathom, sound, plumb; measure completely, to the end of.

　　a. estimate, conjecture, appraise.

　　b. interpret, construe; understand, appreciate.

3. limpid, clear.

4. (med.) interrogation by torture.

畟　cè　MC tsrhik

1. rdup., keen and sharp, esp. of plowshare.

2. (med.) well-ordered, clearly laid out.

策　cè　MC tsrheak

1. bamboo slips used for writing and then bound together with cords.

　　a. written document; record.

2. divining slips, esp. yarrow-stalks (蓍 *shī*) used in *Yijing* divination.

　　a. forecast, prognosticate, predict.

3. riding-whip, crop, quirt, made of thin bamboo strips bound together.

　　a. to whip, switch, lash.

4. counting slips or rods, for figuring numbers.

5. bamboo staff.

　　a. lean on a staff; e.g. ～杖 *cèzhàng*, propped on a staff.

6. plan for action, stratagem, scheme, intrigue; intervention.

7. thin branch, stick; these bound together, fagot.

8. ⊙ 冊 *cè* 2, imperial patent of nobility or appointment to high office.

9. (med.) sgl. or ～問 *cèwèn*, questions posed on civil-service exam.

　　a. (med.) 對～ *duìcè*, candidate's answer to exam question.

筴　cè　MC tsrheak

1. ⊙ 策 *cè* 1, bamboo slips used for writing; written document, record; 2, divining slips, esp. yarrow-stalks (蓍 *shī*) used in *Yijing* divination; forecast, prognosticate, predict; 3, riding-whip, crop, quirt, made of thin bamboo strips bound together; 6, plan for action, stratagem, scheme, intrigue.

籷　cè　MC tsrheak

1. (med.) rice dumpling wrapped in reeds or bamboo leaves.

　　sè　MC sreak

1. (med.) mix rice or barley with other ingredients in stew.

cén

岑　cén　MC dzrim

1. crag, pinnacle; narrow and pointed peak.

　　a. (bn.) ～崟 *cényín* (MC dzrim-ngim), peaked and pointed, sharp and steep.

　　b. lofty, aloft, beetling.

　　c. peak, summit.

2. riverbank.

3. a surname.

涔　cén　MC dzrim

1. downpour, deluge, inundation, torrential rain.

　　a. rdup., ceaseless spate, continual downpour; also, streaming flood, of tears or sweat; also (med.), intensifying affliction, chronic complaint.

2. standing water in the road, pondlet, plashet, large puddle.

céng

層　céng　MC dzong

1. layer(ed), tier(ed).

　　a. overlap, superpose.

2. storey or level of building, terrace, etc.

嶒　céng　MC dzing

1. (bn.) ～崚 *céngróng* (MC dzing-hjwaeng), 崚～ *língcéng* (MC ling-dzing), rising tier upon tier, soaring steeply upward.

曾　céng　MC dzong

1. pre-vв modifier indicating past tense: once; e.g. 孟嘗君～待客夜食 *mèngchángjūn céng dài*

kè yèshí, Lord Mengchang once treated a guest to an evening meal; ～隨織女渡天河 *céng suí zhīnǚ dù tiānhé* once followed the Weaving Maid, crossing over the Sky-River (Milky Way).

   a. modified by the aspectual negative GP *wèi* 未: not yet once > never; e.g. 君子所未 ～聞 *jūnzǐ suǒ wèicéng wén*, what a man of noble status has never once heard; 蟲未～生 *chóng wèicéng shēng*, bugs are never born.

   b. 何～ *hécéng*, intensified rhetorical question: however, whenever (could one) . . .?; e.g. 爾何～比予於管仲 *ěr hécéng bǐ yú yú guǎn zhòng*, however could you compare me with Guan Zhong? 何～須臾同失 *hécéng xūyú xiāngshī*, whenever did we even for a moment lose track of each other?

2. ⊙ 層 *céng*, tier, layer; storey.

   zēng   MC tsong

1. increase, add to.

2. pre-VB modifier indicating a further increase beyond what was stated or expected: even more, all the more, still more, go as far as; e.g. 梁王以此怨盎，～使人刺盎 *liángwáng yǐ cǐ yuàn àng, zēng shǐ rén cì àng*, the king of Liang because of this had an aversion to Ang, he even sent someone to assassinate Ang; 其於我也，～若是乎 *qí yū wǒ yě, zēng ruòshì hū*, as for his relation to us, it is even like this !

   a. frequently, preceding a negated VB-phrase: not even, still not even, etc.; e.g. ～未入其地 *zēngwèi rù qí dì*, they have not even yet entered into his territory; ～不能決也 *zēng bùnéng jué yě*, he is not even able to determine it.

3. after all, in fact, actually, truly now it is that . . .; adding emphasis to factual statement (in med. times often expanded to ～是 *zēngshì*, ant. 斷無 *duànwú*); ～是無心雲 *zēngshì wúxīnyún*, I am indeed an aimless cloud.

4. prefix indicating relational separation of 2 generations between parties; e.g. ～祖 *zēngzǔ*, great-grandfather.

5. a surname.

cèng

蹭   **cèng   MC tshongH**

1. (bn.) ～蹬 *cèngdèng* (MC tshongH-dongH), flounce and flounder, wallow and welter; baffled and foiled, beyond hope.

chā

叉   **chā   MC tsrhae**

1. interlace fingers; cross (hands, legs, arms).

2. point of bifurcation, fork (of road, tree-branches, etc.).

3. 2-pronged fork, for impaling food; bident, pitchfork, 2-pronged spear, for impaling game or as weapon.

   a. impale, spear.

4. pincer formation or movement, in war.

差   **chā   MC tsrhae**

1. differ(ence), differentiate; deviate, deviation.

2. proportion(ate), comparative(ly); according to rank or degree; e.g. ～次 *chācì*, ～等 *chāděng*, ～序 *chāxù*, order, sequence, hierarchy, ranking.

   a. slightly, a little, somewhat; e.g. ～可 *chākě*, quite adequate.

3. mistake, err(or), mishap; e.g. ～忒 *chātè*, blunder, faux pas.

   chāi   MC tsrheaj

1. choose, select(ive); e.g. ～論 *chāilún*, single out.

   a. distinct(ion).

2. send, despatch.

   a. impost, required tax or labor service; e.g. ～發 *chāifā*, taxes and levies; ～科簿 *chāikèbù*, register of imposts and requisitions.

   chài   MC tsrheaH

1. recover from illness, originally Chu dialect term.

   cī   MC tsrhje

1. rdup., or (bn.) ～池 *cēnchí* (MC tsrhje-drje), syn. (bn.) 參～ *cēncī*, → 參 *cēn* (*cān*).

   chà   MC tsrheaH

1. (med.) unusual, uncommon, remarkable; e.g. ～人 *chàrén*, an extraordinary person.

扠   **chā   MC tsrhea**

1. pronged fork-shaped item, esp. for spearing or impaling fish or game.

2. fork, of tree branches.

插   **chā   MC tsrheap**

1. insert, stick into, poke into; mix in, mingle, intersperse; e.g. ～箭 *chājiàn*, nock an arrow into bowstring; ～花 *chāhuā*, pin or stick flower in hair.

2. a spade, scoop; ⊙ 鍤 *chā* 1.

杈　chā　MC tsrhae
1. (bn.) ～枒 chāyā (MC tsrhae-ngae), like bifurcating branches, split and spread apart.
2. pronged spear, esp. for impaling fish.

齄　chā　MC tsrheap
1. a spade, scoop; ⊙ 鍤 chā 1.
2. insert, stick into; mingle, mix in, intersperse; ⊙ 插 chā 1.

叉　chā　MC tsrhae　⊙ 艖 chā.

艖　chā　MC tsrhae
1. small boat, bark; flatboat.

荖　chā　MC tsrhae
1. ⊙ 差 chā 1, differ(ence), differentiate; deviate.

鍤　chā　MC tsrheap
1. a spade, scoop.
2. long needle, for sewing clothes.

chá

察　chá　MC tsrheat
1. scrutinize, investigate, examine, search into; take a hard look at, look at closely, perscrutate.
2. select for appreciation or appointment after examination.
3. manifest, make known.
4. rdup., pristine purity, unsullied whiteness; also, down to the smallest detail.

查　chá　MC dzrae
1. wooden raft, ⊙ 楂 chá 1.
2. (med.) (bn.) ～牙 cháyá (MC dzrae-ngae), jutting and jagging out.
　　zhā　MC tsrae
1. ⊙ 樝 zhā 1, lesser quince; 2, hawthorn.

楂　chá　MC dzrae
1. wooden raft.
2. (med.) rdup., onom. of chitter-chaffer of birds.
　　zhā　MC tsrae
1. ⊙ 樝 zhā 1, lesser quince; 2, hawthorn.

槎　chá　MC dzrae
1. lop off; fell, hew.
2. logs, esp. logs lashed together to make a raft, ⊙ 楂 chá 1.

a. (med.) heavy tree-limbs, boughs.
b. ～頭 chátóu, loggerhead, kind of bream (鯿 biān) that is a local delicacy of Xiangyang 襄陽, Hubei.

瑳　chá　MC dzrae
1. err, mistake, go wrong; be at fault.

茶　chá　MC drae
1. (med.) tea (Camellia sinensis), the bush and the beverage; old form of graph is → 荼 tú.

荼　chá　MC drae　→ 荼 tú.

督　chá　MC tsrheat　⊙ 察 chá.

chà

侘　chà　MC trhaeH
1. (bn.) ～傺 chàchì (MC trhaeH-trhjejH), depressed with despair, futile and forlorn, overcome with melancholy.
2. ⊙ 詫 chà 1, vaunt, brag.

刹　chà　MC tsrhae(t)
1. trsc. Skt. kṣa(t), kṣe(t).
　　a. (Budd.) abb. trsc. of Skt. kṣetra, land, world; also with Ch. semantic addition, ～土 chàtǔ.
　　b. (Budd.) ～那 chàné (MC tsrhae-naH), trsc. of Skt. kṣaṇa, instant(aneous), moment(ary), ephemeral, quick as a thought.
2. (Budd.) stupa, pagoda; esp. the wheel symbol on pagoda's spire; ～末 chàmò, spire of pagoda.
　　a. (Budd.) by synecdoche, Budd. monastery; also, same but with Ch. semantic addition: ～寺 chàsì; e.g. ～竿 chàgān, monastery flagpole.

刹　chà　MC tsrhaet　⊙ 刹 chà.

妊　chà　MC trhaeH　⊙ 姹 chà.

姹　chà　MC trhaeH
1. young girl, lass, nymph.
　　a. ～女 chànǔ, same as preceding; also, "mercurial, or volatile, girl," esoteric name for mercury in alchemical preparations (< next).
2. charming, enchanting, bewitching (of women).
　　a. mercurial, volatile; shimmering.

衩 **chà** MC tsrheaH
1. (med.) lateral slits or side-vents of long robe, from knee downward.
2. (med.) ～衣 *chàyī*, informal dress, casual garb.

詫 **chà** MC trhaeH
1. vaunt, boast, brag about, bluster; exaggerate.
2. mislead, fool, cozen, gull; delude.

chāi

釵 **chāi** MC tsrhea
1. aigrette, (forked) hair-ornament, for women.

chái

儕 **chái** MC dzreaj
1. kind, category, class.
2. equal, alike, same.
3. (al)together, collectively, jointly.
   a. join in marriage.

柴 **chái** MC dzrea
1. brushwood, firewood, scrapwood; fagots.
   a. brushwood-gatherer.
2. burnt sacrificial offering to Heaven.
3. (med.) ～胡 *cháihú*, thorowax (*Bupleurum chinense*), root used medicinally.
   zhài MC dzreaH
1. stockade, barricade, palisade, stakewall; military encampment.
   a. defend, protect; pen in.
2. close off, obstruct; hedge.
   cī MC tsrhje
1. (bn.) ～池 *cīchí* (MC tsrhje-drje), syn. 參差 *cēncī*, → 參 *cēn* (*cān*).

犲 **chái** MC dzreaj   ⊙ 豺 *chái*.

紫 **chái** MC dzrea
1. burnt sacrificial offering to Heaven; ⊙ 柴 *chái* 2.

豺 **chái** MC dzreaj
1. dhole, Asian wild dog (*Cuon alpinus*); N.B. not a "jackal."

chài

蠆 **chài** MC trhaejH
1. scorpion; syn. 蠍 *xiē*.

2. (bn.) ～介, ～芥 *chàijiè* (MC trhaejH-keajH), rancor and venom stored in one's heart, blocked bitterness.

chān

佔 **chān** MC trhjem
1. ～畢 *chānbì*, recite and explain a text that one only understands superficially.
2. rdup., speak low, sotto voce.
3. transmit orally.
4. be in possession of, dominate.

幨 **chān** MC tsyhem
1. lappets of robe.
2. carriage curtain.
   a. bed curtain; cloth partition; e.g. ～幌 *chānhuàng*, thick or heavy curtain.

襜 **chān** MC tsyhem
1. apron, skirt covering one's front.
   a. saddle-cloth, caparison.
2. carriage curtain; ⊙ 幨 *chān* 2.
3. ～褕 *chānyú*, short informal jacket.
4. rdup. or ～如 *chānrú*, flapping and fluttering, waving in the wind.

覘 **chān** MC trhjem
1. steal a look at, peek at; spy on, glance at.
   a. inspect, observe.
2. to look after.

闖 **chān** MC trhjem   ⊙ 覘 *chān*.

chán

儳 **chán** MC dzream
1. mixed, mingled; messed; uneven, disorderly.
2. careless, perfunctory, cursory; haphazard.
   chàn MC dzreamH
1. interrupt (speaking), interpose; cut in, break in.
   a. (take) shortcut; (go by) sideroad.

劖 **chán** MC dzraem
1. (med.) bore into, poke; pierce, puncture.

嬋 **chán** MC dzyen
1. (bn.) ～媛 *chányuán* (MC dzyen-hjwon), attractive and alluring; also, prolonged and drawn out, reluctant.

2. (bn.) 〜娟 *chánjuān* (MC dzyen-ʻjwien), charming and comely, lovely and delightful.

孱　chán　MC dzrean

1. weak(ling), feeble; limp; ineffective, powerless.
   a. shallow, superficial.
   b. mean, base; worthless, sorry, abject.
2. compelled, forced, pressed.
   a. close upon one, come near to.
3. timid, timorous, overcautious; fearful; cowardly, pusillanimous.
4. (bn.) 〜顔 *chànyán* (MC dzrean-ngaen), ⊙ 巉巖 *chányán*, → 巉 *chán*.

嶃　chán　MC dzraem

1. ⊙ 巉 *chán*, crag(gy), steep, scarp(ed).
   zhān　MC dzream
1. (med.) eminent, lofty, high-rising.

巉　chán　MC dzraem

1. rdup. or (bn.) 〜巖 *chányán* (MC dzraem-ngaem), cragged and jagged, peaked and pinnacled, steeply scarped.

廛　chán　MC drjen

1. household plot, land occupied and worked by a family.
   a. populace of town or settlement.
2. warehouse, of merchant's goods.
   a. stall or shop in the marketplace.

攙　chán　MC dzream

1. pierce, penetrate.
2. (bn.) 〜搶 *chánlún* (MC dzream-lwon), tailed comet.

槞　chán　MC dzream

1. (bn.) 〜檀 *chántán* (MC dzream-dan), trsc. Skt. *candana*, sandalwood, → 檀 *tán* 2.
2. (bn.) 〜槍 *chánchēng* (MC dzream-tsrhaeng), "sharpened spearhead," comet.

潺　chán　MC dzrean

1. (bn.) 〜湲 *chányuán* (MC dzrean-hjwen), purl and ripple, lap and plash, of running water; also, well and trickle, of tears.
2. rdup., gurgling, babbling, chuckling rush, chatter and fret, of running water; also, falling and flowing down, of tears.

澶　chán　MC dzyen

1. (bn.) 〜湉 *chántián* (MC dzyen-dem), calm and smooth, peaceful and placid (of water).

　dàn　MC danH

1. (bn.) 〜漫 *dànmàn* (MC danH-manH), at one's whim, as easy as can be; also, ample and expansive, spaciously spread out; also, waving in the wind, trembling in the breeze (esp. of bamboo).

瀺　chán　MC dzream

1. pour into, gush.
   a. (bn.) 〜瀹 *chánzhuó* (MC dzream-dzraewk), plash and splash, of rushing waters; also, sink and float, plunge and drift.

禪　chán　MC dzyen　→ 禪 *shàn*.

纏　chán　MC drjen

1. bind(ing), wrap(ping); lace (up), tie.
2. entwine; involve(ment).
   a. entangle(ments); ties of the senses, passions, or social responsibilities.
3. ⊙ 躔 *chán* 3, celestial transit; station of sun, moon, planets on ecliptic.
4. (med.) (bn.) 〜綿 *chánmián* (MC drjen-mjen), with exacting attention to detail, scrupulously particular; also, dizzy and dazed, wrapped in a haze.

蟬　chán　MC dzyen

1. cicada, various species, esp. noted for its loud song or "clitter" produced by the males' tymbals located on either side of the abdomen; emerging from nymphal state they shed their skins, leaving their exuvia behind, which becomes a potent image for the Dao. adept who leaves behind his physical body (or simulacrum of it) upon transcending to higher realms.
2. sgl. or 〜冠 *chánguān*, name of cap worn by court officials.
3. (med.) sgl. or 〜鬢 *chánbìn*, woman's hairdo styled after cicada's wings.
4. (bn.) 〜聯, 〜連 *chánlián* (MC dzyen-ljen), continuously connected, persistently proceeding, endlessly linked.
5. ⊙ 嬋 *chán*, in bns. 〜媛 *chányuán*, 〜娟 *chánjuān*, → 嬋 *chán*.

蟾　chán　MC dzyem

1. sgl. or (bn.) 〜蜍 *chánchú* (MC dzyem-dzyo), toad, the name onom. of its croaking.
   a. the mythological toad that is said to exist in the moon; by metonymy, the moon itself.

讒 chán **MC dzream**
1. denigrate, vilify, malign, run down, speak ill of, slander.

躔 chán **MC drjen**
1. passage, course, route taken.
2. tracks, traces; spoor.
    a. follow in the tracks of; pursue; imitate.
3. sgl. or ～次 *cháncì*, celestial transit; station of sun, moon, planets on ecliptic.

鄽 chán **MC drjen** ⊙ 廛 *chán*.

鋋 chán **MC dzyen**
1. short spear.
    a. impale, pierce.

鑱 chán **MC dzraem**
1. sharp, keen-edged, pointed; needle-sharp.
2. needle, probe; gimlet; e.g. 天～ *tiānchán*, Heaven's needle, i.e. comet.
    a. pierce, puncture.
3. (med.) spade; plowshare.

饞 chán **MC dzream**
1. (med.) ravenous, gluttonous.
    a. (med.) voracious; greedy, insatiable.

chǎn

弗 chǎn **MC tsrheanX**
1. (med.) skewer, for roasting meat.

剗 chǎn **MC tsrheanX**
1. to plane, scrape, level, pare down, trim, whittle; ⊙ 鏟 *chǎn*.
2. edgeway, cliffway, railing, wooden walkway cantilevered out from the face of a cliff, ⊙ 棧 *zhàn*.
3. (med.) merely, only, just.

燀 chǎn **MC tsyhenX**
1. cook, heat.
    a. give off heat, warm up; radiate.
2. light a fire; flare up, flame, enkindled.
    a. blaze, scorch.
    b. fever(ish).

產 chǎn **MC sreanX**
1. generate, give life to, propagate; produce.
    a. supply, furnish, deliver.

2. product, yield, output.
    a. goods, property.

剗 chǎn **MC trhjenX**
1. resolve, dispose of; compose, reconcile, settle.
    a. conclude, finish, complete.

諂 chǎn **MC trhjemX**
1. play up to, fawn on, glaver(y), flatter(y), truckle; obsequious behavior of all kinds (cf. 諛 *yú*, esp. flattery with words).
    a. cajole, wheedle, gloze.
    b. flatterer, losenger.

譠 chǎn **MC trhjemX** ⊙ 諂 *chǎn*.

鏟 chǎn **MC tsrheanX**
1. a plane, scraper.
    a. to plane, scrape, level; pare down.
2. scrape off, raze; eradicate, eliminate.

闡 chǎn **MC tsyhenX**
1. open to view, bring to light, reveal; throw open, make accessible, expose.
    a. be or make manifest, evident, patent.
2. elucidate, expound; clarify, explain.
3. develop, carry forward; expand, augment.

chàn

懺 chàn **MC tsrhaemH**
1. (med.) repentance, regret, confess(ion); ask for forgiveness; originally trsc. Skt. *kṣamā*, as practiced by monks, but soon adopted elsewhere incl. in certain Dao. rituals.

孱 chàn **MC tsrhaenH**
1. (med.) scramble, muddle, confuse, confound, mix together.
2. (Budd.) ～提 *chàntí* (MC tsrhaenH-dej), trsc. Skt. *kṣānti*, patience as a positive virtue shown toward persons or circumstances that might not deserve it; acceptance, forbearance.

韂 chàn **MC tsyhemH**
1. (med.) caparison; saddle-cloth.

chāng

伥 chāng **MC trhjang**
1. rdup., blindly, recklessly, with complete unconcern for others.

倡　chāng　MC tsyhang

1. professional performer, actor, singer, dancer (male or female); artiste; ranging from professional court performers to those privately employed.

　　　chàng　MC tsyhangH

1. precentor, cantor, lead singer (of song) or chanter (of text).
2. initiate, propose; proclaim.
　　a. advocate; recommend.

娼　chāng　MC tsyhang

1. female performer, artiste; trained songstress or dancer, ranging from professional court performers to those privately employed; NOT a prostitute, nor a "sing-song girl."

昌　chāng　MC tsyhang

1. splendid, shining, brilliance; glory, glorious.
2. flourishing; prosperous.
3. positive; exact; e.g. ～言 chāngyán, straightforward or veracious words.
4. ～披 chāngpī, free-handed indiscretion, imprudence, impulsiveness, impropriety.

猖　chāng　MC tsyhang

1. (bn.) ～狂 chāngkuáng (MC tsyhang-gjwang), careless and heedless, daft and deranged; also, harsh and violent, wild and rampageous.
2. (bn.) ～獗, ～蹶 chāngjué (MC tsyhang-kjwot), wanton and reckless, supremely self-indulgent; also, overturn, subvert, turn upside-down.

菖　chāng　MC tsyhang

1. ～蒲 chāngpú, sweet flag (*Acorus calamus*), calamus, sweetly scented wetland grass, often used apotropaically; sometimes ref. to cattail (*Typha latifolia*) or bulrush (*Typha minima*).

閶　chāng　MC tsyhang

1. (bn.) ～闔 chānghé (MC tsyhang-hap), "opening and closing gate," portal's fores, grand gate, esp. mythological Heaven's Portal; astrologically the opening south of the eastern and western screens of the constellation Purple Tenuity (→紫微 zǐwēi) which leads to the seat of Heaven's god-king.
　　a. flattering ref. to principal gate of imperial palace.
　　b. old name of west wind.

2. (med.) ～門 chāngmén, name of west city-gate of Gusu 姑蘇 in state of Wu 吳.

cháng

倘　cháng　MC dzyang　→ 倘 tǎng.

償　cháng　MC dzyang

1. repay, recompense, requite; compensate, compensation, make good on, make restitution for; indemnify.
2. realize (an aim), fulfill, satisfy.
3. (med.) react(ion); respond, reply, answer.

嘗　cháng　MC dzyang

1. to taste.
　　a. try, attempt; experiment with, get a foretaste of.
　　b. experience, encounter, an occurrence of.
2. pre-VB modifier indicating past tense: once; e.g. 吾友～從事於斯矣 wú yǒu cháng cóngshì yú sī yǐ, my friend has once attended to affairs in this respect; 牛山之木～美矣 niúshān zhī mù cháng měi yǐ, the trees of Ox Mountain were once beautiful.
　　a. modified by the aspectual negative GP wèi 未: not yet once > never; e.g. 未～飽也 wèicháng bǎo yě, he never ate his fill; 未～有所不受也 wèicháng yǒu suǒ búshòu yě, there was never something that I did not accept.

場　cháng　MC drjang

1. open area on which specified action is carried out; e.g. sgl. or ～圃 chángpǔ, threshing floor.
　　a. sacrificial space, altar; area for sanctioned ritual; e.g. 道～ dàocháng, place of practice, arena of the Way, sanctuary, Budd. or Dao. chapel.
　　b. terrain; battlefield.
2. arena, field of action for a number of people, incl. figurative usage; e.g. 文～ wéncháng, the literary arena.
3. tract, yard; plot; clearing.
4. (med.) measure-word for occurrences.

　　　chǎng　MC drjang

1. location, locale, place.
2. market-stall, merchant's shop.

嫦　cháng　MC dzyang

1. (bn.) ～娥 cháng'é (MC dzyang-nga), Chang'e, "persistent beauty," name of legendary lady said

to have stolen elixir of immortality and fled to the moon, hence goddess of moon; originally called 恆娥 Héng'é, 1st syllable changed to avoid taboo on personal name of Liu Heng 劉恆, Han Wendi 漢文帝 (r. 180-157 BCE).

常   cháng   MC dzyang

1. constant, recurrent; persistent, enduring, permanent; prevalent, steady.
   a. long-lasting, long-customed, long-vested, time-honored, time-worn.
   b. frequent, often; in med. texts usu. means "always."
2. conventional, ordinary, commonplace; routine, forewonted; make a regular practice of.
3. 〜棣 chángdì, variously identified as species of cherry, plum, pear, or quince, gorgeously flowering; perhaps kerria (*Kerria japonica*) showing large yellow flowers in springtime; suggested rendering either "kerria" or "sweet-plum"; associated in lit. with fraternal feeling; syn. 棠棣 *tángdì*.
4. a measure of 16 ft. (*chi* 尺), equiv. 2 *xun* 尋.

徜   cháng   MC dzyang

1. (bn.) 〜徉 chángyáng (MC dzyang-yang), shilly-shally, shift back and forth, havering and wavering

腸   cháng   MC drjang

1. intestines, bowels.
2. more generally, innards > innermost feelings; e.g. 〜斷 chángduàn, with innards rent, often paraphrased as "broken-hearted."

萇   cháng   MC drjang

1. (bn.) 〜楚 chángchǔ (MC drjang-tsrhjoX), kiwi fruit, Chinese gooseberry (*Actinidia chinensis*); syn. 羊桃 *yángtáo*, 獼猴桃 *míhóutáo*.

裳   cháng   MC dzyang

1. lower garment, skirt (for men and women).
   a. underskirt.
2. by synecdoche, clothing, garb, attire.

長   cháng   MC drjang

1. of space: long, length(en); stretch, tall; e.g. 〜跪 chángguì, "long-kneeling," kneel with hams not touching back of heels, with torso held upright as sign of respect; 〜門 chángmén, long (i.e. tall) gate; 〜天 chángtiān, long (i.e. far-stretching) sky; 〜谷 chánggǔ, long valley; also, Dao. esoteric name for nose.
2. of time: prolong(ed), lasting, enduring; e.g. 〜庚 chánggēng, "prolonger of the *geng*-hour," Venus seen as evening star; 〜恨 chánghèn, lasting regret; 〜行 chángxíng, regular; 〜行旨符 chángxíngzhǐfú, permanently applicable directive.
3. be good at, excel in; "long suit," forte, strong point; e.g. 〜才 chángcái, specialty, métier.

zhǎng   MC trjangX

1. grow, develop; increase, swell.
   a. cause to grow, raise; cultivate, nurture.
2. senior, in age; e.g. 〜子 zhǎngzǐ, eldest son; 〜少 zhǎngshǎo, seniors and juniors, older and younger.
3. of principal importance; first in status; eminent.
   a. leader, headman (of village), alderman.
4. treat with special respect, honor.
5. (Budd.) 〜者 zhǎngzhe, householder; also, rich merchant.

zhàng   MC trjangH

1. (med.) many, much; more, surplus; e.g. 〜物 zhàngwù, extra things.

鱨   cháng   MC dzyang

1. golden catfish (*Pseudo-bagrus aurantiacus*).

chǎng

廠   chǎng   MC tsyhangX

1. (med.) open yard, crude enclosure.
   a. (med.) hut, shanty, without self-standing walls.

惝   chǎng   MC tsyhangX

1. disconcerted, unsettled, perturbed.
2. (bn.) 〜怳 chǎnghuǎng (MC tsyhangX-xjwangX), fazed and fretted, ruffled and rattled, discomfited.

敞   chǎng   MC tsyhangX

1. spacious, expansive; broadly spread.
2. lay open, disclose; open out widely or grandly.
3. (bn.) 〜怳 chǎnghuǎng (MC tsyhangX-xjwangX), faint and fuddled, vague confusion, mixed muddle, indistinct obscurity, humming hush.

昶　chǎng　MC trhjangX

1. extended daylight, prolonged day; long shining (of sun).
2. ⊙ 暢 *chàng* 1, unobstructed, unimpeded; 2, clear, patent; 3, euphoric, fulfilled.

氅　chǎng　MC tsyhangX

1. feather fringe, feathered trim of coat or cloak, usu. of crane's plumes.
    a. pelisse, coat or cloak trimmed with feathers or fur.
2. (med.) feather-trimmed standard or ensign of imperial honor-guards.
3. (med.) ⊙ 鷩 *biè*, the golden pheasant (*Chrysolophus pictus*).

chàng

唱　chàng　MC tsyhangH

1. precentor, lead singer or chanter.
    a. take the lead, speak up first; raise (an issue), propose; advance, advocate.
2. sing.
    a. play a musical instrument, making it "sing."
    b. chant, recite aloud.
    c. sing out, say loudly, proclaim.
3. praise, commend, extol.
4. (Budd.) ⊙ 磬 *qìng*, bowl-shaped copper percussion instrument in a monastery, struck to call the assembly to attention.

悵　chàng　MC trhjangH

1. dissatisfied, chagrined; despondent; unrequited.
    a. (bn.) ～望 *chàngwàng* (MC trhjangH-mjangH), to long despondently.
    b. (bn.) 惆～ *chóuchàng*, → 惆 *chóu*.

暢　chàng　MC trhjangH

1. unimpeded, unobstructed; unqualified, unmitigated; thoroughgoing.
    a. unfold, extend; smooth out; e.g. ～達 *chàngdá*, easy and smooth, facile.
    b. long, lengthy; e.g. ～轂 *chànggǔ*, "lengthy wheel-hubs," a large war-chariot.
    c. understand thoroughly and without qualification; explain or express oneself completely.
2. clear, patent; recognizable, evident, manifest.
3. open-hearted; euphoric, joyful; fulfilled.
    a. alert, expressive, animated, dynamic; spirited, vivacious.
4. profuse, proliferating; flourishing; full, all-encompassing.
5. ⊙ 觴 *shāng*, wine goblet.

韔　chàng　MC trhjangH

1. bow-case.
    a. put a bow into its case.

鬯　chàng　MC trhjangH

1. aromatic wine used in sacrificial offerings; hippocras, nectar.
2. ～草 *chàngcǎo*, wild turmeric (*Curcuma aromatica*), or common turmeric, saffron, yellow ginger (*Curcuma longa*), syn. 鬱金香 *yùjīnxiāng*.
3. ⊙ 韔 *chàng*, bow-case; 暢 *chàng* 1, unobstructed, clear; 4, profuse, flourishing.

chāo

弨　chāo　MC tsyhew

1. unstring a bow; unstrung bow.
2. (med.) gen. term for a bow.

怊　chāo　MC trhjew

1. sad(dening), cheerless; bleak.
    a. (bn.) ～悵 *chāochàng* (MC trhjew-trhjangH), distraught and downcast, sadly distressed.

抄　chāo　MC tsrhaew

1. take by force, seize; confiscate, plunder, take possession of; take control of.
2. claw up, squeeze up.
3. measure of capacity, a handful, equiv. one-tenth of a "ladle" (*shao* 勺).
4. (med.) scoop up, as with spoon or gourd.
5. (med.) progress or come at something from the side, in an indirect manner.
6. (med.) make an extract of a text, epitomize; copy out (usu. not word-for-word); transumpt.
    a. (med.) make an extract of, quote from.

鼂　chāo　MC tsraew

1. seine, for catching fish; catch fish with same.

鈔　chāo　MC tsrhaew

1. clamor, tumult, uproar, hubbub, cacophony.

2. cunning, wily; resourceful; calculating, scheming.

3. quick (of mind, word, or body); nimble.

超   chāo   MC trhjew

1. leap over, vault over; outstride.
   a. traverse; pass beyond, go beyond.
2. surpass, exceed; outdo, leave behind.
   a. transcend, esp. in sense of world-escaping.
3. far off, far distant; yonder.

鈔   chāo   MC tsrhaew

1. ⊙ 抄 *chāo* 1, take by force, seize; confiscate, plunder, take possession of; take control of; 6 (med.), copy out a text (usu. not word-for-word), transcribe; transumpt; make an extract of, quote from.

   miǎo   MC mjiewX

1. ⊙ 杪 *miǎo* 1, tip or end of a branch; nib, stub; endpoint, last bit of; 2, minute, small bit; slight, mere; mite, speck.

cháo

嘲   cháo   MC traew

1. mock, deride, ridicule; tease; chide.
2. (med.) chant, intone; hum.

巢   cháo   MC dzraew

1. nest, cote.
   a. nestle.
2. lair, den.

晁   cháo   MC drjew

1. ⊙ 鼂 *cháo* 2, a surname.
   zhāo   MC trjew
1. ⊙ 朝 *zhāo* 1, morning, from sunrise to the first meal; 2, daytime.

朝   cháo   MC drjew   → 朝 *zhāo*.

樔   cháo   MC dzraew

1. ⊙ 巢 *cháo* 1, nest(le), cote.
   zhāo   MC tsraew
1. ⊙ 罩 *chāo*, fish-net, seine.
   jiǎo   MC tsjewX
1. sever, cut off.

潮   cháo   MC drjew

1. tide, tidewater, tidal flow.
   a. stream, current, flow; waves.
   b. tidal bore.
2. damp(ness), moist(ure).

謿   cháo   MC traew   ⊙ 嘲 *cháo*.

鼂   cháo   MC drjew

1. leatherback sea-turtle (*Dermochelys coriacea*).
2. a surname.
   zhāo   MC trjew
1. ⊙ 朝 *zhāo* 1, morning, from sunrise to the first meal; 2, daytime.

chǎo

吵   chǎo   MC tsrhaewX

1. (med.) cry out, bellow; raise a ruckus; tumult, commotion; strepitous, strepitant, racket, bedlam.

炒   chǎo   MC tsrhae

1. stir-fry, stir-roast.

麨   chǎo   MC tsyhewX

1. parched grain.

chē

硨   chē   MC tsyhae   → 硨 *jū*.

車   chē   MC tsyhae

1. wheeled vehicle, incl. carriage, chariot, wagon.
2. ref. various wheeled or wheel-shaped implements; e.g. 緯～ *wěichē*, "weft-reel," quilling-reel.
3. (med.) jaw, mandibles.
   jū   MC kjo
1. (med.) (bn.) ～渠 *jūqú* (MC kjo-gjo), mother-of-pearl, nacre, nacreous; also, giant clam (*Tridacna gigas*).

chè

呫   chè   MC tsyhep

1. (bn.) ～囁 *chèniè* (MC tsyhep-ngep), whisper, speak in hushed tones; sibilance, susurrus.
2. (med.) rdup., babble on, chatter, prattle.

坼   chè   MC trhaek

1. crack, split open; rend, split apart.
   a. partition, divide.
2. cracks produced for divination on "oracle bones."
3. burst forth, burgeon (of plants).

徹　chè　MC trhjet

1. go all the way through, thorough(-going); pervasive; penetrate; plunge onward.
   a. completely, from first to last; to the very end.
2. follow through with; accord with from point to point.
3. penetrating; clear, translucent; discerning; ⊙ 澈 *chè*.
4. clear away, remove; eliminate; ⊙ 撤 *chè*.
5. reclaim (wasteland); bring to right form.
6. wheel-ruts; ⊙ 轍 *zhè* 1.

掣　chè　MC tsyhejH

1. drag, pull; tug along; e.g. ～頓 *chèdùn*, lead on, draw after one.
   a. pull out; select, choose out.
2. keep back, retain, hold back.
3. (med.) pass quickly, in a moment; e.g. ～電 *chèdiàn*, in a flash, flicker past.

撤　chè　MC trhjet

1. clear away, remove; eliminate, do away with.
   a. cast off, expel; cancel, strike out.

澈　chè　MC drjet

1. clear, translucent, esp. of water; able to see through to the bottom.
   a. discern(ment), discerning, ascertain(-ment); piercingly understand.
2. penetrating, thorough(-going).

chēn

嗔　chēn　MC tsyhin

1. ⊙ 瞋 *chēn*, glare, in anger, belligerence, or surprise; with dilated eyes, wide-eyed, pop-eyed; infuriated, enraged, incensed, indignant.

tián　MC den

1. rdup., onom. of drumbeats, "dun-dun."

琛　chēn　MC trhim

1. costly, valuable; treasure(d), cherished; ref. gems or other special items.

瞋　chēn　MC tsyhin

1. glare, in anger, belligerence, or surprise; with dilated eyes, wide-eyed, pop-eyed.
   a. infuriated, enraged; incensed, indignant.

綝　chēn　MC trhim

1. halt, pause; stop.

shēn　MC srim

1. (bn.) ～纚 *shēnxǐ* (MC srim-srjeX), ～縿 *shēnshān* (MC srim-sraem) dangling fringe, feathered tufts (of clothing), softly tufted, trailing downward.

lín　MC lim

1. full, full adornment.
   a. (bn.) ～纚 *línlí* (MC lim-lje), lush and dense (vegetation).

腪　chēn　MC tsyhin

1. distend(ed), bloat(ed), swollen.

chén

塵　chén　MC drin

1. dust.
   a. dust particles, smallest amount; e.g. (Budd.) ～劫 *chénjié*, kalpas (equal to the number) of dust particles.
   b. traces, exemplar; e.g. 清～ *qīngchén*, pure traces < dust raised by carriage-wheels of admirable person.
2. worldly, mundane; esp. (Budd.) the sensual world; e.g. ～勞 *chénláo*, worldly sufferings; ～累 *chénlèi*, worldly entanglements; ～表 *chénbiǎo*, extramundane; also (med.), be of transcendent (unworldly) character.

宸　chén　MC dzyin

1. eaves, edges of roof, esp. of Son of Heaven's palace.
2. region of the Pole Star > divine source of (en)light(enment) > sanctum, adytum (of a god or god-king), sacrosanct area.
   a. palace precincts or inner sanctum of emperor; ruler's private apartments.

忱　chén　MC dzyim

1. sincere, unfeigning, ingenuous.
2. trustworthy, believable, dependable.

晨　chén　MC dzyin

1. early morning, esp. time of cock-crow; dawn-source.
   a. ～風 *chénfēng*, morning breeze; also, poetic name for the merlin (*Falco columbarius*).

沈   chén   MC drim

1. sink, plunge into water; e.g. ～浮 *chénfú*, plunging and drifting, follow the current; euph. for succeed and fail; also, life's vicissitudes.
   a. drown, submerge; inundate(d).
2. immerse oneself in, sink into, be lost in, wallow in, indulge in; e.g. ～酣 *chénhān*, drunk with the thought of, besotted with; ～吟 *chényín*, "lost in stammers," unable to make up one's mind, hesitate; also, deep in thought, sunk in musing.
   a. deeply taken with, consumed by, given over to; e.g. ～憂 *chényōu*, consumed by sadness.
3. hide, lie low, conceal(ed).
4. rdup., deep and cavernous, sunken in the deeps of distance (alt. pronounced *tántán* [MC dom-dom]); also (med.), endless rain, drowning downpour.
5. ～香 *chénxiāng*, "sinking aromatic" (because heavier than water), i.e. aloeswood, agarwood (*Aquilaria agallocha*), heavy, dark, diseased wood of *Aquilaria* trees, esp. prized as incense.

   shěn   MC syimX

1. a surname.

沉   chén   MC drim

1. ⊙ 沈 *chén*; but not used for *shěn*, surname.

臣   chén   MC dzyin

1. subject, servant, vassal, liegeman; often in conjunction with 君 *jūn*, sovereign, suzerain, liegelord, ruler.
   a. humble self-ref. in 3rd-person: your subject, your servant, your vassal.
   b. regard as subject, treat or act as inferior.
2. important public servant, great vassal; magnate, courtier.
3. slave (male).

蔯   chén   MC drin

1. (bn.) 茵～ *yīnchén* (MC 'jin-drin), capillary wormwood (*Artemisia capillaris*).

諶   chén   MC dzyim

1. trustworthy, believable; put one's faith in.
2. reliable, definitely so; true; indeed so.

辰   chén   MC dzyin

1. time, esp. propitious time.
2. celestial body; sun, moon, and stars, esp. as indicators of time in various contexts; chronogram.

   a. 北～ *běichén*, the Pole Star; ～星 *chénxīng*, the planet Mercury.
   b. one of the 28 lunar lodgings, comprised of 3 stars, α (Antares), σ, τ Scorpii, in the eastern quadrant (*qinglong* 青龍 or *canglong* 蒼龍) of the sky; alt. names 心 *xīn*, 商 *shāng*.
   c. conjunction of sun and moon.
   d. space of 30° along celestial sphere; > 12 zodiacal stations on the ecliptic.
3. 5th of the 12 earthly branches, associated with the dragon as emblematic animal.
   a. 5th double-hour of the day, from approximately 7 to 9 a.m.
4. ⊙ 晨 *chén*, early morning, dawn-source; 宸 *chén* 2, sanctum, adytum, esp. palace precincts of emperor.

陳   chén   MC drin

1. arrange, place, dispose in order, lay out, deploy, marshal; set forth, display; e.g. ～力 *chénlì*, put forth one's efforts, marshal one's strength.
2. state, announce; declare, give notice of, make known; avow, affirm; e.g. ～情 *chénqíng*, state one's feelings outright.
3. stale, timeworn, outmoded, outworn; hackneyed, over-familiar; obsolete, dessicated.
   a. stale, unfresh, tasteless; withered, moldy, musty.
4. passage connecting main gate and great hall of state.
5. name of feudal state in Zhou times, located in eastern portion of Henan and northern portion of Anhui; granted as appanage by King Wu of Zhou to the reputed descendants of sage-king Shun 舜; absorbed by the state of Chu 楚 at the end of Chunqiu period.
6. name of med. "southern" dynasty (557-589), with capital at Jiankang 建康 (Nanjing).
7. a surname, notably that of the ruling family of the Chen (557-589) dynasty.

   zhèn   MC drinH

1. deployment of troops, to marshal troops, battle array, battle formation.

chěn

磣   chěn   MC tsrhimX

1. (med.) grit in food.
2. (med.) ～黷 *chěndú*, confused, chaotic, askew, awry.

跈　chěn　MC trhimX　⊙ 蹍 *chěn*.

蹍　chěn　MC trhimX
1. (bn.) ～踔 *chěnchuō* (MC trhimX-trhaewk), wamble and wobble, lurch and falter, stumble and list; also, quickly growing, shooting up speedily.

chèn

傶　chèn　MC tsrhinH　⊙ 襯 *chèn*.

櫬　chèn　MC tsrhinH
1. inner coffin, which holds the corpse.
   a. gen. term for coffin.
2. hibiscus, shrubby althaea (*Hibiscus syriaca*), syn. 木槿 *mùjǐn*.

疢　chèn　MC trhinH
1. fever(ish).
2. malady; distress, trouble.
   a. defect, flaw, shortcoming.

襯　chèn　MC tsrhinH
1. (med.) undergarment.
   a. (med.) inner lining; to line (garment).
2. (med.) enhance by contrast, set off, serve as background or complement, make stand out.
3. give alms, donate, donation, offering, charity, esp. to Budd. monk; trns. Skt. *dakṣīna*.

讖　chèn　MC tsrhimH
1. predict(ion), prophesy, prognostication regarding good or ill fortune.
   a. ～緯 *chènwěi*, "predictive weft-texts," prophetic apocrypha, texts composed anonymously as prophetic supplements and esoteric interpretations added to the "warp-texts" (*jing* 經, classics).
   chàn　MC tsrhaemH
1. (med.) ⊙ 懺 *chàn*, repentance, regret, confess(ion); ask for forgiveness.

趁　chèn　MC trhinH
1. pursue, follow, trail.
   a. (med.) ～迭 *chèndié*, catch up with or to.
2. (med.) proceed to, advance toward; push toward.
   a. (med.) follow out, persevere in.
3. (med.) avail oneself of, take advantage of; make use of, profit from.

趂　chèn　MC trhinH　⊙ 趁 *chèn*.

亂　chèn　MC tsrhinH　⊙ 齔 *chèn*.

齔　chèn　MC tsrhinH
1. shedding of baby-teeth.
   a. time of same, childhood.

chēng

噌　chēng　MC tsrheang
1. (bn.) ～吰 *chēnghóng* (MC tsrheang-hweang), onom. of pealing, chiming bells.

樘　chēng　MC trhaeng
1. inclined strut, brace, truss, diagonal post resting on top of rafter.
   a. prop, support.
2. pole a boat, punt.

撐　chēng　MC trhaeng　⊙ 樘 *chēng*.

掌　chēng　MC trhaeng
1. variant form of → 樘 *táng*, diagonal post resting on top of rafter; strut.

琤　chēng　MC tsrheang
1. onom. of jades or other items striking together.
   a. (med.) rdup., "chyeng-chyeng," onom. of tinkling jades or gems; also, of lapping, plashing water; also, of plucked, vibrating zither strings.

瞠　chēng　MC trhaeng
1. stare at, regard fixedly, fix one's gaze on.

稱　chēng　MC tsyhing
1. weigh; evaluate, assess; consider.
2. raise; take up, adduce; take as pretext.
   a. raise up, lift up, recommend; advance.
3. esteem, acclaim, extol.
   a. defer to, bow to.
4. declare, speak of, state; profess, claim.
   a. designate, call, name, denote; designation, appellation.
   chèng　MC tsyhingH
1. steelyard, scales, for weighing.
2. (med.) measure of weight, equiv. 15 "catties" (*jin* 斤).

chèn   MC tsyhingH

1. fit, match, agree with, compatible with, correspond to; e.g. 〜心 *chènxīn*, accord with one's feelings (aims, thoughts); 〜物 *chènwù*, match up with the object.

蟶   chēng   MC trhjeng

1. (med.) razor-clam (*Novaculina constricta*).

頳   chēng   MC trhjeng

1. light-red, flushed, rosy.
   a. blush(ing); e.g. 〜桐花 *chēngtónghuā*, "blushing paulownia," the glorybower (*Clerodendron kaempferi*).

頳   chēng   MC trhjeng   ⊙ 頳 *chēng*.

䞓   chēng   MC trhjeng   ⊙ 頳 *chēng*.

chéng

丞   chéng   MC dzying

1. assist(ant), aid(e), often used in official titles to indicate subordinate status, usu. as last element in title.

2. 〜相 *chéngxiàng*, prime minister, chancellor, highest-ranking civil official; usu. 2 holding the rank at same time, distinguished by prefix *zuo* 左 "left" or *you* 右 "right."

3. sgl., 2nd-ranking official (to the *ling* 令 "magistrate") in a district (*xian* 縣), adjuvant, vice-magistrate; in Tang times informally called 贊府 *zànfǔ*, assistant repositor (cf. magistrate's informal title, 明府 *míngfǔ*, enlightened repositor).

4. ⊙ 承 *chéng* 1, receive, accept; 拯 *zhěng*, rescue, relieve.

乘   chéng   MC zying

1. mount (horse, carriage), board (boat); climb into or onto; ascend onto.

2. ride; be borne on or by; e.g. 〜槎 *chéngchá*, ride a raft; 〜興 *chéngxīng*, borne on an impulse or whim; 〜醉 *chéngzuì*, buoyed by intoxication.

3. avail oneself of, take advantage of; make use of, profit from; e.g. 〜勢 *chéngshì*, rely on circumstances.

4. prevail over, get the better of; impose on, preponderate over; vanquish.

5. pursue, chase, "ride down."

6. calculate, reckon.

shèng   MC zyingH

1. vehicle, esp. quadriga, 4-horse team; e.g. 〜從 *shèngcóng*, carriage and attendants.
   a. in early times, a war-chariot bearing 3 armored knights (*shi* 士) with contingent of 72 foot-soldiers.
   b. 〜輿 *shèngyú*, ruler's carriage of state; also, metonymy for ruler; also, common horse(s) and carriage.

2. (Budd.) a "vehicle" of teaching; e.g. 大〜 *dàshèng*, Great Vehicle, trns. Skt. *mahāyāna*; 小〜 *xiǎoshèng*, Lesser Vehicle, trns. Skt. *hīnayāna*; 三〜 *sānshèng*, the 3 Vehicles, trns. Skt. *triyāna*, i.e. (1) 聲聞乘 *shēngwénshèng*, vehicle of the "voice-hearers" (*śrāvakayāna*), (2) 緣覺乘 *yuánjuéshèng*, vehicle of those "awakened by conditionality" (*pratyekabuddhayāna*), (3) 菩薩乘 *púsàshèng*, vehicle of those "intent on achieving enlightenment" (*bodhisattvayāna*), the latter belonging to the Mahāyāna, the first 2 to the Hīnayāna.

呈   chéng   MC drjeng

1. to present (for observation or inspection), appear, manifest, make evident; emerge.

2. (med.) proffer, give from inferior to superior.

3. 程 *chéng* 1, standard, measure(ment), norm.

城   chéng   MC dzyeng

1. wall, of settlement; esp. inner wall dividing city from outskirts (cf. 郭 *guō*, outer city-wall).
   a. to wall in, enclose.
   b. boundary wall.

2. walled city; enceinte.
   a. citadel; fort.

塍   chéng   MC zying

1. raised path between rice-fields, balk; field-dyke.

懲   chéng   MC dring

1. punish, discipline.
   a. reprove, reprehend.

2. take warning from, learn a lesson.
   a. hold in check, contain oneself.

3. suffer from, be troubled by.

成   chéng   MC dzyeng

1. complete, accomplish, achieve; effect(ive).
   a. fulfill, realize; e.g. 〜禮 *chénglǐ*, fulfill the rites.

b. full round of a tune, full measure of a dance, perform(ance).

c. accomplished at, apt at, good at.

2. whole(ness), make whole; fully formed; mature; consummate.

3. to form, shape; become, develop (into); develop fully.

4. cause to conform; reconcile, accommodate.

a. calm down, compose; allay; suppress.

5. level, layer; degree, gradation, extent; e.g. 九～之臺 *jiǔchéng zhī tái*, 9-layered terrace.

6. ancient measure of 10 square miles.

7. (med.) be like, similar to, resemble; usu. in parallel structure with 如 *rú* or 似 *sì*.

承　chéng　MC dzying

1. receive, accept (from above); be visited with; inherit, heritor.

2. assent to, acquiesce in, acknowledge; e.g. ～伏 *chéngfú*, accept blame.

a. relieve, alleviate, allay, palliate.

3. accede to, succeed to; continue, carry on.

a. undertake, take up.

4. obstruct, forestall.

5. (med.) sgl. or ～聞 *chéngwén*, hear(d) it said that . . .

6. (med.) ～前 *chéngqián*, heretofore, prior to this.

7. ⊙ 丞 *chéng* 1, assist, aid; 乘 *chéng* 3, avail oneself of, make use of, take advantage of.

根　chéng　MC draeng

1. doorposts, doorjambs, on either side of door or gate.

2. provoke, rouse; activate, agitate; stir to action.

3. (med.) rdup., "dre-e-ng, dre-e-ng," onom. of zither strings vibrating.

4. ⊙ 橙 *chéng*, sweet orange, coolie orange (*Citrus sinensis*).

桭　chéng　MC zying

1. mount, ride on, direct (esp. horse, carriage); original form of 乘 *chéng*.

shèng　MC zyingH

1. war-chariot.

橙　chéng　MC dreang

1. sweet orange, coolie orange (*Citrus sinensis*); cf. 柑 *gān*, sweetpeel tangerine (*Citrus nobilis*), 橘 *jú*, sourpeel tangerine (*Citrus reticulata*).

dèng　MC tongH

1. (med.) bench, stool, footstool.

檉　chéng　MC trhjeng

1. tamarisk, saltcedar (*Tamarix chinensis*), syn. 河柳 *héliǔ*.

澂　chéng　MC dring　⊙ 澄 *chéng*.

澄　chéng　MC dring

1. clear and still water, transparent.

2. pellucid, limpid; pure, unsullied.

3. bathe pure, cleanse.

dèng　MC dongH

1. remove impurities from water; decant alcohol.

程　chéng　MC drjeng

1. standard, measure(ment); norm; rule, regulation; e.g. ～式 *chéngshì*, measures and models, proper patterns.

2. weigh, consider, judge, evaluate.

3. to present, make evident, show, manifest; ⊙ 呈 *chéng* 1.

4. (med.) stage, of journey; route, road ahead.

a. (med.) document of safe-conduct, pass(port).

5. a surname.

腥　chéng　MC drjeng

1. fine cut of meat, savory meat.

䋵　chéng　MC drjeng

1. naked, nude, unclothed.

2. belt with pendants or seals attached to it.

誠　chéng　MC dzyeng

1. conforming to reality, genuine; sincere, honest, uncontrived.

a. moral wholeness, integrity.

2. (ADV) verily, truly; actually, really, e.g. 臣～知不如徐公之美 *chén chéng zhī bùrú Xú gōng zhī měi*, Actually I realize I'm not as handsome as Mr. Xu.

3. conditional marker: if indeed, if in fact . . ., e.g. ～如是, 漢室興矣 *chéng rú shì, Hàn shì xīng yǐ*, Were it indeed like this, the House of Han would be restored.

醒　chéng　MC drjeng

1. hangover, from drink; hungover, muzzy-headed, crapulent.

a. (med.) to sober up.

騬　chéng　MC zying

1. geld a horse; a gelding.

chěng

逞   chěng   MC trhjengX
1. gratified, satisfied; smug; contented, fulfilled.
2. gratify one's desires, carry out to the fullest one's wishes; indulge, give license to.
   a. impulsive, impetuous; presumptuous.

騁   chěng   MC trhjengX
1. gallop, give rein to; dash, hie, whisk, bound.
2. give rein to one's desires, unbridled; impetuous, charging.

chèng

秤   chèng   MC tsyhingH
1. steelyard, scales, for weighing, ⊙ 稱 chèng 1 (chēng).
2. (med.) measure of weight, equiv. 15 "catties" (jìn 斤), ⊙ 稱 chèng 2 (chēng).

chī

吃   chī   MC kit
1. stammer, stutter.
   a. do or act haltingly.
N.B. not used for 喫 chī, eat, until post-Tang times.

喫   chī   MC khek
1. (med.) eat; drink; take in, consume.
2. (med.) receive, accept; e.g. ～虧 chīkuī, be injured, suffer, fail.

嗤   chī   MC tsyhi
1. ridicule, jeer, sneer at, mock; treat with contempt.

媸   chī   MC tsyhi
1. (med.) ugly, misshapen, malformed; repulsive, repellent.

摛   chī   MC trhje
1. lay out, set forth; display, show.
   a. express; publish, spread, circulate.

痴   chī   MC trhi   ⊙ 癡 chī.

癡   chī   MC trhi
1. idiot(ic), moron(ic); featherbrain; booby, ninny, simpleton.

2. demented, unhinged, out of one's wits.
   a. deluded, benighted, confounded.
3. (med.) obsessed, infatuated with, fixed on; possessed.

瞝   chī   MC trhje
1. survey completely, gaze all around, look everywhere, search high and low.

笞   chī   MC trhi
1. beat with bamboo cane (in Han times) or thorn-switch (post-Han), as judicial punishment, lighter punishment than 杖 zhàng 3.
   a. flog, whip.

絺   chī   MC trhij
1. fine-textured kudzu or hemp cloth.
   a. gen. term for fine cloth.
      zhǐ   MC trijX
1. ⊙ 黹 zhǐ, embroidery, fine needlework.

蚩   chī   MC tsyhi
1. ignorance, stupid(ity).
   a. rdup., untutored and uncouth; also, in chaos and confusion.
2. ugly, unsightly, unshapely; repulsive, repellent.
3. insult, treat with contempt; misprize; make light of.
   a. ridicule, jeer, sneer at, mock; ⊙ 嗤 chī.
4. unidentified sea-monster.
5. ～尤 chīyóu, name of mythical rebel who fought against and was defeated by the Yellow Emperor.

螭   chī   MC trhje
1. wyvern, a footed winged dragon with serpent's tail, often figured on pillars and stepways of palace and throne-hall; cf. 虬 qiú, spirax. N.B. The gloss "hornless (or horned) dragon" is not reliable.
2. ⊙ 魑 chī, sgl. or ～魅 chīmèi, mountain goblin.

魑   chī   MC trhje
1. sgl. or ～魅 chīmèi, mountain goblin or demon.

鴟   chī   MC tsyhij
1. gen. term for various owls and kites.
   a. 角～ jiǎochī, horned owl, Scops owl (genus *Otus*); ～鵂 chīxiū, eagle-owl, great horned owl (*Bubo bubo*); ～鴞 chīxiāo, horned and hornless owls, collective term for owls, esp. as symbols of unfiliality.

2. ～尾 *chīwěi*, "owl's tails," ridge ornaments on palace roofs.

3. 蹲～ *dūnchī*, "crouching owl," a kind of giant taro from Shu.

chí

匙　chí　MC dzye

1. spoon; if large, ladle.

坻　chí　MC drij

1. islet, cay; reef.
2. embankment.

zhǐ　MC tsyeX

1. stop, cease; pause.
2. molehill.
3. foundation, base of building, esp. palace.

dǐ　MC tejX

1. ⊙ 阺 *dǐ* 1, mountain slope; incline, gradient; hillside.

墀　chí　MC drij

1. entrance staircase in front of hall or palace, usu. lacquered.
   a. stairway, stairs, of finer than usual appearance.
2. by metonymy, parvis, courtyard, portico in front of building.

弛　chí　MC syeH

1. slack bow, unpulled or unbent bow; ant. 張 *zhāng* 1.
2. slacken, relax(ed), release tension, relieve, let up.
   a. defer, delay, suspend, postpone, hold off.
3. remove, do away with, abolish.

持　chí　MC dri

1. hold in hand, grasp; e.g. ～劍 *chíjiàn*, wield a sword; ～衡 *chíhéng*, hold the scales, evaluate a matter.
   a. uphold, support, bear up.
2. maintain, sustain; hold onto, hold fast.
3. take charge of, have (a matter) in hand; direct; e.g. 相～ *xiāngchí*, gain the upper hand, outdo.
   a. foster, take care of, attend to with care; e.g. ～養 *chíyǎng*, nurture, look after.
4. hold off, hold back, hold in check, restrain; e.g. ～久 *chíjiǔ*, hold at bay; ～心 *chíxīn*, restrain one's mind.
   a. cautious, prudent, discreet.

5. bear or hold in mind, retain, remember; e.g. (Budd.) 總～ *zǒngchí*, trns. Skt. *dhāraṇī*, collect and keep in mind > magic spell, mystical formula.

6. stand opposed to.

7. (Budd.) sgl. or ～以 *chíyǐ*, in early translated texts, an instrumental pre-vb, similar to 以 *yǐ*: making use of, with, by means of.

池　chí　MC drje

1. pool, pond, reservoir of still water; lake (with exaggeration); e.g. ～魚 *chíyú*, a fish in a pond, also (med.) euph. for being constrained by official duties.

2. moat, filled with water (cf. 隍 *huáng*, dry moat, fosse).

3. downspout, of roof.

4. ornamental trim on clothing.
   a. same on other objects, such as carriage, coffin.

5. (Dao.) used in esoteric names for several parts of body; e.g. 玄～ *xuánchí*, "murky pond," the bladder; 玉～ *yùchí*, "jade pool," the mouth; 中～ *zhōngchí*, "central pond," gall bladder.

6. (med.) reservoir of sound, esp. 龍～ *lóngchí*, "dragon pool," sound-hole of zither (*qin* 琴).

漦　chí　MC zri

1. sputum, slime, saliva of dragon or fish.

篪　chí　MC drje

1. short (ca. 30 cm.) bamboo cross-flute with both ends sealed and 5 finger-holes laid out in triangular pattern around mouthpiece.

踟　chí　MC drje

1. (bn.) ～躕 *chíchú* (MC drje-drju), fuss and fidget, dilly-dally, vacillate; go back and forth, shilly-shally, haffle-caffle.

遲　chí　MC drij

1. slow, dilatory; circuitous; tedious.
   a. tardy, late(r), late-coming.
   b. dawdle, procrastinate, lag, loiter.
2. extended length of time, a long while.
   a. draw out, protract.
3. slow-witted, dull, backward.
4. (med.) sgl. or cmpd. ～疑 *chíyí*, hesitate, mark time, hang back.

zhì　MC drijH

1. wait for, await.
   a. (med.) look forward to, expect, have in prospect.

鎚   **chí**   MC dzye   → 鎚 *dī.*

馳   **chí**   MC drje
1. gallop; tantivy, ride tantivy.
    a. courser, swift horse.
2. hurry, speed, race (toward), rush to, pursue with urgency; e.g. ～道 *chídào,* imperial causeway, reserved solely for emperor so he may progress as quickly as desired.
    a. flee, run away.
3. spread, disseminate, circulate.

chǐ

侈   **chǐ**   MC tsyheX
1. extravagant, prodigal, immoderate; waste(ful), squander, dissipate; e.g. 奢～ *shēchǐ,* nimiety and waste.
    a. excessive; superfluous, extraneous; e.g. ～靡 *chǐmí,* excessive and inordinate.
2. exaggerate, overdo(ne), overstate.

哆   **chǐ**   MC tsyheX
1. with mouth wide open, agape, agog; also ref. eyes.
    a. babble, prattle.
2. ～然 *chǐrán,* loosely, slackly, laxly, sloppily, indiscreetly.
3. ⊙ 侈 *chǐ,* extravagant, immoderate; waste(ful), squander; excessive, superfluous.

尺   **chǐ**   MC tsyhek
1. measure of length, "foot," equiv. 10 *cun* 寸, "inches"; exact measurement varied over time: Eastern Zhou, Qin, Han, 9.1 Western inches; Sanguo, Jin, 9.5; Nanchao 9.7; Beichao, early 10.1, late 11.8; Tang 12.
    a. 大～ *dàchǐ* = 1 "foot" plus 2 "inches," i.e. 12 *cun* 寸.
    b. 5 "feet" = 1 "pace" or "double-step" (*bu* 步).
    c. foot-measure, ruler.
2. ～鷃 *chǐyàn,* "meager quail," "mere quail," small turnix.
3. (bn.) ～蠖 *chǐhuò* (MC tsyhek-'wak), inchworm, looper, larva of geometer-moth.

恥   **chǐ**   MC trhiX
1. shame(ful), ashamed, to shame, shamefaced.
    a. abash(ed), humiliate(d); discomfit(ed); chagrined.

蚇   **chǐ**   MC tsyhek
1. (bn.) ～蠖 *chǐhuò* (MC tsyhek-'wak), inchworm, looper, larva of geometer-moth.

褫   **chǐ**   MC trhiX
1. denude, undress, disrobe, strip (clothing).
2. strip off or away, deprive of, take from, remove; e.g. ～魄 *chipó,* bereft of spirit.
3. relax, mitigate, abate; lessen.
4. decline, deteriorate; e.g. ～氣 *chǐqì,* lose one's nerve.

豉   **chǐ**   MC dzyeH
1. fermented soy sauce, used as seasoning in the south.

齒   **chǐ**   MC tsyhiX
1. incisors, front teeth.
    a. by synecdoche, teeth in gen.; e.g. ～壯 *chǐzhuàng,* sturdy in the teeth, i.e. in good health.
2. in order, lined up neatly (like teeth).
3. judge the age of horse or ox by its teeth.
    a. age in years, of human.
    b. seniority; rank.
4. latch, clasp, fastening.
5. employ, engage; take on.
6. (med.) from Tang onward, dice; e.g. 快/惡～ *kuài/èchǐ,* good/bad throws of dice.

chì

偛   **chì**   MC trhjejH
1. (bn.) 侘～ *chàchì,* → 侘 *chà.*

勅   **chì**   MC trhik   ⊙ 敕 *chì.*

勑   **chì**   MC trhik   → 勑 *lài.*

叱   **chì**   MC tsyhit
1. revile, rave at, curse, rail at, abuse.
2. bellow, thunder; shout.
    a. call to, bawl.
3. (med.) ～拔 *chìbá* (MC tsyhit-beat), trsc. Sog. *cherpādh,* quadruped, esp. used for exceptional horses.

啻   **chì**   MC syeH
1. merely, only, just; usu. coupled with 不 *bù* or a question-word; e.g. 不～ *bùchì,* not only, not merely; 豈～ *qǐchì,* surely not just . . .; 何～ *héchì,* why only . . .?

彳 chì MC trhjek
1. take small steps.
    a. (bn.) ～亍 chìchù (MC trhjek-trhjowk), starting and stopping, advancing haltingly, toddle and totter, halt and hitch.

敕 chì MC trhik
1. rectify; organize.
2. advise, counsel; recommend.
    a. (med.) imperial decree containing guidance regarding current policy; encyclical.

斥 chì MC tsyhek
1. reject, rebuff, turn aside; scorn, spurn.
    a. dismiss, repudiate; exclude.
2. decry, condemn; censure, reproach; call to account.
3. point to, point out; refer.
4. open out, enlarge, expand.
5. spy out, look at from the side; reconnaissance.
6. saline soil, salt-flat.
7. ～鷃 chìyàn, ⊙ 尺～ chǐyàn, "meager quail," "mere quail," small turnix.

熾 chì MC tsyhiH
1. burn(ing), blaze.
2. brilliant; illustrious; splendid.

瘛 chì MC tsyhejH
1. sgl. or bn. ～瘲 chìzòng (MC tsyhejH-tsjowngH), convulsions of hands or feet.
    瘈 zhì MC tsyejH
1. ⊙ 猘 zhì, rabid dog; rabid, mad, out of control.

眙 chì MC trhiH
1. stare at, be fixated on.

糦 chì MC tsyhiH　⊙ 饎 chì.

翅 chì MC syeH
1. wings, of bird or insect; esp. long narrow wings.
    a. flap the wings.
2. ⊙ 啻 chì, merely, only, just.

赤 chì MC tsyhek
1. red; the broad mid-range of red, not as deep or saturated as 絳 jiàng, scarlet, or 朱 zhū, vermilion.
    a. fire-red, flame-red, blood-red, bare-red, the red of a just-born child, incarnadine; e.g. ～子 chìzǐ, new-born child.
    b. redden, incarnadine; burn; make bare.
2. bare, exposed; e.g. ～地 chìdì, bare ground, denuded of vegetation; (med.) ～骨 chìgǔ, bare bones, i.e. naked.
    a. unfeigned, fully revealed; sincere; e.g. ～心 chìxīn, one's true heart.
    b. with nothing held back, unrestrainedly; e.g. (med.) ～吹 chìchuī, spew out everything > slander, defame; (med.) ～盡 chìjìn, completely finished, all done, nothing left.
3. ～瑾 chìjǐn, sorrel (*Rumex acetosa*); ～膠 chìjiāo, "red resin," lac; ～豆 chìdòu, azuki bean (*Vigna angularis*); ～小豆 chìxiǎodòu, rice-bean (*Vigna calcaratus*).
4. (Dao.) ～城 chìchéng, "red enceinte," esoteric name for the heart.
5. ～鳥 chìniǎo, red bird, emblematic animal of summer; also ref. the southern quadrant of the sky.

飭 chì MC trhik
1. straighten up, put in order, arrange properly.
    a. orderly, carefully set, well-prepared.
2. ⊙ 敕 chì 2a, imperial order of guidelines or prohibitions, encyclical; 飾 shì 2, enhance(ment), adorn(ment), embellish(ment).

饎 chì MC tsyhiH
1. food and drink, provisions.
2. cooked millet, for sacrificial offering.

鶒 chì MC trhik
1. (bn.) 鸂～ xīchì, → 鸂 xī.

chōng

充 chōng MC tsyhuwng
1. full, filled.
    a. whole, complete; abundant; plenitude.
    b. (med.) filled out, of body; e.g. ～壯 chōngzhuàng, fat, fleshy, rotund.
2. fill (up), make whole or complete.
    a. fill an official position, serve as, often in addition to one's normal office; e.g. ～選 chōngxuǎn, fill the appointment, be appointed to an office or for a task.
3. fit in, fit with, accord with, satisfy; e.g. 攻～其言 gōng chōng qí yán, his actions agree with his words.
4. (bn.) ～斥 chōngchì (MC tsyhuwng-tsyhek), swarm and spread, run riot.

冲 chōng MC drjuwng ⊙ 沖 *chōng*.

忡 chōng MC trhjuwng
1. sgl. or rdup., downcast, saddened, uneasy, troubled, agitated.
2. of ornament, dangling, trailing, hanging.

憃 chōng MC trhaewng
1. dense, stupid, thick-headed, duncish, lumpish.

憧 chōng MC tsyhowng
1. rdup., dithering and undecided, circling round and round, swinging back and forth; also, moving on without interruption, ceaseless activity; also, onom. of carriages trundling.
2. (med.) (bn.) ～憬 *chōngjǐng* (MC tsyhowng-kjwaengX), wistfully wishing, imagine with yearning.
    zhuàng MC draewngH
1. witless, empty-headed, foolish.

舂 chōng MC syowng
1. beat against, strike; ram.

沖 chōng MC drjuwng
1. surge, rise up (to), heave; rush upward; e.g. ～天 *chōngtiān*, surge up to the sky.
    a. bubble up, swell.
    b. infuse, saturate, pour into.
2. empty, emptied.
3. sublime, exalted.
4. unassuming, modest, retiring; obliging, amenable, conciliatory; e.g. ～和 *chōnghé*, agreeably moderate.
5. very young, callow, inexperienced, immature.
6. deep-seated, far into.
7. rdup., onom. of chipping and chopping at ice; also, of ornaments, dangling down; also, surging swiftly upward, heaving on high.

舂 chōng MC syowng
1. pound or grind grain with mortar and pestle to remove the husk; e.g. (med.) 下～ *xiàchōng*, when the pounding stops, i.e. sunset.
    a. mortar, in which grain is hulled.
2. ⊙ 衝 *chōng* 2, run against, run into, butt, collide with, rush against, charge into.
3. (bn.) ～容 *chōngróng* (MC syowng-yowng), crash and collide; also (med.), poised and polished, balanced and composed, esp. of lit. style; also (med.), stroll and saunter, swing along easily.

4. ～鋤 *chōngchú*, "pounding hoe," colloquial name for the egret (*Egretta garzetta*, 鷺 *lù*) because bobbing movement of the bird's head when wading was reminiscent of the action of pounding grain or dabbing of hoe.

橦 chōng MC tsyhowng
1. (bn.) 艨～ *méngchōng*, → 艨 *méng*.

衝 chōng MC tsyhowng
1. thoroughfare, avenue, major road or highway; strategic line of communication.
    a. (med.) principal, major; important.
    b. (med.) correspond or communicate with, correspondence, communication.
2. run against, run into, butt, collide with, rush against, charge into.
3. siege engine, moved on wheels.
    a. assault, attack.
4. (med.) toward, up against, upon, hard by.
    chǒng MC tsyhowngX
1. (bn.) ～樅 *chǒngzǒng* (MC tsyhowngX-tsuwngX), jumbled and jostling together.

chóng

崇 chóng MC dzrjuwng
1. high, elevated, raised, exalted, eminent.
    a. exalt, raise, elevate; honor, esteem, place on high, revere.
2. add to, expand, enlarge, magnify.
3. fill up, as wine in a cup.
4. complete, experience all of, to the highest degree; e.g. ～朝 *chóngzhāo*, all morning, the whole forenoon.

蟲 chóng MC drjuwng
1. gen. term for insects; e.g. ～豸 *chóngzhì*, creepy-crawlers, insects and bugs.
    a. (med.) plague of insects.
2. sgl. or ～子 *chóngzi*, gen. term for creatures of all kinds, incl. humans.

重 chóng MC drjowng → 重 *zhòng*.

chǒng

寵 chǒng MC trhjowngX
1. favor, honor, prefer(ment).

a. favored, preferred; indulged, doted on, coddled (usu. by ruler or other influential person).
2. do as one will, give oneself up to, revel in.

chōu

妯　chōu　MC trhjuw
1. act(ive), unsettled, uneasy; unquiet.
　　zhóu　MC drjuwk
1. cmpd. ～娌 zhóulǐ, collective term for older and younger brothers' wives.

抽　chōu　MC trhjuw
1. draw out, pull out.
　　a. unwind, unreel, ⊙ 紬 chōu 1 (→ chóu).
2. set forth, extrude, project, push out, esp. sprouts or leaves.
　　a. advance, promote, put forth.
3. express, speak out.
4. take out, take off, get rid of; e.g. ～簪 chōuzān, set aside (official) hatpin, i.e. give up office.
5. (med.) pull back, recoil, retreat.
6. (med.) extract a part from the whole; levy.

搊　chōu　MC tsrhjuw
1. (med.) pluck a stringed instrument.
2. ⊙ 抽 chōu 1, pull out, draw out; unreel.

瘳　chōu　MC trhjuw
1. recover from illness.
　　a. cure(d), heal(ed).
2. improve; ameliorate.

篘　chōu　MC tsrhjuw
1. (med.) decanter, for wine.
　　a. (med.) to decant or strain wine.

chóu

仇　chóu　MC gjuw
1. counterpart; companion.
2. opposite number, enemy, adversary.
　　a. enmity, animosity, aversion; vendetta.
　　qiú　MC gjuw
1. ⊙ 1 above.
2. a surname.

儔　chóu　MC drjuw
1. of the same kind or class.
　　a. compeer, colleague, fellow, comrade, companion (in pre-Han times usu. written 疇 chóu).

幬　chóu　MC drjuw
1. bed-curtain or canopy.
2. curtain used on carriage or boat.
　　dào　MC dawH
1. cover, hang over, overlay; veil.

惆　chóu　MC trhjuw
1. frustrated, disappointed, disheartened.
　　a. (bn.) ～悵 chóuchàng (MC trhjuw-trhjangH), despairing and despondent, downcast and disheartened, frustrated and unrequited, desolate heartbreak.

愁　chóu　MC dzrjuw
1. sad, woeful, plaintive, rueful.
　　a. grieving; mestive, mournful; somber.
　　b. (med.) (bn.) ～疾 chóují (MC dzrjuw-dzit), sadly sorrowful.
2. cheerless, bleak, descriptive of scene or objects that make one sad or melancholy; e.g. ～雲 chóuyún, gloomy clouds.

疇　chóu　MC drjuw
1. plowed field; arable land.
　　a. cultivate a field.
2. interr. pronoun: who(m)?
3. organize by category; of the same kind.
4. ～昔 chóuxī, in times past, days gone by.
5. ⊙ 儔 chóu 1a, compeer, colleague, comrade, fellow, companion (in pre-Han texts); 酬 chóu 2, repay, requite, return.

稠　chóu　MC drjuw
1. thickset, dense; clump(ed), compact(ed).
　　a. thickly gathered; numerous, multifold.
2. thick, heavy, of soup, porridge, etc.
　　tiáo　MC dew
1. ⊙ 調 tiáo 1, attuned, well-adjusted, in accord with, tempered.
　　diào　MC dewH
1. (bn.) ～嶅 diào'aó (MC dewH-ngaw), shake and quake, sway and waver.

籌　chóu　MC drjuw
1. counting rods, made of bamboo or wood.
　　a. tally, marker; e.g. 更～ gēngchóu, tally of the (night) watches, the o'clock of the night, ref. the marking arrows of clepsydra.
2. tally up, calculate; plan out, devise, contrive.
3. divinatory slips; e.g. 墮～ duòchóu, draw (divination) lots.

4. bamboo arrows for use in ancient game of pitch-pot.

紬   chóu   MC drjuw
1. raw silk; unwound thread from cocoon.
chōu   MC trhjuw
1. unwind, unreel, draw out.
2. draw together; collect, compile.

綢   chóu   MC drjuw
1. bind round; plait.
   a. (bn.) ～繆 *chóumóu* (MC drjuw-mjuw), wrap round, bind closely about; also, tightly tied, closely connected (in feeling or relationship).
2. (med.) bombycine, dense-woven silk fabric; sometimes, tussah silk.
3. ⊙ 稠 *chóu*, tightly packed, dense.

裯   chóu   MC drjuw
1. bed-sheet, unpadded bed-covering to lie on.
2. (med.) padded or lined coverlet to lie under.
dāo   MC taw
1. (bn.) 袛～ *dīdāo*, → 袛 *dī*.

讎   chóu   MC dzyuw
1. reply, respond, make answer to.
   a. contradict, rebut; rejoin.
2. correspond with, be a counterpart of, relative of; of the same kind as.
3. respond in kind, reciprocate, repay, requite.
4. compare texts, place texts side-by-side; e.g. ～校 *chóujiào*, compare and collate.
5. ⊙ 仇 *chóu* 2, opposite number, enemy, adversary; enmity, animosty; 酬 *chóu* 1, wine-toast of guest by host.

躊   chóu   MC drjuw
1. (bn.) ～躇 *chóuchú* (MC drjuw-drjo), halting and hesitant, hesitant but expectant, nervously on tiptoe; also, lingering complacently, dawdling in delight, easy-going and aimless.

酬   chóu   MC dzyuw
1. wine-toast of guest by host (cf. 酢 *zuò*, of host by guest).
2. repay an obligation, requite; reciprocate, rejoin.
   a. respond to; acknowledge.
   b. (med.) (lit.) reciprocate a poem addressed to you with one of your own, or present a poem to a guest, usu. the first word in poem title.

3. (med.) achieve, realize, make manifest (goal or aspiration).

鮋   chóu   MC drjuw
1. sharpbelly, sawbelly, wild carp (*Hemiculter leucisculus*).

chǒu

丑   chǒu   MC trhjuwX
1. 2nd of the 12 earthly branches, associated with the ox as emblematic animal.
   a. 2nd double-hour of the day, approx. 1 a.m to 3 a.m.

醜   chǒu   MC tsyhuwX
1. unsightly, malformed; blemished; ugly.
   a. repulsive, repugnant.
2. shameful, mortifying; odious.
   a. detest(able), loathe, loathful.
3. of the same kind, alike, similar to; compare, comparable.

chòu

臭   chòu   MC tsyhuwH
1. malodorous, fetid; reeking, stinking; e.g. ～椿 *chòuchūn*, "malodorous mahogany," common name for 樗 *chū*, ailanthus.
xiù   MC xjuwH
1. odor, smell.
   a. to smell, sniff.

chū

出   chū   MC tsyhwit
1. go or come out (from), come or go forth; issue (from), emerge(nt); e.g. (med.) ～身 *chūshēn*, ～家 *chūjiā*, one who has gone forth from his home, either to follow an official career or to become a Budd. monk.
2. produce, yield, emanate; put forth, bring forth.
   a. send out, bring out.
3. expel, oust; turn out.
4. go or reach beyond; exceed, surpass; e.g. 不～三日 *bùchū sānrì*, not beyond (no more than) 3 days; 古之聖人，其～人也遠矣 *gǔ zhī shèngrén, qí chū rén yě yuǎn yǐ*, in their surpassing of other men the sages of old went far indeed.

5. (med.) flower-petals (< emerging from bud); e.g. 六〜 *liùchū*, 6-petalled (flower), i.e. snowflake.

6. (med.) one turn or bout of "pure conversation," incl. 1 clarification (*tong* 通) of the topic and 1 objection or rebuttal (*nan* 難).

初　chū　MC tsrhjo

1. (at the) beginning, originally; first-reft; e.g. 〜度 *chūdù*, original passage (into the world), i.e. birthday.

    a. initial, inaugural, primary; e.g. 〜學 *chūxué*, elementary studies.

2. first, earliest (in a sequence); first part of; e.g. 〜夜 *chūyè*, first watch of the night.

    a. earlier (than the present), previous(ly), antecedent(ly).

    b. in historical texts, as initial particle indicates "at some (unspecified) earlier time."

3. just now, just then, only then; e.g. 天下〜定又復立國是樹兵也 *tiānxià chū dìng yòu fùlì guó, shì shùbīng yě*, to re-establish feudal states with the empire only just now secure, this is to sow the seeds of war.

4. (med.) then, thereupon, at that time (equiv. 乃 *nǎi* 1a); esp. in med. poetry this is most common meaning.

5. (med.) intensifying ADV before negative VB-phrase, usu. with time element: never, not once, certainly not; e.g. 那得〜不見君教兒 *nǎdé chūbùjiàn jūn jiāo ér*, How come I have never once seen you instruct your sons?; 羣臣〜無是言也 *qúnchén chūwú shìyán yě*, there have never been words like these (issuing) from the host of vassals.

樗　chū　MC trhjo

1. tree of heaven, ailanthus (*Ailanthus altissima*).

2. short for the dicing game 〜蒲 or 摴蒲 *shūpú* (MC trhjo-bu), derived from the Indian game of *chaupar*.

    a. to game or gamble.

貙　chū　MC trhju

1. leopard-cat (*Felis bengalensis*), small spotted wildcat.

chú

儲　chú　MC drjo

1. store up, conserve, keep in reserve, lay in.

2. to aid, assist, second.

    a. successor to or heritor of the throne, heir-presumptive; esp. in cmpds. 〜君 *chújūn*, 〜貳 *chú'èr*, 〜副 *chúfù*.

3. ready, waiting.

4. (bn.) 〜與 *chúyǔ* (MC drjo-yoX), cramped and constricted, pinched and puckered; also, shifting to and fro, roving and roaming; also, progress on one's own principles, without direction of an exterior force.

5. a surname.

廚　chú　MC drju

1. kitchen.

    a. the cook, i.e. head of the kitchen.

2. (Dao.) cuisines, various practices of Tianshi and later groups incl. communal rituals and meditation techniques, usu. involving a time of purification and then consumption of exclusively vegetarian food and moderate amounts of wine.

3. (med.) chest, cabinet.

篨　chú　MC drjo　⊙ 蒢 *chú*.

芻　chú　MC tsrhju

1. cut hay, mow weeds.

    a. straw-gatherer, forager; common fieldhand > commonplace, simple.

2. straw; hay, fodder.

    a. provide fodder for animals.

    b. by metonymy, animals that subsist on fodder.

蒢　chú　MC drjo

1. sgl. or cmpd. 黃〜 *huángchú*, cutleaf groundcherry, fisalia (*Physalis angulata*).

2. (bn.) 蒢〜 *qúchú*, → 蘧 *qú* 4.

蜍　chú　MC dzyo

1. (bn.) 蟾〜 *chánchú*, → 蟾 *chán*.

躇　chú　MC drjo

1. step on, tread.

2. sgl. or (bn.) 躊〜 *chúchú* (MC drju-drjo), vacillate, shilly-shally, go back and forth, halt and hesitate.

    a. (bn.) 躊〜 *chóuchú*, → 躊 *chóu*.

躕　chú　MC drju

1. (bn.) 〜躇 *chúchú* (MC drju-drjo), 跙〜 *chíchú* (MC drje-drju), fuss and fidget, dilly-dally, vacillate; go back and forth, shilly-shally, haffle-caffle.

鉏 chú MC dzrjo
1. ⊙ 鋤 *chú*, a hoe; to hoe.
    jǔ MC dzrjoX
1. (bn.) 〜語 *jǔyǔ* (MC dzrjoX-ngjoX), unfitted to the form, inapt and unsuited, ⊙ 齟齬 *jǔyǔ*.

鋤 chú MC dzrjo
1. hoe (implement).
    a. to hoe, weed; dig, scrape.

除 chú MC drjo
1. stairs, stairway leading to main hall of palace or residential compound.
    a. plank passageway; vestibule.
2. remove, eliminate, rid(dance); expel, expulsion; e.g. 〜喪 *chúsāng*, 〜服 *chúfú*, remove one's mourning clothes (after completing the mourning period); 〜夕 *chúxī*, the night that expels the year, i.e. last night of year, New Year's eve; 〜差 *chúchā*, 〜愈 *chúyù*, get rid of ailment, cure disease.
    a. set(ting) aside X, besides X, outside of X; often completed with 以外 *yǐwài* following the OBJ of 〜(了) *chú(le)*.
3. well-arranged, to order well (< clean out, expel the unwanted).
    a. prepare an altar or special area for ritual ceremony.
4. appoint to office.

雛 chú MC dzrju
1. nestling, fledgling.
    a. youngling, tyke; youth.
2. (bn.) 鵷〜 *yuānchú*, species of "phoenix," → 鵷 *yuān*.

鶵 chú MC dzrju ⊙ 雛 *chú*.

chǔ

杵 chǔ MC tsyhoX
1. pestle, used in hulling rice.
2. small mallet, used in fulling clothes.
3. to beat, pound.

楚 chǔ MC tsrhjoX
1. thornbush (*Vitex negundo, V. cannabifolia*), root and leaves used medicinally; syn. 牡荊 *mǔjīng*.
    a. thornbrake, thicket, copse, bosk; e.g. 平〜 *píngchǔ*, level thicket, dense forest as seen from above looking like flat green plain.
    b. thorny, brambly, spiny.
2. bramble-rod; scourge, switch (for punishment).
3. suffering, pain(ful).
4. arranged in rows, lined up.
5. vivid, gaily-colored; attractive, charming.
    a. rdup., vivid and vivacious, appealingly attractive; also, thickly clustered, of vegetation; also (med.), painfully plaintive, of music.
6. (med.) common, vulgar, homely, coarse.
7. name of one of the 7 major states of the Warring States period, centered on the middle Yangzi region, incl. area of present-day Hunan and parts of Hubei, Anhui, and Jiangxi, traditionally associated with "the south."

楮 chǔ MC trhjoX
1. paper-mulberry tree (*Broussonetia papyrifera*), used medicinally but bark used esp. as fiber in paper-making.
2. (med.) by metonymy, ref. paper.

礎 chǔ MC tsrhjoX
1. plinth, stone foundation of column, pillar, platform.

處 chǔ MC tsyhoX
1. pause, stop, cease (from).
    a. remain (behind), stay.
2. stay at, rest in, dwell in.
    a. stay secluded, sequestered; e.g. 〜士 *chǔshì*, private gentleman, who does not seek or have an official position; 〜女 *chǔnǚ*, sequestered maiden, unwed daughter living at home.
    b. associate with, place oneself with.
3. fix a place for, situate, locate.
    a. dispose, arrange.
4. assess, judge; do justice to, sentence.
5. occupy; hold; control.
    chù MC tsyhoH
1. place, location, site, spot; physical presence; e.g. 何〜 *héchù*, at what place? where?
    a. rdup., from place to place, everywhere, everyplace.
    b. (Budd.) trns. Skt. *āyatana*, site of perception > senses.
2. situation, circumstance(s).
    a. stage, state, aspect.

3. (med.) time, occasion (considered as though a physical place); e.g. 別～長 biéchù cháng, times of parting are long;. 何～ héchù, at what time? when?

4. (med.) when following a VB-phrase indicates the preceding is the reason for an action or thought: on account of VB-phrase, for the sake of VB-phrase.

    a. (med.) 何～ héchù, on account of what? why?

chù

丁　chù　MC trhjowk

1. toddle, walk unsteadily with short steps.
    a. (bn.) 彳～ chìchù, → 彳 chì.
2. trot, pace, stride, esp. of horses.

俶　chù　MC tsyhuwk

1. begin(ning), commence(ment); undertake, set in motion.
2. construct, build.
    a. repair, keep in order.
3. (med.) ～爾 chù'ěr, suddenly, abruptly.

    tì　MC thek

1. (bn.) ～儻 tìtǎng (MC thek-thangX), unexampled, sui generis, rare and unparalleled, extraordinary, unwonted.

忸　chù　MC trhwit

1. afraid, frightened.
    a. anxious, worried, nervous; restless.
2. alarmed; on guard, watchful.

    xù　MC swit

1. seduce, lure, lead astray, entice.

潃　chù　MC trhjuwk

1. gather, mass, converge (of water).
2. rapid run, rush (of current).
3. swiftly changing, in a rush.

畜　chù　MC trhjuwH

1. livestock; farmyard animals; e.g. 六～ liùchù, the six husbanded animals: horse, ox, sheep, chicken, dog, pig.

    xù　MC xjuwk

1. husband(ry); rear; feed.
    a. nourish; raise, train; foster, provide for, attend to, tend (not only animals).
    b. restrain, discipline.

    c. 小～ xiǎoxù, "lesser domestication," name of 9th hexagram of Yijing; 大～ dàxù, "greater domestication," name of 26th hexagram.

2. garner, store up, keep in store; impound.

矗　chù　MC tsrhjuwk

1. stretch out straight.
2. rise abruptly; soar up straight, stand sheer.
3. sternly straightforward, upright; candid, bluff.

絀　chù　MC trwit

1. insufficient, inadequate, deficient, short of.
    a. reduce, diminish, pare down.
2. bent, crooked; curled (up); ⊙ 詘 qū 2.
3. dismiss, oust (from office), degrade; ⊙ 黜 chù 1.
4. to sew.

觸　chù　MC tsyhowk

1. butt; run into or against, collide with; e.g. ～藩 chùfān, ram into a hedge.
    a. confront, encounter, face; e.g. ～諫 chùjiàn, admonish to one's face; ～目 chùmù, cast one's eyes on.
    b. (med.) pertain to, bear upon; usu. in collective sense; e.g. ～類 chùlèi, relating to all kinds, i.e. in every respect, every single thing; ～處 chùchù, ～地 chùdì, everyplace, everywhere.
2. accost; go counter to; affront, offend.
3. touch, move; elicit, trigger; e.g. ～撓 chùrǎo, disturb, harass.

黜　chù　MC trhwit

1. dismiss, oust (from office), expel; demote, degrade (in rank); banish, send away (from capital).
    a. remove, banish, expel, get rid of (problems, hindrances, etc.).
2. deplete, reduce.

chuǎi

揣　chuǎi　MC tsrhjweX

1. measure, estimate; calculate.
    a. surmise, guess; infer.
2. sound out; probe; bring out.

    zhuī　MC tsywij

1. hammer, sharpen (metal).

tuán   MC dwan

1. ⊙ 團 *tuán* 2, cluster, aggregate, gather together, bunch.

chuài

喁 **chuài   MC tsrhwaejH**

1. bite, eat.
2. gorge, devour.
3. suck up, lap up.

chuān

川 **chuān   MC tsyhwen**

1. river, watercourse; stream.
2. (med.) level terrain, level countryside.

穿 **chuān   MC tsyhwen**

1. bore through; pierce, puncture, perforate, thirl.
2. pass(age) through, push through, push forward; force one's way.
3. worn through, riddled (with); staved in; undermined.
4. string together, thread.
5. grave-pit.
6. (med.) wear (clothing); Tang usage.

chuán

傳 **chuán   MC drjwen**

1. transmit, pass along; hand on, hand down; circulate, spread, during the present time or over generations.
   a. transfer, hand over; move from one place to another or from one person to another.
   b. convey or transmit by relays.
2. pass on orally, relate.
3. impart, express, make known, disclose.
   zhuàn   MC drjwenH
1. tradition, what has been transmitted.
   a. traditions recorded in writing; when pertaining to an individual, conventionally translated as "biography"; e.g. 紀〜 *jìzhuàn*, annals and biographies, the 2 main sections of dynastic histories.
   b. traditions of interpretation relative to a particular text or teaching, conventionally translated as "commentary"; e.g. 左〜 *zuǒzhuàn*, Mr. Zuo's commentary [to the *Chunqiu* 春秋]; 經〜 *jīngzhuàn*, canon (or base-text) and commentary.

2. relay station, post-station < place to change horses or transmit messages.
   a. (med.) state-operated guest-houses; e.g. 停〜 *tíngzhuàn*, rest house; 〜舍 *zhuànshè*, travelers' inn.

橡 **chuán   MC drjwen**

1. base-rafter, usu. long poles set parallel to each other for supporting roof-tiles or sheathing.
2. wooden stick.

船 **chuán   MC zywen**

1. ship, usu. of fair size and used for transporting goods; sometimes beyond the coast (cf. 舟 *zhōu*, usu. smaller and only inland use); this graph in common use only from 3rd century BCE on.
   a. to ship, transport.
2. (med.) 〜杯 *chuánbēi* or 酒〜 *jiǔchuán*, boat-shaped elliptical drinking-bowl, Iran. *kashti*.

遄 **chuán   MC dzywen**

1. in haste, hasten, hurry; move with pace.
   a. hustle; scamper.

chuǎn

喘 **chuǎn   MC tsyhwenX**

1. to pant, huff; wheeze; gasp for breath.
   a. rdup., huffing and puffing.

舛 **chuǎn   MC tsyhwenX**

1. diverge(nt), contrary, oppose(d), counter.
2. err(or), stray, deviate; amiss; wrong.
3. (med.) disturbed, difficult; in dire straits; complicated.

莑 **chuǎn   MC tsyhwenX**

1. (med.) late-picked tea-leaves.

踳 **chuǎn   MC tsyhwenX** ⊙ 舛 *chuǎn*.

chuàn

串 **chuàn   MC tsyhwenH**

1. (med.) string together, connect.
   guàn   MC kwaenH
1. ⊙ 慣 *guàn*, accustomed to.

釧 **chuàn   MC tsyhwenH**

1. bangles; bracelet.

chuāng

籾　chuāng　MC tsrhjang　⊙ 創 *chuāng*.

創　chuāng　MC tsrhjang
1. wound, laceration; injury; contusion, bruise.
   a. to wound, injure, lacerate.
   　chuàng　MC tsrhjangH
1. create; originate, initiate; make.
2. reprimand, reprove.

摐　chuāng　MC tsrhaewng
1. strike, beat, esp. a drum.
2. rise high, stand tall.
3. rdup., (med.) cluttered and jumbled, mixed and many-faceted; also, onom. of twang of stringed instruments.

憽　chuāng　MC tsrhaewng　⊙ 窗 *chuāng*.

摠　chuāng　MC tsrhaewng　⊙ 窗 *chuāng*.

瘡　chuāng　MC tsrhjang
1. imposthume, abscess.
2. ⊙ 創 *chuāng*, wound, laceration; injury.

窗　chuāng　MC tsrhaewng
1. window; fenestral; opening.
   a. 天～ *tiānchuáng*, cupola (not skylight); also, fissure in cliff or cave that lets in light.

窻　chuāng　MC tsrhaewng　⊙ 窗 *chuāng*.

chuáng

幢　chuáng　MC draewng
1. (med.) pennant, streamer, gonfalon.
2. (Budd.) stone pillar, esp. for inscribing *sūtra*, *dhāraṇī*, etc.
3. ⊙ 橦 *chuáng*, wooden pole, pillar, e.g. 尋～ *xúnchuáng*, pole-climb(er).
   zhuàng　MC draewngH
1. (med.) hanging screen over boat or carriage windows.
   tóng　MC duwng
1. (med.) rdup., sway and waver, tilt and trail; also, blink and flicker.

床　chuáng　MC dzrjang　⊙ 牀 *chuáng*.

橦　chuáng　MC draewng
1. wooden pole or pillar, ranging from flag-pole to ship-mast.
   chōng　MC tsyhowng
1. clash, strike against; stab.
2. siege-engine.
   tóng　MC duwng
1. cotton-tree, from the downy flowers of which a kind of cotton was made; identification uncertain, perhaps *Bombax malabaricum* though disputed because that tree's fruit capsules (not flowers) yield cottony fibers.

牀　chuáng　MC dzrjang
1. bed, usu. curtained.
2. raised dais for sitting; couch; bench.
   a. stool; e.g. (med.) 胡～ *húchuáng* "foreign stool," folding stool with soft seat; (med.) 繩～ *shéngchuáng*, "cord-wrapped stool," fixed-frame chair with plank seat, a back, and armrests.
3. railing round the mouth of a well, wellhead.
4. riverbed.

chuàng

創　chuàng　MC tsrhjangH　→ 創 *chuāng*.

愴　chuàng　MC tsrhjangH
1. dejected; heartsore; woeful, woe-laden, grief-laden.
   chuǎng　MC tsrhjangX
1. (bn.) ～悅 *chuǎnghuǎng* (MC tsrhjangX-xjwangX), distraught and disappointed.

chuī

吹　chuī　MC tsyhwe
1. blow, puff, expel air sharply with lips barely opened; huff.
   a. blowing, piping of wind instruments; e.g. 鼓～曲 *gǔchuīqǔ*, tunes for drumming and piping, i.e. for drum and flute.
2. gust, blast, bluster (wind); e.g. ～散 *chuīsàn*, blown all over, blown to bits.

炊　chuī　MC tsyhwe
1. cook (food).

chuì   MC tsyhweH

1. (bn.) 〜累 *chuìlèi* (MC tsyhweH-ljweH), dust adrift on the wind, randomly shifting.

歔   chuī   MC tsyhwe   ⊙ 吹 *chuī*.

chuí

垂   chuí   MC dzywe

1. hang down, depend, let fall; e.g. 〜綸 *chuílún*, let fall a fishing-line, euph. for being in reclusion; 〜涕 *chuítì*, falling tears.
   a. droop, dangle, trail; headlong; e.g. 〜帶 *chuídài*, hanging or trailing sash; 〜拱 *chuígǒng*, trailing (robe) and folded (hands), all that a sage-ruler need do while ruling from the throne as if by charisma and moral power alone.
2. come down, descend (in space or time), downward; e.g. 〜老 *chuílǎo*, descending old age; 〜名 *chuímíng*, fame that descends to later times.
3. condescend to; deign to . . ., be so kind as to . . .; e.g. 〜愛 *chuí'ài*, condescend to show concern for.
   a. vouchsafe, impart; assent to.
4. be on the brink of; to brink; e.g. 〜堂 *chuítáng*, the brink of the hall, i.e. under the eaves; to "brink the hall," standing carelessly under the eaves where danger might befall one.
   a. close to, approximate(ly); e.g. 〜盡 *chuíjìn*, nearly done; 〜暮 *chuímù*, almost sunset.
5. rdup., gradually, little by little.

捶   chuí   MC tsyweX

1. to strike; beat, thrash.
   a. to hammer, pound.
2. ⊙ 錘 *chuí* 1, hammer; 箠 *chuí*, whip, switch.

搥   chuí   MC drwij   ⊙ 捶 *chuí*.

棰   chuí   MC tsyweX

1. cudgel.
2. ⊙ 捶 *chuí* 1, strike, beat; pound; 箠 *chuí*, whip, switch.

椎   chuí   MC drwij

1. hammer, mallet.
   a. to hammer; bludgeon.
2. blunt, dull; dense; obtuse.

槌   chuí   MC drwij

1. hammer.
   a. pound, hammer down; beat down.

   zhuì   MC drjweH

1. wooden posts that are the framework from which are suspended the rush-mats used in rearing silkworms.

箠   chuí   MC tsyweX

1. whip, switch; esp. for horse.
   a. to whip, switch; flog.
2. cudgel, beat, as punishment.

   chuí   MC dzywe

1. unidentified species of bamboo particularly favored for making switches for imperial chariots.

錘   chuí   MC drjwe

1. hammer, mallet.
   a. mace.
2. ancient measure of weight, variously defined: equiv. 8 scruples (*zhu* 銖), i.e. one-third of an ounce (*liang* 兩), or equiv. 12 ounces.

鎚   chuí   MC drwij

1. hammer, mallet; mace; ⊙ 錘 *chuí* 1.
   a. to hammer, bludgeon.

陲   chuí   MC dzywe

1. borderland, frontier, marchland.
2. edge, rim, margin, brink, periphery.
   a. far point; terminus.

chūn

春   chūn   MC tsyhwin

1. springtime, the first 3 months of the year; vernal; season corresponding to the agent wood, the east, the liver, the color green.
   a. 〜秋 *chūnqiū*, spring(s) and autumn(s), synecdoche for a year; also, year-by-year historical chronicle of the state of Lu 魯 from 722 to 481 BCE or somewhat later, attributed to Confucius, and conventionally called *Spring and Autumn Annals*; also, name given retrospectively (because of preceding text) to the Zhou-dynasty period covering those years.
2. vigor, vitality; youth(fulness), sexual desire.
3. (med.) in Tang times a euphemism for wine; used as final element in names of many different types of wine.

杶　chūn　MC trhwin
1. cedrela, fragrant cedar (*Cedrela sinensis*), ⊙ 椿 *chūn* 2.

椿　chūn　MC trhwin
1. cedrela, fragrant cedar (*Cedrela sinensis*).
    a. legendary tree of same name for which 8,000 years counted as 1 springtime and another 8,000 years as 1 autumn (< *Zhuangzi* 1); hence longevity considered a special trait of the common cedrela.

輴　chūn　MC trhwin
1. sledge, for use on muddy terrain.
2. funeral carriage, for transporting of coffin to tomb; hearse.

chún

脣　chún　MC zywin　⊙ 脣 *chún*.

淳　chún　MC dzywin
1. of a single kind, simple, whole.
2. pure, unadulterated, unmixed, untainted, uncorrupted; ⊙ 純 *chún* 2.
3. of full or rich flavor; ⊙ 醇 *chún* 1.
    a. rich in yield, fertile.
        zhūn　MC tsywin
1. soak, moisten; dampen, bedew; irrigate, enrich.

漘　chún　MC zywin
1. banks of river or stream.

純　chún　MC dzywin
1. silk thread all of one color.
2. pure, taintless, untainted, unadulterated, unmixed, uncombined; perfect.
3. genuine; of complete integrity; uncorrupted.
4. completely, entirely, all of.
5. ancient measurement of length, equiv. 15 "feet" (*chi* 尺).
        zhǔn　MC tsywinX
1. border or edging of clothes, footwear, headwear (those of criminals had none).
        tún　MC dwon
1. wrap(ping), enclose, bundle.
2. measure of length for silks or cloth, a "bolt," equiv. → 匹 *pǐ*.

肫　chún　MC dzywin　→ 肫 *zhūn*.

脣　chún　MC zywin
1. lips; labial.
2. (med.) edge, border; e.g. 鬢～ *bīnchún*, hairline.

蒓　chún　MC dzywin
1. (med.) ⊙ 蓴 *chún*, water-mallow, watershield (*Brasenia schreberi*).

蓴　chún　MC dzywin
1. water-mallow, water-shield (*Brasenia schreberi*), with floating green leaves and small murreycolored flowers.

醇　chún　MC dzywin
1. rich-tasting wine, full of flavor, ambrosia(l).
2. ⊙ 淳 *chún* 1, all of one kind, simple, whole; 純 *chún* 2, pure, unadulterated, untainted, unmixed, uncorrupted.

錞　chún　MC dzywin
1. sgl. or ～于 *chúnyú*, mallet-struck bell of copper, in shape of pottery cylinder with swollen top, surmounted by handle in animal shape (often a tiger), developed in Chunqiu period and often used to rouse troops in battle.
2. border on, skirt, lie near to.
        duì　MC dwojH
1. shaft-end of spear, glaive, or pike.

鶉　chún　MC dzywin
1. quail, colin (*Coturnix japonica*).
2. ～首 *chúnshǒu*, Quail's Head, name of one of 12 Jupiter stations, comprising the lunar lodgings *jing* 井 and *gui* 鬼; ～火 *chúnhuǒ*, Quail's Fire, another of the 12 Jupiter stations, comprising the lunar lodgings *liu* 柳, *xing* 星, and *zhang* 張; ～尾 *chúnwěi*, Quail's Tail, another of the 12 Jupiter stations, comprising the lunar lodgings *yi* 翼 and *zhen* 軫. Together these 3 stations make up the southern quadrant (*chiniao* 赤鳥) of the sky.

chǔn

蠢　chǔn　MC tsyhwinX
1. wriggle, like worm or reptile; writhe, squirm.
    a. crawl, creep.
2. disturb, upset, agitate.
    a. rise against, rebel(lious); insubordinate, defiant; obstinate.

3. stupid, ignorant, boorish.
4. rdup., wriggle and writhe, twist and squirm, kim-kam; also, jumbled and tumbled, topsy-turvy, mishmash; also, unrest and upset, helter-skelter; also, insolent and impudent, tactless and indiscreet.

chuō

趠   chuō   MC trhaewk
1. ⊙ 逴 *chuō* 1, far, remote, distant; far journey; 踔 *chuō* 1, gambol, leap, hurdle, bound, rise over, surmount.
    zhuō   MC traewk
1. ⊙ 卓 *zhuō* 1, high-looming; outstanding, salient, excellent.

踔   chuō   MC trhaewk
1. hurdle, bound, leap, throw oneself over.
    a. cross above, rise over, surmount.
    b. frisk, gambol.
2. (med.) ～厲 *zhuōlì*, stirring and inspiring, of words or actions.
    zhuō   MC traewk
1. ⊙ 卓 *zhuō* 1, high-looming; outstanding, prominent; excellent.
2. far off, distant; far beyond.

逴   chuō   MC trhaewk
1. sgl. or rdup., far, distant, afar, far off, remote.
2. (bn.) ～躒 *chuōluò* (MC trhaewk-lak), far surpassing, paramount, outstandingly eminent; (med.) bound and spring over, leap above.

chuò

啜   chuò   MC tsyhwet
1. eat, sup; feed on, chew.
2. drink; suck up, swill.
3. sob, gulp down tears.
4. stew; soup.

婼   chuò   MC tsrhaewk
1. careful, exacting, finicky.
    a. rdup., ⊙ 齪齪 *chuòchuò*, painstakingly precise, exactingly attentive.
2. organize, put in order.

惙   chuò   MC trjwet
1. rdup., overcome with sorrow, wretched and woebegone.

2. worn out, exhausted.
3. ⊙ 輟 *chuò*, stop, suspend, interrupt.
    chuì   MC trhjwejH
1. short of breath, panting.

歠   chuò   MC tsyhwet
1. swill; suck up, drink down, guzzle.
2. potation, draft.

綽   chuò   MC tsyhak
1. serene, well-composed; poised, imperturbable; indulgent.
    a. nonchalant, relaxed, easy-going, unruffled.
    b. (bn.) ～約 *chuòyuē* (MC tsyhak-'jak), even-tempered, obliging and ungrudging, relaxed and restrained, tender and ductile.
2. (med.) grab or clutch with the hand.
3. ～菜 *chuòcài*, "relaxing plant," bogbean, bog-myrtle (*Menyanthes trifoliata*), root slightly narcotic; syn. 睡菜 *shuìcài*, 瞑菜 *miàncài*.

輟   chuò   MC trjwet
1. stop, suspend, interrupt.
2. (med.) give up, abandon, lay aside.

齪   chuò   MC tsrhaewk
1. rdup., attentive to the smallest detail, meticulous, painstakingly precise.

錣   chuò   MC traewt
1. iron point or tip on end of whip.

cī

疵   cī   MC dzje
1. blemish, discoloration, stain, blot, smutch.
    a. flaw, shortcoming; defect; infirmity.
2. find fault, pick holes in, take exception to; critique.

cí

慈   cí   MC dzi
1. loving-kindness, tenderness, merciful care, tender-hearted(ness).
    a. compassion, benevolence.
2. instinctive affection of parent for child, storge; esp. maternal love.
    a. (med.) laudatory epithet for mother, "the merciful (or tender-hearted) one."
3. solicitude, dutiful regard of child for parent.

4. 〜烏 *cíwū*, black jackdaw (*Corvus monedula*).

5. ⊙ 磁 *cí* 1, in 〜石 *císhí*, magnet, lodestone.

瓷　cí　MC dzij

1. ceramics, crockery; stoneware.
   a. (med.) jar, crock, pitcher.

磁　cí　MC dzi

1. 〜石 *císhí*, magnet, lodestone.
2. stoneware, crockery.

祠　cí　MC zi

1. offer sacrifice; originally springtime oblation.
   a. offer cult, cultic sacrifice, particularly to ancestors, local gods, or local heroes.
2. shrine, fane, place where cultic rituals are performed.
   a. enshrine; make a place of worship.

茨　cí　MC dzij

1. tackweed, goathead, bullhead, burnut (*Tribulus terrestris*), weedy plant whose fruit yields spiky nutlets that are painful to touch; syn. 蒺藜 *jílí*.
2. to thatch a roof using reeds or cogon grass.

詞　cí　MC zi

1. word(s); utterance, expression.
   a. diction, choice of words.
2. lyrics, words set to music.
   a. (med.) (lit.) name of a particular genre of poetry, developing from late 8th or 9th century on, in which verses are written to fit pre-existing tunes, often in lines of varying length.

辭　cí　MC zi

1. words, phrase.
   a. express(ion), utter(ance).
2. explain, lay out in words .
   a. legal testimony, deposition.
   b. accusation, confession (depending on perspective).
3. decline, demur; turn down, reject, refuse.
4. bid farewell, take leave.
5. lyrics, words set to music, ⊙ 詞 *cí* 2.
6. (med.) answer, reply.

雌　cí　MC tshje

1. female, of birds; hen.
   a. female of smaller quadrupeds.

2. "the feminine," feminine traits; submissive, docile, weak.

3. 〜黃 *cíhuáng*, "hen-yellow," orpiment; when ground with water into liquid esp. applied to paper as vermicide; because orpiment was also employed to smudge out words to be altered in writing, the term was also used by metonymy for correcting or changing a text; also, to needlessly or captiously criticize someone.

餈　cí　MC dzij

1. rice-cake, millet-cake.

鷀　cí　MC dzi

1. (bn.) 鸕〜 *lúcí*, → 鸕 *lú*.

cǐ

佌　cǐ　MC tshjeX

1. petty, paltry, piddling; trifling, worthless.

此　cǐ　MC tshjeX

1. "near" demonstrative pronoun, often referring to a token (cf. 彼 *bǐ*, "far" demonstrative pronoun): this, these, here; e.g. 賢者亦樂〜乎 *xiánzhě yì lè cǐ hū*, do worthy people also take pleasure in this?; 〜文王之勇也 *cǐ wénwáng zhī yǒng yě*, This was the courage of King Wen; 彼一時〜一時也 *bǐ yīshí cǐ yīshí yě*, That was one time, this is another time; 所敬在〜所長在彼 *suǒjìng zài cǐ suǒzhǎng zài bǐ*, the one shown respect lies here, the one shown honor as an elder lies there.

2. (med.) also ref. to time: at this time, now, at present; e.g. 及〜見君歸 *jícǐ jiàn jūn guī*, when now I see you return . . .

泚　cǐ　MC tshjeX

1. run fresh, run clear (of waterway).
2. fresh and bright, in appearance, ⊙ 玼 *cǐ* 1.
3. sweat, perspire, run with sweat.
4. (med.) 〜筆 *cǐbǐ*, moisten a writing-brush (with ink, in preparation for use).

玼　cǐ　MC tshjeX

1. fresh and bright in appearance, like lustrous jade.

　　cī　MC dzje

1. speckling on jade.
   a. flaw, defect, blemish.

茈   cǐ   MC tsjeX

1. gromwell (*Lithospermum arvense*), from the root of which a purple dye was produced, syn. 紫草 *zǐcǎo*; in med. times also syn. sapanwood (*Caesalpina sappan*, 蘇枋目 *sūfāngmù*), from heartwood juice of which a like dye was produced.
2. ～其 *cǐqí*, flowering fern, royal fern (*Osmunda japonica*).

chái   MC dzrea

1. thorowax (*Bupleurum chinense*), root used medicinally, ⊙ 柴 *chái* 3.

cì

佽   cì   MC tshijH

1. to second, assist.
2. well-ordered; one after another.

刺   cì   MC tshjek

1. pierce, stab; prick.
   a. pierce to the quick, kill.
2. goad, incite, stimulate; e.g. (med.) (bn.) ～促 *cìcù* (MC tshjek-tshjowk), prick and prod, provoke.
   a. poke, probe, pry into.
   b. pick out from, select.
   c. ～史 *cìshǐ*, official title, from Han to Sui "regional inspector" in charge of personnel of at least 1 and usu. more than 1 *zhou* 州; in Tang "prefect," highest central-government appointee in a prefecture (*zhou* 州), equiv. *taishou* 太守 in a commandery (*jun* 郡).
3. poke holes in, pick apart, criticize; protest against.
   a. irritate, annoy, irk.
4. pole or punt a boat.
5. sgl. or 名～ *míngcì*, calling-card, name-card.
6. (med.) rdup., piercing and penetrating, sharp and stinging, of cold wind; also, prolix and verbose.

cì   MC tshjeH

1. ⊙ 束 , spine, spike, thorn(y).

束   cì   MC tshjeH

1. spine, spike, thorn(y); spiny, spiky, barb, tine, sharp point.
   a. ～桐 *cìtóng*, "spiny *tong*," coral tree, flame tree (*Erythrina orientalis, E. variegata*), subtropical flowering plant whose bright-colored blooms are coral-shaped; ～柏 *cìbó*, "prickly cypress," i.e. juniper; ～榆 *cìyú*,

thorn-elm, prickly-elm (*Hemiptelea davidii*); ～薊 *cìjì*, "thorny thistle," mountain thistle (*Cirsium segetum*).

次   cì   MC tshijH

1. the next in sequence.
   a. 2nd in sequence, after whatever is regarded as starting-point; e.g. ～子 *cìzǐ*, 2nd son (in seniority).
   b. 2nd or inferior in quality, mediocre.
2. sequence, sequential; e.g. 相～ *xiāngcì*, in regular order; ～第 *cìdì*, one after another.
   a. imbricate(d), overlapping in order.
3. positions of the 12 Jupiter stations, divisions of Jupiter's synodic period (each 11 years, 315 days; approx. 12 years) along the ecliptic.
   a. position of sun or moon on ecliptic.
4. a stage of an army's march; stage of a journey; make a stage.
5. stay over at temporary stop for more than 2 nights.
6. (med.) written opinion exchanged between officials.
   a. halting-place, stopping-place.
   b. lodging-place; esp. hut when in mourning for father or mother.
7. time-marker; e.g. 彈棋～ *dànqícì*, when they were playing *go*; 泊舟～ *bózhōucì*, when I moored the boat.
8. measure-word for occurrences; e.g. 三～ *sāncì*, thrice.

賜   cì   MC sjeH

1. bestow(al), confer(ral); grant, vouchsafe; give, present; usu. from superior to inferior, or of unusual worth.
   a. impart favor or kindness.
2. complete an action, do fully.

cōng

怱   cōng   MC tshuwng

1. rdup., rushed and abrupt, hurried and flurried.

悤   cōng   MC tshuwng   ⊙ 怱 *cōng*.

樅   cōng   MC tshjowng

1. fir-tree described as having pine leaves and cypress trunk, perhaps Momi-fir (*Abies firma*).
2. serrated or dentate face-board (crossbeam) of bell-frame, from which bells were hung.

璁 cōng　MC tshuwng
1. green-gem, green-jade.
2. (med.) (bn.) 瓏～ *lóngcōng*, → 瓏 *lóng*.

瞛 cōng　MC tshjowng
1. (med.) flashing, sparkling, esp. of eyes.

聰 cōng　MC tshuwng
1. keen or unimpaired hearing, keen-eared; hear clearly.
2. quickness of perception, astute; e.g. ～明 *cōngmíng*, keen-eared and clear-sighted > perceptive and insightful.

葱 cōng　MC tshuwng
1. scallion (*Allium fistulosum*); cf. 韭 *jiǔ*, chive, leek (*Allium tuberosum*), 薤 *xiè*, shallot (*Allium chinense*).
2. (bn.) ～蘢 *cōnglǒng* (MC tshuwng-luwng) or 蘢～ *lǒngcōng*, lush and luxuriant, clumped and crowded, gobbed and knotted; also, verdant and virescent; also ⊙ 朣朧 *tónglóng*, glimmering glow of light.
3. ～嶺 *cōnglǐng* (MC tshuwng-ljengX), the Pamir plateau.

蒽 cōng　MC tshuwng　⊙ 葱 *cōng*.

鏦 cōng　MC tshjowng
1. short spear.
    a. to spear, lance; pierce, stab.
    chuāng　MC tsrhaewng
1. to drum, strike, rap.

驄 cōng　MC tshuwng
1. dappled or pied black-and-white horse.

cóng

叢 cóng　MC dzuwng
1. collect(ion); assemble, amass.
    a. multitude, numerous, accumulation.
    b. (med.) (bn.) ～殘 *cóngcán* (MC dzuwng-dzan), in a jumble, miggle-maggle; scrip-scrap, odds and ends.
2. thicket, copse, bosk, brake, tussock; jungly.

從 cóng　MC dzjowng
1. follow, go with, attend upon; come or go after, consequent; go by.

2. follow the dictates of, obey, conform to, comply with, go along with; give allegiance to.
    a. attach oneself to; participate in or with; e.g. ～事 *cóngshì*, be involved or take part in affairs.
3. from (place or time), coming from; by way of, by means of.
4. secondary, consequent; esp. (med.) lower subdivision of grades 4 through 9 in the 9-grade (*jiupin* 九品) official hierarchy, contrasted with upper subdivision called 正 *zhèng*, standard, proper.
5. (med.), go on toward, advance to; e.g. 宛馬又～東 *yuānmǎ yòu cóng dōng*, once again the Ferghana steeds are proceeding eastward.
    a. (med.) locative marker: at or in (this place); e.g. 偶～池上醉 *ǒu cóng chíshàng zuì*, by chance I became drunk at pondside.
    b. when prefixed to specific kinship term, ref. paternal collateral relatives (cf. 表 *biǎo*, for maternal); e.g. ～父 *cóngfù*, father's elder brother.
    cōng　MC tshjowng
1. (bn.) ～容 *cōngróng* (MC tshjowng-yowng), aimlessly at ease, informal and easy-going, in idle indifference; also, accept and accommodate, mediate and ameliorate, make peace; also, instigate, rile up, incite to contrary action.
    zòng　MC dzjowngH
1. follower, adherent; supporter, attendant; in the retinue of; fellow-traveler.
    a. pawn, peon, minion.
    b. suite, retinue.
2. ⊙ 縱 *zòng* 1, release(d), unleash, let loose, set aside constraints.
    zōng　MC tsjowng
1. ⊙ 縱 *zōng* 1, perpendicular, longitudinal, vertical, north-south direction.

憁 cóng　MC dzowng
1. joy, heart-warming happiness; e.g. 無～ *wúcóng*, unrelieved by joy.
2. (med.) heartfelt expectation; anticipation, longing.

潀 cóng　MC dzowng
1. cascade, waterfall.
2. rdup., onom. of steady streaming of water, coursing cascade, welling rush, splash and spread.

shuàng   MC sraewngH
1. drain into; discharge; sluice; filter.

潨   cóng   MC dzowng
1. confluence, convergence of waters.
2. rdup., ⊙ 潨潨 *cóngcóng*, onom. of rushing water, steadily streaming.

灇   cóng   MC dzowng
1. ⊙ 潨 *cóng* 1, onom. of rushing water, steady streaming; 潨 *cóng* 1, confluence, convergence of waters.

琮   cóng   MC dzowng
1. hollow jade cylinder, shaped like a wheel-hub; often used as valued gift in diplomatic or marriage exchange.

còu

湊   còu   MC tshuwH
1. pool together, converge; gather together.
2. run toward, rush after.
   a. proceed to, go to.
3. ⊙ 腠 *còu*, fine lines or lineaments of the skin, cracks and wrinkles.

腠   còu   MC tshuwH
1. sgl. or ～理 *còulǐ*, fine lines or lineaments of the skin, cracks and wrinkles; cmpd. also gen. term for structure, arrangement, design.

cū

粗   cū   MC tshu
1. unpolished rice; ant. 精 *jīng*, finest bleached rice.
2. coarse, rough; crude.
   a. dross, waste matter.
   b. rough, sketchy.
   c. coarse, thick, unruly (hair).
3. (med.) improper, irresponsible; e.g. ～行 *cūxíng*, unbefitting conduct, esp. of Budd. monk neglecting the prohibitions.
4. massive, bulky; gross; ant. 細 *xì*, fine, fine-set, delicate.
5. (ADV) more or less, pretty much, fairly; e.g. ～立 *cūlì*, more or less established.
6. (med.) lash, buffet; rough, of wind.
   a. (med.) (cause to) tumble.

䴢   cū   MC tshu   ⊙ 粗 *cū*.

cú

徂   cú   MC dzu
1. advance toward, go to.
   a. arrive at.
2. ⊙ 殂 *cú*, pass away; die, decease.

殂   cú   MC dzu
1. pass away; die, decease.

cù

促   cù   MC tshjowk
1. hasten, hurry.
   a. urge(nt), press(ing), of action and also sound; e.g. (med.) ～管 *cùguǎn*, the "urgent pipe," i.e. cross-flute (笛 *dí*).
2. pressing against, close by; hard by; e.g. ～席 *cùxí*, sitting mats placed close together or touching.
   a. cramped, crowded, tight together; e.g. ～狹 *cùxiá*, strait and narrow.
3. tighten, as zither strings.
   a. shorten, reduce; contract.
4. of short duration; hasty, rapid; e.g. ～節 *cùjié*, brief period.
   a. (med.) short in length, stubby.
5. (bn.) 偓～ *wòcù*, → 偓 *wò*.

猝   cù   MC tshwot
1. (med.) dash out or on, dart, bolt, in a rush.
   a. (med.) all of a sudden, without warning, out of the blue.

簇   cù   MC tshuwk
1. (med.) ⊙ 蔟 *cù* 1, silkworm spinning-frame; 3, gather; clump, cluster.
2. (med.) halt, pull up, bring to a stop, esp. horse.

蔟   cù   MC tshuwk
1. silkworm spinning-frame, of various designs but usu. supported by structural framework inside and covered by straw or matting on outside.
2. nest.
3. gather together, clump, cluster.

趗   cù   MC tshuwk
1. (bn.) 趢～ *lùcù*, → 趢 *lù*.

蹴　cù　MC tsjuwk

1. (bn.) 〜踃 *cùjí* (MC tsjuwk-tsjek), discomfited, nonplused; attentive but anxious, polite but fretful.

2. ⊙ 蹙 *cù* 1, wrinkled, cramped; 2, pressing, imminent; 蹴 *cù* 1, trample; 2, kick.

dí　MC dek

1. rdup., broad and level, flat and smooth.

蹙　cù　MC tsjuwk

1. wrinkle, scrunch; contracted, cramped; e.g. 〜額 *cù'é*, furrow the brow; 〜金 *cùjīn*, ornamental embroidery with (wrinkled-looking) gold thread, gold-passement.

2. pressing; urgent, imminent.
  a. force, compel.

3. sgl., rdup., or 〜然 *cùrán*, discomposed, discomfited, tied up in knots, uneasily, anxiously.

4. ⊙ 蹴 *cù* 1, trample, tread; 2, kick.

蹴　cù　MC tsjuwk　⊙ 蹙 *cù*.

踃　cù　MC tshjuwk

1. trample, tread on.

2. kick.

3. 〜然 *cùrán*, startled, unsettled, astonished.

醋　cù　MC tshuH

1. vinegar.
  a. sour-tasting.

zuò　MC dzak

1. ⊙ 酢 *zuò*, guest's toast to host; reciprocate; offer libation (of which 醋 was original form).

cuán

巑　cuán　MC dzwan

1. (bn.) 〜岏 *cuánwán* (MC dzwan-ngwan), sheer and steep, sky-scaling; also (med.), shrink back, quail at.

攢　cuán　MC dzwan

1. bring together, assemble; concentrate; join, make a joinery of.
  a. cluster, bunch up; e.g. 〜峰 *cuánfēng*, massed peaks; 〜眉 *cuánméi*, scrunch up one's eyebrows.
  b. (bn.) 〜雜 *cuánzá* (MC dzwan-dzop), clumped and clustered.

2. clutch, hold in the hand.

3. (med.) temporary encoffining, while awaiting later burial.

zuān　MC tswan

1. ⊙ 鑽 *zuǎn* 1, pierce, perforate; bore, drill.

cuàn

爨　cuàn　MC tshwanH

1. to cook.

2. cooking-stove.

3. (med.) name of tribe of the Man peoples in Guizhou and Yunnan.

竄　cuàn　MC tshwanH

1. hide away, cover up, conceal oneself; skulk, couch.
  a. hiding-hole, covert; den.

2. flee, hie, run off; scurry, scuttle; slink away.

3. be banished, exiled, relegated (< be ousted, run off from one's official position).

4. emend, alter a text.

5. arrange, dispose; set in place.

6. fumigate, with medicinal herbs.

篡　cuàn　MC tsrhwaenH

1. seize, take forcibly, wrest from.
  a. dispossess, usurp, esp. vassal usurping his lord's power and position.

2. perineum (human only).

cuī

催　cuī　MC tshwoj

1. compel, provoke; induce; urge, press.

2. hasten, impel; propel.

崔　cuī　MC dzwoj

1. rdup. or (bn.) 〜嵬 *cuīwéi* (MC dzwoj-ngwoj), tall and towering, sublimely spiring.

2. a surname.

摧　cuī　MC dzwoj

1. push aside, push backward.
  a. swipe off, brush away.

2. break apart, snap.

3. demolish, dash (to pieces).
  a. collapse, crumble; topple, overthrow.

4. cast down, humble, humiliate.
  a. frustrate; foil, thwart.

5. overwhelmed with sadness; grieved; woeful.
    a. (bn.) ～藏 *cuīcáng* (MC dzwoj-dzang) or 藏～ *cángcuī*, also ～殘 *cuīcán* (MC dzwoj-dzan), onom. for sad sounds, sound of fulling-block, sad animal cries, plaintive music; also (med.), curb and check, keep in check.

    cuò   MC tshwaH
1. ⊙ 莝 *cuò*, cut fodder; to fodder, provide hay for animals.

榱   cuī   MC srwij
1. rafter, syn. 椽 *chuán*; e.g. ～題 *cuītí*, rafter-tip or finial, projecting from under the eaves.

縗   cuī   MC tshwoj
1. (med.) unhemmed hemp bib or chemisette, worn in mourning.
2. (med.) weave egret feathers into clothing.

cuǐ

漼   cuǐ   MC tshwojXs
1. deep-looking, pooling (of water).
2. tearful, teary, watery, weeping.
3. broken, damaged, ⊙ 摧 *cuī* 2.

    cuī   MC dzwoj
1. (bn.) ～澄 *cuīyí* (MC dzwoj-ngj+j), layered and thick-lying, of frost and snow.

璀   cuǐ   MC tshwojX
1. (bn.) ～璨 *cuǐcàn* (MC tshwojX-tshanH), gleam and glitter, with lustrous light; also, grand and glorious.
2. (bn.) ～錯 *cuǐcuò* (MC tshwojX-tshak), joined layer upon layer; also, in rich profusion.

cuì

倅   cuì   MC tshwojH
1. assistant, aide; secondary, auxiliary, subsidiary.
    zú   MC tswot
1. ⊙ 卒 *zú* 1, foot-soldiers, troops; company of 100 soldiers.

悴   cuì   MC dzwijH
1. grief-stricken; despondent, despairing.
    a. dishearten, dispirit, discourage.
2. wan, pallid; worn out; drained, debilitated, haggard.
    a. (bn.) 憔～ *qiáocuì*, → 憔 *qiáo*.

毳   cuì   MC tshjwejH
1. down of birds or quadrupeds.
    a. downy; fleecy, woolly; tuft(ed).
2. ⊙ 脆 *cuì* 1, fragile, friable; 2, frail, flimsy, tender; delicate, dainty (to taste).
    qiāo   MC khjew
1. ⊙ 橇 *qiāo*, sledge, for traveling through muddy land.

淬   cuì   MC tshwojH
1. temper steel, by plunging in water; e.g. ～勵 *cuìlì*, temper and sharpen, prepare for ordeal; win out through adversity.
2. douse or extinguish fire.
3. bathe, soak; wet, moisten.
4. undergo; bear up to, brave.

焠   cuì   MC tshwojH
1. temper steel, by plunging into water, ⊙ 淬 *cuì* 1.
    a. to heat, fire, burn.
    b. "tempering," conjunction of Mars (fire) and Mercury (water).
2. infuse with.

瘁   cuì   MC dzwijH
1. overworked, weary; feel strained, depleted; haggard.
    a. pained at heart, troubled in mind, distressed.
2. overwhelmed, ruined, collapsed.

窜   cuì   MC tshjwejH
1. chasm, cave(rn).
    a. den, of animal.
2. grave-pit.

粹   cuì   MC swijH
1. of a single essence, whole as it is; pure, purified; unmixed.
    a. choice selection of, pure summation.
2. gathering, grouping, assemblage, ⊙ 萃 *cuì* 1.
3. ⊙ 碎 *suì*, shatter, splinter, fall apart, go to pieces.

縩   cuì   MC tswojH
1. multicolored, variegated, mottled.
2. (bn.) ～縩 *cuìcài* (MC tshwojH-tshojH), ～粲 *cuìcàn* (MC tshwojH-tshanH), onom. of rustle of silk, swish and whisper, frou-frou.

翠   cuì   MC tshwijH
1. sgl. or in bn. 翡～ *fěicuì* (MC bj+jH-tshwijH), the kingfisher, halcyon (*Halcyon smyrnensis;*

Alcedo bengalensis), small riverine bird, valued for its iridescent bright blue feathers which were woven into many items of aristocratic décor, e.g. hair ornaments, curtains, coverlets, canopies, etc.

2. halcyon-hued, alcedine, bright blue (similar to turquoise). N.B. When describing jade it is not the green jade associated with the term in post-medieval times.

　　a. (bn.) ～微 *cuìwēi* (MC tshwijH–mj+j), the blurred-bluish mist of mountain heights or of distant mountains, "halcyon haze."

3. elegant variation for the azure of the sky.

4. deep blue-green, the color of lush, dense vegetation.

5. blue-black, pertaining to eyebrow pigment.

6. old Chu dialect word for "brightly colored, brilliant."

胞 cuì　MC tshjwejH　⊙ 脆 *cuì*.

脆 cuì　MC tshjwejH
1. brittle, friable, crumbly, frangible.
2. frail, fragile, flimsy; tender.
　　a. delicate, dainty (to taste).
3. (med.) sharp, high-toned, of music or voice.

萃 cuì　MC dzwijH
1. swath, culled grouping, batch.
　　a. choice selection, pure summation, ⊙ 粹 *cuì* 2.
2. concentrate, group together; assemble, collect.
3. come to rest; halt, pause, stay momentarily.
4. "gathering," name of 45th hexagram of the *Yijing*.
5. ⊙ 悴 *cuì* 1, grief-stricken, despondent, discouraged.

顇 cuì　MC dzwijH
1. worn out, sadly bowed, wearied; discouraged.
2. (bn.) 憔～ *qiáocuì*, → 憔 *qiáo*.

cūn

村 cūn　MC tshwon
1. village.
2. rustic, countrified; simple, homely.

皴 cūn　MC tshwin
1. chapped or cracked skin, chafed, raw.
　　a. crinkly, fissured.
2. (med.) texture-strokes in painting.

cún

存 cún　MC dzwon
1. exist materially, be present, survive, remain (ant. 亡 *wáng* 4, defunct, perish, gone).
　　a. keep safe, preserve.
2. keep in one's mind, preserve the thought of.
3. (Dao.) visualization technique of focused intention by which particular energies or deities are made sensibly present and actualized to a practitioner.
4. look for, seek; inquire after.
　　a. do the same with intention of providing aid or comfort, usu. from superior to inferior.

cǔn

忖 cǔn　MC tshwonX
1. turn over in one's mind, ponder.
　　a. surmise, conjecture, infer.

cùn

寸 cùn　MC tshwonH
1. measure of length, "inch"; exact measurement varied over time: Eastern Zhou, Qin, Han, .91 Western inches; Sanguo, Jin, .95; Nanchao .97; Beichao, early 1.01, late 1.18; Tang 1.2.; 10 *cun* "inches" equiv. 1 *chi* 尺 "foot."
　　a. ～心 *cùnxīn*, square inch of heart, one's true feelings.
2. thumb, thumb's-breadth; cf. 膚 *fū* 3, breadth of 4 fingers.

cuō

搓 cuō　MC tsha
1. (med.) roll between the hands or in a hand, ball up.
　　a. (med.) rub the hands; crumble in the hands.
2. (med.) jab, poke; chuck.

撮 cuō　MC tshwat
1. pick up by pinching between fingers, pluck up.
2. bunch up, scrape together, scoop up.
　　a. gather up, compile (texts).
3. measure of capacity: a pinch, tiny amount of, equiv. one-tenth of a "handful" (*chao* 抄).

瑳 cuō   MC tsha
1. lustrous glow, as of jade; whitely gleaming.

磋 cuō   MC tsha
1. to polish; e.g. 切～ qiēcuō, cut and polish (gemstones); also, debate and discuss from various angles (see next).
2. roll an idea around, try out different views.

蹉 cuō   MC tsha
1. lose one's footing, stumble and fall; e.g. (bn.) ～跎 cuōtuó (MC tsha-da), unsteady and unsure, with shuffling step; (bn.) ～跌 cuōdiē (MC tsha-det), trip and tumble, put one's foot wrong > make a slip, be off the mark, err, blunder.
    a. lose track of time, miss an opportunity, slip past the right moment, waste time.
2. press down, esp. with the foot.
3. (med.) stop at, stop by (to visit).
4. (med.) topple, knock over; disarrange.
5. (med.) side-path.

cuó

嵯 cuó   MC tsha
1. (bn.) ～峨 cuó'é (MC tsha-nga), upborne and abrupt, jutting and jagging, gnaw-toothed and saw-toothed, looming above; also, cliff and bluff.

痤 cuó   MC dzwa
1. acne; pimple.
2. blister; pustule, boil.

瘥 cuó   MC dza
1. contagion, epidemic.
2. (med.) exhausted, spent, played out.
    chài   MC tsrheaH
1. heal, cure (disease).

矬 cuó   MC dzwa
1. dwarf(ish); stunted.

醝 cuó   MC dza
1. white-colored (i.e. clear) wine.
2. ⊙ 鹺 cuó, salty, saline.

鹺 cuó   MC dza
1. (med.) salt(y), saline.

cuò

剒 cuò   MC tshwaH
1. damage, destroy; break up, reduce to pieces.
2. (med.) tear apart, rip up; mince.
3. (med.) file, rasp; to file.

削 cuò   MC tshak
1. rough-hew, shape out.
    a. trim, pare.
2. carve; rive; apportion.
    zhuó   MC tsrjak
1. ⊙ 斲 zhuó, chop, cut; sever.

厝 cuò   MC tshak
1. grindstone.
2. to place, position, deposit.
3. bury the dead.
    a. provisional burial in shallow grave, prior to formal burial at chosen gravesite.

挫 cuò   MC tswaH
1. crush, press down; raze; e.g. ～氣 cuòqì, crush the spirit of.
    a. break up, destroy.
2. check, arrest.
    a. frustrate; weaken, cripple.
    b. put under strain.
3. abase, humble, bring low, take down; humiliate.

措 cuò   MC tshuH
1. to place, position where desired; dispose, arrange.
2. lay aside, set aside or apart, reject; leave alone, abandon.
3. deal with, manage; competence (in).
    a. implement, put into effect, execute, take measures; perform, proceed with.
4. (med.) involved, engaged in, concerned about.
    zé   MC tsraek
1. squeeze; press, force.

莝 cuò   MC tshwaH
1. cut fodder; to fodder, provide hay for animals.

銼 cuò   MC tshwaH
1. small earthenware wok, cookpan.
2. ⊙ 挫 cuò 1, crush, press down; break up, destroy.

錯 cuò   MC tshak
1. inlay with gold, silver, jade, etc.
    a. adorn, embellish, trim.

2. grindstone, ⊙ 厝 *cuò* 1.

    a. to polish, dress (jade or other precious stones).

3. intercrossed, interlaced, intermingled; imbricated.

    a. regularly alternating.

4. disparate, diverse; miscellaneous, varied, mixed; in disorder.

    a. (bn.) 〜莫 *cuòmò* (MC tshak-mak), unevenly irregular > troubled and baffled, disappointed and disquieted.

5. (med.) incorrect, mistake(n), err(or); miscue, blunder.

6. ⊙ 措 *cuò* 1, to place, position, dispose; 2, set aside, abandon; 3, deal with, manage, implement, put into effect.

鯌　cuò　MC tshak

1. (med.) fish from whose skin sword-scabbards were made; identification uncertain but perhaps a species of shark.

D

dā

搭　dā　MC top

1. (med.) strike, smite, hit.

2. (med.) hang, suspend; e.g. sgl. or 〜護 *dāhù*, "hanging shelter," long sleeveless cloak.

    a. (med.) wear or throw over the shoulders.

dá

妲　dá　MC tat

1. 〜己 *dájǐ*, Da Ji, notorious consort of Zhou 紂, the bad last king of the Shang dynasty; 1st of many *femmes fatales* credited with turning rulers away from proper government.

怛　dá　MC tat

1. sad, downhearted; disconsolate; pained.

2. startle, frighten.

    a. (med.) scare off; threaten.

3. 〜羅斯 *dáluósī* (MC tat-la-sje), Talas, name of Central Asian oasis city on northwestern edge of the Tianshan 天山 mountain range in present-day Kyrgyzstan; also, the river that flows past it, which was the site of important battle in 751 when forces of the Abbasid caliphate defeated the Chinese, ending Tang expansion westward and confirming Arab superiority which would then increase in Central Asia.

答　dá　MC top

1. respond, reply, answer.

    a. return the favor, reply in kind; repay, recompense.

2. answer affirmatively, consent to, agree.

荅　dá　MC top

1. rice-bean (*Vigna umbellata*), short-lived vine legume or pulse producing small beans that were mainly used for fodder.

2. ⊙ 答 1, respond, reply; return the favor, answer in kind; 2, consent to, answer affirmatively.

3. crass, crude.

    tá　MC thop

1. 〜然 *tárán*, 〜焉 *táyān*, hopelessly, dejectedly.

達　dá　MC dat

1. move beyond the surface level; come into the open, get or break through; penetrate through or beyond; get through, come through.

    a. insight, intuition; come to comprehend, understand(ing); broad-minded.

    b. arrantly, comprehensively, thoroughly; collectively.

    c. succeed, get on, reach one's goal; attain (-ment) (ant. 窮 *qióng*, stranded, fail, be at a dead end); e.g. 〜命 *dámìng*, attain one's desired course of life.

2. unimpeded, untrammeled; free from physical or moral inhibition; free-spirited.

3. clear away, remove blockage or impediment.

    a. communicate, get one's idea across; convey.

4. a plant's sprouting, breaking through the surface of the ground.

    a. prominent, striking.

5. aperture, opening that allows access or view between two areas.

    a. measure-word for windows or gates.

6. (med.) 〜干 *dágān* (MC dat-kan) or 〜官 *dáguān* (MC dat-kwan), trsc. Turk. *tarqan*, Türkic

aristocratic/administrative title often held in conjunction with other titles.

7. ～奚 *dáxī*, a disyllabic surname.

靼   dá   MC tat

1. supple or pliant leather, dressed leather.
2. (med.) (bn.) 韃～ *dádá*, → 韃 *dá*.

韃   dá   MC that

1. (med.) ～靼 *dádá* (MC that-tat), Tatar (NOT "Tartar"), in Tang times name of a tribe of the Türkic confederation; later ref. to Mongols.

dǎ

打   dǎ   MC tengX

1. strike, beat, batter, hit; pound; pummel, thrash.
2. attack, set upon, assail.

dà

大   dà   MC daH

1. big, large; great.
    a. in large measure, greatly, broadly, widely.
2. enlarge, aggrandize.
3. (Budd.) elements, elementary qualities, esp. 四～ *sìdà*, the elements of earth, fire, water, wind, which make up corporeal world.

dài   MC dajH
1. (med.) ⊙ 代 *dài* 3, dynasty, epoch.

tài   MC thajH
1. ⊙ 太 *tài* 1, greatest, grand(est), maximum, most; 2, marker of seniority, age, or importance; 泰 *tài* 1, majestic, lordly, sublime; peace of mind, equanimity.

dài

代   dài   MC dojH

1. in place of, in X's stead, in lieu of, on behalf of.
    a. replace, substitute.
2. alternate(ly); successive, one following another; e.g. ～喜 *dàixǐ*, respond with joy.
    a. continual, chronic; e.g. ～序 *dàixù*, chronic sequence (of seasons); ～謝 *dàixiè*, succeed in turn.
3. dynasty; epoch, era, age.
4. from early Tang a taboo-substitute for 世 *shì* (to avoid element in personal name of emperor Tang Taizong 唐太宗, Li Shimin 李世民 [r. 626-

649]): a generation, period of 30 years; also, the world.

埭   dài   MC dojH

1. (med.) man-made embankment or slope.

岱   dài   MC dojH

1. paramount, alt. name of Mount Tai 泰山 in Shandong, chief and easternmost of the "5 Marchmounts" (*wuyue* 五嶽).

帶   dài   MC tajH

1. belt (usu. leather); sash, waistband (usu. silk, with varicolored trim), cincture.
    a. (en)gird, belt, encircle, surround; spread over or around.
2. hang items from belt or sash, such as objects of ornamentation (e.g. jade pendants) or honor (e.g. seals of office); wear as accessories, be girded with.
    a. (med.) carry or bring along with.
3. invested with (an office or responsibility); beset with (cares or troubles).
    a. involve, include, be attached to or related with; e.g. 連 A～B, *lián* A *dài* B, including both A and B.
    b. draw near (to), draw into.
4. surrounding area, zone, region.
5. (med.) glint or illuminate in a band of light.

待   dài   MC dojX

1. wait for, await, abide; expect(ant).
    a. prepare for; take precautions.
    b. make provision for.
2. wait on, attend upon, abide; entertain, welcome; handle, treat.
3. be dependent or reliant on, sustained by, contingent on; e.g. 有～ *yǒudài*, something to rely on.
    a. need, require < must wait for, cannot do without.

怠   dài   MC dojX

1. indolent, apathetic, idle; negligent, indifferent; offhanded.
2. insolent, unmannerly; disrespectful, contemptuous.
3. tired, fatigued.

戴   dài   MC tojH

1. carry or wear on the head.
    a. be laden with.

2. cap; to cap, put on top.
   a. praise highly, esteem; support, endorse.
3. protect against, forfend.

殆　dài　MC dojX

1. danger(ous), endanger, risk, peril(ous), imperil, hazard(ous), harm; e.g. 不～ *bùdài*, unscathed.
2. be close to, on the verge of; approximately, nearly, virtually; likely, probably; e.g. ～不可復 *dài bùkě fù*, probably it cannot be recovered; ～不可伐 *dài bùkě fá*, nearly unassailable; ～非 *dàifēi*, virtually not (so), not at all; ～於 不可 *dài yú bùkě*, close to being unacceptable; 夫子～將病 *fūzǐ dài jiāng bìng*, Confucius was on the verge of becoming ill.
   a. get close to (as judgment), had better; e.g. 君～去之 *jūn dài qù zhī* you, my lord, had better leave here; ～無願天下人之議之 *dài wúyuàn tiānxià rén zhī yì zhī*, you had better not wish the people of the subcelestial realm to discuss it.
3. ⊙ 怠 *dài*, indolent, apathetic, indifferent.

玳　dài　MC dojH　⊙ 瑇 *dài*.

瑇　dài　MC dojH

1. (bn.) ～瑁 *dàimào* (MC dojH-mawH), hawksbill turtle (*Eretmochelys imbricata*); also, tortoise-shell, bits of carapace of the preceding used in ornamentation.

紿　dài　MC dojX

1. hoodwink, fool, dupe; defraud.

袋　dài　MC dojH

1. (med.) sack, bag; wallet; pouch, satchel.

詒　dài　MC dojX　→ 詒 *yí*.

貸　dài　MC thojH

1. lend goods or cash; loan.
   a. furnish, provide, impart.
2. borrow.
3. absolve, exempt; forgive; excuse.
   tè　MC thok
1. ⊙ 忒 *tè* 2, err(ing), fault, deviant; mistake; be off the mark, out of line

軑　dài　MC dajH

1. axle-cap, hollow outer bearing of bronze at juncture of carriage's wheel and axle, around which the hub projects.

迨　dài　MC dojH

1. ⊙ 逮 *dài* 1, come to, reach a point in place or time; extend to, catch up to; when, by the time of; until; 2a, seize the moment for, take advantage of.

逮　dài　MC dojH

1. come to, reach a point in place or time; extend to, up to.
   a. measure up (to standard), be equally matched; catch up to
   b. when, by the time of; until; keep on till.
2. nab, seize; apprehend, arrest; attain, acquire, obtain.
   a. seize the moment for, catch the chance of; take advantage of.
   dì　MC dejH
1. sgl. or rdup., decorous and dignified, seemly, with grace and elegance.

靆　dài　MC dojH

1. (bn.) 靉～ *àidài*, → 靉 *ài*.

黛　dài　MC dojH

1. kohl, finely powdered antimony sulfide, used to give blue-black tint to women's eyelids or eyebrows.
   a. by metonymy, women's eyebrows.
2. kohl-blue, as color word applied to objects of similar hue.

dān

丹　dān　MC tan

1. cinnabar; e.g. ～鉛 *dānqiān*, cinnabar and lead-powder > correction of texts, criticism, collation, because cinnabar writing-pigment and lead-powder paintover used in revising manuscripts.
   a. (Dao.) by synecdoche, elixir of transcendence or immortality, because cinnabar was one of chief ingredients in mineral-based concoctions; also, often used as adjective indicating connection of item with Dao. transcendence.
2. cinnabar-red, vermilion; e.g. ～青 *dānqīng*, red and green, i.e. painting (< pigments made from cinnabar and malachite); ～書 *dānshū*, "cinnabar document," written with pigment made from cinnabar, usu. ref. special importance, e.g. heaven-sent text, order of emperor, Dao. esoteric text.

a. sun-flushed, burning-red, esp. in scenic descriptions.

3. bare, exposed; unfeigned, authentic; e.g. 〜心 *dānxīn*, one's true heart (equiv. 赤心 *chìxīn*).

4. 〜桂 *dānguì*, depending on context, may ref. red-flowered osmanthus (*Osmanthus fragrans*), red-barked cinnamon (species of *Cinnamomum cassia*), or either as associated with Dao, immortality.

儋   **dān**   MC tam   ⊙ 擔 *dān*.

單   **dān**   MC tan
1. single, sole (ant. 雙 *shuāng*, pair); exclusive, isolated; alone.
   a. single-layered, unlined, as of clothing; e.g. 〜絞 *dānjiǎo*, unlined robe of yellow-green silk.
2. insubstantial, flimsy; weak.
   a. deficient, insufficient.
   b. wanting, impoverished; e.g. 〜門 *dānmén*, poor household.
3. ⊙ 殫 *dān*, use up, deplete; 憚 *dàn*, quail at, shrink from.

   chán   MC dzyen
1. (bn.) 〜于 *chányú* (MC dzyen-hju), title of the Xiongnu supreme leader; also written 禪于.

擔   **dān**   MC tam
1. carry across the shoulders with a pole.
2. bear a burden; assume responsibility for.

   dàn   MC tamH
1. load, burden.
2. measure of weight, equiv. 100 "catties" (*jīn* 斤).

殫   **dān**   MC tan
1. use up, deplete, reach the end of.
   a. entirely, all of.
2. ⊙ 憚 *dàn*, quail at, shrink from.

甔   **dān**   MC tom
1. small-mouthed large pottery jar, crock.
   a. (med.) esp. wine-jug.

眈   **dān**   MC tom
1. rdup., peer at piercingly, consider severely; also, deep and cavernous.

簞   **dān**   MC tan
1. bamboo food-basket.
   a. rice-bin.
2. bin, caddy.

耽   **dān**   MC tom
1. pendulous ears, long-lobed.
2. extended, prolonged.
   a. chronically involved with; addicted to, immersed in, in deep with, wholly taken up with.

聸   **dān**   MC tham
1. large and long-lobed ears.
2. ⊙ 耽 *dān* 2a, addicted to, taken up with, dote on, in deep with.
3. personal name of Laozi 老子.

酖   **dān**   MC tom
1. given over to drink, souse, toper, addicted to wine.
2. hedonist, pleasure-seeker.
   zhèn   MC drimH
1. ⊙ 鴆 *zhèn* 1a, poisoned wine.

dǎn

亶   **dǎn**   MC tanX
1. genuine, true; sincere.
   a. truly, actually, really.
2. ⊙ 但 *dàn* 1, only, merely, just.

疸   **dǎn**   MC tanX
1. jaundice.

紞   **dǎn**   MC tamX
1. stopper-cord, attached to earplugs at either side of ceremonial cap.

膽   **dǎn**   MC tomX
1. gall bladder.
2. gall, audacity; daring, courage.

黕   **dǎn**   MC tomX
1. spot, blot; stain, smirch, smudge; dirt(y).
2. dark; swart, black.

黵   **dǎn**   MC tomX
1. blotch, stain.
   a. smear over; alter.
2. deep blue-black color.
3. 〜面 *dǎnmiàn*, punishment in which a prisoner condemned to death but amnestied has a character (usu. 卻 *què*, "pardoned") carved on his face and filled in with blue-black ink; judicial branding.

dàn

但　dàn　MC danX
1. (ADV) only, merely, just; it is just that . . . (< bare, exposed).
2. (ADV) in vain, vainly, futilely.
3. (med.) in 5th century begins occasionally to be used as conjunction: but, however.
4. (med.) (ADV) without delay, promptly, directly; just then.

啖　dàn　MC damX
1. eat with pleasure; devour.
    a. feed, provide with sustenance.
2. whet the appetite, give a taste; coax; entice(ment), blandish(ment)

啗　dàn　MC damX　⊙ 啖 dàn.

彈　dàn　MC danH　→ 彈 tán.

憚　dàn　MC tanH
1. quail at, shy away from, shrink from, flinch; draw in one's horns.
    a. be wary of, beware, be careful.
2. frighten(ed), daunt(ed); unquiet.
3. ⊙ 癉 dàn 1, exhaustion, debilitation.
    #### dá　MC tat
1. ⊙ 怛 dá 2, startle, alarm.

憺　dàn　MC damX
1. calm, serene, peaceful; unruffled, composed.
2. heart-struck, dispirited, dismayed.
3. ⊙ 憚 dàn 1, quail at, flinch from; 2, frightened.

旦　dàn　MC tanH
1. sunrise, dawn, when night ends with the rising sun; cf. 朝 zhāo 1, morning.
    a. ～夕 dànxì, dawn and dusk; everyday, day after day; also, imminent (in the time between dawn and dusk).
    b. sgl. or in cmpd. ～望 dànwàng, first day of the month.
    c. rdup., everyday, day after day; also, in earnest, candidly.

淡　dàn　MC damX
1. bland, plain, tasteless, insipid; mild.
    a. with positive connotations in *Laozi* and *Zhuangzi*: tranquil, unconcerned, contented with simplicity, indifferent to desire, happy only with what is plainly necessary, without strong emotions; e.g. ～泊 dànbó, placid and at rest.
2. pale, pallid, light (color); faded, etiolated.
    a. rdup., palely faded, thin and fine; also, uninterested and impassive (toward others); also, limpid and lucent; also, calm and full; also, deep and cavernous.
3. (med.) (bn.) ～沱 dànduò (MC damX-daX), clear and calm, of springtime light.

澹　dàn　MC damX
1. rdup., rough and rolling (waves), rippling, undulating.
    a. (bn.) ～淡 dàndàn (MC damX-damX), shuddering and shaking, tossing and tumbling (waves); also, sway and swing, drift and glide.
    b. (bn.) ～蕩 dàndàng (MC damX-dangX), raddled and restless; also, irenic and unruffled (see 2).
    c. (bn.) ～灩 dànyàn (MC damX-yemH), splash and lap, purl and run.
2. placid, tranquil, calm, mild; e.g. ～泊 dànbó, calm and at rest.
3. ⊙ 淡 dàn 2, pale, pallid, faded, light (color).
4. (bn.) ～澉 dànhǎn (MC damX-kamX), bathe and lave, wash and cleanse.
    #### shàn　MC dzyemH
1. ⊙ 贍 shàn 1, well-provided, sufficient.

癉　dàn　MC tanH
1. exhaustion; enervation.
2. ⊙ 疸 dǎn, jaundice; 癉 chǎn 2c, fever(ish).
    #### dān　MC tan
1. diabetes.

菡　dàn　MC domX
1. (bn.) 菡～ hàndàn (MC homX-domX), unopened lotus, lotus-knop (*Nelumbo nucifera*); cf. hé 荷, fúróng 芙蓉, fúqú 芙蕖, lián 蓮.

誕　dàn　MC danX
1. preposterous, excessive, overdone; unreasonable, groundless.
    a. nonsensical talk; bombast, bravado, hyperbole; blather, twaddle.
    b. cozen; bamboozle, delude.
2. broad, expansive.
    a. diffuse, disperse; spread, scatter.
3. unchecked, self-indulgent; dissipated, dissolute.
4. (med.) give birth to, bear.

髧   **dàn**   MC domX
1. thick mane of hanging hair, heavy thatch.
   a. hang down; hover.

dāng

瑒   **dāng**   MC tang
1. finial, decorative tip of projecting rafter.
2. cap ornament of military official in Han times; term afterward associated esp. with eunuchs.
3. women's earring.
4. (med.) girdle chimes, ouches.

當   **dāng**   MC tang
1. be apposite.
   a. pertinent, appropriate; apposite to do > aux. VB of imperative: ought to, should; may be expected to, e.g. 何～ *hédāng*, when shall, how shall . . .; why not?
   b. (med.) marks Skt. future tense in trns. of Budd. texts: shall or will (be so) with reasonable certainty. Then used commonly elsewhere as aux. VB of future tense, e.g. ～復 *dāngfù*, is going to . . ., is about to. . . .
   c. (Budd.) used in question to mark emphasis, e.g. ～復 *dāngfù*, how (who, what) on earth?
2. to appose, foreset, confront; attend to, undertake responsibility for, be accountable for; attend to, be the intendant of, manage, control; e.g. ～路 *dānglù*, "those who control the roads," those with influence or power; ～鑪 or ～爐 *dānglú*, "one who attends to the brazier," vintner, wine-shop owner, sometimes used of female servants in wineshops; ～世 *dāngshì*, those responsible for the age, in control of government; ～盧 *dānglú*, frontlet, decorative piece on forehead of horse.
   a. as locative marker, in X-place, at X-time, e.g. ～時 *dāngshí*, at the said time; also, in the past; also, right this minute, straightaway; ～世 *dāngshì*, in the present age; ～來 *dānglái*, in future; ～身 *dāngshēn*, (for, by) oneself; 何～ *hédāng*, sooner or later; how will (must) it be?; when will it be?; even more so.
   b. impede, block; face off, ward off, ⊙ 擋 *dǎng*.
   c. ～歸 *dāngguī*, "ought-to-return plant," angelica (*Angelica sinensis*), perennial herb which flowers in autumn; so named because when it flowers, it is time for a traveler to return home.

dàng   MC tangH
1. suitable, well-adapted, on point; match, fit, befit; equal, equally matched, correspond to, e.g. ～時 *dàngshí*, accord with the times.
   a. stand in place of, be equivalent to; have the value of, rank with, match; take as, regard as, treat as; act as pawn.

襠   **dāng**   MC tang
1. seat or crotch of trousers.

鐺   **dāng**   MC tang
1. (bn.) 銀～ *lángdāng*, → 銀 *láng*.
2. rdup., onom. of metal being struck, also of plunk-plunk of clepsydra.
   chēng   MC tsrhaeng
1. (med.) cookpot, iron wok; also, pot for warming wine.

dǎng

欓   **dǎng**   MC tangX
1. prickly-ash (*Zanthoxylum ailanthoides*), pungently fragrant tree whose fruit was used in making hot pepper and whose small pale-yellow flowers were gathered esp. on *chongyang* 重陽 (9/9) day to attach to household doorway as protective against malignant spirits; sometimes ref. euodia or evodia (*Tetradium ruticarpum*), aromatic deciduous small tree or large shrub that produces clusters of red rounded seed pods, in which case syn. 茱萸 *zhūyú*.

讜   **dǎng**   MC tangX
1. accordant with what ought to be said; candor, frank speech, forthright talk; plain-spoken.

黨   **dǎng**   MC tangX
1. in Zhou times administrative grouping of 500 households.
   a. class, category.
2. clan members, kin.
3. confederates, combining for attainment of same goals.
   a. faction, party, cabal; partisans (with negative connotation).
4. be partial to, side with; protect or favor improperly; biased.
5. ⊙ 讜 *dǎng*, candor, frank speech.
6. (med.) ～項 *dǎngxiàng* (MC tangX-haewngX), Tangut, a pastoral nomadic people to the northwest in Tang times.

dàng

宕 dàng MC dangH
1. cavern(ous), cave.
  a. quarry.
2. run, course out, flow; get all the way through; traverse.
3. unrestrained, on one's own terms, at liberty; boisterous; profligate.
4. (bn.) ～冥 *dàngmíng* (dangH-meng), blurred, dim and dark.

盪 dàng MC dangX
1. ⊙ 蕩 1, shake, dislodge, unmoor, raddle, convulse, overwhelm; heave, budge; 2, let loose, unchecked, unrestrained, willful, wanton; 3, wash clean, scour, drench; sweep away, eliminate; 4, immense, vast, illimitable.
2. assail, throw oneself against.

碭 dàng MC dangH
1. veined or striated stone.
2. surge, overrun; overflow.
  a. (bn.) ～突 *dàngtú* (MC dangH-thwot), in (less than) no time, pell-mell, before one knows; syn. 唐突 *tángtú*.
3. far edges, immensity (area).

菪 dàng MC dangH
1. (bn.) 莨～ *làngdàng*, → 莨 *làng (láng)*.

蕩 dàng MC dangX
1. shake(n); unsettle(d); dislodge(d), unmoor(ed); disarrange(d), raddle(d), convulse(d); overwhelm(ed), swept away.
  a. heave, bounce; budge, move.
2. ungoverned, unbridled, unchecked, without restraint, let loose, willful(ness); wanton(ness), dissipated.
  a. lay waste, wreak havoc; ravage; devastate.
  b. waste; drain off, spill; throw away, dissipate.
3. wash clean, scour; drench.
  a. sweep away, clear away; liquidate, eliminate.
4. immense, vast, tremendous; illimitable, inexhaustible; far-spreading.
5. calm, unruffled, undisturbed, unstirred, composed; e.g. 坦～ *tǎndàng*, candid and relaxed.
6. rdup., various applications of all above, depending on context: incalculable and indeterminate; immense and infinite; vastly grand and great; also, flooding far and unconfined, roiling ever onward, all-spreading and omnipotent;

also, wantonly willful, doing what one will; also, overwhelmed and overpowered, thrown into thoughtlessness; also, mild and unmoved, placid and unstirred.

遏 dàng MC dangH
1. stumble, trip; stagger, lurch; falter.
  táng MC dang
1. shake, jar, convulse; buffet.

dāo

刀 dāo MC taw
1. single-bladed weapon; sword, saber, broadsword, falchion, knife; e.g. 橫～ *héngdāo*, short sword girded on by soldier; 陌～ *mòdāo*, long sword of infantryman; 儀～ *yídāo*, ceremonial or processional sword, usu. ornamented with gold and silver.
2. sgl. or cmpd. ～幣 *dāobì*, knife-money, coins in knife shape, in use 7th to 3rd centuries BCE, esp. in northern and eastern states.
3. ⊙ 舠 *dāo*, small boat, knife-like canoe.

忉 dāo MC taw
1. sgl. or rdup., heart-stabbed, emotionally wounded, grieved, dismayed and disconsolate.
  a. (bn.) ～怛 *dāodá* (MC taw-tat), painful and plaintive, hopelessly hapless.

舠 dāo MC taw
1. small boat, knife-like canoe.

dǎo

導 dǎo MC dawH
1. lead, lead the way, show the way; conduct, guide.
  a. lead out; extricate.
2. instruct; coach, advise.
3. open a passage, clear the way.

島 dǎo MC tawX
1. island, seamount, usu. of substantial size and in large lake or sea.

搗 dǎo MC tawX
1. (med.) ⊙ 擣 *dǎo*.

擣 dǎo MC tawX
1. pound, beat with a pestle.
  a. sgl. or ～衣 *dǎoyī*, beat (clothes) with a fulling mallet, process of shrinking and thick-

ening woolen cloth causing the fibers to felt; esp. done in preparation for winter.
2. strike, smite; attack, assault.

禱   dǎo   MC tawX
1. pray to gods or spirits, supplicate, implore, entreat.
    a. imprecate.

蹈   dǎo   MC dawH
1. tread, step on, set one's foot on.
    a. step up, clamber; set out on, trek.
    b. tread the steps of someone, follow the example of.
2. step or stamp to rhythm, dance.

dào

倒   dào   MC tawH
1. overturn, upend, reverse; upside-down, topsy-turvy, inverse.
2. (med.) on the contrary < upended, reversed.
    dǎo   MC tawX
1. fall down, collapse.

到   dào   MC tawH
1. reach, arrive at, get to a place or a time (usu. transitive with stated OBJ; cf. 至 *zhì*).
    a. to complete, perfect, round off.
    b. (med.) ～底 *dàodǐ*, ～了 *dàoliǎo*, to the bottom, to the end, i.e. finally, at last.
2. ⊙ 倒 *dào* 1, overturn, upside-down; 2, (med.) on the contrary; 道 *dào* 6, speak, say.

悼   dào   MC dawH
1. downhearted, heavy-hearted, dolorous, woeful.
2. lament or bear in mind the dead; mourn, grieve.
    a. feel or show commiseration for, pity; consolation, condolence; e.g. 自～ *zìdào*, self-commiseration.
3. tremble, quake; shake with fear.

燾   dào   MC dawH
1. cover over, overtop, overlay.
2. (bn.) ～幬 *dào'ào* (MC dawH-ngawH), tower proudly upward.

盜   dào   MC dawH
1. steal, rob.
    a. robber, thief, brigand.
    b. stealth(il)y, furtive(ly), surreptitious(ly); illicit(ly).

2. take by force what is not yours; sack, loot; raid; despoil, ravage.
3. murder(er).
4. sly, wily; deceive, by sycophancy or slander.

稻   dào   MC dawX
1. rice (*Oryza sativa*), primarily *sinica* species (glutinous, short-grained) cultivated in dry fields; post-Han also *indica* species (non-glutinous, long-grained) cultivated in paddies in subtropical areas.

纛   dào   MC dawH
1. banneret with yak-tail tassel or tuft of pheasant plumes held by dancers performing for court or nobles, also used to decorate the emperor's carriage.
    a. (med.) banner with same, used by army and by imperial honor-guard.

翿   dào   MC dawH
1. banneret of pheasant feathers held by dancers.

道   dào   MC dawX
1. way that leads somewhere, road, route, pathway, passage.
2. the Way; as image suggesting how things actually exist, fundamental reality, a constant Way in which the diverse ways of living and relating are essentially balanced and whole.
    a. conceptual term used by all schools of thought, with same root metaphor but varying connotations: Confucian "Way" incl. norms of social responsibility and personal conduct exemplified by ideal worthies such as King Wen of the Zhou, the Duke of Zhou, etc.; Dao. "Way" points to absolute and ineffable reality behind flux and modalities of the world, and advisability of taking it as model; Budd. "Way" incl. possibility of release from the round-of-birth-and-death (*saṃsāra*) and recognition of contingent and impermanent nature of human existence.
    b. ～士 *dàoshì*, gentleman of the Way, exemplar of the Confucian "Way"; also, expert in the Way, specialist in occult or mantic practices, syn. 方士 *fāngshì*; also (med.), Daoist adept, usu. associated with an organized Dao. community (see 5a below), priest. N.B. Contrast these with (med.) ～人 *dàorén*, man of religion, a Budd. monk (not Dao.).

3. way of doing something, course of action, method, proper procedure, practice; e.g. 所以求之之〜 *suǒyǐ qiú zhī zhi dào*, the means by which one seeks it; 〜場 *dàocháng*, place of practice, arena of the Way, altar, Budd. or Dao. chapel.

   a. guiding road, rule of conduct, principle, guidelines.

   b. doctrine, tenets, dicta; teachings.

   c. (Budd.) the Buddha-path, path to enlightenment.

4. skill or art of a particular kind, specialization.

5. ideas and teachings esp. associated with the texts *Zhuangzi* and *Laozi* (or *Daodejing*); e.g. 〜家 *dàojiā*, lineage of the Way, bibliographic category ref. to these and related texts, often defined as "philosophical Daoism" in contrast to next.

   a. practices esp. associated with movements and texts relating to masters of self-cultivation, pursuit of immortality, and various organized religious communities, esp. those ultimately deriving from the Way of the Celestial Masters (*tianshidao* 天師道) founded in mid-2nd-c. CE; e.g. (med.) 〜教 *dàojiào*, teaching of the Way, from early 5th-c. CE a term assoc. with groups and texts just described, often defined now as "religious Daoism."

6. say, speak; express, communicate orally; cue.

7. circuit, administrative area outside the usu. prefecture/district (*junxian* 郡縣) structure; in Han times ref. frontier areas mainly populated by non-Chinese; in Tang times also ref. frontier area but from 706 on more importantly to large units of province size throughout the state, each of which (10 at first) incl. many prefectures and governed by special commissioners (*shi* 使).

8. (med.) understand, be aware of; think, presume.

   a. (med.) expect; have a sense that X is likely to happen.

     dǎo　MC dawH

1. ⊙ 導 *dǎo* 1, lead, show the way, conduct, guide.

dé

得　　dé　MC tok

1. obtain, attain(ment), acquire(ment); gain, get; win; e.g. 〜職 *dézhí*, obtain one's due.

   a. have control of, possess; satisfied in; e.g. 自〜 *zìdé*, self-possessed, complacent.

   b. get by ear, hear.

2. as auxiliary VB: get to VB, be able to VB, find it possible to . . ., manage to . . .

   a. as auxiliary VB followed by 而 *ér*; the occurrence of *ér* seems to be a vestigial marker suggesting that *dé* in its auxiliary function is in orgin ADV; the meaning is not effectively different from the preceding; e.g. 吾不〜而見之矣 *wú bùdé ér jiàn zhī yǐ*, I have been unable to see such.

3. (med.) modal ADV indicating uncertainty, possibility, or mild suggestion: might; e.g. 〜無 *déwú*, might it not be that . . ., wouldn't you agree that . . ., isn't it that . . .?; syn. 將無 *jiāngwú*.

4. (med.) to have, own; there is, there are; e.g. 避暑〜名園 *bìshǔ dé míngyuán*, to escape the summer heat you have (there is) a famed garden.

5. (med.) preceding a time-word indicates the stated amount of time has passed: already, after; e.g. 〜七日 *dé qīrì*, after 7 days.

德　　dé　MC tok

1. innate power, potency, efficacy; sometimes thought of as projection of the *dao* 道 (Way) in the sensible world, hence cmpd. 道〜 *dàodé*, the Way and its Power (Force, Working, Process); a potency vouchsafed by Heaven, so providing connection with Heaven, and permitting one who possesses it to influence charismatically but without overt effort the behavior of others in the same direction; esp. associated with sages, ideal rulers, exemplary figures who live in harmony with all elements of existence. Traditionally translated as "virtue," but having no religious overtones.

   a. merits, essential properties.

   b. distinctive qualities.

2. moral power, quality conducing to proper action in realm of social or community interaction.

3. kindness, favor, gracious treatment; (Budd.) blessing, blessed.

4. (Budd.) 大〜 *dàdé*, trns. of Skt. *bhadanta*, most virtuous, an honorific term for Budd. mendicant or monk.

dēng

甋　　dēng　MC tong

1. (med.) (bn.) 甋〜 *tàdēng*, → 甋 *tà*.

燈　　dēng　MC tong

1. lantern, lamp.

   a. (Budd.) image for the Dharma, truth; e.g. 傳〜 *chuándēng*, transmission of the lamp, handing on the teachings from master to disciple.

登   **dēng**   MC tong

1. climb, ascend, rise; (sur)mount.
   a. on high, elevated.
2. rise in official position, advance, be promoted.
3. increase, add to, pile up.
4. proffer, hand upward.
5. ripen, mature, of grain (< grow to full height).
6. inscribe, register.
7. (med.) as time-marker; e.g. ～時 *dēngshí*, immediately, pronto; also, just then, at that time.
8. (bn.) ～利 *dēnglì* (MC tong-lijH), trsc. Turk. *tängri*, heaven(ly) > god of heaven, esp. epithet attached to the title *kaghan*.

簦   **dēng**   MC tong

1. conical bamboo rain-hat with handle, similar to umbrella.

登   **dēng**   MC tong

1. vessel for ritual offerings.

鐙   **dēng**   MC tong

1. bronze oil-lamp.
2. ⊙ 登 *dēng*, vessel for ritual offerings.
   dèng   MC tongH
1. (med.) stirrup.

děng

等   **děng**   MC tongX

1. equal, same as, at the same level; of the same generation; e.g. 一～ *yīděng*, wholly in step with, one and the same; (med.) ～頭 *děngtóu*, likewise, the same.
   a. (al)together.
   b. with equanimity.
   c. (med.) common(ly), normal(ly); casual(ly); e.g. ～閒 *děngxián*, commonplace, regular, as usual, ordinary.
2. step, grade, rank, class; category; e.g. (med.) 及～ *jíděng*, make the grade, i.e. pass the civil-service exam.
   a. step, of stairway.
3. compare, evaluate.
4. following pronoun or noun(s), indicates plurality or inclusion of unnamed others of the same kind: . . . and others, et al., etc.; e.g. 彼～ *bǐděng*, those (persons), they; 某～ *mǒuděng*, we; 樵漁～ *qiáoyúděng*, woodcutters, fishermen, and others.
5. (med.) (a)wait (late Tang usage).

dèng

凳   **dèng**   MC tongH

1. (med.) bench, stool, footstool.

墱   **dèng**   MC tongH

1. edgeway, footbridge on mountainside.
   a. stone steps, stairway, ⊙ 隥 *dèng* 2.
2. drainage ditch.

瞪   **dèng**   MC dreangH

1. stare, look at straight-on.
   a. (med.) glare at, in anger.

磴   **dèng**   MC tongH

1. ledge on a mountain.
2. stone stairway.
   tèng   MC dongH
1. draining of small streams into larger waterway.

蹬   **dèng**   MC dongH

1. (bn.) 蹭～ *cèngdèng*, → 蹭 *cèng*.
2. bench, stool; footstool.
3. step, stair(way).

隥   **dèng**   MC tongH

1. slope, of hillside.
   a. ramp.
2. stone steps, stairway.

dī

低   **dī**   MC tej

1. low(ly); beneath, under.
   a. to lower, droop, stoop; come down to.
2. (bn.) ～佪 *dīhuái* (MC tej-hwoj), ⊙ 徘佪 *páihuái* → 徘 *pái*.

堤   **dī**   MC tej   ⊙ 隄 *dī*.

滴   **dī**   MC tek

1. to drip, fall drop by drop; drizzle, trickle, sprinkle.
   a. drop(let).
   b. (bn.) ～瀝 *dīlì* (MC tek-lek), 瀝～ *lìdī*, dribbling droplets.

羝   **dī**   MC tej

1. male sheep, ram, tup.

袛   **dī**   MC tej

1. (bn.) ～裯 *dīdāo* (MC tej-taw), short singlet, short unlined chemise.

鍉　dī　MC tej

1. basin, pan, esp. used in early times for blood-oaths.
2. lancet or needle used in medicine.

　　dí　MC tek

1. ⊙ 鏑 dí 1, arrowhead; shoot (arrow); 2, by metonymy, gen. term for weapons, arms.

　　chí　MC dzye

1. small spoon.
2. key.

隄　dī　MC tej

1. dike, embankment; dam.
　　a. to dam, block up; prevent, guard against.
　　b. to limit, bar.

鞮　dī　MC tej

1. leather shoes.
2. ～譯 dīyì, 狄～ dídī, interpreter, translator.

dí

嫡　dí　MC tek

1. principal wife; e.g. ～子 dízǐ, son(s) of principal wife, heritor.

敵　dí　MC dek

1. enemy, rival, opponent.
2. oppose, resist, stand against.
3. be a match for, correspond to.

汥　dí　MC dek　→ 汥 yóu.

滌　dí　MC dek

1. wash, rinse; scour (mostly implements).
　　a. cleanse, purify.
2. rinse out; sweep away; eliminate, do away with.
3. alter, shift, modify.
4. in early times, stable where animals designated for use in sacrifical offerings were raised.
5. rdup., bare and burned out, sear and parched, of drought conditions.

狄　dí　MC dek

1. pejorative name for northern non-Hua peoples, "dog-tribes," barbarians.
2. lowly servant, subaltern.
3. ⊙ 翟 dí, Reeves's pheasant (Syrmaticus reevesii).

　　tì　MC thek

1. ⊙ 剔 tì, shave, scrape off hair; dress, put in order.

甋　dí　MC tek

1. (bn.) 瓴～ língdí, → 瓴 líng.

笛　dí　MC dek

1. bamboo cross-flute, with 5 or 7 stopped holes and a thin membrane over a non-stopped hole which produces a reedy timbre.

篴　dí　MC dek　⊙ 笛 dí.

糴　dí　MC dek

1. to buy grain, lay in grain.

翟　dí　MC dek

1. Reeves's pheasant (Syrmaticus reevesii), large long-tailed pheasant, brightly colored with gold, white, and copper-hued plumage.
　　a. pheasant feathers held by dancers in ritual ceremonies of ancient times.
　　b. clothing, vehicles, items of luxury decorated with pheasant feathers.
2. ⊙ 狄 dí, pejorative name of northern non-Hua peoples.

　　zhái　MC draek

1. a surname.

荻　dí　MC dek

1. Chinese silvergrass, miscanthus (Miscanthus sacchariflorus), a kind of rush esp. used for sitting-mats.
2. a surname.

覿　dí　MC dek

1. see; notice, regard.
　　a. meet, come face-to-face with.
2. appear, be seen, manifest.

踧　dí　MC dek　→ 踧 cù.

蹢　dí　MC tek

1. hoof, of quadruped.

　　zhí　MC drjek

1. (bn.) ～躅 zhízhú (MC drjek-drjowk), ⊙ 躑躅 zhízhú, → 躑 zhí.
2. throw away, cast aside; pitch, toss.

迪　dí　MC dek

1. follow a road, go along a path, advance, go forward, esp. with sense of following the right path (ant. 逆 nì 2, go against, go backward).

a. road or path being taken, course, guideway.
b. follow after; abide by, adhere to.
2. lead along, direct to goal or achievement.
a. redirect; improve, better, amend.
3. carry out, execute; effect, realize, reach one's goal.
4. euphonic phrase-initial particle in *Shangshu*.

鏑   dí   MC tek

1. arrowhead.
a. shoot (arrow).
2. by metonymy, gen. term for weapons, arms.

dǐ

底   dǐ   MC tejX

1. bottom, lowest part, base.
a. under(neath), beneath, below.
b. droop, lower, stoop.
2. reach, arrive at (hoped-for end or goal).
a. come to a stop, bring to an end; halt, cease.
3. (med.) interr., esp. in poetry: how? what? e.g. 終朝有～忙 *zhōngzhāo yǒu dǐ máng*, what is it that keeps one busy all morning?

弝   dǐ   MC tejX

1. carved bow, reputedly of the sage-king Shun.

抵   dǐ   MC tejX

1. push away, push off, resist.
2. strike with the forehead, butt, ram; oppose, collide with.
3. deny, disavow, repudiate.
a. cast aside, turn out; throw off.
4. compensate, make good on, requite.
a. equivalent to, of similar value, come up to; be worth X.
5. reach, arrive at.
   zhǐ   MC tsyeX
1. strike from the side; smack, clap.

柢   dǐ   MC tejX

1. taproot of tree; gen. term for roots.
a. firmly rooted part; base, foundation.

氐   dǐ   MC tejX

1. base, foundation.
a. bottom.
2. in general, generally, mainly, roughly; usu. 大～ *dàdǐ*.

3. "Base," one of the 28 lunar lodgings, comprised of α, β, γ, ι Librae, in the eastern quadrant (*qinglong* 青龍) of the sky.

牴   dǐ   MC tejX

1. strike with the forehead; butt, ram.
a. oppose, collide with; confront; e.g. (med.) ～牾 *dǐwǔ*, contradict(ory), contravention.

砥   dǐ   MC tsyijX

1. whetstone.
2. hone; polish.
a. hone or polish a skill; cultivate a goal; refine to perfection.
3. smooth; level.

觝   dǐ   MC tejX   ⊙ 牴 *dǐ*.

詆   dǐ   MC tejX

1. disparage, belittle, decry, derogate, deprecate.

邸   dǐ   MC tejX

1. residence at capital of prince who is posted elsewhere, for when he attends required court levees; state apartment.
2. mansion, manor, or sometimes office headquarters, of noble, high dignitary, or powerful official; e.g. ～第 *dǐdì*, lordly mansion.
3. pull up, bring to halt (horse or carriage).
4. screen, esp. bed-screen.
5. (med.) guesthouse, inn, hostel.
6. (med.) granary, storehouse.

阺   dǐ   MC tejX

1. mountain slope; incline, gradient; hillside.
2. overhang, ledge, on hill or mountain.

dì

地   dì   MC dijH

1. earth, esp. as paired with "heaven" (*tian* 天).
a. (Budd.) ～獄 *dìyù*, "earth-prison," hell; ～黃 *dìhuáng*, "yellow of earth" or ～髓 *dìsuǐ*, "marrow of earth," foxglove (*Rehmannia glutinosa*), medicinal herb, the roots a dye-source for "imperial yellow" in med. times; ～節 *dìjié*, "nodes of earth," alternate name for 萎蕤 *wěiruí*, sealwort (*Polygonatum odoratum*), medicinal herb; ～骨 *dìgǔ*, "bones of earth," wolfberry (*Lycium chinense, Lycium barbarum*), syn. 枸杞 *gǒuqǐ*; (Dao.)

～關 *dìguān*, "earthly barrier," Dao. esoteric term for feet; (Dao.) ～戶 *dìhú*, "earthly door," Dao. esoteric term for nose.
2. earth, as land, soil; ground.
  a territory.
  b. place, locality, site.
  c terrain, topography.
  d. (med.) ～子 *dìzǐ*, Tang tax on produce of land.
3. floor; e.g. ～衣 *dìyī*, "floor-clothing," i.e. carpet.
4. position, state or stage (of being), condition, situation; (Budd.) trns. Skt *bhūmi*, stages (ten) of a bodhisattva's development.
  a. base, foundation.
5. (med.) consanguineous relations.
6. (med.) suffix giving ADV sense; e.g. 白～斷肝腸 *báidì duàn gāncháng*, so white (white enough) that it (the moon) breaks my heart.
7. (med.) suffix following intransitive VB, suggests continuative sense; e.g. 立～看天坐～吟 *lìdì kàntiān zuòdì yín*, standing and looking at the sky, sitting and chanting poetry.
8. ⊙ 第 *dì* 4, only, merely; (med.) 的 *dì*, target, aim.

娣　dì　MC dejX

1. younger sister married to same man as her older sister.
  a. gen. term for younger sister.
2. younger concubine (unrelated to others).
3. younger of sisters-in-law who are married to different brothers.

嵽　dì　MC dejH

1. (bn.) 岧～ *tiáodì*, → 岧 *tiáo*.

帝　dì　MC tejH

1. highest god.
  a. gen. term for gods, such as those of particular directions or certain Dao. divinities.
2. highest of earthly rulers, traditionally rendered "emperor," of whom the first to adopt the title was Qin Shihuang 秦始皇 (r. 221-210 BCE); if regarded as closely connected with or partaking of the power (*de* 德) of Heaven, possibly "thearch" (i.e. god-king).

弟　dì　MC dejX

1. younger brother.
  a. one who adopts deferentiality expected of younger brother; e.g. ～子 *dìzi*, retainer, disciple, student.

2. ⊙ 第 *dì* 1, sequence, series, place in a series; 4, merely, just only.

  tì　MC dejH

1. ⊙ 悌 *tì* 1, respectful deference toward elder brother(s), acting as a younger brother should; adelphic.

棣　dì　MC dejH

1. sgl., 常～ *chángdì*, 棠～ *tángdì*, variously identified as species of cherry, plum, pear, or quince, gorgeously flowering; perhaps kerria (*Kerria japonica*) showing large yellow flowers in springtime; suggested rendering either "kerria" or "sweet-plum"; associated in lit. with fraternal feeling.

  dài　MC dojH

1. rdup., graceful and refined, decorous and dignified.

玓　dì　MC tek

1. (bn.) ～瓅 *dìlì* (MC tek-lek), glittering glint, twinkling sparkle, esp. of precious stones.

的　dì　MC tek

1. target, butt, in archery.
2. bright dot of light; (bn.) ～皪 *dìlì* (MC tek-lek), sparkling spangles, as moonlight, pearls, fireflies, white birds, sails against dark background.
  a. mouche, beauty-spot, often pink, painted on woman's face.
3. sgl. or rdup., vivid, bright; clear, distinct.
4. (med.) certainly, surely; e.g. ～畢 *dìbì*, ～當 *dìdāng*, indeed, necessarily, certain to.

睇　dì　MC dejH

1. glance from the corner of one's eye; look askance at, peer at questioningly or judgmentally.

禘　dì　MC dejH

1. grand sacrifice offered by ruler triennially to founding ancestor of his line.
2. in early times, summer sacrifice of feudal lords to ancestors.

第　dì　MC dejH

1. sequence, series, place in a series.
  a. rank, grade, degree; e.g. 及～ *jídì*, "make the grade," pass the civil-service examination.
  b. order, put in order, arrange (by sequential order), organize.

2. manor, mansion; state apartment, residence (of nobles or court officials), e.g. ～舍 *dìshè*, mansion-house, domal residence.

3. ordinal number marker.

    a. (med.) ～一 *dìyī*, by all means, certainly; also, in the highest degree.

4. simply, merely, just, only.

締   dì   MC dejH

1. knot or bind up unalterably.

2. establish, form, conclude; e.g. ～交 *dìjiāo*, form an unbreakable friendship.

葯   dì   MC tek

1. seed-cup of lotus.

蔕   dì   MC tejH

1. peduncle, stalk of an inflorescence of fruit, melon, flower; scape, internode forming the base or whole of peduncle.

蝃   dì   MC tejH   ⊙ 蝭 *dì*.

蝭   dì   MC tejH

1. (bn.) ～蝀 *dìdōng* (MC tejH-tuwng), rainbow.

諦   dì   MC tejH

1. examine with care, look into closely.

    a. scrupulous(ly), attentive(ly), careful(ly); e.g. ～聽 *dìtīng*, listen attentively.

2. (Budd.) incontrovertible truth, esp. the four noble truths: 1, life is suffering (*dukkha*); 2, the origin of suffering is craving; 3, there can be an end to craving; 4, that end can be accomplished through following the eightfold path.

踶   dì   MC dejH

1. kick, strike with the foot.

    a. tread, walk, place the foot on.

    chí   MC drje

1. ⊙ 馳 *chí*, gallop, hie.

    zhì   MC drjeX

1. (bn.) ～跂 *zhìzhī* (MC drjeX-tsye), straining on tiptoe to reach, trying with all one's might.

遞   dì   MC dejX

1. change in succession, alternate(ly), progressive(ly), successive(ly), one after another.

2. (med.) post-station, where horses are changed on journey.

3. (med.) hand along, transfer, transmit; syn. 傳 *chuán* 1.

釱   dì   MC dejH

1. foot-shackle.

    dài   MC dajH

1. ⊙ 軑 *dài*, axle-cap.

diān

厧   diān   MC ten

1. to fall ill.

    a. malady, illness.

2. convulsions; epilepsy.

    a. dementia; madness.

巓   diān   MC ten

1. mountaintop, summit, crest, peak; apex, apogee; crown.

癲   diān   MC ten

1. convulsions; epilepsy, "falling sickness"; esp. ref. those older than 10 (cf. 癇 *xián*); ⊙ 厧 *diān* 2.

2. demented, crazy; madness; out of one's head.

蹎   diān   MC ten

1. stumble, trip.

2. rdup., slowly and sedately, staid and deliberate.

顛   diān   MC ten

1. crown of the head; top, topmost part.

    a. apex, summit.

2. head-over-heels, upside-down; upturn; fall over, topple.

    a. fall off, drop.

3. rdup., focused concentration, steady attention.

4. out of one's head; demented, crazy; madness; ⊙ 癲 *diān* 2.

    tián   MC den

1. ⊙ 闐 *tián* 1, filled, fill up; brimming, abounding.

2. rdup., depressed and crestfallen, in the dumps.

diǎn

典   diǎn   MC tenX

1. authoritative text, canon; testament.

2. standard, norm; prescript, institute, regulation; statute.

    a. codified, authoritative; monumental.

3. (attested) precedent; exemplar.

4. have authority over, preside over, in charge of; esp. as prefix in many official titles; e.g. ～客 *diǎnkè*, director of guests, i.e. manager of state visits; ～設 *diǎnshè*, intendant of arrange-

men[=s] (of imperial harem); ～午 *diǎnwǔ*, informal equiv. of 司馬 *sīmǎ*, supervisor of military affairs, ranging from army major to prefectural marshal (because *dian*, preside over, syn. *si* 司], and *wu* is the earthly branch [*dizhi* 地支] associated with "horse," *ma* 馬).

5. (med.) lend or supply cash for needed expenses; e.g. (Budd.) ～坐 *diǎnzuò*, bursar, in monastery.

    a. (med.) to pawn, mortgage, give in pledge for full value.

點　diǎn　MC temX

1. black dot, spot.
    a. speck(le), fleck, stipple; check; point.
    b. mite, mote, particle, iota.
2. tinge; touch up, retouch; dot with writing-brush > revise.
3. to touch lightly or briefly, dab, come into momentary contact with.
4. to nod, bob (head).
    a. (med.) mark or beat time rhythmically.
5. driblet, drop of liquid.
    a. distill(ate), tincture.
6. (med.) appoint, designate.
7. (med.) light a fire or lamp; flare up (from small point).
8. (med.) sgl. or 更～ *gēngdiǎn*, the o'clock of the night-watches, each of the five 2-hour watches of the night being divided into 5 *dian*.

diàn

坫　diàn　MC temH

1. stand or sideboard on which inverted cups (after drinking) were placed by honored guests, a prerogative of feudal lords.
    a. the same near kitchen, for emptied food-bowls.

墊　diàn　MC temH

1. overwhelm(ed); throw(n) down, quash; e.g. ～隘 *diàn'è*, overtaxed, vanquished, depleted (of strength or resources).
2. sink into, drown; submerge, be swamped.
    a. depression (in ground), indentation, dip; hole, hollow.
3. dig out, scoop out; dredge.

奠　diàn　MC denH

1. lay out offerings of food and wine for sacrifice.
    a. sacrificial offerings.

2. to offer, proffer.
3. put in place, dispose; set out, set up.

店　diàn　MC temH

1. (med.) a shop, stall.
2. (med.) inn, hostel.

殿　diàn　MC denH

1. throne-hall, royal hall, ceremonial hall for formal occasions.
    a. basilica, for offerings to spirits, gods, or (in monastery) to the Buddha.
2. palace compound.
    a. elaborate residence; e.g. ～宇 *diànyǔ*, mansion.
3. rearguard, of army; bring up the rear.
    a. protect, cover, guard, defend.
4. censure, consider unsatisfactory, in assessment of official or military matters (cf. 最 *zuì* 1a, commend[able]).

淀　diàn　MC denH

1. swamp, bog, morass, quagmire, slough.

澱　diàn　MC denH

1. sediment, silt.
2. ⊙ 淀 *diàn*, swamp, marsh, bog, morass, quagmire.
3. indigo (plant) (*Indigofera tinctora*); replaced in late-imperial times by graph 靛 *diàn*.

玷　diàn　MC temH

1. flaw in jade.
    a. blemish, spot, speck.
2. to stain, sully, smudge; mar, mark; spoil.
3. (med.) self-depreciatory ADJ or ADV: my shameful(ly) . . ., disgraceful(ly) . . .; ⊙ 忝 *tiǎn*.

甸　diàn　MC denH

1. royal domain, the territory surrounding the capital (ideally extending for a thousand *li* 里) in fealty to the ruler.
    a. far-flung outskirts.
2. products of the fields.
3. bring under royal control.

tián　MC den

1. ⊙ 畋 *tián* 2, take to the fields, engage in a hunt.
2. rdup., "dunn-dunn," onom. of rumbling of carts, chariots, etc.

簟　diàn　MC demX

1. sitting-mat made of bamboo or reeds.
    a. bedmat made of same.

鈿   diàn   MC denH

1. gold or silver filigree hair-ornaments, often inlaid with pearls or lacquered kingfisher feathers.
   a. any filigree work.
2. inlay with gold, silver, jade, etc.

阽   diàn   MC yem

1. on the verge (of danger); impending, looming.

電   diàn   MC denH

1. lightning, lightning-flash, levin; fulgurant.
2. flash, quick moment.

驔   diàn   MC demX

1. shag-shinned horse.
2. (bn.) 驂~ *cāndiàn*, → 驂 *cān*.

diāo

凋   diāo   MC tew

1. wilt(ed), wither(ed), marcid.
   a. fading, decaying; decline, languish; flag, weaken.

刁   diāo   MC tew

1. rdup., flutter and flitter, quiver and shiver.
2. ~斗 *diāodǒu*, cookpot-clappers, copper pots in which soldiers cooked food in the morning and beat the watch-hours at night.
N.B. This graph is not used with the sense "devious, cunning, wicked, meschant" until late-imperial times.

彫   diāo   MC tew

1. ⊙ 雕 *diāo* 1, carve, engrave, incise, sculpt; 2, embellish, elaborate, adorn, trim; 凋 *diāo*, wilt, wither, fade, decline, languish.

琱   diāo   MC tew

1. carve, engrave (jade or other precious stones), ⊙ 雕 *diāo* 1.

貂   diāo   MC tew

1. marten, sable (*Martes zibellina*); if white, ermine, stoat (*Mustela erminea*); e.g. ~蟬 *diāochán*, sable-tail and cicada-wing, ornamentation of cap worn by close attendants of emperor; also, metonymy for such officials; (med.) ~錦 *diāojǐn*, sable-fur and damask-cloak, metonymy for richly attired warrior.

雕   diāo   MC tew

1. carve, engrave (jade or other precious stones); incise; sculpt; glyptic.
2. embellish, elaborate, esp. lit. writings; adorn, trim.
3. eagle (*Aquila*, various species, esp. *A. chrysaetos*).

鵰   diāo   MC tew

1. eagle (*Aquila*, various species, esp. *A. chrysaetos*), ⊙ 雕 *diāo* 3.

diào

吊   diào   MC tewH   ⊙ 弔 *diào*.

弔   diào   MC tewH

1. condole(nces); commiserate; sympathize, pity.
   a. grieve, lament, mourn.
   dì   MC tek
1. come to, arrive.

掉   diào   MC dewH

1. shake; wag; bob; jiggle, jounce; swing round.
   a. tremble, quiver.
2. (med.) throw aside, cast off, fling away.

篍   diào   MC dewH

1. bamboo basket for carrying cut weeds.
   dí   MC dek
1. basket for carrying grainseed.
   tiào   MC thew
1. yellow-dock, curly-dock (*Rumex crispus*).

藋   diào   MC dewH

1. goosefoot, melde (*Chenopodium album*), a weed with stalked, opposite leaves which may be eaten when young; the stalk when full-grown and aged can be made into a staff; syn. 藜 *lí*.
2. ~粱 *diàoliáng*, sorghum (*Sorghum vulgare*), syn. 高粱 *gāoliáng*.
3. by graphic confusion, also ⊙ 菫 *jìn* (*jǐn*) 1, aconite; 2, violet.

調   diào   MC dewH   → 調 *tiáo*.

釣   diào   MC tewH

1. to fish, angle (with hook and line).
   a. fish-hook.

2. angle for a desired outcome, to bait, lure, scheme, plot.

魡　diào　MC tewH　⊙ 釣 diào.

diē

跌　diē　MC det

1. lose one's footing, stumble; trip and fall.
2. put a foot wrong, (commit a) faux pas; blunder, slip up, err(or), miscarry; go too far, fault of commission.
3. sole of the foot.
4. (med.) (bn.) ～宕, ～蕩, diēdàng (MC det-dangH), carousing unconstrained, ran-dan, do whatever one wants, brash and irresponsible, carefree and reckless.

dié

叠　dié　MC dep　⊙ 疉 dié.

喋　dié　MC dep

1. rdup., babble and blather, yammer and yak, yadda-yadda; also, ceaseless flow, spurting flow.
2. cmpd. ～血 diéxuè, bloodletting, bloodshed, slaughter.
　　zhá　MC draep
1. (bn.) 唼～ shàzhá, → 唼 shà.

垤　dié　MC det

1. anthill.
2. mound, hillock, monticule.

堞　dié　MC dep

1. merlon, of battlement; solid part between crennels; by synecdoche, battlement, parapet.

嵽　dié　MC det

1. (med.) (bn.) ～嵲 diéniè (MC det-nget), hilly heights, crowning cusp.

慄　dié　MC dep

1. with one's heart in one's mouth, scared, frightened.

昳　dié　MC det

1. westering sun, declining day; afternoon.
　　yì　MC yit
1. ～麗 yìlì, handsome, good-looking, fair and comely.

氎　dié　MC dep

1. (med.) fine-woven damask or linen.

牒　dié　MC dep

1. wooden writing-tablet, being a thin and short board.
2. official letter, between colleagues; notification, of official appointment; certificate.
　　a. office document, report, memorandum, account book.
　　b. written accusation (legal), allegation.
3. genealogical records.
4. ⊙ 疉 dié, repeat, double; pile up.

疉　dié　MC dep

1. repeat, double.
　　a. fold, pleat; layered; pile up.
　　b. fluff up.
2. musical refrain, reprise.
3. beat a tattoo, lightly tap a drum; resound.
　　a. (cause to) shake, vibrate; jar, unsettle; tremble.
4. mountain ledge, shelf.

経　dié　MC det

1. mourning band, worn around head or waist.

耋　dié　MC det

1. octogenarian, aged, elderly; superannuated, grizzled.

艓　dié　MC dep

1. (med.) small boat, skiff.

蝶　dié　MC dep

1. (med.) sgl. or (bn.) 蝴～ húdié (MC hu-dep), 蛺～ jiádié (MC kep-dep), butterfly.

裸　dié　MC dep

1. unlined clothing, singlet; originally Chu usage.

褶　dié　MC dep

1. mourning robe.
　　a. outer robe.
　　xí　MC zip
1. (med.) riding attire, esp. of cavalryman; breeches.
　　zhě　MC tsyep
1. (med.) folds or pleats of clothing.

諜　dié　MC dep

1. reconnoiter, scout out; spy.

2. genealogical records, ⊙ 牒 *dié* 3.
3. ⊙ 喋 *dié*, rdup., babble and blather, ramble and jabber.

蹀   dié   MC dep

1. stamp, paw the ground; tap.
    a. (bn.) ～躞 *diéxié* (MC dep-sep) or 躞～ *xiédié*, advance inchmeal, with small and measured steps, painstakingly; pace lightly, prance daintily, quickly and mincingly.
    b. rdup., same as preceding; also, swaying atremble (as of girdle-pendants), fluttering atremble (as of leaves).

迭   dié   MC det

1. alternate(ly), in turns, one after the other.
    yì   MC yit
1. ⊙ 軼 *yì* 1, overtake, overrun, outdo; 3, invade, raid.

dīng

丁   dīng   MC teng

1. robust, full-bodied, strong; healthy.
    a. (med.) adult male, esp. as liable for corvée duty.
2. come across, encounter; incur
3. 4th of the 10 heavenly stems; used for "D" in a sequential order.
4. ADJ to describe anything shaped like the graph, nail-like; e.g. ～香 *dīngxiāng*, "nail-aromatic," clove (*Syzygium aromaticum*).
    zhēng   MC treng
1. rdup., onom. of axe-blows to tree, "jhung-jhung."

dǐng

瀎   dǐng   MC tengX

1. (bn.) ～濘 *dǐngníng* (MC tengX-nengX), pellucidly clear, crystal-clear.
    tìng   MC thengH
1. (bn.) ～濙 *tìngyǐng* (MC thengH-'wengX), shallow shoals.

酊   dǐng   MC tengX

1. (bn.) 酩～ *mǐngdǐng*, → 酩 *mǐng*.

頂   dǐng   MC tengX

1. crown of the head.

a. (Budd.) protuberance on crown of Buddha's head, *uṣṇīṣa*, being one of the 32 major marks of a buddha.
    b. point the head at; e.g. (Budd.) ～禮 *dǐnglǐ*, prostrated with head and hands at the feet of the one being reverenced.
2. topmost part of object; crest, summit, vertex; cusp.
    a. be the best of, be the crown or summit of, to cap.
3. (med.) bear or carry on the head.
    a. (med.) support, bear up.

鼎   dǐng   MC tengX

1. 3-footed (or 4-footed) bronze ritual vessel, rectangular or bowl-shaped with upright handles, used for offerings of food; tripod, cauldron.
    a. symbol of dynastic or clan strength and solidity, since ritual tripods were passed down from one generation (ruler) to the next; e.g. ～臣 *dǐngchén*, vassal of the (dynasty's) tripods, minister of state, esp. the "3 Dukes" (*sāngōng* 三公) at apex of court hierarchy.
    b. "Tripod," name of 50th hexagram of the *Yijing*.
2. honored, worthy of using hereditary ritual items.
3. in one's prime, in robust health; powerful.
4. at that time, just then.

dìng

定   dìng   MC dengH

1. to set in desired place, fix in definite fashion; make fast, make secure, make sure (of).
    a. settle a situation, put a stop to disturbance or uncertainty.
    b. settled down, composed; fixity, fixedness.
2. decide, determine; establish; certify; stipulate.
    a. certain(ly), decided(ly), definite(ly); (med.) when all is said and done, in the end.
3. concentrate, fix on, focus on.
    a. (Budd.) concentrated meditation, trns. Skt. *samādhi*; e.g. ～無極 *dìngwújí*, infinitude (perfection) of meditation.
    MC tengH
1. alt. name of the lunar lodging "House" → 室 *shì* 6.
2. forehead.
3. ready-cooked food.

訂 dìng　MC dengX
1. give an opinion, pass judgment, evaluate, appraise.
2. edit, emend, revise (text).

鋌 dìng　MC dengX
1. metal shaft.
 a. (med.) ingot, measure-word for gold or silver bars, usu. equiv. 5 or 10 "ounces" (*liang* 兩).
 b. barb of an arrow; tang of a sword or knife.
2. pig iron, raw copper, unworked metals.
  tǐng　MC thengX
1. run quickly, fly, haste(n).

飣 dìng　MC tengH
1. (med.) sgl. or (bn.) ～餖 *dìngdòu* (MC tengH-duwH), lay out a sumptuous spread of food, not for eating but for conspicuous display; also, heap up and pile.

dōng

冬 dōng　MC towng
1. winter, final three months of the year; brumal; season corresponding to the agent water, the north, the kidneys, the color black.

東 dōng　MC tuwng
1. east, eastern, eastward, easterly; in *wuxing* correspondences associated with the agent wood, season of spring, color green, new growth, etc.
2. symbolically associated with heir-designate, future ruler, e.g. ～宮 *dōnggōng*, Eastern Palace (of the Crown Prince).

蝀 dōng　MC tuwng
1. (bn.) 螮～ *dìdōng*, → 螮 *dì*.

dǒng

董 dǒng　MC tuwngX
1. oversee, direct, manage.
2. rectify, set right.
3. deeply reserved, deeply contained.
4. a surname.

董 dǒng　MC tuwngX
1. lotus-root.

2. (bn.) ～蓈 *dǒngláng* (MC tuwngX-lang), fountain-grass, foxtail-grass (*Pennisetum alopecuroides*); syn. 狼尾草 *lángwěicǎo*.
3. a surname.

dòng

凍 dòng　MC tuwngH
1. freeze; frozen, gelid; icy.
 a. ice-cold, frigid.

動 dòng　MC duwngX
1. move(ment), act(ion), activity; ant. 靜 *jìng*, stillness.
 a. set in motion, bestir; incite, stimulate, moved to (do X); quicken, animate, excite.
 b. stir the sentiments; feel moved emotionally, heart-felt.
 c. agitation of light, esp. twinkling of stars.
2. shift, change.
3. (ADV) at every movement, always, everytime.
4. (med.) take up arms, rise up, revolt; invade.

棟 dòng　MC tuwngH
1. ridgepole, main-beam; e.g. ～宇 *dòngyǔ*, ridgepole and roof; ～梁 *dòngliáng*, ridgepole and roofbeams, main girders; also, euph. pillars of state.

洞 dòng　MC duwngH
1. grotto, cave(rn); ordinarily ref. caverns deep in limestone mountains.
 a. cavernous, spelaean; recessed, deep-cut; tunneled.
 b. (Dao.) ～天 *dòngtiān*, grotto-heaven; separate expansive world of radiant light within a holy mountain, with its own sun and moon, usu. the subcelestial seat of a particular *zhenren* 真人 (Realized Person); classified in Tang times into 10 major and 36 minor grotto-heavens, each communicating with others through secret subterranean channels.
2. duct, vent, channel; e.g. ～簫 *dòngxiāo*, vented syrinx, panpipes of open-ended bamboo tubes of different lengths; some evidence indicates that in Han times ref. a wide-bored notched vertical-flute.
 a. aperture, opening.
3. give unobstructed passage to, open a passage, be a conduit for.

a. pierce, penetrate (to the end of), reach the core or other side of, go deeply into; understand completely; permeated with, fraught with.
b. penetratingly, clearly; e.g. ～視 *dòngshì*, see clearly, see through it all.

潼　dòng　MC tuwngH

1. mother's-milk, human or animal.
2. onom. of drum sound, "toong!"

胴　dòng　MC duwngH

1. large intestine.

dōu

兜　dōu　MC tuw

1. (bn.) ～鍪 *dōumóu* (MC tuw-mjuw), casque, war-helmet in shape of iron pot with turned-back lip.
2. mislead, deceive, blind one to the truth.
3. (Budd.) ～率(陀) *dōushuài(tuó)* (MC tuw-srwit-da) or ～術(陀) *dōushù(tuo)* (MC tuw-zywit-da), trsc. Skt. *tuṣita*, name of the heaven where Maitreya, the "next" Buddha resides at present while awaiting the time for his messianic mission; the Tuṣita Heaven is the home of Maitreya's "Pure Land" (*jingtu* 淨土), a rebirth goal of many Chinese devotees.
4. ～子 *dōuzi*, from late Tang times a chair-litter, high-back chair suspended between 2 shafts with a bearer at each shaft-end.

dǒu

抖　dǒu　MC tuwX

1. (med.) (bn.) ～擞 *dǒusǒu* (MC tuwX-suwX), shudder and shake, quake and quaver; also (Budd.), alt. term for *dhūta*, austerities, ascetic practices (usu. 頭陀 *tóutuó*).

斗　dǒu　MC tuwX

1. measure of capacity, "peck," equiv. 10 "pints" (*sheng* 升).
2. ladle or dipper, for serving wine.
    a. (med.) flagon.
3. Northern Dipper (*Ursa Major*); the most important of all constellations; also plays a major role in Shangqing Dao. meditation/visualization practices.

4. Southern Dipper, composed of 6 stars in Sagittarius; one of the lunar lodgings, in the northern quadrant (*xuanwu* 玄武) of the sky; a common pairing is ～牛 *dǒuniú*, [Southern] Dipper and Ox, the 2 constellations that occupy the Jupiter station *xingji* 星紀.
5. (med.) suddenly, unexpectedly.
6. ⊙ 枓 *dǒu*, bearing-block for roof-bracket; 抖 *dǒu*, shake, tremble, vibrate.

枓　dǒu　MC tuwX

1. bearing-block or carrying-post for bracket, in roof construction; e.g. ～栱 *dǒugǒng*, block and bracket, i.e. the whole bracket construction.

蚪　dǒu　MC tuwX

1. (med.) (bn.) 蝌～ *kēdǒu*, → 蝌 *kē*.

dòu

竇　dòu　MC duwH

1. duct, drain, culvert, scupper.
2. aperture, opening, orifice; gap, crack; hole; gate, door.
3. a surname.

脰　dòu　MC duwH

1. neck; nape.

荳　dòu　MC duwH

1. (bn.) ～蔻 *dòukòu* (MC duwH-xuwH), cardamom (*Amomum cardamomum*).

豆　dòu　MC duwH

1. gen. term for bean, legume; leguminous, fabaceous.
    a. 大～ *dàdòu*, broadbean; 小～ *xiǎodòu*, soybean; ～粒 *dòulì*, beansprout; 赤～ *chìdòu*, azuki bean (*Vigna angularis*); 赤小～ *chìxiǎodòu*, rice-bean (*Vigna calcaratus*); (med.) 澡～ *zǎodòu*, "bath-beans," small pellets made from ground dried peas and mixed with fragrant herbs for use as bath-soap.
2. tazza; stemmed bowl for food, sometimes with cover or with annular handles.
    a. platter, round plate without stand, shaped like broadbean.
3. measure of capacity, equiv. 4 "pints" (*sheng* 升).
4. measure of weight, equiv. 16 "grains" (*shu* 黍), approx. .0067 of an "ounce" (*liang* 兩).

逗　dòu　MC duwH

1. stay, stop at; remain, pause at.
2. punctuate a sentence by parsing it grammatically with inserted pauses, ⊙ 讀 dòu (dú).
3. (med.) cater to, humor.
    a. (med.) induce, blandish, provoke (to action).
4. (med.) arrive at, come to.
    a. (med.) catch up to, reach.

餖　dòu　MC duwH

1. (med.) (bn.) 飣～ dìngdòu, → 飣 dìng.

鬥　dòu　MC tuwH　⊙ 鬭 dòu.

鬭　dòu　MC tuwH

1. fight, contend; engage, battle, contest; e.g. 雞～ jīdòu, cockfight.
    a. wrangle, dispute; e.g. ～變 dòubiàn, brawl, private quarrel.
2. come across, encounter, be at the same place as.
    a. conjunction of 2 planets.

dū

督　dū　MC towk

1. inspect, examine; e.g. ～核 dūhè, inspect and assess.
    a. supervise, oversee; superintend, take command of; e.g. 都～ dūdū, intendant-in-chief, usu. of regional military administration; 都～府 dūdūfǔ, the area directed by the preceding.
2. correct, rectify; redress.
3. reprimand, chastise; censure.
4. ⊙ 裻 dū, back seam of cloak.

裻　dū　MC towk

1. back seam of cloak or robe.

都　dū　MC tu

1. principal city in the fief of a feudal noble, where he establishes his primary residence and ancestral temple; primary seat, see.
    a. metropolis, metropolitan, often the capital city of a realm; to establish a city as the capital; pertaining to the capital; e.g. ～官 dūguān, provincial offices staffed and controlled by central government.
2. dwell, reside in; citizen.
    a. (med.) term for a local official not appointed by the court.

3. aggregate, converge, constellate, come together; gather, collect, assemble, bring together.
    a. (med.) lead a combined military force; "head N" (～N), "chief N" (～N), as part of military title.
    b. (med.) military unit consisting of a thousand men.
    c. leader of a group endeavor, e.g. ～講 dūjiǎng, lecturer in school or academy; also (Budd.) preacher; ～維那 dūwéinà (Budd.), deacon or general overseer of monastery, being third in influence after the abbot and chief monk, trns. Skt. karmadāna.
4. serene, quiet in disposition; comely, attractive.
5. exclamation of praise.
6. (med.) measure-word for occasions, events, occurrences.

都　dōu　MC tu

1. collectively; in all, altogether; all, in entirety, entirely; with modal negatives: (not) at all, (not) in the least. Usage as ADV becomes more common in med. period, esp. Tang times.

闍　dū　MC tu

1. barbican, fortified watchtower on either side of city-gate.

闍　shé　MC dzyae

1. trsc. Skt. ja, jā, ca, cā; e.g. (阿)～梨, ～黎 (ā)shélì (MC ['a-]dzyae-lej), (trsc. or) abb. trsc. of Skt. ācārya, religious teacher, master.

dú

匵　dú　MC duwk　⊙ 櫝 dú.

嬻　dú　MC duwk

1. treat disrespectfully, affront; rude, uncivil.

櫝　dú　MC duwk

1. coffer, box, chest.
    a. box up, store away, put in a coffer.
2. casket, coffin.

殰　dú　MC duwk

1. miscarriage, spontaneous abortion.
    a. abortion; stillborn.
2. damaged, destroyed.

毒　dú　MC dowk

1. medically potent, esp. with negative effects.
2. poison(ous); venom(ous)

a. bane(ful); noxious; pernicious; e.g. 丹〜 *dāndú*, redbane, i.e. erysipelas.

3. endanger, imperil.

a. maltreat, abuse; bring calamity upon.

4. deplore; loathe, execrate.

dài   MC dojH

1. (bn.) 〜冒 *dàimào* (MC dojH-mawH), ⊙ 瑇瑁 *dàimào*, hawksbill turtle; tortoise-shell.

瀆   dú   MC duwk

1. drainage trough, culvert; canal.

a. conduit, esp. of trade, ref. to large river.

2. overflow, inundate.

a. damage, destroy.

3. ⊙ 嬻 *dú*, be disrespectful to, affront.

牘   dú   MC duwk

1. long and narrow writing tablet of wood, usu. for official documents or personal correspondence.

2. written document(s).

犢   dú   MC duwk

1. calf; veal; e.g. 〜褌 *dúkūn*, calf-nose drawers, loincloth draped in 2 loops.

獨   dú   MC duwk

1. solitary, lone, sole, single.

a. alone, lonely.

b. aged and childless.

c. companionless, friendless.

2. unique, distinctive, unmatched.

3. on one's own, of one's own accord, independent(ly).

4. only, merely, just.

5. (med.) still, and yet; e.g. 帷曉〜垂 *wéi xiǎo dú chuí*, the curtains are still lowered in the morning.

6. (med.) especially, most of all.

7. interr. suggesting disbelief, similar to 豈 *qǐ*: is it possible that . . .? how can it be that . . .? is it really that . . .?; e.g. 王〜不見之 *wáng dú bùjiàn zhī*, how can the king not see it?

8. douc langur (various species of *Pygathrix*).

9. 〜孤 *dúgū*, 2-syllable surname (< 屠各 *túgè*, name of a noble Xiongnu tribe).

讀   dú   MC duwk

1. recite a text aloud; declaim.

a. read, esp. aloud; by med. times gradually ref. more often to silent reading.

dòu   MC duwH

1. punctuate a sentence by parsing it grammatically with inserted pauses.

讟   dú   MC duwk

1. vilify, imprecate; speak ill of, denounce; be spiteful toward.

a. complain, cavil, grumble.

櫝   dú   MC duwk

1. pouch for storing milfoil stalks used in divination.

韇   dú   MC duwk

1. quiver, for arrows.

髑   dú   MC duwk

1. (bn.) 〜髏 *dúlóu* (MC duwk-luw), skull.

黷   dú   MC duwk

1. sully, stain; defile, pollute, corrupt.

a. blacken, darken.

b. indecent; outrage.

2. denigrate (person), defame; besmirch; slander.

3. covet, thirst after; lust after; wallow or bask in; e.g. 〜武 *dúwǔ*, over-ready to take up arms, wallow in warfare; 〜貨 *dúhuò*, lust after goods or profits from trade.

dǔ

堵   dǔ   MC tuX

1. unit measure of earthen wall, usu. understood as 5 版 *bǎn* (equiv. 40 尺 feet) long and 1 丈 *zhàng* (equiv. 10 feet) tall; some sources say 10 feet long and 10 feet tall.

a. gen. term for earthen wall.

2. (med.) 阿〜 *ādǔ*, 6 Dynasties colloquialism for "this (kind of)"; e.g. 阿〜物 *ādǔwù*, these objects, this stuff.

睹   dǔ   MC tuX   ⊙ 覩 *dǔ*.

篤   dǔ   MC towk

1. genuine, guileless; honest.

a. generous, whole-hearted(ly).

2. devoted to, intent on, single-minded(ly), dedicated, committed to; relentless.

a. staunch, loyal, faithful.

3. to an extreme degree; quite serious(ly), profound(ly), deep(ly), complete(ly).

覩 **dǔ** MC tuX

1. regard (with eyes), behold; pay attention to, keep in view; observe.

    a. consider, take in; understand.

賭 **dǔ** MC tuX

1. gamble; wager, bet.

    a. venture, risk, hazard.

2. compete for, match oneself against.

dù

妒 **dù** MC tuH

1. jealous(y); envy, envious, spite(ful); usu. of one woman toward another.

2. wary, guarded; suspicious, distrustful.

妬 **dù** MC tuH ⊙ 妒 *dù*.

度 **dù** MC duH

1. measure(ment); measured movement, degree of measurement.

    a. measured music, rhythm, beat.

2. lineament(s), lineation; measurement or configuration that provides the contours or framework of a larger whole; e.g. 九～ *jiǔdù*, 9 Lineaments, i.e. the 9 heavens.

    a. rule, guideline, decided limit of acceptability; keep within bounds; e.g. ～矩 *dùjǔ*, ruler and L-square, norm and standard; 節～ *jiédù*, to moderate and rule, keep in check, control, bring into line; 不～ *bùdù*, unruly, undisciplined.

3. pass(age), transit(ion), cross over, go beyond; e.g. ～江 *dùjiāng*, cross the river; 七～ *qīdù*, 7 Transitors, i.e. 7 stars of the Dipper.

4. cross a line from one condition to another; rite of passage; reach a goal.

    a. religious ordination, ordain as new member of initiate community, consecrate, invest; (Budd.) ～牒 *dùdié*, ordination certificate.

    b. salvation, deliverance, term used both in Budd. and Dao. to signify crossing over into desired state of enlightenment or of transcendence; e.g. (Budd.) ～門 *dùmén*, gate of salvation; (Dao.) ～世 *dùshì*, cross beyond (attain deliverance from) this world.

    c. (Budd.) trns. Skt. *pāramitā*, perfection, a consummate virtue or quality displayed by a bodhisattva, esp. 六～ *liùdù*, 6 Perfec-

tions, i.e. charity (*dāna*), morality (*śila*), forbearance (*kṣānti*), effort (*vīrya*), meditation (*dhyāna*), wisdom (*prajñā*).

5. bearing, manner; behavior, conduct.

6. (med.) measure-word for occurrences; e.g. 兩～ *liǎngdù*, 2 times.

     duó MC dak

1. measure, calculate; consider; plan.

    a. infer, conjecture, assume.

杜 **dù** MC duX

1. sgl. or in cmpd. ～梨 *dùlí*, dancer flowering pear, birchleaf pear (*Pyrus betulifolia*); → 棠梨 *tánglí*, 甘棠 *gāntáng*.

2. sgl. or ～若 *dùrùo*, pollia (*Pollia japonica*), herbaceous perennial that grows from stems of 1 to 3 feet; produces small, white flowers; also, ginger-lily (*Alpinia officinarum*) .

    a. ～蘅 *dùhéng*, asarum (*Asarum forbesii*), with kidney-shaped leaves and small reddish-brown flowers, fragrance similar to ginger-root; in lit. an image of sweet-smelling purity.

3. to block, obstruct; put a stop to.

4. dissemble, misrepresent.

5. (bn.) ～鵑 *dùjuān* (MC duX-kwen), hawk-cuckoo (*Hierococcyx sparverioides*), in lit. specially associated with Shu 蜀 because legendarily a posthumous avatar of an ancient Shu king, syn. 子規 *zǐguī*; also, azalea (*Rhododendron molle*).

6. a surname.

渡 **dù** MC duH

1. cross a river or stream.

    a. cross over, go beyond, transit(ion).

2. (med.) sgl. or ～頭 *dùtóu*, ～口 *dùkǒu*, ferry-point, crossing.

肚 **dù** MC duX

1. belly, stomach; gut.

蠹 **dù** MC tuH

1. wood-boring insect; termite; bookworm; vermin; maggot.

2. bore into, eat away.

    a. harm, destroy.

3. (bn.) 蠅～ *pīdù*, → 蠅 *pī*.

鍍 **dù** MC duH

1. to gild, gold-plate(d), gilt.

duān

端　**duān**　MC **twan**
1. point of true beginning, clue; alpha of, key to; rudiment; taproot.
   a. a prompting; new shoot or sprout rising above the ground, acrospire; bud, bud-like beginning; e.g. 四～ *sìduān*, 4 promptings, i.e. compassion which leads to fellow-feeling (*ren* 仁), shame which leads to dutifulness (*yi* 義), deference which leads to propriety in behavior (*li* 禮), and a sense of right and wrong which leads to wisdom (*zhi* 智).
2. tip, extremity, edge, end-point.
   a. aspect, facet; e.g. 異～ *yìduān*, different angle, irregular approach, deviating from the true.
   b. contingency, eventuality; e.g. 萬～ *wàn-duān*, myriad contingencies.
   c. at last, in the end; truly.
3. straight, upright; correct; exactly placed; e.g. ～拱 *duāngǒng*, stand straight with hands crossed, usu. applied to ruler who follows path of *wuwei*; ～坐 *duānzuò*, sit upright; ～門 *duānmén*, meridional gate, main gate placed exactly at due-south point in palace compound or city-wall.
   a. equable, placid; stolid, staid; e.g. ～心 *duānxīn*, sternly concentrated on.
4. ceremonial clothing, for formal rites.
5. careful(ly), in detail, considering all angles or eventualities.
6. especially, particular(ly).
7. measure of length for silks or cloth, equiv. 2 "staves" (*zhang* 丈), 20 "feet" (*chi* 尺), half of a "bolt" (*pi* 匹).

duǎn

短　**duǎn**　MC **twanX**
1. short, brief (time or space).
2. come up short, shortcoming, deficient, unsatisfactory; meager.
   a. find fault with, criticize, speak cuttingly of.

duàn

斷　**duàn**　MC **dwanX**
1. break apart, break off; tear apart, tear off, sheer off.
   a. sever, cut off, cut short.
   b. put a stop to, check, arrest.

twanH
1. break an impasse, decide, pass judgment.
   a. decidedly, certain(ly).

段　**duàn**　MC **dwanH**
1. to batter, hammer.
2. break apart, break in pieces.
   a. section, segment, portion; component, part.
   b. fragment, particle, flake, wisp.
3. a surname, notably that of the Türkic ruling family of the Northern Liang (北涼, 401-439) dynasty.
4. ⊙ 鍛 *duàn*, to forge (metal); 緞 *duàn*, silks; 碫 *duàn*, addled egg.

碫　**duàn**　MC **dwanH**
1. addled egg.

碫　**duàn**　MC **twanH**
1. grindstone.
2. anvil.

緞　**duàn**　MC **dwanX**
1. gen. term for silks; N.B. does not ref. satin, as in ～紋 *duànwén*, until Southern Song.
2. leather reinforcement attached to heel of footwear.

腶　**duàn**　MC **twanH**
1. dried meat spiced with ginger and cinnamon.

踹　**duàn**　MC **twanH**
1. stamp the foot, kick the ground.

鍛　**duàn**　MC **twanH**
1. to forge (metal).
   a. batter, hammer.
2. sgl. or ～煉, ～練 *duànliàn*, to temper, refine (metal, character, literature, etc.); also, frame for a crime, cook up charges against (< strike blows against).
3. 碫 *duàn* 2, anvil; 腶 *duàn*, dried meat spiced with ginger and cinnamon.

duī

堆　**duī**　MC **twoj**
1. small hill, hillock, mound; knoll, tump.
   a. barrow, cairn.
2. mound up, pile up, heap.

磓 duī MC twoj
1. (med.) to pound, batter.
2. (med.) crash down, fall.
3. (med.) pile up, heap, mound up; ⊙ 堆 duī 2.

䭔 duī MC twoj
1. (med.) Shu dialect word for → 餅 bǐng.

duì

兑 duì MC dwajH
1. glad(ness), joy(ous), delight.
2. one of the 8 fundamental trigrams under-lying the *Yijing*'s 64 hexagrams, made up of 2 unbroken lines topped by a broken line.
   a. "joy," name of 58th hexagram of the *Yijing*.
3. open a passage; get through.
   a. opening, hole; cave.
4. (med.) exchange, barter, trade.
   yuè MC ywet
1. ⊙ 悦 yuè, pleased, relaxed, happy, content.
   ruì MC ywejH
1. ⊙ 銳 ruì 1, sharp-edged, sharp-pointed, acute.

對 duì MC twojH
1. confront, contrapose(d); to face, be face to face; in the face of.
   a. to address, respond, reply; respondent (in court case).
   b. be on the opposite side, stand against; oppose, antagonist(ic).
2. match up, form a pair, pair up; correspond with; counterpart.
   a. of literary composition: parison, parallel to, be in parallel; of physical activities: per-form alternately.
   b. relative, relativity, e.g. 絕～ juéduì, "sur-passing the relative," absolute.
   c. (med.) similar to, same as.
3. (med.) ruler's summons to audience.
4. (med.) collective measure-word for upper and lower clothing.

憝 duì MC dwojH
1. loathe, abhor, abominate.
2. loathsome, abhorrent, noxious; iniquitous, malevolent.

憞 duì MC dwojH
1. ⊙ 憝 duì, loath(som)e, abhor(rent), de-test(able).
   dūn MC dwon
1. (bn.) ～溷 dūnhún (MC dwon-hwon), dizzy and dazed, muddled and muzzy.

碓 duì MC twojH
1. pestle, for hulling rice.

譈 duì MC dwojH ⊙ 憝 duì.

隊 duì MC dwojH
1. troop or company of soldiers, detachment, squad.
   a. formation, assembly.
2. accompanying group, retinue, suite, cortege.
   zhuì MC drwijH
1. ⊙ 墜 zhuì, drop, fall off, shed; topple, tumble; dangle, hang.
   suì MC zwijH
1. ⊙ 隧 suì 1, underground passage, tunnel.

䨴 duì MC twojH
1. scudding, skimming swiftly, esp. clouds.
2. sgl. or in bn. 黮～ tǎnduì (MC thomX-twojH), grim and gloomy, somber and sullen, bleak and black.

dūn

墩 dūn MC twon
1. knoll, mound, tump; Wu dialect word for → 堆 duī.
   a. barrow, cairn.

惇 dūn MC twon
1. sgl. or rdup., honest and sincere, true-hearted; dedicated, devoted to a worthy cause.
2. ⊙ 敦 dūn 3, to honor, hold in high regard, esteem; 4, sedulous, painstaking; serious about, wrapped up in.

憞 dūn MC twon → 憞 duì.

敦 dūn MC twon
1. complete in oneself, intact; (moral) solidity, firmness.
   a. genuine, honest, sincere.

2. generous, ample.

3. to honor, hold in high regard, esteem.

4. sedulous, painstaking; serious about, wrapped up in.

5. ⊙ 驐 *dūn*, geld(ed).

tún　MC dwon

1. ⊙ 屯 *tún* 1 (*zhún*), gather, assemble, mass.

燉　dūn　MC dwon

1. rdup., blazing bright, burning brilliantly.

tūn　MC thwon

1. ⊙ 暾 *tūn*, dawning sun-flash; warm up.

蹲　dūn　MC dzwon

1. squat, sit without touching the ground; crouch.

cún　MC tshwin

1. rdup., sway to and fro, move to the music, rhythmically bob, flutter and flounce; also, measured and steady, deliberate and intentional.

驐　dūn　MC twon

1. geld(ed), of horse.

dùn

沌　dùn　MC dwonX

1. rdup., nescient and benighted, unaware and unknowing, absolutely amorphous.

2. (bn.) 混～ *hùndùn* (MC hwonH-dwonX), → 混 *hùn*.

tún　MC dwon

1. rdup., waves heaving and hoving, rolling and rippling.

盾　dùn　MC dwonX

1. shield, buckler, targe.

遁　dùn　MC dwonH　⊙ 遯 *dùn*.

遯　dùn　MC dwonH

1. run away, flee, make off, get away, abscond, escape.

　a. withdraw, retreat; pull back, pull out; e.g. ～世 *dùnshì*, withdraw from the world.

　b. "withdrawal," name of 33rd hexagram of the *Yijing*.

2. hide away, conceal.

3. keep the truth from one, delude, deceive, trick.

　a. equivocate, put off, hem and haw.

鈍　dùn　MC dwonH

1. dull(ed), blunt, unsharpened; ant. 銳 *ruì*, pointed, sharp, 利 *lì*, keen, edged.

2. obtuse, dull-witted, blockhead, stupid.

　a. cloddish, maladroit, inept, clumsy.

頓　dùn　MC twonH

1. knock, tap; e.g. ～首 *dùnshǒu*, knock one's head on the ground, esp. used figuratively at beginning and/or end of letters to express respect; ～足 *dùnzú*, stamp or tap the foot, to show grief or impatience.

2. shake, shake out to make presentable or usable, or to smooth out, as when shaking out clothing before wearing, or shaking out a fish-net to spread over the water.

　a. prepare, arrange, set out.

3. pause, stop; e.g. ～措 or ～挫 *dùncuò*, mark time (music), neatly measured phrases (lit.), nod and bob, check and catch, neat and pointed, measured and modulated.

　a. stopping-place on a journey; inn, lodge; a halt, stage, gest (the latter esp. for royal progress).

4. tired out, exhausted, worn out.

　a. brought to one's knees, defeated; ruined; harmed, damaged; broken; wounded.

5. collapse, topple over.

6. immediate(ly), instantaneous(ly); e.g. (Budd.) ～悟 *dùnwù*, sudden enlightenment.

7. (med.) set up camp, erect fortifications.

8. (med.) measure-word for occurrences, incidents.

9. ⊙ 鈍 *dùn* 1, blunt, dull.

duō

剟　duō　MC twat

1. cut off, cut away; pare away.

　a. scrape off, scrape away, efface; remove.

　b. delete, abridge (text).

2. pierce, prick.

咄　duō　MC twat

1. rail at, berate, bellow at.

2. rdup., gasp at in surprise, "whoa!"; also, sigh of dissatisfaction, "well now . . ."; also, expression of impatience, "tut-tut."

多　duō　MC ta

1. accrete, accrue, multiply.
   a. many, much; multiple, multitude.
   b. abound, abundant, prolific.
2. exceed, surpass; be greater than, superior to.
   a. make much of; deem important, significant, or valuable; highly esteem or praise; e.g. ～方 *duōfāng*, inflate and diverge > by all means; 不為～ *bùwéiduō*, not amount to much.
3. for the most part, mostly; in med. times occurs in various cmpds. with this meaning, e.g., ～恐 *duōkǒng*, ～是 *duōshì*, ～應 *duōyìng*.
   a. most of the time, often.
4. merely, simply, indeed.

duó

奪　duó　MC dwat

1. take by force, confiscate, take away from, wrest from; deprive of, divest; despoil.
   a. abduct, carry off.
   b. (med.) compel, force to do.
2. lose, forfeit.
   a. omit, exclude, leave out; omission, lacuna.
3. (med.) go counter to; reject, repudiate; take exception to.
   a. (med.) persuade, convince, talk around to a different position, talk over to, prevail upon.

掇　duó　MC twat

1. pick up, collect.
   a. cull, select, choose out.
2. plunder, sack; carry off.
3. ⊙ 剟 *duō* 1, cut off, pare away; scrape away; delete.

鐸　duó　MC dak

1. clapper-bell with large round shank, used as hand-bell for the military and for announcement of government proclamations.
2. (med.) wind-bell, wind-chime.

duǒ

嚲　duǒ　MC taX

1. (med.) droop, dangle, hang down.

垛　duǒ　MC dwaX

1. crenellations of parapet.
2. lateral walls to either side of gate leading to hall.
3. (med.) target, for arrows.

埵　duǒ　MC twaX

1. dike, embankment.
2. air chamber of bellows.

朵　duǒ　MC twaX

1. flower-bud.
   a. spray, cluster of flowers.
2. measure-word for flowers.
3. move; e.g. ～頤 *duǒyí*, move the jaws, to munch, eat.

嚲　duǒ　MC taX　⊙ 嚲 *duǒ*.

duò

剁　duò　MC twaH

1. (med.) chop, hew.
   a. (med.) chop up, mince, hash.

墮　duò　MC dwaX

1. fall, fall off or into, drop; let fall.
   a. falter, decline.
2. ⊙ 惰 *duò* 1, apathetic, indolent, lazy; 2, careless, nonchalant, irreverent; remiss.
   huī　MC xjwie
1. bring down, overthrow, ruin, destroy.

惰　duò　MC dwaX

1. apathetic, indolent, lazy, dissipated.
2. careless, nonchalant, irreverent; remiss.

柂　duò　MC daX

1. rudder, helm, of boat.
   a. (med.) measure-word for boats.

E

ē

婀　ē　MC 'a

1. (bn.) ～娜 ē'nuǒ (MC 'a-naX) or 娜～ nuǒ'ē, soft and delicate, attractive and lovely; (med.) also, drifting and dangling, quivering tremulously.

阿　ē　MC 'a

1. mountain slope, talus, sloping face of mountain; hillside; high ridge.
2. sloping riverbank, embankment.
3. anfractuosity of hillside or riverbank; hern, corner, nook (of mountain); bight (of river); angle, bend, crook (of either).
4. buttress, prop; brace, strut.
   a. support, maintain; shore up.
5. be partial to, side with; inclined to, biased toward.
   a. cater to, pander to, truckle to; losenge(r).
6. fine, thin silk.
   a. soft, delicate, ⊙ 婀 ē.

ā　MC 'a

1. familiar prefix to terms of relationship or unspecified pronoun; e.g. ～母 āmǔ, mother; ～姊 āzǐ, sis(ter); ～誰 āshuí, who(m)ever; ～奴 ānú, "slavey," pet name for younger brothers.
2. (med.) ～堵 ādǔ, colloquialism for "this, these," demonstrative pronoun.
3. trsc. of Skt. a, ā.
   a. (Budd.) ～含 āhán (MC 'a-hom), trsc. Skt. āgama, gen. term for those scriptures attributed to the Buddha and his closest disciples; ～難 ā'nán (MC 'a-nan), trsc. of Skt. Ānanda, name of one of the chief disciples of Gautama Buddha, the putative source of many early scriptures because of his keen memory of the Buddha's words; ～修羅 āxiūluó (MC 'a-sjuw-la), trsc. Skt. asura, spirit, esp. demon; ～彌陀 āmítuó (MC 'a-mjieX-da), trsc. Skt. amita, boundless, infinite, the Chinese trns. of the term being 無量 wúliàng, hence 無量光 wúliàngguāng, (buddha of) boundless light < Skt. Amitābha, and 無量壽 wúliàngshòu, (buddha of) infinite life < Skt. Amitāyus; ～毘曇 āpítán (MC 'a-bjij-dom), trsc. Skt. abhidharma, gen. term for Budd. exegetical works usu. of highly technical nature; ～拏 ā'ná (MC 'a-nrae),

trsc. Skt. aṇu, impartite bit of matter, atom; ～闍梨 āshélí (MC 'a-zyaelej), trsc. Skt. ācārya, religious teacher, master.
   b. ～麻勒 āmálè (MC 'a-mae-lok), trsc. Skt. āmalika, emblic myrobalan, Indian gooseberry (Emblica officinalis), astringent fruit used medicinally, esp. for reputed anti-aging properties.
   c. ～耆尼 āqíní (MC 'a-gij-nrij), trsc. Skt. agni, Agni or Argi, ancient name of Karashahr, city-state on northern route of Silk Road at north-central edge of Taklamakan Desert.
4. (med.) ～濫堆 ālànduī, the North China skylark (Alauda arvensis).

é

俄　é　MC nga

1. shortly, presently, erelong, in a little while.
   a. for a while, briefly, not for long.
2. inclined, slanted, skewed.

吪　é　MC ngwa

1. act(ive), (be)stir, budge.
2. change, alter; reform, convert.

哦　é　MC nga

1. (med.) chant, recite; declaim; sing out.

圔　é　MC ngwa

1. decoy (bird, for hunting).
2. (med.) matchmaker, go-between.

娥　é　MC nga

1. of transcendent or fairy-like beauty, beautiful, lovely; e.g. ～眉 éméi, lovely eyebrows.
2. (bn.) ～皇, ～媓 éhuáng (MC nga-hwang), "Fairy Radiance," name of one of sage-king Yao's 堯 2 daughters who were wives of Shun 舜.
3. (bn.) 恆～ héng'é (MC hong-nga), Heng'e, or 嫦～ cháng'é (MC dzyang-nga), Chang'e, "Persistent Beauty," name of legendary lady said to have stolen elixir of immortality and fled to the moon, hence goddess of moon.

峨　é　MC nga

1. upborne, steeply high, looming above.
   a. ～然 é'rán, standing out like a lone peak.
   b. (bn.) 嵯～ cuó'é, → 嵯 cuó.

é

峩 é MC nga ⊙ 峨 é.

睋 é MC nga
1. look out at, gaze.

莪 é MC nga
1. flixweed (*Descurainia sophia*), member of the mustard family, used in food and medicinally.

蛾 é MC nga
1. moth.
    a. sgl. or ～眉 *é'méi*, moth-eyebrows, descriptive of the long and arching eyebrows of a lovely woman; by synecdoche, a beauty.
2. ⊙ 俄 *é* 1, shortly, presently, in a while; for a while, not long.
        yǐ MC ngjeX
1. old form of 蟻 *yǐ*, ant.

訛 é MC ngwa ⊙ 譌 é.

譌 é MC ngwa
1. falsehood, falsify, prevaricate, lie, mendacity.
    a. fraud(ulent), misguide, cheat, deceive.
2. sway, convert, change; cajole, wheedle.
3. ⊙ 吪 *é* 1, act(ive), (be)stir, budge.

頟 é MC ngaek
1. old form of 額 *é*, forehead.
2. rdup., incessant, going on and on; also (med.), high as can be, exceedingly tall.

額 é MC ngaek
1. forehead; e.g. ～勒 *élè*, browband (of horse's bridle); (med.) ～黃 *éhuáng*, yellow lead-based cosmetic applied by well-to-do women to their foreheads.
2. front of a stele.
3. architrave, facade.
    a. (med.) placard, inscribed horizontal board placed above gateway or entrance.
4. (med.) quota, fixed number.

ě

騀 ě MC ngaX
1. (bn.) 駊～ *pǒě*, → 駊 *pǒ*.

è

魻 è MC 'op
1. (med.) (bn.) ～葉 *èyè* (MC 'op-yep), woman's decorated hairwrap, bandeau, headscarf.

厄 è MC 'eak ⊙ 戹 è.

咢 è MC ngak
1. beat a drum with one's hand but not sing.
2. (med.) square-edged tail-rafter under the eaves.
3. ⊙ 諤 è, straight talk, candor; 鍔 è, blade of sword or knife; 愕 è, startled, shocked; 砐 è, high and tall.

噩 è MC ngak
1. fright(ful), scare, alarm(ing); e.g. ～夢 *èmèng*, nightmare.

堊 è MC 'ak
1. plaster, to plaster; whitewash.
2. white clay, kaolin.

堨 è MC 'at
1. earthen dam, dike, weir.
        ài MC 'ajH
1. dirt, grime, dust.

塄 è MC ngak
1. shore, bank; edge, margin; border.
    a. raised balk at edge of field.

崿 è MC ngak
1. mountain bluff; scarp, steep cliff.
    a. (bn.) 岞～ *zuó'è*, → 岞 *zuó*.

惡 è MC 'ak
1. malefic, malevolent, iniquitous, pernicious.
2. abhorrent, hateful, detestable.
    a. noxious, odious, ugly, offensive, highly unpleasant either in behavior or appearance.
3. (med.) abomination, category of worst judicial offenses.
        wù MC 'uH
1. abhor, detest, hate; feel revulsion for, be revulsed by.
    a. obloquy, revulsion.
2. denounce, deprecate, inveigh against.
3. averse to, aversion.

wū　MC ʻu

1. preverbal interr. pronoun: how...? where...?; e.g. 由此觀之〜有不戰者乎 *yóu cǐ guān zhī wū yǒu bùzhànzhě hū*, Looking at it from this perspective, how is it that there are those who would not fight?; 〜出兵 *wū chū bīng* How would you send forth troops?; ⊙ 烏 *wū* 3.

愕　è　MC ngak

1. startled, shocked, dumbfounded; astonished.
2. ⊙ 諤 *è*, frank talk, candor.

厄　è　MC ʻeak

1. narrow pass, defile; strategic point; ⊙ 阨 *è* 1.
   a. blocked, thwarted; frustrated.
2. difficulty, impediment; in straits, in reduced condition.
   a. squeeze, put pressure on; make difficult.
3. ⊙ 軛 *è*, yoke, placed on neck of horses or oxen pulling carriage.

扼　è　MC ʻeak

1. seize, clamp, hold fast, grip, throttle.
   a. restrain; control.
2. guard, be firmly entrenched in.
3. ⊙ 軛 *è*, yoke, for horse or ox.

捉　è　MC ʻeak　⊙ 扼 *è*.

搤　è　MC ʻeak　⊙ 扼 *è*.

砐　è　MC ngop

1. (med.) rdup., towering tall, looming above.

萼　è　MC ngak

1. calyx, collectively the sepals forming the outermost part of flower.
   a. the petals collectively, corolla.

諤　è　MC ngak

1. sgl. or rdup., frank and straightforward speech, uncompromising candor.

軛　è　MC ʻeak

1. yoke, placed on neck of horses or oxen pulling carriage.

輒　è　MC ʻeak　⊙ 軛 *è*.

遏　è　MC ʻat

1. prevent, hold back, check; obstruct.
   a. stop, break off.

遻　è　MC ngak

1. go against, the reverse of, counter to.
2. happen upon, encounter, be faced with.

鄂　è　MC ngak

1. name of district (*xian* 縣) under Qin, commandery (Jiangxia jun 江夏郡) under Han, prefecture (*zhou* 州) in Sui and Tang, located near modern Wuhan, Hubei.
2. ⊙ 堮 *è*, shore, bank, margin, border; 愕 *è*, startled, shocked; 諤 *è*, frank talk, candor; 萼 *è*, calyx, petals.

鍔　è　MC ngak

1. blade of sword or knife; edge.
2. shore, bank; margin, border; ⊙ 堮 *è*.

閼　è　MC ʻat

1. block(age), plug up; impede, bar.
2. dam, dike.

阨　è　MC ʻeak

1. to cease, stop; close off, delimit.
2. in dire straits, poverty-stricken.

　　　　ài　MC ʻeaH

1. ⊙ 隘 *ài* 1, narrow, strait(ened); closed in; constrained; 2, narrow pass, defile; strategic point.

頞　è　MC ʻat

1. bridge of the nose.

餓　è　MC ngaH

1. famished, starving, starveling (more severe and individual than 飢 *jī*).

鰐　è　MC ngak

1. crocodile (*Crocodylus porosus*); attested from Fujian southward through Tang times, increasingly rare afterward and now extinct in China.

鱷　è　MC ngak　⊙ 鰐 *è*.

鶚　è　MC ngak

1. osprey, fish-hawk, river-hawk (*Pandion haliaetus*).

齃　è　MC ʻat　⊙ 頞 *è*.

ēn

恩　ēn　MC 'on

1. kindness or favor bestowed by a superior; grace, gracious; largess.
   a. kind-hearted, kindly, beneficient; e.g. ～光 ēnguāng, kindly light (of springtime); aura of beneficence (of gracious ruler).
2. affection(ate), caring.

ér

兒　ér　MC nye

1. child; esp. son.
2. a youth, youngster.
   a. self-reference of young girl.
3. (med.) vernacular enclitic; e.g. 花～ huā'ér, blossom.
4. (med.) ～茶 érchá, gum arabic, imported from West Asia.

呃　ér　MC nye

1. (bn.) 嚅～ rú'ér, → 嚅 rú.

　　wā　MC 'wea

1. (bn.) ～嘔 wā'ōu (MC 'wea-'uw), prate and prattle of children, jibber-jabber.

栭　ér　MC nyi

1. uppermost member on top of a bracket-arm, capital, cap-block.
2. sgl. or ～栗 érlì, chinquapin (Castanea seguinii), tree and nut.

洏　ér　MC nyi

1. boil(ing).
2. hot tears; unstoppable weeping.

而　ér　MC nyi

1. vb-phrase conjunction, occurs between two vb-phrases subordinating the former to the latter, indicating generally that the action or state of the second vb-phrase occurs under the circumstances or conditions of the first, thus typically conveying a sequential, temporal, or implied causal relation; cog. nǎi 乃 "only then," zé 則 "then." This can be expressed in a variety of ways, such as:
   a. "vb-phrase 1, and then vb-phrase 2"; e.g. 王顧左右～言他 wáng gù zuǒyòu ér yán tā, The king looked over at his attendants and then spoke of something else; 歸～求之 guī ér qiú zhī, Return home and then seek it.
   b. "having (done) vb-phrase 1, then vb-phrase 2"; e.g. 不遠千里～來 búyuàn qiānlǐ ér lái, Not having considered a thousand li too great a distance, you have come; 坐～言 zuò ér yán, Having sat down, then he spoke.
   c. "after vb-phrase 1, (then) vb-phrase 2"; e.g. 見其禮～知其政 jiàn qí lǐ ér zhī qí zhèng, After having seen their rituals, then you will know about their government; 孔子登東山～小魯 kǒngzǐ dēng dōng shān ér xiǎo lǔ, After ascending the Eastern Mountain, Confucius looked upon the state of Lu as small.
   d. "when vb-phrase 1, (then) vb-phrase 2"; e.g. 子生～色赤 zǐ shēng ér sè chì, When the child was born its color was red; 見之～心醉 jiàn zhī ér xīn zuì, When he saw it his feelings were as if intoxicated.
   e. "if vb-phrase 1, then vb-phrase 2"; e.g. 彼白～我白之 bǐ bǎi ér wǒ bǎi zhī, If those are white, then I treat them as white; 不得～非其上 bùdé ér fēi qí shàng, If someone does not get [what he wants], then he faults his superiors.
   f. ～已 éryǐ, at end of a vb-sentence, results in the rhetorical coda "and that is the end of it, and that's all there is to it, and that's that"; e.g. 九人～已 jiǔrén éryǐ, nine people, that's all; 食粟～已 shísù éryǐ, I eat millet and that's it; 志於仁～已 zhì yú rén éryǐ, incline yourself toward humaneness, and that's all there is to it. (The coda ～已 éryǐ is very often followed by the perfective-aspect final GP 矣 yǐ for additional rhetorical effect.)
2. as a particular sense of the general subordinating function, the construction can also have an adversative sense: "but," "yet"; e.g. 士無事～食 shì wúshì ér shí, The official is devoid of service, but eats [all the same]; 位卑～言高 wèi bēi ér yán gāo, His status was low, yet he talked of exalted things; 可以言～不言 kěyǐ yán ér bùyán, He could have spoken, but he didn't speak.
3. occurring after a noun or noun-phrase and before a vb-phrase, gives a mild adversarial or ironic sense; e.g. 匹夫～有天下 pǐfū ér yǒu tiānxià, A simple chap, yet he possesses the sub-celestial realm.

4. ⊙ 爾 *ěr* 1, 2nd-person pronoun, esp. as SUBJ or possessive, "you, your"; e.g. 余知～無罪也 *yú zhī ěr wúzuì yě*, I know that you are free of misdeeds; 必使～君 *bì shǐ ěr jūn*, it is necessary to send your lord.

髵   ér   MC nyi

1. facial hair, beard, mustache, goatee.

nài   MC nojH

1. ⊙ 耐 *nài* 3, judicial punishment of shaving the beard and temples.

胹   ér   MC nyi

1. boil, heat up.
   a. boil till tender, tenderize.

輀   ér   MC nyi

1. hearse, coffin-wagon.

髶   ér   MC nyi

1. whiskers of animal.
   a. shaggy-haired.
2. (bn.) 髵～ *pīér*, → 髤 *pī*.

鮞   ér   MC nyi

1. fish roe.

ěr

尒   ěr   MC nyeX   ⊙ 爾 *ěr*.

毦   ěr   MC nyiH

1. ornament made with bird plumes or animal fur.
2. hairy panicles of various grasses.

爾   ěr   MC nyeX

1. 2nd-person pronoun: you; e.g. 非～所及也 *fēi ěr suǒjí yě*, it is not what you have reached; 盍各言～志 *hé gè yán ěr zhì*, why doesn't each of you speak of your goals? ～欲吳王我乎 *ěr yù wúwáng wǒ hū*, Do you wish to treat me like the king of Wu?
2. ADV suffix (akin to 然 *rán*): like this, so, -ly, such a . . .; e.g. 僕僕～亟拜 *púpú ěr qì bài*, annoyingly to (have to) pay frequent obeisance; 糟糠～哉 *zāokāng ěr zāi* such dregs-and-husk-like (food)!
   a. adverbial VB-phrase suffix redundantly followed by 而 *ér*: VB-phrase ～ 而 *ěrér*; e.g. 嘑～而與之 *hù ěrér yǔ zhī*, menacingly to

offer something to someone; 渾～而就 *hún ěrér jiù*, get to a place in a muddled way.
   b. typically sentence-final or penultimately final: like this, thus, so; e.g. 所惡勿施～也 *suǒwù wùshī ěr yě*, as for what is despised, do not disseminate it so; 何善～ *hé shàn ěr*, what good was this, so?; 居處、言語、飲食衎～ *jūchǔ, yányǔ, yǐnshí kàn ěr*, in repose and at rest, in speaking and conversing, in drinking and eating one should be content, so.
   c. 曰X云～, *yuē X yún ěr*, indicates imagined or hypothetical speech: say . . ., speaking thus, speaking in this (that) way; e.g. 女奚不曰其為人也 . . . 不知老之將至云～ *rǔ xī bùyuē qí wéirén yě . . . bùzhī lǎo zhī jiāngzhì yún ěr*, why did you not say "as for the way he behaves in his person . . . he does not recognize that old age is about to arrive," speaking in this way?; 其心曰是何足與言仁義也云～ *qí xīn yuē shì hézú yǔ yán rényì yě yún ěr*, in their hearts they say "how is he worthy enough to be talked with about humaneness and propriety," speaking thus.
3. (med.) preceding a VB-phrase to indicate time; e.g. ～來 *ěrlái*, from that time on; ～乃 *ěrnǎi*, at that time, then.
4. (med.) ～所 *ěrsuǒ*, translation idiom in early Budd. texts: so many, so much.
5. (med.) ～朱 *ěrzhū*, bisyllabic surname, of Türkic origin; usu. written with alt. form (尒) of the present graph.

珥   ěr   MC nyiX

1. ear-stud or earring, of jade or other gem.
   a. hang from the ear.
2. sword-guard between hilt and blade, protruding to either side like ears.
3. parhelion (pl. parhelia) or parselene (pl. parselenae), sundog(s) or moondog(s), bright disc on either side of halo round sun or moon.
4. dress a cap with ornament (plume, pin, etc.)

耳   ěr   MC nyiX

1. ear.
   a. give ear to, listen, hear.
2. sentence-final single-syllable equivalent (and phonetic fusion) of the rhetorical coda phrase 而已 *éryǐ* "and that is the end of it, and that's all there is to it, and that's that"; e.g. 前言戲之～ *qiányán xì zhī ěr*, my earlier comments were only in jest about it, that's all there is to it; 直不百步～

zhí bù bǎibù ěr, they simply did not go a hundred paces, that's all. (As with the coda 而已 *éryǐ*, 耳 *ěr* is also very often followed by the perfective aspect final GP 矣 *yǐ* for additional rhetorical effect.)

邇　ěr　MC nyeX
1. nigh, nearby.
    a. come near, approach.
2. simple, easy to understand, shallow.

餌　ěr　MC nyiX
1. rice-flour cakes; tasty morsel, delicacy, dainty, tidbit.
    a. eat with pleasure.
2. bait, for fish.
    a. to bait, lure, entice.
3. nostrum, panacea, curative.

èr

二　èr　MC nyijH
1. the numeral two; second; double; twice; both.

2. the other(s); another.
3. not of just one type, in pejorative sense; of 2 or more kinds, different; e.g. ～心 *èrxīn*, not single-minded, potentially disloyal or deceitful; ～三子 *èrsānzǐ*, the many of you, all of you.

佴　èr　MC nyiH
1. to second, assist.
2. be in a subordinate position.

刵　èr　MC nyiH
1. take as trophy the left ear of animal killed in hunt.
2. judicial punishment of cutting off criminal's ears.

貳　èr　MC nyijH
1. secondary, accessory; cf. 正 *zhèng* 4, principal.
    a. to second, assist(ant).
2. second (time); double.
3. not of all one type; esp. not devoted only to one ruler or guiding principle; changeable.
4. not the same, of a different kind.

F

fā

發　fā　MC pjot
1. shoot, let fly (arrow); go out, go forth.
    a. set out, set forth, start out (on journey).
    b. send, despatch.
2. emit; effuse, effusion; come out, break forth, blow (blossom), emerge.
    a. express(ion); manifest(ation); show, evince, reveal.
    b. avow, profess; announce, issue.
    c. broach, begin, launch; propose, open up.
    d. motive beginning.
3. turn over or throw up a furrow, plow a furrow.
    a. throw over, dislodge(ment), remove; cast off.

fá

乏　fá　MC bjop
1. short of, bereft of, depleted.

    a. lack(ing), esp. in food or other resources; indigent, poor.
2. exhaust(ed), weary.
    a. give up, give over.
3. fall into disuse, neglect.

伐　fá　MC bjot
1. hew, hack at, lop.
    a. strike, smite.
2. attack (military), descend upon; punitive expedition.
    a. denounce, condemn, attack verbally.
3. boast, brag, self-praise; vaunt.
    a. prideful, vainglorious; self-satisfied.

垡　fá　MC bjot
1. (med.) turn up the soil, till; tilled land.

栰　fá　MC bjot　⊙ 筏 *fá*.

瞂　fá　MC bjot
1. pelta, small shield.

筏   fá   MC bjot
1. (med.) raft, made of bamboo or wood.

罰   fá   MC bjot
1. punish(ment) legally, chastise(ment), chasten, usu. lighter penalty than 刑 *xíng*.
2. commute penalty with a fine; redeem, ransom.
3. offense, misdeed, transgression, wrongdoing.

罸   fá   MC bjot   ⊙ 罰 *fá*.

茷   fá   MC bjot
1. bursting with foliage, leafy, lush.
    pèi   MC bajH
1. ⊙ 斾 *pèi* 1, banner, esp. vertical banner ending in swallowtail shape; 2, decorative fringe; rdup., ripple or wave richly in the wind.
    bá   MC pat
1. tangled foliage, winding, intertwined.

閥   fá   MC bjot
1. left-hand gate-column of influential family, carrying half of parallel inscription regarding family's ancestral merits and rank (cf. 閱 *yuè*, right-hand column).
    a. hence, influential or aristocratic family, esp. in cmpds. 〜閱 *fáyuè*, 門〜 *ménfá*.

fǎ

法   fǎ   MC pjop
1. law, legal; rule, regulation; statute, ordinance.
2. objective standard, norm(ative); model, pattern.
    a. take as model or standard; emulate, imitate.
    b. previous model, precedent; prototype, archetype; exemplar.
    c. formal(istic), ceremonial; e.g. 〜駕 *fǎjià*, ceremonial carriage (of emperor).
3. method(ical), system(atic); procedure, technique; e.g. 〜度 *fǎdù*, systematic measures.
4. bibliographic classification of certain pre-Han texts, esp. those valued by or seemingly accordant with the political practices favored in the Qin dynasty.
5. teaching, doctrine, incl. associated practices; e.g. 〜師 *fǎshī*, (Budd.) dharma master, monk (see next); (Dao.) ritual master (see 7).
6. (Budd.) trns. Skt. *dharma*, enormously important and multivalent term whose references and implications point *inter alia* to: Budd. teaching, doctrine; fundamental physical or mental constituents of existence, phenomena; auspicious qualities or characteristics of the Buddha; common descriptive epithet for all manner of Budd. objects.
7. (Dao.) pertaining to rites and protocols; e.g. 〜信 *fǎxìn*, ritual pledge, pledge offering given to master for transmission of sacred texts or teachings; 〜曲 *fǎqǔ*, ritual music, esp. savored by Tang Xuanzong 玄宗 (r. 712-756) who established special ensemble of court musicians to perform it.

灋   fǎ   MC pjop
1. ancient-script form of → 法 *fǎ*.

fà

髮   fà   MC pjot
1. hair of the head, locks, tresses, fax; pileous.
2. hundredth part of an inch; 10 *hao* 毫 equiv. 1 *fà*, 10 *fà* equiv. 1 *fen* 分.

fān

帆   fān   MC bjom
1. a sail.
    a. synecdoche for boat.
    fàn   MC bjomH
1. to sail.

幡   fān   MC phjon
1. pennon, streamer, gonfalon.
    a. dangling decoration, festoon(ed), hanging garland.
2. rdup., flap and flutter, adangle and aswing; also, light and frivolous.
3. 〜然 *fānrán*, changeably, fluctuant.

旛   fān   MC bjon   ⊙ 幡 *fān*.

番   fān   MC phjon
1. alternate, succeed in place; e.g. 〜休 *fānxiū*, periodic rest; 〜次 *fāncì*, recognizable sequence, incl. time.
2. measure-word for a turn, a time, an occurrence.
3. ⊙ 藩 *fān* 1, paling, hedge, bulwark; 2, beyond the pale, foreign, barbarous.

bō　MC pa

1. rdup., brave and bold, martial and mighty.
2. (med.) 吐～ *tŭbō* (MC thuX-pa) or *tŭfān* (MC thuX-phjon), Tibet; also ref. later to Tarim Basin.

pó　MC ba

1. rdup., white as can be, silvery white, of hair.

翻　**fān**　MC phjon

1. wheel, flutter, flap (of birds); e.g. ～翰 *fānhàn*, flap the quills; ～飛 *fānfēi*, wheel and wing.
2. turn over, invert, roll; e.g. ～覆 *fānfù*, upside-down, over-and-under > vicissitudes; ～波 *fānbō*, tumbling waves; ～情 *fānqíng*, tumultuous feelings.
   a. turn, shift of same action by different persons.
3. (med.) on the contrary, nevertheless, despite (the foregoing).
4. convert into, turn into; change, alter, revise (text), rework.
   a. (med.) fit new lyrics to existing tune.
5. (med.) translate.

藩　**fān**　MC pjon

1. hedge; fence, paling; border.
   a. buffer, defense; bulwark, protective.
   b. protect, guard, screen.
2. what is beyond the pale, in the hinterland(s); foreign, barbarous; e.g. ～紅花 *fānhónghuā*, foreign redbloom, i.e. saffron.
3. fiefdom, given by ruler to feudal lord; dependency, vassal state.
   a. (med.) ～鎮 *fānzhèn*, "dependent stronghold," regions of special strategic importance in Tang times, first with military matters and later all matters administered by specially appointed *jiedushi* 節度使, "commissioner who rules with [plenipotentiary] credentials."
   b. (med.) the one whose fief is outside the capital (i.e. dependent, by the paling), usu. ref. younger brother of crown prince.
4. carriage screened on all sides.

轓　**fān**　MC phjon

1. mudguard or screen, attached to lateral sides of carriage chassis.
   a. by synecdoche, the carriage itself.

飌　**fān**　MC bjom

1. rdup., galloping fast as the wind, fleet of foot.
2. ⊙ 帆 *fān* 1, a sail, a boat; 2, to sail.

飜　**fān**　MC phjon

1. ⊙ 翻 *fān* 1, wheel, flap, flutter; 2, turn over, invert, roll; turn, shift of same action by different persons.

fán

凡　**fán**　MC bjom

1. sentence modifier indicating that the statement is to be understood as a generalization: in general, overall, in every case of; whenever, whatever, whoever, whichever; e.g. ～音之起由人心生也 *fán yīn zhī qǐ yóu rénxīn shēng yě*, In general when (musical) sounds come forth they arise from the feelings within a person; ～婦人從其夫之爵位 *fán fùrén cóng qí fū zhī juéwèi*, In general wives follow the rank and station of their husbands; ～人之所以為人者禮義也 *fán rén zhī suǒyǐ wéi rén zhě lǐyì yě*, In general a person's wherewithal for behaving in the way expected of a person is a matter of ceremony and propriety.
   a. as modifier to numbers: in all, *in toto*; e.g. ～三道者 *fán sāndàozhě*, these three methods in all; ～四十八山 *fán sìshíbā shān*, forty-eight mountains in all.
   b. as totalizer: all of, every; e.g. ～時 *fánshí*, ～是 *fánshì*, everything, every one of . . .
2. the general scope; e.g. 喪禮之～ *sānglǐ zhī fán*, the general scope of mourning rites.
3. common, ordinary, quotidian, homely; e.g. ～民 *fánmín*, ～人 *fánrén*, everyday people.
   a. (med.) secular, mundane; e.g. ～世 *fánshì*, the mundane (i.e. not transcendent) world.

墦　**fán**　MC bjon

1. grave, tomb.

樊　**fán**　MC bjon

1. raddle, branch interwoven with others to make a fence.
   a. fence, hedge, screen.
2. cage, coop (birds or animals); e.g. ～籠 *fánlóng*, slatted cage; also, coop and cage.
3. side(s); next to, adjacent to.
4. in confusion, pell-mell; e.g. ～縕 *fányūn*, every which way.

瀿　**fán**　MC bjon

1. overflow, freshet, outpouring, gushing.

煩   **fán**   MC bjon

1. vex(atious), irk(some), annoy(ance), irritate, peeve, aggravate.
    a. trouble(some), bother(some); e.g. ～惱 *fánnǎo*, afflictions.
2. confusingly or unnecessarily many, overmuch; overcomplicated, loaded with trivia.
    a. weighed down, unncessarily laden; e.g. ～重 *fánzhòng*, cumbersome.
3. weary; listless, sluggish; enervated.

燔   **fán**   MC bjon

1. burn; set on fire.
2. meat open-roasted, for sacrifice; to roast.

璠   **fán**   MC bjon

1. jewel, gem; treasure.
    a. 璵～ *yúfán*, ancient prized gem, → 璵 *yú*.

礬   **fán**   MC bjon

1. (med.) alum; used medicinally, also in dyeing and tanning.
    a. (med.) ～石 *fánshí*, native alum, kalinite; 白～ *báifán*, 明～ *míngfán*, "white" or "bright alum," recrystallized alum; 黃～ *huángfán*, "yellow alum," crude halotrichite, feather alum; 黑～ *hēifán*, "black alum," prob. glockerite.

繁   **fán**   MC bjon

1. profuse, prolix, profusion; replete, full.
    a. exuberant, lush, teem(ing).
    b. multiple, manifold; multiply.
    c. added together, condensed, thick; e.g. ～露 *fánlù*, incrassate dew.
2. to tend crops or animals, so they will multiply.
3. troublesomely many or frequent.
    a. compound, complex; difficult, vexatious; involved, overdone.
    pán   MC ban
1. girth-strap, cinch of horse, ⊙ 鞶 *pán* 2.

膰   **fán**   MC bjon

1. meat open-roasted for sacrifice, ⊙ 燔 *fán* 2.

蕃   **fán**   MC bjon

1. profuse, prolific, thriving, teeming, exuberant growth (of plants).
2. propagate, produce.
    a. breed, rear.
    fān   MC pjon
1. ⊙ 藩 *fān* 1, paling, hedge, bulwark; 2, beyond the pale, foreign, barbarous.

    bō   MC pa

1. (med.) 吐～ *tǔbō* (MC thuX-pa) or *tǔfān* (MC thuX-pjon), Tibet; also ref. later to Tarim Basin.

蘋   **fán**   MC bjon

1. larger species of → 莎 *suō*, nutgrass; distinguish as "nut-sedge."

蘩   **fán**   MC bjon

1. various species of artemisia, esp. beach-wormwood (*A. stelleriana*).

袢   **fán**   MC bjon

1. plain undergarment worn in summertime.
2. humid, muggy, sultry.
3. (bn.) ～延 *fányán* (MC bjon-yen), damp and muggy, steamy and sticky; also, sop up sweat with plain cloth; also, wear clothing slack and loose in summertime.

蹯   **fán**   MC bjon

1. paws, footpads of animals.

fǎn

反   **fǎn**   MC pjonX

1. turn over, invert, turn upward; e.g. ～唇 *fǎnchún*, turn up the lip, sneer at; sass, talk back; ～宇 *fǎnyǔ*, upturned eaves.
2. turn back, reverse, go back, revert, return, turn round; e.g. ～經 *fǎnjīng*, return to guiding principles, go back to the classics; ～手 *fǎnshǒu*, hands tied behind the back.
    a. repeat, do again.
3. go counter to, contrary, opposite, oppose; rebel, revolt.
4. look inside, introspection; e.g. ～過 *fǎnguò*, examine one's mistakes.
5. on the contrary, nevertheless; despite (the foregoing).
    fān   MC phjon
1. annul, reverse, overturn (a decision).
    fàn   MC pjonH
1. ⊙ 販 *fàn*, trade, peddle, traffic in, buy cheap and sell dear.

返   **fǎn**   MC pjonX

1. ⊙ 反 *fǎn* 2, turn back, reverse, go back, revert, return, turn round; repeat, do again.

fàn

梵　fàn　MC bjomH
1. trsc. Skt. *brahman*, pure, holy, sacred.
    a. pertaining to Budd. matters; e.g. 〜修 *fànxiū*, Budd. devotions; 〜宇 *fànyǔ*, 〜家 *fànjiā*, Budd. monastery.
2. pertaining to India, Sanskrit, or to Indic matters; e.g. sgl. or 〜文 *fànwén*, Sanskrit; 〜土 *fàntǔ*, India; 〜人 *fànrén*, Indic person; 華〜 *huáfàn*, China and India.

氾　fàn　MC phjomH
1. overflow, flood; inundate.
    a. (bn.) 〜瀾 *fànlán* (MC phjomH-lan), flooded with tears, tears swelling and surging.
2. float, buoy.
3. widespread, extensive; everywhere.
    a. in general, broadly, widely.

汎　fàn　MC phjomH
1. ⊙ 泛 *fàn* 1, (a)float, (a)drift, buoyed up, on water or wind; 氾 *fàn* 1, overflow, flood; 3, widespread, everywhere, broadly.
2. thrum, run the fingers lightly over a stringed instrument.
    　　　　fěng　MC pjowngX
1. ⊙ 覂 *fěng*, overturn, topple.
    　　　　fá　MC bjop
1. (bn.) 〜渫 *fájié* (MC bjop-tsjep), rushing and raging, splashing and slapping (of waves)

泛　fàn　MC phjomH
1. float(ing), buoy(ed) up, (a)drift, on water or wind.
2. inconstant, unsettled; fluctuate, waft.
3. (med.) amplification or forced prevention of vibration of chordophone strings; e.g. 〜聲 *fànshēng*, 〜音 *fànyīn*, harmonics, lightly stopping an acoustic node at moment when zither (*qin* 琴) string is excited.
4. ⊙ 氾 *fàn* 1, overflow, flood, inundate; 3, widespread, everywhere, broadly.
    　　　　fěng　MC pjowngX
1. ⊙ 覂 *fěng*, overturn, topple.

犯　fàn　MC bjomX
1. trespass, transgress.
    a. violate, infringe on; offend against, affront.
    b. conjunction or near-conjunction of star or planet with constellation.

2. invade, attack.
    a. vanquish, conquer.
3. commit a crime, criminal offense, violate the law.
4. 〜引(國) *fànyǐn*(*guó*) Bamiyan (MC bjomX-yinX).

範　fàn　MC bjomX
1. casting mould, pattern; template, prototype.
    a. standard, criterion, norm.

范　fàn　MC bjomX
1. casting mould, pattern, template, protoype; ⊙ 範 *fàn*.
2. ⊙ 氾 *fàn* 1, overflow, flood; 3, widespread, broadly.
3. bee.
4. a surname.

販　fàn　MC pjonH
1. buy and sell; buy to resell, buy cheap and sell dear; deal in, traffic in.

飯　fàn　MC bjonX
1. eat.
    a. to serve others with food; feed animals.
    b. pertaining to meals; e.g. 〜會 *fànhuì*, fête, banquet.
2. place jade, grains of rice, or other object in mouth of corpse.
    　　　　fàn　MC bjonH
1. cooked rice or other grains.

fāng

坊　fāng　MC pjang
1. residential area in city, bounded by lanes or alleys; ward, usu. walled.
    a. quarter(s) in a city or in palace compound, set off for state business whether civil or military.
2. (med.) shop, store, stall.
    a. (med.) atelier, workshop.
3. commemorative monument.
    　　　　fáng　MC bjang
1. ⊙ 防 *fáng* 2, guard against, defend; forestall.

方　fāng　MC pjang
1. square; square-shaped.
    a. square measurement of area; e.g. 〜百里 *fāngbǎilǐ*, 100 *li* square.

2. by metonymy, earth (opp. [round] heaven).

    a. earthly, mundane; finite, confined; e.g. ～外 *fāngwài*, ultramundane, beyond the confines [of the world].

3. foursquare, proper, morally right; regular tendencies; e.g. ～廉 *fānglián*, foursquare and incorruptible; 行～ *xíngfāng*, act on the square, without partiality.

4. direction, quarter; region, area; locus, position, place(ment); e.g. 四～ *sìfāng*, the 4 directions, the 4 quarters; 有/無～ *yǒu/wúfāng*, with/without fixed direction; (Budd.) ～等 *fāngděng*, equal in all directions, ～廣 *fāngguǎng*, broad in all directions, trns. Skt. *vaipulya*, "breadth of scope," ref. broad scope of Mahāyāna.

    a. aspect, facet, side; scope, extent, limit; e.g. 大～之家 *dàfāngzhījiā*, school of the broader scope.

    b. side, partiality; diverge(nt).

    c. by the side of, close to; round about.

5. parallel, side-by-side (< 2 boats lashed together or proceeding together); compare, juxtapose; comparable, similar.

    a. equable; agreeable.

6. means, method, device; e.g. ～士 *fāngshì*, master of methods, specialist in one or more esoteric practices, incl. divination, astrology, medicine, alchemy, immortality, etc.; (Budd.) ～便 *fāngbiàn*, trns. Skt. *upāya*, skillful means, expedient devices, teaching adapted to the level of practitioners, a key Mahāyāna concept; (med.) in non-Budd. contexts, opportunity, advantageous condition; also, manner of behavior, custom, etiquette.

    a. formula, design; recipe, prescription; technique, procedure; often implying something secret or cryptic; e.g. ～術 *fāngshù*, techniques based on esoteric skill, cryptic arts.

7. (ADV) just now, just then; e.g. 趙～西憂秦 *zhào fāng xī yōu qín*, Zhao is just now concerned about Qin in the west; 昨日～歸 *zuórì fāng guī*, yesterday when I had just returned home.

    a. just > just so > exactly, precisely; e.g. 天下～亂 *tiānxià fāng luàn*, the subcelestial realm is exactly in a state of disorder; 邯鄲～盛 *hándān fāng shèng*, Handan is at the peak of prospering.

8. introducing a noun-phrase or a nominalized VB-phrase: just at the moment of; e.g. ～天之休 *fāng tiān zhī xiū*, just at the moment when heaven was agreeable; ～此時也 *fāng cǐshí yě*, just at this time.

9. (ADV) marker of future action expected soon to occur: just about to, will soon; e.g. ～與將軍會獵於吳 *fāng yǔ jiāngjūn huì liè yū wú*, just about to join the general in a battle at Wu; (med.) often compounded as ～須 *fāngxū*, will surely.

10. VB-phrase 1 ～VB-phrase 2: only after VB-phrase 1, then VB-phrase 2: only then; e.g. 向見雷將軍～知足下軍令矣 *xiàng jiàn léi jiāngjūn fāng zhī zúxià jūnlìng yǐ*, Only after meeting with General Lei would you then know your general's commands; 故覽之者初疑其易，而為之者～覺其難 *gù lánzhī zhě chū yí qí yì, ér wéizhī zhě fāng jué qí nán*, To be sure, when one first peruses it, one suspects it is easy; when one tries to do it, only then does he sense its difficulty.

枋   fāng   MC pjang

1. 蘇～ *sūfāng*, sappanwood (*Caesalpinia sappan*), small to medium-size shrubby tree, produces a reddish-purple dye.

2. rafter-plate, horizontal timber carrying rafters or trusses.

    fǎng   MC pjangH

1. ⊙ 舫 *fǎng* 2, bamboo or wooden raft.

芳   fāng   MC phjang

1. scented, sweet-smelling, fragrant, redolent; of scents and also euph. for admirable actions or traits.

    a. (bn.) ～菲 *fāngfēi* (MC phjang-phj+jX), fragrant and flourishing, redolent loveliness.

    b. ～香 *fāngxiāng*, angelica, syn. → 芷 *zhǐ*.

fáng

妨   fáng   MC phjang

1. hamper, impede, obstruct(ion), obstacle, hindrance, hinder.

2. cause difficulty for; do damage to, harm.

房   fáng   MC bjang

1. room, chamber; alcove.

    a. wing, of building; quarters.

2. by synecdoche, house, dwelling, habitation.

3. housing, anything that houses or contains something else; casing; calyx (of flower); pod (of legume).

4. (med.) office, in name of various subordinate agencies, esp. those in the Tang secretariat-chancellery (*zhongshu menxia sheng* 中書門下省) from the early 8th-c. on.

5. branch of a clan.

6. "Chamber," one of the 28 lunar lodgings, comprised of β, δ, π, ρ Scorpii, in the eastern quadrant (*qinglong* 青龍) of the sky.

　　páng　MC bang

1. (bn.) ～皇 *pánghuáng* (MC bang-hwang), ⊙ 徬徨 *pánghuáng*, → 徬 *páng*.

2. 阿～ *ēpáng* (MC 'a-bang), name of famous palace complex built by Qin Shihuang.

防　fáng　MC bjang

1. dike, dam; dam up, stop up.

2. guard against, stand against, defend, fend off, hold off, forestall; e.g. ～風 *fángfēng*. wind screen, partition; also, water-mallow.

　　a. wary of, chary.

魴　fáng　MC bjang

1. white bream (*Parabramis pekinensis*); black bream (*Megalobrama terminalis*).

fǎng

仿　fǎng　MC phjangX

1. imitate, copy; emulate.

2. (bn.) ～佛 *fǎngfú* (phjangX-phjut), ⊙ 彷彿 *fǎngfú*, → 彷 *fǎng*.

　　páng　MC bjang

1. (bn.) ～徨 *pánghuáng* (MC bjang-hwang), ⊙ 徬徨 *pánghuáng*, → 徬 *páng*.

倣　fǎng　MC pjangX

1. imitate, copy, ⊙ 仿 *fǎng* 1.

彷　fǎng　MC phjangX

1. (bn.) ～彿 *fǎngfú* (MC phjangX-phjut), vague shape, vaguely resembling, almost as though, seems somewhat; faded and vague.

　　páng　MC bang

1. (bn.) ～徨 *pánghuáng* (MC bang-hwang), ⊙ 徬徨 *pánghuáng*, → 徬 *páng*.

瓬　fǎng　MC pjangX

1. pottery, earthenware.

紡　fǎng　MC phjangX

1. spin, reel (thread); e.g. ～車 *fǎngchē*, spinning-wheel.

　　a. sgl. or ～條 *fǎngtiáo*, roving, relatively fine fibrous strands used in later stages of carding; also, an untwisted rope.

2. silk-stuff.

舫　fǎng　MC pjangH

1. 2 boats lashed together; barge.

　　a. 2 boats proceeding in tandem.

　　b. double-hulled boat, sometimes with deck-house.

2. bamboo or wooden raft.

訪　fǎng　MC phjangH

1. ask of, inquire of (information or counsel).

2. (med.) call on, pay a visit to; look up, look in on.

3. (med.) search out, be in quest of; examine, find out.

髣　fǎng　MC phjangX　⊙ 彷 *fǎng*.

fàng

放　fàng　MC pjangH

1. abandon(ment); expel, oust, banish(ment), exile.

　　a. throw off, throw away, cast aside.

　　b. put down, set down, lay aside.

　　c. emit, cast forth.

2. release, let go, dismiss; set loose, spare, set free; e.g. (med.) ～朝 *fàngcháo*, release from obligation to attend court; (Budd.) ～生 *fàng-shēng*, release of (caught) animals, esp. birds and fish, as act of merit.

3. act with no constraints, independent(ly); e.g. (bn.) ～浪 *fàngláng* (MC pjangH-lang), ～蕩 *fàngdàng* (MC pjangH-dangX), carefree, free and easy; wild and unbridled, running where one will, coursing unchecked; ～意 *fàngyì*, let one's thoughts run, however fancy leads one.

4. be revealed fully, laid open or expressed to full extent, as in blooming of flowers, singing of song, declaiming praise, etc.

　　a. heart(il)y, lust(il)y, ebullient(ly); extravagant(ly).

5. (med.) sgl. or cmpd. ～教 *fàngjiāo*, bring about, to effect, cause to do, allow, let.

fēi

妃　fēi　MC phj+j

1. wife, spouse.

2. imperial consort; usu. highest-ranking or most favored woman, apart from the "heir-giver," mother of heir-designate ([*huang*]*hou* [皇]后).

　　a. consort of prince of the blood.

3. final element in name of some goddesses.

pèi   MC phwojH

1. ⊙ 配   *pèi* 1, match, mate, counterpart; 2, matched in marriage, spouse.

扉   fēi   MC pj+j

1. leaf of door, panel of window.
   a. single-leaved door, usu. suggesting simplicity.

緋   fēi   MC pj+j

1. (med.) stammel, medium-bright rich red with less orange than scarlet; in Tang times the color of robes of those in the 4th and 5th (of 9) bureaucratic grades.

裶   fēi   MC phj+j

1. rdup., full and flowing, long and trailing (robes); full and billowing (banners).

霏   fēi   MC phj+j

1. sgl. or rdup., heavy fall of snow or rain; fully falling, flurried, pelting.
2. blurred, filmy, of clouds or mist.

非   fēi   MC pj+j

1. negate, deny, gainsay; consider wrong.
2. generic negative GP for nominal sentences, negates an identity: (is) not; e.g. 回也～助我者也 *húi yě fēi zhù wǒ zhě yě*, Hui is not someone who aids me; 我～生而知之者也 *wǒ fēi shēng ér zhīzhīzhě yě*, I am not someone who knows about it from birth.
   a. negates a category identification in nominal sentences: (is) not [of a certain category or kind]; e.g. 殺一無罪～仁也 *shā yī wú zuì fēi rén yě*, killing even one innocent person is not [a kind of] humaneness; ～人所能也 *fēi rén suǒnéng yě*, it is not the kind of thing that a person is able to do.
   N.B. the distinction between 1 and 1a is often subtle; e.g. ～周公之行，～孔子之言也 *fēi zhōugōng zhī xíng, fēi kǒngzǐ zhī yán yě*, it is neither the behavior of the Duke of Zhou nor the speech of Confucius, i.e. it is not the Duke of Zhou's kind of behavior nor Confucius's kind of speech.
   b. negates an associative identification in nominal sentences: (is) not to be associated with, is not due to; e.g. 無是非之心～人也 *wúshìfēi zhī xīn fēi rén yě*, a heart that lacks a sense of right and wrong is not associated with a humane person; 王之不王～不能也

wáng zhī búwàng fēi bùnéng yě the king's not ruling as a proper king is not due to not being able to.

3. coming between the subject and predicate of a verbal sentence, negates the propositional substance of the sentence: it is not that; e.g. 我～愛其財也 *wǒ fēi ài qí cái yě*, It is not that I begrudged its material value; 池～不深也 *chí fēi bùshēn yě*, it is not that the pond is not deep;
4. marks a negative exclusionary clause: except for; e.g. ～祭肉不拜 *fēi jìròu bùbài*, except for [a gift of] sacrificial meat, he does not bow in respect; ～其君不事 *fēi qí jūn bùshì*, except for his lord, he does not provide any service; ～聖人而能若是乎 *fēi shèngrén ér néng ruò shì hū*, except for being a sage, then, would he have been able to do it like this? cf. 微 *wéi*, 唯 *wéi*.
5. negative noun prefix: non-; e.g. ～禮之禮～義之義 *fēilǐ zhī lǐ fēiyì zhī yì*, non-ceremonial ceremony, non-proprietous propriety; ～人所為之火 *fēi rén suǒwéi zhī huǒ*, non-man-made fire.
6. negates attribute of adjective; e.g. ～常 *fēicháng*, ～分 *fēifēn*, ～甚 *fēishèn*, extraordinary, exceptional (< not the ordinary; not just as normally allotted; not just very much but more).

飛   fēi   MC pj+j

1. fly, flight, to wing; airborne, aloft.
2. fleet, winged, rapid; volatile.
3. lofty, elevated, soaring, sky-high.
4. flighty, flimsy, ungrounded, baseless.
5. ～廉 *fēilián*, name of ancient god of the wind; also, plumeless thistle (*Carduus crispus*).

騑   fēi   MC

1. trace-horses of a team of four; syn. 驂 *cān* 2.
   a. team of horses.
2. rdup., striding steadily onward (horses).

féi

痱   féi   MC pj+j   ⊙ 痹 *féi*.

痹   féi   MC bj+j

1. torpor; numbness.
   fèi   MC bj+jH
1. prickly heat.

肥   féi   MC bj+j

1. fat, corpulent, well-fed, fleshed-out; burly; thick, bulky.

a. well-nourished, well-supplied, comfortable; e.g. ～遯 *féidùn*, hide away at ease (from the world), withdraw contentedly.
2. greasy, blubbery, pinguid; flabby.
3. replete, flush, uberous, exuberant (vegetation).
4. rich, fertile, bountiful (land).

腓　féi　MC bj+j
1. calf of the leg.
2. withered, wilted.
　a. (en)feeble(d), weak, torpid.
3. cover, shelter; protect.

fěi

匪　fěi　MC pj+jX
1. ⊙ 非 *fēi* 2, (is) not; 3, it is not that.
2. ⊙ 彼 *bǐ* 1, demonstrative pronoun indicating the one implied, understood, or singled out: that, those, the other.
3. (med.) ne'er-do-well, good-for-nothing, miscreant.

悱　fěi　MC phj+jX
1. frustrated by being at a loss for words, inarticulate, tongue-tied, dumbstruck.

斐　fěi　MC phj+jX
1. colorful, multi-hued, variegated
　a. ornate, adorned; prinked; polished.

朏　fěi　MC phj+jX
1. moon(light) of first 3 days of month, faint sliver.
　a. by metonymy, first 3 days of month.
　b. faintly appearing stars or starlight, just coming out.
2. ～明 *fěimíng*, first hint of sunrise, barely dawn(ing).

棐　fěi　MC pj+jX
1. assist, supplement.
2. ⊙ 菲 *fěi* 2, frail, weak, paltry; 榧 *fěi*, nutmeg-yew (*Torreya grandis*); 篚 *fěi*, round bamboo basket.

榧　fěi　MC pj+jX
1. (med.) nutmeg-yew (*Torreya grandis*), large conifer with nutmeg-like edible seeds and yew-like foliage.

篚　fěi　MC pj+jX
1. round bamboo basket.

翡　fěi　MC bj+jH
1. (bn.) ～翠 *fěicuì*, → 翠 *cuì*.

菲　fěi　MC phj+jX
1. radish (*Raphanus sativus*).
2. sgl. or ～薄 *fěibó*, frail and lowly, feeble, insignificant, meager, wretched; slim, sparing, modest.
　　fēi　MC phj+j
1. rdup., redolent and aromatic, sweetly scented, fragrant fullness; also, mixed and mingled, tangled together; also, anxiously unquiet, restless and fretful.
2. (bn.) ～薇 *fēiwēi* (MC phj+j-mj+j), profusely proliferous, lushly luxuriant (vegetation).
　　fèi　MC bj+jH
1. ⊙ 屝 *fèi*, straw sandals.

蜚　fěi　MC pj+jH
1. crop-eating insect of uncertain identification, perhaps a species of locust or flying cockroach.
　　fēi　MC pj+j
1. ⊙ 飛 *fēi*, all meanings.

誹　fěi　MC phj+jX
1. decry, find fault with, criticize, disparage, run down.
2. criticize without grounds, slander, traduce, calumniate, smear.

fèi

刜　fèi　MC bj+jH　⊙ 跳 *fèi*.

吠　fèi　MC bjojH
1. onom. of dog's bark, yelp; latrant.

屝　fèi　MC bj+jH
1. straw shoes, straw sandals.

廢　fèi　MC pjojH
1. discard, abandon.
　a. dismiss, discharge; depose, supersede.
　b. abolish, put an end to; remove, dispense with.

2. regard as useless, vitiate, invalidate; omit, neglect.
  a. disabled, weakened, brought to the end.
3. use up, waste; destroy.
4. ⊙ 癈 *fèi*, sickly, wasted, incurable.

柿   fèi   MC phjojH
1. wood-shavings; to shave or pare wood.
  a. euph. for intimacy; e.g. ～附 *fèifù*, the closeness of wood-shavings (to wood).
N.B. Do not confuse this graph with 柿 *shì*, persimmon.

沸   fèi   MC pj+jH
1. bubble up, effervesce; churn, heave, turbulent.
  a. boil, seethe.
  b. foam, froth.
  c. (bn.) ～渭 *fèiwèi* (MC pj+jH-hjw+jH), ～潰 *fèipēn* (MC pj+jH-phwon), seethe and spume, frothing and foaming, heave and tumble (waves).
2. gush, push forth.
  a. gurgle, gurge.
3. hubbub, turmoil, pother.

狒   fèi   MC bj+jH
1. rdup., moulin langur, golden snub-nosed monkey (*Rhinopithecus roxellana*), syn. 梟羊 *xiāoyáng*, 狨 *róng*.

癈   fèi   MC pjojH
1. sickly, wasted, incurable; invalid.

肺   fèi   MC phjojH
1. lungs.
  a. (med.) by metonymy, what is in one's chest, innermost feelings.
2. ⊙ 柿 *fèi*, wood-shavings.

芾   fèi   MC pj+jH
1. burgeoning, flourishing, thriving (of vegetation).
2. (bn.) 蔽～ *bifèi*, → 蔽 *bì*.
  fú   MC pjut
1. ⊙ 韍 *fú* 1, knee-coverings worn by nobles at sacrificial offerings in early times.

費   fèi   MC phj+jH
1. squander, waste, dissipate, run through.
  a. expend, consume, use up, use all one's resources.

陫   fèi   MC bj+jX
1. hidden in shame, retired in lowly circumstances, living meanly or wretchedly.

跀   fèi   MC bj+jH
1. judicial punishment of amputation of foot.

fēn

分   fēn   MC pjun
1. divide, separate; split, divert; e.g. ～合 *fēnhé*, divide and join; ～別 *fēnbié*, to separate and part from one another; (Budd.) ～段之鄉 *fēnduàn-zhixiāng*, realm of transmigration; ～頭 *fēntóu*, separately, severally.
  a. differentiate, distinguish, discriminate, demarcate; e.g. ～別 *fēnbié*, differentiate, analyze; also (Budd.), conceptualization, the application of thought-categories and names to the real, the imputed aspect of experience; also, explain, show, proclaim; understand, comprehend; (med.) ～張 *fēnzhāng*, pull apart, distinguish; also, pull away, part from.
  b. discern(ible), make out, distinct(ly); reveal(ed); e.g. ～明 *fēnmíng*, sharp and luminous; distinct and clear; clear-cut and vivid.
2. apportion, allot, parcel out, mete out.
3. equinox, vernal (*chunfen* 春～) and autumnal (*qiufen* 秋～).
4. measure-word for one-tenth of various items; e.g. one-tenth of "inch" (*cun* 寸); one-tenth of "acre" (*mu* 畝).
  fèn   MC bjunH
1. allotment, portion, parcel, segment.
  a. constituent, element, attribute.
2. allocated duty or responsibility, assignment.
  a. position in arrangement of ranks or grades.
3. presume, infer, deduce; e.g. 自～已死久矣 *zifèn yǐsǐ jiǔyǐ*, I presumed you had died long ago.
4. affection, goodwill; e.g. 在遠～日親 *zàiyuǎn fèn rìqīn*, though distant, our affection daily becomes closer.

氛   fēn   MC phjun
1. vapors, exhalation, perfusion, often of ominous nature; if malign: mephitic airs.
  a. fog, fumes, miasma.
2. (bn.) ～氲 *fēnyūn* (MC phjun-ʼjun), perfused and saturated, laden and swollen, blanketing overcast full of vapors, snow, odors, etc.

紛　fēn　MC phjun

1. streamers (of flag or pennon).
2. sgl. or rdup., tangled threads.
   a. rdup. or (bn.) ～綸 fēnlún (MC phjun-lwin), ～紜 fēnyún (MC phjun-hjun), sundry, motley; profuse, confusion, swarming, flurry and blur; also, irksome; muddled and flustered; purblind; staggered and reeling, milling about; also, diffuse(d), scattered; (bn.) ～葩 fēnpā (MC phjun-phae), profusely spread, in full flower.
3. bewildered, bewildering; confused.
4. amply, fully, profusely.
5. (med.) even more, extremely; for long; to keep up, keep on vb-ing; repeat(edly).

籿　fēn　MC phjun

1. rdup., float and flutter, drift with the wind (of birds).

芬　fēn　MC phjun

1. fragrant, sweet-smelling.
   a. agreeable, alluring.
   b. euph. of admirable reputation.
2. succulent, inviting, of food.
3. sgl. or rdup., ⊙ 紛 fēn 2, sundry, various; mixed, motley.

衯　fēn　MC phjun

1. long and trailing, full and flowing (of robes).

雰　fēn　MC phjun

1. cloudy haze, fog.
   a. rdup., snow-frosted air, falling snow-shimmer, snow-swollen haze; also, syn. (bn.) 氛氲 fēnyùn, → 氛 fēn.

fén

墳　fén　MC bjun

1. piled-up earth; cairn, mound, tomb; e.g. ～窟 fénkū, cairn-grotto, catacombs.
2. "landmark" texts, esp. 三～ sānfén, attributed to legendary 三皇 sānhuáng, Three August Ones (i.e. Fuxi 伏羲, Shennong 神農, Huangdi 黃帝).
   a. respectful term for ancient document(s).
3. ⊙ 濆 fén 1, embankment, riverbank.

幩　fén　MC bjun

1. cloth or silk attached to outside edges of horse's bit, for ornamentation and to wipe slaver.

枌　fén　MC bjun

1. elm tree, syn. 榆 yú.
2. ⊙ 棻 fén, purlin.

棻　fén　MC bjun

1. purlin, one of horizontal timbers supporting rafters.
2. sgl. or rdup., ⊙ 紛 fén 2, sundry, various; mixed, motley.

汾　fén　MC bjun

1. name of important river in Shanxi, tributary to Yellow River.
2. (med.) swell, bulge.

濆　fén　MC bjun

1. embankment, riverbank (higher than 濱 bīn, margin, shore); cog. 墳 fén, piled-up earth; cairn; 憤 fèn, raise one's qi, be excited or vehement about; fume.

　　pēn　MC phwon

1. spout, gush, burst forth. (bn.) ～薄, ～礴 pēnbó (MC phwon-bak), spout and spurt.

　　fèn　MC bjunH

1. bubble furiously; break loose, as stones or earth under the force of rushing water.

焚　fén　MC bjun

1. set alight, set fire to, ignite, burn.

菎　fén　MC bjun

1. (bn.) ～菌 fényūn (MC bjun-ʻjun), ⊙ 氤氲 yīnyūn, → 氤 yīn.

　　pén　MC bwon

1. black raspberry (Rubus coreanus).

賁　fén　MC bjun

1. fructiferous, fecund, proliferous.
2. hemp-seeds (edible).

蚡　fén　MC bjun

1. ⊙ 鼢 fén, Temminck's mole.
2. (bn.) ～縕 fényùn (MC bjun-ʻjun), mingle and merge, twist and tangle.

豶　fén　MC bjun

1. neutered pig.

隫　fén　MC bjun

1. ⊙ 濆 fén 1, high riverbank, embankment; 墳 fén 1, cairn, tomb.

豟   fén   MC bjun
1. syn. 鼴 *yǎn*, Temminck's mole, Japanese mole (*Mogera wogura*), large, generally solitary mole.

fěn

粉   fěn   MC pjunX
1. powder(y); flour.
    a. to powder, pulverize.
    b. fine, dusty, granulated.
2. face-powder, make-up, cosmetic, usu. of white lead, ceruse.
    a. adorn(ment), gloss, enhance(ment).
3. to whitewash, with plaster.

fèn

僨   fèn   MC pjunH
1. fall over; fall or lie on one's face, prostrate.
    a. fall down dead.
2. bring down; put to rout.
3. excite(d); tense, strained; jumpy.

坋   fèn   MC bjunX
1. dust, ash.
2. dust with, sprinkle over, strew.

奮   fèn   MC pjunH
1. spread the wings, beat wings (upon takeoff).
    a. rise up, jump off; rouse, put in motion, excite(d); break out.
2. exert oneself; strain, strenuous(ly); act with energy, strive; enthusiastic, zealous.
3. exaggerate, inflate; brag, boast.

忿   fèn   MC phjunH
1. (en)rage(d), wroth; angry, ire, irate, wrath(-ful), furious.

憤   fèn   MC bjunX
1. raise one's *qi*, be excited or vehement about; impassioned.
    a. fume, furious; choleric; indignant, infuriated.
2. exasperated, frustrated, dissatisfied, testy.
    a. put out, rankled, nettled.

漢   fèn   MC pjunH
1. gush out from a subterranean source, bubble up.
    a. underground spring.
2. soak into, infiltrate.

3. multiple effluents from a single source, multi-fluent; multi-influential.

糞   fèn   MC pjunH
1. clear away dirt or filth, sweep away impurities, muck out; cleanse.
    a. muck, filth, dirt.
    b. lowly condition, execrable; shameful, disgraceful.
2. dung, feces, manure, excrement, ordure; fecal, stercorean.
    a. to manure, fertilize (fields).

膹   fèn   MC bjunX
1. meat-stew, hash.
2. sliced meat.

fēng

丰   fēng   MC phjowng
1. flourishing, bountiful, luxuriant (of vegetation).
    a. (bn.) ～茸 *fēngróng* (MC phjowng-nyowng), lush and luxuriant, richly proliferous.
2. generously or bountifully endowed, in appearance; either shapely and refined or plump and full-bodied.

封   fēng   MC pjowng
1. earthen mound.
    a. raise a mound to use as tumulus or on which to plant trees; heap up; entomb.
2. enfeoff, bestow fedual title and appanage on; anciently incl. bestowal of lump of earth symbolizing granting of the fief and the mound on which altar to local gods of grain and soil stood.
    a. enfeoff a (usu. local) divinity with a title.
    b. (med.) provided with imperial sanction; e.g. ～刀 *fēngdāo*, entrusted with sword symbolizing imperial authority to decree capital punishment.
3. imperial ceremony of sacrifice to heaven, to be conducted in conjunction with the 禪 *shàn* sacrifice to earth when there is harmony throughout the realm resulting from ideal government; traditionally carried out at Mt. Tai 泰山, with the *shan* performed at nearby Mt. Liangfu 梁父山 or Mt. Sheshou 社首山.
4. boundary, border.
5. seal up, close up; e.g. ～函 *fēnghán*, sealed envelope, for letter; ～事 *fēngshì*, "sealed matter," private letter to ruler; ～裹 *fēngguǒ*, wrap up, ball up.
    a. block, obstruct.

6. (med.) measure-word for anything sealed, esp. letter.

7. large in size, huge; hulking; giant; e.g. ～豕 *fēngshǐ*, giant boar.

峯　fēng　MC phjowng

1. mountain peak, summit, mountaintop.
   a. by synecdoche, a mountain, a peak.

峰　fēng　MC phjowng　⊙峯 *fēng*.

楓　fēng　MC pjuwng

1. sgl. or ～香 *fēngxiāng*, sweet-gum, liquidambar (*Liquidambar acalycina*), a southern tree of the lowlands, yielding a fragrant resin, with large and spiny egg-shaped seeds, and palmate leaves that are blush-red in spring, turn green during summer, then red-orange in autumn. This is the *fēng*-tree that is usu. meant by the sgl. term in poetry; red leaves are less noticed in lit. than its green, sadly rustling leaves in spring or summer. The resin (also termed *fēngxiāng*), is "storax."

2. maple tree (*Acer*, various species), mainly a northern tree, not fragrant, autumnal red leaves only occasionally noted in lit. where this tree is less common than the preceding.

烽　fēng　MC phjowng

1. beacon-fire, to be lit on border watchtowers in event of enemy incursion; the watchtower for such a beacon-fire.
   a. the beacon-fire lit at night; cf. 燧 *suì*, beacon lit in daytime.

2. set afire, kindle.

芉　fēng　MC phjowng　⊙丰 fēng.

葑　fēng　MC pjowng

1. turnip, rape-turnip (*Brassica rapa*).

豐　fēng　MC phjuwng　⊙葑 *fēng*.

蜂　fēng　MC phjowng

1. wasp; hornet.

2. hive, swarm, band; e.g. ～起 *fēngqǐ*, rise up in a swarm (as of wasps), esp. euph. for banding together to take military action against ruling power.

3. (med.) (lit.) ～腰 *fēngyāo*, wasp's waist, name of prosodic fault in which 2nd and 5th words in a line of pentasyllabic verse have the same tone (2nd word comes immediately before caesural pause and 5th word is the last of end-stopped line, hence with same tone they "squeeze" the middle of the line, just as a wasp's waist looks squeezed).

4. (med.) ～臺 *fēngtái*, Budd. pagoda, because shape resembles wasp's nest.

豐　fēng　MC phjuwng

1. plentiful, copious, bounteous; abundant, luxuriant.
   a. full, replete; generous; sumptuous, lavish.
   b. rich, pleasing to the senses.
   c. of finest quality, choice; opimous.
   d. bountiful or bumper harvest.

2. sleek; glossy.
   a. plump, fat, chubby.

3. serving-tray on which to place vessels of sacrificial wine in early times.

4. "Fullness," name of 55th hexagram of *Yijing*.

酆　fēng　MC phjuwng

1. name of capital of capital or chief city of King Wen of Zhou 周文王, located near present-day Huxian 戶縣, Shaanxi; often paired as ～鄗 *fēnghào*, Hao being the name of capital founded nearby by King Wu 武王, southwest of present-day Xi'an; together Feng and Hao stand for the Zhou dynasty, esp. Western Zhou.

鋒　fēng　MC phjowng

1. point or tip of a weapon.
   a. by synecdoche, a weapon.

2. point or tip of anything that can be said to have one, such as writing-brush.
   a. pointed, spiked, sharp.

3. leading edge or salient portion of an army, vanguard.

風　fēng　MC pjuwng

1. wind(y), breeze(y); air(y), gust(y), wind-blown, wind-swept; e.g. 春～ *chūnfēng*, spring breeze, with connotations of renewed vitality, freshness, often (esp. in poetry) erotic suggestiveness; ～塵 *fēngchén*, wind-blown dust, usu. suggesting cares, vicissitudes, and transience of human life.
   a. by synecdoche, weather, climate; e.g. ～景 *fēngjǐng*, wind and sunlight, the feel of the air, (fine) weather and scenery.
   b. fleet, quick as the wind.

2. prevailing atmosphere, aura, pervading influence; spiritual tenor; general feeling; e.g. ～聲 *fēngshēng*, "prevailing voice," contemporary reputation.

    a. climate of custom, manners, mores.

    b. vogue; mode, style, fashion(able).

    c. (med.) ～流 *fēngliú*, term of much importance and positive regard in describing the behavior of certain persons: natural dignity with flair, a gentleman's polished indifference to polish, *sprezzatura*, cultivated manners, stylish manner, stylishly cultivated, stylishly refined, panache and urbanity, flowing charm, "a drifter with the wind" (N.B. do not translate as "romantic").

3. (lit.) air, in 國～ *guófēng*, "Airs of the States," collective name for odes in 1st section of *Shijing*, traditionally regarded as expressing the sentiments of the commonfolk of the various feudal states of Zhou.

4. (med.) (lit.) the style, temper, or mood of a composition, its animating force directed outward, often paired with *gu* 骨 (underlying structure or argument).

5. wind in an etiological role, thought to cause various illnesses; to strike with malign or debilitating influence, resulting in stroke, heart attack, paralysis, dizziness, migraine, etc.; e.g. ～癲 *fēngdiān*, epilepsy, grand mal seizure.

    fĕng   MC pjuwngH

1. ⊙ 諷 *fĕng*, criticize indirectly.

féng

縫   **féng   MC bjowng**

1. sew, stitch, do needlework.

    a. sew up, mend, patch; restore; close up, bridge.

    fèng   MC bjowngH

1. seam; juncture, joint.

2. (med.) split, breach; crack, fissure.

逢   **féng   MC bjowng**

1. meet, encounter; happen on, chance on.

2. welcome; receive; accept.

    a. cooperate with, join with.

3. to divine, prognosticate.

    péng   MC buwng

1. rdup., onom. of booming of drum.

    páng   MC baewng

1. a surname.

馮   **féng   MC bjuwng**   → 馮 *píng*.

fĕng

覂   **fĕng   MC pjowngX**

1. overturn, turn upside-down (carriage, fate).

2. be thrown off (horse).

    fá   MC bjop

1. (med.) ⊙ 乏 *fá* 1, bereft of, lacking; 2, used up, consumed.

諷   **fĕng   MC pjuwngH**

1. criticize by indirection, allusion, or hint.

    a. suggest in a veiled way.

2. recite (text) from memory; intone, declaim.

3. (med.) take in the breeze, enjoy the breeze.

fèng

俸   **fèng   MC bjowngH**

1. official's salary.

奉   **fèng   MC bjowngX**

1. (ADV) respectfully, deferentially, obligingly.

2. respectfully offer, proffer; hand up or hold up to a superior with both hands.

    a. give over, present; entrust.

3. attend upon deferentially, defer to; oblige, be obliging; observe respectfully; follow, obey.

    a. prefix to many official titles: "Deferential(ly)…"

4. receive with deference; undertake deferentially.

    a. be charged or entrusted with responsibility for; trustee of.

5. respect, esteem, hold in highest regard; believe in.

6. ⊙ 俸 *fèng*, official's salary.

桻   **fèng   MC phjowng**

1. (med.) ～子 *fèngzi*, peddler who carries his goods in a bamboo basket on his shoulders.

賵   **fèng   MC phjuwngH**

1. burial gifts in early times, esp. horses and chariots.

鳳   **fèng   MC bjuwngH**

1. sgl. or (bn.) ～凰 *fènghuáng* (MC bjuwngH-hwang), fabulous animal, traditionally rendered as "phoenix" but without the self-immolating and regenerative features of the Western mythological bird. A composite animal, described as having the front torso of a "unicorn" (*lin* 麟) and hind parts of a deer, a serpent's neck and fish's tail, the markings of a "dragon" (*long* 龍) and carapace of a turtle, a swallow's bill and chicken's beak, with feathers of all hues. Chief among feathered creatures, its charisma causes other birds to flock to it; one of the "four numinous animals" (*siling* 四靈).

    a. emblematic of imperial influence and dignity.

    b. ominous of good fortune and sageliness.

fó

佛　**fó**　MC bjut

1. abb. of ～陀 *fótuó* (MC bjut-da), trsc. of Skt. *buddha*, the Buddha, enlightened one; Buddhist, Buddhism.

    fú　MC phjut

1. (bn.) 仿～ *fǎngfú*, → 仿 *fǎng*.

    bì　MC bit

1. ⊙ 弼 *bì* 2, assist(ant), aid(e); sustain, uphold.

fóu

紑　**fóu**　MC pjuw

1. sleek, spruce, appearance of silk clothing.

fǒu

否　**fǒu**　MC pjuwX

1. "no," in answer to a question; e.g. 王許之乎曰～ *wáng xǔ zhī hū, yuē fǒu*, Would the king agree to this? He said, "no" (i.e. "not so").
2. "or not?" in expressing the negative counterpart to a preceding VB-clause; clause-final (with optional interrog. GP); e.g. 可～ *kě fǒu*, Is it allowable or not?; 動心～乎 *dòngxìn fǒu hū*, Does this bestir your feelings or not?

    pǐ　MC bijX

1. block(age), stoppage; stagnation, lack of movement or progress; e.g. ～泰 *pǐtài*, stagnation and exaltation, adversity and prosperity.

    a. "stoppage," name of 12th hexagram of the *Yijing*.

2. misprized; base, vile; e.g. 臧～ *zāngpǐ*, prized and misprized, better and worse, gain and loss.

缶　**fǒu**　MC pjuwX

1. pottery urn or jar for holding liquids, large-bodied and small-mouthed.
2. measure of capacity, equiv. 16 "pecks" (*dou* 斗).
3. earthenware musical percussion instrument.

瓺　**fǒu**　MC pjuwX　⊙ 缶 *fǒu*.

衃　**fǒu**　MC pjuwX

1. (bn.) 蚍～ *pífǒu*, → 蚍 *pí*.

fū

夫　**fū**　MC pju

1. gen. term for adult man.

    a. husband; e.g. ～婦 *fūfù*, husband and wife.

    b. ～人 *fūrén*, respectful term for wife of official, dignitary, or nobleman: Lady (X), Her Ladyship; when used for wife of someone of lower status, Madame.

2. sentence-final rhetorical interr. GP: "no?," "isn't it?," "n'est-ce pas?," "nicht wahr?"; e.g. 固矣～ *gù yǐ fū*, it has become certain, hasn't it?; 亡之命矣～ *wáng zhī mìng yǐ fū*, bringing about his demise, clearly it is Fate, isn't it?

3. noun suffix to words referring to people; e.g. 匹～耕之 *pǐfū gēng zhī*, the lads will plough it; 彼丈～也，我丈～也 *bǐ zhàngfū yě, wǒ zhàngfū yě*, he is (just) a fellow, and I am (just) a fellow.

    fú　MC bju

1. sentence-initial modifier indicating that the substance of the sentence applies to any individual case or any instance of the sentence topic or subject: it is a fact that . . ., in any particular case, in any particular instance, in any respect > however you look at it; e.g. ～蚓上食槁壤下飲黃泉 *fú yǐn shàng shí gǎorǎng, xià yǐn huángquán*, in any particular case of an earthworm, above it eats from dried leaves and dirt, below it drinks from the Yellow Springs; ～人幼而學之 *fú rén yòu ér xué zhī*, in any given instance, when a person is young he studies it; ～仁政必自經界始 *fú rénzhèng bì zì jīngjiè shǐ*, however you look at it, a humane government inevitably starts from laying out proper boundaries.

    a. indication similar to clearing the throat preparatory to speaking.

2. demonstrative pronoun indicating the one implied, understood, or singled out, also the one further removed or less obvious: that (one,

kind of . . .), those; mostly pre-imperial, used afterward largely for archaic effect, being usu. replaced by 彼 *bǐ*.

孚   fū   MC phju
1. brood over eggs, to nest, hatch, ⊙ 孵 *fū*.
2. reliable, trustworthy.
    a. guardian(ship); custody, safekeeping.
3. 中～ *zhōngfū*, "Inner Trust," name of 61st hexagram of *Yijing*.

孵   fū   MC phju
1. brood over eggs, to nest, hatch.

敷   fū   MC phju
1. spread out, spread open, lay out; e.g. ～衽 *fūrèn*, spread open the lapels, i.e. bare one's breast; ～花 *fūhuā*, blowing flowers.
2. spread widely, disseminate, distribute, diffuse, scatter.
    a. far and wide, everywhere, all around.
3. to elaborate, expand, develop.
    a. set forth, deploy; display, exhibit; perform.
    b. express, expose; assert, present.
4. (med.) readied, well-fixed, well-disposed; well-turned-out.

尃   fū   MC phju   ⊙ 敷 *fū*.

柎   fū   MC pju
1. foot of drumstand or bellstand, legged drum-stand.
    a. gen. term for foot of objects.
2. seed-chamber, of flower; sepal; calyx.
3. cap-block, cushion timber, cross-timber on a bearing-block.
    MC phju
1. ⊙ 泭 *fū*, small raft of wood or bamboo.
    fǔ   MC phjuX
1. ⊙ 弣 *fǔ*, midsection of a bow's grip.
    fù   MC bjuH
1. wooden board, for writing on in early times; wooden plank, on which to place corpse in coffin.

泭   fū   MC phju
1. bamboo or wooden raft, of relatively small size.

玞   fū   MC pju   ⊙ 砆 *fū*.

砆   fū   MC pju
1. (bn.) 碔～ *wǔfū*, → 碔 *wǔ*.

稃   fū   MC phju
1. chaff or glume of grain.

膚   fū   MC pju
1. skin, derma, flesh of humans.
2. skin-deep, superficial; shallow; slick, only for outward show.
3. informal measure of length, equiv. breadth of 4 fingers, approx. 4 inches; e.g. ～寸 *fūcùn*, hand's-width (width of 4 fingers plus thumb), mere handful, wee, paltry.

荴   fū   MC phju
1. disseminate, scatter, diffuse, distribute.

趺   fū   MC pju
1. ⊙ 跗 *fū* 1, back of foot; 2, base or foot of ca-lyx; 3, foot of standing object.
2. sgl. or cmpd. ～坐 *fūzuò*, 跏～ *jiāfū*, (Budd.) sit in lotus position for meditation, legs crossed with upturned feet on opposite thighs; trns. Skt. *āsana*.

跗   fū   MC pju
1. back of the foot.
2. base of calyx, calyx-foot, ⊙ 柎 *fū*.
3. foot or base of standing object such as stele, bell-stand, frame, etc.

鈇   fū   MC pju
1. lever-knife, for cutting chaff.
    a. hinged dagger, similar to a switchblade.
2. axe, for executions.
    fǔ   MC pjuX
1. ⊙ 斧 *fǔ*, axe, mainly for treework.

麩   fū   MC phju
1. ground wheat-husks, bran.
2. crumb, small bit, flake.

fú

伏   fú   MC bjuwk
1. prostrate; humbly.
    a. cower, lout low; succumb to, submit, subject(ion); e.g. ～罪 *fúzuì*, acknowledge a crime, submit to punishment.
    b. crouch, lean forward; huddle, curl up; e.g. ～翼 *fúyì*, (one with) huddled wings, i.e. bat.
2. lie low, stay apart; hide, lie hidden; e.g. ～匿 *fúnì*, hide away, conceal; ～甲 *fújiǎ*, soldiers in ambush.
    a. brood, incubate (of birds and fowl).

3. (med.) laden (with); service(able); e.g. ～手 *fúshǒu*, ready to hand, available for use.

4. dog-days of summer, days of greatest heat, esp. as ～日 *fúrì*, also 三～ *sānfú*, ref. last 2 months of summer and first month of autumn.

　　a. high-summer sacrifice in early times, parallel to winter all-hallows sacrifice, hence usu. in parallel construction ～臘 *fúlà*.

5. throw aside, discard.

6. crossbar at front of carriage, on which one leans.

7. ～羲 *fúxī*, mythological figure responsible for invention or regularization of many aspects of traditional culture, e.g. invention of the eight trigrams (*gua* 卦) of *Yijing*, of hunting, fishing, cooking, etc.

俘　fú　MC phju

1. prisoner, captive.

　　a. take as prisoner, capture.

刜　fú　MC phjut

1. lop off or hew with a sword.

匐　fú　MC bjuwk

1. (bn.) 匍～ *púfú* (MC bu-bjuwk), creep and crawl, drag along.

坿　fú　MC bju

1. quartz, syn. 白石英 *báishíyīng*; e.g. 白～ *báifú*, milky quartz.

第　fú　MC bjut

1. (bn.) ～鬱 *fúyù* (MC bjut-'jut) or 鬱～ *yùfú*, tortuously turning, crookedly looping, of heavily ridged mountains.

帗　fú　MC pjut

1. hand-held streamer made of varicolored bands of silk, used by dancers.

2. ⊙ 韍 *fú*, knee-coverings worn by nobles at sacrificial offerings in early times.

幅　fú　MC pjuwk

1. width of cloth or silk; in Han times equiv. 2 feet (*chi* 尺) and 2 inches (*cun* 寸).

　　a. selvage, border, band; e.g. 裙～ *qúnfú*, skirt band.

2. measure-word for rolled items, e.g. cloth, scrolls.

弗　fú　MC pjut

1. generic negative for VBS and VB-phrases that typically incorporates an implicit direct OBJ pronoun: not . . . it (. . . her, . . . him, . . . them, etc.); e.g. ～得則死 *fú dé zé sǐ*, if one does not obtain it, then he will die; 不可以～識也 *bùkěyǐ fú shì yě*, I cannot not recognize it.

　　a. as a variant of 不 *bù*: not; e.g. 民～去 *mín fú qù*, the people will not leave; ～忍虛也 *fú rěn xū yě*, he cannot bear that it be empty.

2. (med.) emphatic negative, often without implied OBJ: not (X) at all.

彿　fú　MC phjut

1. (bn.) 彷～ *fǎngfú*, → 彷 *fǎng*.

怫　fú　MC bjut

1. (bn.) ～鬱 *fúyù* (MC bjut-'jut), uneasy and unsettled, dejected and dolorous, disconsolate.

2. ～然 *fúrán*, infuriated, in high dudgeon.

fèi　MC bj+jH

1. (bn.) ～憒 *fèiwèi* (MC bj+jH-wojH), grumbling and grieving, lagging and faltering.

bèi　MC bwojH

1. ⊙ 悖 *bèi* 1, contrary, counter; willful, recalcitrant.

扶　fú　MC bju

1. hold by the arms, support, hold up, prop up, brace, help up or along.

　　a. sustain, bolster, shore up, reinforce.

　　b. assist, boost, back up; help, facilitate.

2. go along with, go beside; stand by, be by; cleave to, lean against.

　　a. alongside, by the side of; to edge.

3. (bn.) ～搖 *fúyáo* (MC bju-yew), whirlwind (< rising up and shaking); ascend rapidly.

4. (bn.) ～疏 *fúshū* (MC bju-srjo), thick foliage, thickly leaved, spreading luxuriantly.

5. measure of length, equiv. breadth of 4 fingers, approx. 4 inches, ⊙ 膚 *fū* 3.

6. ～桑 *fúsāng*, mythical tree on easternmost edge of the world, upon which the sun rises; (med.) name for Japan; also, local name in far south for 朱槿 *zhūjǐn*, vermeil rose-mallow (*Hibiscus rosa-sinensis*).

7. ～南 *fúnán* (MC bju-nom), pre-Angkor kingdom in Cambodia (< Old Khmer *bnom*, 'mountain'; equiv. modern Khmer *phnom*).

pú　MC bu

1. (bn.) ～伏 *púfú* (MC bu-bjuwk), ⊙ 匍匐 *púfú*, → 匍 *pú*.

拂   fú   MC phjut

1. brush away, brush off; dust, wipe off, whisk; shake out; e.g. ～筵 *fúyán*, brush off (i.e. arrange) sitting-mats; ～羽 *fúyǔ*, shake out feathers (prior to flight).
   a. rdup., lambent brushing, as of gentle breeze.
   b. be close to, near; e.g. ～曙 *fúshǔ*, close to sunrise.
2. flail, implement for threshing.
   a. to flail; beat.
3. defy, resist; be contrary to.
   bì   MC bit
1. ⊙ 弼 *bì* 2, assist(ant), aid(e).

服   fú   MC bjuwk

1. undertake, take on, take up; apply oneself to; accept responsibility for.
   a. put in order; dispose, arrange.
2. submit to, capitulate; succumb to, yield.
   a. acquiesce; comply with; acknowledge.
   b. adapt, fit; be accustomed to.
   c. acknowledge as superior, admire, esteem.
3. harness, be harnessed; pay deference to or bring to deference.
   a. shaft-horses, thill-horses, inside pair of a 4-horse team.
4. garment, garb, apparel; attire for specific occasion (court, military, esp. mourning).
   a. be garbed, attired, dressed; don, wear.
5. ingest, consume, esp. medicine.
   a. a dose, potion.

枹   fú   MC bjuw

1. mallet, drumstick.
   bāo   MC paew
1. silkworm-oak (*Quercus glandulifera*), smaller species of sweet oak, 樸 *pú* (*Quercus dentata*).

柎   fú   MC bjuw

1. eave-purlin, short ridgepole projected under the eaves.
2. ⊙ 泭 *fú*, small raft of wood or bamboo; 枹 *fú*, mallet, drumstick.

榑   fú   MC bju

1. ⊙ 扶 *fú* 5, in ～桑 *fúsāng*, → 扶 *fú*.

洑   fú   MC bjuwk

1. backflow, eddy, gurge, whirlpool.
2. (med.) flow underground, subterranean course.

浮   fú   MC bjuw

1. float, drift, primarily on water but also on other liquids or in the sky; buoyant; e.g. ～雲 *fúyún*, drifting clouds; ～蟻 *fúyǐ*, "floating ants," bits of sediment floating in unfiltered wine.
   a. to sail, drift a boat; follow the current.
   b. pass over, pass beyond; surpass, exceed; excessive.
2. insubstantial, airy; frothy, flimsy, frivolous, superficial; floss, fluff; whimsical.
   a. inconstant, impermanent, fleeting; e.g. ～生 *fúshēng*, "this floating/fleeting life."
3. be untied from any particular place; e.g. ～人 *fúrén*, a drifter, gadabout; ～逃 *fútáo*, leave behind one's place of household registration, i.e. irresponsible and untaxable.
4. inflict penalty of drinking specified amount of wine on loser of a drinking game; e.g. ～白 *fúbái*, pay a forfeit by drinking a full cup; (med.) drink one's fill, drink freely.
5. (med.) douse, soak; immerse, drench.
6. (Budd.) ～陀 *fútuó* (MC bjuw-da), ～屠 *fútú* (MC bjuw-du), Buddha, Buddhist; also, stupa.
7. ⊙ 罘 *fú* 2, (bn.) ～思 *fúsī*, → 罘 *fú*; 蜉 *fú* 1, (bn.) ～蝣 *fúyóu*, → 蜉 *fú*.

犕   fú   MC bjuwk

1. yoke an ox or horse.
   a. (med.) saddle a horse.
2. submit to; obey.

袚   fú   MC phjut

1. purge, expel, remove, drive out, esp. evil spirits; exorcise.
   a. rite of exorcism, expulsion, purgation.
2. cleanse, purify.

福   fú   MC pjuwk

1. good fortune; favored; propitious; blessed, bless(ing).
   a. (Budd.) merit, favorable karma; e.g. ～行 *fúxíng*, ～施 *fúshī*, acts that produce merit.
2. meat and wine used in sacrificial offerings.

符   fú   MC bju

1. tally, two-halved bamboo or wooden segment, one half given to each of two individuals as credential for legitimating proper transmission of military or official orders.
   a. auspicious token indicative of Heaven's favor or approval, in imperial or dynasty-

legitimating contexts; transcendent token of sovereignty.

b. talisman used in med. Daoist rituals to confirm partnership with or control of certain gods.

2. to fit together, like the two halves of a tally.

絨　fú　MC pjut

1. silk ribbon to tie pendant gems or seal-cords to waistband.

2. ⊙ 韍 *fú*, knee-coverings worn by nobles at sacrificial offerings in early times.

紼　fú　MC pjut

1. sturdy rope, esp. coffin-ropes.

2. ⊙ 絨 *fú* 1, silk ribbon to tie pendant gems or seal-cords to waistband.

緈　fú　MC pjut

1. ⊙ 紼 *fú*, sturdy rope, esp. coffin-ropes.

2. (med.) informal term for imperial proclamation (which pulls one after it).

罘　fú　MC bjuw

1. netting to catch birds or land animals, esp. rabbits; rabbit-snare.

2. (bn.) ～罳 *fúsī* (MC bjuw-si), "covert for second thoughts," screened area outside the doorway to court where a subject might have a last, private moment of introspection (復思 *fùsī*) before entering for audience with the ruler; also (med.), netting set on the eaves of a roof or over a window to repel birds.

芙　fú　MC bju

1. (bn.) ～蕖 *fúqú* (MC bju-gjo), lotus (*Nelumbo nucifera*); cf. ～蓉 *fúróng*, 荷 *hé*, 蓮 *lián*, 菡萏 *hàndàn*.

2. (bn.) ～蓉 (MC bju-yowng):

a. lotus, esp. fully opened, ⊙ ～蕖 *fúqú*.

b. cottonrose hibiscus, cotton rosemallow, confederate rose (*Hibiscus mutabilis*), also called 木～蓉 *mù fúróng*, a deciduous shrub with pink, white, and red flowers. N.B. If in water, ～蓉 ref. the lotus, if on land the hibiscus.

茮　fú　MC bjuw

1. (bn.) ～苢 *fúyǐ* (MC bjuw-yiX) Chinese plantain, arnoglossa (*Plantago asiatica*), an herbaceous perennial the leaves of which arise from the root.

2. (bn.) 芘～ *pífú*, → 芘 *pí*.

苻　fú　MC bju

1. climbing nightshade, bittersweet (*Solanum lyratum*, *S. dulcamara*); also, trumpet-vine (*Campsis grandiflora*).

2. ～蘺 *fúlí*, angelica (*Angelica dahurica*), perennial plant that grows along riverbanks and streams; roots and leaves highly fragrant; in lit. symbolic of high morality and integrity; syn. 芷 *zhǐ*.

3. ⊙ 荸 *fú*, interior pellicle of reed-stem; synecdoche for reed, cattail.

4. a surname.

荓　fú　MC phjut

1. overgrowth, plants overruning a path, wild growth.

a. (bn.) ～鬱 *fúyù* (MC phjut-'jut), feel oppressed and put upon, gloomy discontent.

2. clear away weeds, eradicate, uproot; get rid of.

3. screen for front and back of high-ranking lady's carriage.

4. ⊙ 福 *fú*, good fortune, favored; 紼 *fú*, sturdy rope; coffin-rope.

茯　fú　MC bjuwk

1. ～苓 *fúlíng*, pine-truffle (*Pachyma cocos*) or poria (*Poria cocos*), a fungus esp. used in Dao. dietary regimens.

2. 土～苓 *tǔfúlíng*, China-root, sarsparilla (*Smilax glabra*), root used medicinally; do not confuse with preceding.

荸　fú　MC phju

1. interior pellicle of reed-stem.

a. synecdoche for reed, cattail.

b. reed-membrane for flute.

2. (med.) rind of fruit or vegetable.

piǎo　MC bjewX

1. ⊙ 殍 *piǎo*, die from starvation.

蕧　fú　MC bjuwk

1. (bn.) 蘆～ *lúfú*, 萊～ *láifú*, 蘿～ *luófú*, → 蘆 *lú*.

蒚　fú　MC pjuwk

1. hedge bindweed (*Calystegia sepium*), twining plant with showy white flowers.

蚹　fú　MC bju

1. ～母 *fúmǔ*, 青～ *qīngfú*, water-beetle (*Dityscidae* family, esp. *Cybister chinensis*); because tradition had it that the mother water-beetle never leaves her offspring, it was thought that if a water-beetle's blood were smeared on a string of cash and another's on a 2nd string, the 2 would seek each other out; hence the name (*fúmǔ* or *qīngfú*) was used in med. times as slang for "cash," often with connotation of growing wealth.

蜉   fú   MC bjuw

1. (bn.) ～蝣 *fúyóu* (MC bjuw-yuw), mayfly (*Ephemeroptera*), which lives only a day; metaphor for what is short-lived, ephemeral.
2. (bn.) 蚍～ *pífú*, → 蚍 *pí*.

蝠   fú   MC pjuwk

1. sgl. or as (bn.) 蝙～ *biānfú* (MC pen-pjuwk), bat (*Chiropterae*); symbolic of good fortune because homonymous with → 福 *fú*.
2. sgl. or ～蛇 *fúshé*, poisonous snake, viper.

輻   fú   MC bjuwk

1. spokes of a wheel.

郛   fú   MC phju

1. 2nd or outer wall of city or fortified settlement.
   a. outlying area.

韍   fú   MC pjut

1. knee-coverings worn by nobles at sacrificial offerings in early times.
2. ⊙ 紱 *fú* 1, silk waistband upon which to tie pendant gems or seal-cords.

髴   fú   MC phjut   ⊙ 佛 *fú*.

鳧   fú   MC bju

1. wild-duck; cf. 鶩 *wù*, domesticated duck; e.g. ～趨 *fúqū*, "duck-run," scurry like ducks, scurry in a rush.
2. ～茈 *fúcí*, water-chestnut (*Eleocharis dulcis*), sedge whose corms (not actually nuts) are eaten.

鵩   fú   MC bjuwk

1. houlet, Chu dialect word for 鴞 *xiāo*, short-eared or hornless owl; bird of ill omen.

黻   fú   MC pjut

1. labris pattern embroidered in black and dark-blue on ceremonial robe of ruler.
2. ⊙ 韍 *fú*, knee-coverings worn by nobles at sacrificial offerings in early times; 紱 *fú* 1, silk waistband upon which to tie pendant gems or seal-cords.

fǔ

俛   fǔ   MC pjuX   → 俛 *miǎn*.

俯   fǔ   MC pjuX

1. lower the head, bow the head; e.g. ～仰 *fǔyǎng*, lower and raise the head, esp. the time it takes to lower and raise the head, i.e. the briefest of moments.
   a. lower oneself, to lout, bow.
   b. hunch down; shrivel up.
2. honorific ADV used for those of higher status: deign to do X, condescend to do, see fit to do.
3. hibernate; curl up in extended rest.

吙   fǔ   MC pjuX

1. chew into small pieces, crunch to bits, masticate.

嘸   fǔ   MC phjuX

1. ～然 *fǔrán*, aghast, astonished; flabbergasted, stunned.

府   fǔ   MC pjuX

1. repository (of valuables), archive (of documents).
   a. storehouse, treasury; depot.
2. princely headquarters, administrative center of prince's establishment; palatin(at)e.
3. residence of noble or high dignitary.
4. (med.) prefectural administration in a capital city or strategic location; precincts.
5. (med.), sgl. or ～兵 *fǔbīng*, in Tang times a military garrison, esp. in the militia system operating to rotate soldiers throughout the state.
6. 開～ *kāifǔ*, important title from Han through Tang, varying in application but indicating that holder was permitted to open a headquarters with its own staff; in med. times often a military title.
   a. (med.) element in various informal official titles; e.g. ～君 *fǔjūn*, lord repositor, i.e. grand warden of a commandery (*juntaishou* 郡太守); also, respectful term for a deceased; 明～ *míngfǔ*, enlightened repositor, i.e. district magistrate (*xianling* 縣令); 贊～ *zànfǔ*, assistant repositor, i.e. district adjuvant (*xiancheng* 縣丞); 少～ *shǎofǔ*, deputy repositor, i.e. district constable (*xianwei* 縣尉).
7. receptacles, set of inner organs of the human body, complementary to the 5 "viscera" (*zang* 臟); e.g. 六～ *liùfǔ*, the 6 receptacles, i.e. stomach (*wei* 胃), large and small intenstines (*da/xiao-*

chang 大/小腸), gall bladder (*dan* 膽), urinary bladder (*pangguang* 膀胱), and "triple burner" (*sanjiao* 三焦, variously identified).

柎　fǔ　MC pjuX

1. midsection of a bow's grip.

拊　fǔ　MC phjuX

1. ⊙ 撫 *fǔ* 1, touch lightly, stroke, brush against; 2, comfort, solace, placate; 4, strike, clap, tap.

撫　fǔ　MC phjuX　⊙ 撫 *fǔ*.

撫　fǔ　MC phjuX

1. touch lightly, lay a hand on; stroke gently, fondle, caress; brush against, skim, graze.
   a. (med.) gen. term for playing stringed instrument; e.g. ～琴 *fǔqín*, play (stroke, caress) the zither.
2. comfort, solace, console, soothe; placate, conciliate.
   a. come to terms with, assent, comply with; e.g. ～運 *fǔyùn*, accede to fate; ～期 *fǔqī*, in due time.
   b. brush one's mind over, think pensively on.
3. grasp, hold, grip; e.g. ～劍 *fǔjiàn*, take hold of one's sword.
   a. take possession of, have control over, esp. territory.
4. strike, beat; clap, slap; tap; e.g. ～襟 *fǔjīn*, beat one's breast.

斧　fǔ　MC pjuX

1. axe, mainly for treework.
   a. chop, hew, lop off.
2. battle-hatchet, battle-axe.

甫　fǔ　MC pjuX

1. honorific suffix added in early times to a male's given name or byname; also written 父.
2. for the first time, beginning.
   a. just now, just at that time.
3. large; great.

簠　fǔ　MC pjuX

1. pannier, trencher, grain-hamper; square or oblong with steeply sloping sides forming a round interior, to hold boiled grain for sacrificial offering or banquet (cf. 簋 *guǐ*, round pannier).

脯　fǔ　MC pjuX

1. salted dried meat, usu. in strips.
2. (med.) preserved fruit or melon.

腐　fǔ　MC bjuX

1. rotten, putrid, decayed, decomposed; curdled.
   a. stale, spoiled; corrupt.
2. castration, as judicial punishment.

輔　fǔ　MC bjuX

1. side-supports, props, bulwark of cart.
2. buttress, prop, stabilize, sustain; assist, aide, second; help(er).
   a. euph. for loyal ministers and dedicated vassals.
3. near vicinity or near suburbs of capital city; vicinage, adjunct region.
4. (med.) in Tang times, 1st of 4 special categories designating selected prefectures (*zhou* 州) that, because of their importance were given special standing (in descending order of prestige: ～*fǔ* [buttressing], 雄 *xióng* [dominant], 望 *wàng* [honored], 緊 *jǐn* [important]) outside the usual trilevel ranking (上, 中, 下) of prefectures.
5. "Sustainer," name of one of the 2 supplementary or "hidden" stars of the Northern Dipper (the other is → 弼 *bì*), identified with Alcor in Western astronomy, being a companion star to Mizar which is the penultimate star of the Dipper's handle.

釜　fǔ　MC bjuX

1. cooking-pan, similar to a wok.
2. measure of capacity, equiv. 64 "pints" (*sheng* 升), 6.4 "pecks" (*dou* 斗).

頫　fǔ　MC pjuX　⊙ 俯 *fǔ*.

黼　fǔ　MC pjuX

1. double-headed axe pattern in black and white embroidered on ceremonial robe of ruler; often paired as ～黻 *fǔfú*, double-headed axe and labris patterned embroidery, prerogative of ruler; cmpd. also used in gen. ref. to "elegant embroidery," incl. by med. times as euph. for elegantly dignified lit. style.

fù

付　fù　MC pjuH

1. give to, turn over to, present to; lend.

俯　fù　MC bjuwX

1. in compliance with, accordant with.
   a. imitate, copy, take as model.
2. ⊙ 負 *fù* 3, count on, rely on.

傅　fù　MC pjuH

1. mentor, tutor; advise(r), counsel(or); e.g. grand mentor (太～ *tàifù*) one of the 3 highest-ranking court titles (along with *taibao* 太保 and *taishi* 太師), given to individual of great prestige who may be called on by emperor for advice.
2. entrust, commit to (the care of); rely on, depend on.
3. ⊙ 附　*fù* 1, attach, append; 2, close to, adjoin(ing); 敷 *fù* 1, spread out, lay out; 2, disseminate, distribute; everywhere, all around.
4. a surname.

副　fù　MC phjuwH

1. assist(ant), second(ary), deputy, auxiliary.
2. conform, coincide, match.
    a. transcript, copy (text).
3. false hair, wig of noblewomen in early times.
4. measure-word for a pair of, or a set of.
5. (med.) hand over to, deliver, consign.

pì　MC phik

1. to tear, break open or apart, rend, split.

婦　fù　MC bjuwX

1. wife, married woman.
2. gen. term for mature woman, adult woman; matron.
3. daughter-in-law.

富　fù　MC pjuwH

1. wealth(y), rich; rich in.
    a. opulent; abundant, plentiful.
2. ⊙ 福 *fú* 1, good fortune, propitious, blessed.

復　fù　MC bjuwk; bjuwH (as ADV)

1. go back over the same road, retrace; return, repair to.
    a. repeat(edly), duplicate; again, once more.
    b. resume, restart, start over.
    c. (med.) do at length, in detail, go over and over a task.
2. return to earlier state, restore, renew.
    a. reprieve; remit (taxes or corvée).
3. reply to, respond.
4. (med.) after all, in the next (or last) analysis.
5. (med.) often a simple continuative for narration, "and then," not implying repetition; also, a simple connective, "and also"; e.g. 江路險～永 *jiānglù xiǎn fù yǒng*, the river road is steep and also stretches long.

    a. (med.) or, usu. indicating simple choice between opposites; e.g. 傾榼濁～清 *qīngkē zhuó fù qīng*, pouring from the wine-vessel whether muddy or clear.
6. (Budd.) 雖～ *suīfù*, in Budd. texts equiv. concessive 雖 *suī*, even though, although, even if.
7. "Return," name of 24th hexagram of *Yijing*.
8. ⊙ 複 *fù* 2, doubled, compound, layered; 覆 *fù* 1, covered.

榑　fù　MC bjuwH

1. cloth-beam of loom, cylinder on which cloth is rolled as it is woven.

父　fù　MC bjuX

1. father.
2. honorific term for males of older generation.
    a. suffix in kinship terms for males of same generation as father; e.g. 從～ *cóngfù*, father's elder brother.

fǔ　MC pjuX

1. honorific term for more experienced or veteran colleagues; e.g. 田～ *tiánfǔ*, "patriarch of the fields," farmer.
2. honorific suffix added in early times to a male's given name or byname; also written 甫.

祔　fù　MC bjuH

1. sacrifice to newly deceased ancestor and his predecessors in ancestral shrine.
2. joint burial, shared entombment.

縛　fù　MC bjak

1. tie up, bind up; truss.
    a. binding thread or rope.
2. bundle, bunch.

腹　fù　MC pjuwk

1. stomach, belly.
2. inner or interior part, of object, territory, etc.
3. inner feelings; care for, care about.

蜉　fù　MC bjuwX

1. (med.) (bn.) ～蝂 *fùbǎn* (MC bjuwX-paenX), dung-beetle (*Scarabaeidae*, various species).

蝮　fù　MC phjuwk

1. sgl. or ～蛇 *fùshé*, pit-viper (various species of *Trimeresurus* and *Gloydius*), e.g. ～虺 *fùhuǐ*, pit-viper and bamboo-snake, both poisonous.

複　fù　MC pjuwk

1. lined garment, doubled in thickness.

2. doubled; folded; compound, complicated.
    a. layered, tiered; double-decked, storeyed.
3. repeated; duplicate.

覆　fù　MC phjuwk

1. cover(ed), coverture, extend over; e.g. 天～地載 *tiānfù dìzài*, heaven covers us and earth bears us up; ～道 *fùdào*, covered walkway.
    a. layer(ed), tier(ed).
2. turn over, overturn, turn upside-down; e.g. ～盆 *fùpén*, overturned basin; also, euph. for suffering unjust treatment (as though under a basin that one cannot remove); also, Chinese raspberry (*Rubus coreanus*).
    a. overwhelm, overthrow, subvert; prevail over, overcome.
3. hide, put or be under cover; protect, shelter; e.g. ～兵 *fùbīng*, troops in ambush; ～露 *fùlù*, shelter, safeguard.
    a. guard, protect.
4. examine in detail (< turn over and under), scrutinize fully.
    a. examine or interrogate prisoner.
5. on the contrary, quite the opposite, on the other hand.
6. respond, reply to.
7. again, once more; e.g. ～思 *fùsī*, ⊙ 覄思 *fúsī*, → 覄 *fú*.

訃　fù　MC phjuH

1. announce someone's death.
2. break (news) to someone.

負　fù　MC bjuwX

1. carry on the back, to bear; pack, pack in.
    a. shoulder a responsibility or task, undertake.
    b. bear up under, submit to; accept, accede to.
2. compensate; pay for, indemnify.
3. count on, rely on.
4. turn the back on, turn away; shrug off, ignore, snub, disregard, cold-shoulder; repudiate; betray.
5. undergo a loss; vanquished, subdued, beaten down.
    a. demerit; failing; e.g. ～特 *fùtè*, fail to live up to, unworthy of, disappoint.
    b. owe, be in arrears.
6. throw on or across one's back (clothing).

賦　fù　MC pjuH

1. levy taxes, esp. land-tax or levy on produce.
    a. gen. exacted duties, incl. military service (or contribution for support) and corvée.
2. contribute, distribute; bestow, endow, give to. natural endowments, innate gifts.
3. spread out, diffuse, extend.
    b. display, exhibit.
4. (lit.) traditional poetic trope in *Shijing* usu. defined as narration or description.
5. (lit.) particular genre of verse, one of the 2 major forms from Han through Tang times (the other being *shi* 詩), characteristics incl. lines of unequal length, expansive vocabulary, extensive synonymy, exhaustive description, ranging from long "display" pieces to shorter lyrical compositions; some early examples have brief prose insets but these are not a continuing feature; rhyme at end of alternating lines and (by med. times) preference for varying 4-word and 6-word meter is normal. If translation of the term is needed, use "rhapsody" (do not use "rhymeprose" or "prose-poem," as it is not "prose" of any sort).
6. to recite verse; also, to compose verse.
    a. (med.) (lit.) ～得 *fùdé*, "when *composing*, I *get* (i.e. am given) [X topic or rhyme-scheme]"; term often attached to poem-titles at group occasions where individuals are assigned different topics and/or rhyme-schemes for extemporaneous verse composition.

赴　fù　MC phjuH

1. proceed to, betake oneself to.
    a. hurry to, hasten to.
2. throw oneself into (task, idea).
    a. carry out, follow through on.
3. announce a death, ⊙ 訃 *fù*.

鍑　fù　MC pjuwH

1. covered pot with large mouth.

阜　fù　MC bjuwX

1. mound, hurst, toft.
2. fertile, rich, productive.
    a. burgeon(ing), proliferate; grow; abundant; multiply, increase.

附　fù　MC bjuH

1. attach, append; (ad)join; connect.
    a. annex, add to; include.
2. be nearby, close to, adjoin(ing).
3. attach oneself to, adhere to; depend on, subordinate to, submit to another's authority.
    a. ingratiate oneself with, get on the right side of; win over.

4. (med.) carry along, take with.
5. ～子 *fùzǐ*, aconite (*Aconitum carmichaeli*).

馥   fù   MC bjuwk

1. richly fragrant, odoriferous, balmy, aromatic.
   a. to scent, exhale a fragrance.
      bì   MC bik
1. "byok!" onom. of arrow striking its target.

駙   fù   MC bjuH

1. extra horse(s) added to a team.

2. ～馬都尉 *fùmǎdūwèi*, chief commandant of appended cavalry (escort to the emperor), Han dyn. office that soon became a supernumerary title; in med. times the abb. term ～馬 *fùmǎ* ref. imperial sons-in-law.

鮒   fù   MC bjuH

1. golden carp (*Carassius auratus*).

鰒   fù   MC bjuwk

1. abalone (*Haliotis gigantea*).

G

gāi

侅   gāi   MC koj

1. mired; stuck.
2. 奇～ *qígāi*, unusual, anomalous.

垓   gāi   MC koj

1. outer territory bounding all of space; periphery, perimeter; e.g. 九～ *jiǔgāi*, the 9 peripheries, the whole world, i.e. the far reaches of the ancient 9 provinces that defined the Chinese world; also, all of heaven, ninefold heaven.
   a. boundary, limit, edge, terminus.
2. layer, level, stage.
3. a myriad myriads, ten thousand times ten thousand.
4. ⊙ 陔 *gāi* 1, steps of stairway.

晐   gāi   MC koj   ⊙ 垓 *gāi*.

胲   gāi   MC koj

1. big toe.
2. hoof, of animal.
   gǎi   MC kojX
1. flesh of the cheek.

荄   gāi   MC koj

1. radicle of a plant, its embryonic root.
2. Alliaceous bulbs and corms.

該   gāi   MC koj

1. all complete, ready; whole, wholly; e.g. ～博 *gāibó*, comprehensively learned.

   a. contain(ing), inclusive, embracing; e.g. ～藏萬物 *gāicáng wànwù*, including all of the myriad things.
   b. full(y); undivided.
2. (med.) ought to, should, deserving of; e.g. ～死 *gāisǐ*, deserving of death, conventional self-deprecation in communication with emperor.

賅   gāi   MC koj

1. complete, inclusive, all-contained.

陔   gāi   MC koj

1. steps of stairway (to platform, terrace, dais).
   a. degree(s), stage(s); e.g. 九～ *jiǔgāi*, nine-layered heaven.
2. slope, terraced earth.
   a. ridges between farmfields.

gǎi

改   gǎi   MC kojX

1. change, alter, modify.
   a. recast, replace.
   b. amend, correct, improve.

gài

丐   gài   MC kajH

1. beg, solicit, implore.
2. give to, bestow; donate.

匄   gài   MC kajH   ⊙ 丐 *gài*.

概　**gài**　MC kojH

1. strickle, wood used to level off grain in a measure.
    a. scrape off, level off; plane down.
    b. measure(ment), gauge; standard, norm.
2. (ADV) in large measure, in general, for the most part; in all likelihood.
    a. summary; summarize.
3. the general picture, scene, situation; condition, prospects.
4. moderation, sense of proportion.
5. fidelity, integrity.
    a. personal magnetism, charisma.

溉　**gài**　MC kojH

1. irrigate; wetten, moisten.
2. wash, cleanse, scour.

蓋　**gài**　MC kajH

1. thatch a roof, roofing; put on top.
2. canopy, baldachin, awning, parasol; covering; lid; e.g. 車〜 *chēgài*, carriage canopy; 〜天 *gàitiān*, canopy-heaven, i.e. the heavens seen as hemispherical dome covering the earth.
    a. cover; protect, shield.
3. overarch, overhang, overtop; overshadow, dominate.
4. uphold; respect, venerate.
5. crest(ed), comb, esp. of animals.
6. sentence-initial GP that on the one hand indicates a measure of uncertainty and on the other expresses a measure of confidence in the statement: undoubtedly, probably, presumably; e.g. 〜有之矣，我未之見也 *gài yǒu zhī yǐ, wǒ wèi zhī jiàn yě*, undoubtedly there have been such things, but I have not yet seen such; 〜去者半，入者半 *gài qùzhe bàn, rùzhe bàn*, probably those who departed were half, those who joined in were half.
    a. expresses suggestion or admonition made with the same combination of certainty and guardedness as when sentence-initial: ought; e.g. 敝〜不棄 *bì gài bùqì*, a tattered cloth ought not be discarded.
    b. introduces explanatory clause with the same combination of certainty and guardedness as when sentence-initial: for the purpose or reason, probably because, likely, presumably, undoubtedly for (a certain reason); e.g. 喪服兄弟之子猶子也〜引而進之也 *sāngfú xiōngdì zhī zǐ yóu zǐ yě gài yǐn ér jìn zhī yě*, when it comes to mourning garments, the sons of one's brothers are as one's own sons—likely for the purpose of drawing close to them; 仲尼之嘆〜嘆魯也 *zhòngní zhī tàn, gài tàn lǔ yě*, Confucius's sighing was presumably sighing for the state of Lu.

> **hé**　MC hap
> 1. ⊙ 盍　*hé*, negative interr., equiv. 何不 *hébù*, why not?

gān

乾　**gān**　MC kan　→ 乾 *qián*.

坩　**gān**　MC kham

1. earthenware crock.

奸　**gān**　MC kan

1. offend; challenge; oppose, controvert.
    a. infringe; intervene, meddle.
2. pursue, seek out; importune for favor or advancement.

> **jiān**　MC kaen
> 1. (med.) ⊙ 姦 *jiān* 1, faithless, perfidious, scheming.

干　**gān**　MC kan

1. shield, buckler, targe; e.g. 〜戈 *gān'gé*, shield and glaive, implements of war.
2. affront, offend, go against, violate.
    a. force, encroach upon, impinge on.
    b. importune, press, beset; e.g. 〜謁 *gānyè*, importune with visit (seeking patronage).
3. intervene, interfere; involve oneself, concern oneself with.
    a. entreat, implore.
4. riverbank.
5. flats or dells between hills (mainly in Jiangnan).
6. abb. of 天〜 *tiān'gān*, ref. the 10 "heavenly stems" used in counting and classifying.

忓　**gān**　MC kan

1. ⊙ 干 *gān* 2, affront, offend, go against; encroach on, impinge on, beset.

柑　**gān**　MC kam

1. sweetpeel tangerine (*Citrus nobilis*); cf. 橘 *jú*, sourpeel tangerine (*Citrus reticulata*), 橙 *chéng*, sweet orange, coolie orange (*Citrus sinensis*).

玕　**gān**　MC kan

1. (bn.) 琅〜 *lánggān*, → 琅 *láng*.

甘 gān MC kam

1. sweet to the taste; savory, tasty; succulent.
   a. pleasant, appealing, agreeable (to eye or ear).
2. willingly, with pleasure, gladly, readily.
   a. fond of, avid for.
3. loose, relaxed; mellow.
4. ～蔗 gānzhè, sugarcane (*Saccharum officinarum*); ～蕉 gānjiāo, plantain (*Musa paradisiaca*); ～松香 gānsōngxiāng, "sweet pine aromatic," nard, spikenard (*Nardostachys jatamansi*).

竿 gān MC kan

1. pole; rod, cane; esp. fishing-pole.
2. (med.) measure-word for bamboo, slender trees.

gǎn MC kanX

1. arrow-shaft.

肝 gān MC kan

1. the liver.
   a. euph. for inner feelings, e.g. ～膽 gāndǎn, liver and gall-bladder, euph. for intrepid spirit, daring and gall.

gǎn

感 gǎn MC komX

1. to move (emotionally), rouse, stir; affect, influence, induce; attract(ion); e.g. ～應 gǎnyìng, stimulus and response; spiritual resonance; also, sympathetic response (see 2 below), esp. to spiritual stimulus.
   a. feel, respond to, react(ion), be moved by, moved to.
2. be sensible of, sympathetic toward; feel empathy for, empathetic; e.g. ～會 gǎnhuì, sympathetic communion; ～通 gǎntōng, sensible of spiritual emanations that penetrate the earthly realm or that allow one to communicate with higher realms.
3. deep feelings, heart-felt; e.g. ～慨 gǎnkǎi, deep-felt melancholy.
4. feel grateful, indebted to; gratitude.

hàn MC homX

1. ⊙ 撼 hàn, shake, move (physically); 憾 hàn, resent(ful), dissatisfied.

敢 gǎn MC kamX

1. dare, venture to; presume to, make bold to, beg leave to.
   a. be able to, capable of.

2. as rhetorical question: how could I dare to . . .? i.e. surely I cannot venture to . . .
3. daring, intrepid(ity), courage.

橄 gǎn MC kamX

1. (med.) (bn.) ～欖 gǎnlǎn (MC kamX-lamX), Chinese olive, canarium (*Canarium album*), not related to the Western olive (*Oleaceae*).

奸 gǎn MC kanX

1. livid, discolored; esp. pigmented mark on skin, lentigo.

礆 gǎn MC komX

1. (med.) stone coffer in which the emperor's jade tablets presented at the *feng* 封 and *shan* 禪 ceremonies are placed.

秆 gǎn MC kanX ⊙ 稈 gǎn.

稈 gǎn MC kanX

1. stalk of grain.
   a. stubble.
   b. straw, thatch.

笴 gǎn MC kanX

1. arrow-shaft.

簳 gǎn MC kanX

1. a small bamboo, prob. similar to 箭 jiàn, fountain-bamboo (*Fargesia nitida*).
2. culm, stalk, stem.
3. arrow-shaft.

趕 gǎn MC kanX

1. (med.) chase, pursue.
   a. (med.) catch up to, overtake.
2. (med.) chase off, drive out; oust, expel.

鱤 gǎn MC komX

1. the yellowcheek (*Elopichthys bambusa*), syn. 鰥 guān.

gàn

幹 gàn MC kanH

1. trunk of a tree, bole.
   a. trunk of a (human) body.
2. main supporting structure, framework.
3. capacity, ability.
4. manage, handle; bring under control.

5. commonly miswritten form of 斡 *wò* 2, suspension-ring of chime-bell.

旰　gàn　MC kanH

1. the declining sun; dusk, early evening.

斡　gàn　MC kanH

1. wooden boards used as longitudinal supports in the process of building a rammed-earth wall; buttress.
   a. to buttress, bolster, support.
2. trunk of a tree, ⊙ 幹 *gàn* 1.
   a. base, supporting or underlying element.
3. railing around a well; wellhead.
4. silkworm-thorn, cudrania (*Cudrania tricuspidata*), syn. 柘 *zhè*.

紺　gàn　MC komH

1. deep purplish-blue, ranging from dark magenta (more red-tinged) to deep ruby (purplish-brown) to damson (darker purplish-black).
2. (Budd.) ～園 *gànyuán*, magenta garden, ～宇 *gànyǔ*, magenta precincts, both ref. Budd. monastery.

gāng

亢　gāng　MC kang

1. gullet, throat, pharynx, esophagus.
2. "Gullet," one of the 28 lunar lodgings, comprised of ι, κ, λ, μ Virginis, in the eastern quadrant (*canglong* 蒼龍) of the sky.

kàng　MC khangH

1. high, haughty; overbearing; lift(ed) high.
   a. inflexible, intractable.
2. excessive; exaggerated.
3. resist, withstand; oppose.
   a. protect; shelter.

剛　gāng　MC kang

1. rigid, unyielding, unbending, inflexible; adamant(ine); firm, strong.
2. (med.) steel.
3. (med.) just at that point, just at that time; just now.
4. ⊙ 犅 *gāng*, bull.

岡　gāng　MC kang

1. ridge or spine of a hill.
   a. by synecdoche, a hill.

崗　gāng　MC kang

1. (med.) ⊙ 岡 *gāng*, ridge or spine of a hill.

扛　gāng　MC kaewng

1. lug, lift or carry a heavy object with both hands.

杠　gāng　MC kaewng

1. transverse board at front of a couch or bench.
2. flagpole; pole of carriage's canopy.
3. single-plank bridge.

犅　gāng　MC kang

1. a bull; male ox.

綱　gāng　MC kang

1. headrope, guiderope, mainstay, major cord of a net to which all other strings are attached; cable, cord(age); e.g. 帆～ *fàn'gāng*, yard, long spar to support and spread a sail or lateen; ～紀 *gāngjì*, mainstay and strands, cables and skeins > network, nexus, organization, ordering principles, bring order and support to; ～維 *gāngwéi*, stays and braces, similar to preceding.
   a. euph. for guiding principle, central element that gives structure or organization to the rest; e.g. 三～ *sān'gāng*, 3 mainstays, the 3 most important social relationships (i.e. ruler/subject, father/son, husband/wife).
2. orb, circular or curving path of celestial transit.
3. bind, tie together.
4. (med.) convoy of merchant vessels.

缸　gāng　MC haewng

1. long-necked earthenware jar, amphora.
   a. pitcher, ewer; vase.
2. (med.) oil-lamp.

罡　gāng　MC kang

1. sgl. or 天～ *tiān'gāng*, the (3 stars of the) handle of the Northern Dipper.
   a. by synecdoche, the Dipper itself.
2. ⊙ 岡 *gāng*, ridge or spine of a hill.

肛　gāng　MC kaewng

1. anus, asshole.

釭　gāng　MC kaewng

1. axle-cap, hollow outer bearing of bronze at juncture of carriage's wheel and axle, around which the hub projects; ⊙ 軑 *dài*.

a. anything of similar hub-like shape, such as gilded wood-disc projecting as ornament from a wall; englobed.

2. (med.) oil-lamp.

gǎng

港 **gǎng** **MC kaewngX**

1. (med.) coomb, narrow valley or hollow; e.g. ～洞 *gǎngdòng*, coomb and cavern.

a. (med.) narrow estuary, inlet; channel.

2. only from late Tang times, anchorage, (usu.) shallow harbor.

hòng **MC huwngH**

1. (bn.) ～洞 *hòngdòng* (MC huwngH-duwngH), closely connected, adjacently joined.

gāo

槹 **gāo** **MC kaw**

1. sgl. or (bn.) 桔～ *jiégāo* (MC ket-kaw), well-sweep, shadoof, counterbalanced bailing-bucket to draw up water.

皋 **gāo** **MC kaw**

1. high bank at waterside; embank(ment).

2. depressed wetland surrounded by embankments; marsh, bog, swamp; pool.

a. paddy, for rice-growing.

3. extended cry or call; long-drawn sound.

a. announce, call out.

4. alt. name for 5th lunar month.

5. ～比 *gāobǐ*, tigerskin.

6. ～陶 *gāoyáo*, name of reputed minister of punishments under legendary sage-king Shun 舜.

7. ☉ 高 *gāo* 1, tall, high, elevated.

皐 **gāo** **MC kaw** ☉ 皋 *gāo*.

篙 **gāo** **MC kaw**

1. bamboo-pole for propelling a small boat by pushing against the riverbed below, boat-pole; to punt, pole.

羔 **gāo** **MC kaw**

1. eanling, lambkin; kid (somewhat older).

膏 **gāo** **MC kaw**

1. fat(ty), greasy (softer and more oily than 脂 *zhī*); e.g. ～環 *gāohuán*, greasy ring-cake.

2. unguent, ointment; embrocation.

3. fatty tissue at tip of the heart; e.g. ～肓 *gāo-huāng*, region situated just below the tip of the heart and the diaphragm, a reservoir of vitality.

4. fecund, fertile.

gào **MC kawH**

1. (be)smear, spread, coat; grease, oil up.

a. moisten; saturate.

高 **gāo** **MC kaw**

1. tall; high, lofty; elevated.

a. above the common run or normal concerns, e.g. ～居 *gāojū*, lodge on high, above it all.

2. lofty in character or reputation; eminent, exalted; high-minded.

a. esteem, exalt, hold in high regard.

3. loud to the ear; e.g. ～聲 *gāoshēng*, loud-voiced, loud-sounding.

4. elevated in age, older.

5. ～粱 *gāoliáng*, sorghum (*Sorghum vulgare*), grain alternative to wheat; ～粱姜 *gāoliáng-jiāng*, "gaoliang ginger," i.e. galangal (*Alpinia galanga, A. officinarum*), the root dried and used medicinally and as seasoning in cooking.

6. ～麗 *gāolì* or ～句麗 *gāogōulì* (MC kaw-[kuw-]lejH), Koguryǒ, kingdom controlling northern and central areas of Korea as well as part of southern Manchuria from ca. 1st-c. BCE to 668 CE at which time defeated by rival kingdom of Silla (Xinluo 新羅); (med.) ～昌 *gāochāng*, Qočo, Karakhoja, oasis city on the northern Silk Road in the Tarim Basin, also called Xizhou 西州 in Tang times.

gǎo

暠 **gǎo** **MC kawX**

1. rdup., gleaming aglitter, glint and glitter.

hào **MC hawX**

1. pure-white, gleaming white.

杲 **gǎo** **MC kawX**

1. sgl. or rdup., glimmer, glint, break into light like the just-rising sun; brightening.

2. ascend in the distance.

槀 **gǎo** **MC kawX** ☉ 槁 *gǎo*.

槁 **gǎo** **MC khawX**

1. dried-out wood; withered; desiccated.

2. lifeless, defunct; rotten.

3. rap; strike, knock against.

稾 gǎo　MC kawX　⊙ 稿 *gǎo*.

稿 gǎo　MC kawX
1. culm of cereal grains; stem, stalk.
  a. esp. stalk of arrow-bamboo (箭 *jiàn*, *Fargesia nitida*).
  b. ～人 *gǎorén*, by verbal connection with preceding, "arrow-man," i.e. archer.
2. draft, of writing; preliminary form, sketch.

縞 gǎo　MC kawX
1. undyed close-textured silk.
2. plain-white.

藁 gǎo　MC kawX　⊙ 稿 *gǎo*.

gào

告 gào　MC kawH, kowk
1. announce, proclaim, send word to; esp. superior to inferior.
  a. report, inform; esp. inferior to superior.
  b. ～身 *gàoshēn*, certificate of credentials.
2. exhort, encourage, urge on.
3. request, entreat, beseech.
4. accuse, lodge an accusation (legal), denounce.
5. short vacation, leave, for an official; take leave.
  a. resign from official position.
6. accuse of crime.

誥 gào　MC kawH
1. proclaim, proclamation; announce(ment); from med. times exclusively superior to inferior.
  a. royal proclamation conferring noble title or special recognition; entitlement.
  b. (med.) announcement from retired emperor.
2. exhortation; advisory instruction to subordinate, monition.
3. oracle, announcement from a divinity.

gē

割 gē　MC kat
1. cut with a knife; sever, carve; cut apart.
  a. cut up, carve up, divide, apportion (esp. territory).

哥 gē　MC ka
1. (med.) elder brother, informal syn. of 兄 *xiōng*.

戈 gē　MC kwa
1. glaive, pole-ax, bill, dagger-ax; pike with crescent-blade attached near the top.

擱 gē　MC kak
1. (med.) to place (on), set on.

歌 gē　MC ka
1. sing; carol; trill.
  a. cry out, call out.
  b. sing the praises of, laud, extol.
2. song, words set to music.

胳 gē　MC kak
1. armpit.
  gé　MC kaek
1. hindleg; haunch (of animal).

袼 gē　MC kak
1. armpit-seam of clothing; sleeve-hole, armhole.

鴿 gē　MC kop
1. pigeon (*Columba*, various species).
2. "dove-hawk," nestling hawk.

gé

愅 gé　MC keak
1. change, alter.
  a. (bn.) ～詭 *géguǐ* (MC keak-kjweX), modify and remold, adapt and recast.

格 gé　MC kaek
1. frame(work), structure, scaffold(ing).
  a. layout, configuration; e.g. 窗～ *chuānggé*, latticework grid of window.
  b. conceptual grid, coordinated framework for understanding.
  c. well-framed; coordinated, organized; e.g. 有恥且～ *yǒuchǐ qiě gé*, have a sense of shame and be properly adjusted (to moral principles).
2. established custom or law, precedent, protocol; e.g. ～儀 *géyí*, protocol and formalities; 無～ *wúgé*, unprecedented, unparalleled.
  a. (med.) legal regulations concerned with general matters (cf. 式 *shì*, ordinances, administrative rules that were part of the legal code and concerned with limited areas of law).
3. bring to (proper) pattern, systematize; frame, put together, coordinate.

a. (med.) (lit.) formal pattern or structure of a composition; also, style, general character and manner deriving from author's disposition.
4. cabinet, chest; shelving.
5. grapple with, fight barehanded.
　　a. oppose, withstand; block(age).
6. deal with, come to grips with, come to terms with.
7. arrive at, reach, come upon.
8. target for archery; butt.
9. long tree-branch, bough.
10. (med.) railing, balustrade.
11. (med.) 〜是 *géshì*, ⊙ 隔是 *géshì*, it being the case that . . ., now it is that . . ., already.

榓　gé　MC keak
1. yoke of a large cart or wain.
　　hé　MC heak
1. ⊙ 核 *hé*, stone of a drupe.

膈　gé　MC keak
1. the diaphragm.
2. stand or framework from which chime-bells are suspended.

葛　gé　MC kat
1. kudzu, bean-creeper (*Pueraria thunbergiana*, *P. lobata*), climbing vine whose fibers were used for making cloth; the root is arrowroot, used as starch; e.g. 〜巾 *géjīn*, headwrap made of kudzu-cloth; 〜藤 *géténg*, kudzu and wisteria, climbing vines > entanglements, complications.
　　a. 野〜 *yěgé*, "wild kudzu," gelsemium root (*Gelsemium elegans*), extremely toxic.
2. (med.) 〜羅祿 *géluólù* (MC kat-la-luwk), Qarluq, usu. ref. to as the "3 Qarluq," group of Turkic tribes in the Altai Mountain area, first subordinated to Tang rule in 657.

蛤　gé　MC kop
1. shellfish; term for clams, cockles, mussels, etc.; e.g. 〜蜊 *gélì*, trough-shell, duck-clam, bivalve mollusk (*Mactridae*, various species).
2. (med.) (bn.) 〜蚧 *géjiè* (MC kop-keajH), gecko (*Gekko gecko*).
　　há　MC hae
1. sgl. or (bn.) 〜蟆 *hámá* (MC hae-mae) frog.

觡　gé　MC kaek
1. mature antler of deer, without down or velvet.

閣　gé　MC kak
1. raised passageway between buildings; gallery.
　　a. plankbridge attached to flank of mountain, edgeway, railing; similar to → 棧 *zhàn*.
2. balcony, projecting from wall of a building and usu. surrounded by a railing; a gallery.
　　a. pavilion with balcony or gallery.
3. room or building for storing books or other valuable (esp. religious) items; gallery.
　　a. cabinet, cupboard; chest.
4. sideboard, for placing food and utensils for service.
　　a. pantry.
5. (med.) to place (on), set on.
6. (med.) 〜老 *gélǎo*, "veteran in office," informal Tang designation for long-serving drafter (舍人 *shèrén*) in Imperial Secretariat (中書省) or Chancellery (門下省).
7. ⊙ 閤 *gé* 1, postern, secondary or side-gate; 2, apartment, private quarters; 3, office, for government business.

閤　gé　MC kop
1. postern, secondary or side-gate.
2. apartment, private living quarters.
3. office, for government business.
4. (med.) rdup., onom. of frog's croaking.

隔　gé　MC keak
1. separate, divide, partition, cut off, sever.
　　a. separated from, cut off by; isolated; insulated from; e.g. 〜生 *géshēng*, 〜命 *géming*, cut off from the living (from life), the quick and the dead are separated.
　　b. part from; be at a distance from.
2. interjacent, adjacent.
3. discordant; differ(ent), diverge(nt), deviate; e.g. 〜并 *gébing*, unbalanced *yin* and *yang*.
4. ⊙ 膈 *gé*, the diaphragm.
5. (med.) grid-like pattern; esp. latticework grid of window.
6. (med.) 〜是 *géshì*, ⊙ 格是 *géshì*, it being the case that . . ., now it is that . . ., already.

革　gé　MC keak
1. depilated animal hide; when tanned, leather.
　　a. animal hide, skin.
2. human skin.
3. leather armor, cuirasse.

a. metonomy for implements of warfare; e.g. ～車 *géchē*, war chariot; 兵～ *bīnggé*, weapons and armor > warfare.

b. to skin, fleece, strip off, flay; remove; deprive of, divest, e.g. ～命 *géming*, remove the mandate from, revolt, rebel(lion).

c. molt; change, modify; denature.

4. musical instruments made from leather or hide, esp. drums.

5. "Recast," name of 49th hexagram of *Yijing*.

jí　MC kik

1. urgent, in haste; hurried, quick.

a. severe(ly).

鞈　gé　MC kop

1. cuirasse, leather chest-armor; ⊙ 革 *gé* 3.

2. sturdy, hard; inflexible.

tà　MC thop

1. ⊙ 鞳 *tà*, onom. of rapid drum-sound, drum-roll.

骼　gé　MC kaek

1. bones of birds or beasts.

a. gen. term for bones, skeleton.

2. ⊙ 胳 *gé* (*gē*), hindleg; haunch.

鬲　gé　MC keak　→ 鬲 *lì*.

gě

哿　gě　MC kaX

1. acceptable, agreeable; desirable.

舸　gě　MC kaX

1. large boat; barge.

gè

个　gè　MC kaH

1. ⊙ 個 *gè* 1, individual, single, just one; item, piece.

2. side-rooms of main hall.

個　gè　MC kaH

1. individual, single, just one.

a. item, piece.

b. rdup., every one (of), each and every.

2. (med.) demonstrative pronoun: this, that; e.g. ～人 *gèrén*, this (or that) person; ～時 *gèshí*, (at) this time; ～中 *gèzhōng*, here, in this place.

各　gè　MC kak

1. VB-phrase modifier indicating the distribution or scope of the meaning of the VB-phrase relative to the stated or implied topic, "each case, each instance, each one"; akin to 或 *huò*, 莫 *mò*, 孰 *shú*; often translatable as "each; each one"; e.g. ～言其志 *gè yán qí zhì*, in each case state one's inclinations; ～欲正己 *gè yù zhèng jǐ*, in each case they wish to correct themselves; 物～從其類 *wù gè cóng qí lèi*, creatures each follow their own kind.

a. rdup., each and every.

箇　gè　MC kaH　⊙ 個 *gè*.

gēn

根　gēn　MC kon

1. root; trunk; foundation, base, basis; basic, fundamental; e.g. (Dao.) 復～ *fùgēn*, return to the root, revert to original uncorrupted state of being; (Dao.) 靈～ *línggēn*, numinous root, esoteric name for the tongue.

2. root out, eradicate, completely remove.

3. (Budd.) sense-organ, sense-faculty.

跟　gēn　MC kon

1. heel.

2. (med.) follow; e.g. ～武 *gēnwǔ*, tread on the heels of, in the tracks of, heel-to-toe.

gèn

亙　gèn　MC kongH

1. from head to tail, all the way through, go through; e.g. ～古 *gèngǔ*, ～代 *gèndài*, straight through from distant ages, for all time.

a. complete(ly), thorough(ly); continuous, connected.

b. everywhere, all over; e.g. ～天 *gèntiān*, the whole sky, throughout the heavens.

2. draw out, lead; extend.

3. cross over, run crosswise.

xuān　MC sjwen

1. whirlpool, vortex.

a. gyre; revolve.

2. ⊙ 宣 *xuān* 1, spread, diffuse; 2, exhibit, display, show openly.

亙 gèn MC kongH ⊙ 亙 *gèn*.

艮 gèn MC konH
1. one of the 8 fundamental trigrams underlying the *Yijing*'s 64 hexagrams, made up of 2 broken lines topped by an unbroken line.
   a. "Keeping Still," name of 52nd hexagram of *Yijing*.
2. unstirring, still; in repose; stay, stop.
   a. resist(ant), immovable.
3. the direction northeast.
4. (med.) ref. 2nd double-hour of the day, approx. 1 a.m. to 3 a.m.

gēng

庚 gēng MC kaeng
1. 7th of the 10 heavenly stems.
2. inferior, below average; e.g. ～癸 *gēngguǐ*, (7th and 10th heavenly stems >) lower-end goods, inferior items.
3. road, path, route (archaic usage).

更 gēng MC kaeng
1. change, alter, amend.
   a. improve, better.
2. replace, take the place of, supplant; take one's turn, in turn, alternate(ly), successive(ly).
   a. compensate, make amends; make good on; requite; e.g. ～賦 *gēngfù*, scutage tax, paid in lieu of army service.
3. experience, undergo; pass (a period of time); e.g. ～歷 *gēnglì*, experiences, happenings; ～漏 *gēnglòu*, pass the markings of the clepsydra, passage of time; also, hours of the night (see next).
4. night-watches, 5 double-hours extending from approx. 7 p.m. to 5 a.m.; e.g. ～號 *gēnghào*, call out the night-watches.
5. (Budd.) contacts, of the sense-organs with their objects.
   gèng MC kaengH
1. (ADV) again, (once) more; additional(ly); e.g. ～復 *gèngfù*, once again.
   a. connective indicating narrative succession: next, and then.
   b. further; furthermore.
   c. (an)other; e.g. ～何人 *gènghérén*, what other person? who else?; (med.) ～諸 *gèngzhū*, all the rest.
2. increase, add to.

秔 gēng MC kaeng ⊙ 粳 *gēng*.

粳 gēng MC kaeng
1. round-grained non-glutinous rice, unsuitable for wine-making.

絚 gēng MC kong ⊙ 緪 *gēng*.

緪 gēng MC kong
1. roughly twisted cord.
   a. large rope, cable.
2. tied up, "strung out," wrought up; tense, strained.
   gèn MC kongH
1. ⊙ 亙 *gèn* 1, from first to last, completely, thorough(ly).

羮 gēng MC kaeng
1. stew, with meat and vegetables; ragout.
2. (med.) soup, broth.

耕 gēng MC keang
1. to till, plow.
   a. (engage in) farmwork.
2. "till the field" of whatever work one pursues, ply one's trade.

賡 gēng MC kaeng
1. continue, succeed.
2. match with, complement.
   a. recompense, pay back.

鶊 gēng MC kaeng
1. (bn.) 鶬～ *cānggēng*, → 鶬 *cāng*.

gěng

哽 gěng MC kaengX
1. choke, gag; stifle.
2. block(age), obstruct(ion).

梗 gěng MC kaengX
1. thorn, spike, spine.
   a. sgl. or ～榆 *gěngyú*, thorn-elm, prickly-elm (*Hemiptelea davidii*); syn. 樞 *ōu* (*shū*), 刺榆 *cìyú*.
2. leaf-stalk, petiole; pedicel.
3. obstacle, obstruct(ion).
   a. distress; difficulty.

4. firm, unbending, inflexible, unwavering.
5. (bn.) 〜概 *gěnggài* (MC kaengX-kojH), roughly speaking, in rough outline, in general.

綆　gěng　MC kaengX
1. well-rope.

耿　gěng　MC keangX
1. gleaming; glowing, flaring.
2. steadiness of character; integrity; e.g. 〜介 *gěngjiè*, unbending integrity, unwavering integrity.
3. rdup., fitful and restless, aflit and aflimmer, of glimmering lights or of uneasy thoughts; also, "I am concerned (uneasy) about you," formulaic phrase in personal letters; also, steady integrity, resolute integrity.

鯁　gěng　MC kaengX
1. fish-bones.
2. fish-bones or other items stuck in one's throat; blockage, obstacle.
3. poke, pierce; harm.
　a. difficulty; calamity.
4. inflexible, intransigent, unyielding.
　a. ubending; straightforward.
5. ⊙ 哽 *gěng* 1, choke, gag; stifle.

gèng

魥　gèng　MC kongH
1. (bn.) 〜鱴 *gèngmèng* (MC kongH-mongH), beaked sturgeon, paddlefish, syn. 鱘 *xún*.

gōng

供　gōng　MC kjowng
1. provide for, furnish, supply.
　a. be hospitable, supportive, accommodating; e.g. 〜侍 *gōngshì*, provide for and attend to, treat hospitably.
2. ⊙ 恭 *gōng*, respect, revere(nce); do honor to.
　gòng　MC kjowngH
1. offer in deference or devotion; donate, contribute; e.g. 〜上 *gòngshàng*, offer to one's superior; (Budd.) 〜養 *gòngyǎng*, devotional offering.
2. arrange, dispose properly, set out.
　a. provisions, food or goods arranged for use.
3. discharge responsibilities; e.g. 〜職 *gòngzhí*, carry out official duties.

公　gōng　MC kuwng
1. impartial, just, fair, equitable, even-handed.
2. common, public.
　a. public-spirited.
　b. the public good, commonweal.
　c. communal; mutual; joint; altogether.
　d. make public, do publicly.
3. 1st of the 5 ranks of nobility, usu. translated "duke."
4. honorific term of address or ref.: Your Lordship, His Lordship, Excellency.
　a. high dignitary; e.g. 〜卿 *gōngqīng*, dignitaries and high officials; 三〜 *sāngōng*, 3 Dukes or 3 Dignitaries, highest ranks of official status usu. for persons of great prestige, most often designating *taishi* 太師, *taifu* 太傅, and *taibao* 太保.
5. male of quadrupeds.

功　gōng　MC kuwng
1. work, occupation; labor.
2. achievement, accomplishment; e.g. 〜業 *gōngyè*, legacy of achievement.
　a. feat, exploit; honorable service, merit(orious); e.g. 立〜 *lìgōng*, establish meritorious exploits (for the good of the state).
　b. (Budd.) merit-producing deeds (producing good karma); e.g. 〜德 *gōngdé*, pious works, meritorious actions; 〜報 *gōngbào*, result of meritorious acts; 〜課 *gōngkè*, meritorious devotions (daily chanting of scriptures, honoring the Buddha, etc.).
3. deserving, commendable, creditable; providing a claim to (status, achievement, etc.).
4. excellence, distinction, merit; efficacy.
5. levels of distinction for mourning rites; e.g. 大〜 *dàgōng*, 9 months' mourning; 小〜 *xiǎogōng*, 5 months' mourning.

宮　gōng　MC kjuwng
1. dwelling-place, habitation; esp. in cmpd. 〜室 *gōngshì*, houses and habitations.
2. dwelling-place of ruler; palace.
　a. palace compound, incl. all buildings residential, ceremonial, or for pleasure.
　b. gen. term for the court, incl. present officials, servitors, and servants.
3. ancestral shrine.
　a. shrine or temple of a divinity.
　b. main temple or temple complex of Budd. monastery or Dao. abbey.

4. name of one of the notes of the pentatonic scale, the 1st or lead note, symbolically associated with the "earth" phase of the *wuxing* 五行, the middle, color yellow, etc.

工   gōng   MC kuwng

1. work, labor; public works.
   a. workman, laborer.
2. workmanship, craft, skill, artistry, expertise; well-crafted, skillful.
   a. artisan, craftsman; expert (in).
   b. weaving, embroidery, women's fine work.
3. operate, manipulate.

弓   gōng   MC kjuwng

1. bow; e.g. ~矢 *gōngshǐ*, bow and arrow.
   a. sgl. or ~人 *gōngrén*, bowman, archer.
2. bow-shaped; arc, crescent; curved.

恭   gōng   MC kjowng

1. respect, revere(nce); mainly ref. externally evinced display (cf. 敬 *jìng*, internally held sentiments).
   a. esteem; show regard, do honor to.

攻   gōng   MC kuwng

1. attack, assail, set upon.
2. assail verbally, revile, rail against; impugn; discredit.
3. attack medicinally; attend to, minister to; alleviate; remedy.
4. work at, ply; apply oneself to, delve into, occupy oneself with.
5. craftsmanship, workmanship, expertise; ⊙ 工 *gōng* 2.
6. governmental exaction, impost.
7. well-built, sturdy, strong.

肱   gōng   MC kwong

1. arm, esp. upper arm; brachial.
   a. support, hold up; e.g. 股~ *gǔgōng*, thighs and upper-arms > arms and legs > supporting members > ministers of a ruler.

蚣   gōng   MC kuwng

1. 蜈~ *wúgōng*, centipede, scolopendrid (*Scolopendra morsitans*).

觥   gōng   MC kwaeng

1. elongated covered-pitcher of zoomorphic form, for offerings of wine.

2. rdup., dauntless and indomitable, steady and resolute, stalwart and steadfast.

觵   gōng   MC kwaeng   ⊙ 觥 *gōng*.

躬   gōng   MC kjuwng

1. human body, esp. torso.
2. one's (own) person, oneself; personally, in person.
3. ⊙ 窮   *qióng* 1, come to the end of, use up completely, consume utterly.

軀   gōng   MC kjuwng   ⊙ 躬 *gōng*.

龔   gōng   MC kjowng

1. provide for, furnish, supply; ⊙ 供 *gōng* 1.
2. respect, revere(nce), do honor to; ⊙ 恭 *gōng*.
3. a surname.

gǒng

拱   gǒng   MC kjowngX

1. fold the hands at breast level, in quiet or respectful manner; e.g. ~垂 *gǒngchuí*, with folded hands and hanging robes, the manner in which a sage-king rules without overt action.
   a. salute with joined hands and bowing.
2. arm-spanning, the space enclosed by arms with hands joined; e.g. ~木 *gǒngmù*, arm-spanning (i.e. large) trees, esp. ref. graveyard trees.
3. encircle, encompass; surround.
4. (med.) bump or push with the head.
5. ⊙ 栱 *gǒng*, bracket, bracket-arm, truss.

桊   gǒng   MC kjowngX

1. wooden manacles; put in manacles, as punishment.

栱   gǒng   MC kjowngX

1. bracket, bracket-arm, truss, in roof support; e.g. 令~ *lìnggǒng*, longitudinal bracket; 慢~ *màngǒng*, larger 2nd longitudinal bracket on top of 1st.

汞   gǒng   MC huwngX

1. quicksilver, mercury.
2. flowing round, eddying.

珙   gǒng   MC kjowngX

1. large ceremonial jade-disc.

蛬　*gǒng*　MC kjowngX

1. (med.) field-cricket; syn. 蟋蟀 *xīshuài*.

鞏　*gǒng*　MC kjowngX

1. bind with leather strips; truss.
2. secure, close up; solidify; consolidate.
3. ⊙ 恐 *kǒng* 1, fear(ful), afraid.

gòng

共　*gòng*　MC gjowngH

1. join, connect; cooperate, combine.
2. in common, together, jointly; united.
    a. inclusive; include.
    b. ～然 *gòngrán*, thus the same, equally so, share and share alike.
3. respect, revere(nce), do honor to; esp. in pre-Han texts, ⊙ 恭 *gōng*.

**　*gǒng*　MC kjowngX**

1. ⊙ 供 *gǒng* 1, provide for, furnish, supply; 拱 *gǒng* 1, fold the hands.

貢　*gòng*　MC kuwngH

1. offer as tribute.
    a. tribute item; e.g. (med.) 鄉～ *xiānggòng*, tribute from the parishes, sent up to court as new year's offering, incl. local goods and also candidates to sit for civil-service exam.
2. commend, recommend to one's superiors; speak highly of.

贛　*gòng*　MC kuwngH

1. confer, bestow, impart; present; consign.
2. a surname.

**　*zhuàng*　MC traewngH**

1. naïve, credulous; guileless, innocent.

gōu

勾　*gōu*　MC kuw

1. hook, curve, bend, angle.
    a. curling frond; e.g. ～芒 *gōumáng*, curling fronds and spikelets, name of tutelary divinity of springtime.
    b. hook or barb of fishing-line.
2. caught, entangled, snagged.
    a. entice, seduce.
3. stay behind, linger.
4. (med.) forfeit or penalty of wine-drinking.
5. (med.) ～押 *gōuyā*, sign or endorse an official document.

**　*gòu*　MC kuwH**

1. ～當 *gòudāng*, handle, manage; conduct, transact.

句　*gōu*　MC kuw　→ 句 *jù*.

溝　*gōu*　MC kuw

1. ditch, canal.
    a. drain, gutter.
2. moat, fosse.

**　*kòu*　MC kuwH**

1. (bn.) ～瞀 *kòumào* (MC kuwH-muwH), dumb and dull-witted, simple and stupid.

簼　*gōu*　MC kuw

1. bamboo or wicker basket.
    a. censing-basket.
    b. lantern-basket.

緱　*gōu*　MC kuw

1. cord-wrap around hilt of sword.

鈎　*gōu*　MC kuw　⊙ 鉤 *gōu*.

鉤　*gōu*　MC kuw

1. hook, barb.
    a. gaff, grapnel.
    b. fish-hook; belt-hook; curtain-hook; bell-hook.
2. to hook, catch, snare; draw upward; entangle.
    a. lead on, seduce; entice.
3. curved, bent, crooked; hooked.
4. sickle, scythe.
5. drawing-compass.
6. curved wood-strip placed between the chassis and axletree of a carriage
7. siege-ladder, scaling-ladder.
8. restrain, restrict.
9. (med.) explore, probe, follow the curvings of.
10. (med.) (bn.) ～輈 *gōuzhōu* (MC kuw-tsyuw), onom. of chukar's cry.

韝　*gōu*　MC kuw　⊙ 韝 *gōu*.

韝　*gōu*　MC kuw

1. gauntlet, leather arm-guard to protect left arm in archery or either arm in falconry.

gǒu

枸　*gǒu*　MC kewX　→ 枸 *jǔ*.

狗　gǒu　MC kuwX

1. dog, esp. smaller dog (cf. 犬 *quán*, larger dog); cur; e.g. (med.) ～突 *gǒutū*, dog-door.
   a. hunting-dog, hound.

笱　gǒu　MC kuwX

1. fish-trap, trap-basket, made of bamboo.

耇　gǒu　MC kuwX　⊙ 耉 *gǒu*.

耉　gǒu　MC kuwX

1. sgl. or 胡～ *húgǒu*, long-lived, person of considerable age; wizened.

苟　gǒu　MC kuwX

1. meager, slight, minimal.
2. sgl. or ～且 *gǒuqiě*, with scant attention to, not in the least concerned; careless, haphazard; frivolous(ly), casual(ly); make do.
3. marks conditional clause where the specified condition is not just a minimal condition, but typically the only thing of consequence: if, irrespective of anything else; if only, if at all; ～志於仁矣，無惡也 *gǒu zhì yú rén yǐ, wú è yě*, if, irrespective of anything else, one's inclination were set on humaneness, there would be no ugliness; ～為後義而先利 *gǒu wéi hòuyì ér xiānlì*, if, apart from anything else, you relegate propriety to a second place, and instead give precedence to profit; ～行王政，四海之內皆舉首而望之 *gǒu xíng wángzhèng, sìhǎi zhī nèi jiē jǔshǒu ér wàng zhī*, if, apart from anything else, he would enact a royal government, within the four seas people in all cases would lift up their heads to look at him.
4. ～杞 *gǒuqǐ*, wolfberry, boxtree, boxthorn (*Lycium chinense, Lycium barbarum*).

gòu

冓　gòu　MC kuwH

1. structure or carpentry of building; e.g. 中～ *zhōnggòu*, interior room, private chamber, alcove.

垢　gòu　MC kuwX

1. dirt(y), filth(y); waste deposit; silt; e.g. 塵～ *chén'gòu*, dust and dirt; 耳～ *ěrgòu*, cerumen.
   a. foul, unclean, vile; impure; e.g. ～污 *gòuwū*, foul and stained.
   b. nasty; base, of low quality.
2. defile; disgrace; humiliate.

夠　gòu　MC kuwH

1. many, much, great quantity, abundant.
2. (med.) enough, sufficient.

姤　gòu　MC kuwH

1. come across, meet with, encounter; ⊙ 遘 *gòu* 1.
   a. "Meeting," name of 44th hexagram of *Yijing*.
2. join with; esp. sexually, copulate.
   a. salacious.
3. ugliness, ill-favored; evil; e.g. ～嫭 *gòuhù*, ugliness and beauty, evil and goodness.

媾　gòu　MC kuwH

1. remarry.
   a. gen. term for marriage, joining 2 families.
2. agree on pact, covenant, contract.
3. conciliate, reconcile; bring together.
4. join sexually, copulate; salacious; ⊙ 姤 *gòu* 2.
5. treat with special favor, indulge(nce).

彀　gòu　MC kuwH

1. draw a bow to the full.
   a. sgl. or ～中 *gòuzhōng*, bow-range; e.g. 入～中 *rù gòuzhōng*, pass into range of one's bow, come under the power of.
   b. shoot with bow, let fly (arrow).

搆　gòu　MC kuwH

1. ⊙ 構 *gòu*, all meanings.
2. ⊙ 媾 *gòu* 4, join sexually.

構　gòu　MC kuwH

1. to frame, construct, build, join pieces together, assemble (building, roof; also, plan, composition).
   a. framework; building, structure, edifice; joinery.
2. create, form(ation); complete, conclude.
3. join, link up, unite; couple.
4. plan, scheme, plot.
5. drive a wedge between, sow discord; provoke.

覯　gòu　MC kuwH

1. see by chance; come upon; discover.
   a. unforeseen, unexpected, unmet, unanticipated.
2. behold, descry; take notice of.
3. ⊙ 構 *gòu* 2, create, form; complete, conclude.

詢　gòu　MC xuwH

1. revile(d), execrate, imprecate.
2. humiliate(d), disgrace(d).

詬　gòu　MC xuwH　⊙ 詢 *gòu*.

購　gòu　MC kuwH

1. put a price on, offer a reward for, set a bounty.
   a. reward, award, bestow(al).
2. ⊙ 媾 *gòu* 3, conciliate, reconcile.

遘　gòu　MC kuwH

1. come across, meet with, encounter.
2. ⊙ 構 *gòu* 2, create, form; complete, conclude.

雊　gòu　MC kuwH

1. onom. of a pheasant's cry.

gū

姑　gū　MC ku

1. father's sister, paternal aunt.
2. husband's mother, wife's mother-in-law.
   a. husband's sister, wife's sister-in-law.
3. gen. term for young woman; damsel, maid(en).
4. gen. term for wife or adult woman; dame.
5. (ADV) meanwhile, for the moment, for the time being.
6. (med.) tolerant, easy-going; e.g. 〜息 *gūxī*, casual, laid-back.
7. 〜獲 *gūhuò*, nightjar (various species of *Caprimulgis*).

孤　gū　MC ku

1. fatherless at an early age; orphan.
2. alone, solitary, lone(ly).
   a. unaffiliated, unattached; disengaged.
   b. unique; aloof.
3. humilific self-ref. for ruler, "I, the solitary one."
4. unworthy, undeserving.

沽　gū　MC ku

1. sell, vend, esp. liquor.
   a. buy, pay for.
2. angle for; advertise; e.g. 〜名 *gūmíng*, advertise one's notoriety.

　gǔ　MC kuX

1. wine-vender.
2. roughly, generally, approximate(ly).

箛　gū　MC ku

1. reed-pipe, sideblown single-reed flute of Central Asian origin; syn. 笳 *jiā*.
2. unidentified species of bamboo, reputedly used in making whips for imperial chariots.

罛　gū　MC ku

1. fish-net, seine, dragnet, purse-net.

苽　gū　MC ku

1. ⊙ 菰 *gū*, wild rice, water-bamboo (*Zizania latifolia*).

　guā　MC kwae

1. ⊙ 瓜 *guā*, melon, gourd.

菇　gū　MC ku

1. mushroom.

菰　gū　MC ku

1. wild rice, water-bamboo (*Zizania latifolia*); syn. 蔣 *jiāng*.

蛄　gū　MC ku

1. sgl. or 螻 〜 *lóugū*, mole-cricket (*Gryllotalpa orientalis*), omnivorous pest, esp. damaging to crop-roots, emerges from its burrows at night and can fly.
2. (bn.) 蟪 〜 *huìgū*, → 蟪 *huì*.

觚　gū　MC ku

1. tall beaker, for offerings of wine; drinking-horn.
2. angular.
3. sword-grip.
4. wooden writing-tablet.

辜　gū　MC ku

1. crime, offense; guilt; e.g. 伏 〜 *fúgū*, admit guilt; 〜負 *gūfú*, beg pardon, excuse oneself.
2. dismemberment, as judicial punishment.
3. (med.) unworthy of, undeserving; unworthily, undeservedly.
4. ⊙ 故 *gù* 1, reason, cause, purpose of.

酤　gū　MC ku

1. wine that is fermented for only one night.
   a. gen. term for wine.
2. buy or sell wine.

鴣　gū　MC ku

1. (bn.) 鷓 〜 *zhègū*, → 鷓 *zhè*.

gǔ

估　gǔ　MC kuX

1. (med.) price, cost, value of goods.
    a. (med.) estimate, figure, esp. price of goods.
2. (med.) merchant, dealer.

古　gǔ　MC kuX

1. old, of old, in historical terms (ant. 今 *jīn*, modern); ancient, aged, of a past age, pristine, classical; antiquity.
    a. possessing the positive virtues of the past, olden, priscan; e.g. ～德 *gǔdé*, virtues (of the virtuous men) of olden times; also (Budd.), monk of deep-seated sanctity; (med.) (lit.) ～意 *gǔyì*, subgenre of *shi*-poetry seeking to embody "olden attitudes" or on an "olden motif," sometimes called ～風 *gǔfēng*, "olden airs" with suggestion of moral suasion traditionally imputed to the "Guofeng" 國風 section of *Shijing*.

嘏　gǔ　MC kaeX

1. good fortune, felicity; propitious, providential.
    a. sgl. or ～辭 *gǔcí*, "providential words," benediction; in ancient sacrifices, the message from spirits to worshippers, uttered by the invocator (*shi* 尸); also, usu. at end of bronze inscriptions, auspicious statement representing the words one hopes to hear from the ancestors in response to ritual sacrifice, uttered by the invocator.

扢　gǔ　MC kwot

1. wipe clean, wipe off; swipe.

qì　MC xj+t
1. excited, enthused, elated, worked-up.

榖　gǔ　MC kuwk

1. paper-mulberry tree (*Broussonetia papyrifera*), syn. 楮 *chǔ*.

汩　gǔ　MC kwot

1. dredge, deepen a waterway so it flows more easily in its channel.
2. to swamp, flood.
3. churn up, agitate, disturb.
4. quickly; soon.
5. rdup., run rapidly (water), flooding flow; also, onom. of rushing water, gush and gabble; also (med.), turning and tumbling, jounced and jostled; also (med.) grandly magnificent, at the highest level.

yù　MC hwit
1. race along, hurry, dash away.

hú　MC hwot
1. break out, burst out; gushing springwater.

淈　gǔ　MC kwot

1. stir up, agitate, churn up; e.g. ～泥 *gǔní*, stir up the mud.
2. plunge into, immerse oneself in.
3. rdup., spume and spurt, gush and gurgle (water); also, troubled and turbulent.

牯　gǔ　MC kuX

1. male water-buffalo, esp. neutered > bullock, steer.

鹽　gǔ　MC kuX

1. raw salt.
2. crude, unrefined; of poor quality, shoddy, inferior.
    a. infirm, shaky, unstable; fragile.
3. pause, cease.
4. drink, sip.

瞽　gǔ　MC kuX

1. eyeless, sightless, blind.
2. music-master, musician, because in ancient times often blind.

穀　gǔ　MC kuwk

1. gen. term for grains, cereals, also for common foodcrops; e.g. 六～ *liùgǔ*, the 6 grains, i.e. rice, glutinous millet, non-glutinous millet, foxtail millet, wheat, wild rice; 五～ *wǔgǔ*, the 5 crops, i.e. glutinous millet, non-glutinous millet, foxtail millet, barley or wheat, soybeans; 辟～ *bìgǔ*, abstention from cereals, part of dietetic regimen that sought to eliminate the harmful "worms" or "corpses" residing in the epigastrial region and the brain which bring about bodily decay.
2. nourishment; nurture, provide for.
3. euph. for official salary, emoluments.
    a. prosperity, plenty.
4. to live, be alive.
5. old Chu dialect word for nipple, teat.
6. ⊙ 榖 *gǔ*, paper-mulberry tree (*Broussonetia papyrifera*), syn. 楮 *chǔ*.

罟　gǔ　MC kuX

1. gen. term for net used to catch fish, birds, or small game.
   a. to net, catch, enmesh.

羖　gǔ　MC kuX

1. a black ram.

股　gǔ　MC kuX

1. thigh; e.g. ～弁 *gǔbiàn*, ～栗 *gǔlì*, ～戰 *gǔzhàn*, thighs trembling, greatly frightened.
   a. synecdoche for leg.
   b. support, brace; e.g. ～肱 *gǔgōng*, thighs and upper-arms > arms and legs > supporting members > ministers of a ruler.
2. inner part of a wheel-spoke that joins the hub.
3. extended L-shaped suspension rack for bell-chimes.
4. section, part, portion; band, group(ing).

蠱　gǔ　MC kuX

1. poison concentrated from the venom of various insects and reptiles, usu. associated with the south.
2. black magic, sorcery used for harmful intent, usu. with goal of practitioner's illegitimate personal benefit, often controlled by shamans (*wu* 巫).
   a. noxious influence or harassment, bring or call evil down upon.
3. daze, entrance; derange, stupefy; disorient.
4. "Harm to be Allayed," name of 18th hexagram of *Yijing*.
5. flying insect produced from stale grain, unidentified.

詁　gǔ　MC kuX

1. explicate a text by glossing difficult words; paraphrase in current language.

谷　gǔ　MC kuwk

1. valley, vale; e.g. ～風 *gǔfēng*, valley wind, also ref. east wind; (Dao.) ～神 *gǔshén*, valley spirit, epithet for the Dao 道.
   a. glen, slade, dale.
2. chasm, cave.
3. impasse; dead-end, cul-de-sac.
4. ⊙ 穀 *gǔ* 1, gen. term for grains.

yù　MC yowk

1. 吐～渾 *tùyùhún*, the Tuyuhun peoples, a semi-nomadic branch of the Särbi (Xianbei 鮮卑), → 吐 *tù* (*tǔ*).

lù　MC luwk

1. (bn.) ～蠡 *lùlí* (MC luwk-lje), Xiongnu title given to kings in 3rd rank of tribal hierarchy, below *chanyu* 單于 and *xianwang* 賢王 (or *tuqiwang* 屠耆王).

賈　gǔ　MC kuX

1. buy; sell.
   a. engage in trade; tradesman; merchant, shopkeeper.
2. seek, try to find; strive for.

jià　MC kaeH

1. price; put a price on; evaluate.

jiǎ　MC kaeX

1. a surname.

轂　gǔ　MC kuwk

1. wheel-hub.
   a. synecdoche for carriage, cart.

鈷　gǔ　MC kuX

1. (med.) (bn.) ～鉧, ～鐞 *gǔmǔ* (kuX-muwX), flatiron; also, wok.

骨　gǔ　MC kwot

1. bone; bones of human or animal, as individual items or skeletal structure.
2. (med.) basic character of person or idea, as an articulated whole.
3. (med.) (lit.) underlying structure or argument of a composition, forceful but spare in style, often paired with *feng* 風 (temper, mood, animating force directed outward).

鶻　gǔ　MC kwot　→ 鶻 *hú*.

鼓　gǔ　MC kuX

1. drum.
2. to drum; strike, beat.
   a. striking area of bell-chime.
3. play a stringed instrument, thrum.
4. bulge, protrude; protuberant, convex; e.g. ～帆 *gǔfān*, billowing sail, to hoist sail.
5. vibrate; sway, rock; e.g. ～舞 *gǔwǔ*, swaying and swirling.
6. sounding of drum to indicate the 5 watches (*geng* 更) of the night.

gù

固   gù   MC kuH

1. fastness, secure place, stronghold; fortified; e.g. 山河之～ *shānhé zhi gù*, a fastness of mountains and rivers.
2. solid; firm, secure, steadfast; consolidate(d).
3. firmly, certainly, assuredly, definitely, in fact.
4. set in one's ways, inflexible, unyielding, resolute.

故   gù   MC kuH

1. reason, cause, purpose; e.g. 無～ *wúgù*, for no good reason, without cause; 君以弄馬之～ *jūn yǐ nòngmǎ zhi gù*, the sovereign, because of his love of horses . . .
   a. grammaticalized to phrase-initial attributive GP meaning "for this reason" > "therefore"; e.g. 吾少也賤，～多能鄙事 *wú shǎo yě jiàn, gù néng bǐshì*, when I was young, we were impecunious, therefore I became adept at many menial services; 所惡有甚於死者，～患有所不辟也 *suǒ wù yǒu shèn yú sǐ zhě, gù huàn yǒu suǒ bùbì yě*, among things that I detest there are those worse than dying, therefore, as for grievous sufferings, there are things I will not run away from.
   b. therefore > assuredly, affirmedly, certainly, surely; e.g. ～王之不王，不為也，非不能也 *gù wáng zhī bùwàng, bùwéi yě, fēi bùnéng yě*, Most assuredly, the king's not ruling like a proper king is a matter of simply not doing it, it is not a matter of his not being able; ～二十取一而足也 *gù èrshí qǔ yī ér zú yě*, to be sure, taking (a tax of) one part in twenty, that is sufficient.
   c. 是～ *shìgù*, 以～ *yǐgù*, as sentence- or phrase-initial: for this reason, on this account; e.g. 是～惡夫佞者 *shìgù wù fú nìng zhě*, For this reason I detest anyone of those glib-tongued people; 其言不讓，是～哂之 *qí yán bùràng, shìgù shěn zhī*, his words were not deferential, on account of this I smiled at him.
   d. (med.) 因 . . . ～ *yīn* X *gù*, 由 . . . ～ *yóu* X *gù*, 用 . . . ～ *yòng* X *gù*, because of X, for the reason of X.
   e. (med.) in Budd. translations, occurring at end of statement to indicate it is affirmed as so—"truly thus; indeed."
2. be intent on (doing X), intentionally, purposefully, deliberately.

3. event, happening; esp. unforeseen event, accident, mishap.
4. old, familiar, long-time (ant. 新 *xīn*, new, fresh); e.g. ～人 *gùrén*, old friend (in closeness of friendship, not in chronological age); ～事 *gùshì*, precedents, former occurrences.
   a. (med.) sgl. or ～自 *gùzì*, still, yet (< as of old).
   b. (med.) usually, normally, most often.
5. deceive, deceit(ful), esp. in early texts regarding character assessment.

桍   gù   MC kowk

1. manacles.
2. constrain, take into custody.

牿   gù   MC kok

1. pen, for horse or ox.
2. wooden crosspiece attached to ox's horns to prevent it from goring.

痼   gù   MC kuH

1. chronic illness, persistent affliction.

錮   gù   MC kuH

1. plug a crack in cast metal.
2. obstruct, stop.
   a. restrict, restrain; prevent; forbid, prohibit; esp. to exclude an opposing faction from governmental office or influence.
3. take into custody; imprison, jail.
4. exercise sole control, monopolize.
5. ⊙ 痼 *gù*, chronic illness.

雇   gù   MC kuH

1. hire(ling), engage for payment, employ.

顧   gù   MC kuH

1. look back, look behind (space or time); turn the head to see.
   a. look at, regard.
   b. on the verge of departing (and looking back), e.g. ～命 *gùmìng*, testamentary command before death.
2. look after, attend to, be concerned about, care about.
   a. consider, contemplate.
   b. (med.) be present at; e.g. 光～ *guānggù*, attend, be present (at this moment).
3. call on; inquire after.
4. (ADV) on the other hand, conversely, to the contrary; however.

5. rhetorical interr., syn. 豈 *qǐ*, how could it be that . . .?, i.e. of course it is not, surely not.
6. ⊙ 雇 *gù*, hire(ling), engage for pay, employ.

guā

刮 guā MC kwaet
1. scrape, grate; thwite, whittle; shave.
2. (med.) wind sweeping over the ground, gust, bluster.

瓜 guā MC kwae
1. gen. term for melons, gourds.

緺 guā MC kwae
1. violet-colored silk band or ribbon.

騧 guā MC kwae
1. black-muzzled sandy horse.

鴰 guā MC kwaet
1. 鶬～ *cāngguā*, 麋～ *míguā*, gray crane (*Grus lilfordi*).

guǎ

寡 guǎ MC kwaeX
1. few, scanty; deficient, lacking in; e.g. ～欲 *guǎyù*, having few desires; ～人 *guǎrén*, humilific self-ref. used by feudal lords, by ruler, and by (med.) military commanders, "I, the deficient one," usu. explained as abb. of ～德之人 *guǎdézhirén*, I, a person lacking in virtue.
   a. lessen, reduce, diminish.
2. widow(er), in early times ref. to man or woman, later mostly to woman.
   a. alone, solitary.

guà

卦 guà MC kweaH
1. the trigrams of the *Yijing*, 3-line configurations made up of 8 different combinations of broken (*yin*) and unbroken (*yang*) lines; the fundamental elements that, when combined into 6-line forms, comprise the 64 hexagrams (also called *guà*).
2. to divine, esp. with milfoil stalks; divination.

挂 guà MC kweaH ⊙ 掛 *guà*.

掛 guà MC kweaH
1. suspend, hang up; hitch up; pin on.
   a. droop, hang down.
2. be concerned about, worried, anxious, "hung up on."
3. catch (on), snag, snare, entangle.
4. (med.) drape (clothes) over one, wear, put on, don.
5. (med.) enroll, add one's name to.

絓 guà MC hweaH
1. snag, catch (on); snare, entangle.
   a. embroil, involve.

罣 guà MC kweaH
1. catch fish in a net.
   a. enmesh, ensnare, entangle.

詿 guà MC kweaH
1. embroil, involve against one's will or better interests.
   a. mislead, delude, gull.

guāi

乖 guāi MC kweaj
1. contrary, perverse, counter to; discordant; inconsistent, paradoxical.
2. turn aside, (de)part from; deviate.
3. divide, differentiate; split.

guài

夬 guài MC kwaejH
1. divide; breach, break through.
2. sgl. or rdup., decidedly, resolutely.
3. "Resoluteness," name of 43rd hexagram of the *Yijing*.

廥 guài MC kwajH
1. barn, garner, fodder-pen, for storing hay and grass.

怪 guài MC kweajH
1. eccentric, curious, uncommon, peculiar; oddity, curiosity.
   a. astonishing, stunning.
2. bizarre, grotesque(ry), fantastic.
   a. uncanny, weird, freakish, monstrous.
3. blame; complain, grumble; bear a grudge against.

4. (med.) rhetorical sentence- or phrase-initial exclamation: no wonder that . . . ! of course it would be . . . !

guān

倌   **guān**   MC kwan

1. ～人 *guānrén*, minor servant assigned to the stables; groom, ostler, stableman.

冠   **guān**   MC kwan

1. cap, usu. formal; e.g. ～蓋 *guān'gài*, cap and (carriage) canopy, those with cap and coach, those of high status; ～帶 *guāndài*, cap and sash, those with an official's cap and a sash with seal of office, a member of the bureaucracy; also, a young man who has participated in the capping ceremony (see *guàn* 2, below).
   a. crest, tuft, of certain birds and fowl.
     guàn   MC kwanH
1. to wear a cap; offer a cap to someone else.
2. the "capping ceremony" of a young man at age 20 *sui* during which he receives a cap and sash signifying entry into adulthood.
3. be at the head of, above all others; "the cream of . . .," "the crown of . . ."; e.g. ～軍 *guànjūn*, at the head of the army, in overall command; ～時 文士 *guàn shíwénshì*, be the crown of (dean of) that time's men of letters.

官   **guān**   MC kwan

1. office, building for transaction of government business.
   a. organ of government housed in preceding.
2. official(dom), staff employed by and in preceding or in comparable offices throughout the state.
   a. bureaucracy, higher-level officials usu. appointed by or with direct connection to central government.
   b. functionary, low-level official usu. appointed locally and outside the bureaucracy.
3. official rank in the bureaucracy, office to which one is appointed (cf. 職 *zhí*, official duties or responsibilities of office).
4. governmental; governance.
   a. public, in sense of being used by officials for the public good; public service.
   b. put into public service.
5. sense-organs of human body; e.g. 五～ *wǔguān*, the "5 offices" (eyes, ears, mouth, nose, heart).

6. (Dao.) 三～ *sānguān*, the "3 offices" of Heaven, Earth, and Water, originating in the Celestial Master (Tianshi) movement as destinations for confessional petitions; variously described at different times but mainly responsible for keeping registers of the good and evil acts of humans and correlating these with the fates of the living, posthumous fates of their ancestors, and future fates of descendants.

擐   **guān**   MC kwaen

1. pierce, puncture; stab, run through.
     xuān   MC sjwen
1. ⊙ 揎 *xuān*, roll up, turn up.

棺   **guān**   MC kwan

1. coffin, esp. inner coffin where body is placed.
     guàn   MC kwanH
1. encoffin.

瘝   **guān**   MC kwean

1. illness, malady, indisposition.
   a. sufferer, victim; invalid.
2. neglect, ignore; misuse, throw aside.

莞   **guān**   MC kwan

1. said to be a kind of reed or bulrush, but more likely skimmia (*Skimmia japonica, S. reevesiana*), evergreen shrub with leathery leaves that were plaited to make sitting mats.
     wǎn   MC hwaenX
1. ～爾 *wǎněr*, lightly smiling.

觀   **guān**   MC kwan

1. look intently, look with purpose.
   a. observe; surview; contemplate; consider, meditate (on).
   b. outlook, vista, view; panorama.
2. look with appreciation, hold in high regard; behold, descry, mark.
3. make visible, exhibit, display, manifest.
4. point of view, vantage point, perspective; consideration.
5. "Surview," name of 20th hexagram of *Yijing*.
     guàn   MC kwanH
1. watchtower, lookout tower, usu. on either side of main gate of palace, shrine, walled city; syn. 闕 *què*.
   a. elevated or storeyed structure for taking in a view, belvedere, mirador.
2. (Dao.) Dao. monastery or abbey.

a. (Dao.) insight meditation, ref. several different practices, most important of which is 內〜 *nèiguān*, inward observation, focused on visualization of body gods and energies.

3. (Budd.) trns. Skt. *vipaśyanā*, insight or direct intuition, resulting from *śamatha* meditation (→ 止 *zhǐ* 3b), of the 3 basic marks of all phenomena (i.e. impermanence, suffering, non-selfhood).

關　guān　MC kwaen

1. bar of a gate; to bar(ricade), close, shut.
   a. synecdoche for gate(way), passage.
   b. close in on oneself, fold up (like wings of a bird).
2. barrier (geographic), esp. strategic pass.
   a. passport, credentials for travel.
3. customhouse, tollhouse.
4. juncture, point of contact.
   a. key point, critical point.
   b. key junctures in human body at which movement of blood and *qi* may be facilitated or blocked, such as articulations of joints.
5. connection, relation(ship).
   a. be involved with, concerned with or about, touch upon, have to do with.
6. communicate to, inform, notify, announce.
   a. (med.) a communication between officials regarding an affair.
7. standard, currently used (archaic usage).
8. rdup., onom. of osprey's cry, 1st words of 1st poem in *Shijing*.
9. a surname.

鰥　guān　MC kwean

1. widower; bachelor of advanced age.
2. yellowcheek (*Elopichthys bambusa*), freshwater fish related to the carp; syn. 鱤 *gǎn*.

gǔn　MC kwonX

1. ⊙ 鯀 *gǔn*, name of father of the legendary sage-king Yu 禹.

guǎn

斡　guǎn　MC kwanX　→斡 *wò*.

筦　guǎn　MC kwanX　⊙ 管 *guǎn*.

管　guǎn　MC kwanX

1. flute without holes, usu. of bamboo.
   a. gen. term for wind instruments; e.g. 〜弦 *guǎnxián*, pipes and strings, aerophones and chordophones.

2. hollow tube, pipe; e.g. 〜見 *guǎnjiàn*, look through a pipe, narrow view.
   a. anything of tubular shape.
   b. shaft of writing-brush > the writing-brush itself.
3. key; e.g. 〜鑰 *guǎnyào*, keys and cotters.
4. manage, take charge of; administer.

館　guǎn　MC kwanX

1. official guesthouse or residence, hostel, for officials on state business.
2. guesthouse, inn (privately owned).
3. detached lodge, temporary residence for pleasure outings.

guàn

丱　guàn　MC kwaenH

1. twin tufts gathered in a child's hair.
   a. by metonymy, a child.

悹　guàn　MC kwanH

1. despondent, desperate; weighed down.
   a. bereft, with no one to rely on.

慣　guàn　MC kwaenH

1. accustomed, habituated to, used to, familiar with; experienced in, practiced in.

摜　guàn　MC kwaenH

1. accustomed, habituated to, used to, familiar with; experienced in, "an old hand at"; ⊙ 慣 *guàn*.
2. wear, put on; e.g. 〜甲 *guànjiǎ*, don armor.

涫　guàn　MC kwanH

1. bubble, boil; seethe.

灌　guàn　MC kwanH

1. irrigate, water, douse.
   a. sprinkle, e.g. (Budd.) 〜頂 *guàndīng*, "sprinkle the crown of the head," trns. Skt. *abhiṣeka*, anointment, consecration, ritual of taking bodhisattva vows.
2. pour into, run into; immerse in.
   a. cast a mold (liquid metal).
3. pour a libation to the spirits at start of sacrifice.
   a. pour wine for a guest; encourage to drink.
4. waterspout.
5. clump or cluster of small trees or bushes, brush.

huàn   MC hwanH

1. rdup., flooding full, flowing widely; also, earnest and eager, devotedly diligent.

爟   guàn   MC kwanH

1. fire lit at sacrificial ritual.
2. ～火 *guànhuǒ*, fire lit to eliminate noxious influences; also (med.), beacon-fire.

瓘   guàn   MC kwanH

1. jade tablet; possibly, jade vessel.

盥   guàn   MC kwanH

1. wash the hands.
   a. wash-basin, hand-basin.
2. ⊙ 祼 *guàn* 1, make a libation to the spirits.

祼   guàn   MC kwanH

1. make a libation to the spirits.
2. formal offering of wine to guests.

罐   guàn   MC kwanH

1. (med.) vessels for drawing or storing water, jug, crock, jar; flask, ewer.

貫   guàn   MC kwanH

1. the string on which coins were strung.
   a. measure-word for a string of cash, equalling 1,000 coins.
   b. pass through the center of.
2. thread together, link up; connect, unite.
   a. from first to last, thorough(ly), comprehensive(ly).
3. continue, succeed; unbroken.
4. one's place of official registry (usu. where ancestors had lived for successive generations).
5. accustomed, habituated to, used to; experienced, practiced in; ⊙ 慣 *guàn* 1.

wān   MC ʼwaen

1. ⊙ 彎 *wān* 1b, bent, curved, crooked.

雚   guàn   MC kwanH

1. ⊙ 鸛 *guàn*, stork.

huán   MC hwan

1. ⊙ 萑 *huán* 1, metaplexis.

鸛   guàn   MC kwanH

1. white stork (*Ciconia ciconia*).

guāng

光   guāng   MC kwang

1. light(ed), shining, glow(ing); e.g. 夜～ *yèguāng*, noctilucent, night-shining, esp. items made from fluorite (fluorspar); 三～ *sānguāng*, the 3 Lights, i.e. sun, moon, stars.
   a. sheen, gloss(y); luster, lustrous; aura.
2. cast light on, illumin(at)e; beam.
3. glorious, splendid; e.g. ～塵 *guāngchén*, splendid dust, honorific ref. to one of noble station or character and his traces.
4. time; a moment of time; e.g. 一寸之～ *yīcùn-zhiguāng*, an inch of light, brief moment; ～景 *guāngjǐng*, the light of passing time; or read as *guāngyǐng*, the (alternating) light and shadow of passing time; (med.)～顧 *guānggù*, be present (at this moment).
5. (med.) sleek, smooth (< glossy).
6. (med.) bare, stark.

桄   guāng   MC kwang

1. (bn.) ～榔 *guāngláng* (MC kwang-lang), sugar-palm, feather-palm (*Areca saccharifera, A. pinnata*), yields sago (palm starch), jaggery (unrefined sugar).

guàng   MC kwangH

1. (med.) wooden slats placed horizontally in the building of wagons, gates, boats, benches, etc.

洸   guāng   MC kwang

1. sparkling water, light-flecked, glinting.
2. rdup., brave and bold, intrepid.

huàng   MC hwang

1. (bn.) ～洋 *huàngyáng* (MC hwang-yang) or rdup., shoreless sea, unbounded ocean.

胱   guāng   MC kwang

1. (bn.) 膀～ *pángguāng*, → 膀 *páng*.

guǎng

廣   guǎng   MC kwangX

1. broad(en), wide(n); spacious, widespread; extensive; e.g. ～衍 *guǎngyǎn*, broadly extended; ～開 *guǎngkāi*, open wide; ～莫 *guǎngmò*, broad blast, old name for north wind.
   a. breadth, expanse; extent, scope; amplitude.

2. broad-minded, accepting; generous.

3. (med.) abb. for Guangzhou 〜州.

4. 〜木香 *guǎngmùxiāng*, putchuk (*Saussurea lappa, S. costus*), originally brought from north India, fragrant root used in incense and perfume; syn. 雲木香 *yúnmùxiāng*.

guàng　MC kwangH

1. measure of distance on east-west axis (cf. 運 *yùn*, north-south).

2. company of 15 war-chariots in Chu army of early times.

kuàng　MC khwangH

1. ⊙ 曠 *kuàng* 4, barren, bleak, waste(d); wasteland, desert.

獷　guǎng　MC kwaengX

1. feral, beastly; fierce, vicious; fell.

2. churlish, gross; coarse, vulgar, unmannered.

guàng

狂　guàng　MC gjwangX

1. rdup., wild haste, terror-stricken.

kuáng　MC gjwang

1. (bn.) 〜攘 *kuángráng* (MC gjwang-nyang), tumult and turmoil, crazed and deranged.

guī

傀　guī　MC kwoj

1. grand, gigantic; magnificent.

2. strange, unusual, uncommon; bizarre.

kuǐ　MC khwojX

1. (med.) (bn.) 〜儡 *kuǐlěi* (MC khwojX-lwojX), puppet, wooden figurine, effigy.

圭　guī　MC kwej

1. jade tablet or scepter, square-bottomed and round or pointed at the top, given by ruler in early times to trusted ministers or vassals; e.g. 〜璋 *guīzhāng*, scepter and demi-scepter; also, scepter and insignia.

2. cruse, a wine vessel square-bottomed and round at the top; e.g. 〜瓚 *guīzàn*, jade cruse and ladle for ritual libations.

3. sgl. or 土〜 *tǔguī*, gnomon template to measure the sun's shadow.

4. ancient measure of capacity, equiv. one-fourth of a "pinch" (*cuo* 撮), the merest speck.

歸　guī　MC kjw+j

1. return home, go to where one belongs.

　a. return whence one came, originally or recently; go back to, retreat to; come full circle.

　b. recede; withdraw; e.g. 〜遠 *guīyuǎn*, recede into the distance, 〜山 *guīshān*, withdraw to the mountains (seclude oneself); also (med.), resort finally to the mountains, i.e. die and be buried in a tumulus (see next).

2. take refuge with, as though going home; bring allegiance to; find haven with, resort to.

　a. settle down in, regard as final destination; retire(ment); commit oneself to.

　b. ending-spot, outcome, result.

3. a daughter going to her new home in marriage.

　a. 〜妹 *guīmèi*, "Marrying Maiden," name of 54th hexagram of *Yijing*.

4. give back, return to its proper place or owner; restore, make restitution; e.g. 〜納 *guīnà*, restore and install (in proper category).

　a. devolve to or upon.

5. (med.) admire, appreciate; praise, extol.

kuì　MC gwijH

1. ⊙ 饋 *kuì* 1, present food to someone or as sacrifice to spirits.

珪　guī　MC kwej

1. ⊙ 圭 *guī* 1, jade tablet or scepter, square-bottomed and round or pointed at the top, given by ruler in early times to trusted ministers or vassals.

瑰　guī　MC kwoj

1. sgl. or (bn.) 玫〜 *méiguī*, semi-precious stone, dark mica, biotite, often red-tinted.

2. rare, exceptional, extraordinary.

　a. of unusually fine quality, sterling.

瓌　guī　MC kwoj　⊙ 瑰 *guī*.

皈　guī　MC kjw+j

1. (med.) (Budd.) cmpd. 〜依 *guīyī*, take refuge (in the Buddha, the *dharma*, and the *saṁgha*).

窐　guī　MC kwej

1. opening, hole; mouth; flue.

yāo　MC 'aew

1. (bn.) 〜寥 *yāoliáo* (MC 'aew-laew), vast void, far-reaching and infinite.

袿   **guī**   MC kwej
1. paletot, woman's light cape or mantle.
2. chemise, woman's light undergarment.

規   **guī**   MC kjwie
1. compass, for drawing circle; often paired with 矩 *jǔ*, L-square.
    a. draw a circle.
    b. circle, disc(-shaped).
2. guide-rule, guideline; model, pattern, standard; norm, rule; custom, program.
3. outline, plan, design, plot.
    a. calculate; surmise.
4. give counsel, advise about course of action; caution, admonish.
    a. demand, insist on; require.
5. 子～ *zǐguī*, hawk-cuckoo (*Hierococcyx sparverioides*), with plaintively insistent call, esp. associated with Shu 蜀 as legendarily the posthumous avatar of an ancient king, also harbinger of winter when sounding at autumnal equinox; syn. 杜鵑 *dùjuān*.
6. ⊙ 窺 *kuī* 1, look into, peer at, spy upon.

閨   **guī**   MC kwej
1. interior or secondary door leading to inner apartments, rounded at the top like a *gui*-scepter.
2. inner quarters, women's quarters, boudoir, gynaeceum.
    a. maidenly, virginal, modest; privy, off-limits.

鮭   **guī**   MC kwej
1. puffer, globefish, blowfish (*Spheroides vermicularis*); syn. 河豚魚 *hétúnyú*, 鮐 *tái*.
    xié   MC hea
1. (med.) nonesuch fish, gen. term for rare or colorful species of fish, esp. as culinary delicacies.

龜   **guī**   MC kwij
1. gen. term for turtle, tortoise; symbolic of longevity and immutability; image of the cosmos, its carapace replicating the vaulted heaven and its underside the flat earth. One of the "four numinous animals" (*siling* 四靈); conjoined with snake wrapped round it as the "dusky warrior" (*xuanwu* 玄武), emblematic of the north, the color black, wintertime, and the *wuxing* phase of water.
2. turtle shell, usu. the plastron but sometimes the carapace, used in divination; after the dried shell was prepared, a red-hot poker was applied to a designated point and the resulting cracks (卜 *bǔ*) interpreted; the process and practice of cheloniomancy; the species used seem mainly to have been turtles, not tortoises, esp. *Mauremys sinensis* and *Geoclemmys reevesi*.
3. turtle or tortoise shell used as currency in various places in pre-imperial times.
4. humped or arched backbone of certain mammals, such as deer.
    jūn   MC kwin
1. ⊙ 皸 *jūn*, chapped or cracked skin.
    qiū   MC khjuw
1. (bn.) ～茲 *qiūcí* (MC khjuw-dzi), Kucha, oasis city on the northern Silk Road in the Tarim Basin, esp. important in Tang times for popularity of its music and musical instruments brought to China.

guǐ

佹   **guǐ**   MC kjweX
1. perverse; disagreeable, cantankerous.
    a. unscrupulous, cunning.
2. bizarre, queer; incongruous.

匭   **guǐ**   MC kwijX   ⊙ 簋 *guǐ*.

垝   **guǐ**   MC kjweX
1. crumble, give way, fall to pieces; broken down, deteriorated; esp. of a wall.

娝   **guǐ**   MC kjweX
1. (bn.) ～嬘 *guǐhuà* (MC kjweX-hweak), modest reserve, demure diffidence, comely control.

宄   **guǐ**   MC kwijX
1. renegade, traitor, internal dissident.
    a. outlaw; villain, fiend.

庋   **guǐ**   MC kjweX
1. store up, collect, lay by, put by.
2. cupboard.

庪   **guǐ**   MC kjweX
1. ⊙ 庋 *guǐ* 1, store up, put by; 2, cupboard.
2. bury ritual items after sacrificing to a mountain.

恑 guǐ MC kjweX
1. trick, dupe; betray, inveigle; trim the truth, lead on.

晷 guǐ MC kwijX
1. shadow cast by the sun.
    a. moment(s) of time.
2. sundial; esp. the gnomon; e.g. 〜刻 guǐkè, a notch of the sundial's shadow.
3. ⊙ 軌 guǐ 3, route, course; trajectory of planet.

氿 guǐ MC kwijX
1. springwater that emerges in narrow channels from the side of the font.
2. parched land by a riverside.

癸 guǐ MC kjwijX
1. 10th and last of the heavenly stems.
2. of lowest quality.

簋 guǐ MC kwijX
1. round pannier, grain-hamper (cf. 簠 fǔ, square or oblong pannier), usu. with 2 or 4 handles, sometimes with cover, mounted either on 3 small feet or a square base, to hold boiled grain for sacrificial offering.
2. (med.) petition-box, at court, basket for complaints regarding official misconduct or submission of self-recommendations.

詭 guǐ MC kjweX
1. calculating, crafty; deceitful, unscrupulous, chicanery.
2. dissemble, feign; simulate, pretend; pass off as.
    a. wheedle, flatter; blandish, gloze; e.g. (bn.) 〜隨 guǐsuí (MC kjweX-zjwe), slavering and glavering.
3. anomalous, incongruous; improbable; weird, peculiar.
    a. extraordinary, exceptional.
    b. (bn.) 〜譎 guǐjué (MC kjweX-kwet) aberrantly bizarre; transfigured, metamorphosed.
4. contrary, froward; refractory, antithetical; clashing.

軌 guǐ MC kwijX
1. carriage-gauge, distance between wheels on either side.
2. cart-ruts, wheel-ruts, groove, imprint; track.
    a. follow in the track or path of, follow the example of.

3. route, sustained course.
    a. trajectory; orbit of planet.
4. standard, criterion; scale, guide; example.
    a. rule, law; convention, custom.
    b. conform with, correspond to.

陒 guǐ MC kjweX ⊙ 恑 guǐ.

鬼 guǐ MC kjw+jX
1. returning spirit of the dead, revenant, ghost, specter; often associated with the carnal-soul (魄 pò) that is tied to the earth.
2. animistic spirits of natural objects and phenomena; e.g. 山〜 shānguǐ, a mountain spirit.
3. demon, malevolent spirit.
4. ghostly, eerie; uncanny; of seemingly inhuman character; e.g. 〜才 guǐcái, uncanny genius.
    a. hidden, secret(ive), covert; e.g. (med.) 〜市 guǐshì, "ghost market," nighttime gathering that disperses by dawn.
5. "Revenant," one of the 28 lunar lodgings, comprised of γ, δ, η, θ Cancri, in the southern quadrant (chiniao 赤鳥) of the sky.

guì

劌 guì MC kwajH
1. cut in two, sever; cleave.

劇 guì MC kjwejH
1. to wound, stab, puncture, prick.

桂 guì MC kwejH
1. cinnamon tree (*Cinnamomum cassia, C. pedunculatum*), medium to tall subtropical evergreen tree, assoc. in lit. with longevity, immortality, and reclusion; part of the laurel family, having slightly fragrant bark (viz. cassia) and white odorless flowers; the cinnamon's tall trunk was sometimes used as building material, but no part of the tree was used medicinally nor was its spice used through med. times. When ref. is to fragrant wood, aromatic leaves, or inconspicuous and nearly odorless flowers in spring or summer, it is to the cinnamon. Refs. to 肉〜 ròuguì, "fleshy guì," are also to the cinnamon, and the legendary guì-tree in the moon is the cinnamon. The phrase "cinnabar guì," 丹〜 dānguì, may ref. to a red-barked variety of cin-

namon, but more often signifies the osmanthus (see next). N.B. When ref. the tree, better not to translate *gui* as "cassia," which, as also the name of a genus, belongs to a different family.
2. osmanthus, sweet-olive tree (*Osmanthus fragrans*), small evergreen tree of warm to temperate climes, with highly fragrant white or yellowish-white flowers that bloom in autumn; when ref. is made to the *gui*'s redolence or its autumn-blooming, it is the osmanthus that is meant; often used in private gardens. Also assoc. in lit. with reclusion, esp. Budd. reclusion. The phrase "cinnabar *gui*," 丹～ *dānguì*, usu. ref. to a red-flowered variety of osmanthus.

檜   guì   MC kwajH
1. Chinese juniper (*Sabina chinensis*), with spreading needle-like leaves like those of the cypress.
2. ornamentation on a coffin-lid.

襘   guì   MC kwajH
1. joining point of a collar's 2 sides at front of a garment.

貴   guì   MC kjw+jH
1. costly, expensive, dear.
2. valuable, precious.
   a. prize(d), esteem(ed), honor(ed).
3. noble, of noble station or status.
4. (med.) (ADV) need to, is necessary to, will certainly; e.g. ～欲 *guìyù*, intend to.

跪   guì   MC gjweX
1. kneel, with hams not touching back of heels, with torso held upright (cf. 坐 *zuò* 1, with hams on heels, "Japanese-style"); e.g. 長～ *chángguì*, "tall-kneeling," same as preceding, sign of respect.
2. foot.

鱖   guì   MC kjwejH
1. mandarin-fish, rock-bass (*Siniperca*, various species; but not a perch, despite its scientific name).

gǔn

滾   gǔn   MC kwonX
1. (med.) rdup., roll and roil, run ceaselessly on and onward (water).

緄   gǔn   MC kwonX
1. woven sash.
2. cord, twine, rope.
3. a bundle, packet.

袞   gǔn   MC kwonX
1. ceremonial robes of ruler and the 3 Dukes (*sangong* 三公).
   a. imperial robes.
   b. imperatorial.
2. (med.) rdup., inexorable advance, ceaseless and unstopped.

鯀   gǔn   MC kwonX
1. name of father of the legendary sage-king and flood-tamer Yu 禹; he failed in his attempt to quell the Great Flood.

guō

聒   guō   MC kwat
1. sgl. or rdup., deafening din, clamor(ous), cacophony, barrage of sound, racket, raucous.
2. rdup. also (med.), onom. of waves slapping and smacking.

蟈   guō   MC kweak
1. (bn.) 螻～ *lóuguō*, → 螻 *lóu*.

郭   guō   MC kwak
1. outer wall of city area, enclosing the suburbs; outskirts (cf. 城 *chéng*, inner city-wall, separating city from outskirts).
2. outer fortification; barbican; rampart.
3. periphery, rim of an object.
   a. outline, limn; e.g. ～塡 *guōtián*, outline and fill in (in making facsimile manuscript),
4. (med.) (bn.) ～郎 *guōláng* (MC kwak-lang), puppet, stooge.
5. a surname.

鍋   guō   MC kwa
1. northeast dialect syn. of 釭 *gāng* 1, axle-cap.
2. (med.) cooking-pan, fry-pan, wok.

guó

國   guó   MC kwok
1. girtland, territory.
2. territory under governmental control.

a. governmental polity, state, kingdom; domain.

b. in pre-imperial times, a feudal state, vassal state; by the Zhanguo period virtually independent.

c. in Han and W. Jin times, a principality, usu. administered by a prince of the dynastic family.

3. capital city of a state.

幗　guó　MC kwojH

1. woman's hair-ornament, hairpin with dangling gem.

聝　guó　MC kweak　⊙ 馘 *guó*.

馘　guó　MC kweak

1. cut off the left ear of a defeated enemy as proof of victory.

a. the ear thus cut off.

xú　MC xwek

1. face, visage.

guǒ

果　guǒ　MC kwaX

1. fruit, edible tree-fruit.

a. fruit tree.

2. fruition or result of an action, actual outcome, effect; e.g. (Budd.) 因～ *yīnguǒ*, cause and effect, i.e. karma.

a. to result in, end in.

3. sgl. or ～然 *guǒrán*, actually, indeed.

a. as expected, as predicted.

4. bring an action to completion, achieve or realize a goal; e.g. 未～尋病終 *wèiguǒ xún bìngzhōng*, before doing it he soon took ill and died.

5. decided, determined, resolute, firm; bold, intrepid; e.g. ～剛 *guǒgāng*, firm and inflexible.

椁　guǒ　MC kwak

1. outer coffin, enclosing smaller coffin in which the corpse is laid.

槨　guǒ　MC kwak　⊙ 椁 *guǒ*.

猓　guǒ　MC kwaX

1. ～然, ～猭, *guǒrán*, proboscis monkey (*Nasalis larvatus*).

蜾　guǒ　MC kwaX

1. (bn.) ～蠃 *guǒluǒ* (MC kwaX-lwaX), sphexwasp, digger-wasp (*Ammophila infesta*), uses toxin to paralyze insect-prey which it stockpiles in hole dug in the ground or a pre-existing hole, then deposits eggs in this nest so that the hatched larvae can feed on the insects.

裹　guǒ　MC kwaX

1. wrap up, bundle; swathe.

a. package, packet, parcel.

2. fruit of a plant; ovary of plant.

輠　guǒ　MC kwaX

1. in early times, grease-pot carried on cart with oil to grease the axles.

huà　MC hwaeX

1. revolve, rotate.

guò

過　guò　MC kwaH, kwa

1. pass by, pass through (space or time); e.g. ～庭 *guòtíng*, cross through the courtyard.

2. go beyond, exceed, surpass; e.g. ～望 *guòwàng*, exceed expectations.

a. excessive(ly), inordinate(ly), more than normal; e.g. ～老 *guòlǎo*, of much advanced age.

b. 大～ *dàguò*, "Greater Preponderance," name of 28th hexagram of *Yijing*; 小～ *xiǎoguò*, "Lesser Preponderance," name of 62nd hexagram of *Yijing*.

3. trespass, transgress(ion), error of commission, lapsus; mistake, wrongdoing; e.g. ～法 *guòfǎ*, break the law.

a. find fault with, criticize for actions.

4. to stop at, stop by, visit (esp. in med. poem titles); e.g. ～山人居 *guò shānrén jū*, stopping by the hermit's dwelling; (med.) ～堂 *guòtáng*, visit the official hall (for a legal case, a celebration, ceremony, etc.).

5. (med.) hand over, pass from one person to another.

6. (med.) measure-word for occurrences, incidents.

a. (med.) VB-complement indicating completed or past action; e.g. 杏花開～ *xínghuā kāiguò*, the almond blossoms have opened.

7. ～利 *guòlì*, Khorasmia.

H

hāi

哈   **hāi**   MC xoj
1. laugh at, hoot at, mock, deride.
2. (med.) (bn.) ～台 *hāitái* (MC xoj-doj), onom. of snoring, snore with might and main.

hái

孩   **hái**   MC hoj
1. infant's smile; e.g. ～提之童 *háití zhi tóng*, child held in arms who has just learned to smile.
2. (med.) infant, child.

還   **hái**   MC hwaen   → 還 *huán*.

骸   **hái**   MC heaj
1. shinbone, shank.
2. bones; skeleton.
3. body, corporal form.

hǎi

海   **hǎi**   MC xojX
1. sea, ocean; e.g. 四～ *sìhǎi*, ～內 *hǎinèi*, the 4 seas, (the land) within the (4) seas, "the seagirt land," i.e. China, imagined as land bounded by water on all sides.
    a. marine, maritime.
2. any relatively large freshwater lake whose far shore cannot be seen, called such to emphasize its size.
3. (med.) euph. for large mass or multitude; e.g. 雲～ *yúnhǎi*, sea of clouds.
4. (Budd.) the mundane world; e.g. 苦～ *kǔhǎi*, the sea of woe, sea of suffering, to the "other shore" of which one would like to cross in order to be released from the round of birth and death.
5. ～棠 *hǎitáng*, variously identified but prob. a species of pink-flowering crabapple (*Malus spectabilis*).

醢   **hǎi**   MC xojX
1. meat-pickle, mixture of meat, ferment, salt, steeped in wine and allowed to ferment.

hài

亥   **hài**   MC hojX
1. 12th and last of the earthly branches, associated with the pig as emblematic animal.
    a. 12th double-hour of the day, approx. 9 to 11 p.m.

害   **hài**   MC hajH
1. harm, hurt, damage; injure, wound, mar; bring woe to.
    a. maim; murder.
    b. destroy, devastate.
2. catastrophe, cataclysm, disaster.
3. misuse, abuse, mistreat; interfere with.
4. inimical; averse to, antipathetic.
    a. envious of, jealous.
5. be struck with a disease.
6. (med.) to trouble, cause one concern or worry (without severity of 1, 3, 4).
    hé   MC hat
1. ⊙ 曷 *hé* 1, why? how? (early usage).

駭   **hài**   MC heajX
1. horse's shying out of fear.
    a. frightened, scared, shy away from, panicked.
2. astonish(ed), shock(ed), jolt(ed).
3. tingle, with fear or excitement.
4. stir up, rouse, throw up; rise up quickly.

hān

憨   **hān**   MC xam
1. idiotic, silly, simple-minded.

谽   **hān**   MC xeam
1. (bn.) ～谺 *hānxiā* (MC xeam-xae), gaping and gap-toothed, wide open.

酣   **hān**   MC ham
1. tipsy, from wine; cocked, lit, "high."
    a. drink one's fill.
2. euphoric, exhilarated; fully aroused, stimulated, in high spririts.

3. at the highest point; to the full extent; e.g. ～戰 *hānzhàn*, fighting to the hilt.

    a. deeply, fully.

鼾　hān　MC xan

1. snore.

    a. snort, snuffle.

hán

函　hán　MC hom

1. contain, enclose, envelop.

    a. sheath for sword, scabbard.

2. armor, soldiers' protective covering.

3. (med.) envelope for letter or official communication, sealed silk or paper; also, by metonymy, letter, missive.

4. (med.) coffer, casket, box.

5. abb. name of Hangu Pass ～谷關, important pass roughly midway between Chang'an and Luoyang, near present-day Lingbao 靈寶, in extreme western Henan.

含　hán　MC hom

1. hold in the mouth

    a. in early times, to place a jade or gem in the mouth of the deceased for burial.

2. hold in, hold back, withhold, restrain; e.g. ～情 *hánqíng*, contain one's feelings.

    a. mute(d), suppress, stifle; e.g. ～蓄 *hánxù*, muted and reserved.

3. enclose, contain, hold; embody, incorporate; e.g. 窗～西嶺 *chuāng hán xīlíng*, the window frames (< contains) the western peaks; ～氣 *hánqì*, contain or embody the breath of life.

    a. be full of, filled with; e.g. ～笑 *hánxiào*, wreathed in smiles; ～怒 *hánnù*, filled with anger.

4. tinctured, infused, tinted with; esp. color.

寒　hán　MC han

1. cold; frigid, frore.

    a. season of cold, wintertime; wintry.

2. chill(y), cool(ing).

3. lacking in material resources or in prestige.

    a. of mean background, ignoble; e.g. ～門 *hánmén*, family of humble lineage; ～人 *hánrén*, commoner.

    b. of minor status but not necessarily poor; e.g. ～士 *hánshì*, man of humble background; also (med.), minor official or member of the minor gentry.

4. lacking in affection or enthusiasm, cold-tempered, aloof.

涵　hán　MC hom

1. drench, soak, saturate.

    a. immerse, douse, wash; freshen, bedew.

2. contain, enclose, envelop, ⊙ 函 *hán* 1.

虷　hán　MC han

1. (bn.) ～蠻 *hánmán* (MC han-maen), "mosquito minnows," prob. mosquito larvae, possibly shrimpies.

韓　hán　MC han

1. name of one of the 7 major states in Warring States period, comprising the area of present-day southeast Shanxi and central Henan, originally part of the Jin 晉 state.

2. a surname.

hǎn

罕　hǎn　MC xanX

1. long-handled bird-net.

2. rare in occurrence, sparse, scarce, scant(y); seldom, rarely.

3. banner, flag.

hàn

唅　hàn　MC homH

1. in early times, to place a jade or gem in the mouth of the deceased for burial, ⊙ 含 *hán* 1a.

悍　hàn　MC hanH

1. fearless, unintimidated, intrepid; courageous, valiant.

2. ruthless; domineering, tyrannical.

3. aggressive, harsh; violent, forceful.

    a. impetuous, headlong, uncontainable.

憾　hàn　MC homH

1. regret(ful), remorse(ful), rue(ful).

2. resent(ment); dislike, regard with displeasure; bear malice toward.

扞　hàn　MC hanH

1. fend off, ward off; withstand, stand against, resist.

2. shelter, shield; protect, guard, defend.

3. leather armlet worn by archer on bow-gripping (usu. left) hand.
4. affront, offend; oppose, go against.
5. fearless, unintimidated, brave; ⊙ 悍 *hàn* 1.

捍　hàn　MC hanH　⊙ 扞 *hàn*.

撼　hàn　MC homX
1. stir, shake, rouse; move.

旱　hàn　MC hanX
1. drought, extended rainless period.
   a. parched, arid, dried out.

暵　hàn　MC xanH
1. dried out, sun-dried.
   a. parched, arid; scorched, seared.
2. turned-over soil.

汗　hàn　MC hanH
1. sweat; exude; e.g. ～青 *hànqīng*, "sweat out the green," process by which fresh-cut bamboo-strips to be used as a writing medium are fire-dried so as to remove moisture; also, euph. for completing a composition; (med.) ～衫 *hàn-shān*, undershirt.
2. (bn.) ～漫 *hànmàn* (MC hanH-manH), endless and interminable, borderless and unbounded (area); far-flung freedom, far-flooded vastitude (area and attitude); also (med.), incalculable, unfathomable, endlessly applicable (idea).
3. (bn.) 可～ *kèhàn* (MC khaek-hanH), kaghan, trsc. Turk. title for supreme ruler or sovereign.

漢　hàn　MC xanH
1. name of a major river that rises in Shaanxi and flows through Hubei to join the Yangzi River near present-day Wuhan.
2. the Han River in the sky, i.e. the Milky Way, sgl. or cmpd. 天～ *tiānhàn*, the Han in the sky, or 星～ *xīnghàn*, the starry Han, or doubled with the Yellow River (equally identified with the Milky Way) as 河～ *héhàn*, the He and Han (in the sky).
3. name of several dynasties, most importantly the Western or Former Han 西～ *xīhàn*, 前～ *qiánhàn* (206 BCE-9 CE) and Eastern or Latter Han 東～ *dōnghàn*, 後～ *hòuhàn* (23-220 CE), and the Shu-Han 蜀～ dynasty (221-263 CE) of the 3 Kingdoms Period centered in Sichuan.

4. (med.) fellow, chap, usu. informal or ref. someone of lower status.

瀚　hàn　MC hanH
1. of oceanic extent, shoreless, limitless, boundless, interminable; e.g. 浩～ *hàohàn*, of endless extent, immense and immeasurable; ～海 *hàn-hǎi*, shoreless sea, in Han times reputedly a large lake in the far north; also, oceanic sea of sand, boundless desert; in Tang times ref. specifically Gobi Desert, gen. to the desert wastes of all Central Asia.

熯　hàn　MC xanH
1. fire-dried, parched, seared; sun-dried.
   a. dried out, brittle.
2. grill, burn, scorch.
   　　rǎn　MC nyenX
1. respect, revere, honor.

睅　hàn　MC hwaenX
1. protruding eyes, with eyes abulge, eyes bugging out.

翰　hàn　MC hanH
1. quill, feather-shaft.
2. quill-brush, writing-brush made from a quill.
   a. gen. term for any writing-brush.
3. written matter, literature.
   a. personal letter, missive.
4. red-feathered pheasant.
5. fly high, soar.
6. ⊙ 榦 *gàn* 1, wooden boards used as longitudinal supports in the process of building a rammed-earth wall; buttress

菡　hàn　MC homX
1. (bn.) ～萏 *hàndàn* (MC homX-domX), unopened lotus, lotus-knop (*Nelumbo nucifera*); cf. 荷 *hé*, 芙蓉 *fúróng*, 芙蕖 *fúqú*, 蓮 *lián*.

閈　hàn　MC hanH
1. gate of a lane or alley; wicket.
   a. gen. term for gate.
2. village, hamlet, dorp.
3. enclosing wall; enceinte.
4. (med.) to bar, defend against, hold off.

頷　hàn　MC homX
1. lower jaw, jawbone; chin.
2. slightly nod or incline the head.

頤　hàn　MC homX
1. lower jaw, jawbone; chin; ⊙ 頷 *hàn* 1.
2. (bn.) 〜淡 *hàndàn* (MC homX-damX), roil and rage, slosh and splash (water).

馯　hàn　MC hanH　⊙ 騝 *hàn*.

騝　hàn　MC hanH
1. mettlesome horse, spirited steed, untamed.
   a. valiant, vigorous.
2. to bolt, dash, career; follow one's head, un-reined.

háng

杭　háng　MC hang
1. cross a river, cross over.
   a. ferry; ferry-boat.
2. (bn.) 〜莊 *hángzhuāng* (MC hang-tsrjang), broad and level-spreading, evenly extended.
3. (med.) clothes-horse.

䀑　háng　MC hang
1. swoop, sweep down, plummet, of birds; if raptor, stoop.

航　háng　MC hang
1. boats joined at their sides; double-boat.
   a. pontoon-bridge, made of boats tied together.
2. gen. term for boat.
3. go by boat, cross by boat; navigate.

行　háng　MC hang　→ 行 *xíng*.

迒　háng　MC hang
1. animal tracks, spoor, paw-track.
   a. animal path, paw-path, pathway.
2. tracks of carriage or cart.

頏　háng　MC hang
1. (bn.) 頡〜 *xiéháng*, → 頡 *xié*.

hàng

沆　hàng　MC hangX
1. nighttime mist.
   a. (bn.) 〜瀣 *hàngxiè* (MC hangX-heajH), cold northern fogs, nighttime damps, coldest damps of midnight.

2. (bn.) 〜漭 *hàngmǎng* (MC hangX-mangX), rolling on to the farthest reaches (waves), boundlessly beyond.

hāo

嘄　hāo　MC xaew
1. cmpd. 〜矢 *hāoshǐ*, whistling arrow; by med. times euph. for a beginning, first hint of (because a whistling arrow is heard before it arrives).

蒿　hāo　MC xaw
1. gen. name for various kinds of artemesia or wormwood.
2. overgrown, worthless; e.g. 〜里 *hāolǐ*, "wormwood village," i.e. land of the dead, where nothing is cultivated; (lit.) name of a funeral song.
3. ⊙ 耗 *hào* 1, to waste, use up; 槁 *gǎo*, grain stalk.

薅　hāo　MC xaw
1. mow a field, cut down weeds, to weed.

háo

嗥　háo　MC haw
1. howl, roar, scream, bellow, etc. of wild animal.
2. cry, bawl (human).

壕　háo　MC haw
1. (med.) moat, for city-wall.
   a. (med.) ditch, gutter.

毫　háo　MC haw
1. fine hair; down(y), wisp(y), tuft(ed); 〜芒 *háománg*, hair-tips; also, to split hairs.
   a. the down on plants.
2. the slightest bit, a hair's breadth.
   a. intensifier before negative VB-phrases; e.g. 〜不 *háobù*, not in the slightest, not at all; 〜無 *háowú*, without the least wisp (speck, iota) of, utterly lacking.
3. writing-brush, by metonymy from the fine hairs that form it; e.g. 〜翰 *háohàn*, writing-brush and quill, i.e. written matter.
4. measure of length, a "sliver, whit," the tenth part of a smidgen (*li* 釐), thousandth part of an inch (*cun* 寸).
   a. measure of weight, thousandth part of a single cash (*qian* 錢).

豪　háo　MC haw

1. porcupine.
    a. quill of porcupine; bristly, prickly.
2. standing out, conspicuous, prominent, elite.
    a. in position of authority or renown; power-ful, prestigious.
3. bold, unreserved, forward; open, direct, au-dacious; confident; e.g. ～放 *háofàng*, free and unreserved, bold and powerful (of character, ac-tion, or lit. style).
4. presumptuous, swaggering; overweening, domineering; despotic, unyielding.
5. wealthy, opulent; sumptuous.
    a. extravagant, prodigal, wasteful, profligate.
    b. be ostentatious, show off, flaunt.
6. ⊙ 毫 *háo* 1, down(y), wisp of hair; 2, slightest amount.

hǎo

好　hǎo　MC xawX

1. attractive, handsome, pleasing.
2. excellent, excellence; remarkable.
3. pleasant, fine; agreeable, satisfying.
4. on good terms with, amicable; intimate.
5. (med.) suitable for, befit(ting).
6. (med.) as VB-complement indicates the ac-tion of VB is completed.
7. (med.) rdup., work hard at, diligent(ly), serious(ly).
8. (med.) ～得 *hǎodé*, how can it be that . . .?, is it possible that . . .?
9. (med.) ～看 *hǎokān*, ～與 *hǎoyǔ*, pay atten-tion to, be careful about.
10. (Budd.) secondary characteristic (Skt. *anu-vyañjana*), detail, as opposed to generic or defin-ing characteristic (相 *xiàng*).

hào　MC xawH

1. to like, be fond of; incline toward, have a pref-erence or penchant for; e.g. ～事 *hàoshì*, an am-ateur of the matter in question, someone with a special interest in it, enthusiastic about, aficio-nado, votary, devotee.
    a. (med.) eager (to do X), look forward to.
2. the hole of a jade disc or of a coin.

hào

昊　hào　MC hawX

1. epithet used only with or in ref. to *tian* 天, sky, heaven; primal light; sublime; splendorous, glorious.

晧　hào　MC hawX　⊙ 皓 *hào*.

浩　hào　MC hawX

1. surge forth, flood; uninhibited, unrestrict-ed; e.g. ～然之氣 *hàoránzhiqì*, flood-like vital breath; ～蕩 *hàodàng*, lurch and pitch, rolling surge (of waves), flooding afar; also, vast and unlimited, spacious and unmeasured (sky); also, wayward and inconstant, unchecked and con-fused (thoughts).
    a. rdup. or (bn.) ～汗, ～瀚 *hàohàn* (MC hawX-hanH), of endless extent, immense and immeas-urable, spaciously spreading; also, surging and streaming onward, welling and swelling.
    b. (med.) rdup. also, tumult and turmoil, bel-low and bray.

滈　hào　MC hawX

1. ceaseless rain, deluge.
2. rdup., gleaming and glistening, sun-flecked shimmer (of water).
3. (bn.) ～汗 *hàohàn*, ⊙ 浩汗 *hàohàn*, → 浩 *hào*.

灝　hào　MC hawX

1. limitless, unbounded.
    a. (bn.) ～漾 *hàoyǎo* (MC hawX-yewX), broad and boundless, surging shorelessly; also, shining sheets of water, aqueous waste.
    b. rdup., ⊙ 浩浩 *hàohào*, → 浩 *hào*.
2. ⊙ 皓 *hào*, candent, gleaming white, shim-mering.

皓　hào　MC hawX

1. bright white, esp. candent white of the moon, also of rising sun.
    a. gleaming or shimmering white, of smooth surfaces; delicate white, of a lady's skin.
2. white hair of age, hoary-headed, white-haired; gray-bearded.
3. ⊙ 昊 *hào*, primal light of heaven, sublime, splendorous, glorious.

皜　hào　MC hawX　⊙ 皓 *hào*.

皞　hào　MC hawX

1. pure-white; unmarked, stainless.
    a. rdup., shining and shimmering; also, cheer-ful and unclouded, completely contented.

耗　hào　MC xawH

1. waste, use up, consume.
2. diminish, reduce, lessen.
3. (med.) tidings, news; message, letter.

mào　MC mawH

1. ⊙ 眊 *mào* 1, blurred, bleary; confused, in disarray.

　　máo　MC maew

1. depleted, spent; devoid of.

號　hào　MC hawH

1. designate, name; designation.
2. command, give an order.
3. announce, declare.
4. sobriquet, agnomen, nickname given to oneself.
5. to mark, note; sign, notation.

　　háo　MC haw

1. call out, shout, cry out (human).
　　a. chant, invoke (a text).
2. calls or cries of animals.
3. howling of the wind.
4. weep mournfully, keen.

鄗　hào　MC hawX

1. name of capital or chief city of King Wu of Zhou 周武王, located southwest of present-day Xi'an; often paired as 酆～ *fēnghào*, Feng being name of the capital founded nearby by King Wen 文王, located near present-day Huxian 戶縣, Shaanxi; together Feng and Hao stand for the Zhou dynasty, esp. Western Zhou.

鎬　hào　MC hawX　⊙ 鄗 *hào*.

顥　hào　MC hawX

1. shining white, brilliant white; esp. of sunlight, the western sky, clouds.
　　a. rdup., candid and lambent, vividly white, sublimely resplendent.

鰝　hào　MC hawX

1. crayfish (*Cambaroides japonicus*).

hē

呵　hē　MC xa

1. berate, excoriate.

　　hè　MC xaH

1. strong exhalation of breath with mouth wide open and throat tightened, snort.

訶　hē　MC xa

1. rail at, bellow, shout in rage.
2. (med.) ～梨勒 *hēlílè* (MC ha-lij-lok), chebulic myrobalan (*Terminalia chebula*), tree and astringent fruit (Skt. *harītakī*, Pers. *halīla*), originally an import from Central and Southeast Asia, one of 3 ingredients of *sanle* 三勒 (→ 勒 *lè*).

hé

何　hé　MC ha

1. gen. interr. pronoun for things (as opposed to persons): what, how, why; e.g. ～必改作 *hé bì gǎizuò*, why is it necessary to alter and remake it?; ～先～後 *hé xiān hé hòu*, what first, what last?; ～助於人 *hé zhù yū rén*, how does he provide assistance to another person?
　　a. ～為 *héwèi*, on account of what > why?; e.g. ～為不行 *héwèi bùxíng*, why does he not put it into practice?; 予～為不受 *yú héwèi bùshòu*, why should I not have received it?
　　b. ～以 *héyǐ*, by means of what > how ?; e.g. ～以別乎 *héyǐ bié hū*, how is it distinct from (something)?; ～以利吾國 *héyǐ lì wúguó*, how will you bring profit to my state?
　　c. ～如 *hérú*, to be like what, have what significance; do something in what way > how ?; e.g. 好樂～如 *hàoyuè hérú*, what is it like, to be fond of music?; 敢問～如 *gǎnwèn hérú*, I dare to ask, what is it like?
　　d. 如之～ *rúzhīhé*, make it like what?, what is to be done about it? > how should it be managed?; e.g. 君使臣臣事君如之～ *jūn shǐ chén chén shì jūn rúzhīhé*, as for a lord engaging a vassal or a vassal serving a lord, how should it be done?; 年饑用不足如之～ *nián jī yòng bùzú rúzhīhé*, the year is one of scarcity and what is available for use is insufficient, what is to be done about it? N.B. the construction 如～ *rúhé* is a somewhat archaic equivalent of *hérú* (1c) and not the equivalent of *rúzhīhé*.
2. exclamatory "how X!" expressing surprise at or appreciation of what follows.

　　hè　MC haX

1. carry on one's shoulder, ⊙ 荷 *hè* 1 (*hé*); e.g. ～戈 *hègē*, carry a pole-ax.

劾　hé　MC hok

1. subjugate by means of exorcistic instruments.
2. investigate (crime), bring offense to light.
　　a. challenge (formally), denounce, charge with offense.
3. condemn, convict.

合   hé   MC hop

1. (con)join, fit together, match; bring together, unite, combine; e.g. ～符 *héfú*, join the 2 halves of a tally; (Budd.) ～掌 *hézhǎng*, bring hands together in salutation.

   a. correspond(ing), coordinate(d); e.g. 六～ *liùhé*, 6 Coordinates or Conjunctions, the 4 directions plus zenith and nadir, i.e. the whole world.

   b. converge(nt), coincide(nt); concord(ant); e.g. ～氣 *héqì*, proportionate vapors, well-balanced *yin* and *yang*; also (Dao.), "joining of vital breaths," Tianshi ritual of highly choreographed intercourse between unmarried couple, modeled on cosmic concordance.

   c. come together; blend, mingle; collect; e.g. ～藥 *héyào*, to compound drugs; (bn.) ～沓 *hétà* (MC hop-dop), blending and building, mingling and massing; also, lapped and layered; also, bunched and bulking; ～釀 *héjù*, drinking party at which everyone has pooled money for wine; ～曲 *héqǔ*, play a tune together.

2. conjunction of 2 celestial bodies.

3. meet, accost; engage; e.g. ～戰 *hézhàn*, join battle.

4. close up, shut (door, box, mouth, etc.); e.g. ～昏 *héhūn*, "closing-at-dusk," the mimosa, because its leaves fold up at twilight.

   a. enclose; surround, environ.

5. conclude, bring to closure, bring everything together, set to rights; e.g. ～約 *héyuē*, agree on a pact, conclude an agreement.

6. of a kind with, similar(ity).

7. (med.) fitting, proper (to do X), ought to, should; be mete for.

8. (med.) conjunctive particle: and, and also, along with.

9. (med.) all of, the whole of; e.g. ～朝 *hézhāo*, the whole morning.

10. (med.) rdup., jammed and jumbled, crushed and crowded.

11. ⊙ 盒 *hé*, small box, pyxis, caddy.

   gě   MC kop

1. measure of capacity, a gill, equiv. one-tenth of a "pint" (*sheng* 升).

和   hé   MC hwa

1. harmonious, of sound; in harmony with, accordant; euphonious.

   a. accord with; comport with; be attuned to.

2. bring into harmony, balance, temper.

   a. congruent, concinnous, concordant; compatible.

3. agreeable, mellow; pleasant; gentle.

4. comfortable; calm, peaceful; congenial.

   a. conciliate, reconcile.

5. front board of outer or inner coffin.

6. carriage bells, croatals.

7. (med.) go in company with, go along with; associate, partner with, comport with.

8. (Budd.) ～尚 *héshàng*, "Your (His) Reverence," honorific term for monk of advanced standing, trns. Skt. *upādhyāya*, preceptor.

   hè   MC hwaH

1. accompany in song, harmonize with.

2. (lit.) compose a matching poem, on the same theme as the one being responded to, sometimes using same rhyme categories but not necessarily in same order.

嗑   hé   MC hap

1. 噬～ *shìhé*, → 噬 *shì*.

   xiā   MC khaep

1. ～然 *xiārán*, guffaw, heehaw.

   gě   MC kap

1. rdup., gabble, yap, prattle.

曷   hé   MC hat

1. interr. pronoun for things (as opposed to persons): when?, what?, how?, why?; cf. 何 *hé*, 奚 *xī*, 胡 *hú*, 盍 *hé*; e.g. ～足以美七尺之軀哉 *hé zúyǐ měi qīchǐ zhī qū zāi*, how is this at all sufficient to adorn a person's seven-*chǐ* frame?; ～謂至足 *hé wèi zhìzú*, what does the phrase "perfect adequacy" refer to?

   a. ～為 *héwèi*, on account of what > why?; e.g. ～為先言王而後言正月 *héwèi xiānyán wáng ér hòuyán zhēngyuè*, why first speak of the king and only then speak of the first-month ritual? 子～為泣也 *zǐ héwèi qì yě*, why are you weeping?

   b. ～以 *héyǐ*, by means of what > how ?; e.g. ～以知舞之意 *héyǐ zhī wǔ zhī yì*, how do you know the meaning of dancing? 吾～以識此 *wú héyǐ shì cǐ*, how will I recognize this?

2. ⊙ 盍 *hé*, why not?

核   hé   MC heak

1. stone, of drupe; pit.

   a. drupe, fruit with single stone, e.g. plum, cherry, peach.

2. kernel, core; nucleus.

3. gist; solid truth or reality.
4. examine into, investigate to the core.

氎　hé　MC hat

1. shag-wool; shaggy.
   a. (bn.) 氎〜 *lǚhé*, → 氎 *lǘ*.
2. ⊙ 鶡 *hé*, Manchurian snow-pheasant.

河　hé　MC ha

1. specifically the Yellow River; when used alone, simply transliterate "the He" or render as "the River."
2. gen. term for river; e.g. 〜上 *héshàng*, by (not "on") the river; river-dweller; (med.) 〜頭 *hétóu*, same as preceding.
   a. riverine, riparian, fluvial.
3. the Yellow River in the sky, i.e. the Milky Way, sgl. or cmpd. 天〜 *tiānhé*, the He in the sky, the sky river, or 銀〜 *yǐnhé*, the silver river, or doubled with the Han River (equally identified with the Milky Way) as 〜漢 *héhàn*, the He and Han (in the sky).

涸　hé　MC hak

1. dried out, desiccated, exsiccated.
2. use up, exhaust completely.
3. ⊙ 沍 *hù*, frozen, congealed, frigid.

盒　hé　MC hop

1. small box, pyxis, caddy; cosmetic case.

盍　hé　MC hap

1. interr. pronoun for things (as opposed to persons): why not?; historically equivalent to 何不 *hébù* or 胡不 *húbù*; cf. 何 *hé*, 奚 *xī*, 胡 *hú*, 曷 *hé*; e.g. 〜各言爾志 *hé gèyán ěr zhì*, why doesn't each of you speak of your goals? 〜反其本 *hé fǎn qí běn*, why not revert to one's basics?

禾　hé　MC hwa

1. standing grain.

紇　hé　MC hot

1. (med.) (bn.) 回〜 *huíhé* (MC hwoj-hot), Uighur, Turkic tribe that established a steppe empire centered on the Orkhon valley in 744 and lasting for nearly a century, greatly aided the Tang during the An Lushan rebellion and treated with special favor thereafter.
2. given name of Confucius's father.

翮　hé　MC heak

1. pinion, quill; wing coverts.

a. primary feather.
b. by synecdoche, the bird itself.
2. mouth-organ, pipe (< hollow tube).

荷　hé　MC ha

1. lotus (*Nelumbo nucifera*), also lotus leaf; cf. 蓮 *lián*, 芙蕖 *fúqú*, 芙蓉 *fúróng*, 菡萏 *hàndàn*. The roots of the lotus are planted in the mud at the bottom of a pond or river, and the leaves float on the water surface, with the stems of the flowers rising above the leaves. The rhizome (藕 *ǒu*) is used in cooking, and the root is used in medicine.
   a. (Budd.), a symbol of purity.
   b. 薄〜 *bóhé*, "thin lotus," field mint (*Mentha arvensis*).

hè　MC haX

1. carry on the shoulders, to shoulder, bear a burden, assume, maintain; wield, handle.
   a. burdensome, heavy.
2. lift with two hands.
3. receive, esp. favor or blessings.
4. gratitude.

kē　MC xa

1. ⊙ 苛 *kē*, punctilious.

蝎　hé　MC hat

1. roundheaded borer, wood-grub, various coleopterous beetles.

xiē　MC xjot

1. ⊙ 蠍 *xiē*, scorpion.

覈　hé　MC heak

1. perscrutate, examine in detail.
   a. assess, check the facts of; verify.
2. the facts, proven situation.
   a. actual, real.
3. ⊙ 核 *hé* 1, pit, stone of drupe; 麧 *hé* 1, bran, outer covering of cereal grain, husk.

貉　hé　MC hak

1. raccoon-dog (*Nyctereutes procyonoides*), heavy-bodied and thickly furred, ⊙ 狸 *lí* 1.
2. ferret-badger (*Helictis moschata*), mainly southern resident.

mò　MC maek

1. ⊙ 貊 *mò* 1, term for non-Chinese people to the north and northeast.

閡　hé　MC hok

1. obstruct(ion), block(age), bar(rier).

2. boundary, limit; e.g. 九～ *jiǔhé*, nine-bordered heaven.

    a. contain, keep within.

闔   hé   MC hap

1. leaves or fores of door or gate.

2. (bn.) 闔～ *chānghé*, → 閶 *chāng*.

3. close up, bar.

4. combine, converge, match, conjoin, fit; ⊙ 合 *hé* 1.

5. all, every, the whole of; e.g. ～四境之內 *hé sìjìng zhi nèi*, everywhere within the four borders.

6. ⊙ 盍 *hé*, interr. pronoun for things (as opposed to persons): why not?; historically equivalent to 何不 *hébù* or 胡不 *húbù*.

鞨   hé   MC hat

1. (med.) (bn.) 靺～ *móhé*, → 靺 *mó*.

    mò   MC maet

1. ～巾 *mòjūn*, headwrap, headkerchief, esp. for boys.

鶡   hé   MC hat

1. sgl. or ～雞 *héjī*, brown-eared pheasant, Manchurian snow-pheasant (*Crossoptilon mantschuricum*), dark brown with dark-tipped white tailfeathers, the tailfeathers often being used as decoration for caps.

2. ～旦 *hédàn*, flying fox, flittermouse (*Pteropus pselaphon*).

鴠   hé   MC 'aet

1. identification uncertain but said to resemble a smaller shrike (伯勞 *bóláo*).

2. (bn.) 鴠～ *xiáhé*, → 鴠 *xiá*.

麧   hé   MC hot

1. bran, hard outer covering of cereal grain; husk.

2. coarse fare.

齕   hé   MC hot

1. munch, chomp.

觮   hé   MC hwa   ⊙ 和 *hé*.

hè

喝   hè   MC xat

1. threaten, intimidate.

2. excoriate, berate; yell at, bellow.

    yè   MC 'eajH

1. sob, weep; wail.

    a. be hoarse.

嗃   hè   MC xak

1. rdup., cruel and ruthless, grim and grisly, strict and severe.

    xiāo   MC xaew

1. onom. of bamboo flute: "hyeeh!"

    xiào   MC xaewH

1. blare, blast; shriek.

嚇   hè   MC xaek

1. huff at in anger, intimidation, or exasperation; hoot at; shoo away.

2. puff, pant, blow breath.

壑   hè   MC xak

1. riverbed and nearby land; river valley, strath.

    a. gorge, ravine, gully.

皬   hè   MC hak

1. rdup., glitter and gleam, albescently candent.

皜   hè   MC howk

1. glossy white; rdup., glossily glistening.

褐   hè   MC hat

1. hodden, coarse wool tabby; kersey, burlap; homespun.

    a. coarse clothing made of preceding; by metonymy, plain fellow, simple folk, commoner.

2. dull-brown (color); drab.

賀   hè   MC haH

1. offer a present as expression of felicitation.

    a. congratulate, felicitate; compliment.

2. surname.

    a. ～蘭 *hèlán*, ～拔 *hèbá*, ～若 *hèruò*, all bisyallabic surnames.

赫   hè   MC xaek

1. fire-red; ruddy; rubescent, rubicund; rufous, rutilant.

2. vivid, evident; manifest; blazon(ed); (ef)fulgent.

3. redden with anger; choleric, irascible, quick-tempered, fiery.

    a. frightening, formidable.

4. rdup., superbly splendid, nobly majestic, awe-inspiring (as of person or building).

鶴　hè　MC hak

1. gen. term for crane (*Grus*), incl. common crane (*Grus grus*) and hooded crane (*Grus monachus*), but esp. Siberian crane (*Grus leucogeranus*) and red-crowned crane (*Grus japonensis*) as symbol of longevity, Dao. transcendence and immortality; the white feathers signifying purity and the red patch on red-crowned crane seen as visible mark of the cinnabar-based elixir of immortality (*dan* 丹).

   a. because of association with heaven, often used as emblematic of imperial court; e.g. 〜板 *hèbǎn*, "crane placard," i.e. summons to court.

2. (med.) (lit.) 〜膝 *hèxī*, crane's knee, name of prosodic fault in which 5th and 15th words in pentasyllabic lines of verse have the same tone, thus the 10th word (a rhyme-word) that ends the intervening even line seems to "bulge" between them, like a crane's knobby knee.

hēi

黑　hēi　MC xok

1. the color black, carbon-black, lamp-black; associated in *wuxing* correspondences with the phase or agent of water, the season of winter, direction north, etc.

   a. symbolic of complete ascendance of *yin* prevailing over *yang*.

2. physical but also moral, political, cultural darkness; inability to see or understand clearly.

hén

痕　hén　MC hon

1. scar; wound.

2. tracks, traces; e.g. 淚〜 *lèihén*, tear-tracks.

hěn

很　hěn　MC honX

1. disobey; disagree(able); fractious, querulous; ⊙ 狠 *hěn* 1.

很　hěn　MC honX

1. disobey, defy, contravene; fractious, querulous.

2. contest, dispute; esp. lawsuit.

hèn

恨　hèn　MC honH

1. regret, remorse.

2. rancor, malice; resent(ful), vengeful.

   a. disfavor, have no use for, feel hostile toward.

hēng

亨　hēng　MC xaeng

1. extend throughout, pervade, prevalence; penetrate.

2. success(ful), prosper(ous).

   xiǎng　MC xjangX
   1. ⊙ 享 *xiǎng* 1, sacrificial feast; regale with banquet.

   pēng　MC phaeng
   1. cook, by boiling.

héng

姮　héng　MC hong

1. 〜娥 *héng'é*, "persistent beauty," Heng'e, name of mythological goddess of the moon who reputedly fled there with elixir of immortality stolen from her husband Yi 羿.

恆　héng　MC hong

1. persist(ent), constant; perseverance.

   a. long-lasting, enduring; perpetual.

   b. "Constancy," name of 32nd hexagram of *Yijing*.

2. prevalent; ordinary, routine; habitual, normal, make a regular practice of.

   gèng　MC kongH
   1. waxing crescent of the moon.
   2. extend, expand; spread out.
   3. (med.) Ganges River; e.g. 〜沙 *gèngshā*, the sands of the Ganges.

恒　héng　MC hong　⊙ 恆 *héng*.

桁　héng　MC haeng

1. purlin, crossbeam of roof.

   háng　MC hang
   1. foot-chains, fetters; to fetter.

   a. cangue; to pillory.

2. pontoon bridge.

橫   héng   MC hwaeng

1. horizontal, crosswise, east-west direction; ant. 縱 zōng (zòng); e.g. 縱～ zōnghéng, this way and that, across and athwart; also, sophistical eloquence in political matters and those who practice it, persuaders who can argue one way or another; also, 2 alliances during the late Warring States period, zōng being that of 6 states against Qin 秦, héng being that of 6 eastern states allied with Qin

   a. transverse; athwart; e.g. ～吹 héngchuī, blow (flute) sideways, a cross-flute, transverse flute.

   b. sideways; alongside; e.g. ～潰 héngkuì, flood over along the banks, burst the banks.

2. cut across, go athwart.

3. spread across, spread throughout, spread wide; e.g. ～空 héngkōng, across the sky; ～波 héngbō, spreading waves; also, tears crisscrossing the face.

   a. fill up, pervade; e.g. ～世 héngshì, fill the world.

4. thwart, balk, contravene.

   hèng   MC hwaengH

1. contrary, perverse, at cross-purposes; unmannerly, harsh, offensive; arbitrary, unruly, unchecked.

2. untimely, unexpected; e.g. ～死 hèngsǐ, untimely death (premature), unanticipated death (suicide).

珩   héng   MC haeng

1. girdle pendant of jade longer horizontally than vertically, of rectangular or trapezoidal shape.

2. crosspiece of jade, fitted across head to hold on cap.

胻   héng   MC haeng

1. shinbone, shankbone.

   a. calf of the leg.

脝   héng   MC xaeng

1. (med.) (bn.) 膨～ pénghéng, → 膨 péng.

蘅   héng   MC haeng

1. sgl. or 杜～ dùhéng, asarum (Asarum forbesii), with kidney-shaped leaves and small reddish-brown flowers, fragrance similar to ginger-root; in lit. an image of sweet-smelling purity.

衡   héng   MC haeng

1. balance-arm of steelyard, balance-beam.

   a. weigh, trutinate; e.g. ～量 héngliàng, weigh and measure.

   b. compendium, compendious.

   c. equilibrium, equipoise, balance.

   d. fairness, justice, equity.

2. transverse, horizontal, crosswise; e.g. ～門 héngmén, crossbeam gate, indicative of simplicity; also, metonymy for recluse.

   a. transverse astronomical sighting-tube.

   b. sgl. or 玉～ yùhéng, Jade Transverse, name of 5th star (Alioth) of the Northern Dipper; by synecdoche, the Dipper itself; e.g. ～漢 hénghàn, Jade Transverse (= Dipper) and the Heavenly Han (= Milky Way).

3. crosspiece of wood with which to cap the horns of an ox (esp. sacrificial ox) to keep it from goring.

4. balustrade, railing.

   a. crossbar at front of carriage.

5. crosspiece of jade, fitted across head to hold on cap; ⊙ 珩 héng 2.

6. top of the shank of a chime-bell.

hōng

嵤   hōng   MC xweang

1. (bn.) 岭～ línghōng, → 岭 líng.

烘   hōng   MC xuwng

1. bake, roast.

2. dry at the fire.

硡   hōng   MC xweang

1. (bn.) ～隱 hōngyǐn (MC xweang-'j+nX), onom. of drums, bang and rumble, roll and resound.

薨   hōng   MC xwong

1. in pre-imperial times, honorific term for death of a noble lord; obdormition.

   a. in imperial times, used for death of high-ranking official, e.g. in Tang times for those holding grade-three ranks (sanpin 三品) and above.

訇   hōng   MC xweang

1. (med.) onom. of overpowering sound: boom, crash.

輷   hōng   MC xweang

1. onom. of rumble of thunder or heavy carriages, ⊙ 轟 hōng.

a. (bn.) ～輘 *hōnglíng* (MC xweang-long) or 輘～ *línghōng*, → 輘 *líng* (*léng*).

轟　hōng　MC xweang

1. sgl. or rdup., onom. of rumble-mutter of thunder or trumble-rumble of heavy carriages.
　　a. onom. of any loud noise: bang, crash, boom.

hóng

吰　hóng　MC hweang

1. (bn.) 嚌～ *chēnghóng*, → 嚌 *chēng*.
2. ⊙ 宏 *hóng*, capacious, ample, expansive.

宏　hóng　MC hweang

1. capacious, ample; prodigious.
　　a. extensive, widespread; universal.
2. expand, enlarge, broaden; amplify.
3. far-sounding, sonorous, resounding.

弘　hóng　MC hwong

1. broad, great; capacious; accrescent; e.g. ～遠 *hóngyuǎn*, vastly distant.
2. stretch outward, accrete, expand, broaden.
　　a. dilate; enhance, promote.
3. go beyond, exceed; rise above; e.g. ～慮 *hónglù*, transcend concerns, dispel care.

汯　hóng　MC hweang

1. rdup., swashing and splashing, lapping and plashing (water).
2. (bn.) 泓～ *hónghóng*, → 泓 *hóng*.

泓　hóng　MC 'weang

1. deep water, deeply layered.
　　a. deep pool, fathomless pool.
2. (bn.) ～宏 *hónghóng* (MC 'weang-heang), deep and resonant, deep-toned and throbbing (music).
3. (bn.) ～汯 *hónghóng* (MC 'weang-heang), gyring and spiralling, whirling and swirling (water).

洪　hóng　MC huwng

1. overflooding, overwhelming; e.g. ～水 *hóngshuǐ*, overwhelming waters, inundation.
　　a. awash, drowned in; e.g. ～醉 *hóngzuì*, awash in drink, utterly soused.
2. vast, immense; extensive, wide-spreading; universal, all-encompassing; e.g. ～荒 *hónghuāng*, chaotically commingled, distantly mixed; ～儒 *hóngrú*, broadly learned scholar; ～鈞 *hóngjūn*, the all-fashioning potter, i.e. Heaven as creative force.

竑　hóng　MC hweang

1. to measure, reckon.

篊　hóng　MC huwng

1. (med.) bamboo fish-weir.

紅　hóng　MC huwng

1. gen. term for light to medium-deep red, usu. lustrous, not dark reds; esp. (increasing in deepness) pink, cerise, rose, crimson; e.g. ～粉 *hóngfěn*, pink powder (of women's makeup); ～顏 *hóngyán*, rosy-faced, i.e. young and healthy; ～淚 *hónglèi*, tears of blood-red, normal tears all cried out and now weeping blood; ～塵 *hóngchén*, red dust, of the tumultuous mortal world.
2. ～藍 *hónglán*, "pink indigo," safflower (*Carthamus tinctorius*); ～花 *hónghuā*, safflower flowers, used medicinally.
3. ～嘴烏 *hóngzuǐwū*, red-billed daw, red-billed chough (*Pyrrhocorax pyrrhocorax*).

　　gōng　MC kuwng

1. (med.) ⊙ 工 *gōng* 2b, weaving, embroidery, women's fine work.

紘　hóng　MC hweang

1. chin-strap, to tie on ceremonial cap.
2. cord with which to suspend a chime-bell.
3. cord with which to tie several items together; e.g. 八～ *bāhóng*, 8 Cordings, i.e. bounds of the 8 directions.
　　a. tie together, attach; link up.
4. cords of a net for catching game; the net itself.
5. ⊙ 宏 *hóng* 1, capacious, ample; extensive, widespread.

耾　hóng　MC hweang

1. rdup., roar and rumble, sound and resound.

虹　hóng　MC huwng

1. rainbow; primary rainbow; traditionally considered "male" in contrast to the "female" 霓 *ní*, secondary rainbow; e.g. ～霓 *hóngní*, rainbow and iris, double-term for rainbow.
　　a. circular or bow-shaped bright atmospheric phenomena; e.g. 白～ *báihóng*, white nimbus (round the sun or at edge of sun's arc), sun-dog, parhelion.
2. bow-arched bridge.

　　hòng　MC huwngH

1. (bn.) ～洞 *hòngdòng*, ⊙ 澒洞 *hòngdòng*, → 澒 *hòng*.

谹 hóng   MC hweang

1. sgl. or rdup., echo of mountain valley, sound and resound, swelling echo.
2. ⊙ 宏 hóng 1, capacious, ample; extensive, widespread.

閎 hóng   MC hweang

1. alley-gate; gate to a lane, wicket; small gate.
   a. gen. term for gate.
2. ⊙ 宏 hóng 1, capacious, ample; extensive, widespread.

鴻 hóng   MC huwng

1. swan-goose (*Anser cygnoides*), largest of wild-geese, a winter migrant from Siberia and Mongolia, hence an image of far traveling; e.g. ～漸 *hóngjiàn*, gradual ascent of the swan-goose, euph. for official advancement; ～鵠 *hónghú*, swan-goose and swan; also, just swan (*Cygnus cygnus*).
   a. (med.) ～臚寺 *hónglúsì*, "office of arrangements for swan-geese," Tang office in charge of foreign visitors and tributary envoys.
2. vast; universal; all-encompassing; magnificent; ⊙ 洪 hóng 1; e.g. ～烈 *hóngliè*, all-encompassing brilliance; also, magnificent accomplishment; ～鐘 *hóngzhōng*, large bell, also onom. (MC *huwng-tsyowng*) of the swelling, enveloping sounding of the bell.
   a. (bn.) ～蒙 *hóngméng* (MC huwng-muwng), vast vagueness, vaporous opacity, all-encompassing mist, swirling chaos before creation; ～洞 *hóngdòng* (MC huwng-duwngH), limitless immensity, capacious chaos.

黌 hóng   MC hwaeng

1. school, lyceum.

hòng

澒 hòng   MC huwngX

1. eddying water, flowing round.
   a. (bn.) ～洞 *hòngdòng* (MC huwngX-duwngX), billowing and building up (clouds); also, swirling and whirling (water); also, as in 2, inconceivable chaos.
2. (bn.) ～濛 *hòngméng* (MC huwngX-muwng), commingled chaos, vast opacity, as before separation of heaven and earth; all-encompassing mist.
gǒng   MC huwngX
1. ⊙ 汞 *gǒng*, quicksilver, mercury.

訌 hòng   MC huwng

1. dissent; disrupt(ion), disturb(ance), discompose; upheaval.

鬨 hòng   MC huwngH

1. dispute, contention, quarrel, conflict.
   a. tumult, embroilment, turmoil.
2. pandemonium, uproar; clamor, din; commotion, clatter.

hōu

齁 hōu   MC xuw

1. snuffle, snort, snurt.

hóu

侯 hóu   MC huw

1. archery target, butt, mark, scope.
2. 2nd of the 5 ranks of nobility, usu. translated "marquis" or "marquess."
3. honorific term applied in pre-imperial times to all rulers of states, regardless of actual rank; e.g. 諸～ *zhūhóu*, the various nobles, feudal lords, vassal lords; (med.) ref. governors of prefectures and regions.
4. (med.) honorific epithet among literati or gentry.
5. line-initial or line-middle rhythmic particle in *Shijing*.

喉 hóu   MC huw

1. sgl. or (bn.) ～嚨 *hóulóng* (MC huw-luwng), throat; trachea, windpipe.

猴 hóu   MC huw

1. (bn.) 獼～ *míhóu*, macaque, → 獼 *mí*.

矦 hóu   MC huw   ⊙ 侯 hóu

箜 hóu   MC huw

1. (bn.) 箜～ *kōnghóu*, → 箜 *kōng*.

糇 hóu   MC huw

1. dry provisions, for travel.

翭 hóu   MC huw

1. calamus of feather.
   a. measure-word for feathers.
2. ⊙ 鍭 *hóu*, metal-tipped arrow with clipped feathers.

鍭　hóu　MC huw

1. metal-tipped arrow with clipped feathers, thus heavier in front, used for near targets.

鯸　hóu　MC huw　⊙ 鍭 *hóu.*

hǒu

吼　hǒu　MC xuwX

1. (med.) roar or cry of wild animal.
2. (med.) loud cry, shout, wail of human or rumble, clatter, racket of vehicle.

hòu

候　hòu　MC huwH

1. observe atmospheric conditions for sign or portent, look out for significant changes.
   a. sign, omen, portent.
2. watch for untoward movement of enemy at frontier.
   a. watchman, observer, scout, scan.
3. watch out for and wait on something expected or desired, look out for; bear witness to.
4. ask after someone's health or general condition.
5. ⊙ 堠 *hòu* 1, watch-post, observation post.
6. period of 5 days, pentad of days.

厚　hòu　MC huwX

1. thick (ant. 薄 *bó*, thin); e.g. ～顏 *hòuyán*, thick-skinned.
   a. full of a particular quality, rich in character; e.g. ～酒 *hòujiǔ*, rich wine, fully flavored.
2. substantial, solid; of a certain magnitude.
   a. important, significant; material, necessary.
3. substantive; authentic, genuine.
4. wealthy, prosperous, rich; flush, thriving; e.g. ～地 *hòudì*, bountiful earth; ～載 *hòuzài*, richly bearing, substantively supporting (the myriad things), i.e. the earth.
5. full-hearted; generous, lavish; thoroughly sincere.
   a. deep or profound feelings; e.g. ～善 *hòushàn*, deep-seated friendship.
   b. do a favor for.

后　hòu　MC huwX

1. ruler, sovereign, of empire or of feudal state.
   a. ～土 *hòutǔ*, sovereign earth, name of divinity of earth; also, honorific term for earth, esp. when paired with 皇天 *huángtiān*, august heaven.
2. mother of heir-designate, i.e. of the (currently) designated successor; often translated as "empress," though title is dependent on continuing status of heir-designate.
   a. dowager empress, mother of reigning emperor.

堠　hòu　MC huwH

1. watch-mound, watch-post, observation post; beacon-mound.
2. (med.) landmarks, hummocks of heaped earth marking distances along well-traveled routes, early on every *li* in some areas, by Tang times every 5 *li*.

後　hòu　MC huwX

1. behind, at the back, in the rear, rearward (space); ant. 前 *qián*, in front of, before, front, fore.
   a. backward, go back; go after, take or bring up the rear; latecomer.
2. after, afterward (time); later, latter(ly); ant. 前 *qián*, former, earlier.
   a. (Dao.) ～天 *hòutiān*, latter Heaven, or subsequent to Heaven, the world as currently known, in contrast to 先天 *xiāntiān*, prior Heaven, or prior to Heaven, primal stage of the cosmos; (Dao.) ～聖 *hòushèng*, saint of the latter age, a category in Shangqing hierarchy above *zhenren* 真人 (Perfected), also divinized Laozi as the messiah expected in various med. Dao. movements.
3. those who come afterward; later generation; descendants; e.g. ～生 *hòushēng*, those born in a later time; also, young person.

逅　hòu　MC huwH

1. sgl. or (bn.) 邂～ *xièhòu* (MC heaH-huwH) come upon by chance, run across, → 邂 *xiè.*

鱟　hòu　MC huwH

1. horseshoe-crab, king-crab (*Tachypleus tridentatus*).

hū

乎　hū　MC hu

1. interr. final GP for verbal sentences; e.g. 可得聞～ *kě dé wén hū*, Can it be heard about?; 王許之～ *wáng xǔ zhī hū*, Does the king agree with this?

a. exclamatory final GP for verbal sentences, often including a rhetorical interr. sense; e.g. 其無後～ *qí wúhòu hū*, He really ought not have any descendants!; 若是其大～ *ruòshì qí dà hū*, really as big as this!?
b. exclamatory suffix to nouns or predicate adjectives; e.g. 眇～*miào hū*, so minute!; 神～*shénhū*, how divine!
2. "in relation to," "vis-à-vis" (hence, any indirect or prepositional relation); e.g. 及陷～罪 *jí xiàn-hū zuì*, when one falls into a wrongdoing; 莫大～尊親 *mò dà hū zūnqīn*, Nothing is more important than esteeming one's family intimates; 楚人生～楚 *chǔrén shēng hū chǔ*, People of Chu are born in Chu; cog. *yú* 於, in relation to, vis-à-vis.

呼   hū   MC xu
1. exhale forcefully, with mouth open (ant. 吸 *xī*, inhale, draw breath).
2. call out, shout, cry.
3. cry up, praise, extol.
4. call (as), name, refer to as.
5. (med.) regard as, take as, consider as.

嘑   hū   MC xu
1. ⊙ 呼 *hū* 2, call out, shout, cry.
hù   MC xuH
1. ～爾 *hùěr*, sneer insolently, jeer scornfully.

幠   hū   MC xu
1. cover over, overlay.
2. great, substantial, significant.
3. misprize, disdain.
   a. disregard, ignore.

忽   hū   MC xwot
1. ignore, disregard; be oblivious of, indifferent.
   a. careless of, disdain(ful).
2. swift(ly), quick(ly).
   a. sudden(ly), all at once, abrupt(ly); unawares.
3. rdup. or (bn.) ～荒 *hūhuāng* (MC xwot-xwang), swiftly and suddenly, unawares and evanescent; also, dazed and hazy, bleared and blurry; also, dourly depressed.
4. measure of length, infinitely short, one-millionth of a "foot" (*chǐ* 尺).
   a. infinitesimal, imperceptible, inconceivably small.

5. (med.) ～如 *hūrú*, just like, just the same as, quite the same.
6. (med.) consequently, in the end.

惚   hū   MC xwot
1. (bn.) ～恍, ～怳 *hūhuǎng* (MC xwot-xwangX) or 恍～, 怳～ *huǎnghū*, dazed and distracted, distracted and delirious, muddled and murky, blurred and smeared, hazy maze.

滹   hū   MC 'wot
1. run off, wash away.
   a. decline, wane; erode.
2. (bn.) ～决 *hūyǎng* (MC 'wot-'jangX), running and rushing, scurrying and scudding.

膴   hū   MC xu
1. fish cut in large pieces (cf. 膾 *kuài*, minced).
2. deboned dried meat.
wǔ   MC mjuX
1. substantial; significant, important.
2. rdup., fresh and fertile (land).

譹   hū   MC xu
1. ⊙ 呼 *hū* 2, call out, shout, cry.

hú

壺   hú   MC hu
1. ewer, flacket, flagon, jug, for wine; urn, vase, for water; e.g. 投～ *tóuhú*, pitch-pot, game in which arrows are thrown at narrow opening of jug.
2. ⊙ 瓠 *hù*, bottle-gourd, calabash.

弧   hú   MC hu
1. wooden bow.
   a. bow-shaped, arc, crescent.
2. bend, twist; veer, deviate.

搰   hú   MC hwot
1. dig out, dig up; unearth, bring to the surface.
kū   MC khwot
1. rdup., with might and main, exerting great effort, working hard at.

斛   hú   MC huwk
1. measure of capacity, bushel, equiv. 10 "pecks" (*dou* 斗).

槲　hú　MC huwk

1. sweet-oak, daimyo-oak (*Quercus dentata*).

湖　hú　MC hu

1. lake, lacustrine
    a. large pool, reservoir; basin.

狐　hú　MC hu

1. fox, red-fox (*Vulpes vulpes*); e.g. ～疑 *húyí*, wary as a fox, hesitant, watchful, careful.
2. 短～ *duǎnhú*, "short-bodied fox," i.e. sand-spitter, syn. 蜮 *yù*, 射影 *shèyǐng*.

瑚　hú　MC hu

1. (bn.) ～璉 *húlián*, ritual vessel for sacrifical offerings of grain in ancestral temple; sometimes used as symbolic of a person of worth and ability.
2. (bn.) 珊～ *shānhú*, coral, → *shān* 珊.

糊　hú　MC hu

1. (med). to paste, attach.
    a. (med.) paper a window.
2. (med.) ⊙ 餬 *hú*, gruel, congee.

縠　hú　MC huwk

1. crepe, crepe-gauze, very thin and light silk.

胡　hú　MC hu

1. dewlap.
    a. beard.
2. curved blade on underside of glaive or guisarme.
3. far-reaching; considerable, great; e.g. ～休 *húxiū*, great beneficence; ～考 *húkǎo*, ～耇 *húgǒu*, long-lived, person of considerable age.
4. term for northern (i.e. Turkic, proto-Mongol) and western (i.e. Central Asian, Turkic, Iranian) "barbarians"; depending on context, translate as: foreign(er), north(ern), western(er), nomad(ic), Hun(nish), barbarian, uncouth.
    a. ～麻 *húmá*, "western hemp-seeds," i.e. sesame (*Sesamum orientale*) or flax (*Linum usitatissimum*); ～桃 *hútáo*, "foreign peach," i.e. walnut (*Juglans regia*); ～蕙 *húhuì*, "western melilot," i.e. cocklebur (*Xanthium strumarium*), mainly from India.
    b. (med.) ～孫 *húsūn*, "foreign grandson," vernacular term for macaque (獼猴 *míhóu*).
5. interr. pronoun: what?, how?, why?; cf. 何 *hé*, 奚 *xī*, 曷 *hé*, 盍 *hé*; e.g. ～不遄死 *hú bùchuán sǐ*,

why should he not hasten to die? 余～弗知 *yú hú fúzhī*, why do I not know of it? ～可比也 *hú kěbǐ yě*, how can he be compared with?
    a. ～為 *húwèi*, on account of what > why ?; e.g. ～為其不可以反宿也 *húwèi qí bùkěyǐ fǎn sù yě*, why might he not be able to return it to its repose? 君～為有憂色 *jūn húwèi yǒu yōu sè*, why do you, my lord, have such a concerned look?

葫　hú　MC hu

1. garlic (*Allium sativum*), syn. 蒜 *suàn*.
2. (bn.) ～蘆 *húlú* (MC hu-lu), bottle-gourd, calabash (*Lagenaria siceraria*); often in lit. an image of a secretly enclosed but infinitely expandable world or separate universe.

蝴　hú　MC hu

1. (med.) (bn.) ～蝶 *húdié* (MC hu-dep), butterfly.

觳　hú　MC huwk

1. goblet, wine-vessel.
2. measure of capacity in early times, equiv. 1 "peck" (*dou* 斗) and 2 "pints" (*sheng* 升). N.B. Do not confuse with 斛 *hú*, "bushel."
3. ～觫 *húsù* (MC huwk-suwk), trembling in terror, shaking with fright; wary and worried.
    què　MC khaewk
1. thin, emaciated, lean; bony; spindly.
    jué　MC kaewk
1. pit one's strength against, test of strength; grapple, struggle with.

醐　hú　MC hu

1. (bn.) 醍～ *tíhú*, → 醍 *tí*.

餬　hú　MC hu

1. gruel, made with barley or millet; congee, rice-porridge; e.g. ～□ *húkǒu*, give sustenance to; also, make a living.

鵠　hú　MC howk

1. sgl. or 鴻～ *hónghú*, swan (*Cygnus cygnus*, *C. bewickii*).
2. swan-white.
    gù　MC kowk
1. center of target, bullseye.

鶘　hú　MC hu

1. (bn.) 鵜～ *tíhú*, → 鵜 *tí*.

鶻   **hú**   MC hwot
1. (med.) falcon, esp. peregrine falcon (*Falco peregrinus*); syn. with earlier term 隼 *sǔn*.
   gǔ   MC kwot
1. (bn.) ～鵃 *gǔzhōu* (MC kwot-trjuw), Loochoo green pigeon (*Treron permagna*).

hǔ

澔   **hǔ**   MC xuX
1. waterside; riverbank, lakeside.

琥   **hǔ**   MC xuX
1. jade tablet in shape of tiger.
2. (bn.) ～珀 *hǔpò* (MC xuX-phaek), amber.

虎   **hǔ**   MC xuX
1. tiger; symbolic of ferocity, agility, courage; e.g. ～賁 *hǔbēn*, agile as tigers, epithet for soldiers.
   a. emblematic animal of the west.
2. (bn.) ～落 *hǔluò* (MC xuX-lak), palisades, constructe d of wood or bamboo, as military protection.

hù

互   **hù**   MC
1. reciprocal(ly), reciprocate; mutual(ly); one another, each other.
   a. in exchange, back-and-forth.
2. crisscross; interlace, interlock.
3. rack for hanging meat, esp. for animals killed during a hunt.

嫭   **hù**   MC huH   ⊙ 嫮 *hù*.

嫮   **hù**   MC huH
1. beautiful, handsome; beauty, attractive(ness).
   a. goodness.
2. prettify, embellish; flaunt, boast.

岵   **hù**   MC huX
1. wooded hill, carpeted with plants and trees.

怙   **hù**   MC huX
1. lean on, rely on, depend on.
   a. euph. for father; e.g. ～恃 *hùshì*, rely and depend on; (med.) father and mother, whom one can count on.

戶   **hù**   MC huX
1. single-leaved door.

a. doorway; measure-word for household, esp. for census and taxation purposes; e.g. (med.) ～部 *hùbù*, Department of Revenue (< household imposts), one of the 6 departments operating under the Bureau of State Affairs (*shangshu sheng* 尚書省) in Sui-Tang times.
2. opening, hole, for insect or small creature to get to its nest.
3. inner door, usu. to living quarters; ingress, entrance.
4. prevent, stop, obstruct.
5. (med.) capacity for wine.

扈   **hù**   MC huX
1. escort, follow; retinue, esp. of emperor.
2. restrain, constrain; moderate, keep within bounds.
3. caped, mantled, covered.
4. button-quail (*Coturnix chinensis*).

旿   **hù**   MC huX
1. distinct, clear.
2. rdup., lustrously lambent, shining sleekly.

柜   **hù**   MC huH
1. barricade of poles, erected as protection before official headquarters or encampment; palisade.

楛   **hù**   MC huX
1. thorn-tree.
2. clump, rank growth.
   kǔ   MC khuX
1. crude, unpolished, unrefined; inferior, of poor quality; shoddy.
   a. unstable, shaky; fragile, weak.

冱   **hù**   MC huH
1. frozen, congealed.
   a. frigid, freezing; gelid; cold.

滬   **hù**   MC huX
1. (med.) fish-weir, fish-garth, made of bamboo.

瓠   **hù**   MC huH
1. bottle-gourd, calabash (*Lagenaria siceraria*); e.g. ～瓜 *hùguā*, gourd; also, Gourd-star, constellation comprising α, β, γ, δ, ζ Delphini, near celestial equator in northern sky.
   hú   MC hu
1. earthenware vase, urn, pitcher.

huò　MC hwak

1. (bn.) ～落 *huòluò* (MC hwak-lak), uselessly unwieldy.

祜　**hù**　MC huX

1. blessings; favor, good fortune.

笏　**hù**　MC xwot

1. tablet, usu. of bamboo, held by officials at court audience, on which notes might be taken.

苄　**hù**　MC huX

1. Chinese foxglove, rehmannia (*Rehmannia glutinosa*), used medicinally.

　　xià　MC haeH

1. cattail, bulrush (*Typha latifolia*), used in weaving of mats.

薝　**hù**　MC huX

1. (bn.) 萑～ *huánhù*, → 萑 *huán*.

護　**hù**　MC huH

1. keep watch over; maintain, preserve safely; e.g. ～念 *hùniàn*, keep in mind.
   a. take good care of, treasure, cherish.
2. protect, guard, ward; defend.
3. (med.) harbor, cover up, keep secret; e.g. ～失 *hùshī*, conceal one's mistakes.
4. oversee, manage, be in control of, esp. military.

鞾　**hù**　MC huH

1. leather loop or strap with which to suspend sword from a belt.
2. tie up, bind.

鳸　**hù**　MC huX

1. gen. term for quails (*Coturnix*, various species).

huā

花　**huā**　MC xwae

1. (med.) blossom, flower, (ef)florescence, esp. of woody plants (cf. 榮 *róng*, esp. of herbaceous plants); floriate, floriferous.
2. (med.) euph. for beautiful woman, esp. courtesan or performer.
3. (med.) spotted, dappled, pied, stippled, marked; e.g. ～馬 *huāmǎ*, piebald horse; 三～ *sānhuā*, tri-spotted, horse's crenelated mane done up in 3 blocks.

4. (med.) muddled, blurred, mixed, confused.
5. (med.) adorn, trim, embellish; e.g. ～子 *huāzi*, mouche, patch of black powder worn on woman's face.

huá

嘩　**huá**　MC xwae　⊙ 譁 *huá*.

滑　**huá**　MC hweat

1. sleek, slick; oily, slippery.
   a. smooth, glossy, polished.
2. of character, slippery, shifty, tricky; crafty, wily; glib.
   a. shrewd; resourceful, ingenious.
3. sgl. or ～石 *huáshí*, soapstone; talc.

　　gǔ　MC kwot

1. ⊙ 汨 *gǔ* 3, churn up, agitate, disturb; 4, rdup., run rapidly (water), flooding flow; also, onom. of rushing water, gush and gabble.
2. (bn.) ～稽 *gǔjī* (MC kwot-kej), wine-pot fitted with siphon for constant sipping, wine-hookah; also, font of endless drollery, droll and diverting, cleverly comical, glibly glabrous, carefree wag, glibly loquacious; also, slick and slippery, oily and unctuous.

猾　**huá**　MC hweat

1. crafty, wily; sly, shrewd; shifty, tricky.
2. disarray, dishevel; upset, shake up, throw into disorder.
3. (med.) miniature dog, "toy" dog.

華　**huá**　MC hwae

1. splendor, splendid; glorious.
   a. often as honorific descriptive.
2. brilliant, of high gloss, luster, lustrous.
3. illustrious; eminent, esteemed.
4. beauty, elegance; beautiful, elegant; of physical objects, women, lit. style.
   a. the best of, "the flower of," the glory of.
5. luxurious, sumptuous.
   a. extravagant, wasteful, prodigal.
6. showy, vain display, ostentatious; superficial, flashy; ornate.
7. women's make-up, esp. face-powder.
8. ancient name for the people and land of the Central Plain (*zhongyuan* 中原) or the Central States (*zhongguo* 中國); often paired as ～夏 *huáxià*, Hua-Xia.

a. civilized, born and bred in the land of superior culture (indeed of the only culture worthy of the name) and heir to the traditions of the sage-kings of old.

huā   MC hwae

1. blossom, flower, (ef)florescence, esp. of woody plants (cf. 榮 *róng*, esp. of herbaceous plants); floriate, bloom(ing).

huà   MC hwaeH

1. a surname.
2. name of mountain in Shaanxi, the Western Marchmount.

譁   huá   MC xwae

1. racket, row; bedlam, commotion; bawling, fuss, hubbub; shouting.

驊   huá   MC hwae

1. (bn.) ～騮 *huáliú*, "dappled roan" (?), name of fabulous horse who could run 1,000 *li* in a day > superlative steed.

huà

劃   huà   MC hweak

1. slice, cut through, cleave, skive.
    a. carve out, block out; sculpt, chisel.
2. (med.) ⊙ 畫 *huà* 1, delineate, delimit, mark out.
3. (med.) sgl. or ～然 *huàrán*, suddenly, abruptly, at one cut; also, clearly, cleanly, distinctly.

化   huà   MC xwaeH

1. transform(ation), change, transmute, permutate; e.g. 造～ *zàohuà,* Fashioner of Change, Shaper of Mutations, the selecting and synthesizing principle of Nature.
    a. provide the trigger or reason for change, catalyze; persuade, suasive.
2. bring round to new perspective or understanding, convert; e.g. 教～ *jiàohuà*, teach and transform, change by inculcation of moral expectations and responsibilities, esp. in the populace through the agency and example of government officials; (med.) ～胡 *huàhú*, conversion of the barbarians, legend that Laozi, after departing China, went to India where he taught (or became) the Buddha; (Budd.) ～度 *huàdù*, convert and cross over (to "other shore" beyond impermanence); (Budd.) 導～ *dǎohuà*, guide and convert (to the dharma path).
3. (Budd.) acting in the world of phenomenal experience for the benefit of living beings; e.g.

～迹 *huàjī*, manifested activities, traces of the Buddha.
    a. (Budd.) make manifest an ultimately unreal phenomenon for the sake of "expedient means" (*fangbian* 方便, → 方 *fāng* 6), call up as if by magic, phantasmal; e.g. ～城 *huàchéng*, conjured city, famous parable in 7th chapter of *Lotus Sutra*.
4. euph. for death, dying, the ultimate transformation.

嬅   huà   MC hweak

1. attractive modesty, reserve.
    a. (bn.) 媿～ *guǐhuà*, → 媿 *guǐ*.
2. (bn.) 徽～ *huīhuà*, → 徽 *huī*.

樺   huà   MC hwaeH

1. birch, white birch (*Betula platyphylla*).

畫   huà   MC hweaH

1. draw the borders of a field, delineate, delimit; mark out, outline.
2. draw(ing), sketch.
    a. design, plan; draw up, map out; devise.
3. (med.) sign one's name, autograph, endorse.

繣   huà   MC hweaH

1. cord, tie; tie up, fasten.
2. onom. of tearing or splitting, like tiles breaking, ice crumbling: "kwahh!"

話   huà   MC hwaejH

1. what one says, spoken words, speech; in early texts usu. with sense of words that have some importance or consequence.
2. (med.) converse, conversation, everyday talk.
3. (med.) story, tale, account, anecdote.

huái

徊   huái   MC hwoj

1. turn round; waver.
    a. upset; wrenched, twisted.
2. (bn.) 徘～ *páihuái*, → 徘 *pái*.

懷   huái   MC hweaj

1. bosom, chest.
2. embrace, clasp to one's bosom.
    a. harbor, cherish.
    b. surround, encircle, environ (geography).
3. hold to or in one's heart, hold dear, hold fast to; close-held feelings, deepest feelings, heart-held.

a. feel sympathy or affection for, warm-hearted, cordial.
b. placate, comfort, solace.
4. be concerned for; muse over.
    a. reminisce, be nostalgic for, long for; regret the absence of, to miss.
5. be attracted to, turn to, incline toward; give one's allegiance to.
6. (med.) think of a way, come up with a plan.
7. (med.) tolerate, condone, be patient with.

槐　huái　MC hweaj
1. sophora, pagoda-tree (*Sophora japonica*), medium-sized broad-spreading tree with creamy-white flowers blooming in late summer; in lit. often associated punningly with 懷 *huái*, symbolizing heart-held feelings, longing, memories.

淮　huái　MC hweaj
1. name of important river that rises in southern Henan, crossing Anhui, to empty into Lake Hongze 洪澤湖 in western Jiangsu; delimits a rough climatological division, with wheat and coarse grains generally grown north of the Huai, rice generally grown south of it; during Nanbeichao period, the Huai River often marked the rough political boundary between northern and southern dynasties.

踝　huái　MC hwaeX
1. ankle.

huài

壞　huài　MC hweajH
1. collapse, fall to ruin, fall in; founder, disintegrate.
    a. damage, destroy, demolish, ruin; spoil, wreck.
2. quash, rout; vanquish, conquer, defeat, scatter.
3. decline, wane; subside.
4. defective, deficient; e.g. ～色 *huàisè*, secondary or intermediate colors between the 5 primary colors.

huān

嚾　huān　MC xwan
1. call, cry out, shout, bawl.

懽　huān　MC xwan　⊙ 歡 *huān*.

歡　huān　MC xwan
1. joy(ous), rejoice, enjoyment; delight, delectation; pleasure, take pleasure in.
2. be on friendly terms with, amiable, amicable.
3. (med.) (lit.) in *yuefu* 樂府 poetry an affectionate term of address between lovers: "you, my love."

貛　huān　MC xwan
1. sgl. or cmpd. 豬～ *zhūhuān*, Asian badger, sand-badger (*Meles leucurus, M. amurensis*); syn. 獌 *tuān*.

讙　huān　MC xwan
1. tumult, pandeomonium, din, racket.
2. ⊙ 歡 *huān* 1, joy(ous), rejoice, delight, take pleasure in.

貛　huān　MC xwan　⊙ 貛 *huān*.

驩　huān　MC xwan
1. manageable horse, tame.
2. ⊙ 歡 *huān* 1, joy(ous), rejoice, delight; 2, ami(c)able.

huán

圜　huán　MC hwaen
1. encircle, enclose, surround.
2. confine, imprison.
    yuán　MC hjwen
    1. ⊙ 圓 *yuán*, round, circular, circle; 2, by metonymy, heaven.

垸　huán　MC hwan
1. mixture of varnish and lime used as whitewash for walls.
2. turn around; turn over, revolve.

寰　huán　MC hwaen
1. royal domain, traditionally with a circumference of 1,000 *li*; the empire seen as territory of the ruler; e.g. ～區 *huánqū*, the confines of the domain.
    a. the capital or metropolitan precinct.
2. sphere of activity; e.g. 人～ *rénhuán*, the sphere of man.

桓　huán　MC hwan
1. post or pillar on which announcements are placed, signpost; guidepost.

2. rdup., martial and mighty, fearless and formidable.
3. wind round, coil, wrap round.
4. a surname.

桄　huán　MC hwan

1. soapnut tree (*Sapindus mukorossi*), with leathery-skinned drupe; similar to 訶梨勒 *hēlílè*, chebulic myrobalan (*Terminalia chebula*).
2. scrape; rub, polish.

kuǎn　MC khwanX
1. small buffet, sideboard.

澴　huán　MC hwaen

1. whirlpool, gurge, vortex, maelstrom; swirling, eddying.
  a. (bn.) 旋～ *xuánhuán*, → 旋 *xuán*.

狟　huán　MC hwan

1. ⊙ 獾 *huān*, badger.
2. small raccoon-dog (*Nyctereutes procyonoides*).

獂　huán　MC hwan

1. porcupine (*Hystrix brachyura*).

環　huán　MC hwaen

1. jade bracelet.
  a. other similarly shaped objects of adornment: ring, bangle, earring, armlet.
2. encircle, surround; contain within.
3. (med.) everywhere, all over; in detail, thoroughly.

綄　huán　MC hwan

1. wind-vane, weather-cock, usu. bearing 5 pairs of cockfeathers, hence called in Chu 五兩 *wǔliǎng*.

繯　huán　MC hwaenH

1. hangman's noose.
  a. strangle, choke.
2. cord attached to flag or banner.
3. net for catching game.

獂　huán　MC hwan　⊙ 獂 *huán*.

狟　huán　MC hwan　⊙ 狟 *huán*.

轘　huán　MC hwaenH

1. Chunqiu-period judicial punishment of dismemberment by pulling limbs off simultaneously amidst 4 chariots.

還　huán　MC hwaen

1. turn round, come round; go back, come back, return to previous location or to original condition; e.g. ～京 *huánjīng*, return to the capital; ～車 *huánchē*, turn round the carriage, retrace one's route.
  a. (re)cycle, revert; e.g (Dao.) ～丹 *huándān*, cycled or reverted elixir, gen. term for Dao. alchemical elixirs because most involve several stages of firing, the result of each stage symbolizing a reversion to the essential state and increasing refinement of the key ingredients.
2. send back, send in return; answer; e.g. ～翰 *huánhàn*, return letter; ～恩 *huán'ēn*, repay a favor.
  a. give back, remit; redeem; recompense; restore; e.g. ～蘇 *huánsū*, regain consciousness, return to life; ～税 *huánshuì*, remit taxes; (Budd.) ～願 *huányuàn*, redemption of vows.
  b. rebound against one, come round again (whence it began).
3. turn one's head, look back to or on.
  a. remember, think back on, recollect.
4. ⊙ 環 *huán* 2, encircle, surround, contain.
5. (med.) ～如 *huánrú*, conditional term: if, supposing that.

xuán　MC zjwen
1. ⊙ 旋 *xuán* 1, rotate, turn back on oneself, pivot, coil; 3, immediately, right away, soon after.

hái　MC hwaen
1. on the other hand, to the contrary; instead.
2. (med.) as usual, as always, still.
  a. (med.) once again, once more.
3. (med.) moreover, and what's more, and also, and yet.

鐶　huán　MC hwaen　⊙ 環 *huán*.

闤　huán　MC hwaen

1. wall surrounding city's marketplace.
2. ～闤 *huánhuì* (MC hwaen-hwojH), market wall and gate; the marketplace itself, within the wall and gate.

萑　huán　MC hwan

1. metaplexis (*Metaplexis japonica, M. stauntonii*), reed-like member of the milkweed family.
2. (bn.) ～薍 *huánhù* (MC hwan-huX), variously versicolored, marbled and multi-hued.

3. (bn.) 〜蘭 *huánlán* (MC hwan-lan), tears falling fast, flooded with tears.

鬟　**huán**　**MC hwaen**
1. hair-coil, bun; chignon; hairdo.

huǎn

緩　**huǎn**　**MC hwanX**
1. loose, slack; baggy, hanging; e.g. 〜帶 *huǎndài*, loose(n) belt; 〜耳 *huǎn'ěr*, pendulous ears.
2. indulgent; relaxed, mellow, languid.
3. slow(ly), tardy; easy-going.
    a. in a measured way; e.g. 〜步 *huǎnbù*, measured gait.
4. defer, postpone, put off.
    a. languish; dilatory, sluggish; listless.

huàn

喚　**huàn**　**MC xwanH**
1. call up, invoke, summon; call upon.
    a. (med.) invite, request.
2. (med.) designate, call (by the name of).

奐　**huàn**　**MC xwanH**
1. abundant, numerous; ample.
    a. bountiful, rich, plentiful, exuberant.
2. (bn.) 〜衍 *huànyǎn* (MC xwanH-yenX), lushly layered, piled profusely.
3. sgl. or rdup., bright, brilliant, vibrant and vivid.

宦　**huàn**　**MC hwaenH**
1. servant of aristocratic family (early usage).
2. itinerant scholar.
3. (med.) office-holder.
    a. (med.) official on assignment away from the capital.
4. eunuch.

幻　**huàn**　**MC hweanH**
1. illusory, illusion; phantasmal, imaginary; unreal, mirage, hallucination; specious.
2. delude, mislead; deceive, trick.
3. change by magic, conjure, transform, transfigure; magician, conjuror.

患　**huàn**　**MC hwaenH**
1. cares, troubles, vexation.
    a. troubled, vexed, disturbed, bothered by; worried by, on one's mind.

2. misfortune, calamity; mischance, mishap; suffering.
3. malady, affliction; illness.

換　**huàn**　**MC hwanH**
1. exchange, trade.
    a. substitute, replace.
2. change, alter.
3. to attire, dress, put on clothing, don.

浣　**huàn**　**MC hwanX**
1. wash, launder, esp. clothes (if dirtier, by foot; less soiled, by hand); wash away, scour.
    a. expunge, wipe out; e.g. 〜雪 *huànxuě*, expunge a stain on reputation (< wipe clean as snow).
2. bathe, lave, wash clean.
    a. (med.) sgl. or 〜沐 *huànmù*, in Tang times scheduled rest-day for officials ("for bathing and hair-washing") every 10th day, i.e. 1 day per week.

渙　**huàn**　**MC xwanH**
1. disperse, spread into; suffuse.
    a. dissolve, dissipate, melt away, vanish.
2. rdup., broad and brimming, welling and swelling; also, vibrant and vivid, shining with scintillance.
3. "Diffusion," name of 59th hexagram of *Yijing*.

溴　**huàn**　**MC hwanH**
1. smudge(d), blear(ed), efface(d); erode(d); (bn.) 漫〜 *mànhuàn* (MC manH-hwanH), effaced and obliterated.

澣　**huàn**　**MC hwanX**　⊙ 浣 *huàn*.

煥　**huàn**　**MC xwanH**
1. iridescent; sparkling, shimmering, dazzling, scintillant; e.g. 〜發 *huànfā*, flash of iridescence.
    a. suffused with light; vivid, vibrant.

睆　**huàn**　**MC hwaenX**
1. ⊙ 睅 *hàn*, protruding eyes, with eyes abulge, agape.
2. brilliant, bright; alight, glowing.
    a. glossy, sleek; vivid.
3. perfectly round, spherical, orblike; esp. of fruit.
4. beautiful, handsome; fine-looking.
    a. (bn.) 睍〜 *xiànhuàn*, → 睍 *xiàn*.

豢   **huàn**   MC hwaenH
1. feed pigs and dogs; look after domestic animals.
    a. animal husbandry, raise animals.
2. provide sustenance or resources for, sustain.
3. win over through blandishments, bribes.

逭   **huàn**   MC hwanH
1. run away, run off, flee.
    a. escape from; avoid, evade.

鯇   **huàn**   MC hwaenX
1. orphe, ide, grass-carp (*Ctenopharyngodon idella*), the roe planted in paddies, fed on weeds till grown.

huāng

肓   **huāng**   MC xwang
1. diaphragm, vital area between chest and abdomen.

荒   **huāng**   MC xwang
1. weed-choked, overgrown with weeds.
    a. waste(land), wilderness.
2. uncared for, abandoned, deserted; neglected, desuetude.
    a. fallow, gone to seed; uncultivated, unkempt.
3. desolate, barren.
    a. lean year, famine year.
4. unconstrained, undisciplined, self-indulgent, on a loose tether; intemperate, dissolute; reckless, riotous; e.g. ～宴 *huāngyàn*, indulge in revelry.
    a. (bn.) ～唐 *huāngtáng* (MC xwang-dang), catch-as-catch-can, any which way; also, unchecked and exaggerated, farfetched and fantastic, preposterous; also, open and unbounded, remote and far-ranging.
5. expansive, far-spread, extend to; far-reaching, remote; e.g. 八～ *bāhuāng*, the 8 expanses, i.e. 8 directions.
6. cover over.
    a. occupy, in possession of.
7. ceremonial cloth cover of coffin.
    huǎng   MC xwangX
1. (bn.) ～忽 *huǎnghū* (MC xwangX-xwot), dazed and distracted, muddled maze, indistinct and indefinite; ⊙ 恍忽 *huǎnghū*.

huáng

凰   **huáng**   MC hwang
1. (bn.) 鳳～ *fènghuáng*, phoenix; →*fèng* 鳳.

喤   **huáng**   MC hwang
1. rdup., onom. of infant crying: "wah-wah"; also, onom. of tintinnabulation of bells.

媓   **huáng**   MC hwang
1. (bn.) 娥～ *éhuáng*, → 娥 *é*.

徨   **huáng**   MC hwang
1. rdup., unsettled, jumpy, fretful; concerned and worried.
2. (bn.) 徬～ *pánghuáng*, → 徬 *páng*.

惶   **huáng**   MC hwang
1. unsettled, nervous; frightened, fearful; trepidation; rdup., fearful and fretful, anxious and unsettled, trembling in trepidation.

潢   **huáng**   MC hwang
1. deep pool; lake; reservoir.
    MC hwangH
1. (med.) to dye paper yellow.
    huàng   MC hwangX
1. ～然 *huàngrán*, in a deluge, overrunning, overflowing, flooding; ⊙ 滉然 *huàngrán*.
2. rdup., spreading broad and far.
    guāng   MC kwang
1. ⊙ 洸 *guāng* 2, rdup., brave and bold, intrepid.

煌   **huáng**   MC hwang
1. rdup., glittering and gleaming, sparkling and glistening; also, majestic and magnificent.

璜   **huáng**   MC hwang
1. jade demi-disc, used for ritual purposes or as ornament suspended from belt.

皇   **huáng**   MC hwang
1. august, majestic, sublime; dazzling with glory, illustrious, resplendent; of sovereign character; e.g. ～帝 *huángdì*, august emperor, resplendent thearch, title first taken by Qin Shihuangdi in 221 BCE; 三～ *sānhuáng*, the 3 (legendary) august ones, 3 high sovereigns, usu. Fuxi 伏羲, Shennong 神農, Huangdi 黃帝, but sometimes other trios.

a. descriptive of items belonging to or associated with the emperor; e.g. ～門 *huáng-mén*, imperial gates (to the palace).
b. honorific epithet for spirits, celestial deities, ancestors, deceased parents; ～考 *huángkǎo*, my illustrious deceased father.
2. rdup., splendid and sublime, majestic and magnificent; also, splendidly shining, beautifully brilliant; also, airy and open, clear and uncovered.
3. horse of mixed fulvous and white.
4. ⊙ 惶 *huáng*, unsettled, nervous; 遑 *huáng* 1, time to spare, leisure; 凰 *huáng*, phoenix; 況 *kuàng*, all the more so.

篁　huáng　MC hwang

1. bamboo-brake, bamboo thicket, densely packed bamboo grove.
2. thicket-bamboo, an esp. hard type with short internodes, found in high and dry locations.

簧　huáng　MC hwang

1. reed of wind-instrument, originally bronze; e.g. 鳴～ *mínghuáng*, vibrating reed.
　a. by synecdoche, a wind-instrument, reed-pipe; esp. 笙 *shēng*, reed-organ.
2. (med.) speak with a false tongue, say one thing but think another, speak falsely, dissemble.

蝗　huáng　MC hwang

1. gen. term for locust, various species.
2. plague of locusts.

遑　huáng　MC hwang

1. time to spare, leisure.
2. move on, pass on (to another activity); e.g. 不～ *bùhuáng*, not ready to (do X), not avid for.
　a. rest in, content with, e.g. ～安 *huáng'ān*, rest easy.
3. ⊙ 惶 *huáng*, unsettled, nervous, frightened.

鎤　huáng　MC hwang

1. rdup., onom. of tintinnabulation of bells; singly, of a single chime.
2. ceremonial battleaxe with crescent-shaped blade, used as symbol of authority.

隍　huáng　MC hwang

1. dry moat, fosse.

黃　huáng　MC hwang

1. yellow; ranging from sallow to flax, amber, gold, xanthic, fulvous, tawny, and brown.

a. ～門 *huángmén*, Yellow Gate(s), palace gates and those of imperial mausolea; also, in Han times imperial gatekeeper; also, phrase prefixed to certain titles indicating service in the palace.
b. (med.) color of paper used for imperial proclamations, from Jin times through Tang.
2. children 2 years and under; e.g. ～口 *huángkǒu*, "yellow-mouth," suckling infant (with crusted milk on its mouth); ～男 *huángnán*, infant boy.
　a. (med.) in Tang times, usu. color of winding-sheet used to wrap corpse.
3. ～連 *huánglián*, goldthread (*Coptis chinensis*), root used medicinally; ～精 *huángjīng*, "yellow-germ," polygonatum, solomon's seal (*Polygonatum sibiricum*, *P. falcatum*), root a favored item in Dao. macrobiotics; ～芝 *huángzhī*, "yellow mushroom," sealwort, fragrant solomon's seal (*Polygonatum odoratum*), syn. ＝ 萎蕤 *wěiruí*; ～櫨 *huánglú*, smoke-tree, fustet (*Cotinus coggygria*), from which a yellow dye was made; 地～ *dìhuáng*, rehmannia (*Rehmannia glutinosa*), root used medicinally, also dye-source for "imperial yellow" in med. times.
4. ～精 *huángjīng*, "yellow-germ," also ～牙 *huángyá*, "yellow ivory," and ～龍 *huánglóng*, "yellow dragon," all massicot used as pigment > litharge; 雄～ *xiónghuáng*, "cock-yellow," realgar; 雌～ *cíhuáng*, "hen-yellow," orpiment.
5. ～袍 *huángpáo*, "yellow-robe," i.e. oriole.

huǎng

怳　huǎng　MC xwangX　⊙ 恍 *huǎng*.

恍　huǎng　MC xwangX

1. (bn.) ～忽、～惚 *huǎnghū* (MC xwangX-xwot), dazed and distracted, confused and unclear, muddled and murky, blurred and smudged.

慌　huǎng　MC xwangX

1. (bn.) ～惚 *huǎnghū* (MC xwangX-xwot), ⊙ 恍惚 *huǎnghū*, → 恍 *huǎng*.

晃　huǎng　MC hwangX

1. fulgent, fulgid; rdup., brightly radiant, bright and brisk.
　a. (bn.) ～朗 *huǎnglǎng* (MC hwangX-langX), fair and fulgent, beaming and clear.

焜 huǎng MC xwangX

1. (bn.) 〜爛 *huǎnglàn* (MC xwangX-lanH), lustrous light, raying radiance; (bn.) 爌〜 *kuàng-huǎng*, → 爌 *kuàng* (*huǎng*).

爌 huǎng MC xwangX

1. brighten, illuminate, shine on.

kuàng MC khwangH

1. (bn.) 〜焜 *kuànghuǎng* (MC khwangH-xwangX), broad and bright, far-reaching radiance.

謊 huǎng MC xwangX

1. nonsense, exaggerated, farfetched, groundless, crazy.

huàng

幌 huàng MC hwangX

1. curtain, window curtain.
    a. hanging, drape.
2. (med.) wineshop sign; façade.

滉 huàng MC hwangX

1. 〜然 *huàngrán*, (bn.) 〜瀁 *huàngyǎng* (MC hwangX-yangX), overrunning and overflowing, shoreless and immeasurable, vastly spreading, flooding fast.
2. (bn.) 〜漾 *huàngyàng* (MC hwangX-yangH), bouncing and bobbing, pitching and plunging.

huī

徽 huī MC xjw+j

1. beautiful, comely; handsome; well-favored.
    a. excellent; admirable, choice.
2. cord, strand, braid.
    a. to braid, entwine, bind; tie up, bundle.
3. braided cords that fasten zither (*qín* 琴) strings to stops; e.g. 急〜 *jíhuī*, tighten the stops.
    a. zither's inlaid studs, usu. of jade, ivory, or mother-of-pearl, that indicate acoustic nodes (the half, thirds, fourths, fifths, sixths, and eighths of the string length) on the instrument's upper board.
    b. by metonymy, to play the zither.
4. emblem, insignia; standard.
    a. to signal, make a sign.
5. ribbons of woman's upper garment.
6. (bn.) 〜嫿 *huīhuà* (MC xjw+j-xweak), go at a gallop, lickety-split, speedily scudding.

恢 huī MC khwoj

1. extensive, vast, expansive, broad, wide-spread.
    a. expand, increase; broaden, magnify.
2. broad-meshed net.
3. be ready, prepared, complete.

揮 huī MC xjw+j

1. wave; brandish, flourish.
2. signal with the hand, indicate.
3. flick away, throw off; sprinkle, scatter.
4. wipe away (water, tears, sweat).
5. "sweep," brush zither strings, a right-hand movement; play the zither.
6. (bn.) 〜霍 *huīhuò* (MC xjw+j-xwak), vibrant velocity, rashly dashing, with alert alacrity.

撝 huī MC xjwe

1. cut, rip, tear open or apart.
2. brandish, signal with hand or flag.
3. modest, diffident, reticent; reluctant, verecund.

暉 huī MC xjw+j

1. radiant, gleam(ing); vividly white, candent.
    a. gloze, spread light; dazzle.

灰 huī MC xwoj

1. ashes, cinders, dead embers; cinereous.
    a. reduce to ashes, crush, turn to dust.
    b. dejected, feeling crushed, broken; lifeless.
2. ashen color, dull, wan.

輝 huī MC xjw+j

1. firelight, radiant illumination, glow.
2. splendor, splendid; brilliance.

xūn MC xjun

1. ⊙ 熏 *xūn* 4, to cense, envelop in fragrant smoke.

hún MC hwon

1. rdup., fire-red, blazing brightly.

yùn MC hjunH

1. ⊙ 暈 *yùn* 1, solar or lunar halo, nimbus, usu. with grayish-white haze and a faint band of prismatic colors around outside of ring.

睢 huī MC xjwie

1. gaze upward at, lift one's eyes to; gaze upon.
    a. rdup., dimly descry.

suī MC swij

1. glare at, look at angrily.

翬　huī　MC xjw+j

1. koklass pheasant (*Pucrasia macrolopha*).
2. soaring, winging.

褘　huī · MC xjw+j

1. ceremonial robe of empress, decorated with embroidered pheasants.
2. apron, cloth garment wrapped around waist and hanging over the knees.

yī　MC 'je

1. beautiful; excellent; perfect.

詼　huī　MC khwoj

1. jest, banter, quip, joke; badinage.

豗　huī　MC xwoj

1. onom. of waves crashing and colliding with each other or against rocks: "chwaay!"
    a. deafening din, broil, furor, rampage.

輝　huī　MC xjw+j

1. (med.) ⊙ 煇 *huī* 1, firelight, radiant illumination, glow; 2, splendor, brilliance; ⊙ 暉 *huī*, radiant, gleam(ing), vividly white; gloze, dazzle.

隳　huī　MC xjwie

1. bring down, overthrow, ruin, destroy; ⊙ 墮 *huī* (*duò*).

麾　huī　MC xjwe

1. ensign, standard, banner, signal-flag; e.g. ～下 *huīxià*, under the (army's) standard; troops under (a general's) command, "under the aegis of."
2. brandish, signal with hand or flag; ⊙ 撝 *huī* 2.

huí

回　huí　MC hwoj

1. turn round; revolve, rotate.
    a. vortex, whirl(ing); e.g. ～風 *huífēng*, whirlwind.
2. turn away from, change course, reverse.
3. deviate, wrong-headed; irregular, aberrant; contrary; e.g. 不～ *bùhuí*, undeflected.
4. (med.) go back to, return.
5. (med.) exchange, trade; e.g. ～博 *huíbó*, ～易 *huíyì*, barter.
    a. (Budd.) transfer karmic merit.
6. (med.) measure-word for occurrences that may be repeated, a turn.

7. (med.) ～惑 *huíhuò*, halting and hesitant, irresolute.
8. (bn.) ～紇 *huíhé* (MC hwoj-hot), Uighur, Türkic tribe that established a steppe empire centered on the Orkhon valley in 744 and lasting for nearly a century, greatly aided the Tang during the An Lushan rebellion and treated with special favor thereafter.

佪　huí　MC hwoj

1. rdup., confused and confounded, turned back to front.
2. (med.) ～惶 *huíhuáng* (MC hwoj-hwang), filled with fright, scared stiff, completely consternated.

洄　huí　MC hwoj

1. whirlpool, gurge; vortex.
2. swerving rivercourse, side-run.

迴　huí　MC hwoj

1. ⊙ 回 *huí*, all meanings except 3.

huǐ

悔　huǐ　MC xwojX

1. remorse(ful), self-reproach; repent(ance); contrite.
2. ill favor, misfortune; inauspicious, infelicitous.
3. the upper trigram of each of the 64 *Yijing* hexagrams (cf. 貞 *zhēn*, the lower trigrams).

椒　huǐ　MC xjweX

1. fagara plant, also its seeds (*Zanthoxylum bungeanum*), deciduous shrub of medium height, seeds used as condiment ("Sichuan pepper").

毀　huǐ　MC xjweX

1. damage, dismantle, demolish; fall apart, break apart.
2. damage one's health by excess in mourning austerities.
3. defame, run down, derogate, denigrate, hold up to scorn.

燬　huǐ　MC xjweX

1. blazing fire, conflagration.
2. burn up; reduce to ashes, incinerate.

虺　huǐ　MC xjw+jX

1. bamboo-snake, bamboo-viper (*Trimeresurus stejnegeri*), venomous snake related to but somewhat smaller than the pit-viper (→ 蝮 *fù*).
    a. any large or fearsome snake.

huī   MC xwoj

1. rdup., rumbling and rolling of thunder.
2. (bn.) ～隤 *huītuí* (MC xwoj-dwoj), haggard and staggered, totally wayworn.

huì

匯   **huì   MC hwojX**

1. confluence, flowing together.

卉   **huì   MC xjw+jH**

1. flora, gen. term for plants.

喙   **huì   MC xjwojH**

1. snout, of animals; beak or bill, of birds; mouth, yap, of persons.
2. pant, wheeze; short of breath.

嘒   **huì   MC xwejH**

1. sparkle, gleam, flicker; scintillance of stars.
2. onom. of cicadas, throbbing drone, chirr and murmur; onom. of carriage grelots, chink-chink; onom. of pipes or flutes, shrill and shriek.

彗   **huì   MC zjwejH**

1. broom; besom (made of twigs).
   a. sweep.
2. broom-star, sweeper-star, perihelial (tailed) comet (cf. 孛 *bèi*, tailless comet).

彙   **huì   MC hjw+jH**

1. collocate, arrange items of similar kinds; collocation; categorize, classify.
   a. assemblage, concentration, collection.
2. clustered, clumped, dense, lush (of vegetation).

恚   **huì   MC 'jwieH**

1. irate, indignant; wrath(ful); ire(ful); livid, impassioned.
   a. angr(il)y, cross(ly).

惠   **huì   MC hwejH**

1. gracious(ness), largess, favor; from superior.
   a. benevolent, kind(ness), considerate.
2. gentle, mild; docile, complaisant.

慧   **huì   MC hwejH**

1. intelligence, percipience, cognizance; discerning, discriminating, acute.
2. (Budd.) trns. Skt. *prajñā*, wisdom, discernment, gnosis, insight, understanding of reality

and discrimination of dharmas that surpasses ordinary intelligence.

晦   **huì   MC xwojH**

1. last day of the lunar month, when the moon cannot be seen at night; darkfall.
2. dark, lightless, unlit; murky, dull, dim.
3. hidden, veiled, concealed; obscure; unseen; e.g. ～迹 *huìjī*, conceal one's tracks, i.e. go into reclusion.

會   **huì   MC hwajH**

1. come together; gather(ing), meet(ing); esp. in early times a concourse of noble lords to establish alliance.
   a. assemblage; association; community.
   b. reception; audience.
2. face-to-face meeting with friend(s).
3. aggregate, aggregation; bring objects, items, ideas, texts, etc. together; e.g. ～要 *huìyào*, collected essentials.
4. junction, meeting-place, meeting-point, gathering spot.
   a. do together, jointly; e.g. ～友 *huìyǒu*, join in friendship; ～葬 *huìzàng*, joint interment.
5. coincide, concur; suit, fit with; e.g. ～心 *huìxīn*, suit one's mind.
6. opportune moment (that coincides with need or desire), opportunity; chance.
   a. (ADV) by chance, as chance would have it.
7. (med.) comprehend, take it all in, understand; intuit(ive); e.g. ～意 *huìyì*, understand the meaning (of a text).
8. (med.) (ADV) sgl. or ～當 *huìdāng*, will definitely, must, surely; e.g. ～有時 *huì yǒushí*, surely there will come the right time.

   kuài   MC kwajH

1. reckon accounts, put figures together, calculate.
2. seam or "gathering" of a cap.

槥   **huì   MC hjwejH**

1. provisional coffin, for conveying home the remains of soldiers who died in battle; smaller and lighter than burial coffin.

沬   **huì   MC xwojH**

1. wash the face.
   mèi   MC mwojH

1. ⊙ 昧 *mèi* 1, dim, dull; somber, lackluster.

滙   **huì   MC hwojX**   ⊙ 匯 *huì*.

濊　huì　MC xwajH
1. deep water, bottomless.
2. ⊙ 穢 *huì* 2, filth(y), foul, polluted.

　　huò　MC xwat
1. rdup., onom. of fish-nets being dropped in water, splat-plat!

穢　huì　MC 'jwojH
1. overgrown with weeds, weeds run wild.
2. adulterated; filth(y), foul, vile.
　　a. pollute(d), besmirch(ed), defile(d); impure.
3. promiscuous, licentious.
4. (med.) euph. for feces.

篲　huì　MC zjwejH
1. ⊙ 彗 *huì* 1, broom.

繢　huì　MC hwojH
1. fringe, tassel; shag.
2. ⊙ 繪 *huì*, draw, paint(ing), esp. with colors.

繪　huì　MC hwajH
1. colors neatly coordinated and complementing each other, esp. in embroidery, figured silk.
2. (med.) painting with color.

翽　huì　MC xwajH
1. rdup., onom. of flap and flutter of bird's wings, lap and flap.

蕙　huì　MC hwejH
1. Thai basil, sweet-basil (*Ocimum basilicum*).
2. melilot, sweet-clover (*Melilotus indicus*).
3. sweetly-scented, aromatic, fragrant (as are both of the preceding); > emblematic of fine virtue, pure character.

薈　huì　MC 'wajH
1. flourish, grow in profusion.
　　a. (bn.) ～蔚 *huìwèi* (MC 'wajH-'jw+jH), lushly proliferating, thickly flourishing, of plants; also, surging and swelling, billowing and building up, of clouds.

蟪　huì　MC hwejH
1. (bn.) ～蛄 *huìgū* (MC hwejH-ku), short-lived small cicada (*Platypleura kaempferi*) that according to tradition emerges and sings in the 4th and 5th months and dies before autumn; also, mole- cricket, → 螻 *lóu*.

誨　huì　MC xwojH
1. instruct(ion), teach, guide; counsel.
2. appeal to, attract; engage, invite, induce.

諱　huì　MC xjw+jH
1. abstain from referring to someone or something by name, out of respect.
　　a. ineffable, not to be spoken, taboo.
2. taboo-names, esp. personal names of emperors.
3. avoid, eschew, shun; refrain from, forbear.
　　a. (med.) disgusted with, want no more of.
　　b. (med.) turn one's back on, disregard.

譓　huì　MC hwejH　⊙ 譓 *huì*.

譓　huì　MC hwejH
1. perceptive(ness), discern clearly.
2. submit to, yield to.

賄　huì　MC xwojX
1. goods, property of value.
2. present goods to.
3. (med.) bribe with valuables.

闠　huì　MC hwojH
1. (bn.) 闤～ *huánhuì*, → 闤 *huán*.

靧　huì　MC xwojH　⊙ 沫 *huì*.

顪　huì　MC xjwojH
1. goatee, billy-goat beard.

hūn

婚　hūn　MC xwon
1. take a wife, marry.
2. families related by marriage.

惛　hūn　MC xwon
1. unclear, indistinct, blurred, muddled.
2. rdup., fuddled and confused, dull-witted and dim, in a stupor; also, silent and soundless, muffled and mute.

昏　hūn　MC xwon
1. dusk, twilight, eventide, past sundown but before nightfall.
　　a. dusky, shadowy, lowering; gloomy, tenebrous.

2. of individual: benighted, dim, "in the dark"; muddled, dim-witted; stupid.
   a. of political or social group: in a dark age, unsettled, in unrest, scrambled, in turmoil.
3. blurry, dimmed, dull, of eyesight.
4. ⊙ 婚 *hūn*, take a wife, marry; 暋 *mǐn* 2, exert oneself, strive, put one's might into.

殙 hūn MC xwon
1. wrought up, anxious, flustered, on edge, a nervous wreck.
   mèn MC mwonH
1. expire, die.
   a. death of infant before being named.

葷 hūn MC xjun
1. strong-odored or pungent vegetables, esp. onion, garlic, leek.
2. (med.) meat, animal flesh (as food), when regarded as unclean or polluting to one's spiritual being and therefore to be avoided.

闍 hūn MC xwon
1. warder, gatekeeper, sentinel.
2. (med.) palace-gate, portal.

hún

渾 hún MC hwon
1. heaving water, agitated waves; rdup., pitching and lurching, heaving and hoving, rolling and roiling, trolling and tumbling.
2. roiled, stirred up; muddy, murky, miry.
3. whole, complete(ly); uncut, undivided; e.g. ～家 *húnjiā*, the whole household.
   a. integral; spherical totality, all-encompassing, coalesced; e.g. ～元 *húnyuán*, Integral Origin, time of cosmic wholeness before differentiation of phenomena, perfect oneness.
4. (med.) (ADV) nearly, almost, pretty much, on the point of; barely, hardly; e.g. ～欲不勝簪 *húnyù bùshēngzān*, hardly able (nearly unable) to support a hatpin.
   a. ～脫 *húntuō*, "skinned-whole," felt hat.
   hùn MC hwonX
1. muddled, mixed together, jumbled.
   a. (bn.) ～沌 *hùndùn* (MC hwonX-dwonX), inchoate chaos, absolutely amorphous; most often written 混沌, → 混 *hùn* 2a for fuller discussion.

魂 hún MC hwon
1. "cloud-soul," spiritual or ethereal soul, strongly associated with person's non-material elements and propensities; upward-tending and drawn to natural home in the heavens, where it disperses upon person's bodily death; in early times object of ritual to "summon back the soul" (*zhaohun* 招～) of deceased, before formal acceptance of person's demise; seen as able to depart from body during dreams; representative of *yang* in contrast with the *yin*-derived 魄 *pò* ("white-soul," carnal or material soul, which returns to earth upon person's death); often said to be 3 in number (cf. 7 for *po*).
2. emblematic of one's mental and emotional properties, one's "spirit" in figurative sense.

鼲 hún MC hwon
1. sand-rat, gerbil (*Meriones unguiculatus*).
   a. Daurian ground-squirrel (*Spermophilus dauricus*).

hùn

圂 hùn MC hwonH
1. pigpen, pigsty.
2. latrine, privy (because often positioned above pigsty).

㥯 hùn MC hwonH
1. anxious, uneasy, unquiet, troubled.
2. alarm, disturb, trouble, discomfit.
3. distracted; perplexed, bewildered.

混 hùn MC hwonX
1. ⊙ 渾 *hún* 1, heaving water; 2, roiled, muddy, murky.
2. confused, jumbled, confounded, mixed together.
   a. (bn.) ～沌 *hùndùn* (MC hwonX-dwonX), inchoate chaos, absolutely amorphous, the primordial closed and utterly dark entity containing all potential forms and which ceases to exist when "opened"; has Dao. symbolic connections with enclosed worlds of grotto-heavens (*dongtian* 洞天), bottle-gourds (*hulu* 葫蘆), and suggestive phonetic similarity with the cosmic mountain Kunlun 崑崙; note also semantic overlap (and possible identity) with 渾 *hún* 3, whole, uncut, undivided, integral, spherical totality, all-encompassing.

溷　**hùn**　MC hwonH

1. muddy, miry, roiled.
    a. unclean, impure, foul, filthy.
2. thrown together, jumbled, confused.
3. ⊙ 圂 *hùn* 1, pigpen, pigsty; 2, latrine, privy.

huō

騞　**huō**　MC xwaek

1. onom. of cleaver cutting meat, hwoock!; also (med.), of quick movement such as bird's wings cutting through the air, whoosh!

huó

佸　**huó**　MC hwat

1. meet with, have contact with, see each other.

活　**huó**　MC hwat

1. to live; lively, vital.
2. (med.) livelihood, means of living.
    guō　MC kwat
1. rdup., running and rushing, lilting and lapping (water); also (med.), onom. of walking in mud, khwot-khwot.

huǒ

夥　**huǒ**　MC hwaX

1. many, much; numerous; multitude, multitudinous.
    a. lots of, plenty of (a low-register term).
2. 〜頤 *huǒyí*, exclamatory term: ho-ya!

火　**huǒ**　MC xwaX

1. fire; fiery, ablaze.
    a. start a fire, set fire to, enkindle.
    b. torch, brand, firebrand.
2. one of the 5 "agents" or "phases" in *wuxing* theory, having symbolic correlations with the direction south, the season summer, the color red, planet Mars, etc.
3. sgl. or 〜星 *huǒxīng*, fire-star, Antares; also, alt. name for *xin* 心, "Heart," constellation, one of the 28 lunar lodgings, comprised of 3 stars, α (Antares), σ, τ Scorpii, in the eastern quadrant (*qinglong* 青龍 or *canglong* 蒼龍) of the sky. N.B. In early texts and through med. times 〜星 *huǒxīng* does not ref. Mars (which is *yinghuo* 熒惑).

a. 大〜 *dàhuǒ*, Grand Fire, same as preceding, and also name of one of the 12 Jupiter stations, comprising the lunar lodgings *di* 氐, *fang* 房, and *xin* 心.
4. (med.) a squad of soldiers.
5. (med.) 〜尋 *huǒxún* (MC xwaX-zim), 〜辭彌 *huǒcímí* (MC xwaX-zi-mjie), Khorasmia.

huò

惑　**huò**　MC hwok

1. deceive, delude, mislead; fool, entrap.
    a. puzzle, confuse, perplex.
    b. (Budd.) delusions, of the impermanent world of the senses.

或　**huò**　MC hwok

1. VB-phrase modifier indicating the distribution or scope of the sense of the verb phrase relative to the stated or implied topic, "in some cases, in some instances, sometimes"; akin to 各 *gè*, 莫 *mò*, 孰 *shú*; often translatable as "some, someone"; e.g. 〜死 〜不死 何也 *huò sǐ huò bùsǐ hé yě*, in some cases they died, in some cases they did not die (some died, some did not); why?; 〜百步而後止 *huò bǎibù érhòu zhǐ*, in some cases they went a hundred paces (some went . . .) and then stopped; 臣〜弒其君 *chén huò shì qí jūn*, vassals sometimes assassinate their lords.
    a. indefinite singular sense, often implying uncertainty or speculation: "in some case, in some instance," "perhaps"; e.g. 宋人〜得玉 *Sòngrén huò dé yù*, Perhaps a person from the state of Song obtains a piece of jade (Suppose someone from the state of Song obtains a piece of jade); 今人〜入其央瀆 *jīn rén huò rù qí yāngdú*, Now a person at some time enters into the main drainage trough (Suppose someone goes into the main drainage trough.)
2. (med.) suddenly, all at once; e.g. 在於路上〜見一人 *zàiyúlùshàng huò jiàn yīrén*, suddenly on the road he saw another person.

濩　**huò**　MC hwak

1. boil, stew.
2. water streaming, sluicing.
3. (bn.) 〜落 *huòluò* (MC hwak-lak), watery waste; also, empty and endless, deserted and desolate; also, hugely useless, impracticably unserviceable; also (med.), with all hope drained away, despairingly disappointed.

hù　MC huH
1. (bn.) 布～ *bùhù*, → 布 *bù.*

獲　huò　MC hwak
1. catch or capture game in a hunt.
    a. take prisoner, capture (enemy), seize.
2. obtain, acquire; procure.
3. hit the center of target, shoot with perfect aim.
4. wench, derogatory term for maidservant.
5. ⊙ 穫 *huò*, gather in crops, reap the harvest.

矆　huò　MC xjwak
1. look with wide eyes, stare aghast.

矐　huò　MC xak
1. go blind.
    a. to blind, make someone blind.

禍　huò　MC hwaX
1. unavoidable misfortune, disaster, calamity, catastrophe.
    a. adversity, tribulation, trial.
2. bring harm upon, afflict; harrow.
3. offense, fault.

穫　huò　MC hweak
1. gather in crops, reap the harvest.

膔　huò　MC xowk
1. braise; sear and then simmer in its own juices.

蒦　huò　MC ʻwaek
1. measure out; calculate.

藿　huò　MC xwak
1. bean leaves.
2. (med.) patchouli (*Pogostemon cablin*).

蠖　huò　MC ʻwak
1. sgl. or 尺～, 蚇～ *chǐhuò*, inchworm, looper, larva of geometer-moth.

yuè　MC hjwak
1. ～略 *yuèlüè* (MC hjwak-ljak), inch along, snail-paced, advance inchmeal.

豁　huò　MC xwat
1. broad valley, vale, dale.
2. open breadth, wide-open, agape; unobstructed; spacious, expansive.
    a. unfold, spread out; pass freely through.
    b. (bn.) ～落 *huòluò* (MC xwat-lak), open and unobstructed, free and unhindered.
3. open-minded, uninhibited; e.g. ～蕩 *huòdàng*, open to anything, let come what may.
    a. generous, magnanimous, open-handed.
4. (med.) sweep away, clear away, set loose, set free; dissipate, scatter; e.g. ～情 *huòqíng*, give vent to one's emotions.
5. (med.) fair, cloudless, bright (weather).

huō　MC xwat
1. (med.) be short of, deficient in, lacking; sparse, scarce; e.g. 稀～之處 *xīhuò zhi chù*, where it is scarce and lacking.
    a. (med.) worn through, ragged; damaged.
2. (med.) abandon, cast away, throw away, give up.

貨　huò　MC xwaH
1. material goods, resources.
    a. merchandise, commodities.
2. money, cash, coin.
3. bribe, induce with goods or cash.
4. (med.) sell, deal in, traffic in, peddle.

鑊　huò　MC hwak
1. heavy-bodied cauldron or cookpot.

臒　huò　MC ʻwak
1. vermilion, as pigment obtained from cinnabar; vermeil.

霍　huò　MC xwak
1. onom. of bird's swift flight, cutting through air, whoosh!
    a. (bn.) ～繹 *huòyì* (MC xwak-yek), whoosh and whizz.
2. rdup., in a flash and flicker, in a twinkling; also, onom. of sharpening a sword, whook-whook.
3. ⊙ 藿 *huò* 1, bean leaves.
4. a surname.

J

jī

几　jī　MC kijX
1. low table for use when seated on floor, taboret.
    a. armrest.

劍　jī　MC kje
1. (bn.) ～剧 *jījué* (MC kje-kjwot), curved chisel, bevel-edge chisel, graver's knife, burin; (med.) also, carved printing-block.
2. ravage, plunder; despoil.

勣　jī　MC tsek
1. achievement, accomplishment; merit(orious); ⊙ 績 *jī* 2.

唧　jī　MC tsik
1. rdup., onom. of sigh of sadness; also, of admiration; (med.) also, onom. of birds chirping; also, of crickets stridulating, cicadas buzzing.
    a. (bn.) 啾～ *jiūjī,* → 啾 *jiū.*

嘰　jī　MC kj+j
1. nibble at, take a small bite, eat sparingly.
2. onom. for sighing in sadness or grief.

基　jī　MC ki
1. base, foundation, platform; rudiment; ground, substratum.
    a. basic, fundamental.
2. to found, establish.
    a. undertake; commence(ment); install(ation).

墼　jī　MC kek
1. unfired brick.

奇　jī　MC gje　→ 奇 *qí.*

姬　jī　MC ki
1. surname, traditionally of Yellow Emperor; also, of the royal family of Zhou 周 dynasty.
2. honorific term for wife.
3. concubine.
    a. in Han times, title of palace lady of 2,000-bushel status.
4. (med.) courtesan; houri; grisette; barmaid.

屐　jī　MC gjaek
1. (med.) cleated wooden clogs or pattens (Jpns. *geta*), esp. favored in Nanbeichao period by Southern elite; Xie Lingyun 謝靈運 (385-433) adapted them to mountain-climbing by making the "teeth" or cleats removable—removing the front ones for ascending, the back for descending.

稽　jī　MC hej
1. a surname (pronunciation should properly be *xī*).

幾　jī　MC kj+j
1. latent; invisible, imperceptible.
    a. sign, omen, portent; faint stirring, small beginning; incipience.
2. almost, nearly, approximate(ly); little more than, not far from.
    a. near to, nearby, close to.
3. imminent danger.
4. general affairs; circumstances.
5. time, duration.
    a. opportune, opportunity.
        jǐ　MC kj+jX
1. how much (interr. or rhetorical); so much.
    a. (med.) how? in what way? why? for what reason?
2. small amount, few; not much; e.g. ～許 *jǐxǔ,* ～所 *jǐsuǒ,* ～何 *jǐhé,* not much, only some; ref. uncertain number or place.
        jì　MC kijH
1. ⊙ 冀 *jì,* hope (for); expect.
        qǐ　MC khj+jX
1. ⊙ 豈 *qǐ,* how could it be that . . .? (rhetorical); surely not . . .; hard to believe that . . .

擊　jī　MC kek
1. strike, beat.
2. strike against, assault, assail.
    a. maul; slay, dispatch.
3. come into contact with, touch; encounter.
    a. accost, confront.
        xí　MC hek
1. ⊙ 覡 *xí,* shaman.

朞　jī　MC ki
1. complete period of time; e.g. ～年 *jīnián,* a full year, complete solar year; ～月 *jīyuè,* complete month.

2. sgl. or cmpd. 〜服 *jīfú*, mourning attire worn for a full year; a year of mourning.

枅   jī   MC kej

1. capital, square wooden block at top of column.
2. horizontal balance-beam of scales.

機   jī   MC kj+j

1. trigger mechanism of crossbow.
   a. trigger, catch, trip, latch; e.g. 〜辟 *jībì*, spring-net, trigger-snare.
   b. contrivance, mechanism; e.g. 天〜 *tiānjī*, Heaven's workings; natural spontaneity.
2. key, turning point; hinge, crux, crucial; exigency; e.g. 時〜 *shíjī*, critical moment, timely circumstances.
   a. opportunity, opportune moment; fit(ting); conducive; advantageous.
3. motive (power), stimulus, impulse, impetus; synapse; incipience, leading action > foretoken(ing); e.g. 見〜 *jiànjī*, "see the springs of action," i.e. clairvoyant.
   a. energy; faculty; function(al), action.
   b. operative; effective, efficient.
4. dexterity, skill; ingenuity, ingenious; cleverness.
   a. perspicacity; judgment.
   b. calculating, contriving; e.g. 無(亡)〜 *wújī*, guileless.
5. loom (weaving); e.g. 〜杼 *jīzhù*, loom and shuttle; also, conception and arrangement of literary composition.
6. ⊙ 璣 *jī* 3, sgl. or in cmpd. 天〜 *tiānjī*, "Heaven's Armil," 3rd star of Big Dipper (γ Ursae Majoris, = Phecdra); 〜衡 *jīhéng*, abb. of 璇〜玉衡 *xuánjī yùhéng*, "Jadestone Armil and Jade Transverse," the bowl and handle of the Dipper; also, reputedly the ancient armillary sphere and sighting tube; also > the dome of heaven.

激   jī   MC kek

1. spurt, dash, spout, of water under pressure; outburst; hurtle.
   a. set in motion, incite, stimulate, set off; provoke, excite.
   b. energize, animate, pump life into, invigorate.
2. fervid; impassioned, high-strung; sharp; furious; tumult(uous).
   a. (med.) one-sided, prejudiced.
3. to dam, dike; hold back.
4. high-pitched treble (of sound); e.g. 〜越 *jīyuè*, sharply swelling, high and lasting.

璣   jī   MC kj+j

1. small or irregularly shaped pearl.
2. ancient astronomical device, supposedly made at behest of sage-king Shun 舜, reputedly similar to an armillary sphere.
3. sgl. or in cmpd. 天〜 *tiānjī*, "Heaven's Armil," 3rd star of Big Dipper (γ Ursae Majoris, = Phecdra).
   a. 〜衡 *jīhéng*, abb. of 璇〜玉衡 *xuánjī yùhéng*, "Jadestone Armil and Jade Transverse," the bowl and handle of the Dipper; also, reputedly the ancient armillary sphere and sighting tube; also > the dome of heaven.

畸   jī   MC kje

1. odd parcel of land, left out of well-field (*jingtian* 井田) arrangement.
   a. remnant, oddment; leftover, remainder.
2. irregular; peripheral; lopsided; biased, uneven.
3. odd number.
   qí   MC gje
1. ⊙ 奇 *qí*, singular, uncommon; remarkable.

畿   jī   MC gj+j

1. royal or imperial domain, area surrounding capital under direct control of ruler.
   a. appanage of high feudal lord.
2. territory, region; domain, dominion.
   a. (med.) boundary, frontier.
3. (med.) in Tang times, 2nd of 4 special categories designating selected districts (*xian* 縣) that, because of their importance were given special standing (in descending order of prestige: 赤 *chì* [crimson = imperial], 〜 *jī* [metropolitan], 望 *wàng* [honored], 緊 *jǐn* [important]) outside the usual trilevel ranking (上, 中, 下) of districts.
4. door-sill; inside a gate.

磯   jī   MC kj+j

1. shoreside rocks beaten by water.
   a. rocky projection at waterside; jetty.
2. promontory; foreland.
3. enrage, infuriate; offend.
   a. oppose, go against.

禨   jī   MC kj+j

1. supplicate ghosts or spirits for good fortune.

稽   jī   MC kej

1. delay, retard; put off, defer.
   a. prevent; hinder, forestall.

2. arrive at, reach, come to.
3. examine, scrutinize, study closely.
    a. consult, deliberate.
    b. dispute, contend; haggle over, argue.
4. conform to, similar; agree with, concord(ant).

    qǐ　MC khejX

1. ～首 *qǐshǒu*, touch head to ground while kneeling and with folded hands also touching ground, in respect.
2. ⊙ 綮 *qǐ* 2, wooden halberd with attached flag or streamer, carried before officials as standard of honor when traveling.

積　jī　MC tsjek

1. pile up grain, mow, rick, stack, heap; garner, store up.
2. accumulate, amass; collect, gather.
    a. multiply; multitude, much; overmuch.
3. accumulated time; inveterate, longstanding; ingrained, entrenched.
    a. frequent, ofttimes.
4. block, obstruct; clump.
5. ⊙ 績 *jī* 2, achievement, accomplishment; merit.

筓　jī　MC kej

1. hairpin (women's); hatpin.
2. coming-of-age ceremony for young girl, in which her hair is bound up on top or back of head; usu. at 15 *sui*.
    a. eligible girl, of marriageable age.

箕　jī　MC ki

1. winnowing basket.
    a. to winnow, sift.
    b. Winnowing Basket, one of the 28 lunar lodgings, comprised of γ, δ, ε, and η Sagittarii, in the eastern quadrant (*qinglong* 青龍) of the sky; also called "Heaven's Ford" (*tianjin* 天津) and "Heaven's Cockerel" (*tianji* 天雞).
2. flat wicker tray.
3. sit sprawling, spraddled, with legs stretched out or spreadeagled (in shape of this character); a sign of disrespect.

緝　jī　MC tsip　→ 緝 *qī*.

績　jī　MC tsek

1. twist into a skein (hemp or silk); spin thread, enfilade; e.g. ～羽 *jīyǔ*, down-spun (textile).
    a. join together; continue, succeed.
2. achievement, acomplishment; merit(orious).

羈　jī　MC kje　⊙ 羈 *jī*.

羈　jī　MC kje

1. bridle; e.g. ～縻 *jīmí*, bridle(d) and halter(ed); also, ref. barbarian areas under Chinese control but nominally ruled by native chiefs.
    a. to bridle, curb, restrain; leash.
    b. leash of hunting birds.
2. travel or lodge away from home, sojourn(er), voyage(r), wayfarer; when felt more intensely: exile(d).
    a. migratory (of birds).

肌　jī　MC kij

1. skin-surface of humans, incl. flesh, skin.

芨　jī　MC gip

1. sgl. or 白～ *báijī*, ground orchid, bletilla (*Bletilla striata*), orchidaceous plant of south whose root was used in preparation of paper to increase viscosity and insecticidal effect; syn. 白及 *báijí*.
2. ～～草 *jījīcǎo*, achnatherum (*Achnatherum splendens*), a perennial needlegrass of the north, used esp. for fodder, also stem and flowers used medicinally.

藄　jī　MC tsej　⊙ 蘁 *jī*.

蹟　jī　MC tsjek

1. (bn.) 襞～ *bìjī*, → 襞 *bì*.

觭　jī　MC khje

1. asymmetrical horns, one curved up, one down.
    a. diverge(nt); aberrant.

    jī　MC kje

1. ⊙ 奇 *jī* (*qí*), single, unitary; only, merely.

    qí　MC gje

1. ⊙ 奇 *qí*, singular, uncommon; remarkable, extraordinary.

譏　jī　MC kj+j

1. deride, ridicule, jeer, mock, fleer.
    a. vilify, denounce; imprecate.
2. interrogate, examine.

賷　jī　MC tsej　⊙ 齎 *jī*.

賷　jī　MC tsej　⊙ 齎 *jī*.

跡　jī　MC tsjek　⊙ 迹 *jī*.

蹟 jī   MC tsjek   ⊙ 迹 *jī*.

躋 jī   MC tsej
1. ⊙ 隮 *jī* 1, ascend (to); climb, scale; rise up, mount; 3, fall off; topple.

迹 jī   MC tsjek
1. footprint; tracks, traces.
   a. vestiges, surviving evidence; relics; revealment; trademark.
   b. (Budd.) overt, visible act; outward manifestation.
2. follow in the tracks of; put oneself in the shoes of; emulate.
   a. seek out, follow up, search into.

鐖 jī   MC kj+j
1. curved barb of fish-hook.
2. ⊙ 機 *jī* 1, trigger mechanism of crossbow; catch.

    qí   MC gj+j
1. large scythe.

隮 jī   MC tsej
1. ascend (to); climb, scale.
   a. rise up, mount up; swell, esp. rising mist.
2. rainbow < rising arc.
3. fall off; topple.

雞 jī   MC kej
1. chicken; cock; fowl; gallorine.
2. (med.) ～頭 *jītóu*, "chicken's head," prickly waterlily (*Euryale ferox*), since flowers resemble cock's-comb; syn. 芡 *qiàn*; ～舌香 *jīshéxiāng*, "chicken's-tongue aromatic," clove (*Syzygium aromaticum*).

轙 jī   MC kj+j
1. bit, of horse's bridle.

鲞 jī   MC tsej   ⊙ 齏 *jī*.

飢 jī   MC kij
1. hunger (more general, less severe than 餓 *è*); in want.
   a. hunger for, crave.
2. famine; poor harvest, crop failure; dearth; ⊙ 饑 *jī* 1.

饑 jī   MC kj+j
1. famine; poor harvest, crop failure; dearth; scarcity.
2. hunger; want; ⊙ 飢 *jī* 1.

鶺 jī   MC tsjek
1. (bn.) ～鴒 *jīlíng* (MC tsjek-leng), wagtail (*Motacill flava, Motacilla alba*); in lit. symbolic of brotherly attentiveness (< Ode 164) because of characteristic tail-jerking and head-bobbing which in groups gives impression that each is attending to the others.

鷄 jī   MC kej   ⊙ 雞 *jī*.

齎 jī   MC tsej
1. bestow, give, present to.
   a. furnish, provide with.
2. carry in one's heart.

    zī   MC tsij
1. ⊙ 資 *zī* 1, resource(s); property, material at one's disposal; means.

齏 jī   MC tsej
1. chopped meat or vegetables marinated in vinegar and used as condiments.
   a. pickled, minced, hashed.

jí

赴 jí   MC kik
1. urgent, in haste; hurried, quick.
   a. severe(ly).

    qì   MC khiH
1. frequently, often.

佶 jí   MC git
1. strong; stout, robust.
2. (med.) (bn.) ～屈 *jíqū* (MC git-khjut), jarring and jangling, scraggy and grating (of lit. style).

即 jí   MC tsik
1. marks a noun or vʙ-phrase as being exactly or precisely what is meant: exactly, precisely, just (so), the very; e.g. ～不忍其觳觫 *jí bùrěn qí húsù*, It was precisely that I could not bear its quivering in fear; 進～兩楹間 *jìn jí liǎngyíng jiān*, advance to a spot precisely between the

two posts; (Budd.) 色〜是空, 空〜是色 *sè jíshì kōng, kōng jíshì sè*, "form is exactly emptiness, emptiness is exactly form," famous phrase from *Heart Sutra*.

2. introduces conditional clause: if; e.g. 〜受魚必有下人之色 *jí shòu yú bì yǒu xiàrén zhī sè*, If I had accepted the fish there inevitably would have been a reaction among the underlings; 〜不幸而不起此病 *jí bùxìng ér bùqǐ cǐbìng*, if unfortunately you do not recover from this affliction; 〜使 *jíshǐ*, if it came about that, if it were that . . .

3. to take up, take over, assume; approach; e.g. 即位 *jíwèi*, accede to the throne.

4. (ADV) forthwith, instantly, immediately, promptly.
　　a. (med.) preceding a noun: at the very (time, place); e.g. 〜今 *jíjīn*, 〜日 *jírì*, right now, at this moment; 〜事 *jíshì*, on the spot, at the scene (esp. in poem titles).

5. (med.) adversative particle: to the contrary, conversely, on the other hand.

及　*jí*　MC gip

1. reach (to), arrive (at).
　　a. attain, accede to; e.g. (med.) 〜第 *jídì*, make the grade, i.e. pass the civil-service exam.
　　b. pass on to, succeed; esp. to younger son or collateral relation.
　　c. associate with, attach(ment).

2. catch up with, catch up to.
　　a. come up to, compare favorably with; applicable.

3. preceding nominalized VBs and VB-phrases: reaching up to (the time of), coming down to (a particular time); at the arrived at (later) time, when; e.g. 〜其壯也 *jí qí zhuàng yě*, when he became robust; 〜陷於罪 *jí xiàn yú zuì*, when they have fallen into wrongful conduct.
　　a. when it comes to the matter of > as for; e.g. 〜其使人也 *jí qí shǐ rén yě*, when it comes to the matter of his employing others; 〜行事 *jí xíng shì*, as for putting these matters into practice.

4. conjoining nouns and noun phrases: reaching to and including, together with, and also, as well as; e.g. 予〜女偕亡 *yú jí rǔ xié wáng*, we with you as well will perish together; 其所不愛〜其所愛 *qí suǒbùài jí qí suǒài*, what he does not take good care of together with what he does take good care of.

　　a. conjoining negated VBS or VB-phrases: nor; e.g. 毋發室屋〜起大眾 *wú fā shìwū jí qǐ dàzhòng*, do not throw open the homes or rooms, nor arouse the thronging masses.

5. (med.) apprehend; understand, be clear about.

6. (med.) 白〜 *báijí*, "white connector," bletilla (*Bletilla striata*), syn. → 笈 *jí*.

吉　*jí*　MC kjit

1. auspicious, propitious (ant. 凶 *xiōng*); e.g. 〜凶 *jíxiōng*, weal and woe.
　　a. favorable, fortunate.

2. benign(ant), life-supporting.

3. excellent; of the first order.

4. 1st day of lunar month.

5. 〜了 *jíliǎo*, hill myna (*Gracula religiosa*), with green-glossed black plumage, yellow beak and wattles.

6. 〜利草 *jílìcǎo*, "life-profiting plant," stick-orchid (*Luisia teres*), orchidaceous plant reputedly effective against *gu* 蠱 poison; 〜祥草 *jíxiángcǎo*, pink reineckea (*Reineckea carnea*), flowering grass with pink to lavender blooms; 〜貝 *jíbèi*, kapok tree, silk-cotton tree (*Ceiba pentandra*), > cotton.

7. (med.) 〜蔑 *jímiè* (MC kjit-met), Khmer, name of empire corresponding to most of present-day Cambodia, Laos, and part of Vietnam, supplanting Zhenla 真臘 (Chinrap, Viet. *Chân Lạp*) in 802.

聖　*jí*　MC tsit

1. fired brick; stonework, masonry.

2. candle-end, fag-end; > cinder(s).

3. ⊙ 疾 *jí* 2, hate, detest, loathe.

嫉　*jí*　MC dzit

1. envy; jealous(y); nithe, nithful.

2. find fault with; feel malice toward, hate; be hostile, averse to.

岌　*jí*　MC ngip

1. extremely tall or high.
　　a. rdup., reaching upward, rising high; also, precariously perilous, precipitously vulnerable.

伋　*jí*　MC kip

1. urgent; hasty, hurried; ⊙ 急 *jí* 1.

急　*jí*　MC kip

1. urgent; in haste, hurried; keen, surging; sudden; expedite, speed up, quicken the pace of.
　　a. unrelenting, unflagging.

2. pressing, acute; in a critical state.

   a. ～如令 *jí rú lìng*, "treat with the urgency due the statutes," concluding statement of certain governmental instructions in Han times, adopted in some Dao. petitions and admonitions.

3. irritable, irascible, prickly.

   a. rash, impatient; brusque.

   b. high-strung; intense.

4. (med.) solicitous, anxious for or about.

悋　*jí*　MC kik

1. urgent; hasty.

戢　*jí*　MC tsrip

1. lay up, lay by, set aside, put up, esp. weapons.

   a. store up; reserve, husband; put under wraps, stash.

2. collect, bring together; accumulate, amass.

3. (med.) interrupt, arrest; halt, discontinue; stop; stay.

4. (med.) rdup., move en masse, act altogether; also, even and regular, well-ordered, well-balanced.

极　*jí*　MC gjep

1. pack-frame, for transporting items on donkey.

棘　*jí*　MC kik

1. jujube, red date (*Zizyphus jujuba*), medium-sized tree or shrub with thorny branches, whose fruit is a single-stoned drupe, wrinkled, and of dark-red or reddish-brown color; usu. ref. only to the tree (cf. 棗 *zǎo*).

2. thorn(y), spiny, prickly; bramble.

   a. rough, harsh; asperity.

3. ⊙ 急 *jí* 2, acute, pressing; 3, irritable, prickly, impatient; 戟 *jǐ* 1, guisarme; 瘠 *jí* 2, barren, sterile; effete.

楫　*jí*　MC tsjep

1. oar, paddle; to row.

   a. (med.) by synecdoche, a boat.

2. copse, bosk, small grove of trees.

3. ⊙ 輯 *jí* 2, compile, bring together, edit.

極　*jí*　MC gik

1. ridgepole.

   a. standard, principle.

2. high-point, summit, zenith; pinnacle; apogee, apex; e.g. (Budd.) 有～ *yǒují*, summit of being.

   a. culmen; culmination, end-point toward which all tends; culminate, go all the way to,

reach the end; e.g. 天～ *tiānjí*, ends of the sky > ends of the earth; 情～ *qíngjí*, at wit's end; ～目 *jímù*, see to the limits of vision, as far as one can see.

   b. extremity; supreme; e.g. 無～ *wújí*, infinite, immeasurable; paramount.

3. extreme(ly), exceed(ingly); farthest; most; best, utmost, to the Nth degree; e.g. ～成 *jíchéng*, highest achievement, culminating accomplishment; ～浦 *jípǔ*, farthest shore.

   a. worked to the last point, worn out; exhaust(ed).

4. sgl. or 北～ *běijí*, Pole-star.

5. (med.) tend fully toward; resemble in particular.

6. ⊙ 亟 *jí*, urgent, in haste.

檝　*jí*　MC tsjep

1. ⊙ 楫 *jí* 1, oar, paddle; to row.

殛　*jí*　MC kik

1. kill, slay; slaughter; execute, put to death.

汲　*jí*　MC kip

1. draw water from a well.

2. draw forth, lead out.

   a. recommend; forward, for approval or advancement.

3. rdup., precipitate, impatient and over-hasty, scurry after, rush round; also, worked up, nervous, on tenterhooks, overly anxious.

潗　*jí*　MC tsrip

1. flow out; rush out, flood.

2. rush, dash, whisk; shoot, speed.

3. rdup., bunched together, massed and marshaled, crowded and clustered.

疾　*jí*　MC dzit

1. illness, indisposition; malady.

   a. infirm(ity); unwholesome; diseased.

2. underlying disease, cause of disease, etiology (cf. 病 *bìng*, symptoms).

3. nervous; hasty, quick-moving.

   a. rapid; urgent; e.g. (med.) ～路 *jílù*, short-cut.

4. ⊙ 嫉 *jí* 1, envy, jealous(y); 2, find fault with, feel malice toward, hostile to.

瘠　*jí*　MC dzjek

1. thin, emaciated; lean, spare; gaunt.

   a. enfeebled; effete.

2. barren, fruitless; played out; sterile, arid.

　　　zì　MC dzjek

1. ⊙ 骴 *zì*, rotting corpse.

笈　*jí*　MC gip

1. book-box, carried on back.
   a. book-bag, book-satchel.
2. dossier, portfolio.

籍　*jí*　MC dzjek

1. register, roster, roll, log, record-book, e.g. of population, tax obligations, accounts, clan ancestry, harvest, etc.
   a. cartulary, charter.
2. written documents; books; writings.
3. ⊙ 藉 *jí* (*jiè*) 1, strewn with, cluttered; 6, sacred field where emperor carries out ritual of first plowing in early spring.

級　*jí*　MC kip

1. degree, rank, class, grade; step or level in hierarchy.
2. step(s), stairs.
3. sgl. or 首～ *shǒují*, number of enemy heads captured or slain and accordant level of honor.

耤　*jí*　MC dzjek

1. sacred field where emperor carries out ritual of first plowing in early spring.

　　　jiè　MC dzjaeH

1. ⊙ 藉 *jiè* 4, borrow, lend.

膌　*jí*　MC dzjek

1. ⊙ 瘠 *jí* 1, thin, emaciated; lean, spare; enfeebled, weak.

蒺　*jí*　MC dzit

1. (bn.) ～藜 *jílí* (MC dzit-lej), tackweed, goathead, bullhead, burnut (*Tribulus terrestris*), weedy plant whose fruit yields spiky nutlets that are painful to touch; syn. 茨 *cí*; also, red-headed centipede (*Scolopendra morsitans*), large centipede that bites with two fangs located on either side of its head.

葴　*jí*　MC tsrip

1. heartleaf, fishwort (*Houttuynia cordata*), perennial herb used medicinally; syn. 葅 *zū*, 魚腥草 *yúxīngcǎo*.

藉　*jí*　MC dzjek　→ 藉 *jiè*.

蝍　*jí*　MC tset

1. (bn.) ～蛆 *jíjū* (MC tset-tsjo), centipede, scolopendrid (*Scolopendra morsitans*), used dried medicinally; syn. 蜈蚣 *wúgōng*.

襋　*jí*　MC kik

1. coat collar, lapel.

踖　*jí*　MC dzjek

1. march ahead, tread onward.

　　　jí　MC tsjek

1. sgl. or rdup., step respectfully, advance carefully.

蹐　*jí*　MC tsjek

1. take small steps, tread mincingly, step neatly.

輯　*jí*　MC dzip

1. compartment of a carriage (< gathering point).
2. gather, collect; esp. compile, bring together, edit (writings); reconstruct (lost texts).
3. arrange, put in order.
4. sgl. or rdup., amicable, concordant, mild and genial, placid and affable.

集　*jí*　MC dzip

1. to perch (bird).
   a. to pause, rest.
2. to flock, congregate, cluster; gather(ing), concentration (of).
3. collect(ion), esp. of writings.
   a. (med.) bibliographic classification, largely of belles-lettres, works not grouped as classics (*jing* 經), history (*shi* 史), or philosophy (*zi* 子).
4. accomplish(ment); bring to completion (< resting-spot) the various aspects of a task.
5. settle(d); stable, stabilize.

jǐ

己　*jǐ*　MC kiX

1. 6th of the 10 heavenly stems.
2. reflexive pronoun, may occur as SUBJ or OBJ of VB or attributive to noun (cf. 自 *zì*, only occurring as ADV and only ref. SUBJ of VB); self, oneself, itself; by or for oneself or itself; in itself; one's own; ant. 人 *ren*, other(s): e.g. 不患人之不～知，患不知人也 *bùhuàn rén zhi bùjǐzhī, huàn bùzhī rén yě*, it is not that I'm troubled by others not appreciating myself, but that I'm troubled by

my not appreciating others; 〜所不欲勿施于
人 *jǐ suǒbùyù wùshī yú rén*, what you would not
want for yourself, do not put upon others.
3. (med.) 3rd-person pronoun, esp. when SUBJ
of preceding sentence becomes OBJ in immediately following sentence : him, her, that person.

幾   **jǐ**   MC kj+jX   → 幾 *jī*.

戟   **jǐ**   MC kjaek
1. guisarme, 2-pronged halberd, pole-weapon
with curved (sometimes notched) blade and
back-hook.
2. (med.) provoke, prod, stimulate.

掎   **jǐ**   MC kjeX
1. catch hold of, seize; secure; grip.
   a. grab from the side or behind.
   b. pull aside, set to the side; separate.
2. launch, cast; propel, initiate.

撠   **jǐ**   MC kjaek
1. stab, pierce; run through.
2. engage, come in contact with.
3. hold tightly, grasp firmly.

擠   **jǐ**   MC tsejX
1. push over, into, or out.
2. expel, repulse, get rid of.

給   **jǐ**   MC kip
1. well-supplied, well-provided.
   a. supply, provide (for); furnish.
2. take care of, look after.
3. well-spoken, articulate, fluent; glib.

脊   **jǐ**   MC tsjek
1. spine, backbone, chine.
2. ridge, crest.
3. strong support for, good grounds for; with
reason, justification; order(ly).

蟣   **jǐ**   MC kj+jX
1. nit, egg of louse; e.g. 〜蝨 *jǐshī*, nit-lice.
   a. insignificant, trivial.
2. froth or bubbles on top of wine.

鮆   **jǐ**   MC dzejX   ⊙ 鱭 *jǐ*.

鱭   **jǐ**   MC dzejX
1. anchovy (*Coilia mystus*); also, large anchovy
(*Coilia ectenes*), syn. 刀魚 *dāoyú*, "knife-fish."

麂   **jǐ**   MC kijX
1. muntjac (*Muntiacus reevesi*), small member
of deer family, with short antlers and striped
markings on face.
   a. 〜目 *jǐmù*, "muntjac-eye," a type of apricot.

jì

伎   **jì**   MC gjeX
1. ⊙ 技 *jì*, technique, skill, knack, deft(ness); artisan, craftsman; 妓 *jì*, artiste, performer; geisha.

偈   **jì**   MC gjejH   → 偈 *jiē*.

冀   **jì**   MC kijH
1. hope (for), fancy; look forward to.

劑   **jì**   MC dzejH
1. clip, pare, shave, trim; curtail, cut off; cut in
half.
2. mix, blend, compound (flavors, medicinal ingredients, etc.).
   a. condiments, seasoning.
   b. medicinal dose; medicament.

嚌   **jì**   MC dzejH
1. taste, savor.
     jiē   MC keaj
1. rdup., squawk and screech, squall and sob.

堅   **jì**   MC gijH
1. chink up or smooth out a roof with clay.
2. pick up, take up.
3. rest, repose.

妓   **jì**   MC gjeX
1. artiste, performer; geisha, woman profession-
ally skilled in song and dance; NOT a prostitute.
2. entertainment, amusement.

季   **jì**   MC kjwijH
1. youngest in a sequence of brothers.
2. last (i.e. youngest, 3rd) month of a season.
   a. last years of a reign or dynasty.
3. 3-month period, season of the year; e.g. 四〜
sìjì, the 4 seasons.
4. (med.) nubile, just reaching marriageable age
(girl).

寂   **jì**   MC dzek
1. hushed, soundless, silent; still; e.g. 〜寥 *jìliáo*,
still and undisturbed > unattainable, unimaginable.

a. (bn.) 〜寞 *jìmò* (MC dzek-mak), 〜歷 *jìlì* (MC dzek-lek), silent stillness, still and null, hushed and alone, silent solitude, bleak and forlorn.
b. (Budd.) tranquil, serene; e.g. 〜滅 *jìmiè*, serene extinction, i.e. *nirvāṇa*; 〜志 *jìzhì*, (one with a) tranquil mind, trns. Skt. *śramaṇa*.
2. forlorn; solitude, solitary.

寄 **jì** MC kjeH

1. lodge at temporarily, stop over.
    a. take refuge in; be dependent on.
    b. attach to; e.g. 〜生 *jìshēng*, parasite; also, rump ornament for horse.
    c. (lit.) metaphor, betokening, impart (< lodge temporarily) an other than literal meaning.
2. entrust to, confide to, commit to, project (onto); e.g. 〜言 *jìyán*, lodge in words > confide to words.
    a. deposit, leave with.
3. send, give for delivery to; convey, transfer to; impart; e.g. 〜詩 *jìshī*, send a poem to.
    a. give over to; e.g. 〜傲 *jì'ào*, give oneself up to disdain for the world.

忌 **jì** MC giH

1. antipathy, aversion.
    a. averse to, antagonistic, hostile; spite(ful), hate(ful).
2. eschew, shrink from, dread(ful), be on guard against; abstain from, shun; e.g. 〜日 *jìrì*, "dread day," day on which one's parent(s) died; any inauspicious day.
3. taboo; proscribe, prohibit(ion); interdict(ion).
4. verse-ending rhythmic particle, esp. in *Shijing*.

悸 **jì** MC gjwijH

1. panic-stricken, dismayed.
    a. heart palpitating, throbbing.

惎 **jì** MC giH

1. do grave harm to; maim; wound.
2. feel malice toward; pernicious, oppugn(ant); hate, despise.
3. counsel, advise; teach.

技 **jì** MC gjeX

1. technique, technical; skill(ful), knack; deft(-ness), expert(ise).
    a. artisan, craftsman.

既 **jì** MC kj+jH

1. completely, fully, wholly.
2. aspectual attributive to VB-phrases indicating recent completion of an action: having just, just now, just after, already, as soon as; etymologically the affirmative counterpart to 未 *wèi*; e.g. 兵刃〜接 *bīngrèn jì jiē*, as soon as the weapons and blades were joined (in battle); 〜富矣 *jì fù yǐ*, having just become wealthy; 舊穀〜沒，新穀〜升 *jiùgǔ jì mò, xīngǔ jì shēng*, the old grain has already died, the new has already risen.
    a. sgl. or 〜而 *jì'ér*, for not long, rather soon; e.g. 〜而悔之 *jì'ér huǐ zhī*, not long afterward (soon) he regretted it.
    b. (med.) as long as, since (< now that it is so, it now being so); e.g. 〜與人同樂亦不得不與同憂 *jì yǔ rén tónglè yì bùdé bùyǔ tóngyōu*, since he shares the pleasures of others, he cannot but likewise share their worries.
3. 〜A且B *jì A qiě B*, 〜A又B *jì A yòu B*, both A and B; simultaneously with A, also B; as soon as A, B also.

暨 **jì** MC gijH

1. and, with, together with, as well as.
2. attain, reach, get to, arrive.
3. rdup., firm and fast, intent and steadfast, determined, decided.

洎 **jì** MC gijH

1. fill up a cooking pot with water; to stew.
    a. broth, esp. meat-sauce.
2. soak into, permeate; dampen.
3. reach to, arrive at, come up to (space or time).
4. as well as, and also, together with.
5. (med.) sgl. or 〜合 *jìhé*, nearly, almost.

濟 **jì** MC tsejH

1. cross a river, get to the opposite shore.
    a. cross over, get across; ferry.
2. arrive at a goal, succeed, achieve(ment).
    a. terminate, come to the end of, stop.
3. help across or over, carry across; rescue, deliver(ance); relieve, alleviate; aid, assist; succor, sustain.
    a. be of service to, contribute, useful; benefit, profit; improve.
4. 既〜 *jìjì*, "Completed Crossing," name of 63rd hexagram of the *Yijing*; 未〜 *wèijì*, "Incomplete Crossing," name of 64th hexagram of the *Yijing*.

jǐ   MC tsejX

1. rdup., manifold and multiple; also, impressively imposing; also, merry and convivial, reveling.

瘵   jì   MC gjwijH

1. palpitations of the heart, from fear; panic(-stricken).
   a. troubled in sleep, dretch(ed).

祭   jì   MC tsjejH

1. sacrifice; (make an) oblation; esp. sacrifices to spirits or ancestors with wine and meat.
   a. ～酒 jìjiǔ, libationer, official title from Han times on with various applications, from subordinate positions in bureaus to honorific designation for high dignitaries, to head of foremost capital academy or directorate of education; also (Dao.), term for priests within early Celestial Master organization.

稷   jì   MC tsik

1. foxtail millet (*Setaria italica*), the most important of the "5 grains," used for food; syn. 粟 *sù*.
2. god of millet (metonymy for all grains), esp. in the cmpd. 社～ *shèjì*, gods of the soil and of grain.
   a. ancient designation for director of agriculture.

   zè   MC tsrik

1. ⊙ 昃 zè, sun slanting westward; afternoon hours.

稄   jì   MC tsjejH

1. non-glutinous millet.

概   jì   MC kijH

1. thick, dense; clustering, massed.

穧   jì   MC dzejH

1. reap grain.
   a. sheaf, bundled but unstored grain.

紀   jì   MC kiX

1. strand; filament of silk, thread, or cord; e.g. ～綱 jìgāng, strands and mainstays, skeins and cables, > network, nexus, organization.
   a. grouping of strands, skein.
2. unravel, distentangle, comb out.
   a. arrange, prepare; put in order, organize.

3. main point, principle.
   a. standard, norm; rule.
4. cycle of yearly time, period(icity).
   a. cycle of 12 months > 1 year.
   b. synodic revolution of Jupiter > period of 12 years (11.86 years).
   c. cycle of 20 → 蔀 *bù* (= 4 Callippic cycles, each cycle 76 years) > period of 1520 years.
   d. era, 1 generation.
5. chronicle, annals, year-by-year account of events centered on emperor and court; the 1st section of every "official history" (*zhengshi* 正史); e.g. ～傳 jìzhuàn, annals and biographies, the 2 main sections of official histories.
6. (med.) ancestral sequence, lineage, genealogy.
7. (med.) affirm for the record, attest, notarize.
8. ⊙ 記 *jì* 2, to record, write down; record, account, document.

繼   jì   MC kejH

1. tie together, connect.
   a. add to; increase, augment.
   b. extend, amplify; e.g. ～天 jìtiān, serve as an extension of Heaven.
2. continue, succeed, ensue; e.g. ～武 jìwǔ, continue in the footsteps of.
   a. carry on, take the place of; inherit.
   b. follow, accede to; adopt, accept as one's own.

罽   jì   MC kjejH

1. haircloth; coarse felt.
2. (med.) (bn.) ～賓 jìbīn (kjejH-pjin), old name for Kashmir (< Skt. *kaśmīra*, Tib. *kaspara*), also incl. much of Gandhāra and nearby areas of northwest India.

芰   jì   gjeH

1. water chestnut, caltrop (*Trapa bispinosa*); syn. 菱 *líng*.

薊   jì   MC kejH

1. gen. term for thistle, incl. various species of *Cirsium* or *Echinops*.
2. a surname.

薺   jì   MC dzejX

1. heart's-weed, shepherd's-purse (*Capsella bursa-pastoris*), common herb used for eating.

2. (bn.) 〜苨 *jìnǐ* (MC dzejX-nejX), root of pan-icled lady-bells (*Adenophora remotiflora*), used medicinally.

cí　MC **dzij**

1. tackweed, goathead (*Tribulus terrestris*), syn. 茨 *cí*.

藋　jì　MC kjejH

1. (bn.) 〜蕠 *jìrú* (MC kjejH-nrjo), osmorhiza (*Osmorhiza aristata*), summer-blooming grass, with small white umbelliferous flowers, used medicinally.

覬　jì　MC kijH

1. hope to gain, crave, desire; scheme for, look out for; e.g. 〜覦 *jìyú*, yearn for desperately, cov-et what is not one's due; unbefitting plans, un-warranted aims, undeserving expectations.

計　jì　MC kejH

1. calculate, reckon; plan, figure.
   a. plot, design, formulate.
2. render or settle accounts.
   a. account-books, esp. of tax obligations; e.g. 〜帳 *jìzhàng*, tax registers.
   b. official charged with presenting local account books annually at the capital; used in various official titles.
3. sum up, add up; appraise, assess, take stock of, take into consideration.
   a. survey, scan; take note of, observe.
   b. (med.) indicative of personal comment: one might say (assume, suppose) that . . .
4. (med.) (bn.) 〜都 *jìdū* (MC kejH-tu), trsc. Skt. *ketu*, name of invisible planet signifying in Vedic astronomy (adopted in Tang times) the descending lunar node, where moon on south-erly course crosses the ecliptic (cf. ascending, northerly node *rahu* [*luohou* 羅睺], thought of as complementary invisible planet).

記　jì　MC kiH

1. retain in memory, keep in mind (ant. 忘 *wàng*, forget, ignore).
2. to record, make or take note of; mark; write down.
   a. gen. term for public record or document.
   b. memorandum, note to subordinate; sometimes, petition to superior.
   c. (lit.) prose genre giving an account of a specific topic, incident, or person.

3. (Budd.) 無〜 *wújì*, the Undeclared, the In-expressible, the 14 questions that the Buddha deemed incapable of definition either as exist-ent or non-existent or as both or neither.

記　jì　MC giH

1. warn(ing), admonish, monition; prohibit(ion), interdict(ion).

跽　jì　MC gijX

1. kneel, respectfully with torso held upright; syn. (長)跪 (*cháng*)*guì*.

際　jì　MC tsjejH

1. juncture, interface, connecting spot between 2 contiguous segments; abutment.
   a. seam; connection.
   b. (med.) among, amidst.
2. margin, border, boundary, limit.
   a. delimit, define.
   b. (med.) draw near to, come close to, next to, border on.
3. point in time, connecting former with later.
   a. at that moment, then; at the time when, at the juncture of; e.g. 唐虞之〜 *Táng Yú zhi jì*, in the period of Tang and Yu (i.e. Yao and Shun).
   b. occasion, opportunity, chance, opening for.
4. amidst or among this and that; e.g. 君臣之〜 *jūnchén zhi jì*, between lord and vassal.
5. (med.) happen on, meet up with.

霽　jì　MC tsejH

1. clearing sky, after rain or clouds move off; fair(ing), fair weather.
2. dissipating anger, clearing mind.

驥　jì　MC kijH

1. sgl. or 騏〜 *qíjì*, thoroughbred steed, fine charger, long-galloping and tireless courser.

髻　jì　MC kejH

1. chignon, bound-up hair.

jié　MC **kjit**

1. name of spirit of the stove.

鰿　jì　MC tsjek

1. golden carp (*Cyprinus auratus*).

鯽　jì　MC tsjek　⊙ 鰿 *jì*.

齎　jì　MC dzejH

1. flare up, boil up, act impetuously.

jiā

佳 *jiā* MC kea

1. seemly; pleasing, good(ly); e.g. 〜人 *jiārén*, seemly one, term applied to man or woman of respected or desired connection; also, a man of parts, talented person.

   a. becoming, handsome, attractive, fair; comely.

   b. conforming to good taste, decorous; gratifying.

   c. satisfying, delightful; e.g. 〜境 *jiājìng*, realm of delight.

加 *jiā* MC kae

1. place upon.

   a. confer on (title, position), assign, impart to.

   b. inflict on, execute (punishment, tax claim).

   c. adduce; apply (to); put into practice.

2. add to, increase; augment; improve.

   a. more so, increasingly, yet more.

   b. acquire.

3. align the disk and base of a divining-board (*shi* 式).

4. (med.) deign (to do).

5. (med.) 〜諸 *jiāzhū*, speak falsely, misrepresent (Tang colloquial).

嘉 *jiā* MC kae

1. estimable, admirable, praiseworthy.

   a. favored, fine(st), excellent.

   b. praise, commend.

   c. favorable, favonian; promising, timely.

夾 *jiā* MC keap

1. occupy both sides of.

   a. hold between two fingers, pinch, squeeze (between).

   b. hem, clamp.

2. pincer, tweezer.

3. cling to, hold tight(ly), keep safe; preserve.

4. (med.) insert between, e.g. 〜紵 *jiāzhù*, "inserted ramie," dry-lacquering, for statues, etc.

5. (med.) bundle of Indic palm-leaf (*pothi*) writing.

6. ⊙ 狹 *xiá*, narrow, strait; 鋏 *jiá* 1, sword-hilt.

家 *jiā* MC kae

1. residence, home, domicile.

2. household, family; relations living in same residence, esp. for census and tax purposes.

   a. blood relations of same surname.

   b. dynastic line; e.g. 漢〜 *hànjiā*, the House of Han.

3. honorific prefix, used in terms of address to family members older than oneself in same generation or of earlier generation: our (family's) . . .; e.g. 〜兄 *jiāxiōng*, our older brother (cf. 舍 *shè* for younger persons).

4. term of address between husband and wife.

5. (med.) sgl. or 〜人 *jiārén*, wife, spouse.

6. fief or appanage given a high dignitary by the ruler.

7. as suffix following profession, name of teacher, or school of thought: practitioner of, specialist (in X particular tradition); lineage, tradition of interpretation.

   a. (Budd.) sect, usu. paying special honor to a particular sūtra or tracing lineage to particular founding teacher.

   b. (med.) suffix added to pronoun as enclitic; e.g. 儂〜 *nóngjiā*, I, I myself.

8. 〜人 *jiārén*, "Family," name of 37th hexagram of the *Yìjing*.

gū MC ku

1. 大〜 *dàgū*, respectful term for woman; e.g. 曹大〜 *cáo dàgū*, the lady Cao; (med.) also, term of address used by children of concubine for father's legal wife; (med.) also, palace attendants' term of reference for (not address to) emperor.

枷 *jiā* MC kae

1. flail, threshing implement.

2. cangue, wooden yoke fastened around neck as punishment.

   a. (med.) to collar, leash.

3. ⊙ 架 *jià*, frame, cabinet.

梜 *jiā* MC kaep

1. chopsticks.

2. book-box, book-chest.

浹 *jiā* MC tsep

1. moisten(ed), dampen(ed); steep(ed) in, soak into, drench.

2. perfuse, penetrate, go all the way through; reach all the way to; flow everywhere, spread widely.

   a. pervasive, complete, from one end to the other; e.g. 〜日 *jiārì*, full decade of days using successively all of the heavenly stems, i.e. 10-day "week"; 〜辰 *jiāchén*, full dozen of days using successively all of the earthly branches.

b. common, universal, general, thoroughgoing.

c. (med.) (bn.) 〜洽 *jiáqià* (MC tsep-heap), extending everywhere.

3. make contact with, communicate.

xiá　MC heap

1. (bn.) 〜渫 *xiádié* (MC heap-dep), ceaselessly streaming, swell and spread (of waves or tears); spaciously laced (of continuous waves).

猳　jiā　MC kae

1. male pig, boar, ⊙ 豭 *jiā*.
2. (med.) long-tailed monkey.

珈　jiā　MC kae

1. woman's hairpin with hanging gems.

痂　jiā　MC kae

1. mange; scab(by), crust(y).

笳　jiā　MC kae

1. reed-pipe, sideblown single-reed flute of Central Asian origin; said according to one legend to have been invented by Laozi during his stay with barbarians after leaving China.

篍　jiā　MC kae　⊙ 笳 *jiā*.

茄　jiā　MC kae

1. petiole or leaf-stalk of lotus; lily-stem.

qié　MC gja

1. eggplant (*Solanum melongena*).

葭　jiā　MC kae

1. reed; young reed sprouts.
2. ⊙ 笳 *jiā*, reed-pipe.

xiá　MC hae

1. ⊙ 遐 *xiá*, far.

袈　jiā　MC kae

1. (Budd.) 〜裟 *jiāshā* (MC kae-srae), trsc. Skt. *kaṣāya*, cassock, monk's "turbid-colored" robe, usu. brownish-yellow, ochre, or saffron.

豭　jiā　MC kae

1. male pig, boar.

跏　jiā　MC kae

1. (Budd.) 〜趺 *jiāfū*, sit in lotus position for meditation, legs crossed with upturned feet on opposite thighs; trns. Skt. *āsana*.

迦　jiā　MC kae

1. (Budd.) transcription graph for Skt. *ka, kā, ga, gā*; e.g. (僧)〜藍(摩) (*sēng*)*jiālán*(*mó*) (MC song-kae-lam-ma), trsc. of Skt. (*saṅ*)*ghārām*(*a*), "pleasance of the priestly assembly," i.e. monastery; 〜葉 *jiāyè* (MC kae-yep), trsc. Skt. *kāśyapa*, Kasyapa, name of one of Buddha's principal disciples; 〜陵(頻伽) *jiālíng*(*pínqié*) (MC kae-ling-bjin-gja), Skt. *kala*(*viṅka*), sweetest-voiced of all birds whose song, even before it hatches, brings other birds to it, symbolic of bodhisattva; 〜樓羅 *jiālóuluó* (MC kae-luw-la), trsc. Skt. *garuḍa*, golden-winged bird (trns. 金翅鳥 *jīnchìniǎo*), one of 8 mythical classes of nonhuman beings who pay homage to the Buddha.

2. 〜師 *jiāshī* (MC kae-srij), Kashgar.

xiè　MC heaX

1. (bn.) 〜逅 *xièhòu* (MC heaX-huwH), ⊙ 邂逅 *xièhòu*, chance upon, run across, unlooked for, meet up with unexpectedly; happenstance, coincidence; also (med.), some time or other, if by any chance.

麚　jiā MC kae　⊙ 麚 *jiā*.

麚　jiā　MC kae

1. male deer, stag.

jiá

怒　jiá　MC keat

1. indifferent, uncaring, oblivious of, negligent.

戛　jiá　MC keat

1. pike, halberd.
2. tap, rap; bump.

a. play (a musical instrument), make sound.

3. constant rule; norm(al), usual.

4. (med.) pad, plod; pace, walk on.

5. (med.) break open, break apart.

6. (med.) sgl. or rdup., onom. of sudden tearing, splitting, wrenching; also (rdup.), hard and arduous, trying and tiring.

7. (med.) ～～斯 *jiájiásī* (MC keat-keat-sje), name for Kirghiz, a Türkic people known from Han times, originally centered on upper Yenisei River valley, who became powerful force in the Tang; syn. 結骨 *jiégǔ*, 監昆 *jiānkūn*.

碣　jiá　MC keat

1. (bn.) 碣～ *jiéjiá*, → 碣 *jié*.

荚　jiá　MC kep

1. casing of grains or vegetables with their "fruit": husk, pod, shell.

蛱　jiá　MC kep

1. (med.) (bn.) ～蝶 *jiádié* (MC kep-dep), butterfly; syn. 蝴蝶 *húdié*.

袷　jiá　MC keap

1. lined wrap without padding, for informal wear.
    a. lined, doubled (of clothing).
2. secondary; auxiliary, ancillary.
        jié　MC kjaep
    1. ⊙ 祫 *jié*, overlapping collar or lapels.

袷　jiá　MC keap

1. (med.) ⊙ 袷 *jiá* 1, lined wrap without padding.

跲　jiá　MC keap

1. trip, stumble.
    a. blunder, bungle (orally).

鋏　jiá　MC kep

1. sword-hilt.
2. (med.) pincers; tongs.

頰　jiá　MC kep

1. cheek(s), of human or animal; e.g. ～帶 *jiádài*, cheek-band (of bridle).

jiǎ

假　jiǎ　MC kaeX

1. borrow, use temporarily.
    a. make use of; rely, depend on; by means of, thanks to.
    b. provisional in nature, marker of merely temporary holding of appointment (when preceding official title); e.g. ～名 *jiǎmíng*, provisional words or expressions.

2. introduces conditional clause: suppose that . . ., granted that . . ., if . . .
    a. 1st element of concessive hypothetical cmpd.; e.g. ～使 *jiǎshǐ*, ～饒 *jiǎráo*, even if, though, granted; ～如 *jiǎrú*, even if, though; (med.) also, for example.
3. concede, tolerate; pardon, let off; lenient.
    a. grant, bestow; give to.
4. false, delusive, untruthful; inauthentic, sham, fraudulent; simulated, counterfeit (ant. 真 *zhēn*); N.B. these meanings not common until Han, usu. represented earlier by 偽 *wěi*.
    a. pretend, simulate.
5. (med.) must, necessarily.
6. (med.) to commission or engage with responsibility for.
        jià　MC kaeH
    1. (take a) leave of absence, furlough, leave.
        xiá　MC hae
    1. ⊙ 遐 *xiá*, far-advanced, far distant.

蝦　jiǎ　MC kaeX　→ 蝦 *gǔ*.

岬　jiǎ　MC kaep

1. hill-gap, notch.
    a. mountain flank.

斝　jiǎ　MC kaeX

1. ritual wine vessel used in early times, bronze, 4-legged or tripod with 2 upright handles, similar to 爵 *jué* but larger.

榎　jiǎ　MC kaeX　⊙ 檟 *jiǎ*.

檟　jiǎ　MC kaeX

1. catalpa tree (*Catalpa bungei*); syn. 楸 *qiū* (cf. 梓 *zǐ*, another species [*Catalpa ovata*]).
2. mallotus tree (*Mallotus japonicus*).
3. (med.) tea-tree, camellia (*Camellia sinensis*).
4. (med.) (bn.) ～楚 *jiǎchǔ* (MC kaeX-tsrhjoX), to switch and scourge, whip with slender stick or rod.

甲　jiǎ　MC kaep

1. outer integument of sprouting vegetation; sheath.
2. shell, carapace, plate; hard outer covering of various animals.
    a. category of animals with shells.
    b. nail, claw, talon.

3. armor, protective covering for soldiers, usu. lamellar, made of small plates of lacquered leather, less often iron or steel; buffcoat, cuirasse.
  a. metonomy for soldier.
4. 1st of the 10 heavenly stems; used for "A" in a sequential order.
5. first-order, first-rate.
6. anonymous pronoun used for unknown or fictional figure: such-a-one.
7. (med.) ～香 *jiǎxiāng*, "plate aromatic" or ～煎 *jiǎjiān* "plate decoction," onycha, incense derived from the plate or lid of a snail-like mollusk mixed with aloeswood and musk; ～煎粉 *jiǎjiānfěn*. onycha paste, aromatic lipstick made of preceding mixed with beeswax and ashes of fragrant fruit-flowers.
8. ⊙ 狎 *xiá*, close to, familiar with, intimate.

瘕　jiǎ　MC kaeX
1. various stomach ailments, incl. conglomerations.
  a. unusually severe fetal movements.
    xiá　MC hae
1. (med.) ⊙ 瑕 *xiá*, flaw, fault; act(ing) out of order, infraction, misdeed, offense.

胛　jiǎ　MC kaep
1. shoulder-blade.

賈　jiǎ　MC kaeX　→ 賈 *gǔ*.

jià

價　jià　MC kaeH
1. value, price; worth.
2. (med.) reputation, estimation.

嫁　jià　MC kaeH
1. give a daughter to wive; marry (of a woman), go to another (i.e. one's husband's) home; cf. 娶 *qǔ*, take to wife, marry a wife.
2. proceed, move ahead, go forward.
3. shift or transfer (esp. blame or misfortune) to another, implicate; pawn off.

幏　jià　MC kaeH
1. a cloth presented as tribute in Han times by tribes of the Southern Man 蠻.

架　jià　MC kaeH
1. frame(work), scaffold, (under)girding; shelf, stand; rack, trellis, perch, pergola; branched structure to support something, such as the stepped horizontal beams supporting a roof.
2. to frame, construct, organize.
3. shelve, place on, set on or aside.
  a. ⊙ 駕 *jià* 3, place oneself above, exceed, surpass.

稼　jià　MC kaeH
1. sow grain; sow the seed.
  a. farming, farmwork.
2. grain, crops.
  a. sheaf of grain.

駕　jià　MC kaeH
1. harness, hitch, yoke horse to carriage.
  a. yoked carriage, equipage, rig.
  b. the imperial equipage; cortege; metonymy for the emperor, esp. when traveling.
2. drive a carriage; control, direct.
  a. harness for one's own purposes, put to use, avail oneself of.
3. override; place oneself above; exceed, surpass.
4. disseminate, spread.
5. the distance a horse and carriage can travel in a day.
6. ⊙ 架 *jià* 2, to frame, organize.
    jiā　MC kae
1. ⊙ 加 *jiā* 2, add to, increase, augment.

jiān

兼　jiān　MC kem
1. 2 or more things held or brought together in combination; equipoise(d); combine(d), conjoin(ing).
  a. concurrent, esp. in official titles when appointee holds 2 substantive positions; simultaneous(ly), at the same time.
2. doubled; together; > multiple, many; e.g. ～功 *jiāngōng*, double one's efforts; ～味 *jiānwèi*, multi-flavored.
  a. two, twice; e.g. ～年 *jiānnián*, 2 years.
3. (X) and also (Y), (X) as well as (Y), in addition.
  a. (X) and still (Y), (X) and yet (Y).
  b. the same as, equal to.

4. impartial, indiscriminate, unselective, without distinction; e.g. 〜愛 *jiān'ài*, impartial caring, concern for all alike; 〜忘 *jiānwàng*, indiscriminately oblivious, unaware of distinctions.

5. add(ed) to, annex(ed), esp. territory; e.g. 〜天下 *jiān tiānxià*, incorporate the whole world.

6. (med.) (ADV) even more, more so, to a higher degree.

堅   jiān   MC ken

1. solid, firm, hard, substantial; tough, resistant; durable, obdurate; impregnable; e.g. 〜剛 *jiān'gāng*, firm and rigid; 〜白 *jiānbái*, hard and white, rhetorical example of items independent of each other, not co-occurring.

2. stand firm about; insist on, persist in; e.g. 〜戰 *jiānzhàn*, persevere in warfare.
   a. resolved; stable, secure; e.g. 〜臥 *jiānwò*, rest securely.

3. 〜昆 *jiānkūn*, early name (from Han times) for the Kirghiz, a Turkic people centered on upper Yenisei River valley, becoming powerful force during the Tang; syn. 結骨 *jiégǔ*, 戛戛斯 *jiájiásī*.

奸   jiān   MC kaen   → 奸 *gān*.

姦   jiān   MC kaen

1. faithless, treacherous, perfidious; hypocritical, sly, scheming; meschant.

2. prurient, concupiscent; adulterous; illicit intercourse.

尖   jiān   MC tsjem

1. (med.) tapering to a point, point(ed), tip(ped), peaked, sharp, cuspidate.

2. (med.) piercing, shrill, sharp, of music or the wind.

3. (med.) curious, queer, peculiar, novel, offbeat (< standing out), esp. of written style.

戔   jiān   MC dzan

1. rdup., a great number, manifold; (med.) explicitly evident, patent and apparent.

械   jiān   MC keam

1. wooden receptacle; coffer, case, box; container.
   a. cup, goblet.
      hán   MC hom
1. ⊙ 函 *hán*, contain(er), envelop(e).

櫼   jiān   MC tsjem

1. lever, the horizontal arm on which bracket-constructions carrying the eaves were placed.

殱   jiān   MC tsjem

1. annihilate, reduce to nothing, exterminate, obliterate, destroy completely.

湔   jiān   MC tsjen

1. wash, cleanse with water.
   a. wipe away, wipe clean.
      jiàn   MC tsjenH
1. ⊙ 濺 *jiàn*, spatter, splash, spray.

瀸   jiān   MC tsjem

1. soak, splash, imbue.
   a. moisten; enrich; affect, influence; infect.
   b. agreeable, congenial.

2. intermittent flow of a wellspring.

3. ⊙ 殱 *jiān*, annihilate, extinguish.

煎   jiān   MC tsjen

1. dry-fry, roast; parch.

2. cook with water; decoct, reduce liquid content by heating.
   a. simmer in slight oil or water.

3. (med.) anxious, apprehensive, in a "slow burn."
   a. (med.) 〜蹇 *jiānjiǎn* (MC tsjen-kjenX), maimed with misery, exasperated, aggravated.

熸   jiān   MC tsjem

1. go out, die out, be extinguished (of fire).
   a. recede, wane, disappear.

2. put to rout, overrun, vanquish.

牋   jiān   MC tsen

1. (med.) official memorandum or report stating an opinion, usu. to member of imperial family.
   a. (med.) letter, missive, usu. from inferior to superior.

2. (med.) fine notepaper.

犍   jiān   MC kjon

1. bullock, gelded bull; castrated bovine.
   a. geld(ed), castrate(d).

監   jiān   MC kaem

1. look from above to below, oversee, supervise; superintend; observe, inspect.
   a. 1st element in many official titles: overseer of . . ., supervisor of . . ., inspector of . . .
   b. keep watch over; e.g. 〜守 *jiānshǒu*, guard.

jiàn　MC kaemH

1. fill a basin with water to use as mirror.
   a. (bronze) mirror, ⊙ 鑑 *jiàn*.
   b. draw a lesson from, use reflected image as guide or warning.
2. final element in official titles, indicating the institution for which a superintendant or inspector (*jiān* 1a) has responsibility; e.g. (med.) 國子〜 *guózǐjiàn*, Inspectorate of the Sons of the State, in Tang times the central agency that oversaw the capital-city colleges.
3. sgl. or 太〜 *tàijiàn*, palace eunuch.

礛　jiān　MC kaem

1. (bn.) 〜諸 *jiānzhū* (MC kaem-tsyo), buffstone, for polishing jade or other precious stones.
2. ⊙ 剴 *jiàn*, sharp, keen; cutting.

箋　jiān　MC tsen

1. annotation, commentary (to a text).
2. (med.) 〜布 *jiānbù*, sheer cloth, costly fabric produced in Sichuan area; syn. 黃潤 *huángrùn*, yellow luster.
3. ⊙ 牋 *jiān* 1, (med.) official memorandum or report; letter, usu. from inferior to superior; 2, (med.) fine notepaper.

緘　jiān　MC keam

1. cord, strap, for securing chest, coffer, sealing-board, etc.
2. bind up, bind securely; tie up, wrap.
3. seal up, stop up; close, close off.
   a. (med.) close the mouth; unspeaking, taciturn.
4. (med.) letter, missive (< sealed communication).
5. store up, store away.

縑　jiān　MC kem

1. double-threaded and tightly-woven silk, dimity, usu. beige or light-colored.

肩　jiān　MC ken

1. shoulder.
   a. in quadrupeds, the area to either side of the withers.
2. to shoulder, take up; bear responsibility for; reinforce, strengthen.
   a. assign a task to, appoint; put to use, bring to bear, employ.

xián　MC hen

1. rdup., lean and lanky, scrawny and spindly.

艱　jiān　MC kean

1. difficult(y), arduous, demanding.
2. dangerous, formidable, redoubtable.
3. grief of mourning for a parent.

菅　jiān　MC kaen

1. sgl. or 〜茅 *jiānmáo*, themeda (*Themeda gigantea*), rough-bladed grass with well-developed spikelets, can be thatched for roof-covering, plaited for sandals or mats, entwined for cord.

蒹　jiān　MC kem

1. eared reed, a reed that has not yet put forth its long spikelets or catkins.

蔪　jiān　MC tsjem

1. awn or beard of wheat.

jiǎn　MC dzjemX

1. thick growth of plants, rife, lush, burgeon(ing), entwining.

shān　MC sraem

1. ⊙ 芟 *shān*, cut down grass, mow; eliminate, eradicate.

蕑　jiān　MC kean

1. old term for eupatory, thoroughwort, agrimony, boneset (*Eupatorium japonicum, Eupatorium fortunei*); syn. 蘭 lán 1.

豣　jiān　MC ken

1. wild boar of 4 years (3 *suì*) old.

間　jiān　MC kean

N.B. This graph a med. development, taking place of → 閒 *xián* for *jiān/jiàn* readings.
1. interstice of space, interval, the space of . . .; space between.
   a. in between, among, in the midst of.
2. interstice of time, a while; interval, intermission; e.g. 〜者 *jiānzhe*, a while ago, after a while; 病〜 *bìngjiān*, remission of illness.
   a. sgl. or 之〜 *zhījiān*, following a VB or VB –phrase: when, at the point when VB.
3. measure-word, "bay," indicating span or space between two pillars of a building.

4. (Budd.) 無～ *wújiān*, "interminable," trns. Skt. *avīci*, name of lowest and most baleful of hell-realms, syn. 阿鼻 *ābí*.

jiàn　MC keanH

1. lie or place between; interpose; interspaced with; e.g. ～色 *jiànsè*, intermediate color, such as purple, between primary colors.

   a. put in the midst of; participate.

2. take as an opening to; use as a pretext.

   a. furtive(ly), covert(ly), e.g. ～語 *jiànyǔ*, speak with privately, speak apart.

   b. spy on; reconnoiter; peer into.

3. pick apart, criticize; cavil; find fault with.

4. set apart, differ; separate.

5. alternate(ly), in turn.

6. onom. of various sounds, e.g. ～關 *jiànguān* (MC keanH-kwaen), thundering trundle of carriage wheels, or the calling cries of birds.

軒　jiān　MC kean

1. 軨～ *líjiān*, → 軨 *lí*.

鞬　jiān　MC kjon

1. bow-and-arrow caddy attached to horse's saddle.

韉　jiān　MC tsen

1. saddle-blanket.

鰜　jiān　MC kem

1. flat-fish, spiny-finned fish, various species of flounder.

鶼　jiān　MC kem

1. paired birds of coupled wings and eyes, each reputedly having only one apiece and so needing the help of the other to fly.

jiǎn

儉　jiǎn　MC gjemX

1. restrain(t), moderate, moderation; prudent, prudence (ant. 奢 *shē*, improvident, immoderate; wasteful, profligate).

   a. frugal, thrifty; if excessive, stingy.

2. scarce, scarcity; dearth; inadequate.

3. meager harvest, crop failure.

剪　jiǎn　MC tsjenX

1. (med.) ⊙ 翦 *jiǎn*.

帴　jiǎn　MC tsjenX

1. narrow, strait; cinched.

jiān　MC tsen

1. (med.) baby's swaddling-clothes.

2. (med.) ⊙ 韉 *jiān*, saddle-blanket.

戩　jiǎn　MC tsjenX

1. favorable, good fortune; fortunate, auspicious.

2. ⊙ 翦 *jiǎn* 1, cut off, shear, trim; 2, cut away, eradicate.

揀　jiǎn　MC keanX

1. ⊙ 柬 *jiǎn* 1, choose, select, distinguish between alternatives; glean, cull, sort.

揃　jiǎn　MC tsjenX

1. cut off, cut down.

2. cut away, clear away; eliminate, extirpate.

3. cut up, rend, sever; divide, separate, partition.

撿　jiǎn　MC kjemX

1. restrain(t), reserve; constrain(t), curb.

2. investigate, try to ascertain; root around in.

柬　jiǎn　MC keanX

1. choose, select, distinguish between alternatives; glean, cull.

2. (med.) note, brief letter; memorandum.

3. ⊙ 簡 *jiǎn* 1, bamboo-slip, for writing on.

檢　jiǎn　MC kjemX

1. measure(ment), standard, criterion; rule.

   a. regularly recurring action, incl. musical rhythm.

2. restrain, limit, moderate; curb.

   a. measured deportment, restraint; integrity, moderation.

3. investigate, examine, inspect; check over.

4. collect, gather in.

   a. arrest, take into custody.

5. sealing-board for letters, fastened with cords that were passed through indentation in boards and sealed with clay; (med.) also, by metonymy, letter, missive.

6. book-tag, label, carrying title of book, inserted to hang down from volumes when stacked.

減　jiǎn　MC keamX

1. reduce, decrease, diminish; lessen, subtract.

   a. less than, smaller than; inferior to.

2. alleviate, mitigate; relieve; retrench.
   a. (med.) donate, contribute; tender, extend.
3. (med.) about, approximately, nearly.
4. (med.) right of reduction for judicial punishment.

瞼　jiǎn　MC kjemX
1. eyelid.
2. conserve, store up.

筧　jiǎn　MC kenX
1. (med.) bamboo pipes for conveying water, bamboo aqueduct.

簡　jiǎn　MC keanX
1. bamboo-slip, for writing.
   a. written document, screed.
2. simple, uncomplicated.
   a. brief, concise; sketchy.
   b. frugal, chary; scant.
3. negligent, neglect(ful), ignore, be remiss, cursory.
   a. unceremonious, unrefined; indelicate, tactless.
4. choose, select; glean, cull; ⊙ 柬 *jiǎn* 1.
5. inspect, examine.
6. (med.) single line of poem.

繭　jiǎn　MC kenX
1. silkworm cocoon.
   a. ～栗 *jiǎnlì*, cocoon- and chestnut [-shaped], descriptive of the budding horns of a young calf offered for sacrifice; > any young calf; > buds of flowers.
2. floss-silk, with little or no twist.
   a. clothing embroidered or padded with floss-silk.
3. (med.) ⊙ 趼 *jiǎn*, callus on hand or foot.

翦　jiǎn　MC tsjenX
1. cut off, shear; trim, clip; prune, crop.
2. cut away, clear; root out, eradicate, eliminate.
   a. weaken, deplete; reduce.
3. (med.) scissors, shears.

襇　jiǎn　MC kenX
1. garment embroidered or padded with new floss-silk.

謇　jiǎn　MC kjenX
1. stammer, stutter.

2. sgl. or rdup., frank, forthright, straightforward; outspoken, without reticence; faithful.
3. rhythmic verse-initial particle used in some *Chuci* 楚詞 poems.

謭　jiǎn　MC tsjenX
1. shallow, superficial, insubstantial.
   a. facile, glib (of language).

趼　jiǎn　MC kenX
1. callus on hand or foot; callosity.

蹇　jiǎn　MC kjenX
1. lame, halt(ing); limp(ing), hobble.
   a. hack, nag; lame, worn-out, or inferior horse or ass.
2. rough, ragged; bumpy, uneven; uphill.
   a. toilsome, wearisome; difficulty in advancing.
   b. (bn.) ～產 *jiǎnchǎn* (MC kjenX-sreanX), worn with woe, strained and twisted, bent and bowed; also, swerve and veer.
   c. congeal, coagulate; stagnate.
3. "Hard Going," name of 39th hexagram of the *Yijing*.
4. ⊙ 謇 *jiǎn* 1, stammer, stutter; 3, rhythmic verse-initial particle used in some *Chuci* 楚辭 poems; 褰 *qiān* 2, pull up, pluck up, lift or hitch up one's clothes, furl curtains.

鹻　jiǎn　MC keamX
1. (med.) alkaline, saline.

鹼　jiǎn　MC keamX　⊙ 鹻 *jiǎn*.

<h2 style="text-align:center">jiàn</h2>

件　jiàn　MC gjenX
1. (med.) divide, separate.
2. (med.) measure-word for items, articles.
3. (med.) action items, noted for official business.

俴　jiàn　MC dzjenX
1. shallow.
   a. superficial, trifling.
2. thin mail, light armor.

健　jiàn　MC gjonH
1. strong, healthy; sturdy, sound; formidable, powerful.
   a. ～兒 *jiàn'ér*, militiamen, soldiers.

2. rigid, inflexible.
3. able, talented; of many parts.
4. (med.) one's "strong suit," one's forte; particular(ly) skill(ed).
    a. (med.) extremely, especially (< with force).

僭   jiàn   MC tsemH

1. overstep one's rights; usurp, arrogate (title, position); misappropriate, accroach; presumptuous(ly).
2. fraudulent, false, spurious.

劍   jiàn   MC kjomH

1. double-edged sword, used for combat and ceremoniously, of various lengths but the most valuable usu. about a yard long with incised characters or designs.
    a. ensiform, sword-shaped.
2. run through; wound or kill with sword.

劒   jiàn   MC kaem

1. sharp, keen; cutting.

建   jiàn   MC kjonH

1. establish; set up; install.
    a. enact; appoint, invest with office or title, create.
    b. set out, set forth; e.g. ～言 *jiànyán*, set out in words, offer opinion, advocate.
2. erect, build, construct.
    a. standing upright; e.g. ～鼓 *jiàngǔ*, a standing drum.
3. determine, determinate.
4. sector of sky (indicated by one of the 12 earthly branches) toward which the handle of the Big Dipper points; e.g. ～寅 *jiànyín*, sky-sector toward which Dipper's handle points at dusk in 1st month, hence name for 1st month; ～子 *jiànzǐ*, sky-sector toward which Dipper's handle points at dusk in 11th month, hence name for 11th month.

捷   jiàn   MC gjonH   → 揵 *qián*.

栫   jiàn   MC dzenH

1. fence in, with logs or boughs.
    a. hedge, hedge in.
2. dam, dam up; fish-garth, stream dammed with logs.

揵   jiàn   MC gjonX

1. door-bar; bolt of a lock; e.g. 拔～ *bájiàn*, pull back the bar, pick the lock.
2. wooden posts or piles reinforcing a dike.
    a. block up, dam.
    jiǎn   MC kjenX
1. ⊙ 謇 *jiǎn* 2a, difficulty in advancing.

槛   jiàn   MC haemX

1. pen, fold, enclosure, cage, for domesticated or wild animals.
2. railing, balustrade.
3. cage, pen, holding cell, for prisoners.
    a. cage-cart, for transporting prisoners.
4. rdup., "djem-djem," onom. of carriage or wagon movement.

洊   jiàn   MC dzenH

1. repeat(ed), again; successive(ly).

漸   jiàn   MC djzemX

1. drop-by-drop, drop-wise, stillatim; gradual(ly), incremental(ly), bit-by-bit.
    a. in sequence, one after another.
    b. (med.) at last, all at once (after a gradual sequence).
2. ever more, intensify; e.g. ～X, ever more X, increasingly X.
3. sign, indication; portent.
    a. precondition, premise.
4. "Gradual Advance," name of 53rd hexagram of the *Yijing*.
5. 大～ *dàjiàn*, discommoded, dangerously ill.
    jiān   MC tsjem
1. dip down into; moisten; imbue, soak into.
    a. flow into; influence.
2. cheat; swindle.
    qián   MC dzjem
1. ⊙ 潜 *qián* 1, submerge(d); latent; 2, hide, conceal.

澗   jiàn   MC kaenH

1. beck, gill, swiftly running stream with steep banks.
2. ravine, clough, gorge, canyon; gill used also in this meaning.

磵   jiàn   MC kaenH   ⊙ 澗 *jiàn*.

箭　*jiàn*　MC tsjenH

1. arrow, feathered shaft; made of bamboo (cf. 矢 *shǐ*, made of wood); this graph not common till imperial times.
    a. long dart used in old game of "pitch-pot" (*touhu* 投壺).
2. indicator-rod of clepsydra, marker-rod, borne on a float.
3. ～竹 *jiànzhú*, "arrow-bamboo," fountain-bamboo (*Fargesia nitida*), clump-forming bamboo in mountain areas; 赤～ *chìjiàn*, "red-arrow," gastrodia root (*Gastrodia elata*), used medicinally.

腱　*jiàn*　MC gjonH

1. tendon, sinew.

艦　*jiàn*　MC haemX

1. bulwark-boat, warship with protective planking around deck.

荐　*jiàn*　MC dzenH

1. fodder, for animals.
2. straw mat of double thickness; palliasse, straw pallet.
    a. to cushion; prop, support.
3. once and again, repeated(ly).

薦　*jiàn*　MC tsenH

1. to present; make offering, esp. sacrificial; proffer.
2. recommend; speak highly of, endorse; promote, advance.
3. ⊙ 荐 *jiàn*, all meanings.

見　*jiàn*　MC kenH

1. see, look at.
2. perceive, perception; understand(ing).
    a. see it as, regard as, consider as; be of the opinion that; have an impression of.
    b. (med.) perceive by sound; hear, listen to.
    c. (med.) encounter, experience, meet up with.
3. (GP) preceding VB or VB-phrase as passive marker, indicating object of an action: . . . is seen to be VBed, . . . is exposed to VB, . . . is subject to VB; e.g. ～笑 *jiànxiào*, be laughed at, be exposed to laughter; ～殺 *jiànshā*, be killed.
4. (med.) intend, propose, aim to (do).
    xiàn　MC henH
1. appear, be visible, show forth; be seen, glimpsed; ⊙ 現 *xiàn* 1.
2. (inter)view, be granted (or grant) an audience; (be) receive(d).

諓　*jiàn*　MC dzjenX

1. glib, smooth-tongued.
    a. rdup., slick-talking and suave, shrewdly unctuous.

諫　*jiàn*　MC kaenH

1. admonish, remonstrate; take issue, protest; advise against.

賤　*jiàn*　MC dzjenH

1. of little worth, cheap; humble.
2. lowly, base, mean, lacking dignity, of low repute.
    a. insignificant, nugatory.
3. lacking (basic) resources, impecunious.
4. disrespect, contemn, misprize; mistreat.
5. self-depreciatory ref.: my worthless . . ., my lowly . . .

踐　*jiàn*　MC dzjenX

1. tread, step on; trample.
    a. walk to; come to, arrive.
2. climb up to, mount (on)to.
    a. take possession of, occupy.
3. perform, fulfill, carry out.
4. follow, align with; abide by.
5. situate, site.
6. ⊙ 餞 *jiàn*, farewell ceremony with wine and food; 翦 *jiǎn* 2, cut away, eradicate, eliminate.

鍵　*jiàn*　MC gjonX

1. door-bar.
2. bolt of a lock, cotter; locking spring.
    a. key.
3. linch-pin of wheel-axle.

鐗　*jiàn*　MC kaenH

1. metal axle-fitting between wheel and linchpin.

鑑　*jiàn*　MC kaemH

1. (bronze) mirror.
2. to mirror, reflect; usu. does not take direct-OBJ immediately, often needing complementary 於 *yú* (cf. 鏡 *jìng*).
    a. draw a lesson from, use as guide or warning to reflect on current or future action.
    b. shine about in dark, give off light.
3. discern(ment), perceptive(ness).
4. speculum, anciently basin of water or ice used as reflecting implement.
    a. basin used to collect dew in the moonlight.

鑒   **jiàn**   MC kaemH   ⊙ 鑑 *jiàn*.

餞   **jiàn**   MC dzjenH
1. farewell ceremony for departing friend with wine and food.
   a. to see off.

jiāng

僵   **jiāng**   MC kjang   ⊙ 殭 *jiāng*.

姜   **jiāng**   MC kjang
1. a surname, traditionally of the clan of Shen-nong 神農.
   a. ～原 *jiāngyuán*, Jiang Yuan, mother of legendary first ancestor of the Zhou 周 people, Houji 后稷.
2. ⊙ 薑 *jiāng*, ginger.

將   **jiāng**   MC tsjang
1. take in hand, take hold of; have in hand.
   a. give a hand to; support; protect.
2. use, employ; apply.
   a. (med.) sgl. or ～為 *jiāngwéi*, ～謂 *jiāng-wèi*, take as, regard as, consider as.
3. take along, bring along.
   a. escort, accompany, attend on; see off.
   b. (med.) ensuing, consequently.
4. modal ADV marking future action or intent: about to, will, intend to; e.g. 吾～問之 *wú jiāng wèn zhī*, I am going to ask about it; 子～奚先 *zǐ jiāng xī xiān*, you intend to put what first?; ～以釁鐘 *jiāng yǐ xìn zhōng*, we are going to use it to consecrate a bell; 其～何辭以對 *qí jiāng hécí yǐ duì*, he will likely respond with what words?
   a. in the offing, impending.
5. (med.) modal ADV indicating uncertainty, possibility, or mild suggestion: might; e.g. ～無 *jiāngwú*, might it not be that . . ., wouldn't you agree that . . ., isn't it that . . .?; syn. 得無 *déwú*.
6. or, otherwise, alternatively.
   a. (med.) and, together with, likewise; in parallel phrases often matched with synonyms 共 *gòng*, 與 *yǔ*, etc.; e.g. 暫伴月～影 *zhàn bàn yuè jiāng yǐng*, for a while accompanying the moon and my shadow.
   jiàng   MC tsjangH
1. lead, head, command; be in charge of; e.g. ～軍 *jiàngjūn*, leader of the army, general.

橿   **jiāng**   MC kjang
1. sweet oak, blue oak (*Quercus glauca*), small to medium-sized oak whose leaves are first deep crimson, then turning green above with glaucous blue-green undersides.
2. handle of a hoe.

殭   **jiāng**   MC kjang
1. stiff, rigid (as corpse); corpse-like.
   a. lifeless; unfeeling, insensate.
2. fall over backward.

江   **jiāng**   MC kaewng
1. the Long River (Yangtze).
2. gen. term for river.
3. a surname.

漿   **jiāng**   MC tsjang
1. sour-flavored liquid; e.g. ～水 *jiāngshuǐ*, vinegar leaven.
2. rice-water.
   a. sauce, syrup, broth.
3. gluten.

畺   **jiāng**   MC kjang   ⊙ 疆 *jiāng*.

疆   **jiāng**   MC kjang
1. boundary of land, limit, border; mark out a field boundary.
2. frontier, borderland, marchland; periphery.
3. territory, area, region.

礓   **jiāng**   MC kjang
1. gravel, pebbles, shingle.

繮   **jiāng**   MC kjang
1. reins; halter.

薑   **jiāng**   MC kjang   ⊙ 薑 *jiāng*.

蔣   **jiāng**   MC tsjang
1. wild rice, water-bamboo (*Zizania latifolia*); syn. 菰 *gū*.

薑   **jiāng**   MC kjang
1. ginger (*Zingiber officinale*).
   a. ～黃 *jiānghuáng*, wild turmeric (*Curcuma aromatica*) or turmeric, saffron, yellow ginger (*Curcuma longa*); syn. 鬱金香 *yùjīnxiāng*.

薑　jiāng　MC kjang　⊙ 薑 *jiāng*.

螿　jiāng　MC tsjang
1. sgl. or 寒～ *hánjiāng*, small cicada that sings in late autumn or early winter (*Cosmopsaltria opalifera*).

jiǎng

槳　jiǎng　MC tsjangX
1. (med.) an oar.

獎　jiǎng　MC tsjangX
1. encourage, exhort, urge on; embolden.
2. support, prop up; assist, abet, bestead.
3. (med.) reward, award.
   a. (med.) praise, commend; extol.

講　jiǎng　MC kaewngX
1. discuss, converse; deliberate over.
   a. pay close attention to, be particular about.
2. practice, exercise; e.g. ～武 *jiǎngwǔ*, military exercises.
3. explain, elucidate; lecture (about).
   a. resolve, (be) reconcile(d), conciliate, compose differences.

顜　jiǎng　MC kaewngX
1. explain, clarify.
   a. speak straightforwardly.

jiàng

匠　jiàng　MC dzjangH
1. craftsman, artificer, artisan, opificer.
   a. craft; artful.
2. carpenter, builder.
   a. to build, construct; frame; fashion.

弶　jiàng　MC gjangH
1. (med.) trap, snare, net, for catching birds or beasts.

洚　jiàng　MC kaewngH
1. flood, inundate, overflow the banks.
   a. (bn.) ～洞 *jiàngdòng* (MC kaewngH-duwngH), stretching endlessly, shorelessly spreading.

絳　jiàng　MC kaewngH
1. scarlet, lustrous or glossy red.
   a. bright red tinted with bright yellow: rose-gold; orange (made from rouge and gamboge); yellow-red.

醤　jiàng　MC tsjangH
1. meat-sauce.
2. various sauces mixed with beans and grains.
   a. bean-pickle; pickle(d).

降　jiàng　MC kaewngH
1. descend, come down, bring down (ant. 升 *shēng*).
   a. condescend to, deign to confer a favor upon, as a superior visiting or passing along a boon to a subordinate, e.g. the med. Daoist divinities when revealing themselves to adepts in this world.
   b. bring down, compel to take a lower position, degrade.
2. a princess's leaving the palace to be married.
3. ～婁 *jiànglóu*, name of one of the 12 Jupiter stations, comprising the lunar lodgings *kui* 奎, *lou* 婁, and *wei* 胃.

   xiáng　MC haewng
1. accept or acknowledge subordinate position; surrender, give up, yield, submit to, capitulate.

jiāo

交　jiāo　MC kaew
1. intersect, cross, crisscross, intertwine; e.g. ～手 *jiāoshǒu*, salute or bow with folded hands at breast.
   a. come in contact with, engage; e.g. ～兵 *jiāobīng*, (at) the clash of arms, battle engaged.
   b. point or time of contact; e.g. 九月十月之～ *jiǔyuè shíyuè zhi jiāo*, at the junction of the 9th and 10th months.
2. interchange, relations, intercourse; exchange, communication.
   a. associate with, connect(ion); befriend, friendly relations; cohort; e.g. ～善 *jiāoshàn*, close friendship, on the best of terms with.
   b. join with, combine with; mate with, copulate (esp. animals).
3. transfer from hand to hand, hand over.
4. mutually, reciprocally.
   a. altogether, alike; e.g. ～口 *jiāokǒu*, unanimously.

5. one after another, successively; e.g. ～代 *jiāodài*, in sequence, progressively.
6. (med.) cause, bring about, make (happen).
7. ～河 *jiāohé*, Yarkhoto.
8. (med.) ⊙ 教 *jiào*, teach.

僬   jiāo   MC tsjew

1. (bn.) ～僥 *jiāoyáo* (MC tsjew-ngew), name of legendary country of pygmies; also, term for the inhabitants of said country or of other very small persons, "wren-people" (cog. 鷦鷯 *jiāoliáo*, wren).

jiào   MC tsjewH

1. rdup., scurry and scuttle, scud and scamper.

姣   jiāo   MC kaewX

1. handsome, becoming, beautiful.

xiáo   MC haew

1. dissolute; salacious, licentious.

嬌   jiāo   MC kjew

1. delicately lovely; tender; charming, attractive.
   a. (bn.) ～嬈 *jiāoráo* (MC kjew-nyew), dainty and delicate, graceful and gentle, tender and dear.
2. dote(d) on, indulge(d); pamper(ed), coddle(d), pet(ted), cosset(ed).
3. fragile, weak; squeamish.

嶕   jiāo   MC dzjew

1. (bn.) ～嶢 *jiāoyáo* (MC dzjew-ngew), tall and towering.

憍   jiāo   MC kjew

1. ⊙ 驕 *jiāo* 2, proud, imperious, self-assured, willful.

教   jiāo   MC kaew   → 教 *jiào*.

椒   jiāo   MC tsjew

1. Sichuan pepper (*Zanthoxylum bungeanum*), spicy pepper.
2. 胡～ *hújiāo*, "foreign pepper," black pepper (*Piper nigrum*), first brought from India during Han dynasty.
3. mountaintop.

澆   jiāo   MC kew

1. to water, irrigate; sprinkle, asperge; (Budd.) consecrate.
   a. pour out of or into.
   b. wash, douche.

2. dilute, thin out; weaken.
   a. adulterate, degenerate; debase, pollute.
   b. deficient, defective.

nào   MC nraewH

1. whirlpool, vortex, eddy; whirl round.

焦   jiāo   MC tsjew

1. scorch, singe, burn; scald, torrefy.
   a. smell of scorched object.
2. bake, grill.
   a. parch(ed), exsiccate(d), dry out; desiccated, dried.
3. anxious, worried, on tenterhooks; worked up, agitated, nervous.
4. burning-points, 3 foci of heat in human body: in esophagus, stomach, intestines.
5. singed color, brown.

燋   jiāo   MC tsjew

1. torch; bring fire to.
2. ⊙ 焦 *jiāo* 1, scorch, singe, burn; 2, bake, grill, dry out by firing; 3, anxious, worried, agitated.

qiáo   MC dzjew

1. 憔 *qiáo*, in (bn.) ～悴 *qiáocuì*, → 憔 *qiáo*.

zhuó   MC tsyak

1. burn, scorch, roast.

膠   jiāo   MC kaew

1. glue, paste; adhere(nt), stick(y); viscid, gum(my), resin(ous), tacky; 赤～ *chìjiāo*, "red resin," lac.
2. fast, firm, fixed; steady, secure.
   a. immovable; intractable, obstinate; persistent, dogged.
3. close in on, crowd in.
4. cheat, deceive.
5. rdup., onom. of cock-crow: kukkaow!

jiǎo   MC kaewX

1. rdup., bustle and bother, meddle and muddle.

茭   jiāo   MC kaew

1. ～白 *jiāobái*, wild rice, water-bamboo (*Zizania latifolia*); syn. 菰 *gū*.
2. dried animal fodder.
3. a rope made of bamboo strips or reeds.

jī   MC kek

1. device for holding a crossbow in position; syn. 綮 *qíng*.

蕉   jiāo   MC tsjew

1. sgl. or cmpds. 芭～ *bājiāo*, 香～ *xiāngjiāo*, banana (*Musa basjoo*), stem used medicinally

and, when retted, for making cloth; also planted for decorative purposes; e.g. ～葛 *jiāogé*, banana cloth, made from banana stalks retted until they form fine threads; ～衣 *jiāoyī*, clothing made from preceding.

2. ⊙ 燋 *jiāo*, roast, grill; dry by fire.

qiáo　MC dzjew

1. ⊙ 樵 *qiáo*, firewood, brushwood; 憔 *qiáo*, in (bn.) ～悴 or ～萃 *qiáocuì*, → 憔 *qiáo*.

蛟　jiāo　MC kaew

1. a species of dragon that usu. embodies the destructive or perfidious aspects of water, as opposed to the usu. beneficent aspects represented by the 龍 *lóng*-dragon; often a producer of floods, flood-dragon; in med. times also a shape-changer with ability to take on alluring feminine form. Translate as "lamia," which has some similar features in Western mythology. (N.B. Do not translate as "kraken," whose chief characteristics are enormous size and monstrous appearance like a giant squid, totally unlike the *jiāo*-dragon.)

　a. ～絲 *jiāosī*, "lamia-silk," fine pongee supposedly woven by ～人 *jiāorén*, "lamia-people" of coastal regions, actually cloth woven from the byssus of the pinna mussel, equiv. Greek *pinikon*.

2. ⊙ 鮫 *jiāo*, shark.

蟂　jiāo　MC kew

1. spawn of a snake and a ring-necked pheasant, 4-footed harmful snake, basilisk.

蟭　jiāo　MC tsjew

1. (med.) ～螟 *jiāomíng*, brow-mites (that reputedly nest in eyelashes of mosquitoes).

轇　jiāo　MC kaew

1. rdup. or (bn.) ～轕 *jiāogé* (MC kaew-kat), spacious and capacious, far and full; also, twisting and twining, scrambled and entangled, miggle-maggle, back and forth.

郊　jiāo　MC kaew

1. land surrounding a city; suburbs.

　a. ceremonies in suburbs where ruler sacrificed to Heaven (south) and Earth (north); the altars of those ceremonies.

2. outlying or uncultivated land; moor(s); outlands, of country.

　a. meadow; pasturage.

3. (Dao.) collective name for the 5 viscera.

鐎　jiāo　MC tsjew

1. warming-pot, esp. for soups and broths, usu. a copper tripod with handle, of capacity of 1 *dou* 斗, hence also called ～斗 *jiāodǒu*.

2. cooking-pot for soldiers, also used to beat the watches of the night; syn. 刁斗 *diāodǒu*.

驕　jiāo　MC kjew

1. mettlesome, in fine fettle, high-spirited (esp. of horses).

　a. vigorous, energetic; great-hearted; dashing.

2. proud; imperious, lordly; self-assured, willful; (em)bold(en); e.g. (bn.) ～傲 *jiāo'ào* (MC kjew-ngawH), peremptory proudness.

　a. extravagant, exorbitant; e.g. ～奢 *jiāoshē*, sumptuous, wasteful.

3. favored, preferred; indulged, coddled, cosseted; e.g. ～子 *jiāozǐ*, favored son; ～矜 *jiāojīng*, given free rein, allowed to follow one's own lead.

4. rdup., tall and thick, robust and overfull (of vegetation).

鮫　jiāo　MC kaew

1. shark.

2. ⊙ 蛟 *jiāo*, lamia.

鵁　jiāo　MC kaew

1. (bn.) ～鶄 *jiāojīng* (MC kaew-tsjeng), black-crowned night-heron (*Nycticorax nycticorax*).

鷦　jiāo　MC tsjew

1. (bn.) ～鷯 *jiāoliáo* (MC tsjew-lew), northern wren (*Troglodytes troglodytes*).

2. ～鵬 *jiāomíng*, splendrous gryphon, fire-bright bird, legendary supernatural bird akin to a "phoenix."

鷮　jiāo　MC kjew

1. long-tailed pheasant (species of *Syrmaticus*).

jiǎo

佼　jiǎo　MC kaewX

1. ⊙ 姣 *jiāo*, handsome, becoming, beautiful; 狡 *jiǎo* 1, crafty, cunning; 2, strong, energetic.

jiāo　MC kaew

1. ⊙ 交 *jiāo* 2, interchange, relations, intercourse; exchange, communication, connection.

傲   jiǎo   MC kewX

1. ⊙ 傲 *jiǎo* 1 (*jiào*), ～倖 *jiǎoxìng*, trust to luck, gamble; *jiào* 2, outline, edge, periphery, border; 邀 *yāo* 1a, intercept and attack.

剿   jiǎo   MC tsjewX   ⊙ 勦 *jiǎo*.

剽   jiǎo   MC tsjewX

1. to pare, shear off, cut off.
2. eliminate, annihilate, abolish; ⊙ 勦 *jiǎo* 2.

勦   jiǎo   MC tsjewX

1. to overwork, weary, wear out, wear down; overwhelm; harass.
2. cut off, destroy; eliminate, annihilate, abolish.

chāo   MC dzraew

1. to copy, parrot, plagiarize; fake, forge.
2. nimble, agile, spry.

撟   jiǎo   MC kjewX

1. lift up, raise; move upward; e.g. ～首 *jiǎoshǒu*, raise one's head.
    a. pick up, glean, collect.
2. feign, simulate, pass off as; dissemble, "stretch" the truth.
3. bend, to desired shape or to conform with one's will; mold; subdue, master.
    a. correct, rectify.
4. strong, sturdy; staunch, resolute, inflexible.

攪   jiǎo   MC kaewX

1. disturb, disorder, trouble; ruffle; roil.
    a. (med.) mix up, stir together, blend.

狡   jiǎo   MC kaewX

1. crafty, wily, sly, cunning; astute, canny.
2. sport with, play; caper; joke, quip.
3. strong, vigorous; healthy, hale.
    a. lusty; bold, stout-hearted.
4. pup(py), whelp.

皎   jiǎo   MC kewX

1. bright moonlight; candent, candicant; gleaming.
    a. immaculate; pure, speckless.
    b. clear, lucid, transparent (of meaning).

皦   jiǎo   MC kewX

1. white; shining, glowing.
    a. clear; understandable; distinct, well-defined, clear-cut.
2. pure; clean.
    a. impeccable, unstained (character).

矯   jiǎo   MC kjewX

1. bend, to desired shape or to conform to one's will; mold; subdue, master; ⊙ 撟 *jiǎo* 3.
    a. straighten out, set right; correct, rectify; emend (text).
2. force, press(ure), lean on.
    a. daunt, overawe.
3. conceal, cover up the actual situation.
    a. feign, fake; fabricate; meretricious.
    b. affected, pretentious.
4. raise, rise, mount.
    a. offer up to, hand up.
    b. rdup., superb and poised, high and lofty; also, mutate and change.

絞   jiǎo   MC kaewX

1. hank, warp-threads in coiled form as produced by a warping-reel or warping-board.
2. wrap a cord around; twist, wrench.
    a. interlace, interweave; e.g. ～構 *jiǎogòu*, criss-cross beams, synecdoche for fine dwellings.
    b. wind round, enwrap; winding-sheet for corpse.
3. strangle, garrote.
4. extrude, squeeze; force, press out.
5. impatient, brusque; in haste.

繳   jiǎo   MC kewX   → 繳 *zhuó*.

脚   jiǎo   MC kjak

1. calf of the leg; esp. in pre-imperial texts.
2. foot; e.g. ～手 *jiǎoshǒu*, hand and foot; also, actions of same > conduct, behavior.
    a. lower part of various objects, base, foot, foundation, leg, peduncle, etc.; e.g. 日～ *rìjiǎo*, "sun's leg," i.e. shaft of sunlight (descending through clouds).
3. (med.) messenger, carrier, courier (< footman).
    a. (med.) delivery fee, payment for transmission.

腳   jiǎo   MC kjak   ⊙ 脚 *jiǎo*.

角   jiǎo   MC kaewk

1. horn, of animal.
    a. object shaped like or reminiscent of a horn; e.g. 羊～ *yángjiǎo*, ram's-horn, i.e. whirlwind.
2. frontal eminence or protuberance.
    a. to butt; attack from the front or (2-horned) from both sides.

b. 2 tufts of hair bound on youngster's forehead.

3. corner, angle; nook; e.g. 城～ *chéngjiǎo*, corner of city-wall; 風～ *fēngjiǎo*, divination by angle (i.e. direction) of the wind.

a. cape, point (geographical).

4. musical instrument, esp. used by army.

5. "Horn," one of the 28 lunar lodgings, comprised of α and ξ Virginis, in the eastern quadrant (*qinglong* 青龍) of the sky.

6. (med.) measure of liquid capacity equiv. 4 "pints" (*sheng* 升).

7. (med.) wrap, bundle, pack(age).

jué　MC kaewk

1. name of one of the notes of the pentatonic scale, corresponding symbolically to wood, springtime, the color green, etc.

2. dispute, contend, fight over.

a. ～抵 *juédǐ*, wrestle, tussle; tumble.

3. tripod wine-flagon, similar to 爵 *jué* but with 2 opposed spouts.

gǔ　MC kuwk

1. (med.) rdup., onom. of pheasant's cry: "gooh-gooh!"

銨　jiǎo　MC kaewX

1. (med.) shear(s), scissor(s), pare, blade.

2. (med.) gild, decorate with gold.

jiào

叫　jiào　MC kewH

1. cry out, call (human or animal); shout.

2. (bn.) ～ 條 *jiàotiáo* (MC kewH-dew), passing all measure, illimitable; deeply distant.

喌　jiào　MC kewH

1. ☉ 叫 *jiào*, call, cry out.

2. large ocarina or vessel-flute (→ 塤 *xūn*).

噍　jiào　MC dzjewH

1. chew, masticate; munch, nibble.

a. beings that chew, i.e. living persons or animals.

jiāo　MC dzjew

1. rdup., onom. of pheasant-cry.

2. hasty, hurried; swift.

jiū　MC tsjuw

1. (bn.) 啁～ *zhōujiū*, → 啁 *zhōu* (*zhāo*).

噭　jiào　MC kewH

1. sgl. or rdup., onom. for high-pitched cry, like the howling of gibbons or a keening wail, "keei-keei."

a. call out loudly.

b. wail, cry with grief.

2. (bn.) ～咷 *jiàotiáo* (MC kewH-dewX), old Chu dialect term for incessant crying of babies; also, to sing full-throatedly, call loudly.

徼　jiào　MC kewH

1. make the rounds, patrol, follow a course.

a. border or stockade defense line, esp. with southern barbarians.

2. outline, general lineaments; outer edge, periphery, perimeter; e.g. 觀其～ *guān qí jiào*, observe its outlines, survey its contours.

a. to outline, delimit; limn, describe.

3. sideroad, by-road; path.

jiǎo　MC kewX

1. ～倖 *jiǎoxìng*, gamble, trust to luck, hope for the best, syn. 僥倖 *jiǎoxìng*.

yāo　MC 'jiew

1. seek, solicit.

a. require; insist on, demand.

教　jiào　MC kaewH

1. teach(ing), instruct(ion); usu. suggesting inculcation of particular behavior.

a. when the agent is a government official, implies instructing by example those under one's authority in order properly to improve their morals and sense of social responsibility; often cmpd. ～化 *jiàohuà*, "teach and transform."

b. counsel, advise.

2. school (of thought), sect.

3. convey, transfer, hand on.

4. (med.) an order or "instruction" from a prince(ss) of the blood.

jiāo　MC kaew

1. bring about, to cause, to effect; enable, cause to do; allow, let; syn. 令 *lìng* 6, 使 *shǐ* 2.

斠　jiào　MC kaewk

1. skimmer, with which one removes excess grain when filling a measured container.

2. ☉ 校 *jiào* 1, collate, compare (texts).

校　jiào　MC kaewH

1. compare, collate (esp. texts); classify; examine closely, audit.

a. (med.) proportionate(ly); somewhat (more or less), rather (more or less); ⊙ 較 *jiào* 2.

2. dispute, argue, haggle; set in confrontation with; oppose, resist; e.g. ～獵 *jiàoliè*, competitive hunting.

3. reckon, tally, count; evaluate.

4. wooden enclosure for animals; e.g. ～獵 *jiàoliè*, barricade hunt, in which a certain area of land with animals to be hunted is closed off with palisades.

a. wooden stocks, cangue, for miscreants.

xiào   MC haewH

1. schools in counties and on nobles' estates, academies.

2. military formation of 500 men.

a. cmpd. ～尉 *xiàowèi*, title of military officer below 將軍 *jiàngjūn* ("General"), usu. rendered as "Colonel."

3. (med.) heal(ed), make better.

4. ⊙ 效 *xiào* 1, imitate.

潐   jiào   MC tsjewH

1. rdup., keen and discerning, understand entirely.

皭   jiào   MC tsjewH

1. pure white, albescent.

2. pure, purify; unsullied; clean; pure-minded.

窌   jiào   MC kaewH

1. cave; cellar, pit; subterranean.

2. (bn.) ～條 *jiàotiáo* (MC kaewH-dew), passing measure, illimitable; deeply distant.

liáo   MC laew

1. (bn.) 廖～ *xiáoliáo*, → 廖 *xiáo*.

窖   jiào   MC kaewH

1. cave; cellar, pit; subterranean; ⊙ 窌 *jiào* 1.

a. put into earthen excavation; bury, inter; hide, secrete.

b. deep-kept, deep-tucked.

趭   jiào   MC dzjewH

1. run, fly, flee, hustle.

較   jiào   MC kaewH

1. match, compare, juxtapose; size up.

2. proportionate(ly); somewhat (more or less), rather (more or less); comparatively, relatively.

jué   MC kaewk

1. curved handrails running from back to front of carriage-box.

2. ⊙ 角 *jué* 2 (*jiǎo*), contend, dispute, fight over.

轎   jiào   MC gjewH

1. small cart used for travel in the mountains, a mule-litter. (N.B. This graph not used for palanquin, sedan-chair, until post-Tang times.)

酵   jiào   MC kaewH

1. leaven, used in fermenting wine or soysauce, raising dough, etc.

醮   jiào   MC tsjewH

1. pledge or offer a cup of wine to a young man at his capping ceremony or at his wedding.

a. by metonymy, reaching adulthood or becoming married.

b. (med.) give a daughter in marriage.

2. offer a libation to the spirits.

a. solemn, sacred.

3. (Dao.) ceremony of cosmic renewal, deriving from southern occult traditions and adapted variously within Lingbao liturgy, by Tang times involving large-scale offerings and functioning as the concluding segment of the → 齋 *zhái* ritual.

醨   jiào   MC tsjewH

1. drain a cup, drink every drop, toss off.

jiē

偈   jiē   MC khjet

1. swift, fast-moving, rushing.

jié   MC gjet

1. combative, forceful; staunch; valiant.

jì   MC gjejH

1. (Budd.) abb. of ～陀 *jìtuó* (MC gjejH-da), trsc. Skt. *gāthā*, Budd. verse or ode, esp. versified portion of sūtra.

qì   MC khjejH

1. ⊙ 憩 *qì*, rest, repose, catch one's breath.

喈   jiē   MC keaj

1. rdup., onom. of bird calls: "keeyeh-keeyeh!"; also, of harmonious music, tuneful euphony; also, of brisk brushing of wind.

嗟   jiē   MC tsjae

1. sigh of despair: oh no!

a. sigh of appreciation: ah my!

2. call, summon: hey!

接　jiē　MC tsjep

1. come into contact with, touch, be in touch with; meet.
2. (con)join, connect; associate; go along with.
   a. continue, link; succeed (to).
3. near, touching; contiguous, by the side of.
4. receive, accept.
   a. admit, welcome.
5. (med.) action of birds catching insects; snap up.
6. (bn.) ～給 *jiējǐ* (MC tsjep-kip), repartee, quick wit.

揭　jiē　MC kjot

1. lift, raise.
   a. pick up, take up; pull up and back, cock(ed); e.g. ～竿 *jiēgān*, cock a fishing-line.
   b. erect; poise(d); e.g. ～驕 *jiējiāo*, proud pleasure.
2. (med.) sound rising in intensity or loudness.
3. uncover, unveil, disclose, reveal, show, expose, lay open.
4. indicate, indication; mark.
5. rdup., stretching upward and lengthening, extended and elongated.
6. ～車 *jiēchē*, "cart-halt," gooseneck loosestrife (*Lysimachia clethroides*), summer-flowering, used in food and medicine.

　　qì　MC khjejH

1. lift one's skirt (to the knees), to avoid getting wet.

椄　jiē　MC tsjep

1. cmpd. ～檿 *jiēxí*, bolt or wedge that locks manacles and fetters.

楷　jiē　MC keaj　→ 楷 *kǎi*.

湝　jiē　MC keaj

1. rdup., rushing tumble of river or stream.

　　xié　MC heaj

1. rdup., cold and chill, frore and frigid.

瘊　jiē　MC keaj

1. intermittent fever (cf. 痁 *shān*, lingering fever).

皆　jiē　MC keaj

1. occurs as a modifier to VB-phrases in verbal sentences, typically after an expressed SUBJ or topic, and as a modifier to noun predicates in nominal sentences, in both cases indicating that the action or state described in the VB-phrase or the noun predicate of the nominal sentence pertains to all cases of the subject or topic: "in all cases"; e.g. 國人～曰不可 *guórén jiē yuē bùkě*, People of the state in all cases said "it's not okay"; 古之人～用之 *gǔ zhī rén jiē yòng zhī*, People of antiquity in all cases took advantage of it; 是～僻陋之國也 *shì jiē pìlòu zhī guó yě*, These are in all cases rustic and uncultivated states.
2. (med.) compare, liken.

秸　jiē　MC keat

1. grain-stalk.

街　jiē　MC kea

1. intersection of 4 roads; road-crossing.
   a. roadway, thoroughfare; street.
2. marketplace; meeting-place.
3. conduits or pathways for circulation of *qi* 氣 in the body.

階　jiē　MC keaj

1. steps, stairs, stairway.
   a. to scale, mount.
2. upper platform of a 2-tier hall (cf. 陛 *bì* 2, lower platform).
   a. dais, where honored person sits.
3. ladder, rungs, of official or noble hierarchy.
   a. advancement up said ladder; e.g. ～緣 *jiēyuán*, attach oneself to (someone influential) for purpose of advancement.
4. starting-point, jumping-off point; origin; cause.
   a. rely on; based on.
5. 泰～ *tàijiē*, Sublime Stairway, constellation also called 三台 *sāntái*, → 台 *tái*.

jié

偞　jié　MC dzjep　⊙ 婕 *jié*.

傑　jié　MC gjet

1. salient, prominent, outstanding; egregious, not of the common flock or herd, apart from the crowd.
   a. of choice or select quality; elite, distinguished.

劫　jié　MC kjaep

1. pillage, plunder, despoil; rob; take by force; e.g. ～略 *jiélüè*, annex, appropriate.
2. imperil, menace, threaten; assault, raid; beset.

3. (Budd.) abb. of ～波 *jiébō* (MC kjaep-pa), trsc. Skt. *kalpa*, unit of measurement of cosmological time, esp. a "great kalpa" (*mahākalpa*) covering the creation and dissolution of the universe, itself divided into four eons of 20 intermediate kalpas each; used mainly as hyperbole for an unimaginably long time.

4. (med.) rdup., hurry after urgently; also, age after age.

婕   *jié*   MC tsjep

1. (bn.) ～妤 *jiéyú* (MC tsjep-yo), "preferred helpmeet, favored beauty," title of palace lady, usu. of imperial favor and high rank—2nd of 14 ranks in the Han ideal arrangement, 3rd of 8 in the Tang.

孑   *jié*   MC kjet

1. by oneself, singly, alone.
   a. rdup., sole and solitary; also, unique and unmatched, standing out alone; (med.) also, exacting, fastidious and finicky.
2. leftover, remainder.
3. ⊙ 戟 *jǐ* 1, guisarme, halberd.

峬   *jié*   MC dzet

1. coign, corner, angle (of mountain).
2. sharp-peaked.

嶻   *jié*   MC gjet

1. jut upward, stick out, protrude.

巀   *jié*   MC dzet

1. (bn.) ～嶭 *jiéniè* (MC dzet-ngjet), sheer and sharp, crisply carven.

巀   *jié*   MC dzet

1. cut, sever, section; amputate.
   a. stem, intercept; prevent; e.g. ～流 *jiéliú*, stem the tide.
2. regularly divided, even; well-balanced, in good order; arrange; orderly, organize(d).
3. cut straight through or along; plow (ahead).

拮   *jié*   MC ket

1. (bn.) ～据 *jiéjū* (MC ket-kjo), hold onto with difficulty, give oneself great pains, do everything one can, wear oneself out doing X.

   jiá   MC keat
1. force, compel, press (to do).

捷   *jié*   MC dzjep

1. vanquish, triumph.
   a. spoils of war, booty.
2. succeed, gain desired result; achieve(ment), success.
3. nimble, quick, lively (of mind or body); agile, frisky, fleet-footed; alert, vivacious, sharp.
4. (take a) short-cut, side-road, by-path.
5. (bn.) ～獵 *jiéliè* (MC dzjep-ljep), intricately imbricated, interlocked; layered and folded; also, piled together, mish-mash.
6. (bn.) ～給 *jiéjǐ* or ～急 *jiéjí* (MC dzjep-kip), repartee, quick wit.

桀   *jié*   MC gjet

1. roost, perch, for birds or fowl.
2. fierce, truculent; fell; brutal.
3. lift up, raise up.
4. salient, prominent, outstanding; select, choice, elite; ⊙ 傑 *jié*.
5. rdup., thick and teeming, lush and full (of vegetation).
6. name of despicably cruel last ruler of Xia dynasty.

桔   *jié*   MC ket

1. (bn.) ～槔 *jiégāo* (MC ket-kaw), wellsweep, shadoof, implement to draw up water.
2. (bn.) ～梗 *jiégěng* (MC ket-kaengX), balloon-flower, Chinese bellflower (*Platycodon grandiflorus*), herbaceous perennial, blue-flowering in late summer; 山～ *shānjié*, bellfruit bush (*Glycosmis citrifolia*), producing small translucent pinkish berries.

楬   *jié*   MC gjot

1. marker-post, sign-post; marker-stone.

   qiá   MC khaet
1. wooden instrument that is struck to indicate conclusion of musical performance; syn. 敔 *yǔ*, tiger-box, tiger-scraper.

禼   *jié*   MC tset

1. cap-block or capital of a building column.

榤   *jié*   MC gjet

1. roost, perch, for birds or fowl; ⊙ 桀 *jié* 1.

櫛   *jié*   MC tsrit   → 櫛 *zhì*.

渫　*jié*　MC tsjep

1. (bn.) 汎 *fájié*, → 汎 *fá* (*fàn*).

潔　*jié*　MC ket

1. unsullied, pure, immaculate.
   a. clean(se), purify.
2. of spotless character, impeccable; probity, honesty.

眹　*jié*　MC tsjep　⊙ 睫 *jié*.

睫　*jié*　MC tsjep

1. eyelash; e.g. 眼前之～ *yǎnqiánzhijié*, the eyelash before the eye, i.e. quick as a wink, in the blink of an eye.

   zhǎ　MC tsreap
1. blink, wink; flicker.

碣　*jié*　MC gjet

1. stele, upright stone slab with inscription, commemorative stele; usu. with rounded head (cf. 碑 *bēi*, square-topped stele).
   a. the inscription on such a stone
2. boundary-marker.
3. lone-standing, prominent.
4. (bn.) ～磍 *jiéjiá* (MC gjet-keat), in full rage, raging and roaring (like a tiger).

竭　*jié*　MC gjot

1. dried up (water), parched; run dry, drain.
2. end(ing), close, finish; complete(ly), utterly.
   a. exert, use up, expend, exhaust, run through.
3. (Budd.) (bn.) ～諦 *jiédì* (MC gjot-tejH), trsc. Skt. *gate*, "gone."

節　*jié*　MC tset

1. node or joint of bamboo.
   a. knot, juncture, joint; articulation.
2. segment, section; portion.
   a. "nodes" of the year, originally 8 (equinoxes, solstices, beginning of each season), then 24 fortnightly (ca. 15-day) periods (～氣 *jiéqì*).
   b. festival, celebration at regular seasonal or annual interval; e.g. ～會 *jiéhuì*, holiday feast; also, section of musical performance.
3. measure(d), regular(ity); to moderate, temper, limit(ation); e.g. 合～ *héjié*, matched measures.
   a. degree, rank, class; ordered item or article.
4. temperate, moderate in character; forbearing, steadfast in moral principles, composure; precise, punctilious; discreet, chaste; economical; e.g.

～中 *jiézhōng*, prudently centered, not given to extremes.

5. verge; credentials, insignia; tally, rod, or staff borne as sign of (usu. delegated) authority; e.g. ～旄 *jiémáo*, credentialed with yak-tail pennant, legate invested by emperor with life-and-death authority.
6. ～度 *jiédù*, to moderate and rule, keep in check, control, bring into line; in 3rd century the official title for provisioner of the army (< regulate [provisions] punctiliously); (med.) ～度使 *jiédùshǐ*, in Tang times official title of military commissioner responsible for control of strategically important area or of territory comprising several provinces (< commissioner who rules with [plenipotentiary] credentials).
7. bamboo clappers, used to mark the rhythm in music.
8. "Well-Measured," name of 60th hexagram of the *Yijing*.
9. (med.) (bn.) ～兒 *jié'ér* (MC tset-nye), trsc. Tib. *rtse rje*, town prefect.

結　*jié*　MC ket

1. knot, knot up (knot that cannot be untied, cf. 紐 *niǔ*); e.g. ～髮 *jiéfà*, knot up the hair, esp. of youth; also, the marriage night; also (med.), ref. a concubine.
   a. tie up; fasten, attach; conjoin; e.g. ～綬 *jiéshòu*, attach a seal-cord (to one's belt), i.e. take office.
   b. associate with, connect with; e.g. ～親 *jiéqīn*, make friends, cultivate friendship.
2. intertwine; plait; thatch.
3. knotted up, tangled; constricted, pent-up, unable to be released or resolved; esp. of troubled feelings or difficult affairs.
   a. bunch together, clot; cohere; crystallize; e.g. ～眉 *jiéméi*, knot the brows.
   b. circle round, wrap, spiral; e.g. ～架 *jiéjià*, ～跏 *jiéjiā*, "wrapped cross-legged," seated in meditation.
4. form (out of lesser constituents); construct; organize; e.g. ～廬 *jiélú*, build (or thatch) a hut; ～構 *jiégòu*, knotted or joined beams > form and construction (of a building, written composition, etc.); ～宇 *jiéyǔ*, build a roof.
   a. to set, bear (fruit).
5. contract, agree to; e.g. ～契 *jiéqì*, make a pact.
6. come to a final result, conclude; outcome.
   a. give final judgment, sentence; e.g. ～正 *jiézhèng*, declare lawful judgment.

7. (bn.) ～遼 *jiéliáo* (MC ket-lew), hill myna (*Gracula religiosa*).

8. (bn.) ～骨 *jiégǔ* (MC ket-kwot), Kirghiz, common Tang name of a Türkic people centered on upper Yenisei River valley, known from Han times and becoming a powerful force during the Tang; syn. 監昆 *jiānkūn* (earlier, Han name), 戛戛斯 *jiájiásī*.

羯   jié   MC kjot

1. wether, a castrated ram.

2. name of northern tribe once subject to the Xiongnu, settled in southeast Shanxi in 3rd century and from which came Shi Le 石勒, founder of Later Zhao (Hou Zhao 後趙, 319-351) dynasty.

3. (med.) ～鼓 *jiégǔ*, wether-drum, small 2-sided strap-braced drum, played with small beaters; originally from India, esp. popular in China in 8th century.

衱   jié   MC kjaep

1. overlapping collar or lapels.

袺   jié   MC ket

1. fold or tuck up the lappet of a robe or the flap of a skirt, esp. to place something in it.

訐   jié   MC kjet

1. expose or denounce another's faults, secrets, crimes; inform on.

   a. tattle; gossip.

詰   jié   MC khjit

1. investigate, call to account; interrogate, question; cross-examine.

   a. accuse, charge; reprehend.

2. obligate oneself to spirits by means of written document; subject to (spiritual) scrutiny.

3. ～朝 *jiézháo*, ～旦 *jiédàn*, the next day.

4. (bn.) ～詘 *jiéqū* (MC khjit-khjut), twist and turn, wrap and wind, curve and coil.

jiě

姐   jiě   MC tsjaeX

1. (med.) elder sister.

2. (med.) term of endearment for wife or female entertainer of tender age.

解   jiě   MC keaX

1. untie, unknot, unbind, loosen, release; e.g. ～佩 *jiěpèi*, untie one's girdle pendants, esp. seal-cord of office (i.e. resign official position); ～驂 *jiěcān*, unharness the trace-horses; ～携 *jiěxié*, let go of (clasped) hands, i.e. part, say farewell.

   a. doff, take off; e.g. ～薜 *jiěbì*, put aside one's garb of creeping-fig; ～巾 *jiějūn*, put aside one's (informal) headwrap; ～褐 *jiěhè*, doff one's hodden clothing; all 3 preceding ref. come out of reclusion to take up an official post.

2. disjoint, dismember.

   a. dissect; analyze, take apart.

3. remove, eliminate.

   a. resolve; (find a) solution, work out (a problem).

4. deliver from, release, liberate, free oneself from; emancipate; e.g. (Budd.) ～脫 *jiětuō*, released and extricated (from the round of birth-and-death); (Dao.) 尸～ *shījiě*, "deliverance by means of a [simulated] corpse," in which the adept's supposed corpse is buried but is actually substituted with a personal object (sword, staff, etc.) that temporarily takes on the appearance of the corpse, thus allowing one to escape from the bureaucracy of death; a lower-level means of transcendence; ～駕 *jiějià*, get free of the harness, i.e. leave this world behind.

5. dissipate, dissolve; disperse; dispel; e.g. ～酲 *jiěchéng*, ease a hangover (by further drinking), equiv. "hair of the dog."

6. open out; unfurl, unfold; reveal; e.g. ～顏 *jiěyán*, relax one's expression, break into a smile.

7. explain, expound; exposition.

   a. understand, comprehend; know how to; know about.

   b. (med.) able to do X, can do X.

8. (med.) (lit.) stanza of a song or poem.

jiè   MC keaH

1. (med.) in Tang times, to send off from his home prefecture a candidate for *jinshi* exam at the capital.

xiè   MC heaX

1. "Release," name of 40th hexagram of the *Yi-jing* (meaning as in 4 above, but pronounced differently).

2. ⊙ 懈 *xiè*, indolent, sluggish; negligent, offhand, uncaring; 廨 *xiè*, government office (place), seat, headquarters.

jiè

介　jiè　MC keajH

1. boundary between 2 territories, limit; border, edge; shore; ⊙ 界 *jiè*.
    a. to separate; demarcate, set a borderline.
2. position(ed) between 2 things; intermediate.
    a. intermediary, go-between; messenger.
    b. mediator, intercessor; introduce(r).
    c. herald, forerunner; harbinger.
    d. small intermediate stages (of larger entity or experience).
3. increase, add to.
4. aid, help, assist(ant); deputy.
    a. have the aid of, draw support from; rely on, depend on; protect(ed).
5. isolated, separate; aloof; conspicuous, set apart; not follow fashion.
    a. single, sole, with connotation of insignificant; e.g. 一～書生 *yījiè shūshēng*, lone paltry scholar.
6. integrity; intactness; resolute, principle(d).
7. shell, hard outer casing, testaceous; plating; carapace; crustacean; gen. term for animals with shelly covering.
8. plate armor, of soldiers; armored.
9. ⊙ 芥 *jiè* 1a, tiny; petty, trifling.

借　jiè　MC tsjaeH

1. use temporarily; borrow; lend, vouchsafe.
    a. adopt, adapt.
    b. rely on; on the strength of.
2. conditional marker, esp. of subjunctive: were it (not) that . . ., if it were (not) . . . (< adopting momentarily the supposition that . . .).
3. aid, contribute to.

屆　jiè　MC keajH

1. arrive at a goal, reach desired limit.
2. set a term or time.
3. (med.) sequence, succession.
    a. (med.) measure-word for occurrences.

戒　jiè　MC keajH

1. take precautions against, put on guard; warn(ing), monition.
    a. prohibit(ion), proscription.
    b. purify oneself before religious ceremony, by prescribed actions such as bathing, fasting, meditation, etc.
2. precept(s), injunction(s), directive(s), behest(s).
    a. (Budd.) (Dao.) sets of rules for regulating religious behavior, ranging from quotidian and private activity to monastic and ritual regimens.
    b. instruct(ions), command(ments).
    c. ordain, ordination.
3. (lit.) prose genre (sometimes with verse) offering moral maxims and behavioral advice to younger family members or women, esp. from fathers to sons.

犗　jiè　MC kaejH

1. bullock, castrated ox.
    a. castrate, geld, neuter.

玠　jiè　MC keajH

1. large jade tablet, symbol of distinction bestowed by ruler when enfeoffing feudal lord.

界　jiè　MC keajH

1. boundary between fields or farmplots.
    a. boundary between 2 territories, limit; border, edge; ⊙ 介 *jiè* 1.
2. bounded area, territory, region, realm; section, zone, tract.
    a. by synecdoche, the world.
3. demarcate; set boundary, limit.
    a. to separate, divide; distinguish.
4. contiguous, adjoined.
5. (Budd.) trns. Skt. *dhātu*, element; basic component, object, or consciousness of sensory experience; also, realm of existence; e.g. 三～ *sānjiè*, the triple world, 3 realms of existence (i.e. of sensuous form, subtle materiality, and formlessness).

疥　jiè　MC keajH

1. scabby itch.
2. ⊙ 痎 *jiē*, intermittent fever.

砎　jiè　MC keajH

1. (med.) hard, solid; unyielding; adamant.

芥　jiè　MC keajH

1. mustard-plant (*Brassica juncea*).
    a. sgl. or ～子 *jièzǐ*, mustard-seed > tiny, petty, insignificant, trifle, trifling.

藉　jiè　MC dzjaeH

1. grass- or reed-woven mat, esp. on which sacrificial offerings or ceremonial objects are placed.
    a. gen. term for mat; pad, pallet, cushion.

2. spread out a mat.
    a. sit, stretch out, lie down on mat or couch.
3. rely, depend on; by means of, on the strength of.
    a. take as a pretext for; allege, adduce.
4. use temporarily, borrow, lend.
    a. aid, contribute to.
5. tread on, trample; abuse, humiliate.
6. conditional marker, esp. of subjunctive: were it (not) that . . ., if it were (not) . . . (< adopting momentarily the supposition that . . .).

    jí   MC dzjek
1. strewn with; e.g. 狼～ *lángjí*, strewn in a clutter, littered and jumbled, in a total mess, in disarray; rdup., same as preceding.
2. impost, esp. corvée labor.
3. (pr)offer, lay before.
4. tie up, attach with a cord.
5. (med.) look back to or upon.
6. ⊙ 耤 *jí*, sacred field where emperor carries out ritual of first plowing in early spring.

蚧   jiè   MC keajH
1. a kind of mussel.
2. (med.) (bn.) 蛤～ *géjiè*, → 蛤 *gé*.
3. ⊙ 疥 *jiè*, scabby itch.

誡   jiè   MC keajH
1. warn(ing), (pre)caution; put on guard.
2. precept(s); monition(s); also, set of religious prohibitions and tenets.
    a. (lit.) prose genre (sometimes with verse) offering moral maxims and behavioral advice to younger family members or women, esp. from fathers to sons.
N.B. In all meanings virtually identical with 戒 *jiè*.

魪   jiè   MC keajH
1. flounder, various flat-fish incl. sole, dab; syn. 比目 *bǐmù*.

髻   jiè   MC keajH
1. dressed hair; combed, coifed, arranged.

jīn

今   jīn   MC kim
1. the present time, at present, now.
2. introduces shift in temporal focus in narrative accounts, often after aphoristic or didactic statement or historical reference: now, back to the present; back to the matter at hand; so now it is that . . .; e.g. 臣聞爭名者於朝，爭利者於市；～三川周室天下之市朝也, *chén wén zhēngmíngzhě yú cháo, zhēnglìzhě yú shì; jīn sānchuān zhōushì tiānxià zhī shìcháo yě*, Your vassal has heard that those who contend for name do so at court, those who contend for profit do so in the marketplace; now, the region of the Three Rivers and the House of Zhou are both the court and marketplace of the subcelestial realm.
3. introduces conditional phrase: if (now) it is that . . .; e.g. ～攻梁梁必破 *jīn gōng liáng, liáng bì pò*, if you attack Liang, Liang will inevitably be smashed.

巾   jīn   MC kin
1. cloth or silk kerchief.
    a. cloth for wiping or wrapping.
2. headkerchief, headwrap, headcloth; e.g. (med.) ～卷 *jīnjuàn*, one with headcloth and scrolls, i.e. scholar.
3. sgl. or ～箱 *jīnxiāng*, small box or coffer for holding kerchiefs, writing implements, small documents.
4. cover, veil with cloth or silk; e.g. ～車 *jīnchē*, covered cart.
    a. wrap, truss in cloth or silk.

斤   jīn   MC kj+n
1. axe, hatchet.
    a. chop, hack; hew; strike down, fell.
2. mattock, hand-hoe.
3. measure of weight: catty, equiv. 16 "ounces" (*liang* 兩).
4. rdup., keen and perspicacious, shrewd and penetrating; also, intent and exacting, painstaking and meticulous.

津   jīn   MC tsin
1. ford, crossing-point of river.
    a. channel; passage.
2. key point or person; e.g. (med.) ～要 *jīnyào*, narrow passage (water or land); also, critical point, crux, of action or event; also, person of decisive influence.
3. to cross over; ferry over.
4. riverbank, shoreline.
5. moisten, dampen; imbrue.
6. bodily fluids; secretion; saliva.
7. rdup., overflow with, brim over; also (med.), enthused and elated, exhilarated.

矜　jīn　MC king

1. sympathy, fellow-feeling; compassion.
   a. discommoded, uncomfortable; chagrined.
2. respect; esteem; show regard for.
   a. emphasize, stress, consider important; dote on.
   b. apply oneself to, concentrate on.
3. prudent, cautious, discreet; reserved.
   a. serious, grave; solemn; grim.
4. hold oneself above or aloof; self-important.
   a. vaunt, flaunt; flatter oneself, brag; orgulous.
5. peril, danger, hazard, jeopardy.

　　qín　MC gin

1. handle or grip of a lance.

　　guān　MC kwean

1. ⊙ 鰥 *guān* 1, widower; bachelor of advanced age.

祲　jīn　MC tsim

1. ill-omened aura; esp. solar nimbus.
2. make full; pervade, permeate.

筋　jīn　MC kj+n

1. tendon, sinew; muscle.
2. (med.) line(age), pedigree.
   a. (med.) tendencies, inclinations.

紟　jīn　MC kim

1. sash, cincture, waistband.

衿　jīn　MC kim

1. collar, of robe.
2. lappets, lapels; front flaps of robe which cross over the chest; ⊙ 襟 *jīn* 1.

　　jìn　MC kimH

1. tie up, knot up, fasten.

襟　jīn　MC kim

1. lappets, lapels; front flaps of robe which cross over the chest.
   a. by metonymy, the front of a robe.
2. human breast, bosom, chest; esp. feelings harbored in one's breast (heart).
   a. (med.) breast, chest, of bird.

觔　jīn　MC kj+n

1. ⊙ 筋 *jīn* 1, tendon, sinew; muscle; 斤 *jīn* 3, measure of weight: catty, equiv. 16 ounces (*liang* 兩).

金　jīn　MC kim

1. metal(lic).
   a. hard, durable, lasting; impenetrable, indivisible; often metaphor for what is or can be considered enduring, unchangeable, invulnerable; e.g. ～堤 *jīndī*, "metal" dike, i.e. as strong as metal (not actually made of it).
   b. one of the 5 "agents" or "phases" in *wuxing* theory, having symbolic correlations with the direction west, the season autumn, the color white, planet Venus, etc.
   c. every metal, but esp. bronze, for making various implements, weapons, musical instruments, etc.
2. "the" metal, the finest metal, i.e. gold; golden (substance and color), auric. N.B. When placed in parallel phrasing with 玉 *yù*, jade, almost always to be translated as "gold" (not "metal").
3. ～剛 *jīn'gāng*, "hardness of gold," i.e. diamond; ～精 *jīnjīng*, "germ of gold," realgar, orpiment; ～公黃 *jīngōnghuáng*, massicot; ～牙 *jīnyá*, "metallic teeth," i.e. iron pyrites.
4. (bn.) ～橘 *jīnjú* (MC kim-kjwit), ～柑 *jīn'gān*, kumquat (*Fortunella japonica*); ～錢松 *jīnqiánsōng*, golden larch (*Pseudolarix kaemperi*).
5. ～紫 *jīnzǐ*, gold and purple, auriporphyrian, i.e. gold seal and purple ribbon; in med. times part of title ～紫光祿大夫 *jīnzǐguānglùdàfū*, Grand Master of Splendid Favor with Gold Seal and Purple Ribbon, high prestige title in Sui and Tang; ～吾 *jīnwú*, "golden apotropaion; golden defender," fabulous bird supposed to protect against evil > gold-tipped baton > imperial insignia.
6. cymbals.
7. measure of cash weight; pre-Han equiv. 20 "ounces" (*liang* 兩), Han through Tang equiv. 16 ounces (1 catty).

釿　jīn　MC kj+n

1. ⊙ 斤 *jīn* 1, axe, hatchet; hack, hew, fell.

jǐn

僅　jǐn　MC ginH

1. sgl. or rdup., merely, just, hardly, scarcely, no more than.
   a. only just manage to (do X), do with difficulty.

jìn　MC gj+nH

1. (med.) almost, about, not quite (N number).

儘　**jǐn**　MC tsinX

1. (med.) entirely, completely, to the utmost, as much as possible.
   a. (med.) always, every time.

堇　**jǐn**　MC kj+nX

1. rdup., hardly, scarcely, merely, just; ⊙ 僅 *jǐn*.
2. ⊙ 菫 *jǐn*, yellow-leaved buttercup; *jǐn* 1, aconite; 2, violet.

　　qín　MC gj+n

1. marl, lime-rich clayey soil.

㞏　**jǐn**　MC kj+nX

1. nuptial winecup in early times, made of half-gourd or shaped as such; e.g. 合～ *héjǐn*, join the nuptial cups, newly married husband and wife exchanging cups at wedding ceremony (the 2 half-gourds becoming one).

厪　**jǐn**　MC ginH

1. merely, just, no more than; ⊙ 僅 *jǐn*.

　　qín　MC gj+n

1. ⊙ 勤 *qín* 1, to toil, labor, work hard at; 2, zealous, assiduous.

槿　**jǐn**　MC kj+nX

1. shrubby althea, rose-of-sharon, rose-mallow (*Hibiscus syriacus*), bearing large pink flowers that bloom only for a day, hence metaphor for fleeting time.
   a. 朱～ *zhūjǐn*, vermeil rose-mallow (*Hibiscus rosa-sinensis*), also called 扶桑 *fúsāng* in med. far south, with rich-red flowers; 黃～ *huángjǐn*, yellow rose-mallow (*Hibiscus tiliaceus*), yellow flowers turning orange and then red during one-day bloom.

瑾　**jǐn**　MC kj+nX

1. jadestone, gemstone; jade-like luster; e.g. ～瑜 *jǐnyú*, jade-like gloss and sheen, euph. for virtuous character.

箽　**jǐn**　MC kj+nX

1. white-sheathed bamboo; identification uncertain.

緊　**jǐn**　MC kjinX

1. tighten, taut(en), tense; esp. of stringed instruments or bowstring.
   a. contract, retract.
   b. (bn.) ～紊 *jǐnjuàn* (MC kjinX-kjwonH), tense and distressed, keyed up (of feelings).
2. intense; concentrate one's attention on.
3. pressing, urgent; exigent; severe.
   a. important, necessary.
4. quick, prompt; vital, vigorous.
   a. brisk, crisp, bracing (of wind).
5. (med.) in Tang times, 4th of 4 special categories designating selected districts (*xian* 縣) that, because of their importance were given special standing (in descending order of prestige: 赤 *chì* [crimson = imperial], 畿 *jī* [metropolitan], 望 *wàng* [honored], ～ *jǐn* [important]) outside the usual trilevel ranking (上, 中, 下) of districts.

菫　**jǐn**　MC kj+nX

1. celery-leaved buttercup (*Ranunculus sceleratus*).

　　jìn　MC ginH

1. aconite (*Aconitum carmichaelii*), flowering violet-blue, toxic but used medicinally with care; syn. 烏頭 *wūtóu*, "crow's-head."
2. violet (*Viola verecunda*), usu. flowering violet or white, used medicinally.

謹　**jǐn**　MC kj+nX

1. reticent; taciturn, close-mouthed.
2. circumspect, prudent; watchful, vigilant; on guard against.
3. respect(ful), honor(ed); considerate, regardful.

錦　**jǐn**　MC kimX

1. polychrome patterned compound tabby or (by Tang times) twill; usu. rendered by the general term "brocade."
2. (med.) richly figured, highly patterned; descriptive of elegant lit. composition, richly decorated musical instrument, elegant item of decor.

饉　**jǐn**　MC ginH

1. dearth, scarcity, famine, want of both maturing crops and wild plants.
2. ⊙ 殣 *jìn* 1, die of starvation.

jìn

僸　**jìn**　MC kimH

1. name of music or dances of the northern barbarians, in Han times.

yǐn　MC ngimX

1. raise or lift one's head.

唫　jìn　MC gimH

1. ⊙ 噤 *jìn*, close-mouthed; 吟 *yín* 1, intone, recite.

噤　jìn　MC gimH

1. close the mouth; close-mouthed.
    a. (bn.) ～吟 *jìnyín* (MC gimH-ngim), deformed jaws, unevenly clenched mouth.
2. shut firm and fast, as a gate.

墐　jìn　MC ginH

1. smear with mud or plaster, esp. to fill gaps or patch holes; to plaster, rough-cast.
2. bury, cover over; ⊙ 殣 *jìn* 2.
    qín　MC gin
1. marl, lime-rich clayey soil; ⊙ 墐 *qín* (*jǐn*).

寖　jìn　MC tsimH

1. leak; seep.
    qīn　MC tshim
1. drop-by-drop, bit-by-bit, gradually.

搢　jìn　MC tsinH

1. insert, put in; push into, thrust into; e.g. ～紳 *jìnshēn*, those with (tablet of office) thrust into their sash, i.e. officialdom, bureaucracy.
2. shake, agitate; joggle.

晉　jìn　MC tsinH

1. advance, progress.
    a. to present, for audience with superior.
2. insert, put in; push into, thrust into; ⊙ 搢 *jìn* 1.
3. "Advance," name of 35th hexagram of the *Yijing*.
4. name of a feudal state during Zhou times, located in southern Shanxi and Hebei and central Shaanxi, with ruling seat in Fen River valley (Shanxi); partitioned in early Zhanguo period into 3 states of Han 韓, Zhao 趙, and Wei 魏.
5. name of med. dynasty (265-420), divided into Western Jin (265-317) with capital at Luoyang and then Eastern Jin (317-420) with capital at Jiankang; ruling family, the Sima 司馬.

殣　jìn　MC ginH

1. die of starvation.

---

a. unburied corpses by roadside, dead from starvation.
2. bury, cover over.

浸　jìn　MC tsimH

1. leak; seep (into).
2. soak, immerse.
    a. flood, inundate.
3. irrigate, moisten.
    a. refresh, invigorate; enhance, esp. with ruler's favor or largess.
4. drop-by-drop, bit-by-bit, gradually.
    qīn　MC tshim
1. (bn.) ～淫 *qīnyín* (MC tshim-yim), drench and douse, soak and swash; also, slowly spread, imperceptibly advance.

燼　jìn　MC zinH

1. cinders, ashes.
    a. debris, residue.
2. conflagration; total burning.

盡　jìn　MC dzinX

1. use(d) up, consume(d), deplete(d), expend all of, exhaust(ed); e.g. ～力 *jìnlì*, expend all of one's strength; ～言 *jìnyán*, use up one's words, say everything one wishes to.
2. reach the end of, end in, get through (to); complete, achieve; consummate; e.g. ～命 *jìnmìng*, fulfill one's allotted lifespan; 林～水源 *lín jìn shuǐyuán*, the grove extended all the way to the river's source.
    a. last, final, ending; e.g. ～月 *jìnyuè*, last moon (of the month), final sliver.
3. wholly, completely, all of, in every respect, totally, thoroughly; to the utmost, utterly; e.g. ～善 *jìnshàn*, thoroughly good.

禁　jìn　MC kimH

1. forbid(dance), prohibit(ion), interdict(ion), taboo, proscription.
2. place forbidden to all but privileged or specially permitted persons, inner sanctuary, adytum; e.g. 宮～ *gōngjìn*, palace adyta, private grounds of emperor and family.
3. secret; arcane.
4. take into custody, incarcerate.
    a. jail, guardhouse.
    b. holding-pen, for animals; fold, corral, coop.
    jìn　MC kim
1. able to endure, able to stand.

縉 jìn   MC tsinH
1. pale-red color (of dyed silk).
2. ⊙ 搢 *jìn* 1, insert, put in; push into, thrust into.

藎 jìn   MC zinH
1. small carpgrass, joint-head grass (*Arthraxon hispidus*), source of yellow dye, when harvested just before flowering.
2. ⊙ 進 *jìn*, to offer up (oneself), devoted, loyal; 妻 or 燼 *jìn*, residue, remainder.

覲 jìn   MC ginH
1. in early times, for a feudal lord to have audience with the ruler, esp. in autumn; later, gen. term for audience with ruler.
2. have an interview with; pay one's respects to someone of higher status.

贐 jìn   MC zinH
1. farewell gifts to traveler.
2. (med.) tribute gifts to ruler.

近 jìn   MC gj+nX
1. near (to), nearby, close (to); near at hand.
  a. come close, draw near.
  b. nearly; prone to.
2. recent, near in time; e.g. ～年 *jìnnián*, recent years.
3. simple, ordinary; evident, obvious.
4. near to in quality or character, approximately, seem (to be).

  jìn   MC gj+nH
1. be on close terms with, intimate with; those who are close, esp. to ruler or influential person; favored.
2. closely related (object or idea); similar, comparable.

進 jìn   MC tsinH
1. advance, go forward (ant. 退 *tuì*, retreat); e.g. ～止 *jìnzhǐ*, advance and halt, i.e. activity, movement, behavior; also, orders, commands, esp. imperial instructions.
  a. go farther (toward particular goal), improve; e.g. ～學 *jìnxué*, further one's studies.
  b. direct planetary movement, i.e. eastward.
2. bring forward, for presentation; present, for recognition; e.g. (med.) ～士 *jìnshì*, "Presented Scholar," name of most prestigious and demanding of Tang civil-service examinations.
  a. promote, urge forward; recommend.

3. (med.) enter, go into.
4. income, revenue.
5. ⊙ 贐 *jìn* 1, farewell gifts to traveler.

靳 jìn   MC kj+nH
1. leather breast-strap of shaft-horses (of team of 4).
2. niggardly, stingy; tight-fisted, grudging; cheap.
3. deride; mock, scoff at; sneer at.

齺 jìn   MC gimH
1. (med.) ～齘 *jìnxiè*, gnash and grind one's teeth.

jīng

京 jīng   MC kjaeng
1. capital city, capitoline; e.g. ～兆 *jīngzhào*, the capital municipality; ～都 *jīngdū*, the capital metropolis, or capital and metropolis.
2. artificial hill or mound; gen. term for hill or mound.
  a. granary, in shape of large mound.

競 jīng   MC king
1. rdup., strong and stout, in fine fettle; also, cautious and careful, wary and leery.

旌 jīng   MC tsjeng
1. standard with yak's tail and varicolored plumes.
2. gen. term for standard, ensign, flag, banner.
  a. to signal, show; honor, commend; e.g. ～表 *jīngbiǎo*, standard of distinction, given as honorary bestowal.
  b. dangle, flutter; e.g. ～心 *jīngxīn*, dangling heart, i.e. unsettled.

斿 jīng   MC tsjeng   ⊙ 旌 *jīng*.

晶 jīng   MC tsjeng
1. brilliant, glitter(ing).
  a. crystal-clear, crystalline.
2. sgl. or 石～ *shíjīng*, rock-crystal, clear colorless quartz.

涇 jīng   MC keng
1. flow through, run through.
  a. straight-breaking waves.
2. name of important river in Shaanxi which joins with Wei 渭 River and flows into Yellow River.

睛 jīng MC tsjeng
1. eyeball.
    a. sight, vision.

秔 jīng MC kaeng ⊙ 稉 *jīng*.

稉 jīng MC kaeng
1. lowland rice (*Oryza sativa*, sp. *indica*), long-grained and non-glutinous.

粳 jīng MC kaeng ⊙ 稉 *jīng*.

精 jīng MC tsjeng
1. essence; purest, most highly concentrated element (< finest bleached rice).
    a. pith, marrow, gist.
2. germinal essence, life-germ contained in the Dao.
    a. the energy that nourishes the human body and is esp. attached to sexuality (semen, menstrual fluid); seminal; vital; seed(ling).
3. quintessence; purest, finest, most characteristic, very best of.
    a. concentrate(d), condensed, consolidated; ～志 *jīngzhì*, concentrate one's attention.
    b. subtle; delicate, fine.
4. fine points, niceties, details; detailed, precise.
5. intently focused (on); specially versed in; e.g. ～進 *jīngjìn*, zeal, assiduous(ness); ～童 *jīngtóng*, sharp-witted child.
6. elementals, spirits that are emanations from trees, rocks, etc.; wraiths, phantoms.
7. (Budd.) ～舍 *jīngshè*, place of purest activity, i.e. monastery, chapel.

經 jīng MC keng
1. the warp threads in weaving, which are placed vertically on loom as the ground through which are drawn horizontally the weft or woof threads (緯 *wěi*) to create pattern and design.
    a. hence, basic framework on which to construct organization; fixed; underlying; reliable.
2. guideline; norm, standard; guiding principle; e.g. 無～ *wújīng*, without direction or standards.
3. classic(s), canon(s), foundational texts recognized as incorporating the basic teachings of and providing stable shape to civilization and culture, in early times numbering 5 but by Tang times 9 which were the main texts used on civil-service exam; commentaries to a "classic" are *zhuan* 傳.
    a. (Budd.) sutra(s) (Skt. *sūtra*), the scriptures supposedly spoken by the Buddha, all of which begin with "Thus I have heard" (*rushi wo wen* 如是我聞), forming first and most important of 3 major divisions of Budd. canon (*tripiṭaka*), along with vinaya texts of monastic discipline (*lü* 律) and commentaries or explications of doctrine (*lun* 論).
    b. (Dao.) scripture(s), sacred and pre-cosmic texts issuing from the void and formed from primordial *qi* (*yuanqi* 元氣), transcribed into celestial script by the divinities and eventually revealed in vulgar human script to select persons.
4. align, regularize, arrange, organize; be fundamentally concerned with; e.g. ～國 *jīngguó*, bring the state into proper (political and moral) alignment; ～濟 *jīngjì*, organize and relieve (the world and its people); ～綸 *jīnglún*, lay out basic web, for regularization (of government, ideas, etc.); ～營 *jīngyíng*, arrange with care.
5. meridians, north-south orientation of route or area.
    a. basic circulatory channels or conduits of *qi* (pneuma) and blood in body, often paired with 絡 *luò* (as "ducts and links").
    b. guideways, pathways, layout of rivers forming geographical organization of territory.
6. passage, of time or through space or experience; e.g. 三年之～ *sānnián zhi jīng*, after a passage of 3 years; ～過 *jīngguò*, pass through (a place or an experience); also (med.), pay a call on, stop by, visit; also (med.), the moment at hand, the immediate experience.
7. to hang oneself.
8. (Budd.) early trns. for Skt. *dharma* (usu. 法 *fǎ* 6).

荊 jīng MC kjaeng
1. thorns, thorny bush or tree, esp. ～球花 *jīngqíuhuā*, needle-bush (*Acacia farnesiana*).
    a. thorny or difficult situation.
2. ref. various species of the orchid-tree (*Bauhinia*) or chaste-tree (*Vitex*) or redbud (*Cercis*), medium-sized to large trees with showy flowers and whose wood was used in making various items: e.g. 紫～ *zǐjīng*, Chinese redbud (*Cercis chinensis*); 牡～ *mǔjīng*, five-leaved chaste-tree (*Vitex negundo*); 金～ *jīnjīng*, yellow-bell orchid-tree (*Bauhinia tomentosa*)

3. term used by husband to refer to his wife (usu. pejorative).

4. variant name for the ancient state of Chu 楚.

莖   jīng   MC heang

1. culm of grasses; stem, stalk.

   a. shaft, shank; tongue, that part of a sword on which the grip and pommel are fixed; hilt, handle.

   b. pole, rod.

2. (med.) measure-word for long, thin objects, such as strands of hair.

菁   jīng   MC tsjeng

1. leekflower.

   a. blossom, flower.

2. sgl. or 蕪～ *wújīng*, 蔓～ *mànjīng*, field mustard, turnip-rape (*Brassica campestris*).

3. watergrass.

4. rdup., lushly leaved, in full profusion.

5. (med.) ⊙ 精 *jīng*, quintessence, esp. in ～華 *jīnghuá*, the very best of.

蜻   jīng   MC tsjeng

1. (bn.) ～蜊 *jīnglí* (MC tsjeng-lij), cricket; syn. 蟋蟀 *xīshuài*.

   qīng   MC tsheng

1. (bn.) ～蜓 *qīngtíng* (MC tsheng-deng), dragonfly.

驚   jīng   MC kjaeng

1. skittish, jumpy (as a frightened horse), restive.

   a. startled; flighty; on the verge of or actually bolting.

2. startle, surprise; stun; frighten.

   a. alarm, alert.

3. precipitate, headlong; hasty.

鯨   jīng   MC gjaeng

1. whale, leviathan.

2. metaphor for great rebel or miscreant; also in cmpd. ～鯢 *jīngní*, male and female whales > monsters in general.

鶄   jīng   MC tsjeng

1. sgl. or bn. 鳷～ *jiāojīng* (MC kaew-tsjeng), black-crowned night-heron (*Nycticorax nycticorax*).

麖   jīng   MC kjaeng

1. tufted deer (*Elaphodus cephalophus*), with short antlers often concealed by tufts of long hair.

jǐng

井   jǐng   MC tsjengX

1. a well, from which one draws water.

   a. a pit, shaft, for mining or for extracting salt.

2. descriptive of having the shape of this character; e.g. ～田 *jǐngtián*, "well-field," idealized farming system in which each of 8 families farms equal-sized plots around a central plot that is their communal responsibility for producing crops to pay taxes in kind; 方～ *fāngjǐng*, "square well," caisson (in ceiling of hall) formed by beams crossed in the shape of this character.

3. rdup., well-ordered, orderly, neat, systematic.

4. "Well," one of the 28 lunar lodgings, comprised of 8 stars of Gemini, in the southern quadrant (*chiniao* 赤鳥) of the sky.

5. "The Well," name of 48th hexagram of the *Yijing*.

儆   jǐng   MC kjaengX

1. ⊙ 警 *jǐng* 1, warn, alert; 2, be on guard, vigilant, wary; 3, urgent, critical, exigent.

剄   jǐng   MC kengX

1. cut the throat.

幜   jǐng   MC kjwaengX

1. (med.) silk mantle or cloak worn by noblewomen when on outing, to protect against dust and dirt.

憬   jǐng   MC kjwaengX

1. travel afar, go thither; wayfare(r).

2. awaken to, realize.

3. (med.) (bn.) 憧～ *chōngjǐng*, → 憧 *chōng*.

憼   jǐng   MC kjaengX   ⊙ 儆 *jǐng*.

景   jǐng   MC kjaengX

1. sunlight, sunshine.

   a. any sky-light emanating from celestial bodies, incl. starshine.

2. light, bright, luminescent (incl. *the* luminescent, i.e. the sun), effulgent.

3. daylight; fine weather, a fine day; e.g. ～風 *jǐngfēng*, "sunny wind," old name for south wind.

4. scene, spectacle; pageant.

   a. spectacular, usu. suggesting good fortune; auspicious; e.g. ～雲 *jǐngyún*, spectacular cloud, usu. multicolored and regarded as good omen; ～征 *jǐngzhēng*, auspicious (military) expedition.

b. great, grand; e.g. (Budd.) ～模, ～摸 *jǐngmó*, great standard, code, great canon.

5. (Dao.) luminescent objects, divinities, points; esp. 八～ *bājǐng*, 8 Effulgences: externally, sun, moon, 5 naked-eye planets, and Northern Dipper, also carriages of light that are conveyances of divinities (cf. 八素 *bāsù*, cloud-carriages being *yin* counterparts); internally, 3 sets of 8 inner divinities (body-gods) important in various visualization practices.

6. look up to, admire.

yǐng　MC 'jaengX

1. ⊙ 影 *yǐng* 1, shadow (produced by light), light-image, silhouette; the 2 graphs represent complementary aspects of light, with ～ *jǐng* often suggesting both, esp. in contexts ref. passage of time (daylight = lifetime).

窜　jǐng　MC dzjengX　⊙ 阱 *jǐng*.

警　jǐng　MC kjaengX
1. warn, alert; notify, give notice.
2. be on guard, alert, vigilant, wary; take precautions.
3. urgent, critical, exigent.
4. (med.) astute, wide-awake, discerning, quick to understand.

阱　jǐng　MC dzjengX
1. pitfall, trapfall, for catching animals.

頸　jǐng　MC kjiengX
1. the neck; esp. front of throat.
    a. neck-shaped.
2. isthmus.

jìng

倞　jìng　MC gjaengH
1. strong(ly), vigorous(ly), robust(ly); ⊙ 傹 *jìng* 3.

傹　jìng　MC gjaengH
1. ⊙ 竟 *jìng*, done, finished, finally; 倞 *jìng*, strong(ly), vigorous(ly).

勁　jìng　MC kjiengH
1. sturdy, strong; forceful, potent.
2. upright; straightforward.

境　jìng　MC kjaengX
1. end-point of territory, limit, margin, boundary.
2. precincts, tract, region, territory.
    a. domain, realm (physical place or of particular activity).

婧　jìng　MC dzjengH
1. delicate beauty, dainty; attractive, alluring, charming, engaging.

徑　jìng　MC kengH
1. footpath, pathway.
    a. gen. term for roadway.
2. take the most direct or quickest route, go straight to or through; straight-cut, through-way.
    a. straight line, direct(ly).
    b. exactly, precisely.
3. pass through, get across; go by way of, via.
4. diameter.
5. (bn.) ～廷 *jìngtíng* (MC kengH-deng), wild and wide of the mark, errant in the extreme.

敬　jìng　MC kjaengH
1. respect(ful), revere(nce), regard with honor (ant. 慢 *màn* 3, contemptuous); mainly ref. internally held sentiments (cf. 恭 *gōng*, the same attitude evinced in outward display).
2. serious; solemn, grave; reflective, somber.
3. warn, make one aware.

淨　jìng　MC dzjengH
1. pure, purify; clean(se); unsoiled, unblemished, unmixed; (Budd.) ～人 *jìngrén*, lay servant (of monastery); ～土 *jìngtǔ*, Pure Land, paradise in the west of bodhisattva Amitābha (阿彌陀 *āmítuó*), identified with but not trns. of Skt. Sukhāvatī, "Land of Bliss."

獍　jìng　MC kjaengH
1. (med.) mythical animal said to resemble a small tiger and, when newborn, to eat its mother; a manaphagous wildcat.

竟　jìng　MC kjaengH
1. at last, in the end, finally; reach the end, done, finished.
2. end of a territory, limit, margin, boundary; ⊙ 境 *jìng*.
3. from first to last, all the way; entirely, fully.
4. examine thoroughly, get to the bottom of.

諍　jìng　MC dzjengX
1. ⊙ 靜 *jìng* 1, still, quiet, in repose, calm.

競　jìng　MC gjaengH
1. strive, vie, compete, contend, rival.
2. argue, dispute, controvert, bicker.
3. strong(ly), vigorous(ly), lusty, robust(ly).

脛　jìng　MC hengX
1. shin, shinbone.
kēng　MC kheang
1. rdup., straight-lined and stubborn, set in one's ways, inflexible; ⊙ 硜 *kēng* 2.

逕　jìng　MC kengH　⊙ 俓 *jìng*.

鏡　jìng　MC kjaengH
1. (bronze) mirror.
2. to mirror, reflect; takes direct-OBJ immediately (cf. 鑑 *jiàn*); but usage as VB less common than syn. 鑑 *jiàn*, the latter also often metaphorical (draw a lesson from, use as guide or warning to reflect on current or future action) which ～ *jìng* never is.

靖　jìng　MC dzjengX
1. stable, settled; still, at rest.
2. bring to a pause, cease; calm down, subdue.
3. respectful, polite.
4. tiny, fine; delicate.
jīng　MC tsjeng
1. ⊙ 旌 *jīng* 2a, to signal, show; commend, honor.

靚　jìng　MC dzjengH
1. make up one's face (woman), apply cosmetics, rouge.
    a. prink, adorn, embellish, trim.
2. ⊙ 靜 *jìng* 1, quiet, still, tranquil, calm.

靜　jìng　MC dzjengX
1. still(ness), motionless, immobile (ant. 動 *dòng*, move[ment]); assuage, placate.
    a. quiet(ness), in repose; serene, tranquil(ity), placid(ity), ataraxy, impassive; (be)calm(ed), subude(d); concentration; e.g. ～思 *jìngsī*, sober reflection; ～室 *jìngshì*, ～舍 *jìngshè*, quiet chamber, private retreat for study and reflection; also (Dao.), meditation chamber, abode of concentration, oratory, originally place for Tianshi parishioners to beseech the gods, later place for Shangqing private visualizations; also (Budd.), monastery, temple, also room for private meditation.
2. ⊙ 淨 *jìng*, pure, purity.

jiōng

坰　jiōng　MC kweng
1. outlying area, hinterland, march(es), far-distant.
    a. steppeland (north), desert (far west); if nearer, moorland, heath.

扃　jiōng　MC kweng
1. door-hasp, door-bar, door-fastening, latch, to secure door from outside.
    a. by synecdoche, door(way), gate; passage; also, mountain-pass.
    b. to bar, close up, secure.
2. carrying-rod, to insert through handles of cauldron.
3. frame-lock, for securing banner to chariot; also, weapon-stand at front of chariot.
jiǒng　MC khwengX
1. rdup., piercingly perceptive, sharp and shrewd.

駉　jiōng　MC kweng
1. pasture(land).
2. rdup., in fine fettle, flush and well-fed, sleek and strong (of horses).

jiǒng

冏　jiǒng　MC kjwaengX
1. rdup., glowing gloriously, glinting and gleaming.

洄　jiǒng　MC hwengX
1. far-stretching, faraway, remote; ⊙ 迥 *jiǒng* 1.
2. far-fathomed, depths of sea or river, "the deep."

炅　jiǒng　MC kwengX
1. radiant, brilliant; blaze; resplendent; sunshine.

炯　jiǒng　MC kwengX
1. firelight.
    a. gleam, glare; flash, spark.
2. light up, make evident, manifest; understand clearly.
3. rdup., ⊙ 耿耿 *gěnggěng*, splendidly shining, aflit and aflicker; also, fitful and restive, fretful and

restless, uneasy and concerned; ⊙ 耿介 *gěngjiè*, resolute integrity, unbendingly honorable.

煚　jiǒng　MC kjwaengX

1. (med.) ⊙ 炅 *jiǒng*, sunshine, radiance, resplendent; esp. in given names.

熲　jiǒng　MC kwengX

1. firelight; incandescent; searing light; full light.

窘　jiǒng　MC gwinX

1. in straits, distressed; come to grief.
2. constrain(ed), put upon; coerce, compel.
3. bereft; indigent, poverty-stricken.

絅　jiǒng　MC khwengX

1. unlined cloak, mantle, greatcoat, dust-cloak.

褧　jiǒng　MC khwengX

1. women's unlined hemp or silk cloak, mantle, for wearing out of doors to protect against dust.

迥　jiǒng　MC hwengX

1. far-stretching, faraway, remote.
2. far from the same, deeply different.

逈　jiǒng　MC hwengX　⊙ 迥 *jiǒng*.

jiū

啾　jiū　MC tsjuw

1. rdup., onom. of gibbons wailing, tigers roaring; also, of carriage bells rattling; (med.) also, of rain spattering, of horses' hooves clopping.
   a. (bn.) ～唧 *jiūjī* (MC tsjuw-tsik), onom. of dry leaves rustling; (bn.) ～嘈 *jiūcáo* (MC tsjuw-dzaw), onom. of shrill and skirl of musical pipes.

揪　jiū　MC tsjuw

1. (med.) ⊙ 摮 *jiū*, gather, collect; draw in, harvest.

摮　jiū　MC tsjuw

1. gather, collect; draw in, harvest.

摎　jiū　MC kjuw

1. twist, bind together, (en)twine; coil.
2. look for, search out; pursue.

jiǎo　MC kaewX

1. (bn.) ～蓼 *jiǎoliǎo* (MC kaewX-lewX), draw forth, drag out; induce, lead on; ⊙ 糾蓼 *jiǎoliǎo*.

樛　jiū　MC kjiw

1. drooping or downturning branches.
   a. bent, turned, curving.
2. twist, bind together, (en)twine; ⊙ 摎 *jiū* 1.

究　jiū　MC kjuwH

1. go to the end of, get to the bottom of; extend throughout, pervade.
   a. after all, in the end; e.g. ～竟 *jiūjìng*, finally; also, ultimate, utmost, supreme.
   b. thorough(ly), complete(ly).
2. delve (into), penetrate, probe; go deeply into; scrutinize.
3. think through with goal in mind; draw up plans, design, devise.
4. (med.) endpoint of a mountain stream's rock-filled rapids, quiet end, placid turn.

糾　jiū　MC kjiwX

1. binding-rope or cord; draw together, bind together.
   a. (bn.) ～蓼 *jiūliǔ* (MC kjiwX-lewX), draw forth, drag out; induce, lead on.
2. bring together, gather.
3. correct, rectify; tie together; emend (text).
4. supervise, superintend.
5. reprehend; denounce faults.

蟉　jiū　MC dzjuw

1. (bn.) ～蛑 *jiūmóu* (MC dzjuw-mjuw), giant sea-crab.

赳　jiū　MC kjiw

1. rdup., stout and stalwart, doughty and daring.

鳩　jiū　MC kjuw

1. pigeon, culver, various types of dove (*Columbidae*, *Streptopeliae*).
   a. 雄～ *xióngjiū*, 青～ *qīngjiū*, Loochoo green pigeon (*Treron permagna*).
   b. 鳲～ *shījiū*, the cuckoo (*Cuculus canorus*).
2. (bn.) 雎～ *jūjiū*, → 雎 *jū*.
3. collect together; flock.
4. stable, quiet(en), settle(d); set to rights.
5. a sand-sled.
6. abb. of 鷞～ *shuāngjiū*, goshawk, esp. in *Liji*.

jiǔ

久 jiǔ MC kjuwX
1. (temporally) enduring, for a long time; quite a while; longstanding.
   a. persistent, protracted; age-old.

九 jiǔ MC kjuwX
1. nine(fold), ninth.
   a. numerologically representative of *yang*, as in *Yijing* where lines with value of 9 are "strong" or "moving" *yang* lines.
2. though still translatable as "nine," used in some contexts not as exact number but as gen. term for: many, numerous, totality of; e.g. ～重 *jiǔchóng*, 9-layered (walls of imperial palace); ～死 *jiǔsǐ*, 9 deaths, i.e. "a thousand deaths, die a thousand times."

灸 jiǔ MC kjuwX
1. moxibustion; cauterize with moxa (艾 *ài*).
2. to make stand, prop, support.

玖 jiǔ MC kjuwX
1. jetstone, darkstone, dark-colored gem said to be slightly less precious than jade.

酒 jiǔ MC tsjuwX
1. gen. term for alcoholic beverages produced through fermentation, incl. those with infusions or spices that sometimes lend various colors such as rose-pink or amber. Although most drinks designated by this word are made from cereals and are thus akin to beer, from Western Han times it also ref. grape-wine (first brought from Central Asia) and "burnt-wine" (brandy), the former becoming esp. popular during Tang times; use "wine" as preferred rendering for its inclusiveness; to use "ale" is misleading as it ref. only to a specific type of beer (as do stout, lager, porter, bitter, pilsner, etc.) and cannot properly cover all types of *jiǔ*, "ale" being actually most similar to → 醴 *lǐ*.
2. ～泉 *jiǔquán*, "Wine Springs," also called Fulu 福祿 or Suzhou 肅州, outpost near the Jade Gate (Yumen 玉門) in western Gansu.

韭 jiǔ MC kjuwX
1. garlic-chive, Chinese chive, Chinese leek (*Allium tuberosum*), variously rendered but all ref. same plant which is closer to a leek than a chive; cf. 薤 *xiè*, shallot (*Allium chinense*), 蔥 *cōng*, scallion (*Allium fistulosum*).

jiù

僦 jiù MC tsjuwH
1. hire, engage the services of.
   a. hire out, rent, let out.
2. expense or fee for same.

咎 jiù MC gjuwX
1. calamitous, ruinous; ill-fated, unlucky; e.g. ～徵 *jiùzhēng*, ill-starred omen, calamitous manifestation.
2. fault, failing, blame; odium (incurred for action); e.g. 引～ *yǐnjiù*, adduce one's faults.
   a. repent, regret one's failings.
3. find fault, accuse, impute blame, castigate, condemn; disparage, brand.
      gāo MC kaw
   1. ～繇 *gāoyáo*, Gao Yao, name of legendary minister of sage-king Shun 舜 esteemed for his judgment and wisdom, also reputed ancestor of the Eastern Yi 夷 people; ⊙ 皋陶 *gāoyáo*.

就 jiù MC dzjuwH
1. go toward, (be)take oneself to; approach, draw near to; tend toward, turn or return to; e.g. ～日 *jiùrì*, tend toward the sun, i.e. approach the emperor; ～食 *jiùshí*, go to eat; ～列 *jiùliè*, join the ranks (of officialdom); also (med.), seek one's livelihood.
   a. attend to, attend on; take on; e.g. ～時 *jiùshí*, attend to the moment, take advantage of opportunity.
   b. close to, near to, hard by (place); close to, nearly, almost (situation).
2. tendency, bent, proclivity.
   a. change to, gradually become.
3. attain, reach a goal, bring to completion; e.g. 成～ *chéngjiù*, completion achieved, satisfied accomplishment; ～名 *jiùmíng*, attain fame.
4. (med.) sgl. or ～使 *jiùshǐ*, even if, were it the case that...; e.g. ～能破之 *jiù néng pò zhī*, even if one could defeat them...

廄 jiù MC kjuwH
1. stable, for horses; mews.

廏 jiù MC kjuwH ⊙ 廄 *jiù*.

救 jiù MC kjuwH
1. relieve, provide relief, aid, succor.

a. deliver, rescue, save; e.g. ～物 *jiùwù*, extricate oneself from material things, or from phenomena such as ghosts.

2. cure or remedy illness.

3. prevent, arrest, put a stop to; prohibit, ban.

枢　jiù　MC gjuwH

1. coffin (with corpse).

疚　jiù　MC kjuwH

1. chronic or persistent illness.

2. sick with sadness, heart-stricken, desolate, bereft; esp. in grieving for the dead.

3. destitute; straitened, in want; depleted; indigent.

臼　jiù　MC gjuwX

1. mortar, esp. in which rice is hulled by pounding or grinding.

舅　jiù　MC gjuwX

1. maternal uncle, mother's brothers.

2. husband's father, father-in-law.

a. sgl. or 外～ *wàijiù*, wife's father, father-in-law. *

3. wife's brother, brother-in-law.

a. in early times, ruler's term of ref. for nobles of different surname than his, or by feudal lord for magnates of different surname than his.

舊　jiù　MC gjuwH

1. old; known or in existence for a long time (ant. 新 *xīn*, new, fresh).

a. old-time, bygone, past, former; long-past, old-fashioned.

b. familiar, something one is used to and appreciates.

c. (med.) originally, as it used to be; e.g. 沙～白 *shā jiù bái*, the sand used to be white.

2. person of longstanding acquaintance, dear friend.

3. (med.) ADV marker of past action; e.g. 京中～見 *jīngzhōng jiùjiàn*, in the capital I saw it.

鷲　jiù　MC dzjuwH

1. large raptor, often eagle, more often vulture.

a. (Budd.) (靈)～山 (*líng*)*jiùshān*, Vulture Peak, trns. Skt. Gṛdhrakūṭaparvata, mountain outside Rājagṛha where the Buddha is said to have delivered many important Mahāyāna sutras, incl. Lotus Sutra and "perfection of wisdom" (*prajñāpāramitā*) sutras.

齨　jiù　MC gjuwX

1. mortar-tooth, scooped-out (either with cavity or worn with use) tooth of aged person.

jū

居　jū　MC kjo

1. site(d), situate(d), place(d).

a. seat, central place of activity or authority.

2. reside(nce), dwell(ing), lodge(ment); in private life, at home; e.g. ～山 *jūshān*, residing in the mountains; ～士 *jūshì*, gentleman in retirement, staying out of office; (Budd.) trns. Skt. gṛhapati, householder, i.e. lay devotee, also plural term of address used by the Buddha, "gentlemen."

a. occupy; inhabit; ensconce(d).

3. sit down; stay a while.

a. rest oneself, take repose; settle (down in); put at ease; e.g. ～心 *jūxīn*, rest easy (in mind).

4. set aside, put in reserve, stock up on.

a. acquire, attain, obtain.

5. sgl. or ～常 *jūcháng*, ordinar(il)y, from day to day, normal(ly).

6. (med.) ～然 *jūrán*, peacefully, composed, serenely, placidly; also, clearly, obviously, manifestly, saliently; also, unexpectedly, on the contrary.

7. preceding a term ref. duration, indicates time during or after which an action "takes place"; e.g. ～有頃 *jūyǒuqǐng*, ～頃之 *jūqǐngzhī*, for some time, for a while, ～久之 *jūjiǔzhī*, for a good while, for a long while, ～無幾何 *jūwújǐhé*, for who knows how long.

jù　MC kjoH

1. ⊙ 倨 *jù* 1, contemptuous, rude; self-regarding; 粔 *jù*, ring-cake.

岨　jū　MC tshjo

1. stony, rock-strewn, shingly hill.

jǔ　MC tsrjoX

1. (bn.) ～嵎 *jǔyú* (MC tsrjoX-ngjoX), unmatched and uneven, jutting and jagged, rough and unruly; ⊙ 齟齬 *jǔyǔ*.

zǔ　MC tsrjoX

1. ⊙ 阻 *zǔ* 1, impasse, cul-de-sac, dead-end.

拘　jū　MC kju

1. seize, grasp.

a. apprehend; detain, arrest.

2. restrain, restrict, limit.

a. be "stuck on," a stickler for.

gōu　MC kuw

1. bent, buckled; crinkle, contort, warp.

抹　*jū*　MC kju

1. fill a basket with earth, for use in building; carry such a basket.

　　qiú　MC gjuw

1. curved, bent.

　　jiù　MC kjuwH

1. ⊙ 救 *jiù* 1, relieve, aid, succor; rescue.

据　*jū*　MC kjo

1. (bn.) 拮～ *jiéjū*, → 拮 *jié*.

　　jù　MC kjoH

1. ⊙ 據 *jù* 2, according to, on the basis of, depending on; 倨 *jù* 1, contemptuous; haughty.

掬　*jū*　MC kjuwk

1. to cup in the hands, hold with both hands.
　　a. a double-handful.

椐　*jū*　MC kjowk

1. litter for being carried when in mountains.

　　jū　MC kjuwk

1. sod-carrier.

梮　*jū*　MC kjo

1. identification uncertain, possibly ⊙ 欅 *jǔ*, zelkova (*Zelkova serrata*), tall well-formed deciduous tree, though this does not match well with traditional descriptions of it having bulging bamboo-like nodes that are used for making walking-staffs and riding-switches; also suggested as ref. snowflake-bush (*Viburnum plicatum*), medium-sized shrub with yellow flower-clusters surrounded by white-petalled florets, yields blue-black drupe in autumn.
2. rdup., consecutively continuous, one after another.

狙　*jū*　MC tshjo

1. monkey, identification uncertain; sometimes said to be alt. name for 獼猴 *míhóu*, macaque, rhesus monkey (*Macacus tcheliensis*).
　　a. (bn.) ～猱 *jū'náo* (MC tshjo-naw), golden snub-nosed monkey (*Rhinopithecus roxellana*).
2. be alert for; watch for; lie in wait for.

琚　*jū*　MC kjo

1. jade or jeweled girdle-pendant, sash-pendant.

疽　*jū*　MC tshjo

1. deep-rooted ulcer or abscess.

痀　*jū*　MC kju

1. (bn.) ～僂 *jūlǔ* (MC kju-ljuX) crookbacked, hunchbacked.

硨　*jū*　MC kjo

1. (med.) (bn.) ～磲 *jūqú* (MC kjo-gjo), mother-of-pearl, nacre, nacreous; also, giant clam (*Tridacna gigas*); ⊙ 車渠 *jūqú* (→ 車 *chē*).

罝　*jū*　MC tsjo

1. net or snare for catching birds or beasts.

腒　*jū*　MC kjo

1. strips of dried bird- or fowl-meat.

苴　*jū*　MC tsjo

1. female hemp plant (*Cannabis sativa*), of which the seeds are used in medicine and food (cf. 枲 *xǐ*, male hemp plant).
　　a. hemp seeds.
2. grass shoe-padding; straw-padding, cushion; to pad; to repair.
3. to wrap, esp. with straw.
4. (bn.) ～蒪 *jūpò* (MC tsjo-phak) or 蒪～ *pòjū*, myoga ginger (*Zingiber mioga*); syn. 蘘荷 *ránghé*.

　　chá　MC dzrjae

1. withered plant.

　　bāo　MC paew

1. ancient non-Han state in eastern Sichuan; perhaps a variant of Bā 巴.

裾　*jū*　MC kjo

1. front lappet of robe; lap.
　　a. (med.) skirt or train of robe.
2. full or ample robe, caftan, stole.

　　jù　MC kjoH

1. ⊙ 倨 *jù* 1, haughty, proud, arrogant; 據 *jù* 2, rely on, depend on; based on.

賮　*jū*　MC kjo

1. (med.) stockpile, store up, hoard; deposit.

趄　*jū*　MC tshjo

1. (bn.) 趑～ *zījū*, → 趑 *zī*.

雎　*jū*　MC tshjo

1. (bn.) ～鳩 *jūjiū* (MC tshjo-kjuw), osprey, fish-hawk (*Pandion haliaetus*).

鞠　jū　MC kjuwk
1. leather ball, for game of foot-ball or kick-ball.
2. bend, turn, curve, flex; contorted, warped.
　　a. (bn.) ～躬 *jūgōng* (MC kjuwk-kjuwng), bow abjectly, lout low, show great respect; also, considerately conscientious, minutely meticulous.
3. nurture, provide for; raise; nourish.
4. child(ish), young, youth, immature.
5. entirely, all of, completely.
　　a. used up, depleted, exhausted.
6. admonish, exhort; call on for better effort.
7. (med.) overgrown, wild.
8. ⊙ 鞫 *jū* 1, interrogate (criminal); 菊 *jú*, chrysanthemum.

鞫　jū　MC kjuwk
1. interrogate (criminal), interrogation, question(ing).
　　a. examine thoroughly, probe, investigate.
2. go to an extreme, push on to the end.
　　a. depleted, used up; in extremis; destitute.
3. far bank of a river, land beyond the other shore.

駒　jū　MC kju
1. colt, young horse; if very young, foal, weanling.
　　a. gen. term for young of various quadrupeds, also euph. for human youngster.

鵰　jū　MC tshjo　⊙ 雎 *jū*.

鶋　jū　MC kjo
1. (bn.) 鵷～ *yuánjū*, → 鵷 *yuán*; (bn.) 鴡～ *bēijū*, → 鴡 *bēi*.

jú

局　jú　MC gjowk
1. curled up, bent inward; contracted, cramped; narrow, limited.
　　a. (bn.) ～促 *júcù* (MC gjowk-tshjowk), ⊙ 跼蹐 *júcù*, → 跼 *jú*.
2. nearby, near to, close to; vicinity; close quarters.
3. chessboard, gameboard.
4. configuration, layout; situation, condition; general circumstances.
5. part, portion, section, sector.
6. (government) service, office, bureau, division, usu. of subordinate importance and responsible for domestic matters of imperial family; e.g. 宮門～ *gōngménjú*, service of the palace gatekeepers.
7. tolerance, open-minded(ness).

橘　jú　MC kjwit
1. sourpeel tangerine (*Citrus reticulata*); cf. 柑 *gān*, sweetpeel tangerine (*Citrus nobilis*), 橙 *chéng*, coolie orange, sweet orange (*Citrus sinensis*).
2. (bn.) 金～ *jīnjú* (MC kim-kjwit), kumquat (*Fortunella japonica*); 盧～ *lújú* (MC lu-kjwit), loquat (*Eriobotrya japonica*).

菊　jú　MC kjuwk
1. chrysanthemum (*Chrysanthemum morifolium*), autumn-blooming, so a symbol of longevity.
2. 藍～ *lánjú*, "indigo chrysanthemum," aster (*Callistephus chinensis*).

趜　jú　MC gjuwk
1. end, terminate; go to the extreme.
2. humpbacked.
　　a. unable to stretch one's limbs.
3. discreet, prudent.
4. aspergillum, used to sprinkle purifying water in ritual ceremonies.

跼　jú　MC gjowk
1. contracted, cramped; curled up, bent inward.
　　a. (bn.) ～蹙 *júcù* (MC gjowk-tsjuwk), restrained and restricted, cramped and close; (bn.) ～躅 *júzhú* (MC gjowk-drjowk), shuffle and shy, nitter-natter, stuck in one's tracks; (bn.) 跧～ *quánjú*, → 跧 *quán*.

輂　jú　MC kjowk
1. horse-drawn dray.
2. hod-carrier; sod-carrier.

鵙　jú　MC kwek
1. various species of shrike (*Laniidae*).

jǔ

咀　jǔ　MC dzjoX
1. nibble, peck at; munch.
　　a. (bn.) ～嚼 *jǔjué* (MC dzjoX-dzjak), munch and chew, nibble and gnaw; also, ruminate, mull over.
2. to savor, taste.

枸   *jǔ*   MC kjuX

1. betel plant, betel pepper (*Piper betel*), evergreen creeper, leaves yield a mild stimulant; syn. 蒟 *jǔ* 1.
2. sgl. or cmpd. 枳～ *zhǐjǔ*, honey-tree, oriental raisin-tree (*Hovenia dulcis, H. acerba*), medium to tall summer-flowering tree, fruit-stalks (rachis) and drupes edible and used medicinally.

枸   *gǒu*   MC kuwX

1. ～機 *gǒujī*, ～忌 *gǒujì*, ～杞 *gǒuqǐ*, wolfberry, boxtree, boxthorn (*Lycium chinense, Lycium barbarum*), syn. 地骨 *dìgǔ*.
2. ～櫞 *gǒuyuán*, bitter citron (*Citrus medica*).

枸   *gōu*   MC kuw

1. curved, bent, crooked.

椇   *jǔ*   MC kjuX

1. sgl. or 枳～ *zhǐjǔ*, honey-tree, oriental raisin-tree (*Hovenia dulcis, H. acerba*), medium to tall summer-flowering tree, fruit-stalks (rachis) and drupes edible and used medicinally.
2. small table on which to place ritual food offerings.

欅   *jǔ*   MC kjoX

1. zelkova (*Zelkova serrata*), tall well-crowned deciduous tree, wood used for making various items.
2. ～柳 *jǔliǔ*, Chinese wingnut (*Pterocarya stenoptera*), with long hanging catkins in summer.

沮   *jǔ*   MC dzjoX

1. end, terminate, stop; arrest.
   a. prevent; obstruct; prohibit.
2. destroy, ruin.
3. dispirited, hopeless, despairing; listless, apathetic.

沮   *jù*   MC tsjoH

1. bog(gy), marsh(y), fen; mire.

沮   *jū*   MC tsjo

1. a surname.
2. ～渠 *jūqú*, bisyllabic surname of Central Asian origin.

矩   *jǔ*   MC kjuX

1. carpenter's-square, L-square.
   a. square-shaped, right-angled.
2. rule, norm, measure(ment), guide; standard, criterion; principle.

3. mark off, lay out, outline.
   a. mark down, note, underline.

筥   *jǔ*   MC kjoX

1. round bamboo basket; round canister (cf. 筐 *kuāng*, square-shaped same).
   a. round-shaped, round-framed.
2. sheaf of grain, equiv. ca. 4 handsful.

舉   *jǔ*   MC kjoX

1. lift up, raise up; bear up, hoist; elevate.
   a. adduce, raise for discussion; offer up for consideration, proffer.
   b. raise name for advancement, recommend; promote.
2. undertake, begin, start up, activate, launch; take the lead; instigate, rouse, stir.
   a. undertaking, enterprise.
   b. hold a feast (at court).
3. cultivate; develop; rear, foster, raise.
4. expose, bring to light; report on, inform against.
5. overcome, conquer; occupy, take over.
6. all of, the entirety of, fully; e.g. ～國 *jǔguó*, the entire state; ～世 *jǔshì*, the whole world.
7. (med.) borrow or lend money (with interest).
8. (med.) ～似 *jǔsì*, tell to, bring to the attention of.
9. (med.) ～要 *jǔyào*, in short, briefly.

蒟   *jǔ*   MC kjuX

1. betel plant (*Piper betel*), evergreen creeper, leaves yield a mild stimulant; e.g. ～醬 *jǔjiàng*, betel sauce; sometimes, black pepper, hot pepper (*Piper nigrum*).
2. ～蒻 *jǔruò*, devil's-tongue, elephant-foot, Jpn. konnyaku (*Amorphophallus rivieri, A. konjac*), subtropical single-leaved plant with long protruding spadix; syn. 蒻頭 *ruòtóu*.

踽   *jǔ*   MC kjuX

1. rdup., advance alone, proceed by oneself; self-sufficient, relying only on oneself.
2. (bn.) ～僂 *jǔlǚ* (MC kjuX-ljuX), hunchbacked, crookbacked.

齟   *jǔ*   MC dzrjoX

1. (bn.) ～齬 *jǔyǔ* (MC dzrjoX-ngjoX), irregularly fitting teeth, unmatched and uneven; jutting and jagged; also, discordant, unfitted to the form, inapt and unsuited.

jù

俱 **jù** MC kju

1. altogether, in all; completely, the whole of; generally; ⊙ 具 *jù* 4.
2. together with, accompany(ing), in common.
3. comprehend, understand.

倨 **jù** MC kjoH

1. contemptuous, insolent, with no regard for others; self-regarding, arrogant.
2. slightly bent, curved.
3. ⊙ 踞 *jù* 1, squat, sit on one's heels; also, sit with legs splayed.

具 **jù** MC gjuH

1. arrange, set out, provide, esp. food and drink.
   a. provender; viands, foodstuffs; beverages.
2. equip, prepare for, preparations.
3. paraphernalia, equipment; apparatus, accouterments; implements, items.
   a. furnishings, outfitting; make-up, arrangement, constitution; e.g. 勝～ *shèngjù*, superb make-up, i.e. good health.
4. completely, altogether, the whole of; generally; e.g. ～告 *jùgào*, report everything; ～足 *jùzú*, full(y), perfect(ly).
   a. ～然 *jùrán*, contentedly, pleased, satisfiedly.
5. (med.) special ability, capacity, forte, facility.
6. (med.) state, set forth in writing; itemize, tabulate.
7. (med.) comprehend, understand.

㝡 **jù** MC dzjuH

1. collect, amass, accumulate, group; ⊙ 聚 *jù* 1.

劇 **jù** MC gjaek

1. intense(ly), severe(ly), to an extreme measure or acute degree.
   a. intensify; impel; make more acute.
2. difficulty, problem; predicament; ordeal.
   a. trouble(d), greatly agitate(d).
   b. consider terrible; denigrate.
3. speed up, accelerate; drive on.
   a. sudden(ly), abrupt(ly); rapid(ly).
   b. smooth, slick, freely moving; quick-tongued, glib.
4. (med.) entertain(ment), amuse(ment).

句 **jù** MC kjuH

1. meaningful phrase of text; line of verse.
   a. end-stopped phrase; e.g. (med.) ～讀 *jùdòu*, punctuate a text by marking full-stops (*jù*) and pauses (*dòu*).
2. meaningful musical phrase, incl. measure of duration.

gōu MC kuw

1. ⊙ 勾 *gōu* 1, hook, curve, bend; curling frond; 2, caught, entangled, snagged, entice; 3, stay behind, linger.

gòu MC kuwH

1. ⊙ 彀 *gòu*, draw a bow fully.

婁 **jù** MC gjuX ⊙ 寠 *jù*.

屨 **jù** MC kjuH

1. straw sandal or shoe.
2. tread on, trample; march over.

岠 **jù** MC gjoX

1. distance from, ⊙ 距 *jù* 4.
2. repel, resist, ward off, ⊙ 拒 *jù* 1.
3. large mountain.

巨 **jù** MC gjoX

1. gigantic, gargantuan; beyond measure; immense.
2. graph associated with autumn, west, etc.
3. ⊙ 矩 *jǔ* 1, carpenter's-square.

懅 **jù** MC gjoH

1. shame(d), embarrass(ed); disgrace(d).
2. anxious, uneasy, fretful.
   a. frightened, startled, surprised.

懼 **jù** MC gjuH

1. faint-hearted, timid, timorous; frighten(ed), startle(d) (less strong than 畏 *wèi*, dread).

拒 **jù** MC gjoX

1. resist, withstand, oppose; repel, parry, fend off.
2. decline, reject; repudiate.
3. (med.) reach, arrive at.

jǔ MC kjuX

1. defensive square (battle formation).

據 **jù** MC kjoH

1. rely on, depend on; lean on or against.

a. according to, based on.
b. evidence, proof, substantiation.
2. seize, grasp, take in hand.
a. tangible, palpable.
3. take possession of; occupy, take over.
4. nearby, hard by, nestle against.

距 *jù* MC gjoX

1. surmount; traverse, cross over (to).
2. ⊙ 拒 *jù* 1, resist, oppose, withstand, fend off.

炬 *jù* MC gjoX

1. torch, made of bundled reeds.
a. to torch, set fire to.
2. (med.) wax candle.

瞿 *jù* MC kjuH

1. sgl. or rdup., look to either side; frightened glance, fearful(ly), panic-stricken; also, with extra caution, taking care, circumspect.

qú MC gju

1. weapon similar to a guisarme.
2. ⊙ 蘧 *qú* in ～麥 *qúmài*, → 蘧 *qú* 1.
3. (Budd.) used to trsc. Skt. voiced and voiceless gutturals; e.g. ～曇(摩) *qútán(mó)* (MC gju-dom[-ma]), trsc. Skt. *Gautama*, surname of the Buddha; hence, 瞿 *qú* often used to mark Budd.-related words.
4. a surname.

秬 *jù* MC gjoX

1. black variety of 黍 *shǔ*, broomcorn or glutinous millet (*Panicum miliaceum*), used in making wine.

窶 *jù* MC gjuX

1. straitened, in need; impoverished.
2. unmannerly, uncultivated; boorish, vulgar.
3. (bn.) ～數 *jùshù* (MC gjuX-srjuH), straw-pad, placed underneath item carried on top of head.

簴 *jù* MC gjoX

1. wooden bell-frame, bell-stand, esp. the vertical part (cf. 簨 *sǔn*, crossbeam of bell-stand).

粔 *jù* MC gjoX

1. (bn.) ～籹 *jùnǔ* (MC gjoX-nrjoX), ring-cake or dough-twist, dipped in honey-water mixture and fried.

聚 *jù* MC dzjuX

1. collect(ion), assemble, gather together, group(ing); (a)mass, accumulate; e.g. ～散 *jùsàn*, gather and disperse; also, transitory.
2. assembly of 3 or more celestial bodies in the same lunar lodging.
3. community, populace; settlement; e.g. ～落 *jùluò*, small settlement.
4. (Budd.) living beings.

苣 *jù* MC gjoX

1. torch, made from bundled reeds, ⊙ 炬 *jù*.
2. (med.) 萵～ *wōjù*, asparagus lettuce, → 萵 *wō*.

菹 *jù* MC tsrjoH → 菹 *zū*.

虡 *jù* MC gjoX ⊙ 簴 *jù*.

詎 *jù* MC gjoX

1. rhetorical interr., similar to 豈 *qǐ*: how (could it be that . . .)?, surely not . . .; e.g. ～可聞 *jù kěwén*, how could I ever hear it?
2. abruptly, suddenly; quickly, all at once.
3. conditional marker: if it were that . . ., supposing that . . .

距 *jù* MC gjoX

1. talon of bird; claw of fowl; spur of game-cock.
a. gen. term for foot (of plant, furniture, etc.).
2. hook-shaped blade or barb on halberd or other weapon.
3. reach, arrive at, come to.
4. distance from, separated from; e.g. ～墓十里 *jù mù shílǐ*, 10 *li* from the tomb; ～今九日 *jù jīn jiǔrì*, 9 days from today.
5. ⊙ 拒 *jù* 1, resist, oppose; 2, decline, reject; 巨 *jù*, gigantic, immense; 詎 *jù* 1, rhetorical interr.: how (could it be that . . .)?

踞 *jù* MC kjoH

1. squat; sit on one's heels.
a. sgl. or 箕～ *jījù*, sit with legs splayed, sit spraddled (impolite).
b. (Budd.) ～食 *jùshí*, sit on low stool or chair to eat, with legs spread.
2. lean on, rely on; near to, hard by.
3. ⊙ 倨 *jù* 1, insolent, contemptuous; arrogant; 鋸 *jù* 1, a saw.

踞　jù　MC kjoH

1. occupy, take possession of; squat on.
2. squat, sit on one's heels; ⊙ 踞 *jù*.

遽　jù　MC gjoH

1. hurried(ly), rapid(ly), hast(il)y; urgent(ly).
   a. quicken, rouse; bring life or vitality to.
2. fast courier or messenger, or the horse or carriage that conveys him.
   a. relay-station, post-station, dispatch-station.
3. alarm, fright, sudden fear; panic, terror.
4. 何～ *héjù*, 豈～ *qǐjù*, is it possible that . . .?, how could it be that . . .?

醵　jù　MC gjoH

1. drinking session or feast for which the participants each contribute to the cost; subscription party.
   a. group contributions.

鉅　jù　MC gjoX

1. hard iron.
2. fish-hook, barb.
3. ⊙ 巨 *jù* 1, gigantic, immense; 詎 *jù* 1, rhetorical interr.: how (could it be that . . .)?

鋸　jù　MC kjoH

1. a saw; dentate, saw-toothed, serrated.
2. to saw, saw off.
   a. as punishment, to cut off leg or penis.

鐻　jù　MC gjoX

1. bell-stand, bell-frame, ⊙ 簴 *jù* 1.
2. narrow bell in shape of tiger or other fierce animal.
   qú　MC gjo
1. gold or silver earring; ⊙ 璩 *qú*.

颶　jù　MC gjuH

1. (med.) hurricane, typhoon.
   a. (med.) ～母 *jùmǔ*, colored clouds or nimbus presaging hurricane.

駏　jù　MC gjoX

1. offspring of a molly (female mule) and a stallion (male horse).
2. (bn.) ～驉 *jùxū* (MC gjoX-xjo), usu. 蛩蛩～驉 *qióngqióngjùxū*, → 蛩 *qióng*.

juān

娟　juān　MC ʼjwien

1. (bn.) 嬋～ *chánjuān*, → 嬋 *chán*; 娸～ *piánjuān*, → 娸 *pián*.
2. rdup., lovely and lissome, fair and winsome.

捐　juān　MC ywen

1. cast aside, throw away; relinquish; reject, renounce, expel.
2. abolish, eliminate; extirpate.
3. contribute, donate; offer assistance.

朘　juān　MC tsjwen

1. reduce, contract; draw inward, recoil.
2. meat-stew with small amount of broth; casserole; ⊙ 臇 *juǎn*.
   zuī　MC tswoj
1. genitalia of baby boy.

涓　juān　MC kwen

1. brooklet, streamlet, rivulet.
   a. rdup., burbling and bubbling, lapping lazily.
2. pure, clean; purify, cleanse; wash.
3. select, choose; e.g. ～吉 *juānjí*, choose an auspicious day (to do something).
   xuàn　MC ʼjwienH
1. ～然 *xuànrán*, (of tears) running, flowing, trickling.

钃　juān　MC kwen

1. dispense with, rid oneself of
   a. abrogate, rescind; waive.
   b. mitigate, palliate (disease).
2. manifest, distinct, (make) evident.
   a. clear; translucent.
3. purify, cleanse, purge.

鋗　juān　MC kwen

1. ⊙ 涓 *juān* 2, pure, clean; purify, cleanse; wash.
   xuān　MC xwen
1. onom. of soft sound of tapped jade.

鐫　juān　MC tsjwen

1. carving or sculpting tool for wood or stone; gouge, scauper, burin.
   a. carve, sculpt.
2. advise with intention of molding behavior to a standard, hew closely to principle.

鵑 juān MC kwen

1. (bn.) 杜～ *dùjuān* (MC duX-kwen), hawk-cuckoo (*Hierococcyx sparverioides*), in lit. specially associated with Shu 蜀 because legendarily a posthumous avatar of an ancient Shu king; also, azalea (*Rhododendron molle*).

juǎn

卷 juǎn MC kjwenX

1. roll up, furl, curl up; wrap.
   juàn   MC kjwenH
1. scroll, rolled-up document.
   a. division of text, fascicle, chapter, originally a single scroll.
   quán   MC gjwen
1. curled; crinkled; rolled, clenched.

捲 juǎn MC kjwenX

1. roll up, furl, curl up; wrap; ⊙ 卷 *juǎn* 1.
   quán   MC gjwen
1. fist, closed hand; clench(ed); ⊙ 拳 *quán*.

臇 juǎn MC tsjwenX

1. highly seasoned meat-stew with small amount of broth; ragout; casserole.

juàn

倦 juàn MC gjwenH

1. weary, fatigued, tired, worn out.
   a. tired of, bored with, fed up with, exasperated, have enough of.

券 juàn MC gjwenH   ⊙ 倦 *juàn*.

圈 juàn MC gjwonH

1. pen, fold, enclosure for containing animals.
2. outline, circumscribe; e.g. 籠～ *lóngjuàn*, "encage and enclose," i.e. delineate.
   quān   MC khjwen
1. ⊙ 棬 *quān*, bowl or plate made of wicker.
2. (med.) ring, circle.

帣 juàn MC kjwenH

1. pouch, sack.
2. bound-up or tied-up sleeve.

悁 juàn MC kjwienH

1. (med.) (bn.) ～急 *juànjí* (MC kjwienH-kip), irritably impatient, peevish and perverse, captious and crabby.
   yuān   MC 'jwien
1. short-tempered, irascible, touchy, volatile; in a pet.

惓 juàn MC gjwenH

1. critically ill; enfeebled; enervated.
   quán   MC gjwen
1. rdup., hold tight to, keep close to one; zealous, earnest, ardent; ⊙ 拳 *quán* 3.

羷 juàn MC kjwenH

1. nose-ring of ox, to attach a leading-rope.

狷 juàn MC kwenH

1. prudent, self-contained; wary, uncommitted.
2. nervous, impatient, quick-tempered; impetuous, hasty; uncompromising.

獧 juàn MC kwenH   ⊙ 狷 *juàn*.

眷 juàn MC kjwenH

1. look back at (fondly), turn one's gaze (affectionately) on, regard with favor.
   a. kind attention, goodwill, beneficence.
2. fond feeling, pang of affection; e.g. 罔～ *wǎngjuàn*, without a pang of feeling, totally indifferent.
   a. rdup., (with) loving longing, fond affection.
   b. (bn.) ～戀 *juànliàn* (MC kjwenH-ljwenH), near and dear.
3. someone dear to one, beloved.

睊 juàn MC kwenH

1. rdup., squint sideways at in anger, peer at peevishly.

睠 juàn MC kjwenH

1. look back at (fondly); kind attention, goodwill; ⊙ 眷 *juàn* 1.

絭 juàn MC kjwonH

1. bind up, knot up.
2. cord, binding, twisted braid.
3. bowstring; string of zither or other chordophone.

絹　juàn　MC kjwien
1. tabby silk, plain-weave; pongee, thin tabby.
　　　juàn　MC kwienH
1. tie up, knit together; ⊙ 罥 *juàn* 1.

罥　juàn　MC kwenH
1. tie up, knit together; net.
2. hang up, suspend.
3. net, for catching birds or small game.
　　a. snag, snare, catch.

羂　juàn　MC kwenH
1. net, for catching birds or small game; ⊙ 罥 *juàn* 3.

儁　juàn　MC dzjwenX
1. plump, fleshy, stout (esp. of birds); podgy, fat.
2. rich (to taste), savory; delectable.
　　　jùn　MC tswinH
1. ⊙ 俊 *jùn*, superior in talent, outstanding; eminent.

jué

倔　jué　MC gjut
1. unbending, intractable, unsubmissive; stiff-necked; obdurate.
2. stick out, protrude, protuberant; obtrude, obtrusive.

劂　jué　MC kjwot
1. (bn.) 剞 ~ *jījué*, → 剞 *jī*.

厥　jué　MC kjwot
1. pronoun, usu. 3rd-person: (s)he, they, his, her, its, theirs.
2. marker of successive action: and then . . .
3. (bn.) 突 ~ *tūjué*, → 突 *tū*.
4. suddenly lose consciousness, faint, swoon.
5. ⊙ 掘 *jué* 1, dig out, scoop out; 橛 *jué* 1, short post, stake.
6. (med.) ~ 摩師 *juémóshī*, die, pass away (Tang colloquialism).

嚼　jué　MC dzjak
1. chew on, gnaw on; nibble at.

屩　jué　MC kjak
1. sandals made of straw or hemp fiber.

崛　jué　MC gjut
1. rise up sharply; protrude, protuberance.

懅　jué　MC gjwak
1. ~ 然 *juérán*, shocked, dumfounded; unsettled, staggered; appalled, paralyzed with fear.

抉　jué　MC kwet
1. gouge out, scoop out, pull out; dredge out.
2. run through with weapon, stab; carve up, butcher, hack to pieces.
3. raise, lift up, pull up, esp. latch or door-bar.
　　a. bring out (into the open), cast light on, esp. in finding fault.
4. (med.) draw out, choose, select.
5. archer's protective thumb-ring.

掘　jué　MC gjwot
1. dig out, hollow out, gouge, scoop out; the physical act that creates a 缺 *quē*, gap.
　　a. excavate, unearth, dig up.
　　b. indentation, hollow, recession.
2. use up, exhaust; devoid of, deplete(d).
3. rise up sharply, protrude; ⊙ 崛 *jué*.
　　　kū　MC khwot
1. ⊙ 窟 *kū*, cavern, grotto, den.

撅　jué　MC kjwot
1. pull up, pull out.
2. dig out, scoop out; excavate; ⊙ 掘 *jué* 1.
3. (med.) strike, hit, smite.
　　a. (med.) attack, assail.

攫　jué　MC kjwak
1. seize in claws or talons, clutch, clench; pounce on.
　　a. carry off, pluck up; catch.

桷　jué　MC kaewk
1. square beam, girder.
2. tile-lath (for roof tile).

橛　jué　MC kjwot
1. short wooden post, stake.
2. stubble, short growth remaining in field after harvest.
3. wooden bit (horse's).
4. (med.) ⊙ 撅 *jué* 3, strike, hit.

蹶　jué　MC gjwot　⊙ 橛 *jué*.

決   jué   MC kwet
1. breach, in dike or dam; flow out, burst forth, overflow the banks.
    a. run out, run into a channel.
    b. open out.
2. break out, break away from, break through; escape.
    a. break off, sever, cut off; split.
3. decide(dly), decisive, definitive; determine(d), certain(ly); resolve, resolute(ly).
4. decide punishment, execute a sentence.
5. take leave, part, break off from; bid farewell.
6. ⊙ 抉 *jué* 1, gouge, scoop out, dredge; 6, archer's protective thumb-ring.

潏   jué   MC kwet
1. bubble up, froth; gush, rush, flow fast.

爝   jué   MC tsjak
1. torch, flambeau.
2. light a bundle of reeds to use in ceremonial purging of noxious influences.

爵   jué   MC tsjak
1. beaker; tripod cup with thick extended front spout, narrow extended tail, and 2 upright handles, for sacrificial offerings of wine, mainly Shang dynasty, use diminishing in Zhou.
2. ranks of nobility (i.e. *gong* 公, duke; *hou* 侯, marquess; *bo* 伯, count or earl; *zi* 子, viscount; *nan* 男, baron); e.g. ～里 *juélǐ*, rank and place of enfeoffment.
    què   MC tsjak
1. ⊙ 雀 *què* 1, small bird, birdling, sparrow.

玃   jué   MC kjwot
1. (bn.) 猖～ *chāngjué*, → 猖 *chāng*.

玃   jué   MC kjwak
1. described as a large blue-black macaque but identification uncertain, perhaps a hoolock.

玦   jué   MC kwet
1. C-shaped disk of jade or nephrite suspended from belt as ornament; esp. given as token upon leave-taking.

珏   jué   MC kaewk
1. paired or matching jades.

珏   jué   MC kaewk   ⊙ 珏 *jué*.

瑴   jué   MC kaewk   ⊙ 珏 *jué*.

矍   jué   MC kjwak
1. look to either side in fear, look round anxiously; gape in amazement.
    a. frightened, anxious, fear-struck, on edge.
    b. rdup., scared and skittish, with eyes jumping everywhere; also (med.), exigent and pressing, imperatively needed.
2. (med.) (bn.) ～鑠 *juéshuò* (MC kjwak-syak), hale and hearty in old age.

穱   jué   MC tsraewk
1. early ripening grain.

絕   jué   MC dzjwet
1. break off, cut off, sever, sunder; cut through.
    a. break with, separate from, leave behind; abjure, renounce; strip(ped) of.
2. sheer (height), steep, brant.
3. superlative (< cutting off all competition), superb, excellent; unsurpassed, incomparable; distinct(ive).
    a. distinctively, especially; decidedly, definitely.
    b. (med.) as intensifier following VB: VB in the extreme.
4. cut across, cross over; traverse (land or water).
    a. (med.) pass a period of time; e.g. ～時 *juéshí*, after a while.
5. (med.) fall down, topple over; swoon, lose consciousness; e.g. ～倒 *juédǎo*, knocked flat, bowled over; also, bend to, submit.

臄   jué   MC gjak
1. much disputed but variously said to be cheek, palate, or tongue of ox (as sacrificial offering of meat); most likely, tongue.

蕝   jué   MC tsjwet
1. ancient practice for court ceremonies of erecting fasces of floss-grass to mark where particular people should stand in order of precedence.
    a. mark(er), signal.

蕨　jué　MC kjwot

1. bracken (*Pteridium excelsum*), symbolic of simple eating fare of those who have retired from society; syn. 蒝 *yuán* 2.

蟨　jué　MC kjwot

1. Siberian jerboa, kangaroo-rat (*Allactaga sibirica*), desert rodent with long hindlegs, short forelegs, long tail, and moves quite quickly by hopping like a kangaroo; sometimes paired with the → 蛩蛩駏驉 *qióngqióngjùxū* as symbolic of 2 creatures that need each other to function adequately.

蟩　jué　MC kjwot

1. mosquito larvae.

蠼　jué　MC kjwak

1. ⊙ 玃 *jué*, large macaque-like animal, perhaps a hoolock; 躩 *jué* 2, leap, bound, jump.

　　qú　MC gju

1. (bn.) ～蒐 *qúsōu* (MC gju-srjuw), earwig (*Forficula auricularia*).

覺　jué　MC kaewk

1. be(come) conscious of, aware of, sense, perceive.
　　a. discover, realize; awaken to, esp. awaken from dream-state.
2. (Budd.) awaken(ing), wake up spiritually, enlightenment, e.g. 獨～ *dújué*, "awakened on one's own," pratyekabuddha; also, initial thought.
3. make known, bring to the attention of; show, indicate.
4. lofty and straight (of pillars).

　　jué　MC kaewH

1. awaken from sleep. N.B. The meaning "to sleep, nap" is not found till post-Tang times.
2. comparatively, approximately, relatively; ⊙ 較 *jiào* 2.

觖　jué　MC kwet

1. dissatisfied, discontented; e.g. ～如 *juérú*, ungratified, displeased; ～望 *juéwàng*, resentful, embittered.
2. ⊙ 抉 *jué* 3a, bring into the open, find fault with.

　　kuì　MC khwiejH

1. hope for, anticipate with desire.

觼　jué　MC kwet　⊙ 钁 *jué*.

訣　jué　MC kwet

1. valediction, words spoken upon parting or when bidding final farewell to the dead.
2. acroama, private instructions or teachings intended only for initiates; esp. in titles of Dao. texts.

譎　jué　MC kwet

1. deceptive, changeable, unreliable; evasive, dodgy, shifty; specious.
　　a. deceive, mislead, delude, defraud.
2. altered, changed; e.g. ～詭 *juéguǐ* or 詭～ *guǐjué*, improbable, anomalous; transfigured, metamorphosed.

趹　jué　MC kwet

1. race along, gallop, tear, fly (esp. of horse); speed, hurry.

　　guì　MC kwejH

1. kick with hind-legs (horse, donkey, mule).

蹶　jué　MC kjwot

1. stumble, trip, lose one's footing, falter.
　　a. tumble, fall over, topple over.
2. trample, tread on.
　　a. spread apart with feet.
3. kick.
4. move rapidly; run.
　　a. agile, nimble; alert.
5. exhausted, spent; worn out; dried up.

　　guì　MC kjwejH

1. shake, joggle; convulse; dislodge.

蹷　jué　MC kjwot　⊙ 蹶 *jué*.

躩　jué　MC kjwak

1. briskly stepping, making haste but in dignified manner.
2. to bound, leap, jump.

钁　jué　MC kwet

1. latch, buckle, clasp, lock.
　　a. lock up, keep secure.

钁　jué　MC kjwak

1. large hoe; pick, pick-axe.
2. dig out, uproot.

駃 **jué**   MC kwet
1. (bn.) 〜騠 *juétí* (MC kwet-dej), a "blood-sweating" horse from Ferghana; also, hinny, offspring of a stallion and a jenny (female donkey).
    kuài   MC khwaejH
1. quick, fleet of foot.

鴂 **jué**   MC kwet
1. (bn.) 鷦〜 *níngjué*, wren, → 鷦 *níng*.
2. shrike (*Laniidae*), ⊙ 鶪 *jú*; e.g. 〜舌 *juéshé*, shrike-tongued, i.e. incomprehensible, babbling.

jūn

君 **jūn**   MC kjun
1. sovereign, suzerain, liegelord, ruler; lord (of noble rank).
    a. 〜子 *jūnzi*, son of a lord, lordling; gentleman; from Warring States period on, most often philosophical term ref. someone not noble-born but whose behavior conforms with the moral ideal of what a nobleman's should be: gentleman, man of noble character or disposition.
2. honorific 2nd-person pronoun, used when addressing someone of higher status or of equal status to whom one wishes to show respect: you milord, you sir.
3. mistress, when used as designation of female spirit or deity; e.g. 湘〜 *xiāngjūn*, Mistress of the Xiang (River).
4. (bn.) 〜遷 *jūnqiān* (MC kjun-tshjen), ⊙ 裙 樾 *jūnqiān*, → 裙 *jūn*.

均 **jūn**   MC kjwin
1. equal, even.
    a. likewise, uniform(ly), equally, in every instance.
2. regulate, bring into regular gradation; equalizing pivot, equipoise, balance; harmonize, tune; modulate.
    a. assess(or), e.g. taxes.
3. ⊙ 鈞 *jūn* 1, potter's wheel; 2, measure of capacity, equiv. 30 catties (*jin* 斤); 4 *jūn* = 1 picul (*shi* 石).
4. tuning-board, ancient stringed instrument 7-ft. long, used sympathetically to determine pitch of bells.

    yùn   MC hwinH
1. harmonic scale of each of the 12 musical modes that accord with the 12 pitch-pipes (*lü* 律).
2. ⊙ 韻 *yùn*, rhyme, harmony.

裙 **jūn**   MC kjun
1. (bn.) 〜樾 *jūnqiān* (MC kjun-tshjen), date-plum (*Diospyros lotus*).

皸 **jūn**   MC kjun
1. chapped or cracked skin.

軍 **jūn**   MC kjun
1. army, collective name for largest military unit, usu. prefixed with identifying designation.
    a. army-group, traditionally numbering 12,500 men; because the Son of Heaven in Zhou times supposedly had a sixfold army, while feudal lords were allowed only a threefold army, the phrase 六〜 *liùjūn*, "6 armies," was commonly used later to ref. the emperor's army, not meaning 6 different armies.
    b. troops, soldiers.
2. encamp(ment); bivouac.
3. (med.) in Tang times, frontier garrison.

鈞 **jūn**   MC kjwin
1. potter's wheel.
    a. by metonymy, a potter; e.g. 洪〜 *hóngjūn*, the all-fashioning potter, i.e. Heaven as creative force.
2. measure of capacity, equiv. 30 catties (*jin* 斤); 4 *jūn* = 1 picul (*shi* 石).
3. equal, even.
    a. likewise, uniform(ly), equally, in every instance.
    b. equidistant, equally spaced; midmost; e.g. 〜天 *jūntiān*, midmost heaven, middle of the ninefold heavens.
4. regulate, bring into regular gradation; equalizing pivot, equipoise, balance; harmonize, tune; modulate.

麇 **jūn**   MC kwin   ⊙ 麕 *jūn*.

麕 **jūn**   MC kwin
1. roe-deer (*Moschus chinloo*).
    a. (med.) river-deer (*Hydropotes inermis*).

qún　MC gjun

1. ⊙ 羣 *qún*, host of, group of, gathering of; teeming, sundry, diverse.

jùn

俊　jùn　MC tswinH

1. of exceptional quality or ability; paragon.
   a. outstanding, excellent; extraordinary, prodigious; eminent.

傶　jùn　MC tswinH　⊙ 俊 *jùn*.

峻　jùn　MC swinH

1. exalted, pinnacle(d); e.g. ～極 *jùnjí*, pinnacled apogee.
   a. precipitous; steep-sided.
2. stern, severe; grim; e.g. ～急 *jùnjí*, stern and unrelenting.
3. ⊙ 駿 *jùn* 2, rapid, light-footed.

捃　jùn　MC kjunH

1. pick up; gather, collect; reap, harvest.

攈　jùn　MC kjunH　⊙ 捃 *jùn*.

浚　jùn　MC swinH

1. dredge, dig out, deepen (waterway, canal, well).
2. deep, profound; penetrating.
3. demand, exact; extract from, appropriate.

濬　jùn　MC swinH

1. ⊙ 浚 *jùn* 1, dredge, deepen; 2, deep, penetrating.

焌　jùn　MC tswonH

1. burn; set on fire, enkindle, ignite.
   a. apply point of searing implement to "oracle bone" in order to produce cracks for divination.

畯　jùn　MC tswinH

1. sgl. or 田～ *tiánjùn*, official title in Zhou times, inspector of fields.

竣　jùn　MC tshwin

1. retreat, retire, turn away from; cease doing.
2. finish up, wrap up, complete.

箘　jùn　MC gwinX

1. sgl. or (bn.) ～簬 *jùnlù* (MC gwinX-luH), species of bamboo, not convincingly identified, but used in the making of arrows.

菌　jùn　MC gwinX

1. gen. term for mushroom.
2. mold, fungus; mildew.
3. ⊙ 箘 *jùn*, arrow-bamboo.

郡　jùn　MC gjunH

1. administrative unit: commandery, coordinating several *xian* 縣 "districts" or "counties"; through 3rd century smaller than a *zhou* 州 "prefecture"; in Sui-Tang times alt. designation for "prefecture"; chief administrative officer a *taishou* 太守.

陵　jùn　MC swinH

1. defile, narrow gorge or valley, steep-sided.
2. harsh, grim, fearsome; cruel, ruthless.

餕　jùn　MC tswinH

1. leftovers of meal, incl. remnants of sacrificial offerings.
   a. eat leftovers.

駿　jùn　MC tswinH

1. exceptional horse, fine steed, bayard.
   a. person of exceptional talent or quality, paragon, ⊙ 俊 *jùn* 1.
2. rapid, fleet, light-footed; e.g. ～疾 *jùnjí*, in a flash, evanescent.
3. ⊙ 峻　*jùn* 1, tall, exalted; precipitous, steep-sided; 2, stern, severe; grim.

鵔　jùn　MC swinH

1. (bn.) ～鸃 *jùnyí* (MC swinH-ngje), the golden pheasant (*Chrysolophus pictus*), with golden crest and rump and bright-red body; also, according to some med. commentators, a kind of "phoenix" (鳳 *fèng*).

K

kāi

揩 kāi MC kheaj
1. wipe, swipe.
2. rub together.

開 kāi MC khoj
1. open.
    a. unfold, uncover, expose.
    b. clear (land); clear away.
    c. to separate, spread apart, spread open.
2. begin, start; inaugurate; found.
    a. broach; introduce; set out.
    b. lay open; vent (feelings).
3. open-minded; enlightened.
4. remove, relieve; find diversion in.
5. expand, widen, enlarge.
6. (Budd.) 〜士 *kāishì*, "adept who opens [the Way]," early ref. to bodhisattvas, by extension to monks; 〜山 *kāishān*, "open a mountain [retreat]," found a monastery; 〜素 *kāisù*, "engage in plain [eating]," take a vegetarian meal.

kǎi

凱 kǎi MC khojX
1. triumphal music, celebrating military victory.
    a. triumphant, in glory; e.g. 〜風 *kǎifēng*, "triumphal wind," balmy southern wind betokening comfortable days.
    b. bask in the warmth of good feeling, > warmth of fine weather, balmy.
2. ⊙ 愷 *kǎi* 1, joy, jubilant; gratified, content.

剴 kǎi MC ngoj
1. sickle, scythe, reaping-hook.
2. pertinent, to the point; exact; e.g. 〜切 *kǎiqiè* MC ngoj-tshet, precisely on point.
3. show the point of, give instructions to; advise.
    a. admonish.
    b. caustic, mordant; make cutting remarks about.

塏 kǎi MC khojX
1. dry upland, arid plateau.

愷 kǎi MC khojX
1. (en)joy(ment), jubilant; gratified; exultant.

    a. (bn.) 〜悌 *kǎitì* (MC khojX-dejX), contented and carefree, satisfied and at ease.
2. ⊙ 凱 *kǎi*, triumphal music.

慨 kǎi MC khojH
1. desolate, disappointed; melancholy; sigh forlornly.
    a. deeply stirred, with strong feeling; fortitudinous; bearing up; brave.
    b. (bn.) 慷〜 *kāngkǎi*, → 慷 *kāng*.

楷 kǎi MC kheajX
1. model, pattern; outline.
    a. take as a model; copy.
2. regular, standard script; normal four-square calligraphic style used most commonly.
    jiē MC keaj
1. pistachio tree (*Pistacia chinensis*), hardwood used in furniture making; unlike the *Pistacia vera* brought from Persia in later times, the native tree did not yield nuts prized for eating.
    a. sturdy, tough, hardy; rigorous; stalwart.

鍇 kǎi MC kheajX
1. iron; esp. fine-quality iron.

鎧 kǎi MC khojX
1. armor, mail (for soldiers), usu. cut pieces of rhinoceros hide tied together; cf. 甲 *jiǎ* 3.

闓 kǎi MC khojX
1. ⊙ 開 *kāi*, open; 愷 *kǎi*, (en)joy(ment), jubilant, gratified.

飀 kǎi MC khojX
1. ⊙ 凱 *kǎi* 1a, "triumphal" or balmy south-wind.

kài

愒 kài MC khojH
1. indignant, resent(ful); piqued, provoked.
2. onom. sigh of exasperation or discontent.

欬 kài MC khojH
1. cough, clear the throat; hawk; hack; e.g. 〜逆上氣 *kàinìshàngqì*, reflexive coughing with rising *qi*.

kān

刊 **kān** **MC khan**

1. cut down, hew; raze.
2. edit; revise or "cut down" a text.
3. cut into stone, carve.

勘 **kān** **MC khom**

1. (med.) collate, compare (texts).
2. (med.) investigate, examine; esp. judicial inquiry.

堪 **kān** **MC khom**

1. bear, sustain; endure.
   a. able to bear, tolerate, put up with; is willing to do X.
   b. (med.) indifferent to, unconcerned, passive about.
2. right for, suited to, equal to.
   a. qualified, competent, capable.
3. (med.) shall, will; soon; is about to.
4. canopy of carriage, esp. in cmpd. ～輿 *kānyú*, "canopy and chassis," i.e. heaven and earth.

嵁 **kān** **MC khom**

1. (bn.) ～嚴 *kānyán* (MC khom-ngaem), craggy cliffs, ragged ridges.

戡 **kān** **MC khom**

1. overcome, conquer; suppress, put down.
2. stab; skewer; hack down, cut to pieces; slaughter.

龕 **kān** **MC khom**

1. (Budd.) stūpa, esp. for housing relics.
   a. (Budd.) niche, sacrarium, in which relics are deposited.
2. cavity (in stone), vug; grotto.
3. crock, for containing food.
4. victor(ious), triumph(ant); overcome.

kǎn

侃 **kǎn** **MC khanX**

1. outspoken, unreserved; candid, frank.
   a. rdup., affable and easygoing, congenial, open and aboveboard.

偘 **kǎn** **MC khanX** ⊙ 侃 *kǎn*.

坎 **kǎn** **MC khomX**

1. sink-hole; pit; hollow; cleft.
   a. (bn.) ～坷 or ～軻 *kǎnkě* (MC khomX-khaX), pitted with problems, rough road, rough going; also, rough and ragged, bumpy and stubbled.
2. onom. of striking an object (drum, pan, etc.).
3. rdup., kam-kam, onom. of drumming, most likely a briskly moving, high-pitched drumbeat; also, empty and unfilled; also, sunk and pitted; (med.) also, placid and pleased.
4. one of the 8 fundamental trigrams of the *Yijing*, made up of an unbroken line between two broken lines.
   a. sgl. or 習～ *xíkǎn*, name of 29th hexagram of the *Yijing*.

埳 **kǎn** **MC khomX**

1. ⊙ 坎 *kǎn* 1, sink-hole; pit, cavity; hollow, cleft.
2. dissatisfied, despairing, as though one's heart is hollowed out.

欿 **kǎn** **MC homX**

1. displeased with oneself, self-reproachful.
   a. modest, diffident, feel insufficient.
2. crave, ardently desire.
3. ⊙ 坎 *kǎn* 1, sink-hole, pit, cavity.

轗 **kǎn** **MC khomX**

1. (bn.) ～軻 *kǎnkě* (MC khomX-khaX), ⊙ 坎坷 *kǎnkě*, → 坎 *kǎn*.

顑 **kǎn** **MC khomX**

1. (bn.) ～頷 *kǎnhàn* (MC khomX-hanX), famished and sallow-faced, careworn and weakened.

kàn

看 **kàn** **MC khanH**

1. look, look about, see.
   a. look upon, regard (as).
2. (med.) look for, look to do (in future) > shall, will.
   a. (med.) (ADV) soon, in a moment.
   b. (med.) expect, presume; plan on.
   c. (med.) figure, reckon, suppose.
   kān **MC khan**
1. look after, keep watch over, take care of, tend; protect, comfort.

瞰   kàn   MC khamH

1. catch sight of; see afar.
   a. see from above, surview, overview.
2. glimpse, glance at; peek, spy on.

矙   kàn   MC khamH   ☉ 瞰 kàn.

衎   kàn   MC khanH

1. pleased; satisfied, content.
   a. rdup., gratified and gladdened; also, forth-right and frank, open and aboveboard.

瞰   kàn   MC khamH

1. observe, view; esp. regard from a height, see what is below one.
   ### hǎn   MC xeamX
   1. ～如 hǎnrú, ～然 hǎnrán, like a tiger's (onom.) roar or growl; fearsome, forceful.

kāng

康   kāng   MC khang

1. (bn.) ～㝗 kāngláng (MC khang-lang), ～梁 kāngliáng (MC khang-ljang), empty inside; hollowed out.

康   kāng   MC khang

1. well-being, peace of mind; at ease, tranquil; e.g. 小～ xiǎokāng, basic well-being, as brought about under sage-kings of old.
   a. settle, bring to stability.
2. health(y), hale(ness), fit(ness); vigor, strength, robust(ness).
   a. prosper(ous), fullness.
   b. overfull; wild; excess(ive).
3. grand; inclusive, expansive; e.g. ～莊 kāngzhuāng, spacious avenue; also, crossroads where several roads meet.
   a. magnify, approve enthusiastically, hail; e.g. ～歌 kānggē, sing the praises of, song of praise.
4. empty, hollow; e.g. ～瓠 kānghù, empty gourd.
5. ～居 kāngjū, Sogdiana; (med.) esp. Samarkand.
   a. (Budd.) sgl., when used as surname for monk, ethnonym indicating Sogdian ancestry.
6. (med.) a surname, usu. for Sogdians originally hailing from Samarkand.

忼   kāng   MC khang   ☉ 慷 kāng.

慷   kāng   MC khang

1. strong-hearted, great-hearted.

2. (bn.) ～慨 kāngkǎi (MC khang-khojH), passionate intensity, brave forbearance, sorrowful but strong, desolate defiance, righteous fortitude, earnestly indignant, sternly strong-hearted, vehement, fervent.

糠   kāng   MC khang

1. bran, chaff, husk of grain.
   a. glume, of grass.

kǎng

骯   kǎng   MC khangX

1. (bn.) ～髒 kǎngzǎng (MC khangX-tsangX), fat and fleshy, well-fed, burly and bulky, hulking; also, outright, downright, blunt and bluff; also, firm and forceful, staunch and strong.

kàng

亢   kàng   MC khangH   → 亢 gāng.

伉   kàng   MC khangH

1. complement; match, equal; counterpart.
   a. ～儷 kànglì, wife; (med.) also, husband and wife.
2. withstand, stand opposed to; resist.
3. inflexible, staunch; strong.
4. high; haughty.
   a. to the highest degree; excessive.

抗   kàng   MC khangH

1. withstand, stand opposed to; be a match for; resist; contend with, grapple with.
   a. intractable, inflexible, unyielding; intransigent.
   b. (bn.) ～髒 kàngzǎng (MC khangH-tsangX), firm and forceful, staunch and strong.
2. protect; shield, shelter.
3. raise up, lift; hold aloft, brandish.
   a. high, tall; elevated; e.g. ～殿 kàngdiàn, lofty palace; ～言 kàngyán, elevated or high-spirited talk.

炕   kàng   MC khangH

1. dry by fire; oven-bake; grill.
   a. parched, sered.
2. ☉ 抗 kàng 3, raise up, lift, elevated, lofty.
N.B. This graph not used for the kang-bed (heatable brick platform for sleeping) until post-med. times; in the Tang, the graph 坑 kàng (→ kēng) was used for that meaning.

閌　**kàng**　MC khangH
1. towering upward, stretching aloft; esp. of gates and mountains.

kāo

尻　**kāo**　MC khaw
1. buttocks, rump, haunches.

kǎo

拷　**kǎo**　MC khawX
1. (med.) flog, whip, thrash; esp. prisoners, criminals.

攷　**kǎo**　MC khawX
1. ⊙ 考 *kǎo* 3, examine, analyze, research, study; 5, strike, pound.

栲　**kǎo**　MC khawX
1. euscaphis (*Euscaphis japonica*), medium-height deciduous shrub, spring-flowering.
   a. also identified as syn. 樗 *chū*, ailanthus (*Ailanthus altissima*).
2. (med.) (bn.) ～栳 *kǎolǎo* (MC khawX-lawX), basket or hamper made of willow withes, wicker-basket.
3. (med.) ⊙ 拷 *kǎo*, flog, whip.

考　**kǎo**　MC khawX
1. advanced in years, old.
   a. experienced; veteran.
2. deceased father (cf. 妣 *bǐ*, deceased mother).
3. examine; analyze, research; put to the test.
   a. study intently, pore over.
4. complete, accomplish.
5. strike, pound, esp. drum.
   a. ⊙ 拷 *kǎo*, flog, whip, thrash, esp. prisoners.
6. flaw, imperfection in jade or other precious stone.

藁　**kǎo**　MC khawX
1. dried food.
   a. stale; withered, limp.

kào

犒　**kào**　MC khawH
1. feast victorious troops.
   a. requite, compensate, reward; esp. regale with food and wine.

靠　**kào**　MC khawH
1. lean on, rely on, count on; depend(ing) on, based on.
2. lean against, be near to, close to.
   a. put back to back, next to.

kē

唂　**kē**　MC khop
1. (med.) (bn.) ～匝 *kēzā* (MC khop-tsop), twine round about, circle round, enfold.

柯　**kē**　MC ka
1. axe-handle.
2. limb, branch; stem; stalk.
3. schima (*Schima superba*), very tall evergreen hardwood, glossy green lanceolate leaves, with new growth in spring being red-bronze, lavender to white-flowering.

榼　**kē**　MC khap
1. wine-jar, wine-vessel, carafe; water-jar.
2. bin, coffer.
   a. trough, for fodder.

珂　**kē**　MC kha
1. horse's bridle ornament, made of white agate or chalcedony.
   a. (med.) by metonymy, a fine horse.

疴　**kē**　MC khaeH
1. afflict(ion), adversity, illness; infirm(ity), weak(ness).

痾　**kē**　MC 'a
1. itch; annoy(ance), irritate.
   a. constant sore > feud, old grudge.
2. trial; adversity, misadventure; calamity.

瞌　**kē**　MC khap
1. (med.) drowsy, nodding; groggy.

磕　**kē**　MC khap
1. bump, knock against.
2. sgl. or rdup., onom. of slapping, plashing, striking, knocking, smacking, clashing (water against rocks, one object against another, carriage wheels over road, pounding at doors, etc.).

礚　**kē**　MC khap　⊙ 磕 *kē*.

科   kē   MC khwa

1. class(ification), category; section, division; type.
   a. classify; assess; esp. for taxation.
2. article in legal code; ordinance; e.g. ～律 *kēlǜ*, regulations.
   a. judge, pass judgment in accordance with law; adjudicate.
3. protocol; behavioral framework or organizational structure; rules, regulations.
4. (med.) examination, esp. exam-type, usu. appended to exam-name, such as *jinshike* 進士～, *boxuehongcike* 博學鴻辭～.
   a. (med.) sit for exam.
   b. (med.) course of study.
5. (med.) requisition, levy; e.g. ～取 *kēqǔ*, appropriate by command or law.
6. hole, pit; burrow.
   a. hollow; empty; esp. wood.
7. bald.
   a. bare-pated, capless.

稞   kē   MC khwa

1. (med.) sgl. or 青～ *qīngkē*, highland oats, from the plateaus of the far northwest.

窠   kē   MC khwa

1. burrow, nook, niche; den, lair; nest, covert; berth; retreat.
2. (med.) outlined or blank spaces of a seal-carving.
   a. (med.) embroidered motif.

苛   kē   MC ha

1. punctilious; captious, cavil(ling).
   a. (med.) eke out, elaborate (in overfine detail).
2. reproach(ful), irascible.
   a. cruel, mistreat; harass, persecute; pitiless.
      hē   MC xa
1. rail at, denounce, inveigh against; decry.

蝌   kē   MC khwa

1. (med.) (bn.) ～蚪 *kēdǒu* (MC khwa-tuwX), tadpole; also, "tadpole-script," ancient script-form that resembles tadpoles in shape.

軻   kē   MC kha

1. trundle-cart, barrow-cart, small cart placed atop axletree made of two lengths of wood.
2. ⊙ 柯 *kē* 1, axe-handle.
      kě   MC khaX
1. (bn.) 轗～ *kǎnkě*, → 轗 *kǎn*.

頦   kē   MC hoj

1. (med.) lower jaw; chin.

顆   kē   MC khwaX

1. grain, granule; pellet.
   a. measure-word for small round items.
2. clod of earth, lump, clump.

髁   kē   MC khwa

1. thighbone, femur.
2. (bn.) 謑～ *xíkē* (MC hej-khwa), uncaring of what is right, acting however one feels; offensive(ly).

ké

咳   ké   MC khojH

1. ⊙ 欬 *kài*, cough, clear the throat; hawk, hack.
      hái   MC hoj
1. onom. of child's laugh, or of adult laughing with child.
2. ⊙ 孩 *hái*, child.

殼   ké   MC khaewk   → 殼 *qiào*.

kě

可   kě   MC khaX

1. possible, permissible, feasible; allow(able); admit; bear, brook.
2. as auxiliary VB, indicates VB that follows should be construed in the passive; e.g. ～食 *kěshí*, edible; ～食 *kěsì*, can be fed; ～治 *kězhì*, can be brought to order.
   a. ～以 *kěyǐ* VB, can be used to VB, can be the agent to VB, possible to VB; the addition of 以 *yǐ* restores the active force of the VB that follows.
3. interr.: could one . . .? could it be that . . .? might one . . .? how is it that . . .?; e.g. ～能 *kěnéng*, how could one . . .? surely one could not . . .
4. as conjunction: nevertheless, however, on the contrary.
5. (med.) (ADV) probably, most likely.
   a. (med.) just so, exactly so; suitable; exactly then, right then.
      kè   MC khaek
1. (bn.) ～汗 *kèhàn* (MC khaek-hanH), kaghan, trsc. Turk. title for supreme ruler or sovereign.

2. (bn.) 〜敦 *kèdūn* (MC khaek-twon), trsc. Turk. *khatun*, wife, woman < Sog. *khwāten*, queen.

坷　kě　MC khaX

1. (bn.) 坎〜 *kǎnkě*, → 坎 *kǎn*.

嵑　kě　MC khat

1. (bn.) 巆〜 *kěkě*, → 巆 *kě*.

巆　kě　MC khat

1. (bn.) 〜嵑 *kěkě* (MC khat-khat), scarped and sloped (of mountains).

渴　kě　MC khat

1. thirst(y).
    a. thirst for, crave, avid for.
2. (med.) permeable.

    jié　MC gjet

1. dried up (water), parched; run dry.
2. end(ing), close, finish; complete(ly), utterly.

kè

厺　kè　MC khap

1. grotto, hillside cave(rn).

克　kè　MC khok

1. prob. a fusion of 可得 *kědé*, "can effect …"; capable of, able to, liable to; carry off, bring about, achieve.
2. vanquish, subdue, overcome; subordinate, bring to heel.
3. agree upon, fix, set (a date).

刻　kè　MC khok

1. carve, engrave, incise.
    a. hone, sharpen.
2. notch, graduated mark on timekeeping device (sundial, clepsydra), indicating the hundredth part of a day, 14.4 minutes.
    a. stipulate, fix, set (a time).
3. cutting, piercing; caustic.
    a. cruel; severe; flinty; e.g. 〜薄 *kèbó*, treat with severe disapproval.
4. constrain, restrain; pare down.
    a. fastidious, finicky, fussy.

剋　kè　MC khok

1. ⊙ 克 *kè* 1, able to, capable of, liable to; carry off, bring about, achieve; 2, vanquish, subdue, overcome; subordinate; 3, agree upon, fix, set (a date); 刻 *kè* 1, carve, incise; 3, cutting, cruel.

勊　kè　MC khok　⊙ 剋 *kè*.

咯　kè　MC khaek　⊙ 喀 *kè*.

喀　kè　MC khaek

1. cough up, vomit.
    a. spit blood, cough up blood.

堁　kè　MC khwaH

1. dust.
2. earth-mound, hump; knob; swell.

客　kè　MC khaek

1. guest, visitor.
    a. treat with respect, as due a guest.
    b. occupy honored position vis-à-vis one's host.
    c. (med.) interlocutor at a session of "pure conversation" (*qingtan* 清談).
2. retainer, client, recognizing and submitting to another's authority; esp. in feudal relationship with one's lord.
3. stranger, outsider; not native to the place visited; e.g. 〜舍 *kèshè*, 〜店 *kèdiàn*, inn, lodging for strangers (privately owned); 〜星 *kèxīng*, stranger star, i.e. nova; sometimes, comet.
    a. royal or aristocratic descendant from a different dynasty.
4. farmer, peasant.

尅　kè　MC khok　⊙ 剋 *kè*.

愙　kè　MC khak

1. respect(ful); circumspect, scrupulous.

溘　kè　MC khop

1. sudden(ly); unexpected(ly), at unawares.
2. (med.) lean against; close by, close to.
3. waves, breakers.
4. rdup., onom. of waves sloshing and slapping, suck and swash; also, shiveringly frigid, bitterly biting.

帤　kè　MC khaek　⊙ 喀 *kè*.

課　kè　MC khwaH

1. examination, test on set topic.
    a. examination topic, subject for study.
2. (med.) discharge, fulfill, carry out (task).
3. (med.) impost or levy, such as tax or corvée.
4. (med.) to divine by means of plant-stalks.

kěn

墾　**kěn**　MC khonX
1. clear or break new land.
   a. till; delve; work the land, labor.
2. break up; split, sunder; damage.

懇　**kěn**　MC khonX
1. earnest, sincere; heart-felt, deep-felt.
   a. determined; assiduous.
2. entreat(y), implore.

肎　**kěn**　MC khongX　⊙ 肯 *kěn*.

肯　**kěn**　MC khongX
1. willing(ly), consent to, assent to, accepting(ly).
   a. admit, acknowledge.
   b. able to, capable of.
2. (med.) interr: is it possible that . . .? could it be . . .?
3. tendon; ligament.
4. (med.) able to, manage to.

齦　**kěn**　MC khonX　→ 齦 *yín*.

kēng

坑　**kēng**　MC khaeng
1. ditch, trench; ravine, corrie.
   a. (med.) mine; pit.
2. bury alive.
   kàng　MC khangH
1. (med.) kang-bed, heatable brick platform for sleeping.

硜　**kēng**　MC kheang
1. onom. of stone being struck: "khong!"
2. rdup., rigid and obstinate, stupidly stubborn, set in one's ways.

硁　**kēng**　MC kheang　⊙ 硜 *kēng*.

誙　**kēng**　MC kheang
1. rdup., make a mad dash for, proceed instinctively, act unthinkingly.

鏗　**kēng**　MC kheang
1. onom. of sounding bell ("khahng!"), of tinkling pendants ("kling!"), of plucked zither strings ("khunng").

a. (bn.) ～鍧 *kēnghōng* (MC kheang-xweang), onom. of clanging and crashing of bells; (bn.) ～鏘 *kēngqiāng* (MC kheang-tshjang), onom. of sound of musical instruments.

阬　**kēng**　MC khaeng
1. ⊙ 坑 *kēng* 1, ditch, trench; ravine, corrie; 2, bury alive.
   kàng　MC khangH
1. (bn.) ～衡 *kànghéng* (MC khangH-haeng), tilt toward and tangle with one another (trees), stand one's ground, resist and withstand.
   gāng　MC kang
1. ⊙ 岡 *gāng*, ridge of a hill.

kōng

悾　**kōng**　MC khuwng
1. (bn.) ～侗 *kōngtóng* (MC khuwng-duwng), dunderhead, dunderpate; inane and idiotic, emptyheaded.
   kǒng　MC khuwngX
1. (bn.) ～傯 *kǒngzǒng* (MC khuwngX-tsuwngX), overcome with anguish, care-laden and concerned, deeply disquieted, hard-pressed; also, multitude, multiplicity, a whole host of.

崆　**kōng**　MC khuwng
1. (bn.) ～峒 *kōngtóng* (MC khuwng-duwng), cavernous void, name of mountain in far west where Yellow Emperor was said to have visited the sage Guangchengzi 廣成子; (Dao.) term for a mountain of transcendents; also, central realm of space below the Pole-star and Dipper > correlated with Luoyang on earth, hence sometimes ref. to it.
   a. (bn.) ～嶸 *kōngyáng* (MC khuwng-ngaewng), cragged and crannied, crested and caverned.

悾　**kōng**　MC khuwng
1. rdup. or (bn.) ～款 *kōngkuǎn* (MC khuwng-khwanX), innocent and simple-hearted, naïve, artless.

空　**kōng**　MC khuwng
1. empty, void; vacant, unoccupied.
   a. hiatus, blank; gap.
   b. uninhabited area, wilderness; e.g. ～閑 *kōngxián*, wasteland, desert.

2. space; the sky, the air; e.g. 碧～ *bìkōng*, the cyan void, elegant variation for 青天 *qīngtiān*, blue sky; (Dao.) 太～ *tàikōng*, Grand Emptiness, locus of Dao. stellar mansions.

　　a. (bn.) ～同 or ～洞 *kōngtóng* (MC khuwng-duwng), the hollow (of) space, hollow and cavernous.

3. hollow; insubstantial, immaterial; e.g. (Budd.) trns. of Skt. *śūnya*, *śūnyatā*, the essential insubstantiality and illusoriness of all phenomena; ～無 *kōngwú*, emptiness and nothingness.

　　a. with nothing added, just as one purely is.

4. vapid(ly), in vain, to no avail, pointless(ly).

5. (med.) (ADV) do no more than VB, to VB and nothing else; e.g. ～飲 *kōngyǐn*, just drink; drink it straight.

　　a. (med.) sgl. or ～自 *kōngzì*, personally, by oneself; alone.

　　b. (med.) simple, plain, with nothing added; e.g. ～飯 *kōngfàn*, a plain meal.

6. transparent, sheer (of water).

　　kòng　MC khuwngH

1. empty out; deprive(d of), devoid of OBJ.

箜　kōng　MC khuwng

1. (bn.) ～篌 *kōnghóu* (MC khuwng-huw), in Han texts the term usu. refers to a kind of zithern (*se* 瑟); in med. times, harp, a small vertical chordophone held in lap and played with both hands, of Central Asian origin; cog. Uighur *qunqqau*.

kǒng

孔　kǒng　MC khuwngX

1. small hole, perforation, thirl; opening, aperture; e.g. ～竅 *kǒngqiào*, bodily orifices (nostrils, ear-holes, etc.); also, the heart; ～穴 *kǒngxué*, cave(rn).

2. penetrate, perforate; go through; pervade.

　　a. communicate with; affect; comprehend.

3. large; encompassing; spacious; e.g. ～道 *kǒngdào*, broad road, thoroughfare; also, the Way of Confucius (see 5); ～德 *kǒngdé*, all-pervading Potency, vastly reaching Inner Power.

　　a. very much, considerable, a great deal of; e.g. ～陽 *kǒngyáng*, much sunlight.

4. sgl. or (bn.) ～雀 *kǒngquè* (MC khuwngX-tsjak), peacock; e.g. ～翠 *kǒngcuì*, peacock and kingfisher (feathers).

5. honorific appelation of Confucius, Kongzi ～子 *kǒngzi*; e.g. ～門 *kǒngmén*, school of—or disciple(s) of—Confucius; ～墨 *kǒngmò*, Confucius and Mozi.

　　a. surname (post-Confucius).

恐　kǒng　MC khjowngX

1. fear(ful), afraid.

2. perhaps, probably; it may be that . . .; I think that . . .

kòng

控　kòng　MC khuwngH

1. draw a bow; draw in, esp. rein in, draw up the reins.

2. control; master, dominate, command; take the lead.

3. make a complaint against, accuse; denounce.

4. throw; throw down, throw off.

　　qiāng　MC khaewng

1. strike, hit.

鞚　kòng　MC khuwngH

1. a bridle.

　　a. by metonymy, a horse.

kōu

弸　kōu　MC khuw

1. bow-notch, notch at either end of a bow in which the bowstring is attached.

2. (med.) ring, circlet, bracelet.

摳　kōu　MC khuw

1. lift, raise, esp. the edge or hem of a robe.

2. throw away, throw off; pitch.

N.B. This graph does not carry the meaning "dig out, scrape out" until Ming times.

芤　kōu　MC khuw

1. scallion, green onion (*Allium fistulosum*).

2. (med.) ref. medically to certain kind of pulse that feels hollow within but supple without, like a scallion.

kǒu

口　kǒu　MC khuwX

1. mouth, of person or animal.

a. mouthful; (to) taste; flavor; savor.
b. to mouth, to speak; oral; speaking ability, glib(ness).
2. an opening (of door, cave, jar, etc.); orifice, aperture.
a. place from which one may enter or exit a mountain or river.
b. gap or opening in a mountain, mountain-pass.
3. measure-word or euph. for a person: "a mouth," esp. with regard to group counts; also, an individual as distinct from group or something belonging to an individual; e.g. 〜分田 *kǒufēntián*, personal-share land.
4. edge of a sword-blade or knife-blade.

kòu

叩　**kòu**　MC khuwH
1. strike, knock against; e.g. 〜門 *kòumén*, knock on a gate; (Dao.) 〜齒 *kǒuchǐ*, gnash or clack the teeth together, action preparatory to meditation or visualization by which one calls spirits to alert.
a. supplicate, implore < 〜頭 *kòutóu*, strike one's forehead on the ground in submission or supplication, kowtow.
2. examine thoroughly; interrogate, inquire into.
3. to grab, take hold of; ⊙ 扣 *kòu* 1.
4. 〜頭蟲 *kòutóuchóng*, "kowtow-bug," click-beetle, elater-beetle (*Elateridae*, various species).

寇　**kòu**　MC khuwH
1. maraud(er), pillage(r), plunder(er); despoil(er); brigand.
a. border-raid(er), encroach across border.

怐　**kòu**　MC khuwH
1. (bn.) 〜愁 *kòumào* (MC khuwH-muwH), blocked and bitter at heart, failed and foolish, gulled and gudgeoned, flounder foolishly.

扣　**kòu**　MC khuwH
1. grab, take hold of; hold onto; esp. horse's head, in order to halt its advance.
2. strike, knock against; ⊙ 叩 *kòu* 1.

蔻　**kòu**　MC xuwH
1. (bn.) 豆〜 or 荳〜 *dòukòu*, → 豆 or 荳 *dòu*.

釦　**kòu**　MC khuwX
1. gild the lip or edge of a vessel; edge an item with jade.
2. (med.) button, knob.
3. ⊙ 叩 *kòu* 1, strike, knock against.

鷇　**kòu**　MC khuwH
1. nestling, baby bird awaiting mother to bring it food; fledgling.

kū

刳　**kū**　MC khu
1. cut open; esp. gut, disembowel.
a. slaughter, esp. for sacrifice.
2. hollow out, scrape clean; scoop out, dig out, excavate.

哭　**kū**　MC khuwk
1. weep, cry, sob.
2. keen, lament, bemoan the deceased.

堀　**kū**　MC khwot
1. ⊙ 窟 *kū*, cavern, grotto; den.
2. scoop up or out.

枯　**kū**　MC khu
1. deadwood; withered, dried up.
a. decayed, deteriorated; hardened; worn.
2. careworn, flagging; haggard.

矻　**kū**　MC khwot
1. rdup., toil untiringly, firmly focused on the task at hand; drudge away at, persist and persevere.

窟　**kū**　MC khwot
1. cavern, grotto; den.
a. storage cave, for valuable items.

kǔ

楛　**kǔ**　MC huX　→ 楛 *hù*.

苦　**kǔ**　MC khuX
1. bitter(-tasting); e.g. 〜酒 *kǔjiǔ*, wine vinegar.
2. anguish(ed), wretched, miserable; distress(ed); troubled; suffer(ing); e.g. (Budd.)

〜諦 *kǔdì*, the Truth of suffering, 1st of 4 Noble Truths (life is suffering); (Budd.) 〜海 *kǔhǎi*, Sea of Misery, i.e. life.

    a. sore(ly), pain(ed).

3. take pains to (do X); worry about.

    a. strict(ness), stringent; exacting; e.g. (Budd.) 〜行 *kǔxíng*, exacting practices, askesis.

4. (med.) persistent(ly), incessant(ly); frequently, e.g. 〜雨 *kǔyǔ*, steady, continuous rain.

5. sgl. or 〜菜 *kǔcài*, sow-thistle (*Sonchus oleraceus*); 〜竹 *kǔzhú*, "bitter bamboo," amarus bamboo (*Pleioblastus amarus*), shoots bitter and inedible, new culms powdery white and eventually yellow-green; 〜參 *kǔshēn*, "bitter-root" (*Sophora flavescens*), low evergreen shrub with paired pinnate leaves, root used medicinally; 〜樹 *kǔshù*, Chinese ash-tree (*Fraxinus rhynchophylla*), medium-sized, late to leaf in spring and early to color in autumn.

    gǔ　MC kuX

1. ⊙ 鹽 *gǔ* 1 raw salt; 2, crude, shoddy.

kù

譽　kù　MC khowk

1. name of 3rd of the 5 legendary rulers of prehistoric times; also ref. as Gaoxin shi 高辛氏.

庫　kù　MC khuH

1. armory, arsenal, for weapons and war-chariots.

2. storehouse, repository for any collection of items; treasury, archive, granary.

硞　kù　MC khowk

1. (med.) (bn.) 碌〜 *lùkù*, → 碌 *lù*.

    kè　MC kheak

1. (med.) (bn.) 礐〜 *quèkè*, → 礐 *què*.

綺　kù　MC khuH　⊙ 袴 *kù*.

袴　kù　MC khuH

1. trousers, pants, breeches.

    kuà　MC khwaeH

1. ⊙ 胯 *kuà*, crotch, between the legs.

酷　kù　MC khowk

1. full-bodied, heavy (of alcohol); pungent, intense (flavor).

    a. (med.) intensely, acutely; vehemently, desperately.

2. truculent, brutal; ruthless, cruel.

3. (med.) heavy-laden; pained; aggrieved.

kuā

夸　kuā　MC khwae

1. excessive, overdo(ne); exaggerate(d).

2. flaunt, show off; boast(ful).

3. ⊙ 姱 *kuā*, charming, fetching, well-favored.

姱　kuā　MC khwae

1. charming, fetching; pretty.

    a. well-favored, seemly.

誇　kuā　MC khwae

1. flaunt, vaunt, show off.

    a. boast(ful), brag; thrasonical.

2. laud, extol, magnify; hail; applaud.

3. ⊙ 姱 *kuā*, charming, fetching, well-favored.

kuà

胯　kuà　MC khwaeH

1. between the legs or thighs; crotch, groin.

2. hip-bone.

3. (med.) jade-studs as ornamentation on leather belt.

跨　kuà　MC khwaeH

1. straddle, bestride.

    a. overstep; go beyond, exceed; surpass.

2. sit astride, ride.

3. occupy, hold; dominate.

4. ⊙ 胯 *kuā*, crotch, groin, between the legs.

kuǎi

䕯　kuǎi　MC khweajH

1. bulrush, woolgrass (*Scirpus eriophorum*).

2. a surname.

kuài

儈　kuài　MC kwajH

1. middleman, broker (for trade).

噲　kuài　MC khwaejH

1. snout, beak, bill, of animal.

2. rdup., lightsome and bright, broadly lit.

3. ⊙ 快 *kuài* 1, pleasing, pleasant; cheerful.

塊   **kuài**   MC khwojH

1. clod of earth, lump, clump of soil, glebe; e.g. 大～ *dàkuài*, "greatest ball-of-earth," i.e. the world, nature.
2. sgl. or ～然 *kuàirán*, alone, independent(ly), on one's own.

快   **kuài**   MC khwaejH

1. please(d), pleasant; cheerful.
   a. untroubled, carefree; comfortable, easeful.
2. (med.) fast, speedy; prompt; with alacrity.
   a. (med.) quick at, good at.
3. (med.) sharp, keen.
   a. (med.) incisive, decisive.

膾   **kuài**   MC kwajH

1. ensign, standard, esp. one raised for battle.
2. (med.) catapult, ballista.

澮   **kuài**   MC kwajH

1. irrigation ditch between fields.
   a. channel, gully.

   huá   MC hweat

1. confluence of 2 streams, flow together; intermingle.

膾   **kuài**   MC kwajH

1. fish or meat cut in thin slices, minced (cf. 軒 *xiàn* [*xuān*], in large slices; 胾 *zì*, in large chunks).
   a. to slice, mince.

鱠   **kuài**   MC kwajH

1. mince(d) or dice(d) fish (cf. 膾 *kuài*, mincemeat, incl. minced fish).

kuān

寛   **kuān**   MC khwan

1. broad, wide; spacious, ample.
   a. extend, stretch out.
2. let go, release, loose(n); relieve; e.g. ～泰 *kuāntài*, relieved, free from worry.
3. large-minded; magnanimous, generous; liberal.
   a. tolerant, tolerate; make allowance(s) for, excuse, forgive.

髖   **kuān**   MC khwan

1. hipbone.
   a. haunch(es).

kuǎn

款   **kuǎn**   MC khwanX

1. earnest, sincere; devoted, faithful.
2. knock, rap, esp. at door.
   a. arrive at, reach (destination).
3. (med.) treat cordially, entertain; e.g. 情～ *qíngkuǎn*, liaison (sexual).
4. (med.) slow(ly), without haste, deliberate(ly); e.g. ～段馬 *kuǎnduànmǎ*, a slow-gaited horse.
5. rdup., earnest and ardent, staunch and sincere; (med.) also, measured and gradual, unhurried, slow-going.
6. inscription carved in intaglio; esp. in cmpd. ～識 *kuǎnzhì*, inscriptions carved in intaglio and relief.
7. ⊙ 窾 *kuǎn* 1, gap, vent; hole, opening.

窾   **kuǎn**   MC khwanX

1. gap, fissure, vent; hole, opening; orifice.
   a. hollow, empty; concave.
2. hollow out, scrape out.

kuāng

劻   **kuāng**   MC khjwang

1. (med.) (bn.) ～勷 *kuāngráng* (MC khjwang-nyang), hurried and hasty; also, uneasy and anxious.

匡   **kuāng**   MC khjwang

1. straighten; rectify, correct.
   a. return to order, redress.
2. assist, aid; succor; save.
3. eye-socket, ⊙ 眶 *kuàng*.
   a. surround, envelop, encircle.
4. ⊙ 枉 *wǎng*, bent, crooked; 恇 *kuāng*, scared, frightened; 筐 *kuāng*, square basket.

恇   **kuāng**   MC khjwang

1. scared, frightened; alarmed, shaken.
   a. timid, faint-hearted; nervous, apprehensive.

筐   **kuāng**   MC khjwang

1. square bamboo-basket; square canister; pannier (cf. 筥 *jǔ*, round-shaped same).
   a. square-shaped, square-framed.
2. pack in, stuff into, fill.

誆   **kuāng**   MC gjwangH

1. lie, make up, prevaricate; deceive, delude, distort; falsify, defraud.
   a. mendacious; deceitful; untrustworthy.

kuáng

狂 **kuáng MC gjwang**
1. rabid; mad, crazy; daft; deranged, unbalanced.
    a. manic, mania(cal); frantic, frenzied; mad-cap.
    b. uncontrollable, impractical; reckless, rash.
    c. fervent, over-eager, urgent.
2. enraged, raging, infuriated.
    a. wild, violent.
3. irregular; unnatural.
4. fatuous; swaggering, self-important; dogmatic.

誑 **kuáng MC kjwangH**
1. falsehood, lie; mendacity, falsify; deceive, feign.
2. unbalanced, unsteady, off-kilter.

kuǎng

懭 **kuǎng MC khwangX**
1. (bn.) 〜悢 *kuǎnglǎng* (MC khwangX-langX), dissatisfied and disappointed, dejected and discontent, despairing and past hope.

kuàng

壙 **kuàng MC khwangH**
1. underground tunnel or passageway.
    a. access tunnel to tomb; by metonymy, tomb-vault, grave-pit.
    b. adit, to mine; by metonymy, the mine itself.
2. uncultivated land, wilds; barrens.
    a. barren; neglected.
3. far off, far-stretching (space).
    a. long ago, long distant (time).
    b. (bn.) 〜埌 *kuànglàng* (MC khwangH-langH), broad and boundless, open and unobstructed.

曠 **kuàng MC khwangH**
1. brilliant; clear; bright; vivid.
2. set off, set apart.
    a. far-ranging, far-reaching, stretch(ed) out; spacious(ness); broad scope, broad extent; extended time.
    b. (bn.) 〜蕩 *kuàngdàng* (MC khwangH-dangX), ranging far and free.
3. unconfined, unrestricted, untrammeled.
    a. expansive; far-sighted, clear-sighted.
4. barren, bleak; waste(d); wasteland, desert.

5. neglect(ed); be of no use.
    a. (med.) in vain, futile(ly).

況 **kuàng MC xjwangH**
1. compare with; be equal to, equal with.
2. even more; e.g. 〜厚之 *kuànghòu zhī*, treat him even more lavishly, reward even more.
    a. marker of rhetorical comparison: how much more (or less) is it so that . . .; even more (or less) is it that . . .; X, let alone Y; e.g. 困獸猶鬬，〜國相乎 *kùnshòu yóu dòu, kuàng guóxiàng hū*, if a beast when trapped will still fight, how much more should a minister of state?
3. (med.) situation, condition(s).

爌 **kuàng MC khwangH**
1. (bn.) 〜熀 *kuànghuǎng* (MC khwangH-xwangX), broad and bright, amply illumined.
        huǎng MC xwangX
1. radiant, brilliant; glow(ing).

眶 **kuàng MC khjwang**
1. eye-socket.

礦 **kuàng MC kwaengX**
1. mineral ore.
    a. coarse, unrefined; e.g. (bn.) 頑〜 *wánkuàng*, crude and coarse.
2. stone-wrought needle for medical use.

絖 **kuàng MC khwangH** ⊙ 纊 *kuàng*.

纊 **kuàng MC khwangH**
1. floss-silk, high-gloss silk.
    a. silk wadding.

貺 **kuàng MC xjwangH**
1. bestow(al), confer; present; reward; gift.

鑛 **kuàng MC kwangH** ⊙ 礦 *kuàng*.

kuī

刲 **kuī MC khwej**
1. slice open or off; cut open.
    a. slaughter, butcher (animal); kill by bleeding.
2. annex (territory); expropriate.

歸 **kuī MC khwij**
1. tall and prominent; salient, standing out, protruding upward.

悝 kuī MC khwoj

1. ridicule, mock, laugh at.
   a. banter, twit.

窺 kuī MC khjwie

1. look into or out of a small opening.
   a. peer; descry; glimpse, steal a look at.
   b. spy upon, keep an eye out for; pry into.
2. cast one's eyes toward, in anticipation or hope of attainment.

kuĭ MC khjwieX

1. one step, half of a "pace" (*bu* 步), ⊙ 跬 *kuĭ*.

莙 kuī MC khwej

1. Chinese raspberry (*Rubus chingii*); syn. 覆盆子 *fùpénzi*.

藱 kuī MC khwij

1. curly mallow, vegetable mallow (*Malva crispa*), syn. 葵 *kuí*.

虧 kuī MC khjwe

1. diminish; deficient; reduce(d); abate.
   a. lack, be missing; wane (of moon); fail(ure).
2. damage; loss.
3. (med.) fortunate(ly), luck(il)y.

闚 kuī MC khjwie

1. ⊙ 窺 *kuī* 1, look into or out of small opening; peer, descry, catch a glimpse of, steal a look at, spy upon, search out.

kuí

夔 kuí MC gwij

1. mythological creature, variously described but usu. with distinguishing feature of only one leg, a unipede.
   a. elemental spirit or imp of mountain grove.
2. rdup., reverent and respectful, be in awe of and pay homage to.
3. name of reputed music-master during time of sage-king Yao 堯.

奎 kuí MC khwej

1. crotch; space between thighs or legs.
   a. straddle, spraddle.
   b. stride, take long steps.
2. "Strider," one of the 28 lunar lodgings, comprised of 9 stars in Andromeda and 7 in Pisces describing the sole of a shoe, in the western quadrant (*baihu* 白虎) of the sky.

戣 kuí MC gwij

1. ancient weapon, dagger-lance, pike-dagger.

揆 kuí MC gjwijX

1. measure, gauge; to orient.
   a. measurement, standard, principle; orientation.
2. infer; surmise, conjecture.
3. dab hand; adept at; e.g. 不～ *bùkuí*, inept.
   a. take in hand, manage, take charge of.
   b. put in order; govern; (med.) esp. ref. to actions of chief minister or grand councilor (*zaixiang* 宰相).

睽 kuí MC khwej ⊙ 暌 *kuí*.

暌 kuí MC khwej

1. opposed, contrary; conflict(ing); discord(ant).
   a. diverge(nt), variant; discrepant; separate, differ(ent).
   b. "contrary," name of 38th hexagram of the *Yijing*.
2. rdup. or (bn.) ～睢 *kuíhuī* (MC khwej-xjwie), glare and glower, fix a stare upon.

葵 kuí MC gjwij

1. curled mallow, vegetable mallow (*Malva crispa*).
   a. 蜀～ *shǔkuí*, "Shu mallow," hollyhock (*Althaea rosea*); 龍～ *lóngkuí*, "dragon mallow," sunberry, black nightshade (*Solanum nigrum*); 落～ *luòkuí*, vine-spinach, Malabar nightshade (*Basella rubra*); 水～ *shuǐkuí*, "water mallow," water-shield (*Brasenia schreberi*), syn. 蓴菜 *chúncài*.
2. 蒲～ *púkuí*, Chinese fan palm, fountain palm (*Livistona chinensis*).

蹞 kuí MC gwij

1. (bn.) ～跜 *kuíní* (MC gwij-nrij), quivering and trembling, agitated and stirred, shaken and squirming, coiled and wriggling; also, hunkering low.

逵 kuí MC gwij

1. crossroads; convergence, juncture.
   a. thoroughfare, throughway, causeway.

kuí

頄　**kuí**　MC gwij
1. cheekbone, ⊙ 頯 *kuí* 1.

頯　**kuí**　MC gwij
1. cheekbone.
2. plain, simple-looking; clear (of brow), broad (of forehead).

頯　**kuí**　MC gwij　⊙ 逵 *kuí*.

騤　**kuí**　MC gwij
1. rdup., (of horses), stately and strong, advancing awesomely, splendidly striding.
2. (bn.) 〜瞿 *kuíjù* (MC gwij-kjuH), race off in alarm, scatter in surprise, stampede and flee.

魁　**kuí**　MC khwoj
1. ladle, dipper, scoop.
   a. the 4 stars making up the bowl of the Northern Dipper; also, ref. specifically to the 1st star, Dubhe.
2. leader, foremost, chief; principal.
   a. prominent, remarkable; outstanding; imposing.
3. mound, monticule.
       kuài　MC khwojH
1. ⊙ 塊 *kuài* 2, alone, independent(ly), on one's own.

kuǐ

傀　**kuǐ**　MC khwojX　→ 傀 *guī*.

磈　**kuǐ**　MC khwojX
1. (bn.) 〜磊 *kuǐlěi* (MC khwojX-lwojX), uneven and irregular, gnarled and knurled.
       wěi　MC 'jw+jX
1. (bn.) 〜硊 *wěiwěi* (MC 'jw+jX-ngjweX), massively mountainous, perilously peaked.

跬　**kuǐ**　MC khjwieX
1. one step, half of a "pace" (*bu* 步).
   a. a very short distance, or short period of time.

蹞　**kuǐ**　MC khjwieX　⊙ 跬 *kuǐ*.

頍　**kuǐ**　MC khjwieX
1. cleft-band of cap, tied at back of neck.

kuì

匱　**kuì**　MC gwijH
1. be short of, lack; deficient, wanting, inadequate.
2. ⊙ 簣 *kuì*, bamboo basket or hod, for carrying earth.
       guì　MC gwijH
1. cupboard, armoire, cabinet; chest, trunk.

喟　**kuì**　MC khwijH
1. onom. of sighing, "khee-ee"; heave a sigh.

媿　**kuì**　MC kwijH　⊙ 愧 *kuì*.

愧　**kuì**　MC kwijH
1. abashed, ashamed, shamefaced; out of countenance, embarrassed; lose face; self-reproachful; can sometimes take OBJ (cf. 慚 *cán*, which rarely does).

憒　**kuì**　MC kwojH
1. distracted, bewildered, flustered; nonplussed; disconcerted, discomfited; irk(some).

潰　**kuì**　MC hwojH
1. water breaking through a dike or dam.
   a. overflow; overwhelm, smash; overrun, rout; vanquish.
   b. break out, from military encirclement.
   c. in furor, impetuous(ly); passion, rage.
2. break up, scatter, disperse; disband.
3. collapse, fall apart.
4. fester, ulcerate.

簣　**kuì**　MC gwijH
1. bamboo basket, for carrying earth; pannier, hod.

聵　**kuì**　MC ngweajH
1. deaf, from birth.
2. mixed up, fuddled; stupefied, dumfounded.

蕢　**kuì**　MC gwijH
1. straw-basket.
       kuaì　MC khweajH
1. amaranth (*Amaranthus mangostanus*), ⊙ 莧 *xiàn*.

饋　**kuì**　MC gwijH
1. to present food to someone or as sacrifice to spirits.

a. supply with food, provision; maintain, nurture.
b. food, provisions.
2. eat; take sustenance.
3. ⊙ 匱 *kuì* 1, be short of, lack; deficient, wanting; inadequate.

kūn

坤   **kūn   MC khwon**
1. indicative of all images and qualities identified with *yin*: the receptive, quiescent, fecund; latent; latency; feminine; earth; darkness, cold, etc.; ant. 乾 *qián*; e.g. 乾～ *qiánkūn*, potent and latent, generative and receptive, Caelum and Terra.
2. one of the 8 fundamental trigrams underlying the *Yijing*'s 64 hexagrams, made up of 3 broken lines.
a. 2nd of the *Yijing*'s 64 hexagrams; represents supreme *yin*.

崑   **kūn   MC kwon**
1. (bn.) ～崙 *kūnlún* (MC kwon-lwon), name of mythical mountain in far west, usu. associated with Dao. goddess Xiwangmu 西王母; also, of an actual mountain range running along south side of Tarim Basin westward to the Pamirs, so named from Han dynasty on, but most refs. in texts through med. times are to the mythical mountain; (Dao.) also, esoteric name for the head; (med.) also, ref. peoples of Indochina and Indonesia.
a. ～山 *kūnshān*, abb. ref. to Mt. Kunlun; (med.) also, gen. ref. to far-distant mountain.
2. very tall, towering.

輝   **kūn   MC kwon**   ⊙ 褌 *kūn*.

昆   **kūn   MC kwon**
1. elder brother.
2. last in a sequence.
a. posterity, descendants.
3. together, conjoint(ly), collective(ly).
a. group(ed), mass; numerous, many of.
4. ～布 *kūnbù*, sweet tangle (*Ecklonia kurome*), brown kelp.
5. (bn.) ～崙 *kūnlún*, ⊙ 崑崙 *kūnlún*, → 崑 *kūn*.
6. (bn.) ～吾 *kūnwú* (MC kwon-ngu), vulcan stone, adamant; also, official in charge of smelting and founding.

hún   MC hwon
1. (bn.) ～侖 *húnlún* (MC hwon-lwon), integral totality, undifferentiated wholeness, ⊙ 渾淪 *húnlún*.

晜   **kūn   MC kwon**
1. elder brother, ⊙ 昆 *kūn* 1.
2. ～孫 *kūnsūn*, 5th-generation descendant.

焜   **kūn   MC hwon**
1. bright, shining; warm glow.

琨   **kūn   MC kwon**
1. semi-precious stone, perhaps jasper.
2. (bn.) ～珸 *kūnwú*, ⊙ 昆吾 *kūnwú*, → 昆 *kūn*.

褌   **kūn   MC kwon**
1. full-bottomed pants, drawers, breeches.
2. (med.) underpants, loincloth.

髡   **kūn   MC khwon**
1. shave the head.
a. judicial punishment of having head shaved.
b. (med.) bald-pate(d), a Budd. monk.
2. prune branches from a tree.

鯤   **kūn   MC kwon**
1. fabulous fish of gigantic size in the Northern Main 北溟, from opening passage of *Zhuangzi* 莊子; transforms into the enormous → 鵬 *péng*-bird.

鵾   **kūn   MC kwon**
1. ～雞 *kūnjī*, if silent, "kun-fowl," painted stork (*Mycteria leucocephala*), or common white stork (*Ciconia ciconia*); if giving voice, demoiselle crane (*Grus virgo*).
a. ～弦 *kūnxián*, "stork strings," zither or lute strings made from *kun*-fowl sinews.

鶤   **kūn   MC kwon**   ⊙ 鵾 *kūn*.

kǔn

壼   **kǔn   MC khwonX**
1. corridor in palace or passage-way between palaces.
a. by metonymy, the inner palace, esp. women's quarters.

悃　kǔn　MC khwonX
1. sincere; honest, trustworthy.
   a. (bn.) 〜款 *kǔnkuǎn* (MC khwonX-khwanX), true-hearted and trustworthy, devoted and dependable.

捆　kǔn　MC khwonX
1. to baste thread, sew temporarily with long stitches; plait, truss; esp. in making sandals.
2. to hammer so as to make fast or secure.

梱　kǔn　MC khwonX
1. doorpost, gatepost, placed where 2 leaves meet to keep them from swinging back.
   a. by metonymy, door-sill, border between inner and outer.
2. strike, knock, beat against.
   　　kùn　MC khwonH
1. make uniform, equalize.

稇　kǔn　MC khwonX
1. bind or truss up with twine, esp. in sheaves or bundles.

閫　kǔn　MC khwonX
1. threshold, of gate; esp. of city-gate.
2. ⊙壼 *kǔn*, corridor in palace or passage-way between palaces; the inner palace, esp. women's quarters.

kùn

困　kùn　MC khwonH
1. constrain(ed), constrict(ed); bound up; restrict(ed), hem(med) in.
   a. in difficulty, hard-pressed; arduous.
2. exhausting, wearisome, tiresome; trying.
3. in straits, straitened, pinched; in want, poor.
4. "Obstruction," name of 47th hexagram of the *Yijing*.

kuò

廓　kuò　MC khwak
1. vast, extensive, immense; broad; grand(eur); excess(ive).
   a. immeasurable, unlimited; infinite.

2. enlarge; broaden, extend.
   a. open(ed) out, spread out; patent.
3. empty; desert(ed); uncultivated; unpeopled.
4. sweep clear, remove unwanted objects or problems.
5. ⊙郭 *guō* 1, outermost wall of city area, outskirts.

彍　kuò　MC xwak
1. bend or pull a bow.

括　kuò　MC khwat
1. attach, bind; lash together; tie up, wrap up.
2. include, contain; comprise, comprehend; draw together.
3. seek, search, hunt for.
4. arrive, come to.
5. rear tip of arrow, notch of arrow; by synecdoche, arrow; ⊙栝 *kuò* 2.

擴　kuò　MC khwak
1. broaden, widen; expand; extend, spread.
   a. patulent, patulous.

栝　kuò　MC kwat
1. Chinese juniper (*Sabina chinensis*), ⊙檜 *guì*.
2. rear tip of arrow, notch of arrow.
3. binder, for straightening objects (e.g. arrows).
   a. carpenter's square.

闊　kuò　MC khwat
1. far-divided, far-separated (from), far off.
   a. distance oneself from; estrange; ignore.
   b. far from reality, unrealistic; impractical.
2. commodious, capacious, vast, extensive.
   a. broadly spread; loose-fitting.
3. loosen, release; let go.
   a. excuse; exempt from, remit.
4. far back, ages ago.

鞟　kuò　MC khwak　⊙鞹 *kuò*.

鞹　kuò　MC khwak
1. shorn pelt, depilated hide; leather.
2. wrap round or bind up with leather.

髺　kuò　MC kwat
1. bind up the hair, esp. in top-knot

L

lā

拉 lā MC lop
1. break, snap in two, split; fracture, splinter.
2. (med.) drag; tow, haul.

擸 lā MC lop
1. ⊙ 拉 *lā* 1, break, snap.

摺 lā MC lop → 摺 *zhé*.

là

剌 là MC lat
1. perverse, refractory; fractious, contumacious; disagreeable.
2. (med.) rdup., onom. of gusting or lapping wind; (bn.) 撥～ *bōlà*, → 撥 *bō*.

臘 là MC lap
1. 12th-month sacrifice to all ancestors on 8th day of month, preceded by the → 儺 *nuó* exorcism.
2. sgl. or ～月 *làyuè*, All-Hallows month, 12th month.
    a. gen. ref. to end of year.
3. (Budd.) end of the monastic year coinciding with the end of summer retreat in the 6th month; marks the end of year when counting a monk's religious age, i.e. years since taking monastic vows.

菈 là MC lop
1. (med.) (bn.) ～擸 *làlà* (MC lop-lap), burst apart, crack, split open; also, crashing din.

蠟 là MC lap
1. any waxy or greasy effusion from animal, plant, or mineral; cere, cereous.
2. wax, beeswax.
    a. (med.) abb. for ～燭 *làzhú*, wax-candle.
3. ～梅 *làméi*, "wax-mume," wintersweet (*Chimonanthus praecox*), medium to tall deciduous shrub, with scented flowers blooming in winter.
4. maggot.

辣 là MC lat
1. (med.) spicy, peppery; piquant.

鑞 là MC lap
1. (med.) solder; fuse lead and tin.
    a. (med.) pewter.

lái

來 lái MC loj
1. wheat (archaic usage).
2. come, come to, arrive (ant. 往 *wǎng*, go); e.g. ～往 *láiwǎng*, come and go, back and forth; also, contacts or meetings between people; ～去 *láiqù*, arrive and depart, also ref. life and death.
    a. cause to come; summon; bring along.
3. the future, what is coming.
    a. combined with 以 after a specified time or event, indicates from that time or event forward, coming from that time or event to the future, after the specified time; e.g. 漢興以～ *hànxīng yǐlái*, from the restoration of the Han onward.
4. (med.) when following time-period or action X: during, while X; e.g. 夜～ *yèlái*, during the night; 興～ *xīnglái*, when in the mood.
5. (med.) (GP) from Tang times, when following VB indicates continuing action (cf. modern *zhe* 着) or change of status (cf. modern *le* 了).

崍 lái MC loj
1. 邛～ *qiónglái*, name of mountain range in Sichuan.

徠 lái MC loj
1. ⊙ 來 *lái* 2, come, come to; cause to come, bring along, summon.
        lài MC lojH
1. ⊙ 勑 *lài*, encourage; comfort, console.

萊 lái MC loj
1. goosefoot, melde (*Chenopodium album*), a weed with stalked, opposite leaves; syn. 藜 *lí*.
2. gen. term for weeds; e.g. 蒿～ *hāolái*, wormwood and weeds.
    a. weed-choked, infested with weeds.
    b. to weed, clear out; eradicate.
3. land beyond the outskirts of a city that has gone uncultivated, weedland.

騋　lái　MC loj

1. a horse more than 7 *chi* 尺 ("feet") tall, a stately horse.

lài

勑　lài　MC lojH

1. encourage; comfort, console.

　　chì　MC trhik

1. ⊙ 敕 *chì* 1, rectify, organize; 2, advice, counsel, recommendation; (med.) imperial decree.

瀨　lài　MC lajH

1. riffle(s); brisk, chattering flow over sandbank or stones.
　　a. shallows.
　　b. rapids.

癩　lài　MC lajH

1. leprosy; leprous, scabrous.

睞　lài　MC lojH

1. squint; skew; peer at.
2. look sideways or askance at, out of the corner of one's eye.

籟　lài　MC lajH

1. sounding-pipes.
　　a. pipings, sounds emitted from sounding-pipes (whether man-made or natural).

藾　lài　MC lajH

1. pearly everlasting (*Anaphalis sinica*), a small evergreen perennial shrub with silvery-gray leaves, many-petaled flowers, and fruits that are achenes; syn. 萩 *qiū*.
2. to shade, cover, protect.

賚　lài　MC lojH

1. bestow on, grant, confer.
　　a. (med.) give, in general.

賴　lài　MC lajH

1. profit, benefit, take advantage of.
　　a. accruing to the good, beneficial(ly), fortunately, luckily.
2. rely on, depend on.
　　a. put one's trust or confidence in; dependable; e.g. 無～ *wúlài*, not to be trusted, undependable, without certainty.
　　b. lay a task or responsibility on.
3. (med.) go back on one's word, renege.

lán

棽　lán　MC lom

1. covet(ous), greed(y), avaricious, cupidinous; insatiable.
　　a. rdup., greedy and grasping.
　　b. (med.) impatient, restive, yearning for; e.g. ～尾 *lánwěi*, "restive tail," the last guest to drink when wine is passed round at a banquet.

嵐　lán　MC lom

1. aura of the hilltops; mountain fog or vapor; windgap-mist.
　　a. mist of mountain grove.
2. gale, gust.

惏　lán　MC lom

1. ⊙ 棽 *lán*, covet(ous), greedy; insatiable.
　　lín　MC lim

1. (bn.) ～悢 *línlì* (MC lim-lejH), joyless and mournful, doleful and downcast, woebegone.

攔　lán　MC lan

1. (med.) bar, obstruct; block off, cut off.

斕　lán　MC lean

1. (med.) (bn.) ～斑 (MC lean-paen) or ～編 *lánbān* (MC lean-pean), or 編～ *bānlán*, vividly various, diversely dazzling.

欄　lán　MC lan

1. pen for domestic animals.
　　a. stable, corral (for horses).
2. sgl. or (bn.) ～杆 *lán'gān* (MC lan-kan), railing, balustrade, barrier; also, criss-cross(ed), interlace(d); also, crack and cleave.

瀾　lán　MC lan

1. rolling or welling waves; swells, billows, breakers.
　　a. surge, swell; undulate; e.g. (bn.) ～汗 *lánhàn* (MC lan-hanH), swell and surge, swash and crash.
　　b. (med.) rdup., welling tears, waves of tears.
　　làn　MC lanH

1. (bn.) ～漫 *lànmàn* (MC lanH-manH), flinging oneself around freely, with casual unconcern, willfully wanton; also, elated and exultant, at the height of happiness; also, glossily gleaming, glisteningly aglow; also, (med.) spreading into space, far-flung.

籃   **lán**   MC lam
1. (med.) wicker basket or hamper.
2. (med.) sgl. or cmpd. ～輿 *lányú*, wicker or bamboo sedan-chair.

籣   **lán**   MC lan   ⊙ 韊 *lán*.

藍   **lán**   MC lam
1. indigo (*Polygonum tinctorium*), the leaves of which are a source of blue dye; the dye-color produced from the plant was usu. ref. to as *qing* 青.
   a. indigo-blue, as color, relatively rarely used through med. times.
   b. 紅～ *hónglán*, safflower (*Carthamus tinctorius*).
2. (bn.) ～縷 *lánlǚ* (MC lam-ljuX), ragged and tattered, ⊙ 襤褸 *lánlǚ*.
3. ⊙ 籃 *lán*, esp. as abb. of 籃輿 *lányú*, wicker or bamboo sedan-chair.

蘭   **lán**   MC lan
1. thoroughwort, agrimony, eupatory, eupatorium (*Eupatorium japonicum, Eupatorium fortunei*), flowers white or very light purple; a genus of the aster family that includes chrysanthemums and daisies; (lit.) often symbolic of purity of character, redolent integrity.
   a. ～若 *lánruò*, cmpd. ref. to *láncǎo* ～草, thoroughwort, and *dùruò* 杜若, pollia.
2. ～花 *lánhuā*, "superior sword orchid" (*Cymbidium ensifolium*). N.B. This meaning for *lán* not attested until the Song period; for pre-Song texts, *lán* is invariably *Eupatorium*, not "orchid."
3. 木～ *mùlán*, laurel magnolia, lily tree (*Magnolia denudata*); 紫玉～ *zǐyùlán*, lily magnolia (*Magnolia liliflora*), syn. 辛夷 *xīnyí*; 黃～ *huánglán*, champak (*Magnolia champaca*), syn. 蕾蔔 *zhánbó*, → 蕾 *zhán*.
4. (Budd.) ～若 *lánrě*, abb. of 阿～若 *ālánrě* (MC 'a-lan-nyaeX), trsc. of Skt. *araṇya*, quiet refuge, hermitage; ～闍 *lánshé* (MC lan-dzyae), abb. trsc. Skt. *rañjanī*, "good cheer," Budd. greeting.
5. (bn.) ～單 *lándān* (MC lan-tan), fatigued, tired; worn and weary.
6. ⊙ 闌 *lán* weapon rack; 欄 *lán* palisade; balustrade.

襤   **lán**   MC lam
1. unhemmed garments.
2. (bn.) ～褸 or ～縷 *lánlǚ* (MC lam-ljuX), ragged and tattered, shabby and ragged, scrappy and tattered.

襴   **lán**   MC lan
1. (med.) sgl. or cmpd. ～衫 *lánshān*, long, flowing robe that trails and billows.

讕   **lán**   MC lan
1. repudiate, deny.
   a. renege on a promise.
2. accuse falsely, bear false witness, traduce; defame, slander.

闌   **lán**   MC lan
1. bar(rier), railing, balustrade; ⊙ 欄 *lán* 2.
   a. bar, obstruct; separate, divide.
   b. (bn.) ～干 *lán'gān* (MC lan-kan), railing, balustrade; also, criss-cross(ed), interlaced; also, crack and cleave; ⊙ 欄杆 *lán'gān*.
2. abate, wane; wear away; finish, end; e.g. 星～ *xīng lán*, the stars faded; 夜～ *yè lán*, the night wore on.
3. unauthorized, unsanctioned, esp. of entering and exiting restricted places.
4. (med.) ～單 *lándān* (MC lan-tan), weary and worn-out, exhausted.

韊   **lán**   MC lan
1. quiver, for arrows.

lǎn

嬾   **lǎn**   MC lanX
1. (med.) ⊙ 懶 *lǎn*.

懶   **lǎn**   MC lanX
1. (med.) sloth(ful), lethargic; torpid; inactive, passive.
   a. (med.) otiose; unambitious; careless, shiftless.

㩜   **lǎn**   MC lamX
1. ⊙ 攬 *lǎn* 1, grasp, clasp; hold.
2. ～涕 *lǎntì*, wipe dry one's tears.

攬   **lǎn**   MC lamX
1. grasp, clasp; hold.
   a. take charge of, control.
2. gather in, gather up; cull.
3. adopt, take up.

欖   **lǎn**   MC lamX
1. (med.) (bn.) 橄～ *gǎnlǎn*, → 橄 *gǎn*.

纜   **lǎn**   MC lamH
1. (med.) hawser, heavy cable for mooring or towing a boat.

覽　lǎn　MC lamX

1. look broadly at, canvass; scan; vista.
   a. look over; peruse.
2. recognize, appreciate.
3. adopt, take up; ⊙ 攬 *lǎn* 3.

làn

濫　làn　MC lamH

1. brim over, overflow; flood; e.g. ～觴 *lànshāng*, overflow a goblet, ref. the insignificant source of a river, esp. the Yellow River; > imperceptible beginning, trifling onset.
   a. drift away; spread out.
2. excessive(ly), extravagant(ly); overfull; immoderate.
   a. (med.) abuse; presume (wrongly) to do X.

燷　làn　MC lamH

1. (bn.) ～焱 *lànyàn* (MC lamH-yemH), roaring fire, flames flaring.

爛　làn　MC lanH

1. soften by boiling or stewing.
2. disintegrate(d), deteriorate; fall apart; (un-) loose(ned), fray(ed).
   a. decompose(d), rotten, overripe; molder.
3. burn up, burn through.
4. glisten(ing), scintillant, phosphorescent; glittering, sparkling; rdup., flashing and flaring.
5. (bn.) ～漫 *lànmàn* (MC lanH-manH), free and unfettered, in total abandon; also, wholly and fully, extravagantly; also, fresh and bright, vividly various, fully displayed or flaunted.

láng

筤　láng　MC lang

1. (bn.) 康～ *kāngláng*, → 康 *kāng*.

廊　láng　MC lang

1. covered corridor or area attached to a building; portico, arcade, veranda.
2. structures surrounding a palace hall; e.g. ～廟 *lángmiào*, gen. term for the court.

桹　láng　MC lang

1. (med.) beating-pole, struck on the sides of a boat to drive fish into a net.
   a. (med.) rdup., onom. of wood striking wood, thump-thump.

2. (bn.) 桄～ *guāngláng*, → 桄 *guāng* (*guàng*).

槵　láng　MC lang

1. (med.) beating-pole, struck on the sides of a boat to drive fish into a net.
2. (med.) ～榆 *lángyú*, Chinese elm (*Ulmus parvifloria, Ulmus chinensis*).
3. (med.) (bn.) 檳～ *bīnláng*, → 檳 *bīn*; 桄～ *guāngláng*, → 桄 *guāng*.

狼　láng　MC lang

1. wolf.
2. ～尾草 *lángwěicǎo*, foxtail grass, fountain-grass (*Pennisetum alopecuroides*); syn. 菫郎 *dǒngláng*.
3. cmpd. ～籍, ～藉 *lángjí*, strewn in a clutter, littered and jumbled, in a total mess; (med.) cmpd. ～狽 *lángbèi*, fall stupidly out of step, stumble and blunder unwittingly; disconnected(ly), disconcerted(ly) (< 2 animals, 1 with front legs too short, 1 with back legs too short, who must lean on each other to go forward).

琅　láng　MC lang

1. (bn.) ～玕 *lánggān*, gemstone-jade (MC lang-kan), prob. ref. originally to malachite, but regularly used as name of gemstone from distant lands or supernal regions, appropriate to decorate persons of special beauty or power, to nourish transcendent beings, to grow as trees in paradise realms.
2. rdup., onom. of tinkle or clink of pendants, bells, other metallic objects; also, (med.) sterling distinction, ref. outstanding person.
   a. (Dao.) ～玕華 *lánggānhuá*, efflorescence of gemstone-jade, astro-alchemical concoction involving absorption of stellar essences, a Shangqing practice.
3. (bn.) ～當 *lángdāng* (MC lang-tang), onom. of tink-clink of pendants, bells, etc.; also, shackles, iron chains, onom. of clank-lank of same; rdup., onom. of clear tones of stone-chimes: ling-ling.

硠　láng　MC lang

1. onom. of a rockslide, a mountain collapsing
   a. rdup., onom. of rocks grinding and grating together; also, staunch and strong.

稂　láng　MC lang

1. ryegrass, darnel, tare.

筤 láng MC lang
1. (med.) fresh bamboo-shoots.

舼 láng MC lang
1. (med.) sea-going vessel, ship.

莨 láng MC lang
1. foxtail grass (*Pennisetum alopecuroides*), syn. 狼尾草 *lángwěicǎo*.

làng MC langH
1. (bn.) ～菪 *làngdàng* (MC langH-dangH), henbane (*Hyoscyamus niger*).

蓈 láng MC lang
1. (bn.) 蕫～ *dǒngláng*, → 蕫 *dǒng*.

螂 láng MC lang
1. (bn.) 蜣～ *qiāngláng* (MC khjang-lang), → 蜣 *qiāng*; (bn.) 螗～ *tángláng*, → 螗 *táng*; (bn.) 蟑～ *zhāngláng*, → 蟑 *zhāng*.

郎 láng MC lang
1. gentleman, person of respect; used in various titles at court; e.g. 侍～ *shìláng*, "officiant gentleman," from Han to Tang usu. mid-level attendant or secretary, in Tang the 2nd-ranking position in the Imperial Secretariat (*zhongshusheng* 中書省) and Chancellery (*menxiasheng* 門下省) carrying with it appointment as a grand councilor (*zaixiang* 宰相); ～中 *lángzhōng*, "gentleman of the inner court," from Han to Tang usu. a servitor awaiting appointment, in Tang the head of a sub-office (*si* 司) of a department (*bu* 部) in the Bureau of State Affairs (*shangshusheng* 尚書省).
2. (med.) donzel, esquire, young gentleman.
    a. (med.) gen. term for a courtier or servitor.
3. (med.) term of address for husband by wife, for master by slave: my sir, my master; for son-in-law: master; with exaggerated courtesy for young boys: young sir, young master.
    a. (med.) 女～ *nǚláng*, term of endearment used toward young girl: lass(ie).
4. (med.) (ADV) truly, really, doubtless.

鋃 láng MC lang
1. (bn.) ～鐺 *lángdāng* (MC lang-tang), shackles, iron chains; to link together, chain.

閬 láng MC lang
1. grand or high gate.

2. spacious, far-extended.
    a. rdup., yawning, gaping, hollow.
3. fell(s), elevated stretch of wild land, moorland ridge; e.g. ～風 *lángfēng*, "Wind-on-the-Fells," name of a peak on Mt. Kunlun 崑崙山.
4. dry moat.

lǎng MC langX
1. (bn.) 儴～ or 燺～ *tǎnglǎng*, → 儴 *tǎng*.

liǎng MC ljangX
1. (bn.) 罔～ *wǎngliǎng*, → 罔 *wǎng*.

lǎng

朗 lǎng MC langX
1. sgl. or rdup., brilliant, luculent, glowing; transparently luminous, brightly gleaming.
    a. bright, intelligent, far-sighted, enlightened.
2. sgl. or rdup., loud and clear, resonant, sonorous.
3. (med.) serene, poised; e.g. ～豫 *lǎngyù*, serenely tranquil.

烺 lǎng MC langX
1. (med.) rdup., brilliant and dazzling; striking and distinct.

làng

埌 làng MC langH
1. (bn.) 壙～ *kuànglàng*, → 壙 *kuàng*.
2. tomb-vault, grave-pit.

浪 làng MC langH
1. whitecap, breaking wave, billow; comber, surf.
    a. surge up, rise; billow.
2. reckless, unrestrained; carefree, negligent(ly); insouciant; e.g. ～語 *làngyǔ*, crazy talk; ～人 *làngrén*, drifter, someone attached to no place.
    a. (med.) as one will, however one likes, casually, indifferently.
    b. (med.) expansive, effusive, exuberant.
    c. (med.) (bn.) ～漫 *làngmàn* (MC langH-manH), carefree and unconstrained, extravagantly expansive; also, vibrant and bright.
3. (med.) vain(ly), in vain, pointless, useless(ly); e.g. ～語 *làngyǔ*, pointless speech; ～死 *làngsǐ*, die for naught.
4. (med.) tap, strike against, drum; e.g. ～枻 *làngyì*, drumming oars.

láng MC lang
1. (med.) rdup., coursing incessantly, of river or prolonged rain.

láo

勞　láo　MC law

1. (be)labor, struggle, put under strain; take trouble with.
    a. travail, toil, moil; trouble(some), strenuous.
    b. troubled at heart, depressed, overborne.
2. contribution, accomplishment; credit, merit.

lào　MC lawH

1. comfort, console; assuage; reassure, commiserate; encourage, hearten.
2. acknowledge, recognize, or express thanks for one's labors.
    a. remunerate, compensate, pay off; requite with gifts; reward.
3. trouble oneself to entertain, provide food and drink for.

撈　láo　MC law

1. (med.) dredge up, drag out of water, drag for.

浒　láo　MC law

1. (bn.) 〜浪 *láolàng* (MC law-langH), raise and rouse (esp. game), rummage and ransack, search out and scare up.

牢　láo　MC law

1. pen for domestic animals; coop; stockade.
    a. pen up, enclose; cage.
2. collective term for animals used in sacrifices, indicating the type of sacrifice; e.g. 大〜 *dàláo*, suovetaurilia (sacrifice of pig, sheep, and ox); 小〜 *xiǎoláo*, suoveilia (of pig and sheep).
3. prison, pen for criminals; N.B. this meaning rare in pre-Han times.
4. public granary; food supplied from government storehouses.
5. firm, secure.
6. (bn.) 〜落 *láoluò* (MC law-lak), desolate and deserted, silent and set apart; scattered and strewn; withered and fallen.

lào　MC lawH

1. (med.) (bn.) 搜〜 *sōulào*, → 搜 *sōu*.

lóu　MC luw

1. reduce in the middle of the fist; roll in the hand, knead; e.g. 〜丸 *lóuwán*, kneaded dough-ball.

笒　láo　MC law

1. unspecified poisonous variety of bamboo, native to Wu area, may be shaped into a lance to kill wild animals at a touch.

醪　láo　MC law

1. unstrained wine, still with lees; usu. ref. a rich ale, sweeter than 醴 *lǐ*.

lǎo

栳　lǎo　MC lawX

1. (med.) (bn.) 栲〜 *kǎolǎo*, → 栲 *kǎo*.

潦　lǎo　MC lawX

1. heavy rain, rainstorm, torrent(ial).

lào　MC lawH

1. flooded roads; inundation.

liǎo　MC lew

1. (med.) (bn.) 〜倒 *liǎodǎo* (MC lew-tawX), undisciplined, incorrigible, willful and incurable; also, dispirited and depressed.

老　lǎo　MC lawX

1. old, elder(ly), aged, advanced in years (cf. 舊 *jiù*, of long standing; 古 *gǔ*, of long ago).
    a. elder; venerable: sgl. or in various combined terms showing respect for seniority or rank.
    b. sgl. or cmpd. 〜身 *lǎoshēn*, humble self-reference: this oldster.
    c. aging; waning, declining.
    d. old age, senescence, end of life; die of old age.
    e. (med.) prefixed to surname or to birth-rank in generation or family, showing friendship or intimacy.
    f. 〜人星 *lǎorénxīng*, "Old Man Star," Canopus, 2nd brightest star in sky, only visible below 34° N latitude.
2. superannuated; outmoded, obsolete; stale.
    a. retire(d), withdraw(n), estivate(d).
3. experienced (in), versed (in), masterly, devoted to; practiced (in), proficient (at); knowledgeable (of).

轑　lǎo　MC lawX

1. curved pole of a carriage canopy.
    a. by synecdoche, arched canopy of carriage.

liǎo　MC ljewX

1. ⊙ 橑 *liǎo*, upswept eaves of roof; 燎 *liǎo*, controlled burn; burn up, enflame.

lào

嫽　lào　MC lawH

1. (med.) tentiginous, lust(ful).
    a. (med.) jealous of, greedy for; clinging, tenacious.

憥 lào   MC lawH

1. (bn.) 懊～ *àolào*, → 懊 *ào*.

澇 lào   MC lawH

1. drenched, flooded from rain; waterlogged, inundated.

    láo   MC law

1. cresting wave, heaving wave.

酪 lào   MC lak

1. kumiss, fermented mare's milk (also cow's or sheep's), < Khotan-Saka *ragai* (with metathesis).
   a. yogurt, milk curdled by bacteria.

lè

勒 lè   MC lok

1. bit, mouthpiece of bridle.
   a. pull on the bit; rein in, pull up; restrain.
2. control; lead, direct.
3. compel, force, exercise pressure.
4. carve, engrave (text on stone).
   a. (med.) outline, limn; transcribe.
5. (med.) trsc. Tokharian *rak*, fruit, in "3 fruits" 三～ *sānlè* (Skt. *triphalā*), medicinal tonic of 3 myrobalans from Central Asia/Northern India: 毗梨～ *pílílè* (MC bij-lij-lok), belliric myrobalan (*Terminalia bellirica*, Skt. *vibhītakī*), 訶梨～ *hēlílè* (MC xa-lij-lok), chebulic myrobalan (*Terminalia chebula*, Skt. *harītakī*), 菴摩～ *ānmólè* (MC 'om-ma-lok), emblic myrobalan (*Emblica officinalis*, Skt. *āmalaka*).
6. (med.) (bn.) 蘿～ *luólè*, → 蘿 *luó*.

    lēi   MC lok

1. (med.) bind up; tie, fasten, twist together; tighten.

扐 lè   MC lok

1. spaces between the fingers; esp. for holding divining-stalks.

樂 lè   MC lak   → 樂 *yuè*.

泐 lè   MC lok

1. split along veins of stone.
   a. erode; wear away from exposure.
2. (med.) ⊙ 勒 *lè* 4, engrave.

肋 lè   MC lok   → 肋 *lèi*.

芳 lè   MC lok

1. (bn.) 蘿～ *luólè*, → 蘿 *luó*.
2. ⊙ 扐 *lè*, spaces between the fingers; esp. for holding divining-stalks.

阞 lè   MC lok

1. veins of earth; creases and depressions reflecting structure of mountains, rivers, etc.

léi

儽 léi   MC lwoj

1. fatigued, worn out.
   a. enfeebled, weak.
2. discomfit(ed); destroy, wreck, damage; overthrow.
3. rdup., listless and dispirited, dour and depressed.

    lěi   MC lwojX

1. (med.) (bn.) 傀～ *kuǐlěi*, → 傀 *kuǐ* (*guī*).

㯌 léi   MC lwij

1. litter, for being conveyed in mountains.

    lěi   MC ljweX

1. (med.) plate, with internal partitions.
   a. (med.) lacquered box with partitions, boxes often in pairs to fit together.

欙 léi   MC lwoj   ⊙ 纝 *léi*.

縲 léi   MC lwij

1. ropes or bonds to restrain a prisoner.
   a. be bound; in bonds; > imprisoned.

纝 léi   MC lwij

1. cord, rope, line.
   a. put in bonds, as prisoner.
2. encircle, engird, encompass.
   a. framed, wrongly accused.
3. rdup., continuously connected, clustered and commingled, joined and jumbled; also, bewildered, dejected.

    lěi   MC lwojX

1. piled up, heaped up; aggregate, accumulate.

    lèi   MC lwijH

1. rope in, implicate, involve, entangle.

罍　léi　MC lwoj
1. wine-vase, with a large body, made of copper or pottery.
    a. (med.) cannikin, drinking vessel.

贏　léi　MC ljwe
1. emaciated, thin, gaunt.
    a. feeble, weak.
    b. fade away, attenuate; decline; falter.
2. exhausted, weary; haggard; peaked.
    a. outworn, timeworn; shoddy.
3. ruin; undermine.
4. bind up, tie up; encircle, wrap up.

虆　léi　MC lwij
1. creeping grapevine, species of liana (*Vitis flexuosa*).
    a. bind round, wind round, envelope.
2. basket or pannier, esp. for carrying earth.
3. ⊙ 樏 *léi*, litter, to be carried on amidst mountains.

藟　léi　MC lwij　⊙ 虆 *léi*.

轠　léi　MC lwoj
1. butt against, collide with; strike, batter.
2. rdup., onom. of thundering rumble, rumble and rattle, of carts or carriages.
3. (bn.) ～轤 *léilú* (MC lwoj-lu), bound and linked together, completely connected.

雷　léi　MC lwoj
1. thunder(ous), thunderclap.
    a. beat or strike thunderously, esp. a drum.

靁　léi　MC lwoj　⊙ 雷 *léi*.

lěi

儽　lěi　MC lwojX
1. sgl. or rdup., tired and overtaxed, fatigued, worn out, done in, exhausted; listless and dispirited, lethargic, depressed.

儽　lěi　MC lwojX　⊙ 儽 *lěi*.

壘　lěi　MC lwijX
1. earthworks, military defences incl. rampart, entrenchment, fortification, bulwark.
2. build up, pile up, pile on.

    a. rdup., piled higher and higher, heaped and massed, more and more.
3. (bn.) ～塊 *lěikuài* (MC lwijX-khwojH), rough and rugged, gnarled and knotty.
    léi　MC lwij
1. truss up, bind.
    lèi　MC lwojH
1. shower stones on enemy from above, ⊙ 礧 *lèi*.

磊　lěi　MC lwojX
1. piled-up rocks.
    a. amassed; gigantic.
    b. rdup., massed and mounded, heaped and huddled, stacked and scrambled, hugger-mugger; also, (med.) clear-cut and complete; wholly candid, open and aboveboard.
2. shingle, talus; rubble.
    a. (bn.) ～落 *lěiluò* (MC lwojX-lak), rough and rugged, flintlike; pebbled and piled, massive boulder > outstandingly impressive, highly distinguished; (bn.) ～砢 *lěiluǒ* (MC lwojX-laX), gnarled and knotty, rugged and hubbly; (bn.) ～塊 *lěikuài* (MC lwojX-khwojH), same as preceding.

礧　lěi　MC lwojX　⊙ 磊 *lěi*.

礨　lěi　MC lwojX
1. cave, hollow; den.
    lèi　MC lwojH
1. ⊙ 礧 *lèi*, shower rocks or roll logs on an enemy from above.

累　lěi　MC ljweX
1. pile up, heap up; stack, mound; cluster(ed); e.g. ～重 *lěichóng*, massed; tiered; ～足 *lěizú*, one foot on top of another, i.e. immobile, transfixed.
    a. clump(ed); pebbled; e.g. ～丸 *lěiwán*, "pebbly pellet," fungus that resembles pebbles (*Omphalia lapidescens*), used medicinally.
2. gather up, collect together; hoard, store, set aside; accumulation; e.g. ～辭 *lěicí*, hoard of words, verbose; ～息 *lěixī*, bated breath.
    a. repeat(edly), successive; continuous; frequent; e.g. ～日 *lěirì*, many days in succession.
    b. increase(d), add(ed) to; augment, pile on.
    lèi　MC ljweH
1. trouble(some), bother(some).
    a. overwork(ed), tire(d).

2. tie up, rope; bind up, bind round; entangle (-ment).
   a. complication; quandary, predicament.
   b. rope in; involve, implicate(d); compromise(d); shackled.

耒   lěi   MC lwijX
1. digging-stick, 2-pronged; plowstick > plow; e.g. ～耜 *lěisì*, plows and plowshares, plowsticks and square-frame plows.

藟   lěi   MC lwijX
1. creeping grapevine, liana (*Vitis flexuosa*); ⊙ 蘽 *léi* 1.
2. wind round; entangle.

誄   lěi   MC lwijX
1. eulogize the deeds and character of the dead.
   a. (lit.) eulogy, verse form of solemn nature, usu. heptametric and with a prose preface giving the circumstances of composition.

lèi

淚   lèi   MC lwijH
1. tears; teardrop.
   a. tearful, lachrymose; weep(ing).
      lì   MC lejH
1. cold; glacial.
2. (med.) rdup., intensely forceful, vehement.

礧   lèi   MC lwojH
1. in war, shower rocks or roll logs on enemy from above.
      lěi   MC lwojX
1. crash against, collide with.
      léi   MC lwoj
1. (med.) rdup., distinct and well-defined, stand out clearly.

纇   lèi   MC lwojH
1. knot in silk thread; knotty.
2. kink; rough spot; defect, drawback; deformation, scar.
   a. perverse; disagreeable.

肋   lèi   MC lok
1. rib(s); sides of chest.

酹   lèi   MC lwojH
1. pour a libation on the ground.

類   lèi   MC lwijH
1. category, class, kind, type, sort; e.g. ～聚 *lèijù*, collection or gathering grouped by category.
2. akin to, conform to; be of the same category, etc.
   a. analogy; analogize.
3. arrangement, disposition; criterion, standard.
4. (ADV) for the most part; in general, in the main.
5. (GP) (Budd.) following a personal pronoun or a noun ref. to a person, forms plural.

léng

棱   léng   MC long
1. (med.) square-edged log.
   a. (med.) angle(d), edge; ridge(d).
2. (med.) severe, formal; stiff, austere.
3. (med.) stately, dignified; imposing, majestic.
4. (med.) rdup., bitter and biting, of wind; also, stately and solemn, austere and severe; (bn.) ～層 *léngcéng* (MC long-dzong), tiered and towering, of mountains; also, cruel and ruthless, of appearance.

楞   léng   MC long
1. (med.) ⊙ 棱 *léng* 1a, angle, edge.
2. (Budd.) ～伽 *léngqié* (MC long-gja), trsc. Skt. Laṅka, name of mountain in Ceylon where Buddha reputedly preached the *Laṅkavatāra sūtra*.
3. (med.) (bn.) ～層 *léngcéng* (MC long-dzong), cruel and ruthless, of appearance.

碐   léng   MC ling
1. (med.) (bn.) ～磳 *léngzēng* (MC ling-tsong), rugged and craggy, rough and broken, of uneven hills.

稜   léng   MC long   ⊙ 棱 *léng*.

輘   léng   MC long
1. (bn.) ～輷 *lénghōng* (MC long-xweang), onom. of rumble and rattle of carriages or thunder.
      líng   MC ling
1. (bn.) ～轢 *línglì* (MC ling-lek), crush and flatten, as a wagon rolls over what is in its path; ride roughshod over; also, force and compel, oppress and overbear.

lěng

冷　lěng　MC laengX
1. cold, chill(y); frore, frigid.
2. cool (to), indifferent; neutral; detached, unconcerned.
    a. out-of-the-way, secluded; abandoned, neglected, forlorn; e.g. ～宮 lěnggōng, cold, forgotten palace where an out-of-favor consort lives.
    b. lonely, "left in the cold," lone(some).
3. rdup., plink, plink! onom. of zither playing; clear and melodious notes, giving a sense of cold and chill.

lí

劙　lí　MC li
1. cut or pare with a knife; e.g. ～面 límiàn, pare skin from the face, custom of some Central Asian tribes to show devotion and loyalty to the ruler esp. in mourning.
    a. cut open, slice open.

剗　lí　MC lje
1. partition, divide, separate (with knife); dismember.

嫠　lí　MC li
1. widow.

梨　lí　MC lij　⊙ 黎 lí.

黎　lí　MC lij
1. pear (Pyrus pyrifolia), spring-flowering tree, with round fruit.
    a. 白～ báilí, white pear (Pyrus bretschneideri), spring-flowering, fruit narrow at top.
2. partition, dismember, separate.

漓　lí　MC lje
1. water seeping or soaking into the ground.
    a. (med.) dripping water; dribble, patter, trickle; drizzle.
    b. (med.) (bn.) 淋～ línlí, → 淋 lín.
2. (med.) thin; light.

嫠　lí　MC li　→ 嫠 chí.

灘　lí　MC lje
1. water soaking, seeping into the ground; ⊙ 漓 lí 1.

犁　lí　MC lej　⊙ 犂 lí.

犂　lí　MC lej
1. plow.
2. brindled, dappled, mottled.
    a. liver-spots appearing in old age.
3. arrive at or reach a particular time; e.g. ～明 límíng, just at daybreak; ～老 lílǎo, someone who has become old.
4. explicit(ly), definite(ly).
5. ～軒 líjiān (MC lej-kean), Hyrcania, → 犛 lí 2.
6. ⊙ 黎 lí 1, black(ish), sable.

犛　lí　MC li
1. yak (Bos grunniens).
2. ～軒 líjiān (MC li-kean), trsc. Old Pers. Wrkāna > Gk. Hyrcania, region comprising the southern and southeastern shore of Caspian Sea, important area of Persian Empire; in Eastern Han misidentified with 大秦 dà Qín, Roman Empire in Asia Minor. N.B. Identification with Seleucia is incorrect (→ 條 tiáo 10).

狸　lí　MC li　⊙ 狸 lí.

璃　lí　MC lje
1. (med.) (bn.) 玻～ bōlí, → 玻 bō.
    a. (med.) (bn.) 琉～ liúlí, → 琉 liú.

籬　lí　MC lje
1. (med.) bamboo fence or paling; hedge.

縭　lí　MC lje
1. belt, cincture.

纚　lí　MC lje　→ 纚 xǐ.

罹　lí　MC lje
1. encounter, meet with (unfortunately).
    a. mischance, mishap.

羅　lí　MC lje
1. (med.) 2nd element in compounds ref. to 2 particular caps: 接～ jiēlí, cap decorated with long white head-plumes of the egret, usu. worn by men in informal settings; 冪～ mìlí, full-body-length garment draped from one's head (with face open) for protection against wind and dust, usu. made of silk, similar to an Arab chador; originally worn by both men and women in Central Asia, but in China worn as

exotic import only by women in Tang times, usu. when going on an outing, esp. on horseback.

藜 lí MC lej

1. goosefoot, melde (*Chenopodium album*), a weed with stalked, opposite leaves which may be eaten when young; the stalk when full-grown and aged can be made into a staff; syn. 藋 *diào*.
2. 蒺〜 *jílí*, → 蒺 *jí*.

蘺 lí MC lje

1. 茳〜 or 江〜 *jiānglí*, lovage (*Ligusticum chuanxiong*), herbaceous perennial often found near riverbanks, with umbels of yellow or greenish-yellow flowers. Often paired or conflated in lit. with 蘼蕪 *míwú*, selinea.

蜊 lí MC lij

1. (bn.) 蜻〜 *jīnglí*, → 蜻 *jīng*.

褵 lí MC lje

1. belt, cincture; (med.) serviette or scent-pouch worn by a bride at her waist; e.g. 結〜 *jiélí*, join cinctures, i.e. to marry.
2. (med.) (bn.) 〜襹 *líshī* (MC lje-srje) or 襹〜 *shīlí*, fluffy and flossy, of young birds' feathers; flocculently feathered, prettily plumed.

貍 lí MC li

1. raccoon-dog (*Nyctereutes procyonoides*).

mái MC meaj

1. bury, inter; ⊙ 埋 *mái*.

邌 lí MC lej

1. (med.) slowly, gradually.

醨 lí MC lje

1. thin wine.
   a. (med.) watered-down; insipid, bland; tasteless.

釐 lí MC li

1. govern, administer; manage; regulate.
   a. (med.) reform, correct; modify, change.
2. give to, bestow on.
3. thousandth part of a "foot" (*chi* 尺) or "ounce" (*liang* 兩), hundredth part of an "inch" (*cun* 寸) > tiny portion or quantity, smidgen, mite, bit.
4. ⊙ 嫠 *lí*, widow; 來 *lái* 1, wheat.

xī MC xi

1. meat used in sacrifice.
2. auspicious, well-favored.

離 lí MC lje

1. to part from, separate; leave; e.g. 〜緒 *líxù*, emotions at parting; 〜居 *líjū*, leave one's home; also, live apart; 〜位 *líwèi*, give up one's post.
   a. disengage(ment), detached; distinct from, distinct(ive);disjunct(ion);divide(d);e.g.〜宮 *lígōng*, detached palace; 〜合 *líhé*, divide and join; 〜群 *líqún*, apart from the flock, on one's own, with implication of loneliness or superiority; 〜俗 *lísú*, avoid the everyday world, disengage from the vulgar.
   b. stray from, astray; estrange(ment); divorce oneself from; be or get free of; e.g. 〜落 *líluò*, aimlessly astray, drifting rootlessly; 〜書 *líshū*, bill of divorce; 〜結 *líjié*, free from bonds; (Budd.) 〜垢 *lígòu*, free from impurities.
2. dispose(d), set out, array(ed), align(ed).
3. pass through, experience.
   a. encounter, meet with (unfortunately); mishap, mischance; ⊙ 罹 *lí*; e.g. (lit.) 〜騷 *lísāo*, "Encountering Sorrow," 1st and chief poem of the *Chuci* 楚辭 collection.
4. pair(ed) with; side-by-side; e.g. 火〜 *huǒlí*, (the bird) paired with fire, i.e. phoenix.
   a. (bn.) 〜樓 *lílóu* (MC lje-luw), latticed and interlaced, entwined tightly.
5. rdup., distant and dense; also, divorced and disjoined, split and splintered; also, distinctly disposed; also, in ample array; also, hanging heavy (of grain).
6. (bn.) 〜靡 *límí* (MC lje-mje), tightly tangled, continuously connected; (bn.) 〜披 *lípī* (MC lje-phje), scattered far and wide.
7. trsc. of Skt. *li, lī, le, re*.
8. ⊙ 蘺 *lí*, lovage; 褵 *lí* 1, bride's scent-pouch; 2, (bn.) 〜襹 *líshī*, fluffy and flossy.

lì MC lejH

1. attach(ed) to, tie(d) to; cling, cohere; ⊙ 麗 *lì* 2.
   a. "Cohering," name of 30th hexagram of the *Yijing*.
2. orbit of the moon.

驪 lí MC lje

1. horse of deep-black color.
2. deep-black, jet; glossy black.

3. in tandem, paired; side-by-side; parallel.

4. ⊙ 離 *lí* 1, to part from, separate.

鸝　lí　MC lje

1. sgl. or 黃～ *huánglí*, oriole, esp. black-naped oriole (*Oriolus chinensis*), esp. associated with summer; syn. 鶯 *yīng*, 黃鳥 *huángniǎo*, 倉庚 *cānggēng*.

黎　lí　MC lej

1. numerous, many, multitude; e.g. ～民 *límín*, ～氓 *líméng*, ～元 *líyuán*, ～烝 *lízhēng*, multitudinous folk, common people.

2. sable; glossy black of animal fur; blackish; swart(hy); ⊙ 黧 *lí*.

3. ⊙ 犁 *lí* 3, reach a particular time, at the time when, at the moment of.

黧　lí　MC lej

1 sable; glossy black of animal fur; blackish; swart(hy); ⊙ 黎 *lí* 2.

lǐ

俚　lǐ　MC liX

1. churlish, boorish; vulgar, uncouth; rustic, roughcast.

2. rely on, depend(able); use as a resource.

娌　lǐ　MC liX

1. cmpd. 妯～ *zhóulǐ*, collective term for wives of older and younger brothers.

李　lǐ　MC liX

1. plum (*Prunus salicina*), with thin, hard, crisp pulp; cf. 梅 *méi* (*Prunus mume*) with thick, soft pulp.

2. 行～ *xínglǐ*, emissary, envoy (early usage).

3. a surname, notably that of ruling family of the Tang (618-907) dynasty.

理　lǐ　MC liX

1. inherent or informing pattern in an object, action, or idea; natural order, natural process; cf. 文 *wén*, pattern overlaid on or external to basic stuff 質 *zhí*; cog. 裏 *lǐ*, internal.

2. configuration, delineation, venation, texture.

　　a. structure, organization, system(atize).

　　b. order, cosmic order; in accord with understandable order, reasonable, systematic; ground of argument.

3. to manage, arrange, bring order to, attend to.

　　a. apply reason to a situation, bring to systematic disposition; argue from systematic principle; e.g. 自～ *zìlǐ*, defend oneself (from accusation), exonerate.

　　b. as element in official titles, usu. indicates connection with legal matters.

　　c. reason, excuse, justification (for).

4. (Budd.) associated with Skt. *prajñā*, gnosis raised to an ontological level; sometimes equated with the *xuanxue* concept of 本無 "fundamental nullity" or 至無 "ultimate nullity"; the noumenal, the thing-in-itself, as opposed to the phenomenal 事 *shì* or 相 *xiāng*.

　　a. Truth, as absolute.

禮　lǐ　MC lejX

1. ritual, rites; ceremonial form (cog. 體 *tǐ*, one's physical frame, form, body), prescribed behavior at religious or other solemn ceremony; usu. paired in Ruist texts with 樂 *yuè*, music, as the 2 basic activities of social coordination.

　　a. ritual ceremony.

2. good form; formality, etiquette; expected social behavior appropriate to one's family standing, social rank, or official position; behavior appropriate to the particular occasion (whether prescribed or not).

　　a. do or pay reverence to, as formally expected.

3. formal present or gift.

蠡　lǐ　MC lejX

1. worm-eaten.

　　a. dilapidated, falling apart, in ruins.

　　lí　MC lje

1. calabash split in two, used as dipper.

　　luó　MC lwa

1. ⊙ 蠃 *luó*, gastropod, snail, whelk; conch, used as musical instrument.

裏　lǐ　MC liX

1. inner lining of clothing.

　　a. within, inside, inner; enclosed in.

邐　lǐ　MC ljeX

1. rdup. or bn. ～迤 *lǐyǐ* (MC ljeX-yeX) or 迤～ *yǐlǐ*, continuously twisting and turning, one after another.

醴 lǐ   MC lejX

1. sweet liquor, sweet wine, made from a short fermentation with malt (*nie* 糵) and glutinous millet (*shu* 黍), so retaining more sugar; somewhat similar to mead, but without honey as an ingredient; the better equivalent is "ale."
2. wine that has fermented for one night.
3. fountain or spring of sweet water.

里 lǐ   MC liX

1. residential compound, anciently thought equiv. 25 households (*jia* 家); in Tang times equiv. 100 households, a hamlet, village, with 5 *li* making up 1 "parish" (*xiāng* 鄉).
2. measure of length, up to Tang equiv. 300 paces or double-steps (*bu* 步, equiv. 6 "feet" [*chi* 尺]), but in Tang when double-step was shortened to 5 feet the *lǐ* became equiv. 360 *bu*; approx. 1/3 mile; often translated loosely as "league" (but a league = 3 miles).
   a. 百～ *bǎilǐ*, an area 100 *li* in circumference, metaphor for district (縣 *xiàn*).

鯉 lǐ   MC liX

1. the carp (*Cyprinus carpio*). During the Tang a protected fish, because homophonous with Li 李, family name of the dynastic house.

鱧 lǐ   MC lejX

1. snakehead mullet, murrel (*Ophiocephalus argus*).

鱺 lǐ   MC lejX   ⊙ 鱧 *lǐ*.

lì

例 lì   MC ljejH

1. example, instance (of); of the same type or class as.
   a. precedent, model; usage.
   b. (med.) according to example X, based on . . .
2. rule, regulation; norm.
   a. layout, arrange(ment).
3. (med.) sgl. or ～皆 *lìjiē*, wholly, completely, all of a piece, entirely.

儷 lì   MC lejH

1. pair with, go together, couple; in tandem; balanced, parallel, symmetrical; ⊙ 麗 *lì* 2.

利 lì   MC lijH

1. sharp edge of a blade (cf. 銳 *ruì*, sharp point of blade).
   a. sharpen, whet.
2. gain an "edge," take advantage, exploit.
   a. profit(able), benefit; gain(ful).
   b. successful, favorable.
   c. (med.) covet, greedy or avid for.
3. sharp in movement, swift, rapid.
   a. agile, well-trained; active.
4. sharp of thought; pointed, keen-witted, clever.
5. smooth; effortless.
   a. facile in speech, glib; convincing or smooth in behavior.
6. 痢 *lì*, dysentery.

力 lì   MC lik

1. strength, power(ful); force(ful); vigor(ous), strenuous.
   a. ability, potency.
   b. strongly, firmly, resolutely, diligently.
2. give one's strength to; exert or make an effort, apply oneself to, labor in or toward.
   a. exacted or enforced labor, corvée.

勵 lì   MC ljejH

1. exert, expend; strive, strain.
   a. apply to the utmost, as one's best.
2. encourage, urge; inspire, stimulate.
3. esteem, regard highly.

厲 lì   MC ljejH

1. a hone, whetstone.
   a. to hone, whet, sharpen, acuminate, grind to an edge.
   b. be "on the edge," in danger, peril.
   c. sharp sound, rasping, grating.
2. incite, stimulate; urge, encourage.
3. raise up, lift up; exert effort; e.g. ～翼 *lìyì*, beating of wings, exert oneself.
4. sharp, severe; harsh; strict, vehement; e.g. ～精 *lìjīng*, ardent vehemence.
   a. malicious, cruel; unrelenting, implacable.
   b. malign, malevolent; harmful; horrid.
5. cross a stream when fully clothed.
   a. crossing-point, ford.

吏 lì   MC liH

1. in pre-imperial times, gen. term for officials of all ranks.

a. from Qin-Han onward, ref. low-level government employees such as clerks; in Tang times, esp. ref. local functionaries (i.e. not appointed by central government) in prefectures and districts, such as bailiffs, lictors, runners, messengers, similar to the Roman apparitor or servant of a magistrate.

唳　lì　MC lejH
1. (med.) crunkle, call of a crane.
　　a. (med.) trumpet, bugle; clarion call.

悷　lì　MC lejH
1. (bn.) 㑦～ *línlì*, → 㑦 *lín* (*lán*).

慄　lì　MC lit
1. tremble, shake with fear; quaver, quake with fright; apprehensive; ⊙ 栗 *lì* 4.
2 rdup., quake and quaver, in fear and trembling, intimidated, overawed; also, frore and frigid, shiveringly cold.

戾　lì　MC lejH
1. ungovernable, unmanageable; rebellious, contrary, froward.
　　a. perverse; obstreperous.
2 violent, cruel; brutal, savage; do violence; strong(ly), forceful(ly).
3. crime; transgress(ion), infringe(ment).
4. secure, stable; unshakable.
5. arrive, come.
　　liè　MC let
1. (med.) turn, rotate.

捩　lì　MC lejH　→ 捩 *liè*.

攦　lì　MC lejH
1. break, crack; split, rend.

曆　lì　MC lek
1. calender; calendrical system.
　　a. calendrical system; calculate the courses of sun, moon, stars, esp. in establishing correct calendar; chronometry.
　　b. calculation of influence of preceding on human actions or destiny; predestined likelihood of occurrences or length of life-span.
　　c. almanac, containing calendrical information and astro-calendrical predictions.
2 ⊙ 歷 *lì* 3, successive, continuous.

栗　lì　MC lit
1. chestnut (*Castanea mollissima*), tree and fruit.
2. solid, firm, hard.
3. solemn, serious.
4. tremble, shake from fear; ⊙ 慄 *lì*.
5. rdup., a great many, many and more; also, shaking and shuddering.
6. (bn.) ～烈 *lìliè* (MC lit-ljet), frore and frigid, shiveringly cold.

櫟　lì　MC lek
1. oak-tree, esp. serrated or sawtooth-oak (*Quercus acutissima*); ⊙ 櫪 *lì* 1.
2. railing, balustrade.
3. scrape a pot to get everything out, making a rasping sound.
4. attack, strike at.

櫪　lì　MC lek
1. oak-tree, esp. serrated or sawtooth-oak (*Quercus acutissima*); ⊙ 櫟 *lì*.
2. stable, for horses.

欐　lì　MC lejH
1. ridgepole, roofbeam.
2. small boat, dinghy, pram.
3. rdup., many-massed, thronging together.

歷　lì　MC lek
1. pass through (space), fare past.
　　a. surpass, exceed, outstrip.
2. pass through (time); experience, undergo; e.g. ～運 *lìyùn*, fortuitous or chance happening.
3. successive(ly), in series; continuous(ly); one by one, in order.
　　a. rdup., successively evident, distinct and well-defined, vividly clear.
4. wholly, entirely, completely, universally.
5. calculate, reckon.
6. calendrical system, calendar; chronometry; ⊙ 曆 *lì*.
7. select, choose.
8. interspersed, spaced apart; e.g. ～齒 *lìchǐ*, gap-toothed.
9. (med.) ～落 *lìluò* (MC lek-lak), honest and upright.
10. ⊙ 櫪 *lì* 2, horse stable; 鬲 *lì*, tripod with hollow legs, for food offerings.

沴   lì   MC lejH

1. unbalanced pneumas of *yin* and *yang*.
   a. disturbing vapors, miasmal air; disordered auras.

冽   lì   MC lijH

1. rushing water, in spate, coursing.
2. rapid(ly), quick(ly), urgent(ly).

灑   lì   MC ljejH

1. cross a stream fully clothed; ⊙ 厲 *lì* 5.
   a. cross or ford a stream.

瀝   lì   MC lek

1. drip, fall drop by drop; trickle; esp. last drops, dregs.
   a. (bn.) ～滴 *lìdī* (MC lek-tek), 滴～ *dīlì*, dribbling droplets.
2. (bn.) 淅～ *xīlì*, →淅 *xī*.
3. clear wine.
4. reveal, show, disclose.

猁   lì   MC lijH

1. (bn.) 猞～ *shēlì*, → 猞 *shē*.

瓅   lì   MC lek

1. (bn.) 玓～ *dìlì*, → 玓 *dì*.

痢   lì   MC lijH

1. dysentery.

癘   lì   MC ljejH

1. pestilence, plague; infectious illness.
2. leprosy, from Han times onward.
3. (med.) malignant boil, imposthume.

皪   lì   MC lek

1. (bn.) 的～ *dìlì*, → 的 *dì*.

蠫   lì   MC lejH

1. ⊙ 戾 *lì* 1, ungovernable, froward; perverse, obstreperous; 2, cruel, brutal, savage; do violence; 綟 *lì*, small carpetgrass (*Arthraxon hispidus*); olive color produced as dye from this plant.

礪   lì   MC ljejH

1. whetstone; whet, hone, sharpen, grind; ⊙ 厲 *lì* 1.
   a. grind away at; work diligently or obsessively, overdo.

礫   lì   MC lek

1. pebbles, gravel, shingle.

立   lì   MC lip

1. stand, stand straight.
   a. stand firm, stand on one's own feet, take a stand.
   b. (med.) bring to a standstill, stop, cease, interrupt.
2. set up; (be) establish(ed); e.g. ～功 *lìgōng*, establish one's deeds.
   a. confirm; install, instate, esp. in high position or rulership.
   b. fortnightly period that is the onset or advent of each of the 4 seasons; e.g. ～節 *lìjié*, "nodes of onset," i.e. advent of spring (*lìchūn* ～春), of summer (*lìxià* ～夏), etc.
3. instant(ly), quick(ly), immediate(ly); prompt; e.g. ～成 *lìchéng*, quickly fulfilled, immediately accomplished; also, handbook or manual, for quick mastery.
4. (med.) exist, be.

笠   lì   MC lip

1. wide-brimmed conically-shaped bamboo or straw rainhat.

簛   lì   MC lit

1. (bn.) 薜～ *bìlì*, → 薜 *bì*.

粒   lì   MC lip

1. kernel, clevel, of rice or other grain-crops.
   a. (med.) a grain (of rice, etc.), as measure of capacity.
2. have a meal.

糲   lì   MC ljejH

1. grain coarsely husked.
2. coarse, rough; inferior.

綟   lì   MC lejH

1. small carpetgrass, joint-head grass (*Arthraxon hispidus*).
   a. olive color produced as dye from this plant.

苙   lì   MC lip

1. pigpen, pigsty.
2. (med.) Chinese angelica (*Angelica dahurica*), ⊙ 茝 *zhǐ*.

荔　lì　MC lejH

1. Chinese woad (*Isatis indigotica*), from which an indigo-colored dye is extracted.
2. (bn.) 薜～ *bìlì* (MC bejH-lejH), creeping fig (*Ficus pumila*).
3. (bn.) ～枝 or ～支 *lìzhī* (MC lejH-tsye), lychee (*Litchi chinensis*).
4. ～挺 *lìtíng*, purple iris (*Iris ensata*).

苙　lì　MC lijH

1. look down on from a height, overlook.
    a. oversee, preside over, manage, supervise.
2. verge on, approach, arrive, be present at; esp. arrive at one's post, take office, attend to.
3. rdup., onom. of coursing water: splash and plash, burble and bubble, rush and whoosh.

莉　lì　MC lijH

1. (med.) (bn.) 茉～ *mòlì*, → 茉 *mò*.

茘　lì　MC lijH　⊙ 苙 *lì*.

蒚　lì　MC lek

1. (bn.) 葶～ *tínglì*, → 葶 *tíng*.

蠣　lì　MC ljejH

1. (med.) sgl. or cmpd. 牡～ *mǔlì*, oyster.

詈　lì　MC ljeH

1. curse, revile, rate, rail at.
    a. blame, reprove; upbraid.
N.B. Used more often than syn. 罵 *mà* in pre-imperial texts, gradually replaced by it from Han onward.

躒　lì　MC lek

1. stride, length of a step.
2. stride over, bound over.
    a. surpass, outdo, exceed, excel.
        luò　MC lak
1. (bn.) 逴～ *chuōluò*, → 逴 *chuō*.

轢　lì　MC lek

1. roll over on, crush, flatten, as carriage wheels.
    a. (bn.) 輘～ *línglì*, → 輘 *líng* (*léng*).
2. bully, mistreat, oppress.
3. tap, as the spokes of a carriage to speed it up.

鑗　lì　MC lek

1. large tripod, for cooking.

隸　lì　MC lejH

1. low-ranking subordinate, servitor, subaltern; runner; lackey, servant; houseman; turnkey.
    a. laborer, esp. at corvée.
2. (med.) attached to, dependent on; client, dependent.
3. examine closely, audit.
4. "clerical" style of calligraphy.
        yì　MC yijH
1. ⊙ 肄 *yì* 1, exercise, train, practice; rehearse.

靂　lì　MC lek

1. (bn.) 霹～ *pīlì*, → 霹 *pī*.

颲　lì　MC lep

1. gust, gale, blast of wind; raging of wind.

鬲　lì　MC lek

1. tripod with hollow legs, used for food offerings in sacrificial ritual.
2. lower part of a steamer or double-boiler.
        gé　MC keak
1. hinder, block, separate; hindrance.
        è　MC 'eak
1. hold or control by hand.
2. yoke or collar placed on neck of horses or oxen pulling a carriage; ⊙ 軛 *è*.

麗　lì　MC lejH

1. gorgeous, ravishing, beauty that is outwardly or sensually striking; applicable to people, clothing, architecture, etc.; artful beauty.
2. paired, in tandem, yoked together; advance together.
    a. parallel; balanced, symmetrical; esp. of literary style.
3. tie(d) to, tether(ed); attached tightly; clinging; cleave to.
4. apply, exert (effort).
5. ⊙ 欐 *lì*, roofbeam; 歷 *lì* 2, passage of time, experience(d).
        lí　MC lje
1. ⊙ 罹 *lí*, encounter, meet with (unfortunately).

lián

奩　lián　MC ljem

1. (med.) vanity-case, for woman's combs, makeup, etc.; also, mirror-case.
2. (med.) gen. term for case, coffer, sheath.

帘　lián　MC ljem

1. (med.) wineshop flag.
2. (med.) half-curtain.

襝　lián　MC ljem

1. cloth curtain.
2. (med.) tight-woven pongee or tabby.

廉　lián　MC ljem

1. incorruptible; irreproachable, blameless; probity, integrity; scrupulous; disinterested.
2. grave reserve, keep one's own counsel.
   a. (med.) withdraw(n), retreat; yield.
3. side-portions of a hall or large room.
   a. angle, corner > pointed in attention or intelligence.
4. inspect, scrutinize; examine, investigate.

憐　lián　MC len

1. sympathize, be in sympathy with; solace.
   a. be moved, touched, affected by; feel sorry for, have one's heart go out to; lament.
2. have tender feelings for, love, be dear to one's heart.
   a. find appealing or engaging.
   b. (med.) think of tenderly, long for, remember fondly.
3. admire, appreciate.
   lán　MC lan
1. ⊙ 瀾 lán, rolling wave, breaker, swell, billow.

溓　lián　MC lem

1. (med.) still, tranquil, esp. of water.
   a. (med.) rdup., thinly frozen ice.
   nián　MC nrjem
1. ⊙ 黏 nián, adhere, bind; fasten, attach, paste to.

漣　lián　MC ljen

1. ripples, riffles of water, laplets.
   a. (bn.) ～漪 liányī (MC ljen-'je), wimpled waves.
2. rdup., or ～洏 lián'ér, flowing tears, unstoppable weeping.

簾　lián　MC ljem

1. drop-curtain made of bamboo or cloth.

聯　lián　MC ljen

1. connect(ed), join(ed); link(ed) with; joint.
2. (bn.) ～卷 liánquán (MC ljen-gjwen), curved and curled, sinous swirl, wavy; (med.) (bn.) ～娟

liánjuān (MC ljen-'jwien), closely curved, as of woman's eyebrows; gracefully curved; curved and coiled; arabesque.
3. (med.) (lit.) couplet of verse.

蓮　lián　MC len

1. lotus (*Nelumbo nucifera*), also lotus leaf, lotus seed; cf. 荷 *hé*, 芙蓉 *fúróng*, 芙蕖 *fúqú*, 菡萏 *hàndàn*. The roots of the lotus are planted in the mud at the bottom of a pond or river, and the leaves float on the water surface, with the stems of the flowers rising above the leaves. The rhizome (藕 *ŏu*) is used in cooking, and the root is used in medicine. In Budd. a symbol of purity. Often associated punningly in lit. with 憐 *lián*, affection, sympathy.
   a. 青～ *qīnglián*, "blue lotus," Indian waterlily (*Nymphaea caerulea*, Skt. *nīlotpala*), esp. associated with the bodhisattva Mañjuśrī.
   b. 睡～ *shùilián*, "sleeping lotus," pygmy waterlily (*Nymphaea teragona*), white-flowered.
2. 木～ *mùlián*, "woody lotus," manglietia (*Manglietia fordiana*), stately evergreen tree similar to magnolia, with white or straw-yellow blossoms that resemble lotus blossoms, hence the name; also ⊙ 薜荔 *bìlì*, climbing fig.

蠊　lián　MC ljem

1. cockroach.

謰　lián　MC ljen

1. (bn.) ～謱 liánlóu (MC ljen-luw), gibber-jabber, blither and blather; also, inarticulate, tongue-tied.

連　lián　MC ljen

1. link up with, connect with, join with, adjoin(ing); join to, attach; e.g. ～璧 liánbì, paired jade-discs, also euph. for intimate friends or for persons or items of similar beauty or value; (med.) sgl. or ～紙 liánzhǐ, paste a piece of blank paper to a document received in an administrative office so that the relevant authority could write on it his decision or judgment.
   a. merge with, blend into.
   b. draw(n) into, implicated with; hemmed in by.
2. sgl. or rdup., continuous(ly), in succession; unbroken, uninterrupted.
   a. (bn.) ～軒 liánxuān (MC ljen-xjon), continual and constant, in ceaseless succession;

(bn.) ～卷 *liánquán* (MC ljen-gjwen), sinuous swirl; swerve and curl.

3. get, obtain, or capture simultaneously.
4. linked or related by marriage.
5. anciently, administrative grouping of 4 villages (*li* 里) providing soldiers.
6. raw lead.

鎌　lián　MC ljem
1. scythe, sickle.

鐮　lián　MC ljem　⊙ 鎌 *lián*.

鬑　lián　MC ljem
1. rdup., sparse and straggly beard.

鰱　lián　MC ljen
1. the silver carp, whitefish (*Hypophthalmichthys molitrix*), syn. 鱮 *xù*.

liǎn

㩭　liǎn　MC ljenX
1. (med.) bear, shoulder, carry as burden.

斂　liǎn　MC ljemX
1. collect; lay up; gather, glean, take in.
   a. levy, collect taxes or imposts.
2. contract, pull in, draw back, fold back; put away; restrain, bring into order or composure; e.g. ～衽 *liǎnrèn*, pull in one's lappets or sleeves, in gesture of humility or admiration; ～容 *liǎnróng*, compose one's features; ～策 *liǎncè*, lay aside one's whip, i.e. give up office; ～翼 *liǎnyì*, scantle or fold one's wings; (Budd.) ～心 *liǎnxīn*, turn one's mind within.
3. reduce; decrease.
4. prepare body for funeral, ⊙ 殮 *liàn*; e.g. ～日 *liǎnrì*, the day the body is placed in crypt.

璉　liǎn　MC ljenX
1. ritual vessel for sacrificial offerings of grain in ancestral temple, usu. 瑚～ *húliǎn*.

　lián　MC ljen
1. ⊙ 連 *lián* 1, join, connect, link up.

臉　liǎn　MC ljemX
1. (med.) features, of face; visage.

liàn

戀　liàn　MC ljwenH
1. (med.) be enthralled by, enamored of; hold dear, think fondly of.
   a. (med.) crave, long for.
   b. (med.) (bn.) ～眷 *liànjuàn* (MC ljwenH-kjwenH) or 眷～ *juànliàn*, near and dear.

楝　liàn　MC lenH
1. sgl. or 苦～ *kǔliàn*, chinaberry tree, Persian lilac (*Melia azedarach*), decidious tree of medium height, purple or lilac flowers, yielding small drupe fruit; syn. 紫花樹 *zǐhuāshù*, purple-blossom tree.

殮　liàn　MC ljemH
1. (med.) prepare a corpse for burial; ⊙ 斂 *liǎn* 4.

澰　liàn　MC ljemH
1. riverbank, strand, where waves expire.
2. tumble, roll, roil (of waves).
   a. (med.) (bn.) ～灩 *liànyàn* (MC ljemH-yemH), rolling and roiling, tossing and tumbling (waves); also, brimful and bursting, overflowing and flooding.

煉　liàn　MC lenH　⊙ 鍊 *liàn*.

練　liàn　MC lenH
1. boil silk to soften and whiten it.
   a. purify; refine; lustrate.
2. new-dressed silk, white silk.
3. train, drill; practice(d), experienced.
4. select, choose.
5. smelt, fuse together, ⊙ 鍊 *liàn* 3.

鍊　liàn　MC lenH
1. purify by removing dross, esp. when refining metals.
   a. refined, purified; e.g. (Dao.) ～師 *liànshī*, Refined Master (or Mistress), one freed of the impurities of the world, most exalted title of a Dao. priest(ess).
2. mold or shape under fire.
   a. discipline, train to preferred condition.
3. smelt, fuse together.

liáng

俍   liáng   MC ljang
1. deft, adept at.

lǎng   MC langX
1. (bn.) ～倡 *lǎngchāng* (MC langX-tsyhang), ～傍 *lǎngpáng* (MC langX-bang), step askew, thrown off the track, unsteady and insecure.

梁   liáng   MC ljang
1. bridge; plankbridge; sometimes pontoon bridge.
2. roofbeam, ridgepole.
    a. rafter; transversal crossbeam.
    b. lintel, of door or window.
3. fishing-sluice, fish-weir.
    a. dam.
4. (bn.) ～昌 *liángchāng* (MC ljang-tsyhang), lose one's footing, fall from favor; also, shaky and indecisive; in perilous straits.
5. 大～ *dàliáng*, name of one of the 12 Jupiter stations, comprising the lunar lodgings *mao* 昴 and *bi* 畢; also, name of the capital of feudal state of Liang or Wei, see next.
6. name of a feudal state (also ref. as Wei 魏) during Zhou times, originally part of the Jin 晉 state, located in northern Henan and southwest Shanxi, with capital near present-day Kaifeng; one of the 7 major states during the Warring States period.
7. name of med. "southern" dynasty (502-557), with capital at Jiankang 建康 (Nanjing).
8. a surname.

椋   liáng   MC ljang
1. largeleaf dogwood (*Cornus macrophylla*), smallish tree, flowering in late summer.

涼   liáng   MC ljang
1. refreshingly or comfortably cool; slightly cold.
2. cold; chilly; bleak.
    a. cold-hearted; indifferent, passive.
3. slight, weak; thin; e.g. ～德 *liángdé*, weak in virtue.

liàng   MC ljangH
1. assist, aid.
2. (med.) dry in the open air, set in the wind to dry; ⊙ 晾 *liàng*.

梁   liáng   MC ljang
1. foxtail millet (*Setaria italica*), the most common millet.

2. finest of rice; e.g. ～肉 *liángròu*, finest of rice and meat, best viands.

糧   liáng   MC ljang
1. provisions, esp. dried food for travel.
    a. gen. term for grains, everyday food.

良   liáng   MC ljang
1. goodly, seemly; matching the ideal; innately good; e.g. ～知 *liángzhī*, goodly or innate knowledge, conscience; also, (med.) close friend, who inherently understands one.
    a. term of ref. used by wife for husband; e.g. ～人 *liángrén*, my goodman.
2. well-bred, well-born, of good lineage; patrician.
    a. respectable, deserving; estimable; of the best quality.
3. moderate, conciliate; coordinate, compose.
4. very much so, quite; e.g. ～久 *liángjiǔ*, a good long while.
    a. surely, certainly.
5. ～耀草 *liángyàocǎo*, "finely shining plant," rock-orchid, dendrobium (*Dendrobium*, various species).
6. ⊙ 埌 *làng* 2, tomb-vault.

輬   liáng   MC ljang
1. coach used for longer journeys and in which one could lie down, with curtains that could be rolled up to allow play of fresh breezes.
    a. (med.) a hearse, coffin-carriage.

liǎng

兩   liǎng   MC ljangX
1. pair, make a pair; both.
    a. 一～ *yīliǎng*, one of a pair, as of shoes, carriage wheels, etc.
    b. from Han onward, often used in numbering objects that are not natural pairs: two (but never used ordinally).
2. measure of weight, an "ounce," equiv. 1/16 of "catty" (*jin* 斤).
    a. (med.) 大～ *dàliǎng*, "large ounce," equiv. 3 ounces.
3. measure of length for silks or cloth, equiv. 1 "bolt" (*pi* 匹), 40 "feet" (*chi* 尺).
4. (med.) in every case, all of, everything, every one.

liàng   MC ljangH
1. measure-word for carriages, carts, wagons, ⊙ 輛 *liàng*.

魎 liǎng MC ljangX
1. (bn.) 魎～ *wǎngliǎng*, → 魍 *wǎng*.

liàng

亮 liàng MC ljangH
1. bright(ness), brilliant; gleam(ing), beam; glow(ing).
   a. light up; reveal, make manifest or evident; clarify.
   b. clearly, evidently, obviously.
2. (med.) bright-minded, intelligent.
3. (med.) clear-toned, vibrant (sound).
4. ⊙ 諒 *liàng* 1, believe, trust in, have confidence in; 3, expect, presume; 4, tolerate, condone.

悢 liàng MC ljangH
1. disconsolate, downhearted; discouraged, depressed.
   a. rdup., pained and despondent, woeful and forlorn; also, (med.) preserve and hold dear.
      lǎng MC langX
1. (bn.) 懭～ *kuǎnglǎng*, → 懭 *kuǎng*.

諒 liàng MC ljangH
1. trust, believe in, have confidence that . . .; put full, unconditional faith in.
   a. uncompromising, unwavering; pertinacious; obstinate, stubborn.
2. trustworthy, reliable; authentic, true.
   a. truly, surely.
3. expect, presume; reckon X will be so.
4. tolerate, condone, pardon, excuse; abide generously, make allowance for.

踉 liàng MC ljangH
1. sgl. or (med.) (bn.) ～蹡 or ～蹌 *liàngqiāng* (MC ljangH-tshjang), stagger, stumble, sway, fall out of step.

輛 liàng MC ljangH
1. measure-word for carriages, carts, wagons.

量 liàng MC ljangH
1. measure(ment), quantity; e.g. 無～ *wúliàng*, measureless, ormete; immense; excessive.
   a. standard, criterion; limit.
2. capacity; amplitude, magnitude.
   a. receptivity, tolerance.
3. evaluation; calculate; consider(ation).

liáng MC ljang
1. to measure, by a set standard of length, weight, capacity, etc; measure out.
2. take the measure of, gauge; appraise; deliberate.

liáo

僚 liáo MC lew
1. colleague(s), associate(s), esp. bureaucratic.
2. official functionary.

嘹 liáo MC lew
1. (med.) (bn.) ～亮 *liáoliàng* (MC lew-ljangH), sonorously echoing; (bn.) ～唳 *liáolì* (lew-lejH), vibrantly clear, of song or musical instrument.

寥 liáo MC lew
1. deserted, empty, untenanted, featureless; undisturbed, unperturbed; silent.
   a. rdup., empty stillness, undisturbed solitude; also, no more than, the merest mite of.
   b. (med.) (bn.) ～落 *liáoluò* (MC lew-lak), untenanted and unattainable, echoless emptiness, beyond earthly limits; also, fading faraway; (bn.) ～廓 *liáokuò* (MC lew-khwak), endless expanse, unmeasured infinity or immensity, infinity's outskirts, empty space; (bn.) ～戾, ～唳 *liáolì* (MC lew-lejH), ～亮 *liáoliàng* (MC lew-ljangH), pentratingly clear, distantly or endlessly resonant (of sound).

寮 liáo MC lew
1. small window.
2. ⊙ 僚 *liáo*, official colleague; functionary.

嶚 liáo MC lew
1. steep, precipitous; scarp(ed).

憀 liáo MC lew
1. ⊙ 聊 *liáo* 1, rely on, depend; 嘹 *liáo*, in bns. describing clear and sonorous tones.
2. (med.) sad thoughts, melancholia; (bn.) ～慄 *liáolì* (MC lew-lit), grim and gloomy, in the doldrums.

撩 liáo MC lew
1. manage, attend to; put in order.
2. (med.) throw away, cast off.
   a. (med.) stir up, agitate; toy with; e.g. ～亂 *liáoluàn*, stir up trouble.

3. (med.) draw forth, induce; summon; e.g. 〜撥 *liáobō*, entice, attract.

敹 liáo MC lew
1. stitch a seam, sew up a tear.

澋 liáo MC lew
1. limpid, clear, pure, pellucid; transparent.
2. flow through, run through.
    a. (bn.) 〜浰 *liáolì* (MC lew-lijH), coursing quickly.
3. aggrieved, saddened; disturbed, bothered.
4. ⊙ 寥 *liáo*, deserted, empty; silent; endless; esp. in bns.

獠 liáo MC lew
1. hunt at nighttime by torchlight.
    a. gen. term for hunting excursion.
        lǎo MC lawX
1. (med.) southern or southwestern barbarian tribes.
    a. (med.) derogatory term derived from preceding, used as insult: hyena, mongrel, cur.

療 liáo MC ljewH
1. cure, heal illness; palliate.
    a. take care of trouble, relieve, deliver from; succor.

繚 liáo MC lew
1. tie up, wrap up; bind.
    a. encircle, curl round; reel, coil; e.g. (bn.) 〜繞 *liáorào* (MC lew-nyewH), reeling and wheeling.
2. (med.) measure-word for a strand of hair ("twist, curl") or of silk ("skein").

聊 liáo MC lew
1. rely on, depend; e.g. 無〜 *wúliáo*, with nothing to rely on, without relief.
    a. contented, comfortable; assured.
2. (bn.) 〜浪 *liáoláng* (MC lew-lang), frisk and frolic, romp and revel, cavort and carouse; also, muddle through, hugger-mugger.
3. for a while, for a moment, for a spell; tentatively; temporarily, in the meantime.
4. (med.) ADV indicator of decided future action: shall, will.
5. tinnitus, ringing in the ear.

瞀 liáo MC lew ⊙ 膋 *liáo*.

膋 liáo MC lew
1. fat around the intestines.
2. (med.) caul, amniotic sac covering head of newborn infant.

遼 liáo MC lew
1. distant, faraway.
2. (med.) lengthy, protracted; esp. prolonged rains, flooding.

鐐 liáo MC lew
1. fine silver.

飂 liáo MC lew
1. rdup., rush and gust, rush and roar, of high wind; also, blank and empty.
    a. (med.) (bn.) 〜戾 *liáolì* (MC lew-lejH), whizzing and whooshing, rapidly passing; also, onom. of wind, soughing sibilance.

飍 liáo MC lew
1. (med.) sgl. or rdup., light breeze, breezy, riffle and ruffle.
    a. (med.) (bn.) 〜厲 *liáolì* (MC lew-ljejH), lilt and lift, of wind; clear and resonant, of song or music.

鷯 liáo MC lew
1. (bn.) 鷦〜 *jiāoliáo*, → 鷦 *jiāo*.

liǎo

了 liǎo MC lewX
1. complete, finish(ed), end; e.g. (Budd) 〜義 *liǎoyì*, "completed rightness," i.e. perfected doctrine, definitive meaning.
    a. (ADV) completely, fully, either pre-verbal or post-verbal.
2. (med.) understand clearly, grasp the meaning of; thoroughly master.
    a. (med.) rdup., quick and perceptive.

憭 liǎo MC ljewX
1. explain, make clear.
    a. perspicacious, intelligent.
        liáo MC lew
1. (bn.) 〜慄 *liáolì* (MC lew-lit), grim and gloomy, in the doldrums.

橑　liǎo　MC lewX

1. upswept eaves of roof.
2. ⊙ 轑 *lǎo*, arched support of carriage canopy.
3. firewood, brushwood.

潦　liǎo　MC lew　→ 潦 *lǎo*.

燎　liǎo　MC ljewX

1. brushfire, burn off dead or unwanted vegetation; controlled burn.
   a. burn up, enflame.
2. roast; cook.

liáo　MC ljew

1. torch; flare.

瞭　liǎo　MC lewX

1. clear-eyed, bright-eyed.
   a. gen. term for bright(ness), shining.
2. clarify, explain.

蓼　liǎo　MC lewX

1. knotweed, knotgrass, smartweed (various species of *Polygonum* or *Persicaria*); used in lit. metaphorically for difficulties, vexations.
   a. 水～ *shuǐliǎo*, "water-knotweed," i.e. water-pepper (*Polygonum hydropiper*).

lù　MC ljuwk

1. sgl. or rdup., large-sized, tall and grand.

liǔ　MC lewX

1. (bn.) 糾～ *jiūliǔ*, → 糾 *jiū*.

liào

料　liào　MC lewH

1. measure out, count; calculate, evaluate; consider closely; e.g. ～視 *liàoshì*, count and check on; also, consider, take into account, look after; (med.) ～理 *liàolǐ*, same as preceding; also, arrange, deal with, handle; also, repair, mend, put in order; also, attack, harass.
2. anticipate, estimate; presume.
3. supply, provide; (med.) supplemental stipend or provisions allocated to officials, beyond their set salary.
   a. (med.) gen. term for material, resources, stuff.
4. (med.) cost, expenses.

liáo　MC lew

1. pat, touch lightly.

liè

冽　liè　MC ljet

1. icy, gelid; stingingly cold; freezing.

列　liè　MC ljet

1. split, break up; divide, partition.
   a. (bn.) ～缺 *lièquē* (MC ljet-khwet), "shattering crack(s)," i.e. lightning.
2. rank, order; array.
   a. to array, arrange in ranks or sequence; line up, align(ment); set out.
   b. enlist(ment), rally.
3. pre-nominal marker of plural.
4. (med.) report, give an account of.
5. ⊙ 烈 *liè* 2, ardent, fervent; intense; devoted to a person or principle, resolute.

劣　liè　MC ljet

1. weak, powerless.
2. inferior, poor or lacking in desired quality; lowly; abject, sorry.

埒　liè　MC ljet

1. low wall or embankment, esp. surrounding particular area; enclosure; paddock.
   a. bounded, enclosed, delimited.
2. banked-up irrigation channel.
   a. mountain stream.
3. equal to, equivalent of (< in the same channel or course as), tantamount to.
4. (med.) sgl. or cmpd. 馬～ *mǎliè*, riding-course, beaten track, piste.

捩　liè　MC let

1. (med.) fold, bend, crook.
   a. (med.) twist, wring.
2. (med.) turn against, go contrary to.

lì　MC lejH

1. plectrum, used for playing the lute (*pipa* 琵琶).

擸　liè　MC ljep

1. hold, grip; pick up, grasp.
   a. arrange properly by turning, twisting or untwisting; tweak, smooth out.

là　MC lop

1. (med.) 菈～ *làlà*, → 菈 *là*.

栵　liè　MC ljet

1. Chinese chinquapin (*Castanea seguinii*), small shrublike chestnut, bearing small sweet nuts.

洌   liè   MC ljet
1. crystal-clear, of water.
2. (bn.) 澥～ *piēliè*, → 澥 *piē* (*pì*).
3. ⊙ 冽 *liè*, cold, frigid.

烈   liè   MC ljet
1. blazing, burning; fiery.
   a. set afire.
   b. raging, furious; violent; merciless.
2. ardent, fervent; vehement, impassioned, spirited; intense, zealous.
   a. devoted to a person or principle, resolute, stalwart; possessing integrity.
   b. principled or meritorious service, high achievement.
3. brightly lit, brilliant; illustrious, glorious.
   a. celebrated, famous.
4. thick and strong, intense, pungent (as of smells).
5. rdup., blazing fiercely; also, brassy and harsh, relentlessly formidable; also, resolute and determined, steadfast and unwavering; also, toweringly eminent, sharply salient; also, in ardent agony, burning with sorrow; also, cold and chill (< burned out).
6. ⊙ 列 *liè* 2, rank, order, array; arrange in order.

獵   liè   MC ljep
1. hunt, engage in a hunt, esp. an excursion hunt for wild game.
   a. hunt for, search out, scare up.
2. attack, assail, move against, do battle with; invade; plunder.
3. (med.) rdup., onom. of gusting, blustery wind.
4. ⊙ 躐 *liè*, trample on; move through or over; 擸 *liè*, hold, grip; arrange by turning this way or that, tweak, smooth out.

胅   liè   MC ljwet
1. rib-meat of animals.

茢   liè   MC ljet
1. common reed (*Phragmites communis*), esp. used to make brooms for sweeping away evil or impure influences.

蜊   liè   MC ljet
1. (bn.) 蜻～ *jīngliè*, → 蜻 *jīng* (*qīng*).

裂   liè   MC ljet
1. rip apart, rend, tear, split open, cut open.
   a. burst, rupture; crack.
   b. (bn.) ～缺 *lièquē* (MC ljet-khwet), ⊙ 列缺 *lièquē*, "shattering crack(s)," i.e. lightning.
2. dismember, pull apart; esp. judicial punishment of dismembering by pulling apart limbs with 4 chariots.

躐   liè   MC ljep
1. trample on or down, tread on.
   a. step over, move through or over.
2. ⊙ 擸 *liè*, grasp, pick up; arrange by twisting or untwisting, tweak, smooth out.

迾   liè   MC ljet
1. obstruct, impede, esp. arrest the free flow of traffic around palace compound or on streets where ruler or high dignitaries are traveling.
2. ⊙ 列 *liè* 2, align, array, set out in order.

颲   liè   MC ljet
1. sgl. or rdup., fierce wind, wild wind, cruel and pitiless wind.

鬛   liè   MC ljep
1. beard, whiskers of man.
   a. bristly, stivery.
2. mane, of horse; bristles, of pig; barbel, of fish or dragon; tuft, of bird; scales, of snake; needles, of pine-tree.
3. sweep away, whisk away.

鴷   liè   MC ljet
1. woodpecker, wryneck (various species of *Picinae, Jynginae*); syn. 啄木 *zhuómù*.

lín

嶙   lín   MC lin
1. (bn.) ～峋 *línxún* (MC lin-swin), towering tier upon tier, with overlapping cliffs.
   a. (bn.) 岭～ *línglín*, → 岭 *líng*.

惏   lín   MC lim   → 惏 *lán*.

林   lín   MC lim
1. forest, grove.
   a. sylvan, bosky.

2. metaphorically a category of particular people or things; e.g. 羽～ *yǔlín*, Plume Grove, name of the military company constituting the emperor's personal guard, or the palace guard, or the honor guard.

    a. rdup., a veritable forest of . . ., tree after tree of . . .; many and more; row upon row.

淋　lín　MC lim

1. pour out, pour down.

    a. drench, soak, imbue with.

    b. (bn.) ～灕 *línlí* (MC lim-lje), soaked and steeped, sluicing and spewing; (med.) also, closely clustered, mass and slew.

    c. rdup., streaming and sluicing, dash and spatter.

2. spray, sprinkle.

    a. drip drop-by-drop.

3. ⊙ 霖 *lín*, copious, steady rain.

潾　lín　MC lin

1. (med.) rdup., limpid and lucid, crystalline clarity, esp. of water.

猋　lín　MC lin

1. will-o'-the-wisp, ignis fatuus; esp. flicker of luminescent fungi infecting rotten wood, cadavers, etc.

燐　lín　MC lin

1. ⊙ 猋 *lín*, will-o'-the-wisp, ignis fatuus.

    a. (bn.) ～亂 *línluàn* (MC lin-lwanH), flicker and flutter.

2. light of firefly.

琳　lín　MC lim

1. blue-gem; sapphire.

2. (med.) (bn.) ～琅 *línláng* (MC lim-lang), onom. of tinkling of gems; also, dazzling and scintillant, glinting and glittering, standing forth in brilliance.

璘　lín　MC lin

1. luster or brilliance of jade; splendent; sheen; often descriptive of moonlight.

    a. (bn.) ～彬 *línbīn* (MC lin-pin), ～班 *línbān* (MC lin-paen), sparkling splendor, glitter and glisten (of gems).

    b. (Dao.) 結～ *jiélín*, "bundled luster," Dao. esoteric name of the moon.

瞵　lín　MC lin

1. fix the gaze on, stare at.

2. (bn.) ～彬 *línbīn* (MC lin-pin), lustrously flecked, brilliantly dappled.

琳　lín　MC lim

1. rdup., deep and plunging, profound and bottomless.

磷　lín　MC lin　⊙ 粼 *lín*.

粼　lín　MC lin

1. rdup., clear-cut, distinct and well-defined, like stones in a clear stream.

    lìn　MC linH

1. become thin, wear away; flake off; e.g. ～石 *lìnshí*, "flake-stone," mica of purest white.

臨　lín　MC lim

1. overlook, look out at from above.

    a. look downward; e.g. ～目 *línmù*, eyes cast down, lower one's gaze.

2. oversee, supervise; preside over; e.g. ～政 *línzhèng*, preside over the government.

3. be on the verge of, appoach(ing) (place or time); e.g. ～淵 *línyuān*, at the edge of an abyss; ～終 *línzhōng*, approaching the end, on the verge of death.

    a. lean into; in the face of, confront; e.g. ～風 *línfēng*, facing the wind.

4. (med.) make a copy of, copy from (calligraphy or painting).

5. "Overseeing," name of 19th hexagram of the *Yijing*.

6. siege machine from which one could shoot down on defenders.

    lìn　MC limH

1. pay respects to the dead; lament for the dead, keen(ing).

轔　lín　MC lin

1. rdup., onom. of the thunder of carriage wheels.

2. threshold of door or gate.

    lìn　MC linH

1. crush under wheels of chariot; ⊙ 輷 *lìn*.

    a. (bn.) ～轢 *línlì* (MC lin-lek), crush and squash, flatten.

鄰　lín　MC lin

1. neighborhood, anciently a residential division of 5 households (*jia* 家), sometimes also said as 4 or 8.
    a. neighbor(s).
    b. neighboring, near to; adjoining (< sharing a wall).
    c. mutual security group.
2. approximate, approximation, "in the neighborhood of."
3. rdup., ⊙ 轔轔 *línlín*, onom. of movement of many carriages or wagons.

霖　lín　MC lim

1. copious or steady rain, continued for at least 3 consecutive days.

驎　lín　MC lin

1. 騏～ *qílín*, → 麟 *lín* 1.

鱗　lín　MC lin

1. fish-scales.
    a. strip or remove scales.
2. by synecdoche, scaly creatures, fish and dragons.
3. scaly, squamous.
    a. overlapping, imbricated; shingled; arranged in connected layers.

麟　lín　MC lin

1. sgl. or (bn.) 麒～ *qílín* (MC gi-lin), fabulous animal, traditionally rendered as "unicorn" though with few similar characteristics. Described as having the body of a roe-deer, tail of an ox, feet of a horse with round hooves, light brown in color, and with a single horn whose tip is not of bone but of flesh (thus incapable of harming other animals). Chief among hooved creatures. One of the "four numinous animals" (*siling* 四靈). Emblematic of humaneness (*ren* 仁); said to appear when a sage-king is on the throne or a sage exists to recognize it.
2. rdup., brightly shining.
3. ⊙ 鱗 *lín*, scales of fish.

lǐn

凜　lǐn　MC limX

1. rdup., stinging chill, numbing(ly) cold, shivering; also, quaking with fear.
2. ～然 *lǐnrán*, severely, coldly, forbiddingly.

廩　lǐn　MC limX

1. granary.
    a. grain rations, esp. as official salary.
2. rdup., ⊙ 懍懍 *lǐnlǐn*, quail and quiver.

懍　lǐn　MC limX

1. dismayed, unmanned; in fear or dread.
    a. rdup., quail and quiver, flinch and blench.

lìn

吝　lìn　MC linH

1. chary of, stint, sparing, grudging; stingy, costive, niggardly.
2. disgrace, shame.

橉　lìn　MC linH

1. various species of rosewood (*Dalbergia*), white-flowering and with extremely hard wood, syn. 檀 *tán*.

　　lǐn　MC linX

1. threshold of door or gate.

藺　lìn　MC linH

1. soft rush (*Juncus effusus*), esp. used for making mats.
    a. 馬～ *mǎlìn*, → 馬 *mǎ*.
2. trample, crush; ⊙ 躪 *lìn*.

賃　lìn　MC nrimH

1. work for hire, hired labor
    a. pay (for hired work), commission.
2. let out, lease, rent; hire.

躙　lìn　MC linH　⊙ 躪 *lìn*.

躪　lìn　MC linH

1. sgl. or (med.) (bn.) ～轢 *lìnlì* (MC linH-lek), trample on, crush, ride roughshod over.

輴　lìn　MC linH

1. roll over, with carriage or chariot wheels; wheel through.
    a. (bn.) ～轢 *lìnlì* (MC linH-lek), flatten and crush, grind down, ride roughshod over.
2. (med.) trample, tread on.
    a. (med.) exceed, surmount; move past.

遴　lìn　MC linH

1. troublesomely, with difficulty.
2. ⊙ 吝 *lìn*, chary of, stingy.

閵　lín　MC ljeng
1. (med.) choose out, carefully select, esp. a person for a task.

閵　lìn　MC linH　⊙ 蹸 lìn.

líng

伶　líng　MC leng
1. musician, esp. at court; performer of music, song, dance.
2. (med.) messenger, envoy.
3. (med.) (bn.) ～俜 língpīng (MC leng-pheng) or 俜～ pīnglíng, all on one's own, single solitary, one and only; also, stagger unsteadily.

凌　líng　MC ling
1. iced up, iced over; ice-block.
2. mount upon, ride.
3. climb up to or over, surmount, escalade; traverse; skim over.
　a. (bn.) ～歷 línglì (MC ling-lek), traverse and transit.
4. confront, brave.
　a. (med.) come near to, draw near to; e.g. ～曉 língxiǎo, getting on toward daybreak.
5. affront, violate; override, trangress, infringe on.
6. strict, severe.
7. frightened, in dread; quavering; (bn.) ～兢 língjīng (MC ling-king), trembling terror; also, contentious and querulous.

囹　líng　MC leng
1. (bn.) ～圄 língyǔ (MC leng-ngjoX), prison; esp. pre-Han usage.

岭　líng　MC leng
1. (bn.) ～嶝 línghōng (MC leng-xweang), deep and steep, precipitously plunging.
2. (bn.) ～嶙 línglín (MC leng-lin), lying in layers; also, ringing resonantly.

崚　líng　MC ling
1. (med.) (bn.) ～嶒 língcéng (MC ling-dzing), rise up layer upon layer.

悢　líng　MC ling
1. fright(ened), scared; atremble.

櫺　líng　MC leng
1. latticework, of window or railing.

痠　líng　MC ling
1. (med.) (bn.) ～殑 língqíng (MC ling-ging) or 殑～ qínglíng, worn out and done in, dead tired, fagged out, played out; also, as if one's soul has gone, spiritless.

泠　líng　MC leng
1. coolly indifferent, nonchalant; insouciant.
2. (med.) clear, limpid.
　a. (med.) clear-witted.
3. rdup., fresh and cool, esp. of wind; also, clear and resounding, of sounds.

淩　líng　MC ling
1. surmount, climb beyond; traverse.
　a. skim over, skim past; graze the top of.
2. mount upon, ride.
3. override, transgress; infringe on; affront; violate.
　a. trip up, dupe, play for a fool.
4. (med.) confront, brave, come face-to-face with.

玲　líng　MC leng
1. (med.) (bn.) ～瓏 línglóng (MC leng-luwng), goffered, honeycombed, like openwork weave; also, tintling tinkle of gems; also, clear and transparent.
　a. (med.) rdup., tintling tinkle of gems.

瓴　líng　MC leng
1. water-jar in shape of urn, urn-jar.
2. (bn.) ～甋 língdí (MC leng-tek), square brick for tiling, cobblestone.

綾　líng　MC ling
1. figured light-twill, damask twill.
　a. figured chiffon, esp. before ca. 5th century.

羚　líng　MC leng
1. (med.) goral (various species of *Naemorhedus*), serow (various species of *Capricornis*, larger and less agile than *Naemorhedus*), Asian mountain-goat. N.B. Although some species may resemble small antelopes, they are not antelopes and should not be called such.

翎　líng　MC leng
1. (med.) pinion, flight-feather.
　a. (med.) plume, esp. tailfeather.

聆　líng　MC leng
1. give ear to, bend an ear to, harken; attend to.
2. rdup., understand fully, apprehend clearly.

舲　líng　MC leng
1. small boat or bark with windowed cabin, fenestrated barge.

苓　líng　MC leng
1. cocklebur (*Xanthium sibiricum*), fall-flowering, syn. 蒼兒 *cāng'ér*.
2. abb. 茯～ *fúlíng*, pine-truffle (*Pachyma cocos*), a fungus esp. used in Dao. dietary regimens.
3. clematis (*Clematis chinensis*), a climbing vine or liana, producing showy flowers; syn. 微靈仙 *wēilíngxiān*.
4. ⊙ 蘦 *líng*, Chinese licorice (*Glycyrrhiza uralensis*), esp. used medicinally; syn. 甘草 *gāncǎo*.
5. (bn.) ～落 *língluò* (MC leng-lak), flutter and fall, wilt and wither (of leaves); ⊙ 零落 *língluò*.
　　　lián　MC
1. ⊙ 蓮 *lián*, lotus.

菱　líng　MC ling
1. caltrop (*Trapa bispinosa*); syn. 芰 *jì*.
　　a. (med.) ～花 *línghuā*, "caltrop-adorned," i.e. bronze mirror, because back often multi-cornered like caltrop.

蘦　líng　MC leng
1. Chinese liquorice (*Glycyrrhiza uralensis*), esp. used medicinally; syn. 甘草 *gāncǎo*, 苓 *líng* 4.

蛉　líng　MC leng
1. (bn.) 蜻～ *qīnglíng*, → 蜻 *qīng*.
2. (bn.) 螟～ *mínglíng*, → 螟 *míng*.
3. (bn.) ～窮 *língqióng* (MC leng-gjuwng), scutigera, spider-centipede (*Cermatiae*); syn. 蚰蜒 *yóuyán*.

詅　líng　MC leng
1. (med.) call out or cry one's wares.

軨　líng　MC leng
1. carriage-rail or horizontal wood-slats of grill-work, which runs around front and both sides of carriage-box.
2. carriage mudguard, made of red oiled silk and fastened to end of axle.

3. ～軒 *língxuān*, carriage with enclosed and windowed chaise; also, windowed small room or portico.
4. ⊙ 舲 *líng*, small bark with windowed cabin.

輘　líng　MC ling　→ 輘 *léng*.

醽　líng　MC leng
1. (med.) mead, made with fermented honey, water, and grains; sweet wine.
　　a. (med.) (bn.) ～醁 *línglù* (MC leng-ljowk), metheglin, spiced mead.

鈴　líng　MC leng
1. grelot, folly-bell, croatal, jingler, small clapper-bells used on horses or carriages.
　　a. onom. of sound of preceding.
2. (med.) ～鼻 *língbí*, grommet, eyehole, for attaching an object with string.

陵　líng　MC ling
1. large earthen (not rocky) mound, knoll; slope.
　　a. tomb-mound, tumulus, barrow; esp. burial mounds for emperors.
　　b. ～遲 *língchí*, wearing away over time, like a mound erodes and levels down; gradual(ly) decline; (med.) also, persecute, torment, pick away at.
2. ascend, climb, mount.
　　a. mount upon, ride on.
3. climb past, skim over, skim past; graze; scandent; escalade.
　　a. cross over, traverse.
4. transgress; override, infringe on, encroach on.
　　a. insult, humiliate.
5. wane, decline; fall apart; e.g. ～替 *língtì*, fade away and be replaced, fall into desuetude.
6. strict, rigorous, severe.
7. hone, sharpen.
8. ～藁 *línggǎo*, spurge (*Euphorbia kansui*), syn. 大戟 *dàjǐ*.

零　líng　MC leng
1. fine rain, drizzle; douse.
　　a. gentle, muted, quiet; e.g. ～粲 *língcàn*, muted scintillation.
2. fall gently (rain, snow, dew, leaves).
　　a. fade, wither, die out; e.g. (bn.) ～落 *língluò* (MC leng-lak), withered and wasted, sere and stripped, devastated; in vain disarray.

3. fall apart, crumble, crumple.

　　a. (med.) fragment(ed), fraction, sliver; left-over.

4. (bn.) ～丁 *língdīng* (MC leng-teng), sole and solitary, alone and apart, all unattached; also, missing-person notice.

5. ～陵香 *línglíngxiāng*, "aromatic from Lingling," sweet basil (*Ocimum basilicum*); syn. 蕙 *huì*.

靈　líng　MC leng

1. numinous, sacred; spiritual power or efficacy; potency of the disembodied world.

　　a. ethereal, supernatural; preternatural, un-earthly; sublime.

2. life principle, vital principle, embodied realization of the numinous, one's inner spirit.

　　a. potency of this principle that may survive the body's demise, incl. spiritually potent remains of the deceased (i.e. the corpse), also perhaps postmortem consciousness.

3. seemingly divine intelligence or awareness.

　　a. inherent responsiveness or quickness to other beings and entities.

4. providential, divinely ordained; auspicious, favorable.

5. ～香草 *língxiāngcǎo*, lysimachia (*L. foenum-graecum*), summer-flowering.

鯪　líng　MC ling

1. mud-carp (*Cirrhina molitorella*).

2. (med.) (bn.) ～鯉 *línglǐ* (MC ling-liX), pango-lin, scaly anteater (*Manis pentadactyla*).

鴒　líng　MC leng

1. sgl. or (bn.) 鶺～ *jílíng* (MC tsjek-leng), wagtail (*Motacill flava, Motacilla alba*); in lit. symbolic of brotherly attentiveness (< Ode 164) because of characteristic tail-jerking and head-bobbing which in groups gives impression that each is attending to the others.

齡　líng　MC leng

1. years of life; age, seniority; e.g. 弱～ *ruòlíng*, of tender age.

lǐng

嶺　lǐng　MC ljengX

1. mountain pass, high pass; mountain ridge, ridge-line.

　　a. mountain range.

2. (med.) ref. the 5 Passes in Hunan, Guangxi, and Guangdong that were mountain routes into the deep south; e.g. ～外 *lǐngwài*, beyond the passes, i.e. the Lingnan ～南 area.

領　lǐng　MC ljengX

1. neck.

　　a. collar.

　　b. neckband.

2. take by the neck, lead(er), guide; direct(or), manage(r).

3. measure-word, esp. for clothes.

4. (med.) endow(ed with), possess(ed of); be mandated to have.

　　a. (med.) claim, accept.

5. (med.) understand, comprehend; take in.

6. (med.) nominal(ly), ref. official appointment; e.g. 遙～ *yáolǐng*, appointed in absentia.

7. ⊙嶺 *lǐng*, mountain pass, ridge.

lìng

令　lìng　MC ljengH

1. issue a command, usu. with intention of bringing about particular action; direct(ive), order, command.

　　a. (med.) an order from the heir-designate.

2. official title indicating person in charge of particular area, group, or agency: commandant, director, etc.; e.g. 縣～ *xiànlìng*, district magistrate; 中書～ *zhōngshūlìng*, Director of Imperial Secretariat.

3. commanding, of distinguished or impressive quality, esteemed, finest, noble; e.g. ～聞 *lìngwén*, a commanding reputation; ～酒 *lìngjiǔ*, the finest wine.

　　a. respected, esteemed, honorific applied to relations or possessions of addressee.

　　b. pretentious, purporting, of falsely or improperly used quality.

4. season, particular time or occasion.

5. administrative statutes (cf. 律 *lù*, criminal code).

　　a. rules of behavior, appropriate manner; e.g. 辭～ *cílìng*, manner of speech; (med.) 酒～ *jiǔlìng*, drinking customs, incl. drinking games.

6. bring about, to cause, to effect; enable, cause to do; allow, let; syn. 使 *shǐ* 2.

　　a. (GP) conditional particle, impersonally introducing supposition, often in cmpd. 若～

ruòlìng: if it were (brought about) that . . .; supposing that . . .; in the event that . . .; let it be that . . .

b. (GP) optative particle, used when expressing a wish: may it be that . . .

7. (med.) 〜上 *língshàng*, transcendent level of existence; (med.) 〜達 *língdá*, transcendently free.

liú

劉   liú   MC ljuw

1. battle-axe.

a. slaughter, hew, cut to pieces; massacre; kill.

2. declining, waning; dilapidated.

3. a surname, notably that of ruling family of the Han dynasty (206 BCE-220 CE) and of the Song (420-479) dynasty.

斿   liú   MC ljuw

1. decorative fringe or indentations or scalloping at bottom of flag or banner; also, strung gems hanging from rulers' or nobles' ceremonial cap; ⊙ 旒 *liú*.

yóu   MC yuw

1. float, drift; ⊙ 游 *yóu* 1.

旒   liú   MC ljuw

1. decorative fringe or indentations or scalloping at bottom of flag or banner.

2. strings of small gems hanging from front and back of rulers' or nobles' ceremonial cap.

榴   liú   MC ljuw

1. sgl. or in cmpd. 石〜 *shíliú*, pomegranate (*Punica granatum*), which is abb. of 安石〜 *ānshíliú*, "*liú* from Parthia," because brought to China from Iran; also called 五月〜 *wǔyuèliú*, "*liu* of the fifth month," because blooms in midsummer; also 若〜 *rěliú* (MC nyak-ljuw), trsc. Sog. *n'r'kh* < Skt. *kremeru(ka)*, red.

a. 海〜 *hǎiliú* or 海石〜 *hǎishíliú*, camellia, winter-rose, red-flowering tea-tree (*Camellia japonica*); N.B. post-Tang often used for pomegranate (*shíliú*), but before that invariably camellia.

b. 山石〜 *shānshíliú*, red barberry, Japanese barberry (*Berberis thunbergii*).

流   liú   MC ljuw

1. flow, drift, course, glide, run, stream.

a. current, course (of river).

b. fluid; fluent.

2. follow the current, go with the flow; trend(y), in vogue; e.g. 〜風 *liúfēng*, "drift(er) with the wind," stylish manner, flowing charm, stylishly cultivated, urbanity, refinement.

a. adrift, aimless, undirected; vagabond; rove.

3. circulate, distribute, spread.

a. stimulate, excite.

4. tributary, branch (off from).

a. sect, class, group, school; common run of.

5. (send to) penal exile, banish(ment) to farthest reach of empire.

6. (bn.) 〜連 *liúlián* (MC ljuw-ljen), so swept away (with music, idea, happiness) that one is oblivious of the world; give oneself up to, charmed and enchanted; also, wander wantonly, drift directionless.

7. 〜黃 *liúhuáng*, sulphur.

瀏   liú   MC ljuw

1. deep and clear, of water.

a. transparent, lucid; sheen, sheer.

b. (bn.) 〜亮 *liúliàng* (MC ljuw-ljangH), lambent and lucid, lambent luster.

2. keen wind, crisp wind, zephyr; rdup., blowing hard and swift.

a. swiftly running; urgent, quick.

琉   liú   MC ljuw

1. (bn.) 〜璃 *liúlí* (MC ljuw-lje), opaque colored glass, glazed glass, sometimes colored ceramic glaze, native to China and also imported in med. times from west and south; "paste," imitation gemstones often confused with natural minerals, esp. lapis lazuli and turquoise; (Budd.) in Budd. texts, beryl (< Skt. *vaidūrya*), one of the 7 treasures (*saptaratna*).

鎏   liú   MC ljuw   ⊙ 旒 *liú*.

留   liú   MC ljuw

1. remain, stay behind, wait; abide; retain; e.g. 〜守 *liúshǒu*, "abiding warden," *locum tenens* in charge of capital when emperor is elsewhere.

a. linger, tarry; pause, wait; e.g. 〜連 *liúlián*, linger and loiter, saunter and stroll, relax; also, be stalled and stuck; 〜行 *liúxíng*, pause en route.

2. detain, stall, delay, check, keep back; e.g. ～難 *liúnàn*, thwart, make difficult for.
　　a. belated, dilatory, tardy.
3. protect, keep safe, be safe from; keep watch over, be attentive to; e.g. ～意 *liúyì*, keep one's own counsel, be careful.
4. (med.) present upon parting, esp. a poem; leave as keepsake.
5. (bn.) ～落 *liúluò* (MC ljuw-lak), balked from attaining one's goal.
6. ～求子 *liúqiúzi*, Chinese honeysuckle, Rangoon creeper (*Quisqualis indica*), ligneous vine, red-flowering, used medicinally; syn. 使君子 *shǐjūnzi*.
7. ～夷 *liúyí*, flowering peony (*Paeonia lactiflora*), syn. 芍藥 *sháoyáo*.
8. ⊙ 騮 *liú*, black-maned roan horse.

瘤　liú　MC ljuw
1. tumor, unusual swelling.

硫　liú　MC ljuw
1. sulphur; also ～黃 *liúhuáng*, 石～黃 *shíliúhuáng*.

蟉　liú　MC ljiw
1. (bn.) ～虯 *liúqiú* (MC lijw-gjiw), coiling and curling, writhing and winding.

膠　liú　MC ljuw
1. (bn.) ～觓 *liúqiú* (MC ljuw-gjuw), curved and cornute, twisted like horn, curved and contoured.

飀　liú　MC ljuw
1. rdup., onom. of gentle wind: lhooh-lhooh.
　　a. (bn.) 飀～ *sōuliú*, → 飀 *sōu*.

騮　liú　MC ljuw
1. roan horse with black mane and tail.
　　a. (bn.) 驊～ *huáliú*, → 驊 *huá*.

鶹　liú　MC ljuw
1. (bn.) ～鷅 *liúlì* (MC ljuw-lit), short-eared or hornless owl.
2. (bn.) 鵂～ *xiūliú* (xjuw-ljuw), nightjar, nighthawk; also, pygmy owl.

liǔ

懰　liǔ　MC ljuwX
1. fine-looking, attractive; lovely.

飗　liú　MC ljuw
1. (bn.) ～慄 *liúlì* (MC ljuw-lit), sadly shaken, woefully faltering.
2. hold back, keep back; arrest, reserve.

柳　liǔ　MC ljuwX
1. willow (various species of *Salix*, also incl. sallows, osiers).
　　a. ～柏 *liǔbó*, "willow cypress," weeping cypress (*Cupressus funebris*), medium-sized to tall cypress with pendulous slender leaves.
2. "Willow," one of the 28 lunar lodgings, comprised of δ, ε, ζ, η, θ, ρ, σ, ω Hydrae, in the southern quadrant (*chiniao* 赤鳥) of the sky.
3. ⊙ 瘤 *liú*, tumorous swelling.
4. a surname.

綹　liǔ　MC ljuwX
1. bundle of silk threads; skein; hank.

罶　liǔ　MC ljuwX
1. bamboo fish-trap.

liù

六　liù　MC ljuwk
1. six(th).
　　a. numerologically representative of *yin*, as in *Yijing* where lines with value of 6 are "strong" or "moving" *yin* lines.
　　b. ～時 *liùshí*, 6 double-hours, i.e. beginning, middle, and end of both day and night; ～出 *liùchū*, 6-pointed [blossom], i.e. snowflake; ～合 *liùhé*, 6 coordinates or conjunctions, cardinal directions plus above and below; (Budd.) ～趣 *liùqù*, 6 states of existence; ～度 *liùdù*, 6 *pāramitās* or perfected practice leading to Buddhahood; (Dao.) ～天 *liùtiān*, 6 demonic heavens

溜　liù　MC ljuwH
1. spout, gush, flow; outrush, runoff, spill over.
　　a. trickle, plash, flow gently.
2. curved downspouts under roof-eaves.

霤　liù　MC ljuwH
1. water runoff from roof.
　　a. water-run, overflow.
2. impluvium, eaves-trough; also, runoff culvert.
　　a. by metonymy, roof-eaves.

餾 liù   MC ljuwH
1. (med.) to steam rice.

鰡 liù   MC ljuw
1. (bn.) 沙～, 紗～ shāliù, → 沙 shā.

鷚 liù   MC ljuwH
1. sgl. or 天～ tiānliù, 阿～ èliù, skylark (*Alauda arvensis*).
2. pheasant chick, poult.

lóng

嚨 lóng   MC luwng
1. sgl. or (bn.) 喉～ hóulóng (MC huw-luwng), throat, gullet.

巄 lóng   MC luwng
1. (bn.) ～㙡 lóngsǒng (MC luwng-sjowngX), arching aloft, sharply spiring.
2. steep gully, ravine.

曨 lóng   MC luwng
1. (med.) (bn.) 曈～ tónglóng, → 曈 tóng.

朧 lóng   MC luwng
1. faint glow of moonlight.
    a. rdup., filmy and faint, palely flickering.
    b. (bn.) 曈～ tónglóng, → 曈 tóng; (bn.) 朦～ ménglóng, → 朦 méng.

櫳 lóng   MC luwng
1. pen, paling, corral, cage (for animals).
2. latticed window.

瀧 lóng   MC luwng
1. rdup., rain pelting and pouring, falling in continuous cascade.
        MC laewng
1. (med.) streaming onward, fast flow of river.

瓏 lóng   MC luwng
1. (med.) (bn.) ～玲 lónglíng (MC luwng-leng) or 玲～ línglóng, also ～璁 lóngcōng (MC luwng-tshuwng), tintling tinkle, of gems.

癃 lóng   MC ljuwng
1. infirm, enfeebled by age.
    a. doddering, tottering.
    b. ischuria, urine retention.

礱 lóng   MC luwng
1. grind, sharpen; grindstone.
    a. hull rice; rice-huller.
2. (med.) examine or explain in detail, get below the surface of.

籠 lóng   MC luwng
1. bamboo basket, cage, panier, coop, of any size to contain or enclose various objects or animals.
    a. items shaped like basket; e.g. (med.) ～冠 lóngguān, basket-hat, high close-fitting semi-transparent headwear made of lacquered woven material, worn as court attire.
2. encage, enfold, envelop, englobe, encircle; e.g. ～裙 lóngqún, wraparound skirt.
    a. (en)trap, trick.
3. circumscribe, include; embrace; e.g. ～圈 lóngjuàn, delineate, delimit.
4. (med.) ～連 lónglián (MC luwng-ljen), flit and flicker, of light.

聾 lóng   MC luwng
1. deaf; hard of hearing.
2. insensible, stupified; nonplussed.

蘢 lóng   MC luwng
1. ～草 lóngcǎo, ～葛 lónggé, cayratia, bush-killer (*Cayratia japonica*).
2. ～古 lónggǔ, polygonum, knotgrass (*Polygonum orientale*).
        lǒng   MC luwngX
1. (bn.) ～茸 lǒngróng (MC luwng-nyowng), lush and luxuriant, rank and rampant; clumped and crowded, gobbed and knotted; ～葱 lǒngcōng (MC luwng-tshuwng) or 葱～ cōnglǒng, same as preceding; also, verdant and virescent.

隆 lóng   MC ljuwng
1. prominent; ascendant; arched, raised; high, lofty; e.g. ～準 lóngzhǔn, arched or aquiline nose.
    a. heighten, raise; increase.
    b. (bn.) ～穹 lóngqióng (MC ljuwng-khjuwng) or 穹～ qiónglóng, arched and angled, steeply vaulted, high and humped.
2. hold in high regard; revere, venerate; attach high value to.
3. in the ascendant, triumph(ant); prosperous, flourishing; bring prosperity to; e.g. ～替 lóngtì, rise and fall, glory and decline.
4. to a high or extreme degree; e.g. ～冬 lóngdōng, the height of winter, severe cold.

龍　lóng　MC ljowng

1. mythological animal of divine provenance, traditionally rendered as "dragon," though lacking generally frightful aspects of Western counterpart. Pictured as having scales, whiskers, and five claws per foot. Quintessence and incarnation of the power of water, but a *yang* symbol equally associated with the heavens; at home in earthly pools and rivers and also in the clouds upon which it depends to rise aloft. Mutable and transformative in nature, a symbol of universal dynamism. Chief among scaly creatures; one of the "four numinous animals" (*siling* 四靈); associated with the east, the color *qing* 青, and correspondences related with the phase or agent of wood.
    a. emblematic of celestial and imperial power; e.g. ～風 *lóngfēng*, dragon (i.e. imperial) aura.
    b. euph. for an exceptional horse.
    c. euph. for Jupiter, the "year-star" (歲星 *suìxīng*), because Jupiter associated in *wuxing* correspondences with phase of wood, whose emblematic animal is the dragon.
2. (Budd.) trns. of Skt. *nāga*, serpent; e.g. cmpd. with *xiàng* 象 "elephant," metaphor for most important monks in a monastery.
3. collectively referring to the seven lunar lodgings in the eastern quadrant of the sky, *qinglong* 青～ or *canglong* 蒼～.
4. (bn.) ～鍾 *lóngzhōng* (MC ljowng-tsyowng) weakened, frail and failing; also, displeased, dissatisfied, frustrated and unfulfilled; also, proceed unsteadily, faltering and haltingly; also, descriptive of tears flowing and falling.
5. (med.) (bn.) ～鯉 *lónglǐ* (MC ljowng-liX), pangolin, scaly anteater (*Manis pentadactyla*); syn. 鯪鯉 *línglǐ*.
    chǒng　MC trhjowngX
1. ⊙ 寵 *chǒng*, divinely or imperially favored.
    máng　MC maewng
1. ⊙ 尨 *máng* 2, motley, parti-colored.

lǒng

壠　lǒng　MC ljowngX

1. hummock, hill, knoll; down(s).
2. grave-mound, barrow-down.
3. baulk of earth dividing fields; farmworkers' path.
    a. irrigation channel, dike.

攏　lǒng　MC luwngX

1. gather, bring together; coalesce.
2. draw alongside, come near to; accost.
3. (med.) comb out, dress.
4. (med.) picking or plucking a stringed instrument, esp. a left-hand movement, "gathering."

隴　lǒng　MC ljowngX

1. hillock, mound, down(s); highland; dune; long or large slope.
    a. ～斷 *lǒngduàn*, broken ridge of hills.
2. ⊙ 壠 *lǒng* 2, grave-mound, barrow-down; 3, baulk dividing fields; irrigation ditch, dike.
3. (bn.) ～種 *lǒngzhǒng* (MC ljowngX-tsyowngX), defeated and dispersed, overrun and scattered (of troops); frail and failing.

lòng

哢　lòng　MC luwngH

1. (med.) warble, twitter, trill (of birds).
    a. (med.) (bn.) 喑～ *ānlòng*, → 喑 *ān*.

lóu

婁　lóu　MC luw

1. "Harvester," one of the 28 lunar lodgings, comprised of α, β, γ Arietis, in the western quadrant (*baihu* 白虎) of the sky.
    lǘ　MC lju
1. drag, pull; trail.
    lǚ　MC ljuX
1. pull-rope for oxen, leading-rope; tether.
    lǜ　MC ljuH
1. ⊙ 屢 *lǜ*, frequently, often.

慺　lóu　MC luw

1. rdup. or cmpd. ～誠 *lóuchéng*, respectful and deferential, careful and courteous, attentively assiduous, truly dedicated.

㨨　lóu　MC luw

1. pull along, drag after one.

樓　lóu　MC luw

1. multi-storeyed building (2 storeys or more), loft-building, tiered pavilion; the common translation "tower" wrongly gives the impression of narrow verticality but is often hard to replace.
    a. double-decked (of boats, wagons, etc.).

耬   lóu   MC luw
1. seed-drill, funnel-shaped implement for delving and sowing.

膢   lóu   MC luw
1. early festival of eating and drinking, the celebratory date of which is given differently in different sources (2nd month, 7th month, 8th month); often spoken of on equal footing with the *la* 臘 festival; died out after the Han.

艛   lóu   MC luw
1. tiered boat, double-decked or carrying a 2-storey cabin.

蔞   lóu   MC luw
1. mugwort, wormwood (*Artemisia vulgaris*).

螻   lóu   MC luw
1. sgl. or ～蛄 *lóugū*, mole-cricket (*Gryllotalpa orientalis*), omnivorous pest, esp. damaging to crop-roots, emerges from its burrows at night and can fly.
2. (bn.) ～蟈 *lóuguō* (MC luw-kweak), frog.

謱   lóu   MC luw
1. (bn.) 謰～ *liánlóu*, → 謰 *lián*.

驢   lóu   MC luw
1. onager, Asian wild ass (*Equus hemionus*), brought to China from Central Asia.

髏   lóu   MC luw
1. (bn.) 髑～ *dúlóu*, → 髑 *dú*.

lǒu

塿   lǒu   MC luwX
1. (bn.) 培～ *pǒulǒu*, → 培 *pǒu* (*péi*).

lòu

瘻   lòu   MC luw
1. enlarged lymph-nodes; esp. neck lumps

漏   lòu   MC luwH
1. leak, seep; drip.
   a. discharge, exude; e.g. ～瘡 *lòuchuāng*, running sores.
   b. (Budd.) contaminating outflows, which derive from the mind and affect one's interaction with the world, both mental and sensual, trns. Skt. *āsrava*.
2. clepsydra, waterclock; e.g. ～刻 *lòukè*, graduated time-markings of clepsydra, carved on side; 夜～ *yèlòu*, the o'clock of the night.
3. divulge, let slip; reveal; release.
4. ～蘆 *lòulú*, globe-thistle (*Echinops dahurica*), showing spiny globe-shaped blue or violet flower-heads.

鏤   lòu   MC luwH
1. incise(d), engrave(d), chase(d); inlay, inlaid.

陋   lòu   MC luwH
1. out-of-the-way, geographically.
   a. far-removed from the norm and inferior, intellectually or behaviorally; uncultured, uncouth, uncivil; graceless; provincial, (c)rude, crass; mean, ignoble, base, low; ugly, vulgar.
   b. narrow, confined; exiguous, scant(y), trifling, piddling, esp. in one's knowledge of and perspective on the world.
2. disdain(ful), contemptible; hold in low regard.
3. (med.) be depressed at or over.

lú

壚   lú   MC lu
1. black hard-packed earth.
2. earthen stand on which stored wine is placed in wineshop > by synecdoche, wineshop, tavern.
3. ⊙ 爐 *lú*, stove, furnace; brazier.

廬   lú   MC lu
1. hut, cottage, little house; cabin; a dwelling smaller and simpler than a normal residence, usu. at a distance from city or neighborhood, often in countryside or (during spring and summer) in farm-fields; tugury, tigurye.
   a. hovel, depreciatory term for one's residence, even if more elaborate than the word suggests.
2. mourning hut, by a tomb.
3. lodging, inn, resting place, hostel for travelers.
   a. apartment, overnight lodging for officials on night service.

櫨   lú   MC lu
1. smokebush, smoketree (*Cotinus coggygria*), small bush producing pinkish-purple wispy flower clusters, leaves turning yellow or scarlet in autumn; similar to sumac.

2. bearing-block or king-post of bracket construction that supports roofbeams, structural member running vertically between apex and base of a triangular roof truss, often in bn. 欂～ *bólú*.

爐　lú　MC lu

1. furnace, stove.
    a. brazier, esp. for warming wine; e.g. 當～ *dānglú*, one who attends the wine, wineshop-girl, barmaid; also, cassolette, for keeping food warm.
    b. reaction vessel, for alchemical processes.
2. to temper; incl. one's character.

盧　lú　MC lu

1. earth-black, soot-black.
    a. pupil of eye > front-face; e.g. 當～ *dānglú*, decorative piece on forehead of horse.
    b. "Blackie," legendary swiftest hunting hound in the world.
    c. all-black, best throw in game of chaupar (*shupu* 樗蒲).
2. brazier, esp. for warming wine; cassolette, for keeping food warm.
    a. stove, furnace; ⊙ 爐 *lú*.
    b. earthen stand on which stored wine is placed in wineshsop > wineshop, tavern; ⊙ 壚, 罏 *lú*.
3 grip or handle of lance.
4 cranium, skull, of live person or animal.
5 (Budd.) 都～ *dūlú*, all, all of; entire(ly), total(ly) (Budd. vernacular).
6. (bn.) ～橘 *lújú* (MC lu-kjwit), loquat (*Eriobotrya japonica*).
7. ⊙ 欂 *lú* 2, bearing-block, king-post; 盧 *lú*, hut, cabin.
8. a surname.

矑　lú　MC lu

1 pupil of eye > eyeball, orb; front-face; ⊙ 盧 *lú* 2.

繿　lú　MC lu

1 bleached hempen threads.
    a. twisted hempen threads, prepared for bast weaving.
2. ramie, white ramie (*Boehmeria nivea*), bark of the stalks used for weaving.

鑪　lú　MC lu

1 small-mouthed wine-jar, amphora (early usage).

2. ⊙ 壚 *lú* 2, earthen stand on which wine is stored in wineshop > wineshop.

臚　lú　MC ljo

1. skin, outer part of flesh.
    a. rind, peel.
2. forehead.
3. expose, make known, make evident; inform.
4. lay out, arrange; dispose.

艫　lú　MC lu

1. front of a boat, where oars are set > stem, prow; e.g. 舳～ *zhúlú*, stern to stem, ships in tight convoy.
    a. by synecdoche, boat.

蘆　lú　MC lu

1. common reed (*Phragmites communis*), also cmpd. ～葦 *lúwěi*; one text says *wěi* is a reed that has flowered, *lú* is one that has not.
2. (bn.) ～菔 *lúfú* (MC lu-bjuwk), daikon, white radish (*Raphanus sativus*); syn. 萊菔 *láifú*, 蘿菔 *luófú*.
3. (drinking-)straw.

轤　lú　MC lu

1. (bn.) 轆～ *léilú*, → 轆 *léi*.

鑢　lú　MC lu　⊙ 爐 *lú*.

顱　lú　MC lu

1. cranium, skull, of live person or animal; ⊙ 盧 *lú* 4.
2. forehead.

髗　lú　MC lu

1. (med.) ⊙ 顱 *lú* 1, cranium, skull, of living being; 2, forehead.

鱸　lú　MC lu

1. sea-perch, sea-bass (*Lateolabrax japonicus*).

鸕　lú　MC lu

1. sgl. or (bn.) ～鷀 *lúcí* (MC lu-dzi), (fishing) cormorant (*Phalacrocorax carbo*).

lǔ

擄　lǔ　MC luX

1. (med.) take captive, capture; ravage, pillage; ⊙ 虜 *lǔ* 1.

櫓   lǔ   MC luX

1. large shield; pavis.
2. lookout tower.
3. stern-oar, scull, sweep.
4. (med.) brushwood dwelling.

艣   lǔ   MC luX

1. (med.) stern-oar, scull, sweep; ⊙ 櫓 lǔ 4.

虜   lǔ   MC luX

1. take captive, capture.
   a. carry off, pillage, ravage.
2. prisoner, captive.
   a. slave.
3. caitiff, recreant; term of contempt used for military enemies, esp. outlanders.

魯   lǔ   MC luX

1. slow-witted, thick-witted, stupid; backward; coarse, oafish.
2. name of small feudal state in Zhou times, located in area of present-day southern Shandong.

      lǔ   MC ljoX

1. lodging-house, inn for travelers; ⊙ 旅 lǔ.
2. make known; announce, proclaim; display.

鹵   lǔ   MC luX

1. saltflat, saltland; alkaline soil.
   a. rock salt, product of preceding; salty, saline.
2. ～莽 lǔmǎng, brusque, rash, incivil; also, saltland weeds; overgrown, weed-grown; (med.) also, indistinct, faint, vague, dim.
3. (med.) ～簿 lǔbú, escort of honor, esp. to accompany emperor or heir-apparent on outings.
4. ⊙ 櫓 lǔ, 1, large shield; 魯 lǔ, slow-witted, stupid; coarse; 擄 lǔ, capture; ravage, pillage.

lù

僇   lù   MC ljuwk

1. ⊙ 戮 lù 1, slaughter, massacre; expose corpse to view; 2, humiliate, dishonor, treat with contempt; 勠 lù, cmpd. ～力 lùlì, join forces, exert all one's effort.

勠   lù   MC ljuwk

1. cmpd. ～力 lùlì, join forces, unite; also, put all one's strength into, exert every effort.

戮   lù   MC ljuwk

1. slaughter, butcher, kill; massacre; carnage.
   a. expose corpse to view as sign of conquest.
2. humiliate, shame; mortify; dishonor, treat with contempt.
3. ⊙ 勠 lù, cmpd. ～力 lùlì, join forces; exert all one's effort.

摝   lù   MC luwk

1. shake, move to and fro; esp. of bells.

淥   lù   MC ljowk

1. vitreously clear; translucent.
2. (med.) clear green wine made with water from Lu River ～水 in eastern Hunan; perhaps one could say it is the Falernian wine of med. China.
3. (med.) bubbles.

漉   lù   MC luwk

1. drain away, drain dry; dredge.
   a. run off; leak, trickle away.
2. strain; filter; decant; sift, sieve.
3. (med.) scoop up (from liquid), draw off.

瑮   lù   MC luwk

1. rdup., polished luster (of jade).

璐   lù   MC luH

1. jewel, unidentified; gemstone, bijou.

盝   lù   MC luwk

1. ⊙ 漉 lù 1, drain away, drain dry, dredge; run off, trickle; 2, strain, filter; decant.
2. small box or case, for holding makeup, seals, etc.

睩   lù   MC luwk

1. sgl. or rdup., examine with extreme care, scrutinize searchingly.

碌   lù   MC luwk

1. rdup., rough and unworked (of stones or gems); also, crude and common, banal and ordinary; (med.) also, onom. of grumble and groan of cart-wheels, creak and rattle.
2. (med.) (bn.) ～硞 lùkù (MC luwk-khowk), scraped and scored, appearance of rocks heavily battered by waves.

祿   lù   MC luwk

1. favor(able), good fortune; benefice(nt).

2. official salary, emolument, e.g. 不～ *bùlù*, "[have] no more emolument," canonical expression for death of a serviceman (士 *shì*).
3. rdup., rough and unworked; crude and common, banal and ordiinary; ⊙ 碌碌 *lùlù*.

稑　lù　MC ljuwk
1. grain that is planted late but ripens early (cf. 穜 *tóng*, grain planted early that ripens late).

簏　lù　MC luwk
1. cylindrical bamboo basket; bin, hamper.

簬　lù　MC luH
1. (bn.) 箘～ *jùnlù*, → 箘 *jùn*.

籙　lù　MC ljowk
1. prophetic document presaging a founding emperor's accession to the throne, patent of investiture.
2. register, record-book.
3. (Dao.) ordination register, patent certifying holder as initiate at various levels in Dao. religious community, incl. catalogue of divinities with whom the adept is now on familiar terms and over whom (s)he has invocatory power, to be received only from an accredited master in ceremonial ritual.

菉　lù　MC ljowk
1. small carpgrass (*Arthraxon hispidas*), syn. 藎 *jìn*.

賂　lù　MC luH
1. bestow a gift on, present to; bestowal, gift, present.
   a. reward, award, honor with.
2. (med.) bribe, with goods or money.

趢　lù　MC luwk
1. (bn.) ～趗 *lùcù* (MC luwk-tshuwk), petty and paltry, trifling and trivial; (med.) also, clipped and mincing, pussyfooting, esp. of gait.

路　lù　MC luH
1. road, roadway, pathway.
   a. travel, journey, proceed on the way to destination.
2. route, course.
   a. path or course of action; process, method.
   b. career path.

3. grand, impressive; e.g. ～寢 *lùqǐn*, ruler's main apartment, sometimes euph. for audience-hall.
4. conveyance, esp. carriage of state; ⊙ 輅 *lù*.

踛　lù　MC ljuwk
1. spring, bound, leap.

輅　lù　MC luH
1. wagon, wain; esp. royal conveyance of imposing size for king or emperor.
2. harness, yoke.

逯　lù　MC ljowk
1. advance circumspectly, proceed with care.
   a. rdup., jumpy and jittery, apprehensive, nervous and leery.
2. unbeknownst, unrecognized; on one's own recognizance, in one's own manner.

醁　lù　MC ljowk
1. (med.) sgl. or (bn.) 醽～ *línglù* (MC leng-ljowk), metheglin, spiced mead.

錄　lù　MC ljowk
1. to record, make a record of; indite, make note of; copy down.
   a. enroll, register; admit, accept.
2. record (of actions, words, accounts, comments), register (of persons, items, techniques); roster (of persons); ledger (of accounts, methods).
3. employ, take on; recruit.
   a. collect, gather; save up; select.
   b. take possession of; seize, arrest.
4. supervise, superintend; direct.
   a. intendant, used in official titles or to indicate supervisory responsibility; e.g. ～事 *lùshì*, intendant of affairs; ～尚書事 *lùshàngshūshì*, intendant of affairs of the Magistry of Documents (State Affairs).
5. order, sequence; one after the other.
6. rdup., ⊙ 碌碌 *lùlù*, crude and common, banal and ordinary; also, be without a definite view, follow the crowd.
   lǜ　MC ljoH
1. examine prisoner's dossier, to determine sentence.

陸　lù　MC ljuwk
1. flatland; dry land.
2. roadway; route, course.

a. 北～ *běilù*, Northward Route, alt. name for the lunar lodging "Barrens" (→ 虛 *xū* 7); 西～ *xīlù*, Westward Route, alt. name for the lunar lodging "Mane" (→ 昴 *mǎo*).

3. leap, bound.

a. (bn.) ～梁 *lùliáng* (MC ljuwk-ljang), leaping and lurching, skip and bound; also, run rampant, rash and ruthless.

4. (bn.) ～離 *lùlí* (MC ljuwk-lje), pell-mell, mixed and mussed, diverse and varied; also, scattered and dispersed, helter-skelter; also, swinging and trailing, daggling and dangling; (med.) also, sightly and stunning.

5. a surname.

露   lù   MC luH

1. dew; dewy, roscid, roral; usu. symbolic of the transience of life.

a. bedew, irrorate; moisten, freshen.

b. condense in droplets; e.g. ～珠 *lùzhū*, dew-bead, dewdrop; in lit. dew is often associated with the moon, both having watery *yin* essence.

2. euph. for delicious drink, nectar.

a. (Dao.) beverage drunk by transcendents, conducive to their spiritually refined being.

3. expose, reveal, lay bare; let appear openly, make public; e.g. ～布 *lùbù*, unsealed government document or order; also, military call-to-arms, usu. incl. denunciation of enemy, syn. 檄 *xí*; (med.) also, triumphal proclamation of successful military campaign, announcement of victory.

a. outdoors, in the open air; e.g. ～坐 *lùzuò*, sit in the open.

4. ruined, destroyed.

a. weak(ened); in decline, failing.

5. ～甲 *lùjiǎ*, ～申 *lùshēn*, winter daphne (*Daphne odora*), evergreen shrub with pink or white fragrant blooms in late winter or early spring; ～葵 *lùkuí*, "dew-mallow," curly mallow, vegetable mallow (*Malva crispa*).

6. ⊙ 輅 *lù*, conveyance, esp. carriage of state.

鷺   lù   MC luH

1. sgl. or (med.) (bn.) ～鷥 *lùsī* (MC luH-si), egret (*Egretta garzetta*), invariably the white or snowy egret, esp. prized for the long plumes of its head and back which were plaited into sun-visors, used to decorate carriages and caps, military insignia, etc. In lit. egrets in well-ordered array were a classical image of court gentlemen; the aloof egret in natural habitat often a smaller and more approachable cousin of the Dao. transcendents' white crane.

鹿   lù   MC luwk

1. deer, gen. term for cervine animals; e.g. ～裘 *lùqiú*, deer-hair cloak, worn in winter.

a. specifically, sika deer, spotted deer (*Cervus nippon*); in lit. often a symbol of unfettered freedom.

2. euph. for ruling authority, seat of power; e.g. 逐～ *zhúlù*, "chase the deer," i.e. pursue or contend for the throne.

3. common, unrefined; inferior; e.g. ～布 *lùbù*, (someone clothed in) common cloth.

4. granary.

5. ～竹 *lùzhú*, "deer-bamboo," polygonatum, Solomon's seal (*Polygonatum chinense, Polygonatum sibiricum*), rhizome used medicinally, esp. favored in Dao. dietetics, syn. 黃精 *huángjīng*; ～角 *lùjiǎo*, "deer-horn," red seaweed, red algae (*Gloiopeltis furcata*), used medicinally; ～腸 *lùcháng*, "deer innards," yellow patrinia, golden valerian (*Patrinia scabiosifolia*) yellow-flowering from midsummer through autumn.

6. ⊙ 麓 *lù*, foot of a mountain.

麓   lù   MC luwk

1. foot of mountain or hill.

2. grove of trees growing at mountain's foot.

a. keeper or guardian of forest preserve.

lú

氈   lú   MC lju

1. (bn.) ～毼 *lúhé* (MC lju-hat), wool, as textile fabric; worsted.

蘆   lú   MC ljo

1. (bn.) 茹～ *rúlú*, → 茹 *rú*.

閭   lú   MC ljo

1. alley-gate; village gate.

a. wicket, small gate leading to fields.

b. gen. term for gate.

2. anciently, group of 25 households (*jia* 家), same as 里 *lǐ*; village, hamlet.

3. ～丘 *lúqiū*, bisyllabic surname.

驢   lú   MC ljo

1. donkey, ass (*Equus asinus*), as domesticated animal.

lǚ

侶 lǚ MC ljoX
1. companion; associate, colleague; compeer.
   a. accompany, be in company with, associate with.

僂 lǚ MC ljuX
1. bend at the waist, incline toward.
   a. bend; flex; curve, crook.
2. hunchbacked, crookbacked.
3. speedy, in a rush; quickly, fast.

呂 lǚ MC ljoX
1. the series of 6 pitch-pipes (→ 律 *lǜ*) associated with the *yin* principle, incl. the notes *dalǚ* 大～, *jiazhong* 夾鐘, *zhonglǚ* 中～, *linzhong* 林鐘, *nanlǚ* 南～, *yingzhong* 應鐘.
2. backbone.
3. a surname.

屢 lǚ MC ljuH
1. frequently, many times, often.
2. have one's fill of, weary of, bored with the repetition of.

履 lǚ MC lijX
1. sandal, single-soled slipper with upturned toe; leather shoe.
2. step, pad, tread; stroll; tramp.
3. proceed on the course of, act on, do; execute, perform, put in practice.
   a. behavior, conduct; esp. right behavior, proper conduct (cog. 禮 *lǐ*, prescribed behavior, ritual).
4. emoluments; dignity.
5. "Treading," name of 10th of the 64 hexagrams of the *Yijing*.

旅 lǚ MC ljoX
1. travel(er), sojourn(er).
   a. lodge, inn, guesthouse; lodger, guest.
   b. on a temporary basis, temporarily.
2. battalion, of 500 soldiers.
   a. gen. term for army.
3. numerous; group(ed), mass(ed).
   a. altogether, as a group, collectively.
4. set out in order, arrange; dispose.
   a. in sequence, in order, one after another.
5. "Traveler," name of 56th hexagram of the *Yijing*.

柗 lǚ MC ljoX
1. eaves of roof.
2. (med.) fruit growing in the wild.

櫚 lǚ MC ljo
1. sgl. or 花～ *huālǚ*, Burmese rosewood, amboine, narra (*Pterocarpus indicus* and some other *Pterocarpus* species); sometimes yellow rosewood, ormosia (*Ormosia henryi*).
2. 棕～ *zōnglǚ*, windmill palm, coir palm (*Trachycarpus fortunei*).

穭 lǚ MC ljoX
1. (med.) wild-growing grain.
   a. (med.) wild, uncultivated.

縷 lǚ MC ljuX
1. filament, fiber, strand; wisp.
   a. wispy, gossamer.
2. bit-by-bit, to the finest detail; item-by-item.
3. (med.) measure-word for long, thin items.
4. (med.) 襤～ *lánlǚ*, → 襤 *lán*.

膂 lǚ MC ljoX
1. backbone.
   a. bodily strength, brawn.
   b. pluck, grit; intrepid(ity).

褸 lǚ MC ljuX
1. sgl. or (bn.) 襤～ *lánlǚ* (MC lam-ljuX), ragged, tattered, shabby and ragged, scrappy and tattered.

lǜ

崜 lǜ MC lwit
1. (bn.) ～崒 *lǜzú* (MC lwit-dzwit), precipitously piled, loftily layered.

律 lǜ MC lwit
1. pitch-measure, regulated harmonics, in music and applied figuratively elsewhere, such as in calendrics, metrology, poetry, etc.; e.g. ～歷 *lǜlì*, musical pitches and calendar, name of monograph on these subjects in many of the official histories.
2. pitch-pipes, 12 bamboo tubes of graduated length (alternately two-thirds and four-thirds the length of the preceding pipe, producing

a gamut of ascending fifths and descending fourths), marking the fundamental pitches of Chinese music, a gamut of 12 semitones.

　　a. the series of 6 pitch-pipes associated with the *yang* principle (cf. 呂 *lǚ*, those associated with the *yin* principle), incl. the notes *huang-zhong* 黃鐘, *dacou* 大蔟, *guxian* 姑洗, *ruibin* 蕤賓, *yize* 夷則, *wuyi* 無射.

3. rule, regulation, law, esp. criminal code (cf. 令 *lìng*, administrative statutes).

　　a. uniform, regular(ity), according to rule.

4. (med.) in lit. certain forms of verse, incl. ～詩 *lǜshī*, regulated verse, of 8 lines and expecting alternations of level (*ping* 平) and deflected (*ze* 仄)-tone words in particular places, plus grammatical parallelism between the lines of each of the middle two couplets, and 排～ *páilǜ*, regulated lines in ordinem, poem constructed of couplets of parallel lines (except for final couplet) with tonal alternations.

5. (Budd.) trns. Skt. *vinaya*, monastic discipline or regulations; e.g. ～師 *lǜshī*, vinaya master; (Dao.) rules of discipline for Dao. initiates.

慮　lǜ　MC ljoH

1. ponder, think on, muse on; pensive, reflect on; meditate, contemplate; consider(ate).

　　a. infer(ence); anticipate, foresee; project, expect, look forward to.

2. as one might expect; most likely, in all likelihood; probably.

3. (med.) apprehension, anxiety; uneasy about; foreboding, presentiment; concern(s).

4. (med.) interrogate, press a prisoner.

濾　lǜ　MC ljoH

1. (med.) to filter, strain; run through, pass through; drain.

率　lǜ　MC lwit　→率 *shuài*.

綠　lǜ　MC ljowk

1. gen. referring to the chlorophyllous range of color from bright to heavily saturated green; bright-green, virid, virescent; lime-green, reseda; esp. the color of newly burgeoning plants and leaves.

　　綠　lǜ　MC ljowk

1. ⊙ 籙 *lù* 1, prophetic document presaging accession to the throne; 菉 *lù*, small carpgrass.

鑢　lǜ　MC ljoH

1. burnish, polish, buff; file or rub to smoothness and luster.

　　a. improve, refine, temper one's character or reputation.

luán

孿　luán　MC srwaenH

1. twin-born, twins.

　　a. twinned, doubled.

巒　luán　MC lwan

1. tor, rocky pinnacle.

　　a. sharp-cut hills; long and narrow stretch of hills.

2. mountain spine, ridge.

攣　luán　MC ljwen

1. attach, connect(ion); continuous, link(ed).

2. contracted, balled-up, coiled; bent, twisted; crooked, contorted; gnarled, warped.

欒　luán　MC lwan

1. goldenrain tree, chinaberry (*Koelreuteria paniculata*).

2. corners of the lenticular opening of a bell.

3. bracket, curved wood connecting bearing-block to rafter.

4. rdup., wasted and emaciated, gaunt.

5. ⊙ 鑾 *luán*, harness-bells, simurgh-bells; 孿 *luán*, twin-born.

灓　luán　MC lwan

1. seep, soak into the ground.

臠　luán　MC lwan

1. mince(d), dice(d), finely cut meat or fish; morsel.

2. apportion; partition, separate, divide; split, sunder.

鑾　luán　MC lwan

1. harness-bells, small carriage-bells, croatals, attached to yoke or crossbar; jingler.

　　a. simurgh-bells, small harness-bells in shape of simurgh (鸞 *luán*) and imagined to suggest the bird's cry, esp. on carriage of ruler.

　　b. by synecdoche with preceding, a ruler's carriage.

鸞　luán　MC lwan

1. "simurgh," fabulous bird similar to the "phoenix" (*fenghuang* 鳳凰) in occupying a position of high status and dignity among feathered creatures, though traditionally considered of somewhat less charisma; often symbolic of cultural elegance, literary talent, conjugal harmony; sometimes associated with feminine beauty and grace; e.g. 〜鳳 *luánfèng*, simurgh and phoenix, men of comparably high worth and capacity, well-matched husband and wife; 〜鏡 *luánjìng*, simurgh mirror, i.e. mirror of lovely lady.

2. ⊙ 鑾 *luán*, harness-bells, esp. simurgh (-shaped)-bells, croatals; ruler's carriage.

luǎn

卵　luǎn　MC lwanX

1. egg, of bird or insect.
   a. brood, sit on or hatch eggs.
   b. (med.) 〜色 *luǎnsè*, ivory or pale-yellow color, esp. of sky.
2. testicle.

kūn　MC kwon

1. fish-roe.

luàn

亂　luàn　MC lwanH

1. disorder(ly), disarray (ant. 治 *zhì*); chaos.
   a. dishevel(ed); disrupt(ed), unsettl(ed); disturb(ed).
   b. trouble(d); confuse(d), blur(red); jumble(d), mix(ed) up.
2. rebel, revolt; riot; unrest; lawless(ness).
3. cross river or stream against the current.
4. (lit.) finale, envoi, concluding section of a *fu* 賦, usu. incl. recapitulative summary.
   a. put the finishing touch on.
5. bring to order, govern; < graphic confusion with 乿 *zhì*, ancient-script form of 治 *zhì*.

薍　luàn　MC lwanH　→ 薍 *wàn*.

lüè

掠　lüè　MC ljak

1. carry off, take away, plunder, loot; rob; ravish, rapacious; annex.
   a. take to oneself; hug.

2. cudgel, beat with a stick.
3. fell, hew, chop down.
4. (med.) brush, graze, touch lightly.
   a. (med.) (bn.) 〜削 *lüexuē* (MC ljak-sjak), comb carefully.

擽　lüè　MC ljak

1. strike, beat against.
2. run against, in battle; assault, attack.
3. stern, steadfast.

略　lüè　MC ljak

1. boundary, border; outline, measure; draw an outline, trace out, sketch.
   a. make the rounds of a territory for inspection.
2. margin(al), sketchy, slight(ly); e.g. 〜相 *lüèxiàng*, marginal basis for evaluating; 〜無 *lüèwú*, not in the least, completely without.
   a. in general, in sum, roughly; attend to generally; utterly.
   b. (med.) for the time being, for a while.
3. an abstract, summary; epitome; précis, sketch.
   a. define; definition of.
4. maneuver, plan; contrive, scheme; operate.
   a. gambit, tactic; coup.
5. carry off, plunder, loot; rob; take away, annex, seize; ⊙ 掠 *lüè* 1; e.g. 〜地 *lüèdì*, annex territory.
6. neglect, negligent; remiss.
7. sharp, cutting; keen, trenchant; e.g. 〜刃 *lüèrèn*, a keen blade.

lún

倫　lún　MC lwin

1. relationship, affinity, relative place in hierarchy or natural order; e.g. 人〜 *rénlún*, human relationships; 五〜 *wǔlún*, the 5 key social relationships: ruler/subject, husband/wife, father/son, elder and younger brothers, friends.
   a. prescribed, fixed, or morally approved principle.
   b. category, class; rank; order; system(atic), sequence, hierarchy.
2. comparable to, equal, on a par with.

崙　lún　MC lwon

1. (bn.) 崑〜 *kūnlún*, → 崑 *kūn*.

掄 lún MC lwon

1. select, pick out, choose.
2. (med.) brandish, wave, revolve the hand on high while holding an object.

淪 lún MC lwin

1. wavelet, ripple, laplet.
2. immerse, submerge; engulfed.
   a. subside, sink; lapse, settle; e.g. ～隱 *lúnyǐn*, retire into seclusion.
   b. seep into, soak; fall into, slide into, slip into.
3. founder; sink into nothingness; disappear, be lost; die.
   a. (med.) (bn.) ～落 *lúnluò* (MC lwin-lak), fall foundering, swirl and sink; also, drift aimlessly, eddy about; also, wiped out and worn away, expunged.
4. ～胥 *lúnxū*, involved together, swept up as one; also, lost, ruined.

綸 lún MC lwin

1. silken cord, usu. dark-blue, tied around waist and to which an official's seal of office may be attached.
2. interweave, interlace; network; texture; twist together, pull together; e.g. 經～ *jīnglún*, lay out basic web, weave a pattern, weave the warp and threads of order > organize government policy.
   a. descriptive of emperor's fine-spun words; e.g. ～語 *lúngào*, "textured declaration," imperial decree.
3. fishing-line of silk thread.
   guān MC kwean
1. ～巾 *guānjīn*, cap trimmed with blue thread, supposedly first worn by Zhuge Liang 諸葛亮 (181-234) in reclusion, so symbolic of elegant freedom.

艤 lún MC lwin

1. (med.) small boat, vessel, pram.

輪 lún MC lwin

1. wheel of carriage, cart, wagon.
   a. by synecdoche, wheeled vehicle.
   b. euph. for any circular- or disc-shaped object, e.g. the moon.
2. revolve, rotate, turn round; rotation, cycle.
   a. (med.) by turns, in turn.
   b. (med.) in lute (*pipa* 琵琶) and zither (*qin* 琴) playing, repeated striking of a string with different fingers in sequence.
3. length, north-south measurement (cf. 廣 *guǎng*, breadth, east-west measurement).

a. circumference, perimeter.
4. high-soaring, high-wheeling, overtopping.
   a. (med.) brandish, wave, revolve the hand on high while holding an object; ⊙ 掄 *lún* 2.
5. (Budd.) ～迴 *lúnhuí*, round of life-and-death, cycle of rebirth, trns. Skt. *saṃsāra*; ～王 *lúnwáng*, wheel-turning king, trns. Skt. *cakravartin*, universal monarch who turns the dharma wheel, also defined as whose chariot rolls everywhere.

鯩 lún MC lwin

1. yellowcheek carp (*Elopichthys bambusa*).

lùn

論 lùn MC lwonH

1. discuss critically, debate or weigh the merits of.
   a. pronounce judicial sentence.
2. (lit.) prose genre: discourse, disquisition, examination of a subject according to its structure and qualities.
   a. (lit.) prose genre: appraisal, summary evaluation sometimes placed at end of chapter in historical texts.
3. (Budd.) trns. Skt. *śāstra*, exposition of or instruction in the philosophy of a *sūtra* (經 *jīng*), commentary according with doctrine; one of the 3 major divisions of Budd. canon (*tripiṭaka*), along with sutras and vinaya (*lü* 律) texts.
4. theory, statement; claim, advocate.
5. (med.) according to, by means of; e.g. ～劫 *lùnjié*, by kalpas, endlessly.
   lún MC lwon
1. so pronounced in title of ～語 *Lúnyǔ*.
2. ⊙ 倫 *lún* 1b, rank, order, sequence, hierarchy; 掄 *lún* 1, select, pick out, choose.

luō

捋 luō MC lwat

1. take in the hand; handful; gather; pluck.
2. rub, stroke with hand.

luó

羅 luó MC la

1. bird-net, bird-snare; web, mesh, retiary.
   a. ensnare(d), net(ted), enmesh(ed); catch, capture.

2. silk-gauze or chiffon in net weave; gossamer.
   a. veil(ed); filmy; finely stretched; e.g. (Dao.) 大～天 *dàluótiān*, Grand Veil Heaven, in Lingbao texts the heaven where the great god Celestial Worthy of Primordial Commencement (Yuanshi tianzun 元始天尊) holds court and which hangs like a veil over the lower heavens, incl. those of the 3 Clarities (*sanqing* 三清).
3. spread out; stretch out; array, set out; rdup., loosely spreading.
   a. set around, lie around; envelop.
4. (Budd.) ～漢 *luóhàn* (MC la-xanH), abb. trsc. of Skt. *arhat* 阿～漢 *āluóhàn* (MC 'a-la-xanH), saint, one who has attained enlightenment; ～剎 *luóchà* (MC la-tsrhae), trsc. Skt. *rākṣasa*, demon.
5. (med.) (bn.) ～睺 *luóhóu* (MC la-huw), trsc. Skt. *rāhu*, name of invisible planet signifying in Vedic astronomy (adopted in Tang times) the ascending lunar node, where moon on northerly course crosses the ecliptic (cf. descending, southerly node *ketu* [*jidu* 計都], thought of as complementary invisible planet).
6. (med.) ～師 *luóshī*, irrelevant, have nothing to do with.
7. ⊙ 罹 *lí*, encounter, confront.

蘿　luó　MC la

1. various twining vines, incl. bindweed (*Convolvulus arvensis*), beard-lichen (*Usnea longissima*); e.g. 女～ *nǚluó*, "lady-vine," same as preceding, beard-lichen; 松～ *sōngluó*, "pine-moss," pine-lichen, same as preceding.
2. (bn.) ～芳, ～勒 *luólè* (MC la-lok), sweet basil (*Ocimum basilicum*); syn. 蕙 *huì* 1.
3. (bn.) ～蔔 *luóbó* (MC la-bok), radish (*Raphanus sativa*), syn. 菲 *fěi*.

螺　luó　MC lwa

1. (med.) ⊙ 蠃 *luó*, gastropod; snail, whelk, periwinkle.
   a. (med.) wine vessel made of large sea-snail shell.
   b. (Budd.) abb. 法～ *fǎluó*, "dharma conch," musical instrument made of same, to harmonize with gong; also 法蠡 *fǎlí*.
   c. (med.) abb. ～髻 *luójì*, "snail chignon," woman's hair dressed in snail-whorls.
   d. (med.) abb. ～墨 *luómò*, snail ink, made from snail secretion.

蠃　luó　MC lwa

1. gastropod; snail, whelk, periwinkle.

覶　luó　MC lwa

1. (med.) (bn.) ～縷 *luólǚ* (MC lwa-ljuX), detail bit-by-bit, express in painstaking detail, relate circumstantially, precise and punctilious.

覼　luó　MC lwa　⊙ 覶 *luó*.

邏　luó　MC la

1. patrol, make the rounds of; inspect, survey.
   a. reconnaisance troops, scouts, patrol.
2. (med.) edge, margin; border.
3. (med.) ～娑 *luósuō* (MC la-sa), ～些 *luósuò* (MC la-saH), Lhasa.

騾　luó　MC lwa

1. mule, offspring of a jack (male donkey) and a mare (female horse).

luǒ

倮　luǒ　MC lwaX　⊙ 裸 *luǒ*.

砢　luǒ　MC laX

1. (bn.) 磊～ *lěiluǒ*, → 磊 *lěi*.

蠃　luǒ　MC lwaX

1. ⊙ 裸 *luǒ*, naked, bare, stripped; 騾 *luó*, mule.

苽　luǒ　MC lwaX

1. winter-melon, wax-gourd (*Benincasa hispida*).
2. fruit of herbaceous plants.

蠃　luǒ　MC lwaX

1. (bn.) 蜾～ *guǒluǒ*, → 蜾 *guǒ*.

裸　luǒ　MC lwaX

1. nude, stripped, naked; bare, expose(d).

躶　luǒ　MC lwaX　⊙ 裸 *luǒ*.

luò

洛　luò　MC lak

1. name of important river in He'nan, tributary to the Yellow River.

a. sgl. or ～陽 *luòyáng*, important city on the north side of the Luo River, often serving as the capital.

犖   luò   MC laewk

1. brindled ox.
   a. pied, parti-colored; flecked, speckled.
2. rdup., manifestly evident; (med.) also, conspicuous, outstanding, pronounced.
3. (med.)(bn.) ～确 *luòquè* (MC laewk-khaewk), buried and bristling with rocks, rugged and ragged; also, fixed fast, solid and stiff.

珞   luò   MC lak

1. rdup., hard as stone; also, onom. of stone-chimes.

絡   luò   MC lak

1. reel thread, spin.
   a. ～絲 *luòsī*, to "throw" thread, i.e. twist together several single yarns into one thread in a direction opposite to that in which they themselves are twisted.
2. web, (en)mesh, net(work); reticulate.
   a. wind round, envelop; encircle; contain.
   b. (bn.) ～繹 *luòyì* (MC lak-yek), continuously connected, threaded throughout, unbroken and uninterrupted.
3. veins, in human body; often paired as 2nd member of cmpd. with 經 *jīng* (basic circulatory channels of *qi* and blood) as "ducts and links."
   a. metaphorically, network of veins, as in the earth.
4. headstall, of horse.
5. (med.) ～緯 *luòwěi*, katydid (*Mecopoda elongata*), named from seemingly continuous ("unbroken reeling") chirr of its stridulation; syn. 莎雞 *shājī*.

落   luò   MC lak

1. fall, let fall; drop off or away; shed (of leaves); cast down; tumble; e.g. ～木 *luòmù*, leaf-stripped trees, trees gone bare.
   a. (med.) drop-off, depths; e.g. (Dao.) 碧～ *bìluò*, Cyan Drop-off, distant deep-blue reaches of the sky, also abb. name of a Dao. heaven where the chief Lingbao scripture, *Duren jing* 度人經, is stored; 八～ *bāluò*, 8 Depths, 8 directions of space.
2. fall away; fade, wilt, waste away; decline; go downhill; die.
   a. (bn.) 零～ *língluò*, → 零 *líng*.

b. (med.) suffer, sustain harm, pass through difficulty; lag behind, fall behind; tumble down; e.g. ～虧 *luòkuī*, suffer loss, come to grief; ～第 *luòdì*, fail the (*jinshi* 進士) exam.
3. thread of water, thready drip, trickle, drip down; e.g. ～泉 *luòquán*, trickling fountain.
   a. (med.) sprinkle widely; scatter afar, strew; dissipate; e.g. (bn.) ～拖 *luòtuō* (MC lak-tha), ～魄 *luòtuò* (MC lak-thak), ～泊 *luòbó* (MC lak-bak), aimless and unrestrained, take liberties; also, desolate and alone, down and out, downcast and dispirited, sad and bedraggled.
4. rdup., steadily fall away, bereft and forlorn of; also, long separated, far apart, estranged and alienated; also, expansive and independent, stalwart and stately.
5. suspend, call off; settle.
   a. stay for a time, stop over.
6. small settlement, thorp, hamlet; e.g. 村～ *cūnluò*, village and thorp.
   a. encampment, esp. of "barbarian" nomads.
7. (med.) expel, dispense with; e.g. ～藉 *luòjí*, strike off from a list.
8. (med.) skirt, sidle; move by.
9. commence, inaugurate; e.g. ～筆 *luòbǐ*, set the writing-brush to paper, begin writing.
   a. ritual to inaugurate a newly finished hall or palace.
   b. ancient ritual in which a newly cast bell is anointed with blood.
10. bamboo hedge, wicker fence.
11. ⊙ 絡 *luò*, unwind thread; web, (en)mesh, net; envelop, encircle; veins, in human body; headstall of horse.
12. ～下 *luòxià*, a bisyllabic surname.

酪   luò   MC lak   → 酪 *lào*.

雒   luò   MC lak

1. white-maned black horse.
2. ⊙ 洛 *luò*, name of important river in Henan, tributary to the Yellow River; sgl. or ～邑 *luòyì*, Luo City, important city on north side of Luo River, often serving as capital, Luoyang ～陽.

駱   luò   MC lak

1. black-maned white horse.
2. (bn.) ～駝 *luòtuó* (MC lak-da), camel (*Camelus bactrianus*), the 2-humped bactrian camel.
3. (bn.) ～漠 *luòmò* (MC lak-mak), riding at full speed, swiftly striding.
4. a surname.

M

má

蟆 **má** MC mae
1. (bn.) 蛤～, 蝦～ *hámá* (MC hae-mae), frog.
　　mò MC mak
1. gnat.

麻 **má** MC mae
1. hemp (*Cannabis*, various species), esp. bast fibers used in weaving and seeds and oil used in food products; e.g. ～仁 *márén*, white seeds of hemp with pericarp removed, eaten as tonic cereal; ～油 *máyóu*, hemp-seed oil, the seeds when pressed to form a drying oil used for waterproofing paper and cloth.
　　a. ～黃 *máhuáng*, "hemp yellow," ephedra, thistle (*Ephedra sinica*), yellow-flowering, with stems used medicinally; 胡～ *húmá*, "western hemp-seeds," i.e. sesame (*Sesamum indicum*).
2. mourning garments, esp. cap and belt, made of hemp cloth.
3. (med.) imperial fiat or order, by synecdoche because in Tang times these were written on white or yellow hemp-fiber paper.
4. (med.) (bn.) ～荼 *máchá* (MC mae-drae), muddled and fuddled, in a daze, in a stupor.

麼 **má** MC mae　→ 麼 *mó*.

mǎ

瑪 **mǎ** MC maeX
1. (med.) (bn.) ～瑙 *mǎ'nǎo* (MC maeX-nawX), agate, also carnelian.

碼 **mǎ** MC maeX　⊙ 瑪 *mǎ*.

馬 **mǎ** MC maeX
1. horse (*Equus caballus*); equine; e.g. 兵～ *bīngmǎ*, war-horse, a blonk.
2. (bn.) ～腦 *mǎ'nǎo* (MC maeX-nawX), "horse brains," ⊙ 瑪瑙 *mǎ'nǎo*, agate, also carnelian.
3. (med.) ～牙(消) *mǎyá(xiāo)*, "horse-tooth (powder)," purified form of crude sodium sulphate (*puxiao* 朴消).
4. ～(齒)莧 *mǎ(chǐ)xiàn*, purslane, verdolaga, pigweed (*Portulaca oleracea*).

　　a. ～蘭 *mǎlìn*, ～薤 *mǎxiè*, purple iris (*Iris ensata*), syn. 荔挺 *lìtǐng*.
5. (Dao.) 天～ *tiānmǎ*, heaven's horses, esoteric name for hands.
6. counter, made of bamboo-strip.
7. a surname.

mà

禡 **mà** MC maeH
1. sacrifice made by army on expedition, to solicit good fortune in battle.

罵 **mà** MC maeH
1. execrate, imprecate, curse; revile, inveigh against; impugn, traduce.

mái

埋 **mái** MC meaj
1. bury, inter; hide in the ground; cover over with soil; compact(ed).
　　a. hide away unseen; hide in one's heart

薶 **mái** MC meaj
1. original form of → 埋 *mái*.
　　wō MC 'woj
1. contaminate, defile, pollute.

霾 **mái** MC meaj
1. dust-storm, windstorm; kick up dust, whirl up dust.
2. dense, impenetrable to sight; dim; confused.
3. ⊙ 埋 *mái*, bury, inter; hide in the ground; hide away unseen, conceal.

mǎi

買 **mǎi** MC meaX
1. buy, purchase, acquire by means of cash.
　　a. hire; engage, contract with.
　　b. obtain desired actions or statements through money or other means, bribe, suborn; blandish(ment).

mài

勱 **mài** MC maejH
1. exert one's strength, put forth effort; strive, drive; apply oneself; take pains.

脈 **mài** MC meak
1. blood vessels; veins, arteries; ducts.
   a. things connected like blood vessels, e.g. veins of leaves or insect wings
2. pulse, esp. as indicator of health.
   a. diagnose illness by examining the pulse, e.g. 〜學 *màixué*, sphygmology.
3. subterranean water currents, aquifers.
   mò MC meak
1. ⊙ 眽 *mò*, rdup., gaze longingly at, with intense gaze; inexpressibly united.

脉 **mài** MC meak → 脈 *mài*.

賣 **mài** MC meaH
1. sell, vend, exchange for cash; offer for sale.
   a. sell out, betray; deliver desired statements or actions for cash.
2. show off, advertise, promote.

邁 **mài** MC maejH
1. step forward, stride, advance (toward).
   a. get ahead, move forward
   b. get on in time, advancing in years; aging.
2. ruler going on a tour of inspection.
3. stride across or over, traverse; exceed, get beyond.
4. rdup., displeased, disapproving.
5. ⊙ 勱 *mài*, exert oneself.

霡 **mài** MC meak
1. (bn.) 〜霂 *màimù* (MC meak-muwk), light drizzle, mizzle; (med.) also, shining with sweat.

麥 **mài** MC meak
1. wheat.
   a. barley.

mán

妎 **mán** MC mam
1. (med.) older woman; dowager, matron.

怋 **mán** MC man
1. confused; lost, muddled.
2. troubled; depressed, melancholy.

měn MC mwonX
1. indifferent, unconcerned, oblivious.

懣 **mán** MC man
1. mixed-up, muddled; distracted, absent-minded; perplexed.

槾 **mán** MC man
1. trowel.
   a. rough-cast, parget.
   wàn MC mjonH
1. vitex (*Vitex trifolia*), syn. 蔓荊 *mànjīng*.

檽 **mán** MC man
1. Chinese elm (*Ulmus parvifloria, Ulmus chinensis*), syn. 櫨榆 *lángyú*.
2. ooze, seep out, esp. sap from tree.

瞞 **mán** MC man
1. with eyes closed; unseeing; blear-eyed; blinkered; lower one's eyelids; wink.
2. deceive, hoodwink; trick, dupe; mask one's feelings; ⊙ 謾 *mán* 1.
   mén MC mwon
1. ashamed; chagrined; blush with embarrassment.

蠻 **mán** MC maen
1. the Man people, aboriginal non-Han tribes in southeast and southern regions.
   a. general term for non-Han people beyond the borders of the Chinese state, "barbarians."
2. coarse, boorish, uncouth, brutish; aboriginal.
3. wilderness; remote, uncivilized regions.
4. (med.) rdup., "mwan-mwan," onom. of small birds calling.

謾 **mán** MC man
1. cheat, hoodwink, deceive.
2. deny, repudiate, disavow, disown, renege.
   màn MC manH
1. gibe, jeer; slander.
2. (med.) in vain, futile(ly).
3. (med.) do not, by no means.
4. ⊙ 慢 *màn* 3, contemptuous, arrogant, slighting; shiftless; 漫 *màn* 2, unrestrained, profuse.

鞔 **mán** MC man
1. upper, of shoe or boot; vamp, part that covers instep and toes.
   a. by synecdoche, gen. term for footwear.

2. cover the top of something with leather.

    a. (med.) stretch leather over drum as sounding surface.

        mèn　MC **mwonX**

1. ⊙ 懑 *mèn*, troubled, depressed, despondent; annoyed, vexed.

饅　**mán**　MC **man**

1. (med.) steamed rice-cake.

    a. (med.) 〜頭 *mántóu*, steamed bun with filling inside, equiv. 蠻頭 *mántóu*, "head of a Man (barbarian)."

髮　**mán**　MC **maen**

1. fair of hair.

    a. (med.) flower garland, chaplet, floral headdress, < Skt. *mālā*, garland.

mǎn

滿　**mǎn**　MC **manX**

1. full, brimming; fullness, plenitude; to swell, well up, fill up.

    a. permeate, suffuse; all over X; completely.

2. fulfill, complete.

    a. reach a time limit.

3. contented, satisfied.

4. be "full of oneself," self-satisfied, boast(ful), proud, conceited.

5. the full moon.

6. in arrow-shooting, the moment the bowstring is fully drawn.

7. taboo-substitute from early 2nd-c. BCE for 盈 (to avoid given name of Han Huidi 惠帝, r. 194–187).

8. ⊙ 懑 *mèn* troubled, depressed; 謾 *mán* 1, cheat, deceive.

彎　**mǎn**　MC **maenX**

1. look, view; see.

2. put on, place over, cover with.

màn

慢　**màn**　MC **maenH**　⊙ 慢 *màn*.

墁　**màn**　MC **manH**

1. plastered or roughcast wall.

    a. to plaster, parget, roughcast; to coat, smear.

2. trowel.

嫚　**màn**　MC **maenH**

1. to disrespect.

    a. despise, scorn.

    b. insult, offend, humiliate.

2. arrogant, haughty.

3. ⊙ 慢 *màn* neglectful, lax, indolent.

        yuān　MC **'jwon**

1. rdup., tender, gentle, elegant, languid.

幔　**màn**　MC **manH**

1. curtain, screen; awning; tent.

    a. cover with a screen; veil.

2. (med.) flag in front of a tavern.

慢　**màn**　MC **maenH**

1. neglect(ful), indolent, lax, at one's own whim.

    a. shiftless, undisciplined; sketchily, superficially, slackly.

2. at one's own pace, unhurriedly, dilatory, slow.

    a. (med.) not up to the standard of, inferior.

3. boast(ful); contemptuous, arrogant, conceit(ed) (ant. 敬 *jìng*, respectful).

4. ⊙ 墁 *màn*, coat, smear, plaster.

曼　**màn**　MC **manH**

1. extend(ed), long, lengthy.

    a. stretch out, lengthen; expand; cast afar, spread, draw(n) out; diffuse.

    b. (bn.) 〜衍 *mànyǎn* (MC manH-yenX), ever and endless transformations; also, continuously connected, ceaseless linkage, constant conjunctions; (bn.) 〜羨 *mànxiàn* (MC manH-zjenX), lost to sight, fading away to vagueness.

2. svelte, slender; delicate, graceful; fine-looking.

3. (Budd.) 〜陀羅 *màntuóluó* (MC manH-da-la), trsc. Skt. *mandāra*, fragrant flower that grows in heaven, with white trumpet-shaped blooms whose appearance brings joy; also, coral tree (*Erythrina indica*); 〜殊沙花 *mànshūshāhuā* (MC manH-dzyu-srae-xwae), trsc. Skt. *mañjusaka*, cluster-amaryllis, red spider-lily (*Lycoris radiata*).

4. (med.) (GP) time-marker, chiefly in Budd. texts: when, while, e.g. 〜時 *mànshí*, at the time when, during the time when.

漫　**màn**　MC **manH**

1. overflow, spillover; wash out to, flow away to.

2. widespread, diffuse.

a. all around, everywhere, to all quarters; omnipresent, boundless; unrestricted.
b. completely, wholly, in all respects.
3. desultory; indiscriminate(ly), random(ly); rambling.
a. leisure(ly), relaxed, easy-going; reckless(ly); borne on one's own tide.
b. negligent, haphazard; unconventional.
4. rdup., endlessly extended, disperse limitlessly; also, flow with one's fancies, sate one's cravings; also, confused and carried away, dazed and distracted.
5. smudge(d), efface(d); blur(red), obscure(d); dim, filmy; e.g. (bn.) ～漶 *mànhuàn* (MC manH-hwanH), effaced and obliterated.
a. (med.) smear, spread over the surface of.
6. (med.) to no avail, futilely, vainly.
7. ⊙ 慢 *màn* 1-2, indolent, shiftless; 謾 *mán* 1, cheat, deceive.

縵   màn   MC manH
1. plain, unpatterned silk.
a. gen. term for unpatterned, unadorned.
2. rdup., depressed and disheartened; at the end of one's rope; also, continuously connected, lengthening out.
3. (med.) surround, circle about.
4. ⊙ 慢 *màn* 2, slow; 幔 *màn* 1, curtain.

蔓   màn   MC manH
1. vines, plant tendrils, creepers.
a. gen. term for creeper plants, e.g. kudzu, rattan, liana, etc.
b. ～荆 *mànjīng*, vitex (*Vitex trifolia*); ～菁 *mànjīng*, field mustard, turnip-rape (*Brassica campestris*), syn. 蕪菁 *wújīng*; ～華 *mànhuá*, goosefoot, melde (*Chenopodium alba*), syn. 藜 *lí*.
2. diffuse, spread out; extend(ed), stretch(ed), draw(n) out; ⊙ 曼 *màn* 1.

máng

厖   máng   MC maewng
1. enormous; massive, mighty.
a. ample; thick.
2. mixed, motley; varied.
a. disorderly; unruly; turmoil.

尨   máng   MC maewng
1. shaggy or tufted-haired dog.
a. shaggy, fuzzy.
2. motley, multi-colored.

méng   MC muwng
1. (bn.) ～茸 *méngróng* (MC muwng-nyowng), rough and ragged, mishmash, jumbled and muddled, simsam, befuddled and fuzzy.
páng   MC baewng
1. (med.) ⊙ 龐 *páng*, sizable, hefty.

忙   máng   MC mang
1. (med.) pressed, occupied; troubled with.
a. (med.) over-stretched, busy; taken up with.

宋   máng   MC mang
1. roofbeam.

盲   máng   MC maeng
1. blind, sightless.
2. dim, hazy.
a. dim-witted; purblind, slow or deficient in understanding, imagination, or vision
3. ⊙ 望 *wàng*, gaze into the distance,

芒   máng   MC mang
1. eulalia, Chinese silvergrass (*Miscanthus sinensis*), grows in dense clumps, with waving awns.
2. arista, awn, beard, of grain or grass.
a. spike, barb, sharp point of a weapon.
b. extremely small, infinitesimal; insignificant.
3. sharp point or spikelet of light; glitter(ing).
4. rdup., extensive, vast, wide, spacious.
5. indistinct, blurred, obscure; ⊙ 茫 *máng*)
6. rapid, hurried, hasty; busy (⊙ 忙 *máng*); rdup., weary and worn out, tired, fatigued.
7. (med.) abb. ref. to Mount Beimang 北邙山, hills north of Luoyang famous as burial ground.
huǎng   MC xwangX
1. (bn.) ～忽 *huǎnghū* (MC xwangX-xwot), muddled and murky, blurred and smudged, dazed and distracted; ⊙ 恍惚 *huǎnghū*.

茫   máng   MC mang
1. vast, expansive; boundless, undetermined; illimitable; to the limits of vision, lost to sight; e.g. ～然 *mángrán*, blindly lost, dazed, in a haze.
a. rdup. or (bn.) ～昧 *mángmèi* (MC mang-mwojH), ～洋 *mángyáng* (MC mang-yang), vague and vast, stretching farther than eye can see, lost in the distance, measureless and indeterminate, afar and aloof.

邙   máng   MC mang
1. 北～山 *běimáng shān*, hills north of Luoyang famous as burial ground.

鋩　máng　MC mang

1. point, tip, barb, esp. sword-point; ⊙ 芒 *máng* 2a.

駹　máng　MC maewng

1. horse with white blaze on forehead.
2. blue-black horse.
3. motley, brindled, particolored.

mǎng

漭　mǎng　MC mangX

1. vast, expansive, esp. of water.
   a. rdup., fathomless expanse.
   b. (bn.) ～漾 *mǎngyàng* (MC mangX-yangX), far-flooded flow; also, confused and fuddled, hugger-mugger, topsy-turvy.
2. ⊙ 莽 *mǎng* 2, tangled; indistinct.

莽　mǎng　MC mangX

1. tiger-grass (*Thysanolaena maxima*), tight-clumping perennial grass.
   a. 宿～ *sùmǎng*, sloughgrass (*Beckmannia syzigachne*).
2. brush, undergrowth; thicket.
   a. tangled, clumped; indistinct.
3. sgl. or rdup., dense and teeming, profuse, spreading, overgrown, unbounded.
   a. (bn.) ～蒼 *mǎngcǎng* (MC mangX-tshangX), distantly indistinct, faint and far-off, blurred and boundless.
4. (med.) interr. and exclamatory "how," "what."
5. ～草 *mǎngcǎo*, illicium, anise tree (*Illicium lanceolatum*), small evergreen shrub or tree, with light pink to orange-pink aromatic flowers; stems and leaves used medicinally.

蟒　mǎng　MC mangX

1. Burmese python (*Python bivittatus*); more rarely, black-tailed python (*Python molurus*).

māo

貓　māo　MC maew

1. cat, most often domestic.

máo

旄　máo　MC maw

1. yak-tail or ox-tail pennant, as symbol of authority or as ornament.

2. back-sloping hill, high in front and low behind.

　　mào　MC mawH

1. ⊙ 耄 *mào*, octogenarian; aged.

毛　máo　MC maw

1. hair or down of animals; pelt, fleece, fur, pelage, coat; plumage, contour feathers.
   a. pileous, pileated; furry, fuzzy.
   b. scalp-hair and eyebrow-hair of humans.
2. furry-looking growth on surface of earth, euph. for plants and trees.
3. to be without, not have, lack.

氂　máo　MC maw

1. yak-tail.
2. long hair.
　　lí　MC li

1. ⊙ 犛 *lí* 1, yak; 3, hundredth part of an inch.

矛　máo　MC mjuw

1. spear, lance, pike.
   a. (med.) ～盾 *máodùn*, cutting reply, sharp riposte.
2. name of seventh star of Big Dipper (Ursa major), alternatively called 招搖 *zhāoyáo* (→ 招); also, by synecdoche the Big Dipper.

茅　máo　MC maew

1. floss-grass, cogon (*Imperata cylindrica*), often used in thatching roofs.
   a. ～香 *máoxiāng*, "cogon aromatic," citronella; ～坑 *máokēng*, latrine pit.
2. name of three-peaked mountain in southern Jiangsu, holy locale in Shangqing 上清 Dao.
3. sometimes ref. milfoil, for divination.

蝥　máo　MC maew

1. (bn.) 螌～ *bānmáo*, → 螌 *bān*.
　　MC mjuw

1. ⊙ 蟊 *máo*, sgl. or cmpd. ～賊 *máozéi*, grubs that eat the roots of grain.

蟊　máo　MC maw

1. sgl. or cmpd. ～賊 *máozéi*, grubs that eat the roots of grain; also, euph. for destroyers of state or person.

酕　máo　MC maw

1. (med.) (bn.) ～醄 *máotáo* (MC maw-daw), dead-drunk, feeling no pain.

髦   **máo**   MC maw
1. flowing mane of horse.
   a. long tresses.
2. obtrusive; remarkable; outstanding.
   a. pick out from the crowd.
3. child's hair parted into 2 tufts hanging from forehead to eyebrows.
4. ～頭 *máotóu*, topknot.
5. ⊙ 旄 *máo*, ox-tail pennant.

貌   **máo**   MC maewH   ⊙ 貌 *mào*.

mǎo

卯   **mǎo**   MC maewX
1. 4th of the 12 earthly branches, associated with the hare as emblematic animal.
   a. 4th double-hour of the day, from approximately 5 a.m. to 7 a.m.

昴   **mǎo**   MC maewX
1. "Mane," one of the 28 lunar lodgings, comprised of the 7 stars of the Pleiades, in the western quadrant (*baihu* 白虎) of the sky. The translation "Mane" is based on an alternate name, referring to an ox-tail spear. The word *mao* itself indicates the completion of the growing season and reflects the sun setting on a closed gate; it is also the time in autumn when criminals were punished or executed. A better rendering would perhaps be "Concluder." N.B. Do not confuse with 昂 *áng*.

茆   **mǎo**   MC maewX
1. water-shield (*Brasenia schreberi*), a watermallow with floating bright-green leaves and small purple flowers; syn. 蓴 *chún*, 水葵 *shuǐkuí*.
2. ⊙ 茅 *máo*, floss-grass, cogon.

mào

冒   **mào**   MC mawH
1. cover(ing), overlay.
   a. cover up, hide, conceal; veil.
   b. (en)shroud, for corpse.
2. spread out over; (of water) flood, inundate.
3. to brave, risk; contend with, hazard, venture, make bold to.
   a. presume to do, defy; reckless, rash, rush into; affront, offend; e.g. ～昧 *màomèi*, rash and hasty, crude and indiscreet.
   b. covet(ous); usurp(atious).

4. mask, feign; make a pretense of; act or speak falsely; sham.
5. to see, look.
6. ⊙ 瑁 *mào*, ruler's scepter; 媢 *mào*, jealous(y), envy.

媢   **mào**   MC mawH
1. jealous(y); envy.

帽   **mào**   MC mawH
1. cap, hat; headgear (usu. less formal than 冠 *guān*).
   a. to cap, place on; cover with.

愗   **mào**   MC muwH
1. (bn.) 恂～ *kòumào*, → 恂 *kòu*.

懋   **mào**   MC muwH
1. put one's heart into, try hard.
   a. enhearten, embolden; encourage, urge.
2. grand, magnificent.
   a. fine(ly); handsome(ly), lovely.
3. satisfied, pleased.

楙   **mào**   MC muwH
1. flowering quince (*Chaenomeles speciosa*), shrub and fruit.
2. ⊙ 茂 *mào* 1, in full bloom, luxuriant, thriving; 2, excellent, consummate, perfect; 貿 *mào* 1, trade, commerce, barter; sell, vend.

䫉   **mào**   MC mawH
1. (med.) (bn.) ～䫉 *màosào* (MC mawH-sawH), chapfallen and hapless, longfaced and low-spirited, woebegone.

瑁   **mào**   MC mawH
1. jade scepter held by ruler when receiving feudal lords, with which he symbolically "caps" the batons (珪 *guī*) held by them.
2. (bn.) 瑇～ *dàimào*, → 瑇 *dài*.

眊   **mào**   MC mawH
1. clouded vision, blurred, bleary.
   a. addled, baffled; distraught, confused, in disarray.
2. ⊙ 耄 *mào*, octogenarian; aged, superannuated.

瞀   **mào**   MC muwH
1. dim-sighted, dull-eyed, troubled vision; myopic.

a. rdup., lower the eyes, out of embarrassment or humility.
2. dazed, dizzy; deluded.
    a. puzzled, mystified; in a fog.
3. dim, obscure, dark, blurred.
    a. unknowing, ignorant.

耄　mào　MC mawH
1. octogenarian.
    a. superannuated, long in years.
2. befuddled, daft; senile.

耄　mào　MC mawH
1. pick, cull vegetables; select, choose.
    máo　MC maw
1. greens, vegetables; plants.

茂　mào　MC muwH
1. in full bloom, flourishing, luxuriant, thriving; ripe(ned), mature.
2. excellent, choice, sensational.
    a. consummate, perfect.
3. ⊙ 懋 *mào* 1, put one's heart into; encourage, urge.

袤　mào　MC muwH
1. length (north-south) of a tract of land.
    a. length(wise).

貌　mào　MC maewH
1. appearance, look of; semblance, guise.
    a. bearing, mien; manner.
    b. having the sense or meaning of, approximating to.
2. demeanor, deportment; behavior.
3. apparent; external, outer; on the surface, superficial.
4. (med.) apparition, phantom.
    MC maewk
1. (med.) ⊙ 邈 *miǎo*, far-reaching, distant, remote.
    mò　MC maewk
1. (med.) to outline, limn, copy; portray (painting).

貿　mào　MC muwH
1. trade; commerce; barter.
    a. sell, vend.
    b. seek to gain or profit from.
2. change, alter, modify; rearrange.
    a. mix(ed) up, jumble(d), disarrange(d).

méi

塵　méi　MC mwoj
1. dust(y).
    a. rdup., drifting dust.

媒　méi　MC mwoj
1. marriage go-between, matchmaker.
    a. intercessor, intermediary; mediator.
2. leaven, barm, ferment, of alcoholic drinks.
3. (med.) provoke, foment.
    mèi　MC mwojH
1. rdup., dark and dull, dim and begloomed.

徵　méi　MC mij
1. rdup., following in the footsteps of, one right after the other.

枚　méi　MC mwoj
1. tree-trunk, stalk of shrub.
    a. stem, branch, twig.
    b. board, plank.
2. inner purlins of roof that extend outward to the eaves.
3. measure-word for small objects.
    a. one-tenth of an "inch" (*cun* 寸).
4. gag, restraint, placed in mouth of soldiers and horses engaging in night attack to keep them from making noise.
5. (ADV) one-by-one, individually.
    a. a single one of.
6. rdup., in full and fine detail, in minute completeness.
7. the bosses on the face of a chime-bell.
8. (med.) leaf or sheet of paper.
9. a surname.

梅　méi　MC mwoj
1. plum (*Prunus mume*), tree and its fruit with thick, soft pulp; cf. → 李 *lǐ* (*Prunus salicina*) with thin, hard, crisp pulp; the *mei*-plum is actually more similar to the apricot; its 5-petaled white blossoms are the earliest flower of the year, sometimes blowing before the last snowfalls, and are thus the first symbol of springtime. To distinguish from the *li*-plum, translate as "prunus" or "mume."
2. 楊～ *yángméi*, bayberry, wax-myrtle, box-myrtle (*Mryica rubra*).
3. rdup., dim and dusky, faint and faded.
4. (med.) dialect word in Jiangnan area denoting summer rain.

楣 méi   MC mij

1. lintel of door.
2. rafter or crossbeam supporting the eaves of a roof.

湄 méi   MC mij

1. riverbank or streamside with waterplants.
   a. verge, edge, brink; brow.

煤 méi   MC mwoj

1. soot(y).
   a. black(en); euph. for ink.

玫 méi   MC mwoj

1. (bn.) ～瑰 *méiguī* (MC mwoj-kwoj), dark mica, biotite; also, rose (*Rosa rugosa*), with sweetly scented deep-pink flowers that bloom in late summer or early autumn.

mín   MC min

1. ⊙ 珉 *mín*, semi-precious stone.

眉 méi   MC mij

1. eyebrow.
2. verge, edge, brink; brow.
   a. upper margin of a page.

禖 méi   MC mwoj

1. divine intermediary whom one supplicates for a son.

胇 méi   MC mwoj

1. meat on either side of backbone.
2. (med.) ～胎 *méitāi*, unrestrained, uncurbed; intemperate; cut loose.

腜 méi   MC mwoj

1. rdup., fertile and fecund, fat and fruitful, richly productive.

莓 méi   MC mwoj

1. berries, of various sorts.
2. liverwort; moss; lichen.
   a. rust, mold.
3. rdup., rich and lush, thick and thriving, of vegetation.

鋂 méi   MC mwoj

1. collar, with sounding rings attached, for hunting dog.

黴 méi   MC mij

1. swart(hy), dark-colored; dark-skinned.
2. black mould, mildew blight.

měi

燆 měi   MC mijX   ⊙ 美 *měi*.

抺 měi   MC mwojX

1. covet, desire.
2. old Jin 晉 area dialect word for ashamed, humiliated.

每 měi   MC mwojX

1. each time, every time, whenever.
   a. nearly always, most of the time; very often.
2. even though, even if.

浼 měi   MC mwojX

1. soil, make impure, sully; defile; despoil.
2. rdup., flow gently, proceed placidly.

美 měi   MC mijX

1. handsome; lovely, fair; attractive, beautiful.
   a. fine(st), of best quality, excellent; well-regarded, praise(worthy), commend(able), admirable.
2. flavorful, tasty; to relish; sweet.

mèi

妺 mèi   MC mwojH

1. younger sister.
   a. young girl, lass.
2. the last, of a series.

媚 mèi   MC mijH

1. fawn on, play up to; flatter, gloze; toady to, curry favor; entice.
2. appealing, amiable; charming, alluring; bewitch; seduce.

寐 mèi   MC mjijH

1. to (go to) sleep; sleep, be asleep; cf. 眠 *mián*, close the eyes in rest, 睡 *shùi*, nod off, fall asleep.
   a. repose.
   b. euph. for death.

昧　mèi　MC mwojH

1. dim; faintly outlined, indistinct; obscure, lacking brightness, lackluster, dull; somber, drab.
   a. bedimmed, clouded vision.
   b. ～爽 *mèishuǎng*, ～旦 *mèidàn*, ～明 *mèimíng*, almost but not quite sunrise, false dawn.
2. be in the dark about; unknowing, ignorant; dull-minded, dunderhead(ed); purblind.
   a. color-blind.
3. rdup., dim and dull; also, dim and disoriented; also, in a brown study, mulling over, lost in thought; also, pure and honest, unfeigned; also, purblind gropers.
4. to risk, hazard; make bold to, venture; e.g. ～死 *mèisǐ*, to brave death.
5. (bn.) ～莫 *mèimò* (MC mwojH-mak), widespread and spacious.
6. (Budd.) 三～ *sānmèi* (MC sam-mwojH), trsc. Skt. *samā[dhi]*, concentration preparatory for meditation; also, often used for latter.

眛　mèi　MC mwojH

1. clouded vision.
2. hid(d)e(n), deceive.

蝐　mèi　MC mijH

1. identification uncertain but prob. hermit-crab.

袂　mèi　MC mjiejH

1. sleeve, of garment.
   a. sleeve-cuff, sleeve-band.

靺　mèi　MC mwojH

1. leather dyed purplish-red or garance, from madder.
2. madder (*Rubia cordifolia*), root yielding a purple-red pigment used in dyeing; syn. 茜 *qiàn*.

髍　mèi　MC mijH

1. bogy, sprite, goblin, maleficent spirit of natural object ill-disposed toward humans; ⊙ 魅 *mèi*.

魅　mèi　MC mijH

1. demon, goblin, essence of a natural object (e.g. tree, mountain) that has become rancorous with age.
   a. unnatural being that is ill-disposed toward humans, troll, bogy, sprite.
2. bewitch, mesmerize; seduce, lure.

mén

靐　mén　MC mwon　→ 靐 *wěi*.

捫　mén　MC mwon

1. lay hold of, hold, grasp; hent.
   a. touch, stroke, run one's hands over; feel one's way along or through.
2. smear away, wipe away, clean away.

璊　mén　MC mwon

1. russet, auburn, reddish-brown.

虋　mén　MC mwon

1. red-stalked proso millet (*Panicum miliaceum*).

門　mén　MC mwon

1. gateway, usu. with two leaves; portal, outer door; entrance (cf. 戶 *hù*, single-leaved or inner door); e.g. ～人 *ménren*, ～子 *ménzǐ*, ～徒 *méntú*, gatekeeper; (Dao.) 天～ *tiānmén*, celestial gate, esoteric term for mouth.
   a. access, approach to; key, solution to a situation or problem; means, way to do something.
   b. orifice, sense-organ.
2. family, group, faction, sect, community associated with particular individual or teaching; e.g. ～人 *ménrén*, ～子 *ménzǐ*, ～徒 *méntú*, retainer, disciple; ～附 *ménfù*, a dependent; (med.) 道～ *dàomén*, the Daoist community.
3. class, category; section.

měn

悗　měn　MC mwonX　→ 悗 *mán*.

mèn

懑　mèn　MC mwonH

1. troubled, depressed, despondent; ⊙ 悶 *mèn* 1.
2. discontented, annoyed, vexed; indignant.

悶　mèn　MC mwonH

1. troubled, worried; melancholy; depressed.
   a. rdup., dull and dour, despondent; stupid-seeming.

mén　MC mwon

1. stuffy, obstructed flow of air; stifled, suffocating.
2. taciturn, silent.

méng

幪 méng MC muwng
1. cloak, wrap; muffler; hood.
2. (med.) cover, veil, overlay; e.g. 帲～ *píng-méng*, drapes and curtains; also, cover(ing), screen(ing), shelter; protection, patronage.
    měng MC muwngX
1. rdup., thick and dense growth, thickly thriving.

懞 méng MC muwng
1. artless, genuine, unfeigning.
2. (med.) (bn.) 忪～ *sōngméng*, → 忪 *sōng*.

曚 méng MC muwngX
1. (med.) (bn.) 瞳～ *tóngméng*, → 瞳 *tóng*.

朦 méng MC muwng
1. (bn.) ～朧 *ménglóng* (MC muwng-luwng), scarrow-shine, diffused moonlight, shining faintly as through clouds, veiled in clouds, dimly diffuse(d); (bn.) 瞳～ *tóngméng*, → 瞳 *tóng*.

氋 méng MC muwng
1. (med.) (bn.) 氃～ *tóngméng*, → 氃 *tóng*.

甿 méng MC meang
1. (common) people; in Tang used esp. as taboo-substitute for 民 *mín* (to avoid personal name [Shimin 世民] of Tang Taizong 太宗 [r. 626-49]).
    a. peasants, rustics, country people.
    b. people who have come from outside to settle in a community.

濛 méng MC muwng(X)
1. drizzling mist, mizzle; fine moisture.
    a. rdup., steaming mistily, drizzly-mizzly; (in) showering spray(s); filmy blur.
2. (bn.) ～澒 *ménghòng* (MC muwngX-huwngX) or 澒～ *hòngméng*, vaporous opacity, vast opacity, as before separation of heaven and earth; all-encompassing mist.
3. diffuse, widespread light; luminous haze; auroral shimmer.

甍 méng MC meang
1. purlin, longitudinal member in roof-frame for supporting rafters.
    a. by synecdoche, roof.
2. extended eaves at 4 corners of roof.

甿 méng MC meang ⊙ 甿 *méng*.

盟 méng MC mjaeng
1. blood-oath sworn to divinities or among men (cf. 誓 *shì*, unilateral oath without blood sacrifice).
    a. swear an oath.
2. a bond, covenant; to forge a covenant, join in alliance.

瞢 méng MC mjuwng
1. dim of sight; dull, darkened, shadowed.
    a. befuddled, benighted.
    b. senseless, foolish, fatuous; witless.
    c. (med.) (bn.) ～腾 *méngténg* (MC mjuwng-dong), dazed and dizzy, disoriented, addled and boggled, with head swimming.
2. ashamed, abashed.
    mèng MC mjuwngH
1. ⊙ 夢 *mèng*, dream.

矒 méng MC muwng
1. blear-eyed; purblind.
2. bleary, filmy, foggy.
    a. dim-witted, unknowing, ignorant.

矇 méng MC muwng
1. (bn.) ～艟, ～衝 *méngchōng* (MC muwng-tsyhowng), a warship like a cutter or corvette, long and narrow, covered with cowhide and with holes for oars, and equipped with a ram; first used by the state of Wu at Battle of Red Cliff in 208.

萌 méng MC meang
1. to sprout, bud, germinate, of plants and of endeavors.
    a. sprouts, buds, shoots; the very beginnings, first appearance.
2. to hoe weeds
3. the common people; ⊙ 甿 *méng*.
    a. (Budd.) ～類 *mínglèi*, sentient beings.

蒙 méng MC muwng
1. dodder (*Cuscuta chinensis*), parasitic vine, syn. 菟絲 *tùsī*, 女蘿 *nǚluó*; used in lit. metaphorically to suggest unwavering love, tightly held friendship.
2. cover, envelop, encompass; hooded; e.g. ～朧 *ménglóng*, densely enveloped; 大～ *dà méng*, "Great Shroud," home of the setting sun; rdup., dim and dark.
    a. misty, hazy, filmy, ⊙ 濛 *méng*.
    b. hoodwink, delude.

3. unenlightened; simple, rudimentary; ignorant; innocent, young, immature, inexperienced; e.g. 童～ *tóngméng*, childlike simplicity.

   a. "Immaturity," name of 4th hexagram of the *Yijing*.

   b. humble self-designation

4. suffer, meet with; confront, withstand, brave, face (adversity).

   a. accept; receive.

   b. incur, fall into.

5. ⊙ 尨 *máng* 1, shaggy; 2, multi-colored.

蝱　méng　MC maeng　⊙ 蟲 *méng*.

虻　méng　MC maeng　⊙ 蟲 *méng*.

蟲　méng　MC maeng

1. horsefly, gadfly.

2. fritillary (*Fritillaria*, various species), used medicinally; syn. 茼 *yóu*.

雺　méng　MC muwng

1. ⊙ 霿 *méng*, lowering or leaden skies, overcast, beclouded.

   wù　MC mjuH

1. ⊙ 霧 *wù*, fog, rouk, haze, mist.

霿　méng　MC muwng

1. lowering or leaden skies, overcast, beclouded.

   mào　MC muwH

1. dull-minded, dim-witted.

   wù　MC mjuH

1. ⊙ 霧 *wù*, fog, rouk, haze, mist.

餸　méng　MC muwng

1. replete, filled with; profuse.

鸏　méng　MC muwng

1. (med.) (bn.) ～鶇 *méngtóng* (MC muwng-duwng), great hornbill (*Buceros bicornis*), syn. 越王鳥 *yuèwángniǎo*, "Bird of the King of Viet."

měng

㦩　měng　MC muwngX　⊙ 懵 *měng*.

懵　měng　MC muwngX

1. (med.) purblind; insensible, witless.

   a. (med.) deficient in, ignorant of.

猛　měng　MC maengX

1. brute, brutish; in uncivilized state.

2. fierce, forceful; violent, savage; cruel, ruthless.

3. severe, stern, vehement; intense; e.g. (med.) ～利 *měnglì*, extremely acute, of intelligence.

4. stout, strenuous, staunch, orped, valiant, vigorous.

䖌　měng　MC maengX

1. (med.) (bn.) 舴～ *zéměng*, → 舴 *zé*.

蠓　měng　MC muwngX

1. (bn.) ～蠛 *měngmiè* (MC muwngX-met) or 蠛～ *mièměng*, biting midges, blackflies and sandflies.

黽　měng　MC meangX

1. toad.

   mǐn　MC mjinX

1. ⊙ 僶 *mǐn*.

mèng

夢　mèng　MC mjuwngH

1. dream.

   a. illusion, fantasy.

2. old Chu dialect-word for 澤 *zé* 1, marshland; 6, grassland, heath.

孟　mèng　MC maengH

1. principal, first, eldest.

   a. first-born, eldest child

   b. first month of a season, e.g. ～春 *mèngchūn*, 1st month of spring.

2. pristine, in original state.

3. to exert oneself, e.g. ～進 *mèngjìn*, forge ahead zealously.

4. exaggerate(dly); (bn.) ～浪 *mènglàng* (MC maengH-lang), intemperate and impetuous, crass and insouciant.

5. ⊙ 猛 *měng* 1, brutish.

6. a surname.

鱛　mèng　MC mongH

1. (bn.) 鮔～ *gèngmèng*, → 鮔 *gèng*.

mí

彌　mí　MC mjie

1. pervade, permeate; pervasive, (all-)inclusive; throughout; e.g. ～天 *mítiān*, all-pervading heaven.

   a. complete, consummate; full, filled with; e.g. ～日 *mírì*, the whole day.

   b. close up, bridge, join together.

2. spread out, far-spread; span.

    a. extensive, in time or distance; e.g. 〜留 *míliú*, lingering incurable illness.

3. (ADV) more, even more.

4. a surname.

    mǐ   MC mjieX

1. ⊙ 弭 *mǐ* 1, check, restrain, hold back, pause.

瀰   mí   MC mjie

1. sgl. or rdup., extended expanse of water, watery waste, overfull and flooding.

    a. (med.) (bn.) 〜漫 *mímàn* (MC mjie-manH), endless expanse, vast and limitless, farspread and shoreless.

䵘   mí   MC mje

1. splinter(ed), fragment(ed), shred(ded), section, chip, piece.

    a. ruin(ed), destroy(ed).

獼   mí   MC mjie

1. (bn.) 〜猴 *míhóu* (MC mjie-huw), macaque, rhesus monkey (*Macacus tcheliensis*).

    a. 〜猴桃 *míhóutáo*, "macaque's peach," Chinese gooseberry (*Actinidia chinensis*).

糜   mí   MC mje

1. rice- or millet-gruel (thicker than 粥 *zhōu*, congee).

    a. (med.) 〜沸 *mífèi*, "bubbling gruel," i.e. seethe with rebellion.

2. crush, mash, reduce to pulp; break into pieces.

    a. dissolve; rotten.

3. waste, squander; extravagant.

縻   mí   MC mje

1. ox's leading-rope, attached to nose-ring.

    a. halter (horse).

2. tie up; fetter, restrain; control, conduct.

3. squander, waste; throw off, run through, use up.

靡   mí   MC mje

1. (bn.) 〜蕪 *míwú* (MC mje-mju), hemlock-parsley, selinea (*Conioselinum chinense*), most often found along riverbanks, has fragrant umbels of white flowers; (lit.) often paired or conflated with 芷蘺 or 江蘺 *jiānglí*, lovage.

2. 薔〜 *qiángmí*, → 薔 *qiáng*.

迷   mí   MC mej

1. lose one's way, go astray; lost; e.g. 〜藏 *mícáng*, hide-and-seek (game).

2. bewilder(ed), perplex(ed), beguile(ment); mislead, confuse(d), delude(d); riddle.

    a. (bn.) 〜密 *mìmì* (MC mej-mit), moiling maze, bewildering complexity.

3. infatuated with, possessed by, spellbound, transported by.

4. (med.) ⊙ 彌 *mí* 1a, complete, full, whole of.

醾   mí   MC mje

1. (med.) (bn.) 酴〜 *túmí*, → 酴 *tú*.

麋   mí   MC mij

1. elaphure, Père David's deer (*Elaphurus davidianus*); e.g. 鹿 *mílù*, elaphurine deer; also, gen. term for deer when 2-word term is needed for parallelism.

    a. 〜舌 *míshé*, "elaphure-tongued," dicot plants, with cotyledons resembling glossy elaphure tongues.

2. 〜鴣 *míguā*, gray crane (*Grus lilfordi*); syn. 鶬鴣 *cāngguā*, 鶬雞 *cāngjī*.

3. ⊙ 蘼 *mí*, selinea, hemlock-parsley; 糜 *mí* 1, gruel; 湄 *méi*, riverbank, streamside; 眉 *méi*, eyebrow.

麛   mí   MC mej

1. fawn, calf, young deer.

    a. gen. term for young animals; yearling.

mǐ

嬤   mǐ   MC mjeX

1. (bn.) 〜密 *mǐmì* (MC mjeX-mit), collected and composed, serenely self-possessed.

弭   mǐ   MC mjieX

1. check, restrain, hold back, repress; slow down; stop, pause; e.g. 〜節 *mǐjié*, halt the pace, with slow pace.

2. curved ends of a bow.

3. calm, assuage, quieten, still, compose.

    a. complaisant, amenable, submissive, agreeable.

4. be oblivious of, put out of mind, forget.

敉   mǐ   MC mjieX

1. soothe, calm; settle down; placate, pacify.

2. consummate, achieve.

渳 **mǐ** **MC mjieX**
1. wash a corpse with fragrant millet-wine, for purification.

瀰 **mǐ** **MC mjieX**
1. rdup., richly ample, spilling over (in appearance or quantity); flowing on and on (of water).
2. (med.) (bn.) ～迤 *mǐyǐ* (MC mjieX-yeX), smooth and gently sloping, stretching gently onward.

眯 **mǐ** **MC mejX**
1. get something (a foreign object) in the eye, have trouble seeing.
mì **MC mjijH**
1. nightmare.

米 **mǐ** **MC mejX**
1. uncooked rice.
2. hulled grain, dehusked and polished.
   a. a grain of, smidgen, bit.
3. (med.) surname, usu. of Sogdians.

芈 **mǐ** **MC mjieX**
1. onom. of bleating of sheep.
2. a surname.

靡 **mǐ** **MC mjeX**
1. negative particle: not; not have; e.g. 天命～常 *tiānmìng mǐ cháng*, Heaven's decree is not permanent. Often used as emphatic negative: there is absolutely not . . .; no X whatever; e.g. 物～不得其所 *wù mǐ bùdé qí suǒ*, Not a single thing was not in its place.
2. collapse, fall down, knocked over.
   a. draw back, pull back, retreat; be overborne, blown back (plants by strong wind, army by stronger adversary, etc.).
3. minute; delicate, intricate.
   a. exquisite; beautiful.
4. edge, margin; e.g. 江～ *jiāngmǐ*, riverside, riverbank.
5. accumulate; add up.
6. rdup., slowly and steadily, follow complacently; also, lazing and lascivious; also, swaying and waving; also, crowded in clusters.
mí **MC mje**
1. disperse, separate, disband; destroy; e.g. ～軀 *míqū*, to the detriment of one's own person > in utmost or selfless sincerity.
   a. splinter, break apart, shiver, fragment, chip.
2. waste, squander; be prodigal with, not stint.

mì

塓 **mì** **MC mek**
1. apply a coat of plaster or paint on a wall.

宓 **mì** **MC mjit**
1. tranquil, calm; unworried, composed; ⊙ 密 *mì* 4.
2. confidential, circumspect; secret; ⊙ 密 *mì* 2.
3. a surname.
fú **MC bjuwk**
1. used in various proper names; e.g. ～羲 *fúxī*, Fuxi, ⊙ 伏羲, legendary culture-hero; ～妃 *fúfēi*, Consort Fu, goddess of the Luo 洛 River.

密 **mì** **MC mit**
1. snug, close; compact, tight(ly meshed); condense(d), consolidate(d).
   a. (bn.) ～勿 *mìwù* (MC mit–mjut), put forth one's complete, finely coordinated effort, ⊙ 僶俛，黽勉 *mǐnmiǎn* (MC mjinX–mjenX), do all and everything one can; perforce, willy-nilly.
   b. close-fitting; close-set, thick-set (as of trees).
2. closely held; private, confidential, circumspect, secret, hermetic.
3. retired, place of retirement.
4. calm, quiet; stable; circumspect.

幂 **mì** **MC mek**
1. cloth cover, for cauldrons, goblets, vases, etc.
2. drapes, hung from above; veil, pall, sheet.
   a. to veil, cover over, mantle.
   b. tent.
3. (med.) rdup., thickly laden, heavily covered, blanketed with.

冪 **mì** **MC mek** ⊙ 幂 *mì*.

幎 **mì** **MC mek**
1. cover a corpse with a shroud, pall, winding-sheet.
   a. gen. term for cover over, overlay.
2. ⊙ 幂 *mì*, drapes, hung from above; veil, mantle; tent.
3. (med.) (bn.) ～歷 *mìlì* (MC mek-lek), hooded hiding-place, dense underbrush, copsy covert.

幦 **mì** **MC mek**
1. dust-screen hung from carriage's front-crossbar.

汨   mì   MC mek

1. ～羅 *mìluó*, name of upper reaches of Mi River in northeastern Hunan, tributary to the Xiang 湘, in which Qu Yuan 屈原 is said to have drowned himself.

汩   mì   MC mit

1. hide, conceal; secrete.
2. (bn.) ～潏 *mìjué* (MC mit-kwet), bubbling forth from a fountainhead.

    wù   MC mjut

1. (bn.) ～穆 *wùmù* (MC mjut-mjuwk), slight and subtle, fine and faint.

祕   mì   MC pijH

1. secret, private, confidential; privy to.
    a. reserved for the royal family; e.g. ～府 *mìfǔ*, imperial library.
    b. esoteric, for the initiated only; e.g. ～教 *mìjiào*, esoteric teachings.
2. to hoard, store away, treasure.
    a. rare, exceptional.

秘   mì   MC pijH   ⊙ 祕 *mì*.

蔤   mì   MC mit

1. white root of lotus, which lies in the mud.

蜜   mì   MC mjit

1. honey, sweet; possibly pre-Han loanword from Tocharian B *mit*.
2. sgl. or 木～ *mùmì*, hovenia (*Hovenia acerba*, *Hovenia dulcis*); e.g. ～香 *mìxiāng*, hovenia incense.
    a. (med.)   ～香紙   *mìxiāngzhǐ*, "honey-fragrance paper," made from the paper-mulberry.

覓   mì   MC mek

1. seek out, look for, hunt up.
2. choose between, select the better.

覛   mì   MC mek

1. ⊙ 覓 *mì* 1, seek out, look for, hunt up.

    mò   MC meak

1. examine into, investigate; look into.

謐   mì   MC mjit

1. soothe, placate; comfort(able); quiet(en); peaceful, placid.

鼏   mì   MC mek

1. lid of a cauldron.
2. cloth cover of wine goblet, for ceremonial occasions.

mián

嬵   mián   MC mjien

1. charming, captivating, inviting, esp. of eyes.
2. look at with envy; jealousy.

棉   mián   MC mjien

1. (med.) cotton-tree, silk-cotton tree (*Gossampinus malabarica*, *Bombax malabarica*), brought from India and southeast Asia.
    a. fibers yielded by this tree, similar to kapok.
    b. wadding.

橌   mián   MC mjien

1. short beam upholding eaves of roof.

眠   mián   MC men

1. doze, slumber; repose, lie at rest; half-awake, half-asleep; stupor.
    a. close one's eyes, fall asleep.
    b. hibernate (animals).
2. feign death.
3. (med.) to lay (oneself or something) down.
    a. (med.) lie down spread-eagled.
4. (Budd.) latent proclivities or tendencies that lead to new cravings, trns. Skt. *anuśaya*.

矊   mián   MC mjien

1. flashing eyes, vivacious look.
2. (bn.) ～眇 *miánmiǎo* (MC mjien-mjiewX), gazing and gaping, facing from afar.

綿   mián   MC mjien

1. floss silk; cotton.
    a. soft, downy, delicate.
    b. silk or cotton wadding.
2. fine-spun thread, thin-threaded.
    a. far-stretched, stretching long into the distance; long-drawn-out, continuous, uninterrupted; prolonged; e.g. ～貌 *miánmào*, far-extended (drawn out) in space or time; rudp., far and finely threaded.
3. twisted, entangled.

緜   mián   MC mjien   ⊙ 綿 *mián*.

miǎn

俛　miǎn　MC mjenX
1. incline or lower the head.
2. ⊙ 勉 *miǎn* 1, exert oneself.
　　fǔ　MC pjuX
1. bend down, lower, bow the head, ⊙ 俯 *fǔ* 1.

偭　miǎn　MC mjienX
1. turn toward, face.
2　turn away from; oppose, go against.

免　miǎn　MC mjenX
1. avoid, evade, elude.
　　a. shirk, refrain from; dispense with.
　　b. escape, get away from.
2　relieve; remove, dismiss; remit, exempt.
3　⊙ 娩 *miǎn*, to bear a child; childbirth.
　　wèn　MC mjunH
1　mourning cap, swath of hempen cloth wrapped around the head.

冕　miǎn　MC mjenX
1. ceremonial cap, worn by grandees and above.
　　a. coronet, for ruler.

勉　miǎn　MC mjenX
1. make an effort, exert oneself, apply oneself, strive.
　　a. force oneself to do everything in one's power.
　　b. 僶 ～ *mǐnmiǎn*, → 僶 *mǐn*.
2. encourage, urge on; exhort.
　　a. hasten, hurry.

勔　miǎn　MC mjenX　⊙ 勉 *miǎn*.

娩　miǎn　MC mjenX
1. parturition, childbirth; bear a child.

沔　miǎn　MC mjenX
1. name of the upper reaches of the Han River 漢水, in Shaanxi.
2. brimming full, swelling; full-flowing.
3. ⊙ 湎 *miǎn*, abandoned to a habit or vice, wallowing in, indulging in.

湎　miǎn　MC mjenX
1. abandon oneself to drink; besotted.
　　a. abandon oneself to any habit or vice, indulge in, wallow in.

2. rdup., drifting and shiftless, adrift and untied, vagrantly roving.

眄　miǎn　MC menX
1. to look sideways, look askance at, give a side-long glance; slanted glance, half-glance.
　　a. ogle, leer.
2. look for with anticipation, watch out for; hope for.

絻　miǎn　MC mjenX　→ 絻 *wèn*.

緬　miǎn　MC mjienX
1. thin strand of silk, finely spun.
　　a. slight, flimsy, airy; delicate
2. thin-threaded, far-stretched; drawn out, extended; distant, remote.
　　a. distant in time, long ago.
3. (med.) thin-threaded thought, attached to something not before one at present; e.g. ～懷 *miǎnhuái*, pensive, absorbed in thought; musing on the past.

miàn

面　miàn　MC mjienH
1. face, visage.
　　a. to face, turn toward; e.g. 南～ *nánmiàn*, south-facing.
　　b. face to face, directly confronting; in the face of, in the presence of.
2. outer surface.
　　a. front, topside, marked side (of an object); outward appearance, aspect, facet.
　　b. façade, exterior.
　　c. flat, two-dimensional.
3. facial expression; arrangement of features; countenance.
　　a. "face," reputation, dignity; value or standing in the eyes of others.
4. (med.) turn toward to examine; observe, survey; inspect.
5. measure-word for long, flat objects.

麪　miàn　MC menH
1. flour, from wheat.
　　a. (med.) dough(y).
　　b. (med.) noodles.

麵　miàn　MC menH
1. (med.) ⊙ 麪 *miàn*.

miáo

描 **miáo** **MC mjew**

1. (med.) to trace, copy (calligraphy or illustration); follow an outline or model; e.g. ～真 *miáozhēn*, draw a likeness (portrait).

苗 **miáo** **MC mjew**

1. sprout, shoot, of a plant; pamping, young tendril of a vine.
   a. gen. term for something in first growth or just showing.
2. symptom; sign, presage.
3. sgl. or cmpd. ～裔 *miáoyì*, ～胤 *miáoyìn*, ～緒 *miáoxù*, ～末 *miáomò*, offshoots, descendants, posterity.
4. summertime hunt.

miǎo

杪 **miǎo** **MC mjiewX**

1. tip or end of a branch.
   a. nib, stub; endpoint, last bit of; e.g. ～春 *miǎochūn*, the stub of springtime.
2. minute, small bit; slight, mere; mite, speck.

淼 **miǎo** **MC mjiewX**

1. waters spreading widely.
   a. in various bns., ⊙ 渺 *miǎo*.

渺 **miǎo** **MC mjiewX**

1. sgl. or (bn.) ～茫 *miǎománg* (MC mjiewX-mang), ～漫 *miǎomàn* (MC mjiewX-manH), ～瀰 *miǎomí* (MC mjiewX-mje), endless expanse (esp. of water), boundlessly spreading, flooding afar, cresting and coursing, infinite overflow.
2. rdup., far and ever farther, dimly in the distance.

眇 **miǎo** **MC mjiewX**

1. make one eye small, squint.
   a. peer at a very small object; focus(ed) intently.
2. something so far away or so small that it cannot be seen clearly.
   a. mite, minim(al); infinitesimal, subliminal; insignificant.
   b. to the utmost, endmost.
   c. subtle; exquisite.
   d. rdup., nebulous nowhere, impalpable infinity, faintness of infinity; minute and muted.

miào

秒 **miào** **MC mjiewH**

1. ⊙ 妙 *miào*, marvelous, miraculous; wonderful.

秒 **miào** **MC mjiewX**

1. awn or beard of grain.
2. endpoint, last tip, narrowing down to almost nothing; mite, smallest speck, merest part of.
   a. 1 second of time (1/60th of minute); 1/10,000th of an inch.

緲 **miào** **MC mjiewX**

1. lightly blurred, fading, faded; esp. (bn.) 縹～ *piāomiǎo*, → 縹 *piāo*.

藐 **miào** **MC mjiewX**

1. unripe, immature; young, frail; sprig.
   a. puerile, child(ish), youngling.
   b. innocent, naïve.
2. hold in slight regard; misprize, contemn.
3. ⊙ 邈 *miǎo*, remote, distant.
   mào **MC maewk**
1. gromwell (*Lithospermum arvense*), white-flowering plant from whose root a purple dye is made, syn. 茈 *zǐ*.

邈 **miǎo** **MC maewk**

1. remote, distant, far afield.
   a. far beyond, surpassing by far, much superior to.
2. long past, long ago, long separated (time).
3. aloof; bemused.
4. ⊙ 藐 *miǎo* 2, hold in slight regard, misprize, contemn; (med.) 描 *miáo*, trace, copy, draw after a model.

miào

妙 **miào** **MC mjiewH**

1. marvel(ous), miraculous, mirific(ent); sublime.
2. inscrutable; subtle(ty), barely perceptible; infinitesimal; subliminal (ant. 徼 *jiǎo* 2, outline, general lineaments); e.g. 觀其～ *guān qí miào*, observe its subtleties.
   a. fine, delicate; exquisite.
3. small of age, young; e.g. ～齡 *miàolíng*, few of years.

廟 **miào** **MC mjewH**

1. ancestral temple.
2. (post-Han) shrine or fane, for worship of various spirits.
   a. sanctuary.

miè

幭 miè MC met
1. screen, often of tiger-skin, hung from front railing of carriage.
2. headwrap.

懱 miè MC met
1. scorn, disdain; contemn.
2. (bn.) ～爵 *mièjué* (MC met-tsjak), old dialect word from Qin area for wren → 鷦鷯, *jiāoliáo*.

滅 miè MC mjiet
1. snuff out, damp out, quench, extinguish (fire).
    a. flood, inundate.
2. exterminate, abolish, eliminate; remove; cessation.
    a. disappear, vanish; pass away, cease to exist; destroy.
    b. (Budd.) sgl. or ～度 *mièdù*, trns. Skt. *nirvāṇa*, pass into extinction.
3. lack, be deficient in.
4. (med.) 明～ *míngmiè*, intermittent or shifting light, gleam fitfully.

矊 miè MC met
1. swollen or puffy eye, red eye, sore eye.

篾 miè MC met
1. rind of bamboo; also of reed, or sorghum.
    a. thin strip, lath, splint, slat.
2. weaver's bamboo (*Bambusa textilis*); syn. 桃枝竹 *táozhīzhú*, "peach-branch bamboo."

蔑 miè MC met
1. regard as nothing, disdain; scorn, ignore; despise, flout.
    a. discard, throw aside, toss away; make as nothing, dispense with, reject; destroy.
2. negative particle of the perfective: had not, have not, will have not; similar to 末 *mò* and often accompanied by perfective-final 矣 *yǐ*; mostly found in *Zuozhuan* 左傳 and *Guoyu* 國語, later mainly for archaic effect; e.g. 寧事齊楚, 有亡而已, ～從晉矣 *níngshì Qí Chǔ, yǒu wáng éryǐ, miècóng Jìn yǐ*, Better to serve Qi and Qi, lest we simply perish, and [better] not to have followed Jin.

3. not to have, lack; there are no . . .
4. (bn.) ～蒙 *mièméng* (MC met-muwng), rapidly running, quickly flitting; also, drifting aloft, uplifting loftiness.
5. ⊙ 矊 *miè*, swollen or puffy eye, red eye.

蠛 miè MC met
1. (bn.) ～蠓 *mièměng* (MC met-muwngX) or 蠓～ *měngmiè*, biting midges, blackflies and sandflies.

巘 miè MC met
1. stain or befoul with blood.
    a. defile, denigrate; besmear, sully.

mín

忞 mín MC min
1. with all one's will, strive hard; take pains, force oneself to do X; endeavor.
    wěn MC mjun
1. rdup., murky and misunderstood, continuous confusion.

旻 mín MC min
1. heaven, high heaven.
    a. compassionate or merciful heaven.
2. autumn(al) sky

旼 mín MC min
1. rdup., moderate and merciful, gentle and gracious.

民 mín MC mjin
1. commonfolk, commoner; peasant.
2. people, humankind.

珉 mín MC min
1. semi-precious stone, unidentified, similar to but inferior to jade.

緍 mín MC min
1. fishing-leader, drop-line.
2. cord for stringing coins together.
    a. by synecdoche, a string of coins.
3. fit a string to a bow.
    a. deploy; enfilade.

mǐn

僶   mǐn   MC mjinX
1. (bn.) ～俛 or ～勉 *mǐnmiǎn* (MC mjinX-mjenX), do all and anything one can, exert every possible effort; perforce, obliged to, willy-nilly; (med.) also, in the merest nodding of the head, in the blink of an eye.

慜   mǐn   MC minX
1. pained at heart; exasperated, dismayed.
    a. grieved, despondent.
2. sympathize, care for; solicitous of; commiserate with, compassion(ate).
3. misfortune, trouble; suffering.

憫   mǐn   MC minX
1. depressed, downhearted; heartache.
2. compassion(ate), pity; concern(ed) for, worry over.
    a. be moved by, touched by; sympathize with.

敏   mǐn   MC minX
1. quick-witted, keen, sharp-minded; alert, attentive; e.g. ～給 *mǐnjǐ*, witty, glib.
    a. intelligent, ingenious; apt, deft; ready; capable, competent; sensible.
2. rapid, quick, swift.
3. diligent, devoted; conscientious, intent on; intense.
4. big toe.

䫟   mǐn   MC minX
1. cruel; violent, brutal.
    a. surly, arrogant.
2. exert oneself, strive, put one's might into.
    mín   MC min
1. ⊙ 憫 *mín*, depressed, melancholy; worried over, concerned for.

泯   mǐn   MC mjinX
1. sweep away, put an end to, do away with; destroy, ruin.
2. rdup., mixed and muddled, thrown together, mingmang; also, extinguish utterly, finish off, wipe out of existence, make gone, leave no trace of.

湣   mǐn   MC minX
1. ⊙ 閔 *mín*, solicitous, caring, concerned for; sympathize with, compassionate.
2. rdup., trouble and turmoil, wambling welter.

3. ⊙ 泯 *mǐn*, do away with, sweep away, destroy, put an end to.
    miàn   MC menH
1. (bn.) 眩～ *xuànmiàn* (MC hwenH-menH), → 眩 *xuán*.

瘝   mǐn   MC min
1. affliction, malady, ailment; indisposition, disability.

皿   mǐn   MC mjaengX
1. plate, platter; trencher.

閔   mǐn   MC minX
1. be solicitous of, concerned for; compassionate, merciful; have one's heart go out to, sympathize with; pity.
    a. rdup., mild and merciful, calm and clement; also, concerned and caring of, anxious and uneasy about; also, muddled and muzzled.
2. grieved, sorrow(ing) over; lament.
3. (bn.) ～勉 *mǐnmiǎn*, ⊙ 僶勉, → 僶 *mǐn*.
4. ⊙ 䫟 *mín*, violent, brutal; surly, arrogant.

míng

冥   míng   MC meng
1. dark-cast light; darkling, darksome; gloom(y); tenebrity; tenebrous, caliginous; rdup., as dark as can be.
    a. faint(ness), imperceptible; e.g. (bn.) ～寞 *míngmò* (MC meng-mak), faint and far.
    b. covert, undercover, unseen; e.g. ～合 *mínghé*, covert connection or correspondence.
    c. rdup., gloomy and glowering, bleak and brooding, dim and dull.
2. the unseen realm, as of spirits, the dead, or of the depths of the heavens; e.g. ～報 *míngbào*, requital from the unseen realm, i.e. post-mortem recompense for kindness or restitution for misdeeds; ～鴻 *mínghóng*, heaven-soaring swan-goose; (Dao.) ～通 *míngtōng*, communication with the unseen realm of gods and spirits.
3. (med.) twilight state of mystical intuition; to connect with or touch unseen the source of truth; mystical darkness, mystically indistinct or undifferentiated (from); merge into or with, identify imperceptibly with—an esp. important word in *xuanxue* 玄學 writings.
4. deep and dark sea, darkest gulf, the main; ⊙ 溟 *míng*.

5. time of darkness, nighttime.
6. mental darkness, narrow-minded, dull.
7. efface, black out; strike out.

名　míng　MC mjieng

1. name, term; designation, (to) call (as), denominate; titular; word; e.g. 〜物 *míngwù*, names and things; 正〜 *zhèngmíng*, "get the words right," rectify terms so that names match properly with what they signify; (med.) 〜理 *mínglǐ*, Names and Principles, the practice of the foregoing, esp. in *xuanxue* 玄學 discourse or debate.

   a. personal name, given at birth, usu. used by family members and oneself; cf. 字 *zì*, byname, polite or public name, taken at marriageable or procreating age, used by non-family members; e.g. 〜刺 *míngcì*, (med.) 〜紙 *míngzhǐ*, name-card, calling-card.

2. name, character for which one is known; reputation, fame; e.g. (med.) 〜場 *míngchǎng*, "arena in which one makes a name," the examination ground of *jìnshì* 進士 degree.

   a. renown(ed), repute(d), acclaim(ed); notable, noted, well-known; e.g. (med.) 〜士 *míngshì*, gentleman of repute, usu. who has not taken public office.

3. moral, conforming to proper social and political expectations; e.g. 〜教 *míngjiào*, the Moral Teaching (< Doctrine of Names), principles favored by people in public life, world-oriented philosophies, esp. Ruism, generally opposed to ideas of "naturalness."

明　míng　MC mjaeng

1. light, luminous, bright(ness); diffusely bright, shed light on, illuminate; e.g. 〜珠 *míngzhū*, luminous pearl or gem; 〜滅 *míngmiè*, shifting or intermittent light; 〜堂 *míngtáng*, "Hall of Light," building symbolic of perfect government and of ideal harmony with gods, spirits, and cosmic order, supposedly originating with Yellow Emperor; specific use and construction differed in various dynasties—hall where ancestors are venerated, where monthly or seasonal rituals are performed to guarantee cosmic harmony, where government decisions are promulgated, etc.; but may also mean "Sanctified (or Sacred) Hall," → 5 below; (Dao.) also, esoteric name for space one inch behind spot between eyebrows.

   a. world of the living, of light; e.g. 幽〜 *yōumíng*, realms of the dark (dead) and the light (living).

2. evident, clear; manifest.

   a. make evident or clear, explain, expound; promulgate.

   b. celebrate(d); renown(ed).

3. perceptive, perspicacious; insight(ful), clear-seeing, clear-sighted, discern(ment).

   a. enlightened, wise; intelligent; e.g. 〜主 *míngzhǔ*, enlightened ruler.

   b. trns. Skt. *vidya*, wise, wisdom, e.g. (Budd.) 無〜 trns. Skt. *avidya*, ignorance.

4. next in order after the present, succeeding; e.g. 〜年 *míngnián*, next year.

5. sanctified, consecrated, having to do with rites or sacrifices pertaining to the spirits, or to the actions of gods or spirits; e.g. 〜衣 *míngyī*, "sanctified clothing," worn during sacrificial ceremonies; 〜器 *míngqì*, "consecrated vessels," grave-goods buried for enjoyment of deceased in afterlife.

瞑　míng　MC mengH

1. (med.) gloam(ing), dark-cast light of dusk, dimmet; dimming.
2. (med.) rdup., lone and forlorn, abandoned and alone, single and solitary.

   MC meng

1. ⊙ 冥 *míng* 1, dark-cast light; darkling, darksome; gloom(y); tenebrity; tenebrous, caliginous.

溟　míng　MC meng

1. deep and dark gulf of the sea, the main; gen. ref. far-stretching sea; e.g. 〜渤 *míngbó*, "caliginous surge," undersea deep, i.e. the Great Sea.
2. (med.) (bn.) 〜濛 *míngmǎng* (MC meng-mangX), far-fathomed main.
3. (bn.) 〜沐 *míngmù* (MC meng-muwk), mizzle and drizzle, dribbling drop(let)s.

   mǐng　MC mengX

1. (bn.) 〜涬 *mǐngxìng* (MC mengX-hengX) or 涬〜 *xìngmíng*, broad and boundless, shoreless sweep; also, misted murk, obscure opacity, infinite obscurity.

眳　míng　MC mjieng

1. eyelid, space between eyebrow and eyelash, esp. ref. to beauty of woman's eyes or glance.

瞑　míng　MC meng

1. eyes shut.

   a. sightless; blind.

   mián　MC men

1. "shut-eye," close one's eyes in sleep.

2. ～菜 *miáncài*, "eye-closing plant," bogbean, bog-myrtle (*Menyanthes trifoliata*), root slightly narcotic; syn. 睡菜 *shuìcài*, 綽菜 *chuòcài*.

  miàn   MC menH

1. (bn.) ～眩 *miànxuàn* (MC menH-hwenH), seeing spots before the eyes, dizzy, woozy; stunned and dazed.

茗   **míng   MC mengX**

1. (med.) tea-leaves; ～汁 *míngzhī*, tea as a drink, hot water infused with tea-leaves.

  a. (med.) late-picked tea-leaves.

2. (bn.) ～邈 *míngmiǎo* (MC mengX-maewk), sky-high and soaring, rearing up loftily.

3. (bn.) ～苧 *míngtīng* (MC mengX-theng), ⊙ 酩酊 *mǐngdǐng*, → 酩 *mǐng*.

蓂   **míng   MC meng**

1. sgl. or in cmpd. ～莢 *míngjiá*, name of a legendary auspicious plant; syn. 歷莢 *lìjiá*.

  mī   MC mek

1. sgl. or in (bn.) 菥～ *xīmì* (MC sek-mek), field pennycress, stinkweed (*Thlaspi arvense*), small, leafy white-flowering weed.

螟   **míng   MC meng**

1. cerambycid larvae, wood-boring larvae.

  a. (bn.) ～蛉 *mínglíng* (MC meng-leng), bollworm, grain-earworm (*Helicoverpa armigera*), larvae that feed disastrously on crops, eventually transforming to moths; in med. times also ref. pejoratively to adopted children.

銘   **míng   MC meng**

1. engrave, on stone or wood; carve, incise.

  a. inscription, text engraved on stone.

  b. (lit.) inscription, verse genre, usu. commemorating place or deceased person and meant to be engraved on stone; of person, often placed at end of prose epitaph.

2. imprint, as on mind, memory, etc.

鳴   **míng   MC mjaeng**

1. call or cry of birds and beasts; translate according to specific animal (e.g. caw of crow, hoot of owl, roar of tiger, chirr of cicada, neigh of horse, etc.).

2. give voice, sound(ing) of various objects; translate accordingly (e.g. crack of whip, chime of jade pendants, sounding of zither, etc.).

3. call out to, hail.

鵬   **míng   MC mjaeng**

1. sgl. or cmpd. 鷦～ *jiāomíng*, gryphon or splendrous gryphon, legendary supernatural bird akin to a "phoenix."

mǐng

酩   **mǐng   MC mengX**

1. (bn.) ～酊 *mǐngdǐng* (MC mengX-tengX), besotted(ness), soused and besotted, fully flown, inebriated, crapulent; also, mawkish and maudlin.

mìng

命   **mìng   MC mjaengH**

1. call on one to do X; give orders to; bid(ding); direct(ive).

  a. command, ordain; decree; injunction, mandate.

  b. exhortation; advice, counsel.

2. to name, call (as).

  a. confer a title on, bestow a dignity.

3. "what is appointed," heaven-ordained duration of life, life-span; course of life; e.g. ～終 *mìngzhōng*, end(ing) of one's life.

  a. heaven-ordained circumstances of life, fate, destiny; "calling," vocation, mission; also, official mission.

詺   **mìng   MC mjiengH**

1. (med.) give a name to something, designate by name.

miù

繆   **miù   MC mjiwH**

1. ⊙ 謬 *miù* 1, err(or), mistake(n), fallacious; baseless, groundless, undeserved; absurd(ity), preposterous, irrational; 2, twist the truth, gull, cozen, sucker.

  móu   MC mjuw

1. (bn.) 綢～ *chóumóu*, → 綢 *chóu*.

  jiū   MC kjiw

1. coil(ed), twist(ed).

  a. crisscross, interlock(ing).

2. ⊙ 糾 *jiū*, straighten out; correct < tie together separate strands.

  mù   MC mjuwk

1. ⊙ 穆 *mù* 1, well-disposed, reverent(ial); 2, tablets on right-hand side of ancestral shrine, being the odd-numbered ancestors.

謬　miù　MC mjiwH
1. blunder, err(or), mistake(n); fallacious.
    a. baseless, groundless; undeserved.
    b. absurd(ity), preposterous; irrational, illogical
2. gull, cozen; lead on; defraud; sucker.

mō

摸　mō　MC mak
1. touch with the hand; stroke, feel; fondle, caress.
    a. examine by touch, palpate; e.g. ～索 *mōsuǒ*, probe, feel one's way; grope.
2. ⊙ 摹 *mó*, model, pattern; imitate.

mó

劘　mó　MC ma
1. pare away, cut away.
2. criticize, rebuke, be sharp with.
3. rub, stroke; smoothen; grind.
    a. brush against, come near to.

摩　mó　MC ma
1. rub, scrape; polish, buff, chafe; e.g. ～戛 *mójiá*, rub and bump.
    a. wear away, abrade, erode.
2. touch lightly, graze; rustle against.
    a. stroke; fondle, caress, massage; ⊙ 摸 *mō* 1.
    b. rub up against, get close to.
3. bush-harrow, very light woven harrow that smooths the soil without breaking it up.
4. deliberate, discuss; comb through.
5. (med.) (bn.) ～何 *móhé* (MC ma-ha), indifferently, unconcernedly.
6. (Budd.) trsl. Skt. *ma*, *mā*; e.g. ～尼 *móní* (MC ma-nrij), trsl. Skt. *maṇi*, pearl, jewel, symbolic of truth, esp. associated with the bodhisattva Avalokiteśvara; ～利 *mólì* (MC ma-lijH), abb. trsl. Skt. *mallikā*, Indian jasmine (*Jasminum sambac*), the plant and its fragrant white flower; ～訶 *móhē* (MC ma-xa), trsc. Skt. *mahā*, prefix meaning "great."

摹　mó　MC mu
1. model, pattern.
    a. imitate, copy out, follow the model of; outline.
    b. (med.) depict, portray; describe.

模　mó　MC mu
1. wooden mold, pattern, matrix.
    a. follow a pattern or model; copy, imitate.
2. standard, norm; example.
3. (med.) (bn.) ～糊 *móhú* (MC mu-hu), unclear and ill-defined, fuzzy; also, fuzzy and fuddled, woozy and boozy.

橅　mó　MC mu　⊙ 模 *mó*.

磨　mó　MC ma
1. grind, polish.
    a. pulverize(d); powder(ed), flaked.
2. sharpen, whet.
3. wear away, abrade, work to nothing.
4. grind down; torment, persecute.
    a. (med.) encounter difficulty, come to a grinding halt.
5. grind away at, examine or study diligently.
    mò　MC maH
1. grindstone.
2. quern, hand-operated grinding-mill.

礳　mó　MC ma　⊙ 磨 *mó*.

謨　mó　MC mu
1. plan out, design; formulate; devise, contrive.
2. give an opinion, counsel, advise.

魔　mó　MC ma
1. (med.) demon, evil spirit; < Skt. *māra*, "Maker of Death," the Buddha's antagonist.

麼　mó　MC ma
1. (med.) sgl. or (bn.) ～眇 *mómiào* (MC ma-mjiewH), tiny, teen(s)y.
    ma　MC ma
1. (med.) (GP) from Tang times, post-VB marker of interrogative.

mǒ

抹　mǒ　MC mat
1. (med.) smear, rub, wipe, spread over; smooth out.
    a. (med.) ～摋 *mǒsà* (MC mat-sat), wipe out, sweep away, obliterate.
    mò　MC mat
1. (med.) brush fingers outward when playing zither or lute, "rub," a right-hand movement.

mò

万　mò　MC mok

1. (med.) ～俟 *mòqí*, a bysillabic surname.
2. old-script form of → 萬 *wàn*.

嘿　mò　MC mok　⊙ 默 *mò*.

墨　mò　MC mok

1. ink; atramentous.
   a. inky, ink-black.
2. ink-line, as in calligraphy or ink-drawing.
   a. black line of carpenter's marking ink.
3. blacken; sully.
   a. venal; corrupt; covetous.
4. tattoo, esp. the face, as judicial punishment.
5. burn a field (turn it black), as part of swidden agriculture.
6. ancient measure of 5 "feet" (*chi* 尺).
7. ⊙ 默 *mò*, soundless, silent.

寞　mò　MC mak

1. (bn.) 寂～ *jìmò*, → 寂 *jì*; (bn.) 冥～ *míngmò*, → 冥 *míng*.

末　mò　MC mat

1. branch, of tree (ant. 本 *běn*, root).
2. tip; end of, latter, last, final; e.g. ～流 *mòliú*, "latter current," lower reaches of a river; also, last in sequence; (Budd.) ～法 *mòfǎ*, latter age of the Law (Dharma), 3rd of 3 stages of the Dharma's (d)evolution (the first 2 being *zhengfa* 正法, age of true Dharma, and *xiangfa* 象法, of Semblance Dharma), in which traditional religious practices lose their effectiveness and spiritual capacity erodes.
   a. trimmings, leavings; remnants, residuum; e.g. ～光 *mòguāng*, vestigial light, lingering glow.
3. secondary, non-essential; accessory; peripheral; e.g. ～產 *mòchǎn*, peripheral occupations, i.e. handiwork and commerce.
   a. inferior, lowly, humble.
   b. deviate from the basic.
4. the least bit, least amount; particle; powder.
5. (Budd.) ～伽 *mòqié* (MC mat-gja), trsc. Skt. *mārga*, path or course leading to enlightenment.
6. ⊙ 莫 *mò* 1-4.

歾　mò　MC mwot

1. ⊙ 殁 *mò*, die.
   wěn　MC mjunX
1. ⊙ 刎 *wěn*, cut one's throat.

殁　mò　MC mwot

1. die, descend into nothingness.
   a. come to naught; finish, come to the end.
2. fall, descend; fade away.
   wěn　MC mjunX
1. ⊙ 刎 *wěn*, cut one's throat, esp. suicide.

沒　mò　MC mwot

1. sink, drown, engulf; submerge; subside.
   a. sink into the ground, be buried, cover(ed), conceal(ed).
2. dissolve, sink away; disappear, vanish.
   a. die, ⊙ 殁 *mò* 1.
3. subdue, overcome.
4. confiscate, take possession of; divest.

沫　mò　MC mat

1. foam, froth, spume.
2. saliva.
3. dissolve to an end; dwindle, diminish; run out; finish.

漠　mò　MC mak

1. silent; silence, hush; still(ness); e.g. ～然 *mòrán*, silently, noiselessly.
   a. rdup., still and silent, soundless, hushed and still.
2. silent sands, desert.
3. silent space, beyond the stars.

瘼　mò　MC mak

1. illness, indisposition; affliction, suffering.
   a. malaise, weakness.

眜　mò　MC mat

1. rush against, brave, defy; ⊙ 冒 *mào* 3.

眿　mò　MC meak

1. gaze at.
   a. rdup., eye intently, with intense gaze; look longingly at, inexpressibly united.

秣　mò　MC mat

1. fodder for horses or oxen.
   a. feed grain to same.

纆　mò　MC mok

1. cord or rope plaited from three separate strands.
   a. ligature, binding, bundling.
   b. (bn.) ～綿 *mòmián* (MC mok-mjien), tightly textured.

茉　mò　MC mat

1. (med.) (bn.) 〜莉 *mòlì* (MC mat-lijH), abb. trsc. Skt. *mallikā*, Indian jasmine (*Jasminum sambac*), the plant and its fragrant white flower.

莫　mò　MC mak

1. VB-phrase modifier indicating the distribution or scope of the sense of the VB-phrase relative to the stated or implied topic, "in no case, in no instance"; akin to 各 *gè*, 或 *huò*, 孰 *shú*; often translatable as "none, nothing, no one"; e.g. 民〜敢不敬 *mín mò gǎn bújìng*, the people will in no case dare not to be respectful; 從者病〜能興 *cóngzhě bìng mò néng xìng*, the followers became ill and in no case were they able to arise (. . . and none was able to arise); 養心〜善於寡欲 *yǎngxīn mò shàn yú guǎyù*, for nurturing one's inner senses nothing is better than reducing one's yearnings.
2. (med.) emphatic negative ADV: in no case, no chance that, not at all.
    a. (med.) esp. in early Buddhist texts, prohibitive: do not.
3. to determine > presume; presumably, likely.
    a. (med.) ADV indicating diffidence, hesitancy, less than complete certainty; most likely, probably; e.g. 〜非 *mòfēi*, isn't it [the case] that . . . ?
4. (med.) imperative: must, need to, by all means.
5. rdup., thick and dense, of trees, dust, fog, etc.
6. (bn.) 〜錯 *mòcuò* (MC mak-tshak) or 錯〜 *cuòmò*, unevenly irregular > troubled and baffled, disappointed and disquieted.
7. ⊙ 劖 *mó* 1, to slice, shave; 謨 *mó* 1, to plan, project; 漠 *mò*, expanse.

mù　MC muH

1. ⊙ 暮 *mù* sunset; late; 幕 *mù*, drapes; tent.

袜　mò　MC mat

1. waistband, for woman; usu. for high-waisted dress, hence also breastband.
2. cover up; shield from sight.

wà　MC mjot

1. ⊙ 襪 *wà*, stockings.

貃　mò　MC maek

1. non-Chinese people, esp. to north and northeast; outland "swine."
2. quiet; without fuss.
3. ⊙ 貘 *mò*, giant panda.

貘　mò　MC maek

1. giant panda (*Ailuropoda melanoleuca*). N.B. Does not ref. "tapir" until modern times.

鏌　mò　MC mak

1. (bn.) 〜鋣 *mòyé* (MC mak-yae), name of a legendary sword.

陌　mò　MC maek

1. raised path or balk running east-west (latitudinal) through cultivated fields; cross-path, terry; cf. 阡 *qiān*, longitudinal balk.
    a. small path; footpath, footway.
    b. gen. term for road.

靺　mò　MC mat

1. (med.) (bn.) 〜鞨 *mòhé* (MC mat-hat), name of confederation of Tungusic tribes in Sui-Tang period, located in southern Manchuria; in N. Wei period called Moji 勿吉 (MC mat-kjit), during Song and after Nüzhen 女真; also, name of unidentified red-orange gemstone.

wà　MC mjot

1. ⊙ 襪 *wà*, stockings.

袜　mò　MC mat　⊙ 袜 *mò*.

驀　mò　MC maek

1. gallop, dash, race off.
2. (med.) rise above, surmount, transcend.
    a. (med.) cross over; e.g. 〜水 *mòshuǐ*, cross the river.
3. (med.) 〜地 *mòdì*, in vain, futile(ly).

驚　mò　MC meak

1. shy away from; start, recoil, blench, flinch.

默　mò　MC mok

1. soundless, silent; hushed, mute; wordless; tacit, muffled.
    a. rdup., still and soundless, tacit and tranquil; also, silently desolate; also, wordlessly eloquent.
2. darkened, dimmed; blackened.

móu

侔　móu　MC mjuw

1. equal to, same as, (a)like.
2. ⊙ 牟 *móu* 2, take, carry off; confiscate.

恈   móu   MC mjuw
1. rdup., crave and covet, lust after, eye greedily.

牟   móu   MC mjuw
1. low, bellow (ox).
2. take, carry off; claim for oneself, confiscate; accroach.
3. enlarge; increase, double.
4. ⊙ 侔 *móu*, equal to, same as, like unto; 眸 *móu*, pupil (of eye); 麰 *móu*, barley.

眸   móu   MC mjuw
1. pupil (of the eye).

蛑   móu   MC mjuw
1. (bn.) 蟧~ *jiūmóu*, → 蟧 *jiū*.
  máo   MC maw
1. ⊙ 蟊 *máo*, grubs that eat the roots of grain; also, euph. for destroyers of state or person.

謀   móu   MC mjuw
1. take counsel with, consult; consider opinions or expectations.
  a. advise, counsel.
2. plan, strategize; plot, scheme.
  a. strategy, stratagem; policy, plan of action; design.
3. (med.) ~反 *móufǎn*, plot to rebel, one of 10 judicial "abominations" 惡 *è*.

鉾   móu   MC mjuw   ⊙ 鍪 *móu*.

鍪   móu   MC mjuw
1. iron pot, with turned-back lip.
2. sgl. or (bn.) 兜~ *dōumóu* (MC tuw-mjuw), casque, war-helmet in shape of preceding.
  a. cap, of same shape.

麰   móu   MC mjuw
1. barley.

mǒu

某   mǒu   MC muwX
1. unspecified adjective or (pro)noun: such-and-such, so-and-so; e.g. ~人 *mǒurén*, such-and-such a person.
  a. humble self-ref.; e.g. ~甲 *mǒujiǎ*, just me.

mǔ

姆   mǔ   MC muX
1. preceptress, governess.
2. (med.) nursemaid; housekeeper.

姥   mǔ   MC muX
1. beldam, elderly woman; matron.
2. mother of adult male.

姆   mǔ   MC muX
1. ⊙ 姆 *mǔ* 1, preceptress, governess.
  wǔ   MC mjuX
1. ⊙ 侮 *wǔ*, offend, affront, insult; disgrace(ful), humiliate.

拇   mǔ   MC muwX
1. largest digit of hand or foot; thumb; big toe.

母   mǔ   MC muwX
1. mother; maternal.
  a. matron, dame, ref. elderly woman.
  b. (Budd.) ~邑 *mǔyì*, womankind.
2. female gender.
3. nurture, foster.
4. largest or heaviest portion of currency (the others being called *zi* 子).
  a. capital, of investment (profits or interest called *zi* 子).
5. source, origin(al).

牡   mǔ   MC muwX
1. male of birds or beasts.
2. bolt, of lock.
3. hummock, hump.
4. ~丹 *mǔdān*, tree peony (*Paeonia suffruticosa*).
5. (med.) ~蠣 *mǔlì*, oyster.

畝   mǔ   MC muwX
1. cultivated land, humped with plants; esp. ricefield.
2. land-measure, Chinese "acre," area varying according to period; from Warring States through imperial times equiv. 240 square double-paces (*bu* 步), but since length of the "foot" (*chi* 尺) varied at different times, so did the area of the 畝 *mǔ*, thus in Han approx. 9 *mǔ* per acre, in Northern Dynasties 5-6 *mǔ*/acre, in Tang 8 *mǔ*/acre.

鉧　**mǔ**　**MC muX**
1. (med.) (bn.) 鈷〜 *gǔmǔ*, → 鈷 *gǔ*.

鏻　**mǔ**　**MC muX**　⊙ 鉧 *mǔ*.

mù

募　**mù**　**MC muH**
1. levy; solicit, raise.
   a. recruit, enlist.

墓　**mù**　**MC muH**
1. tomb; grave.
   a. 〜表 *mùbiǎo*, epitaph, engraved on stone tablet erected in front of tomb; 〜誌銘 *mùzhìmíng*, tomb inscription, engraved on stone tablet and buried with coffin.

幕　**mù**　**MC mak**
1. screen, veil (cf. 帷 *wéi*, side-curtain); hanging; bed-curtain.
2. tent; e.g. 〜府 *mùfǔ*, "tent-headquarters," military headquarters in the field; (med.) also, for any military headquarters or office of imperial guard.
3. baldachin, canopy of state over altar or throne; by metonymy, dais.

慕　**mù**　**MC muH**
1. think of ardently, regard fondly.
   a. favor; hanker after, yearn for.
2. admire, esteem; aspire to, emulate.
3. 〜容 *mùróng*, bisyllabic surname of Särbi (Xianbei 鮮卑) origin, notably that of ruling family of the Later Yan (後燕, 384-409) dynasty.

暮　**mù**　**MC muH**
1. sunset, nightfall.
2. late(r).
   a. latter part of a period or of life; e.g. 歲〜 *suìmù*, end of the year; 〜年 *mùnián*, one's later ("sunset") years.

木　**mù**　**MC muwk**
1. wood(en).
   a. one of the 5 "agents" or "phases" in *wuxing* theory, correlated symbolically with the direction east, season of springtime, green-blue color, planet Jupiter, etc.

2. tree.
   a. timber; board.
   b. wooded, timbered.
3. one of the 8 categories of musical instruments, those made of wood (but not strings), esp. 柷 *zhù*, box-rattle, churn-box.
4. stiff, rigid; insensible.
   a. simple(-minded); unhewn; unadorned.
5. 〜蘭 *mùlán*, laurel magnolia, lily tree (*Magnolia denudata*); 〜蓮 *mùlián*, "woody lotus," manglietia (*Manglietia fordiana*), stately evergreen tree similar to magnolia, with white or straw-yellow blossoms that resemble lotus blossoms, hence the name; also ⊙ 薜荔 *bìlì*, climbing fig.

楘　**mù**　**MC muwk**
1. ornamental bands of leather attached to carriage-pole.

瞀　**mù**　**MC muwk**
1. rdup., dim and dull-witted, beclouded; also, shrug and brush, whisk and whisper (of wind).
   mào　**MC mawH**
1. ⊙ 眊 *mào* 1, clouded vision, blurred, bleary; addled, distraught.

沐　**mù**　**MC muwk**
1. wash one's hair; e.g. 〜浴 *mùyù*, wash one's hair and bathe; (med.) also, have the benefit of, be favored with.
   a. sgl. or 休〜 *xiūmù*, scheduled rest-day ("hair-washing break") for officials (in Tang times, every 10th day, i.e. 1 day per week).
2. water in which rice has been washed, often then used for hair-washing.
3. cut off, shear, lop off, dock; strip, remove.

牧　**mù**　**MC mjuwk**
1. (to) shepherd, pastor.
   a. used in various official titles: sgl. as regional commissioner in Han; post-Han to Tang, prefect of a *zhou* 州, then replaced by *cishi* 刺史, though often used informally as title or as verb signifying duties of same; in Tang, title of governer of a superior prefecture (*fu* 府); (med.) in compounds (e.g. *mujian* 〜監) often pertaining to imperial horse pasturage.
   b. to tend, look after; keep in order.
2. pasture, pasture-lands.

目   mù   MC mjuwk

1. eye(s).
   a. eyesight, vision.
2. to "eyeball," regard, look at; see.
   a. indicate intention with movement of eyes, signal with a look.
3. point of view, judgment.
   a. characterization, how one is "seen"; reputation; e.g. 品～ *pǐnmù*, classification and characterization.
4. label, tag; item(ize).
   a. item; entry (in a list or sequence); e.g. ～錄 *mùlù*, table of contents.
5. "eyes" of a net; mesh(es); opening.

睦   mù   MC mjuwk

1. in concord; harmonious.
2. ⊙ 穆 *mù* 2, well-disposed toward others; generous; understanding; on good terms, friendly; rdup., clement and benevolent.

穆   mù   MC mjuwk

1. well-disposed; like rice that is "set," bent over with full ear.
   a. well-ordered, well-set; stately, dignified.
2. well-disposed toward others; generous; understanding; on good terms, friendly.
   a. placid, even-tempered; composed; calm, tranquil.
   b. in concord, harmonious; ⊙ 睦 *mù*.

3. rdup., clement and benevolent; also, spruce and snug.
4. 昭～ *zhāomù*, sequential order of ancestral tablets in family shrine, placed alternately to the left and right of the founder's tablet (facing south), those on the left designated *zhāo* being the even-numbered successors (beginning with 2), those on the right designated *mu* being the odd-numbered successors.
5. Merv, Margiana.

苜   mù   MC mjuwk

1. (bn.) ～蓿 *mùsù* (MC mjuwk-sjuwk), alfalfa (*Medicago sativa*), trsc. Iran. *buksuk or *buxsux; introduced into China by Zhang Qian 張騫 from one of his missions to Central Asia, ca. 128-115 BCE.

蚞   mù   MC muwk

1. (bn.) 蜓～ *tíngmù*, → 蜓 *tíng*.

霖   mù   MC muwk

1. (bn.) 霡～ *màimù*, → 霡 *mài*.

鍪   mù   MC muwk

1. ⊙ 緐 *mù*, ornamental bands of leather, attached to carriage-pole.

   móu   MC mjuw

1. ⊙ 鍪 *móu* 2, sgl. or (bn.) 兜～ *dōumóu* (MC tuw-mjuw), casque, war-helmet in shape of iron pot with turned-back lip.

N

ná

挐   ná   MC nrae

1. draw out, draw forth, pull out.
   a. of music, drawn out, extended.
2. (med.) grip with the hand, seize, hold.
3. ⊙ 挐 *rú* 1, mix up, mingle; muddle, confuse.

nà

納   nà   MC nop

1. enter, pass into.
   a. give entrance to; bring in, introduce.
2. receive, accept, take in, admit; adopt.
   a. include; keep within, store up.

3. install (as).
4. send in, hand in; turn over to, present to.
5. piece in, patch up, sew up, mend, ⊙ 衲 *nà*.

衲   nà   MC nop

1. (med.) patch up, piece in, sew up, mend.
2. (Budd.) "patches," i.e. monk's patchwork robe, because it was to be made of several strips and patches, not a single piece of cloth; also, informal metonymic ref. to or self-referential term for a monk.

軜   nà   MC nop

1. inside reins of a 3-horse team.

那   nà   MC naH   → 那 *nuó*.

nǎi

乃　nǎi　MC nojX

1. when preceding a VB-phrase, emphasizes sequential or temporal relation between prior circumstances and the action or state of the VB-phrase: then, only then (cog. *ér* 而 "then"); e.g. 我～行之 *wǒ nǎi xíng zhī*, Only then did I put it into practice; ～可以長生 *nǎi kěyǐ chángshēng*, Only then can you enjoy a long life.

    a. with that, given that, thereupon; e.g. 客～笑而還 *kè nǎi xiào ér huán*, With that the visitor, laughing, returned; ～比於狂 *nǎi bǐ yú kuáng*, Given that, it is comparable to being crazy.

    b. so, thus; e.g. ～謂我為盜跖 *nǎi wèi wǒ wéi dàozhí*, So they refer to me as Robber Zhi; 王～說之 *wáng nǎi yuè zhī*, Thus the king was pleased with it.

    c. when preceding 今 *jīn*: from now on, henceforth; e.g. 吾～今知之 *wú nǎi jīn zhī zhī*, Henceforth I will know it; ～今可為矣 *nǎi jīn kě wéi yǐ*, From now on it can be done.

2. when preceding noun phrases in nominal sentences, emphasizes the noun predication: indeed, in fact, to be sure; e.g. 是～仁術也 *shì nǎi rénshù yě*, This is, to be sure, the art of humaneness; ～所謂善也 *nǎi suǒwèi shàn yě*, This is indeed what is referred to as goodness.

3. after 無 *wú*, makes a rhetorical negative: really not . . . ?, really nothing . . . ?, really doesn't (isn't, etc.) . . . ?; e.g. 無～不察乎 *wúnǎi bùchá hū*, Is there really nothing to find out about it?; 無～大簡乎 *wúnǎi dàjiǎn hū*, Isn't that really too casual?

4. 2nd-person pronoun: you, your(s); e.g. ～能從我乎 *nǎi néng cóng wǒ hū*, Are you able to follow me?; 余嘉～勳 *yú jiā nǎi xūn*, I much applaud your success in royal service.

5. 無～ *wúnǎi*, nothing other than, no doubt.

嬭　nǎi　MC nreaX

1. breast-milk; suckle.

    a. woman's breast; teat; nipple.

迺　nǎi　MC nojX　⊙ 乃 *nǎi*.

廼　nǎi　MC nojX　⊙ 乃 *nǎi*.

nài

奈　nài　MC najH

1. typically does not occur alone, but only in combinations with 何 *hé* (a. – c. below) or existentially negated (d. below).

    a. ～何 *nàihé* what is it like? what is the explanation?; e.g. 其為人也～何 *qí wéi rén yě nàihé*, as for how he behaves as a person, what is it like?; ～何去宗廟也 *nàihé qù zōngmiào yě*, what is the explanation for departing from one's ancestral temple?; 君子之行～何 *jūnzi zhī xíng nàihé*, as for the movements of a man of noble status, what is it like?

    b. ～之何 *nàizhīhé*, or abb. ～何 *nàihé*, make it like what? > what's to be done about it? what recourse is there?; e.g. 後有大患將～之何 *hòu yǒu dàhuàn jiāng nàizhīhé*, later there will be great distress, what shall be done about it?; 若然者吾～之何 *ruò ránzhe wú nàizhīhé*, if this is what it's like, then what am I to do about it? 吾其～何 *wú qí nàihé*, what ought I do about it?

    c. ～ X 何 *nài* X *hé*, what's to be done about X; e.g. 其奪君名美何 *nài qí duó jūn míngměi hé*, what is to be done about his having misappropriated your reputation and glory?; ～其情何 *nài qí qíng hé*, what's to be done about their feelings? ～前言何乎 *nài qiányán hé hū*, what is to be done about his earlier speech?

    d. negated: (i) 無～何 *wúnàihé*, there is nothing to be done about X, there is no remedy; e.g. 不務知之所無～何 *bùwù zhī zhī suǒ wúnàihé*, do not strive for that in regard to which there is no recourse from one's knowledge; 諸侯兵困力極無～何 *zhūhóu bīngkùn lìjí wúnàihé*, when the arms of the various nobles have been constrained and their energy has reached its limit, there is nothing to do about that. (ii) 無～之何 *wúnàizhīhé*, there is nothing to be done about it, there is no way to deal with it; e.g. 我欲更之，無～之何 *wǒ yù gēng zhī wúnàizhīhé*, I may wish to change it, but there is no way to do that; 夫水勢勝火，章華之台燒，以升勺沃而救之，雖涸井

而竭池，無～之何也 *fú shuǐshì shèng huǒ, zhānghuá zhī tái shāo, yǐ shēngsháo wò ér jiù zhī, suī gùjǐng ér jiéchí, wúnài zhīhé yě*, In any particular respect water has the capacity to overcome fire, yet if the Zhang-hua Palace is aflame, you can try to save it by dousing it with buckets and ladles of water until you drain the wells and dry up the ponds, but there will be no way to deal with it. (iii) 無～ X 何 *wúnài* X *hé*, there is nothing to be done about X, there is no way to deal with X; e.g. 狐欲渡河無～尾何 *hú yù dùhé wúnài wěi hé*, the fox wishes to cross the river, but there is no way to deal with his tail; 孤無～越之先君何 *gū wúnài yuè zhī xiānjūn hé*, what am I to do about the former lords of Yue? 韓必赴無～秦何矣 *hán bì fù wúnài qín hé yǐ*, Han will inevitably rush ahead, but there will be nothing that they can to do against Qin. (iv) 無可～何 *wúkěnàihé*, 無可～ *wúkěnài*, there is nothing that can be done about X; e.g. 夫智不足以見賢，無可～何矣 *fú zhìbùzú yǐ jiànxián, wúkěnàihé yǐ*, in any case where someone's knowledge might be insufficient to recognize merit, there is nothing that could be done about it; 唯無形者無可～也 *wéi wúxíngzhe wúkěnài yě*, especially for those things without a shape, there is nothing that can be done about them. (v) 莫 奈 *mò nài*, in no case a way to deal with something, no way to manage something; e.g. 人莫予奈 *rén mò yú nài*, others have no way to deal with me.
2. ⊙ 柰 *nài*, crab-apple (*Malus pumila*).

柰   nài   MC najH

1. crab-apple, paradise apple (*Malus pumila*).
   a. 素～ *sù'nài*, white crab-apple
2. ～花 *naihuā*, night-blooming jasmine (*Cestrum nocturnum*).
3. ⊙ 奈 *nài*, recourse, as in 柰...何 *nài...hé*, "what recourse is there? what is to be done about X?"

耐   nài   MC nojH

1. endure, (for)bear, put up with; endure, show patience.
2. (med.) (ADV) only, as long as, still.
3. judicial punishment of shaving the beard and temples.

néng   MC nong

1. ⊙ 能 *néng*, ability, capacity; resourceful(ness), prowess.

鼐   nài   MC nojH

1. great-sized cauldron.

nán

南   nán   MC nom

1. south, southern, southward, southerly; in *wuxing* correspondences associated with the agent fire, season of summer, color red, etc.
2. (med.) ～司 *nánsī*, Southern Ministries, in Tang times ref. to higher-level agencies whose offices were located in the capitals' "imperial city" (*huangcheng* 皇城), south of the "palace city" (*gongcheng* 宮城), esp. the Imperial Secretariat (*zhongshusheng* 中書省), Bureau of State Affairs (*shangshusheng* 尚書省), Chancellery (*menxiasheng* 門下省), and Censorate (*yushitai* 御使臺); (med.) ～省 *nánshěng*, in Tang times, informal ref. to Bureau of State Affairs (*shangshusheng* 尚書省); also to the Department of Rites (*libu* 禮部), whose officials were often given editorial duties in the *shangshusheng*.
3. ～天樹 *nántiānshù*, ～天竹 *nántiānzhú*, ～天燭 *nántiānzhú*, nandin tree, ⊙ 楠 *nán*; syn. 琪 *qí*.
4. (Budd.) trsc. of Skt. *nam*; e.g. ～無 *nánwú* (MC nom-mju), ～摸 *nánmó* (MC nom-mu) trsc. of Skt. *namo* "salutations [to OBJ]."

喃   nán   MC nream

1. rdup., "nam-nam," onom. of whispering; also, (med.) of reading aloud in a murmur, mutter; also, (med.) of gabbling birds.

栴   nán   MC nom   ⊙ 楠 *nán*.

枏   nán   MC nom   ⊙ 楠 *nán*.

楠   nán   MC nom

1. sgl. or ～木 *nánmù*, nanmu tree (*Phoebe nanmu*), large straight-trunked evergreen, often used in building because resistant to decay; also, nandina tree (*Nandina domestica*), medium-sized evergreen shrub, white-flowering in early summer.
   a. 紅～ *hóngnán*, bay tree (*Machilus thunbergii*), massive broad-leaved evergreen; like *Phoebe*, belongs to laurel family.

男　nán　MC nom

1. man, male.
2. son.
3. 5th of the 5 ranks of nobility, usu. translated "baron."

諵　nán　MC nream

1. (med.) ⊙ 喃 *nán*.

難　nán　MC nan

1. difficult(y), hard(ship), hardly; impossible, impossibly.
2. unpleasant.

nàn　MC nanH

1. trouble(s), disaster, catastrophe; esp. of war, military conflict.
2. antagonist, foe, enemy.
3. object(ion), argue against, critique; disapprove, disapproval; deprecate, animadvert, take to task.
    a. reject(ion), repel(lent), repudiate.
    b. (med.) rebuttal to the topic first presented in a bout of "pure conversation."

nuó　MC na

1. exorcise; expel or drive away malevolent forces, demons.

nǎn

戁　nǎn　MC nraenX

1. fear(ful), dread; be afraid of.

赧　nǎn　MC nraenX

1. blush, from shame or embarrassment.
    a. flushed, red-faced.

náng

囊　náng　MC nang

1. sack, bag; sachet; gipser, pouch hung from belt or girdle.
    a. to bag, put away; cover up; e.g. ～括 *náng-kuò*, include, enclose, cover.

nǎng

曩　nǎng　MC nangX

1. formerly, in times past.
    a. precursory, precursal.

náo

呶　náo　MC nraew

1. clamor(ous), bawl(ing).
    a. (med.) rdup., yak and gab, meaningless babble; also, (med.) bawl and bray, yap and wail.

恞　náo　MC nraew

1. noisy; blustery, obstreporous.

撓　náo　MC nraewX

1. disturb, bother, trouble, annoy, frustrate.
    a. stir; mix; mess up.
2. bend, twist; flex; e.g. (bn.) ～挑 *náotiāo* (MC nraewX-thew), fluently coiling, meandering, easy circuit.
    a. bend to one's desire, influence, affect; subdue, subjugate.
    b. crooked, warped; unscrupulous.

橈　náo　MC nraew

1. bent, crooked.
    a. rdup., ⊙ 撓挑 *náotiāo*, fluently coiling, meandering, circulating easily.
2. bend to one's will; subdue, cause to yield.
    a. weaken, enfeeble; cripple.
3. annoy, vex; disturb, disorder.

ráo　MC nyew

1. oars; to row.

猱　náo　MC naw

1. a species of gibbon, identification uncertain but perhaps the black-crested gibbon (*Nomascus concolor*) or the northern white-cheeked gibbon (*Nomascus leucogenys*).
    a. 狙～ *jūnáo*, golden snub-mosed monkey (*Rhinopithecus roxellana*).
2. sgl. or cmpd. ～雜 *náozá*, stir up, mix up, confound.

獶　náo　MC naw　⊙ 猱 *náo*.

獿　náo　MC naw

1. ⊙ 猱 *náo*.
2. ～人 *náorén*, plasterer.

nǎo　MC nraewX

1. (bn.) ～獠 *nǎoxiāo* (MC nraewX-xaew), yip and yelp, surprised barking of a dog.

蟯　náo　MC ngew

1. intestinal parasites, helminths.

ráo   MC nyew
1. wriggle, slither.

詉   náo   MC nraew
1. (med.) ⊙ 呶 *náo.*

譊   náo   MC nraew
1. quarrelsome, captious, contentious.
    a. rdup., cross and querulous, blustery, bellicose, disputatious.

鐃   náo   MC nraew
1. shank-mounted bell, upward-facing and mallet-struck, similar to the longer-handled 鉦 *zhēng* 1, and, like it, used to signal a halt or retreat to army troops.
2. ⊙ 撓 *náo* 1, annoy, disturb, vex, frustrate.

nǎo

惱   nǎo   MC nawX
1. be averse to, hostile; detest; angered.
2. worried, anxious, troubled.
    a. (med.) tormented, esp. by love.
3. (med.) provoke, aggravate; chide.
    a. (med.) tease, tantalize.

瑙   nǎo   MC nawX
1. (med.) (bn.) 瑪～ *mǎ'nǎo,* → 瑪 *mǎ.*

腦   nǎo   MC nawX
1. the brain.
    a. (med.) one's head, noggin; also, top part.

nào

淖   nào   MC nraewH
1. mire, muck, slop; sludge; slush.
    a. bespatter, smear, muddy.
   zhào   MC draewH
1. be in accord; temperate, gentle.
   chuò   MC tsyhak
1. (bn.) ～約 *chuòyuē* (MC tsyhak-ʼjak), meek and mild; also, soft and tender.

臑   nào   MC nawH
1. arms of biped, forefeet of quadruped.
   ér   MC nyi
1. ⊙ 胹 *ér,* boil, heat up; tenderize.

nuǎn   MC nwanX
1. (med.) warm, hot.

鬧   nào   MC nraewH
1. noisy, tumult(uous), commotion; boisterous, riotous, bedlam.
    a. roister(ing), excitement, bother, fuss.

nè

訥   nè   MC nwot
1. stutter, stammer; speak haltingly.
2. reticent, tight-lipped, reserved.

něi

餒   něi   MC nwojX
1. famished; ravenous.
2. putrid, of fish.

餧   něi   MC nwojX   ⊙ 餒 *něi.*

nèi

內   nèi   MC nwojH
1. inside, within specified area or topic; interior, inner(most), internal; e.g. 方～ *fāngnèi,* within the confines (of normal life or society), inframundane; (Dao.) ～視 *nèishì,* inward vision, the ability to see clearly and affect the interior of one's body with its viscera and various body-gods, a practice aided by different somatic and meditation techniques.
    a. ref. home or family, in contrast to outer (*wai* 外) larger world; the court, in contrast to the common people and lives outside; one's own thoughts, feelings, and intent, in contrast to one's public actions; e.g. (med.) ～家 *nèijiā,* "inner household," i.e. the court; also ref. palace women.
2. esoteric, comprehensible or suited to the initiated; e.g. ～傳 *nèizhuàn,* esoteric account or biography, providing information not typically reported; ～編 *nèibiān,* "inner chapters," the central or essential sections, or those dealing with topics of relatively more privileged matter; (Budd.) ～典 *nèidiǎn,* "inner canons," Budd. writings, in contrast to secular texts.
    a. intimate, private; intimacy.

3. ref. the persons who normally stay "inside," i.e. wife, concubine, palace woman; e.g. (med.) ～子 *nèizǐ*, wife (also self-referential); (med.) ～人 *nèirén*, palace lady, incl. entertainers.

nà　MC nop

1. ⊙ 納 *nà* (later graph for VB uses of ～), enter, pass into; give entrance to, bring in; accept, take in, admit; include, keep within; install (as); send in, hand in, present, turn over to.

nèn

嫩　**nèn　MC nwonH**

1. (med.) tender, delicate; frail, feeble, not fully developed.

néng

能　**néng　MC nong**

1. capacity, (cap)ability; faculty, prowess; resourceful(ness), potential(ity).
   a. able, talented, capable; competent; e.g. 無 ～ *wúnéng*, good-for-nothing.
   b. (Budd.) ～仁 *néngrén*, "[He who was] Empowered to be Good," trns. of folk etymology for Śākyamuni (*śak*, able to, empowered to be [instead of Śākya, the name of Gautama's clan]; *muni*, goodman, sage); also used as trns. solely of Skt. *muni*, sage.
2. capable of, able to.
   a. practiced in, expert at, knows well how to, proficient in, well-versed in.
3. harmony; amity.
   a. (med.) care for, tend to.
4. reach to, arrive at, get to.
5. (med.) (ADV) only, as long as, still, yet.
   a. (med.) despite, even if.
   b. (med.) nevertheless, but.
6. (med.) (ADV) in this way, like this.

nài　MC nojH

1. ⊙ 耐 *nài*, endure, bear; put up with; 乃 *nǎi* 1, then, only then, thereupon.

ní

倪　**ní　MC ngej**

1. infant; toddler.
   a. child, tyke.
2. terminus; starting-point or end-point.
   a. edge, border, limit.
   b. demarcate, differentiate, define.

nì　MC ngejH

1. ⊙ 睨 *nì*, look at askance; (bn.) 俾～ *pìnì*, → 俾 *pì* (*bǐ*).

妮　**ní　MC nrij**

1. (med.) ～子 *nízi*, affectionate term for a young girl: missy, lass.

尼　**ní　MC nrij**

1. (Budd.) 比丘～ *bǐqiūní* (MC bjijH-khjuw-nrij), trsc. Skt. *bhikṣuṇī*, ordained female monastic, nun; or sgl. as abb. of preceding.
2. ～父 *nífù*, Father Ni, i.e. Confucius, from his byname Zhongni 仲～.

nì　MC nrit

1. obstruct, stop.
2. ⊙ 昵 *nì*, close to, near.

怩　**ní　MC nrij**

1. (bn.) 忸～ *niǔní*, → 忸 *niǔ*.

泥　**ní　MC nej**

1. mud(dy).
   a. clay(ey); paste.
2. (med.) dough(y).

nì　MC nejH

1. lute, packed mud used as sealing agent for elixir-preparing crucible.
   a. to lute, seal up.
2. stuck, obstructed; delay(ed), mired in.
   a. be a stickler for; unchangeable.
   b. (med.) completely entangle(d) in, tie(d) up; infatuated with, wallow in.
3. (med.) search out, look for, seek.
4. (med.) wear away gradually.

nǐ　MC nejX

1. rdup., heavily bedewed, inspissate; soaking wet; also, glossily smooth, sleek and delicate.

niè　MC net

1. stain with black dye.
2. (Budd.) ～洹 *nièhuán* (MC net-hwan), trsc. Skt. *nirvāṇa*.

猊　**ní　MC ngej**

1. 狻～ *suānní*, → 狻 *suān*.

蜺　**ní　MC ngej**

1. ⊙ 霓 *ní*, rainbow, esp. inner rainbow of double.
2. winter cicada.

跒 ní   MC nrij
1. (bn.) 蹊～ *kuíní*, → 蹊 *kuí*.

輗 ní   MC ngej
1. curved collar-bar of large carriage (cf. 軏 *yuè*, for small carriage), bar-lock, attached at end of the thills for yoking horses or oxen.

霓 ní   MC ngej
1. rainbow, iris, esp. secondary or interior bow (with reversed colors) of a double-rainbow; traditionally considered "feminine" rainbow in contrast to the "male" 虹 *hóng*.
   a. iridian, iridescent.

鯢 ní   MC ngej
1. giant salamander (*Andrias davidianus*); syn. 鰡 *tǎ*.
2. female whale, cow.
3. small fish, minnow.
4. ～齒 *níchǐ*, elders with "baby teeth," i.e. those of extreme age who reputedly acquire regrown teeth to replace those they have lost.

麑 ní   MC ngej
1. a fawn.
2. 狻～ *suānní*, → 狻 *suān*.

齯 ní   MC ngej
1. teeth grown in one's 10th decade.
   a. nonagenarian; an old man "new in the tooth."

nǐ

儗 nǐ   MC ngiX
1. ⊙ 擬 *nǐ* 3, model(ed) on, imitate, mimic, copy; (lit.) compose in the manner of, "after X"; compare, liken to.

擬 nǐ   MC ngiX
1. estimate, assess, consider; e.g. ～足 *nǐzú*, measure one's steps, i.e. plan carefully.
   a. propose, plan; aim at, intend to, be intent on.
   b. prepare, get ready.
2. decide, determine; settle, dispose of.
   a. sentence, pronounce judgment.
3. model(ed) on, imitate, mimic, copy; (lit.) compose in the manner of, "after X."
   a. compare, liken to; analogy, analogous.

4. gesticulate, gesture, make the motion of.
   a. (med.) lift up, pull up.

旎 nǐ   MC nrjeX
1. (bn.) 旖～ *yǐnǐ*, → 旖 *yǐ*.

柅 nǐ   MC nrjeX
1. sweetheart tree (*Euscaphis japonica*), medium-sized tree with glossy pinnate leaves, gray bark with white striations, producing heart-shaped pear-like fruit that ripens from green to red.
2. chock, wedge, wooden block placed by wheels to keep a carriage from moving.
   a. obstruct, impede.
3. (bn.) 椅～ *yǐnǐ* (MC 'jeX-nrjeX), swinging and swaying, lithe and lissome, ⊙ 猗狔 *yǐnǐ*.

狔 nǐ   MC nrjeX
1. (bn.) 猗～ *yǐnǐ*, → 猗 *yī* (*yǐ* 1).

禰 nǐ   MC nejX
1. term used for deceased father after his memorial tablet is placed in ancestral temple.
   a. temple of deceased father.
2. spirit-tablet of father carried by son on military expedition.
   mǐ   MC nejX
1. a surname.

苨 nǐ   MC nejX
1. (bn.) 薺～ *jìnǐ*, → 薺 *jì*.

薿 nǐ   MC ngiX
1. rdup., lush and luxuriant, thickly teeming.

nì

匿 nì   MC nrik
1. conceal, hide; seclude.
   a. keep back, under wraps; e.g. 無～ *wúnì*, unreserved, ingenuous.
   b. secretly, clandestine(ly).
      tè   MC thok
1. ⊙ 慝 *tè*, vice, vicious(ness), turpitude; malevolence, malice.

埌 nì   MC ngejH
1. (bn.) 埤～ *pìnì*, → 埤 *pì* (*pí*).

嶷 nì   MC ngik
1. unscalable, sheer.

yí　MC ngi

1. 九～ *jiǔyí*, "Nine Doubts," name of mountain range where sage-king Shun 舜 was reputed to be buried, in present-day southeastern Hunan.

恧　nì　MC nek

1. sadly longing.
2. pained by thought.

昵　nì　MC nrit

1. near to, close; intimate acquaintance; ⊙ 暱 *nì*.

暱　nì　MC nrit

1. near to, close.
   a. intimate acquaintance, close friend.

溺　nì　MC nek

1. sink, drown.
   a. flood, inundate.
2. mired in, wallow in; taken with, infatuated.
   niào　MC newH
1. urine; urinate; ⊙ 尿 *niào*.

睨　nì　MC ngejH

1. look at from the side, glance at, sneak a look at.
   a. (bn.) 睥～ *pìnì*, → 睥 *pì*.
   b. skewed, deflected, off to the side.
2. view, take in, gaze upon.
3. (med.) frown.

膩　nì　MC nrijH

1. oily, greasy; viscous.
   a. fatty, rich.
2. smooth, slick; lustrous, glossy; e.g. ～細 *nìxì* (MC nrijH-sejH), lustrous and lovely.
3. (med.) besmeared, impure, foul(ed), taint(ed).

逆　nì　MC ngjaek

1. welcome, receive; e.g. ～旅 *nílǚ*, "receiver of travelers," an inn (privately owned).
   a. meet straight on, confront, stand opposite.
2. go against, counterpose, contravert; contrary; go backward; against the current, go upstream (ant. 迪 *dí* 1, follow a path forward).
   a. rebel against; refractory.
   b. backwards; inverted; upside-down.
   c. retrograde planetary movement, i.e. westward (cf. 順 *shùn*, direct or eastward movement).
3. anticipate, presume, conjecture.
   a. in advance, beforehand; e.g. ～知 *nìzhī*, foresee.

4. (med.) sedition, one of 10 judicial "abominations" 惡 *è*.

niān

薍　niān　MC ʼjon

1. (med.) withered, wilted, faded, dried out, lifeless.

nián

年　nián　MC nen

1. the time required for a year's harvest to come to fruition (cf. 歲 *suì*, the time it takes Jupiter to move from one sidereal station to the next; a twelvemonth; and 載 *zǎi* [*zài*], legal year, comprising period from any given month to its recurrence, incl. any intercalary month).
   a. gen. term for a year.
2. the years of one's life; one's age.
   a. (Budd.) ～臘 *niánlà*, one's age in religion, years since taking monastic vows; also, metonymy for fellow devotee.

拈　nián　MC nem

1. pick up with the fingertips; pinch; squeeze; tweak.

鮎　nián　MC nem

1. sheatfish, clade (*Siluridae*), a freshwater catfish, syn. 鮀 *tuó* 2.

黏　nián　MC nrjem

1. to paste, stick together.
   a. sticky, tacky, gluey, glutinous, adhesive.
2. 青～ *qīngnián*, sealwort, fragrant solomon's seal (*Polygonatum odoratum*), syn. 萎蕤 *wěiruí*.

niǎn

撚　niǎn　MC nenX

1. take up or hold with the fingers.
2. to twist, pinch; roll in or with the fingers.
   a. (med.) a particular kind of finger-picking movement when playing the lute (*pipa* 琵琶).
3. stamp with the feet.

涊　niǎn　MC nenX

1. sweat; ooze.
2. (bn.) 淟～ *tiǎnniǎn*, → 淟 *tiǎn*.
3. (med.) rdup., roil and moil, mix and muddle.

碾 niǎn   MC nrjenX
1. (med.) ⊙ 輾 niǎn (→ 輾 zhǎn).

輂 niǎn   MC ljenX
1. palanquin, sedan-chair, lifted on lateral poles and hand-carried.
    a. carry, or be carried on, a palanquin.
2. from Han times on, ref. any conveyance of the emperor, incl. horseless carriage pushed or pulled by servants; e.g. ～轂 niǎngǔ, "the conveyance's wheel-hubs," euph. for the emperor; ～下 niǎnxià, "what is below the conveyance," i.e. the capital, the court.
    a. ride in a carriage.
    b. push or pull the imperial carriage.
3. load or convey in a wagon.

輾 niǎn   MC nrjenX   → 輾 zhǎn.

niàn

廿 niàn   MC nyip
1. combined form of 二十 èrshí, twenty.

念 niàn   MC nemH
1. hold in mind, bear in mind, be mindful of; (Budd.) mindfulness, trns. Skt. smṛti.
    a. (med.) have in prospect, expect, earnestly hope.
2. recall, recollect(ions), remember, memories, call to mind, usu. with conscious intent.
    a. mental retention; (Dao.) imprint in mind, fix in mind, visualize.
3. think of, consider, ponder, reflect on, muse on.
4. recite aloud, usu. from memory.
5. (med.) like, love, be fond of; think of fondly, sympathize, empathize with.

莶 niàn   MC nemH
1. (med.) braided bamboo tow-rope, for boats.

niáng

娘 niáng   MC nrjang
1. (med.) sing. or ～子 niángzi, gen. term for woman, esp. maid, young woman, therne; also, wife.
    a. (med.) sing. or rdup., mother.

孃 niáng   MC nrjang   ⊙ 娘 niáng.

niàng

釀 niàng   MC nrjangH
1. to brew, ferment (grain-based alcoholic beverages).
    a. (med.) brew, common term for wine.
2. brew up, foment; incite, stimulate.

niǎo

嫋 niǎo   MC newX   ⊙ 褭 niǎo.

嬝 niǎo   MC newX   ⊙ 褭 niǎo.

嫐 niǎo   MC newX
1. (med.) tease, chaff, poke fun at, banter with; tempt, beguile.
    a. (med.) provoke, pique; annoy, pester, harass.

蔦 niǎo   MC tewX
1. parasitic mistletoe (Loranthus parasiticus), esp. on the mulberry.

裊 niǎo   MC newX
1. (bn.) 姌 ～ rǎnniǎo, → 姌 rǎn.
2. rdup., slender and delicate, lithe and graceful (of vegetation or lovely woman).
    a. (med.) rdup. or (bn.) ～娜 niǎonuǒ (MC newX-naX), drifting and dangling, tenderly trailing, wispy and wafting (of smoke, mist, light clothing); curled and thready, twisting and twining (also of rising smoke); adrift on the breeze, freely floating (of clouds); lingering hauntingly (of drawn-out music or gibbon's cry); thinly threading (all preceding).

褭 niǎo   MC njewX   ⊙ 裊 niǎo.

鳥 niǎo   MC tewX
1. gen. term for birds.
    a. also ref. winged insects.

niào

尿 niào   MC newH
1. (med.) urine; urinate; ⊙ 溺 niào (nì).

niē

捏　niē　MC net

1. (med.) mold from clay or other pliant substance.
   a. (med.) fabrication, sham, fake.
   b. (med.) improper, irregular; e.g. ～怪 *niēguài*, bizarre, unbefitting.
2. (med.) massage, knead; rub, stroke.
3. (med.) ～舌 *niēshé*, loquacious, long-winded, jabber(ing).

捻　niē　MC nep

1. (med.) tweak, nip, pinch.
   a. (med.) roll between the fingers; twist, braid.
   b. (med.) technique of zither (*qín* 琴) playing in which first finger and thumb pull and release string so it strikes resonating table.
2. (med.) press down, knead.
3. close off, block; choke.

nié

茶　nié　MC net

1. ～然 *niérán*, wearied, worn out, exhausted, enervated, listless.

niè

嚙　niè　MC nget　◉ 齧 *niè*.

囁　niè　MC nyep

1. whisper.
2. (bn.) ～嚅 *nièrú* (MC nyep-nyu), speak in hushed tones, sotto voce, breathe a whisper; also, (med.) choke back one's words, stifle oneself from speaking.

孼　niè　MC ngjet　◉ 孽 *niè*.

孽　niè　MC ngjet

1. visitation, curse, plague, affliction, scourge; desecration, profanation.
   a. harm, (en)danger, injure.
2. recalcitrant, perverse; disobedient.
3. son of a concubine.

嶩　niè　MC nget

1. (bn.) 嶫～ *diéniè*, → 嶫 *dié*.

槷　niè　MC nget

1. ◉ 臬 *niè* 1, target, butt; 2, measure(ment), standard; wooden gnomon; 3, (de)limit, bound(ary); 闑 *niè*, door-stake.
2. ～卼 *nièyuè* (MC nget-ngjwot), perilously poised, looming dangerously.

櫱　niè　MC ngat

1. (bn.) 巀～ *jiénniè*, → 巀 *jié*.
2. ◉ 蘗 *niè* 1, sucker, shoot; transplant seedlings; 2, ～木 *nièmù*, Amur corktree.

涅　niè　MC net

1. alum (syn. 礬石 *fánshí*), used in dyeing and tanning.
   a. dye black, blacken; stain.
2. black mud; sludge; sediment.
3. block up, stuff up.
4. (Budd.) ～槃 *nièpán* (MC net-ban), trsc. Skt. *nirvāṇa*

糵　niè　MC ngjet　◉ 蘗 *niè*.

蘗　niè　MC ngjet

1. malt, sprouted grain used in fermenting and brewing 醴 *lǐ*, ale, sweet wine (cf. *qū* 麴, preparation of ferments used in making *jiǔ* 酒, wine).
   a. barm, yeast formed on malt liquors when fermenting.
2. long shoots of growing wheat or beans.

聶　niè　MC nrjep

1. whisper.
2. a surname.
shè　MC syep
1. ◉ 攝 *shè* 2, catch hold of, hold onto; grasp, keep.

臬　niè　MC nget

1. target (for arrows), butt.
2. measurement, standard (moral or physical).
   a. (med.) gnomon, shadow-marker of sundial.
3. reach the end of, delimit; bound(ary).

鮧　niè　MC nget

1. (bn.) ～卼 *nièwù* (MC nget-ngwot), ◉ 杌陧 *wùniè*, shaky and unsteady, teetering on the edge.

蘖 niè   MC ngjet
1. sucker, shoot, new growth from a tree that has fallen or been cut down.
    a. transplant seedlings or cuttings.
2. ～木 *nièmù*, Amur corktree (*Phellodendron amurense*), deciduous tree with thick corky bark and inner layer of bright-yellow bark that is used in dyeing.
3. ～米 *nièmǐ*, rice-malt.

蠥 niè   MC ngjet
1. overwhelming grief, consumed with sorrow.
2. (med.) ⊙ 孽 *niè* 1, affliction, scourge, visitation, calamity.

躡 niè   MC nrjep
1. tread on, step on, usu. with conscious plan and purpose.
    a. place oneself at; e.g. ～足 *nièzú*, "place your feet," take one's stand.
    b. (bn.) ～蹀 *nièdié* (MC nrjep-deap), ⊙ 蹀躞 *diéxiè*, → 蹀 *dié*.
2. march, proceed, go forward on prescribed route; e.g. (Dao.) ～紀 *nièjì*, "marching the strands," another name for esoteric visualization of "pacing the void" (*buxu* 步虛, → 步 *bù*), esp. when undertaken in summer.
    a. follow, walk in the tracks of; ～景 *nièyǐng*, chase the [sun's] shadow, go in haste.
3. mount up, climb.
4. put on or pull on footwear.
5. treadle, of loom.

鑷 niè   MC nep
1. small decorative hairpin.

鑷 niè   MC nrjep
1. (med.) tweezers.
    a. (med.) to pluck; yank out, pull out; esp. depilate.
2. (med.) dangling part of ornamental hairpin.
3. (med.) mails on leashes of a drawloom, with warp-threads passing through each of them, permitting a design of 120 "moves"; may also ref. the treadle that raises and lowers warp-threads.

闑 niè   MC ngjet
1. door-prop, short post in middle of gate against which the 2 leaves come to rest.

陧 niè   MC nget
1. (bn.) 杌～ *wùniè*, → 杌 *wù*.

齧 niè   MC nget
1. gnaw, champ on, munch.
    a. eat away, erode.
2. breach, gap.

níng

凝 níng   MC nging
1. congeal, freeze; e.g. ～花 *nínghuā*, "frozen flowers," i.e. snowflakes.
2. condense, coagulate, clotted; dense; thickened, inspissate.
    a. (af)fix(ed), stuck; e.g. ～滯 *níngzhì*, stuck in place, unmoving; also, trapped, bogged down.
    b. (med.) of colors, deeply saturated, pure and unmixed; e.g. ～碧 *níngbì*, pure deep cyan-blue.
3. concentrate(d), focus(ed), transfix(ed); e.g. ～睇 *níngdì*, intent gaze; ～心 *níngxīn*, concentrate one's mind, focus one's attention.

寧 níng   MC neng
1. peaceful, tranquil, irenic; pacify, calm.
    a. content, complacent.
2. call upon, pay a visit, esp. one's birth-family; e.g. 歸～ *guīníng*, new wife paying a visit to her parents; ～省 *níngxǐng*, call on one's elder kin.
3. be in mourning for one's parents.
        nìng   MC nengH
1. indicates the preferred option in a construction where two choices are given: (would) rather, better (to do X), preferable; e.g. 禮與其奢也～儉 *lǐ yǔqí shē yě nìng jiǎn*, In ritual ceremonies, rather than being extravagant, better to be frugal; 與其棄身，不～棄酒乎 *yǔqí qì shēn bùnìng qì jiǔ hū*, instead of forgoing oneself, would it not be preferable to forgo the liquor? 與其殺不辜，～失不經 *yǔqí shā bùgū nìng shī bùjīng*, rather than executing someone who had committed no crime, better to let someone who did not adhere to the rules get away. Also → 與其 *yǔqí* at 其 *qí* 1d.
2. rhetorical interr.: how could it be that . . .? how is it that . . .? > surely not . . .
3. (med.) ～馨 *nìngxīn*, ～許 *nìngxǔ*, like this, like so, in this way.

獰 níng   MC nraeng
1. (med.) brutal, violent; ferocious, beastly; uncivilized, uncouth.
    a. (med.) (bn.) 儜～ *cāngníng*, → 儜 *cāng*.

甯　níng　MC neng
1. desire, wish, hope for.

　　níng　MC nengH
1. ⊙ 寧 *nìng* 1 (→ *níng*), preferred option in a construction where two choices are given: (would) rather, better (to do X), preferable.
2. a surname.

薴　níng　MC nreang
1. tangled, clumped; muddled, scrambled; in disarray.

鬡　níng　MC nreang
1. (med.) (bn.) 鬡〜 *zhēngníng*, → 鬡 *zhēng*.

鷑　níng　MC neng
1. (bn.) 〜鴂 *níngjué* (MC neng-kwet), wren (*Troglodytes troglodytes*), syn. 鷦鷯 *jiāoliáo*.

nìng

佞　nìng　MC nengH
1. verbally facile, eloquent; glib, fluent.
　　a. clever, cunning, shrewd.
2. casuist(ry), sophist(ry), guile(ful); gloze; specious.
　　a. sycophant(ish), flatter(y), toady.

濘　nìng　MC nengH
1. slush, muck, mire.

　　níng　MC neng
1. (med.) (bn.) 〜溺 *níngnì* (MC neng-nek), muddied and (sub)merged; (bn.) 瀿〜 *dǐngníng*, → 瀿 *dǐng*; (bn.) 汀〜 *dìngníng*, → 汀 *dìng* (*tīng*).

　　nì　MC nejH
1. sink into mire, bog down.

niú

牛　niú　MC ngjuw
1. ox, beeve; bovine; water-buffalo.
　　a. emblematic animal of the 2nd of the 12 earthly stems, 丑 *chǒu*.
2. Ox, one of the 28 lunar lodgings, comprised of α2, β, ξ, ο, π, ρ Capricorni, in the northern quadrant (*xuanwu* 玄武) of the sky.
3. 牽〜 *qiānniú*, Ox-puller, Ox-leader, He who Leads an Ox by a Rope, the star Altair (α Aquilae), often called "Herd Boy," but he has no herd.

4. 天〜 *tiānniú*, longhorn beetle, longicorn (*Cerambycidae*), characterized by extremely long antennae.

niǔ

忸　niǔ　MC nrjuwk
1. (bn.) 〜怩 *niǔní* (MC nrjuwk-nrij), ashamed and abashed.
2. be accustomed, habituated to; practice regularly.

杻　niǔ　MC nrjuwX
1. various species of ilex or holly, esp. *Ilex pedunculosa*.

狃　niǔ　MC nrjuwX
1. be so habituated to that one does not need to pay attention, routine, routinized; habit, regular practice.
　　a. accustomed to, familiar with.
2. covet(ous), envy, have a passion or lust for.
3. assume the role of, accept responsibility for.

紐　niǔ　MC nrjuwX
1. knot, knot up (a knot that can be untied; cf. 結 *jié*).
　　a. fasten(ing), connect(ion), link.
　　b. nexus; connecting or central point; pivot.
2. blood-vessels, veins.
3. the initial consonant of a phoneme.

鈕　niǔ　MC nrjuwX
1. the "nose" or boss of a seal, knob-like protrusion on top of the seal to which may be attached a cord or ribbon for hanging it from one's belt.
2. loop-shaped suspension device on certain bell-chimes.

nóng

儂　nóng　MC nowng
1. (med.) 1st-person pronoun, used in Jiangnan area.
2. (med.) sgl. or cmpd. 渠〜 *qúnóng*, 3rd-person pronoun, in Jiangnan.

濃   **nóng**   **MC nrjowng**
1. inspissate dew, heavy dew.
   a. heavy; deep; thick(en); condense(d); intense.
   b. viscid, viscous.

穠   **nóng**   **MC nrjowng**
1. (med.) dense, thick growth of plants; close-packed, clustered, massed.
2. (med.) of women, statuesque; well-endowed, well-proportioned; voluptuous, gorgeous.

膿   **nóng**   **MC nowng**
1. pus; suppurate, suppuration.
2. (med.) bloated, overweight, fat.
3. (med.) 醲 *nóng*, heavy-flavored wine, rich in taste.

襛   **nóng**   **MC nrjowng**
1. thick fabric, layered clothing.
2. ⊙ 穠 *nóng*, thick, dense growth; clump(ed), massed.

農   **nóng**   **MC nowng**
1. agriculture; to farm; to till and sow.
   a. farmer; peasant.
2. abb. of 神～ *shénnóng*, Divine Tiller, mythic inventor and first teacher of the practice of agriculture.
3. work steadily at, industrious(ly); focus one's efforts on.

醲   **nóng**   **MC nrjowng**
1. heavy-flavored wine, rich in taste.
2. thick, dense, heavy (as of clouds, mist, etc.)
   a. consider weighty, emphasize.

nòng

弄   **nòng**   **MC luwngH**
1. manipulate with the hand; e.g. ～琴 *nòngqín*, play the zither; ～翰 *nònghàn*, manipulate the writing-brush.
   a. handle, treat with.
   b. bring about, manipulate, cause to happen; conjure up; e.g. ～□ *nòngkǒu*, stir things up by what one says.
2. toy with, play with, enjoy(ment), fancy; amuse oneself with, occupy oneself with; ～月 *nòngyuè*, enjoy the moonlight.
   a. try out, test.
3. (med.) a tune, ditty.

lòng
1. alley, alleyway.

nóu

뾟   **nóu**   **MC nuw**
1. leveret, a baby hare.

nòu

檽   **nòu**   **MC nuwH**
1. wood-ear (*Auricularia auricula*), edible fungus that grows on wood; syn. 木耳 *mùěr, mùjùn* 木菌.

耨   **nòu**   **MC nuwH**
1. a hoe.
   a. to hoe, weed; delve into.

鎒   **nòu**   **MC nuwH**   ⊙ 耨 *nòu*.

nú

奴   **nú**   **MC nu**
1. slave.
   a. enslave, treat as a slave; derogatory designation of others.
2. servant, menial.
   a. famulus, esp. serving a scholar or magician.
3. (med.) 1st-person humble pronoun, used by children.

孥   **nú**   **MC nu**
1. child(ren), tyke(s).
   a. wife and child(ren).
   b. (med.) 1st-person humble pronoun, used by children; ⊙ 奴 *nú* 3.

帑   **nú**   **MC nu**   → 帑 *tǎng*.

筶   **nú**   **MC nu**
1. birdcage.

駑   **nú**   **MC nu**
1. an inferior horse, esp. one no longer useful, with spent abilities; an "old warhorse."
   a. any worn-out or useless animal.
   b. person of inferior talent; a mediocrity, dullard.

nǔ

努　nǔ　MC nuX
1. exert one's strength, put forth effort, strive; industrious, moliminous.
2. stick out, protrude; protuberant.

弩　nǔ　MC nuX
1. crossbow, arbalest.
　a. 水〜 *shuǐnǔ*, "water-crossbow," syn. → 蜮 *yù*, sand-spitter.

砮　nǔ　MC nuX
1. flint.
　a. metonymy for arrowhead.

nù

怒　nù　MC nuX
1. angry, infuriated, furious; wrath(ful), wroth; stirred up, (im)passion(ed); exasperated.
　a. impel, force; goad.
2. tense, intense.
　a. vigorous, invigorate(d).
3. conflict, ant. 和 *hé*.

nǔ

女　nǔ　MC nrjoX
1. woman; female gender, feminine.
　a. maiden, unmarried woman; girl.
　b. (Dao.) 〜冠 *nǔguān*, "capeline," Daoist priestess.
2. daughter.
3. possessed of feminine qualities; soft, frail, vulnerable.
4. "Maiden," one of the 28 lunar lodgings, composed of ε, μ, 3, 4 Aquarii, in the northern quadrant (*xuanwu* 玄武) of the sky.
5. 〜青 *nǔqīng*, cinquefoil, potentilla (*Potentilla kleiniana*), yellow-flowering, used medicinally; syn. 蛇含 *shéhán*.
　　nù　MC nrjoH
1. give a daughter in marriage.
　　rǔ　MC nyoX
1. ⊙ 汝 *rǔ*, 2nd-person pronoun: you, your(s).

籹　nǔ　MC nrjoX
1. (bn.) 粔〜 *jùnǔ*, → 粔 *jù*.

nù

恧　nù　MC nrjuwk
1. ashamed; humbled.
2. disconcerted, out of countenance.

朒　nù　MC nrjuwk
1. appearance of the sliver of moon in the east on the first day of the month.
2. deficient, lacking.

衄　nù　MC nrjuwk
1. nose-bleed, epistaxis.
2. frustrate, foil; defeat.
　a. shrink back, recoil; cower.
　b. be humiliated, humbled; disgraced; routed.

nuǎn

暖　nuǎn　MC nwanX
1. pleasantly warm, sweetly warm, temperate.
　a. lew, lukewarm.
　b. warm up; e.g. 〜酒 *nuǎnjiǔ*, warm the wine.
2. drag, lag; lax.
　　xuān　MC xjwon
1. 〜姝 *xuānshū*, self-satisfied, complacently content.

㬉　nuǎn　MC nwanX　⊙ 暖 *nuǎn*.

煖　nuǎn　MC nwanX　⊙ 暖 *nuǎn*.

煗　nuǎn　MC nwanX　⊙ 暖 *nuǎn*.

nüè

瘧　nüè　MC ngjak
1. malaria, paludism.

虐　nüè　MC ngjak
1. cruel, ruthless, brutal; ferocious, ferity; oppressive; violent.
　a. oppress; beset, harry.
2. affliction, ruination; catastrophe; misfortune.
3. excessive, exaggerate(d).

nún

麜　nún　MC nwon
1. (med.) fragrant, sweet-smelling, aromatic.

nùn

嫩   **nùn**   MC nwonH   → 嫩 *nèn*.

nuó

儺   **nuó**   MC na

1. well-regulated conduct, self-disciplined, self-possessed.
2. name of the great exorcistic ritual performed on eve of the 臘 *là* (12th-month New Year festival) to expel demons, pestilences, noxious influences lingering on from the ending year.
    a. exorcise.

捼   **nuó**   MC nwa

1. rub the hands together, roll between the hands.

那   **nuó**   MC na

1. numerous, plenty; considerable, ample.
    a. satisfactory, pleasing.
2. phonetic contraction of 奈何 *nàihé* (MC najH-ha), "what recourse is there?" or 奈 X 何 "what is to be done about X?"

    nǎ   MC naX

1. interr.: how? what?

    nà   MC naH

1. (med.) demonstrative pronoun or adjective ref. to something away from speaker: that (one), those; used beginning in Tang period.
2. transcription of Skt. *na*, *nā*; e.g. ～由他 *nàyóutā* (MC naH-yuw-tha), trsc. Skt. *nayuta*, an unimaginably high number; ～伽 *nàqié* (MC naH-gja), trsc. Skt. *nāga*, serpent, dragon; (Budd.) ～難陀 *nà'nántuó* (MC naH-nan-da), trsc. Skt. Nāḷandā, name of famous Budd. university and center of learning established mid-5th century near Patna.

nuǒ

妸   **nuǒ**   MC nwaX

1. (med.) (bn.) 婐～ *wǒnuǒ*, → 婐 *wǒ*.

娜   **nuǒ**   MC naX

1. (bn.) ～妸 *nuǒ'ē* (MC naX-'a) or 妸～ *ē'nuǒ*, soft and delicate, attractive and lovely; (med.) also, drifting and dangling, quivering tremulously; (bn.) 嫋～ *niǎonuǒ* (MC newX-naX), same as preceding.

nuò

懦   **nuò**   MC nwaH

1. faint-hearted; cowardly, pusillanimous; timorous.
    a. ineffectual, impotent; effete.
    b. weak, powerless.

搦   **nuò**   MC nraewk

1. press down, lean on.
2. rub; scrape.
3. grasp, seize; take; hold.

諾   **nuò**   MC nak

1. assent (to), concur; approve; accept; usu. directed toward inferior (cf. 唯 *wéi*, usu. toward superior).
    a. voiced assent: agreed! yes!
    b. at end of contract or written agreement: pledged! promised!
2. (Dao.) ～皋 *nuògāo*, name of Dao. god of the moon.

O

ōu

嘔   **ōu**   MC 'uw

1. ⊙ 謳 *ōu* 1, sing.
2. (bn.) ～啞 *ōuyǎ* (MC 'uw-'aeX), onom. of various sounds, incl. prate and prattle of children, gibber-jabber of incoherent mumblers, chit-ter-chatter of birds, rumbling trundle of carts, "eeoo-yaa" of wind or string instruments; (bn.) ～軋 *ōuyà* (MC 'uw-'eat), onom. of grinding, creaking, clattering, rattling sounds.

    ǒu   MC 'uwX

1. ⊙ 歐 *ǒu* (*ōu*), gag, retch.

xū　MC xju

1. rdup., sweet and soothing, dulcet and pleasing, easily agreeable.

歐　ōu　MC 'uw

1. ⊙ 謳 ōu, sing; 毆 ōu, strike with a stick, beat.
2. ～陽 ōuyáng, a bisyllabic surname.

ǒu　MC 'uwX

1. gag; vomit, retch; spit up, disgorge.

毆　ōu　MC 'uwX

1. beat with a stick or cudgel, bastinado.
   a. strike, deliver blows.

ǒu　MC 'uwX

1. ⊙ 歐 ǒu (ōu), gag, retch.

qū　MC khju

1. whip up, goad on, urge on, esp. a horse; old form of 驅 qū.

漚　ōu　MC 'uw

1. drought of extraordinary severity, unbearable drought.

甌　ōu　MC 'uw

1. shallow but wide cup or bowl, porringer.
2. (bn.) ～脫 ōutuō (MC 'uw-thwat), Xiongnu word for earthen habitations, perhaps similar to a yurt, housing frontier residents and guards.
   a. by metonymy, the frontier, esp. sparsely populated area.

謳　ōu　MC 'uw

1. sing without musical accompaniment, a capella.
   a. sing the praises of.
2. chant in unison.
3. folk songs, popular songs from particular locales.

鏂　ōu　MC 'uw

1. old measure of capacity equiv. 2 dou 斗 or "pecks."

鷗　ōu　MC 'uw

1. gull, tern, various species Laridae.

驅　ōu　MC 'uw　⊙ 鷗 ōu.

oú

齵　oú　MC nguw

1. sgl. or (bn.) 齵～ zōu'óu (MC tsrjuw-nguw), crooked teeth; mismatched, misaligned, uneven.

ǒu

偶　ǒu　MC nguwX

1. wooden or pottery figurine in the likeness of a person, statue(tte); facsimile, replica.
2. counterpart, match, mate, opposite number.
   a. partner; colleague of equal status, coequal, of the same generation or cohort.
   b. even number, i.e. paired; ant. 奇 qí, odd number, unpaired; e.g. 不～ bù'ǒu, not even, i.e. unlucky.
3. be in accord with, jibe with, match up with.
   a. meet up with a fitting time or opportunity, suit; be in the good graces of.
   b. appropriately, exactly, just right, quite.
   c. (med.) encounter unexpectedly, happen on.
4. perchance, inadvertent(ly), accidentally; for no reason; indeterminate, unmotivated.
   a. casual(ly); for the time being.
5. (med.) unpartnered, by oneself, alone.

耦　ǒu　MC nguwX

1. a 2-man plow.
   a. work as a team of 2, esp. when plowing.
   b. make a pair; be even.
2. ⊙ 偶 ǒu 2, counterpart, match, mate.

藕　ǒu　MC nguwX

1. edible rhizome or rootstock of the lotus (lian 蓮, Nelumbo nucifera).
   a. associated punningly in lit. with 耦 or 偶 ǒu, pair, mate, counterpart.

òu

漚　òu　MC 'uwH

1. saturate, soak, imbrue; ret (flax).
   a. let ferment, let brew or simmer until ready.

ōu　MC 'uw

1. bubbles on water, froth.
2. ⊙ 鷗 ōu, seagull.

P

pā

葩 **pā**　MC phae
1. corolla, outer envelope of flower; petals.
   a. flowery, ornate, bedecked.
2. (bn.) ～華 *pāhuá* (MC phae-hwae), spread and scatter, spread and sprawl; 紛～ *fēnpā*, → 紛 *fēn* 2a.

pá

杷 **pá**　MC bae
1. harrow, rake, scuffle.
   a. comb, rearrange; comb over.
2. scoop up with the hands.
3. (bn.) 枇～ *pípá*, → 枇 *pí*.
   bà　MC paeH
1. handle of implement; helve, shaft.

爬 **pá**　MC bae
1. scratch, scrape with one's fingernails, claw at, rake over.
   a. (med.) (bn.) ～沙 *páshā* (MC bae-srae), scrabble, crawl.
2. (med.) harrow, rake, scuffle; e.g. ～梳 *páshū*, comb through, rake over, put in order.

琶 **pá**　MC bae
1. (bn.) 琵～ *pípá*, → 琵 *pí*.

pà

帕 **pà**　MC phaeH
1. (med.) handkerchief; throat-band, kerchief.
2. (med.) shroud, for a corpse.
3. (med.) saddle blanket, horse-cloth.
   mò　MC maet
1. (med.) hair-wrap, turban.

怕 **pà**　MC phaeH
1. (med.) fear(ful), afraid of; dread.
   bó　MC bak
1. calm, content, at repose.

pāi

拍 **pāi**　MC phaek
1. strike lightly with the palm of the hand; clap, cuff; pat, paddle.
   a. strike forcefully, smack; beat, pound.
2. the beat or rhythm of music; keep time.
   a. clapper, with which one keeps time to music.
3. catapult, ballista, for use in war.

pái

俳 **pái**　MC beaj
1. entertain(ment), amuse(ment); jest.
2. ⊙ 俳 *pái* (～佪 *páihuái*).

徘 **pái**　MC bwoj
1. (bn.) ～佪 *páihuái* (MC bwoj-hwoj), go round and about, back and forth; shilly-shally, aimlessly irresolute, restless but hesitant, loiter and linger, dawdle and delay; also (med.), continuing ceaselessly, of sounds.

排 **pái**　MC beaj
1. push toward, thrust.
   a. push back, repel; resist, oppose; e.g. ～風 *páifēng*, against the wind.
   b. push open, force open; squeeze open.
   c. push aside, thrust aside, squeeze out.
   d. move out of the way; eliminate, exclude; dismiss.
2. put in order, regulate; lay out, dispose; e.g. ～當 *páidāng*, lay out a palace banquet.
   a. arrange, esp. in a line or row; line(d) up, one after another; e.g. (med.) (lit.) ～律 *páilǜ*, "regulated lines in a row," genre of verse in which the lines of all couplets except the first and last follow the syntactic and tonal expectations of "regulated verse" (*lǜshi* 律 詩); (med.) ～方 *páifāng*, closely spaced jade studs lined up as decoration on a belt.
   b. find the best course of action; mediate.

牌 **pái**　MC beaj
1. (med.) signboard, inscription plaque.
   a. (med.) identity tag.

箄　pái　MC bea

1. (med.) large bamboo raft.

bēi　MC pjie

1. (med.) fishing net made from bamboo.

pài

派　pài　MC pheaH

1. branch(ing) stream.
   a. faction, group, school.

湃　pài　MC pheajH

1. (bn.) 澎～, 滂～ *pēngpài*, → 澎 *pēng*.
2. rdup., crashing and battering of waves.

pān

扳　pān　MC phaen

1. ⊙ 攀 *pān*.

bān　MC paen

1. draw toward oneself, pull in.
2. (med.) turn over, twist around; reverse.

拚　pān　MC phan　→ 拚 *biàn*.

攀　pān　MC phaen

1. pull or drag oneself up; clamber; shinny; pull along hand-by-hand.
2. pull down with the hands, pluck down, snatch; e.g. ～花 *pānhuā*, pluck flowers from a tree.
3. catch hold of, clutch; cling to, fasten upon, hang onto, hold fast to; e.g. ～附 *pānfù*, attach oneself closely to (in hope of advancement); ～胸 *pānxiōng*, "breast-clinger," breast-strap of saddle; (Budd.) ～緣 *pānyuán*, caught up in karmic conditions.

潘　pān　MC phan

1. rice-water; water in which one has rinsed rice, sometimes then used for washing hair.
2. overflow of water, run over, gush out.
3. a surname.

pán　MC ban

1. whirlpool, eddy, vortex.

pán

媻　pán　MC ban

1. (bn.) ～姍, ～珊 *pánshān* (MC ban-san), sauntering slowly, lingering languidly, scuffling and shuffling.

pó　MC ba

1. (bn.) ～娑 *pósuō* (MC ba-sa), ⊙ 婆娑 *pósuō*, → 婆 *pó*.

柈　pán　MC ban

1. ⊙ 盤 *pán* 1, plate, tray; pan, basin.

槃　pán　MC ban

1. ⊙ 盤 *pán* 1, 2.
2. (bn.) ～礴 *pánbó* (MC ban-bak), sit with legs outspread.
3. (Budd.) 涅～ *nièpán* (MC net-ban), trsc. Skt. *nirvāṇa*.

盤　pán　MC ban

1. plate, tray for food, ⊙ 槃 *pán*.
   a. pan, basin for holding or pouring liquid; tub for washing.
   b. scale pan.
2. wind round, turn around, coil; wrap round or in, wound up; e.g. ～據 *pánjù*, tightly wound, firmly coiled, well-clasped, securely grounded; ～坐 *pánzuò*, sit cross-legged; ～結 *pánjié*, wound up and knotted, complicated, difficult to explain.
   a. (bn.) ～桓 *pánhuán* (MC ban-hwan), circling round and round, wavering and havering, hemming and hawing, moving from one side to the other; also, wandering and roaming.
   b. (bn.) ～薄 *pánbó* (MC ban-bak), diffused and distended, broad and boundless, expanding outward.
   c. be "wrapped up in," completely absorbed in, indulging oneself in.
3. (med.) move, transport.
4. ⊙ 磐 *pán* 1, stone slab, large flat stone or boulder; flagstone; immovable; broad-faced.

磐　pán　MC ban

1. stone slab; large flat stone or boulder, esp. one that can be sat on; flagstone.
   a. stable, immovable.
   b. broad-faced.
2. sgl. or bn. ～桓 *pánhuán* (MC ban-hwan), ～辟 *pánbì* (MC ban-bjiek), unable to advance, hesitant, havering; moving from one side to the other; reeling round and round.
3. (bn.) ～礴, ～薄 *pánbó* (MC ban-bak), diffuse and distended, broad and boundless; ⊙ 盤薄 *pánbó*, → 盤 *pán*.

蟠 pán MC ban

1. wind round, turn around, coil; wrap round, curl; ⊙ 盤 *pán* 2; e.g. ～龍 *pánlóng*, coiled dragon, which has not yet ascended to the sky; ～桃 *pántáo*, twisted peach-tree, bearing peaches of immortality that fruit once every 3,000 years
2. circle round, encompass; circuit.
3. spread all over, encroach on; pervade; fill up.

　　　　fán MC bjon

1. woodlouse

蹣 pán MC ban

1. (bn.) ～跚 *pánshān* (MC ban-san), ～連 *pánlián* (MC ban-ljen), ～辟 *pánbì* (MC ban-bjiek), sauntering slowly, lingering languidly, slowly shuffling; swaying and staggering, limping lamely, tottering unsteadily; moving from one side to the other; reeling round and round.

鞶 pán MC ban

1. broad leather belt or waistband.
　　a. pouch hung from waistband.
2. girth-strap, cinch of horse.

　　　　　　　pàn

判 pàn MC banX

1. divide in two, halve; separate.
2. discriminate, differentiate, distinguish between.
　　a. (med.) judge, pass judgment on; judgment.
　　b. (med.) "decision," an official document in prose addressing administrative or legal matters; also (lit.), a version of such a document written often as a requirement in the Tang "assessment" (*quanxuan* 銓選) exam held annually to promote lower-level office-holders or those without an appointment.
3. (med.) decidedly, definitely, certainly.
　　a. (med.) absolutely so, extremely.
4. (med.) ～自 *pànzì*, in the natural course of things, naturally, bound to be so, as always.
5. (med.) prefixed to an office or bureau title, indicating that an official with a regular appointment has been assigned temporarily to supervise the affairs of the designated office.
6. (bn.) ～換 *pànhuàn* (MC phanH-hwanH), relaxed, slack, at loose ends.
7. (med.) give up, abandon; e.g. ～命 *pànmìng*, ～死 *pànsǐ*, risk one's life.

叛 pàn MC banH

1. betray, rebel against; fractious.
　　a. desert, abandon.
　　b. throw into disarray, disorder.
　　c. rebut, confute; contradict.
2. blazing light.
3. (bn.) (med.) ～衍 *pànyǎn* (MC banH-yenX), continuously connected, without break; ～換 *pànhuàn* (MC banH-hwanH), fractious and refractory.

拌 pàn MC phanH

1. ⊙ 判 *pàn* 1, halve, separate; break apart.

　　　　pān MC phan

1. (med.) reveal; display.

　　　　bàn MC banX

1. (med.) mix together; stir up.

泮 pàn MC phanH

1. thawing of ice; dissolve, melt away.
　　a. break apart, separate.
2. in early times a place for sons of feudal lords to learn archery > a school, academy.
3. ⊙ 畔 *pàn* 2a, riverbank, riverside.
4. (bn.) ～汗 *pànhàn* (MC phanH-hanH), overflowing flood, waters swelling and surging.

胖 pàn MC phanH

1. divide, portion; e.g. ～合 *pànhé*, rejoin what has been divided, reunite.
　　a. divide in two, halve; half.

畔 pàn MC banH

1. bank between fields, field-balk.
2. boundary, (along)side.
　　a. riverbank, riverside.
　　b. parapet on wall.
3. ⊙ 叛 *pàn*, betray, rebel against; desert; rebut, contradict.

盼 pàn MC pheanH

1. clear-set eyes, with the white and iris distinctly set off.
　　a. something colored both black and white distinctly.
2. (med.) turn one's gaze on, fix the gaze on; look at.
　　a. (med.) discern, make out.
3. (med.) glance sideways at, glimpse; cut one's gaze toward.
4. (med.) look after, attend to.

胖　pàn　MC phanH
1. half the body of an animal presented in a sacrificial ceremony.
   a. thin strips of meat.
  pán　MC ban
1. unfolded, stretched out; at ease.

N.B. The pronunciation *pàng* with meaning of "fat, corpulent" does not arise until after the Tang.

襻　pàn　MC phaenH
1. (med.) frog, braided loop serving to fasten a flap of clothing to a button.

pāng

滂　pāng　MC phang
1. rushing water, torrent(ial).
   a. (bn.) ～沛 *pāngpèi* (MC phang-phajH), rushing and roaring, crashing and dashing of waves; driving deluge or downpour of rain; (bn.) ～沱 *pāngtuó* (MC phang-da), of rain, same as preceding; also a flood or torrent of tears.
   b. (bn.) 淜～ *píngpāng*, → 淜 *píng*.
  pēng　MC phaeng
1. (bn.) ～濞 *pēngpì* (MC phaeng-phijH), crashing and colliding, rushing and roaring of waves; also, thickly thronging, growing densely.

páng

傍　páng　MC bang
1. (med.) ⊙ 旁 *páng*, alongside.
   a. (med.) ～地 *pángdì*, everywhere, all over, the entire ground.
2. (bn.) ～徨 *pánghuáng* (MC bang-hwang), ⊙ 徬徨 *pánghuáng*, → 徬 *páng*.
  bàng　MC bangH
1. nearby, close to.
   a. accompany; follow.

徬　páng　MC bang
1. (bn.) ～徨 *pánghuáng* (MC bang-hwang), walk back and forth, shilly-shally; vacillate, procrastinate; nervously pacing.
  bàng　MC bangH
1. walk alongside of, walk with; accompany.

旁　páng　MC bang
1. the side of, alongside; lateral, peripheral.
   a. askant, crooked; sideways.

   b. (med.) another, other(s); e.g. ～人 *pángrén*, outsiders, others; bystander.
2. pervasive, throughout.
   a. (med.) simultaneous(ly).
3. help, assist, come to one's aid from the side.
4. (bn.) ～魄 *pángbó* (MC bang-bak), boundless and unbroken.
  bàng　MC bangH
1. ⊙ 傍 *bàng*, close by, near to.

磅　páng　MC phang
1. (bn.) ～礴 *pángbó* (MC phang-bak), ～唐 *pángtáng* (MC phang-dang), unlimited, boundlessly wide; also, pervasively full, packed with.
2. (bn.) 砰～ *pēngpáng*, → 砰 *pēng*.

筹　páng　MC bang
1. a poisonous kind of bamboo reputedly used by "barbarians" to kill tigers and leopards.
  péng　MC baeng
1. punish by beating with a bamboo rod, caning.

膀　páng　MC bang
1. (bn.) ～胱 *pángguāng* (MC bang-kwang), the bladder; syn. 脬 *pāo*.
  bǎng　MC pangX
1. (med.) shoulder-bone.

螃　páng　MC bang
1. (med.) (bn.) ～蟹 *pángxiè* (MC bang-heaX), the edible crab (*Brachyura brachyura*).

逢　páng　MC baewng
1. (med.) rdup., onom. of drumming, "bohng-bohng."
2. a surname.

霶　páng　MC phang
1. heavy snowfall, blanket of snow; blizzard.

霶　páng　MC phang　⊙ 霶 *páng*.

龐　páng　MC baewng
1. huge, massive.
   a. substantial; staunch; reliable.
2. (med.) mixed, heterogeneous; motley.
   a. (med.) grizzled, gray-spotted.
3. a surname.
  lóng　MC luwng
1. rdup., sturdy and strong, robust.

pāo

拋   **pāo**   MC phaew
1. (med.) throw, hurl, fling, dash, pitch.
   a. (med.) get rid of, cast aside, throw away.
2. (med.) brandish, wave vigorously.
3. (med.) 〜絲 *pāosī*, to "throw" thread, i.e. twist together several single yarns into one thread in a direction opposite to that in which they themselves are twisted.
   pào   MC phaewH
1. (med.) ballista, for hurling rocks in wartime.

脬   **pāo**   MC phaew
1. the bladder; syn. 膀胱 *pángguāng*.

páo

匏   **páo**   MC baew
1. sgl. or cmpd. 〜瓜 *páoguā*, gourd, calabash; also, Gourd-star, constellation made up of 5 stars in Delphinus.

咆   **páo**   MC baew
1. roaring, howling, bellowing, yowling of wild animals.
   a. (bn.) 〜烋 *páoxiāo* (MC baew-xaew), rage and roar; also, spout and swagger, brag and bluster.

庖   **páo**   MC baew
1. kitchen.
   a. a cook.
   b. a butcher.

炮   **páo**   MC baew
1. grill, roast, esp. in a wrapping; a "wrapped bake."
   a. burn, set on fire.
2. ⊙ 庖 *páo* 1a, a cook.

炰   **páo**   MC baew
1. ⊙ 炮 *páo* 1, roast, wrapped grill.
2. (bn.) 〜烋, ⊙ 咆哮 *páoxiāo* (MC baew-xaew), rage and roar.

袍   **páo**   MC baw
1. long robe, gown; cope.
   a. (med.) battle-cloak.
2. inner robe, usu. quilted with hemp.

跑   **páo**   MC baew
1. of animals, pawing the ground.
   pǎo   MC baew
1. (med.) run, move quickly.

颮   **páo**   MC baew   → 颮 *biāo*.

麃   **páo**   MC baew   → 麃 *biāo*.

麚   **páo**   MC baew
1. Siberian roe-deer (*Capreolus pygargus*).

pǎo

跑   **pǎo**   MC baew   → 跑 *páo*.

pào

泡   **pào**   MC phaew
1. foam, froth; spume; bubbles.
   a. insubstantial, unreal figment.
   páo   MC baew
1. rdup., quickly rippling water.
2. (bn.) 〜溲 *páosǒu* (MC baew-srjuw), foaming and frothing.

疱   **pào**   MC phaewH
1. blister; pustule; pimple.

皰   **pào**   MC phaewH   ⊙ 疱 *pào*.

鮑   **pào**   MC phaewH   ⊙ 疱 *pào*.

pēi

胚   **pēi**   MC phwoj
1. (med.) sgl. or cmpd. 〜胎 *pēitái*, organism in its first stage of growth; foetus, embryo; e.g. 〜運 *pēiyùn*, fecund Cosmic Egg.
   a. (med.) embryonic, rudimentary; origin(al), initial, beginning, not fully formed.

衃   **pēi**   MC phwoj
1. coagulated blood.
2. ⊙ 胚 *pēi*, foetus, embryo(nic).
   fǒu   MC pjuwX
1. (bn.) 蚍〜 *pífǒu*, → 蚍 *pí*.

醅 pēi MC phwoj
1. (med.) unfiltered fermented mash; unfiltered w ne.

péi

坏 péi MC bwoj
1. fill up, block up with clay or plaster.
2. ⊙ 阫 *péi*, back wall of a house.
　　pī MC phwoj
1. unfired ceramic; half-finished product.

培 péi MC bwoj
1. bank up with earth, mound up, hill up.
2. ⊙ 阫 *péi*, back wall of a house.
　　pǒu MC buwX
1. (bn.) ～塿 *pǒulǒu* (MC buwX-luwX), small h ll, monticule, hummock, hillock.

毬 péi MC bwoj
1. (med.) (bn.) ～毸 *péisāi* (MC bwoj-swoj), tensed stretching; bristling one's plumes, having one's back up, raising one's hackles.

裴 péi MC bwoj
1. (bn.) ～徊 *péihuái* (bwoj-hwoj), ⊙ 徘徊 *páihuái*, → 徘 *pái*.
2. a surname.

阫 péi MC bwoj
1 back wall of a house.

陪 péi MC bwoj
1 piled one on top of another; superposed, overlapping.
　　a. augment(ed), increase(d), add(ed); double(d).
2. accompany, associate(d) with, share; e.g. ～陵 *péilíng*, "accompanying tumulus," privilege accorded certain individuals of being buried near the ruler's tumulus, i.e. satellite burial.
　　a. accessory, attendant; auxiliary; complementary.
3. assist, aid; support; come to the side of.

pèi

佩 pèi MC bajH
1. pendants hanging from a sash or belt, incl. jeweled ornaments, cord with seal of office, etc.
　　a. hang from the waist, hang down, dangle.
2. carry with one; take on, accept.
3. girded with, zoned with; surround.
4. admire, esteem.

旆 pèi MC bajH
1. vertical banner ending in swallowtail shape.
　　a. by metonymy, gen. term for banner.
2. decorative fringe; festoon.
3. rdup., wave or ripple richly in the wind.

沛 pèi MC phajH
1. marshy plant-cover, marshy tangle, marsh jungle.
2. watery excess, flood, overflow; surfeit.
　　a. torrent(ial); awash in; teeming with, flush.
3. racing onward, coursing quickly; rapid(ly), rush(ing), fleet(ly); speed, skim.
4. rdup., brimming with energy, vitality.

珮 pèi MC bwojH
1. ⊙ 佩 *pèi* 1, pendants hung from sash or belt, esp. of jade; 1a, hang from the waist, hang down, dangle.

轡 pèi MC pijH
1. reins, traces.
　　a. control, as with reins; guide, direct.

配 pèi MC phwojH
1. match, mate; suit(able), fit(ting).
　　a. partner, counterpart; equal; equivalent to.
2. matched in marriage; marry.
　　a. spouse, usu. the wife.
3. coordinate, cooperate with; coadjutor.
　　a. accompany, join with.
　　b. (med.) also, and, as well as.
4. at sacrificial ceremonies, the assessor who invites the spirit(s) to partake of offerings.
5. (med.) apportion, distribute, assign, allot.
6. (med.) banish to the frontier.

霈 pèi MC phajH
1. (med.) sheets of rain, torrential rain; downpour, deluge; swash, swamp.
　　a. (med.) ～然 *pèirán*, full of, overflowing with; awash in; teeming with.

pēn

噴 pēn MC phwon
1. spurt, spout, spray, squirt, spew; jet, expel with force; shoot forth, burst forth.
　　a. sprinkle, asperse.

2. snort, snuff; blow out, spit out; e.g. ～玉 *pēnyù*, "spitting jade," a horse seeming to snuffle foam because of hard galloping.

    a. breathe out heavily, expire; sneeze; eruct, belch; emit.

3. (bn.) ～薄 *pēnbó* (MC phwon-bak), frenzied fury.

歆　**pēn**　MC phwon　⊙ 噴 *pēn*.

pén

溢　**pén**　MC bwon
1. ⊙ 盆 *pén* 3, inundate, course in flood.

盆　**pén**　MC bwon
1. basin; pot; bowl.
2. old measure of capacity, equiv. 12 pecks (*dou* 斗) and 8 pints (*sheng* 升).
3. inundate, course in flood; burst the banks of.

pēng

怦　**pēng**　MC pheang
1. rdup., distressed and distraught, upset and uneasy, troubled and in turmoil.

抨　**pēng**　MC pheang
1. let loose a drawn bow.
2. (med.) graze or touch lightly, skim; flap.
3. (med.) denounce, accuse.
    bēng　MC peang
1. employ as, depute as.

澎　**pēng**　MC phaeng
1. (bn). ～湃 *pēngpài* (MC phaeng-pheajH), ～滂 *pēngpì* (MC phaeng-phijH), onom. of crashing and colliding, roaring and rushing of waves.

烹　**pēng**　MC phaeng
1. cook, esp. by boiling.
2. boil alive, judicial punishment in early times.

硑　**pēng**　MC pheang
1. sgl. or rdup., onom. of booming, rumbling, thundering, reverberating sounds.

硼　**pēng**　MC pheang
1. (med.) (bn.) ～磕 *pēngkē* (MC pheang-khap), onom. of the rumble of thunder; also, of many instruments sounding in concert.

2. (med.) (bn.) ～隱 *pēngyǐn* (MC pheang-'j+nH), onom. of the booming reverberation of drums.

駍　**pēng**　MC pheang
1. onom. of rumbling of carriages.
2. (bn.) 騯～ *pīnpēng*, → 騯 *pīn*.

péng

弸　**péng**　MC beang
1. powerful or strong bow.
    a. complete, full < a drawn bow.

彭　**péng**　MC baeng
1. (Dao.) surname of the spirits of the 3 Corpses (*sanshi* 三尸) that dwell within one's body and aim to bring about premature death, reporting one's transgressions on the 57th day of every 60-day cycle to the Master of Fate (*siming* 司命); their names are Peng Ju ～倨 who dwells in the head, Peng Zhi ～質 who dwells in the heart, and Peng Jiao ～矯 in the abdomen.
2. ～祖 *péngzǔ*, name of long-lived figure of legend, reputedly with life-span of 700-800 years, often called "the Chinese Methuselah."
3. (med.) mixed, balled-up; e.g. ～星 *péngxīng*, "tangle-star," tailless comet.
    bāng　MC pang
1. rdup., numerous and many; also, advancing steadily; also, robust and vigorous.
    pēng　MC phaeng
1. ⊙ 澎 *pēng*, 1st element in bns. onom. of crashing rocks, roaring waves.

搒　**péng**　MC baeng
1. bastinado, punish by beating with a stick or cudgel.
    bàng　MC pangH
1. ⊙ 榜 *bàng* (→ *péng*), an oar; row a boat.

朋　**péng**　MC bong
1. comrade, partner, associate.
2. band together, form a group or faction; collaborate with.
    a. coterie, set, group, band, contingent.
3. equal, equivalent to; same as, alike; comparable.
4. in early times, a double-string of either 5 or 10 (total 10 or 20) cowry shells used as medium of exchange.

棚　péng　MC baeng

1. mountainside footbridge, made of wood or bamboo.
2. (med.) faction, group.
3. (med.) canopy, awning.
   a. (med.) shed, hut.

榜　péng　MC baeng

1. board for training the wood of a bow into desired shape.
2. ⊙ 搒 *péng*, bastinado, punish by beating with stick or cudgel.

bàng　MC pangH

1. oar; row a boat; e.g. 〜人 *bàngrén*, oarsman, helmsman, bargeman.
   a. by synecdoche, a boat.

bǎng　MC pangX

1. wooden board.
   a. (med.) placard, plate, esp. publicly displayed pass-list of successful exam candidates.
2. pole, post.

篷　péng　MC buwng

1. (med.) awning of a boat, canopy of a carriage.
   a. (med.) by synecdoche, a boat.

膨　péng　MC baeng

1. (med.) bloat(ed), distended, swollen, torous.
   a. (med.) (bn.) 〜脝 *pénghēng* (MC baeng-xaeng), blown and bloated, tumid and torous.

芃　péng　MC buwng

1. rdup., of plants, thickly thriving, teeming with growth.

蓬　péng　MC buwng

1. tumbleweed, tumblebush, any of several plants that when withered disengage from their roots and are pushed along by the wind.
2. bitter fleabane (*Erigeron acris*); also, garland chrysanthemum (*Chrysanthemum coronarium*); both leafy herbs, growing in a tangle.
3. seed-pod, of lotus.
4. wicker, wattle.
5. 〜萍 *péngpíng*, pond-lily, spatterdock.
6. sgl. or rdup., dishevelled, tangled, disarrayed; also, windblown; (bn.) 〜勃 *péngbó* (MC buwng-bwot), 〜茸 *péngróng* (MC buwng-nyowng), lush and leafy, overgrown and rank.

鵬　péng　MC bong

1. fabulous bird of enormous size, from the opening passage of *Zhuangzi* 莊子; transformed from the gigantic *kun* 鯤 fish, it rises 90,000 *li* high and soars from the northern sea to the southern sea in a single flight of six months; symbolic of what seems unimaginable.

pěng

捧　pěng　MC phjowngX

1. hold in both hands.
   a. offer up, hand up.
2. support, hold up; sustain.

pī

丕　pī　MC phij

1. grand; immense, vast; magnificent; majestic.
2. respectfully attend upon.
3. marker of connection or continuation: then, thereupon.

伾　pī　MC phij

1. rdup., stout and sturdy, robust and strapping.

劈　pī　MC phek

1. split in two, cleave, rend.
   a. (med.) differentiate, distinguish; e.g. 〜面 *pīmiàn*, face-to-face, directly, openly.

坏　pī　MC phwoj　→ 坏 *péi*.

坯　pī　MC phwoj

1. ⊙ 坏 *pī* (*pēi*), unfired ceramic; half-finished product.

怶　pī　MC phjij

1. mistake, error; aberration.

批　pī　MC phej

1. strike with the back of the hand, backhand; slap, smack, hit.
2. remove, eliminate; dispel.
3. (med.) peel, slice; pare, sheer off, shave; e.g. 〜竹 *pīzhú*, peel(ed) bamboo, also descriptive of a horse's short and pointed ears; 〜判 *pīpàn*, slice and divide > discriminate between alternatives, judge.

4. (med.) acknowledge receipt of, esp. a superior responding to an inferior.
    a. (med.) note down; memorandum.

披   pī   MC phje(X)

1. break open, split open, rend.
    a. divide in two, separate.
2. reveal, show, disclose.
    a. throw open, spread open.
    b. unroll, open to view, display; unfold.
3. throw over one's shoulders, fling on, invest with; cloaked with.
    a. mantle, cloak, shawl.
    b. carry on one's back, esp. armor.
4. fling away, scatter, bestrew.
    a. (bn.) ～靡 *pīmǐ* (MC phjeX-mjeX), tossed and tumbled on the wind, strewn and scattered; also, overthrown, overturned, discomfited.

狉   pī   MC phij

1. rdup., herd of animals bolting and rushing off, whisking and racing away.

秠   pī   MC phij

1. black broomcorn millet (*Panicum miliaceum*), yields double grains.

紕   pī   MC bjie

1. embroider the edge of (flag, cap, clothing), trim out, garnish.
    a. border, garniture, fringe.
      pī   MC phjij
1. ravel out, shred.
    a. shoddy; unsound; negligent, oversight; mistake(n).

狓   pī   MC phje

1. (med.) spread one's wings.
    a. (med.) spread open, open out.
2. (med.) ⊙ 披 *pī* 4, fling away, scatter, bestrew.

蚾   pī   MC pej

1. (bn.) ～蠹 *pīdù* (MC pej-tuH), large ants; syn. 蚍蜉 *pífú*.

鈹   pī   MC phek   ⊙ 鈹 *pī*.

鈹   pī   MC phje

1. long needle or lancet, for medicinal use such as opening an abscess.
    a. to lance, pierce.

2. ⊙ 鈹 *pī*, double-bladed short sword or dagger.
    a. long lance.
3. ⊙ 披 *pī* 4, fling away, scatter, bestrew.

鈹   pī   MC phij

1. double-edged short sword or dagger.

霹   pī   MC phek

1. (bn.) ～靂 *pīlì* (MC phek-lek), thunderclap, thunderbolt.
    a. (med.) cause to shudder, quake, from overpowering noise, surprise, or fear.

駓   pī   MC phij

1. dappled tawny and white horse.
2. rdup., speed posthaste, at a full gallop.

髬   pī   MC phij

1. (bn.) ～髵 *pī'ér* (MC phij-nyi), bristling coat of fierce animal, hispid and bristling; toss one's shaggy mane.

鈹   pī   MC phek

1. split, cleave, rend; break asunder.
    a. (med.) break apart for examination, analyze.
2. ornamental figuring on a sword.

                       pí

埤   pí   MC bjie

1. increase, add to, augment; increment, layer.
2. ⊙ 陴 *pí*, crenelation; battlement, parapet.
      pì   MC phejH
1. (bn.) ～堄 *pìnì* (MC phejH-ngejH), spy-holes, observation holes along battlements.
      bèi   MC bjeX
1. low-lying wetland.
      bēi   MC pjie
1. ⊙ 卑 *bēi*, low.

枇   pí   MC bjij

1. (bn.) ～杷 *pípá* (MC bjij-bae), loquat, fruit of the Japanese medlar (*Eriobotrya japonica*).
      bì   MC bjijH
1. fine-toothed comb.
    a. comb the hair.
      bǐ   MC pijX
1. long-handled wooden ladle, used in sacrificial ceremonies.

椑　pí　MC bej

1. elliptically-shaped wine container.
   a. gen. term for elliptically-shaped items.

   bì　MC bek

1. inner coffin, containing the corpse.

   bēi　MC pjie

1. Dahurian buckthorn (*Rhamnus davurica*), medium-sized flowering tree.

槐　pí　MC bjij

1. front edging of roof-eaves.

毗　pí　MC bjij

1. adjoin, adjacent, contiguous; juxtapose.
2. support; strengthen.
3. (Budd.) trsc. Skt. *vi, vai*; e.g. ～盧 *pílú* (MC bjij-lu), abb. of ～盧舍耶 *pílúshěyé* (MC bjij-lu-syaeX-yae), trsc. Skt. Vairocana, name of the Buddha of Great Illumination, central figure of the *Avataṃsaka sūtra* (*Huayanjing* 華嚴經) and sometimes regarded as the *dharmakāya* (*fashen* 法身) or bliss body of Śākyamuni Buddha; ～奈耶 *pí'nàiyé* (MC bjij-najH-yae), trsc. Skt. *vinaya*, rules of monastic discipline.
4. (med.) ～梨勒 *pílílè* (bjij-lij-lok), belliric myrobalan (*Terminalia bellirica*), tree and astringent fruit (Skt. *vibhītakī*, Pers. *balīla*), originally an import from Central and Southeast Asia, one of 3 ingredients of *sanle* 三勒 (→ 勒 *lè*).

毘　pí　MC bjij　⊙ 毗 *pí*, esp. 3, in phonetic transcriptions of Skt.

琵　pí　MC bjij

1. (bn.) ～琶 *pípá* (MC bjij-bae), 5-stringed pear-shaped or round (like the loquat 枇杷, *pípá*) lute of Central Asian origin, played with a plectrum; the only instrument rightly called a "lute"; strongly associated with the Western Regions (Xiyu 西域) and the Hu 胡 peoples.

疲　pí　MC bje

1. fatigued, wearied, exhausted; played out.
   a. feeble, on the wane; incompetent, incapable of.

皮　pí　MC bje

1. animal hide, pelt; cf. 肌 *jī*, human skin.
   a. archery target made of stretched and depilated hide.
   b. dressed or tanned hide, leather.

2. integument, outer covering of object, such as bark of tree, rind of fruit, shell of nut, wrapping of dumpling; surface, outside.
3. to skin; scrape or peel off the outer layer.

笓　pí　MC bej

1. (med.) bamboo basket for catching shrimp, crab, etc.
2. (med.) barrier or barricade made of bamboo or thornwood.

羆　pí　MC pje

1. brown bear (*Ursus arctos*).

脾　pí　MC bjie

1. the spleen; with *wuxing* symbolic correlations with earth, yellow, center.
2. ⊙ 膍 *pí*, tripe, stomach lining of ruminants.

   bì　MC bejX

1. ⊙ 髀 1, haunch(es).

膍　pí　MC bjij

1. tripe, stomach lining of ruminants.
   a. third stomach of ruminants.
2. deeply line, generously provide.

芘　pí　MC bjij

1. (bn.) ～芣 *pífú* (MC bjij-bjuw), mallow (*Malva sinensis*); syn. 蚍衃 *pífǒu*, 錦葵 *jǐnkuí*.

   bì　MC bjijH

1. ⊙ 庇 *bì*, shelter, protect, cover.

蚍　pí　MC bjij

1. (bn.) ～蜉 *pífú* (MC bjij-bjuw), large ants.
   a. ～蜉酒草 *pífújiǔcǎo*, cottonweed, Jersey cudweed (*Gnaphalium affine*), biennial herb with yellow florets, used medicinally and in cooking; syn. 鼠曲草 *shǔqǔcǎo*.
2. (bn.) ～衃 *pífǒu* (MC bjij-pjuwX), mallow (*Malva sinensis*); syn. 錦葵 *jǐnkuí*.

裨　pí　MC bjie

1. secondary or indifferent ceremonial garb.
2. subordinate, secondary, assist(ant)
   a. mediocre; inferior.

   bì　MC pjie

1. supplement, fill out; increase; remedy, benefit.

貔　pí　MC bjij

1. sgl. or (bn.) ～貅 *píxiū* (MC bjij-xjuw), "ferine ravener," fabulous animal of great strength and

ferocity, said to resemble an ash-gray tiger, leopard, or bear; > epithet for ferocious company of soldiers.

陴   pí   MC bjie
1. crenelations; battlement, parapet.

鼙   pí   MC bej
1. small military hand-drum, war-drum, used on horseback.
   a. by metonymy, warfare, military affairs.

pǐ

仳   pǐ   MC phjieX
1. separate, part from.
   a. esp. husband setting aside his wife.

匹   pǐ   MC phjit
1. measure of length for silks or cloth, a "bolt," equiv. 4 *zhang* 丈 or "staves" (i.e. 40 *chi* 尺 or "feet" by 1.8 *chi* wide).
   a. (med.) measure-word for a quantity of goods equivalent to the worth of a "bolt."
2. measure-word for horses.
3. single, individual; e.g. 〜夫 *pǐfū*, one person; also, commoners, common people, regular fellow, chap.
4. match, mate; pair.
   a. equal, equivalent to; correlation.
   b. accompany; companion.

圮   pǐ   MC bijX
1. ruin, destroy; bring down, overthrow; collapse.

庀   pǐ   MC phjieX
1. prepare, provide, furnish.
2. put in order; arrange.

痞   pǐ   MC pijX
1. constipation.
   a. stomach blockage or obstruction.

癖   pǐ   MC phjiek
1. chronic enlargement of the spleen or lungs.
   a. chronic, incurable illness.
2. addiction, obsession; excessive attachment to or desire for a particular activity or object; compulsion.

pì

僻   pì   MC phjiek
1. remote, out of the way, far to one side.
   a. separated from, far-removed; rare; isolated; withdrawn, retired.
2. off-center, oblique; divergent; distorted; incorrect; unorthodox; perverted, perverse.
3. (med.) ⊙ 癖 *pǐ*, addicted to, obsessed with.

副   pì   MC phik   → 副 *fù*.

媲   pì   MC phejH
1. to match, mate.
   a. well-matched; equal to.

帔   pì   MC phjeH
1. cape, mantle, robe; long scarf.
2. ⊙ 披 *pī* 3, throw over the shoulders.

揊   pì   MC phik   ⊙ 捭 *pì*.

捭   pì   MC phik
1. slice open, rend; break open.

洈   pì   MC phijH
1. float, glide, of boats.
2. rdup., bunched and abundant.
   pèi   MC phajH
1. rdup., streaming and swinging in the wind, waving and ruffling.

潎   pì   MC phjiejH
1. rdup., of fish, lightly gliding, slipping to and fro.
   piē   MC phjiet
1. (bn.) 〜洌 *piēliè* (MC phjiet-ljet), beating and battering of waves, plashing and splashing.

澼   pì   MC phek
1. (bn.) 洴〜 *píngpì*, → 洴 *píng*.

濞   pì   MC phijH
1. roaring of waves.
   a. (bn.) 澎〜 *pēngpì*, → 澎 *pēng*.

甓   pì   MC bek
1. brick; brickwork; cover with brick.

睤   pì   MC phejH
1. (bn.) 〜睨 *pìnì* (MC phejH-ngejH), look at askance, look at from the side, cut a glance at;

eye disdainfully; spy at, be on the look-out for; also, spy-holes, observation holes in battlements, ⊙ 埤堄 *pìnì*.

譬　pì　MC phjieH

1. draw an analogy or parallel with, make a comparison; exemplify, propose as an example or illustration.
2. (med.) comprehend, understand.
   a. instruct(ion), lead to understanding of.

辟　pì　MC bjiek　→辟 *bì*.

闢　pì　MC bjiek

1. open, open out, swing open; commence(ment), debut.
   a. break open, erupt; debouch; gape, yawn.
2. open for use, reclaim (wasteland).
   a. develop, expand.
3. clear away, get rid of, clear out; expel.
4. (med.) ⊙ 避 *bì*, elude, avoid; withdraw.

piān

偏　piān　MC phjien

1. oblique, inclined to the side, slanted; e.g. (med.) ～提 *piāntí*, "inclined lifter," pipette used for ladling wine.
   a. off-center, lopsided, unmatched; eccentric, capricious; e.g. ～衣 *piānyī*, bicolored vestment, of a different color on either side.
   b. in immoderate or unusual degree, preponderant(ly); (e)special(ly), particular(ly); strange to say.
   c. (med.) only, merely; alone.
2. one-sided, unilateral; partial; incomplete; e.g. (med.) ～孤 *piāngū*, young person who has lost either father or mother.
   a. inclined or disposed to (do) X; bias, predilection, partiality; insist(ent).
   b. portion, part, segment, division; e.g. ～伍 *piānwǔ*, platoon of soldiers.
3. sideways, aside; lateral, peripheral.
   a. sweep aside, swept aside, off to the side > far-removed, remote; e.g. ～棲 *piānqī*, dwelling apart.
4. (med.) by antithesis, wholly; intently, earnestly.
5. ～桃人 *piāntáorén*, almond (*Prunus amygdalus*).

篇　piān　MC phjien

1. bamboo or wooden tablet with writing on it.
2. a literary unit of a certain length, usu. part of a longer work; section, chapter; tract.
   a. measure-word for a poem.

翩　piān　MC phjien

1. sgl., rdup., or in bn. ～飄 *piānpiāo* (MC phjien-phjiew), effortless glide, easy flight; lightsome lightness, freely fluttering; also, facile, smooth, skillfully designed so as to seem effortless, esp. of lit.

鶣　piān　MC phjien　⊙ 翩 *piān*.

pián

婩　pián　MC bjien

1. (bn.) ～娟 *piánjuān* (MC bjien-'jwien), lithe and lissome, gracefully shaped; also, curving and coiling around.

楄　pián　MC ben

1. lath, short square beam attached to the corner-beam of a roof.
2. ～柎 *piánfù*, long board at bottom of coffin, on which the corpse is placed.
3. (med.) flat, bottom part of wooden clog or patten, to which the "teeth" are attached.

緶　pián　MC bjien

1. sew, seam, esp. sew together 2 adjoining pieces.

胼　pián　MC ben

1. ～胝 *piánzhī*, callouses on hands or feet.

諞　pián　MC bjien

1. of talk, captious, cunning, guileful, artful; conniving.

跰　pián　MC ben　⊙ 蹁 *pián*.

蹁　pián　MC ben

1. limp; stagger, hobble; totter; lean to one side, askew.
   a. (bn.) ～躚 *piánxiān* (MC ben-sen), limping and lurching; also, whirling and swirling.

駢   pián   MC ben

1. team of 2 horses.
2. in tandem, paired; esp. (lit.) parison, in parallel, style of writing in which pairs of lines or phrases are composed with parallel grammatical structures.
   a. in regular order.
3. joined, integrated, linked.

piàn

片   piàn   MC phenH

1. slip or strip of bamboo or wood.
   a. small portion of other physical objects: flake, chip; wisp; scantle; spall.
   b. a stretch or swath; e.g. 一～月 *yīpiànyùe*, a swath of moonlight.
2. a least amount > one, individual, only.
   a. small portion of time, a moment, a brief while.
   b. insignificant bit.

騙   piàn   MC phjienH

1. (med.) get on a horse, mount up; e.g. ～石 *piànshí*, mounting block, to stand on when mounting.
   a. (med.) straddle, be astride.
N.B. Meanings associated with cheating, deceiving, etc., are post-Tang developments.

piāo

嫖   piāo   MC phjiew

1. light, airy, buoyant.
   a. (bn.) ～姚 *piāoyáo*, equiv. 飄搖 *piāoyáo*, → 飄 *piāo*; also, equiv. 票姚 *piàoyáo*, → 票 *piào* (*piāo*).
   b. frivolous, flighty.

影   piāo   MC phjiew

1. ⊙ 票 *piào* (*piāo*), agile, lithe, active; prompt, ready, alert; e.g. (bn.) ～搖 *piàoyáo*, equiv. 票姚.
   a. ⊙ 飄 *piāo*, rdup., float and flutter, rise and roll, toss and glide.

漂   piāo   MC phjiew

1. ⊙ 飄 *piāo* 1a, gust, blow; 2, float or toss on the wind; flutter, glide.
2. ～然 *piāorán*, high and far off.

piǎo   MC phjiewX

1. bleach; scour.

piào   MC phjiewH

1. speed(ily), quick(ly), rapid(ly), swift(ly).

票   piāo   MC phjiew

1. leaping flames.
   a. flickering light.
2. buoyant, lightly rising.
3. shake, agitate, rouse, stir.

piào   MC phjiewH

1. agile, lithe; active, "fiery"; alert.
   a. ～騎 or 驃騎 *piàojì*, cavalry on the alert, a military title; (bn.) ～姚 *piàoyáo* (MC phjiew-yew), agile and alert, descriptive epithet used in some military titles.

縹   piāo   MC phjiew

1. (bn.) ～緲 *piāomiǎo* (MC phjiew-mjiewX), vaporous seemings, vaporous mists; far-seeing, distantly descried; hauntingly distant, haunting and ethereal; shading off afar, blurred and bleared.

piǎo   MC phjiewX

1. pale blue silks; pale blue in color.
   a. silvery-blue, like moonlight.

螵   piāo   MC phjiew

1. (bn.) ～蛸 *piāoxiāo* (MC phjiew-sjew), mantis egg-case, used medicinally; also, the cuttlefish.

飈   piāo   MC phjiew

1. ⊙ 飄 *piāo* 1, whirlwind, tempest; gale, squall; gust.

飄   piāo   MC phjiew

1. whirlwind, tempest; gale, squall.
   a. blow, gust; blow off, blow down.
2. float or toss on the wind; flutter, glide.
   a. rdup. or (bn.) ～搖 *piāoyáo* (MC phjiew-yew), wafted aloft, floating and fluttering, gracefully gliding, wind-whirled, tossed and tumbled, whirling and swirling; also (med.) of roads, twisting and turning, hard to travel.

piáo

瓢   piáo   MC bjiew

1. calabash.
   a. ladle-gourd, made from half a calabash.

piǎo

殍　piǎo　MC bjewX
1. die from starvation.

皫　piǎo　MC phjiewX
1. fade(d), dull(ed), dim(med), esp. of a bird's plumage.

瞟　piǎo　MC phjiewX
1. squint at.
2. (bn.) 〜眇 *piǎomiǎo* (MC phjiewX-mjiewX), equiv. 縹緲 *piāomiǎo*, → 縹 *piāo*.

piào

僄　piào　MC phjiewH
1. light, airy.
    a. flighty, frivolous.
    b. (bn.) 〜狡 *piàojiǎo* (MC phjiew-kaewX), brisk and bold, quick and courageous.
2. sudden(ly).

剽　piào　MC phjiewH
1. take by force; confiscate, wrest; rapacious, predatory
    a. seize, grab, snatch.
2. pare, shave; split off.
    a. stab, pierce; assail, beset.
3. extirpate; eliminate; destroy, bring down.
4. ready, prompt, alert, eager.
    biāo　MC pjiewX
1. tip, edge; extremity.

驃　piào　MC phjiewH
1. swift, agile horse; charger.
    a. doughty, brave, intrepid; e.g. 〜騎 *piàojì*, "doughty cavalry," a military title, but 〜 *piào* here short for 票姚 *piàoyáo*, agile and alert, hence the title is understood as "cavalry on the alert."
2. rapid gallop.
    biāo　MC bjiewH
1. dappled roan horse.

piē

瞥　piē　MC phet
1. glance at, throw a glance at, glimpse, catch a glimpse of.

a. sgl. or rdup., in the blink of an eye; an instant; quick, hasty; sudden(ly); in med. times in various cmpds. with preceding meaning, e.g. 〜裂, 〜列 *piēliè*; 〜眼 *piēyǎn*.

piě

撆　piě　MC phet　⊙ 撇 *piě*.

撇　piě　MC phet
1. strike lightly; hit.
    a. brush against.
2. cast aside, throw off.
3. (med.) sidewards, off-center, off the mark.

pīn

驫　pīn　MC phjin
1. (bn.) 〜駍 *pīnpēng* (MC phjin-pheang), clatter and rattle, clamorous racket.

pín

顰　pín　MC bjin
1. ⊙ 矉 *pín*, knit one's brows; scowl.
2. (med.) (bn.) 〜呻 *pínshēn* (MC bjin-syin), groan, moan; also, intone, chant aloud, recite.

嬪　pín　MC bjin
1. "guestmaiden," court serving lady; also, imperial concubine.
    a. title used for deceased wife.
2. give in marriage, esp. a sovereign's daughter.
3. 〜然 *pínrán*, a large group, multitude.

玭　pín　MC bjin
1. pearl, from oyster.

矉　pín　MC pjin
1. stare angrily, glare.
2. ⊙ 顰 *pín*, knit the brows, scowl.

蠙　pín　MC bjin　⊙ 蘋 *pín*.

蘋　pín　MC bjin
1. clover-fern, water-clover, four-leaf clover (*Marsilea quadrifolia*), fern growing near ponds and paddy fields.

貧 pín MC bin
1. poor, impoverished; indigent; in want.
    a. scarce, few; spare, sparing of.

頻 pín MC bjin
1. frequent(ly), persistent(ly); continuous(ly), incessant(ly).
    a. successively, one after another, repeatedly.
    b. (al)together.
2. urgent; at a critical point.
    a. hurry on, rush forward.
3. ⊙顰 pín, sgl. or cmpd. ～蹙, ～顣 píncù, ～眉 pínméi, knit one's brows, furrow the brow, scowl.
4. (med.) (bn.) ～煩 pínfán (MC bjin-bjon), attentively, with care and courtesy; cordially; gallantly.
5. (Budd.) (迦陵)～迦 (jiālíng)pínjiā (MC kae-ling-bjin-kjae), (迦陵)～伽 (jiālíng)pínqié (MC kae-ling-bjin-gja), Skt. (kala)viṅka, sweet-est-voiced of all birds whose song, even before it hatches, brings other birds to it, symbolic of bodhisattva; ～婆 pínpó (MC bjin-ba), trsc. Skt. bimba, pimpon tree, Chinese chestnut, bimba fruit (Sterculia nobilis).
    bīn MC pjin
1. shore, riverbank, brink.
    a. on the brink of, close by.

顰 pín MC bjin
1. sgl. or cmpd. ～蹙, ～顣 píncù, ～眉 pínméi, draw one's eyebrows together, knit one's brows; furrow the brow, scowl.

pǐn

品 pǐn MC phimX
1. class, grade, gradation; rank(ing).
    a. classify, grade, rank; evaluate, judge, sort by quality.
2. quality, degree or grade of excellence; e.g. ～流 pǐnliú, quality and caste.
3. mass, multitude; e.g. ～人 pǐnrén, a throng; ～庶 pǐnshù, the common mass.

pìn

娉 pìn MC phjiengH
1. ⊙聘 pìn 1a, send a representative with gifts to make a marriage agreement; betrothal.

pīng MC pjieng
1. (bn.) ～婷 pīngtíng (MC pjieng-deng), fair of form and manner.

牝 pìn MC bjinX
1. female of animals, ant. 牡 mǔ.
    a. gen. term for female gender, the yin qualities of receptivity and fertility.
2. ravine, valley.

聘 pìn MC phjiengH
1. send a diplomatic mission with gifts, as in seeking to establish or confirm an alliance.
    a. send a representative with gifts, to make a marriage agreement; betrothal.
    b. send a representative with gifts, to request one's presence and service at court; summon respectfully to take up an official position.
2. gen. term for an amicable visit of some formality.

pīng

俜 pīng MC pheng
1. (bn.) ～伶 pīnglíng (MC pheng-leng) or 伶 ～ língpīng, all on one's own, single solitary, one and only; also, stagger unsteadily.

娉 pīng MC phjieng → 娉 pìn.

砯 pīng MC phing
1. (med.) onom. of waves crashing against rocks.
2. (med.) rdup., onom. of bang and clatter of carts or carriages.

頻 pīng MC pheng
1. glossy, shining, of a face or surface.
    pīng MC phengX
1. flushed face; changed expression.

píng

凭 píng MC bing
1. lean on, rest on; rely on, depend on; ⊙憑 píng 1.

屏 píng MC beng
1. screen before or behind a doorway, to block the view or keep out wind.

a. partition.

b. ornamental screen.

bǐng　MC pjiengX

1. to screen off; block; hide, cover.

a. avoid; set off; set back; ward off.

2. set aside; remove; withdraw from; e.g. ～息 *bǐngxī*, bated breath.

bīng　MC pjieng

1. (bn.) ～營 *bīngyíng* (MC pjieng-yweng), waver and haver; hem and haw, fearfully faltering; tense and timid.

帡　píng　MC beng

1. draw-curtain, drape; e.g. (med.) ～幪 *píngméng*, drapes and curtains; also, cover(ing), screen(ing), shelter; protection, patronage.

平　píng　MC bjaeng

1. level, flat; even.

a. even out, level out, level off.

2. equal(ize), equivalent; normal, ordinary; e.g. (med.) ～步 *píngbù*, normal steps, i.e. ordinary actions; ～人 *píngrén*, ordinary people, commonfolk.

a. thoroughgoing, habitual, undeviating; e.g. ～生 *píngshēng*, throughout one's life, one's whole life; also, in the past.

b. fair, just, impartial.

3. tranquil(ity), calm, unruffled; peace(ful), irenic.

a. pacify, quiet; bring to terms, reconcile; subdue, suppress, calm, allay.

4. evaluate, lay out in proper order; esp. (med.) ～章事 *píngzhāngshì*, "evaluate and articulate affairs," title often attached in Tang times to official of the Bureau of State Affairs (*shangshusheng* 尚書省) who also served as a *zaixiang* 宰相, chief minister; abb. of *tong zhongshu menxia sanpin* 同中書門下三品, "coequal with grade-three officials in the Imperial Secretariat and Chancellery."

a. (med.) inlay, esp. ～脫 *píngtuō*, inlay precious metals in a lacquer base (Jpns. *heidatsu*).

5. wasteland, flat and fallow land.

6. (med.) ref. to words of "level," non-oblique tone in the spoken language; binary contrast with 仄 *zè*, "deflected"-tone words incl. those of 上 *shǎng*, 去 *qù*, and 入 *rù* tones.

7. ～仲 *píngzhòng*, gingko (*Gingko biloba*), syn. 銀杏 *yínxìng*.

pián　MC bjien

1. cmpd. ～章 *piánzhāng*, differentiate and mark out the merits of officials, as sage-king Yao 堯 is reputed to have done, in 1st chapter of *Shangshu*; probable source of title in 4 above; rdup., differentiate(d) and rightly order(ed).

憑　píng　MC bing

1. lean on; rely on, depend on.

a. thanks to, by means of, owing to.

b. according to, in conformity with.

c. cmpd. ～陵 *pínglíng*, "depend on dominance," i.e. prevail by bullying or encroaching.

2. tense, unsettled, ajitter, nervous, "hung up."

3. rdup., plentiful and replete, full, crowded with; also (med.), onom. of rumbling of thunder or trundling of carriage.

4. (med.) climb, ascend; scale.

5. cross water without a boat; wade across.

6. (med.) request, solicit.

枰　píng　MC bjaeng

1. gingko (*Gingko biloba*), syn. 銀杏 *yínxìng*, 平仲 *píngzhòng*.

2. (med.) game-board, esp. of *weiqi* 圍棋 (Jpns. *go*).

3. (med.) bed for one person, single bed.

洴　píng　MC beng

1. (bn.) ～澼 *píngpì* (MC beng-phek), bleach silk.

溯　píng　MC bing

1. (bn.) ～滂 *píngpāng* (MC bing-phang), blasting and blustering of wind.

pēng　MC phaeng

1. (bn.) ～湃 *pēngpài* (MC phaeng-pheajH), crashing and battering of waves.

瓶　píng　MC beng

1. jar, vase, ewer, pitcher, urn.

苹　píng　MC bjaeng

1. pearly everlasting, moon's silver (*Anaphalis sinica*); syn. 萩 *qiū*.

2. ⊙ 萍 *píng*, duckweed (*Lemna minor*).

3. rdup., clumped and clustered.

pēng　MC pheang

1. (bn.) ～縈 *pēngyíng* (MC pheang-'jwieng), whirling and twirling.

萍   píng   MC beng

1. duckweed, bayroot (*Lemna minor*), floating plant clustering on surface of still or slow-moving waters.
2. pond-lily, nuphar (*Nuphar lutea*), commonly yellow-flowering; when the word is modified by any color but "green," it is nuphar.

蓱   píng   MC beng

1. ⊙ 萍 *píng*, duckweed (*Lemna minor*); pond-lily (*Nuphar lutea*); 苹 *píng*, pearly everlasting (*Anaphalis sinica*).
2. ～翳 *píngyì*, name of mythological god of rain.

評   píng   MC bjaeng

1. evaluate, weigh, appraise, rate the quality of; (ad)judge, adjudicate; criticize, critique.

軿   píng   MC beng

1. (med.) screened carriage, curtained on all four sides; calèche, phaeton, esp. for use by noblewomen, often a vehicle of Dao. goddesses in the heavens.
   a. (med.) a carriage-curtain.

pēng   MC phaeng

1. (bn.) ～訇 *pēnghōng* (MC phaeng-xweang), deafening din, uproarious racket.

pián   MC ben

1. (med.) (bn.) ～闐 *piántián* (MC ben-den), ceaseless assemblage, unbroken massing, continually collecting.

馮   píng   MC bing

1. ⊙ 憑 *píng* 1-6.
2. ～夷 *píngyí*, name of mythological spirit of the Yellow River, the Count of the He (*Hebo* 河伯).

féng   MC bjuwng

1. a surname.

pō

坡   pō   MC pha

1. flank of a hill, slope; gradient, declivity.
   a. (med.) (bn.) ～陀 *pōtuó* (MC pha-da), hubbly and rugged, broken and bumpy, of mountain contours.

岥   pō   MC pha   ⊙ 坡 *pō*.

潑   pō   MC phat

1. (med.) sprinkle, spatter, spray, sparge; asperse, disperse; spill.

bō   MC pat

1. rdup., onom. of fish flapping their tails or leaping from water, flip-flap, spitter-spatter, splish-splash.

醱   pō   MC phat

1. (med.) twice-fermented wine; e.g. ～醅 *pōpēi*, twice-fermented unfiltered wine.

陂   pō   MC pha   ⊙ 坡 *pō*.

頗   pō   MC pha

1. ADV of degree, ranging from slight to larger: rather, somewhat, fairly, considerably, quite, notably.
   a. (med.) in Budd. texts an interr. particle: could it be that…?
2. slanting, inclined; oblique; veer.
3. ～羅, ⊙叵羅 *pǒluó*, Iranian drinking horn, *pālagh*.

pó

婆   pó   MC ba

1. (bn.) ～娑 *pósuō* (MC ba-sa) of dancing, whirling round, twirling and swirling, cavort and frolic; also, saunter and stroll, linger and loiter; also, straggling and bedraggled; of reflection, to pause and ponder; of vegetation, in leafy foliage, fully flowering.
2. (med.) sgl. or cmpd. 老～ *lǎopó*, term for an older woman, matron.
   a. (Budd.) 老～ *lǎopó*, 老～禪 *lǎopóchán*, 老～心 *lǎopóxīn*, old biddy('s Chan, mind), i.e. overexplain(er) or overcomplicate(r of) Chan practice.
3. (med.) ～律 *pólù* (MC ba-lwit), Baros (< Arabic *bālūs*), settlement on west side of Sumatra, chief place of camphor export; hence ～律香 *pólùxiāng*, "Baros aromatic," i.e. camphor; ～皇 *póhuáng* (MC ba-hwang), Pahang river and state in Malaysia.
4. (Budd.) ～伽～ *póqiépó* (MC ba-gja-ba), trsc. of Skt. *bhagavān*, Exalted One, epithet of the Buddha.

璠 pó MC ba

1. white, as the hair and beard of an oldster; rdup., hoary-headed.
   a. gen. term for white.
2. rdup., in profuse abundance, one upon another.
3. paunch(y); bloated stomach.

pǒ

叵 pǒ MC phaX

1. fusion-word of 不可 *bùkě*, not possible, not permissible.
2. thereupon, and then; thereat.
3. (med.) ～羅 *pǒluó* (phaX-la), Central Asian drinking vessel with a large mouth and shallow base, wine-bowl; perhaps cog. Persian *piyāla*, drinking-bowl; also Iran. drinking horn, *pālagh*.

叵 pǒ MC phaX ⊙ 叵 *pǒ*.

駊 pǒ MC phaX

1. (bn.) ～騀 *pǒě* (MC phaX-ngaX), descriptive of a horse shaking or tossing its head; also, proud hauteur.

pò

珀 pò MC phaek

1. (bn.) 琥～ *hǔpò*, → 琥 *hǔ*.

破 pò MC phaH

1. strike against mightily, smite; lay into, lay on.
   a. crush, smash, mammock; overthrow utterly; destroy, demolish, ruin; lay waste; ravage; breach, broach.
   b. assail; bring down, confute, disprove (a proposition or interpretation).
2. squander, waste; expend recklessly.
3. (med.) concluding section of musical performance, finale, esp. 3rd section of 大曲 *dàqǔ* suite.

粕 pò MC phak

1. lees, dregs, sediment left after fermentation of wine.
   a. euph. for inferior or worthless item.

膊 pò MC phak

1. chop into pieces.
   a. dismember.
2. expose to the open air.

bó MC pak

1. the shoulder.
   a. by synecdoche, upper part of torso.

蕈 pò MC phak

1. (bn.) ～苴 *pòjū* (phak-tsjo) or 苴～ *jūpò*, myoga ginger (*Zingiber mioga*).

趙 pò MC phaek

1. skim over, skim past, flit past.

迫 pò MC paek

1. press near, be at close quarters.
2. impel, compel(ling), drive toward; force, press(ing); prod, urge(nt).
   a. harry, harass, coerce, beleaguer; oblige, obligate.
   b. hasten.
3. narrow, confine(d), restrict(ed).

魄 pò MC phaek

1. "white-soul," carnal or material soul, anima; strongly associated with the body (cf. *shen* 神 with the spirit); in early texts possibly compounded with 魂 *hún* ("cloud-soul," ethereal soul) but by med. times usu. seen as representative of *yin* in contrast with the *yang*-derived *hun* and said to return with a corpse as residuum to the earth, also to be 7 in number (cf. 3 for *hun*); most often symbolic of the earthbound nature of a human being.
2. illuminated portion of the moon.
   a. gen. term for moonlight; glimmer.
   b. faint sliver of the moon during first 3 days of the month; sometimes also last 3 days.
3. ⊙ 粕 *pò*, lees, dregs, residuum.
bó MC bak

1. (bn.) 旁～ *pángbó* (MC bang-bak), boundless and unbroken.
2. onom. of crackling or bursting flames.
tuò MC thak

1. (bn.) 落～ *luòtuò* (MC lak-thak), downcast and dispirited, sad and bedraggled.

pōu

剖 pōu MC phuwX

1. to split, cut open; rend.
   a. lay open, reveal; e.g. ～心 *pōuxīn*, bare one's heart.
2. analyze, break down; discriminate or judge critically.

póu

抔   póu   MC buw
1. take or hold in one's cupped hands.
2. a handful.

掊   póu   MC buw
1. cup soil in the hands.
    a. delve, dig into the earth, with an implement.
2. ⊙ 抔 *póu* 1, take or hold in cupped hands; 2, a handful; 裒 *póu* 1, collect, assemble, amass.
    掊   MC phuwX
1. attack, assault; strike against; destroy.
    bó   MC bok
1. ⊙ 踣 *bó*, topple forward, fall head over heels; upside-down, overturn(ed); also, lay out a corpse.

裒   póu   MC buw
1. assemble, gather, accumulate, amass; collect.
    a. much, many; mass(ed).
2. decrease, reduce, diminish.
3. ⊙ 俘 *fú*, capture, take prisoner.
    bāo   MC paw
1. loose-fitting robe.

pǒu

培   pǒu   MC buwX   → 培 *péi*.

pū

仆   pū   MC bok
1. topple forward; stumble over.

扑   pū   MC phuwk   ⊙ 撲 *pū*.

撲   pū   MC phuwk
1. strike, beat.
    a. slap, whack; thump; buffet; e.g. (med.) ～滿 *pūmǎn*, "break-when-full," container like a piggy-bank for coins which is to be broken when full so the accumulated coins may be used.
2. cudgel, bastinado, esp. for use in physical punishment; to cudgel.
3. lightly tap, knock, rap.
    a. (med.) brush against, skim.
4. (med.) all of, the entirety of; e.g. ～地 *pūdì*, the whole earth, everywhere.
5. (med.) rdup., profuse and full, thick and lush.
6. (med.) place over the top of, cover with.
7. (med.) fall over, trip.

痡   pū   MC phu
1. overwork(ed), exhausted; prostrate from fatigue; fagged out; with all strength sapped, enervated.
    a. exhaustion, debilitation, prostration.
2. do harm to; inflict injury; debilitate; mar, spoil.

鋪   pū   MC phu
1. door-head, animal head carved on a door to hold a link-chain for locking it; also, a knocker.
2. display, exhibit; spread out, spread open, lay out.
    a. arrange, set out: e.g. ～兵 *pūbīng*, encamp troops.
    b. widespread, pervasive.
3. ⊙ 痡 *pū*, overworked, exhausted; enervated.
    pù   MC phuH
1. shop, stall, for selling goods.
2. (med.) inn; tavern.
    a. (med.) □～ *kǒupù*, post-station, customs house.

pú

僕   pú   MC buwk
1. low-level servant, lackey; serving-boy.
    a. humble self-reference: "I who am abject," "this abject person."
2. equerry, groom.
    a. sgl. or ～夫 *púfū*, coachman, carriage-driver.
3. attached to, connected with.
4. rdup., annoying(ly), irritating(ly).
5. ～射 *púyè*, official title; pre-Tang usu. a concurrent administrator of an office whose chief was merely nominal; in Tang the 2 vice-ministers of the Bureau of State Affairs (*shangshusheng* 尚書省) who were the de facto heads of the bureau, since the chief title of director (*ling* 令) was left vacant out of deference to emperor Taizong 太宗 after he assumed the throne, because he had earlier held that position.

匍   pú   MC bu
1. (bn.) ～匐 *púfú* (MC bu-bjuwk), creep and crawl, drag along.

墣   pú   MC phuwk
1. clod or clump of earth.

襥   pú   MC bjowk
1. men's formal headgear in square shape and 2 tiers, the top tier being set back from the front.

2. (med.) ～頭 *pútóu*, men's headwrap consisting of 4 bands of silk, wrapped so as to have 2
bands twisted around the crown of the head and
the tails of 2 bands hanging down in back.
3. kerchief, throat-band.

璞　pú　MC phaewk
1. crude matrix of jade or other precious stone;
unworked, undressed, or uncarved block of a
precious object.
   a. simple, unadorned, unpolished; plain;
   unaffected, natural.
2. dried rat-meat.

菩　pú　MC bu
1. (Budd.) ～薩 *púsà* (MC bu-sat), trsc. of
Skt. *bodhisattva*, a being who has achieved
enlightenment but chooses out of compassion to remain in the world; (Budd.) ～提 *pútí*
(MC bu-dej), trsc. of Skt. *bodhi*, enlightenment, awakened, perfect knowledge of the true
dharma.

葡　pú　MC bu
1. (med.) (bn.) ～萄 or ～桃 *pútáo* (MC
bu-daw), grapevine; grape; grape-wine; all with
exotic associations with the Western Regions
(*xìyu* 西域).
   a. (med.) ～桃髻 *pútáojí*, Tang children's
   hairstyle made up of many small ringlets.

蒲　pú　MC bu
1. sweet-flag (*Acorus calamus*), also 菖～
chāngpú, a wetland grass, used apotropaically;
the latter also cattail (*Typha latifolia*) or bulrush
(*Typha minima*).
2. ～柳 *púliǔ*, purple willow, purple osier (*Salix
sinopurpurea*), deciduous shrub that produces
small purple catkins in early spring.
3. ～葵 *púkuí*, Chinese fan palm, fountain palm
(*Livistona chinensis*).
4. ～桃 *pútáo*, rose-apple (*Syzgium jambos*).
5. (bn.) ～伏 or ～服 *púfú* (MC bu-bjuwk),
creep and crawl; ⊙ 匍匐 *púfú*.

酺　pú　MC bu
1. imperially authorized period of general celebration to indulge in food and drink, connected
with events such as installation of imperial heir,
general amnesties, etc.; days of public celebration or public license, revelment.
   a. refection, widespread drinking.

鏷　pú　MC bowk
1. raw, unpolished, unrefined bronze or iron.

pǔ

圃　pǔ　MC puX
1. vegetable garden; orchard for fruit trees.
   a. gardener, grower.
2. threshing floor, e.g. 場～ *chǎngpǔ*, often of
garden that in autumn was tamped or pounded
hard.

普　pǔ　MC phuX
1. pervasive, widespread; universal; all of, the
entirety of; e.g. ～地 *pǔdì*, the whole earth;
～恆 *pǔhéng*, always; ～及 *pǔjí*, and all, extending to all; ～達 *pǔdá*, reaching everywhere.
   a. impartial, equally; e.g. (Budd.) ～等心
   pǔděngxīn, impartial mind.
2. (med.) ～嵐 *pǔlán* (MC phuX-lom), alt. trsc.
equiv. 拂林 *fúlín* (MC phjut-lim) ref. to eastern
Roman empire, i.e. Byzantium.

朴　pǔ　MC phaewk
1. large section of timber.
   a. large, substantial.
2. ⊙ 樸 *pǔ* 1, plain, simple; unaffected; natural.
3. (med.) (bn.) ～簌 *pǔsù* (MC phaewk-suwk),
falling in profusion; also, onom. of birds' wings
in brisk flight, "pfuut-suut."
   pò　MC phaewk
1. the bark of a tree.
   pū　MC phuwk
1. ⊙ 扑 *pū* 1, strike, beat, cudgel.

樸　pǔ　MC phaewk
1. plain, simple; unadorned, untouched, unaffected; natural, unadulterated; pure.
   a. original condition before influenced or
   affected by anything outside; basic state.
2. unworked wood.
3. sweet oak (*Quercus dentata, Q. obovata*).

浦　pǔ　MC phuX
1. riverbank, river margin.
2. estuary; inlet, bay, cove.
3. (med.) surface of a river.

溥　pǔ　MC phuX
1. large; vast, immense; substantial.
2. ⊙ 普 *pǔ*, widespread, pervasive, all of; 浦 *pǔ* 1,
riverbank.

fū   MC phju
1. ⊙ 敷 *fū*, spread out, lay out; exhibit.

pò   MC phak
1. (bn.) ～漠 *pòmò* (MC phak-mak), clipping and skimming the surface, like the wings of waterfowl; also, broad and boundless.

譜   pǔ   MC puX
1. ledger, systematic written record or register of categorized things, such as genealogy, tax rolls, musical repertoire, *catalogue raisonée*.
    a. (med.) orderly explanatory description of techniques, such as for composing certain styles of verse.

pù

曝   pù   MC buwk
1. expose to the sun, apricate; dry in the sun; adure.
    a. expose, reveal, bring out in the open.

瀑   pù   MC buwk
1. spraying or spewing water; waterfall, cascade; cmpd. ～布 *pùbù*, "sheet of spray," waterfall.

bào   MC bawH
1. spume, froth, foam; spray.

Q

qī

七   qī   MC tshit
1. seven(th).
    a. ～星 *qīxīng*, "seven stars," ～宮 *qīgōng*, "seven palaces," ～闕 *qīquē*, "seven pylons," ～曜 *qīyào*, "seven scintillances," all ref. to the 7 stars of the Dipper, the latter term also ref. to sun, moon, and 5 naked-eye planets; ～元 *qīyuán*, seven principals, i.e. sun, moon, and 5 naked-eye planets; also (Dao.), esoteric term for 2 eyes, 2 ears, 2 nostrils, and mouth; (Budd.) ～垢 *qīgòu*, 7 defilements, i.e. desire, illusion, doubt, contempt, arrogance, sloth, parsimony; (Budd.) ～覺 *qījué*, trns. Skt. *saptabodhyangāni*, 7 means of achieving enlightenment.
2. (lit.) a genre of verse exemplified by Mei Sheng's 枚乘 (d. 141 BCE) "Seven Stimuli" (Qi fa 七發).

傶   qī   MC khi
1. rdup., weave drunkenly, stagger.
2. (bn.) ～丑 *qīchǒu* (MC khi-trhjuwX), hideous, unsightly, ugly; ⊙ 魕 *qī*.

凄   qī   MC tshej   ⊙ 淒 *qī*.

妻   qī   MC tshej
1. wife (cf. 妾 *qiè*, concubine).

qì   MC tshejH
1. give a daughter in marriage.
    a. take as a wife.

娸   qī   MC khi
1. ill-featured; repugnant.
    a. vilify; deface, defame.

悽   qī   MC tshej
1. heartsore; rueful; disconsolate; poignant.
    a. (bn.) ～愴 *qīchuàng* (MC tshej-tsrhjangH), heavy-hearted.

慼   qī   MC tshek
1. anxiety, distress(ed); concern(ed) for; fretful; ⊙ 戚 *qī* 3.

戚   qī   MC tshek
1. battle-axe, held in one hand; smaller than 鉞 *yuè*, two-handed halberd-axe.
2. relatives, kin, e.g. 親～ *qīnqī*, kith and kin.
    a. sgl. or rdup., be close to, on intimate terms with, e.g. ～豎 *qīshù*, a (royal) favorite.
3. anxiety, despair(ing), distress; concern for; rdup. lament(able), fretful, restless, in a dither; also, closely or anxiously concerned for.
4. (med.) (bn.) ～促 *qīcù* (MC tshek-tshjowk), ～草 *qīcǎo* (MC tshek-tshawX), urgent, pressing; hastily > transitory, temporary, ephemeral.

敧   qī   MC khje
1. (med.) (bn.) ～嶇 *qīqū* (MC khje-khju), sloped and slanted; precariously inclined.

攲   qī   MC khje
1. slanting, canted, leaning to the side; inclined; oblique.
    a. askew; unstable, unsteady.

2. (bn.) (med.) ～缺 *qīquē* (MC khje-khwet), cleft and cloven.

期　qī　MC gi

1. stipulated period of time; term; phase.
    a. agreed upon time, fixed date or term; appointment.
    b. set a time to meet, rendezvous, tryst.
    c. fix in advance; promise; specify; e.g. ～心 *qīxīn*, set one's mind on.
2. expect, anticipate; hope, look forward to.
    a. forecast, conjecture; know in advance.
    b. time or place toward which one aims; destination.
3. certainly, surely.
4. rdup., onom. of stammering, stuttering.

jī　MC ki

1. a complete period of time; a full year (⊙ 朞 *jī*), month, or day.
2. mourning attire worn for a full year; a year of mourning.

棲　qī　MC sej

1. roost, perch, of birds; roosting place.
    a. nestle, take refuge in; settle in; rest; resting place; sequester.
    b. (bn.) ～遲 *qīchí* (MC sej-drij), linger long; also (med.), downcast and discouraged, syn. ～惶 *qíhuáng*.

xī　MC tshej

1. rdup., fuss and rush, restless excitement.
2. (bn.) ～屑 *xīxiè* (MC tshej-set), hustle and bustle, scurry and hurry.

槭　qī　MC tsjuwk

1. a kind of maple tree or small maple shrub (*Aceraceae*).

sè　MC sreak

1. (med.) of trees, bare, after leaves have fallen.
2. (med.) rdup., onom. of wind creaking the branches of autumn trees.

欺　qī　MC khi

1. cheat, swindle, deceive; to be mistaken; mistake, error, fault.
    a. take advantage of, bully, mistreat.
2. (med.) overpower, overwhelm; excel, surpass.

淒　qī　MC tshej

1. chill(ed), cool(ing).
    a. stingingly cold; shivering with cold, nithering.
    b. (bn.) ～楚 *qīchǔ* (MC tshej-tsrhjoX), "cold and keen," intense, piercing; poignant; acute.
2. rdup., cool and chilling; also, chilling and numbing with sadness; also, condensation of clouds billowing and building up.

漆　qī　MC tshit

1. lacquer tree, varnish tree (*Rhus verniciflua*).
    a. lacquer, varnish; natural resin with yellow-gold tint (not gold-flecked as in late imperial times).

緝　qī　MC tship

1. twist hemp into a skein.
    a. join together; follow up, continue.
2. sew up, mend; repair.

jí　MC tsip

1. ⊙ 輯 *jí* 1, collect; compile; 2, harmony; amity.

萋　qī　MC tshej

1. lush growth of plants.
    a. rdup., lush and luxuriant, thickly thronging; also, billowing and building up of clouds, ⊙ 淒淒 *qīqī*; also (med.), of literary style, sumptuous, elegantly exuberant, profuse and prodigal.
2. (bn.) ～斐 *qīfěi* (MC tshej-phj+jX) interlocking pattern of color on silkstuff.

諆　qī　MC khi

1. ⊙ 欺 *qī*, cheat, deceive; take advantage of, overpower.

jī　MC ki

1. (med.) scheme, plot; plan out.

踦　qī　MC khje

1. one-legged.
    a. lame, walking with a limp; hobble(d); spraddle.
    b. incomplete, deficient, lacking; unfinished.
2. lay particular stress on, rest heavily on, emphasize.

jī　MC kje

1. single, only, sole.
    a. odd number; not balanced > unfortunate, hapless.

jǐ　MC kjeX

1. shin, tibia.

yǐ　MC ngjeX

1. resist, withstand by crooking the knee; stand fast.
2. lean into; rely on, in accord with.

鏚 qī MC tshek

1. ⊙ 戚 qī 1, battle-axe, held in one hand.

魌 qī MC khi

1. cmpd., 〜頭 qītóu, "hideous head," frightful mask worn by the demon impersonator or exorcist (fangxiangshi 方相氏) who ceremonially expels malevolent spirits in various rituals.

    a. unsightly, monstrous; ugly.

qí

亓 qí MC gi ⊙ 其 qí.

其 qí MC gi

1. pronominal substitute for noun or noun-phrase + 之 zhī.

    a. as a possessive pronoun: his, her, their, its, one's; e.g. 鄉人之善者好之，〜不善者惡之 xiāngrén zhī shànzhě hào zhī, qí búshànzhě wù zhī, the good people of the village like him, its bad people detest him; 事父母能竭〜力 shì fùmǔ néng jié qí lì, in serving their parents, they are able to expend to the fullest capacity their effort; 聽〜言而信〜行 tīng qí yán ér xìn qí xíng, having heard his words, I trusted in his actions; 見〜過 jiàn qí guò, to see one's faults.

    b. standing pronominally for SUBJ + 之 zhī in nominalized sentences; e.g. 〜為人也孝弟 qí wéi rén yě xiào tì, As for his behaving the way a person is expected to behave, he is filial and adelphic; 〜如是 qí rúshì, its being like this; 吾不忍〜觳觫 wú bùrěn qí húsù, I cannot bear its frightened and trembling appearance.

    c. in a partitive construction, refers pronominally to a class a subpart of which is the topic: of them, of that, of those, of these; e.g. 可者與之，〜不可者拒之 kězhě yù zhī, qí bùkězhě jù zhī, for those where it is possible, join with them; for those of them where it is not possible, resist them; 美〜一 měi qí yī, make one of them attractive; 〜誰能睹是 qí shéi néng dǔ shì, who among them is able to observe this?

    d. in the phrase 與〜 yǔqí indicates the less preferred option in a kind of comparison: rather than; e.g. 與〜從辟人之士 yǔqí cóng bìrén zhī shì, rather than following individu-als who shun others; 與〜奢 yǔqí shē, rather than being extravagant; → 寧 nìng (níng).

2. modal GP indicating doubt, uncertainty, supposition, subjectivity, or incredulity, either genuine or as a rhetorical expression of deference or politeness, frequently in rhetorical questions: ought, should, perhaps, likely, must, possibly; e.g. 不在此，〜在異國 búzài cǐ, qí zài yìguó, they are not located here; [I suppose that] they must be in a different state; 人〜賤我乎 rén qí jiàn wǒ hū, are the people likely to disparage us?; 樂〜可知 yuè qí kězhī, perhaps the music can be known; 〜何以免乎 qí héyǐ miǎn hū, how could he possibly avoid it?

圻 qí MC gj+j

1. royal domains; the capital city and environs; ⊙ 畿 jī.

    a. an area 1,000 li in circumference.

2. riverbank, shore.

3. fissure, rift; division.

    yín MC ngj+n

1. ⊙ 垠 yín, limit, boundary.

埼 qí MC gje

1. indented angle of a cliff or riverbank, bight.

奇 qí MC gje

1. singular; uncommon, not to be paired, nonpareil; rare; remarkable; wondrous.

    a. irregular; extraordinary, strange, curious; deviating; ant. 正 zhèng, right, regular.

    jī MC kje

1. odd number; single; ant. 偶 ǒu, even number.

    a. surplus, remainder, fraction(al); leftover; extra.

    b. 數〜 shùjī, bad luck, unlucky; ill-fortuned.

岐 qí MC gjie

1. bend or angle in a mountain; bight.

    a. (bn.) 〜嶷 qíyí, ⊙ 崎嶷 qíyí, → 崎 qí.

2. ⊙ 歧 qí, branching road, forking path; diverge(nt).

崎 qí MC khje

1. sloping, slanting.

    a. (bn.) 〜嶇 qíqū (MC khje-khju), sloped and slanted, precariously inclined, unsteady and uneven; a rugged mountain path > hobble along, rough going.

    b. (bn.) 〜嶷 qíyí (MC khje-ngi), precociously intelligent; also, straddle and stand firm.

憏　qí　MC dzej
1. angry, wrathful.

旂　qí　MC gj+j
1. flag decorated with dragons and with grelots attached to the pole .
2. ⊙ 旗 *qí*, banner, flag; standard.

旗　qí　MC gi
1. banner, flag, streamer.
    a. guidon, standard; rallying point.
    b. sign, emblem, marker; guidepost, indicator.
2. flag decorated with bear and tiger.

萁　qí　MC gi　⊙ 棋 *qí*.

棋　qí　MC gi
1. name of board game, "encirclement chess" (圍 ～ *wéiqí*) or go (Jpns.); to play this game.
    a. the board or stones used in the game; e.g. ～子 *qízǐ*, draughtsmen, go stones; ～峙 *qízhì*, "chessmen-studded," i.e. soldiers everywhere.
    jī　MC ki
1. foundation, basis.

歧　qí　MC gjie
1. branching road, forking path.
    a. branch off, fork; diverge(nt), bifurcate.

琦　qí　MC gje
1. precious or rare stone.
    a. rare, precious; incomparable.
2. ⊙ 奇 *qí*, uncommon, singular; strange, curious.

琪　qí　MC gje
1. white-colored precious stone, snow-gem.
    a. snow-gem tree (of fable); also, syn. 楠 *nán*, nandin tree (*Nandina domestica*), medium-sized evergreen with white flowers in early summer.

瑧　qí　MC gi
1. jade decoration on leather cap.

畦　qí　MC hwej
1. unit of land traditionally equivalent to 50 *mǔ* 畝; a plat.
2. bounded plot of land.
    a. the plantings that demarcate the plot.

疷　qí　MC gjie
1. malady, ill(ness).

碁　qí　MC gi　⊙ 棋 *qí*.

碕　qí　MC gje
1. folded or undulating mountain ridges.
    a. ⊙ 埼 *qí*, cliffside or riverbank bight.
    qǐ　MC khjeX
1. (bn.) ～礒 *qǐyǐ* (MC khjeX-ngjeX), rough and ragged, strewn and scattered, of mountainside rocks.

祁　qí　MC gij
1. grand, vast.
    a. rdup., lushly teeming; also, softly and gently.
2. female elaphure, doe.
3. ～連 *qílián*, Xiongnu word for "heaven"; also, mountain range in southern Xinjiang.

祇　qí　MC gjie
1. chthonian spirits, spirits of the earth.
    zhǐ　MC tsye
1. merely, only, just; still. N.B. Through the Tang this graph (or 祇 *zhī* or 秖 *zhī*) is usu. found for the meaning now associated with 只 *zhǐ* which graph was not commonly used with this meaning until after the Tang.

祈　qí　MC gj+j
1. obsecrate, supplicate, pray for, implore, beseech.
    a. request, ask for; beg for.
2. rdup., slowly and steadily, unhurried.

祺　qí　MC gi
1. good fortune, prosperity; fortunate, lucky.
2. ～然 *qírán*, serenely, calmly, composedly.

綦　qí　MC gi
1. mottled gray, deep gray; pallid.
    a. (med.) pale green, sea-green, pea-green.
2. shoelace; sandal cord.
3. footprint, track.
4. (med.) jade stud or button on front of cap.
5. ⊙ 極 *jí*, extremely, very much, to the highest degree; 忌 *jì*, avoid, shun, be on one's guard against.
6. ～毋 *qíwù*, a bisyllabic surname.

耆 qí MC gij

1. aged, advanced in years, senior; e.g. 〜舊 *qíjiù*, seniors and elders; 〜艾 *qíài*, oldster with moxa-gray hair.
2. strict, rigid; surly.
3. disapprove, disfavor; punish.

shì MC dzyijH

1. ⊙ 嗜 *shì* be fond of, keen on, addicted to, have a weakness for.

zhǐ MC tsyijX

1. reach, achieve, attain.
   a. to send, extend, present, offer up.

臍 qí MC dzej

1. navel, umbilicus.

其 qí MC gi

1. bean-stalks.

jī MC ki

1. fine bean-leaves used for plaiting containers such as quivers.

蘄 qí MC gi

1. angelica (*Angelica sinensis*), autumn-flowering herb, also 白〜 *báiqí*, 山〜 *shānqí*; syn. 當歸 *dāngguī*.
2. horse's bit.
3. ⊙ 靳 *jìn*, breast-strap of horse > harness; 祈 *qí*, obsecrate, supplicate, implore, beseech; 圻 *qí*, limit, boundary.

蚑 qí MC gjie

1. scramble, scuttle, scoot.
2. small, long-legged spider.
3. leech.

蠐 qí MC dzej

1. woodlouse.
2. (bn.) 〜螬 *qícáo* (MC dzej-dzaw), larvae of scarab bettle (*Holotrichia diomphalia*).
3. (bn.) 蠐〜 *qiúqí*, → 蝤 *qiú*.

跂 qí MC gjie

1. an extra toe; a foot with an extra toe.
2. three-pointed, triangle(d).
3. ⊙ 蚑 *qí*, scramble, scuttle, scoot.

qǐ MC khjieX

1. ⊙ 企 *qǐ*, get up on tiptoes, stand on tiptoe in anticipation or desire.

qì MC khjieH

1. sit with one's feet hanging down.

jī MC gjaek

1. ⊙ 屐 *jī*, toothed clogs, *geta* (Jpns).

zhī MC tsye

1. (bn.) 踞〜 *zhīzhī*, → 踞 *zhì* (*dì*).

錡 qí MC gje

1. 3-footed boiler or saucepan.
   a. canted or unbalanced-looking mountain bluffs.
2. chisel.

yǐ MC ngjeX

1. weapon-rack, weapon-stand.

頎 qí MC gj+j

1. imposing in stature.
2. tall and slender; lanky.

kěn MC khonX

1. devoted; profoundly moved.

騎 qí MC gje

1. mount or ride a horse, ride astride.
   a. sit astride, straddle.

jī MC gjeH

1. horseman, rider; cavalier, chevalier; cavalry.
   a. saddled horse; mount.

騏 qí MC gi

1. black-mottled gray horse.
   a. black and gray dappling.
2. 〜驥 *qíjì*, thoroughbred steed, fine courser; 〜驎 *qílín*, long-galloping steed; also, ⊙ 麒麟 *qílín*, "unicorn," → 麒 *qí*.

鬐 qí MC gij

1. mane of a horse or other quadruped.
2. dorsal fin of a fish.

鰭 qí MC gij

1. fish's fin, esp. dorsal fin.

麒 qí MC gi

1. (bn.) 〜麟 *qílín*, "unicorn"; → 麟 *lín*.

齊 qí MC dzej

1. even, of the same rank/height; equal, equitable; in step with.
   a. bring into line, hold even, regulate, make uniform; adjust, compose; arrange, array; determine.
2. ready, complete; altogether; act in concert, make concerted efforts.

3. nimble, agile; quick.

4. ⊙ 臍 *qí*, navel, umbilicus.

5. name of one of the 7 major states of the Warring States period, largely comprising present-day Shandong.

6. name of 2 early medieval dynasties, Southern Qi 南齊, 479–502, and Northern Qi 北齊, 557–81.

jī　MC tsej

1. ⊙ 躋 *jī*, rise, ascend, climb.

2. ⊙ 齏 *jī*, chopped meat or vegetables preserved with salt or soy sauce and used as condiments; pickled, minced, hashed.

3. (bn.) ～給 *jījǐ* (MC tsej-kip), repartee, quick wit.

jì　MC dzejH

1. ⊙ 劑 *jì* 1, clip, curtail; 2, mix, blend ingredients for food or medicine; seasoning; medicinal dose.

2. (de)limit, distinguish, define, differentiate.

zī　MC tsij

1. lower part of a long garment.

   a. ～衰 *zīshuāi*, mourning garb hemmed with rough hemp.

2. ⊙ 粢 *zī*, broomcorn millet (*Panicum miliaceum*), used in ritual sacrifices.

zhāi　MC tsreaj

1. ⊙ 齋 *zhāi*, ritual purification by fasting, bathing, meditation, etc.

qǐ

乞　**qǐ**　MC khj+t

1. beg, beg for; implore, humbly request, beseech.

   a. beggar, mendicant.

   b. needy, destitute, indigent.

qì　MC khj+jH

1. give, grant, provide, supply.

企　**qǐ**　MC khjieX

1. stand on tiptoe and look, esp. in hope or anticipation.

   a. anticipate, expect(ant), look forward to, desire.

2. stand up straight.

啓　**qǐ**　MC khejX　⊙ 啟 *qǐ*.

啟　**qǐ**　MC khejX

1. open; unfold, unroll; unfasten; disclose; e.g. ～明 *qǐmíng*, opener-of-light, Venus as morning star.

   a. open up or develop land.

   b. open out, give guidance, teach; enlighten.

2. start, begin, initiate.

   a. designation for fortnightly period that begins the seasons of spring and summer.

3. expound, expatiate; put forward, announce, declare, inform; show, disclose, reveal, expose.

4. (lit.) a communication in form of a letter, usu. official, from inferior to superior; write such a letter.

   a. thank-you note.

5. kneel resting on one one's haunches or heels with torso upright; kneel upright.

6. left flank of army formation (cf. 肢 *qū*, right flank).

屺　**qǐ**　MC khiX

1. hill or mountain denuded of vegetation, bare mound.

杞　**qǐ**　MC khiX

1. sgl. or ～柳 *qǐliǔ*, purple willow, purple osier (*Salix purpurea*).

2. sgl. or 枸～, 苟～ *gǒuqǐ*, wolfberry, boxtree, boxthorn (*Lycium chinense, Lycium barbarum*).

棨　**qǐ**　MC khejX

1. wooden tally or identification notice allowing passage into or across a guarded location.

2. sgl. or ～戟 *qǐjǐ*, wooden halberd with attached flag or streamer, carried before officials as standard of honor when traveling.

綺　**qǐ**　MC khjeX

1. monochrome, usu. white, patterned tabby-silk; warp-faced tabby with 3/1 twill.

   a. monochrome brocade.

   b. sericeous; damascened.

2. lacework, filigree, tracery patterning; e.g. ～羅 *qǐluó*, filigree and gauze, silks and chiffons; ～窗 *qǐchuāng*, silk-traced window, traceried window.

   a. reticulate(d), delicate, intricate; exquisite; precious, rare in quality or workmanship.

   b. frilly; frivolous, excessive or overdone trim.

腒　**qǐ**　MC khejX

1. calf of the leg, fat of the leg.

豈　**qǐ**　MC khj+jX

1. used in rhetorical questions to imply that the speaker knows that what is being asked or

proposed is unlikely or impossible, or to give the impression that it ought to be unlikely or impossible; in effect, to ask a question, the answer to which the speaker assumes will be some form of "no"; e.g. ～至此哉 *qǐ zhì cǐ zāi*, has it (really) come to this!? (implying "No, it cannot have come to this"); 吾～敢 *wú qǐ gǎn*, how would I dare?; ～有此理 *qǐ yǒu cǐ lǐ*, can there (really) be such a thing/reason? (implying "of course not!"); often translatable as "surely not…!?"

起   qǐ   MC khiX

1. stand up, get up, rise; stand upright; e.g. ～居 *qǐjū*, arising and resting, activity and repose, esp. ref. to emperor's daily affairs; also, gen. term for deportment.
    a. rise, surge, ascend; prosper, flourish.
    b. arise, emerge, appear.
    c. begin, start, launch, initiate, undertake, set about doing.
    d. protrude; raised, elevated; convex, in relief.
    e. set out, embark on a journey.
2. help up, raise, lift up.
    a. heal, cure.
    b. produce, engender; give rise to, set in motion, stimulate, arouse, agitate.
    c. formulate, conjecture.
    d. set up, establish, erect; build, construct.
    e. promote, appoint, call to office, employ.
3. originate, stem from, derive from.
4. (med.) (GP) verbal suffix indicating action of VB has begun or is now possible.
5. (med.) "call up," in Tang times the recalling of an official in mourning to resume his previous post or take on a new position.

芑   qǐ   MC khiX

1. white millet, proso millet (*Panicum miliaceum*).
2. rehmannia, Chinese foxglove (*Rehmannia glutinosa*), syn. 地黃 *dìhuáng*.
3. ⊙ 杞 *qǐ*, purple willow, purple osier (*Salix purpurea*); wolfberry, boxtree (*Lycium chinense, Lycium barbarum*).

跂   qǐ   MC khjieX   ⊙ 企 *qǐ*.

qì

器   qì   MC khijH

1. implement, utensil, instrument.
    a. use as a tool, to implement, apply.
    b. any formed item or thing.

2. vessel, utensil used as a container or receptacle.
    a. capacity, capability, potential; utility, competence, esp. as (potential) minister of state.
    b. intellectual or spiritual capacity; magnanimity.
    c. precious vessel indicating rank or official position, insignia.
    d. assess the value of, appreciate, esteem, regard highly.
    e. internal organs, viscera.

契   qì   MC khejH

1. inscribe with a knife on tortoiseshell or bone.
    a. writing inscribed on tortoiseshell or bone.
    b. carve, engrave; notch; cf. 鍥 *qiè*.
2. written agreement, contract, pact, covenant; tally, proof; certify, certificate; enter into an agreement, make a contract.
    a. form an alliance, agree (upon), cooperate, complement each other; associate, confidant(e), kindred spirit; be meet for, agreeable to; e.g. 吾～ *wúqì*, my own counterparts, those with whom I agree.
    b. bond of affection, shared feelings.
    c. (med.) come to understand, recognize the meaning of; commit oneself to.
3. rdup., separated far and long; also, sad and sorrowful.
4. (med.) juncture, turning point, critical moment.
5. (med.) ～丹 *qìdān* (MC khejH-tan), name of a northern people, Khitan, founders of the Liao dynasty (907–1125). N.B. The word "Khitan" is probably the origin of the word "Cathay."

qiè   MC khet

1. (bn.) ～闊 *qièkuò* (MC khet-khwat), work hard, toil and moil; also, break apart, feeling broken in two or shattered by separation, woebegone and disconsolate; also (med.), fit together, form a bond of friendship.
2. (med.) ⊙ 挈 *qiè* to hold, take.

愒   qì   MC khjejH

1. ⊙ 憩 *qì*, rest, repose; catch one's breath.

kài   MC khajH

1. neglect(ful), waste(ful); idle.
2. covet, desire; impatient for.

hè   MC xat

1. fearful, timorous.

憩   qì   MC khjejH

1. to rest, repose; catch one's breath.

棄　qì　MC khjijH

1. throw away, discard; put aside, leave behind; abandon, forsake; renounce, reject, abolish, get rid of; annul.
2. forget; overlook, disregard.
3. (Budd.) trns. Skt. *pārājika*, eject from the monastic community.

氣　qì　MC khj+jH

1. effluvium, vapor(ous); fumes.
    a. exhalation, breath(e).
2. vital breath, pneuma, energizing breath, life-force, material force. The force, characterized by a blending of *yin* and *yang*, that animates each living creature and also runs through the inanimate universe; regarded as hybrid or dual in nature, described as neither just matter nor just energy, or rather as matter-energy. Different compositions of *qi*, from the most light and rarefied to the most heavy and substantial, make up the "myriad things" (*wanwu* 萬物) that exist; *qi* is the basic constituent element of the universe.
    a. vitality, energy; zest, spirit; zeal, gusto.
    b. inspiration; aspiration.
    c. power, strength; impelling force.
3. air, aura, atmosphere; climate, weather.
    a. any of the 24 fortnightly periods or "nodes" (*jie* 節) of the solar year.
    b. flavor; smell, scent.
4. disposition, mood, spirit; temper(ament); mettle, fortitude.
    a. style, manner, mode, of writing or of behavior, esp. as revealing of individual character.

　　xì　MC xj+jH

1. ⊙ 餼 *xì* 1, present living animals or uncooked grain to someone, to be used as sacrificial offerings.

汔　qì　MC xj+t

1. dry up, run dry; evaporate.
    a. finish, come to an end, complete.
    b. completely, entirely.
    c. finally, after all.
2. almost, nearly, on the point of; cog. 幾 *jǐ*.
    a. (med.) till, until.

泣　qì　MC khip

1. weep, shed tears, esp. silently or softly.
    a. tears.
    b. tearful; flebile.

　　lì　MC lip

1. violent or heavy, of wind.

　　sè　MC srip

1. ⊙ 澀 *sè*, rough, of a person's pulse.

湆　qì　MC khip　⊙ 滊 *qì*.

滊　qì　MC khip

1. gravy, fatty broth.

炁　qì　MC khj+jH

1. ⊙ 氣 *qì* 2, vital breath, pneuma, life force.

甋　qì　MC khjejH

1. (med.) earthenware jug or container.

　　yì　MC ngejH

1. shatter(ed), shiver(ed); crack(ed), smash(ed).

砌　qì　MC tshjeH

1. brickwork, paving; revetment.
2. inlaid work.

磧　qì　MC tshjek

1. shingle-beach, shingles; e.g. (bn.) ～礫 or ～歷 *qìlì* (MC tshjek-lek), shingles and shards, stony shards; also, rock-strewn ridges.
    a. reef; sandbank.
2. ground bare of vegetation, desert.

葺　qì　MC tship

1. to thatch, esp. a roof.
    a. repair, mend, patch up, trim up.
    b. pile up; overlap, overlay; shingle, cover with; layer(ed).

訖　qì　MC kj+t

1. conclude, wind up; finish, cut off, terminate, bring to an end; settle, stop.
    a. entirely, completely.
2. ⊙ 迄 *qì* 1, arrive at, reach, on the point of; till, until, to.

迄　qì　MC kj+t

1. arrive at, reach; on the point of; till, until.
2. ⊙ 汔 *qì* 1a, finish, come to the end of, complete; b, completely; c (med.), finally, after all.

qià

帢　qià　MC kheap

1. conical-shaped headwear usu. made of dimity and worn by soldiers.

帢　qià　MC kheap　⊙ 帢 *qià.*

恰　qià　MC kheap
1. (med.) just so, precisely, exactly; appropriately, suitably.
    a. (med.) just now, at this moment.
    b. (med.) still, yet.
    c. (med.) only, merely.
    d. (med.) on the contrary, nevertheless.

洽　qià　MC heap
1. soak, permeate, imbue.
2. join, combine, unite; cog. 合 *hé,* 協 *xié.*
    a. accord with, conform to, be in harmony, on good terms.
3. general, ordinary, widespread, universal.

qiān

仟　qiān　MC tshen
1. army contingent of 1,000 men.
    a. commanding officer of such a contingent, chiliarch.
2. ⊙ 阡 *qiān,* north-south path between fields; 芉 *qiān,* prolific growth.

僉　qiān　MC tshjem
1. of all sorts, all kinds, every instance; together; all and sundry.
    a. everyone, everybody; unanimous.

千　qiān　MC tshen
1. thousand(s).
    a. countless, a lot, manifold; e.g. (Budd.) 大〜 *dàqiān,* great chilicosm, mega-chilicosm, countless world-systems, abb. of 三〜大〜世界 *sānqiāndàqiān shìjiè* (Skt. *trisāhas-ramahāsāhasralokadhātu*), trichiliomegachilicosm, the ever-expanding immensity of Buddha-fields, implying nearly infinite space and time; infinite universes.

厱　qiān　MC kheam
1. clefts in hill or riverbank.

嵌　qiān　MC khaem
1. pitted, pocked; cratered, notched; scission; gaping or yawning inward.
    a. (bn.) 〜巖 *qiānyán* (MC khaem-ngaem), fissured and sheer.
2. recessed, embedded; inlaid.

愆　qiān　MC khjen
1. offense, err(or), mistake; transgress(ion), violation.
    a. exceed, overstep, surpass; excess(ive).
2. debilitating or pernicious illness.
3. (med.) rowdy, disorderly conduct.

慳　qiān　MC khean
1. (med.) frugal, sparing of; parsimonious, stingy, miserly.
    a. (med.) scant, deficient.

掔　qiān　MC khean
1. firm, solid; make secure.
2. eliminate; abolish; put aside.
3. ⊙ 牽 *qiān,* lead, pull, tug with a rope; lead out, guide, direct.
        wàn　MC 'wanH
1. ⊙ 腕 *wàn,* the wrist.

搴　qiān　MC khjen
1. pick up, pick out; choose, select.
2. ⊙ 褰 *qiān* 2, pull up, pinch together, pluck up; lift up, gather up.

攓　qiān　MC khjen
1. pick out, pull out; select.
2. to slight, neglect; set aside.
3. ⊙ 褰 *qiān* 2, lift the skirts.

樿　qiān　MC tshjen
1. (bn.) 桾〜 *jūnqiān,* → 桾 *jūn.*

汧　qiān　MC khen
1. jetting water; spout, spurt.
    a. pool or small lake where a river's overflow has collected; basin, reservoir.

牽　qiān　MC khen
1. pull, drag, haul, tug with rope or cord; e.g. 〜鈎 *qiāngōu,* tug-o'war.
    a. domestic animals that can be pulled forward with a rope: cattle, sheep, pigs.
    b. to lead forward, guide, conduct.
    c. 〜牛 *qiānniú,* Ox-puller, Ox-leader, He who Leads an Ox by a Rope, the star Altair (α Aquilae), often called "Herd Boy," but he has no herd.
2. draw into, mix up in, implicate, involve; compromise.
3. bind(ing), bind up, bind together.

簽　qiān　MC tshjem

1. ⊙ 籤 *qiān*, bamboo slip > label, tag; counting stick; oracle slip; clepsydra marker.
2. vouch for by signing name, endorse; voucher.

籤　qiān　MC tshjem

1. pointed and inscribed bamboo slip.
   a. label, tab, marker, tag, esp. index-label used for books; also (med.), affixed label on clepsydra with graduated markings indicating durations of time.
   b. counting sticks.
   c. oracle slips used in temples.
2. (med.) insert(ion) with needle-shaped bamboo wand, pierce.

芊　qiān　MC tshen

1. rdup. or ～眠, ～綿 *qiānmián* (MC tshen-men), lushly clustering, thickly thriving, densely proliferating, leafy shade.

騫　qiān　MC khjen

1. trousers, pants, leggings.
   a. lower garment, skirt.
2. pull up, pinch together, pluck up, as lifting or hitching up one's clothes, drawing or furling curtains.
   a. shrink together, contract.
3. (med.) unfold, lay out, open out.

詓　qiān　MC khjen　⊙ 愆 *qiān*.

謙　qiān　MC khem

1. sgl. or rdup., unpretentious, unpresuming, unassuming, unaffected; diffident, acquiescent; verecund(ous).
2. "modesty," name of 15th hexagram of the *Yijing*.
3. ⊙ 嫌 *xián*, demur, be averse to; 慊 *qiè*, pleased, satisfied, contented.

遷　qiān　MC tshjen

1. transfer, relocate, transport.
   a. transport goods to sell.
2. transfer from one official posting to another.
   a. usu. of higher rank; promote, promotion.
   b. transfer to a less desirable posting with demotion in rank > banish, send away in punishment.
3. displace, divert.
   a. separate, disperse.

4. change, transform, modify; reform, change for the better.
   a. be transported in spirit; exhilarated.

鉛　qiān　MC ywen

1. lead (metal).
   a. ～丹 *qiāndān*, minium; ～黃花 *qiānhuáng-huā*, massicot.
   b. (med.) ～華 *qiānhuá*, lead-based yellow-tinted powder cosmetic used on women's forehead.
2. through med. times often syn. 錫 *xī*, tin.

阡　qiān　MC tshen

1. longitudinal path between cultivated fields; balk, cross-path, terry; cf. 陌 *mò*, latitudinal path between fields.
   a. small path; footpath, footway.
   b. by metonymy, fields, countryside.
2. (med.) path leading to a tomb; the tomb itself.
3. (bn.) ～眠, ～綿 *qiānmián* (MC tshen-men), lushly clustering, thickly thriving, densely proliferating, leafy shade; ⊙ 芊 *qiān*, rdup. with this meaning.

騫　qiān　MC khjen

1. defect(ive); fault, flaw.
   a. deficient, wane, be lacking; diminish(ed); impair(ed); perish.
2. arch the head, lift the head.
   a. prance; curvet, frolic.
3. scared, startled; flinch, start.
4. ⊙ 搴 *qiān*, pick up, pick out; choose; 騫 *qiān* 2, lift the skirts; 愆 *qiān*, err(or), offense.

qián

乾　qián　MC gjen

1. indicative of all images and qualities identified with *yang*: the generative, energetic, creative; potent; potency; masculine; light, heat, etc.; ant. 坤 *kūn*; e.g. ～坤 *qiánkūn*, potent and latent, generative and receptive, Caelum and Terra.
   a. esp. associated with heaven > empyreal, supernal.
2. one of the 8 fundamental trigrams underlying the *Yijing*'s 64 hexagrams, made up of 3 unbroken lines.
   a. name of 1st of the *Yijing*'s 64 hexagrams; represents supreme *yang*.

gān   MC kan

1. dry out; dry, arid; ant. 濕 *shī*, wet, moist.
2. (med.) barren; bare, exposed.

前   qián   MC dzen

1. in front of; before, in space; front, fore, fore-front; ant. 後 *hòu*, behind, at the back, in the rear.
   a. frontward, forward; go ahead, go before; advance; guide, lead.
   b. appear before, have audience with.
2. before, in time; former(ly), earlier, prior; past; ant. 後 *hòu*, after, later.

拑   qián   MC gjem

1. tuck under one's arm, clasp, grasp.
2. pinch, clamp, clench as with pincers or tongs.
   a. pinch closed, close off; e.g. ～ 口 *qiánkǒu*, clench one's mouth, i.e. choke back words, bite one's tongue.

捷   qián   MC gjen

1. raise up, lift.
2. plant firmly, set upright; erect, build.
3. place or carry on the shoulders; to shoulder.
   jiàn   MC gjonH
1. close up, shut tight; bury.
2. establish a fiefdom.

潛   qián   MC dzjem

1. submerge(d); below the surface of water or ground.
   a. latent, implicit; unnoticed.
   b. covert, undercover; surreptitious, furtive(ly); stealth(il)y.
   c. lurk beneath, couch; lie in ambush.
   d. (med.) euph. for death; e.g. ～ 逝 *qiánshì*, "swept onward below the current," pass away.
2. hide, conceal; retire from; sink from sight.
3. plunge into water.
   a. plumb the depths; probe.

黏   qián   MC zjem

1. boiled meat.
   shān   MC sraem
1. China fir (*Cunninghamia lanceolata*); syn. 柀 *bǐ*.

箝   qián   MC gjem   ⊙ 拑 *qián*.

虔   qián   MC gjen

1. sgl. or rdup., respect(ful), revere(nce); devout; awe(some).

2. murder, kill, massacre, slaughter.
   a. cut off, slice off; sever; chop.
   b. take away, plunder, loot, capture.
3. a tiger's walk or stalk; menacing.

鈐   qián   MC gjem

1. linchpin or cotterpin holding axle-cap of carriage in place.
2. door-latch, sneck; e.g. ～鎖 *qiánsuǒ*, sneck and lock.
N.B. The meaning "stamp, seal" is found only in late imperial times.

鉗   qián   MC gjem

1. iron collar used as punishment to squeeze a criminal's neck, neck-vise.
   a. wring, twist; constrict, confine.
   b. force, compel by squeezing toward a single alternative.
   c. ⊙ 拑 *qián* 2, pinch together, clench; close off; seal off > tongs, pliers.
2. ⊙ 拑 *qián* 1, tuck under one's arm; clasp, grasp.

錢   qián   MC dzjen

1. coin, cash; round metal currency (usu. of copper alloy) with square hole in the center for threading on string.
   a. money; fortune, wealth.
2. measure of weight: mace; 1 cash or mace usu. equiv. .1 "ounce" (*liang* 兩); in 621 the *qian* was made standard unit of currency, replacing the *wuzhu* 五銖 (→ 銖 *zhū*).
   jiǎn   MC tsjenX
1. metal part of a spade, scuffle, trowel.
   a. by synecdoche, the implement itself.

鱫   qián   MC gjen

1. identification not certain but prob. a kind of loach or perhaps large eel.

黔   qián   MC gjem

1. black; blacken, esp. with soot; dye black, darken.
   a. ～首 *qiánshǒu*, ～黎 *qiánlí*, black-haired, sable-haired, i.e. the common folk.

qiǎn

淺   qiǎn   MC tshjenX

1. shallow, of water; e.g. ～深 *qiǎnshēn*, shallow and deep > pervasive.
   a. superficial, shallow; facile, simple.

2. slight, small; narrow, slim.
   a. insignificant, petty, minor.
3. scant(y), little of, skimpy; negligible; meager; slightly.
4. fading, passing, brief, a drop of time.
5. light, pale, weak, faint, of color.
   jiān　MC tsen
1. rdup., flowing rapidly, plashing and dashing.
   jiàn　MC tsjenH
1. ⊙ 濺 *jiàn*, jet, gush out, splash.

繾　qiǎn　MC khjienX

1. (bn.) ～綣 *qiǎnquǎn* (MC khjienX-khjwonX), near and dear to, inseparably attached; getting on grandly.

譴　qiǎn　MC khjienH

1. censure, reprimand; criticize, reprove, reprehend; cast blame on, denounce.
   a. (med.) degrade in rank, relegate; banish from court.
2. a blameworthy or reprehensible act; offense; fault, crime.

遣　qiǎn　MC khjienX

1. send, despatch; e.g. ～使 *qiǎnshǐ*, despatch an envoy, send a messenger; (med.) ～妾 *qiǎn-qiè*, maidservant sent with the bride.
   a. send off; let go, release.
   b. send away, expel, drive out, banish; demote, relegate.
   c. send away a wife, divorce.
2. (med.) deliver from, eliminate; dispel; unburden oneself from.
   a. (med.) relieve oneself of, esp. feelings; give vent to, get off one's chest; express.
3. (med.) to cause, bring about; allow.
4. (med.) make use of, wield, employ, apply.
   qiàn　MC khjienH
1. convey to the grave, esp. sacrificial goods.

qiàn

俔　qiàn　MC khenH

1. similar to, may be likened to; for example.

倩　qiàn　MC tshenH

1. attractive, charming; winsome.
   a. handsome; pleasing; dignified; gracious, generous.
2. complimentary term for a male: squire, seigneur.

qìng　MC tshjengH
1. ask for something to be done in one's place or as a favor.
2. son-in-law.

傔　qiàn　MC khemH

1. content(ed), pleased; satisfied; ⊙ 慊 *qiè* (*xián*).
2. (med.) follow along with, fall in with; accompany; companion, follower.

塹　qiàn　MC tshjemH

1. moat, trench, fosse; gully; pit, digging.
   a. dig out; hollow.

槧　qiàn　MC tshjemH

1. wooden tablets for writing on; N.B. does not mean "printing block" until after the Tang.

欠　qiàn　MC khjomH

1. yawn; open wide, gape.
   a. showing lack of interest or intelligence.
2. (med.) owe, be in debt to.
   a. to lack, be short of; deficient.

歉　qiàn　MC khjiemX

1. not eat one's fill.
   a. sgl. or rdup., insufficient; inadequate, deficient, lacking, dearth; scant and scarce.
   b. dissatisfied; discontent.
2. crop failure, deficient harvest; dearth of food.

綪　qiàn　MC tshenH

1. ⊙ 蒨 *qiàn* 1a, madder-red, garance, deep reddish-purple; esp. silks dyed this color.
   zhēng　MC tsreang
1. knot up, twist.
   a. turn up, tuck up.

縴　qiàn　MC khenH

1. (med.) rope or cord for leading animals, lead-rope; N.B. does not mean "tow-rope for boats" until after the Tang.

芡　qiàn　MC gjemH

1. prickly waterlily (*Euryale ferox*), with round, very large, spiny leaves that rest on the water's surface, produces bright purple flowers; seeds are edible, also used medicinally; syn. 雞頭 *jītóu*.

茜 qiàn MC tshenH

1. madder (*Rubia cordifolia*), root yielding a red dye, also used medicinally; syn. 蒐 *sōu* 1, 韎 *mèi*.
   a. madder-red, garance, deep reddish-purple.

蒨 qiàn MC tshenH

1. ⊙ 茜 *qiàn*, madder (*Rubia cordifloria*), root yielding a red dye.
   a. madder-red, garance, deep reddish-purple.
2. sgl. or rdup., lushly leaved, greenly growing; also, distinctive, striking.

qiāng

艠 qiāng MC tshjang

1. rdup., onom. of waves crashing against cliff-walls, dashing and battering, in turbulent tumult.

戕 qiāng MC dzjang

1. kill brutally; murder, assassinate.
   a. mutilate, cruelly injure.
2. destroy, ravage, wreak havoc on.

搶 qiāng MC tshjang

1. bump or knock against, butt; collide or clash with.
2. go against, contrary to; struggle against; e.g. ～風 *qiāngfēng*, against the wind; headwind.
   chéng MC dzraeng
1. (bn.) ～攘 *chéngrǎng* (MC dzraeng-nyangX), tumult and turmoil, confusion and chaos, miggle-maggle.

槍 qiāng MC tshjang

1. 2-pronged long-handled wooden staff, usable as weapon or tool.
   a. lance, spear, pike; e.g. 木～ *mùqiāng*, long wooden spears of infantry; 漆～ *qīqiāng*, short lacquered lances of cavalry.
   b. stake, post, pale.
   c. mattock, spiked digging implement.
2. ⊙ 搶 *qiāng* 1, bump against, collide with, clash.
3. (bn.) ～攘 *qiāngxiāng* (MC tshjang-sjang), disordered and unsettled, in disarray; scrambled, hugger-mugger.
   chēng MC tsrhaeng
1. spearhead, esp. as ref. to comet.

瑲 qiāng MC tshjang

1. onom. of tinkling of pendants or of carriage-bells.
   a. (bn.) ～玲 *qiānglíng* (MC tshjang-leng), "ting-a-ling."

羌 qiāng MC khjang

1. ancient name for proto-Tibetan peoples who migrated south from the Kokonor region. In Sui and Tang times the Tibetan Bod peoples were called by the term 吐蕃 *tǔbō* (MC thuX-pa).
2. line-initial exclamatory particle in verse, esp. in *Chuci* 楚辭.

蜣 qiāng MC khjang

1. (bn.) ～蜋 *qiāngláng* (MC khjang-lang), dung-beetle, scarab-beetle, tumble-dung (*Scarabaeidae*).

蹌 qiāng MC tshjang

1. sgl. or rdup., advance or move forward with grace and style, as if to a rhythmic cadence; with a sure step, with assured ease; also, in orderly array, proper sequence. N.B. Meanings associated with speed or unsteadiness do not appear until Song times and later.
2. (med.) (bn.) 踉～ *liàngqiāng*, → 踉 *liàng*.

瑲 qiāng MC tshjang

1. rdup., onom. of rumbling and rattling of chariots; also ⊙ 蹌蹌 *qiāngqiāng*, with assured ease; in orderly array.
2. (med.) (bn.) 踉～ *liàngqiāng*, → 踉 *liàng*.

鎗 qiāng MC tshjang

1. sgl. or rdup., onom. of harmonious sound of bells or other musical instruments; rdup. also ⊙ 蹌蹌 *qiāngqiāng*, move with assured ease; in orderly array, proper sequence.
   a. (bn.) ～玲 *qiānglíng* (MC tshjang-leng), "ting-a-ling."
   N.B. Meanings associated with weapons not attached to this graph till after the Tang.
   chēng MC tsrhaeng
1. (med.) tripod warming pot for food or wine.

鏘 qiāng MC tshjang

1. onom. of clink of metal or jade.
2. rdup., onom. of jing-jangle of carriage-bells, the tink-clink of pendants; also, towering aloft, high in the sky; also, with ease and grace.

qiáng

嬙 qiáng　MC dzjang
1. in pre-Han times, court lady immediately in rank below consort (*fei* 妃), with authority to direct others.

廧 qiáng　MC dzjang　⊙ 牆 *qiáng*.

強 qiáng　MC gjang
1. strong, powerful, vigorous; forceful; ant. 弱 *ruò*, weak.
  a. dominant, prepotent; capable of extensive mastery; e.g. ～記 *qiángjì*, powerful or formidable memory.
  b. strengthen, fortify, reinforce; e.g. (med.), ～處 *qiángchù*, strong point, forte; point to be stressed.
  c. firm, determined, steadfast; capable of enduring; stubborn, rigid.
  d. fearsomely strong, violent, tyrannical.
  e. (med.) with decided purpose, intentionally, particularly.
2. (med.) excess, surplus, more than; X and to spare; e.g. ～半 *qiángbàn*, more than half.
  a. (med.) very much, very many; deeply.
    qiǎng　MC gjangX
1. put strong effort into; forcibly.
  a. strongly urge, impel, force; perforce, oblige(d) to VB.

彊 qiáng　MC gjang　⊙ 強 *qiáng*.

檣 qiáng　MC dzjang
1. mast of a boat.
  a. by synecdoche, a boat.

牆 qiáng　MC dzjang
1. wall of a building, made of earth or brick.
  a. interior wall; screening wall.
  b. fence, fencing.
2. funerary drape, screening off the coffin.

薔 qiáng　MC dzjang
1. (med.) ～薇 *qiángwéi*, multiflora rose, hedgerose (*Rosa multiflora*).

qiǎng

繈 qiǎng　MC kjangX
1. ⊙ 鏹 *qiǎng*, cord on which copper cash is strung; string of cash; 襁 *qiǎng*, wrap or sling for carrying infant on one's back.

襁 qiǎng　MC kjangX
1. wrap or sling for carrying an infant on one's back.
  a. carry in a sling.
2. ～褓 *qiǎngbǎo*, swaddling clothes; wrap an infant in swaddling.
3. (med.) ⊙ 鏹 *qiǎng*, cord on which copper cash is strung; a string of cash.

鏹 qiǎng　MC kjangX
1. (med.) cord on which copper cash is strung; a string of cash.

qiàng

腔 qiàng　MC kjangH
1. anatomical cavity.
  a. thorax, chest, main body-cavity.
2. (med.) main theme of musical composition.
    kòng　MC khuwngH
1. dried mutton.

qiāo

墝 qiāo　MC khaew
1. land with thin topsoil, unfit for farming; barren, unproductive; ant. 肥 *féi*, fertile.

幧 qiāo　MC tshjew
1. sgl. or cmpd. ～頭 *qiāotóu*, cloth band with which men tie up their hair; headband, headwrap.

敲 qiāo　MC khaew
1. beat on, strike, hit; rap, knock.
2. short stick or cane.

橇 qiāo　MC khjew
1. sledge, for traveling through muddy land; Yu 禹 is said to have used one shaped like a winnowing-fan to move about in his flood-quelling activities.

磽 qiāo　MC khaew
1. hard and stony soil, barren soil; cf. 墝 *qiāo*.
  a. solid; unyielding.
2. fruitless, sterile; unavailing; ruin(ous), fail(ed).

繑 qiāo　MC khjiew
1. belt for trouser legs that are worn over leggings.
    jué　MC kjak
1. ⊙ 蹻 *jué* (*qiāo*), sandals made of hemp fiber or straw.

趫   qiāo   MC khjiew

1. proceed nimbly, with alacrity.

蹻   qiāo   MC khjiew

1. raise one's feet.

    jiǎo   MC kjewX

1. sgl. or rdup., imposing, impressive; also, prideful, overweening.

    jué   MC kjak

1. ⊙ 屩 *jué*, sandals made of straw or hemp fiber.

骹   qiāo   MC khaew

1. shank, the part of the leg from knee to ankle; shinbone, tibia.

    a. gen. term for foot of person, also of implements or furniture.

2. tapered end of a wheel-spoke.

    xiāo   MC xaew

1. (med.) whistling arrow; also, onom. of its sound.

qiáo

僑   qiáo   MC gjew

1. ⊙ 喬 *qiáo* 1, high, tall; upturning.
2. live away from one's homeplace.

    a. one who lives abroad.

3. (med.) cmpd. ～假 *qiáojiǎ*, sham, hypocritical; falsify, dissimulate.

喬   qiáo   MC gjew

1. high, tall; upturning; e.g. ～木 *qiáomù*, trees with upturned branches, i.e. magnificent though offering little shade.
2. hook-tipped, as the barb on a spear.
3. (med.) foolish, silly.
4. a surname.

    jiāo   MC kjew

1. ⊙ 驕 *jiāo*, haughty, arrogant, proud.

嶠   qiáo   MC gjew

1. sharp peak; escarpment, scarp.
2. ⊙ 喬 *qiáo* 1, high, tall; upturning.

憔   qiáo   MC dzjew

1. (bn.) ～悴, ～顇 *qiáocuì*, (MC dzjew-dzwijH), careworn; wan and thin, haggard and harried; wearied and worn out, enervated; frayed and failing; ⊙ 蕉萃 *qiáocuì*.

樵   qiáo   MC dzjew

1. firewood, brushwood.

    a. gather firewood; collector of firewood, woodcutter.

    b. burn firewood, for heating or cooking.

2. ⊙ 譙 *qiáo*, lookout-tower, mirador.

橋   qiáo   MC gjew

1. bridge; arch.

    a. arc(ed), bow(ed).

    b. to bridge, connect two points; build a bridge.

2. shadoof, well-sweep, device for fetching up water with a bucket on one end and a weight on the other. N.B. In pre-imperial texts this is the usual meaning of the graph; meaning 1 becomes common only from the Han onward.
3. crossbeam, lintel.
4. name of mountain in Shaanxi where the mythic Yellow Emperor was reputed to be buried; also of mountain in Hebei where there was a shrine to Yellow Emperor and sage-king Yao.
5. (bn.) 屈～ *juéqiáo*, → 屈 *jué* (*qū*).
6. ⊙ 喬 *qiáo* 1, high, tall; upturning.

瞧   qiáo   MC dzjew

1. (med.) dim-sighted, dull-eyed; strained vision.
2. (med.) take a look at, steal a glance at.

翹   qiáo   MC gjiew

1. long tailfeathers.

    a. tail, of bird or of other objects.

2. lift up or raise, esp. the edge or extremity of; flare(d).

    a. rdup., arching upward, sweeping outward; perilously poised.

    b. reveal, uncover.

    c. (med.) hackles > raise one's hackles.

3. outstanding, pronounced, salient.

苀   qiáo   MC gjiew

1. Chinese mallow (*Malva sinensis*).
2. ⊙ 蕎 *qiáo*, buckwheat (*Fagopyrum esculentum*).

蕎   qiáo   MC gjew

1. sgl. or cmpd. ～麥 *qiáomài*, buckwheat (*Fagopyrum esculentum*).

譙   qiáo   MC dzjew

1. watchtower, lookout tower, mirador.

2. rdup., equiv. 憔悴 *qiáocuì*, careworn, haggard and harried; worn out and wearied; frayed and failing.

qiào　MC dzjewH

1. blame, reprove, reprimand, denounce.
   a. ridicule, sneer at, jeer.

趫　qiáo　MC gjew

1. nimble, agile; energetic, active.
2. hale, healthy; prospering, in the best condition.

qiǎo

巧　qiǎo　MC khaewX

1. skill, dexterity, acumen, artistry, craft.
   a. skillful, dexterous, artful, adept, clever, deft; cunning, canny; nimble, ingenious, quick-witted, smart, shrewd; ant. 拙 *zhuó*, clumsy, inept.
   b. winning, charming; e.g. ～笑 *qiǎoxiào*, a winning smile.
2. cheat, swindle, take in.
3. adept at, good at.
4. (med.) just right, right on time, timely; luckily, fortunately.
5. (bn.) ～老 *qiǎolǎo* (MC khaewX-lawX), hollow and open, emptily agape.

悄　qiǎo　MC tshjewX

1. sad, miserable, distressed, despondent.
   a. rdup., sadly distressed, cheerless and downhearted.
2. (med.) silent, still, quiet, tranquil.
   a. rdup., sinkingly soft; sadly silent, whisperingly still.
3. (med.) fully, entirely; truly, really, quite.

愀　qiǎo　MC tshjewX

1. change color, facially; blanch; look sheepish.
2. (bn.) ～愴 *qiǎochuàng* (MC tshjewX-tsrhjangH), downhearted and dejected.

qiào

峭　qiào　MC tshjewH

1. angular, jagged, of mountain cliffs or peaks; precipitous, vertiginous; (e)scarp(ment).
   a. stern, severe, harsh.
   b. (med.) sharp, keen, cutting, piercing, of cold or wind.
   c. (med.) scrawny, scraggy.

2. (med.) (bn.) ～蒨 *qiàoqiàn* (MC tshjewH-tshenH), sharply defined, standing out sharply, strikingly vivid, intensely evident.

帩　qiào　MC tshjewH　⊙ 幧 *qiāo*.

撨　qiào　MC khaewH

1. strike from the side, sideswipe.
   a. poke, prod, jab.

殼　qiào　MC khaewk

1. hard outer skin of object; husk, rind, casing, hull, shell.
   a. (Budd.) ref. unwelcome body of human birth.

竅　qiào　MC khewH

1. aperture, opening, cavity; orifice, esp. orifices of the body; vent-hole; fumarole, of mountain.
   a. dig, bore, drill, or thirl a hole; make an opening, excavate.

蹾　qiào　MC khewH

1. a horse's croup, rump > anus.

鞘　qiào　MC sjewH

1. (med.) sheath, scabbard.

shāo　MC sraew

1. (med.) whip-lash, crack of a whip.

qiē

切　qiē　MC tshet

1. to cut, slice with a knife; e.g. (med.) ～金 *qiējīn*, "cut gold," gold-leaf appliqué (Jpns. *kirikane*).
   a. incise; carve bone or gemstones.

qiè　MC tshet

1. rub, chafe, scour, come in contact with; e.g. ～齒 *qièchǐ*, grind one's teeth.
   a. take a pulse.
2. close to, nearby.
   a. closely; detailed; in depth; e.g. X 之～, X to the extreme.
   b. (med.) suit, fit in.
3. urgent, pressing.
   a. sharp, acute(ly); intense(ly); fierce(ly).
4. incisive(ly); earnest(ly), sincere(ly); heartfelt, "cuts to the quick"; deep(ly), profound(ly); e.g. ～人 *qièrén*, an incisive person.

5. make cutting remarks about; condemn, denounce, criticize.
6. threshold, door-sill.
7. (med.) necessary, important, significant, essential.
  a. (med.) 一～ *yīqiè*, each and every, every one of, the whole of.
8. (med.) rubbed fine > soft, light (of sound); e.g. ～語 *qièyǔ*, quiet conversation, sotto voce; rdup., breathless whispering.
9. ⊙ 竊 *qiè* stealthily, furtively, secretly, in private; humbly, modestly; also, to rob.

qié

伽   qié   MC gja
1. (Budd.) transcription graph for Skt. *ga, gā, gha, ghā, ka, kā*; e.g. (僧)～藍(摩) (*séng*)*qiélán*(*mó*) (MC song-gja-lam-ma), trsc. Skt. (*saṅ*)*ghārām*(*a*), "pleasance of the priestly assembly," i.e. monastery; ～陀 *qiétuó* (MC gja-da), abb. trsc. Skt. *gāthā*, Budd. verse, syn. Ch. trns. 偈 *jì*.
2. ⊙ 茄 *qié* (*jiā*), eggplant.

茄   qié   MC gja   → 茄 *jiā*.

qiě

且   qiě   MC tshjaeX
1. moreover, furthermore, by the same token; e.g. ～子見執政而不違 *qiě zǐ jiàn zhízhèng ér bùwéi*, Moreover, when you see the prime minister you don't turn away; ～不知其在彼乎其在我乎 *qiě bùzhī qí zài bǐ hū, qí zài wǒ hū*, By the same token, I don't know, is it located there or is it located within me?
  a. "even," used as an intensive; e.g. ～不知耳目之所宜 *qiě bùzhī ěrmù zhī suǒyí*, He doesn't even understand what eyes and ears are suitable for.
  b. conjoining predicate adjectives: "both . . . and…" "and…as well"; e.g. 貧～賤 *pín qiě jiàn*, both poor and ignoble; 仁～智 *rén qiě zhì*, humane and knowledgeable as well; 虜多～近 *lǔ duō qiě jìn*, The renegades are both numerous and nearby.
  c. in coordinate verb phrases indicates linked, but non-causal simultaneity or co-occurrence: "in the one case . . . in the other case"; e.g. 子～致我我～言子之奪我珠 *zǐ qiě zhì wǒ, wǒ qiě yán zǐzhi duó wǒ zhū*, You may for your part turn me over [to the authorities]; I for my part will tell of your snatching my pearl; ～引～戰 *qiě yǐn qiě zhàn*, On the one hand leading them away, on the other hand battling with them.
  d. in the second of coordinate VB-phrases indicates an alternative: "or"; e.g. 王以天下為尊秦乎～尊齊乎 *wáng yǐ tiānxià wéi zūn qín hū, qiě zūn qí hū*, Does the king regard the subcelestial realm as esteeming Qin or esteeming Qi?; 是～非耶 *shì qiě fēi yé*, Is it right or wrong?
2. marker of future action: "about to," "shall," "will"; e.g. 我～往見 *wǒ qiě wǎng jiàn*, I shall go to see him; 趙～伐燕 *zhào qiě fá yàn*, Zhao is about to strike at Yan.
  a. about to reach, on the verge of > almost; e.g. 殺其騎～盡 *shā qí jì qiě jìn*, They killed the horsemen almost to a man; 疾～革 *jí qiě jí*, The ailment is on the verge of becoming severe.
    jū   MC tsu
1. numerous, many; ample; manifold.
2. altogether, collectively, in all, completely.
3. dignified; respectful.
4. (lit.) verse-ending particle.

qiè

妾   qiè   MC tshjep
1. concubine; to take a concubine; cf. 妻 *qī*, wife.
  a. female servant, handmaid, attendant, ancilla.
  b. woman's humble self-designation: "your handmaid."

怯   qiè   MC khjaep
1. faint-hearted; timid, timorous, fearful; diffident, shrinking.

愜   qiè   MC khep
1. content(ed), gratified, satisfied; fully at peace; to one's heart's content.
  a. well-disposed, delighted, or eager to do X.
  b. (med.) ～當 *qièdāng*, perfectly arranged, completely apt.
2. (med.) rdup., with all happiness gone, disconsolate and disaffected.

抾   qiè   MC khjaep
1. seize, grasp.

挈　qiè　MC khet

1. take up in the hand; hold suspended.
    a. lift up, raise up.
2. carry with one, take along.
    a. pull along; lead along.
3. rdup., with eager anticipation, nervous excitement; impatiently hurrying.

qì　MC khejH

1. ⊙ 契 *qì* 1, carve, engrave; notch; inscribe on tortoiseshell or bone; 2, written agreement, contract, pact; cooperate, associate, complement.

朅　qiè　MC khjet

1. depart, move away from; leave off, leave behind; quit.
2. stout-hearted, staunch; courage(ous), doughty; full of fight.

hé　MC hat

1. ⊙ 曷 *hé*, interr.: why? what?

竊　qiè　MC tshet

1. steal, rob(ber), snatch, pilfer; thief.
    a. stealthily, furtively, secretly, in private.
    b. encroach on, violate, harm.
2. self-depreciatory adverbial expression of humility: take the liberty of, have the audacity or effrontery to, venture to, be so bold as; with all due respect, with humility or deference.
3. have secret or illicit sexual relations with.

篋　qiè　MC khep

1. small rectangular box with a cover; coffer, case, box, caddy (smaller than a 箱 *xiāng*, chest, cabinet).

踥　qiè　MC tshjep

1. (bn.) ～蹀 *qièdié* (MC tshjep-dep), advance with skittish, jittery steps; impatiently and restively shuffling; trudging drudge-like.

鍥　qiè　MC khet

1. carve, engrave; notch.
2. cut in two.

qīn

侵　qīn　MC tshim

1. invade, attack; intrude on, encroach upon, violate.
    a. to appropriate, arrogate.

b. a celestial body stationary at a certain coordinate earlier than usual and in conjunction or near-conjunction with another situated there, encroach(ment).
2. attack stealthily, without announcement or fanfare (ant. 伐 *fá*, open attack).
3. (advance) by degrees, progressively; slowly, imperceptibly; e.g. (bn.) ～尋 *qīnxún* (MC tshim-zim), bit by bit.
    a. infiltrate, infringe upon, soak into.
4. corrode.
    a. famine year, crop failure.
5. (med.) touching, reaching, near to, closely, e.g. ～夏 *qīn xià*, close on summer, ～夜 *qīn yè*, into the night, toward evening; rdup., packed and piled, massed and bunched.

qǐn　MC tshimX

1. offensively ugly; ill-formed, misshapen.

嶔　qīn　MC khim

1. spiring upward; most precipitous.
    a. (bn.) ～岑 *qīncén* (MC khim-dzrim), ～崎 *qīnqí* (MC khim-khje), steeply climbing, perilously peaked, hazardously high.
2. salient, outstanding; conspicuous.

欽　qīn　MC khim

1. to revere, venerate, hold in awe; esteem, admire.
    a. cautious, circumspect.
2. rdup., onom. sound of a bell, ding-ding; also, troubled and disturbed.
3. twisted, contorted; misshapen.

yín　MC ngim

1. ⊙ 吟 *yín* 2, drone; 3, groan.

衾　qīn　MC khim

1. coverlet, blanket (usu. larger than 被 *bèi*).
2. shroud, winding-sheet of corpse.

親　qīn　MC tshin

1. parents.
2. consanguineous relatives, kin, relationally close; rarely including relatives by marriage.
3. those close to oneself who are practically thought of as kin; emotionally close.
    a. to be close to, fond of, on intimate terms with; akin to; privy to.
4. (ADV) personally, in person.

qìng　MC tshinH

1. ～家 *qìngjiā*, relatives by marriage, in-laws.

駸   qīn   MC tshim

1. rdup., headlong gallop; also, effortless sweep, sweeping rush, hurry-scurry, lickety-split.

qín

勤   qín   MC gj+n

1. to toil, labor, swink; struggle, strain; work till weary; e.g. ～勞 qínláo, toil and travail, swink and sweat.

   a. (Dao.) endeavor, meritorious deeds done for the Celestial Masters community which could be accumulated toward the award of promotion within the church.

2. assiduous, earnest, devoted; zealous, ardor; careful; courteous; e.g. ～懈 qínxiè, at first devoted and then remiss; ～怠 qíndài, first zealous and then idle; (bn.) 慇～ yīnqín, → 慇 yīn.

憅   qín   MC gj+n

1. brave, stout-hearted; intrepid; daring.

勲   qín   MC gj+n   ⊙ 勤 qín.

擒   qín   MC gim

1. to take with force, seize; catch, apprehend, capture; take prisoner.

   a. bring under one's control; captivate.

檎   qín   MC gim

1. (bn.) 林～ línqín (MC lim-gim), red apple (*Pyrus malus*).

琴   qín   MC gim

1. zither, 5- or, most often, 7-stringed instrument without bridges or frets, placed horizontally before one for playing; most often played for oneself or one other person, an instrument to convey one's innermost thoughts; translate as "zither" and distinguish from 瑟 sè ("zithern"), larger zither with bridges, and 箏 zhēng ("cither"), zither of size intermediate between qin and se, with bridges; cmpd. ～瑟 qínsè, "zither and zithern," metaphorical of conjugal harmony or close friendship. N.B. Do not translate any of these as "lute," which is the *pipa* 琵琶, a quite different, round-bodied instrument held before one's chest.

矜   qín   MC gin   → 矜 jūn.

禽   qín   MC gim

1. general ref. to beasts, including quadrupeds, but increasingly in med. period most often birds, avifauna, wildfowl, e.g. ～獸 qínshòu, birds and beasts; 六～ liùqín, "the six fowl" (wildgoose, common quail, eastern quail, pheasant, dove, pigeon).

2. the hunt, to hunt; chase.

3. ⊙ 擒 qín to catch, capture; take prisoner; snare.

秦   qín   MC dzin

1. name of one of the 7 major states in the Warring States period, comprising most of present-day Shaanxi.

2. name of several imperial dynasties, esp. the first (221-206 BCE), assumed to be the source of Central Asian and early European words for "China."

3. 大～ dà Qín, Greater Qin, a "counter-China" in the mythological far west, by Han times confused with the Roman Empire in Asia Minor.

芩   qín   MC gim

1. runner-reed (*Phragmites japonica*), small reed with pinnate leaves, in autumn has white blossoms resembling those of wild rice (*Zizania*).

芹   qín   MC gj+n

1. water-dropwort (*Oenanthe stolonifera*).

螓   qín   MC dzin

1. small cicada with a striped broad head.

2. cmpd. ～首 qínshǒu, descriptive of a woman with attractively broad forehead.

qǐn

寢   qǐn   MC tshimX

1. to lie down to sleep or rest; slumber; to lay down something, let something rest.

   a. to rest, be bedridden.

   b. lay something down, put aside, let it rest, put a halt to.

   c. euph. to be dead, be at perpetual rest.

2. rest-chamber, bedroom, inner chamber; retiring hall.

   a. rear chamber of a (royal) ancestral temple, where ancestor's clothing is kept; main chamber of a royal tumulus.

   b. private apartments.

3. offensively ugly; misshapen.

4. ⊙ 侵 *qīn* 2, gradual(ly).

栔　qǐn　MC tshimX

1. (med.) ～桂 *qǐnguì*, cinnamon tree (*Cinnamomum cassia*), syn. 木桂 *mùguì*.

qìn

沁　qìn　MC tshimH

1. soak into, seep, ooze; penetrate.

2. sound the water, plumb the depths.

qīng

傾　qīng　MC khjwieng

1. incline toward, lean; cant(ed), pitch(ed), tip(ped), slant(ed); e.g. ～危 *qīngwēi*, steeply, sloped, perilously tall; also, hazardous, dangerous.

   a. off-center; improper, incorrect.

   b. lean toward mentally; admire, esteem.

2. overturn, upturn; e.g. ～杯 *qīngbēi*, upturned cup, drink up, "bottoms up."

   a. topple; subvert; e.g. 國～ *guóqīng*, "state-toppler," woman of devastating beauty for whom a ruler might risk everything.

3. pour out, pour down; empty out.

   a. expend, disburse; lay out, give away.

   b. completely, wholly.

4. hold sway over; overpower.

5. (med.) injure, wound > destroy(ed), lost, gone, dead.

卿　qīng　MC khjaeng

1. high official, dignitary.

   a. steward; grandee; "Companion."

2. in early times, respectful term of address: "your lordship."

   a. (med.) term of address from superior to inferior: "you, my dear sir"; also, familiar term of address between equals: "you."

3. ⊙ 慶 *qìng*, felicitous, esp. ～雲 *qīngyún*, felicitous or auspicious clouds.

圊　qīng　MC tshjeng

1. latrine, privy, outhouse.

2. pigsty, often with privy above it.

清　qīng　MC tshjeng

1. clear; free from anything that dims, darkens, or obscures; clarify.

   a. plain, evident, clear-cut, openly discernible; lucid.

   b. limpid, pellucid; transparent.

2. pure; free from impurity or flaw; purify.

   a. rarefied; unmixed, unadulterated; unfiltered.

   b. clean(sed); speckless.

   c. honest; spotless in conduct, irreproachable.

3. fresh(en); bracing.

   a. clear-sounding, vivid.

4. the upper 6 notes of the 12-note gamut of pitches.

5. of excellent, even ideal quality, esp. of government; also, elegant.

6. lucent, luculent; shining.

7. distinctive in isolation; e.g. ～歌 *qīnggē*, unaccompanied song, *a capella*.

蜻　qīng　MC tsheng

1. (bn.) ～蜓 *qīngyán* (MC tsheng-yen), ～蛉 *qīnglíng* (MC tsheng-leng), dragonfly.

　　jīng　MC tsjeng

1. (bn.) ～蛚 *jīngliè* (MC tsjeng-ljet), field-cricket (*Gryllulus chinensis*); syn. 蟋蟀 *xīshuài*.

輕　qīng　MC khjieng

1. light in weight (ant. 重 *zhòng*, heavy).

   a. easily movable; buoyant; airy; lithe, tripsome.

   b. lacking in seriousness; flighty, frivolous.

   c. carefree, however one wishes, casual(ly).

2. treat lightly, make light of, consider of scant importance (ant. 重 *zhòng*, put weight on, consider important); to slight, snub, be rude to; vilipend.

   a. superficial; shallow; slight; of no account; feckless.

3. to smooth, make even or unwrinkled; e.g. ～裾 *qīngjū*, smooth the lapels > "with what composure I can summon."

   a. soothe, lessen the pain or tension of; relieve; e.g. ～暑 *qīngshǔ*, soothe the summer heat.

青　qīng　MC tsheng

1. generally ref. to the glaucophyllous range of color from blue-black to dark-green; associated in *wuxing* correspondences with the phase or agent of wood, the season of spring, direction east, etc.; e.g. ～龍 *qīnglóng*, blue-green dragon, emblematic animal of springtime; also, ref. the eastern quadrant of the sky.

a. dark blue; color of pigment produced from azurite; e.g. 〜丹 *qīngdān*, azurite and cinnabar, blue and vermilion > polychrome painting.
b. blue, azure, as the color of the sky, e.g. 〜天 *qīngtiān*; N.B. 〜雲 *qīngyún*, "clouds in the blue," short for 〜天之白雲 *qīngtiān zhi báiyún*, white clouds in blue sky, not "dark (gray, blue, blue-green) clouds."
c. indigo-blue, color of pigment produced from the indigo (藍 *lán*) plant.
d. blue-glinting, when describing glossy highlights of something luxuriously or deeply black. N.B. *qīng* itself is never "black" or "gray."
2. green, as the color of vegetation, e.g. 〜草 *qīngcǎo*.
3. (bn.) 〜熒 *qīngyíng* (MC tsheng-hweng), palely gleaming, shimmering, twinkling.
4. 〜魚 *qīngyú*, the black carp, black roach (*Mylopharyngodon piceus*; actually dark-green in color); ⊙ 鯖 *qīng*.
5. 〜箱 *qīngxiāng*, celosia, plumed cockscomb (*Celosia argentea*), tropical plant with feathery spikes of usu. red or pink flowers; 〜榨 *qīngzhà*, Père David's maple (*Acer davidii*), small snakebark maple with multiple trunks and long, arching branches; 〜萍 *qīngpíng*, common duckweed (*Lemna minor*).

鯖   qīng   MC tsheng
1. the black carp, black roach (*Mylopharyngodon piceus*; actually dark-green in color).
    zhēng   MC tsyeng
1. (med.) boiled stew of fish and meat.

qíng

勍   qíng   MC gjaeng
1. powerful, strong; fearsome.

情   qíng   MC dzjeng
1. in early texts usu. ref. the genuine or prevailing condition of a subject; disposition (cf. 性 *xìng*, inherent quality, predisposition).
    a. the actual situation; properties; matters; circumstance(s).
2. emotion(s), mood; feelings, sentiments; thoughts; e.g. 無〜 *wúqíng*, insensate, devoid of feeling.

a. affection(s), endearment; liking; e.g. 〜人 *qíngrén*, dear friend.
    b. predilection, tendency, bent; willingness.
3. cognition, sentience; esp. in Budd. contexts, e.g. 有〜 *yǒuqíng*, [all who] have sentience; 〜物 *qíngwù*, sentient beings; 〜照 *qíngzhào*, sentient illumination, i.e. embryonic buddha-nature.

擎   qíng   MC gjaeng
1. lift up, raise; hold up, hold toward.
2. (med.) take away, remove.

晴   qíng   MC dzjeng
1. cloudless, fair(ing) sky, clear(ing); pellucid.

暒   qíng   MC dzjeng   ⊙ 晴 *qíng*.

殅   qíng   MC ging
1. (med.) (bn.) 〜殘 *qínglíng* (MC ging-ling) or 殘〜 *língqíng*, worn out and done in, dead tired, fagged out, played out; also, as if one's soul has gone, spiritless.

黥   qíng   MC gjaeng
1. to brand on the face and color with ink, as judicial punishment.
2. (med.) tattoo, as sign of ownership (as of slaves or concubines) or as voluntary ornamentation.

qǐng

請   qǐng   MC tshjengX
1. request someone to do something or give one something: "I pray you …"
    a. ask instruction of, inquire of.
2. request permission to do something: "permit me to …," "allow me to …" This usage most common in med. times.
    a. (med.) receive, be given, esp. official emolument.
3. pay a call on, pay respects to.
    a. invite, request the presence of.
4. (med.) right of petition regarding judicial sentence.

謦   qǐng   MC khengX
1. 〜欬 *qǐngkài*, cough, clear the throat; also, chatter and laugh.

頃   qǐng   MC khjwiengX
1. hectare, unit of area equiv. 100 *mu* 畝, or to 10,000 square meters (approx. 2.4 acres).

2. interval of time, varying from a short while to a moment (ant. 久 *jiǔ*, a long while).

    a. formerly, some time ago; a while ago, recently, of late, lately.

    qīng　MC khjwieng

1. ⊙ 傾 *qīng* 1, incline toward, lean, slant; off-center, improper.

qìng

清　qìng　MC tshjengH

1. cool; cold.

慶　qìng　MC khjaengH

1. felicitous, felicity; favor accorded by or associated with Heaven, fortuitous.

    a. well-chosen, apt.

2. felicitate, congratulate, celebrate; compliment; wish the best for, salute; acclaim.

磬　qìng　MC khengH

1. lithophone, stone chime, tuned slab of stone shaped like a carpenter's square and suspended from a frame, struck with a mallet, usu. consisting of a group of various sizes and tunings.

    a. ～折 *qìngzhé*, "bent like a lithophone," bow deeply and humbly; also, graceful modulation of mellifluous music.

2. to hang, punishment of death for wrongdoing.

3. (Budd.) bowl-shaped copper percussion instrument in a monastery, struck to call the assembly to attention.

磬　qìng　MC khengH

1. empty (of a container), unfilled; devoid of.

    a. (med.) bare, unaccoutered; e.g ～馬 *qìngmǎ*, untacked horse.

2. use(d) up completely, exhaust(ed), deplete(d), consume(d).

3. ⊙ 磬 *qìng* 1, lithophone, stone chime.

qióng

嬛　qióng　MC gjwieng　⊙ 煢 *qióng*.

㥄　qióng　MC gjwieng　⊙ 煢 *qióng*.

煢　qióng　MC gjwieng

1. brotherless.

    a. alone, by oneself, isolated, unaided; rdup., alone and unaided, on one's own.

璚　qióng　MC gjwieng

1. solar halo; sundog.

    jué　MC kwet

1. ⊙ 玦 *jué*, C-shaped disk of jade or nephrite suspended from belt as ornament; esp. given as token upon leave-taking.

瓊　qióng　MC gjwieng

1. a fine gemstone, usu. reddish in color, perhaps carnelian or sard; other possible renderings: rose-gem, garnet, rhodonite.

    a. descriptive of classic, divine, or fairy beauty; of the highest excellence.

2. (med.) by Tang times often used for whitish gemstone, snow-gem, with connotations of heaven-given purity.

3. ～枝 *qióngzhī*, tallow tree, candleberry (*Sapium sebiferum*), deciduous tree with waxy leaves and waxy-coated seeds; also, cotton tree (*Bombax ceiba*), producing cup-shaped red flowers in early spring, syn. 木棉 *mùmián*.

㷾　qióng　MC gjwieng　⊙ 瓊 *qióng*.

瓊　qióng　MC gjwieng

1. gaze with astonishment; look at with fear.

2. rdup., ⊙ 煢煢 *qióngqióng*, alone and unaided, on one's own.

穹　qióng　MC khjuwng

1. vault(ed), dome(d); arch(ed); lofted in the center with sloping sides; e.g. ～盧 *qióng-lú*, yurt, of northern nomads (MC khjuwng-lu < Sog. *kwn'k'r*, bier, pinnacled building).

    a. the vault of heaven, firmament; e.g. ～蒼 *qióngcāng*, "vaulted cerulean," ～昊 *qióng-hào*, "vaulted brilliance," ～冥 *qióngmíng*, "vaulted gulf"—all ref. heaven, the sky; ～壤 *qióngrǎng*, "firmament and loam," i.e. heaven and earth.

    b. tent(ed); hanging, canopy.

2. deep-cut, plunging; chink(ed).

3. ⊙ 窮 *qióng*, spent, deprived; bereft, destitute; exhaust(ively).

窮　qióng　MC gjuwng

1. go to the end of; come to the last point; end in, end with.

    a. expend(ed), use(d) up; spent, forspent, expire; run through, go(ne) through; complete(ly), thoroughly; utter(ly).

b. consider to the ultimate degree, study with utmost thoroughness.
c. reach the end of one's resources; depleted, destitute, deprived; penury, indigent, in extremity; bereft (of), desperate.
d. at wit's end, at the end of one's rope, last resort.
e. push to the limit; to corner, trap, strand(ed).
f. go on farther and farther toward an ever-receding end; endless; e.g. ～溟 *qióngmíng*, the boundless ocean, Endless Main.
2. adversity, fail(ure).
3. come to the end of, stop, cease.

筇   qióng   MC gjowng
1. (med.) sturdy species of bamboo good for making canes.
   a. (med.) a bamboo cane.

藑   qióng   MC gjwieng
1. ～茅 *qióngmáo*, larger bindweed, hedge bindweed (*Calystegia sepium*).

藭   qióng   MC gjuwng
1. (bn.) 芎～ *xiōngqióng* (MC khjuwng-gjuwng), Szechuan lovage (*Ligusticum chuanxiong*).

蛩   qióng   MC gjowng
1. locust.
2. rdup., Xiongnu name of the wild ass, chigetai; also, fabulous quadruped (usu. ～～駏驉 *qióngqióngjùxū*) said to be swift-running but unable to procure its own food, often paired with 蟨 *jué* whose characteristics are just the opposite, hence they need each other; another explanation says the *qióngqióng* and *jùxū* are 2 animals, one having long forelegs and short hind-legs, the other just the opposite, so one cannot go anywhere without the other; also, sad and sorrowing, hapless and heavy-hearted.
   gǒng   MC kjowngX
   1. (med.) ⊙ 蛬 *gǒng*, field-cricket; syn. 蟋蟀 *xīshuài*.

跫   qióng   MC khaewng
1. onom. of footstep, footfall: "khung," plunk.

邛   qióng   MC gjowng
1. hillock, knoll; mound.
2. melancholy; distress, sadness.
3. ～崍 *qiónglái*, name of moutain range in Sichuan.

qiòng

佢   qiòng   MC khjuwngH
1. small, inconsequential; belittle; be dismissive of, indignant at.

qiū

丘   qiū   MC khjuw
1. hill(ock), mound, rise; esp. smaller hill among larger ones; e.g. (med.) ～樊 *qiūfán*, "hillside fencing," i.e. dwelling of a recluse.
   a. (bn.) ～虛 *qiūxū* (MC khjuw-xjo), hillocky and hummocky; also, ruins and wastes, esp. near tombs (see 2, 3).
2. grave-mound, gravesite; grave, tomb.
   a. "landmark" texts, respectful term for ancient documents, esp. in cmpd. ～墳 *qiūfén*.
3. ruins, desert(ed); barren(s).
4. fields, farmland; e.g. ～民 *qiūmín*, farmer, yeoman; ～落 *qiūluò*, village, thorp; ～里 *qiūlǐ*, hamlet, countryland.
5. bulwark, of fortification or other support.
6. ～兹 or 龜兹 *qiūcí* (MC khjuw-dzi), Kucha, Central Asian oasis kingdom on northern edge of Taklamakan Desert, esp. significant in transmission of Budd. to China.
7. personal name of Confucius; hence → 邱 *qiū* later used in order to avoid this graph out of respect.

楸   qiū   MC tshjuw
1. catalpa tree (*Catalpa bungei*), tall tree with excellent wood used in framing buildings, making boats, tables, etc.; syn. 檟 *jiǎ* (cf. 梓 *zǐ*, another species [*Catalpa ovata*]).
2. mallotus (*Mallotus japonicus*), medium- to tall-sized woody shrub with round leaves and summer-setting pale yellow flowers.
3. cupule, of acorn.

湫   qiū   MC tshjuw
1. grotto, deep cave.
   a. (med.) deep pool.
2. collect, hoard, accumulate, bring together.
   jiū   MC tsjuw
   1. cold, cool(ing).
      a. pure, clean.
   2. put an end to, finish, complete.

jiǎo　MC tsewX

1. low, low-lying, sunken.
    a. to lower, come down.

秋　qiū　MC tshjuw

1. autumn, the third 3 months of the year; season corresponding to the agent metal, the west, the lungs, the color white; e.g. 九～ *jiǔqiū*, the "Autumn Nine," nine 10-day decades of the autumn season; also, last month of autumn, 9th month of year; ～毫 *qiūháo*, "autumn down," fine hair of animals lengthening in autumn > small smidgen, a wisp, a bit.
    a. harvest-tide, esp. of grain crops; harvest.
    b. synecdoche for year.
    c. melancholy, esp. ref. the musical mode (*shang* 商) associated with autumn.
2. sgl. or rdup., swoop and soar (of birds), hover high.

緧　qiū　MC tshjuw　⊙ 鞦 *qiū*.

楸　qiū　MC dzjuw

1. tintinnabulation, ringing in ears; reverberate.

萩　qiū　MC tshjuw

1. pearly-everlasting reed (*Anaphalis yedoensis*), setting clusters of small white flowers.
2. ⊙ 楸 *qiū* 1, catalpa; 2, mallotus.

邱　qiū　MC khjuw

1. ⊙ 丘 *qiū* 1-6, created to avoid graph that writes Confucius's personal name.

鞦　qiū　MC tshjuw

1. breechstrap, crupper, leather strap fastened to the rear of the saddle of a harness and passing in a loop under the tail.

鰌　qiū　MC tshjuw

1. the dojo-loach, weather-loach (*Misgurnus anguillicaudatus*), a slender bottom-dwelling scavenger.

qiú　MC dzjuw

1. press against, lean on; harass.

鰍　qiū　MC tshjuw　⊙ 鰌 *qiū*, dojo-loach, weather-loach.

鶖　qiū　MC tshjuw

1. adjutant stork, the lesser adjutant (*Leptoptilus javanicus*), black-backed and white-chested, with bare neck and head.

qiú

仇　qiú　MC gjuw　→ 仇 *chóu*

俅　qiú　MC gjuw

1. rdup., capped with distinction; reverent and respectful.

囚　qiú　MC zjuw

1. confine(ment), imprison(ment); restrain, fetter; detain.
    a. prisoner; convict, criminal.

毬　qiú　MC gjuw

1. (med.) ball, used for playing games; to play ball, kick a ball.
    a. (med.) ball-shaped, round, sphere, orb.

求　qiú　MC gjuw

1. seek, search out; explore, probe.
    a. look for; invoke.
    b. be avid for, aspire to.
2. beseech, solicit; press for, urge.
    a. require, demand.
    b. (med.) invite, entreat.

泅　qiú　MC zjuw

1. swim(ming).

球　qiú　MC gjuw

1. precious gem, fine jade.
2. jade chime or lithophone.

N.B. The meaning "round, ball, sphere" is not associated with this graph until later times; through med. times the graph → 毬 *qiú* carries that meaning.

璆　qiú　MC gjuw

1. ⊙ 球 *qiú*, fine jade; jade lithophone.
2. onom. of jostling jade pendants.

絿　qiú　MC gjuw

1. pressing, exigent.
    a. precipitate, rash, impetuous, impatient.

芁　qiú　MC gjuw

1. far wilds, remote and uncultivated land.
2. twigs, branches, leafstalks used by birds and beasts in building nests or dens.

jiāo　MC kaew

1. 秦～ *qínjiāo*, "gentian of Qin," large-leaf gentian (*Gentiana macrophylla*), autumn-flowering, the root used medicinally.

茵 qiú MC zjuw

1. polypore mushrooms, ganoderma (*Ganoderma lucidum, Ganoderma japonicum*); syn. 靈芝 *língzhī*, 紫芝 *zǐzhī*, 赤芝 *chìzhī*.

虬 qiú MC gjiw ⊙ 蚪 *qiú*.

蚪 qiú MC gjiw

1. spirax, a dragon distinctive for its coiled, convolute form; cf. 螭 *chī*, wyverne. N.B. The gloss "horned (or hornless) dragon" is not credible.
2. coiled, wrapped; twisted, curled, crinkled; wound, contorted.
    a. (bn.) 蚴～ *yǒuqiú*, → 蚴 *yǒu*; (bn.) 蟉～ *liúqiú*, → 蟉 *liú*.

蝤 qiú MC dzjuw

1. (bn.) ～蠐 *qiúqí* (MC dzjuw-dzej), larvae of longhorn or capricorn beetle (*Cerambycidae*).
    jiū MC tsjuw
1. (med.) (bn.) ～蛑 *jiūmóu* (MC tsjuw-mjuw), blue crab, horse crab (*Portunus trituberculatus*).

裘 qiú MC gjuw

1. fur, fur clothing, fleece, fur-lined; wear a fur(-lined) garment.

觓 qiú MC gjiw ⊙ 觩 *qiú*.

觩 qiú MC gjiw

1. horned, hornlike, cornute, ceratoid, cornual; curved upward.
    a. (bn.) 觓～ *liúqiú*, → 觓 *liú*.

賕 qiú MC gjuw

1. bribe, buy off; suborn, corrupt.

逑 qiú MC gjuw

1. gather, bring together.
2. pair off, pair up; mate, match.
    a. counterpart.

逎 qiú MC dzjuw

1. get close to, move in on; press against, lean on; harass.
2. draw together, collect; consolidate.
3. complete, conclude, finish, bring to an end.
    a. solidify, settle, make stable; strengthen.
4. (med.) bold, vigorous, robust.
    a. (med.) "hit one's stride," do to the best of one's ability.

酋 qiú MC dzjuw

1. old wine, either mellow or stale.
2. wine-master, keeper of the wines, wine-steward.
    a. wine-girl, serving girl.
3. village leader, headman.
4. complete(d), finish(ed), well accomplished; < wine that is mature and ready to be drunk.

銶 qiú MC gjuw

1. adze.
    a. helve, handle of adze or hatchet.

鮂 qiú MC gjuw

1. the scaly mullet.

魗 qiú MC gjuw

1. head-cold; rheumy.
    a. runny nose.
2. cheekbones.

qiǔ

糗 qiǔ MC khjuwX

1. roasted grain, esp. used as dry provisions.

qū

佉 qū MC khja

1. graph used to trsc. Skt. syllables *kha, khā*; e.g. ～闍尼 *qūdūní* (MC khja-tu-nrij), trsc. Skt. *khādanīya*, "chewables," i.e. hard foods; ～盧 *qūlú* (MC khja-lu), abb. trsc. of Skt. *kharoṣṭhī*, script used ca. 3rd-c. BCE to 3rd-c. CE in northwest India to write Gāndhārī and Sanskrit; ～陀羅 *qūtuóluó* (MC khja-da-la), trsc. Skt. *khadira*, acacia tree (*Acacia catechu*).

區 qū MC khju

1. delimit, demarcate, delineate; divide.
2. delimited area, tract; sector, zone.
    a. place, locale; seat.
3. rdup., trifling and trivial, nugatory, of little or no account > self-depreciatory ref.: "my insignificant self."
    ōu MC ʔuw
1. early measure of capacity, equiv. 4 "pecks" (*dou* 斗).
    kòu MC khuwH
1. (bn.) ～霿 *kòumào* (MC khuwH-muwH), bedulled and bedimmed, senseless and stupefied, bewildered.

呿　qū　MC khjo

1. gaping (mouth).

屈　qū　MC khjut

1. bend; curl; e.g. ～伸 *qūshēn*, curl and stretch.
   a. curl up; reduce, diminish; contract.
   b. (med.) ～膝 *qūxī*, "bent hinge," latch for window or door.
2. cause to bend or crouch; subdue, repress.
   a. submit to, yield to; submissive.
   b. condescend to serve in the capacity of.
3. treat unjustly, do wrong to.
   a. be wronged, humiliated.
4. (med.) temporarily, for a while.
5. (med.) invite, solicit.

jué　MC gjut

1. use up, exhaust; spent; come to the end of.
2. (bn.) ～強 *juéqiáng* (MC gjut-gjang), intractable, intransigent; obstinate and unyielding; (bn.) ～橋 *juéqiáo* (MC gjut-gjew), strong and sturdy, stout and stalwart.

嶇　qū　MC khju

1. (bn.) 崎～ *qíqū*, → 崎 *qí*.

毆　qū　MC khju　⊙ 驅 *qū*.

曲　qū　MC khjowk

1. bend, bent; twist(ed), wind(ing); crooked; deflect(ed), indirect (ant. 直 *zhí*, straight, direct); e.g. ～彎 *qūwān*, bent in a curve; 心～ *xīnqū*, "heart's coils," 衷～ *zhōngqū*, "innermost twists [of the heart]," both ref. deep-hidden feelings.
   a. intricate; complicated; involved; e.g. ～成 *qūchéng*, intricately adaptable, accordant with all diversities.
   b. circumspect(ly), thorough(ly), as though following every twist.
   c. tendentious; unreasonable; irregular; e.g. ～赦 *qūshè*, amnesty due to special circumstances.
   d. crossed, curved over; e.g. ～裾 *qūjū*, crossed opening of robe lappets.
2. corner; out-of-the-way place.
   a. section, part(ial); local.
3. feeding basket for silkworms.
4. (med.) ～取 *qūqǔ*, ingratiate oneself with, worm one's way into good graces; also, listen with half an ear, put little faith in; ～受 *qūshòu*, same as preceding.

qǔ

1. musical tune, an air.
   a. (med.) 法～ *fǎqǔ*, pseudo-classical ritual music popular in Tang times, using handbells, cymbalets, large bells, lithophones, streamered syrinxes, and lutes.

祛　qū　MC khjo

1. dispel, drive away; remove; eliminate, do away with.
2. open up; break open, break apart.
   a. to rifle, turn over and paw through hastily.
3. rdup., strong and swift, hardy and spry.

胠　qū　MC khjo

1. part of the body under the armpits; side.
   a. to sidle, come at from the side; indirect(ly).
2. right flank of army formation (cf. 啓 *qí*, left flank).
3. ⊙ 祛 *qū* 2, open up, break open; rifle through; 阹 *qū* 1a, pen in, surround; block escape.

蛆　qū　MC tshjo

1. maggot; larvae of flies.
   a. gen. term for troublesome or loathsome insects.
2. the froth of wine fermentation.
3. vicious or unpleasant talk; rubbish, trash, garbage; filth.

jū　MC tsjo

1. (bn.) 蜘～ *jújū*, → 蜘 *jí*.

袪　qū　MC khjo

1. sleeve; sleeve-opening.
2. raise, lift up; turn up, tuck up.
3. brush off, flick away.
   a. ⊙ 祛 *qū* 1, dispel, drive away; remove.

詘　qū　MC khjut

1. dull or backward of speech, boorish; obtuse.
2. bent, crooked; curl(ed) up.
   a. (bn.) 詰～ *jiéqū*, → 詰 *jié*.
3. cause to bend to; subdue; bring to heel.
   a. submit to, yield to.
4. humiliate, disgrace.
5. reduce, diminish; curtail.

chù　MC trhwit

1. ⊙ 黜 *chù*, demote, degrade; expel, dismiss.

謳　qū　MC khjut　⊙ 詘 *qū* 1-5.

趍　qū　MC tshju　⊙ 趨 *qū* 1-2.

趨　qū　MC tshju
1. hurry forward, run toward, advance hastily, festinate; scurry.
   a. scuttle along with small steps and bowed head as sign of respect, either quickly or more deliberately.
2. incline toward, tend toward, move in the direction of; e.g. ～舍 *qūshè*, advance and retreat > likes and dislikes.
   a. intention, purpose; inclination.
   b. submit to, come under the influence of; truckle to.
    cù　MC tshjowk
1. ⊙ 促 *cù*, hasten, hurry; urge(nt), rapid; cramped, close, tight(en).

軀　qū　MC khju
1. physical body, of human or animal.
   a. fleshly husk, human body seen in pejorative sense.
   b. one's person, oneself; e.g. ～命 *qūmìng*, one's own fate; life, existence.
2. (med.) measure-word for statues, icons, etc.

阹　qū　MC khjo
1. land barrier such as a mountain valley used as a bounded pasture for horses or oxen.
   a. pen in; surround; block the escape of.

匷　qū　MC khju
1. tilted, askew.
   a. (bn.) 敧～ *qīqū*, → 敧 *qī*.

驅　qū　MC khju
1. spur on, goad on, whip up; press ahead, drive or force forward.
   a. battue, driving or chasing game in a hunt; e.g. 三～ *sānqū*, 3-sided battue.
   b. drive away, chase off; expel.
2. gallop; race ahead, haste on, hie; tear along.

鱋　qū　MC khjo
1. (bn.) ～鰨 *qūtà* (MC khjo-thap), flounder, flatfish.

麴　qū　MC khjuwk
1. grain ferment, grain mould, used in making *jiu* 酒, wine (cf. *nie* 蘖, malt, sprouted grain used in fermenting and brewing *li* 醴, sweet wine).

   a. by metonymy, gen. term for wine.
   b. leaven.

qú

劬　qú　MC gju
1. toil(some), labor(ious); travail; grind, drudge(ry) (more severe than 勞 *láo*).
   a. (bn.) ～錄 *qúlù* (MC gju-ljowk), toilsome travail, moil and toil.
2. assuage; recompense.

朐　qú　MC gju
1. bent part of dried meat.
2. ⊙ 軥 *qú*, curved extension of carriage-yoke placed over horses' neck and attached to the transverse bar (衡 *héng*).

欋　qú　MC gju
1. four-toothed rake.
2. tangle or knot of tree roots.

氍　qú　MC gju
1. (bn.) ～毹 *qūshū* (MC gju-srju), carpet or mat woven of felt.

渠　qú　MC gjo
1. canal or channel, man-made; trench.
   a. rill, rivulet, gutter.
2. felloe, rim of wheel into which the spokes are fitted.
3. shield, buckler.
   a. large; substantial.
4. (med.) sgl. or in cmpd. ～儂 *qúnóng*, ～家 *qújiā*, 3rd-person pronoun.
    jù　MC gjoH
1. ⊙ 遽 *jù*, hastily, in a hurry; 詎 *jù*, rhetorical interr.: "how?"; also, emphatic ADV attached to rhetorical interr. 豈 *qǐ*, how indeed!?

璩　qú　MC gjo
1. ear-ring of jade, gold, or silver.
   a. gen. term for jade disk.
2. a surname.

癯　qú　MC gju　⊙ 臞 *qú*.

瞿　qú　MC gju　→ 瞿 *jù*.

磲　qú　MC gjo
1. (bn.) 硨～ *jūqú*, → 硨 *jū*.

籧　qú　MC gjo
1. (bn.) ～篨 *qúchú* (MC gjo-drjo), ⊙ 蘧篨 *qúchú*, → 蘧 *qú* 4.

　　筥　MC kjoX
1. round basket, pannier.

臞　qú　MC gju
1. gaunt, scraggy, skinny, excessively thin.
　　a. recede; diminish, reduce.

蕖　qú　MC gjo
1. (bn.) 芙～ *fúqú*, lotus; → 芙 *fú*.

蘧　qú　MC gjo
1. ～麥 *qúmài*, the fringed pink (*Dianthus superbus*), herbaceous flowering plant, with scented pink to lavender blossoms; also, China pink (*Dianthus chinensis*), with white, red, or pink blossoms.
2. ～蔬 *qúshū*, Manchurian wild-rice (*Zizania caduciflora*).
3. ⊙ 蕖 *qú*, lotus.
4. (bn.) ～篨 *qúchú* (MC gjo-drjo), reed or bamboo matting; also, torso so rigid or paralyzed that one cannot bend; also, flatter and fawn, curry favor.
5. (bn.) ～盧 *qúlú* (MC gjo-lu), stopgap resthouse, overnight lodging; also (Budd.) syn. *upāya*, provisionally expedient.
6. ～然 *qúrán*, with a start, startled, all of a sudden.

衢　qú　MC gju
1. junction of several roads, allowing next movement in any direction; crossroads; e.g. 天～ *tiānqú*, "Crossroads of Heaven," constellation made up of 4 stars in Scorpio marking the intersection of the celestial equator and the ecliptic.
　　a. broad avenue, thoroughfare; e.g. 九～ *jiǔqú*, the 9 thoroughfares, i.e. the many great roads of the capital.
2. forking (as of a tree), prong(ed).

躩　qú　MC gju
1. rdup., advance in a curling and coiling manner, like a dragon.

輢　qú　MC gju
1. curved extension of carriage-yoke placed over horses' neck and attached to the transverse bar (衡 *héng*).
2. ⊙ 軥 *qú* in bn. ～錄, → 軥 *qú* 1a.

鴝　qú　MC gju
1. (bn.) ～鵒 *qúyù* (MC gju-yowk), crested myna (*Acridotheres cristatellus*), primarily black with dullish white bill.

　　gòu　MC kuwH
1. ⊙ 雊 *gòu*, onom. of a pheasant's cry.

鸜　qú　MC gju
1. (bn.) ～鵒 *qúyù* (MC gju-yowk), ⊙ 鴝鵒 *qúyù*, → 鴝 *qú* 1.

　　　　　qǔ

取　qǔ　MC tshjuX
1. take, seize, take away, acquire, capture, anything from a small object to an idea, to a prisoner, to a town; (Budd.) grasp, cling to (existence, desire).
　　a. take up; choose, pick, select; e.g. 相～ *xiāngqǔ*, complement (one another); ～捨 *qǔshě*, select(ion) and reject(ion).
　　b. adopt; accept; take back; e.g. ～容 *qǔróng*, adopt a [pleasing] countenance, i.e. ingratiate oneself; (med.) ～語 *qǔyǔ*, accept advice; also, adopt an opinion.
　　c. give ear to, obey; follow.
　　d. attain, reach to.
2. (med.) altogether > at the most > no more than.
3. (med.) ～次 *qǔcì* or ～此 *qǔcǐ*, normal(ly), ordinary; also, as one will, casual(ly); the latter meaning also for ～便 *qǔbiàn*, ～性 *qǔxìng*.
4. (med.) (GP) verbal suffix indicating completion or realization of VB.
5. (med.) toward, in the direction of.
6. ⊙ 娶 *qǔ*, take to wife, marry a wife.

娶　qǔ　MC tshjuH
1. take to wife, marry (of a man); cf. 嫁 *jià*, give a daughter in marriage.

曲　qǔ　MC khjowk　→ 曲 *qū*.

朐　qǔ　MC khjuX
1. imposing, stately; impressive.

麮　qǔ　MC khjoX
1. sweet wheat-porridge; barley porridge.

齲　qǔ　MC khjuX
1. decayed or rotting teeth.

qù

去   qù   MC khjoH
1. depart (from), go away (from), leave, go off.
   a. (med.) euph. for die.
2. time past; often ref. time just gone; e.g. ～來 *qùlái*, past and future; ～年 *qùnián*, last year.
3. distance from, be distant from.
4. (med.) go to; N.B. this only from 8th c., rare till post-Tang.
5. (med.) (GP) verbal or adjectival suffix indicating completion or continuance.
6. (med.) ～就 *qùjiù*, behavior, manner(s), bearing; also, decorum, courtesy, etiquette.
7. (med.) ref. words of "departing" tone in the spoken language; departing-tone words classified as "oblique" or "deflected" (仄 *zè*), along with those in "rising" (上 *shǎng*) and "entering" (入 *rù*) tones, in binary contrast to those in "level" (平 *píng*) tone.
   MC khjoX
1. get rid of; discard, dismiss; exclude; reject.
   jǔ   MC kjoX
1. store away, store up.

虧   qù   MC tshjoH
1. (med.) ⊙ 覷 *qù*.

覷   qù   MC tshjoH
1. look closely, peer at; spy out.
   a. look upon; behold, espy.

趣   qù   MC tshjuH
1. go quickly (toward), hasten (to).
   a. press on toward, chase after; throw oneself into; be in step with.
2. impulse, urge; inclination, leaning, bent; import; predilection, proclivity; taste for, relish, interest in; purposeful, determined.
   a. attraction, appeal, flair; pleasing, agreeable; delight.
3. (Budd.) destination; e.g. 六～ *liùqù*, 6 destinations of rebirth, 6 paths of existence (hell-beings, hungry ghosts, animals, demons, humans, devas).
   cù   MC tshjowk
1. ⊙ 促 *cù*, urge toward, press to (do X); urgent, pressing; quickly, hastily, in a hurry.

闃   qù   MC khwek
1. quiet(ness), still(ness).

quān

圈   quān   MC khjwen   → 圈 *juàn*.

巻   quān   MC kjwenH
1. arbalest, crossbow.

悛   quān   MC tshjwen
1. make amends; redeem; repent.
   a. repair, mitigate, change for the better.
2. in order, sequential(ly).
   xún   MC swin
1. ⊙ 恂 *xún* 1, rdup., open-hearted and ingenuous, simple and sincere.

桊   quān   MC khjwen
1. bowl or plate made of wicker.
   quán   MC gjwen
1. rdup., energetically, vigorously, forcefully.
   juàn   MC kjwenH
1. ⊙ 桊 *juàn*, nose-ring of ox, to attach a rope.

quán

全   quán   MC dzjwen
1. complete(ly), entire(ly), whole of, all of.
   a. (med.) to the fullest (or a fuller) degree; even more.
2. preserve intact, keep whole.
   a. to perfect, bring to completion.
3. jade of one color (pure) all the way through.

拳   quán   MC gjwen
1. fist, closed hand.
   a. (med.) practice martial arts.
2. powerfully, vigorously.
3. rdup., hold tight to, keep close to one; zealous, earnest, ardent.
4. curled, twisted; rolled up; clenched.

權   quán   MC gjwen
1. balance-weight; e.g. ～衡 *quánhéng*, balance-weight and beam > impartial scales; also, ref. north and south, respectively.
   a. weigh, evaluate.
   b. compar(abl)e; assess; consider specific circumstances and merits.
2. have the balance of power, carry weight; authority; privilege, prestige; e.g. 當～ *dāngquán*, to hold sway; ～門 *quánmén*, gates of the powerful, families of influence.

a. influence, advantage(ous); compel(ling); effect(ive); dominant.
3. flexible, adapt(ive), responsive to circumstances.

    a. expedient, opportune; contingent, relative, conditional; circumstantial, impermanent, provisional; e.g. (Budd.) 〜便 *quánbiàn* or 〜宜 *quányí*, expedient means, trns. Skt. *upāya*, syn. 方便 *fāngbiàn*; (Budd.) 〜慧 *quánhuì*, contingent wisdom; (Budd.) 〜實 *quánshí*, the conditional and the substantial, the phenomenal and the real, provisional and absolute (truth).
4. temporar(il)y, for the moment.
5. 〜輿 *quányú*, blooming of early sprouts (equiv. 藧藇 *quǎnyú* < Ode 135); start up, begin.

泉　quán　MC dzjwen
1. wellspring, freshet; fountain, spring, source.
    a. subterranean water; often with special ref. to 黃〜 *huángquán*, the Yellow Springs, i.e. netherworld, underworld, euph. for death; e.g. 〜壤 *quánrǎng*, mound of the Springs, 〜台 *quántái*, platform of the Springs, both ref. the grave, tomb.
    b. spring-fed.
2. old term for cash; > wealth, riches.

牷　quán　MC dzjwen
1. an ox all of one unmixed color to be used for sacrifice; whole victim, internally sound and externally whole.
2. pure, faultless.

痊　quán　MC tshjwen
1. recover from illness, return to health; heal(ed), convalesce(nt).

筌　quán　MC tshjwen
1. fish-trap made of bamboo.
    a. 〜蹄, 〜罦 *quántí*, fish-trap and rabbit-snare, i.e. means to an end, instruments to attain a goal, often ref. to language; also (Budd.), metaphor for *upāya*, "skillful means."

絟　quán　MC tshjwen
1. fine cloth, lawn.

線　quán　MC tshjwen
1. light orange (color).

荃　quán　MC tshjwen
1. sweet-flag, calamus (*Acorus calamus*), sweetly scented wetland grass; (lit.) in *Chuci* poems often a symbol of purity (sometimes rendered "iris," but this is incorrect); syn. 菖蒲 *chāngpú*, 蓀 *sūn*.
2. ⊙ 筌 *quán*, fish-trap made of bamboo; 絟 *quán*, fine cloth, lawn.

蜷　quán　MC gjwen
1. (bn.) 〜局 *quánjú* (MC gjwen-gjowk), shrink and draw inward, wriggle up, pull into oneself, cringe and contract, shy away from.

蠸　quán　MC gjwen
1. slimebug, said to be voracious eater of melon leaves; syn. 守瓜 *shǒuguā*.

詮　quán　MC tshjwen
1. explicate, explain in detail, interpret.
2. choose with care, select with discernment as to relative worth.
3. underlying principles, criteria, basic standards.

踡　quán　MC gjwen
1. twisted, contorted; rolled in, rolled up.
    a. draw into, contract; e.g. (bn.) 〜跼 *quánjú* (MC gjwen-gjowk), ⊙ 蜷局 *quánjú*, → 蜷 *quán*.

輇　quán　MC dzywen
1. solid spokeless wheels of a carriage.
    MC tshjwen
1. lesser, low (in worth or status); e.g. 〜才 *quáncái*, piddling talents, trifling ability.

銓　quán　MC tshjwen
1. test coins and separate, esp. by weighing, the base from the genuine; shroff.
    a. weigh, evaluate.
2. judge the merits of, assess(ment); (med.) esp. the assessment of candidates in the civil-service exam system and those already in the bureaucracy being considered for reassignment.

顴　quán　MC gjwen
1. cheekbone.

鬈　quán　MC gjwen
1. well-dressed (of hair), well-coiffed.
    a. prettily curled or wavy hair.

2. women's everyday hairstyle, parted in middle with a bun on either side.

齤 **quán**   MC gjwen
1. gap-toothed; crack-toothed.

quǎn

犬 **quǎn**   MC khwenX
1. dog; canine; cur.
   a. pejorative term for a contemptible person, wretch, knave.

甽 **quǎn**   MC kwenX   ⊙ 畎 *quǎn*.

畎 **quǎn**   MC kwenX
1. water channels, irrigation ditches between fields; e.g. ～畝 *quǎnmǔ*, irrigated fields, furrowed fields, farmland.
   a. channel a watercourse; > circulate.
2. small river-valley; coulee; dale.

綣 **quǎn**   MC khjwonX
1. crooked, curved; curled, shriveled.
   a. roll up, tie up.
   b. (bn.) 繾～ *qiǎnquǎn*, → 繾 *qiǎn*.
2. rdup., in all earnestness, with total dedication, faithfully steadfast.

虇 **quǎn**   MC khjwonX
1. Jiangnan area term for reed-sprouts.
   a. gen. term for sprouting plants; e.g. ～蕍 *quǎnyú*, blooming of early sprouts (< Ode 135).

quàn

券 **quàn**   MC khjwonH
1. contract, originally wooden slip or tablet divided in two with each party keeping one half as guarantee or bond.
   a. written agreement, pact, covenant.

勸 **quàn**   MC khjwonH
1. encourage, urge, exhort; motivate, prompt; dispose to do X; strive toward.
   a. to ply, use diligently; e.g. ～筆 *quànbǐ*, ply the writing-brush.
2. (med.) persuade, convince.
   a. (med.) advise, counsel; admonish; dissuade from.

quē

缺 **quē**   MC khwet
1. crack, break; smash.
   a. in pieces; tattered, splintered, in shreds, in scraps.
   b. (bn.) 列～, 裂～ *lièquē* (MC ljet-khwet), "shattering cracks(s)," i.e. lightning.
2. defective, deficient; deficiency, deficit, lacking, short of; (de)fault.
   a. sgl. or rdup., incomplete, imperfect; insufficient.
   b. lying open, gaping; vacant.
3. decline, wane; e.g. ～月 *quēyuè*, waning moon.
   a. detract, diminish; reduce.
4. discard(ed), abandon(ed); useless.
5. ～盆 *quēpén*, thimbleberry, Chinese raspberry (*Rubus parvifolius*); also, ref. bone above the breast, prob. collarbone < "broken basin."

què

却 **què**   MC khjak   ⊙ 卻 *què*.

卻 **què**   MC khjak
1. step back, withdraw; retire, retreat.
   a. hold off, reject; decline; put off, let go.
   b. pardon, commute a death-sentence.
2. (med.) return, come back, go back; revert; often in cmpds., e.g. ～返 *quèfǎn*, ～回 *quèhuí*, ～來 *quèlái*, all with preceding meaning; (Budd.) ～活 *quèhuó*, reincarnation.
   a. (med.) ～後 *quèhòu*, henceforth, from now on.
3. (med.) (GP) mild adversative particle: nevertheless, after all, in spite of all, despite > still, once again.
   a. (med.) (GP) marker of immediate present: just now.
4. (med.) (GP) post-verbal suffix indicating completion (< dismissal) of action.
5. (med.) (GP) after a VB or VB-phrase and before a noun or noun-phrase, indicating comparative sense: than; syn. 於 *yú* 1a.
N.B. This graph sometimes confused with 郤 *xì* 1, cleft, reft; 2, rift, discord; but they are quite distinct.

埆 **què**   MC khaewk
1. poor infertile soil; ⊙ 确 *què* 1.
2. determine; examine; consider.

愨 què MC khaewk ⊙ 愨 què.

愨 què MC khaewk
1. conscientious, scrupulous; dedicated, earnest.

榷 què MC khaewk
1. rap, knock, strike against; onom. of this action: "kock!"
2. consider, deliberate, discuss < bat ideas around.
3. cite, call up (as evidence).
    a. (med.) in general, to sum up.
4. have sole control of, monopolize.

榷 què MC khaewk
1. footbridge; small wooden bridge, plankbridge.
2. have a monopoly, monopolize; exercise special privilege.
    a. concentrated; particular.
3. (med.) 商～ shāngquè, deliberate over, discuss together.

殼 què MC khaewk → 殼 qiào.

确 què MC khaewk
1. rock-strewn sterile soil, fallow land; barren.
    a. (med.) hard, solid; certain, true; ⊙ 碻 què.
2. ⊙ 榷 què, knock, rap, strike against.
    jué MC kaewk
1. ⊙ 角 jué (jiǎo), compete, vie; dispute.

碻 què MC khaewk
1. hard, solid; unyielding; durable; substantial.
    a. staunch, unshakable; reliable; steady, stable.
2. certain, undoubted; true; authentic.

礐 què MC khaewk
1. onom. of waves striking against rocks; crash, slap, smack.
2. (med.) (bn.) ～硞 quèkè (MC khaewk-kheak), onom. of water running over rapids or breaking against rocks.
3. unshakable, unyielding; strong.

闋 què MC khwet
1. close off; conclude, terminate, reach the end of; e.g. 服～ fúquè, come to the end of the mourning period (when one can set aside mourning clothes).
    a. rest, pause (after completion of an act).
    b. measure-word for a bout of "pure conversation" (qingtan 清談), a section of or full performance of music, a stanza of ci 詞 poetry.
2. ⊙ 缺 quē 2, deficient, lacking; incomplete; vacant, waiting to be filled (esp. official position).

闕 què MC khjwot
1. watchtower, gate-tower, guard-tower, flanking city or palace gate; pylons; gatehouse.
    a. by synecdoche, imperial palace, imperial court.
2. pylons with honorific arch flanking road to a tomb or to ancestral shrine; monument(al).
    quē MC khwet
1. ⊙ 缺 quē 2, deficient, wanting, lacking; imperfect; gap(ing), vacant, 3, detract, diminish(ed).
2. fault, error.
3. put to one side, reserve; e.g. ～疑 quēyí, withhold one's doubts.
    jué MC khwet
1. ⊙ 掘 jué, dig, delve (< physical act that creates a gap).

雀 què MC tsjak
1. small bird, birdling, esp. sparrow, tree-sparrow (Passer montanus).
    a. gen. term for all birds but raptors.
    b. abb. of 孔～ kǒngquè, peacock.
2. rufous-colored, brownish-red color of sparrow's pate.

鵲 què MC tshjak
1. magpie; various corvids, esp. Eurasian magpie (Pica pica, Pica sericea) and azure-winged magpie (Cyanopica cyanus).

qūn

囷 qūn MC khwin
1. round granary.
    a. gen. term for granary.
2. (med.) rdup., twisting and turning, curved and winding.

踆 qūn MC tshwin
1. ⊙ 逡 qūn, step back, recede; pull back, shrink from, recoil; defer.

cún MC dzwon

1. kick.

zūn MC tswon

1. sit with legs splayed, sprawl.

逡 **qūn** MC tshwin

1. step back, recede; pull back, shrink from, recoil; defer.

   a. (bn.) ～巡, ～循 *qūnxún* (MC tshwin-zwin), shy from and shrink back, turn away and avoid; hesitate and hang back, dawdle and dally; also, with all due deference.

2. ⊙ 駿 *jùn* 1a, rapid, speed(il)y.

qún

帬 **qún** MC gjun ⊙ 裙 *qún*.

羣 **qún** MC gjun

1. gathering of a large number of objects; e.g. of animals: flock (of sheep), herd (of oxen), gaggle (of geese), etc.

   a. of people: host, group, concourse, horde, company, band, crowd; e.g. ～臣 *qúnchén*, host of vassals, congregated officials; ～季 *qúnjì*, band of youths.

2. teeming, sundry, diverse; e.g. ～黎 *qúnlí*, the teeming multitudes; (Budd.) ～動 *qúndòng*, ～有 *qúnyǒu*, the sundry beings (of this world).

群 **qún** MC gjun ⊙ 羣 *qún*.

裙 **qún** MC gjun

1. skirt: for women, tie-around skirt; also, apron.

   a. for men, lower garment without legs; also, skirting of a long robe.

2. rims of carapace.

3. prepuce.

R

rán

然 **rán** MC nyen

1. burn; light a fire, kindle; ⊙ 燃 *rán*.

2. to be like this, to be so, to be such; to be like something is expected to be, to be natural; e.g. 自～ *zìrán*, what is so-of-itself, naturally so, what is as-it-is (N.B. when used as noun, better not to translate as "nature" or "Nature," to avoid confusion with 性 *xìng*, inborn nature, inherent tendencies).

3. descriptive ADV suffix: -like, -ly; needs to be rendered *ad hoc* according to context; e.g. 俄～覺 *érán jué*, momentarily I awoke; 卒～問 *cùrán wèn*, to ask abruptly; 夫子喟～歎曰 *fūzi kuìrán tàn yuē*, Confucius exasperatedly sighed and said; 孔子泫～流涕 *kǒngzi xuànrán liútì*, Confucius let the tears flow in beaded profusion; 忽～出，勃～動 *hūrán chū, bórán dòng*, emerging suddenly, moving abruptly.

   a. VB-phrase suffix, often with reduplicated verbs, suggesting an expressive, imprecise, impressionistic, or Gestalt sense, likeness, or demeanor; to be rendered *ad hoc* according to context; e.g. 勿視其巍巍～ *wùshì qí wéiwéirán*, do not look at their grandiose-great demeanor; 由由～不忍去也 *yóuyóurán bùrěn qù yě*, calm-and-contentedly, he could not bear to leave; 栩栩～胡蝶 *xǔxǔrán húdié*, a flittering-fluttering butterfly.

   b. adverbial VB-phrase suffix redundantly followed by 而 *ér*: VB-phrase ～而, X *ránér*; e.g. 規規～而求之 *guīguīrán ér qiú zhī*, probingly to seek for it; 囅～而笑 *chǎnrán ér xiào*, to laugh heartily.

   c. redundant suffix to a *ruò* 若 X or *rú* 如 X, 'like X' VB-phrase: 若 X～ *ruò* X *rán* or 如 X ～ *rú* X *rán*, usu. not readily translatable; e.g. 夫道若大路～ *fú dàoruò dàlù rán*, the Way, in any given respect, is like a great path (so); 今言王若易～ *jīn yán wàng ruò yì rán*, now speaking of ruling as a king as being easy (like); 若是小丈夫～ *ruò shì xiǎo zhàngfu rán*, like these petty chaps (so); 如見其肺肝～ *rú jiàn qí fèi gān rán*, it is like seeing one's lungs and liver (so).

4. conjunction, usu. indicating contrast or opposition with preceding VB-phrase: but, however, yet; it being so (as just stated), nevertheless . . .; e.g. 周勃重厚少文～安劉氏者必勃也 *Zhōu Bó zhònghòu shǎowén rán ān Liúshì zhe bì Bó yě*, Zhou Bo is thick-witted and lacking refinement, yet the one who can make the Liu clan secure is certainly Bo.

燃　rán　MC nyen

1. burn; light a fire, kindle; ☉ 然 *rán* 1.

爇　rán　MC nyen

1. burn; light a fire, kindle; ☉ 然 *rán* 1.

蚺　rán　MC nyem

1. ☉ 蚦 *rán*, python.
   tiàn　MC themH
1. (bn.) 〜螮 *tiàntàn* (MC themH-thamH), with tongue protruding, with jaws agape; syn. 舚舕 *tiǎntàn*.

蚦　rán　MC nyem

1. sgl. or cmpd. 〜蛇 *ránshé*, python.

袡　rán　MC nyem　☉ 袇 *rán*.

袇　rán　MC nyem

1. selvedge; hem or border of clothing.

顃　rán　MC nyem　☉ 髯 *rán*.

髯　rán　MC nyem

1. whiskers, beard (human).
   a. bewhiskered or bearded elder.
2. whiskers (animal).

rǎn

冄　rǎn　MC nyemX　☉ 冉 *rǎn*.

冉　rǎn　MC nyemX

1. rdup., advancing apace, steadily approaching, insensible gradualness; also, gently hanging, lithely bending.
2. edge of a turtle's carapace.
3. a surname.

妍　rǎn　MC nyemX

1. (bn.) 〜嫋 *rǎnniǎo* (MC nyemX-newX), slender and slight, tenderly trailing, dainty and delicate.

染　rǎn　MC nyemX

1. to dye; to stain, color; imbue with; suffuse; tinge.
   a. (Budd.) 〜服 *rǎnfú*, dyed clothing, ref. the dark robe of monks.

2. befoul, sully; sullied, smear(ed), taint; e.g. 〜污 *rǎnwū*, defiled; clouded, dulled.
3. (med.) infect(ion), corrupt(ion).

苒　rǎn　MC nyemX

1. rdup., (med.) ☉ 冉冉 *rǎnrǎn*, advancing apace, insensibly approaching; also, gently bending, lithely hanging.
   a. rdup., also, (med.) burgeoning and abounding, flourishing fully.
2. (med.) (bn.) 〜弱 *rǎnruò* (MC nyemX-nyak), supplely graceful, lithe and pliant.
3. (med.) (bn.) 〜荏 *rǎnrěn* (MC nyemX-nyimX) or 荏〜 *rěnrǎn*, imperceptibly passing, gradually going (of time).

ráng

儴　ráng　MC nyang

1. run along, coast along.
   a. abide by, adhere to.
      xiāng　MC sjang
1. (bn.) 〜佯 *xiāngyáng* (MC sjang-yang), wandering and wavering, ambling and meandering.

勷　ráng　MC nyang

1. (med.) (bn.) 劻〜 *kuāngráng*, → 劻 *kuāng*.

攘　ráng　MC nyang

1. extract, pull out; eliminate.
   a. seize by force, take what one wants; purloin, steal.
2. repel, reject; repulse, parry; thrust aside; e.g. 鉤〜 *gōuráng*, "hooked parrier," ancient defensive weapon resembling a bowed shield with hand-grip.
3. roll up or tuck up (sleeves).
4. put up with, tolerate, condone.
5. ☉ 讓 *ràng*, yield, cede, relinquish.
   rǎng　MC nyangX
1. disturb, disarray, throw into confusion.
   a. (bn.) 擾〜 *rǎorǎng*, → 擾 *rǎo*.

瀼　ráng　MC nyang

1. rdup., drenched with dew, heavy with dew; also, (med.) spurting and spouting (of tossing waves).
   nǎng　MC nangX
1. (bn.) 決〜 *yāngnǎng*, → 決 *yāng*.

瓤   **ráng**   MC nyang
1. pulp, flesh of fruits and melons.
   a. pith, inner soft part of seed or nut.

禳   **ráng**   MC nyang
1. deprecatory sacrifice, to ward off misfortune or bad harvest.
2. exorcise; an exorcistic rite.

穰   **ráng**   MC nyang
1. pith of a grain-stalk.
2. rich growth of grain, rich harvest.
3. ⊙ 瓤 *ráng*, pulp of fruits and melons, pith of nuts and seeds.
   rǎng   MC nyangX
1. teeming; thriving, flourishing.
2. ⊙ 禳 *ráng*, sacrifice to ward off misfortune or bad harvest.

蘘   **ráng**   MC nyang
1. ～荷 *ránghé*, myoga ginger (*Zingiber mioga*).

rǎng

壤   **rǎng**   MC nyangX
1. loam(y); friable, rich soil, humus.
   a. loose mould; clod, glebe; mound; e.g. 擊～ *jīrǎng*, break up clods.
   b. gen. term for earth; e.g. 天～ *tiānrǎng*, heaven and earth, syn. 天地 *tiāndì*.
2. territory, region, area.
3. game of chuck-stick or "pegs."
4. ⊙ 攘 *rǎng* 3, disarrayed, disordered, confused.
   ráng   MC nyang
1. ⊙ 穰 *ráng* 2, rich harvest of grain.

ràng

讓   **ràng**   MC nyangH
1. defer(ence), cede, waive, relinquish, acquiesce(nce); deferentially; diffident.
2. deprecate, decry, chide.

ráo

橈   **ráo**   MC nyew   → 橈 *náo*.

蕘   **ráo**   MC nyew
1. brushwood, scrub.
   a. gather brushwood; brushwood-gatherer.
2. turnip-rape, field-mustard (*Brassica rapa*).

饒   **ráo**   MC nyew
1. sufficient, sufficiency; plenty, plentiful, rich; abundance; yield (of crops).
   a. surplus, excess(ive); e.g. ～舌 *ráoshé*, locquacious, garrulous, gabby.
   b. increase, add to, accumulate.
2. fertile, productive; bounteous, copious.
   a. (med.) beautiful, charming.
3. tolerate, pardon, forgive; tolerant, lenient.
4. (med.) yield to, acknowledge superiority of.
5. (med.) (GP) even if, granted that, despite.

rǎo

嬈   **rǎo**   MC nyewX
1. importune, vex; disturb, trouble.
   ráo   MC nyew
1. (bn.) 妖～ *yāoráo*, → 妖 *yāo*.
2. rdup., graceful and gentle, soft and yielding.

擾   **rǎo**   MC nyewX
1. throw into confusion, cause disorder or disarray; beset, harass; trouble; e.g. (bn.) ～攘 *rǎorǎng* (MC nyewX-nyangX), welter of confusion, roiling welter, tumult and turmoil.
2. domesticate(d), tame; bring to docility, make tractable, subdue; e.g. 六～ *liùrǎo*, the 6 domestic animals (horse, ox, sheep, pig, dog, chicken).
3. (med.) (bn.) ～弱 *rǎoruò* (MC nyewX-nyak), tender and gentle, pliant and delicate.

rào

繞   **rào**   MC nyewH
1. enlace, (en)wreathe, wind round, coil.
   a. encircle, surround.
   b. make the round of, make a full circuit; circumscribe, circumambulate.
   rǎo   MC nyewX
1. winding, curved; crooked, distorted.
2. a surname.

rě

惹   **rě**   MC nyaeX
1. (med.) to dye, imbue with.
2. (med.) adhere to, cohere; cling.
3. (med.) provoke, goad, incite; annoy, disturb.
   a. (med.) invite, court, attract, draw in, draw close.

4. (Budd.) 〜那 *rě'né* (MC nyaeX-na), trsc. Skt. *jñāna*, knowledge, wisdom.

rè

熱　**rè**　MC nyet
1. hot; heat.
    a. fever; excess of *yang* vapors.
2. heated, excited, aroused, inflamed, ardent, vehement.
    a. (med.) flare-up, turmoil, fomentation; row, racket, pother.

rén

人　**rén**　MC nyin
1. person, human being, man, mankind; e.g. 〜間 *rénjiān*, the human realm, mortal world; 〜性 *rénxìng*, human nature.
    a. in early texts, sometimes ref. those with surnames, in contrast with 民 *mín*, common-folk.
2. others, the other one(s) (opp. *wo* 我, *wu* 吾, *ji* 己, which ref. oneself).
3. from 7th century on, often a replacement character for 民 *mín*, the latter being tabooed as part of the personal name of Li Shimin 李世民 (Tang Taizong 唐太宗, r. 626-649).
4. kernel, pit, of fruit, ⊙ 仁 *rén* 2.

仁　**rén**　MC nyin
1. humane(ness), human-heartedness , humane empathy; kind(ness), fellow-kindness, fellow-feeling toward others in a more inclusive sense than 義 *yì* (rightness, duty, responsibility), with which it is often paired as the 2 fundamental Ruist moral principles, "humaneness" always coming first in the compound.
    a. (Budd.) 〜者 *rénzhe*, "dear fellow; my good man," respectful form of address, trns. Skt. *bhadra*; 〜王 *rénwáng*, the humane king, ref. the Buddha.
2. kernel, pit, of fruit.

壬　**rén**　MC nyim
1. 9th of the 10 heavenly stems.
2. flatter, cozen; intrigue.
3. grand, great.

rěn

忍　**rěn**　MC nyinX
1. patience, forbear(ance); endure, bear; persevere, perseverance; keep inside one (as feelings); e.g. 〜看 *rěnkàn*, endure the sight of; 〜垢 *rěn'gòu*, put up with disgrace.
    a. be passive or inactive with regard to; e.g. 不〜人之心 *bùrěnrénzhīxīn*, a heart that is not passive with regard to others (< *Mengzi* 2A.6).
    b. (Budd.) sgl. or 〜辱 *rěnrǔ*, trns. Skt. *kṣānti*, patience as a positive virtue shown toward persons or circumstances that might not deserve it; acceptance, forbearance; receptivity; serenity.
2. cruel, ruthless, hard-hearted, unfeeling (< passive); e.g. 〜人 *rěnrén*, a ruthless person.

稔　**rěn**　MC nyimX
1. grain that is ripe; ready for harvest.
    a. a harvest; a year.
2. ripe(ness), at peak stage of readiness; ready to be enjoyed.
3. (med.) familiar with (a topic), well acquainted, fully conversant with.

荏　**rěn**　MC nyimX
1. perilla (*Perilla frutescens*), broad-leaved plant of the mint family, esp. the purple-leaved species, used in cooking and medicinally; perilla oil is expressed from the seeds; syn. 蘇 *sū* 1.
2. pliant, flexible, weak.
    a. (med.) (bn.) 〜苒 *rěnrǎn* (nyimX-nyemX), gracefully supple, lithe and lissome; also, same or 苒〜 *rǎnrěn*, imperceptibly passing, gradually going (of time).
3. 〜菽 *rěnshū*, broad-beans.

rèn

仞　**rèn**　MC nyinH
1. measure of length: fathom, equiv. 7 or 8 "feet" (*chi* 尺).
2. to fathom, sound, attempt to get to the bottom of; take the measure of.
3. ⊙ 牣 *rèn*, full; 韌 *rèn*, supplely resistant; 認 *rèn*, familiar, acquainted with.

任   rèn   MC nyimH

1. duty, responsibility, burden, charge.
   a. fulfill, discharge, take on (duty, responsibility, etc.); take in charge, undertake.
2. burden, load (physical).
3. appoint, assign to a post; e.g. 〜人 rènrén, appoint someone to an official position.
4. competence, aptitude, capacity; e.g. 〜士 rènshì, capable person, a man of parts.
5. repose one's trust in, have confidence in; entrust with; e.g. 〜人 rènrén, put one's trust in someone else.
   a. rely, depend on, trust to; thanks to; e.g. 〜土 rèntǔ, rely on local (physical) conditions.
   b. according to, based on.
6. allow, let, permit; concede, put up with, yield to.
   a. voluntarily, readily.
   b. indulgent(ly), at will; revel in.

      rén   MC nyim

1. flatter, gloze; insinuate; e.g. 〜人 rénrén, fawner, sycophant.
2. a surname.

刃   rèn   MC nyinH

1. blade; sword-blade, knife-edge.
   a. by synecdoche, gen. term for swords, halberds, other bladed weapons.
2. to run through (with a blade), dispatch.
3. ⊙ 仞 rèn 1, fathom (measure).

妊   rèn   MC nyimH

1. gravid, pregnant, with child, heavy with child.

恁   rèn   MC nyimH

1. think about, reflect on; call to mind.

靭   rèn   MC nyinH

1. full, fill(ed) up; stuff(ed).

紉   rèn   MC nrin

1. twist thread; plait, braid.
   a. sew, stitch; join together, connect.
2. thread a needle.
3. ⊙ 靭 rèn, pliantly resistant.

絍   rèn   MC nyimH

1. spin thread; e.g. 〜織 rènzhī, spin and weave.
   a. lead forth, draw out.
2. silk fibers, filaments.
   a. gen. term for silk-stuff.

絍   rèn   MC nyimH   ⊙ 絍 rèn.

衽   rèn   MC nyimH

1. long lappets or overlaps on either side of upper garment, usu. broad at the chest and tapering below; e.g. 右〜 yòurèn, left lapel covering the right, right-covering, standard Chinese style.
   a. skirts of a robe.
2. long hanging sleeves.
3. bed, mattress.
   a. lie down, go to bed; go to sleep.
4. wooden tenon used in securing the lid of a coffin.

訒   rèn   MC nyinH

1. reserved or discreet in speech, guarded, hesitant.

認   rèn   MC nyinH

1. recognize, know; be familiar with, acquainted with.
2. (med.) acknowledge.
3. (med.) regard as, take as, take X to be Y.

靭   rèn   MC nyinH

1. carriage-brake; block, chock.
   a. to brake, chock, bring to a halt.
2. resistant; solid, secure.
3. laggard, sluggish; halting.
4. ⊙ 仞 rèn 1, fathom.

靭   rèn   MC nyinH   ⊙ 靭 rèn.

靭   rèn   MC nyinH

1. supplely resistant, strong but flexible.

餁   rèn   MC nyimH

1. food well or thoroughly cooked.
2. well prepared.

鵀   rèn   MC nyimH

1. 戴〜 dàirèn, hoopoe (Upupa epops), medium-sized, brightly plumed bird with a distinctive crown of feathers (hence the name, crested rèn) and long thin bill; syn. 戴勝 dàishèng.

réng

仍   réng   MC nying

1. carry on as before, follow(ing), continue to; reiterate(ly), repeat(edly).

a. still, at the same time, while continuing to, meanwhile; as always, as normal.
b. sometimes with sense of cause: consequently, therefore.
2. join with, connect.

芿　réng　MC nying
1. (med.) new growth of plants or grasses following on previous uncut growth.
2. (med.) dense thicket, rank, teeming.

rèng　MC nyingH
1. second growth of plants or grasses where previous growth was cut.

陾　réng　MC nying
1. rdup., more and more, much and many.

rèng

扔　rèng　MC nyingH
1. draw toward one, pull, haul, tow.
2. destroy, wreck.

芿　rèng　MC nyingH
1. ⊙ 芿 *rèng* 1 (*réng*), second growth of plants or grasses where previous growth was cut.
2. tangled mass of plants, wild growth.

rì

日　rì　MC nyit
1. the sun; solar.
   a. daytime.
2. a day, diurnal; each day, daily.
3. formerly, past; (at) another time.
   a. (med.) ～者 *rìzhě*, recently, lately.
4. days considered ill-omened, because of various astrological and calendrical relations.
5. ～魂 *rìhún*, "solar cloud-soul," i.e. orpiment; ～及 *rìjí*, "sunrise only," i.e. rose-mallow (*Hibiscus syriacus*), because opens in morning, closes at night, syn. 木槿 *mùjǐn*.

袝　rì　MC nyit
1. underclothes.

駉　rì　MC nyit
1. post-horse, relay-horse.

róng

容　róng　MC yowng
1. countenance; appearance, features.
2. to countenance, accept; receive, be receptive to, accommodate.
   a. permit, authorize, acquiesce.
   b. pardon; tolerate, condone; (med.) make space for; also, ingratiate.
3. (bn.) ～與 *róngyǔ* (MC yowng-yoX), with effortless ease, however one wishes, indulging one's whims; also, wavering and havering, halting and hesitant.
4. rdup., spreading freely, rolling in billows; also, with no set view, undetermined.
5. (med.) ～易 *róngyì*, rashly, carelessly, indifferently; also, ordinarily, regularly; also, hastily, hurriedly.
6. (med.) sgl. or ～許 *róngxǔ*, perhaps, maybe; also, sometime.
7. (med.) rhetorical interr., how could it be that…? > surely not.

嵤　róng　MC hjwaeng　⊙ 嶸 *róng*.

嶸　róng　MC hjwaeng
1. (bn.) 崢～ *zhēngróng*, → 崢 *zhēng*.

戎　róng　MC nyuwng
1. military implements, incl. weapons, war-chariots, etc.
2. soldiers, the military.
3. warfare; battle, clash; conflict, hostilities.
   a. assault, attack; offensive, onslaught.
   b. bellicose, belligerent, combative; aggressive; rowdy, boisterous.
4. gen. term for non-Chinese peoples to the west; savages, barbarians, louts.
5. provide help, assist.

榕　róng　MC yowng
1. laurel-fig, Chinese banyan (*Ficus microcarpa*).

榮　róng　MC hjwaeng
1. (ef)florescence, esp. of herbaceous plants (cf. 華 *huá*, esp. of woody plants); burgeon(ing), fruition; in full glory, in full flower, flourishing.
   a. luxuriant, abundant.

2. glory, glorious; honor(able); e.g. ～辱 *róngrǔ*, honor and dishonor; ～君 *róngjūn*, "my glorious lord."

3. roof-tips; curved ends or "wings" of eaves.

4. mystical name for blood.

溶　róng　MC yowng

1. ample, broad; generous.

   a. rdup., amply adrift; also, surging and billowing (clouds or water); also, vast and ample; also, (med.), pure and pellucid, crystal-clear.

2. (bn.) ～與 *róngyǔ* (MC yowng-yoX), ⊙ 容與 *róngyǔ*, → 容 *róng* 3; (bn.) ～瀷 *róngyì* (MC yowng-yejH), shudder and shake, roll and rumble (of waves).

犾　róng　MC nyuwng

1. (med.) golden snub-nosed monkey (*Rhinopithecus roxellana*).

肜　róng　MC yuwng

1. Shang-period sacrifice of culmination, performed the day following a solemn sacrifice.

2. (med.) rdup., harmonious and concordant, ⊙ 融融 *róngróng*.

荿　róng　MC nyuwng

1. ～葵 *róngkuí*, hollyhock (*Althaea rosea*), syn. 蜀葵 *shǔkuí*.

2. ～菽 *róngshú*, broad-beans.

茸　róng　MC nyowng

1. down(y), covering of soft fibers.

   a. rdup., soft and downy, fluffy and fleecy, soft and shaggy.

   b. (bn.) 檌～ *běngróng*, → 檌 *běng*, also 龍～ *lóngróng*, → 龍 *lóng* (*lóng*); also, 丰～ *fēngróng*, → 丰 *fēng*.

2. freshly sprouted plants or budding flowers.

3. soft animal fur, down, fleece.

   a. velvet of deer antlers.

rǒng　MC nyowngX

1. push in; throw into.

2. ～闒 *rǒngtà* or 闒～ *tàrǒng*, "downy hair and small door," i.e. petty person, good-for-nothing, dummy, moron; also, base, menial, useless.

蓉　róng　MC yowng

1. (bn.) 芙～ *fúróng*, lotus, →芙 *fú*.

融　róng　MC yuwng

1. rising vapor.

   a. vaporize, dissipate.

   b. waft gently; e.g. ～泄 *róngyì*, swing and sway, dissolve and disperse in the wind.

2. melt, liquefy; thaw; e.g. ～風 *róngfēng*, "thawing breeze," the northeast wind of springtime.

3. melt together, fuse.

   a. perfuse, permeate; interfuse; infuse; perfusive, unobstructed.

4. bright(ness), brilliance, shining.

5. rdup., fine and fitting, harmonious and concordant, mild and agreeable; also, (med.) brightly glowing.

6. long-lasting, sustained; e.g. ～裔 *róngyī*, sustained and lingering (of music).

蠑　róng　MC hjwaeng

1. sgl. or ～螈 *róngyuán*, fire-bellied newt (*Cynops orientalis*).

鎔　róng　MC yowng

1. to fuse, melt together.

   a. smelt (metal); refine.

2. mold, matrix for casting.

髶　róng　MC nyowng

1. dishevelled or tangled hair.

rǒng

宂　rǒng　MC nyowngX

1. extraneous, superfluous; supernumerary.

   a. unused; idle.

2. commonplace, tiresome, humdrum; inferior, low-grade.

毧　rǒng　MC nyowngX

1. fleece of quadrupeds, down of birds.

róu

揉　róu　MC nyuw

1. bend, shape (wood); force into new configuration; twist.

   a. (med.) knead; press and roll with hands; rub.

2. bend to one's will, subdue, cause to submit.

3. 糅 *róu*, mix, jumble; confused.

柔　róu　MC nyuw

1. pliant, flexible, bendable, pliable, lithe; e.g. ～枝 *róuzhī*, a springy bough; ～筆 *róubǐ*, pliant writing-brush.
2. soft, tender, gentle.
   a. weak, delicate; ～日 *róurì*, weak days, even-numbered (*yin*) days of the *tian'gan* 天干 cycle (opp. 剛日 *gāngrì*, strong days, odd-numbered [*yang*]).
   b. docile, meek.
3. placate, pacify, conciliate; mollify, molliate; emollient; soften.
4. (med.) ～然 *róurán*, peoples of mixed ethnolinguistic ancestry who conquered the Eastern Steppe and established a kingdom ranging from Karashahr in northwestern Tarim Basin to the borders of north Korea, during 4th-6th centuries, identified with the Avars.

糅　róu　MC nyuw

1. mix(ed), jumble(d); confuse(d), confound(ed).
   a. assorted, motley, varied.
   b. interspaced, interleaved with.

蹂　róu　MC nyuwX

1. trample, stamp with the foot.
   a. tread on, crush.
2. debase, demean; humble, humiliate.
3. ⊙ 揉 *róu* 1a, knead, mold.

輮　róu　MC nyuwX

1. rim or felloe of a wheel.
2. ⊙ 揉 *róu*, to bend, shape, curve; 蹂 *róu*, trample, stamp, tread on.

鞣　róu　MC nyuw

1. to tan or cure leather.
2. (med.) 蹂 *róu*, trample, stamp; tread on.

ròu

肉　ròu　MC nyuwk

1. meat; flesh of animals.
   a. flesh of fruit, pulp.
2. skin, flesh of humans, often used pejoratively (in imperial times; before that, ref. only to animal flesh).
3. fleshy, soft; e.g. ～角 *ròujiǎo*, fleshy horn, of the "unicorn" (*qilin* 麒麟) which does no harm.

rú

儒　rú　MC nyu

1. those trained in the classic "Six Arts" (*liuyi* 六藝: ritual, music, archery, chariot driving, calligraphy, mathematics) of pre-imperial times.
2. those learned in the teachings, esp. ritual teachings, of "classic" texts and who attempt to act accordingly; classicist, traditionalist; sometimes, ritualist.
   a. from mid-Western Han times, those identifying themselves as followers of Confucius' teachings; Ruist (N.B. Better not to translate as "Confucian," because the "Confucian"-ism of such is compact of teachings often not found in, and sometimes at variance with, the reputed words of Confucius.)
   b. a bibliographic category, including works associated with classicist teachings.
3. pedant, pedagogue; used pejoratively or humilifically to describe a book-learner, in contrast to a man of action.
4. weak(ling); docile, timid.

嚅　rú　MC nyu

1. (bn.) ～呃 *rú'ér* (MC nyu-nye), strained smile, smirking laughter.
2. (bn.) 囁～ *nièrú*, → 囁 *niè*.

如　rú　MC nyo

1. follow, comply with, defer to; according to, in light of; e.g. ～武王之意 *rú wǔwáng zhi yì*, complying with (in light of) King Wu's intentions; ～律令 *rúlùlìng*, according to the statutes and documents, phrase that appears at end of Han-time official documents; (Dao.) 急急～律令 *jíjí rúlùlìng*, "promptly, promptly, according to the statutes and documents," expansion of preceding adopted in Dao. ritual petitions to other-worldly officials, borrowed from use in earlier funerary texts .
2. go to, proceed to; e.g. 公將～齊 *gōng jiāngrú qí*, his lordship is about to go to Qi.
3. following a VB or VB-phrase, introduces a descriptive complement: be like, as if, similar to; compare with, be equal to; e.g. 蓋之 ～天 容之～地 *gài zhī rú tiān róng zhī rú dì*, cover them over like the sky, accommodate them like the earth; 養民～子 *yǎng mín rú zǐ*, nurture the people as if they were children; A 不～ B, A does not compare with (is inferior to) B; syn. 若 *ruò* 1.

a. ～何 *rúhé*, 何～ *hérú*, → 何 *hé*.

b. demonstrative pronoun: this, such a(n); syn. 若 *ruò* 4.

c. in this way, so, such as; e.g. ～意 *rúyì*, as you wish; in med. times name of baton or scepter, often in evidence at court, among elegant literati, and used by Budd. monks, in varying symbolic fashion; (Budd.) ～是我聞 *rúshì wǒ wén*, "Thus (like this) have I heard," trns. Skt. *evaṃ mayā śrutam*, beginning phrase of most Budd. sutras, indicating that teachings to follow were heard from the Buddha himself; ～來 *rúlái*, the thus-come-one, epithet of the Buddha, trns. Skt. *tathāgata*; 真～ *zhēnrú*, true suchness, ultimate reality that is always thus and free from distinctions, trns. Skt. *bhūtatathatā*.

4. introduces conditional clause: if, supposing that . . .; e.g. 王～施仁政於民 *wáng rú shī rénzhèng yú mín*, if the king would extend a humane government to the people; ～不可求 *rú bùkě qiú*, if it cannot be sought; syn. 若 *ruò*, 2a.

5. with regard to, concerning, pertaining, as to . . .; syn. 若 *ruò* 5.

6. disjunctive marker of alternative: or rather, or instead; e.g. 予秦地如毋予孰吉 *yú qín dì rú wùyú shú jí*, To give land to Qin or rather not give, which is more favorable?

7. 2nd-person pronoun: you; syn. 若 *ruò* 6.

8. old term for 2nd lunar month.

孺　rú　MC nyuH

1. nursling, babe.

2. in early times, an heir-presumptive born of a concubine.

3. ～人 *rúrén*, term designating wife of a grandee; also used self-referentially by same.

帤　rú　MC nrjo

1. headwrap, made of large band of silk.

2. (med.) shabby, tattered, raggedy.

3. wood-strip reinforcing the grip of a bow.

濡　rú　MC nyu

1. moisten, dampen; soak, drench; immersed in, imbued with; e.g. ～首 *rúshǒu*, juicehead, sot.

a. glossy, lustrous, sleek, smooth.

2. favor or largesse bestowed or given.

3. gentle, soft; yielding, flexible.

4. detain, remain; pause, arrest; e.g. ～迹 *rújī*, stay one's steps, halt.

a. endure, bear with patience; e.g. ～忍 *rúrěn*, forbear, put up with.

繻　rú　MC nyu

1. fine silk gauze, taffeta.

2. safe-conduct pass or travel pass made of silk.

茹　rú　MC nyo

1. to eat, subsist on; swallow.

a. enfold, embrace.

2. gen. term for vegetable.

3. (bn.) ～藘 *rúlú* (MC nyo-ljo), ref. various species of madder (*Rubia*), roots used medicinally and also yielding a pigment used to produce a scarlet dye.

4. to measure, calculate.

a. guess at, conjecture.

5. soft(ened); rotten, putrid.

蕠　rú　MC nrjo

1. (bn.) 薊～ *jìrú*, → 薊 *jì*.

藘　rú　MC nyo

1. ⊙ 茹 *rú* 3, (bn.) ～藘 *rúlú* (nyo-ljo), ref. various species of madder (*Rubia*), roots used medicinally and also yielding a pigment used to produce a scarlet dye.

2. hemp-floss.

rú　MC nrjo

1. to stick, affix, attach to, paste.

蠕　rú　MC nyu

1. sgl. and (med.) rdup., crawl, wriggle, creep, squirm, writhe, worm.

a. move stealthily, skulk, slink.

2. (med.) rdup., the Avars, syn. 柔然 *róurán*, → 柔 *róu* 4.

衼　rú　MC nrjo

1. ball of old rags used to stop up a leak in a boat.

襦　rú　MC nyu

1. singlet, for men, unlined short garment; chemise, simarre, for women; bib, for infants.

2. fine silk gauze, taffeta, ⊙ 繻 *rú*.

醹　rú　MC nyu

1. thick wine, heady wine.

駕 rú　MC nyo

1. a type of small turnix, buttonquail, bustard-quail (*Turnicidae*); syn. 尺鷃 *chǐyàn*.

rǔ

乳 rǔ　MC nyuX

1. woman's breast, teat; nipple; mammary.
   a. to nurse, suckle, breast-feed.
   b. (med.) breast-milk.
   c. mammary-shaped; e.g. ～管 *rǔguǎn*, "nipple tubes," i.e. stalactites; ～香 *rǔxiāng*, "teat aromatic," i.e. frankincense.
   d. the bosses on the face of a chime-bell.
2. newborn, nursling; of birds, hatchling.
3. to nurture, brood, nest.

女 rǔ　MC nyoX　→ 女 *nǔ*.

擩 rǔ　MC nyuX

1. moisten, dampen; imbue, soak.
   a. (med.) to dye, stain.
      ruán　MC nywen
1. (med.) press or squeeze with fingers, knead.

汝 rǔ　MC nyoX

1. 2nd-person pronoun: you, your(s).
2. name of river rising in west-central Henan and running southeastward to join the Huai 淮 River.

辱 rǔ　MC nyowk

1. dishonor, disgrace(ful), ignominy, obloquy, disrepute; disfavor, discredit(ed).
2. humiliate, insult, abase(ment).
3. self-depreciatory ADV: unworthily, unworthy to…, unworthy of…, unsuited for…
4. ⊙ 溽 *rù*, moist, damp, humid.

rù

入 rù　MC nyip

1. enter, pass into, go in.
   a. give entrance to.
2. take in, accept; adopt.
3. pay in, hand in, remit.
4. be involved with, engage in; participate with, join in.
5. accord with, fit, conform to.

   a. combine with, take on the qualities of; e.g. ～神 *rùshén*, unite with the divine, seem as though supernatural.
6. (med.) ref. words of "entering" tone in the spoken language, those ending with a stopped consonant; entering-tone words classified as "oblique" or "deflected" (仄 *zè*), along with those in "rising" (上 *shǎng*) and "departing" (去 *qù*) tones, in binary contrast to those in "level" (平 *píng*) tone.

洳 rù　MC nyoH

1. (med.) wet, soak; low-lying, boggy; (bn.) 沮～ *jùrù*, → 沮 *jù* (*jǔ*).

溽 rù　MC nyowk

1. soak, drench; moist(en), damp(en); steep, immerse.
   a. humid, muggy, swelter(ing), sultry.
2. rich-tasting, savory, succulent.

縟 rù　MC nyowk

1. of ornamentation, elaborate, extravagant, overdone, involved, intricate; embellish(ment).
2. (med.) ⊙ 褥 *rù*, sitting-mat, cushion; pallet.

蓐 rù　MC nyowk

1. spikelet, new growth of plants; e.g. ～收 *rùshōu*, "Reaper (Harvester) of New Growths," name of tutelary deity of autumn and the west.
2. straw mat; cushion.
   a. pallet, mattress.

褥 rù　MC nyowk

1. bed-mat, bed-roll; pallet.
   a. sitting-mat, cushion.

ruán

堧 ruán　MC nywen

1. empty land between the walls of a shrine, palace, or city-wall and the outer surrounding wall; also, empty land by a riverside.

壖 ruán　MC nywen　⊙ 堧 *ruán*.

ruǎn

耎 ruǎn　MC nywenX

1. soft, pliable, supple; weak.
2. recoil, shrink back.

楥   ruǎn   MC nywenX
1. sgl. or ～棗 *ruǎnzǎo*, date-plum, lilac persimmon (*Diospyros lotus*), fruit yellow and juicy.

蝡   ruǎn   MC nywenX
1. (med.) rdup., the Avars, ⊙ 柔然 *róurán*, → 柔 *róu* 4.

軟   ruǎn   MC nywenX
1. weak, feeble.
2. (med.) soft, gentle; lithe, pliant, flexible, supple.
3. (med.) accommodating, agreeable, yielding.

輭   ruǎn   MC nywenX   ⊙ 軟 *ruǎn*.

阮   ruǎn   MC ngjwonX
1. a surname.
2. name of small feudal state in early Zhou times, in present-day southeastern Gansu.

ruí

緌   ruí   MC nywij
1. hanging tassels of knotted capstrings.
   a. ribbons hanging down as decorative tassels.
   b. (med.) rdup., dangling down.
2. gen. term for pennon, guidon.
3. proboscis, esp. of cicada.

蕤   ruí   MC nywij
1. frond; pendulant, droop(ing), esp. of leafage, foliage; festoon(ed).
   a. petals, panicle.
2. (bn.) 葳～ or 葳～ *wěiruí* (MC 'jwe-nywij), sealwort, Solomon's seal (*Polygonatum odoratum*), medicinal herb.

ruǐ

縈   ruǐ   MC nyweX
1. (med.) hang down, dangle, trail.

蕊   ruǐ   MC nyweX
1. (med.) ⊙ 藥 *ruǐ*.

藥   ruǐ   MC nyweX
1. stamen or thrum of a flower; perigynous, situated around the pistil or ovary.

   a. by metonymy, petal, flower.
   b. (Dao.) ～珠經 *ruǐzhūjīng*, Scripture of Stamen and Pearl, esoteric name for the *Scripture of the Yellow Court* (*Huangting jing* 黃庭經).
2. (med.) 玉～ *yùruǐ*, "jade stamens," passionflower (perhaps *Passiflora cochinchinensis*).
3. (med.) rdup., petals drifting down.

ruì

叡   ruì   MC ywejH   ⊙ 睿 *ruì*.

枘   ruì   MC nywejH
1. tenon, peg, pin.
   a. string-anchor, for the *se* 瑟, zither.

汭   ruì   MC nywejH
1. bend of a river, meander.
2. confluence of 2 streams.
3. (med.) riverbank, riverside.

瑞   ruì   MC dzyweH
1. auspicious sign, omen, or token; favorable, propitious, providential.
2. in early times, jade token of investiture (usu. 圭 *guī*, tablet, or 璧 *bì*, disc).

睿   ruì   MC ywejH
1. sagacious, sapient; percipient, farsighted; esp. ref. the emperor.

芮   ruì   MC nywejH
1. floss-silk, waste silk.
2. strap for holding a shield.
3. (med.) rdup., frail and fragile.
4. (med.) ⊙ 汭 *ruì* 1, bend of a river.

蕊   ruì   MC ywejH
1. sprout, bud, shoot, plants just showing above the ground.

蚋   ruì   MC nywet
1. blackfly, simulie.

蜹   ruì   MC nywet   ⊙ 蚋 *ruì*.

鋭   ruì   MC ywejH
1. sharp-edged, sharp-pointed; acute; finely honed.

a. highly trained; crack (troops).
b. punctilious, precise; scrupulous; finely focused.
2. tapered to a point; narrow; slight.
a. insufficient, scant.
3. swift, quick.

rún

犉 **rún** **MC nywin**
1. black-muzzled brown ox.

rùn

潤 **rùn** **MC nywinH**
1. moist(en); luster, lustrous; sheen, sleek.
a. rain; freshen, as with necessary moisture.
2. enrich, embellish, enhance; revise, improve; e.g. ～飾 *rùnshī*, enrich and adorn, esp. lit. composition.

閏 **rùn** **MC nywinH**
1. intercalary or epactic month, added to the calendar 7 times every 19 years in order to reconcile the lunar year with the solar year.
2. surplus, leftover.
a. deputy, substitute; usurp(ed).

ruò

弱 **ruò** **MC nyak**
1. tender, weak, frail, delicate; pliable, supple; e.g. ～湍 *ruòtuān*, gentle current; ～毫 *ruòháo*, supple hairs (of the writing-brush).
a. weaken, debilitate; fail.
b. undeveloped, inexperienced, immature, callow; e.g. ～齡 *ruòlíng*, "of tender age"; ～冠 *ruòguān*, callow (young man not yet capped) and capped (young man who has undergone the capping ceremony in his 20th year), thus gen. term for a youth of approx. 20 years.
2. lessen, reduce, decrease.
a. when following a number: not quite N, less than N.
3. ～水 *ruòshuǐ*, "Weak Water," name of a mythical river said to be near Mt. Kunlun, reputedly unable to bear up even the weight of a swan's feather.

爇 **ruò** **MC nywet**
1. burn; set fire to.

箬 **ruò** **MC nyak**
1. sgl. or ～竹 *ruòzhú*, broad-leaved bamboo (*Indocalamus tessellatus*).
2. an old Chu dialect word for bamboo rind or skin.

篛 **ruò** **MC nyak** ⊙ 箬 *ruò*.

若 **ruò** **MC nyak**
1. (be) like, similar to; compare with.
a. following a VB or VB-phrase, introduces descriptive complement: like, similar to; syn. 如 *rú* 1.
2. comply with, agree, assent to; approve; concordant, compliant; cog. 諾 *nùo*.
3. introduces a conditional clause: if; e.g. 王～隱其無罪而就死地 *wáng ruò yǐn qí wúzuì ér jiù sǐdì*, if the king was pained by its going to its place of death, having committed no wrong; ～時雨降 *ruò shíyǔ jiàng*, if the seasonal rains come (down); syn. 如 *rú* 4.
a. ～夫 *ruòfú*, introduces a topic contrasted with a preceding topic: but if, but as for; e.g. ～夫成功則天也 *ruòfú chénggōng zé tiān yě*, but if you succeed, it is thanks to heaven; ～夫君子所患 *ruòfú jūnzi suǒhuàn*, but as for what a man of noble status regards as a disaster.
4. used attributively to an embedded clause: that sort of, that kind of; e.g. 以～所為求～所欲 *yǐ ruò suǒwéi qiú ruò suǒyù*, to use that sort of act to satisfy that sort of desire.
a. demonstrative pronoun: this, such a(n); syn. 如 *rú* 3b.
5. with regard to, concerning, pertaining, as to ... ; syn. 如 *rú* 5.
6. 2nd-person pronoun: you; syn. 如 *rú* 7.
7. indicative of being undetermined or unspecified, sometimes interr.; e.g. ～干 *ruògān*, so many, so much; ～人 *ruòrén*, some person, someone; (med.) ～個 *ruògè*, which (of them)?
8. (med.) ～復 *ruòfù*, or; and also.
9. sgl. or in cmpd. 杜～ *dùruò*, pollia (*Pollia japonica*), herbaceous perennial that grows from stems of 1 to 3 feet, produces small, fragrant white flowers.
10. name of a sea-god.

11. 〜榴 *ruòliú* (MC nyak-ljuw), pomegranate, trsc. Sog. *n'r'kh*.

rě   MC nyaeX

1. (Budd.) 般〜 or 波〜 *bōrě* (MC pa-nyaeX), trsc. Skt. *prajñā*, wisdom, gnosis; 般〜波羅蜜 *bōrě-bōluómì* (MC pa-nyaeX-pa-la-mit), trsc. Skt. *prajñāpāramitā*, perfection of wisdom; 阿蘭〜 *ālánrě* (MC 'a-lan-nyaeX) or abb. 蘭〜 *lánrě* (MC lan-nyaeX), trsc. Skt. *araṇya*, quiet refuge, hermitage. 2. 〜榴 *rěliú* (MC nyak-ljuw), pomegranate, trsc. Sog. *n'r'kh*.

蒻   ruò   MC nyak

1. broadleaf cattail (*Typha latifolia*).
   a. reed-mat, made from preceding.
2. the part of a lotus root that stands above the mud.
3. 〜頭 *ruòtóu*, "cattail-head," i.e. devil's-tongue, elephant-foot, Jpn. *konnyaku* (*Amorphophallus rivieri, A. konjac*), subtropical single-leaved plant with long protruding spadix; syn. 蒟〜 *jǔruò*.

S

să

撒   să   MC sat

1. (med.) disperse, scatter; distribute; cast afar.

洒   să   MC sreaX

1. ⊙ 灑 *să* 1-3.

xǐ   MC sejX

1. wash, lave; scrub, scour; cleanse. N.B. This graph originally assoc. with this pronunciation and meaning, but became commonly used as substitute for 灑 *să*.

xiǎn   MC senX

1. stern, solemn.
2. sgl. or rdup., crisply cold, coolly chill.

cuǐ   MC tshwojX

1. high and steep.

灑   să   MC sreaX

1. sprinkle, asperse, sparge; spray, spatter; spew forth.
2. disperse, scatter, (be)strew; broadcast, sow; throw off.
   a. cast off restraint, unreserved, free, unhindered.
3. distribute into proper channels; divide, diverge (esp. waterway).

xǐ   MC srjeX

1. wash, lave; scrub; cleanse. N.B. This graph used for this pronunciation and meaning because 洒 *xǐ* (*să*) came to be commonly substituted for 灑 *să* and the substitution was then reciprocated.

纚   să   MC sreaX   → 纚 *xǐ*.

靸   să   MC sop

1. children's heelless slippers.
2. rise lightly, buoyant; float.
3. slop or spill over the side (of bowl or cup).

sà

卅   sà   MC sop

1. combined form of 三十 *sānshí*, thirty.

搬   sà   MC sat

1. strike or slap with the side of the hand; side-swipe.
2. (med.) (bn.) 抹〜 *mǒsà*, → 抹 *mǒ*.

薩   sà   MC sat

1. (Budd.) 菩〜 *púsà*, → 菩 *pú*.

颯   sà   MC sop

1. rdup., onom. of the wind, whooshing and rushing, gusting and blustering; or of falling rain, plashing and splotching, lap-lap; also descriptive of speed, in no time, swift and sudden.
2. (bn.) 〜沓 *sàtà* (MC sop-dop), full and exuberant; (bn.) 〜爽 *sàshuǎng* (MC sop-srjang), with verve and vigor, bluff and hardy, of a strong wind or a commanding individual.
3. to have spent one's force, be "blown out"; be enfeebled, in decline; withering, aging; sere.
4. (med.) sudden(ly), abrupt(ly).

sāi

塞 **sāi** MC sok

1. obstruct, block, plug, close up.
    a. restrain, check, forbid.
    b. to fill, stuff, pervade, saturate with; satiate, satisfy.
    c. to supply, compensate; recompense.

sài MC sojH

1. strategic stronghold, fortress, usu. on the border > gen. term for frontier.
    a. ref. Great Wall e.g. ～外 *sàiwài*, area beyond (north of) the Great Wall.
2. thank-offering to a divinity (cf. 1c above).
3. a board-game: ⊙ 簺 *sài* 1.
4. (Budd.) ～頗胝加 *sàipōdìjiā* (MC sojH-pha-trij-kae), trsc. Skt. *sphaṭika*, quartz crystal, one of the 7 treasures (*saptaratna*)

sè MC sok

1. (med.) northwest dialect reading of 相 *xiāng* 1, 2,

毸 **sāi** MC swoj

1. (med.) (bn.) 毰～ *péisāi*, → 毰 *péi*.

腮 **sāi** MC soj

1. ⊙ 鰓 *sāi*, lower half of the face below the cheekbones; jaws, jowls; 鰓 *sāi*, gills of fish.

鰓 **sāi** MC soj

1. lower half of the face below the cheekbones.
    a. jaws.

顋 **sāi** MC soj ⊙ 鰓 *sāi*.

鰓 **sāi** MC soj

1. gills of fish.

sài

塞 **sài** MC sojH → 塞 *sāi*.

簺 **sài** MC sojH

1. board-game akin to *liubo* 六博; also called 格五 *géwǔ*, "5-square" (because draughtsmen move a maximum of 5 spaces in a turn).
2. (med.) bamboo fish-weir, fish-garth.

賽 **sài** MC sojH

1. sacrificial thank-offering to spirits, usu. made to local tutelary deity.
2. compete, vie, contend, rival.

sān

三 **sān** MC sam

1. numeral three, third; triple; thrice.
    a. important number symbolically, e.g. the triad of heaven, earth, and man, from which many trinities are derived; also in Budd. such as 3 Vehicles, 3 periods, 3 realms of existence, 3 divisions ("baskets") of the canon, etc.; also in Dao. such as 3 heavens of "clarity," 3 abysses, 3 Primes, 3 divisions ("caverns") of the canon, etc.
2. several, many; repeatedly, time and again.

毿 **sān** MC som

1. (med.) rdup., fine-tressed (hair), long-plumed (feathers), lush-leaved (tree branches).

sǎn

傘 **sǎn** MC sanX

1. parasol, sunshade; esp. used as item of regalia.
    a. umbrella, rainguard.

糤 **sǎn** MC somX ⊙ 糝 *sǎn*.

糝 **sǎn** MC somX

1. rice-gruel added to meat, ragout with rice.

纙 **sǎn** MC sanX ⊙ 傘 *sǎn*.

鐖 **sǎn** MC sanX

1. (med.) crossbow trigger.

饊 **sǎn** MC sanX

1. dry-fried sweet doughcake; doughnut.

sàn

散 **sàn** MC sanH

1. scatter(ed), (be)strew(n), shed.
    a. disperse, spread, circulate, diffuse.
    b. squander, dissipate, blow.
2. give up, let go of, turn loose.
3. distract, divert; find diversion in.
4. (med.) ～沬 *sànmò* (MC sanH-mat), sambac, Arabian jasmine (*Jasminum sambac*), trsc. Arab. *zanbaq*, jasmine-oil.

sǎn   MC sanX

1. relax(ed), loose.

   a. unregulated, unassigned; free-style, ordinary; e.g. ～民 *sǎnmín*, ordinary people (opp. 梟民 *xiǎomín*, leading people); ～棋 *sǎnqí*, ordinary draughtsmen (as in board-game).

   b. random, unsystematic; imperfect, partial; e.g. ～質 *sǎnzhì*, imperfect substance.

2. triturate, grind or pound to powder.

   a. powder, esp. of medicinal nature; e.g. (med.) 五石～ *wǔshísǎn*, 5-mineral powder, recreational drug compounded of stalactite, sulphur, milky quartz, amethyst, red bole; also called 寒食～ *hánshísǎn*, cold-food powder (because to be taken only with cold food).

3. melody, tune, esp. of zither music, usu. attached as suffix to particular title.

sāng

桑   **sāng   MC sang**

1. mulberry tree (*Morus alba*), esp. important in sericulture (common women's occupation), as its leaves provide nourishment for the silkworm; hence a symbol of hearth and home, esp. as cmpd. ～梓 *sāngzǐ*, mulberry and catalpa (the latter important in woodworking).

   a. ～田 *sāngtián*, mulberry fields, symbolic of inexorable passage of the centuries, from story of the Eastern Sea changing to mulberry fields (and back again) through the aeons.

sǎng

顙   **sǎng   MC sangX**

1. forehead.

   a. cmpd. 稽～ *qǐsǎng*, to kowtow.

sàng

喪   **sàng   MC sangH**

1. to lose, fail to keep; renounce, abandon.
2. founder, suffer.

   a. be bereft of; be bereaved, mourn.

3. to flee; fugitive.

   sāng   MC sang

1. death; destruction.

   a. obsequies, funeral rites.

   b. encoffined corpse.

2. bereavement, mourning; luctiferous; e.g. ～服 *sāngfú*, mourning attire.

3. fell, baleful.

sāo

搔   **sāo   MC saw**

1. to scratch; rub, chafe, irritate.
2. ⊙ 騷 *sāo* 1, agitated(d).

繰   **sāo   MC saw**

1. to reel silk from cocoons placed in hot or boiling water.

   zǎo   MC tsawX

1. ⊙ 璪 *zǎo*, fringe of beaded pendants on ceremonial headwear; 藻 *zǎo*, literary ornamentation.

臊   **sāo   MC saw**

1. smell of animal meat, gamy, rank; rancid, e.g. ～膏 *sāogāo*, "rancid grease," dog-fat.

   a. stench of a bad reputation.

騷   **sāo   MC saw**

1. agitate(d), disturb(ed); irritate(d).

   a. rdup., of fast-running water, hissing and surging; of heavy wind, gusting and galing, rush and bluster; (bn.) ～屑 *sāoxiè* (MC sawset), of trees in the wind, shaken and shuddering, in tremulous agitation > shaken to splinters, of emotional upset.

2. sgl. or in cmpd. ～體 *sāotǐ*, type of verse associated with the poem 離～ "Lí sāo" attributed to Qu Yuan 屈原, a reputedly banished and unappreciated court official of the ancient state of Chu 楚; in the poem's title the word is traditionally glossed as meaning "sorrow."

   a. ～人 *sāorén*, Qu Yuan, or in gen. any poet.

3. ⊙ 臊 *sāo*, gamy, rancid; 掃 *sǎo*, sweep away.

sǎo

埽   **sǎo   MC sawX   ⊙ 掃 *sǎo*.**

掃   **sǎo   MC sawX**

1. sweep, sweep away; clear away, brush away; whisk off.

   a. get rid of, remove; eliminate.

2. (med.) brush on > paint (eyebrows, makeup).
3. sgl. or (med.) ～地 *sǎodì*, the whole of, all of; thoroughly, completely; without a trace.

sào

毥　sào　MC sawH
1. (med.) (bn.) 毥～ *màosào*, → 毥 *mào*.

sè

嗇　sè　MC srik
1. thrifty, frugal, sparing; chary of, economical.
2. be overly attached to, stingy, miserly, parsimonious; avaricious.
3. ～夫 *sèfū*, husbander, bailiff, low-level functionary (through Han times).
4. ⊙ 穡 *sè*, to harvest, reap.

澀　sè　MC srip
1. (med.) rough, unsmooth, coarse (ant. 滑 *huá*, smooth; glossy).
   a. (med.) rugged, stubbled, hubbly, rough-hewn, of land.
   b. (med.) crabbed, labored, forced, of lit. style; also, of speech, ⊙ 譅 *sè*.
2. (med.) tart, astringent, acrid, of taste.
3. (med.) hard to understand, obscure; unfathomable.

澁　sè　MC srip　⊙ 澀 *sè*.

瑟　sè　MC srit
1. zither-like instrument variously described as having sixteen, (most often) twenty-five, or fifty strings, with movable bridges; translate as "zithern" to distinguish from 琴 *qín* ("zither"), zither of seven strings, without bridges, and 箏 *zhēng* ("cither"), zither of intermediate size, with movable bridges. A more robust and serious instrument than the *qín*; the two together (琴瑟 *qínsè*) often metaphorical of conjugal harmony or close friendship. N.B. Do not translate any of these as "lute," which is the *pipa* 琵琶, a quite different, round-bodied instrument held before one's chest.
2. sedate, solemn, grave; dignified.
3. flourishing, dense, thick, teeming.
4. rdup., onom. soughing and sighing of wind, esp. in autumn; also (med.), a blue-gem, mostly lapis lazuli with some sodalite and possibly sapphire > deep-blue color, deep azure, lapis-blue.
5. (bn.) ～索 *sèsuǒ* (MC srit-sak) or ～縮 *sèsuǒ* (MC srit-srjuwk), coiled and curled, twisted together, gathered and drawn in, shrinking back, narrowing down.

穡　sè　MC srik
1. (to) harvest, reap.
   a. to sow and cultivate, esp. grain.
   b. farmwork in general.
2. ⊙ 嗇 *sè* 1, thrifty, sparing.

色　sè　MC srik
1. hue (from original meanings "form, appearance, complexion"); visual surface quality; manifestation.
   a. appearance, aspect, guise; esp. ref. natural setting or (Budd.) as trns. of Skt. *rūpa*, form, matter, outward appearance.
   b. countenance, facial expression; fair-faced.
   c. desirable appearance or attractiveness of physical objects, surface appeal, sensuality, esp. of feminine beauty; sexual desire.
   d. color(ing).
2. (med.) type, variety, kind.
3. (med.) ⊙ 索 *suǒ* 4, to seek.

譅　sè　MC srip
1. ⊙ 澀 *sè* 1b, crabbed, labored, forced, of speech or of lit. style.

sēn

森　sēn　MC srim
1. heavily wooded, forest(ed), thick-set; densely planted; thicket.
   a. to forest, crowd together like unthinned trees.
   b. rdup., lushly luxuriant, plentifully profuse; densely tufted.

sēng

僧　sēng　MC song
1. Budd. monk, bonze.
   a. abb. trsc. of Skt. *saṁgha*, the Budd. order, community of devotees.
2. (med.) (bn.) ～耆 (MC song-gij), ～祇 *sēngqí* (MC song-gjie), dark-skinned person, trsc. of Arab. *zanj, zanjī*, black person.
3. (Budd.) trsc. Skt. *sam*, completely, e.g. 波羅～竭諦 *bōluósēngjiédì*, Skt. *pārasamgate*, "to the other shore completely gone."

shā

椴　shā　MC sreat
1. ancient name in Chu 楚 for 茱萸 *zhūyú*, prickly-ash; → 茱 *zhū*.

殺　shā　MC sreat
1. terminate.
   a. bring to a close, put an end to, conclude; complete, wrap up.
   b. put to death, kill; slaughter; assail, wound, strip of.
2. fail, be at the end of; decay(ed), wear away; spoil.
3. (med.) following VB or ADJ, extremely, to the maximal extent; e.g. 愁～ *chóushā*, as sad as can be.
   a. (med.) 可～ *kěshā*, extremely, very, exceedingly; e.g. 可～濕 *kěshāshī*, excessively wet.
   ### shài　MC sreajH
1. diminish, reduce, lessen; despoil of.

沙　shā　MC srae
1. sand; sand-grain; granular, powdery; pebble.
   a. abb. of 丹～ *dānshā*, cinnabar granules, i.e. cinnabar.
   b. (bn.) ～鰡 *shāliù* (MC srae-ljuw), sanddab (*Citharichthys*).
   c. ～梨 *shālí*, sand-pear, coarse variety of 梨 *lí*, pear; ～棠 *shātáng*, species of wild pear with yellow flowers, red fruit that tastes like the plum (李 *lǐ*) but without a pit; its wood valued for making boats; reputedly also found on Mount Kunlun 崑崙山.
2. sandshore, strand.
3. sgl. or cmpd. ～汏 *shātài*, sift out (< wash from sand), rinse; winnow, refine; remove the coarse while retaining the fine; (med.) also, gossip (about), criticize, take the shine off.
4. ⊙ 紗 *shā*, plain-weave gauze; tulle.
5. (Budd.) ～門 *shāmén* (MC srae-mwon), trsc. of Skt. *śramaṇa*, ascetic practitioner, mendicant, later used as gen. ref. to monks (*not* a shaman); ～彌 *shāmí* (MC srae-mjie), abb. trsc. of Skt. *śrāmaṇera*, Budd. novice.
   ### suō　MC swa
1. (bn.) ～劘 *suōmó* (swa-ma), fondle, stroke gently.

砂　shā　MC srae
1. (med.) ⊙ 沙 *shā*.

紗　shā　MC srae
1. plain-weave gauze; tulle; e.g. ～羅 *shāluó*, tulle and gauze; also, silk-gauze woven with intersecting diagonal threads.
2. ～鰡 *shāliù*, sanddab; ⊙ 沙鰡 *shāliù*.

莎　shā　MC srae　→ 莎 *suō*.

裟　shā　MC srae
1. (bn.) 袈～ *jiāshā*, monk's robe, *kaṣāya*, → 袈 *jiā*.

鎩　shā　MC sreat
1. long-bladed lance; a rapier.
2. to shear, clip, crop.
3. damaged wings of a bird > become powerless, lose the ability to realize one's ambitions, be past hope, discouraged.

鯊　shā　MC srae
1. the goby fish (*Acanthogobious flavianus*), syn. 鮀 *tuó* 1.

魦　shā　MC srae　⊙ 鯊 *shā*.

shà

唼　shà　MC sraep
1. nibble, peck at; (bn.) ～喋 *shàzhá* (MC sraep-draep), nibble and nacker.
2. ⊙ 歃 *shà*, smear on the mouth, esp. blood of sacrificial offering in ritual of covenant or treaty of alliance.
   ### qiè　MC tshjep
1. sgl. or cmpd. ～佞 *qiènìng*, insinuate, gloze, wheedle, beguile.

嗄　shà　MC sraeH
1. hoarse, raspy, cracked (of voice).

廈　shà　MC haeX
1. stately residence, mansion; ⊙ 夏 *xià* 1a.

歃　shà　MC sreap
1. to drink or smear on the mouth, esp. blood of sacrificial offering as oath in ancient ritual of covenant or treaty of alliance.

煞　shà　MC sreajH
1. spirit of the dead, esp. malignant revenant.

a. (Dao.) malignant earth spirits, death-bringers, which can seize one's *hun* 魂 and *po* 魄 souls.

2. ⊙ 殺 *shā* 3, following VB or ADJ, extremely, to the maximal extent

    shā　MC sreat

1. ⊙ 殺 *shā* 1, terminate, conclude; kill.

箑　shà　MC sreap
1. a fan held in the hand; flabellum.
    a. fan the air to cool off.

霎　shà　MC sreap
1. light rain, soft rain.
    a. rdup., onom. of drumming rain, prap-prap.
2. short period of time, an instant, moment(ary); precipitate; fleeting.

shāi

篩　shāi　MC srij
1. sieve, strainer, sifter, made of bamboo; some-times, winnowing basket.
    a. sift finer elements from coarser; strain.
    b. shake, vibrate.

筛　shāi　MC srje　⊙ 篩 *shāi*.

shài

曬　shài　MC sreaH
1. dry in the sun, expose to the light.
    a. shine, glint (of sunshine).
2. (med.) VB-suffix indicating extreme state, ⊙ 殺 *shā* 3.

shān

刪　shān　MC sraen
1. cut off, cut out, delete, abridge, curtail, expur-gate, esp. of texts.

埏　shān　MC syen　→埏 *yán*.

姍　shān　MC san
1. rdup., walk without haste, in a leisurely way, stroll easily.
    shàn　MC sraenH
1. mock, ridicule, deride; ⊙ 訕 *shàn* 2.

山　shān　MC srean
1. mountain(ous), either single mountain or massif, mountain range.
    a. ～林 *shānlín*, mountain grove; also, her-mitage; (med.) ～朵 *shānduǒ*, "mountain ear," i.e. mountaintop; (med.) ～都 *shāndū*, "mountain citizen," i.e. gibbon.
2. pile up, mound up.

掺　shān　MC sream
1. rdup., dainty and delicate.
    shǎn　MC sreamX
1. pick up; hold on to, carry.
    sēn　MC srim
1. ⊙ 森 *sēn*, densely wooded, thick-set.
    càn　MC tshomH
1. (med.) ～撾 *cànzhuā*, drum-roll, beat a drum rapidly.

杉　shān　MC sream
1. giant evergreen conifer (*Cunninghamia lan-ceolata*), sometimes called China-fir or cedar though it is neither, actually a sweetly-scented cypress whose wood is much valued in building; sometimes also identified as *Cryptomeria fortu-neii* or *japonica* (because conflated with Jpns. *sugi*) but that species not known in China till late med. times and after.

濣　shān　MC sraen
1. tearful(ly), lachrymose, weeping.

䚟　shān　MC sraem　→䚟 *qián*.

煽　shān　MC syen
1. fan a fire, fan the flames.
    a. inflame, incite, impassion, work up.

珊　shān　MC san
1. (bn.) ～瑚 *shānhú* (MC san-hu), coral.
2. rdup., onom. of wind or rain, sa-sa, hish-hish; of tinkling jade, tam-tam.

痁　shān　MC syem
1. lingering fever (cf. 痎 *jiē*, intermittent fever).

羴　shān　MC syen
1. odor of sheep; goatish, hircine, hircose; gamy.
    a. describing anything of similarly unpleas-ant odor; rank, stink; fetid.

膻   shān   MC syen

1. ⊙ 羶 *shān*.

dàn   MC danX

1. bare, exposed(d), open to view; naked.
2. mediastimum.

芟   shān   MC sraem

1. cut down grass, mow.
    a. weed out, prune; eliminate.
2. sickle, scythe.

苫   shān   MC syem

1. anything made with a covering of straw, rushes, thatch, e.g. mats, roofs.
    a. simple thatch-roofed mourning hut.

shàn   MC syemH

1. to thatch, cover with thatch.

衫   shān   MC sraem

1. unlined upper garment, singlet; blouse, chemise; smock; sometimes without sleeves, a vest.
    a. to wear, don; be garbed.

shǎn

搟   shǎn   MC syemX

1. (med.) ⊙ 閃 *shǎn* 2, in a flash, in an instant.

睒   shǎn   MC syemX

1. (med.) ⊙ 閃 *shǎn*.

閃   shǎn   MC syemX

1. glance, glimpse; blink at.
2. flash, flicker.
    a. in a flash, in an instant; fleeting.

shàn

善   shàn   MC dzyenX

1. good; favorable; excellent; benevolent; actions deriving from inner moral power.
    a. advantageous; appropriate.
    b. ameliorate, improve.
2. be good at, excel at, skilled at.
    a. be inclined to, show a pronounced tendency toward.
3. show goodwill, be on good terms with; favor.
    a. well-known, familiar.
4. approve, esp. statement of imperial approval: "Excellent!"

5. (Budd.) 〜權 *shànquán*, skilful means, trns. Skt. *upāya* (syn. 方便 *fāngbiàn*); 〜逝 *shànshì*, "Well-Gone," epithet of a buddha, trns. Skt. *sugata*.

墠   shàn   MC dzyenX

1. flat suburban land prepared for a sacrificial ceremony; a place to perform sacrifice.
2. to clear and prepare land for sacrificial ceremony.
3. ⊙ 禪 *shàn* 1, the imperial *shan* sacrifice to earth.

嬗   shàn   MC dzyenH

1. change, transform, evolve; substitute.
    a. transfer the throne to someone else; abdicate, ⊙ 禪 *shàn* 2.

扇   shàn   MC syenH

1. door leaf; door, usu. made out of bamboo or reed-thatch.
    a. one leaf of a two-part object.
    b. measure-word for doors, windows, etc.
2. a fan, flabellum, for relief from heat.
3. cloth headkerchief, to protect from sunlight or dust.
4. castrate, spay, neuter an animal; replaced in med. period by 騸 *shàn*.

shān   MC syen

1. to fan, producing a current of air > to urge on, encourage to action, incite, foment.

掞   shàn   MC syemH

1. unfold; extend, stretch out.

yǎn   MC yemX

1. (med.) ⊙ 剡 *yǎn*, keen, sharp; acute, pointed; cut off, shear.

yàn   MC yemH

1. (med.) ⊙ 焰 *yàn* 1, flame-tip; ray of light.

擅   shàn   MC dzyenH

1. act on one's own, without consultation with or approval from others; usurp, arrogate, vendicate; dictatorial; stake a claim to.
2. occupy unique position, hold first place in; be expert or skilful in (syn. of verbal use of 專 *zhuān*).
3. ⊙ 禪 *shàn* 2, abdicate the throne.

汕   shàn   MC sraenH

1. wicker-net for catching fish.
    a. to fish with the preceding.

疝　**shàn**　MC sraenH
1. hernia.
   a. gen. ref. various maladies of the lower abdomen or genitalia.

禪　**shàn**　MC dzyenH
1. imperial ceremony of sacrifice to earth, to be conducted in conjunction with the 封 *fēng* sacrifice to heaven when there is harmony throughout the realm resulting from ideal government; traditionally carried out at Mt. Liangfu 梁父山 or Mt. Sheshou 社首山, near Mt. Tai 泰山 where the *feng* was performed.
2. to abdicate or cede, esp. the throne; to replace with, transfer; yield, step away from.
   chán　MC dzyen
1. (bn.) ～于 *chányú* (MC dzyen-hju), title of the Xiongnu supreme leader; also written 單于.
2. (Budd.) sgl. or in bn. ～那 *chánné* (MC dzyen-na) trsc. of Skt. *dhyāna*, meditation, e.g. ～定 *chándìng*, *dhyāna*-concentration; 四～ *sìchán*, the four stages of meditation or the four *dhyāna*-heavens.
   a. in general ref. Buddhism and Budd. practices.
   b. composure, equanimity.

繕　**shàn**　MC dzyenH
1. mend, repair, restore, make whole again; preserve in near-original fashion.
2. make a fair copy of a text or document.

膳　**shàn**　MC dzyenH
1. repast, fine meal; savory dishes; e.g. 六～ *liùshàn*, "the six viands," i.e. beef, mutton, pork, dog, goose, fish.
2. preparation of meals, cooking, esp. to boil meat.

訕　**shàn**　MC sraenH
1. slander, libel, calumniate; vilify; backbite.
2. ridicule, mock, sneer at.

贍　**shàn**　MC dzyemH
1. provide for, supply so as to meet all needs.
   a. well-provided, in all sufficiency; affluent, rich.
   b. rich of language, full-toned, sumptuous in diction.
2. ⊙ 澹 *dàn*, placid, tranquil.

釤　**shàn**　MC sraemH
1. (med.) large sickle, reaping-hook.
   a. (med.) to cut down, mow.
   xiān　MC sjem
1. ⊙ 銛 *xiān* 2, acuminate, pointed, sharp, keen.

鱔　**shàn**　MC dzyenX
1. the mud-eel (*Heterenchelyidae* or *Flutidae*).
   tuó　MC da
1. ⊙ 鼉 *tuó*, alligator.

鱓　**shàn**　MC dzyenX
1. (med.) ⊙ 鱔 *shàn*, mud-eel.

shāng

傷　**shāng**　MC syang
1. wound; harm; injure, impair; hurt(ful).
2. feel pity for, be hurt by; be troubled over.
3. grieve for, lament, mourn.
4. (med.) excessive(ly), too much, more than usual.

商　**shāng**　MC syang
1. merchant, trade(r); peddler; engage in trade; e.g. ～賈 *shānggǔ*, traveling and resident traders; ～旅 *shānglǚ*, itinerant merchant, usu. far from home.
   a. commerce, commercial activity.
2. reckon, figure the numbers of.
   a. consider; deliberate, discuss.
3. graduated markings on a clepsydra.
4. name of note of the pentatonic scale, symbolically associated with autumn > euph. for autumn; e.g. ～歌 *shānggē*, ～聲 *shāngshēng*, song in the *shang* mode, i.e. of sadness, as of autumn when plants wither and die.
5. alt. name for *xin* 心, "Heart," constellation, one of the 28 lunar lodgings, comprised of 3 stars, α (Antares), σ, τ Scorpii, in the eastern quadrant (*qinglong* 青龍 or *canglong* 蒼龍) of the sky.
6. name of dynasty, ca. 1600-ca. 1046 BCE.

殤　**shāng**　MC syang
1. die young.
   a. obsequies for someone who dies young.
2. die in battle.

觴   shāng   MC syang
1. kylix, a shallow, oval-shaped, and stemless wine goblet, usu. with 2 flat handles or "wings" to hold while drinking from one of the vessel's ends, hence often called 羽〜 *yǔshāng*, winged kylix.
   a. drink; drinking together, compotation.
   b. toast, invite to drink.

shǎng

賞   shǎng   MC syangX
1. award, reward for merit.
   a. (med.) gen. term for bestow(al), give (to), grant.
2. esteem, prize, value; praise.
   a. appreciate, recognize the worth of; appraise.
3. (med.) enjoy(ment), take pleasure in; e.g. 〜心 *shǎngxīn*, delight the heart.

shàng

上   shàng   MC dzyangH; dzyangX (when vb)
1. on top, above; on high, higher; up(ward).
   a. respectful term for emperor, "His Highness."
   b. superior in rank, status, or quality; supreme, best, highest; e.g. (Budd.) 〜佛道 *shàngfódào*, supreme Buddha-path; (Budd.) 〜人 *shàngrén*, "superior one," "Your (or His) Eminence," "Your Reverence," respectful epithet for monk; (Dao.) 〜清 *shàngqīng*, "Highest Clarity," name of the heaven whose deities bestowed the revelations of 364-370 and by which those revelations are known.
2. earlier in time (time thought of as descending from higher to lower); former, prior; e.g. 〜世 *shàngshì*, earlier generations; 〜古 *shànggǔ*, high antiquity.
3. first in a sequence, esp. of 2 (〜, 下) or 3 (〜, 中, 下); e.g. 〜卷 *shàngjùan*, first fascicle.
   a. aforementioned, before.
4. present or submit, hand up, offer up a document or offering to someone of higher rank, incl. emperor or spirit.
5. place above, in fact or thought; prefer; exalt; hallow; after mid-Han times usu. replaced in this meaning by → 尚 *shàng*.

shǎng   MC dzyangX
1. go up, ascend, get on (as in climbing a mountain, mounting a horse or carriage, boarding a boat, etc.)
   a. go forward, proceed onward.
2. (med.) ref. words of "rising" tone in the spoken language; rising-tone words classified as "oblique" or "deflected" (仄 *zè*), along with those in "departing" (去 *qù*) and "entering" (入 *rù*) tones, in binary contrast to those in "level" (平 *píng*) tone.

尚   shàng   MC dzyangH
1. place above, in fact or thought; high regard; prefer, attach special importance to, put high, set ahead, give precedence to; exalt; hallow; e.g. 〜志 *shàngzhì*, set one's aims high; 〜書 *shàngshū*, the Hallowed Documents (or 書經 *shūjīng*, Canon of Documents, Book of Documents), though some commentators intepret the modifier in the sense of 3, the Venerable Documents.
2. surpass, go beyond in excellence; ideal, goal; e.g. 微〜 *wēishàng*, inconsiderable ideals (usu. self-depreciatory).
3. far back in time, of the remote past; venerable.
4. marry upward, esp. into the royal family; e.g. 〜主 *shàngzhǔ*, marry a princess.
5. forehandle, forehold, manage, esp. be in charge of a ruler's certain affair; magister (as title); e.g. 〜書 *shàngshū*, magister of documents, originally superintendent of archives, so in Han times 〜書臺 *shàngshūtái*, Tribunal of the Magistry of Documents, was the imperial secretariat; but in Tang times 〜書省 *shàngshūshěng*, Bureau of the Magistry of Documents (usu. ref. to as Bureau of State Affairs), was the chief administrative bureau of central government, with six Boards (*bu* 部) each headed by a 〜書 *shàngshū*, Magister of Documents (the imperial secretariat then being known as *zhongshusheng* 中書省).
6. (ADV) still, yet; even.
   a. almost, nearly, just about.
7. used to express wish, command, or prayer: May (it be that)...

shāo

弰   shāo   MC sraew
1. end-tips of a bow.

捎　shāo　MC sraew

1. brush, stroke, touch lightly in passing, graze; pass over lightly.
2. lift up, raise up; wave, wield, brandish.
    a. strike, hit, club.
3. cut down, mow, weed out.
    a. get rid of, eliminate, remove; abolish, do away with.

梢　shāo　MC sraew

1. tip or end of a twig or branch, nib.
    a. nib or tip of anything long and tapered (lash of a whip, nib of writing-brush, etc.).
2. rudder of a boat.
3. wooden stick, rod.
4. strike down, fell.
5. rdup., onom. of soughing and sighing of wind; also, jutting out, protruding, sticking out.

燒　shāo　MC syew

1. burn, set fire to; cook, heat-roast.

shào　MC syewH

1. burn off vegetation to clear land for planting; swidden.
2. (med.) wildfire.

稍　shāo　MC sraew

1. slightly, a bit, a little, a few, of a small quantity or amount; less significant.
2. bit by bit, little by little, gradually.
    a. (med.) for the time being, for the moment; already.
    b. (med.) somewhat, hardly.
3. tip of an ear of grain.
    a. cmpd., ～食 shāoshí, monthly grain stipend of an official.
4. ⊙ 梢 shāo, nib, tip of a twig or branch; 弰 shāo, end-tips of a bow.

筲　shāo　MC sraew

1. bucket made of bamboo or wood strips, to contain rice or grain; vessel used to contain grain offering in a sacrificial ceremony.
    a. small amount, insignificant; e.g. 斗～ dǒushāo, of slight ability, narrow-minded.

篍　shāo　MC sraew

1. brush made of bamboo, used to scrape the bottom of pot or pan.
2. ⊙ 筲 shāo, bamboo basket, esp. for holding rice or grain.

蛸　shāo　MC sraew

1. (bn.) 蠨～ xiāoshāo (MC sew-sraew), long-legged spider, spume-spinning spider, esp. associated with the South.

xiāo　MC sew

1. (bn.) 螵～ piāoxiāo (MC phjew-sew), mantis egg-case, used medicinally; also, the cuttlefish.

髾　shāo　MC sraew

1. long fringe or hanging frill resembling a swallowtail on a woman's garments.
2. hanging plumes on banner or pennon.
3. (med.) falling tresses.

sháo

勺　sháo　MC dzyak

1. ladle; spoon.
    a. ladle out, spoon out.
2. measure of capacity, equiv. 1/100 "pint" (*sheng* 升).
3. ⊙ 芍 sháo, in bn. 芍藥 sháoyào, flowering peony.

zhuó　MC tsyak

1. ⊙ 酌 zhuó 1, pour into a cup, ladle, esp. wine; shenk.

韶　sháo　MC dzyew

1. music associated with the legendary sage-king Shun 舜; often in the cmpd. 簫～ xiāosháo, hallowed hymnody.
2. (med.) gracious(ness), splendid, lovely.
3. (med.) ～子 sháozǐ, rambutan (*Nephelium lappaceum*), spiny-red tropical fruit, similar to lychee when peeled.

芍　sháo　MC dzyak

1. (bn.) ～藥 sháoyáo, flowering peony (*Paeonia lactiflora*).

shǎo

少　shǎo　MC syewX

1. few, of a small quantity (ant. 多 dūo, many). >
    a. be short of, lacking, wanting, scarce; e.g. ～情 shǎoqíng, wanting in passion.
2. belittle, look down upon, depreciate; despise.
3. slightly, a little; scarcely.
4. for a moment, a short while.

shào   MC syewH

1. young, youth(ful) (ant. 老 *lǎo*, old); e.g. ～年 *shàonián*, young or few in years.
   a. pertaining to the end or near the end in sequence or order.
2. lesser; deputy position, subordinate in status; junior; e.g. ～師 *shàoshī*, junior preceptor; (med.) ～府 *shàofǔ*, "Deputy Repositor," in Tang times informal title of the → 尉 *wèi* in a district (*xian* 縣), 4th-ranking (of 4) centrally appointed officials, responsible for local military and police matters, subordinate to the 令 *lìng* ("commandant," magistrate) who was informally known as 明府 *míngfǔ*, "Enlightened Repositor."

shào

劭   shào   MC dzyewH

1. encourage, exhort, urge.
   a. improve, advance; become better, strengthen.
2. possessed of fine qualities, excellent, admirable.

紹   shào   MC dzyewX

1. continue, carry on, succeed to.
   a. heritage; inherited lot, status, or possessions.
2. wind round, intertwine.
3. introduce, acquaint, bring together, initiate a tie with.

chāo   MC tsyhew

1. leisurely, slow and unhurried, idling.

shē

奢   shē   MC syae

1. wasteful, improvident, extravagant; prodigal, lavish, profligate; nimiety, nimious (ant. 儉 *jiǎn*, restraint, moderation, prudent; thrifty, frugal).
   a. excessive, immoderate; exaggerate(d).
   b. overabundant, superfluous; plethora.

猞   shē   MC syae

1. (bn.) ～猁 *shēlì* (MC syae-lijH), lynx (*Lynx lynx*), medium-sized wildcat.

畬   shē   MC syae   → 畬 *yú*.

賒   shē   MC syae

1. buy or sell on credit.
2. distant, faraway, far off.
   a. far off in time, esp. the future.

3. sluggish, slowly; to slow, proceed slowly.
4. sparse, few and far between, thin; fading; fade, decline.
5. ⊙ 奢 *shē*, wasteful, profligate; excessive.

shé

舌   shé   MC zyet

1. tongue.
   a. words, language.
2. anything in the form of a tongue, e.g. the reed of a reed-pipe, clapper of a bell, small needle, etc.
3. 百～ *bǎishé*, gray starling, white-cheeked starling (*Sturnus cineraceus*).

虵   shé   MC zyae   ⊙ 蛇 *shé*.

蛇   shé   MC zyae

1. snake; ophidian, serpent(ine).
2. ～含 *shéhán*, cinquefoil, potentilla (*Potentilla keiniana*), yellow-flowering, used medicinally; syn. 女青 *nǚqīng*.

yí   MC ye

1. rdup., sure and seeming, easily grand.
2. (bn.) 委～ *wēiyí*, → 委 *wēi* (*wěi*)

鉈   shé   MC dzyae

1. short spear.

shě

捨   shě   MC syaeX

1. let go of, give up, release; set aside; renounce, relinquish, abandon; choose out, exclude; e.g. ～失 *shěshī*, rejection and loss.
   a. (med.) leave behind; quit; part company with, avoid; forgo, be indifferent to.
2. give alms, give in charity, donate.

shè

射   shè   MC zyaeH

1. shoot an arrow; aim at; e.g. ～侯 *shèhóu*, shoot at a target.
   a. the consequence of shooting an arrow: impale.
2. propel, dart; eject, discharge; emit; spurt out.
3. seek after, pursue; e.g. ～利 *shèlì*, pursue profit, esp. engage in trade.
   a. contend for; risk, hazard.

4. forecast, predict; guess at; e.g. ～覆 *shèfù*, "guess what is covered," game in which players guess at objects hidden under an overturned vessel.

yè　MC yaeH

1. 僕～ *púyè*, official of varying responsibilities from Qin through med. times, usu. with broad supervisory duties; in Tang times the 2nd-ranking position in the Bureau of State Affairs (*shangshusheng* 尚書省) but after 626 actually the head of the bureau, because the 1st-ranking position (*ling* 令) was thereafter left vacant out of deference to emperor Taizong 太宗 (r. 626-649) who had earlier occupied it.

yì　MC yek

1. 無～ *wúyì*, name of a pitch-pipe or its pitch, one of the 12 fundamental notes forming the gamut from which scales may be produced in ancient Chinese music.

2. ⊙ 斁 *yì*, weary of, tired of, bored with.

懾　shè　MC tsyep

1. fear, dread, awe; terror.

2. inspire fear or reverence; inspire with awe; bring to submission, e.g. ～服 *shèfú*, succumb in awe of.

攝　shè　MC syep

1. pull in, draw in, gather in;
   a. attract into one's power, lure; conjure.
   b. subsume, assimilate; absorb; unite; (Budd.) ～心 *shèxīn*, collect the mind.

2. catch hold of, hold onto; grasp, keep.
   a. capture, arrest.

3. be in charge of; administer, direct, manage; organize; discipline.

4. provide assistance, aid.
   a. act as agent or substitute of, proxy, in the capacity of, assume the duties of; regent.

5. take care of, maintain in prime condition, guard, protect.

6. be squeezed between opposing forces.

7. ～提 *shètí* or ～提格 *shètígé*, 6 stars in Boötes, 3 on either side of Arcturus, making up a constellation in line with the handle of the Dipper and therefore able to "hold onto and lead" the seasonal rotation of the heavens.

8. ⊙ 懾 *shè*, dread, awe.

niè　MC nep

1. settle(d), peaceful, quiet(ed).

涉　shè　MC dzyep

1. wade through; to ford, cross over (a body of water).
   a. a ford, crossing-point.

2. go through; undergo, experience; venture, hazard.

3. enter into, arrive at.

4. touch on, be involved with, concerned with; be connected or related to, implicated in; engage with.
   a. entail, require.

5. peruse; study, read.

dié　MC tep

1. ⊙ 喋 *dié*, in cmpd. ～血 *diéxuè*, bloodletting, bloodshed, slaughter.

社　shè　MC dzyaeX

1. god of the soil; e.g. ～稷 *shèjì*, gods of the soil and of millet (metonymy for all grains), supplying the natural foundation of the state, hence often used as euph. for the state.
   a. community temple dedicated to the god of the soil, with altar for sacrifices; village shrine, often functioning as community center.
   b. sacrifice to the god of the soil > the particular days in spring and autumn when the sacrifice is carried out.
   c. sacred, describing something on or beside a sacred mound.

2. a basic unit in community organization, usu. defined as consisting of 25 households.

舍　shè　MC syaeH

1. guest-house; stay over at a guest-house.
   a. gen. term for house, a place of rest or ease, lodging.
   b. cottage, quarters, esp. when living apart in mourning.
   c. ～人 *shèrén*, "chamberlain," member of crown prince's household staff; also, someone attached to the staff of a specific bureau, usu. indicating someone with various secretarial or drafting responsibilities.
   d. honorific prefix, used in terms of address to family members younger than oneself in same generation or of earlier generation; e.g. ～弟 *shèdì*, our younger brother (cf. *jia* 家 for older persons).

2. reside, dwell.
   a. rest, repose.
3. retain, save, set aside, reserve for other use.
4. overnight military encampment.
   a. one day's troop movement of 30 *li* 里.
5. (bn.) ～利 *shèlì* (MC syaeH-lijH), the "fish-dragon" in Han ritual processions (< Sillah, kingdom on the Irawaddy River in Burma, from which came performers who dressed as this beast and cavorted as it); also (Budd.), trsc. of Skt. *śarīra*, relics, human remains to be revered; (Budd.) ～利弗 *shèlìfú* (MC syae-lijH-pjut), trsc. of Skt. Śāriputra, name of one of the chief disciples of Gautama Buddha, often understood in sutras.

shě   MC syaeX
1. ⊙ 捨 *shě* 1, give up, release; set aside, relinquish; leave behind, part with; 2, give alms.

設   shè   MC syet
1. place, set, set up, establish.
   a. display, arrange, furnish, set out, lay out, provide; e.g. ～酒 *shèjiǔ*, set out wine.
2. posit, set up hypothetically, implying a condition on which something depends: provided (that)…, supposing (that)…
   a. (lit.) ～論 *shèlùn*, hypothetical discourse, a text in verse or rhythmic prose that usu. consists of a dialogue between the speaker and an imaginary interlocutor in which the former justifies his actions in political or moral terms in response to the latter's questions.
   b. (med.) ～復 *shèfù*, ～使 *shèshǐ*, if it were the case that…, should it be that…
   c. set up for capture, (en)trap.
3. implement, execute, set in motion.
4. complete in setup or furnishing, well-equipped, having all facilities.
5. (med.) trns. of Turk. term for an army detachment.

赦   shè   MC syaeH
1. absolve, pardon, remit punishment, amnesty, esp. on imperial command; imperial act of grace.
   a. to exempt from or reduce tax or other levies.
2. forgo, set aside; cog. 捨 *shě*.

麝   shè   MC zyaeH
1. musk-deer (*Moschus moschiferus*).
   a. sgl. or cmpd. ～香 *shèxiāng*, musk, an aromatic glandular secretion from the musk-deer.

shéi

誰   shéi   MC dzywij
1. interr. pronoun: who? which one?
2. by reversal: everyone, all who …

shēn

伸   shēn   MC syin
1. ⊙ 申 *shēn* 1, stretch out, extend; unroll; 2, to state, declare, extend one's meaning to be clearly understood; state one's case to authority.
2. be freed from blame, vindicated. exonerated, exculpated.

侁   shēn   MC srin
1. rdup., pace or rush to and fro; also, in great numbers.

參   shēn   MC srim   → 參 *cān*.

呻   shēn   MC syin
1. recite; intone.
   a. (bn.) ～吟 *shēnyín* (MC syin-ngim), recite by rote; also, moan piteously, esp. from pain or illness.

娠   shēn   MC syin
1. pregnant, with child.
   a. quickened, fetal movement.

深   shēn   MC syim
1. deep, of water (ant. 淺 *qiǎn*, shallow).
   a. profound, of other physical or mental objects.
2. deep into, all the way into; far back in, in the recesses of; to the extremity of; e.g. ～宮 *shēngōng*, the depths of the palace.
   a. recede, withdraw into; set far inside.
3. describing accumulated time; e.g. 夜～ *yèshēn*, deep in the night; 年～ *niánshēn*, as the years deepen.
4. of significance that reaches far below the surface meaning or appearance; profound; abstruse, mysterious, arcane; deep-lying, deep-reaching.
5. heavily saturated in color.
6. well-versed in, well-advanced or competent in, have mastery of.

申　shēn　MC syin

1. stretch out, extend; unroll (ant. 屈 *qū*, bend, crook).
2. to state, declare, extend one's meaning to be clearly understood, divulge; present one's case to authority.
3. do something repeatedly (used either as VB ref. to previously specified action or as ADV).
4. restrain, constrain, hold back.
    a. warn, admonish, exhort, give urgent advice.
5. 9th of the 12 earthly branches, associated with the monkey as emblematic animal.
    a. 9th double-hour of the day, approximately 3-5 p.m.

眒　shēn　MC syin

1. swift, hurried; sudden.
   shèn　MC syinH
1. (med.) open one's eyes wide; stare, glare.

紳　shēn　MC syin

1. sash, girdle, esp. as mark of official or social status > the begirded class, the gentry or the literati.
    a. to cinch, (be)gird, bind, cincture.

莘　shēn　MC srin

1. length(en); extend, stretch.
2. rdup., en masse, swarming, in groups and droves.

蓡　shēn　MC srim

1. (bn.) 蕭 ~ *xiāoshēn*, → 蕭 *xiāo*.

詵　shēn　MC srin

1. pass along hearsay, gossip, prate; gab.
2. rdup., many and numerous, multitudinous.

身　shēn　MC syin

1. torso of a man or animal, trunk of the body, the body below the neck.
    a. by synecdoche, gen. term for body.
    b. 有 ~ *yǒushēn*, with child, be pregnant.
    c. trunk of a tree.
2. ref. to oneself, one's person; personally, in person; myself, my person.
    a. all one's life, span of one's life; e.g. ~ 後 *shēnhòu*, after death, postmortem.
3. one's integrity, moral quality, ability, behavior.
    a. social status, station, identity.

yūan　MC ywen

1. ~ 毒 *yūandú* (MC ywen-dowk), gen. term for India, trsc. of Iran. *hinduka* (< Skt. *sindhu*, name of Indus River) ref. to people who live beyond the Indus River.

shén

神　shén　MC zyin

1. spirit(ual), divine, god(ly), deity; sacred, ethereal, holy; e.g. ~ 明 *shénmíng*, "divinely luminous essences," all spiritual entities amidst heaven and earth, from spirits of natural objects to body-gods to transcendent beings of practical immortality; also, spiritual essence imparting superior vitality and discernment.
2. actualizing spirit in humans, that power or agency which makes possible interaction and relation with nature and with other beings (cf. 精 *jīng*, germinal or embryonic essence; 氣 *qì*, vital breath, energizing breath, life-force), cog. 申 *shēn*, extend, extension, reach out.
    a. spiritual essence of humans that survives death, which may exercise influence on human affairs, and which may be propitiated.
    b. (Budd.) that element which carries one's spiritual essence from one rebirth to the next.
    c. (Dao.) that quality in humans which may be nurtured and perfected so as to shed one's bodily frame and become a rarefied being all of spirit.
3. of a quality surpassing the normally human or transcending the ordinary categories of *yin* and *yang*; supernal, unearthly; marvelous, miraculous, wondrous, awe-inspiring; e.g. ~ 樂 *shényuè*, otherworldly music; ~ 交 *shénjiāo*, spiritual accord, a friendship that goes beyond common understanding; (Budd.) ~ 通 *shéntōng*, trns. of Skt. *abhijñā*, supernatural power, superknowledge; also, intuitive powers.
4. expression, mien; bearing, one's "air"; e.g. ~ 色 *shénsè*, countenance, composure, appearance.
5. natural order, law of nature.

shěn

哂　shěn　MC syinX

1. smile slightly, with indulgence or with annoyance.

2. ridicule, find ludicrous, laugh at; smile at, poke fun at; raillery.

審   shěn   MC syimX

1. examine closely, scrutinize; study, take careful note of, remark.
   a. be thoroughly familiar with, know perfectly.
2. careful(ly), in detail, meticulous(ly), scrupulous(ly), vigilant.
   a. as expected, indeed, really.
3. clarify, explain, explicate, make distinct, be clear about.
4. (med.) judicial hearing.
5. (med.) 不～ *bùshěn*, colloquial term indicating uncertainty: could one not…? I wonder if…

沈   shěn   MC syimX   → 沈 *chén*.

湵   shěn   MC syimX

1. (med.) brisk; thready; e.g. (bn.) ～爍 *shěnshuò* (MC syim-syak), sometimes written for semantic suggestion as ～躍 *shěnyuè*, jumpy and jittery, shaky and skittish; pulsing and palpitating.

瀋   shěn   MC tsyhinX

1. natural fluids extracted from a plant or a part of a plant, juice, sap; secretion.
   a. liquid; fluid.

矤   shěn   MC syinX

1. (ADV) all the more…, increasingly…, how much more…, a fortiori; let alone…; surely…; indeed (is it not)?
2. also, for X's part; likewise, similarly.
3. gums of the teeth, gingiva.

諗   shěn   MC syimX

1. reprimand, reprove; warn against, admonish.
2. give careful thought to, consider closely, ponder.

shèn

慎   shèn   MC dzyinH

1. attentive, heedful, vigilant; meticulous; prudent, careful, cautious, mindful of.
2. in reality, in fact.
3. be sure to, must; usu. in negative phrases of admonition or warning, e.g., ～勿 *shènwù*, take care not to…, do not by any means…

滲   shèn   MC srimH

1. ooze, seep; bleed out.
   a. dried out, dried up, dehydrated, exsiccated.
2. filter(ed).
3. (med.) rdup., becloud(ed), blot(ted) out, dark and dour.

甚   shèn   MC dzyimH

1. excessive, undue, too much; serious, grave, critical; more serious (than).
2. very, exceedingly, extremely; ～有 *shènyǒu*, possess a considerable amount (of X).
   a. truly, genuinely.
3. (med.) sgl. or ～沒 *shènmò*, interr. pronoun: why? what? (late Tang colloquial usage).

脤   shèn   MC dzyinH   ⊙ 慎 *shèn*.

脤   shèn   MC dzyinX   ⊙ 脤 *shèn*.

脤   shèn   MC dzyinX

1. raw meat offered in sacrifice to god of the soil, usu. awarded after the ceremony to royal clansmen; cf. 膰 *fán*, cooked meat in a sacrificial ceremony.

腎   shèn   MC dzyinX

1. kidneys; loins.
2. urogenital system, esp. in medical texts, where 內～ *nèishèn* = kidneys, 外～ *wàishèn* = testes.

葚   shèn   MC zyimX

1. mulberry fruit.

蜃   shèn   MC dzyinX

1. giant clam, large bivalve mollusk.
2. clam-monster, dragon-mollusk, fabulous creature said to produce from its breath vaporous offshore castles and pavilions; e.g. ～樓 *shènlóu*, clam-monsters' towers; e.g. ～氣 *shènqì*, dragon-mollusk's mirages.
3. the ash-residue of burnt clamshells, anciently used in ceremonies to protect against tidal bores.
4. clam-shaped vessel in which meat-offerings were placed, for use in sacrificial ceremonies.

shēng

升   shēng   MC sying

1. rise, ascend, climb.
   a. climb into (carriage, boat, etc.).

2. advance to a higher official position, be promoted.

3. ripen, mature, of grain (< grow to full height); to harvest.

4. measure of capacity, "pint," equiv. 10 *ge* 合 and to one-tenth of a *dou* 斗 ("peck").

    a. 大〜 *dàshēng*, "larger pint," equiv. 3 pints.

5. bundle of 80 threads of weaving fabric, fine cloth of 80-thread weave.

6. cmpd., 〜平 *shēngpíng*, (time of) peace and prosperity.

7. "rising," name of 46th hexagram of the *Yijing*.

昇　shēng　MC sying

1. rising of the sun.

2. ⊙ 升 *shēng* 1, rise, ascend; climb; 2, advance to a higher official position, be promoted; 6, cmpd., 〜平 *shēngpíng*, (time of) peace and prosperity.

牲　shēng　MC sraeng

1. sacrificial animal, mainly domesticated (ox, sheep, pig).

    a. domesticated animals consumed as food.

狌　shēng　MC sraeng

1. ⊙ 鼪 *shēng*, weasel, stoat.

    xīng　MC sraeng

1. ⊙ 猩 *xīng*, rdup., orangutan.

生　shēng　MC sraeng

1. live, be alive, exist; life (ant. 死 *sǐ*, be dead, die; death); e.g. (Budd.) 〜趣 *shēngqù*, (the 6) states of existence.

    a. living being; e.g. 〜類 *shēnglèi*, various kinds of living things.

    b. the act of living; lifetime, lifespan; e.g. 〜平 *shēngpíng*, all one's life; 他〜 *tāshēng*, next life, afterlife.

2. cause to live, bring into existence, quicken, vitalize; give birth to, bear, engender; originate.

    a. emerge, come forth, appear; to grow, develop.

3. fresh; green; unripe, raw; uncooked (ant. 熟 *shú*, ripe, mature; cooked.)

    a. unfamiliar, unacquainted; hitherto unknown; unskillful, clumsy, inept, awkward, unrefined.

    b. estranged, as if unknown.

4. nature, natural instinct, inherent character, intrinsic quality; cog. 性 *xìng*, inborn.

5. courtesy title ref. a scholar or teacher; student, disciple, adherent; novice, neophyte; for an older person, "sir."

甥　shēng　MC sraeng

1. nephew, niece, child of ego's sister.

2. male cousin, son of a paternal aunt or maternal uncle.

3. brother-in-law; wife's brother or a sister's husband.

笙　shēng　MC sraeng

1. reed-organ, mouth-organ; musical instrument usu. of 17 (originally 13) bamboo pipes of different lengths, each with a bronze or metal reed and a hole near the base for stopping with the fingers, bound around a wooden resonance chamber; when blown, produces continuous chords; cf. 竽 *yú*, larger (and older) reed-organ; 簫 *xiāo*, panpipes, syrinx, pipes of different lengths joined in a row.

2. (med.) bamboo-mat for sitting.

聲　shēng　MC syeng

1. sound, noise; voice.

    a. music, song, melody; musical note; pitch.

2. linguistic tone; 四〜 *sìshēng*, 4 tones, of the spoken language, i.e. 平 *píng* level, 上 *shǎng* rising, 去 *qù* departing, and 入 *rù* entering tones.

    a. abb. for 〜母 *shēngmǔ*, initial of a Chinese syllable; cf. 韻 *yùn* abb. for 韻母 *yùnmǔ*, final.

    b. phonophoric element of a Chinese graph.

3. message, a communication; words, speech, talk.

4. give voice to, make known publicly, publish, noise about, circulate; announce, declare.

    a. (Budd.) 〜聞 *shēngwén*, "voice-hearer," a listener to the Buddha's teachings, a direct disciple, later ref. one who seeks enlightenment on his own without mediation of a bodhisattva trns. Skt. *śrāvaka*.

5. fame, renown, reputation; good name, public respect.

    a. form, appearance, pretext; opp. 實 *shí*, reality, truth.

6. measure-word for a unit of sound, the number of times something is heard or uttered.

陞　shēng　MC sying

1. (med.) advance to a higher official position, be promoted, rise in the ranks; this graph rarely

used before Tang times, then gradually is favored for 升 *shēng* and 昇 *shēng* in this meaning.

鼪 shēng MC sraeng

1. weasel, stoat (*Mustelidae*), esp. used for hunting small animals; syn. 鼬 *yòu*.

shéng

繩 shéng MC zying

1. rope, string, cord; e.g. 〜樞 *shéngshū*, corded door-hinge, euph. for humble dwelling; (med.) 〜牀 *shéngchuáng*, cord-wrapped seat, fixed-frame chair with plank seat (originally rattan, hence the name) and a back and armrests.
2. carpenter's marking-line; plumb-line.
    a. standard, criterion, model.
    b. measure or rectify according to a standard.
    c. guide; confine, restrain.
3. praise, extol, commend, acclaim.
4. continue, go on, keep on.
5. snowparsley (*Cnidium monnieri*).

mǐn MC mjinX

1. rdup., cautious, prudent, taking precautions; also, teeming, boundless, limitless; prolific, fecund, fertile.

shěng

省 shěng MC sraengX → 省 *xǐng*.

眚 shěng MC sraengX

1. corneal opacity; cataract.
    a. film, shroud; veil, muffle, pall.
2. be off-color cosmically, esp. ref. solar or lunar eclipse.
    a. aberration, disorder; disaster, calamity; affliction, suffering.
3. fault, error, mistake; flaw, imperfection.
4. ⊙ 省 *shěng* (*xǐng*) 2, reduce, diminish; abrogate, weaken.

shèng

剩 shèng MC zyingH

1. (med.) ⊙ 賸 *shèng*.

勝 shèng MC syingH

1. surpass, excel, prevail; overcome, conquer; dominate, dominance; be superior to, better than.

a. overcome; conquer, gain the victory, win; triumph over, defeat; e.g. 〜國 *shèngguó*, a superate or conquered state.
2. of superlative quality or degree; surpassing, superb, incomparable; highlight; e.g. 〜語 *shèngyǔ*, exquisite language; 〜境 *shèngjìng*, place of superb natural beauty; (Budd.) 〜義 *shèngyì*, trns. of Skt. *paramārtha*, the Ultimate or Noumenal Reality, Absolute.
3. (ADV) all, fully, totally, completely, exhaustively; syn. 盡 *jìn*.
    a. (med.) to a large extent, greatly.
4. the warp-beam or roller of a loom.
    a. a headdress, often incorporating shape of the warp-beam, typically ref. to woman's headdress (because of connection with weaving), esp. the headdress associated with Xiwangmu 西王母, Queen Mother of the West; e.g. 華〜 *huáshèng*, "bedecked headdress" or 金〜 *jīnshèng*, "gilded headdress," worn by imperial consort, dowager, etc. in silkworm ceremonies.
5. (Dao.) a tri-cornered cap or "crown," often worn by exalted women or Daoist goddesses, the 3 peaks symbolizing the paradise isles of the Eastern Sea.
6. 戴〜 *dàishèng*, hoopoe (*Upupa epops*), medium-sized, brightly plumed bird with a distinctive crown of feathers (hence the name) and long thin bill; syn. 戴鵀 *dàirèn*.

shēng MC sying

1. equal to, capable of; fitted or competent for; able to be borne; often in negative form, e.g. 不〜數 *bùshēngshù*, incapable of being counted, innumerable; 不〜悲 *bùshēngbēi*, insupportable grief.
    a. owing to, because of; e.g. X〜, thanks to X.
2. exult(ing) in.

晟 shèng MC dzyengH

1. bright(ness), shining; vivid, brilliance.
2. prosperous, flourishing, thriving.

盛 shèng MC dzyengH

1. hale, thriving, flourishing; exuberant, vigorous (ant. 衰 *shuāi*, declining, fading, weak).
    a. consummate fullness; prosperous, abundant, ample.
    b. full, brimful; replete with, fraught with.
2. of peak intensity, to a high degree; perfect(ion); e.g. 〜怒 *shèngnù*, be totally furious.

a. to an excessive degree; fulsome, egregious, orotund: e.g. ～稱 *shèngchēng*, overdone praise, extravagant claim.

3. extol, laud, eulogize.

4. (Dao.) in Shangqing texts, regularly used in place of 淨 *jìng*, pure.

chéng　MC dzyeng

1. sacrificial grain placed in a special container.

a. container, utensil, vessel, receptacle.

2. put into a container, pack; stow away, keep safe.

聖　shèng　MC syengH

1. peerless, incomparable, uniquely endowed; paragon.

a. conventional epithet for sovereign; e.g. ～旨 *shèngzhǐ*, imperial directive.

2. possessing wisdom, judgment, and moral excellence.

a. profoundly wise and virtuous; sage(ly), sagacious.

b. (Budd.) holy, sacred; holy person, saint; e.g. ～教 *shèngjiào*, the sacred teaching, Buddha's teaching; ～諦 *shèngdì*, the holy truth.

3. master practitioner of an art; e.g. 草～ *cǎoshèng*, greatest master of cursive-style calligraphy.

4. (med.) quickly, with alacrity.

賸　shèng　MC zyingH

1. surplus, extra; addition(al).

a. leftover, residue; remainder.

2. (med.) again, more; to a large extent, greatly.

3. (med.) very, quite, rather.

shī

失　shī　MC syit

1. lose, forfeit (real or figurative); e.g. ～意 *shīyì*, forfeit one's desires; ～心 *shīxīn*, melancholy; also, heart palpitations, panic attack; ～足 *shīzú*, lose one's footing > lose one's bearings > lose one's dignity, be forgetful of one's position; ～身 *shīshēn*, forfeit one's person, lose one's life.

a. (med.) in negative VB-phrase, 不～VB, not lose out on VB, do no worse than VB, shall still (be able to) VB.

2. be remiss about; lacking in, deficient in; not careful about, neglectful of, waste(ful); lose the opportunity for, let slip, miss out on; e.g. ～言 *shīyán*, remiss in speech, say what one shouldn't or miss the chance to say what one should.

a. ill-done, wrongly done; mistake(n), misplace(d); err(or), slip; (a)stray; e.g. ～望 *shīwàng*, can't imagine, find it inconceivable that...; ～圖 *shītú*, poorly planned.

3. (med.) unable to endure, can't help doing X; e.g. ～喜 *shīxǐ*, can't contain one's delight.

a. (med.) go beyond, surpass.

yì　MC yit

1. ⊙ 逸 *yì*, flee; 佚 *yì*, disregard, reject.

尸　shī　MC syij

1. person serving as a surrogate for the deceased in a sacrificial ceremony, the impersonator.

a. memorial tablet.

2. corpse, lich; cadaver.

a. (Dao.) ～解 *shījiě*, "deliverance by means of a [simulated] corpse," in which the adept's supposed corpse is buried but is actually substituted with a personal object (sword, staff, etc.) that temporarily takes on the appearance of the corpse, thus allowing one to escape from the bureaucracy of death; a lower-level means of transcendence.

b. lay out a corpse; expose a corpse.

3. be in charge of, have the care or supervision of.

a. occupy a position without performing the duties attached to it; e.g. ～位 *shīwèi*, possess a sinecure.

屍　shī　MC syij

1. ⊙ 尸 *shī* 2, corpse, lich; cadaver.

師　shī　MC srij

1. troop of 2,500 soldiers; regiment; e.g. ～旅 *shīlǚ*, regiments and battalions.

a. troops; army; field an army, take the field.

b. multitude, crowd, throng, host.

c. place protected by troops: garrison.

2. gathering place of well-protected multitude, esp. as cmpd. 京～ *jīngshī*, capital city.

3. master, tutor, teacher; preceptor, counselor; e.g. 不～ *bùshī*, untutored.

a. (Dao.) a master of the Celestial Master (*tianshi* 天～) sect.

b. 太～ *tàishī*, grand preceptor, one of the 3 highest-ranking court titles (along with *taifu* 太傅 and *taibao* 太保), given to individual of great prestige who may be called on by emperor for advice.

4. learn from, follow the example of; regard as a teacher.

a. take as an authority.

5. person specially skilled in an art or profession, an authority, expert; maestro, virtuoso; craftsman.
6. name of 7th hexagram of the *Yijing*, "the army; the troops."
7. ⊙ 獅 *shī*, lion.

施   shī   MC sye

1. apply to, extend (outward) to; exert.
   a. practice on, impose on.
   b. (med.) pertain to, relate to, have reference to, compare with.
2. attend to; to implement, carry out; put in practice.
3. set up, arrange; deploy; display, exhibit.
   a. make a show of; flaunt, boast; brandish.
4. spread, disseminate, disperse; distribute.
5. give, render; supply, provide, dispense; bestow.
   a. (Budd.) donate, donation, esp. alms; largess, charity, bounty.
6. rdup., proceed haltingly or slowly, carefully choosing one's way.

   yì   MC yeH

1. to trail, spread; continue, to last through; (bn.) ～靡 *yìmí* (MC yeH-mje), continuous and unbroken.

   yí   MC ye

1. to wind, meander.
2. rdup., complacent and self-content, self-satisfied.

   chí   MC syeX

1. ⊙ 弛 *chí*, slack(en), unstrung; neglect(ful); forsake, discard; replace, change.

湮   shī   MC syip   ⊙ 濕 *shī*.

濕   shī   MC syip

1. humid; moist(en), wet, imbue(d) with; e.g. ～地 *shīdì*, wetland, lowland.
   a. soak(ed), drench(ed), saturate, immerse.
2. rdup., shake and shudder, wamble and wobble.

獅   shī   MC srij

1. sgl. or with enclitic ～子 *shīzi*, lion; pre-Han loanword < Tocharian B *śiśäk*, Tocharian A *secake*.
   a. (Budd.) symbolic of the buddha; e.g. ～子吼 *shīzihǒu*, lion's roar, i.e. the preaching of a buddha; ～子床 *shīzichuáng*, lion's seat, lion's throne, seat of a buddha.

絁   shī   MC sye

1. (med.) coarse bombazine, coarse fabric with twill warp and worsted filling.

葹   shī   MC sye

1. cocklebur, clotbur, burrweed (*Xanthium strumarium*); syn. 蒼耳 *cāng'ěr*.

蓍   shī   MC syij

1. alpine yarrow (*Achillea alpina*), esp. the stalks as used in *Yijing* divination.

虱   shī   MC srit   ⊙ 蝨 *shī*.

蝨   shī   MC srit

1. louse.
2. interfere with, meddle in.
   a. intruder, quidnunc, meddler.

褷   shī   MC srje

1. (med.) (bn.) ～褵 *shīlí* (MC srje-lje) or 褵～ *líshī*, fluffy and flossy, of young birds' feathers; flocculently feathered, prettily plumed.

詩   shī   MC syi

1. generic term for poetry, verse.
   a. poetry par excellence, i.e. the anthology of poems traditionally dated to between 1000 and 600 BCE and known by this word simply as "The Poems" or "The Odes," later *Shijing* ～經, Classic of Poetry or Book of Odes.
   b. a particular genre of verse, normally tetrametric, pentametric, or heptametric with even-numbered lines (and often 1st lines of stanzas) rhyming, though other rhyme-schemes are possible; in contrast to various kinds of prose (*wen* 文) or other genres of verse such as *fu* 賦, *ci* 詞, etc.

釃   shī   MC srje

1. to filter wine, strain off the sediment.
   a. lees of wine.
2. to drain, lead off.

鳲   shī   MC syij

1. (bn.) ～鳩 *shījiū*, the cuckoo (*Cuculus canorus*), syn. 布穀 *bùgǔ*.

shí

什   shí   MC dzyip

1. a decad; a set of ten, e.g. group of 10 households for tax registry, groupings of 10 poems in the "Xiaoya" 小雅, "Daya" 大雅, and "Zhou

song" 周頌 sections of the *Shijing*, a band of 10 soldiers, etc.

    a. tenfold.

2. miscellaneous, assorted, sundry.

3. (med.) ～伐 *shífá* (MC dzyip-bjot), trsc. Sog. *cherpādh*, quadruped, esp. ref. horses.

十　shí　MC dzyip

1. numeral ten, tenth; e.g. ～方 *shífāng*, the 10 directions, i.e. 4 cardinal points, 4 intermediate points, above, below.

2. the whole of, all; total(ly)

塒　shí　MC dzyi

1. nest-hole in house wall for domestic fowl.

寔　shí　MC dzyik

1. ⊙ 實 *shí* 3, real(ly), fact; truly; 6, resumptive pronoun GP, ref. exposed SUBJ: (as for the aforementioned SUBJ)...this, these, he, they.

實　shí　MC zyit

1. fruit, in gen. technical sense, incl. hard fruits, drupes, seeds, nuts, legumes, etc.

    a. the fruition or result of an action; result in; be instrumental in.

2. full; repletion, replete with; to capacity.

    a. abundant; prosperous.

    b. complete; well-rounded.

3. solid, substantial(ity); really existing; reality; actual(ity), fact, what actually is or happens to be (cf. 真 *zhēn*, what is true to its nature or the way it is meant to be).

    a. really, actually, in fact, indeed.

    b. verify, confirm.

    c. honest(ly), sincere(ly).

    d. exemplar, realities to be cited or used as precedents.

4. belongings, possessions; money, property; assets; wealth.

    a. goods and materials; supplies.

5. ～沈 *shíchén*, one of the 12 Jupiter stations, situated in the western quadrant (*baihu* 白虎) of the sky.

6. resuming pronoun placed between an exposed SUBJ and VB or VB -phrase and referring, often with contrastive sense, to the exposed SUBJ: he, they, this, these; e.g. 此二人者～弒寡君 *cǐ èrrén zhě shí shì guǎ jūn*, These two people, they were the ones who assassinated our lord; 宋衛～難 *sòng wèi shí nàn*, Song and Wei, they

are the ones making trouble; 人～有國 *rén shí yǒu guó*, It was others who held control of the state.

    a. resuming the interr. pronoun 何 *hé* (used exceptionally as SUBJ): what/ which is/ are the one(s) that; e.g. 今茲諸侯何～吉何～凶 *jīn zī zhūhóu hé shí jí hé shí xiōng*, Of the various nobles at present, which will be the ones of good fortune, which of bad?

拾　shí　MC dzyip

1. pick, pick up.

    a. retrieve, reclaim; recover; e.g. (med.) ～遺 *shíyí*, "reclaimer of omissions," one of 2 anaplerotic posts at the Tang court (the other being 補闕 *bǔquē*) which, though rather low-ranking, carried some prestige.

2. gather, collect.

3. archer's brassard or armguard (for left arm), made of hide.

時　shí　MC dzyi

1. season of the year; e.g. ～運 *shíyùn*, annual round or cycle of the seasons; ～物 *shíwù*, elements of the seasons (facts, workings, phenomena).

    a. seasonal, seasonable; timely, at the right time; e.g. (med.) ～來 *shílái*, in timely fashion, in good time; ～雨 *shíyǔ*, timely or seasonal rain.

2. double-hour period of the day, "hour" designated by one of the 12 earthly branches.

3. specific period or moment of time; a period, age, era (not often ref. abstract time until late Tang or post-Tang).

    a. trend of the times; fashion, vogue.

4. opportunity, chance, an opportune or favorable time.

    a. one's fate, lot, fortune.

    b. (med.) special(ly), particular(ly).

5. sometimes, at times; rdup., from time to time; also, time after time.

    a. at that moment, then; in those days.

    b. (med.) often, frequently.

6. preclassical demonstrative pronoun: this.

7. ⊙ 蒔 *shì*, transplant; to plant, cultivate, grow; 伺 *sì*, keep watch, watch for, wait for, await, attend on.

梣　shí　MC dzyi

1. standing straight; e.g. 松～ *sōngshí*, pinetree standing straight; also, a stand of pines.

湜 shí MC dzyik
1. rdup., crystal-clear, of water; also (med.), pure and impeccable, of character.

石 shí MC dzyek
1. stone, rock(y); mineral.
   a. upright inscribed stone, stele.
2. finely-sharpened stone needle used in acupuncture; treat a patient with this instrument.
   a. by synecdoche, gen. term for medical implements and nostrums.
3. measure-word for unit of capacity, "bushel," equiv. 10 斗 *dǒu* or 1 斛 *hú*; in Han times officials' salaries were measured in *shi* "bushels," ranging from 100 to 10,000.
   a. unit of weight measurement, "picul," equiv. 120 斤 *jīn* (*shi* used in this meaning because 1 *hu* of unhusked rice weighed 120 *jin*). N.B. alt. pronunciation *dàn* in this usage.
4. one of the 8 categories of materials from which musical instruments were made.
5. ～髓 *shísuǐ*, "stone marrow," stalactite, mammillary calcite; ～青 *shíqīng*, "stone blue," azurite; ～黑 *shíhēi*, "stone black," graphite; ～黛 *shídài*, "stone kohl," usu. graphite, sometimes indigo; ～膽 *shídǎn*, "stone gall," chalcanthite.
6. ～楠, ～南 *shínán*, photinia (*Photinia serrulata*), large shrub with showy blossoms and new red leaves in spring, so named because should be planted "southward of rocky ground"; ～蓴 *shíchún*, sea lettuce, green laver (*Ulva lactuca*); ～檀 *shítán*, "stone rosewood," beak-leaved ash tree (*Fraxinus chinensis*).
7. (med.) ～國 *shíguó*, Chāch, i.e. Tashkent; syn. 柘支 *zhèzhī*.

碩 shí MC dzyek   → 碩 *shuò*.

祏 shí MC dzyek
1. protective stone-coffer for ancestral tablets in ancestral shrine.

蝕 shí MC zyik
1. eat away, gnaw away; erode, corrode; impair, deteriorate.
2. lunar or solar eclipse.

識 shí MC syik
1. familiar with, knowledgeable about, informed about; aware of; recognize; acquainted with; e.g. 常～ *chángshí*, (on terms of) accustomed familiarity.

   a. experience; practical knowledge.
   b. close acquaintance, good friend.
2. discern(ment); insight; (Budd.) consciousness or pure awareness without content, 5th of the 5 *skandha*s (→ 蘊 *yùn*), trns. of Skt. *vijñāna*.
3. (med.) 不～ *bùshí*, sometimes idiomatic for "perhaps."

   zhì MC tsyiH
1. remember, commit to memory, memorize.
   a. to put a mark or sign on; label.
   b. to record, document.
2. inscription carved in relief; esp. in cmpd. 款～ *kuǎnzhì*, inscriptions in intaglio and relief.

食 shí MC zyik
1. to eat; consume.
   a. cooked cereals > food, comestible(s); repast.
2. take in; accept, receive.
   a. receive an official salary or stipend (anciently figured in bushels of grain).
3. eclipse (eating away) of sun or moon, ☉ 蝕 *shí* 2.
4. (med.) 大～ *dàshí*, 'Abbasid caliphate.

   sì MC ziH
1. to feed, give food to; provide with food, supply.
   a. nourish, raise.

鰣 shí MC dzyi
1. Reeves's shad, Hilsa herring (*Macrura reevesii*, *Hilsa reevesii*).

鼫 shí MC dzyek
1. ～鼠 *shíshǔ*, flying squirrel (*Petauristae*); also, mole-cricket, syn. 螻蛄 *lóugǔ*.

shǐ

使 shǐ MC sriX
1. depute, dispatch, commission, send on an errand or to carry a message; e.g. (med.) ～君 *shǐjūn*, commissioned lord, honorific term for chief official of a prefecture, otherwise 刺史 *cìshǐ* or 太守 *tàishǒu*.
   a. (med.) envoy, deputy, legate, agent, erendrake, emissary; messenger.
2. to cause, bring about.
   a. employ, make use of; enable, cause to do.
3. (GP) conditional particle, impersonally introducing supposition, often in cmpd. 若～ *ruòshǐ*: if it were (brought about) that . . .; supposing that . . .; in the event that . . .; let it be that . . .

4. give free rein to, allow unrestricted action; indulge, abandon.

5. ～君子 *shǐjūnzi*, Chinese honeysuckle, Rangoon creeper (*Quisqualis indica*), ligneous vine, red-flowering, used medicinally; syn. 留求子 *liúqiúzi*.

史　shǐ　MC sriX

1. term used for a wide range of functionaries charged with duties pertaining to writing or inscriptions.

    a. ritualist, high dignitary responsible in W. Zhou times for ceremonial presentation of written texts during court rituals; clerk, low-level post responsible in late Warring States and early imperial times for keeping and recording local government documents; scribe, even lower-level post responsible for simple copying of documents.

    b. historian, archivist, astrologer, in early imperial times an official responsible for storing and organizing of documents pertaining to the past and present functioning of government, incl. records of celestial phenomena; by Tang times, more fully a historian, with activities centered in the Historiographical Office (*shiguan* ～官; the latter term also then a gen. ref. to all officials engaged in writing of history, regardless of rank or bureau to which they were assigned).

    c. 內～ *nèishǐ*, variously a royal secretary or, up to Tang times, metropolitan superintendant of capital city; 刺～ *cìshǐ*, up to Sui times an irregularly appointed supervisory official of a specified region; in Sui-Tang times, prefect, chief official of a "prefecture" (*zhou* 州).

2. historical text, historical record; annals; history.

    a. (med.) one of 4 major bibliographic groupings of writings (the other 3 being *jing* 經, *zi* 子, *ji* 集).

3. fussiness in lit. style, pedantry, over-scrupulosity, pretension; e.g. 文勝質則～ *wén shèng zhí zé shǐ*, when ornament prevails over substance, you have pedantry.

4. (med.) surname, usu. of Sogdians from Kish.

始　shǐ　MC syiX

1. begin(ning), esp. organic; inception, initiation, incience; start, outset, onset, commencement, inauguration.

    a. at first, at the start.

b. 未～ *wèishǐ*, not, never; used in front of a negative expression to form a double negative; e.g. 未～不可 *wèishǐbùkě*, have no reason not to, may as well.

2. just now (or then), only now, now for the first time, not until; then and only then.

3. (med.) just, exactly, right; in the process of.

    a. (med.) only, merely, just.

屎　shǐ　MC syijX

1. excrement, dung, feces; manure.

矢　shǐ　MC syijX

1. arrow, feathered shaft; made of wood (cf. 箭 *jiàn*, made of bamboo).

    a. long dart used in old game of "pitch-pot" (*touhu* 投壺).

2. straight; upright, righteous, honest, just.

3. to vow, swear.

4. exhibit, set out; array, dispose.

    a. to present; to state, narrate.

5. ⊙ 屎 *shǐ*, feces, excrement.

豕　shǐ　MC syeX

1. pig, hog, swine; in pre-Qin period only ref. mature pig, later a gen. term.

2. privy, latrine, outdoor toilet, often above pigsty.

駛　shǐ　MC sriH

1. (med.) gallop; bound.

    a. (med.) speed(ily), swift(ly), quick(ly), with alacrity, at a goodly pace.

shì

世　shì　MC syejH

1. generation; traditionally a period of 30 years.

2. period from a father's adulthood to that of his son; e.g. 三～ *sānshì*, 3 generations from grandfather to grandson.

    a. inherit, succeed to; heredit(ar)y; e.g. ～官 *shìguān*, a hereditary office.

    b. from generation to generation; e.g. ～次 *shìcì*, generational sequence.

3. later generations, descendants, posterity.

    a. heir, successor; e.g. ～子 *shìzǐ*, designated heir (usu. but not always eldest son) of ruler.

    b. clan with a series of men retaining power or position in succeeding generations; pedigree of distinction > ruling dynasty.

4. lifetime, one's whole life.

5. era, epoch, age; times; e.g. 〜情 *shìqíng*, the conditions of the time.

   a. current times; e.g. 〜物 *shìwù*, everyday matters; 〜譽 *shìyú*, contemporary fame.

6. the world, the realm, often with overtone of "vulgar"; e.g. 〜士 *shìshì*, a man of the world; (Dao.) 〜度 *shìdù*, deliverance or salvation from the world, i.e. ascending to transcendence; (Budd.) 〜塵 *shìchén*, worldly dust, the defilements of the mortal world.

事   shì   MC dzriH

1. a matter, affair; event, occasion, occurrence, incident (incl. unforeseen event, mishap).

2. be engaged in, concerned with; undertake, devote oneself to; do, work at; do service for or in.

   a. to serve, render service to; do the bidding of, be dutiful toward, serve the interests of.

3. deeds; task, duty; occupation, business; profession; official post.

   a. appoint, employ, assign someone to a post.

4. written document, text.

   a. factual matter > knowledge (of X).

5. (med.) (lit.) allusion, an indirect or implied reference to a person, event, object, precedent, or text presumed to be known to the reader.

6. (Budd.) pertaining to the phenomenal world of karma-producing actions, as opp. to 理 *lǐ*, the noumenal, the thing-in-itself.

7. measure-word for a thing or event.

仕   shì   MC dzriX

1. carry out an assignment, esp. serve in office, hold a position; functionary.

   a. official position.

2. ⊙ 事 *shì* 2, be engaged in, concerned with; perform a task; render service.

侍   shì   MC dzyiH

1. be attentively at the side of a respected person, esp. an elder or senior.

   a. attend upon, wait on; assist with.

   b. attendant, apparitor, officiant, servant; e.g. 〜從 *shìcóng*, attendants and followers.

   c. used in various official titles, e.g. 〜中 *shìzhōng*, "confidential attendant," adviser to the ruler; in Tang times, the head of the Chancellery (*menxiasheng* 門下省); 〜御 *shìyù*, "officiant aurigal," i.e. censor (< with duty to advise the ruler personally).

2. present advice or remonstrance to a superior; expostulate; this meaning often conflated with the preceding.

勢   shì   MC syejH

1. influence, authority, grandeur; power, might, force.

2. force of circumstances, condition(s); line of force, contour of a situation (incl. topographical), "lay of the land."

   a. structure, stance; conformation; fettle.

   b. posture, poise; pose, appearance; gesture.

3. impetus, momentum; tendency, trend, conatus; potentiality; verve, vigor, vitality.

   a. moment of opportunity.

4. male genitalia.

嗜   shì   MC dzyijH

1. have a taste or thirst for; given over to, disposed to; have a penchant for; be addicted to.

   a. have an insatiable desire for, crave; be avid for, covet.

噬   shì   MC dzyejH

1. to bite, gnaw, champ on.

2. 〜嗑 *shìhé*, "biting through," name of 21st hexagram of the *Yijing*.

士   shì   MC dzriX

1. male person, from unmarried young man to adult man.

2. lowest rank of ancient nobility, "knight."

   a. by late Warring States no longer noble, simply "gentleman"; e.g. 〜大夫 *shìdàfū*, gentleman-grandee, usu. an office-holder; 〜庶 *shìshù*, gentlemen and commoners.

   b. serviceman, usu. lowest category of regular officials; noun form of 事 *shì*, "to serve."

3. increasingly in imperial times, a scholar, man of learning.

4. person with a special quality, training, or skill; an adept; e.g. 方〜 *fāngshì*, adept of formulas, man of special methods, expert in occult practices; (Dao.) 道〜 *dàoshì*, a Daoist adept, gentleman of the Way.

5. ordinary soldier; e.g. 〜卒 *shìzú*, soldiers and troops.

6. ⊙ 事 *shì* 2, be concerned with, engaged in, undertake; 仕 *shì*, serve in a government office.

奭   shì   MC syek

1. full(y); complete(ly), thorough(ly); sufficient.

a. 〜然 *shìrán*, unhindered, unhampered; in full force.

2. rich red, deep red.

3. furious, angry, in high dudgeon.

室　shì　MC syit

1. inner chamber, room; cell.

2. living quarters, abode, house.

    a. household, family members.

    b. family line of nobility, incl. ancestors and descendants; e.g. 漢〜 *hànshì*, the House of Han.

    c. family property/assets.

3. wife (< the household person).

    a. marry off one's son or daughter.

4. coffin chamber, pit, tomb.

5. sheath for a bladed weapon; scabbard.

6. one of the 28 lunar lodgings, "House," made up of α, β Pegasi, in the northern quadrant (*xuanwu* 玄武) of the sky.

市　shì　MC dzyiX

1. market, marketplace, where goods are bought and sold; meeting-place; e.g. 〜井 *shìjǐng*, market and meeting-place; also, merchants; also (med.), town, townsmen.

2. to buy in a market.

    a. to deal, bargain, trade.

    b. buy favor, bribe, corrupt.

式　shì　MC syik

1. model, pattern, standard, paradigm; archetype; mode.

    a. emulate, follow the example of, model after.

2. design; (magic) diagram; formula(ry); configuration.

    a. divining-board, a model of the cosmos, made of 2 pieces of fine wood or bronze, consisting of a square bottom ("earth") plate and a top round ("heaven") disk which was rotated in relation to the square plate; the earth plate usu. marked in bands along its sides with directional symbols of the earthly branches and heavenly stems and also the 28 lunar lodgings, the heaven disk usu. marked in bands around circumference with the lunar lodgings as well as *tiangan*/*dizhi* symbols and in its center a representation of the Northern Dipper; aligning the disk, esp. the Dipper's handle, with the plate in different ways suggests auspicious or inauspicious qualities of a situation at a precise moment in time.

3. put to effect; use, ply.

4. (med.) ordinances, administrative rules that were part of the legal code and concerned with limited areas of law (cf. 格 *gé*, regulations concerned with general matters).

5. (GP) phrase-initial particle, used to express bidding: May you . . . ; May it be done that . . .

    a. (GP) phrase-initial particle, used to express mood: How . . . !; e.g. 〜微 *shìwēi*, how few, how much in decline!

6. ⊙ 軾 *shì*, front hand-bar of a chariot; to salute with half-bow from the hand-bar.

弑　shì　MC syiH

1. murder one's father (parricide) or ruler (regicide).

恃　shì　MC dzyiX

1. repose one's confidence in; have faith in; count on; rely on, depend on.

    a. be confident, be sure of; e.g. 自〜 *zìshì*, self-assured, self-confident.

    b. euph. for mother; e.g. 怙〜 *hùshì*, rely and depend on; (med.) father and mother, whom one can count on.

阤　shì　MC dzriX

1. paving stones flanking the stairs to a hall; pavement.

2. (med.) door-sill, threshold.

拭　shì　MC syik

1. to wipe, rub; swipe, sweep.

    a. clean off, swab.

是　shì　MC dzyeX

1. anaphoric demonstrative pronoun, often referring to a type: this, these, that, those; e.g. 〜可忍也 *shì kěrěn yě*, this kind of thing can be tolerated; 小人反〜 *xiǎorén fǎn shì*, petty people are the opposite of this; 〜心足以王矣 *shì xīn zúyǐ wàng yǐ*, this kind of heart would be sufficient to allow one to rule as a king.

    a. resuming pronoun placed between an exposed OBJ and a transitive VB, referring to the exposed OBJ: he, they, this, these, that, those; e.g. 不善不能改〜吾憂也 *bùshàn bùnéng gǎi shì wú yōu yě*, being bad and not being able to change, this is what I am concerned about; 善人〜富 *shànrén shì fù*, the good people, those he enriched.

2. indefinite demonstrative pronoun: any, any such; e.g. 夫子至於～邦也 *fūzi zhì yú shìbāng yě*, when Confucius arrives at any state; 鈞～人也 *jūn shìrén yě*, any such people in all.

3. affirm, assert; prove out, prove to be so (*this* way); be in favor (of this); ant. 非 *fēi*, deny, negate, gainsay.

    a. true, right; what is this way, as it is supposed to be (ant. 非 *fēi*, false, wrong).

4. (med.) in translation of Skt. Budd. texts, used as copula, "is, are"; gradually occurring in Tang vernacular usage.

柿   shì   MC dzriX

1. Asian persimmon (*Diospyros kaki*).

N.B. Do not confuse this graph with 柹 *fèi*, wood-shavings.

氏   shì   MC dzyeX

1. clan, name used by branches of a family with a common surname (*xìng* 姓), tracing lineage to a common ancestor; lineage.

    a. form of address added at the end of the name of a leader or commanding figure from ancient times; e.g. 伏羲～ *fúxīshì*, (the culture-hero) Fuxi.

    b. form of address added to hereditary title of nobility or dynastic name.

2. honorific designation of a celebrated scholar or person of fine repute, added to the surname; e.g. 左～ *zuǒshì*, Mr. Zuo, ref. Zuo Qiuming 左丘明, purported author of *Zuozhuan*; in med. times often a common designation meaning no more than "Mr."

3. née, maiden name of married woman; e.g. 其母鄭～ *qímǔ zhèngshì*, his mother née Zheng.

4. respectful reference to member of an elder generation, added to the form of address; e.g. 舅～ *jiùshì*, mother's brother.

    zhī   MC tsye

1. 月～ *yuèzhī*, Central Asian tribal name, → 月 *yuè* 5.

滍   shì   MC dzyejH

1. riverbank, embankment.

    a. riverside, shore.

示   shì   MC zyijH

1. reveal numinously, revelation, manifest(ation), unveil(ing), make seen; causative mode of 視 *shì*.

    a. to show, display, divulge.

    b. make known to, notify, demonstrate, inform; indicate, express, instruct(ion).

    c. show the way to; guide.

筮   shì   MC dzyejH

1. to divine with yarrow stalks, milfoil sortilege; e.g. 卜～ *bǔshì*, cheloniomancy and milfoil sortilege, the 2 chief forms of ancient divination > gen. term for divination.

舐   shì   MC zyeX

1. lick, brush with the tongue; lap up.

狧   shì   MC zyeX   ⊙ 舐 *shì*.

蒔   shì   MC dzyiH

1. (med.) transplant; to plant, cultivate, grow.

    shí   MC dzyi

1. (med.) (bn.) ～蘿 *shíluó* (MC dzyi-la), cumin, trsc. Skt. *jīra*.

蟴   shì   MC syek

1. sting or bite of a deadly insect or venomous snake, syn. 蜇 *zhé*

    a. pricked, stung, goaded; irritated, angered, piqued.

2. venom, poison.

3. virulent, vicious, violent.

4. (med.) wood-grub's front pincers.

襫   shì   MC syek

1. 襏～ *bōshì*, → 襏 *bō*.

視   shì   MC dzyijH

1. look at, look upon, regard, view, vision.

    a. look upon as, regard as; treat as, take to be; sometimes, looking for but not seeing.

    b. look after, see to; e.g. ～事 *shìshì*, take care of a matter.

    c. (Dao.) 久～ *jiǔshì*, enduring vision, long-lasting sight, i.e. extended life without aging; (Dao.) 內～ *nèishì*, inward vision, the ability to see clearly and affect the interior of one's body with its viscera and various body-gods, a practice aided by different somatic and meditation techniques.

2. compare with; evaluate; look at in the same way.

3. ⊙ 示 *shì*, reveal, show, make known, make seen.

試　shì　MC syiH

1. to use, employ, task.
2. to taste, sample by tasting, savor, try the flavor of.
3. try out, test out, attempt, essay; try one's hand at; ply.
    a. tentative, provisional, pending, probationary.
4. examine, assess; set an examination.

誓　shì　MC dzyejH

1. oath, vow, swear to a pact, pledge, promise solemnly.
    a. to pledge or take an oath en masse before a military expedition or battle; harangue given as collective exhortation by general to his troops.
2. covenant, pact; oath; treaty of alliance; promise, pledge.

諟　shì　MC dzyeX

1. correct, exact; to correct, rectify, put right.

謚　shì　MC zyijH　⊙ 諡 *shì*.

諡　shì　MC zyijH

1. posthumous title bestowed on a member of the royal family, a feudal lord, or eminent official to reflect his or her lifetime deeds.
2. call, name, be referred to as.

貰　shì　MC syejH

1. to take or hold with a promise to pay later, buy on credit; lease.
2. absolve, pardon; excuse, forgive.

軾　shì　MC syik

1. horizontal railing or crossbar to lean on at front of a carriage or chariot
    a. to salute with a half-bow while leaning on the handbar.

逝　shì　MC dzyejH

1. go away, go off, leave, pass onward, depart, be gone.
    a. run away, run off; flee; abscond.
2. to pass away, die.
3. (GP) emphatic phrase-initial particle, "Ah!," esp. in *Shijing*.

4. ⊙ 誓 *shì*, vow, swear, pledge an oath.

適　shì　MC syek

1. go to, get to, arrive at, reach; destination.
    a. turn toward, turn, appeal to; incline to.
2. (of a woman) marry (< move to husband's home), proceed in marriage (to new home); espoused.
3. fit(ting), suit(able), fadge, be suited to; appropriate, apt; becoming.
    a. satisfy, gratify; conform to the desires, needs, demands of.
    b. comfort(able), sooth(ing); at ease with oneself; enjoy.
    c. adjust, bring toward ideal.
4. just then, just when, just in time; exactly, precisely; just now, at this instant.
    a. happen (that), have a chance to; may well be (that).
5. ⊙ 啻 *chì*, only, merely, just.

dí　MC tek

1. be devoted or dedicated to; be fixed on, focus on, target.
2. ⊙ 嫡 *dí*, principal, formal wife; cf. 庶 *shù*, concubine, be born to a concubine.
    a. children born to the primary wife, esp. eldest son of the primary wife.
    b. be close, intimate; show favor, treat with partiality.

MC dek

1. ⊙ 敵 *dí*, be equal, to match; rival; enemy, opponent.

zhé　MC dreak

1. ⊙ 謫 *zhé*, censure, reproach, reprove, blame; be ostracized, relegated in office, banished.

釋　shì　MC syek

1. release, deliver from; set free.
    a. let go, cast aside, discard, get rid of, divest of; dispel.
2. dissolve, melt away.
    a. clear up, clear away, resolve, resolution.
    b. settle; lay out clearly.
3. explain, analyze, disabuse; elucidate; interpret.
4. (Budd.) abb. of ～迦牟尼 *shìjiāmóuní* (MC syek-kae-mjuw-nrij), trsc. of Skt. *śākyamuni*, the ascetic of the Śākya clan, the historical Buddha; hence, an epithet for anything pertaining to Budd.; often used as surname preceding a monk's "religious" name.

yì   MC yek

1. ⊙ 譯 *yì* 2, glad, pleased; elated.

飾   shì   MC syik

1. to wipe; polish, make bright.
2. enhance(ment), decorate, embellish(ment), garnish; adorn(ment), ornament; outfit.
    a. showy, flamboyant.
3. cover up, whitewash, gloss over.
4. make over, revise, modify, alter, amend.

chì   MC trhik

1. ⊙ 飭 *chì*, straighten up, put in order; issue an order, instruct, admonish.

shōu

收   shōu   MC syuw

1. bring in a crop, to harvest, crop(ping).
    a. the crops themselves.
2. take in, collect; gather.
3. put away, put aside, reserve, lay by; put in order.
    a. bind up, restrain; retract, take back.
    b. to close; conclude, end, finish up.
    c. enshroud and bury.
4. receive, take possession of; accept.
    a. capture, occupy; take into custody, arrest; e.g. ～孥 *shōunú*, official servitude imposed on wife and children of a criminal.
5. horizontal floorboards of a carriage-box.
    a. by synecdoche, the carriage-box itself.

shǒu

守   shǒu   MC syuwX

1. keep safe, safeguard; to ward, keep ward.
    a. maintain; protect, defend.
    b. keep watch over; (p)reserve; e.g. ～見 *shǒujiàn*, reserve one's views.
    c. ref. a celestial body found stationary near a constellation or other celestial body.
2. hold to, keep to; abide by, observe.
3. official title, esp. as 太～ *tàishǒu*, grand warden, grand protector, centrally appointed chief official of a commandery (*jun* 郡), equiv. prefect (*cishi* 刺史) of a prefecture (*zhou* 州).

shòu   MC syuwH

1. official post; duty.
    a. serve as "grand warden" of a commandery.

2. marker of provisional office, "maintaining the post of" or "acting"—used between the nominal and substantive office-title when the latter is higher (cf. 行 *xíng*).

手   shǒu   MC syuwX

1. hand.
    a. hand over, hand out, hand down; grab with the hand, seize, clutch.
    b. set one's hand to, take up the task of.
    c. by hand, with one's own hand, personally.
2. master-hand, dab-hand, expert in a particular art or occupation; virtuoso.

首   shǒu   MC syuwX

1. head.
    a. topmost part; peak, apex.
    b. heading; toward, in the direction of, turn to, inclined toward.
2. foremost, chief, archi-, capital.
    a. main point, essential; gist.
3. first, premier; beginning of, initial; capitate beginning.
4. capitulate, bow the head to; submit to, surrender.
    a. admit guilt, acknowledge blame.
    b. chief offender in crime or misdeed.
5. (med.) (lit.) measure-word for verse compositions.

shòu

受   shòu   MC dzyuwX

1. receive, accept.
    a. take in; experience, suffer, sustain.
    b. tolerate, accommodate; acceptance; contents.
2. confer, transfer, transmit, grant, ⊙ 授 *shòu*.
3. (Budd.) feel(ing), react to, sense, sensation (physical or mental), trns. Skt. *vedanā*.

售   shòu   MC dzyuwH

1. sell, offer for sale; dispose of.
    a. seller, monger.
2. spread, distribute, give out; circulate.
3. realize, achieve; bring about.
    a. (med.) make the grade, pass the Tang civil-service exam.
4. (med.) buy, purchase; aquire.

壽　shòu　MC dzyuwX

1. longevity, long life.
    a. a long-lived person.
2. ～星 *shòuxīng*, "Longevity Star," i.e. Canopus, a star rarely visible in winter months in north China and then barely above the horizon, thought to betoken good fortune for the ruler (syn. *laorenxing* 老人星, "Old Man Star"); also, name of one of the 12 Jupiter stations, comprising the lunar lodgings *jiao* 角 and *kang* 亢 which are the first two (hence "eldest") of the 28 celestial mansions.
3. long-life wishes, bestowed in a toast or with a gift.
4. euph. for burial goods prepared before death.
5. (med.) birthday.

授　shòu　MC dzyuwH

1. confer, grant; transfer, transmit, give to, hand over.
    a. pass on, impart; instruct, teach.
2. appoint, assign; employ.

狩　shòu　MC syuwH

1. winter hunt, in early times.
    a. gen. term for hunt.
2. drive game by fire.
3. emperor's tour of inspection, along a planned route.
4. military expedition.

獸　shòu　MC syuwH

1. quadruped; beast, animal.
    a. wild animals.
2. ⊙ 狩 *shòu* 1, hunt, esp. organized for ruler.
3. (med.) taboo-substitute in Tang times for 虎 *hǔ*, "tiger" (to avoid given name of grandfather of Tang Gaozu 高祖 [r. 618-626]).

瘦　shòu　MC srjuwH

1. lean, thin, spare; gaunt, emaciated; skinny, scraggy; lanky.
    a. fine, frail; scant(y), meager; scarce, sparse, skimp(y).
2. barren, arid; infertile, sterile (esp. of unproductive land).

綬　shòu　MC dzyuwX

1. seal-ribbon, ribbon-cord, silk band for tying ornament or esp. seal of office to one's waistband.

shū

倏　shū　MC syuwk

1. (bn.) ～忽 *shūhū* (MC syuwk-xwot), ～眒 *shūshēn* (MC syuwk-syin), swift and sudden, in haste and hurry, in a flash and a flicker.

儵　shū　MC syuwk

1. black, gloomy.
2. white flash in darkness, like lightning or the lambent shimmer of blue-black silks.
    a. ⊙ 倏 *shū*, sgl. or in bn. ～忽 *shūhū* (MC syuwk-xwot), in a flash, swift(ly), abrupt(ly); flash and flicker, haste and hurry, swift and sudden; the bn. also collectively naming the god of the South Sea and god of the North Sea (< *Zhuangzi*).
3. ⊙ 鰷 *tiáo*, hemiculter, minnow, slender white fish, "stick-fish"; "flash-fish" (< sun glinting off the school of these fish when they turn quickly near the water's surface).

叔　shū　MC syuwk

1. gather up, gather in, collect; harvest.
2. 3rd in seniority of a sequence of 3 or 4 brothers (1=伯 *bó*, 2=仲 *zhòng*, 4=季 *jì*).
    a. first element in many bynames or epithets.
3. husband's younger brother.
    a. father's younger brother.
4. (med.) used in specific terms for various collateral male relatives.
5. declining, waning; the last or end of.

姝　shū　MC tsyhu

1. beautiful; comely, fair.
    a. a beauty, a belle.

抒　shū　MC zyoX

1. scoop out, spoon out, ladle off; drain away.
    a. loosen up; remove, get rid of.
2. debouch; emit, let forth; express; convey.

攄　shū　MC trhjo

1. spread out, spread far, extend; disperse, distribute.
2. open out, unroll, unfurl; evince, expose, reveal; express without reservation.
3. leap over, bound.

書　shū　MC syo

1. to write; write down, record.
2. writing, script.
   a. style of writing, calligraphy.
3. document, writ.
   a. the *Documents*, collection of records pertaining to the words and deeds of the earliest rulers, from prehistory to the beginning of the Zhou dynasty, known simply by this word alone or as *Shangshu* 尚～, the Hallowed Documents, or *Shujing* ～經, Classic of Documents, Book of Documents.
   b. (lit.) letter, missive, epistle, written communication usu. of a personal nature sent to a particular addressee or small group.

梳　shū　MC srjo

1. comb.
   a. comb through; e.g. ～理 *shūlǐ*, to card thread, operation preparatory to spinning in which fibers are formed into rope form without twisting.

檋　shū　MC trhjo　→ 檋 *chū.*

樞　shū　MC tsyhu

1. door-hinge, doorpost; pivot.
   a. (un)hinge.
2. key point, axis, pivot, crux.
3. put side-by-side; compare.
4. sgl. or 天～ *tiānshū*, "Heaven's Pivot," 1st star of Dipper (Ursae majoris α, Dubhe), following outward from which one locates the pole-star.
   　ōu　MC ʻuw
1. thorn-elm, prickly elm (*Hemiptelea davidii*).

殊　shū　MC dzyu

1. kill; slaughter; extirpate, eliminate.
2. sever, break off, cut off.
   a. injure but not destroy.
   b. exceed, pass beyond; e.g. ～絶 *shūjué*, surpassingly incomparable (< cut off from comparison).
3. peculiar, different, unusual; special; outlandish, alien; excluded, distinct from.; e.g. ～恩 *shūēn*, special favor, extraordinary graciousness; ～方 *shūfāng*, a different place; also, different method, different approach.
   a. decidedly, particularly; especially; excessively.

殳　shū　MC dzyu

1. a bamboo lance, bound with a ferrule at one end.

魷　shū　MC srju

1. (bn.) 魷～ *qúshū*, → 魷 *qú.*

淑　shū　MC dzyuwk

1. clear, limpid; pure.
2. gentle, mild; fine, admirable.
   a. warming, comforting.

疋　shū　MC srjo

1. the foot, lower appendage.
   　pǐ　MC phjit
1. ⊙ 匹 *pǐ*, length measure for silks and cloth, a "bolt," equiv. 4 *zhang* 丈 or "staves"; also, measure-word for a quantity of goods equal to a "bolt."
   　yǎ　MC ngaeX
1. ⊙ 雅 *yǎ*, correct, decorous, refined.

疎　shū　MC srjo　⊙ 疏 *shū.*

疏　shū　MC srjo

1. wide apart, far between, separate(d); sparse; dilated, teased; distant; e.g. ～散 *shūsàn*, few and far between; ～數 *shūcù*, loose and tight, far and near.
   a. spread apart, put at a distance; ramify; disperse(d), strew(n).
   b. (med.) deserted, unfrequented; e.g. ～索 *shūsuǒ*, empty and out-of-the-way.
2. arrange or set out part-by-part.
3. be estranged, alienated in affections, at a distance psychologically.
   a. ignore, disregard; pay no heed to, be inattentive to, snub.
4. coarse, rough, crude; inferior, not worth paying attention to.
5. license, loose(ness) of behavior or talk; e.g. ～節 *shūjié*, loose morals, lax conduct.
6. clear out, open up, clear away obstructions; e.g. ～觀 *shūguān*, penetrating insight.
7. (med.) ～勒 *shūlè* (MC srjo-lok), trsc. Tib. *śu-liq*, alt. name for Kashgar (迦師 *jiāshī*).
   　shù　MC srjoH
1. amplify, expatiate on in writing, draw out ramifications, esp. a subcommentary.
2. arrange or set out item-by-item in writing.

a. submission of advice to the ruler, recommendation.
b. (lit.) a letter, missive.

紓　shū　MC syo
1. loose(n), slack(en); remiss.
    a. release(d), relax(ed).
    b. let go of, get rid of; let free.
2. ⊙ 抒 shū 2, debouch, emit; express, convey.

練　shū　MC srjo
1. cloth of coarse hemp or jute; burlap, gunny.

舒　shū　MC syo
1. spread out, stretch, expand; unfold.
    a. loose(n), slack(en).
2. leisurely, relaxed; easygoing, slow-paced.
    a. neglect(ful), overlook; careless.
3. at ease; serene; composed.

菽　shū　MC syuwk
1. gen. name for legumes; pulse.
    a. soybean (Glycine max).

蔬　shū　MC srjo
1. vegetables.
    a. plain fare, meatless.
    shǔ　MC srjoX
1. ⊙ 糈 xǔ 2, edible grains.

輸　shū　MC syu
1. to transport, convey.
    a. transfer, move, pass along.
    b. transmit, communicate, make known.
2. hand over, deliver up what is due, remit.
    a. offer up, present to, contribute.
    b. bring together; e.g. ～粟 shūsù, bring in the harvest.
3. to ruin, destroy; exhaust, use(d) up.
    a. (med.) lose, be defeated (gambling, wager, undertaking).

shú

塾　shú　MC dzyuwk
1. the rooms to either side of a residence's main gate.
2. in early times a family school.

孰　shú　MC dzyuwk
1. interrogative vb-phrase modifier indicating the distribution or scope of the sense of the vb-phrase relative to the stated or implied topic, "in which cases?, in which instances?"; akin to 各 gè, 莫 mò, 或 huò; often translatable as "who? which ones?"; e.g. ～不知禮 shú bùzhī lǐ, which one (i.e. who) does not understand the rites?; 弟子～為好學 dìzǐ shú wéi hàoxué, Of the disciples, which ones especially were fond of learning?; ～能禦之 shú néng yù zhī, who is able to forestall them?
2. ⊙ 熟 shú 1-6, all meanings.

熟　shú　MC dzyuwk
1. cooked food.
2. ripe, mature, of vegetation.
    a. harvest, crop.
    b. fully finished or prepared; e.g. (med.) ～紙 shúzhǐ, "matured paper," paper hammered smooth and surfaced with alum.
3. maturely, thoroughly; deeply; carefully, in complete detail.
    a. well-accustomed to, deeply familiar with, thoroughly known; rapt with; e.g. ～友 shúyǒu, a fast friend.
4. cure, treat, bring to desired state (of objects).
5. soundly asleep.
6. (med.) intensifying ADV: very much, extremely.
    a. (med.) overripe, overfull; exaggerated.
7. (med.) used, bespoke; e.g. ～衣 shúyī, clothing made from previously used fabric.

秫　shú　MC zyit
1. gen. term for glutinous rice.
    a. esp. glutinous setaria, used for making wine.

贖　shú　MC zyowk
1. redeem, ransom, buy back; reclaim, regain; secure the return of a person or object by providing goods or cash; avoid or lessen decreed punishment by same or by other specified action.

shǔ

屬　shǔ　MC dzyowk　→ 屬 zhǔ.

暑　shǔ　MC syoX
1. heat; hot(ness).
    a. summer, the hot season; estival.

曙　shǔ　MC dzyoH
1. dawnglow, the flush of morning.
    a. pale glow, faint celestial light.

瘑 shǔ   MC syoX
1. depression, despair; anxiety.
2. scrofula.

署 shǔ   MC dzyoH
1. governmental office (building).
   a. as suffix: the office of . . .
2. to place, arrange; establish.
   a. appoint, invest with (office or responsibility).
3. act as agent, proxy, representative; provisory, ad hoc.
4. sign one's name to, endorse; inscribe.

薯 shǔ   MC dzyoH
1. (med.) (bn.) 〜蕷 shǔyù (MC dzyoH-yoH), Chinese yam (*Dioscorea batatas*), may be eaten raw; syn. 山藥 shānyào.

蜀 shǔ   MC dzyowk
1. name of state in Warring States period and of area thereafter, comprising the western part of present-day Sichuan; often paired with Ba 巴, covering the eastern part of present-day Sichuan.
2. name of early med. dynasty, sometimes called Shu-Han 〜漢 (221-263), one of the "3 Kingdoms"; name of 2 short-lived 10th-century dynasties: Former Shu (Qian-Shu 前〜 907-925) and Later Shu (Hou-Shu 後〜 934-965).
3. old Chu dialect word for 獨 dú, alone, solitary.
4. ⊙ 蠋 shǔ, hawk-moth caterpillar.

蠋 shǔ   MC drjowk
1. hawk-moth caterpillar (*Deilephila elpenor*).

襡 shǔ   MC dzyowk
1. (med.) long singlet, tunic; shirtwaist.
   ### dú   MC duwk
1. store away, save.
2. (med.) bow-case, bow-sheath.

黍 shǔ   MC syoX
1. broomcorn millet, proso millet, glutinous millet (*Panicum miliaceum*), used for food but mainly for making wine; cf. 稷 jì, foxtail millet, chief among millets used for food.
2. early measure-word for very small portions of various sorts.
   a. of length, equiv. 1 *fen* 分, "inch," one-tenth of a *chi* 尺, "foot."

b. of weight, 2,400 *shu*, "grains," equiv. 1 *liang* 兩, "ounce."
c. of capacity, 24,000 *shu*, "grains," equiv. 1 *sheng* 升, "pint."

鼠 shǔ   MC syoX
1. rat, mouse; rodent.
2. ⊙ 瘑 shǔ 1, depression, anxiety; 2, scrofula.

shù

墅 shù   MC dzyoX
1. hut, shack; cabin; farmhouse.
2. villa, country estate; secondary residence.

庶 shù   MC syoH
1. numerous, many; multitude; all kinds of.
2. sgl. or cmpd. 〜人 shùrén, 〜民 shùmín, the multitude of the people, the plebs, commoners.
3. pertaining to a collateral or side-relation of a family, esp. a concubine and the children born to her; non-inheriting offspring.
4. nearly, approximate(ly), almost, quite close to, usu. positive in connotation; e.g. 〜幾 shùjǐ, just about, fairly, almost the same, not far from.
5. sgl. or 〜幾 shùjǐ, in hope that . . .; hopefully; may you . . .; may it be that . . .
   a. (ADV) to VB fully.

恕 shù   MC syoH
1. regarding others' conduct and intentions as one does one's own, likening others to oneself, seeing others in light of how one looks at oneself.
2. forgiving, indulgent; lenient; clemency; tolerant, kind.

戍 shù   MC syuH
1. guard the border, defend the frontier; frontier duty.
   a. a border-guard.
   b. frontier outpost, garrison.

數 shù   MC srjuH
1. number; numeral.
   a. mathematic(al).
2. a number of, a quantity of; several, numerous.
3. numerology, the ability to see analogies among phenomena and their symbolic numbers, incl. with the lines of *Yijing* hexagrams.
   a. appetency, skill; craft, art, technique.

4. decreed fortune, fate (< what can be counted on).

    a. premise(s).

        shǔ　MC srjuX

1. to count out, enumerate; lay out one-by-one; reckon, figure.

2. rebuke; blame, reprove; enumerate the faults of.

3. (med.) permit, allow, accede to.

4. (med.) compare; be equal to, equivalent.

        shuò　MC sraewk

1. frequently, many times, often.

        cù　MC tshjowk

1. close together, dense; tight-meshed, close-stitched.

尤　shù　MC zywit　→ 朮 *zhú*.

束　shù　MC syowk

1. tie in a bundle, bind, bundle, truss; tie up, bring together.

    a. a bundle, a sheaf, a truss.

2. restrict, limit, constrain.

3. measure-word for: a bundle of 10 strips of dried meat, anciently a ceremonial gift, esp. to an academic master; also, a bundle of 5 "bolts" (*pi* 匹) of silk; also, a clutch of arrows; also, 500 sheets of paper.

樹　shù　MC dzyuH

1. tree.

    a. measure-word for trees.

2. to plant.

3. stand upright, erect.

4. door-screen.

漱　shù　MC srjuwH

1. rinse the mouth; gargle.

2. sip, suck up; taste.

    a. draw toward one.

3. wash clean, cleanse; scour; wash away; esp. wash clothes by hand.

澍　shù　MC dzyuH

1. timely rain.

    a. dampen; fructify, enrich.

        zhù　MC tsyuH

1. ⊙ 注 *zhù* 1, pour out, gush; sluice; infuse, imbue.

竪　shù　MC dzyuX　⊙ 豎 *shù*.

腧　shù　MC syuH

1. "conductive" points on the human body, acupuncture points.

        yú　MC yu

1. (med.) ⊙ 腴 *yú* 2, fertile, fruitful, fecund; well-provided.

術　shù　MC zywit

1. procedure, process; method.

2. technique(s); special knowledge or skill, art(s); aptitude; technical, specialized; craft; e.g. 方 ~ *fāngshù*, cryptic or esoteric arts.

    a. practice or show expertise in a specialized craft.

3. divination based on close observation of particular phenomena and their inferred effects; projective calculation; e.g. ~ 數 *shùshù*, extrapolative numerology.

4. roadway, street.

5. ⊙ 述 *shù*, recount, tell of, describe.

        suì　MC zwijH

1. Zhou-dynasty administrative division, "county," equiv. 10 *li* 里, "hamlets."

裋　shù　MC dzyuX

1. coarse-woven plain clothes, sackcloth.

豎　shù　MC dzyuX

1. (im)plant; set upright, erect.

    a. vertical, perpendicular.

2. adolescent boy, uncapped youth; immature fellow.

    a. (med.) sgl. or ~ 子 *shùzi*, pejorative term ref. to someone acting beyond himself: upstart, nobody, pretender.

    b. ~ 儒 *shùrú*, puerile pedant, shallow scholar.

3. young servant-boy, footboy, houselad.

述　shù　MC zywit

1. recount, rehearse; relate, tell of, describe, narrate; review.

    a. (lit.) recapitulation, original heading of the verse appraisals closing each chapter of Ban Gu's 班固 (32-92) *Han shu* 漢書, changed to *zan* 贊 by Fan Ye 范曄 (398-445).

2. follow along; adhere to, stick to (the course of).

鉥　shù　MC zywit

1. long needle.

2. point out, point to; guide, lead.

shuā

刷 **shuā** **MC srwaet**

1. a brush; to brush, daub; apply gently.
   a. brush away, sweep off; clean off, wipe clean; scrape clean.
2. preen, groom, primp, as a bird its plumage or a person carefully dressing.

shuǎ

耍 **shuǎ** **MC sraeX**

1. (med.) play with, toy with.
   a. (med.) make sport of, make fun of, mock, tease.

shuāi

衰 **shuāi** **MC srwij**

1. decline, wane; weaken; abate, let up.
   a. diminish, reduce, lessen; dwindle.

   suō **MC swa**

1. ⊙ 簑 *suō*, straw rain-cloak.

   cuī **MC tshwoj**

1. contrast or difference in level, graduated degree, esp. of diminished or reduced amount or quality.
2. ⊙ 縗 *cuī* 1, unhemmed hemp bib or chemisette, worn in mourning.

shuài

帥 **shuài** **MC srwijH**

1. ⊙ 率 *shuài* (MC srwijH) 2, be at the head of, lead.

   MC srwit

1. ⊙ 率 *shuài* (MC srwit) 1, headman, leader, esp. of army; commander-in-chief; 2, go along, follow.

率 **shuài** **MC srwijH**

1. netting to catch birds; spread out a bird-net; also, long-handled bird-net.
2. be at the head of; lead.

   MC srwit

1. headman, leader, esp. of army; commander-in-chief.
   a. example, model.
2. go along, follow; 〜性 *shuàixìng*, act in accord with one's nature.
3. in the main, on course with, for the most part, in general.

   a. (med.) without exception, totally, categorically; (med.) 〜意 *shuàiyì*, wholly, in every respect.
4. frank, candid; direct; unconcealed, unhidden.
5. 〜然 *shuàirán*, 〜爾 *shuàiěr*, rash, hasty; indiscreet.

   lǜ **MC lwit**

1. norm, standard; limit, quota; proportion, ratio.
2. calculate, reckon.

蟀 **shuài** **MC srwit**

1. (bn.) 蟋〜 *xīshuài*, cricket; → 蟋 *xī*.

shuāng

孀 **shuāng** **MC srjang**

1. a widow.
   a. a woman living alone; lorn.

雙 **shuāng** **MC sraewng**

1. a pair, two of; paired, matched.
2. even (number).

霜 **shuāng** **MC srjang**

1. frost; hoarfrost, rime.
   a. coldly pure.
   b. white-tipped, edged in white.
2. (med.) a type of woman's lead-based white make-up powder.
3. (med.) euph. for a year.

驦 **shuāng** **MC srjang**

1. (bn.) 驌〜 *sùshuāng*, → 驌 *sù*.

鷞 **shuāng** **MC srjang**

1. (bn.) 鸘〜 *sùshuāng*, → 鸘 *sù*.
2. 〜鳩 *shuāngjiū*, goshawk (*Accipiter gentilis*).

鸘 **shuāng** **MC srjang** ⊙ 鷞 *shuāng*.

shuǎng

爽 **shuǎng** **MC srjangX**

1. vivid or fresh in air or appearance; verve; brisk, bracing; e.g. 〜氣 *shuǎngqì*, brisk aura, bracing air (of autumn); 〜朗 *shuǎnglǎng*, fresh and transparent (of personal character).
   a. vivacious, buoyant; lively, quick; frisky.
   b. fulgid, gleaming, sparkling.
   c. forthright, direct.

2. go against, contravene; violate; shirk, disregard; lose sight of.
   a. to dull, blunt; deaden, numb; e.g. □～ *kǒushuǎng*, have one's sense of taste dulled.
   shuāng　MC srjang
1. ～鳩 *shuāngjiū*, goshawk (*Accipiter gentilis*), ⊙ 鷞鳩 *shuāngjiū*.

shuǐ

水　shuǐ　MC sywijX
1. water; liquid, watery, fluid, aqueous; soluble.
   a. one of the 5 "agents" or "phases" in *wuxing* theory, having symbolic correlations with the direction north, the season winter, the color black, planet Mercury, etc.
2. river, a long run of water.
3. flood, inundation.
4. to swim.

shuì

帨　shuì　MC sywejH
1. handkerchief, given by a mother to daughter when the latter leaves home to be married, worn at the waist.

睡　shuì　MC dzyweH
1. sleepy; ready to drop off, unable to keep one's eyes open.
2. (med.) to sleep, go to sleep.
3. ～蓮 *shuìlián*, "sleeping lotus," pygmy water-lily (*Nymphaea tetragona*), white-flowering in the afternoon; ～菜 *shuìcài*, "soporific plant," marsh trefoil, bog-bean (*Menyanthes trifoliata*), its root mildly narcotic, syn. 瞑菜 *miáncài*, 綽菜 *chuòcài*.

稅　shuì　MC sywejH
1. land-tax, property tax; e.g. 戶～ *hùshuì*, Tang tax on value of land.
   a. gen. term for taxes and imposts.
   b. pay or collect an impost.
2. lease, rent.
3. income, derived from farmwork or husbandry.
4. interest, on loan.
5. present as a gift.
6. to release, free, turn loose, liberate.
   tuō　MC thwat
1. ⊙ 脫 *tuō*, discard, cast off; take off, strip off, doff.

說　shuì　MC sywejH　→ 說 *shuō*.

shǔn

吮　shǔn　MC zywinX
1. suck, draw into the mouth; take in; sip.

楯　shǔn　MC zywinX
1. horizontal bar of a railing, hand-rail.
2. ⊙ 盾 *dùn*, shield, buckler.
   chūn　MC trhwin
1. hearse, for conveying coffin to burial site.

shùn

眴　shùn　MC sywinH
1. to motion with the eyes, signal by raising the eyebrows, give a meaning look.
2. look intently at, be transfixed by.
   xuàn　MC hwenH
1. ⊙ 眩 *xuàn* 1, eyesight dimmed, see as in a fog; blurred; unclear; confused.
2. (bn.) ～煥 *xuànhuàn* (MC hwenH-xwanH), bright and shiny, bedazzlingly bright.

瞚　shùn　MC sywinH　⊙ 瞬 *shùn*.

瞬　shùn　MC sywinH
1. blink of an eye; wink.
   a. quick moment of time: in the blink of an eye, in a wink, in the twinkling of an eye, in a flash.

舜　shùn　MC sywinH
1. name of legendary sage-king of high antiquity whose virtue caused Yao 堯 to select him as heir instead of Yao's own son; his clan was called Yu 虞, hence he is often ref. to as Yu Shun; his given name was Chonghua 重華; like Yao, he passed on the throne not to his son but to the most virtuous man in the kingdom, Yu 禹; he reputedly died at Cangwu 蒼梧 and was buried at Mt. Jiuyi 九疑山.
2. sgl. or ～華 *shùnhuā*, hibiscus, shrubby althea (*Hibiscus syriacus*); syn. *mùjǐn* 木槿, *shùn* 蕣.

蕣　shùn　MC sywinH
1. (med.) ⊙ 舜 *shùn* 2, hibiscus (*Hibiscus syriacus*).

順　**shùn**　MC zywinH
1. compliant, compliance; accommodate, accommodating; amenable (to), conform(ing) (with); go along with, accept(ing); submissive.
　　a. follow the course of, go with the current; not make waves.
　　b. direct planetary movement, i.e. eastward (cf. 逆 *nì*, retrograde or westward movement).
2. amiable, agreeable; soothing; gentle(ness).
　　a. soothe, facilitate; expedite.
3. (med.) pass on; e.g. ～世 *shùnshì*, pass away, die, "go the way of the world."

shuō

説　**shuō**　MC sywet
1. talk about, express, tell.
2. explain; discuss.
3. theory; doctrine, dogma.
　　a. assert, claim; argue over.
4. (med.) (lit.) allocution, discussion, prose genre of explanation or assertion.
　　shuì　MC sywejH
1. persuade, exhort; assert(ion), claim; argue for.
　　yuè　MC ywet
1. pleasing, satisfying; ⊙ 悦 *yuè*.

shuò

妁　**shuò**　MC dzyak
1. go-between, intermediary, from the bride's family.

朔　**shuò**　MC sraewk
1. astronomical conjunction, when 2 bodies are coincident in the sky.
　　a. the first day of the lunar month, when sun and moon rise together; neomenic.
2. beginning, inauguration, start.
3. boreal, residing in or coming from the north; e.g. ～風 *shuòfēng*, the boreal (north) wind; ～方 *shuòfāng*, the northern quarter.

槊　**shuò**　MC sraewk
1. (med.) long lance.
2. (med.) "spearmen," a board game.

爍　**shuò**　MC syak
1. sgl. or rdup., flashing, flaring, effulgent, alight, rutilant; splendrous.

2. hot, heated; warm(ing).
3. ⊙ 鑠 *shuò* 1, melt, fuse.
　　luò　MC lak
1. rdup., bare and ruined, stripped and leafless, of trees.

稍　**shuò**　MC sraewk　⊙ 槊 *shuò*.

碩　**shuò**　MC dzyek
1. large, outsize; imposing, grandiose, majestic; powerful.
2. boulder.
　　a. sturdy, firm.
3. well-grounded, well-read, broadly learned.

鑠　**shuò**　MC syak
1. melt, fuse (metal).
　　a. "fusion," conjunction of Mars (fire) and Venus (metal).
2. weaken, soften; come apart, disintegrate; ruin.
　　a. dissolve; seep, leak out.
3. polished, gleaming; shining; glittering, flashing.
4. exclamation of approbation: "splendid!"
5. (med.) (bn.) 矍～ *juéshuò*, → 矍 *jué*.

sī

澌　**sī**　MC sje
1. drifting ice-floe.

司　**sī**　MC si
1. oversee(r), supervise, superintend(ant), watch over; administrate, manage; have authority over, gerent, minister, arbiter; dominate; e.g. 有～ *yǒusī*, 所～ *suǒsī*, those in authority, appointed officials; ～南 *sīnán*, "holding to the south," i.e. a compass.
　　a. often used in titles, divine or official; e.g. ～命 *sīmìng*, arbiter of fate, supervisor of destinies; ～中 *sīzhōng*, superintendant of the palace; ～空 *sīkōng*, minister of (public) works; ～徒 *sītú*, administrator discipulant, minister of instruction; ～馬 *sīmǎ*, administrator equestrian, supervisor of military affairs, title used for positions of various levels from army majors to prefectural marshals.
　　b. (med.) agency, in Tang the 4 sub-offices attached to each of the 6 departments (*bu* 部) of the Bureau of State Affairs (*shangshusheng* 尚書省).

2. inspect, examine, investigate.
3. first element in two-syllable surnames derived from office titles, esp. Sima ～馬, Situ ～徒, the former notably that of ruling family of the Western Jin (265-317) and Eastern Jin (317-420) dynasties.

嘶　sī　MC sej
1. hoarse, husky voice or sound.
2. onom. of neighing of a horse.
3. (med.) onom. of the raucous rasp of buzzing insects or clamoring birds.

廝　sī　MC sje
1. a menial, hireling; domestic, servant, slavey; yeoman.
2. divide, separate.

思　sī　MC si
1. to think, think of, think about, conceive of.
   a. reflect on, think back on; consider, contemplate, meditate on; pensive.
   b. long for, longing, yearn for; feel affection for, love.
   c. mental; thought(ful); action of the mind.
2. rhythmic particle used in verse, esp. in *Shijing*.

sì　MC siH
1. feelings, emotions.

斯　sī　MC sje
1. demonstrative pronoun: this, these; e.g. 君子之至於～也 *jūnzi zhī zhì yú sī yě*, that the men of noble status have reached this; 吾～之未能信 *wú sī zhī wèinéng xìn*, in this I am not yet able to put any credence.
2. vb-phrase conjunction: then; e.g. 觀過～知仁矣 *guān guò sī zhī rén yǐ*, observe someone's faults, then you would know about his humaneness; 再～可矣 *zài sī kě yǐ*, if you do it twice, then it would be acceptable.
3. adv, in this way, thus.
4. ～文 *sīwén*, "our" culture in a broad sense, esp. as represented in texts; (med.) literature, specific writing as well as belles-lettres generally.

澌　sī　MC sje
1. dried out, drained.
   a. used up, done with, finished; worn out; extinguished.
2. cadaver, corpse; dried-up body.

3. (med.) slight trickle of flowing water.
   a. (med.) rdup., onom. of falling rain, "syeh-syeh."
4. ⊙ 嘶 *sī*, husky sounding; onom. of neighing of horse, or buzzing insects, clamoring birds.

禠　sī　MC si
1. rdup., agitated and uneasy, unsettled, disquieted, flustered.

私　sī　MC sij
1. private; oneself only; self-interest(ed), private interest (ant. 公 *gōng*, public).
   a. privately, secretly; privy, confidential, intimate; clandestine.
   b. have a secret relationship with.
2. treat with partiality because of a personal relationship, personally favor.
3. term of address in early times for a woman's brothers-in-law.
   a. (med.) humble self-reference: just I myself.
4. private parts, reproductive organs; e.g. ～白 *sībái*, "blank genitals," i.e. neutered, a eunuch.
5. urinate.
6. everyday clothing.

絲　sī　MC si
1. silk, from silkworm cocoon.
2. filament, thread.
   a. thin, slender; delicate.
   b. extremely slight in size or amount; e.g. ～毫 *sīháo*, the merest slip of.
   c. (lit.) often associated punningly with 思 *sī*, longings, affectionate thoughts connecting to a loved one like a finely stretched silken thread.
3. silkstuff, anything made of silk.
4. strings of a musical instrument such as a zither.
   a. by synecdoche, chordophones, stringed instruments; one of the 8 categories of musical instruments.

緦　sī　MC si
1. fabric of fine-woven hemp, esp. for mourning garments.
2. sgl. or ～親 *sīqīn*, distant relation(s), for whom one wears only 3 months of mourning.

罳　sī　MC si
1. (bn.) 罘～ *fúsi*, → 罘 *fú*.

颸   sī   MC si

1. (med.) cool breeze.
2. (med.) sgl. or 〜風 *sīfēng*, brisk wind; whipping wind.

鷥   sī   MC si

1. (med.) (bn.) 鷺〜 *lùsī*, → 鷥 *lù*.

sǐ

死   sǐ   MC sijX

1. die; dead, lifeless, inert.
   a. lose consciousness.
2. come to an end, be finished.
3. sacrifice one's life for.
4. (med.) necrosis, dead or diseased bodily tissue.
5. (med.) following VB or ADJ, extremely, to the maximal extent (syn. 殺 *shā* 3); "… to die for"; e.g. 喜〜 *xǐsǐ*, lethally happy, happier than one could ever imagine.

sì

伺   sì   MC siH

1. watch over, keep watch on, watch out for.
   a. keep under surveillance; spy on; keep an eye on.
   b. wait for, expect, anticipate.

似   sì   MC ziX

1. resemble, be like, seem(ing), similar to; likeness, (veri)similitude.
2. (med.) can compare with; considerably.
   a. (med.) (GP) marker of the comparative; e.g. 白〜雪 *bái sì xuě*, whiter than snow.
3. (med.) (GP) postverbal suffix of direction away from agent: to, toward; e.g. 說〜他 *shuōsì tā*, explained to someone.
   a. (med.) give to.
4. ⊙ 嗣 *sì* 1, continue, carry on with, succeed to.

俟   sì   MC zriX

1. wait for, wait on, await.
   a. look forward to, anticipate, expect.

qí   MC gj+j

1. (med.) 2nd element in bisyllabic surname, Moqi 万〜.

兕   sì   MC zijX

1. traditionally defined as a rhinoceros, but most often designates the gaur or wild water-buffalo.

嗣   sì   MC ziH

1. continue, carry on with; succeed to, inherit.
   a. successor, heritor, heir; posterity, descendants.
2. follow after; come round to.

四   sì   MC sijH

1. numeral four, fourth.
   a. fourfold; on all sides, in (from, to) the four directions.

姒   sì   MC ziX

1. eldest of a man's concubines.
2. term of address from a younger brother's wife to an elder brother's wife.
3. older sister.

寺   sì   MC ziH

1. government office (place).
2. Budd. monastery, temple (post-Han).
3. 〜人 *sìrén*, early term for eunuch.

巳   sì   MC ziX

1. 6th of the 12 earthly branches, associated with the snake as emblematic animal.
   a. 6th double-hour of the day, from approximately 9 a.m. to 11 a.m.
   b. 上〜節 *shàngsìjié*, springtime purification festival, originally held on the 1st *si* day of 3rd month, by med. times regularized to the 3rd day of 3rd month.

汜   sì   MC ziX

1. branch of a river that returns to the main channel.
2. riverside; river's edge.
3. name of a river in north-central Henan.

泗   sì   MC sijH

1. snivel; snot.
2. name of a river in central Shandong.

涘   sì   MC zriX

1. riverside; riverbank.
2. (med.) edge, boundary; dividing line; limit.

祀   sì   MC ziX

1. ceremonial sacrifice, litation; esp. sacrifices continued for generations.
   a. place of sacrifice.

2. old word for year, used in this meaning later with archaic overtone.
    a. (med.) age, epoch, period.

笥　sì　MC siH
1. bamboo hamper, for food or clothes.

耜　sì　MC ziX
1. plow; plowshare.
    a. square-frame plow, with long flat sole.

殣　sì　MC sijH
1. provisional interment, temporary burial, when not yet possible to convey the coffin to its final resting-place and perform formal obsequies.

肆　sì　MC sijH
1. lay out, dispose, arrange according to plan.
    a. extend, spread out; enlarge.
    b. lay out a corpse (usu. of executed criminal) for public viewing in the marketplace.
2. display, expose, reveal, exhibit to view; clearly visible, manifest.
3. perform, carry out, execute (an action); allow to run its course.
    a. exhaust, use up completely; take to the extreme; do violence to.
4. unbridled, uncontrollable, lax, unrestrained; wanton; impudent.
    a. (med.) give free rein to, do as one wishes.
5. remit (punishment), pardon.
6. market-stall, shop, place to display one's wares.
    a. workshop, atelier.
7. (GP) phrase-initial particle indicating consequential action: "so now it is that . . ."

飤　sì　MC ziH　⊙ 飼 *sì*.

飼　sì　MC ziH
1. to feed, give food to, provide with food; nourish, raise.

駟　sì　MC sijH
1. quadriga, carriage or chariot pulled by a 4-horse team.
    a. alt. name for the constellation → 房 *fáng*, one of the 28 lunar lodgings, made up of the 4 stars β, δ, π, ρ Scorpii.
2. drive, as one would a carriage; ride, as one would a horse.
3. gen. term for horses.
4. ⊙ 四 *sì*, four.

sōng

崧　sōng　MC sjuwng　⊙ 嵩 *sōng*.

嵩　sōng　MC sjuwng
1. lofty, exalted, eminent; tall and large, of a mountain.
2. name of a mountain about 40 miles southeast of Luoyang, in Henan; the "central marchmount" (*zhongyue* 中嶽) of the traditional 5 sacred peaks; also called ～高 *sōnggāo*, "the heights of Song."

忪　sōng　MC sowng
1. (med.) (bn.) 惺～ *xīngsōng*, → 惺 *xīng*.
    zhōng　MC tsyowng
1. (med.) (bn.) ～懞 *zhōngméng* (MC tsyowng-muwng), trembling and terrified.
2. (med.) (bn.) 怔～ *zhēngzhōng*, → 怔 *zhēng*.

松　sōng　MC zjowng
1. pinetree; symbolic of longevity and of steadfastness in adversity (because remains green in winter).
    a. gen. term for evergreen conifers; e.g. 水～ *shuǐsōng*, "water-pine," swamp cypress (*Glyptostrobus pensilis*), a subtropical cypress that can grow in water 2 ft. deep.
    b. (med.) 金～ *jīnsōng*, "golden pine," umbrella-pine, shadow-pine (*Sciadopitys verticillata*).

菘　sōng　MC sjuwng
1. (med.) sgl. or ～菜 *sōngcài*, cabbage, bok-choy (*Brassica chinensis*).

鬆　sōng　MC sowng
1. (med.) disheveled hair, in loose disarray, hanging unbound; unkempt, shaggy.
2. (med.) loosen(ed), relax(ed), slacken(ed).
    a. (med.) careless, negligent; nonchalant, unconcerned.

sǒng

嵷　sǒng　MC sjowng
1. (bn.) 巃～ *lóngsǒng*, → 巃 *lóng*.

悚　sǒng　MC sjowngX
1. fearful, afraid; apprehensive, ruffled; shaking with fright, agitated.
    a. terrified, shocked; panicky.

慫   sǒng   MC sjowngX
1. appalled, affrighted; startled; apprehensive; quaking with fear.

竦   sǒng   MC sjowngX
1. rise up on tiptoe and crane the neck to look afar; raise oneself up.
   a. anticipate, expect(ant).
2. stand straight, stand erect.
   a. (med.) rise up to contend, dispute at full stretch.
3. lift up, raise up, upsweep; brandish; hold aloft.
4. ⊙ 悚 sǒng, fearful, apprehensive, agitated; terrified, shocked; 聳 sǒng 2, respectful, regardful; 4, (a)rouse, incite; encourage, embolden.

聳   sǒng   MC sjowngX
1. upthrust, high-rising, rising up; bold.
2. regard with respect, look up to; esteem(ed), highly regard(ed), regardful.
3. alarmed, shocked; frightened, in dread.
4. (a)rouse, incite; encourage, embolden; stir up, whip up.
5. deaf (physical condition).

sòng

宋   sòng   MC sowngH
1. name of one of the smaller feudal states of the Chunqiu and Warring States periods, in present-day eastern Henan; originally held by descendants of the rulers of the Shang dynasty; its inhabitants often portrayed as simplistic in Warring States philosophical texts.
2. name of imperial dynasties: a medieval southern dynasty, 420-479 (often called Liu-Song 劉～); an early modern dynasty, Northern Song (960-1127) ruling all of China, and Southern Song (1127-1278) ruling only the south.
3. a surname.

訟   sòng   MC zjowngH
1. dispute, argument; argue, contend.
   a. dispute at law; sue; litigation, bring to court; esp. disputes about property.
   b. accuse, accusation; blame, lodge a complaint; repine.
2. "contention," name of 6th hexagram of *Yijing*.
3. make public, say openly.
4. ⊙ 頌 sòng, praise, laud, hymn.

誦   sòng   MC zjowngH
1. pronounce aloud, declaim, recite, speak out; intone, chant, sing through.
   a. an intoned composition, poem, song.
2. state, recount, declare.
3. criticize indirectly with subtle phrasing.
4. ⊙ 訟 sòng 3, make public, say openly.

送   sòng   MC suwngH
1. see off, accompany to a farewell spot someone who is leaving; send off.
   a. follow a departing person or object with one's eyes.
2. accompany, escort, go along with, usu. behind.
3. send to, present to.
   a. deliver; transmit.

頌   sòng   MC zjowngH
1. praise, laud, extol, cry up; sing the praises of, pay tribute to.
   a. (lit.) verse genre: laud, hymn, eulogy.
   b. (lit.) collective name for odes in 4th section of *Shijing*, solemn hymns that were sung and danced to in ritual ceremonies.
2. divinatory pronouncements, oracles.
3. ⊙ 誦 sòng 1, recite, intone, pronounce aloud.
   róng   MC yowng
1. ⊙ 容 róng 1, countenance, appearance, figure, look of; 2, to countenance, tolerate, be indulgent.

sōu

廋   sōu   MC srjuw
1. hide, conceal, cover up, disguise.
2. corner; hollow, indentation; bight, of a mountain or river.
3. ⊙ 搜 sōu 1, search for, seek out.

搜   sōu   MC srjuw
1. search for, go in search of, seek out, look for.
2. dig into, examine thoroughly, probe.
3. onom. of an arrow in flight: syooh!
4. (med.) (bn.) ～牢 sōuláo (MC srjuw-lawH), ravage, pillage, plunder.

艘   sōu   MC srjuw
1. gen. term for boats.
   a. measure-word for boats.

涑　sōu　MC suw

1. wash, cleanse, esp. clothes; wash away, scour.

蒐　sōu　MC srjuw

1. common madder (*Rubia cordifolia*), root used as source of a red textile dye, also used medicinally; syn. 茜草 *qiàncǎo*.
   a. madder-red, garance, deep reddish-purple.
2. springtime hunt, in early times.
3. investigate, examine, look into; pass in review.
4. hide, cover up, conceal.
5. ⊙ 搜 *sōu* 1, search for, seek out.

蒐　sōu　MC srju

1. (bn.) 蠷~ *juésōu*, → 蠷 *jué*.

鎪　sōu　MC suw

1. carve, incise.

颼　sōu　MC srjuw

1. rdup., onom. of blowing of wind or rain: shooh-shooh.
   a. (bn.) ~飀 *sōuliú* (MC srjuw-ljuw), onom. of gentle wind: shooh-lhooh.

sǒu

叟　sǒu　MC suwX

1. an elder, a grisard, old-timer.
   sōu　MC sjuw
1. rdup., onom. of washing rice: shyoo-shyoo.

嗾　sǒu　MC suwX

1. onom. of sound by which one calls or commands a dog.
2. to "sic on," incite to harmful action.

擻　sǒu　MC suwX

1. (med.) (bn.) 抖~ *dǒusǒu*, → 抖 *dǒu*.

溲　sǒu　MC srjuwX

1. soak, drench.
2. mix with water.
   a. make paste, mix flour and water.
   sōu　MC srjuw
1. urinate.

瞍　sǒu　MC sew

1. having eyes but without defined pupils; blind.
   a. in early times, esp. ref. to music-masters, many of whom were blind.

藪　sǒu　MC suwX

1. carr, fenland; marshy ground, with weeds and underbrush; boggy copse.
   a. fetid marsh, morass, camarine, sink, slough.
2. gathering-place for people or objects; preserve, sanctuary; sometimes used humilifically with overtones of 1a.

sòu

嗽　sòu　MC suwH

1. cough, hack.
   shù　MC srjuwH
1. ⊙ 漱 *shù* 1, rinse the mouth, gargle; 2, sip, suck up.

sū

甦　sū　MC su

1. (med.) revive, regain consciousness, return to life from death, ⊙ 蘇 *sū* 6.

稣　sū　MC su

1. ⊙ 蘇 *sū* 6, revive, regain consciousness, return to life from death.

窣　sū　MC swot

1. emerge suddenly, leap forth.
2. (med.) sudden(ly), unexpected, abrupt.
3. (med.) brush against, touch lightly.
   a. (med.) onom. of light whisking.
4. (med.) (bn.) 勃~ *bósū*, → 勃 *bó*.
5. ~利 *sūlì* (MC swot-lijH), Sogdiana.

蘇　sū　MC su

1. perilla (*Perilla frutescens*), broad-leaved plant of the mint family, esp. the purple-leaved species, used in cooking and medicinally; perilla oil is expressed from the seeds; syn. 荏 *rěn* 1.
2. ~合(香) *sūhé(xiāng)*, storax (*Styrax officinalis*), vanilla-scented dark-purple resin, imported from Parthia and Asia Minor, used as fixative in aromatics; in Tang times also ref. to liquidambar, sweetgum (*Liquidambar acalycina, L. formosana*), the tree and its resin.
3. ~方, ~枋 *sūfāng*, or ~木 *sūmù* (MC su-pjang-muwk), sappanwood (*Caesalpinia sappan*), small to medium-size shrubby tree, produces a reddish-purple dye.

4. 〜摩那 *sūmónà* (MC su-ma-na), trsc. Skt. *sumanā*, great flowering jasmine.

5. to cull plants, collect herbs.
   a. herb-gatherer.
   b. plants that have been culled.
   c. pick, pick up; take.

6. revive, regain consciousness; return to life from death; resuscitate; awaken, recover (from illness); rescue, relieve.

7. tail of a bird.
   a. drooping, hanging down; esp. 流〜 *liúsū*, "flowing fringe," decorative hanging ornament of multicolored plumes or silk, esp. for horses.

8. ⊙ 酥 *sū*, fatty matter, as in 〜油 *sūyóu*, butter.

9. a surname.

sù   MC suH

1. toward, in the direction of, tending to.

酥   sū   MC su

1. (med.) kaymak, clotted cream; ghee, clarified butter, butterfat (< Iran. *fšu-*, fat, fatty matter, as in *fšutā-*, cheese).

sú

俗   sú   MC zjowk

1. customs, mores, usual actions; vogue, fashion, mode.

2. customary, commonplace, popular.
   a. plain, simple; vulgar, unrefined.

3. worldly, lay, secular.

sù

傃   sù   MC suH

1. toward, in the direction, tending to.

2. (med.) usual(ly), normal(ly), common(ly).

塑   sù   MC suH

1. (med.) mold from clay.
   a. (med.) fictile, able to be molded.

夙   sù   MC sjuwk

1. early dawn, early morning.
   a. early years, youth.

2. aforetime, erstwhile.
   a. longstanding, abiding; ingrained.

宿   sù   MC sjuwk

1. spend the night, pass the night; stay over, overnight at, sojourn, pernoctate.

a. night-halt, stopping-place, lodging-place, halting-place.

2. indwelling, ingrained; abiding, long-held; e.g. 〜習 *sùxí*, ingrained habit; 〜志 *sùzhì*, long-cherished aim.
   a. in the past; experienced, seasoned, inveterate; aged, superannuated; e.g. 〜火 *sùhuǒ*, smouldering fire, embers; 〜昔 *sùxī*, ever and anon.
   b. (Budd.) pertaining to previous incarnation(s).
   c. predisposed to, predestined, predetermined, pre-ordained; wont to; e.g. (Budd.) 〜對 *sùduì*, predestined recompense, from former life.
   d. ordinarily, habitual(ly).

3. of the previous night; of the previous year.

4. 〜莽 *sùmǎng*, sloughgrass (*Beckmannia syzigachne*).

xiù   MC sjuwH

1. constellations, zodiacal mansions, esp. the 28 lunar lodgings.

愫   sù   MC suH

1. open-hearted, unfeigning; candid, plain-spoken; genuine; artless.

愬   sù   MC suH   ⊙ 訴 *sù*.

泝   sù   MC suH

1. ⊙ 遡 *sù* 1, go upstream, against the current; (med.) follow to the source; 2, face, facing; go toward.

溯   sù   MC suH

1. ⊙ 遡 *sù* 1, go upstream, against the current; (med.) follow to the source; 2, face, facing; go toward.

礸   sù   MC sjuwk

1. (med.) black-colored whetstone.

簌   sù   MC suwk

1. (med.) rdup., weeping copious tears, ceaseless weeping; also, onom. of the scribble-scrabble of mice, the suss-sissing of snakes.

粟   sù   MC sjowk

1. foxtail millet (*Setaria italica*), non-glutinous millet used for cooking; syn. 稷 *jì*.

2. by metonymy, gen. term for all grains, esp. when unhusked.

a. provisions.

b. salary of an official, calculated in measures of grain.

3. descriptive of small, kernel-shaped items, e.g. goose-bumps.

4. ～特 *sùtè* (MC sjowk-dok), ～忒 *sùtè* (MC sjowk-thok), Sogdiana.

素　sù　MC suH

1. unbleached and undyed silk, plainsilk, ecru.

a. color of plainsilk, beige, ecru, light grayish- brown.

2. plain, simple, unornamented, colorless; undyed, unsullied, unblemished, immaculate.

a. original, untouched; unaffected, innocent; blank.

b. having natural worthiness and integrity but without official position.

c. elemental, of basic or indispensable importance.

d. (Dao.) 八～ *bāsù*, 8 Pallors, cloud-carriages for divinities (cf. 八景 *bājǐng*, carriages of light, being *yang* counterparts); also, 8 Immaculates, important Shangqing female divinities.

3. plain fare, simple food; vegetarian, maigre.

4. fine white silk, suitable for writing on.

5. longstanding, habitual(ly).

a. typically, expectedly.

b. wont to, used to.

6. ～馨 *sùxīng*, ～方花 *sùfānghuā*, jasmine (*Jasminum officinale*).

7. ～方 *sùfāng*, tie-beam, rafter-tie connecting the bottom of opposing rafters.

肅　sù　MC sjuwk

1. dignified, stately; in strict order, formal.

2. austere, stern, grave; solemn, staid; self-controlled, self-contained; unmoved, impassive.

3. pay respects to; bow deeply to; revere.

4. shriveled, shrunken; draw back or into, draw together.

5. (med.) clean out and renovate; recondition, put in new order.

6. (med.) rdup., in urgent haste, pressed by need.

蓿　sù　MC sjuwk

1. (bn.) 苜～ *mùsù*, → 苜 *mù*.

蔌　sù　MC suwk

1. gen. term for vegetables, greens.

2. rdup., crass and crude, base and abject; also, roaring and raging, shuddering and shaking, of the wind; also, flying and fluttering, swirled and scattered, of falling blossoms.

觫　sù　MC suwk

1. (bn.) 觳～ *húsù*, → 觳 *hú*.

訴　sù　MC suH

1. complain, repine; deplore, deprecate.

2. accuse, inform on, decry; state the faults of, bring a claim against.

a. speak ill of, defame; vilify, slander.

3. (med.) politely decline, demur.

謖　sù　MC srjuwk

1. arise, rise up; get up.

2. respectful, reverential.

3. rdup., brisk and bracing, of the wind.

速　sù　MC suwk

1. sgl. or rdup., fast, rapid, quick, speedy, swift, apace, immediate.

a. (med.) urgent, pressing; hasten to do.

2. lead to, induce to; beckon toward; invite.

遡　sù　MC suH

1. go upstream, against the current.

a. (med.) follow to the source.

2. face, facing; head(ing) into, go toward.

3. ⊙ 訴 *sù* 2, accuse, inform on; defame.

餗　sù　MC suwk

1. food in a cauldron; comestibles.

a. savory food; viands.

驌　sù　MC sjuwk

1. (bn.) ～驦 *sùshuāng* (MC sjuwk-srjang), bold-spirited steed, stalwart stallion.

鷫　sù　MC sjuwk

1. sgl. or in (bn.) ～鵊 *sùshuāng* (MC sjuwk-srjang), the halcyon kingfisher (*Halcyon smyrnensis*), syn. 翡翠 *fěicuì*.

2. (bn.) a kind of "phoenix" associated with the direction west; also, ⊙ 驌驦 *sùshuāng*, bold-spirited steed.

suān

狻 **suān** MC swan
1. ～猊, ～麑 *suānní*, lion, pre-Han and Han usage; when used in med. times a conscious archaism for 獅子 *shīzi*.

痠 **suān** MC swan
1. (med.) over-fatigued, sore, aching.

酸 **suān** MC swan
1. sour; acid, tart; acerbic.
   a. pickled.
2. pained, biting; troubling, unpleasant, disagreeable.
3. ⊙ 痠 *suān*, (med.) over-fatigued, sore, aching.

suàn

筭 **suàn** MC swanH
1. counting-stick, counting-tally.
2. ⊙ 算 *suàn* 1, calculate, reckon; 2, figure out, plan.

算 **suàn** MC swanX
1. count up; calculate, reckon.
   a. calculation, reckoning.
2. figure out, plan; devise, contrive.
3. chopsticks.
4. ⊙ 筭 *suàn*, counting-stick, counting-tally.

蒜 **suàn** MC swanH
1. sgl. or 大～ *dàsuàn*, garlic (*Allium sativum*).
   a. 小～ *xiǎosuàn*, rocambole, sand-leek (*Allium scorodoprasum*).

suī

睢 **suī** MC swij → 睢 *huī*.

荽 **suī** MC swij
1. coriander, Chinese parsely, cilantro (*Coriandrum sativum*); syn. 香菜 *xiāngcài*, 胡～ *húsuī* (< Iran. *koswi*).

薞 **suī** MC swij
1. ⊙ 荽 *suī*, coriander.
2. flower stamen.

雖 **suī** MC swij
1. preceding either VBS /VB-phrases or nouns/ noun-phrases, marks a concessive clause: (conceding the fact of or that >) although, even though, even, even if; e.g. ～曰未學，吾必謂之學矣 *suī yuē wèixué, wú bì wèi zhī xué yǐ*, although he said "I have not yet learned it," I would inevitably refer to him as learned; ～百世可知也 *suī bǎishì kězhī yě*, even a hundred ages can be known; ～大國必畏之矣 *suī dàguó bì wèi zhī yǐ*, even great states would inevitably stand in awe of him; ～然吾嘗聞之矣 *suīrán wú cháng wén zhī yǐ*, even so, I have already heard it once; ～與之天下，不能一朝居也 *suī yǔ zhī tiānxià, bùnéng yīzhāo jū yě*, even if one gave him the subcelestial realm, he would not be able to retain it for a single morning.

suí

綏 **suí** MC swij
1. strap by which to pull oneself onto a carriage.
2. placate, pacify; calm down, settle.
3. retreat in battle.

隋 **suí** MC zjwe
1. name of a lesser feudal state during the Warring States period, in present-day central Hubei.
2. name of an imperial dynasty, 581-618.
   duò MC dwaX
1. ⊙ 墮 *duò*, fall from; falter; 惰 *duò*, enervated; dissipated, indolent.
   huī MC xjwie
1. ⊙ 隳 *huī*, destroy, ruin.
   tuǒ MC thwaX
1. ⊙ 橢 *tuǒ*, oval; elliptical.

隨 **suí** MC zjwe
1. follow after, pursue; go along with.
2. pursuant to, in due course; along the way, by the way.
   a. to the extent that; mete with, responsive to, in conformity, as much as one can; e.g. ～宜 *suíyí*, as the situation demands; ～分 *suífēn*, according to one's allotted fate, as expected, as before.
3. (med.) tractable, obsequious; e.g. 詭～ *guǐsuí*, slavering and glavering.
4. (med.) ～處 *suíchù*, everywhere, everyplace.
5. "Following," name of 17th hexagram of the *Yijing*.
   duò MC dwaX
1. ⊙ 惰 *duò*, enervated; dissipated, indolent.
   huī MC xjwie
1. ⊙ 隳 *huī*, destroy, ruin.

tuǒ　MC thwaX

1. ⊙ 橢 *tuǒ*, oval; elliptical.

suǐ

瀡　suǐ　MC sjweX

1. slippery, slick; glossy.

髓　suǐ　MC sjweX

1. marrow, pith; medulla; inmost core of.

suì

樣　suì　MC zwijH

1. wild pear, Callery pear (*Pyrus calleryana*), bearing white five-petalled flowers of an unpleasant odor, small fruit hard until softened by frost.

歲　suì　MC sjwejH

1. Jupiter, the "year-star," so called because it remains in each of the 12 Jupiter stations for approx. a year while completing a full orbit of the heavens.
    a. 太～ *tàisuì*, invisible counter-Jupiter which moves opposite to it in orbit.
2. a year, the time it takes Jupiter to move from one sidereal station to the next; a twelve-month.
    a. gen. term for a year.
3. the years of one's life; one's age.
4. a year's harvest.

燧　suì　MC zwijH

1. fire-kindler, e.g. burning-glass or flint; tinder; to kindle, ignite.
2. beacon-fire, esp. the lit beacon in daytime; cf. 烽 *fēng*, beacon.
    a. beacon tower.

璲　suì　MC zwijH

1. jade pendant worn for good luck, lucky charm.

碎　suì　MC swojH

1. shatter, splinter, spall, mammock, crumble, chimble, fall apart, go to pieces; shred, tatter; minutiae; e.g. ～義 *suìyì*, fragmented meaning, incoherent explanation; ～金 *suìjīn*, splintered gold, descriptive of elegant lit. style.

cuì　MC swijH

1. (med.) ～葉 *cuìyè* (MC swijH-yep), Sūyāb, name of Central Asian oasis city on the northern edge of the Tianshan 天山 mountain range, in present-day Kyrgyzstan.

祟　suì　MC swijH

1. an affliction visited by spirits or demons; evil emanation, noxious influence.
    a. plague, bane, scourge.

穗　suì　MC zwijH

1. raceme or spike of grain in ear.
    a. loosely applied to catkins, aments, any longish inflorescence.
    b. tassel, fringe; tuft, puff; floss(y).
    c. (med.) euph. for candle-flame, lamp-flame.

檖　suì　MC zwijH

1. ripe grain, fully in ear, bending under the weight of its ripeness.
2. ⊙ 穗 *suì*, raceme, inflorescence of grain or other plant.
3. (med.) plant-stalk.

繐　suì　MC sjwejH

1. fine open-weave linen cloth, muslin; esp. used for the edging of coffin-curtains and grave-clothes for the dead.

襚　suì　MC zwijH

1. cerements, grave-clothes; shroud, winding-sheet.
    a. clothes for the dead kept in ancestral temple.
2. ribbon or sash to which pendant jades are attached.

誶　suì　MC swijH

1. insult, abuse verbally, impugn, disparage.
    a. denounce, accuse, inform on; denunciation, accusation.
2. criticize, remonstrate with, reprimand.
3. interrogate, question harshly.
4. (lit.) rare term for the concluding section or finale of a *fu* 賦 poem.

晬　suì　MC swijH

1. resources, goods; items of value; property, belongings.

遂 suì MC zwijH
1. to progress, to further.
    a. carry out, follow through with; succeed, achieve; fulfill.
2. do in consequence of, consequently, in due course; thereupon.
3. respond to, comply with.
    a. meet a favorable fate; sequacious.
4. in pre-imperial times an administrative area beyond the capital; distant counties; e.g. 芒〜 *mángsuì*, all the bounds of.
5. trough underneath striking area of chime-bell.
6. ⊙ 燧 *suì*, fire-making tool, flint; 邃 *suì*, deepest recesses of.

邃 suì MC swijH
1. inmost recesses, farthermost range, the quality of spaciousness in depth or distance.
    a. inaccessible, unfathomable, unsoundable; of immense, intense, or far-reaching profundity.

隧 suì MC zwijH
1. an underground passage, tunnel, esp. in a tomb.
    a. to make or excavate a tunnel, to tunnel.
    b. trench, excavation, groundwork (war).
2. passageway, route.
3. drainage ditch.
4. ⊙ 燧 *suì* 2a, beacon tower.
    zhuì MC drwijH
1. ⊙ 墜 *zhuì*, to fall, drop shed; sink; topple, tumble.

sūn

孫 sūn MC swon
1. grandchild.
    a. descendant; posterity.
2. second growth of plant, new shoot.
3. subordinate; show proper respect.
4. a surname, notably that of ruling family of Wu 吳 kingdom (222-280) of Three Kingdoms period.
    xùn MC swonH
1. ⊙ 遜 *xùn* 1, flee from, escape; retire; 2, compliant, submissive, self-effacing, modest(y).

蓀 sūn MC swon
1. sweet-flag, calamus (*Acorus calamus*), sweetly-scented wetland grass; (lit.) in *Chuci* poems a

symbol of purity (often rendered "iris," but this is inaccurate); syn. 荃 *quán*, 菖蒲 *chāngpú*.

飧 sūn MC swon
1. evening meal, supper.
    a. gen. term for cooked food, a meal, repast.
    b. to eat, sup, dine.
2. dilute or liquefy food with water.

殢 sūn MC swon ⊙ 飧 *sūn*.

sǔn

損 sǔn MC swonX
1. diminish, decrease, reduce, cut back, curtail; mitigate.
    a. impair(ment); damage, maim.
    b. relinquish; lose, loss; detriment(al).
2. restrain, suppress.
3. name of 41st hexagram of *Yijing*, "diminishment."

笋 sǔn MC swinX ⊙ 筍 *sǔn*.

筍 sǔn MC swinX
1. bamboo-shoot (edible).
2. ⊙ 簨 *sǔn*, crossbeam of bell-rack.

簨 sǔn MC swinX
1. horizontal rack from which to hang musical bells or stone-chimes, crossbeam of bell-rack (cf. 簴 *jù*, vertical part of bell-frame).

隼 sǔn MC swinX
1. falcon, esp. Han usage; syn. (med.) 鶻 *gǔ*.

sùn

巽 sùn MC swonH → 巽 *xùn*.

潠 sùn MC swonH
1. (med.) spit, spurt; spew; spout, squirt.

suō

傞 suō MC sa
1. rdup., drunkenly reeling, staggering, swaying, lurching; also, twirling, whirling round.

娑 suō MC sa
1. (bn.) 婆〜 *pósuō*, → 婆 *pó*.

2. rdup., flowing fullness.

3. (Budd.) ～訶 *suōhē* (MC sa-xa), ～婆訶 *suōpóhē* (MC sa-ba-xa), trsc. Skt. *svāhā*, exclamation "hail!" pronounced at end of mantra; ～羅 *suōluó* (MC sa-la), trsc. Skt. *śāla*, teak tree, esp. those at the place of the Buddha's *parinirvāṇa*; ～婆世界 *suōpóshìjiè*, the *sahā* world, this world in which suffering must be endured.

梭 suō MC swa

1. shuttle, used in weaving.
   a. a pass of the shuttle.

簑 suō MC swa

1. rain-cloak woven of bamboo or rushes.

縮 suō MC srjuwk

1. contract, draw back, recede, retract; shorten, reduce.
   a. recoil, shrink; withdraw; turn inward, fold in.
2. take out of, withdraw from.
   a. strain or filter sediment from wine.
3. bind together, as in sheaves; draw in, draw together.
4. straight(en), upright; vertical.

莎 suō MC swa

1. coco-grass, nutgrass (*Cyperus rotundus*), a perennial grass often used to make rain hats and raincoats.
   a. ⊙ 蓑 *suō*, straw cloak, strammel-cope.
2. sago palm (*Metroxylon sagu*), a short tree that produces sago, which is used as a food thickener; syn. 欀 *xiāng* 1.
3. ～車 *suōjū*, Han-dynasty name for Yarkand.

shā MC srae

1. ～鷄 *shājī*, katydid (*Mecopoda elongata*); syn. 絡緯 *luòwěi*.

蓑 suō MC swa

1. strammel-cope, straw cloak, used esp. as raingear; ⊙ 莎 *suō* 1a.
2. thatch a roof.

suī MC swoj

1. rdup., to dangle or draggle down.

suǒ

所 suǒ MC srjoX

1. place, spot, site, location.

a. measure-word for buildings and other items at specific site.

2. marker of object nominalization, i.e., when prefixed to a VB makes a noun phrase referring to the object of the VB: that which (X VBs), that which is (VBed by X); e.g. 從心～欲 *cóng xīn suǒyù*, to follow what the heart desires; 察其～安 *chá qí suǒān*, to examine that in which he takes comfort; 君子無～爭 *jūnzi wú suǒzhēng*, there is nothing over which a man of noble status will wrangle.
   a. ～以 *suǒyǐ*, that which is used > wherewithal, means; e.g. ～以養人 *suǒyǐ yǎng rén*, the means for nurturing people; ～以明人倫 *suǒyǐ míng rénlún*, the means for elucidating human relations; 國之～以廢興存亡 *guó zhī suǒyǐ fèixīng cúnwáng*, a state's wherewithal for failing or flourishing, surviving or perishing.
   b. ～以 *suǒyǐ*, that which is used (as a pretext, basis) > reason; e.g. 人之～以求富貴 *rén zhī suǒyǐ qiú fùguì*, a person's reason for seeking wealth and high status; ～以謂人皆有不忍人之心 *suǒyǐ wèi rén jiē yǒu bùrěn rén zhī xīn*, the reason for referring to people as in all cases having a heart that does not brook the suffering of others; (Budd.) ～以者何 *suǒyǐzhe hé*, what is the reason for it? > what do I mean by (saying) that?
   c. ～以 *suǒyǐ*, that which is used (as a means) > thereby; e.g. ～以尊師 *suǒyǐ zūn shī*, thereby they esteemed their teacher; ～以報本 *suǒyǐ bào běn*, thereby recompensing the fundamentals.
   d. ～以 *suǒyǐ*, that which is used (as a pretext, basis, reason) > therefore; e.g. ～以不願人之文繡 *suǒyǐ bùyuàn rén zhī wénxiù*, therefore he does not wish for the patterned embroideries of others.
   e. frequently deleted after 有 *yǒu* and 無 *wú*; e.g. 有以 *yǒu yǐ* (< 有～以 *yǒu suǒyǐ*) to have the means for; 無以言 *wú yǐ yán* (< 無～以言 *wú suǒyǐ yán*) to have no means for speaking.

3. marker of indirect nominalization, i.e., when prefixed to a VB makes a noun-phrase referring to that in relation to which a VB-OBJ clause pertains: that in relation to which or in regard to which > from, where, etc.; e.g. 東日之～出也 *dōngrì zhī suǒchū yě*, the east is (that in relation to which >) where the sun comes up; 有～受

之也 *yǒu suǒshòu zhī yě*, there was something (in relation to which >) from which he received it.

瑣　suǒ　MC swaX

1. sgl. or rdup., slight tinkling sound of jades.
2. small particle or piece, shred, bit, snippet; fractured, fragmented; e.g. ～碎 *suǒsuì*, chimble-chumble, bits and pieces, trifling trivialities; ～言 *suǒyán*, chitchat.
3. finely detailed, intricate; fastidious.
4. (med.) design of linked circlets or chain on a door or latticework window; e.g. 青～ *qīngsuǒ*, "blue-chained," detailed engraving on gates.
   a. (med.) by metonymy, gates of court or nobility.

璅　suǒ　MC swaX　⊙ 瑣 *suǒ*.

索　suǒ　MC sak

1. cord of twisted yarn, rope.
   a. corded, braided; twist strands together, lace up; string together; e.g. ～頭虜 *suǒtóulǔ*, braided-hair caitiffs, northern barbarians.
2. norm, standard, what one is typically bound by; usually, generally.
3. force, exhort; being made to do, bound to do; e.g. ～語 *suǒyǔ*, forced statement.
4. try to connect with, find an attachment to, bind to; seek out; ～隱 *suǒyǐn*, search for something or someone that is hidden.

   a. investigate thoroughly, rummage through, ransack.
5. be unstrung, unconnected; e.g. ～然 *suǒrán*, at loose ends; also, descriptive of tears falling in streams; ～居 *suǒjū*, live all on one's own.
   a. sgl. or rdup., at the end of one's rope, spent; forlorn, lonesome; e.g. (bn.) ～落 *suǒluò* (MC sak-lak), bereft and abandoned.
6. (Budd.) ～訶 *suǒhē* (MC sak-xa), ～婆 *suǒpó* (MC sak-ba), trsc. Skt. *sahā*, ref. this world of suffering which must be endured.

鎖　suǒ　MC swaX

1. chain, links.
   a. manacles, fetters.
2. lock; latch, hasp, clasp.
   a. lock up, close up.
3. (med.) ⊙ 瑣 *suǒ* 4, design of linked circlets as ornamentation for door or latticework, esp. engraving on gates of court or nobility.

鏁　suǒ　MC swaX　⊙ 鎖 *suǒ*.

suò

些　suò　MC saH

1. rhythmic particle placed at end of some lines of verse, esp. certain poems in *Chuci* collection.
   ### xiē　MC sjae
1. (med.) a few, a bit, a little of; somewhat.

T

tā

他　tā　MC tha

1. other, the other, another.
2. (med.) 3rd-person pronoun.

塌　tā　MC thap

1. (med.) sag, sink, cave in; subside, collapse, fall in; crumble, give way.

它　tā　MC tha

1. other, the other, another, ⊙ 他 *tā* 1.

tǎ

塔　tǎ　MC thap

1. (Budd.) trsc. Pāli *thūpa* (< Skt. *stūpa*), stupa, mound-like structure containing sacred relics > pagoda, tiered tower.

獺　tǎ　MC that

1. otter; semiaquatic mammal, various species, incl. Eurasian otter (*Lutra lutra*), Asian small-clawed otter (*Aonyx cinerus*), smooth-coated otter (*Lutrogale perspicillata*).
2. ⊙ 鰨 *tà*, giant salamander.

tà

嗒　tà　MC thap

1. ～然 *tàrán*, ～焉 *tàyān*, in a trance, as though disembodied.

拓　tà　MC thak　→ 拓 *zhí*.

搨　tà　MC thop

1. hang down, dangle.
2. (med.) ⊙ 榻 *tà* 2, make a copy of an inscription through the process of stone rubbing.
3. (med.) to outline or trace written graphs or drawings.

撻　tà　MC t

1. beat with a whip or stick, to whip, flog.
2. swift, speedy, rapid.
   a. hasten, drive on or forward.
3. leather grip at the midpoint of a bow, with indented groove to hold and guide the arrow.
4. (med.) (bn.) ～末 *tàmò* (MC that-mat), Jiangnan-area term for butterfly.

榻　tà　MC thap

1. narrow low platform for 1 or 2 persons, with no side-rests or back, primarily for kneeling on, rarely for sleeping if somewhat longer; banquette, bench, cot, couch-bed.
2. (med.) copy, esp. an ink rubbing of an inscription made by placing thin paper over incised stone and tamping it into the engravings, after which ink is stippled over the paper surface leaving, when the paper is peeled away, everything black except the incised areas which are white.

㯓　tà　MC thap

1. ⊙ 榻 *tà*, low narrow bed, cot; couch.
2. (med.) sloppy, slovenly; shuffling.
   a. (med.) (bn.) ～臈 *tàlà* (MC thap-lap), slippety-slop.

毾　tà　MC thap

1. (med.) (bn.) ～㲪 *tàdēng* (MC thap-tong), small wool rug, luxury item from Persia, trsc. Iran. *tābidān*, spun, woven.

沓　tà　MC dop

1. heap up, pile up; amass; build up, join up, bring together; e.g. (bn.) ～合 *tàhé* (MC dop-hop), blend and build, heap and hoard, collect and accumulate.
   a. profuse, enlarging; rdup., prolix and verbose, tirelessly talkative, babbling bedlam; redundant, reiterative, repetitive; also, quick and keen, hurried and headlong, running rapidly.
   b. (med.) set of 2 lacquered boxes that fit together, a double-set.
2. bubble, boil, burst upward.
3. avaricious, greedy; grasping, rapacious.
4. lackadaisical, indolent; disrespectful.

踏　tà　MC thop

1. stamp (with feet), tramp on; tread; stride, step.
2. (med.) examine on site, in situ; make one's way to for a look.

蹋　tà　MC dap　⊙ 踏 *tà*.

遝　tà　MC dop

1. reach to, get to; come up to, catch up to.
2. (bn.) 雜～ *zátà*, → 雜 *zá*.

譫　tà　MC thop

1. (med.) rdup., open to and tolerant.
2. (med.) ～伯 *tàbó*, free spirit, free-willing, laid back; also, unable or unconcerned to distinguish good from bad.

闒　tà　MC dap

1. upper-storey door, smaller than lower-floor doors.
   a. ～茸 *tàróng*, "small door and downy hair," i.e. petty person, good-for-nothing, dummy, moron; also, base, menial, useless.

闟　tà　MC that

1. small door, esp. leading to inner room; inner entrance.
   a. inner palace door.
2. vestibule, genkan.
3. swiftly, briskly.

鰨　tà　MC thap

1. giant salamander (*Andrias davidianus, A. sligoi*); syn. 鯢 *ní* 1.
2. (bn.) 鱸～ *qūtà*, → 鱸 *qū*.

鞳　tà　MC thop

1. onom. of rapid drum-sound, drum-roll.

tāi

胎 **tāi** **MC thoj**
1. fetus, embryo.
   a. womb.
   b. something encapsuled like a fetus.
2. embryonic, fetal; source, origin; e.g. (Dao.) 〜息 *tāixī*, embryonic breathing, technique of "pneuma circulation" (*xingqi* 行氣) in which an adept breathes in stillness, without using nose or mouth, as when in the womb.
   a. early stage of development; something in an unfinished state.
3. give birth to; spawn.
   a. congenital.

tái

台 **tái** **MC doj**
1. eminent.
   a. 三〜 *sāntái*, Three Eminences, 3 groups of paired stars along the southwest border of our Ursa Major marking 3 of the bear's paws (N.B. not part of the "Dipper"), being lined up (下〜 *xiàtái* = ν, ξ Ursae Majoris; 中〜 *zhōngtái* = λ, μ; 上〜 *shàngtái* = ι, κ) in ascending order between the constellations Grand Tenuity (*taiwei* 太微) and Purple Tenuity (*ziwei* 紫微) which symbolize respectively the southern imperial court and the central, highest imperial court; the *santai* thus stand for steps on the way to high office and are sometimes equated with the 3 Dignitaries (*sangong* 三公: Director of Instruction [*situ* 司徒], Director of Works [*sikong* 司空], and Grand Marshal [*taiwei* 太尉], the supreme officers of state); also called 泰階 *tàijiē*, Sublime Stairway, equated with (上) emperor, (中) princes/dukes and lower ministers/grandees, and (下) scholars and commoners; this is the same set of stars known in Arabic astronomy as the 3 Leaps of the Gazelle.
2. ⊙ 臺 *tái* 1, terrace, platform; 鮐 *tái*, puffer, globefish.

   yí **MC yi**
1. 1st-person pronoun, in early times.
2. interrogative "how?, what?" in early times.
3. consonant, agreeable; congenial, amiable; content; ⊙ 怡 *yí*.

擡 **tái** **MC doj**
1. (med.) raise, lift up, elevate.
   a. (med.) pick up, carry; lift with both hands or from both sides.

煲 **tái** **MC doj**
1. soot.

臺 **tái** **MC doj**
1. terrace, raised platform, estrade.
   a. a stand, to support or hold up object, such as mirror.
2. (med.) elevated, tower-like.
3. tribunal, suffix of various names of central-government agencies; e.g. 中〜 *zhōngtái*, Inner Tribunal, Han-time alternate name for imperial secretariat (*shangshusheng* 尚書省); 御史〜 *yùshǐtái*, Tribunal of Imperial Supervisors, i.e. censorate.
4. in early times, designation for lowly official.
5. capitulum, flower-head.

苔 **tái** **MC doj**
1. moss; lichen; incl. various species of each and of other bryophytes.

薹 **tái** **MC doj**
1. (med.) 蕓〜 *yúntái*, bird-rape, → 蕓 *yún*.

跆 **tái** **MC doj**
1. sgl. or 〜藉 *táijiè*, trample, tread on > ruthless, brutal.

駘 **tái** **MC doj**
1. a horse free of its bit or with loose reins.
2. a horse of inferior quality; worn-out horse, a jade, a hack.
   a. person of mediocre or inferior talent.
3. trample down.
   a. downtrodden; dejected, jaded.

   dài **MC dojX**
1. (bn.) 〜蕩 *dàidàng* (MC dojX-dangX), loose and free, slack and relaxed; unconfined, unrestrained; also, fagged and fatigued, worn and jaded.

鮐 **tái** **MC doj**
1. puffer, globefish, blowfish (*Spheroides vermicularis*); syn. 河豚魚 *hétúnyú*, 鮭 *guī*.
2. (med.) sgl. or 〜背 *táibèi*, an aged man (with maculations on his back like a blowfish), an "old puffer."

tài

太　tài　MC thajH

1. great(est), grand(est); e.g. 〜息 *tàixī*, give a great sigh, long sigh.

    a. indicating extreme, maximum, or superlative status of following word; e.g. (Dao.) 〜上老君 *tàishàng Lǎojūn*, Lord Lao, Most High; (med.) 〜煞 *tàishài*, most extreme, ultimate.

    b. (med.) excessive, undue.

2. honorific marker of seniority, age, or importance; e.g. 〜子 *tàizǐ*, the Grand Heir, Grand Scion, heir-designate; 〜祖 *tàizǔ*, Grand Forefather, usu. indicating a dynasty's founding emperor.

態　tài　MC thojH

1. posture, bearing, carriage, manner; appearance.

    a. demeanor, posturing, pose; attitude; feeling, mood.

2. situation, condition, circumstance.

3. pose as, pretend; affect, assume; impostor; false.

汰　tài　MC thajH

1. rinse, wash; scour, cleanse.

    a. sift; discard, eliminate.

2. wave (of river).

3. exceed, excessive; extravagant.

泰　tài　MC thajH

1. majestic; august, lordly; sublime.

2. peace of mind, contented equanimity, calm, composed.

3. generous, large-hearted.

    a. benefit, bestead; largesse.

4. arrogant, haughty; overweening, supercilious.

5. ⊙ 太 *tài* 1, grand, great; maximum, most; (med.) excessive, undue.

6. "Contentment," name of 11th hexagram of the *Yijing*.

7. name of Mt. Tai, "Paramount," in Shandong, the Eastern Marchmount.

tān

嘽　tān　MC than

1. rdup., panting and snorting, exhausted and spent; also, unnumbered and legion, drawn-out in throngs.

攤　tān　MC than

1. (med.) spread out, lay out; expose, display.

2. (med.) share responsibility for, partake of.

灘　tān　MC than

1. (med.) shoal, shallows.

    a. (med.) rapids, relatively shallow but swift-running section of river.

2. (med.) sandflat, sandbank; strand, shore.

癱　tān　MC than

1. paralysis; immobility.

舑　tān　MC tham

1. (bn.) 〜䑙 *tāntán* (MC tham-thamH), ⊙ 舔䑙 *tiǎntàn*, → 舔 *tiǎn*.

貪　tān　MC thom

1. avid for, greedy, covetous, insatiate, esurient; crave, lust after, pursue obsessively.

    a. avaricious(ness), cupidity; cling to.

    b. (Budd.) trns. Skt. *rāga*, sensual attachment, clinging to desires of this world.

2. (med.) wish to, prefer to (without pejorative implication).

3. ⊙ 探 *tàn* 1, search out; probe.

tán

僤　tán　MC dan

1. 〜佪 *tánhuí*, go back and forth, round and about, pace here and there, tarry and linger.

    tǎn　MC danX

1. rdup., free and easy, relaxed, easy-going.

    shàn　MC dzyenH

1. ⊙ 禪 *shàn* 2, yield, step away from; cede, abdicate.

壇　tán　MC dan

1. raised mound for performance of religious ritual, political ceremony, ancestral sacrifice; altar, sacred stage; estrade.

    a. by metonymy, court (political).

2. banked around the borders; e.g. 〜陸 *tánlù*, "banked lands," seagirt lands.

    dàn　MC danH

1. (bn.) 〜曼, 〜漫 *dànmàn* (MC danH-manH), distantly extended, steadily stretching.

    shàn　MC dzyenH

1. small hall for ceremonies (old Chu usage).

2. inner courtyard (old Chu usage).

彈　tán　MC dan

1. shoot (crossbow) pellets.

2. pluck with fingers, pick, esp. a stringed instrument.

a. snap the fingers > a brief unit of time, an instant, a jiffy.

3. pierce, lance (an abscess).

4. criticize, reproach; denounce, accuse; impeach.

dàn   MC danH

1. pellet of crossbow or stone-bow.

a. by synecdoche, crossbow, arbalest; stone-bow, pellet-bow, goolail.

2. polished stones used in board-game *weiqi* 圍棋; by metonymy, to play *weiqi*.

惔   tán   MC

1. consume by fire, burn up.

dàn   MC damX

1. tranquil, settled, content.

憛   tán   MC dom

1. (bn.) 〜惏 *tántú* (MC dom-thu), avidly craving, deeply covetous.

2. (bn.) 惏〜 *tútán* (MC thu-dom), downcast and disquieted, → 惏 *tú*.

曇   tán   MC dom

1. sgl. or rdup., overcast clouds, dark and densely spread.

2. (Budd.) trsc. of Skt. *d*, *dh*; e.g. 〜磨, 〜摩 *tánmó* (MC dom-ma), trsc. Skt. *dharma*.

檀   tán   MC dan

1. rosewood (*Dalbergia hupeana*, *Dalbergia odorifera*), straight-grained hardwood tree with light brown to mahogany-colored bark, from which a fragrant oil is extracted.

a. lustrous reddish-brown, from the deeper hues of rosewood bark.

2. sandalwood (*Santalum album*), medium-sized semi-parasitic tree with fragrant brownish-yellow bark, from which a fragrant oil is extracted; known under names confusingly employing "rosewood," because both trees are fragrant, e.g. 旃〜 *zhāntán* "oriflamme rosewood" (MC tsyen-dan, trsc. Skt. candana, sandalwood), 真〜 *zhēntán* "true rosewood," 〜香 *tánxiāng* "rosewood aromatic," all ref. sandalwood.

a. 紫〜 *zǐtán*, "purple rosewood," sanders-wood (*Pterocarpus santalinus*).

b. 〜心 *tánxīn* "sandal heart," fawn colored, brownish-yellow or reddish-yellow.

3. 青〜 *qīngtán*, winged hackberry (*Pteroceltis tatarinowii*), a multi-stemmed tree that grows on hot, dry slopes and ravines; bark gray-white to dark gray, used in making paper.

4. (Budd.) alms, almsgiving, trsc. Skt. *dāna*, donation, also 〜施 *tánshī*.

a. 〜越 *tányùe*, almsgiver, combined trsc. and trns. Skt. *dānapati*.

5. (bn.) 〜欒 *tánlúan* (MC dan-lwan), slimly tapering; smoothly supple, gracile(ly), esp. of bamboo.

6. ⊙ 覃 *tán*, lengthy.

diàn   MC tenH

1. eave of a roof.

潭   tán   MC dom

1. Chu dialect word for a deep pool, abyss, syn. 淵 *yuān*.

a. (med.) mountain pool, tarn.

2. deep-seated; profound; unfathomable.

3. rdup., soaked and saturated, immersed and absorbed.

xún   MC zim

1. ⊙ 潯 *xún*, riverside, riverbank.

蕁   tán   MC dom

1. anemarrhena (*Anemarrhena asphodeloides*), liliaceous plant with white night-blooming flowers, the root used medicinally; syn. 知母 *zhīmǔ*.

薄   tán   MC dom

1. date-palm (*Phoenix dactylifera*).

覃   tán   MC dom

1. long, prolong(ed).

2. extend(ed), extensive, stretch; spread, pervade.

3. far-reaching, deep (of thoughts).

4. a surname.

談   tán   MC dam

1. talk, chat, converse, conversation; discuss(ion).

a. (med.) speak about, talk of, raise as a subject of discussion.

譚   tán   MC dom

1. stretch out, extend.

a. exaggerate, aggrandize, stretch the truth.

2. ⊙ 談 *tán*, talk, chat, converse; discuss(ion).

醰   tán   MC dom

1. rich taste of wine, long-lasting, lingering "finish," aftertaste.

a. of finest purity.

2. rdup., mellow and mellifluous, sweet and dulcet (of music).

餤　tán　MC dam
1. serve food; bring in.
 a. advance, put forward.
  dàn　MC damX
1. eat, nibble at.
 a. bait; provoke, induce(ment).

tǎn

坦　tǎn　MC thanX
1. level, flat; smooth.
 a. even-tempered, unflappable.
2. lay open; bare; reveal, expose.
 a. candid, frank, with nothing hidden; honest; e.g. ～蕩 *tǎndǎng*, candid and relaxed.
3. composed, calm.

毯　tǎn　MC thamX
1. tapis; carpet, rug; covering, blanket.

襢　tǎn　MC domX
1. ⊙ 袒 *tǎn* 1, strip to the waist; bare, expose.
 zhàn　MC trjenH
1. colorless; unadorned; in early times, esp. ref. ceremonial clothing of wives of high dignitaries.

菼　tǎn　MC thamX
1. freshly sprouting rush or reed, reed-sprout; sometimes pussy-willow.
 a. pale green (color of preceding).

袒　tǎn　MC danX
1. strip off clothing, esp. from upper part of body; strip to the waist.
 a. naked; bare(d), expose(d).
 b. unadorned, undecorated; plain.
2. (med.) side with, be partial to; make excuses for.

醓　tǎn　MC thomX
1. brine or pickling juice of pickled mincemeat.

黮　tǎn　MC thomX
1. the black of ripe mulberries.
 a. sgl., rdup., or (bn.) ～黣 *tǎndùi* (MC thomX-dwojH), ～暗 *tǎn'àn* (MC thomX-'omH), 黯～ *àntǎn* (MC 'eamX-thomX), grim and gloomy, sullen and somber, bleak and black.

---

 shèn　MC zyimX
1. ⊙ 葚 *shèn*, ripe mulberry fruit.

tàn

蜒　tàn　MC thamH
1. (bn.) 蚰～ *tiàntàn*, → 蚰 *tiàn* (*rán*).

嘆　tàn　MC thanH　⊙ 歎 *tàn*.

探　tàn　MC thomH
1. stretch out one's hand for, reach for, feel for, reach into.
 a. probe into, explore; investigate; search out, scout out; test, try.
 b. inquire after, find out; pursue thoroughly.
2. go forward into, make a foray.

歎　tàn　MC thanH
1. to sigh; gasp.
 a. lament, bewail.
 b. exclaim in admiration, admire; praise, commend.
2. catch one's breath; takes one's breath away.
3. recite, chant aloud, declaim; intone.

炭　tàn　MC thanH
1. charcoal; coal.
 a. ashes, soot.
 b. smirched, smudged, smutched.

惔　tàn　MC thamH
1. (med.) (bn.) 舔～ *tiǎntàn*, → 舔 *tiǎn*.

tāng

湯　tāng　MC thang
1. hot water, boiling water.
 a. thermal springs, hot springs, thermae.
2. medicinal decoction.
3. (med.) soup, hot soup; broth.
4. (med.) rush ahead, rush against, collide with.
5. name of reputed founder of Shang dynasty (ca. 1600-1045), also called 成～ *chéng Tāng*, "Tang the Successful."
 tàng　MC thangH
1. warm or heat with hot water, boil, scald.
2. drift about, unconnected to anyone, unconstrained by convention.

yáng   MC yang

1. ～谷 *yánggǔ,* ⊙ 暘谷 *yánggǔ,* Sunrise Vale, legendarily the valley whence the sun emerges each day.

shāng   MC syang

1. rdup., rushing and roaring (of river current, waves); also, sound of zither's imitation of same.

鏜   **tāng   MC thang**

1. onom. of beaten drum: tahn-tahn.

闛   **tāng   MC dang**

1. onom. of beaten drum: dahn-dahn.

鞺   **tāng   MC thang**   ⊙ 鏜 *tāng.*

táng

唐   **táng   MC dang**

1. central walkway within a court or shrine.
2. boast, brag; exaggerate.
   a. extensive; grand.
3. empty, deserted.
4. dodder (*Cuscuta chinensis*); syn. 菟絲 *tùsī.*
5. black-blotched, black-spotted.
6. (med.) (bn.) ～突 *tángtū* (MC dang-dwot), in (less than) no time, pell-mell, before one knows.
7. name of kingdom associated with legendary sage-king Yao 堯; name of feudal state in Zhou times, located in south-central Shanxi; name of med. dynasty (618-907); name of 2 short-lived 10th-century dynasties: Later Tang 後～ (Hou-Tang, 923-936) and Southern Tang 南～ (Nan-Tang, 937-975).
8. ⊙ 塘 *táng,* embankment, dam, dike; pond, pool.

堂   **táng   MC dang**

1. hall, main building for receptions, ceremony, religious or official business; aulary, aularian.
   a. fore-hall, chief meeting-room for public gathering, main room.
2. dais, raised platform for seating honored persons or placing ritual objects.
3. prefix attached to relational terms indicating descent from patrilineal line, used as such in Tang times; in Nanbeichao period the term used was 同～ *tóngtáng;* in Qin-Han times the term used was 從 *cóng.*
4. plateau, in mountains.
   a. embankment.

5. rdup., broad and limitless; large and lofty; massive and magnificent.

塘   **táng   MC dang**

1. embankment, dam, dike.
2. lake, pond, or stank formed behind a banked barrier; basin, reservoir.

搪   **táng   MC dang**

1. (med.) stand against, protect against; resist; parry; confront.
   a. (med.) ～塞 *tángsè,* deal with, cope with.

棠   **táng   MC dang**

1. ～梨 *tánglí,* 甘～ *gāntáng,* dancer flowering pear, birchleaf pear (*Pyrus betulifolia*), deciduous fast-growing tree with soft-green oval leaves that flutter in the wind, also called 杜梨 *dùlí.*
2. ～棣 *tángdì,* variously identified as species of cherry, plum, pear, or quince, gorgeously flowering; perhaps kerria (*Kerria japonica*) showing large yellow flowers in springtime; suggested rendering either "kerria" or "sweet-plum"; associated in lit. with fraternal feeling; syn. 常棣 *chángdì.*
3. 沙～ *shātáng,* species of wild pear with yellow flowers, red fruit that tastes like the plum (李 *lǐ*) but without a pit; its wood valued for making boats; reputedly also found on Mount Kunlun 崑崙山.
4. ⊙ 樘 *táng,* stave-side, wooden slats forming the sides of a carriage-box.
5. a surname.

糖   **táng   MC dang**

1. bowl; basin.

樘   **táng   MC dang**

1. diagonal post resting on top of rafter; strut; ⊙ 牚 *chēng.*
2. stave-side, wooden slats forming the side of carriage-box.
3. (med.) (bn.) ～突 *tángtū* (MC dang-dwot), run up against, confront, offend, affront; ⊙ 唐突 *tángtū.*

溏   **táng   MC dang**   ⊙ 塘 *táng.*

糖   **táng   MC dang**

1. sugar(ed); candied.

螗   **táng   MC dang**

1. (bn.) ～蜋 *tángláng* (MC dang-lang), mantis (*Mantoidea*).

餹　táng　MC dang　⊙ 糖 *táng*.

tǎng

倘　tǎng　MC thangX
1. perhaps, it might be that.
2. (med.) marker of conditional: should it happen that, should it befall that, in the event of.
3. surprised by, in shock.
cháng　MC dzyang
1. (bn.) ～佯 *chángyáng* (MC dzyang-yang), shilly-shally, shift back and forth, havering and wavering.

儻　tǎng　MC thangX
1. stupefied, in a daze; bewildered, bemused.
2. inadvertent, unexpected; extraordinary.
3. ⊙ 倘 1, perhaps, it might be that; 2, (med.) should it be that, should it happen that, in the event of.
4. (med.) (bn.) ～朗 or ～閬 *tǎnglǎng* (MC thangX-langX), glimmering glow, gloriously ablaze; (med.) (bn.) 倜～ *tìtǎng*, → 倜 *tì*.

帑　tǎng　MC thangX
1. state or national treasury.
   a. currency; valuable property.
nú　MC nu
1. ⊙ 孥 *nú*, child(ren), tyke(s); also, wife and children.
2. bird-tail.

懠　tǎng　MC thangX
1. (bn.) ～慌 *tǎnghuǎng* (MC thangX-xwangX), desperately disappointed, deeply depressed.

曭　tǎng　MC thangX
1. (bn.) ～莽 *tǎngmǎng* (MC thangX-mangX), dulled and dusky, darkly shaded; (med.) (bn.) ～朗 *tǎnglǎng* (MC thangX-langX), glimmering glow.

燙　tǎng　MC thangX
1. (med.) ⊙ 儻 *tǎng* 4, in (bn.) ～朗 or ～閬 *tǎnglǎng*.

tāo

叨　tāo　MC thaw
1. covet(ous), greedy; insatiable; avid for; savor.

2. (med.) pejorative or self-depreciatory term: not worthy (to do X), would be ashamed (to do X), to be favored with.
3. (med.) (bn.) ～沓 *tāotà* (MC thaw-dop), avaricious and shiftless, greedy but negligent.

弢　tāo　MC thaw
1. bowcase; wrapping for bow.
2. ⊙ 韜 *tāo* 2, (en)case, wrap(ping); hide, conceal, cover.

慆　tāo　MC thaw
1. joyous, happy; take pleasure in, delight in.
2. negligent; to slight; insolent.
3. doubtful, dubious, uncertain.
4. hide, conceal; cover up.
   a. slip by unnoticed, pass imperceptibly, esp. of time.
5. rdup., for a long, long time; also, damaged and disordered, chaotically confused.

搯　tāo　MC thaw
1. knock, beat on, strike.
2. (med.) draw out, extract, pull out.

滔　tāo　MC thaw
1. flood, inundate, deluge; overflow.
   a. surge, swell, mount up, rise high (of water).
   b. rdup., swelling and surging, raging torrent, steadily streaming, ever flowing, steadily flowing; also, grand and glorious, majestic, magnificent; also, in turbulent tumult, overwhelmed in disarray.
2. overweening, overbearing; prideful, presumptuous; flamboyant.
3. (med.) rush forward, race toward.

絛　tāo　MC thaw
1. silk cord(on), ribbon, strap, silk band.
   a. jess, in falconry a short strap tied round a leg of falcon or hawk and attached to a leash.

縧　tāo　MC thaw
1. ⊙ 絛 *tāo*, silk cord, strap; 韜 *tāo*, bow-case; wrap(ping), cover(ing).

繛　tāo　MC thaw　⊙ 絛 *tāo*.

諂　tāo　MC thaw
1. doubt(ful), uncertain; hesitant.

韜 tāo   MC thaw

1. sheath(ing), for sword; scabbard; also, ⊙ 弢 *tāo*, bow-case.
2. (en)case, wrap(ping); envelop.
   a. enfold, swathe; e.g. ～世 *tāoshì*, embrace the world.
   b. hide, conceal; cover; e.g. ～光 *tāoguāng*, hide one's light, to not flaunt one's abilities, withdraw from public view.
3. collect, store up; accommodate.
4. abb. of 六～ *liùtāo*, the 6 Sheathings, book of tactics legendarily attributed to Jiang Shang 姜尚 (also known as Taigong 太公), adviser to Kings Wen 文王 and Wu 武王 of Zhou; hence, gen. term for military tactics or strategy.

饕 tāo   MC thaw

1. ⊙ 叨 *tāo* 1, covet(ous), greedy, avid for.
2. (bn.) ～餮 *tāotiè* (MC thaw-thet), "ravening and gluttonous" < legendary figure of insatiable lusts in the time of the Yellow Emperor; name of a 2-eyed face-like decorative motif often found on Shang and early Zhou bronzes.

táo

咷 táo   MC daw

1. (bn.) 號～ *háotáo* (MC haw-daw), wail and weep.

tiào   MC thewH

1. (bn.) 噭～ *jiàotiào* (MC kewH-thewH), old Chu dialect term for incessant crying of babies; also, to sing full-throatedly.

桃 táo   MC daw

1. peach, both tree and fruit (*Prunus persica*); symbolic of springtime (esp. 3rd month), youthful beauty and flowering; the wood of the peachtree was used in various apotropaic items; often paired with 李 *lǐ*, plum (*Prunus salicina*), as suggestive of spring, beauty, love, pulchritude, also (med.) of the spreading shade and fruit (i.e. influence) of followers or disciples.
   a. peach-colored; pink.
   b. 羊～ *yángtáo*, "sheep's peach," Chinese gooseberry (*Actinidia chinensis*); 獼猴～ *míhóutáo*, "macaque's peach," syn. preceding; 含～ *hántáo*, "enclosed peach," cherry, esp. when presented at ancestral temple; 胡～ *hútáo*, "Western peach," walnut.

檮 táo   MC daw

1. (bn.) ～杌 *táowù* (MC daw-ngwot), block of wood, tree-stump; also, legendary malevolent beast or man; also, name of the pre-imperial historical chronicles of the state of Chu.
2. cmpd. ～昧 *táomèi*, blockhead, idiot, moron.
   dǎo   MC tawX
1. ⊙ 擣 *dǎo*, pound, beat with a pestle; strike.

洮 táo   MC thaw

1. pour water; wash; rinse with water to clean; purify, make ablutions; e.g. ～汰 *táotài*, cleanse, scour, wash away impurities; also, eliminate, remove, purge, liquidate.
   a. wash the hands.

淘 táo   MC daw

1. (med.) ⊙ 洮 *táo*.

濤 táo   MC daw

1. surge, swell (of water); billow, comber.

綯 táo   MC daw

1. cord, rope; braid.

萄 táo   MC daw

1. (med.) (bn.) 葡～ *pútáo*, → 葡 *pú*.

逃 táo   MC daw

1. flee, run off.
   a. desert; abscond.
2. evade, elude, avert, avoid; sidestep, shirk.

醄 táo   MC daw

1. (med.) (bn.) 酕～ *máotáo*, → 酕 *máo*.

陶 táo   MC daw

1. pottery.
   a. to fashion pottery; mold in clay.
   b. potter.
   c. kiln; bake in a kiln.
2. to mold, fashion; fabricate; fictile.
   a. educate; cultivate, develop.
3. pleased, contented; untroubled, satisfied, at peace.
4. a surname.
   yáo   MC yew
1. rdup., well-pleased and elated, satisfied and delighted; also, endlessly extended, stretching on and on; also, fleetly galloping, hurriedly hasting.

2. 皋～ *gāoyáo*, Gao Yao, name of legendary minister of sage-king Shun 舜 esteemed for his judgment and wisdom, also reputed ancestor of the Eastern Yi 夷 people.

韜　táo　MC daw　⊙ 鼗 *táo*.

駣　táo　MC daw

1. (bn.) ～駼 *táotú* (MC daw-du), tarpan, Central Asian wild horse used by the Xiongnu and other nomadic tribes.

鼗　táo　MC daw

1. long-handled small hand-drum, double-faced with 2 attached beaters on strings, played by holding the handle and twisting from side to side.

tǎo

討　tǎo　MC thawX

1. inquire into, ask searchingly, sound out.
    a. discuss, examine; confer, parley.
    b. seek into, search out; explore, investigate.
2. denounce, condemn, inveigh against, imprecate.
    a. attack, assail.
    b. chastise, suppress, punish (opposing forces); launch punitive strike; harry.
3. (med.) demand, exact.
    a. (med.) implore, adjure, solicit.

tè

忒　tè　MC thok

1. change, modify; do differently, deviate.
2. err(ing), fault, deviant; mistake; be off the mark, out of line.
3. (med.) excess(ive), exceedingly; nimious, nimiety.

慝　tè　MC thok

1. vice, evil, vicious(ness); turpitude, depravity.
    a. malevolence, malice; pernicious or malign occurrence.
    b. malevolent or noxious influence.
2. ⊙ 忒 *tè*, change, deviate; err, fault, mistake; 匿 *nì*, conceal, hide.

特　tè　MC dok

1. prominent(ly), pointed(ly), marked(ly); (e)special(-ly); outstanding.
    a. in particular, striking(ly), exceptional(ly).
2. sole, individual, single.
    a. only, merely; alone, in itself, of its own accord; e.g. ～為 *tèwéi*, nothing but, nothing other than.
3. spouse (< particular counterpart).
4. a bull > gen. term for oxen or water-buffalo.
    a. sacrificial beast, esp. one 3 or 4 years old.
5. ～勤 *tèqín* (MC dok-gj+n) (often miswritten ～勒 *tèlè*), tegin, trsc. of Turk. *tägin* or *tigin*, Türkic title attachable to junior males of the kaghan's family, often of significant power or influence, usu. subordinate to *yabghu* (*yehu* 葉護); (med.) ～勒 *tèlè*, the Tiele confederation of Türkic tribes during Tang times.

貣　tè　MC thok

1. ask for, ask of; request; solicit, implore.
    a. borrow.
2. (med.) forgive, pardon; absolve.
3. ⊙ 忒 *tè* 2, err; fault, mistake; deviant.

téng

縢　téng　MC dong

1. pouch; pocket; sack.

滕　téng　MC dong

1. of water, to splash up, rise up, mount up, billow up, well up.
2. gush forth, rush outward, pour forth (of water or of words).
3. small state during Warring States period, located in southeastern Shandong.

疼　téng　MC downg

1. pain, ache, sore.

縢　téng　MC dong

1. seal, seal up.
2. tie up, bind; lace up.
    a. cord; lace.
3. leg-wrap, leggings.
4. ⊙ 縢 *téng*, pouch, sack.

藤 téng MC dong

1. climbing or trailing vines, incl. various species of wisteria or liana; when used to make objects, translate as rattan.

  a. 紫〜 *zǐténg*, "purple wisteria" or "purple liana" (*Wisteria sinensis*); 〜蘿 *téngluó*, "wisteria creeper" (*Wisteria villosa*).

  b. 紫〜香 *zǐténgxiāng*, "purple liana aromatic," lakawood, scented heartwood of *Dalbergia parviflora*, used as incense.

  c. 〜黃 *ténghuáng*, "rattan yellow," gumresin of certain species of mangosteen (*Garcinia*); gamboge, the orange-yellow pigment derived from the resin.

謄 téng MC dong

1. transcribe, copy a text.

騰 téng MC dong

1. vault, bound; spring, bounce.

  a. spring up; rise up; mount upward, ascend.

  b. mount up, pile up, accumulate; swell up.

  c. mount up or on (horse or carriage).

2. prance; gambade; rear up.

  a. caper, frisk, cavort, gambol, frolic; swing round.

3. mount beyond, bound over; transcend; move beyond.

  a. overcome; oppress.

4. gallop lightly, dash.

5. transfer; deliver.

  a. send around, circulate.

6. (med.) shift from one place to another; displace.

tī

剔 tī MC thek

1. separate meat from bone.

  a. pick off or apart, esp. with pointed instrument.

  b. scrape, scrape off; grate.

2. dredge (a waterway).

  a. remove obstructions; eliminate, clear away, expunge.

  tì MC thejH

1. shave, scrape off hair; dress, put in order; ⊙ 剃 *tì*.

梯 tī MC thej

1. ladder.

  a. climb up, mount up.

2. lean on or against.

3. foothold.

4. provide a reason for; pretext, what something depends on or derives from.

踢 tī MC thek

1. kick, boot.

tí

嗁 tí MC dej

1. sob; keen.

2. cry out, bawl; shriek, howl; squawk.

媞 tí MC dej

1. rdup., fair and beautiful; also, gracefully easy.

提 tí MC dej

1. take up in the hand; pick up, lift up.

  a. draw up, pull up.

  b. pull out, draw forward; lead forward.

2. raise up, move from lower to higher.

  a. advance, promote.

3. raise, adduce, propose (example, topic, suggestion).

4. throw, fling.

褆 tí MC dej

1. stability, calm; security; unthreatened.

2. ⊙ 祇 *zhǐ*, merely, only, just; still.

稊 tí MC dej

1. barnyard millet (*Echinochloa utilis*), used as fodder.

2. ⊙ 荑 *tí* 1, sprout, shoot; bud.

綈 tí MC dej

1. raw pongee.

緹 tí MC dej

1. tangerine-colored.

  a. silk of orange-red color.

荑 tí MC dej

1. fresh sprout, tender shoot.

  a. show as visible for the first time, bud(ding), sprout.

2. ⊙ 稊 *tí* 1, barnyard millet.

蹄 tí MC dej

1. hoof.

a. tread with hooves, hoof it; gallop (horses), trod (oxen).

b. measure-word for quadrupeds.

2. hare-trap, rabbit-snare.

dì　MC dejH

1. ⊙ 踶 *dì*, kick; trudge.

蹏　tí　MC dej　⊙ 蹄 *tí*.

醍　tí　MC dej

1. (bn.) 〜醐 *tíhú* (MC dej-hu), ghee, clarified butter-fat from cow's milk (< Avestan *tayu-*, sour; cheese); (Budd.) symbolically the quintessential nectar of the Buddha's teaching.

2. fine rose-colored wine.

題　tí　MC dej

1. forehead.

a. capital, of column or pillar.

2. heading, title; label, name.

a. topic, theme.

3. superscription; inscribe on a surface, esp. a wall.

a. caption, epigraph.

b. (lit.) "verses on [particular topic]."

4. (med.) critique, evaluate.

騠　tí　MC dej

1. (bn.) 駃〜 *juétí*, → 駃 *jué*.

鵜　tí　MC dej

1. (bn.) 〜鶘 *tíhú* (MC dej-hu), pelican (*Pelecanus*, various species).

tǐ

體　tǐ　MC thejX

1. limbs, of the body.

a. element, part, component, constituent.

2. one's physical frame, form, body (cog. 禮 *lǐ*, good form in conduct, formality, ritual); one's own person.

a. physical structure, configuration; shape, appearance.

b. embody, incarnate, incorporate.

3. substance, content; constitution; normative form.

a. immanent substance, essential being (cf. 用 *yòng*, functional aspects).

b. substantiate; rely on as basic truth; infer from, conjecture.

c. put into practice or effect; embody.

d. realize; comprehend.

4. put oneself in the place of others; be considerate of, make allowances for.

5. (lit.) genre, particular form of writing.

a. (lit.) style, mode, manner, fashion.

tì

偍　tì　MC thek

1. 〜然 *tìrán*, extraordinary, exceptional, standing out from the crowd; also, faraway, distant, almost beyond reach.

2. (bn.) 〜儻 *tìtǎng* (MC thek-thangX), special and exceptional, sui generis, in a different category; also, careless and unchecked, coolly unconcerned; also, assertive and assured, in complete control.

剃　tì　MC thejH

1. shave, scrape off hair; shear.

a. (Budd.) tonsure; e.g. 〜度 *tìdù*, take the tonsure and become a monk.

嚔　tì　MC tejH

1. snort; snuffle, grunt; sneeze, sternutatory.

屜　tì　MC thejH

1. shelf; pull-out tray, drawer.

悌　tì　MC dejX; deH (when VB)

1. respectful deference toward elder brother(s), acting as a younger brother should; adelphic.

2. (bn.) 愷〜 *kǎitì*, → 愷 *kǎi*.

愻　tì　MC thek　⊙ 惖 *tì*.

惖　tì　MC thek

1. be on guard against, cautious; wary of, leery.

a. (bn.) 〜息 *tìxī* (MC thek-sik), trembling in terror, shuddering with dread.

b. rdup., dread the thought of, faltering with fear.

2. anxious, have misgivings; cavil.

3. alert to, suddenly aware of.

揥　tì　MC thejH

1. comb-hairpin (ornament).

dì　MC tejH

1. discard, set aside; throw away.

擿   tì   MC thek   → 擿 *zhì.*

替   tì   MC thejH

1. abrogate, abolish; nullify.
   a. do away with, put aside, abandon.
2. decline, wane; abate, subside; e.g. 崇替 *chóngtì*, rise and fall, thrive and decline.
3. (med.) replace, substitute; stand in for, take the place of.
4. (med.) ⊙ 屉 *tì*, drawer, pull-out tray; shelf.

孋   tì   MC thejH

1. (med.) detain, keep behind.
   a. (med.) be caught in, trapped by, stuck in; flounder; wallow in.

渧   tì   MC thejH

1. mucus from the nose; snivel; ⊙ 涕 *tì* 2.

涕   tì   MC thejH

1. weep, cry; tears.
2. mucus from the nose; snivel.

睼   tì   MC thejH

1. see straight on, peer intently at, gaze narrowly.

薙   tì   MC thejH

1. cut down weeds or grass, mow, shear.
   a. extirpate, root out, cut down, do away with.
2. barren terrain.

趯   tì   MC thek

1. ⊙ 躍 *yuè*, leap over, jump, vault.
   a. rdup., leap and spring, skitter-scamper (of grasshoppers).
2. (med.) kick, strike with the foot.

逖   tì   MC thek

1. remote, far distant.
   a. move away from, remove.
2. rdup., overcome with fear, dreading the thought of, ⊙ 惕惕 *tìtì.*

鬀   tì   MC thejH   ⊙ 剃 *tì.*

tiān

天   tiān   MC then

1. the sky, the heavens; celestial (as physical quality, paired with the earthly, *dì* 地); e.g. 〜下

tiānxià, the subcelestial realm, the world, the empire; 青〜 *qīngtiān*, the blue sky; 〜河 *tiānhé*, the He River in the sky, sky river, i.e. Milky Way; 〜末 *tiānmò*, 〜際 *tiānjì*, 〜涯 *tiānyá*, the end(s), edge, or shores of the sky, i.e. of the world.
   a. climate, weather; seasons.
2. heaven, as overarching power beyond human comprehension but often responsive to human entreaty and to ritual sacrifice from the ruler.
   a. heaven, as conscious overseer and regulator of earthly matters, given to rewarding and punishing human conduct.
3. heaven-endowed, affirmed or approved of by heaven; e.g. 〜王 *tiānwáng*, heaven-endowed king; (Dao.) 〜師 *tiānshī*, Celestial Master, name of religious movement initiated and the title taken by Zhang Daoling 張道陵 in the mid-2nd-century CE as a covenant with the deified Laozi.
   a. having the qualities associated with heaven; of most unusual or extraordinary ability; 〜馬 *tiānmǎ*, heavenly horses, the "blood-sweating" horses brought from Ferghana in the late 2nd-century BCE which were far superior to those previously known in China.
4. natural, not initiated by or deriving from humans; e.g. 〜道 *tiāndào*, the Way of heaven, the natural course and structure of the world; 〜才 *tiancái*, native genius, heaven-sent ability.
   a. the natural world; e.g. 〜物 *tiānwù*, nature's phenomena, the animals and plants of the physical world; 〜籟 *tiānlài*, nature's sounding-pipes, the "cosmic harmony" of the natural world (< *Zhuangzi* 2).
5. (Budd.) trns. of Skt. *deva*, god, divinity, celestial being; divine.
6. (med.) 〜竺 *tiānzhú*, gen. term for India, but properly read as 祆竺 *xiānzhú* (MC xen-trjuwk), trsc. of Iran. *hinduka* (< Skt. *sindhu*, name of the Indus River) ref. to people who live beyond the Indus River.

添   tiān   MC them

1. (med.) increase, add to; augment, supplement; fill.

酟   tiān   MC them

1. season(ing), balance the flavors of.

tián

佃　tián　MC den

1. ⊙ 畋 *tián* 1, to plant, cultivate a field; 2, engage in a hunt; the chase.

diàn　MC denH

1. (med.) tax-land, fields planted to produce crops in kind.

填　tián　MC den

1. fill, stuff.
    a. stop up, clog; obstruct(ion).
2. fill in, complete.
    a. replenish, fill up, compensate for a lack; e.g. (med.) ～償 *tiáncháng*, ～還 *tiánhuán*, repay, pay back in full.
    b. copy within an outline.
3. rdup., fully satisfied, completely content; also, onom. of the sound of drums.
4. (med.) to color, varnish.
5. (med.) ～置 *tiánzhì*, lay blame on, complain about.

zhèn　MC trinH

1. rdup., grave and dignified, in formal manner.
2. ⊙ 鎮 *zhèn*, press down, quell, restrain.

恬　tián　MC dem

1. tranquil, quiet.
    a. poised, peaceful.
    b. contented, satisfied.
2. carefree, comfortable, leisurely.
    a. unambitious, indifferent, aloof; negligent, careless.

摴　tián　MC den

1. strike, smite; smack, hit.

泏　tián　MC den

1. rdup., far-rolling and running (of river water).

湉　tián　MC dem

1. (bn.) 澶～ *chántián*, → 澶 *chán*.
2. (med.) rdup., placidly pooled, clearly calm (of water).

甜　tián　MC dem

1. sweet-tasting; delicious, luscious.
2. agreeable, pleasurable, likeable; amiable.

田　tián　MC den

1. cultivated field, farmland; paddy field.
    a. to cultivate a field, plant, ⊙ 畋, 佃 *tián* 1.
    b. (med.) ～舍 *tiánshě*, "dweller in the fields," colloquial pejorative term for farmer: peasant, bumpkin, yokel.
2. open field, open country.
    a. to go to the fields, hunt, engage in the chase, ⊙ 畋, 佃 *tiàn* 2.
3. an allotment of land as emolument.
4. (Dao.) 丹～ *dāntián*, cinnabar field(s), 3 sites in the human body of special importance for the cultivation of life-preserving forces; located in the brain, the heart, and just below the navel.
5. (Budd.) a place, or state, for the cultivation of (meritorious) deeds.

畋　tián　MC den

1. to plant, cultivate a field; use a field.
    a. toil(er) in the fields; e.g. ～食 *tiánshí*, tenant farmer.
2. take to the field, engage in a hunt; the chase.

磌　tián　MC den

1. onom. of rocks thunderously falling.
2. pedestal, of column.

闐　tián　MC den

1. filled, fill up; brimming; abounding.
2. rdup., "dunn-dunn," reverberant resonance, onom. of rolling thunder, of the rumbling of carriages, of the sound of drums.
3. (bn.) 于～ *yútián* (MC hju-den), Khotan, oasis city on the southern Silk Road in the Tarim Basin, the main source of nephrite imported to China.

tiăn

忝　tiăn　MC themX

1. dishonor, disgrace, (a)shame(d).
    a. self-depreciatory ADJ or ADV: my shameful (disgraceful)…

殄　tiăn　MC denX

1. exhaust, use up, consume, come to the end of, finish; e.g. ～瘁 *tiăncuì*, ruined and done.
    a. put an end to, conclude, terminate; dispose of.
2. abate, wane, decline, fall off, wear away.
3. stupified, comatose; slow-witted, obtuse.

淟　tiăn　MC thenX

1. muddy, turbid; roiled; sullied.

a. (bn.) ～涊 *tiǎnniǎn* (MC thenX-nenX), muddy and mired, sully and smudge; (med.) also, weak and wavering, shaking and swaying.

腆 tiǎn MC thenX

1. abundant, rich; sumptuous.
   a. splendid, sublime (of physical appearance).

舔 tiǎn MC themX

1. (med.) lick, lick up.
2. (med.)(bn.) ～啖 *tiǎntàn* (MC themX-thamH), tongue lolling and lagging, protruding (usu. of animals), with jaws agape.

靦 tiǎn MC thenX

1. facial appearance, mien; e.g. ～冒 *tiǎnmào*, put on a brave face.
   a. blushing face.
   b. shameful, ashamed.

餂 tiǎn MC themX

1. entice, tempt; bait, lure, snare, hook.
   a. seduce, inveigle.

tiàn

瑱 tiàn MC thenH

1. jade pendants suspended from official cap and hanging beside the ears, symbolizing refusal to hear malevolent words (often mistakenly translated as "earplug").
2. fill up.

zhèn MC trinH

1. ⊙ 鎮 *zhèn*, press down; quell, restrain; guard closely.

tiāo

佻 tiāo MC thew

1. frivolous, flippant; careless, insouciant; impudent.
   a. treat shabbily; ungenerous, insult(ing).
2. pilfer, steal, appropriate.

tiáo MC dew

1. rdup., advancing alone, proceed singly.

tiào MC dewX

1. fleet, fast, in a hurry.

恌 tiāo MC thew

1. ⊙ 佻 *tiāo* 1, flippant, careless, insouciant; ungenerous.

祧 tiāo MC thew

1. ancestral vault, hall to which tablets of distant ancestors are moved in order to make room in main shrine for more recent deceased.
   a. remove tablets to ancestral vault.
2. sometimes, gen. term for ancestral shrine.
3. (med.) be recognized as proper descendant, inherit, succeed to, accede to, come into.

tiáo

岧 tiáo MC dew

1. rdup. or in various binomes, e.g. ～嶤 *tiáoyáo* (MC dew-ngew), ～嵽 *tiáodì* (MC dew-dejH), loftily lifted, toweringly tall, high and far, rearing upward.

條 tiáo MC dew

1. bough, branch, twig.
   a. withe, cane, splint (also used in basketry or wickerwork).
   b. a strip, slip.
2. long, length(y).
   a. measure-word for long, narrow items.
3. openings of a mesh.
4. arrangement, presentation; order(liness), regular(ity); e.g. ～品 *tiáopǐn*, evaluate in orderly sequence.
5. item, entry, section or article of a longer text.
6. reach to, lead to, follow along to; e.g. ～暢 *tiáochàng*, come to an understanding of, alertly comprehending; also, branch and burgeon.
7. catalpa-tree (*Catalpa bungei*).
   a. sometimes, pomelo, shaddock (*Citrus maxima*).
8. mutes, discharged urine and feces, of hunting-hawks and falcons.
9. ～風 *tiáofēng*, old name for the northeast wind of springtime; sometimes, springtime breeze.
10. ～支 or ～枝 *tiáozhī* (MC dew-tsye), abb. trsc. Greek *Seleukia*, Seleucia, the area of the Hellenistic Seleucid kingdom in Mesopotamia and Syria.

苕 tiáo MC dew

1. Chinese trumpet-vine, trumpet-creeper (*Campsis grandiflora*), deciduous creeper showing orange trumpet-shaped blossoms in summer; syn. 凌霄華 *língxiāohuá*, 紫葳 *zǐwēi*.

2. hairy vetch (*Vicia hirsuta*), flowering legume with hairy stem and pod; or milk-vetch (*Astragalus sinicus*), used medicinally, with edible seedpods, subtropical.

3. raceme or spike of reeds.

4. ⊙ 迢 *tiáo*, indicating distance or height, as rdup. or in various binomes.

蜩　tiáo　MC dew

1. gen. term for cicada; sometimes also used for locust; if buzzing, humming, or exuviating—cicada; if swarming—locust.

調　tiáo　MC dew

1. attune, concerted, harmonize, blend; regulate.
   a. accord with, in rapport; adjust(ed), temper(ed); agree(ment); well-adjusted.
   b. ～絲 *tiáosī*, to "throw" thread, i.e. twist together several single yarns into one thread in a direction opposite to that in which they themselves are twisted.
2. tame, train, get under control; ameliorate, mitigate; assuage; ～柔 *tiáoróu*, calm and gentle; (Budd.) ～御 *tiáoyù*, tame(r) and rule(r), harness and drive, i.e. guider of men, epithet for a buddha, trns. Skt. *puruṣadamyasarāthi*.
3. toy with, tease, flirt; make fun of, mock.
   a. provoke, induce; rouse, foment; inspire.
      diào　MC dewH
1. transfer, interchange; move, shift.
   a. requisition, muster, call up (troops).
2. melody-type, mode (musical); tune.
   a. manner, style, mode (behavior).
3. to plan, calculate; contrive, arrange; formulate.
4. (med.) in Tang times, household tax paid in textiles.

迢　tiáo　MC dew

1. rdup. or (bn.) ～遞 *tiáodì* (MC dew-dejX), far and distant, far and farther off, progressively far-removed; also, far into the sky, tall and far-towering.

髫　tiáo　MC dew

1. (med.) child's hanging tufts of hair, usu. dressed on either side of forehead.
   a. (med.) the time of preceding, childhood or adolescence.

鰷　tiáo　MC dew

1. hemiculter, minnow, slender white fish, "stick-fish"; "flash-fish" (< sun glinting off a

school of these fish when they turn quickly near the water's surface, → 鰷 *shū*).

鮡　tiáo　MC dew

1. lose one's baby teeth.
   a. the time for preceding: childhood.
2. ⊙ 髫 *tiáo*, child's bunched tufts of hair.

tiǎo

挑　tiǎo　MC dewX

1. pick out, pull out, poke out. (N.B. to carry with a pole across the shoulders is a post-Tang meaning for this graph.)
   a. choose, select; take.
2. poke at; provoke, challenge, goad, incite.
      tiāo　MC thew
1. (med.) brush fingers toward one when playing zither or lute (cf. 抹 *mò*, brush outward).
2. ⊙ 佻 *tiāo* 1a, treat shabbily; ungenerous, insult(ing).
      tāo　MC thaw
1. (bn.) ～達 *tāodá* (MC thaw-dat), come and go, go back and forth, hem and haw.

朓　tiǎo　MC thewX

1. appearance of the sliver of moon in the west on last day of the lunar month.
2. surplus, extra (< residue, leftover).

窕　tiǎo　MC dewX

1. space to spare, unfilled.
   a. crack, gap.
   b. small, minute.
2. time to spare, interval; leisure.
3. insubstantial, slight; flimsy; fanciful; e.g. ～言 *tiǎoyán*, flighty words.
   a. false, sham; unreliable.
4. 窈～ *yǎotiǎo*, → 窈 *yǎo*.
      tiāo　MC thew
1. ⊙ 佻 *tiāo*, frivolous, flippant; careless, insouciant.
      yáo　MC yew
1. ⊙ 姚 *yáo*, (bn.) ～冶 *yáoyě* (MC yew-yaeX), fine and featly, graceful and seemly

篠　tiǎo　MC thewX

1. (bn.) 窈～ *yǎotiǎo* (MC 'jewX-thewX), → 窈 *yǎo*.

誂　tiǎo　MC dewX

1. lead on, lure, entice; seduce, beguile.

2. make fun of, mock, tease.
3. (bn.) 噭～ *jiàotiǎo*, → 噭 *jiào*.
4. (bn.) ～越 *tiǎoyuè* (MC dewX-hjwot), float lightly on the air, hang in the air.

diào   MC tewH

1. hastily, brusquely, all of a sudden.

tiào

眺 **tiào   MC thewH**

1. gaze at afar, look into the distance, esp. from a high vantage-point.

糶 **tiào   MC thewH**

1. sell grain.

覜 **tiào   MC thewH**

1. audience between feudal lords or between a feudal lord and the king.
2. ⊙ 眺 *tiào*, look at from afar.

跳 **tiào   MC dewH**

1. leap, jumb, bound; jump over; skip.
   a. move up and down, joggle.
2. ～梁 *tiàoliáng* or ～踉 *tiàoliàng*, pounce, spring upon; also, run wild, do whatever one likes.
3. ～頭 *tiàotóu*, transverse bracket, in roof support (cf. 令栱 *lìnggǒng*, longitudinal bracket).

táo   MC daw

1. ⊙ 逃 *táo*, flee, run off; abandon; evade, shirk.

tiē

怗 **tiē   MC thep**

1. submit, submissive; peacable; tractable.

貼 **tiē   MC thep**

1. stick to, affix, attach; paste, glue.
   a. hold closely to, be right next to; e.g. ～裏 *tiēlǐ*, undergarments.
2. (med.) to pawn.
3. (med.) obedient, submit; bring into line.

跕 **tiē   MC thep**

1. walk with trailing or dragging slippers, shuffle, scuff.
   a. tap with the foot.
2. (med.) ⊙ 貼 *tiē* 1, stick to, affix; paste, glue.

dié   MC tep

1. (med.) rdup., diving, lunging, darting down, sweep and swoop.

鮎 **tiē   MC thep**

1. saddle blanket; area covered by same, flank.

dié   MC tep

1. (med.) breastplate.

tiě

鐵 **tiě   MC thet**

1. iron.
2. as strong as iron; hard, unyielding, unbending; stark, grim.
3. iron-gray in color.
4. (med.) ～勒 *tiělè*, the Tiele confederation of Türkic tribes during Tang times.

tiè

帖 **tiè   MC thep**

1. (med.) copybook, of calligraphy or model paintings; rubbing of calligraphy on stone.
2. (med.) brush against, graze, touch lightly.

tiě

1. (med.) card, letter; label, note.
   a. (med.) announcement, official document, diploma.
2. (med.) gathering of 50 sheets of paper.

1. (med.) settle(d), stable, calm; under control.
2. (med.) hang down; e.g. ～耳 *tiē'ěr*, with drooping ears, i.e. completely submissive, obedient.
   a. (med.) commit to writing on silk.
3. (med.) ⊙ 貼 *tiē* 1, stick to, paste, glue; 2, to pawn.

餮 **tiè   MC thet**

1. (bn.) 饕～ *tāotiè*, → 饕 *tāo* 2.
2. (bn.) ～切 *tièqiè* (MC thet-tshet), swiftly sweeping, slightly soughing (of wind).

tīng

廳 **tīng   MC theng**

1. (med.) audience-hall, for government matters below court level; place where one attends to official business; local government office.
   a. (med.) reception-hall, in private residence.

汀 **tīng   MC theng**

1. sandflats, sandspit; sandbank; sandy holm; shoals.

tìng　MC thengH

1. (med.) (bn.) ～瀯 tìngyìng (MC thengH-ywengH), purling and rippling, running crystal-clear.

dìng　MC dengX

1. (bn.) ～濘 dìngníng (MC dengX-neng), mud-flats, mud-muck, mud and slush.

聽　tīng　MC theng

1. listen, hear, give ear to.
    a. (source of) information, intelligence.
2. ⊙ 廳 tīng, audience-hall.

tìng　MC thengH

1. obey, heed, comply with; attend to, pay attention.
    a. acknowledge, agree with or to.
    b. accept; allow.
    c. await (an order).
2. hear a court-case; adjudicate.

芋　tīng　MC theng

1. (bn.) 茗～ míngtīng, → 茗 míng.

鞓　tīng　MC theng

1. (med.) belt made of hide or untreated leather.

tíng

亭　tíng　MC deng

1. watchtower, look-out post at the frontier.
2. precinct, in Qin-Han times an administrative unit below the level of the district (xian 縣), the main functions of which were local peace-keeping and providing accommodations for travelers, in Han times the administrative buildings of precincts were usu. a combination of precinct-house and guest-house and located at intervals of ca. 10 li 里.
3. (med.) pavilion, kiosk, small structure for respite and scene-viewing with a roof supported by columns but no walls; N.B. this meaning not common until 5th/6th century.
4. sgl. or rdup., stand straight, tall and upright, jutting erect; rdup. also, far and remote.
    a. ～午 tíngwǔ, "straight up to the wu-hour or zenith", i.e. precisely noon.
5. rear, raise; ensure the proper shape of.
    a. balance, harmonize, manage justly.
6. ⊙ 停 tíng, stop; 渟 tíng, standing water.

停　tíng　MC deng

1. stop, cease; stay, halt.
    a. pause, suspend; delay.

婷　tíng　MC deng

1. (bn.) 娉～ pīngtíng, → 娉 pīng (pìn).

庭　tíng　MC deng

1. courtyard, in front of main hall.
    a. parvis, esp. in front of sacred buildng.
2. courtyard, in interior section of residential compound.
3. main hall of residential compound.
4. ⊙ 廷 tíng, court, as residential center of ruler or dignitary, or as bureaucratic center of government.

廷　tíng　MC deng

1. court, residential center of the ruler or other dignitary.
    a. court, as bureaucratic center, seat of government.
2. ⊙ 庭 tíng, courtyard, in front of main hall or in interior area of living compound.

梍　tíng　MC deng

1. wild pear (Pyrus calleryana), both tree and fruit.

渟　tíng　MC deng

1. standing water, standing pool; still water, dead water; stagnant.
    a. deep-lying; unsoundable.
2. rdup. or (bn.) ～瀯 tíngyíng (MC deng-'wengX), clear as can be, pellucidly clear, crystal-clear.
3. (bn.) ～濙 tíngyíng (MC deng-yweng), slight shallows; also, eddying whirl.

筳　tíng　MC deng

1. bamboo rods used for divination.
2. spindle, used for spinning thread.

綎　tíng　MC deng

1. silk band or ribbon with which to fasten jade pendants.

莛　tíng　MC deng

1. stalk, stem of plant.
2. stubble, in field.

葶   tíng   MC deng

1. (bn.) ～藶 *tínglì* (MC deng-lek), nasturtium, watercress (*Nasturtium officinale, Rorippa dubia*), a yellow-flowering watercress, hence also yellow-cress.

蜓   tíng   MC deng

1. (bn.) ～蚞 *tíngmù* (deng-muwk), a small cicada (*Platypleura kaempferi*).
2. (bn.) 蜻～ *qīngtíng*, → 蜻 *qīng* (*jīng*).

霆   tíng   MC deng

1. thunderclap, rumble.
2. vibrations of thunder, reverberate; shaking, trembling.
3. lightning.

tǐng

挺   tǐng   MC dengX

1. pull out, pull up; extract.
    a. elicit, draw out from; e.g. 天～ *tiāntǐng*, heaven-endowed elicitations, innate endowments drawn forth by one's proper relationship with the processes of the natural world.
2. stick out, extend outwards, project, protrude, extrude.
    a. outstanding, prominent; conspicuous (for); e.g. ～拔 *tǐngbá*, prominently upthrust.
    b. rdup., honest and upright, straightforward and reliable.
3. stretch out, extend; bend forward, lean out.
    a. straight(en); rigid, stiff.
4. stir, agitate; shake.
5. loosen, relieve; treat with leniency.
6. ⊙ 梃 *tǐng*, stick, staff, club.

梃   tǐng   MC dengX

1. bamboo or wooden stick, staff, club, cudgel.
2. stalk, stem, trunk.
    a. measure-word for plants.
3. doorposts; sides of a window-frame.

珽   tǐng   MC thengX

1. jade tablet held by emperor when at court.

町   tǐng   MC thengX

1. raised footpath between fields, a balk.
    a. field boundary; divide or apportion fields; e.g. ～畦 *tǐngqí*, bounded plots of land; also, bring a conclusion (bounded limit) to a ritual performance.

腆   tiǎn   MC thenX

1. (bn.) ～腄, ～瞳 *tiǎntuǎn* (MC thenX-thjwanX), "tamped and trampled," fallow land given over to animals.

脡   tǐng   MC thengX

1. strip of dried meat.
    a. measure-word for strips of meat.

艇   tǐng   MC dengX

1. small boat, skiff; caïque.

鋌   tǐng   MC thengX   → 鋌 *dìng*.

tōng

恫   tōng   MC thuwng

1. pain, ache, sore(ness), hurt.
    dòng   MC duwngH
1. heartsore, heartstricken.
    a. sore-afraid, painfully anxious.

通   tōng   MC thuwng

1. pass through, go all the way through.
    a. penetrate to or through; permeate; e.g. (Dao.) ～玄 *tōngxuán*, penetrate the mysteries (of the Dao).
2. pass along to desired destination; transmit.
    a. make public, circulate; make clear to, inform, announce; e.g. ～俗 *tōngsú*, circulation among the populace.
    b. (med.) present to, offer to (an elder or superior).
3. have access to or throughout; give passage or access to, give onto; e.g. ～道 *tōngdào*, open up a road.
    a. open(ed), unobstructed, unimpeded; e.g. ～直 *tōngzhí*, direct access (esp. to ruler).
    b. run or go smoothly; e.g. ～變 *tōngbiàn*, continuity and change, coherence and transformation, perpetuate and innovate.
4. attain one's goal, physical or figurative; get through to, make it to the end; e.g. ～陽 *tōngyáng*, "furthest *yang*," place where the sun reaches its apogee at the south pole.
    a. (med.) in the end, finally.
5. communicate with, have free exchange with; association, interchange, contact; conduit; e.g. ～道 *tōngdào*, communication or trade route.
    a. having the ability to understand and exploit the contacts, connections, and influences

between the mortal world and the spirit world; e.g. 神～ *shéntōng*, supernatural powers.

 b. engaging in clandestine or illicit intercourse.

6. comprehensive(ly), arrant; thorough(ly), thoroughgoing; entire(ly), pervasive; e.g. ～道 *tōngdào*, the comprehensive Way, the Way that leads to all (understanding); ～夕 *tōngxī*, all through the night, the whole night.

 a. understand completely, comprehend every sense or implication of; catholic or capacious in intelligence, erudite; e.g. ～人 *tōngren*, person of liberal understanding.

7. in general; consistent(ly); collective(ly), universal; normal(ly), current.

 a. continuity, understandable development.

8. (med.) release from constraint, punishment, or obligation; pardon, forgive; remit.

9. (med.) "clarification" or presentation of the topic in a round of "pure conversation."

10. measure-word for occurrences, instances, bouts, repetitions.

tóng

仝　tóng　MC duwng
1. (med.) ☉ 同 *tóng*.

侗　tóng　MC duwng
1. child, adolescent.
2. immature, juvenile; callow, naïve; fatuous.
 a. (bn.) 倥～ *kōngtóng*, → 倥 *kōng*.

僮　tóng　MC duwng
1. boy, youth, lad.
2. serving-lad, varlet.
3. ☉ 童 *tóng* 4, slave.

同　tóng　MC duwng
1. share with or in; join.
 a. coincide with, conform with.
 b. similar(ity), like(ness); ～心 *tóngxīn*, of like mind.
 c. same(ness), identity; coequal; e.g. ～時 *tóngshí*, at the same time, simultaneously; ～人 *tóngrén*, the same person.
 d. identical to, no more than.
2. together, in concert; e.g. ～坐 *tóngzuò*, sit together.
3. ～人 *tóngrén*, "fellowship," name of 13th hexagram of the *Yijing*.

峒　tóng　MC duwng
1. (bn.) 崆～ *kōngtóng*, → 崆 *kōng*.

彤　tóng　MC downg
1. vermilion, carmine; crimson.
 a. red lacquer, pigmented with minium; red-lacquered.

挏　tóng　MC duwng
1. to churn; e.g. ～馬 *tóngmǎ*, wine made from mare's milk by beating and churning it.

曈　tóng　MC duwng
1. (med.) rdup. or (bn.) ～曚 *tóngméng* (MC duwng-muwng), ～曨 *tónglóng* (MC duwng-luwng), pale rays of the rising sun, growing gleam of sunrise.

桐　tóng　MC duwng
1. paulownia (*Paulownia fortunei*), tall, deciduous hardwood tree with a straight, fine grain, warp-resistant, bearing light purple flowers in spring; certain species were esp. favored for making zithers, chests, and other items.
 a. 油～ *yóutóng*, "oil *tong*," wood-oil tree (*Aleurites fordii*), small to medium-sized deciduous tree, the oil of its seeds traditionally used as fuel for lamps, also in varnish and paint.
 b. 刺～ *cìtóng*, "spiny *tong*," coral tree, flame tree (*Erythrina orientalis*, *Erythrina variegata*), subtropical flowering plant whose bright-colored blooms are coral-shaped.
 c. 胡～ *hútóng*, "Western *tong*," Euphrates poplar (*Populus diversifolia*), medium-sized to tall flowering tree known from the northwest regions.
 d. 梧～ *wútóng* (MC ngu-duwng), parasol tree, phoenix tree (*Firmiana simplex*, *Firmiana plataniflora*), medium-sized to tall deciduous tree, with small greenish-white or greenish-yellow flowers that bloom in the summer, large maple-like leaves, and an elevated crown; reputed to be the only tree on which the phoenix (*fenghuang* 鳳凰) alights; symbolic of love because its name is homophonous with the phrase 吾同 *wútóng*, "we together," and in such contexts may be rendered "the we-together tree."

橦　tóng　MC duwng　→ 橦 *chuáng*.

氋　tóng　MC duwng

1. (med.) (bn.) 〜氃 *tóngméng* (MC duwng-muwng), with a flurry of feathers.

瞳　tóng　MC duwng

1. pupil of the eye
2. sgl. or (bn.) 〜矇 *tóngméng* (MC duwng-muwng), blear-eyed and blind, unknowing, ignorant, dim-witted.

穜　tóng　MC duwng

1. grain that is planted early but ripens late (cf. 穋 *lù*, grain planted late that ripens early).

童　tóng　MC duwng

1. serving-lad, varlet.
2. boy, lad, aged 8 to 19 years (*sui* 歲).
   a. youth, junior; minor.
   b. immature, juvenile; naïve.
3. bare-headed (like an uncapped youth); bald (person), hornless (animal), bare (mountain).
4. slave, of either gender and of any age.
5. ⊙ 瞳 *tóng*, pupil of the eye; 同 *tóng*, share; similar, like; same.

罿　tóng　MC duwng

1. bird-net, most often for official hunts.

朣　tóng　MC duwng

1. (bn.) 〜朧 *tónglóng* (MC duwng-luwng), 〜矇 *tóngméng* (MC duwng-muwng), dimly glimmering, sunlight or moonlight barely breaking through clouds.

赨　tóng　MC downg

1. vivid red, cochineal, color of red dye made from bodies of dried insects.

銅　tóng　MC duwng

1. copper.
   a. 〜精 *tóngjīng*, "germ of copper," i.e. azurite.
2. bronze, latten (copper with tin additive), describing cast objects; e.g. 〜鏡 *tóngjìng*, bronze mirror; 〜壺 *tónghú*, bronze ewer, but most often ref. clepsydra.

鮦　tóng　MC duwng

1. the grass carp, ide (*Ctenopharyngdon idellus*).
2. snakehead mullet (*Ophiocephalus argus*).

tǒng

桶　tǒng　MC thuwngX

1. pail, bucket; cask; tub, tun.
2. measure of capacity, equiv. approx. 6 "pints" (*sheng* 升).

筒　tǒng　MC duwng

1. bamboo tube.
   a. tubular, cannular, vasiform; cylindrical; encase(d); hollow.
      dòng　MC duwngH
1. panpipes, syrinx; syn. → 簫 *xiāo* 2.

箽　tǒng　MC duwngX

1. ⊙ 筒 *tǒng* 1, bamboo tube; tubular, cylindrical; encase(d); hollow.

統　tǒng　MC thuwngX

1. beginning of a ball of a thread, clue, governing thread (what leads to everything else).
2. succession, sequence strung together, series; filiation, filiate, connect(ion).
   a. (provide) continuity, integrate; regular(-ity); generalize, bring together.
3. govern, direct, control; conduct, lead; wield executive power.

tòng

慟　tòng　MC duwngH

1. weep bitterly, sorely grieved, deeply pained.

痛　tòng　MC thuwngH

1. feel pain from sickness or injury; ache, hurt; sore(ness).
2. feel mental pain or anguish.
   a. feel sorrow, be deeply grieved.
   b. feel regret, pity.
   c. hate bitterly.
3. suffer harm, damage, injury.
4. painstakingly, meticulously; do one's best.
   a. intensely, sorely; very.

tōu

偷　tōu　MC thuw

1. negligent(ly), nonchalant(ly), perfunctory.
   a. contemn; disesteem.

2. (med.) stealthy, furtive, underhanded; cunning.
   a. (med.) steal, filch, carry off, pilfer.
3. (med.) compromise(d), acquiesce(nt).

婾 tōu MC thuw → 婾 *yú.*

鍮 tōu MC thuw
1. (med.) brass (copper with zinc additive); perhaps < Pers. *tutiya*, zinc.

tóu

投 tóu MC duw
1. throw, cast; toss, pitch; fling.
   a. throw down, as in sowing seeds.
   b. throw outward, fling sideways; e.g. ～袂 *tóumèi*, shake out one's sleeves, preparatory to taking determined action.
   c. cast forward, hurl, chuck, pelt; project, launch; e.g. ～策 *tóucè*, cast or draw lots; ～壺 *tóuhú*, pitch-pot, game in which arrows are thrown at narrow opening of wine-jug.
   d. cast aside, throw away; e.g. ～戈 *tóugē*, lay aside arms, abandon warfare.
2. "throw in with," take refuge with; rely on.
   a. join, take part in.
3. give as a gift, give up to, surrender to, present.
   a. oblige, agree, cater to; get along with.
4. fall forward, drop down; e.g. ～地 *tóudì*, prostrate oneself.
5. place one's foot forward, tread; e.g. ～迹 *tóujī*, "make tracks," move on; ～足 *tóuzú*, stamp the foot.
6. near to, close to, close by; e.g. ～暮 *tóumù*, close to sunset.
7. dice, ⊙ 骰 *tóu.*
8. (med.) ⊙ 酘 *tóu*, adding charges of steamed rice in the process of fermenting wine.

酘 tóu MC duw
1. (med.) sgl. or cmpd. ～醹 *tóurú*, adding charges of steamed rice in the process of fermenting wine.

頭 tóu MC duw
1. head.
2. top; topmost, uppermost, chief.
   a. best, choice(st); topgrade.
3. first; beginning, start; outset, commencement.
   a. front; forefront, foremost.
4. headland, bluff.

5. (Budd.) ～陀 *tóutuó* (MC duw-da), trsc. Skt. *dhūta*, austerities, ascetic practices.
6. nominal or locative enclitic; e.g. 膝～ *xītóu*, the knee; 日～ *rìtóu*, the sun; 前～ *qiántóu*, in front, before.
7. measure-word for animals.
8. (med.) (lit.) 平～ *píngtóu*, flat head, name of prosodic fault in which 1st and 6th words, or 2nd and 7th, in a couplet of pentasyllabic verse have the same tone, thus "levelling off" (making identical) the start of both lines.

骰 tóu MC duw
1. (med.) ⊙ 投 *tóu* 7, dice.

tòu

透 tòu MC thuwH
1. (med.) leap, bound.
   a. (med.) jump for joy.
   b. (med.) surpass, mount above.
2. (med.) flee, escape.
   a. (med.) let loose; e.g. ～漏 *tòulòu*, leak, divulge; also, talk carelessly.
3. (med.) pass through, penetrate.
   a. (med.) transparent, permeable to; shine through, become visible.
   shū MC syuwk
1. surprised, startled; disturbed by.

tū

凸 tū MC dwot
1. protuberant, convex; protrude; stick up.

禿 tū MC thuwk
1. bald; uncovered; denuded, stripped bare.
   a. (bn.) ～兀 *tūwù* (MC thuwk-ngwot), bald and bare.

突 tū MC thwot
1. spring out (as from a bolt-hole), burst forth, break through.
   a. all of a sudden, abrupt(ly); brusque(ly), impetuous(ly).
2. charge against, run against or into; to brave.
   a. go against, offend; violate.
   b. sudden attack; rampage; e.g. ～門 *tūmén*, sally-port, small gate under city-walls from which quick sorties may be launched against besieging army.

3. stand out; protrude, emerge; e.g. (bn.) ～兀 *tūwù* (MC thwot-ngwot), boldly protruding; in bold, bald relief.

4. dig out; excavate, unearth; burrow.

   a. tunnel, underground passage; cavern.

   b. (med.) low opening; e.g. 狗～ *gǒutū*, dog-door.

5. flue, smoke-hole.

6. ～厥 *tūjué* (MC thwot-kjwot), Türks of central Asia and Mongolia, perhaps descended from a branch of the Xiongnu 匈奴, established an empire in the 6th century that was divided into 2 confederations (east and west) in 582; the Tang defeat of the Eastern Türks in 630 gave the Tang control of the Tarim basin and the Central Asian "Silk Road"; ～騎施 *tūjìshī* (MC thwot-gjeH-sye), the Türgäš, Turgesh, important tribal federation of the Western Türks.

7. ⊙ 塗 *tú*, smear, daub; plaster.

tú

圖 **tú** **MC du**

1. design, array; chart, diagram, plan, map, layout.

   a. illustration, tableau.

   b. pattern, exemplar, paradigm.

2. portray, depict; illustrate.

3. devise, design; chart out, plan, draw up, map out; project, intend to.

   a. assess, evaluate, estimate (the values or prospects of).

   b. counsel, advise.

4. complete the picture of, achieve.

塗 **tú** **MC du**

1. mud(dy); mire.

   a. defile, stain, besmirch.

   b. (Budd.) evil state of existence; e.g. 三～ *sāntú*, 3 Mires, existence in hell (*dìyu* 地獄), as an animal (*xusheng* 畜生), as a hungry ghost (餓鬼).

2. smear, spread; daub.

   a. (apply) plaster or paint.

3. (med.) wipe out, expunge, erase.

4. ～林 *túlín* (MC du-lim), pomegranate (old Iran. name, cognate Skt. *dālima*).

5. ⊙ 途 *tú*, road, route.

屠 **tú** **MC du**

1. butcher, slaughter.

2. (med.) (bn.) ～蘇 *túsū* (MC du-su), a spice-herb; wine infused with this plant and pepper,

cinnamon, and atractylis was drunk on New Year's day to ward off illness in the coming year.

3. (bn.) ～耆 *túqí* (MC du-gj+j), Xiongnu title meaning "worthy; wise" (< Iran. *tukai*, "the great [or good] one"), given to kings in 2nd rank of tribal hierarchy, sometimes used to designate heir of the *shanyu* 單于; term perhaps related to tegin, 特勤 *tèqín*, → 特 *tè*; (bn.) ～各 *túgè* (MC du-kak), noblest of the 19 Xiongnu tribes, from which the *chanyu* was chosen, equiv. bisyllabic surname Dugu 獨孤 *dúgū* (MC duwk-ku).

徒 **tú** **MC du**

1. go on foot.

   a. foot-soldier, infantry.

   b. pawn, peon.

2. disciple, adherent, postulant, follower, apprentice (disciplined to a certain training or goal).

   a. if applied pejoratively, epigone, inferior imitator.

   b. X之～, X *zhitú*, the likes of X, of X's ilk, of the same sort as X.

   c. 司～ *sītú*, administrator discipulant, usu. translated Director of Instruction, one of the 3 traditionally supreme offices of state or *sāngōng* 三公, "3 Dignitaries" (the other 2 being sikong 司空, director of works, and *taiwei* 太尉, grand marshal); also, a bisyllabic surname derived from the office.

3. penal servitude; corvée laborer by force; convict, usu. sentenced to definite period of servitude (< "one to be disciplined"); conscript; e.g. ～隸 *túlì*, hard labor.

4. crowd, group; e.g. ～等 *túděng*, group, party.

   a. colleague, companion.

5. to no avail, in vain, emptily.

6. simply, merely, just, only; e.g. (med.) ～為爾 *túwéiěr*, simply like this, just this way, in reality …

悇 **tú** **MC du**

1. (bn.) ～憛 *tútán* (MC du-dam), downcast and disquieted, sadly suffering.

2. (bn.) 憛～ *tántú* (MC dom-du), avidly craving, → 憛 *tán*.

瘏 **tú** **MC du**

1. fatigue, exhaustion.

稌 **tú** **MC du**

1. rice-plant (*Oryza sativa*), incl. glutinous and non-glutinous varieties.

腯 tú MC dwot

1. well-fed, sleek; lustrous, well-groomed.
    a. stout, strong.

茶 tú MC du

1. sowthistle, hare's thistle (*Sonchus oleraceus*), used medicinally, in cooking, and as fodder.
    a. because of its bitterness, used euph. for foul weed, odious person; e.g. ～毒 *túdú*, bitter and poisonous > injure or suffer cruelly.
2. white-flowering reed or cogon.
3. (med.) ～毘 *túpí*, cremation.
4. ⊙ 塗 *tú*, smear; mud(dy).
        chá　MC drae
1. old form of 茶 *chá*, tea (*Camellia sinensis*).

途 tú MC du

1. roadway, route, course; path.
2. the road ahead, prospects; route to a particular goal.
    a. process, method; course of action.

酴 tú MC du

1. ferment, used in wine-making
2. (med.) sgl. or (bn.) ～醿 *túmí* (MC du-mje), exceptionally fine wine used on special occasions (often at court) in Tang times; (bn.) also, rose-leaf-bramble, thimbleberry (*Rubus rosifolia*).

駼 tú MC du

1. (bn.) 駒～ *táotú*, → 駒 *táo*.

tǔ

吐 tǔ MC thuX

1. spit out, eject; belch, spew, sputter, eruct(ation).
    a. expel, emit, exude, send forth; debouch.
    b. divulge, utter; give forth.
2. ～蛟鳥 *tǔjiāoniǎo*, gray nightjar (*Caprimulgus jotaka*).
3. first element in various foreign place-names or ethnonyms; e.g. ～(火)羅 *tǔ(huǒ)luó* (MC thuX-[xwaX-]la), Tocharia, equiv. 大宛 *dàyuān*, Ferghana; ～番, ～蕃 *tǔfān* (MC thuX-phon) or *tǔbō* (MC thuX-pa), Tibet, later also ref. Tarim Basin; ～谷渾 *tǔyùhún*, the Tuyuhun peoples, a semi-nomadic branch of the Särbi (Xianbei 鮮卑), and the state founded by them that was located on the Mongolian steppe in the northeast section of the Qinghai-Tibetan plateau and Qaidam basin controlling the Qinghai road, a branch of the Silk Road south of the Hexi corridor route; their multi-ethnic state lasted from ca. mid-4th to late-7th centuries and was an important intermediary for trade and diplomacy between Central Asia and China.

tù MC thuH

1. vomit, keck, disgorge.

土 tǔ MC thuX

1. earth; soil.
    a. land, ground.
    b. territory, area.
2. native land, homeground.
    a. local; common; rustic.
3. god of the soil.
4. one of the 5 "agents" or "phases" of *wuxing* theory, earth, correlated symbolically with the center, color yellow, midsummer, Saturn, etc.
5. one of the 8 categories of musical instruments, those made of pottery, esp. the ocarina or 6-holed globular flute (壎 *xūn*), made of fired clay.

tù

兔 tù MC thuH

1. hare; when young, leveret; leporine; also, rabbit; when young, kitten.
    a. legendary hare resident in the moon, where he constantly pounds the elixir of immortality with mortar and pestle; e.g. ～魄 *tùpò*, "hare's glimmer," euph. for moonlight.
    b. emblematic animal of the 4th of the 12 earthly stems (*dizhi*), 卯 *mǎo*.

菟 tù MC thuH

1. ～絲 *tùsī*, dodder, "hare-silk" (because sleek-feeling, like hare's fur), hairweed, angelhair (*Cuscuta chinensis*), parasitic of herbaceous plants, hence symbolic of dependence, connection, servility.
2. ⊙ 兔 *tù*, hare, rabbit.
        tú　MC du
1. (bn.) 於～ *wūtú* (MC 'u-du), old Chu-area name for tiger.

tuān

湍 tuān MC thwan

1. rapid, swift current of water; torrent(ial).
    a. billow.
2. dash against, run up against, clash, collide, smash into.

猯 tuān MC thwan

1. Asian badger (*Meles leucurus, Meles amurensis*); syn. 豬貛 *zhūhuān*.

tuán

剶 tuán MC dwan

1. cut or slice, usu. with sword.
  a. cut into sections.
  b. cut off, curtail.
    zhuān MC tsywen
1. ⊙ 專 *zhuān*, exclusive(ly), specialize(d); have sole charge of, control.

團 tuán MC dwan

1. round, circular; spherical.
  a. roll into a ball, ball up, clump.
  b. encircle, surround.
2. cluster, aggregate, gather together, combine; aggregation, bunch; group, team.
3. (med.) a military unit, regiment.
4. (med.) appraise, estimate, measure.
5. (med.) whole, full(y), complete(ly); en masse; ensemble.

慱 tuán MC dwan

1. rdup., saddened with sorrow, worn with grief, pained with sadness.

摶 tuán MC dwan

1. knead or roll into a ball; mold.
  a. bundle, clump, cluster; e.g. ～風 *tuánfēng*, ～搖 *tuányáo*, bundling the wind, wheeling with the whirlwind.
2. round, circular.
3. spiral, circle round, wheel; rdup., spiral and swirl.
4. hold onto, rely on.
    zhuān MC tsywen
1. ⊙ 專 *zhuān*, exclusive(ly), specialize(d); have sole charge of, control.

漙 tuán MC dwan

1. heavy dew; soaked, weighed down with dew.
2. ⊙ 團 *tuán*, round, full.

tuǎn

畽 tuǎn MC thwonX

1. (bn.) 町～ *tiǎntuǎn*, → 町 *tiǎn* (*tǐng*).

疃 tuǎn MC thwanX

1. (bn.) 町～ *tiǎntuǎn*, → 町 *tiǎn* (*tǐng*).

tuàn

彖 tuàn MC thwanH

1. judgment, the statements in *Yijing* that immediately follow the names of the 64 hexagrams, giving a general sense of the hexagram topic and of its controlling principle; part of the original layer of the *Yijing* text, from ca. 9th century BCE.
  a. ～傳 *tuànzhuàn*, Commentary on the Judgments, part of the 2nd layer of the *Yijing* text, traditionally attributed to Confucius or his followers.

tuī

推 tuī MC thwoj

1. push away; shove.
  a. move; remove; expel, replace a predecessor.
  b. eliminate, dispose of; get rid of.
  c. (med.) decline or cede (a position, prerogative, possession), e.g. ～心 *tuīxīn*, give up one's heart to.
  d. (med.) give an excuse, shirk responsibility.
2. push forward, press toward; carry out; develop; e.g. ～移 *tuīyí*, advance and shift, developing changes in time or situation; ～轂 *tuīgǔ*, push the wheel-hubs forward, promote one's goals or career.
  a. ply, use (a tool, implement); e.g. ～筆 *tuībǐ*, ply the writing-brush.
  b. practice; extend, enlarge; e.g. ～恩 *tuī'ēn*, extend kindness toward.
3. movement of left hand in bending a bow.
  a. sustain, hold fast; support.
4. infer, deduce; extrapolate, calculate; predict; e.g. ～命 *tuīmìng*, extrapolation of destiny; ～機 *tuījī*, extrapolate the instants (or junctions) of a horoscope; ～步 *tuībù*, calculate the positions of the stars.
  a. probe into, examine; e.g. ～問 *tuīwèn*, ～讀 *tuīdú*, investigate, look into.
5. popularize, recognize publicly; esteem; promote, advance, recommend for office; e.g. ～任 *tuīrèn*, hold in high regard, have confidence in.

蓷 tuī MC thwoj

1. Chinese motherwort (*Leonurus heterophyllus*), used medicinally; syn. 益母草 *yìmǔcǎo*.

tuí

隤　tuí　MC dwoj
1. fall down, collapse.
   a. decayed, ruined.
   b. bring down, undermine.
2. stumble, fall over, topple.
3. give way, yield(ing), deferential.
   a. condescend, lower oneself, vouchsafe.
4. docile, peaceable, submissive; complaisant, acquiescent.
5. (bn.) 虺 ~ *huītuí*, → 虺 *huī* (*huǐ*).

頹　tuí　MC dwoj
1. collapse, crumble, cave in.
   a. fail(ing), give way; falter, weaken, lapse; e.g. ~ 波 *tuíbō*, faltering waves.
   b. decline; ruined, dilapidated.
   c. fall down, topple over.
2. run downward (time conceived of as moving from top downward), pass, elapse.
3. descend, fall.
   a. slump; sprawl; e.g. ~ 雲 *tuíyún*, slumped clouds (type of chignon).
4. weak, compliant; submissive.
   a. drawn into oneself, composed.
5. whirlwind; gale; tornado, cyclone.

腿　tuǐ　MC thwojX
1. calf (of leg); shin.
   a. by synecdoche, leg.

tuì

蛻　tuì　MC thwajH
1. shed, cast off, slough off (old skin or shell), molt, exuviate; divest oneself of.
   a. cast-off casing, exuviae.
2. (Dao.) shed, cast off, leave behind one's physical form, in ascending to transcendence; (Budd.) same, in departing current existence for one's next life in the round of birth-and-death.

退　tuì　MC thwojH
1. go backwards, step back.
   a. withdraw (from), retire; resign; decline, refuse.
   b. shrink back, recoil, flinch.
   c. concede, yield, give in; retiring, modest.
   d. recede, disappear.
   e. return, go back; (Budd.) retrogress, regress (to a prior, inferior state).
   f. retrograde planetary movement, i.e. westward.
2. dismiss from office.
3. (med.) ~ 故 *tuìgù*, obsolete, outdated, uselessly old.

tūn

吞　tūn　MC thon
1. swallow whole, gulp down.
   a. devour; consume, take in; imbibe.
   b. (med.) endure or accept without showing outward reaction.
2. embrace, enclose; contain.
   a. to appropriate, annex; overpower.

吨　tūn　MC thwon　⊙ 啍 *tūn*.

啍　tūn　MC thwon
1. talkative, voluble.
2. rdup., jumbled and jangled, noisy and annoying; also, insist(ent) and reiterate(d).

暾　tūn　MC thwon
1. dawn's sunglare, sun-flash, flare up.
   a. the dawn(ing) sun.
   b. showing forth gradually, steadily emerging.
2. rdup., in all brilliance, fully showing.
3. (med.) warm up; vivify.

炖　tūn　MC thwon
1. fire-bright, blazing, flaring up.

焞　tūn　MC thwon
1. brightly shining; radiance, luster.
   　tuī　MC thwoj
1. rdup., palely glinting, faint glimmer; also, grandly arrayed.
   　jùn　MC tswonH
1. heated poker that diviner applies to prepared turtle-shell so as to produce cracks for omen-taking.

tún

屯　tún　MC dwon　→ 屯 *zhūn*.

忳　tún　MC dwon
1. dispirited, saddened; anxious.
   a. rdup., consumed with sorrow, broken and bowed-down.

dùn   MC twonH

1. rdup., addled and senseless, blank and unthinking.

zhūn   MC tsywin

1. rdup., sincere and resolute, deeply devoted.

臀   **tún**   MC dwon

1. rump, buttocks; gluteal.
    a. base, foundation; lower part.

豚   **tún**   MC dwon

1. shoat, pigling, snork; suckling pig.
    a. 河～(魚) *hétún(yú)*, "river shoat," i.e. puffer, globefish, blowfish (*Spheroides vermicularis*); syn. 鮐 *tái*, 鮭 *guī*.
    b. ～耳 *túněr*, "snork's ear," i.e. purslane, little hogweed, pigweed (*Portulaca oleracea*), an annual succulent, eaten as leaf vegetable, syn. 馬齒莧 *mǎchǐxiàn*; ～草 *túncǎo*, ragweed (*Ambrosia artemisiifolia*).

dūn   MC twon

1. ⊙ 墩 *dūn*, knoll, tump, mound.

dùn   MC dwonX

1. ⊙ 遯 *dùn*, hide, conceal; withdraw; escape.

tuō

倪   **tuō**   MC thwat

1. simple, unassuming; genuine.
2. ⊙ 脫 *tuō* 2, get away from, escape, avoid; 悅 *yuè*, pleased, relaxed, content.

tuì   MC thwajH

1. seemly, befitting.

托   **tuō**   MC thak

1. (med.) hold or carry in the palm of one's hand; sustain, support. N.B. This graph not commonly used before the 9th century; most often, ⊙ 託 *tuō* or 拓 *tuò*.

扡   **tuō**   MC tha   ⊙ 拖 *tuō*.

拖   **tuō**   MC tha

1. drag, pull.
    a. drag out; pull down or away; tug; tow; e.g. (med.) ～鉤 *tuōgōu*, tug-o'-war.
2. take away from, wrest from; seize, capture; appropriate.
3. (med.) train, trailing part (of dress, bird's tail, etc.).
4. (med.) delay, put off.

挩   **tuō**   MC thwat

1. remove, take off, strip away, ⊙ 脫 *tuō* 1.
2. strike with a cudgel.

shuì   MC sywejH

1. wipe off, wipe away.

梲   **tuō**   MC thwat

1. wooden cane; club, cudgel.

zhuō   MC tsywet

1. small post placed above the beams to support the rafter.

ruì   MC ywejH

1. ⊙ 銳 *ruì*, sharp(en), acute.

脫   **tuō**   MC thwat

1. strip off, peel away; slip off; e.g. ～簡 *tuōjiǎn*, peel loose matter from and smooth the surface of a bamboo strip for writing; ～甲 *tuōjiǎ*, strip off one's armor; ～粟 *tuōsù*, hulled (but unrefined) spiked millet.
    a. shed, get free of, divest; e.g. (Dao.) ～胎 *tuōtāi*, shed one's fetal ties, leave behind mortal limitations and advance to a transcendent level of being.
    b. fall away, fall off (like trees shedding leaves); fall out, leave out (like characters from a text).
    c. 渾～ *húntuō*, "skinned-whole," felt hat.
2. separate or remove from, extricate; get away from, escape, avoid; e.g. ～身 *tuōshēn*, extricate one's person (from travel, danger, or [Dao.] earthly constraints); (Budd.) ～生 *tuōshēng*, be reincarnated, move on from one life to the next.
    a. come out of, emerge from; e.g. ～口 *tuōkǒu*, (words) escaping from the mouth.
3. take away, remove, deprive; dispossess(ed).
    a. unloose(d), unconstricted; irreverent; e.g. ～然 *tuōrán*, indifferently, casually; (med.) ～略 *tuōlüè*, nonchalant, cavalier about.
    b. (med.) trick, deceive, with intention of acquiring another's possession.
4. (med.) perhaps, maybe; sometimes, at random, unpredictably.
5. (med.) conditional marker: if it happened that..., were it the case that...

tuì   MC thwajH

1. rdup., softly and slowly, with careful regard.

託   **tuō**   MC thak

1. entrust to, commit to the care of, confide to; e.g. ～情 *tuōqíng*, commit one's feelings; ～分

tuōfēn, ～命 *tuōmìng*, cast one's lot; (Budd.) ～生 *tuōshēng*, be reincarnated.

　　a. rely on, bank on; take refuge in; e.g. ～大 *tuōdà*, rely on your greatness, i.e. keep aloof.

　　b. express by metaphor.

2. assume responsibility for something; assumption of.

　　a. ascribe or attribute, esp. authorship.

　　b. borrow; requisition; commandeer.

　　c. (med.) ～若 *tuōruò*, assuming that . . ., if it were the case that . . ., supposing it were . . .

3. set off, serve as a contrast or foil for.

　　a. serve as pretext, justification, rationale; simulate.

4. to commission, engage with responsibility for, as for composing of commemorative inscription.

飥　tuō　MC thak

1. doughy foodstuffs, buns, noodles; pasta.

　　a. (med.) (bn.) 餺～ *bótuō*, → 餺 *bō*.

tuó

佗　tuó　MC da

1. add to, increase.

2. carry on the back, ⊙ 馱 *tuó*.

3. rdup., handsome and well-formed.

4. ⊙ 駝 *tuó*, camel.

**　　**tuō　MC tha

1. ⊙ 他 *tā* 1, other, the other, another.

橐　tuó　MC thak

1. sack, pouch.

　　a. to bag, pack up, stuff.

2. bellows; e.g. ～籥 *tuóyuè*, bellows, esp. euph. of the inexhaustible variety of life amidst heaven and earth.

3. sgl. or (bn.) ～駝 *tuótuó* (MC thak-da), camel (*Camelus bactrianus*), the 2-humped bactrian camel.

　　a. hump-backed.

4. rdup., onom. of the pounding of rammed-earth construction: dahk-dahk.

5. ～吾 *tuówú*, coltsfoot, butterbur (*Tussilago farfara*), sets yellow daisy-like flowers used medicinally.

沱　tuó　MC da

1. tributary, branch-stream.

2. streaming, gushing (of tears); pouring, driving (of rain).

　　a. (bn.) 滂～ *pāngtuó*, → 滂 *pāng*.

**　　**duò　MC daX

1. (med.) (bn.) 淡～ *dànduò*, → 淡 *dàn*.

訑　tuó　MC da　→ 訑 *yí*.

跎　tuó　MC da

1. (bn.) 蹉～ *cuōtuó*, → 蹉 *cuō*.

酡　tuó　MC da

1. flushed face, esp. after wine-drinking; "lit up."

陀　tuó　MC da

1. (bn.) 陂～ *pōtuó*, → 坡 *pō*.

2. (Budd.) ～羅尼 *tuóluóní* (MC da-la-nrij), trsc. Skt. *dhāraṇī*, magic spell or formula composed of Skt. phonemes, imparting certain powers of mind and spirit.

**　　**duò　MC daX

1. collapse, crumble, cave in.

陁　tuó　MC da

1. ⊙ 陀 *tuó* 1, (bn.) 滂～ *pāngtuó*, → 滂 *pāng*.

**　　**yǐ　MC yeX

1. (bn.) ～靡 *yǐmǐ* (MC yeX-mjeX), splaying and spreading.

**　　**zhì　MC drjeX

1. collapse, fall in, tumble down, disintegrate.

馱　tuó　MC da

1. (med.) use a pack-animal to carry a burden.

**　　**duò　MC daH

1. a pack-animal.

　　a. the load carried by preceding.

駝　tuó　MC da

1. sgl. or (bn.) 橐～ *tuótuó* (MC thak-da), 駱～ *luòtuó* (MC lak-da), camel (*Camelus bactrianus*), the 2-humped bactrian camel.

　　a. hump-backed.

2. use a pack-animal to carry a burden on its back.

馳　tuó　MC da　⊙ 駝 *tuó*.

驒　tuó　MC da

1. a dark scale-patterned horse.

diān   MC ten

1. (bn.) ～騱 *diānxī* (MC ten-hej), a wild ass of the Mongolian steppe, perhaps the onager or kulan (*Equus hemionus*).

鮀   tuó   MC da

1. the goby (*Acanthogobious flavianus*), syn. 鯊 *shā*.
2. the sheatfish, clade (*Siluridae*), a freshwater catfish, syn. 鮎 *nián*.
3. ⊙ 鼍 *tuó*, alligator.

鼍   tuó   MC da

1. alligator (*Alligator sinensis*); e.g. ～鼓 *tuógǔ*, drum made of alligator hide.

䶄   tuó   MC da

1. (med.) (bn.) ～䶄 *tuóbá* (MC da-bat), tarbagan marmot (*Marmota sibirica*), known from Mongolia.

tuǒ

妥   tuǒ   MC thwaX

1. sit still.
   a. firmly settled, securely in place.
   b. ～帖 *tuǒtiē* (MC thwaX-thep), fast and firm, sure and secure, stable and steady; also, smooth and tractable
2. (med.) drop, fall down; hang down.

tuò

唾   tuò   MC thwaH

1. spittle, saliva.
2. spit out; sputter.
   a. eject, expel, cast off.
   b. evince disdain or disgust.

拓   tuò   MC thak   → 拓 *zhí*.

柝   tuò   MC thak

1. night-watchman's clapper or rattle.
2. open up, develop; enlarge, expand; ⊙ 拓 *tuò* 2 (*zhí*).

毻   tuò   MC thwaH

1. moulting or shedding of birds and beasts.

籜   tuò   MC thak

1. sheaths of bamboo-shoots.

蘀   tuò   MC thak

1. leaves and bark fallen from plants and trees.
   a. drift down, be shed.

跅   tuò   MC thak

1. cmpd. ～弛 *tuòchí*, however one wants, free of all constraints, following one's whims, on one's own impulse, undisciplined.

W

wā

哇   wā   MC 'wae

1. vomit, retch (onom.).
2. insinuating, seductive, esp. of music.

媧   wā   MC kwea

1. 女～ *nǚwā*, Nüwa, according to mythology the sister of culture-hero Fuxi 伏羲; expert at smelting, said to have patched the sky with fused stones when its northwest supporting pillar was dislodged; reputed inventor of mouth-organ (笙 *shēng*).

洼   wā   MC 'wae   ⊙ 窪 *wā*.

窊   wā   MC 'wae

1. a dalk, small hollow; depression; hole, cavity.
   a. dig out, excavate.
2. under, below, beneath.
   a. slip down, decline.

窪   wā   MC 'wae

1. still pond; puddle.
   a. stagnant water, sink.

wá

娃   wá   MC 'wea

1. fetching, sightly, pretty.
   a. an attractive woman; a "babe."
2. (med.) young girl, lass; belle; nymphet.

wǎ

瓦　wǎ　MC ngwaeX
1. earthenware, pottery.
    a. tile, esp. roof-tile.
    wà　MC ngwaeH
1. to tile a roof.

wà

襪　wà　MC mjot
1. stockings.

韈　wà　MC mjot　⊙ 襪 *wà*.

wài

外　wài　MC ngwajH
1. outside, not within specified area or topic; beyond, outer; external; e.g. 方～ *fāngwài*, beyond the confines (of normal life or society), ultramundane.
    a. ref. to larger world, in contrast to inner (*nei* 內) closed world of home or family; the common people and lives outside the bounds of the court; one's public actions, in contrast to one's thoughts, feelings, and intent.
2. outer surface, exterior.
3. exoteric, comprehensible or suited to the uninitiated; not within the limits and expectations of a specific manner; e.g. ～傳 *wàizhuàn*, exoteric account or biography, not bound by normal limits of official history; ～編 *wàibiān*, "outer chapters," not the central or essential sections, also those dealing with topics of relatively more popular or common matter; (Budd.) ～書 *wàishū*, non-Budd., secular writings.
4. outland(s), hinterland(s); foreign.
5. place outside or at a distance; regard as outside or distant.
6. prefix to relationship terms indicating connection with maternal line or with wife's lineage; e.g. ～妹 *wàimèi*, mother's daughter by a different father than her other children; ～戚 *wàiqī*, emperor's consort families; ～甥 *wàishēng*, nephew, son of a sister; ～孫 *wàisūn*, maternal grandson (equiv. 女子 *nǚzǐ*, "daughter's son," scribal pun for 好 *hǎo*, fine).
7. (med.) wife's term of address for husband.

wān

剜　wān　MC 'wan
1. gouge out, scoop out; dig out; excavate; excise.

彎　wān　MC 'waen
1. pull a bow, bend a bow.
    a. bow-bend, curve; crook(ed), bent, angled.
2. (med.) ⊙ 灣 *wān*, bend in a river, bay, cove.

灣　wān　MC 'waen
1. (med.) bay, cove, bend in a river.

蜿　wān　MC 'jwon
1. curving, bending; e.g. ～虹 *wānhóng*, swelling rainbow.
2. (bn.) ～蜒 *wānyán* (MC 'jwon-yen) or rdup., snake and slither, wriggle and writhe, winding and wreathing, fluent undulation.

豌　wān　MC 'wan
1. sgl. or ～豆 *wāndòu*, garden peas (*Pisum sativum*).

wán

丸　wán　MC hwan
1. small round object, ranging in size from pill to egg to ball.
    a. pellet, shot, used with crossbow.
2. measure-word for round object.
3. enclosure.

刓　wán　MC ngwan
1. file off or pare down corners; round off.
    a. smooth out; polish.

完　wán　MC hwan
1. complete, whole, intact.
    a. finish, complete; conclude, carry through.
    b. make whole, bring to final form; repair.
    c. keep whole, preserve.

岏　wán　MC ngwan
1. (bn.) 巑～ *cuánwán*, → 巑 *cuán*.

忨　wán　MC ngwan
1. covet, crave, lust after.
2. to idle, fritter away one's time.

抏   **wán**   MC ngwan
1. wear down, wear away.
    a. cut back, pare; abate.
2. ⊙ 玩 *wán* 1, toy with, trifle.

挷   **wán**   MC hwan
1. pare, scrape; carve.
2. (bn.) 塼～ *zhuānwán*, → 塼 *zhuān*.

汍   **wán**   MC hwan
1. (bn.) ～瀾, ～蘭 *wánlán* (MC hwan-lan), tears flowing full, dissolved in tears, tears swelling in waves.

玩   **wán**   MC ngwanH
1. toy with, trifle with, dally with, play with, sport with; amuse oneself, divert oneself.
    a. plaything, object of diversion; curio; frivolity.
2. appreciate, enjoy, savor with critical discrimination; be quite familiar with.
    a. ponder, consider or evaluate perceptively.
3. be overly familiar with; monotonous, repetitive; monotony, boring.
    a. negligent; frivolous.

紈   **wán**   MC hwan
1. taffeta, lustrous tight-weave pongee, cambric.
    a. by metonymy, gen. term for silk fabric.
2. calf, young ox.

翫   **wán**   MC ngwanH   ⊙ 玩 *wán*.

芄   **wán**   MC hwan
1. (bn.) ～蘭 *wánlán* (MC hwan-lan), roughpotato, milkweed (*Metaplexis japonica*), a deciduous climbing vine; syn. 蘿藦 *luómó*.

頑   **wán**   MC ngwaen
1. coarse-grained; unpolished, crude; blunt; e.g. ～礦 *wánkuàng*, crude and coarse.
    a. (bn.) ～鈍 *wándùn* (MC ngwaen-dwonH), blunt and dull.
2. coarse, uncouth, crude, crass; oafish.
    a. doltish, stupid; insensate.
3. obstinate, stubborn, intractable; stolid.
4. greedy, covetous, cupidinous.

wǎn

婉   **wǎn**   MC 'jwonX
1. gentle, docile, mild, tender; accommodating, complaisant; e.g. (bn.) ～戀 *wǎnliàn* (MC 'jwonX-ljwenH), gently alluring; also, tender longings.
    a. graceful, charming; supple; e.g. ～麗 *wǎnlì*, ～約 *wǎnyuē*, charmingly attractive, gracefully gorgeous (of lit. style).
2. ⊙ 宛 *wǎn* 1, yielding, pliant; smooth, fluent.

宛   **wǎn**   MC 'jwonX
1. pliant, supple; yielding, give way.
    a. rdup., supplely sweeping, as of graceful bamboo.
    b. (bn.) ～轉 *wǎnzhuǎn* (MC 'jwonX-trjwenX), giving way, yielding; conformably, accommodating, compatibly, responsive; fluently, smoothly, supplely, flexibly, undulant; also, tortuous, devious, twining and twisting, sinuous, flexuous; recessed, indented.
2. sgl. or ～如 *wǎnrú*, quite as if, quite like, rather like.
3. very small, tiny.
    yuān   MC 'jwon
1. 大～ *dàyuān*, name of Central Asian kingdom of Ferghana, esp. famous for superb "blood-sweating" horses; roughly situated at tri-state border region of present-day Uzbekistan, Kyrgyzstan, and Tajikistan.

惋   **wǎn**   MC 'wanH
1. chagrin(ed), vexation; rankle; irritate(d), embitter(ed), resentful.

挽   **wǎn**   MC mjonX
1. pull (in, on, up, out), drag; lead; e.g. (med.) ～轂 *wǎn'gǔ*, "lead on the wheel-hubs," advance a carriage, euph. advance someone's official career.
    a. draw a coffin or hearse with ropes; e.g. (lit.) ～歌 *wǎn'gē*, pallbearer's song, dirge sung by one who leads ("pulls") the hearse.
2. roll up.

晚   **wǎn**   MC mjonX
1. evening; close of day.
    a. night, nighttime.

2. late(r), belated; tardy.
3. declining period, ending time; aftertime.

椀　wǎn　MC 'wanX
1. (med.) ⊙ 盌 wǎn.

琬　wǎn　MC 'jwonX
1. sgl. or ～圭 wǎnguī, round-topped jade tablet.
    a. (bn.) ～琰 wǎnyǎn (MC 'jwonX-yemX), round-topped and pointed jade tablets; jade-stone gems, euph. fine virtue or character; paragon.

畹　wǎn　MC 'jwonX
1. ancient unit of land, differently defined as either 12 *mou* 畝 or 30 *mou*.
    a. by metonymy, gen. term for plot of land, field.

盌　wǎn　MC 'wanX
1. (med.) a bowl, eating vessel.
    a. (med.) bowl-shaped.

碗　wǎn　MC 'wanX
1. (med.) ⊙ 盌 wǎn.

縮　wǎn　MC 'waenX
1. tie together, connect; attach, fasten; to thread, enfilade.
    a. (med.) intertwine, wind together, knot up, coil up.
2. take control of, manage.

莞　wǎn　MC hwaenX　→莞 guān.

菀　wǎn　MC 'jwonH
1. sgl. or 紫～ zǐwǎn, aster (*Aster tartaricus*).
    yuàn　MC 'jwonX
1. ⊙ 苑 yuàn, preserve, park; meadow, glade.
    yù　MC 'jut
1. dense, lush plant growth.
2. (med.) rdup., gently yielding, gracefully supple.

輓　wǎn　MC mjonX
1. convey by cart or wagon.
2. ⊙ 挽 wǎn 1, pull (on, in, up, out), drag; lead; 晚 wǎn 2, late(r), belated.

wàn

卍　wàn　MC mjonH
1. (Budd.) swastika (< Skt. *svastika*, be well), fylfot; symbol of unlimited merit and good fortune; one of the physical marks of a buddha, often placed iconographically on chest (i.e. heart), feet, or palms.
    a. (med.) the foregoing used as an ornamental design; e.g. ～字錦 wànzìjǐn, fylfotted polychrome damask; ～字欄杆 wànzìlán'gān, fylfot-latticed balustrade.

腕　wàn　MC 'wanH
1. wrist.
    a. forearm, wrist, and hand as a unit.

萬　wàn　MC mjonH
1. ten thousand, myriad.
    a. countless, innumerable.
2. absolutely, positively; unequalled; in every case.
3. "scorpion" dance, name of ancient ritual dance, with different accoutrements for military or civil aims.

薍　wàn　MC ngwaenH
1. (med.) just-sprouted silvergrass (→ 荻 dí).
    luàn　MC lwanH
1. root of rocambole or sand-leek (*xiaosuan* 小蒜).

蟎　wàn　MC mjonH
1. (bn.) ～蜒 wànyán (MC mjonH-yen), mythical beast reputedly 800 feet (*chi* 尺) long.

wāng

尪　wāng　MC 'wang
1. crippled, rickety.
    a. lame, halt.
    b. infirm(ity), impair(ment), (en)feeble.

汪　wāng　MC 'wang
1. shoreless, limitless; fathomless; vast, extensive, far-spreading, far-ranging.
    a. (bn.) ～洋 wāngyáng (MC 'wang-yang), ～漾 wāngyàng (MC 'wang-yangH), ～翔 wāngxiáng (MC 'wang-zjang), wide-eyed with

wonder; also, shoreless and far-spreading, unplumbed profundity; vast and profound.

b. rdup., broad and boundless, spreading to the farthest extent; also (med.), shaking with tears, streaming with tears.

2. pool of still water; tank; catchment.

    a. pool of stopped or stagnant water.

wáng

亡   **wáng**   MC mjang

1. flee, run off, run away; abscond; fugitive.

2. disappear; lose.

    a. be absent, be elsewhere.

3. undo, be undone; at a loss for useful action.

4. gone for good; perish, die; defunct, extinct; e.g. ～國 *wángguó*, a moribund state, soon to collapse or be conquered.

    a. bring to an end; destroy.

5. to not have, be without, lack, devoid of; in early texts followed by OBJ only when used causatively, otherwise ref. to relevant preceding noun, e.g. 人皆有兄弟，我獨～ *rén jiē yǒu xiōngdì, wǒ dú wáng*, people all have brothers but only I have none; in Han times and later, may be used transitively when followed by OBJ; in these usages equiv. 無 *wú* and often pronounced as such but that pronunciation not verified in classical or med. texts.

6. ⊙ 忘 *wàng*, forget, be oblivious of, indifferent to.

王   **wáng**   MC hjwang

1. king; in pre-imperial times, supreme ruler of the Chinese ecumene, equiv. *tianzi* 天子, "Son of Heaven"; in imperial times, "prince," prince of the blood, esp. when remaining at court; when installed as virtual ruler of own territory, as often in W. Han and W. Jin times, best rendered "king."

    a. kingly, royal, partaking of the exemplary qualities of a king.

    b. ideally, intermediary between Heaven and Earth.

2. pay homage at the royal court, treat with the ceremony due a king, esp. ref. feudal lords or foreigners.

3. respectful epithet for grandfather (*wangfu* ～父) and grandmother (*wangmu* ～母).

4. a surname.

    wàng   MC hjwangH

1. to rule, govern, act as a king.

wǎng

往   **wǎng**   MC hjwangX

1. go, go toward; wend, fare (ant. 來 *lái*); usu. without OBJ or destination following.

    a. ～來 *wǎnglái*, come and go; also, past and future.

    b. 以～ *yǐwǎng*, ... and onward; e.g. 過此以 ～ *guòcǐ yǐwǎng*, from this time onward.

2. be gone; bygone, past, former(ly); e.g. ～昔 *wǎngxī*, bygone times.

    a. ever, indicating extended period; e.g. ～VB, has ever (always) VB-ed.

    b. rdup., ever and anon, now and again, from time to time.

3. gone forever, dead.

    wàng   MC hjwangH

1. turn toward, incline toward, take refuge with; in this usage may take OBJ.

惘   **wǎng**   MC mjangX

1. sgl. or rdup., disappointed, disillusioned, discouraged, dejected.

枉   **wǎng**   MC ʼjwangX

1. bent, crooked.

    a. perverse, depraved.

2. unjust, illegitimate.

3. deign or condescend to do or accept.

4. (med.) unavailing, bootless, for naught; in vain, futilely.

瀇   **wǎng**   MC ʼwangX

1. (bn.) ～漾 *wǎngyàng* (MC ʼwangX-yangH), shoreless and immeasurable, endless and unbounded, ⊙ 汪漾 *wāngyàng*.

網   **wǎng**   MC mjangX

1. ⊙ 罔 *wǎng* 1, catch-net, fish-net, hunting-net; to net, catch, enmesh, entangle.

    a. collect, pull together, bring in.

2. web, mesh(work), network.

    a. design patterned on meshwork, esp. in lattice-work; grille(d).

罔   **wǎng**   MC mjangX

1. net for catching fish (fish-net, seine), birds (bird-net), quadrupeds (hunting-net, tangle-net, throw-net).

    a. to net, catch; entangle; spread a net for, capture.

2. enmesh, ensnare; deceive; hoodwink, dupe.
　　a. befuddle, confuse, addle.
3. (bn.) 〜閬 *wǎngliǎng* (MC mjangX-ljangX), ⊙ 魍魎 *wǎngliǎng*, malignant spirit of mountain or river, spectral succubus.
4. (med.) malign, accuse falsely.
5. ⊙ 無 *wú* 1, be without, lack, devoid of; e.g. 〜極 *wǎngjí*, without limit, without end; 〜春 *wǎngchūn*, devoid of feeling.
6. pre-verbal negative, equiv. *bu* 不, not.
　　a. imperative negative: do not, don't.
　　b. rhetorical negative: cannot but be that …; cannot be the case that …

蒾　wǎng　MC mjangX
1. "net-vine," swallowwort (*Cynanchum atratum*), a non-succulent climbing vine, slightly toxic but carefully used medicinally.

諣　wǎng　MC mjangX
1. ⊙罔 *wǎng* 2, enmesh, deceive, dupe; befuddle, addle.

輞　wǎng　MC mjangX
1. rim or felloe of a wheel.

魍　wǎng　MC mjangX
1. (bn.) 〜魎 *wǎngliǎng* (mjangX-ljangX), malignant spirit of mountain or river, spectral succubus; also, penumbra, faint outer shadow; also, when regarded as 2 parts of same whole, penumbra and shadow (< *Zhuangzi* 1).

wàng

妄　wàng　MC mjangH
1. haphazard, frivolous; careless, rash; inconsiderate; unseemly; errant.
　　a. irresponsible, not in accord with expected social norms.
2. insubstantial, groundless, fraud(ulent); sham; hallucinatory, phantasm(al).
　　a. preposterous; absurd.
　　b. falsehood; lie, prevaricate.
3. deign to.
4. 无〜 *wúwàng*, "no errancy," name of 25th hexagram of the *Yijing*.
5. ⊙ 無 *wú*, esp. in cmpd. 將〜 *jiāngwàng* (syn. 將無 *jiāngwú*), isn't it that …?, mightn't it be …?

忘　wàng　MC mjangH
1. forget, fail to think of.
　　a. be oblivious of, ignore, disregard, be indifferent to.

旺　wàng　MC hjwangH
1. shining brightly.
2. exuberant, prolific; prosperous; flourishing.
3. (bn.) 〜相 *wàngxiāng* (MC hjwangH-sjang), be in luck, by happy chance, favored by fortune.

望　wàng　MC mjangH
1. look at from afar, gaze afar at, look off at.
　　a. the view from afar, a vista, a prospect of; e.g. 〜中 *wàngzhōng*, within view; 〜外 *wàngwài*, beyond view; unforeseen, unexpectedly.
2. have a hopeful view of, hope; anticipate, expect, have prospects of.
3. be distanced from, estranged from (< regard only from afar).
　　a. resent, disdain.
4. look up to; respect(ed), admire(d), of repute; prestige, prestigious; e.g. 〜族 *wàngzú*, clan of repute.
　　a. (med.) in Tang times, 3rd of 4 special categories designating selected prefectures (*zhou* 州) that, because of their importance were given special standing (in descending order of prestige: 輔 *fǔ* [buttressing], 雄 *xióng* [dominant], 〜 *wàng* [honored], 緊 *jǐn* [important]) outside the usual trilevel ranking (上, 中, 下) of prefectures; also, 3rd of 4 special categories designating selected districts (*xian* 縣) in same manner (in descending order of prestige: 赤 *chì* [crimson = imperial], 畿 *jī* [metropolitan], 〜 *wàng* [honored], 緊 *jǐn* [important]).
5. full-moon day of lunar month, when sun and moon are opposite each other (< regard each other from afar); in a month of 30 days (*dayue* 大月) the 16th, in a month of 29 days (*xiaoyue* 小月) the 15th.
6. turn toward, look toward, incline to.
　　a. in early times, a sacrifice offered to mountains and rivers, or sun and moon, or constellations (upon turning toward them from afar).
7. (bn.) 〜洋 *wàngyáng* (MC mjangH-yang), wide-eyed with wonder.

迋 wàng MC hjwangH

1. go, go to; go on.

guàng MC kjwangH

1. ⊙ 誑 *kuáng*, cheat, deceive; 恇 *kuāng*, frightened, scared, stupefied.

wēi

偎 wēi MC 'woj

1. (med.) snuggle up to, cuddle, nestle; hug; squeeze close to.

危 wēi MC ngjwe

1. precipitous; steep.
   a. erect, upright; e.g. 〜坐 *wēizuò*, sit erect; 〜言 *wēiyán*, speak straightforwardly; 〜行 *wēixìng*, upright conduct.
2. danger(ous), peril(ous), hazard(ous).
   a. imperil, endanger, jeopardize.
   b. take pains to do; e.g. 〜苦 *wēikǔ*, the most painstaking, bend every effort to.
3. queasy, nauseous, esp. because of fear.
4. spine or peak of a roof.
5. "Steep Roof," one of the 28 lunar lodgings, comprised of α Aquarii and θ, ε Pegasi, in the northern quadrant (*xuanwu* 玄武) of the sky.

威 wēi MC 'jw+j

1. overawe, awe-inspiring, awesome; daunt(ing), intimidating; cog. 畏 *wèi*, dread(ful); e.g. 〜儀 *wēiyí*, awesome observances (ref. ritual practices); dignified deportment; also (med.), honor guard; also, 〜遠 *wēiyuǎn*, awesome to the distant, daunt the distant.
   a. dominate, master; authority, authoritarian; imposing, respect-inspiring.
2. 〜靈仙 *wēilíngxiān*, clematis (*Clematis chinensis*), a climbing vine or liana, producing showy flowers; syn. 苓 *líng* 3.

巋 wēi MC 'weaj

1. (bn.) 〜嵬 *wēiwéi* (ngeaj-xwoj), precipitously piled, pinnacled and poised.

微 wēi MC mj+j

1. faint; imperceptible, indiscernible; intangible, tenuous, subtle; efface(d).
   a. what lies between *wú* 無 (of Dao) and *yǒu* 有 (of phenomena).
   b. faded; hidden; inconspicuous, unassuming; secret; e.g. 〜行 *wēixíng*, go incognito, move about inconspicuously.
   c. faint or eclipsed light of sun or moon; e.g. 〜月 *wēiyuè*, first slender crescent of moon, usu. ref. 3rd day after new moon.
   d. gentle, light; wispy; e.g. 〜風 *wēifēng*, gentle breeze.
2. infinitesimal, minute, minuscule; minimal, rudimentary.
   a. humilific modifier, e.g. 〜尚 *wēishàng*, my insignificant ideals, (what I) humbly esteem, my petty goals.
3. modal negative GP for nouns and noun-phrases, negates an identity, typically in a hypothetical or subjunctive sense: were it not for . . .; e.g. 〜禹吾其魚乎 *wéi yǔ wú qí yú hū*, were it not for Yu we would likely be fish; 〜管仲吾其被髮左衽矣 *wéi guǎnzhòng wú qí pīfà zuǒrèn yǐ*, were it not for Guan Zhong, we would likely have loosely hanging hair and lapels closing on the left.

萎 wēi MC 'jwe

1. wilt, droop, bent down; wither(ed), dried up.
   a. (bn.) 〜約 *wēiyuē* (MC 'jwe-'jak), wasted and withered, weak and sickly, frail and feeble.

wěi MC 'jweX

1. (bn.) 〜腰 *wěiněi* (MC 'jweX-nwojX), tender and delicate.
2. (bn.) 〜蕤 *wěiruí* (MC 'jweX-nywij), sealwort, fragrant solomon's seal (*Polygonatum odoratum*), small herbaceous plant with unbranched curved stem and small hanging greenish-white flowers, favors moist areas, used medicinally and in food; syn. 玉竹 *yùzhú*, 黃芝 *huángzhī*.

葳 wēi MC 'jw+j

1. (bn.) 〜蕤 *wēiruí* (MC 'jw+j- nywij), sealwort, Solomon's seal (*Polygonatum odoratum*), medicinal herb; also, full-hanging foliage, riotously lush.

薇 wēi MC mj+j

1. bracken (if young, fiddlehead, which may be eaten), thornfern (*Pteridophyta*); vetch (*Vicia sativa*), leguminous plant often used as livestock fodder.

逶 wēi MC 'jwe

1. bend, curve; wind; approach indirectly.
   a. (bn.) 〜迆 *wēiyí* (MC 'jwe-ye), tortive and twisted, wind and writhe, long and round-about, meandering endlessly, proceeding persistently.

隈　wēi　MC ʼwoj

1. corner, nook; bend.
    a. hollow or depression in mountains.
    b. inlet, bight, cove of river; headland.

wéi

唯　wéi　MC ywij

1. generic assertive particle for noun phrases and nominal sentences, asserts an identity: (it) indeed (is), "only"; e.g. 〜天為大〜堯則之 *wéi tiān wéi dà wéi yáo zé zhī*, indeed heaven is the grandest, only Yao models himself on it; 〜所欲 *wéi suǒyù*, it was indeed what they wished.
    a. initial particle lending archaic copular sense: be you (it, they)…, you (it, they) be…; verily it is…, yea…
2. marks affirmative exclusionary clause (cf. 非 *fēi*, 微 *wēi*): only, nothing but; e.g. 〜水漿不祭 *wéi shuǐ jiàng bù jì*, only the water and sauces were not given as sacrificial offerings; 〜利之求 *wéi lì zhī qiú*, only profit, this he seeks.
3. ADV assertive: only, particularly; e.g. 必慎〜諾 *bì shèn wéi nuò*, one needs be careful [only >] particularly in assenting; 〜救死 *wéi jiù sǐ*, they only strive to escape dying.
4. assent (to), concur; approve; accept; usu. directed toward superior (cf. 諾 *nuò*, usu. toward inferior).
    wěi　MC ywijX
1. stammer; rdup., stammering self-depreciating response, "quite so, quite so."

圍　wéi　MC hjw+j

1. environ(ing), surround(ing); enclose, encompass, encircle; e.g. 〜棋 *wéiqí*, encirclement chess (Jpns. *go*).
    a. lay siege to (a city); beleaguer.
2. circumference, circuit, periphery; girth.
    a. vicinity, environs; e.g. 九〜 *jiǔwéi*, 9 Environs (syn. 九州 *jiǔzhōu*, 9 Provinces), i.e. all the (Chinese) world.
3. double-handspan, distance between tips of small fingers when thumbs are touching.
4. (med.) gather, concentrate in one area.
    a. (med.) hunting preserve or enclosure.

嵬　wéi　MC ngwoj

1. (bn.) 崔〜 *cuīwéi*, → 崔 *cuī*; (bn.) 崴〜 *wēiwéi*, → 崴 *wēi*.

巍　wéi　MC ngjw+j

1. towering; majestic.
    a. rdup. or (bn.) 〜峨 *wéiʼé* (MC ngwj+j-nga), toweringly tall, exaltedly elevated.

帷　wéi　MC hwij

1. drape, draw-curtain, side-curtain (cf. 幕 *mù*, 帳 *zhàng*, drape), usu. screening all 4 sides, without a top gathering.
2. (med.) veil; e.g. 〜帽 *wéimào*, veiled hat, worn by women when riding, the hat itself being round-brimmed and conical with silk mesh falling from the brim to below the chin.

幃　wéi　MC hjw+j

1. perfume sachet.
2. front panel of a skirt.
3. ⊙ 帷 *wéi*, drape, draw-curtain; also (med.) tent, pavilion.

惟　wéi　MC ywij

1. think carefully, ponder over; e.g. 〜省 *wéixǐng*, reflect upon oneself, examine oneself.
    a. understand, realize.
2. be only, be nothing but, ⊙ 唯 *wéi* 2.
3. because of, owing to, deriving from.
4. phrase-initial or mid-phrase particle indicating decisive truth (with archaic overtone) of what follows: verily, yea, ⊙ 唯 *wéi* 1, 1a; 維 *wéi* 3, support, uphold.

桅　wéi　MC ngwoj

1. mast of a boat.

為　wéi　MC hjwe

1. followed by direct OBJ: do; make, contrive; effect; carry out; e.g. 〜舟 *wéi zhōu*, make a boat; 〜政 *wéizhèng*, carry out government; 無〜 *wúwéi*, without effect, without ado, Dao. concept of "doing nothing," (Budd.) the unconditioned, trns. Skt. *asaṃskṛta*.
2. followed by SUBJ complement: act as, serve as, assume the role of; constitute, become; comport; e.g. 〜人 *wéi rén*, (in one's) conduct as a man…, personally he was…; 〜太守 *wéi tàishǒu*, serve as prefect.
    a. serve for, be deemed (as); consider as.
    b. 以(A)〜B, *yǐ* (A) *wéi* B, take the (stated or) unstated OBJ A as B, regard (A) as B.
    c. 〜X 所 VB, *wéi* X *suǒ* VB, to be VBed by X (i.e. passive voice); e.g. 〜敵所擒 *wéi dí*

suǒqín, be taken prisoner by the enemy; ～世所笑 *wéi shì suǒxiào*, be laughed at by the world.

3. ditransitive beneficiary construction, ～X Y, *wéi* X Y: to do or make Y for X; e.g. 吾能～之足 *wú néng wéi zhī zú*, I am able to make feet for it; 王～民父母 *wáng wéi mín fùmǔ*, the king acts as father and mother to the people.

4. with stative VB: especially, particularly, -est; e.g. 魯～小 *lǔ wéi xiǎo*, Lu is particularly small; 唯堯～大 *wéi yáo wéi dà*, Yao alone is the greatest; 不～多 *bùwéiduō*, not amount to much, not be especially numerous.

5. marker of subjunctive: if it were (the case) that…, suppose that…

    wèi   **MC hjweH**

1. sgl. or ～了 *wèile*, on account of…, for the sake of…; because of…

2. in place of, substituting for.

3. ⊙ 謂 *wèi* 3, to call, term, refer to (as), mean.

維   *wéi*   MC ywij

1. stay(s), brace(s), chief support-cords attaching to the mainstay (綱 *gāng*) of net.

2. attach, tie together; truss.

3. support, uphold; e.g. ～新 *wéixīn*, uphold and renew.

4. phrase-initial or mid-phrase particle indicating decisive truth (with archaic overtone) of what follows: verily, yea.

5. (Budd.) (bn.) ～那 *wéinà* (MC ywij-naH), vice-abbot of monastery, overseer, supervises its daily life, trsc. Skt. *vainayika*.

6. ⊙ 惟 *wéi* 1, think carefully, ponder; 唯 *wéi*, pre-classical copula: "be you (it, they)…; you be…; it is that…"; also, be only, be nothing but.

違   *wéi*   MC hjw+j

1. go away from, turn away from; depart from.

    a. be apart from, displaced from.

    b. avoid; parry.

2. go against, go or run counter to; disobey, offend; deviate.

    a. disinclined, reluctant.

    b. abjure, repudiate.

3. wayward; untoward; froward; contrary.

闈   *wéi*   MC hjw+j

1. small interior palace-gate.

    a. 宮～ *gōngwéi*, gate leading to quarters of imperial consorts and concubines; by synecdoche, the women's quarters.

2. (med.) private rooms of one's parents.

3. (med.) exam grounds, locale in Tang times for the *jinshi* 進士 civil-service exam.

韋   *wéi*   MC hjw+j

1. tanned or softened hides; leather.

2. ⊙ 違 *wéi*, turn against, wayward; 圍 *wéi*, circumference, girth; circuit, enclosure; double-handspan.

3. a surname.

鮠   *wéi*   MC ngwoj

1. bagrid, bagrid catfish (various species of genus *Pseudobagrus*).

wěi

亹   *wěi*   MC mj+jX

1. rdup., unstinting and tireless, untiring, indefatigable, earnestly diligent, resolute; compelling, urgent, steadily advancing; ⊙ 娓娓 *wěiwěi*.

    mén   **MC mwon**

1. stretch of river enclosed by steep banks; cleft, gorge, chasm.

偉   *wěi*   MC hjw+jX

1. magnificent; imposing; stately, majestic; awesome.

2. praise, speak highly of; esteem.

偽   *wěi*   MC ngjweH

1. fabricated, artificial, man-made.

2. falsified, feigned, sham; specious; counterfeit, forgery, deception; imposture.

    a. usurp(ation); illegitimate.

委   *wěi*   MC ʼjweX

1. consign, delegate; entrust to; hand over to.

    a. give away, send.

2. make an allowance of or for; e.g. ～分 *wěifēn*, accept one's lot.

3. let go, release; abandon, throw away; strew(n); quit, give up, leave behind.

4. heap up, pile(d); lay up, lay aside; collect.

5. tortive, twisted, tortuous; involuted; involved, intricate; in every way; e.g. ～悉 *wěixī*, minute, punctilious, meticulous; ～曲 *wěiqǔ*, turned and twisted, every twist and turn > vicissitudes > all the fine details.

    a. tort, a wrongful or harmful act.

6. lower reaches of a river.

    a. the far end or last bit of something.

7. indeed, in fact; truly.
8. (med.) have confidence in; regard highly.

　　wēi　MC ʼjwe

1. (bn.) ～蛇 *wēiyí* (MC ʼjwe-ye), wind and writhe, twisted and tortuous, sinuous and serpentine, slip and slide, meander(ing); also, intricately involved, extensively protracted; also, relaxed and free, sure and easy.
2. ⊙ 萎 *wēi*, wilt, droop, hang down, bend down.

娓　wěi　MC mj+jX

1. submit, yield to.
2. rdup., diligent, unstinting and tireless; also, handsomely shaped, beautifully formed.

尾　wěi　MC mj+jX

1. tail.
　　a. tail-end, far end; hinder part, rear.
　　b. final, last.
　　c. lower reaches of a river.
2. animal copulation, coupling.
3. "Tail," one of the 28 lunar lodgings, comprised of ε, μ 2, μ 1, η, θ, ι, κ, λ, υ Scorpii, in the eastern quadrant (*qinglong* 青龍) of the sky.
4. measure-word for fish.
5. (med.) (lit.) 上～ *shàngwěi*, raised tail, name of prosodic fault in which 5th and 10th (successive line-ending) words in a couplet of pentasyllabic verse have the same tone.

暐　wěi　MC hjw+jX

1. sgl. or rdup., bright resplendence, gleam(ing), glow(ing).

煒　wěi　MC hjw+jX

1. swirling or globed flames; bright shimmer.

猥　wěi　MC ʼwojX

1. numerous, ever so many; manifold, multifarious; sundry.
　　a. (al)together, in a group.
　　b. all at once; sudden(ly).
2. heap up, pile up; accumulate.
3. commonplace, ordinary; mediocre; lowly; also used as self-depreciatory adjective.
4. perfunctor(il)y, careless(ly), uncaring(ly).

瑋　wěi　MC hjw+jX

1. bright-beaded, glowing with light.
　　a. precious; jewel-like.

痏　wěi　MC hwijX

1. scar, left from medical treatment.
　　a. puncture point of acupuncture.
　　b. wound, from beating.
2. abscess, ulceration.

痿　wěi　MC ʼjwe

1. enervation, muscular atrophy; consumption.
　　a. paralysis, immobility.

硊　wěi　MC ngjweX

1. (bn.) 磈～ *wěiwěi*, → 磈 *wěi* (*kuǐ*).

緯　wěi　MC hjw+jH

1. the weft or woof threads in weaving, which are drawn horizontally through the warp threads (經 *jīng*) to create pattern and design.
　　a. spool of weft-thread, bobbin.
2. weave (fabrics or words), create text(ure).
　　a. govern, control, knit together various people and opinions into one polity.
3. east-west orientation, as with roads, geographical features, etc.
4. "weft texts," usu. translated as "apocrypha," texts composed anonymously during the Han dynasty as esoteric interpretations of and prognosticatory supplements added to the "warp texts" (*jīng* 經, classics).
5. 五～ *wǔwěi*, Five Wefts, i.e. the 5 naked-eye planets.

萎　wěi　MC ʼjweX　→ 萎 *wēi*.

葦　wěi　MC hjw+jX

1. sgl. or in cmpd. 蘆～ *lúwěi*, common reed (*Phragmites communis*); one text says *wěi* is a reed that has flowered, *lú* is one that has not.

蔿　wěi　MC hjweX

1. foxnut (*Euryale ferox*), a waterlily that produces bright purple flowers.

諉　wěi　MC nrjwieH

1. shift responsibility to, decline responsibility for.
2. shift blame elsewhere; excuse oneself by implicating another.

韙　wěi　MC hjw+jX

1. correct, right, just so.

韡　wěi　MC hjw+jX

1. rdup., vividly dazzling, gorgeously glistening.

骫   wěi   MC ʼjweX
1. bent, curved; crooked.
2. ⊙ 委 *wěi* 4, heap up, pile up; collect, gather together.

鮪   wěi   MC hwijX
1. beaked sturgeon, paddlefish (*Psephurus gladius*); syn. 鱏 *xún*.

wèi

位   wèi   MC hwijH
1. seat, see.
   a. position of authority or influence, incl. noble rank, bureaucratic office, esp. imperial sway; e.g. 即～ *jíwèi*, ascend the see, assume the throne.
2. place, (em)placement; position.
3. rank; bearing, situation.

味   wèi   MC mj+jH
1. taste, savor; flavor.
   a. significance; implication; overtone.

媦   wèi   MC hjw+jH
1. younger sister.

尉   wèi   MC ʼjw+jH
1. palliate; placate, pacificate, bring to terms.
   a. condole with, console, comfort; ameliorate; hearten, encourage; e.g. ～勞 *wèiláo*, console and commiserate with, console and reassure; often, to receive and hail, salute and fête, pay respects to, make comfortable.
2. official title indicative of military or police responsibilities, "one who imposes (or keeps) the peace," constable; (med.) 4th-ranking (of 4) centrally appointed officials in a district (*xian* 縣), in charge of local military and police matters, informally titled 少府 *shàofǔ*, "Junior (Deputy) Repositor," as subordinate to the 令 *lìng* ("commandant," magistrate) who was informally known as 明府 *míngfǔ*, "Enlightened Repositor."
   a. 太～ *tàiwèi*, grand marshal, one of the 3 traditionally supreme officers of state or *sāngōng* 三公, "3 Dignitaries" (the other 2 being *sikong* 司空, director of works, and *situ* 司徒, director of instruction).
3. (med.) gen. term for junior officers.
      yù   MC ʼjut
1. ～遲 *yùchí* (MC ʼjut-drij), a disyllabic surname.

慰   wèi   MC ʼjw+jH
1. ⊙ 尉 *wèi* 1, palliate; placate; comfort, condole with; hearten.

未   wèi   MC mj+jH
1. aspectual negative for VB-phrases: not yet, still not; etymologically the negative counterpart to 既 *jì*; e.g. 我～見力不足者 *wǒ wèijiàn lì bùzúzhe*, I have not yet seen anyone whose strength was insufficient; ～有以對也 *wèiyǒu yǐ duì yě*, he still did not have any way to respond.
   a. not yet, still not > before; e.g. 名實～加於上下 *míngshí wèijiā yú shàngxià*, before fame or fact has spread to the rulers or commoners; ～葬 *wèizàng*, before interment.
2. simple negative: has not (ever) VBed.
3. "or not?" in expressing the negative counterpart to a preceding VB-clause; clause-final; 可以言～ *kěyǐ yán wèi*, may it be spoken or not?
4. 8th of the 12 earthly branches; associated with the sheep as emblematic animal.
   a. 8th double-hour of the day, from approximately 1:00 p.m. to 3:00 p.m.

渭   wèi   MC hjw+jH
1. important river that rises in Gansu, flows through south-central area of Shaanxi near Chang'an, and enters the Yellow River near Tongguan 潼關; because of its proximity to Chang'an usu. calls up thought of the capital.
2. (bn.) 沸～ *fèiwèi*, → 沸 *fèi*.

燹   wèi   MC hjwejH
1. to dry in the sun.

猬   wèi   MC hjw+jH
1. hedgehog (*Erinaceus koreanus*).

畏   wèi   MC ʼjw+jH
1. dreadful, cause dread; frighten.
   a. shrink from, shy away from.
2. hold in awe, awe-inducing; revere; cog. 威 *wēi*, overawe, daunt.
3. exorcise (in pre-Han texts).
4. ⊙ 隈 *wēi* 1b, inlet, cove; 圍 *wéi* 1a, besiege, beleaguer.

磑   wèi   MC ngwojH   → 磑 *ái*.

罻   wèi   MC ʼjw+jH
1. small net or snare, esp. for birds.
   a. to net, snare.

胃 wèi MC hjw+jH
1. stomach.
2. "Granary" (from the shape of the constellation, not "Stomach"), one of the 28 lunar lodgings, comprised of 35, 39, 41 Arietis, in the western quadrant (*baihu* 白虎) of the sky.

蔚 wèi MC 'jw+jH
1. southernwood, averoyne (*Artemisia japonica*); syn. 牡蒿 *mǔhāo*.
2. thickly growing, proliferating, luxuriant.
   a. (lit.) rich, of diction or imagery; copious, lavish; lushly figured.
   b. billow up, swell (ref. clouds or vapors).
   yù MC 'jut
1. deep and clear, as of fathomless abyss.
2. ⊙ 鬱 *yù*, rdup. or ～結 *yùjié*, stifled and smothered, glum and grim, with thoughts bound and knotted.

蝟 wèi MC hjw+jH
1. hedgehog (*Erinaceus koreanus*).

衛 wèi MC hjwejH
1. defend, safeguard; guard.
   a. a guard, a paladin.
2. feathering of arrows.
3. donkey, ass; syn. 驢 *lǘ*.
4. old feudal state during the Zhou dynasty, area roughly approximate to present-day southern Hebei and northern Henan.

謂 wèi MC hjw+jH
1. speak to, address, say, followed by pronominal indirect OBJ which is then usu. followed by quotative 曰 *yuē* introducing direct-OBJ statement; e .g. X ～王曰 ..., X said to the king "..."
2. speak about, tell of, followed by direct OBJ; e.g. 子～子賤君子哉若人 *zǐ wèi zǐjiàn jūnzi zāi ruò rén*, The Master said of Zijian, "A gentleman indeed is such as he!"
3. to call, term, refer to as; to mean; e.g. 中土～中國也 *zhōngtǔ wèi zhōngguó yě*, "The central lands" refers to the central states.
4. sgl. or 以～ *yǐwèi*, regard as . . ., treat as . . ., expect to be . . .
5. introduces conditional situation: If it were said that . . .; Should it be stated that . . .

讆 wèi MC hjwejH
1. misrepresent the character of an unworthy person, praise unjustifiably, exaggerate, embroider, overstate, make too much of, hyperbolize.

轊 wèi MC hjwejH ⊙ 轊 *wèi*.

轊 wèi MC hjwejH
1. axle-cap.

遺 wèi MC ywijH → 遺 *yí*.

鐏 wèi MC zjwejH
1. small cauldron or tripod.

魏 wèi MC ngjw+jH
1. watchtower or lookout tower by palace gates.
   a. by synecdoche, the court or palace, esp. in compound ～闕 *wèiquè*.
2. name of a feudal state during Zhou times, originally part of the Jin 晉 state, located in northern Henan and southwest Shanxi, with capital near present-day Kaifeng; one of the 7 major states during the Warring States period; also ref. as Liang 梁.
3. name of 4 med. dynasties: one of the "3 Kingdoms" (220-265); northern dynasty during the Nanbeichao period, ruled by the Tabgatch (i.e. Tuoba 拓跋) people (386-534); Eastern Wei (534-550), fragmented successor state to preceding; Western Wei (535-556), another fragmented successor state to same.
4. a surname.
   wéi MC ngjw+j
1. stand alone and unmoved.
2. ⊙ 巍 *wéi*, towering; majestic.

wēn

殟 wēn MC 'won
1. lose consciousness, faint.

溫 wēn MC 'won
1. warm, tepid.
2. temperate, moderate; mild, gentle.
   a. congenial, cordial, amiable.
3. rekindle, refocillate, reanimate.
   a. review, practice, revise.
4. intermittent fever, esp. in springtime.

yùn   MC 'junH

1. ⊙ 蘊 *yùn*, accumulate, bundle, aggregate; store up, (p)reserve; pent-up, frustrated.

溫   wēn   MC 'won   ⊙ 温 *wēn*.

瘟   wēn   MC 'won

1. (med.) epidemic; infectious, infection.

薀   wēn   MC 'won

1. water-milfoil (*Myriophyllum*, various species).

輼   wēn   MC 'won

1. sleeping-wagon, screened carriage in which one may lie down during longer travel.
    a. (med.) hearse, for conveying encoffined corpse.

wén

文   wén   MC mjun

1. natural pattern of lines, incl. distinctive markings on animals and natural phenomena.
2. designed or incised pattern, surface ornament, elaboration, as added to (ant.) 質 *zhì*, basic stuff, plainness; cf. 理 *lǐ*, inherent pattern; cog. 紋 *wén*, reticulated, embroidered.
3. ornament(ed); ornate.
4. the refined, civil, or cultured qualities, as opp. to (ant.) 武 *wǔ*, martial attainments or prowess.
    a. culture, and the arts associated with it.
    b. written text; consciously devised pattern of words; literature.
5. well-patterned; artful; e.g. ～章 *wénzhāng*, artful display or design, (med.) esp. literature.
6. a graph consisting of a single component only; cf. *zì* 字, graph consisting of 2 or more components.
7. (med.) rhymed or refined writings, as distinguished from 筆 *bǐ*, unrhymed or utilitarian writings.
8. prose or prosimetric writings, as distinguished from 詩 *shī*, "verse."
9. (med.) a unit of cash; in Nanbeichao period equiv. 10 coins, in Tang usu. equiv. 1 coin.
10. (Budd.) ～殊 *wénshū* or ～殊師利 *wénshūshīlì* (MC mjun-dzyu-srij-lijH), trsc. Skt. Mañjuśrī, bodhisattva esp. associated with wisdom and with Mount Wutai 五台山.
    wèn   MC mjunH
1. to ornament, bedeck, decorate, mark.
    a. gloss over; make acceptable by superficial luster.

紋   wén   MC mjun

1. (med.) patterned design worked into silk fabric; figured textiles; tapestry.
    a. (med.) strips, bands, veins, lines.

聞   wén   MC mjun

1. to hear.
2. make heard, make known, inform.
3. what one hears; rumor, hearsay, commonly transmitted information.
4. (med.) to smell, sniff (only from Tang times and then rarely).
    wèn   MC mjunH
1. repute, reputation; celebrated, renowned.

蚊   wén   MC mjun

1. mosquito.

雯   wén   MC mjun

1. (med.) cloud pattern(ing)s, cloud colorings.

wěn

刎   wěn   MC mjunX

1. cut one's throat, esp. suicide.
    a. cut off, slice off, lop off.

吻   wěn   MC mjunX

1. mouth, incl. both lips.
2. kiss.

抆   wěn   MC mjunX

1. wipe off, wipe away.

穩   wěn   MC 'wonX

1. stable, firm; fixed, secure; close, tight.
    a. (as)sure(ed), certain; dependable.

紊   wěn   MC mjunH

1. (en)tangle, ravel; jumble, scramble, disarray; disorder, confuse.

wèn

問   wèn   MC mjunH

1. ask, inquire.
    a. ask of (someone); inquire about (something).
    b. inquire into, interrogate, investigate, pursue a question; line of inquiry; be curious about.
    c. censure; rebuke.

2. ask after; send one's regards to, send respects.

3. in early times, send a diplomatic mission with gifts to another state.

4. news, tidings, current information.

5. (med.) ask about marriage, propose.

6. ⊙ 聞 *wén* 2, make known, inform; *wèn*, repute, reputation.

搵　wèn　MC 'wonH

1. (med.) immerse, plunge into.

2. (med.) ⊙ 抆 *wèn*, wipe off, rub off.

汶　wèn　MC mjunH

1. name of an important river in north-central Shandong.

mín　MC min

1. alternate graph for name of Min 泯 River in Sichuan.

mén　MC mwon

1. rdup., soiled and stained, muddied and maculate, dirty and defiled; pollution.

璺　wèn　MC mjunH

1. crack, fracture (esp. in pottery); fissure.

緄　wèn　MC mjunH

1. mourning headband, white cloth band tied around the head during mourning.

2. long cloth bands attached to the casket and held by mourners.

miǎn　MC mjenX

1. ⊙ 冕 *miǎn*, ceremonial cap worn by grandees and above; coronet (for ruler).

wēng

翁　wēng　MC 'uwng

1. oldster, gaffer, codger, oldfellow, often as suffix, usu. affectionate or respectful.

　　a. respectfully affectionate term for father (papa) or grandfather (gramps).

2. (med.) statue of human likeness cast from bronze or carved from stone.

wěng

滃　wěng　MC 'uwngX

1. sgl. or rdup., billowing up or massing of clouds.

蓊　wěng　MC 'uwngX

1. full, flourishing, thick, rife, esp. of vegetation.

　　a. (bn.) ～茸 *wěngróng* (MC 'uwngX-nyowng), lush and luxuriant; (bn.) ～鬱 *wěngyù* (MC 'uwngX-'jut), dense and thick, massed and mingled.

wèng

瓮　wèng　MC 'uwngH　⊙ 甕 *wèng*.

甕　wèng　MC 'uwngH

1. large-mouthed earthenware wine-jar; jar-shaped; vat.

　　a. urn, esp. burial urn.

2. ～城 *wèngchéng*, "urn-wall," barbican, moon-shaped defensive wall in front of a city-gate.

灉　wèng　MC 'jowng　→ 灉 *yōng*.

wō

倭　wō　MC 'wa

1. (med.) dwarf(ish), durgen; stunted; pejorative term applied to the Japanese.

wǒ　MC 'waX

1. (bn.) ～墮 *wǒduò* (MC 'wa-dwaX), "swept-fall," women's hairstyle with hair combed over to one side.

wēi　MC 'jwe

1. (bn.) ～遲 *wēichí*, coiling afar, meandering into the distance.

渦　wō　MC 'wa

1. whirlpool, eddy; vortex.

2. (med.) dimple (cheek).

3. (med.) water-worn hole; hiding-place, covert; ⊙ 窩 *wō*.

猧　wō　MC 'wa

1. (med.) small or young dog, pup.

　　a. (med.) ～子 *wōzi*, "pup," parents' affectionate term for child.

窩　wō　MC 'wa

1. (med.) cote, recessed shelter esp. for birds; covert, hole, hiding-place; ⊙ 渦 *wō* 3.

萵　wō　MC 'wa

1. (med.) ～苣 *wōjù*, ～筍 *wōsǔn*, asparagus lettuce (*Lactuca sativa*), introduced from western Asia, esp. cultivated for stems which were eaten raw.

蝸　wō　MC kwae

1. sgl. or in cmpd. 〜牛 *wōniú*, land-snail (perhaps *Euhadra quaesita*).
2. ⊙ 媧 *wā*, in the name 女〜*nǚwā*, → 媧 *wā*.

wǒ

媟　wǒ　MC ʻwaX

1. (med.) (bn.) 〜姽 *wǒnuǒ* (MC ʻwaX-nwaX), soft and delicate, attractive and lovely.

我　wǒ　MC ngaX

1. 1st-person pronoun: I, my, we, our(s); sometimes emphatic: my own . . ., it is I who . . .
2. specific 3rd-person reference: oneself, one (who . . .).
3. (Budd.) trsl. Skt. *ātman*, the illusory sense of ego produced by the 5 *skandha* (→ 蘊 *yùn*).

wò

偓　wò　MC ʻaewk

1. (bn.) 〜促 *wòcù* (MC ʻaewk-tshjowk), vapid and tiresome, dim-witted, small-minded and rigid.

幄　wò　MC ʻaewk

1. awning; tent, pavilion.
2. wooden frame for inner curtained room.

握　wò　MC ʻaewk

1. grasp by or with the hand, grasp tightly, hold firmly; seize, take hold of; hold on to.
2. a handful (of).
3. (bn.) 〜齪 *wòchuò* (MC ʻaewk-tsrhaewk), strait and narrow, cramped and confined.

斡　wò　MC ʻwat

1. turn round, revolve; swirl, whirl.
   a. shift position, change.
2. suspension-ring of chime-bell.
     guǎn　MC kwanX
1. take control, be in charge of.

沃　wò　MC ʻowk

1. irrigate, water; sprinkle.
   a. immerse, submerge, drench; splash.
2. moisten, lubricate.
   a. glossy, smooth.
3. well-watered, fertile.

涴　wò　MC ʻwaH

1. impure, polluted, foul; sullied, stained.
     wǎn　MC ʻjwonX
1. (bn.) 〜演 *wǎnyǎn* (MC ʻjwonX-yenX), sinuously stretching, turning and twisting.

渥　wò　MC ʻaewk

1. soak; dampen, moisten.
2. richly glossed with; rich in; steeped in; slick with.
   a. deep, rich (of color); thick (of liquid); heavy, rich (of taste).

臥　wò　MC ngwaH

1. lie down, lie; recumbent; be abed, off one's feet.
   a. lounge, rest; sprawl(ed); littered.
2. repose; sleep.
   a. sleeping room; sickbed.
3. lay down official responsibilities; retire(ment), retreat; e.g. 高〜 *gāowò*, lofty retirement.

齷　wò　MC ʻaewk

1. (bn.) 〜齪 *wòchuò* (MC ʻaewk-tsrhaewk), ⊙ 握齪 *wòchuò*, → 握 *wò*.

wū

劓　wū　MC ʻuwk

1. execute a high dignitary, usu. within his own grounds instead of publicly in the marketplace.

嗚　wū　MC ʻu

1. onom. element in various compounds.
   a. 〜乎, 〜呼, 〜虖 *wūhū*, sigh of sadness: alas!; ⊙ 烏 *wu* 4.
   b. rdup., onom. of melodious song; also (med.), onom. of comforting: "there, there."
   c. 〜咽 *wūyē*, wailing and keening, choking with tears; also (med.), onom. of swift-flowing water, gurgling and gushing.
2. (med.) kiss, esp. in Budd. translations.

圬　wū　MC ʻu

1. (to) plaster, parget, roughcast.
   a. trowel.

屋　wū　MC ʻuwk

1. roof.
   a. by synecdoche, chamber, dwelling.
   b. house, residence.
2. silk canopy of carriage, awning; covering, cope.

巫　wū　MC mju

1. pre-Han generic term for one involved with sacerdotal functions or with the supernatural; Han and after, often specifically shaman; spirit-medium; N.B. this word is often defined as "female shaman, shamanka," contrasted with 覡 *xí*, supposedly "male shaman," but the word usu. carries no gender distinction.

杇　wū　MC ʻu　⊙ 圬 *wū*.

汙　wū　MC ʻu　⊙ 污 *wū*.

污　wū　MC ʻu

1. stagnant water.
　　a. mud puddle, dirty pool, dub.
2. sinkland, basin; bog.
　　a. lowly, inferior.
　　b. drained, sinking; declining.
3. foul, stale; polluted, putrid; corrupt.
　　a. defile(d), impure; stain(ed), smudge(d), smear(ed).
4. vile, miserable.
5. wipe off, wipe clean; wash, cleanse.

洿　wū　MC ʻu

1. ⊙ 污 *wū* 1, stagnant water; mud pool; 2, sinkland, basin; lowly; 3, foul, polluted; defile, stain; 5, wipe off.
2. boisterous, unruly, out of hand.

烏　wū　MC ʻu

1. crow, daw; raven.
　　a. 山～ *shānwū*, "mountain daw," i.e. yellow-billed chough (*Pyrrhocorax graculus*), syn. 鸄 *zhuó*.
2. crow-black, raven-colored; black.
　　a. ～臼 *wūjiù*, black drongo (*Dicurus macrocercus*), small passerine with distinctly creaking call, often considered a herald of dawn in advance of cock-crow.
　　b. ～賊 *wūzéi*, "black thief," cuttlefish (*Sepia esculenta*).
3. preverbal interr. pronoun: how…?; where…?; e.g. 秦～能與齊縣衡 *Qín wū néng yǔ Qí xiànhéng* How could Qin be on a par in strength with Qi?; 故亂世之主～聞至樂 *gù luànshì zhī zhǔ wū wén zhìlè*, Assuredly, how would the rulers of a chaotic age hear about the ultimate in joys?; ⊙ 惡 *wū* 1 (*è*).
4. ～乎, ～呼, ～虖 *wūhū*, sigh of sadness: alas!

5. (med.) ～爹泥 *wūdiēní*, gum arabic, hardened sap of acacia tree, imported from West Asia.
6. (med.) ～場 *wūcháng* (MC ʻu-drjang), Uḍyāna.

誣　wū　MC mju

1. misrepresent(ation), mislead, delude, cozen; defraud, belie.
2. bear false witness, accuse falsely, traduce, calumniate.

wú

吳　wú　MC ngu

1. name of fedual state in pre-Qin times, located in lower reaches of Yangzi River, largely the area of Jiangsu.
2. name of 3rd-century dynasty, one of the "3 Kingdoms," controlling the middle to lower Yangzi and lands southward (222-280).
3. a surname.

吾　wú　MC ngu

1. 1st-person pronoun: I, my, we, our(s); in pre-Han texts usu. possessive or as SUBJ; by med. times no difference between this and 我 *wǒ*. N.B. This is a grammatical, not a psychological, term.
2. resist, oppose, parry, defend; e.g. 金～ *jīnwú*, "golden apotropaion; golden defender," fabulous bird supposed to protect against evil > gold-tipped baton > imperial insignia.

无　wú　MC mju

1. ⊙ 無 *wú*, without, not have; let there be no…
　　a. always used instead of 無 in *Yijing*; e.g. ～妄 *wúwàng*, "no errancy," name of 25th hexagram.

梧　wú　MC ngu

1. (bn.) ～桐 *wútóng* (MC ngu-duwng), parasol tree, phoenix tree, "we-together tree," → 桐 *tóng* 1d.
2. weight-bearing support; strut, brace, truss.
　　a. encroach on; conflict with.

毋　wú　MC mju

1. prohibitive or voluntative VB-negative: do not, will not, etc.; e.g. ～過禮 *wú guò lǐ*, do not exceed the prescripts of ceremony; 君子安可～敬也 *jūnzǐ ān kě wú jìng yě*, wherein could a man of noble status not be respectful? 民用力～休 *mín yònglì wú xiū*, the people will use all of their strength and will not slack off.

a. often written 無; ⊙ 无; e.g. 〜望民之多於鄰國 *wú wàng mín zhī duō yú línguó*, do not expect that your population will become greater than that of the neighboring states; 王〜罪歲 *wáng wú zuì suì*, King, do not lay fault with the year; 予欲〜言 *yú yù wú yán*, I prefer not to speak.

無　**wú**　MC mju

1. to be without or lack OBJ.

a. there is no OBJ; absence of OBJ; e.g. 〜為 *wúwéi*, no consciously directed actions, Dao. ideal of "doing nothing" against the natural flow.

2. to have nothing; nought.

3. nothing; null(ity); indeterminate, immaterial; e.g. 虛〜 *xūwú*, the nullity of the void. In *xuanxue* 玄學 discourse has the positive connotations of radical potentiality, unlimited possibilities; in pre-Budd. cosmology stands for 〜形 *wúxíng*, "the Formless, or Indeterminate."

4. rhetorically dismissive negative: regardless of OBJ, no matter whether . . .

a. 〜乃 *wúnǎi*, nothing other than, no doubt.

5. (Budd.) 〜所著 *wúsuǒzhuó*, trns. of Skt. *arhat*, one who is free from attachments; 〜為 *wúwéi*, uncreated, uncaused; also early trns. of Skt. *nirvāṇa*, "the unconditioned"; also, first of two stages of *nirvāṇa*, when one is freed from the round of birth-and-death but one's beneficial traces (*ji* 跡) are still active in the world; 〜從生 *wúcóngshēng*, unborn dharmas; abb. of 南〜 *nánwú* (MC nom-mju), trsc. of Skt. *namo* "salutations [to OBJ]" (also written 南摸 *nánmó* [MC nom-mu], 納謨 *nàmó* [MC nop-mu]); 〜上正等覺 *wúshàngzhèngděngjué*, trns. of Skt. *anuttarasamyaksaṃbodhi*, "unsurpassed, complete, and perfect enlightenment."

　　wù　MC mjut

1. ⊙ 毋 *wù*, imperative: let there be no OBJ; do not VB.

珸　**wú**　MC ngu

1. (bn.) 琨〜 *kūnwú*, → 琨 *kūn*.

蕪　**wú**　MC mju

1. weed-choked, weed-grown, weedy; overgrown; rife, rank.

a. grassland, moorland, wold.

2. unkempt; in disrepair, neglected, disused; uncultivated; wasted, ruined.

3. (med.) of lit. style, fussy, fustian, turgid, overdone.

4. 〜菁 *wújīng*, field mustard, turnip-rape (*Brassica campestris*).

蜈　**wú**　MC ngu

1. 〜蚣 *wúgōng*, centipede, scolopendrid (*Scolopendra morsitans*), used dried medicinally; syn. 蝍蛆 *jíjū*.

鼯　**wú**　MC ngu

1. sgl. or cmpd. 〜鼠 *wúshǔ*, flying squirrel (*Petauristae*).

wǔ

五　**wǔ**　MC nguX

1. numeral five; fifth.

a. 〜行 *wǔxíng*, 5 "Agents" or "Phases," i.e. wood, fire, earth, metal, water; esp. as organizing principle for grouping all manner of items.

b. of particular importance numerically as spatial principle indicating 4 cardinal points plus the center.

仵　**wǔ**　MC nguX

1. similar to, same as, of the same sort.

2. go against, rival, oppose(d).

伍　**wǔ**　MC nguX

1. pentad, group of five.

a. small company of 5 soldiers.

b. in early times, group of 5 households associated for mutual defense.

2. confederate, allied; of the same sort.

侮　**wǔ**　MC mjuX

1. offend, affront; insult.

a. disrespect(ful), humiliate, slight; disgrace(ful).

儛　**wǔ**　MC mjuX　⊙ 舞 *wǔ*.

午　**wǔ**　MC nguX

1. criss-cross(ing); this way and that.

a. (mark an) X.

b. go every which way; e.g. 蜂〜 *fēngwǔ*, (like) wasps going every which way (from a disturbed hive).

2. 7th of the 12 earthly branches, associated with the horse as emblematic animal.

 a. 7th double-hour of the day, from approximately 11 a.m. to 1 p.m.; midday (< crossing-point of *yin* and *yang*, zenith of daylight).

3. zenith, high point (< crossing point from ascending to descending); e.g. 月〜 *yuèwǔ*, the moon at zenith.

悟　wǔ　MC nguH　⊙ 忤 *wǔ*.

嫵　wǔ　MC mjuX

1. (bn.) 〜媚 *wǔmèi* (MC mjuX-mijH), winning and winsome, attractively appealing.

廡　wǔ　MC mjuX

1. portico (around a hall or a building), covered gallery, loggia, porch.

 a. by metonymy, building, house.

  wú　MC mju

1. ⊙ 蕪 *wú*, weed-choked, overgrown; rife, rank.

忤　wǔ　MC nguH

1. defy, defiant, oppugn(ant); refractory, contradict(ory); pervicacious; contumacious; willful.

2. breech-birth.

憮　wǔ　MC mjuX

1. rueful; despair(ing), disappointed, despondent; discouraged.

2. ⊙ 嫵 *wǔ*, appealing, likeable.

武　wǔ　MC mjuX

1. pertaining to the military or martial, as opposed to (ant.) 文 *wén*, cultured, civil.

 a. warrior, soldier, fighter.

2. warlike prowess; courageous; militant, aggressive, bellicose; violent.

3. footprint, e.g. 踵〜 *zhǒngwǔ*, walk in the tracks of, follow or imitate closely.

4. length-measure of 3 feet (*chi* 尺), i.e. half of a "pace" (*bu* 步), 1 step.

5. succeed to, continue.

6. a surname.

珷　wǔ　MC mjuX　⊙ 碔 *wǔ*.

碔　wǔ　MC mjuX

1. (bn.) 〜砆 *wǔfū* (MC mjuX-pju), "warrior-stone," semi-precious stone having white streaks on a red background, perhaps flaming opal.

舞　wǔ　MC mjuX

1. dance.

 a. perform, execute; (panto)mime; act(ion).

 b. carry out court ritual, "dance attendance on."

2. play, disport; giddy.

 a. brandish; exhibit; turn to one's own purposes.

迕　wǔ　MC nguH

1. oppugn(ant), resist(ant); defy, oppose; contrary; be at odds with.

2. meet up with, encounter, come up against.

 a. crisscross, interlace; jumble, mix together.

鵡　wǔ　MC mgjuX

1. (bn.) 鸚〜 *yīngwǔ*, → 鸚 *yīng*.

wù

兀　wù　MC ngwot

1. elevated and flat-topped.

 a. plateau, mesa, esp. one treeless and bare of vegetation.

 b. (bn.) 突〜 *tūwù*, → 突 *tū*.

2. bald; uncovered.

3. unknowing, ignorant, unschooled; blank-minded, empty-headed.

4. (med.) rdup., stuck still, motionless, transfixed; also, dazed and befuddled, blank and rigid; also, failure and frustration, suffer in torment.

5. judicial punishment of having one foot amputated.

務　wù　MC mjuH

1. apply oneself to, make an effort to, occupy oneself with, take as a priority; strive, work hard at, exert oneself, be zealous about.

 a. concentrate on, focus on.

2. necessities, fundamentals; requisite.

 a. absolutely, definitely; by all means; must needs.

3. occupation, pursuit; activity; concern(s).

勿　wù　MC mjut

1. prohibitive negative: do not; e.g. 〜憚改 *wù dàn gǎi*, do not shy away from changing; 〜助長也 *wù zhù zhǎng yě*, do not try to assist in its growth.

 a. often implies a pronominal direct OBJ: do not VB it (. . . her, . . . him, . . . them, etc.); e.g. 非禮〜視 *fēi lǐ wù shì*, if it is not proper ceremony, do not observe it; 王請～疑 *wáng qǐng wù yí*, I beg of you, king, do not doubt it.

陒   wù   MC ngwot

1. (bn.) 鵵～ *nièwù*, → 鵵 *niè*.

噁   wù   MC ʼuH

1. (bn.) 喑～ *yīnwù* (MC ʼim-ʼuH), rant and rave.

塢   wù   MC ʼuX

1. protective embankment, earthen barrier, low wall; fortification.
    a. escarpment, rampart; redan.
2. low area within surrounding barrier; basin.
    a. dock, landing-place, quay.
3. bailiwick, fortified district; manor.

婺   wù   MC mjuH

1. ～女 *wùnǚ*, "Serving Maid," one of the 28 lunar lodgings (also called simply 女 *nǚ*, "Maid"), composed of ε², μ, 3, 4 Aquarii, in the northern quadrant (*xuanwu* 玄武) of the sky.

寤   wù   MC nguH

1. awake from sleep, wake up; come to, come around.
    a. awaken to, become aware of; perceive.
2. breech-birth.

屼   wù   MC ngwot

1. bare, denuded hill; bald-top.

悟   wù   MC nguH

1. awaken to, become aware of; realize, understand anew; perceive, perception.
    a. quick-witted, alive to; mindful of; e.g. 不～ *bùwù*, unguarded.
    b. (Budd.) enlightenment, awakening; e.g. 頓～ *dùnwù*, sudden enlightenment.
2. 晤 *wù*, see face-to-face; à deux.

惡   wù   MC ʼuH   → 惡 *è*.

戊   wù   MC muwH

1. 5th of the 10 heavenly stems; used for "E" in a sequential order.
    a. ～夜 *wùyè*, 5th of the 5 night-watches, approx. 3-5 a.m.

晤   wù   MC nguH

1. meet or see face-to-face; à deux; head-on.

2. ⊙ 悟 *wù*, awaken to, become aware of; perceive; quick-witted.

杌   wù   MC ngwot

1. (bn.) ～陧 *wùniè* (MC ngwot-nget), shaky and unsteady, teetering on the edge.
2. sway, shake, move back and forth; waver, fluctuate.
3. tree-stump; denuded tree, stripped of branches.
4. bench, stool.
5. rdup., stupid and senseless, mindless and obtuse, dunderheaded, blockhead.

沕   wù   MC mjut   → 沕 *mì*.

物   wù   MC mjut

1. particolor of animal's coat, esp. cattle; pelt.
    a. variate; mottling; e.g. 雲～ *yúnwù*, cloud-mottlings, shifting shapes of clouds.
    b. color of form; form, aspect.
2. variegated things; matters, material things; phenomena; the exterior world; e.g. 萬～ *wànwù*, the myriad phenomena (of the world); ～華 *wùhuá*, the flowering (burgeoning life) of natural things.
    a. variety; sort(ing) by groups; class, kind, sort.
3. properties, elements, contents.
    a. definable reality, distinctions.
4. living beings (often other than oneself); wight; e.g. 人～ *rénwù*, human beings; (Budd.) 情～ *qíngwù*, sentient beings.
5. topic, matter; posed problem.
6. identify, recognize; choose; consider (as).

矹   wù   MC ngwot

1. (med.) rdup., steeply soaring, boldly up-thrust.

芴   wù   MC mjut

1. violet-cress (*Orychophragmus violaceus*).
    hū   MC xwot
1. ⊙ 忽 *hū* 2, careless; confused; bewildered.

誤   wù   MC nguH

1. mistake(n), error, erroneous; blunder.
2. lead into error, mislead; misinform.
    a. baffle, confuse, perplex, confound.
    b. impair; vitiate.

阢   wù   MC ngwot

1. ⊙ 杌 *wù* 1, in (bn.) ～陧 *wùniè* (MC ngwot-nget), shaky and unsteady, teetering on the edge.

隖　wù　MC 'uX　⊙ 塢 wù.

霧　wù　MC mjuH

1. fog, rouk, haze, mist; brumous; any cloudlike atmospheric phenomena reducing visibility, ranging from heavy to light.

騖　wù　MC mjuH

1. run freely; mad dash, full gallop.

a. sprint, tear, rush; make haste, hurry; speedily, precipitately; briskly.

2. (med.) pursue, strive to; chase after; be zealous for.

鶩　wù　MC mjuH

1. domestic duck (*Anas domesticata*).

　　a. occasionally, the wild duck.

2. scuttle, scurry.

X

xī

傒　xī　MC hej

1. wait for; hope for.

2. (med.) name applied to inhabitants of the Jiujiang 九江 and Yuzhang 豫章 areas of present-day Jiangxi.

3. ⊙ 奚 xī 3, Tätäbi; 繫 xì 1, tie up, bind; 2, attach, conect; 蹊 xī, small footpath.

兮　xī　MC hej

1. (lit.) rhythmic particle placed at the middle or end of lines of some verse, esp. but not only verse in *sao* 騷 style, sometimes functioning to slow the rhythm, or supply a needed metrical beat, or suggest a poignant tone.

吸　xī　MC xip

1. inhale, draw breath through the mouth (ant. 呼 *hū*, exhale through the mouth).

　　a. snuffle, snuff up.

2. imbibe, drink; sip.

唏　xī　MC xj+j

1. onom. for sighing in sadness or grief, syeeh!

嘻　xī　MC xi

1. onom. for sighing (syee) or for laughing (hee).

噏　xī　MC xip

1. inhale, draw in breath.

　　a. draw together, converge; ⊙ 翕 xī 1.

夕　xī　MC zjek

1. dusk, twilight, end of day till stars come out; e.g. 日～ *rìxī*, dusk of day, ～陽 *xīyáng*, evening sunlight, last light of day.

2. evening, night; e.g. 日～ *rìxī*, day and night.

3. pay evening respects at court, evening audience.

4. to face west.

5. on the side, to the side; e.g. ～室 *xīshì*, side-rooms.

6. last decade of the ("waning") month; last season of the ("waning") year.

奚　xī　MC hej

1. gen. interr. pronoun for things (as opposed to persons): what?, where?, how?, why?; cf. 何 *hé*, 曷 *hé*, 胡 *hú*, 盍 *hé*; often equiv. 何 以 *héyǐ*; e.g. 子～不為政 *zǐ xī bùwéi zhèng*, why are you, sir, not active in government?; 子將～先 *zǐ jiāng xī xiān*, what will you give priority to?; ～可以與我友 *xī kěyǐ yǔ wǒ yǒu*, how can you become a friend with me?

　　a. ～為 *xīwèi*, on account of what > why?; e.g. ～為後我 *xīwèi hòu wǒ*, why does he put us last?; 君～為不見孟軻也 *jūn xīwèi bùjiàn mèng kē yě*, why have you, my lord, not gone to see Meng Ke?

　　b. ～以 *xīyǐ*, by means of what > how ?; e.g. ～以敬民 *xīyǐ jìng mín*, how do you show respect to the people?; ～以知之 *xīyǐ zhī zhī*, how do you know it?

2. prisoner condemned to servitude, slave(ry).

　　a. (med.) personal attendant.

3. (med.) name of a Türkic tribe, the Tätäbi, living in the northeast borderlands.

嬉　xī　MC xi

1. divert or amuse oneself; diversion; take joy in, please oneself.

巇　xī　MC xje

1. dangerously high or steep; (bn.) ～險 *xīxiǎn* (MC xje-xjemX) or 險～ *xiǎnxī*, hazardous and high, perilous peaks.

2. crevice, rift, crack.

3. justification (for), pretext.

希 xī MC xj+j

1. sparse, few; scarce, rare.

   a. disperse(d), dilute(d); reduce gradually, dissipate.

2. faint, esp. to the ear, e.g. (bn.) 〜夷 *xīyí* (MC xj+j-yij) mysteriously inaudible and invisible.

3. diaphanous, thin; rarefied.

4. look up to; admire; aspire to, hope for.

徯 xī MC hej

1. wait for; hope for.

2. ⊙ 蹊 *xī*, small footpath.

恓 xī MC sej

1. rdup. or (bn.) 〜惶 *xīhuáng* (MC sej-hwang), 〜屑 *xīxiè* (MC sej-set), perturbed, troubled; agitated, unquiet.

2. ⊙ 悽 *qī*, heartsore.

息 xī MC sik

1. exhale; respiration, suspire, breathe; e.g. 累〜 *lěixī*, bated breath.

2. to desist from, give up; abate, pause, interrupt, suspend, rest; respite.

   a. "blow out," extinguish, put an end to; abandon, lose.

3. (to) comfort, calm, assuage; treat an illness; e.g. 〜心 *xīxīn*, calm oneself, compose one's mind, be of tranquil mind; (Budd.) 〜心侣 *xīxīnlǚ*, "companion of the tranquil mind," trns. of Skt. *śramaṇa*, one who has left passions behind, monk < religious ascetic.

4. to increase, multiply; swell, grow, develop (ant. 消 *xiāo*), e.g. of children or interest on cash.

5. (med.) one's child(ren).

悉 xī MC sit

1. comprehensive(ly), complete(ly), wholly, exhaustive(ly), altogether, all of; ref. OBJ of VB (cf. 皆 *jiē*, ref. SUBJ).

   a. (med.) strongly, violently.

2. comprehend, understand fully.

惜 xī MC sjek

1. care about, care for.

   a. preserve, hold close.

   b. be attached to, chary of, grudging of.

2. regret the (real or potential) loss of, regretful, sad about.

3. (med.) reject, decline.

昔 xī MC sjek

1. formerly, in the past; ago, long ago; yesteryear.

2. ⊙ 夕 *xī* 2, night.

晞 xī MC xj+j

1. dry; to dry, dry out; dry in the sun, expose to sun.

2. faintly brightening sky, dissipating darkness.

晰 xī MC sek

1. clear, white, fair, often of skin.

   a. understand or explain with distinct clarity.

曦 xī MC xje

1. sun-flash, sun-sheen, solar blaze; heliacal; e.g. 赫〜 *hèxī*, rutilant sun-sheen.

析 xī MC sek

1. to split apart, separate, divide, break apart; break open.

   a. analyze, explicate, go into the particulars of.

   b. resolve; dissipate.

2. rdup., onom. for sound of wind in trees, rushing and rustling.

3. 〜木 *xīmù*, "Split Wood," one of the 12 Jupiter stations, incl. stars in the lunar lodgings 尾 *wěi* and 箕 *jī*.

樨 xī MC sej

1. abb. form of 木犀 *mùxī*, sweet olive; → 犀 *xī*.

欷 xī MC xj+j

1. onom. of sighing or sobbing: syehh.

   a. bewail, bemoan.

歙 xī MC xip

1. breathe in, inhale.

2. draw together, collect; narrow down (ant. 張 *zhāng*, draw out).

3. pleased, satisfied.

4. rdup., unbiased and impartial, equitable; also, mutually amenable, complete concord.

   shè MC syep

1. grab, catch, seize.

2. (med.) ～侯 *shèhóu* (MC syep-huw) trsc. Turk. *yabghu* (< Iran. *yāvuka*), Türkic high military title, "troop-assembler."

汐　xī　MC zjek

1. nighttime tide (cf. 潮 *cháo*, tide, general or daytime).
2. ebb-tide.

淅　xī　MC sek

1. to wash rice.
2. onom. in various contexts; rdup. rushing and rustling, of wind-tossed leaves in trees, ⊙ 析析 *xīxī*; also, of rushing water.
   a. (bn.) ～瀝 *xīlì* (MC sek-lek) gurgling and babbling (water); pashing and pattering (falling rain or snow).

溪　xī　MC khej

1. mountain stream, burn, bourn; creek, runnel; torrent.
   a. (med.) stream-bed, watercourse in mountains; gorge, clough; ⊙ 谿 *xī*.
2. (bn.) ～刻 *xīkè* (MC khej-khok), petty and perverse.
3. ～蓀 *xīsūn*, syn. 菖蒲 *chāngpú*, sweet-flag, calamus; also, blood-red iris (*Iris sanguinea*).

熄　xī　MC sik

1. extinguish a fire; quench.
2. ⊙ 息 *xī* 2b, put an end to, bring to a close.

熙　xī　MC xi

1. shine brightly; glitter, sparkle, emicate; emicacious, radiant.
   a. to glory in.
   b. dry out with warmth; parch.
2. serene; satisfied.
   a. content(ed), well-pleased.
3. spring forth, spark; appear, arise.
   a. expand, extend; grow, thrive.
4. onom. of sighing.
5. ⊙ 嬉 *xī*, amuse(ment), divert.

熹　xī　MC xi

1. brilliantly glowing.
   a. to warm, heat, chafe; bake.

燨　xī　MC xi

1. aglow with light, brilliant.

2. firelight; blaze; lend warmth to.
   a. prosper, strengthen; increase, expand.
3. ⊙ 饎 *chì*, roast, bake.

犀　xī　MC sej

1. rhinoceros.
   a. rhinoceros-horn.
2. sharp and solid, well-honed and sturdy.
3. calabash seeds; because white and well-set > euph. for fine teeth.
4. 木～ *mùxī*, sweet-olive, osmanthus (*Osmanthus fragrans*), evergreen shrub or small tree with fragrant yellowish-white flowers syn. 桂 *guì* 2; also, white melilot or white sweet-clover.

犧　xī　MC xje

1. beast (ox, sheep, or pig) used in ancient sacrificial rites, preferably of pure white color.
   a. sacrificial victim.

稀　xī　MC xj+j

1. ⊙ 希 *xī* 1, sparse, few; scarce, rare; disperse(d), dilute(d); 2, faint-sounding; 3, diaphanous, thin; rarefied.

窆　xī　MC zjek

1. ⊙ 夕 *xī* 2 evening; night.
   a. cmpd. 窀～ *zhūnxī*, unfathomable night > inter, inhume, entomb; tomb-pit, grave.
2. (med.) tomb-pit, gravesite.

錫　xī　MC sek

1. fine hemp cloth.
2. bottom hem of lower garment or skirt.

羲　xī　MC xje

1. element in name of mythological figures: abb. for Fu Xi 伏～, legendary figure responsible for invention or regularization of many aspects of traditional culture, e.g. invention of the eight trigrams (*gua* 卦) of *Yijing*; ～和 *xīhé*, charioteer of the sun; also two officials Xi and He, pair of calendrical experts in time of sage-king Yao 堯.
2. breath, vapor; aspire to.
3. ⊙ 曦 *xī*, sun-flash.

翕　xī　MC xip

1. draw together, converge.
   a. concentrate, combine, collect; merge, blend; e.g. (bn.) ～赩 *xīxì* (MC xip-xik), full-flushed red.

b. massed, abundant; flourishing; e.g. ～赫 *xīhè*, grandiose, majestic; illustrious, brilliant. **c.** contract, pull back; e.g. ～然 *xīrán*, in pursed-together manner; also, in thorough or consistent manner.
2. onom. of rustling or brushing of clothing, wind, etc.

翖   xī   MC xip   ⊙翕 *xī*.

肸   xī   MC xit
1. stir up, excite, activate.
a. rdup. or (bn.) ～蠁 *xīxiàng* (MC xit–xjangX), stir and spread everywhere.

腊   xī   MC sjek
1. dried or pickled meat.
a. dried and wrinkled skin.
2. extremely; to a great degree or for a long time.

膝   xī   MC sit
1. knee.
a. to kneel.

菥   xī   MC sek
1. (bn.) ～蓂 *xīmì* (MC sek-mek), pennycress, stinkweed (*Thlaspi arvense*), small, leafy white-flowering weed.
sī   MC sje
1. a type of oat.

蜥   xī   MC sek
1. (bn.) ～蜴 *xīyì* (MC sek-yek), skink, various small lizard species of the family *Scincidae*.

蟋   xī   MC sit
1. (bn.) ～蟀 *xīshuài* (MC sit-srwit), field-cricket (*Gryllulus chinensis*), shiny black in color; also, onom. of its stridulent, chirping sound.

蠵   xī   MC hwej
1. sgl. or (bn.) 觜～ *zīxī*, loggerhead turtle, → 觜 *zī* 2; syn. 靈龜 *língguī*.

裼   xī   MC sek
1. divest oneself of an outer garment, revealing those underneath or one's uncovered body; strip, disrobe, unclothe, expose.
tì   MC thejH
1. infant's swaddling clothes.

西   xī   MC sej
1. west, western, westward, westering; in *wuxing* correspondences associated with the agent metal, season of autumn, color white, etc.
a. place of honor given to respected guest, e.g. ～席 *xīxí*, the west mat.
b. often ref. Central Asia, places along the Silk Road, and beyond; e.g. ～域 *xīyù*, the "Western Regions," gen. term for Chinese Turkestan; (med.) 安～ *ānxī*, "the Pacified West," Tang protectorate controlling city-states of the Tarim Basin.

谿   xī   MC khej
1. stream-bed or watercourse in the mountains (with or without water).
a. narrow valley, gorge, clough.
b. (med.) ⊙溪 *xī*, mountain stream, bourn; creek.

豨   xī   MC xj+j
1. pig, swine.

蹊   xī   MC hej
1. footpath.
2. trudge on foot, pass or press onward.

醯   xī   MC xej
1. vinegar; sour or acrid taste.

錫   xī   MC sek
1. tin; pewter.
a. (Budd.) sgl. or ～丈 *xīzhàng*, Budd. monk's tin-ringed staff (Skt. *khakkara*)
b. tin-colored, smoky-gray.
cì   MC sjeH
1. confer on, bestow(al); gift, present(ation); ⊙賜 *cì* 1.
a. inform, provide information.
2. frontlet, metallic decoration for horse's forehead.
3. ⊙緆 *xī* 1, fine cloth.

騱   xī   MC hej
1. (bn.) 驒～ *diānxī*, → 驒 *diān* (*tuó*).

鸂   xī   MC khej
1. (bn.) ～鶒 *xīchì* (MC khej-trhik), tufted duck (*Aythya fuligula*), larger than the mandarin duck, with more purple in coloring, usu. found in pairs.

xí

席　xí　MC zjek
1. mat, usu. thin and loom-woven, placed on top of undermat of bamboo (筵 *yán*), hence > overmat.
   a. (med.) feast, banquet, entertainment (enjoyed while seated on mat).
2. matting; sail.
3. (med.) official position, or seat of responsibility.
4. rely on, depend on.

楮　xí　MC sjek
1. rugose tree-bark, wrinkled, ridged.

榴　xí　MC zip
1. large bar or wedge that joins the two holes of a cangue.
2. bar of a balustrade.

檄　xí　MC hek
1. incitement, prompture.
   a. military call-to-arms, usu. denouncing and detailing transgressions of the enemy; e.g. 羽〜 *yǔxí*, winged call-to-arms, imperial war summons with bird-plume attached to indicate need for quick action.

習　xí　MC zip
1. to exercise oneself, practice, habituate oneself, rehearse, learn by repeated action; pursue.
   a. teach, exercise, train.
2. habituated to, versed in, familiar with, accustomed to, experienced in.
   a. habitude, regular practice, custom(ary); customarily, regularly; routine(ly).
   b. repeat, redo, reiterate.
3. multitude, mass; repeated number of occurrences, repetition, as of (Budd.) contacts of sense-organs with their objects.
4. close to, intimate with; close acquaintance(s).
5. rdup., onom. of light breeze, softly wafting; also, of the flutter or flapping of a bird's wings.

蓆　xí　MC zjek
1. large, ample, capacious.
   a. abundant; rife.
2. ⊙ 席 *xí* 1, mat.

襲　xí　MC zip
1. add a second layer to clothing; cover.
   a. overclothes; overcoat.
   b. repeat, double; reiterate; return to.
2. put on clothing, dress oneself.
   a. turn down sleeves that were previously turned up.
   b. dress a corpse.
3. measure-word for ensemble of clothing.
4. inherit; perpetuate, continue; hereditary; e.g. 〜封 *xífēng*, inherit a fiefdom; 〜逮 *xídài*, carry on in unbroken fashion.
   a. conform (to), cooperate, accord with, join, associate, go along with.
5. accept, receive, take in.
6. follow along, follow after; e.g. 〜迹 *xíjī*, follow in the traces (of one's predecessors).
7. assail, attack (esp. by surprise), invade; work one's way into, steal into.
   a. appropriate fraudulently; plagiarize.
8. to hide away, cover over.
9. (bn.) 〜雜 *xízá* (MC zip-dzop), in disarray, hodge-podge, ming-mang, simsam, mixed and messed.

覡　xí　MC hek
1. shaman; N.B. this word is often defined as "male shaman," contrasted with 巫 *wū*, supposedly "female shaman," but the two words are most often used interchangeably with no gender distinction.

隰　xí　MC zip
1. lowlands; wetlands, fen.
2. land newly opened for cultivation; dressed or scored field.

xǐ

喜　xǐ　MC xiX
1. delight in, joy(ful), happiness usu. of a temporary nature; light-hearted(ness), glad(ness), mirth(ful).
2. felicitous, well-suited.
3. ⊙ 嬉 *xī*, diverting; 熙 *xī* 1, shine brightly, glory in.

屣　xǐ　MC srjeX
1. single-soled thin slippers, sandals (cf. 舄 *xì*, double-soled slippers).
   a. to scuttle, scoot.
2. gen. term for footwear.

xī　MC xje

1. ⊙ 羲 *xī*, 2nd element in name of the culture-hero Fuxi 伏～.

huī　MC xjwe

1. ⊙ 麾 *huī* 1, military banner or standard.

hū　MC xu

1. ⊙ 呼 *hū*, in exclamatory expression 於～ *wūhū*, ah me!

瀉　xì　MC sjek

1. salt-blanched land; sterile land.
   a. salt-marsh.

盻　xì　MC hejH

1. scowl, glare at.
2. look wide-eyed at; entranced.

禊　xì　MC hejH

1. spring purification ceremony to clean away inauspicious influences, traditionally carried out at riverside on the first *si* 巳 day of 3rd month; later regularized on 3rd day of 3rd month.

系　xì　MC hejH

1. connect(ed) in series; continuum; succession.
   a. filiation, lineage, genealogy.
   b. relationship, connection, association; enlist(ment).
2. bind, tie(d) together, link(ed); truss up.
   a. belt, girdle, band.
3. system(atize).
4. depend(ent), suspend(ed), hang from.
5. (lit.) coda of a *fu* 賦 poem (alt. called *luan* 亂).

細　xì　MC sejH

1. minimal in size, minute, minuscule, tiny (ant. 大 *dà*, large); e.g. (med.) ～末 *xìmò*, powder.
   a. slight, spare; thin, lean.
   b. ～辛 *xìxīn*, wild ginger (*Asarum*, various species).
2. fine, fine-set, close-set; delicate.
   a. precise, detail(ed), go into in detail; meticulous, exact(ing), careful; thorough (syn. 精 *jīng*, fine, essential; ant. 粗 *cū*, bulky, crude).
   b. (med.) excellent, of finest quality; e.g. (bn.) ～膩 *xìnì* (MC sejH-nrijH), lustrously lovely.
3. nice(ty), particular(ity).
4. unsparing, exigent; fastidious, picayune.

5. of minor worth or importance, of no account, not much, nugatory, paltry, as of infertile or low-grade land or of an inconsequential person.
6. of sound, soft, not resonant.
7. (med.) young, youthful; immature.
8. ～草 *xìcǎo*, milkwort (*Polygala tenuifolia*), herb used medicinally, produces lavender to purple flowers; syn. 遠志 *yuǎnzhì*.

綌　xì　MC khjaek

1. coarse or unfinished kudzu cloth.

繫　xì　MC hejH

1. bind, gird, tie(d) together, twist together, braid; link(ed); connect(ed), associate(d).
2. attach(ed), connect(ed) in series; continuum.
   a. associated, related.
3. belt, girdle, band; cord.
   a. truss up, tie together; join together.
4. depend(ent), hang from; bring down.
5. abb. ref. to *Xici* commentary 繫辭傳 on the *Yijing*.

舄　xì　MC sjek

1. double-soled slipper, with upturned toe (cf. 屣 *xǐ*, single-soled slipper).
   a. wood-soled shoe.
2. general term for shoe.
3. base of a pillar.
4. ⊙ 瀉 *xì*, salt-blanched land.

赩　xì　MC xik

1. heavy red, rich red, carmine.

郤　xì　MC khjaek　⊙ 郤 *xì*.

郤　xì　MC khjaek

1. ⊙ 隙 *xì* 1, breach, cleft; 2, riff, discord.
2. a surname.

隙　xì　MC khjaek

1. chink, crack in a wall, cleft; e.g. ～駒 *xìjú*, "colt through a crack," glimpse through a gap in the wall a colt running past, metaphorical for the swift passage of life.
   a. breach, rift, fissure, gap, rent; interruption.
2. divergence, alienation, rift, rupture; discord, dissent.
3. juxtapose; adjoin, contiguous.

灥   xì   MC xj+jH

1. (bn.) 灅~ *yǐxì*, → 灅 *yǐ* (*ài*).

饩   xì   MC xj+jH

1. to present living animals or uncooked grain to someone, to be used as sacrificial offerings.
   a. the items so given.
2. be sated.
3. (med.) official salary.

鬩   xì   MC xek

1. fall out of agreement; contend, fight; compete.

xiā

呀   xiā   MC xae

1. completely empty, gapingly empty.
2. gape-mouthed, agape.

呷   xiā   MC xaep

1. suck up, sip, drink, imbibe; swallow; inhale.

岈   xiā   MC xae

1. (med.) cavernously deep.
2. (med.) deep-delving valley.

瞎   xiā   MC xaet

1. (med.) blind in one eye.
   a. (med.) purblind; regardless, unmindful, heedless.

蝦   xiā   MC xae

1. gen. term for arthropods. esp. crustaceans.
2. ⊙ 鰕 *xiā*, shrimp.
   há   MC hae
1. (bn.) ~蟆 *hámá* (MC hae-mae), small toad.
   xiá   MC hae
1. ⊙ 霞 *xiá*, reddish-pink clouds.

谺   xiā   MC xae

1. (bn.) 谽~ *hānxiā*, → 谽 *hān*.

鰕   xiā   MC xae

1. pink or red crustacean; river-shrimp; prawn.
2. cmpd. 海~ *hǎixiā*, crayfish.

xiá

俠   xiá   MC hep

1. gallant(ry), zeal(ous), esp. to assist those in need or mistreated.

a. resolute, steadfast, unwavering in word and deed; valiant, courageous; chivalrous.
   b. cavalier, gallant, swashbuckler, bravo.
2. ⊙ 夾 *jiā* 1, hem in from both sides, close round.

匣   xiá   MC haep

1. coffer, case, small chest (cf. 箱 *xiāng*, large chest, cabinet).
   a. pyx, for revered articles; pyxis, for toiletries.
   b. to encase in a container.

峽   xiá   MC heap

1. steep-cut river gorge.
   a. often ref. the famous 3 gorges of the upper Yangzi.

暇   xiá   MC haeH

1. interval of unoccupied time; repose, respite, leisure; holiday.
   a. at ease, unhurried, restful, relax(ed); easy-going, carefree.
   jiǎ   MC kaeX
1. ⊙ 假 *jiǎ* 1, avail of, borrow the use of.

柙   xiá   MC haep

1. wooden enclosure for penning wild animals.
   a. encage, imprison.
2. coffer, case, small chest; scabbard.
   a. encase.
   jiǎ   MC kaep
1. (med.) an "aromatic tree," but unidentified.

狎   xiá   MC haep

1. grow accustomed to, become familiar or comfortable with, habituated to.
2. be overly familiar with, too intimate, disrespectful.
   a. impertinent, insolent; frivolous.
   b. toy with, trifle, banter, fiddle with.
3. crowd(ed) together; e.g. (bn.) ~恰 *xiáqià* (MC haep-kheap), at close quarters, hugger-mugger.
4. alternate, one and then the other.

狹   xiá   MC heap

1. narrow, confining, strait(ened); tight, squeezed (ant. 寬 *kuān*, broad; 廣 *guǎng*, spacious).
   a. cramp(ed), limit(ed), restrain(ed); narrow-minded, uptight, illiberal.
   b. mean, humble.
   c. be few, less(ened); small; belittle, disparage.
2. incite, push toward, hurry.
3. (med.) ⊙ 狎 *xiá* 2, close to, overly familiar with.

瑕　**xiá**　MC hae
1. flaw in jade surface; scratch, scar, chip.
　　a. imperfection, defect; blemish, fault; botch, error; shortcoming, weakness.
　　b. leave a mark; scar(red).
2. ⊙ 遐 *xiá* 2, interr.: why?

硤　**xiá**　MC heap　⊙ 峽 *xiá*.

祫　**xiá**　MC heap
1. collective sacrifice to distant and near ancestors, carried out by ruler or nobles at three-year intervals.

蕸　**xiá**　MC hae
1. lotus leaves.

椵　**xiá**　MC hae
1. rubescent, rubicund.
　　a. rose-hued.

轄　**xiá**　MC haet
1. wheel-axle cap with linchpin.
2. (med.) to control, direct, keep steady, govern, regulate.
　　a. (med.) restrain, restrict; force, compel.

遐　**xiá**　MC hae
1. far-advanced, far extent.
　　a. far distant, far off; to go far away.
　　b. lasting in time; e.g. ～齡 *xiálíng*, advanced in years, far extent of age.
2. interr.: why? (in early texts)

鎋　**xiá**　MC haet
1. ⊙ 轄 *xiá* 1, linchpin.

陜　**xiá**　MC heap
1. ⊙ 狹 *xiá* 1, narrow; 峽 *xiá*, gorge.

陿　**xiá**　MC heap　⊙ 陜 *xiá*.

霞　**xiá**　MC hae
1. rose-pink clouds of dawn or dusk; e.g. 碧～ *bìxiá*, rose-pink clouds against the cyan-blue sky.
　　a. dawn-flush; auroral clouds, aurora(e).
　　b. rose-pink, roseate < color of cooked shrimp (蝦 *xiā*).
2. bright-colored or pastel mist.
3. ⊙ 遐 *xiá* 1, far-advanced.

騢　**xiá**　MC hae
1. sorrel horse, with mixed copper-red and white coat, chestnut.
　　a. sorrel-colored.

鶷　**xiá**　MC haet
1. (bn.) ～鷃 *xiáhé* (MC haet-'aet), variously identified, but in lit. always a herald of spring; prob. bush-warbler (*Horornis diphone*), perhaps white-cheeked starling (*Sturnus cineraceus*), or a larger shrike (a species of *Lanius*).

點　**xiá**　MC heat
1. cunning, sly, shrewd; disingenuous, guileful.
　　a. blackguard; malicious, ill-disposed.
2. (med.) ingenious, clever, resourceful.

xià

下　**xià**　MC haeX
1. below, low(er), under; at the bottom; down(ward).
　　a. low(er) in rank or position, lowly, inferior; underling, subaltern.
　　b. humble form of self-reference, "this lowly person."
　　xià　MC haeH
1. go down, descend; get off; decline, fall; condescend; retire, withdraw.
　　a. send down from above, as orders, proclamations.
2. to lower, bring down; throw down, cast down, topple, depose; raze, ruin; reduce.
　　a. look down on; disparage, misprize.
　　b. submit to, abase(ment).
3. second in a series of two, secondary; last in a series of three or more.
　　a. next in time.
　　b. (med.) complete an act or task, do and set it down.
4. measure-word for actions.

夏　**xià**　MC haeH
1. summertime, 2nd three months of the year; estival; season corresponding to the agent fire, the south, the heart, the color red; e.g. ～臘 *xiàlà*, from summer through the twelfth month, metonymy for a year.

xià　MC haeX
1. ancient name of the Han (Chinese) people and their land.
2. grand, vast.
3. ⊙ 廈 *xià*, mansion.
4. ～侯 *xiàhóu*, a bisyllabic surname.
5. 大～ *dàxià*, Bactria.

jiǎ　MC kaeX
1. ⊙ 榎 *jiǎ*, catalpa tree.

廈　xià　MC haeX
1. large, grand house; mansion, manor.
   a. manorial, palatial.

罅　xià　MC xaeH
1. split open; rend.
   a. rift, crevice, crack, fissure.
2. rift, split; rupture; alienation, disaffection.

苄　xià　MC haeH　→ 苄 *hù.*

xiān

仙　xiān　MC sjen
1. (Dao.) transcendent being; one who has moved beyond the needs and limits of the mundane world into the realm of spiritualization or divinity. In Shangqing Dao. exceeded in status and attainment by *zhenren* 真人, "Perfected" or "Realized Persons." N.B. Although extraordinarily long-lived, a *xian* is not "immortal."
   a. transcendent, of character, quality, or beauty; sylphine; of seemingly holy or celestial beauty; light and airy, subtle.
2. rise up, ascend; transcend.
3. (Budd.) trns. of Skt. *ṛṣi*, seer, sage, wise man; 大～ *dàxiān*, great sage, a buddha.

僊　xiān　MC sjen　⊙ 仙 *xiān.*

先　xiān　MC sen
1. former, previous, preceding, prior; premier, pre-; at first, first of all; before in time or space; in front.
   a. predecessor(s); ancestor(s).
   b. (Dao.) ～天 *xiāntiān*, prior Heaven, or prior to Heaven, primal stages of cosmos before the current world (which is 後天 *hòutiān*, latter Heaven, or subsequent to Heaven).

2. of first importance, premier; precedent; leading.
   a. (med.) ～陀 *xiāntuó*, quick-witted, alert; resourceful.
3. (med.) already; originally.
   a. one before the last; e.g. ～日 *xiānrì*, day before yesterday.

xiàn　MC senH
1. precede, go first, go ahead of.
   a. introduce.
2. put or place first; make a priority of; consider of first importance.
   a. take the initiative, lead.

嬐　xiān　MC sjem
1. ⊙ 纖 *xiān* 2, slight, fine; 4, chary, sparing.

qiān　MC tshjem
1. ⊙ 纖 *xiān* 3, crafty, clever; (bn.) ～趨 *qiānqū* (MC tshjem-tshju), cunningly clever, craftily crooked.

忺　xiān　MC xjaem
1. (med.) agree(able), enjoy(able); comfortable, satisfied.

憸　xiān　MC sjem
1. flattering, disingenuous; calculating, designing; perfidious.

掀　xiān　MC xjon
1. lift, raise up; bring up; lift out.
   a. drag out; pull aside.
2. (med.) turn over.

祆　xiān　MC xen
1. (med.) creator-god Ahura Mazda, of Zoroastrianism.
2. ref. to Central or South Asian peoples, for which this reading applied to 天 *tiān* as, e.g. 天竺 *tiānzhú*, → 天 *tiān* 6.

秈　xiān　MC sjen
1. non-glutinous rice that ripens early, in the sixth or seventh month.

纖　xiān　MC sjem
1. fine-woven silk.
2. slight, fine.
   a. slender, thin; delicate, gracile; graceful; rdup. fine and fragile; ～腰 *xiānyào*, slender waist.

3. subtle; crafty, clever.
4. chary, sparing; stingy, niggardly.
5. ～阿 *xiān'à*, alternate name of Wangshu 望舒, mythological charioteer of the moon.

jiān　MC tsjem
1. (med.) sharp, pointed; pierce.
   a. thin, pointed bamboo or wooden cane; bamboo slip; also, toothpick; ⊙ 籤 *qiān*.

躚　xiān　MC sen
1. (bn.) 蹁～ *piánxiān* (MC ben-sen), whirling and swirling.
   a. (med.) rdup., swaying and spinning.

銛　xiān　MC sjem
1. mattock, grubbing-axe.
2. acuminate, pointed, sharp, keen.

鮮　xiān　MC sjen
1. fresh fish.
   a. newly slaughtered animal flesh.
   b. savory, delicious.
2. fresh, new; renewed.
   a. vital, lively, invigorating, salutary.
3. bright, vivid; e.g. ～白 *xiānbái*, pure white.
4. to die before one's time.
5. ～卑 *xiānbēi*, the Särbi, proto-Mongolian tribe that attacked the Xiongnu 匈奴 at the end of the Han and established a confederacy in the north during the next few centuries, the high point being the establishment of the Northern Wei 北魏 dynasty (386-534) by the Tabgach (Ch. Tuoba 拓跋), a tribe within the confederacy.

xiǎn　MC sjenX
1. few; rare; seldom.

xián

咸　xián　MC heam
1. marker of inclusivity usu. ref. to SUBJ: total(ly), in all cases; entire(ly), integral(ly), in toto, complete(ly); universal.
   a. "Entirety," name of 31st hexagram of *Yijing*.
2. all-encompassing; everywhere.
   a. cmpd. ～池 *xiánchí*, all-encompassing pool: name of an ancient musical piece reputedly from the time of Yao 堯; also, name of a mythological pool in the east where the sun reputedly bathes; also, name of constellation made up of ρ, λ Aurigae.
   b. everyone.

嗛　xián　MC haem
1. ⊙ 銜 *xián* 1-4.

qiǎn　MC khemX
1. cheek-pouch of monkey; gizzard of bird.

qiàn　MC khemH
1. ⊙ 歉 *qiàn*, inadequate, deficient.

嫌　xián　MC hem
1. be apprehensive of, doubt, mistrust.
   a. demur; take exception to.
2. be averse to; disinclined toward; find offensive, dislike.
   a. (med.) displeased with, dissatisfied.
3. touch on; be near to.

嫺　xián　MC hean
1. distinguished; refined.
2. well-versed in, well-trained, adept.

嫻　xián　MC hean　⊙ 嫺 *xián*.

弦　xián　MC hen
1. bowstring; taut cord.
   a. straight; taut.
   b. thin, thready, as of pulse.
2. stringed instruments in general; e.g. ～歌 *xián'gē*, singing accompanied by stringed instruments; euph. for proper governing as a district magistrate (< *Lunyu* 17.4).
3. chord of an arc.
   a. first or last quarter ("chord") of the moon, when its face is half-full as if cut straight down the middle.
4. euph. for wife.

慊　xián　MC hem
1. ⊙ 嫌 *xián* 1-3.

qiè　MC khep
1. content(ed), pleased; satisfied.

憪　xián　MC hean
1. leisurely, comfortable.

xiàn　MC heanX
1. uneasy; disturbed.

涎　xián　MC zjen
1. saliva, spittle; sputum.
   a. slime.
2. envious, lustful, in a sweat for, drooling over.
3. ～衣草 *xiányīcǎo*, summer cypress, mock cypress (*Kochia scoparia*), also called 地膚 *dìfū*.

diàn   MC denH

1. rdup., glossy and glowing, dewy and damp.

癇   xián   MC hean

1. convulsions; epilepsy; esp. ref. those 10 years and under (cf. 癲 *diān*).

瞷   xián   MC hean

1. wall-eyed, with abnormal amount of white showing.
2. powerful, mighty; martial; valiant.

jiàn   MC keanH

1. be on watch for, spy out.

礥   xián   MC hen

1. durable; hard; difficult(y); rdup., arduous and wearying.

絃   xián   MC hen

1. string, cord, esp. of chordophone instruments.
2. ⊙ 弦 *xián*.

舷   xián   MC hen

1. (med.) side or flank of a boat.

蚿   xián   MC hen

1. millipede.

諴   xián   MC hen

1. urgent, pressing; imperative.

諴   xián   MC heam

1. accord with, be in harmony; concord, united.

賢   xián   MC hen

1. worthy, esp. in character or virtue; usu. considered 2nd in moral character and charisma only to a sage (*sheng* 聖).
   a. estimable, admirable.
   b. (med.) honorific epithet for deceased.
2. having highest competence, excelling others.
3. (med.) honorific 2nd-person pronoun, "esteemed sir"; e.g. (Budd.) ～者 *xiánzhe*, "my excellent fellow," trns. Skt. *āyuṣmat*, used in addressing persons of same or younger generation.
4. (Budd.) morally good, trns. Skt. *bhadra*; e.g. ～善 *xiánshàn*, benevolent; ～劫 *xiánjié*, the present kalpa (because one in which 5 buddhas are to appear).
5. (med.) ～豆 *xiándòu* (MC hen-duwH), gen. term for India, trsc. of Iran. *hinduka* (< Skt.

sindhu, name of Indus River) ref. to people who live beyond the Indus River.

銜   xián   MC haem

1. transverse bit, snaffle.
2. to snaffle, clench in one's teeth, hold tightly in the mouth.
   a. contain, keep control of.
   b. be in close contact; e.g. ～尾 *xiánwěi*, "holding the tail," nose-to-tail, in continuous order.
   c. interlock(ing), fit together.
3. hold in one's heart or mind; e.g. ～意 *xiányì*, full of thoughts.
   a. conceal, harbor, esp. ill feelings.
4. accept, receive.
   a. (med.) relish, enjoy.
5. (med.) official rank, esp. nominal office, brevet rank.

閑   xián   MC hean

1. barred gate, bar(rier).
   a. railing; pen, corral.
   b. pleasance, imperial pasture for government animals; range.
2. protect, guard against; obstruct.
   a. restrain; train, discipline.
3. ⊙ 閒 *xián* 1, inactive, idle, at leisure, bootless; 2, comfortable with; well-versed in.

閒   xián   MC hean

1. inactive, idle(ness), unoccupied; e.g. ～月 *xiányuè*, fallow month, when no farmwork is done.
   a. relaxed, at leisure, otiant, languid; comfort(able); e.g. ～居 *xiánjū*, dwelling at leisure, unheedful of the larger world; rdup., or 等～ *děngxián*, quite unconcerned.
   b. (med.) useless, bootless, of no value; e.g. ～語 *xiányǔ*, discussion that leads nowhere.
2. comfortable (with), composed, at ease (with).
   a. well-versed (in); well-trained.
3. ⊙ 間 *jiān, jiàn*, in all meanings, for which it was original graph; 閑 *xián* 1, bar(rier); 嫺 *xián*, distinguished, refined.

鷳   xián   MC hean

1. fireback pheasant (*Lophura nycthemera*).
   a. 白～ *báixián*, white fireback, white lophura.
2. sparrowhawk.

鹹　xián　MC heam
1. salty; brine; brackish.
2. acerbic, sarcastic.

麙　xián　MC heam
1. small goat-antelope, incl. serow (*Capricornis miineedwardsii*) and esp. goral (*Nemorhaedus*, various species).

xiǎn

尠　xiǎn　MC sjenX
1. few; rare, seldom; ⊙ 鮮 *xiǎn* (*xiān*).

勫　xiǎn　MC sjenX　⊙ 尠 *xiǎn*.

嶮　xiǎn　MC xjem　⊙ 險 *xiǎn*.

幰　xiǎn　MC xjonX
1. curtain of a carriage.
   a. metonymy for carriage.

毨　xiǎn　MC senX
1. moulted and renewed plumage of bird, shed and regrown coat of beast.
   a. renew; (re)fashion, (re)arrange.

燹　xiǎn　MC senX
1. wildfire, brushfire.
   a. fires of war; incendiary warfare.
2. set fire to, burn up.

獫　xiǎn　MC xjemX
1. long-snouted hunting dog.
2. (bn.) ～狁 *xiǎnyǔn* (MC xjemX-ywinX), northern barbarian tribe known in Zhou period, later regarded as ancestors of the Xiongnu 匈奴; northern hordes.

獮　xiǎn　MC sjenX
1. autumnal hunt, in early times.
   a. to hunt, kill.

玁　xiǎn　MC xjemX　⊙ 獫 *xiǎn*.

蘚　xiǎn　MC sjenX
1. (med.) lichen.

蜆　xiǎn　MC xenX
1. freshwater basket-clam (*Corbicula leana*).

蠌　xiǎn　MC xenX　⊙ 蜆 *xiǎn*.

跣　xiǎn　MC senX
1. barefoot; unshod.

銑　xiǎn　MC senX
1. metallic gloss, polish.
2. bow fitted with metal-tipped ends.
3. pointed spines on the vertical sides of chime-bell.
   a. projecting angles of a bell's mouth.
4. small chisel.

險　xiǎn　MC xjemX
1. a defile, fastness, strategic pass; cramped, constricted; strait, confined.
2. hazard(ous), peril(ous), danger(ous), treacherous; e.g. ～易 *xiǎnyì*, peril and ease; cramped and cleared; (bn.) ～巇 *xiǎnxī* (MC xjemX-xje), perilous peaks, hazardous and high.
3. sinister, treacherous; deceitful, e.g. ～易 *xiǎnyì*, devious and candid.
   a. (med.) provocative, tempting, e.g. ～妝 *xiǎnzhuāng*, seductive makeup.
4. out of the way; unconventional, peculiar; awry.
5. on the point of, almost.
6. (med.) frightful, frightening; shocking.

韅　xiǎn　MC xenX
1. cinch-strap, girth for carriage horse.

顯　xiǎn　MC xenX
1. evident, manifest, apparent; visible.
   a. to manifest, show forth, display, reveal; appear; e.g. ～晦 *xiǎnhuì*, light and dark; act and rest; advance and retreat; take office and retire.
   b. make evident, make clear; demonstrate, explain; e.g. ～布 *xiǎnbù*, proclaim, announce; ～發 *xiǎnfā*, expound, state explicitly.
2. distinguished, prominent; celebrated; illustrious.
   a. honorific ref. to ancestors.
3. (Budd.) miracle, marvel, wonder.

xiàn

倆　xiàn　MC haenX
1. martial mien; virile, manly.
   a. daunting; formidable.

2. open-armed, all-embracing; magnanimous; great-hearted.

3. ⊙ 嫺 *xián*, distinguished; well-versed in.

峴   xiàn   MC henX

1. small but steep mountain, butte, scarp.

2. name of a mountain outside Xiangyang 襄陽 in north-central Hubei.

憲   xiàn   MC xjonH

1. regulation, law, standard; promulgation.
    a. promulgate, publish; explicate.

2. take as a standard; emulate; exemplar(y).

3. (med.) ～司 *xiànsī*, alt. title for censor (*yushi* 御史).

獻   xiàn   MC xjonH

1. proffer, tender, present to; offer up.

2. exhibit, display; show.
    a. celebrate.

3. document.

4. worthy (person), syn. 賢 *xián* 1.
        suō   MC sa

1. method of filtering wine for use in sacrifice.

2. ritual vessel for offering of sacrificial wine.

現   xiàn   MC henH

1. (med.) appear, show forth, make present.
    a. (Budd.) explain, develop; preach.

2. (med.) be present; at present, actual; e.g. ～前 *xiànqián*, now before one, in one's presence; here to hand; ready, emerge(nt).
    a. (Budd.) ～在 *xiànzài*, is present, appear now; right now, at this moment; ～身 *xiànshēn*, one's true body; ～世 *xiànshì*, in the present life.
    b. (Budd.) ～行 *xiànxíng*, manifest(ation); ～相 *xiànxiàng*, present marking; hint; allusion.

3. (med.) act as if.

睍   xiàn   MC henX

1. eyes agape, bug-eyed.
    a. (med.) rdup., fearful glance, peek furtively.

2. (bn.) ～睆 *xiànhuàn* (MC henX-hwaenX), attractively agreeable, prettily pleasing, of appearance or of birdsong.

綫   xiàn   MC sjenH   ⊙ 線 *xiàn*.

線   xiàn   MC sjenH

1. thread, string; filament; line.

a. trifling amount, petty, smitch; inconsequential.

b. ray, as of light; mote.

2. ins and outs, long and short of a matter; circumstances.

縣   xiàn   MC hwenH

1. smallest unit of local administration controlled by appointees from the central government: district, county; e.g. ～官 *xiànguān*, district offices staffed from central government; government in general, esp. the court; Han sometimes ref. to emperor; ～令 *xiànlìng*, district magistrate, chief district official appointed from central government; ～承 *xiànchéng*, district adjuvant, deputy magistrate; ～尉 *xiànwèi*, district commandant, overseer of local military affairs, taxation, etc., lowest centrally appointed official.

        xuán   MC hwen

1. ⊙ 懸 *xuán*, suspend(ed); connect(ed).

2. weigh(t), evaluate.

3. (med.) elongated, far separate, remote; very different.

羨   xiàn   MC zjenH

1. avid (for), hanker (for), covet.
    a. envy; admire.

2. surplus, superabundance; excess; (bn.) ～漫 *xiànmàn* (MC zjenH-manH), run on and on, spread and swell, diffusely dispersed.
    a. exceed, surpass; exaggerate; overdo.
        yàn   MC yenH

1. invite; introduce.
    a. engage in or with.
        yán   MC yen

1. tomb passageway, tomb entrance.

莧   xiàn   MC heanH

1. sgl. or ～菜 *xiàncài*, amaranth (*Amaranthus mangostanus*), small herbaceous plant, in flower late summer to early autumn, used mainly in food but a yellow or green dye can be made from leaves.
    a. ～陸 *xiànlù*, pokeberry (*Phytolacca acinosa*).
    b. 馬～ *mǎxiàn*, → 馬 *mǎ*.
    c. 人～ *rénxiàn*, Asian copperleaf (*Acalypha australis*).

2. ～羊 *xiànyáng*, thin-horned argali, wild sheep.

軒   xiàn   MC xjonH   → 軒 *xuān*.

限　xiàn　MC heanX

1. to (de)limit, bound, demarcate; restrict(ion), include in.
2. limit, boundary, in space or time.
    a. bounded measure, amount; to measure, calculate; (de)term(ine).
    b. limitation; hindrance, obstacle.
3. limit of a building > door-sill, threshold.

陷　xiàn　MC heamH

1. a pit, ditch, trap, as for catching animals.
    a. fall into; trapped in; engulfed in.
2. pitfall; artifice, ploy.
    a. snares of the law.
3. destroy, reduce, as an enemy or a city.
4. fall into error; in fault.
    a. (med.) ～車 xiànchē, wagon for transporting prisoners, tumbril.
5. (med.) embed(ded), as jewels in clothing; involve(d) in.

霰　xiàn　MC senH

1. sleet; graupel.

餡　xiàn　MC haemH

1. (med.) stuffed bun.
2. (med.) stuffed filling, of bun or metaphorically.

xiāng

廂　xiāng　MC sjang

1. lateral or side rooms of a building.
    a. suite of rooms; wing.
2. side portion of a palace.

儴　xiāng　MC sjang

1. (bn.) ～徉 or 相羊 xiāngyáng (MC sjang–yang) roam round and about, stroll and saunter.

欀　xiāng　MC sjang

1. sago palm (Metroxylon sagu).
2. curved prop for a roof-truss.
3. (bn.) 槍～ qiāngxiāng, → 槍 qiāng.

湘　xiāng　MC sjang

1. largest river in Hunan area, emptying into Lake Dongting 洞庭湖, identified with the South, particularly the old state of Chu 楚.
2. to cook by boiling.

瓖　xiāng　MC sjang

1. jade ornamentation on a horse's cinch.

相　xiāng　MC sjang

1. ADV indicating reciprocal or mutual action: in common, each other, one another, respective(ly); e.g. 性～近也，習～遠也 xìng xiāngjìn yě, xí xiāngyuǎn yě, (people) by nature are akin to one another, in practice they become distant from one another.
2. aspectant, anent > ADV indicating transitivity and unidirectionality of following verb, usu. replacing direct object; e.g. ～許 xiāngxǔ, to permit X; ～殺 xiāngshā, to slay X; ～思 xiāngsī, long for X; ～照 xiāngzhào, shine on X. During med. period, this usage becomes more common than 1.
3. rhythm, in music.
    a. (med.) upper unmoveable frets of lute (pipa 琵琶).
4. ～思 xiāngsī, coralwood (Adenanthera pavonia), medium to tall deciduous tree, the red seeds of which (～思豆 xiāngsīdòu) sometimes used as beads for jewelry, symbolic of love and longing.

xiàng　MC sjangH

1. to assist; adjuvant, minister, esp. of government; often short for 丞～ chéngxiàng, prime minister, chancellor, or for 宰～ zǎixiàng, grand councilor, chief minister.
    a. a ministry; governmental organ or physical location associated with ministerial functions.
2. support, enhance, add a supplemental element to; e.g. ～質 xiàngzhì, enhance the substance.
3. appraise, assess, inspect, ken, esp. appraise the inner qualities of a person or animal by means of its physical aspects; somatomancy, similar to physiognomy but involving the whole body, not just the head.
    a. gauge or estimate character or destiny.
    b. someone who is expert in a field.
4. (Budd.) trns. of Skt. nimitta or lakṣaṇa, principal or defining characteristic, as opposed to secondary characteristic (好 hǎo), external mark, appearance, manifested aspect, characteristic mark, physical sign, esp. of a cakravartin or buddha; > the phenomenal, as opp. to the noumenal 理 lǐ.
    a. an attribute, characteristic.
    b. physical appearance, e.g. ～好 xiànghǎo, physical features.

箱 xiāng MC sjang

1. compartment of a carriage, for accommodating persons or cargo.
2. chest, box (larger than 篋 *qiè* or 匣 *xiá*, coffer); cabinet.
3. ⊙ 廂 *xiāng* side-rooms.

緗 xiāng MC sjang

1. blond or cream-colored, shading to very light brown.

纕 xiāng MC sjang

1. sash, cinch, belt.
  a. cinch (for horse).
2. extend bared arms from sleeves.

薌 xiāng MC xjang

1. fragrant aroma of sacrificial grain, esp. millet > pleasant aroma of cooked food; ⊙ 香 *xiāng*.
2. a type of perilla used in flavoring foods.
  xiǎng MC xjangX
1. ⊙ 響 *xiǎng*, resound, echo.

襄 xiāng MC sjang

1. to raise or lift up; ascend, rise to, overtop; ⊙ 驤 *xiāng* 1, raise spiritedly.
  a. tall, high.
2. to accomplish, complete, execute.
  a. to aid, assist, second.
3. distance of 30° which a star passes through in one double-hour.
4. ⊙ 攘 *ráng*, pull up or off; extract, remove.

鄉 xiāng MC xjang

1. land outside city or town; countryside.
  a. parochial, provincial.
2. administrative unit, parish; in Tang times equiv. 5 "hamlets" (*li* 里) but smaller than a "district" (*xian* 縣).
3. sgl. or 故～ *gùxiāng*, one's native place, homeplace, hometown.
4. ⊙ 向 *xiàng* 1, toward; 2, formerly; 響 *xiǎng* echo; 享 *xiǎng*, dapatical sacrifice.

香 xiāng MC xjang

1. scented, aromatic, fragrant; redolent.
2. incense.
  a. when burned for medicinal purposes: suffiment.
3. ～茅 *xiāngmáo*, lemongrass, citronella (*Cymbopogon citratus*); ～櫞 *xiāngyuán*, bitter citron (*Citrus medica*); ～青 *xiāngqīng*, pearly everlasting (*Anaphilis margaritacea*); ～桃 *xiāngtáo*, pomelo (*Citrus grandis*).

驤 xiāng MC sjang

1. to lift up spiritedly; e.g. ～首 *xiāngshǒu*, toss one's head.
  a. gambade, prance.
2. gallop, run high-spiritedly.

xiáng

庠 xiáng MC zjang

1. district school in antiquity; e.g. ～序 *xiángxù*, district and hamlet schools, local lyceums and palestrae.

祥 xiáng MC zjang

1. presage, omen; usu. favorable omen; propitious.
2. ⊙ 詳 *xiáng* detail(ed).

翔 xiáng MC zjang

1. to hover, wheel round; soar.
  a. circle round to alight.
2. to move or walk briskly.
  a. walk with arms spread.
3. ⊙ 詳 *xiáng* detail(ed).

詳 xiáng MC zjang

1. detail(ed), in detail, in particular; particularize.
  a. precise, with precision; care(ful), minute(ly), thorough(ly).
  b. explain or examine carefully, go into the particulars of.
2. ⊙ 祥 *xiáng* propitious; 佯 *yáng* feign.

降 xiáng MC haewng → 降 *jiàng*.

xiǎng

享 xiǎng MC xjangX

1. to offer or partake of a dapatical sacrifice (for gods or ancestors); sacrificial feast or refection.
  a. regale a guest with banquet.
2. be gratified by or enjoy a gift; relish, accept with pleasure.

想 xiǎng MC sjangX

1. to imagine, have a mental vision or image of; think of.

a. have in mind, hold in mind; impression.
b. fancy, to fancy that . . ., e.g. ～象 *xiǎng-xiàng* "seeming semblance."
c. (Budd.) thought, as field of perception.
2. plan to do, hope to do, expect, anticipate; anticipation.

響　xiǎng　MC xjangX

1. echo, countertone.
2. resound; resonant, sonorous.
3. (med.) what has been voiced abroad: reputation, rumor.

餉　xiǎng　MC syangH

1. to give provisions to laborers; military rations; the provisions so given.
2. to provide with, present to.
3. a brief moment, short break.

饗　xiǎng　MC xjangX

1. communal banquet of thanksgiving and offering; regale a guest with banquet; accept a banquet offering with enjoyment; syn. 享 *xiǎng* 1, 2; e.g. (med.) 尚～ *shàngxiǎng*, "May you partake of [the offering(s)] reverently handed up," formulaic phrase closing an offering-text (*jiwen* 祭文) for the dead.

鱶　xiǎng　MC sjangX

1. dried croaker, maigre, percoid (*Sciaenidae* family).

xiàng

像　xiàng　MC zjangX

1. semblance.
   a. appearance; figure; image, icon, statue.
   b. to simulate, model, take as guide.
   c. to resemble, seem as.

向　xiàng　MC xjangH

1. toward, turn toward; anent, over against, give onto < north-facing window.
   a. tend toward, incline toward, on the verge of; go toward.
   b. (to) approximate, more or less.
   c. 一～ *yīxiàng*, utterly, completely.
2. previously, earlier, formerly.
   a. recently, just now.
   b. (med.) ～來 *xiànglái*, immediately.
3. presuming, supposing that.

4. (med.) attack, assault.
5. a surname.
6. ⊙ 響 *xiǎng* echo; 享 *xiǎng* dapatical sacrifice; 饗 *xiǎng* banquet.

嚮　xiàng　MC xjangH

1. turn toward; face, face-to-face.
   a. move toward, tend toward; hasten to.
   b. look out on > window.
2. formerly, previously.
3. presuming, supposing that.
　　　xiǎng　MC xjangX
1. ⊙ 享 *xiǎng* dapatical sacrifice; 響 *xiǎng* echo.

巷　xiàng　MC haewngH

1. alley, alley-way; lane; hutong; also written 衖.

曏　xiàng　MC xjangH

1. erewhile; formerly, previously.
2. to face.

橡　xiàng　MC zjangX

1. sawtooth oak (*Quercus acutissima*).
2. acorn.

缿　xiàng　MC haewngH

1. terracotta container for cash; for presenting legal documents.

衖　xiàng　MC haewngH　⊙ 巷 *xiàng*.

象　xiàng　MC zjangX

1. elephant; ivory.
   a. (Budd.) metaphorical of majestic or commanding qualities; e.g. cmpd. with 龍 *lóng*, "dragon, *nāga*," ref. the chief monks of a monastery.
2. image.
   a. counterpart, replica, semblance, e.g. 想 ～ *xiǎngxiàng*, imagined image, "seeming semblance"; (Budd.) ～教 *xiàngjiào*, "the teaching of semblances" (i.e. illusory nature of phenomenal images); (bn.) ～罔 *xiàng-wǎng* (MC zjangX-mjangX), without trace or thought, subtle and imperceptible.
   b. representation; effigy; icon; analogue, emblem, simulacrum; symbol, e.g. verbal representations and explications of *Yijing* hexagrams, or in *xuanxue* discourse the imagistic stage between fundamental idea and denotative word; ～設 *xiàngshè* or ～室 *xiàngshì*, chamber of the dead, replicating their abode

while alive; also, (Budd.) image hall with statue or icon.

c. phenomenon, apparition, figure, figuration, e.g. 天～ *tiānxiàng*, "celestial phenomena" or 星～ *xīngxiàng*, "sidereal phenomena," i.e. heavenly bodies or stars esp. as associated with earthly events; 無～ *wúxiàng*, out of sorts; also, amorphous; (Dao.) 大～ *dàxiàng*, Great Schemata, unifying patterns that underlie variegated phenomena.

d. simulate, imitate; take as rule or model.

關　xiàng　MC xjangH
1. space between two steps of stairs.

項　xiàng　MC haewngX
1. nape of the neck; neck.
2. engorged, large; e.g. ～領 *xiànglǐng* broad-necked, often with connotation of "stiff-necked."
3. a surname.

xiāo

嘐　xiāo　MC xaew
1. rdup., talk magniloquently, vaunt, exaggerate, blow hard.
　　jiāo　MC kaew
1. rdup., onom. of cock's crow, "cocoroo!"

嘵　xiāo　MC xew
1. sgl. or rdup., exclamation of fright: "hyai!"
　　a. prattle, babble.
2. prate, boast; hyperbolize.
　　a. (med.) insist on; dispute, wrangle; querulous.

囂　xiāo　MC xjew
1. tumult, din, clamor; hue and cry; hubbub, tintamar; rdup., clamorous cacophony.
2. sated, satisfied; content; rdup., well and fully pleased.
　　a. self-satisfied, full of oneself; smug; rdup., arrantly arrogant, smugly snobbish.
　　b. antipathetic, oppugnant; rdup., disturbed by and disapproving of.
　　áo　MC ngaw
1. rdup., brawl and brouhaha; moiling mob; rife and riotous; (bn.) ～藹 *áo'ǎi* (MC ngaw-'ajH), teeming tintamar.

宵　xiāo　MC sjew
1. nighttime (ant. 晝 *zhòu*, daytime).
2. ⊙ 小 *xiǎo*, small; 肖 *xiào*, resemble.

枵　xiāo　MC xjew
1. hollow tree-trunk.
　　a. hollow, empty; barren.
2. 玄～ *xuánxiāo*, alt. name for → 虛 *xū* 7, one of the 28 lunar lodgings.

梟　xiāo　MC kew
1. hornless or short-eared owl (*Asio flammeus*) (cf. 鴟 *chī*, horned owl).
2. spirited, aggressive, audacious; e.g. ～雄 *xiāoxióng*, overpowering; imperious, peremptory; ～羊 *xiāoyáng*, "spirited goat," i.e. moulin langur (*Rhinopithecus roxellanae*), syn. 狒狒 *fèifèi*.
3. chief, head; lead(ing); e.g. ～民 *xiāomín*, leading people; ～棋 *xiāoqí*, leading draughtsmen in the game of *go*.
4. expose criminal's severed head.
　　a. suspend(ed), hang(ing).
5. summit, topmost point.
6. class, category; rank(ing).
7. designation for certain results in *liubo* 六博 and *shupu* 樗蒲 games.

歊　xiāo　MC xjew
1. rising vapor.
　　a. rdup., swelling full; overbearing.
2. warm air; steam; heat.

消　xiāo　MC sjew
1. dissolve, disintegrate; melt, flow; dissipate, thaw.
　　a. dispel, disperse; diminish; reduce; dwindle, wane; e.g. ～伏 *xiāofú*, minimize, suppress.
　　b. slake; consume, use up, wear away; digest.
　　c. cancel, eliminate; efface.
　　d. cmpd., ～息 *xiāoxī*, flow and ebb, tiding(s); vicissitudes; also rest and relax, recuperate; remedy, give treatment.
2. ～石 *xiāoshí*, nitre, saltpetre, potassium nitrate.
　　a. 朴～ *púxiāo* or 芒～ *mángxiāo*, crude sodium sulphate.
3. (med.) enjoy, accept with pleasure.
4. (med.) be worth X.
5. (med.) must, need to.
6. (med.) cmpd., ～瘦 *xiāoshòu*, thin and weak.
7. (med.) ⊙ 痟 *xiāo* 2, diabetes.

瀟　xiāo　MC sew
1. rdup., onom. of wind or light rain, also ⊙ 蕭 2 and 3 in onom. binomes given there.

徙　xǐ　MC sjeX

1. shift or change residence; remove from one's current place; move on; move toward.
　　a. alter one's behavior.
　　b. pass a certain period of time.
2. be transferred to a different official post, usu. of equal status (cf. 遷 *qiān*, usu. to higher post).
3. be conveyed afar as punishment, e.g. 〜邊 *xǐbiān*, banished to the frontier.
4. free oneself, escape from undesired situation.
5. (bn.) 〜倚 *xǐyǐ* (MC sjeX-'jeX), halting and hesitant, troubled and undecided.

枲　xǐ　MC siX

1. male hemp plant (*Cannabis sativa*), used for its fiber in making cloth (cf. 苴 *jū*, female hemp plant).
　　a. gen. term for hemp.

洗　xǐ　MC sejX

1. wash, lave, bathe; esp. feet or hands.
　　a. clean, cleanse, purify, wash away (literally or figuratively); expiate; efface.
　　b. purge, do away with; sweep away; eradicate.
2. wash-basin, for hands or for preserving food and drink.

xiǎn　MC senX
1. 〜然 *xiǎnrán*, in a dignified, grave manner; unperturbed, composed; distinct(ly), clear(ly).
2. 〜馬 *xiǎnmǎ*, clear the way for the horse of one's lord or master; official title for an attendant charged with this responsibility for the royal heir-designate.
3. a surname.

璽　xǐ　MC sjeX

1. seal, signet.
　　a. from Qin dynasty on, ref. imperial seal.

繼　xǐ　MC srjeX

1. in a crowd, mass(ed), amass; group, aggregate.
2. ⊙ 纚 *xǐ* 1, ribbon to tie up hair.

纚　xǐ　MC srjeX

1. silk ribbon to tie up hair.
　　a. rdup., long and fine-looking.
　　b. (bn.) 絼〜 *shēnxǐ*, → 絼 *shēn* (*chēn*).
2. advance together.

lí　MC lje
1. tie up, tie together.
2. (bn.) 絼〜 *línlí*, → 絼 *lín* (*chēn*).

lǐ　MC ljeX
1. connect, link, join, e.g. 〜屬 *lǐzhǔ*, joined in sequence, one after another.

sǎ　MC sreaX
1. fishing net; mesh; continuously meshed, linked.

葸　xǐ　MC siX

1. shrink back, shrink away in fear, draw back; cringe, wince.

葰　xǐ　MC sjeX

1. fivefold.

蟢　xǐ　MC xiX

1. small, long-legged spider, usu. of auburn color.

諰　xǐ　MC siX

1. fear(ful), dread(ful), frightened; flinch, cringe.

謑　xǐ　MC hejX

1. 〜詢 *xǐgòu*, revile; disgrace(d), shame(d), humiliate(d).

xí　MC hej
1. 〜髁 *xíkē*, uncaring of what is right, acting however one feels; offensive(ly).

xì

係　xì　MC hejH　⊙ 系 *xì*.

卅　xì　MC sip

1. combined form of 四十 *sìshí*, forty.

嚱　xì　MC xjeH

1. onom. of sighing or exclamation of surprise, astonishment, or chagrin.

屓　xì　MC xijH

1. (bn.) 贔〜 *bìxì*, → 贔 *bì*; (med.) (bn.) 〜奰 *xìbèi* (MC xijH-bijH), exerting extraordinary force.

屭　xì　MC xijH　⊙ 屓 *xì*.

戲　xì　MC xjeH

1. amuse(ment), sport (with), disport.
　　a. divert; divertissement; enjoy(ment), entertain(ment).
2. pleasantry; joke, mock, toy with.
3. engage in combat with.

2. clear water.

    a. rdup., clear and cool, trickle and run (of flowing rainwater).

    b. ～湘 *xiāoxiāng*, "the clear Xiang," i.e. the Xiang River, in Hunan, traditionally symbolic of the South; sometimes spoken of as two rivers—"Xiao and Xiang"—the Xiao being a tributary of the Xiang in southern Hunan.

庥　xiāo　MC xaew

1. (bn.) 匏～ *páoxiāo* (MC baew-xaew), rage and roar.

獟　xiāo　MC xew

1. brave; fierce.

嫽　xiāo　MC xaew

1. (bn.) 獶～ *nǎoxiāo*, → 獶 *nǎo* (nao).

    qiāo　MC khaew

1. (bn.) 髐～ *xiàoqiāo* (MC haewX-khaew), hustle and bustle, tumultuous tangle, of a noisy throng.

瘄　xiāo　MC xaew

1. wheezing, difficulty in breathing; asthma(tic).

瘹　xiāo　MC sjew

1. migraine, headache.

2. (med.) diabetes.

簫　xiāo　MC sew

1. vertical end-blown bamboo flute, cut on angle at top joint and with holes for stopping.

2. panpipes, syrinx, musical instrument joining in a row 16 or 23 bamboo pipes of different lengths; unsealed at bottom, therefore sometimes called *dongxiao* 洞簫, "vented syrinx," also sometimes called 排簫 *páixiāo*, "lined-up pipes" (cf. 笙 *shēng*, mouth-organ).

3. ～韶 *xiāosháo*, hallowed hymnody, music of the lengendary sage-king Shun 舜.

4. ⊙ 篠 *xiǎo*, dwarf bamboo.

5. end-tips of a bow.

綃　xiāo　MC sjew

1. raw or unprocessed silk, esp. raw silk-gauze or raw tabby.

2. ⊙ 梢 *shāo*, spar, mast.

翛　xiāo　MC sew

1. rdup., onom. of ruffle and flutter of wings; also, of rustle and whisper of wind among trees.

2. ～然 *xiāorán*, natural and detached, casual(ly); brisk(ly) and without fuss.

蕭　xiāo　MC sew

1. averoyne, southernwood (*Artemisia abrotanum*), small bushy shrub with camphor-like odor and yellow flowers.

2. removed from or untouched by outside influences.

    a. somber, grave; sedate; private; e.g. ～牆 *xiāoqiáng*, "solemn screen," partition in palace beyond which are ruler's private quarters; ～肅 *xiāosù*, serene and sedate; ～閒 *xiāoxián*, private and austere; (Dao.) ～閒堂 *xiāoxiántáng*, "Hall of the Secluded and Austere," paradise for male postulants; (bn.) ～灑 *xiāosǎ* (MC sew-sreaX), carefree and detached; also onom. of light rain, softly sprinkling.

    b. desolate, drear(y), bleak; e.g. (bn.) ～條 *xiāotiáo* (MC sew-dew), drear and cheerless, barren and bleak, decaying and desolate, lone and forlorn; also, quiet and calm, idly at ease, living in quietude; → also 3a.

3. cool(ing), draughty; brisk.

    a. onom. of wind in trees and associated feelings, e.g. rdup. or in (bn.) ～森 *xiāosēn* (MC sew-srim) or ～瑟 *xiāosè* (MC sew-srit) or ～索 *xiāosuǒ* (MC sew-sak) or ～率 *xiāoshuài* (MC sew-srwit), sough and sigh, rustle and swish, whistle and wail, drear and doleful, grim and grisly, → also 2b.

4. rdup., snuffle, onom. of horse's neighing; also, onom. of bird's wings in flight, hish-hish.

5. (bn.) ～蔘 *xiāoshēn* (MC sew-srim), closely clustered; also, perilously tall.

6. a surname, notably that of ruling family of the Qi 齊 (479-502) and Liang 梁 (502-557) dynasties.

7. ⊙ 肅 *sù* 1-3, stately; solemn; reverent.

藃　xiāo　MC xjew

1. white angelica, syn. → 芷 *zhǐ*.

虓　xiāo　MC xaew

1. howl or roar of wild beast.

    a. uproar(ious); reverberant.

    b. bellow(ing), rave, rant.

2. fierce, ferocious; brave.

蠵　xiāo　MC kew

1. otter; prob. smooth-coated otter (*Lutrogale perspicillata*).

2. reputedly, spawn of a snake and a ring-necked pheasant; in legend harmful to humans, somewhat similar to Western basilisk; prob. giant salamander (*Andrias sligoi*).

蠨 **xiāo** **MC sew**
1. (bn.) ～蛸 *xiāoshāo* (MC sew-sraew), long-legged spider, spume-spinning spider, esp. associated with the South.

逍 **xiāo** **MC sjew**
1. (bn.) ～遙 *xiāoyáo* (MC sjew-yew), easy and effortless, footloose and fancy-free, free and easy.

銷 **xiāo** **MC sjew**
1. fuse metal; melt together, meld.
2. melt away; disintegrate, fleck away; release, dispel; waste away; e.g. ～落 *xiāolùo*, fail and wither; ～魂 *xiāohún*, delirious, out of one's mind (with grief or happiness); (bn.) ～鑠 *xiāoshuò* (MC sjew-syak), dissolve steadily.
 a. ⊙ 消 *xiāo* 1, dissolve, thaw; eliminate; consume; cancel.
3. short sword; dagger, dirk.
 a. spade.
4. pig iron.

霄 **xiāo** **MC sjew**
1. the welkin, empyrean; the skewes; e.g. 神～ *shénxiāo*, the divine empyrean; ～上 *xiāoshàng*, above in the emyprean; ～極 *xiāojí*, apex of the empyrean, highest heaven; euph. for imperial court; ～漢 *xiāohàn*, the Han (river) in the welkin, sky river, i.e. Milky Way.
 a. clouded sky.
2. snow-mist.
 a. slush, melted snow.
3. solar nimbus, halo, sun-ring.
4. ⊙ 宵 *xiāo*, nighttime; 消 *xiāo*, dissolve, melt.

驍 **xiāo** **MC kew**
1. high-spirited horse; mettlesome; dashing.
 a. valorous, gallant; stout-hearted.
2. (med.) bounce-back or rebound of arrow in game of pitch-pot.

髐 **xiāo** **MC xaew**
1. whistling arrow.

魈 **xiāo** **MC sjew**
1. (med.) mountain forest imp, hob, sprite, goblin.

鴞 **xiāo** **MC hjew** ⊙ 梟 *xiāo*.

xiáo

哮 **xiáo** **MC xaew**
1. (bn.) ～窌 *xiáoliáo* (MC xaew-laew), gaping and gawping, gaping wide.

殽 **xiáo** **MC haew**
1. ⊙ 淆 *xiáo*, mix(ed), mingle(d); confuse(d), agitate(d).
 yáo **MC haew**
1. ⊙ 肴 *yáo*, cates, delicacies.

淆 **xiáo** **MC haew**
1. roil(ed), agitate(d); muddy, turbid.
 a. mix(ed), muddle(d); confuse(d), mingle(d); adulterate(d).

xiǎo

小 **xiǎo** **MC sjewX**
1. small, little.
 a. lesser, in size, importance, or repute; minor; elementary; e.g. ～學 *xiǎoxúe*, lesser studies, esp. lexicology and (med). also phonology and exegesis; (Budd.) ～乘 *xiǎoshèng*, Lesser Vehicle, trns. Skt. *hīnayāna*.
 b. petty, insignificant; low, low-rank(ing); e.g. ～人 *xiǎorén*, commoner, petty person (cf. 君子 *jūnzǐ*, nobleman or man of noble character); ～家 *xiǎojīa*, commoner, peasant.
 c. adolescent, juvenile; jejune; e.g. ～子 *xiǎozǐ*, (med.) "little boy," patronizing form of address to juniors.
 d. of slight ability; e.g. (med.) ～戶 *xiǎohù*, one with slight ability for drink, unable to hold his liquor.
2. make small, lessen, diminish; shrink.
 a. consider or treat as inferior, belittle, slight.

曉 **xiǎo** **MC xewX**
1. daybreak.
 a. daylight; brightness.
2. "see the light," have something "dawn on" one; understand, discern; be (made) aware of; shed light on.
 a. be completely clear about; comprehend fully.

皛 **xiǎo** **MC hewX**
1. blankly white; clear; manifest.

a. rdup. or in (bn.) 〜漾 *xiǎoyǎo* (MC hewX-yewX), finely fulgent, smoothly shining, candid and clear.

pāi　MC phaek
1. pat, slap; strike.

筊　xiǎo　MC sewX
1. dwarf bamboo, esp. *Bambusa multiplex*.

篠　xiǎo　MC sewX　⊙ 筊 *xiǎo*.

xiào

俲　xiào　MC haewH
1. ⊙ 效 *xiào* 1, imitate.

効　xiào　MC haewH　⊙ 效 *xiào*.

嘯　xiào　MC sewH
1. to whistle.
    a. (med.) breathing exercises performed with various vocalizations meant to harmonize one's physical being with the primal *qi* of the natural world.
2. howl(ing), cry(ing) out, of various animals.

孝　xiào　MC xaewH
1. filial devotion, showing required piety and respect toward parents.
    a. 〜廉 *xiàolián*, filial and incorrupt, category used by local officials to recommend men suitable for appointment at court.
2. (med.) be in mourning for a recently deceased parent; wearing mourning garments.

效　xiào　MC haewH
1. imitate, take as a model, copy; conform with or to.
2. bring to, hand over; offer forth, present.
3. make every effort, do one's best.
4. produce an effect, bring about a result; efficacious, efficacy; win out.
    a. effect, result.
5. verify, examine, test.
6. indict(ment); sue or accuse legally.

斆　xiào　MC haewH
1. teach, educate; guide, counsel.
2. intended effect, desired result; proof.

校　xiào　MC haewH　→ 校 *jiào*.

笑　xiào　MC sjewH
1. smile; grin.
    a. display happiness, regard with favor.
2. laugh.
    a. laugh at, ridicule.

肖　xiào　MC sjewH
1. likeness, "kind-ness"; resemble; esp. in cmpd. 不〜 *bùxiào*, discrepant, untoward; incompetent; unlike (one's forebears); unworthy (ant. 賢 *xián*).

肖　xiāo　MC sjew
1. decline, wane; reduce(d), make small; diminish(ed), dwindle.

詨　xiào　MC haewH
1. cry out; cry for.
    a. onom. for cry, shriek.

xiē

些　xiē　MC sjae　→ 些 *suò*.

楔　xiē　MC set
1. cherry tree (*Cerasus pseudocerasus*), syn. 櫻桃 *yīngtáo*.
2. door-jamb.
3. angled block, wedge; peg.

歇　xiē　MC xjot
1. come to the end of, finish, come to nothing; run out, use up.
    a. cease, desist; pause, stop a while; (ar)rest, interrupt; stop, halt; discontinue.
    b. (med.) decline, fade away; disappear.
2. send out, diffuse; distribute, issue.

猲　xiē　MC xjot
1. rdup., pug-nosed dog.
2. ⊙ 喝 *hè*, yell at, threaten.

蠍　xiē　MC xjot
1. (med.) sgl. or 〜子 *xiēzi*, general name for scorpions (*Scorpionidae*).
2. (med.) 〜子 *xiēzi*, dough-stick.

xié

偕　xié　MC keaj
1. act in unison; be together in place or opinion.

a. (al)together; completely, totally; pervasive(ly).

2. (med.) compare, place side by side.

䚩   xié   MC heap   ⊙ 協 *xié*.

協   xié   MC hep

1. concord, unison; agreement of sentiments, aims, sounds, etc.; agree with; fitting; e.g. ～日 *xiérì*, "concordant day," fitting or auspicious for particular event.

a. act or speak in concord, e.g. ～比 *xiébǐ*, collaborate; harmonize, be in accord; > assonant, assonance.

b. bring together, compose (as differences, passions).

叶   xié   MC hep   ⊙ 協 *xié*. N.B. not used for 葉 *yè*.

挾   xié   MC hep

1. take or hold between two fingers, pinch, squeeze.

a. tuck or hold under the arm.

b. clench, clamp, cling to, hold onto.

2. hold or carry close to one; embrace.

a. keep in one's heart; preserve faithfully.

b. count on, rely on; believe in.

c. withhold, keep safe; preserve; hide.

3. press(ure), intimidate, coerce.

jiā   MC keap

1. ⊙ 夾 *jiā*.

携   xié   MC hwej   ⊙ 攜 *xié*.

擷   xié   MC het

1. carry beneath the folded lapels of one's robe.

a. tuck up one's clothing.

b. tuck away, conceal, hide.

2. (med.) clinch(ed); wrest from, carry off, take away.

a. (med.) strip flowers or leaves, pluck, cull, gather.

攜   xié   MC hwej

1. take or lead by the hand; pull along.

a. coupled, e.g. ～襟 *xiéjìn*, coupled lapels > robes.

2. one after another, in succession; follow along; be contiguous to.

3. be estranged (from), be parted.

斜   xié   MC zjae

1. slanted, (a)slant; incline(d), bias(ed); oblique; diagonal(ly); e.g. ～輝 *xiéhuī*, slanting light of early evening before sunset.

a. irregular, unruled; unorthodox. N.B. In med. times applied mainly to things, replaced when applied to people by 邪 *xié*.

b. cmpd. ～紋 *xiéwén*, twill, twill-patterned.

yé   MC yae

1. cmpd., 褒～ *bāoyé*, name of strategically important valley in Shaanxi, of which the south entrance is called Bao and the north entrance Ye.

絜   xié   MC het

1. use a cord to measure the girth of an object, such as a tree.

a. measure; rule, delimit.

b. evaluate, judge; compare, asses; come to a conclusion.

jié   MC ket

1. ⊙ 潔 *jié*, pure, clean; unsullied, honest.

纈   xié   MC het

1. (med.) watered silk, similar to moiré, esp. in flower patterns; flower-skeined.

2. (med.) dazzle(ment), bedazzled; daze(d), bewilder(ed).

脅   xié   MC xjaep

1. flank, side(s), esp. of upper torso; ribs.

2. menace, threaten; compel; press upon.

3. feel threatened, intimidated.

a. pull back, shrink back, contract; restrain oneself; e.g. ～息 *xiéxī*, hold one's breath; have one's breath taken away by fear.

膎   xié   MC hea

1. (med.) preserve(d) meat; store(d) up food.

a. (med.) resources held in reserve.

衺   xié   MC zjae   ⊙ 邪 *xié*.

襭   xié   MC het

1. ⊙ 擷 1, carry or conceal beneath one's robe.

諧   xié   MC heaj

1. conform, agree with; accord with; e.g. 不～ *bùxié*, doesn't conform, won't do.

a. pair (up), couple (with); e.g. ～比 *xiébǐ*, collaborate with closely.

2. good-humored, agreeable.

    a. humorous, jocular; facetious.

3. (med.) consult about; come to consensus, decide after discussion.

    a. complete in accord with one's wishes, accomplish satisfactorily.

邪　xié　MC zae

1. irregular, off-center, off-kilter, inclined; loxotic (cog. 斜 *xié*, aslant).

    a. unorthodox, heterodox.

2. bias(ed); prejudice(d); pervert(ed), perverse.

    a. malefic, pernicious; noxious; e.g. ～瘴 *xiézhāng*, malignant miasmas; ～佞 *xiénìng*, malicious dissembler; ～鬼 *xiéguǐ*, evil spirits.

    yé　MC yae

1. sentence-final interr. GP equiv. to (and phonetic fusion of) *yě* 也 + *hū* 乎, (possibly dialect) variant of 與 *yǔ* in this usage; e.g. 陛下不自知～ *bìxià bùzìzhī yé*, is it that you, good sir, do not yourself know?; 汝將諫～ *rǔ jiāng jiàn yé*, are you going to admonish them?

    a. phrase-final GP implying probable assent interrogatively: "... yes?; ... hmm?"

2. onom. for emphatic exclamation.

鞋　xié　MC hea

1. shoe(s), footwear.

    a. straw sandal.

鞵　xié　MC hea

1. untanned leather shoes or boots.

2. (med.) ⊙ 鞋 *xié*, gen. term for footwear.

頡　xié　MC het

1. (bn.) ～頏 *xiéháng* (MC het-hang), soar and swoop, soaring high and swooping low, darting in and out; also equally matched, almost the same; also, stiff-necked, aloof and arrogant; also, cracked and crazy, esp. of speech.

2. (bn.) ～滑 *xiéhuá* (MC het-hweat), tangled and twisted, fuddled and muddled, involved and embroiled, captious and equivocal.

    jiā　MC keat

1. scrape, pare away.

2. bump, tap, thump.

    jié　MC het

1. 倉～ *cāngjié*, Cang Jie, name of legendary inventor of Chinese script.

xiě

寫　xiě　MC sjaeX

1. move from one place to another, e.g. as water for irrigation; shift, transfer; transplant.

2. pour out, drain; exhaust.

    a. express fully and completely; vent; disburden, unload; confess.

3. copy, imitate, model after.

    a. (med.) limn, draw, trace; depict, portray; describe; divulge.

    b. (med.) transcribe, write out a text, usu. with sense of writing out an exact copy, not "write down."

    c. (med.) seem like, resemble, reflect; suggest a similarity with.

    xiè　MC sjaeH

1. ⊙ 卸 *xiè* 1a, get rid of, remove, eliminate.

xiè

卸　xiè　MC sjaeH

1. (med.) unyoke the carriage and release the horses.

    a. (med.) get rid of, remove, eliminate; throw off, put aside; step back from; e.g. 交～ *jiāoxiè*, leave office for a successor; ～頭 *xiètóu*, take off hairpins, headwear, etc.

媟　xiè　MC sjet

1. debauch, rape; violate.

    a. take liberties with; treat slightingly, disrespect.

屑　xiè　MC set

1. crumb, particle, fragment; morsel; powder(ed); shard, mite; trifle.

    a. sweepings, detritus.

    b. trifling, negligible; rdup., trifling and trivial; 不～ *bùxiè*, pay not the least heed to, disdain, regard as worthless.

2. (med.) freckles; anthers.

3. (med.) in no time, in a jiffy; suddenly; fleetingly.

嶰　xiè　MC heaX

1. recessed area of land in mountain > river basin, combe, coulee; dale (cog. 澥 *xiè*, bight; cf. 澗 *jiàn*, rill, valley-stream).

廨   xiè   MC keaH

1. governmental building, bureau office.

懈   xiè   MC keaH

1. indolent, sluggish; slothful.
    a. negligent, nonchalant; offhand, uncaring.

械   xiè   MC heajH

1. implements, apparatus in general; machine.
    a. implements used in punishment, shackles, manacles.

榭   xiè   MC zjaeH

1. kiosk, small wooden structure built atop a terrace and roofed, mainly used for viewing the surrounding scenery; if high up, similar to an eyrie.

泄   xiè   MC sjet

1. drain, spill out, leak away; run off, disperse.
2. divulge; unveil, reveal.
3. ⊙ 媟 *xiè*, debauch, take liberties.
    yì   MC yejH
1. rdup., gracefully gliding, freely at liberty; also, massed in multitudes; also, wordy and long-winded.

洩   xiè   MC sjet

1. spill(age), leak, ooze; glide away; slip away.
    a. disperse, diverge, divulge; perfuse.
    b. drained, depleted; spent, used up.
    yì   MC yejH
1. rdup., expand, relax; brighten, gladden; also, gliding gracefully.

渫   xiè   MC sjet

1. wash or sluice away impurities; asperge, purge.
    a. disperse, scatter; evacuate.
    b. drain; discharge; excrete.
    c. spent, used up; exhausted.
2. disrespect; disregard.
    dié   MC dep
1. (med.) rdup., or (bn.) 浹～ *xiádié* (MC heap-dep), ceaselessly streaming, of waves or tears.

澥   xiè   MC heaX

1. recessed area of water near shore > bight; gulf, bay; cove, inlet (cog. 嶰 *xiè*, river basin).
2. the sea.

瀉   xiè   MC sjaeH

1. pour out, spill forth, drain; slip away.
    a. excrete, purge; diarrhea.
2. waterless land, drained, desiccated, parched, stripped of vegetation.

灐   xiè   MC heajH

1. (bn.) 沆～ *hàngxiè* (MC hangX-heajH), → 沆 *hàng*.

灺   xiè   MC zjaeX   ⊙ 炧 *xiè*.

炧   xiè   MC zjaeX

1. cinders, ashes; dripped wax of candle, lamp, or burnt residue of incense.

燮   xiè   MC sep

1. bring together, unite; harmonize; concord.
    a. accommodating; docile.

獬   xiè   MC heaX

1. (bn.) ～豸 *xièzhì* (MC heaX-drjeaX), "sagacious stag," fabulous animal resembling a one-horned deer which interposes itself between two fighting animals to determine which has been wronged; > cap worn by judges, because they decide tort cases between disputants.

紲   xiè   MC sjet

1. rope or cord with which to lead an animal.
    a. fasten(ing), strap, tie; link up.
2. put in bonds; chain; shackle, fetter.

絏   xiè   MC sjet   ⊙ 紲 *xiè*.

緤   xiè   MC sjet   ⊙ 紲 *xiè*.

薤   xiè   MC heajH

1. shallot (*Allium chinense*); cf. 葱 *cōng*, scallion (*Allium fistulosum*), 韭 *jiǔ*, chive, leek (*Allium tuberosum*).
    a. (lit.) ～露 *xièlù*, "dew on the shallots," name of a coffin-bearer's song, symbolic of the brief passing of life—as quick as the morning dew dries on the shallots.

蟹   xiè   MC heaX

1. the edible crab (*Brachyura brachyura*).
    a. straitly held, as between a crab's pincers; e.g. ～埞 *xièkè*, narrow ("crab-squeezed") ledge.

褻　xiè　MC sjet

1. underclothes, intimate apparel, private garb.
   a. dishabille, disheveled, careless in appearance.
2. on intimate terms with, thoroughly familiar.
   a. improperly familiar, disrespectful; presumptuous, taking unwarranted liberties.
   b. indecent, unseemly; shameless; vulgar, vile; unclean.

謝　xiè　MC zjaeH

1. renounce, decline; forgo; disclaim, reject.
   a. part with, surrender to; retire from, withdraw; e.g. ～事 *xièshì*, set aside official matters, retire from office.
   b. part with physically, separate; say farewell.
2. apologize, demur, acknowledge fault; beg indulgence (for); make amends; appease, conciliate, placate; e.g. ～慚 *xiècán*, expiate shame.
3. feel grateful for, beholden to, appreciative of.
   a. express regards; inquire after.
4. surrender to time, fade, decline, crumble, decay; e.g. 代～ *dàixiè*, fade in turn, wane successively, like the seasons in continuous cycle.
5. (med.) yield to, give place, acknowledge as better.
6. a surname.

躞　xiè　MC sep

1. (bn.) ～蹀 *xièdié* (MC sep-dep) or 蹀～, advance inchmeal, with small and measured steps; pace lightly, prance daintily; painstakingly.

躠　xiè　MC sjet

1. (bn.) 蹩～ *biéxiè*, → 蹩 *bié*.

邂　xiè　MC heaH

1. (bn.) ～逅 *xièhòu* (MC heaH-huwH), chance upon, run across, unlooked for, meet up with unexpectedly; happenstance, coincidence; also (med.), some time or other, if by any chance.

齘　xiè　MC heajH

1. grind one's teeth, grit one's teeth.

xīn

心　xīn　MC sim

1. the heart, as the center of intellectual and emotional activity; first among the five viscera; in system of *wuxing* 五行 correspondences associated with the agency of fire, color red, season of summer.
   a. intentions, desires, convictions, will; thoughts; feelings, mood, attitude.
2. the center, focal point, or most important part of a multi-part or conglomerate item.
   a. pistil and stamens of a flower; kernel of a nut; pith of wood.
3. (Budd.) the mind, as center and initiator of mental constructs, in contrast to body.
   a. in one's mind, to oneself.
4. one of the 28 lunar lodgings, comprised of 3 stars, α (Antares), σ, τ Scorpii, in the eastern quadrant (*qinglong* 青龍 or *canglong* 蒼龍) of the sky; alt. names 商 *shāng*, 辰 *chén*.

忻　xīn　MC xj+n

1. inspire, stimulate, exhilarate; inspiration, exhilaration.
2. ⊙ 欣 *xīn*, rejoice, delight, take pleasure in.

新　xīn　MC sin

1. new; fresh.
   a. renew, refresh, freshen.
2. recent(ly), just now; latest.
3. first element of bisyllabic surname, Xinyuan ～垣, also written 辛.
4. ～羅 *xīnluó* (MC sin-la), Silla, name of kingdom founded in southeastern part of Korean peninsula in 1st-c. BCE, expanding in medieval times to defeat, with Tang help, the 2 rival kingdoms of Paekche (Baiji 百濟) in 660 and Koguryŏ (Gaoli 高麗) in 668, thus unifying Korea.

昕　xīn　MC xj+n

1. daybreak, dayspring; sunup.
   a. light emerging from darkness, brighten; bright(ness).

　xuān　MC xjon

1. ～天 *xuāntiān*, "tilted heaven," ancient cosmological view which saw heaven as higher in the north, lower in the south.

欣　xīn　MC xj+n

1. rejoice, take pleasure in; be content with, delight(ed), exuberant.
2. (med.) rdup., luxurious exuberance, of plants or flowers.

歆　xīn　MC xim

1. breathe in a smell satisfiedly, like spirits or ancestors delighting in the fumes of a sacrificial offering; snuff up, smell; inhale.

a. feast on, savor; gladly accept, be gratified with, content(ed), well-satisfied.
2. seek, covet.
   a. (med.) heartily admire(d); extol, praise.

莘　xīn　MC sin
1. wild ginger (*Asarum*).

薪　xīn　MC sin
1. brushwood, underwood; firewood, fuel.
   a. to gather same, e.g. ～水 *xīnshǔi*, gather firewood and draw water.
2. wages, pay, for manual or menial work.

訢　xīn　MC xj+n
1. sgl. or rdup., expressly pleased, content with, happy about; exuberant(ly).
2. ⊙ 熹 *xī*, to heat, warm.

辛　xīn　MC sin
1. acrid, bitter(ness); tart(ness), pungent, sour; amarous, amaritude; stringent.
   a. distressful; painful; toilsome.
2. 8th of the 12 heavenly stems.
3. ～夷 *xīnyí*, lily magnolia, red magnolia (*Magnolia liliflora*), esp. the flower buds.
4. first element of bisyllabic surname, Xinyuan ～垣, also written 新.

馨　xīn　MC xeng
1. wafting, far-spreading scent; redolent, odoriferous.
   a. far-spreading renown, fragrant reputation.
2. (med.) sgl. or in cmpd. 寧～ *níngxīn*, in this way, like such (usu. placed after noun or adjective).

xín

鐔　xín　MC zim
1. pommel or hilt of a sword.
2. poniard, skean.

xìn

信　xìn　MC sinH
1. trustworthy, faithful to one's word; reliable, assured.
   a. trust to, believe in, have faith in; attend to or on.

b. in truth, truly, indeed.
   c. (Budd.) religious belief, faith.
2. pledge, gage, token or guarantee of one's word; surety.
   a. evidence, proof; reliable information, e.g. ～風 *xìnfēng*, tidings, news, intelligence.
3. messenger, courier, carrier of trustworthy information.
4. pass two nights in the same place < sojourn with confidence.
5. (med). missive, letter, epistle.
6. (med.) gift, present, bestowal.

囟　xìn　MC sinH
1. fontanel, space covered by membrane between the not-yet knit bones atop a baby's skull.

焮　xìn　MC xj+nH
1. burn, singe; heat up, fire.

釁　xìn　MC xinH　⊙ 釁 *xìn*.

衅　xìn　MC xinH　⊙ 釁 *xìn*.

釁　xìn　MC xinH
1. covenant or sacrificial offering sealed with blood.
   a. to smear, esp. with blood as symbolic sealant.
   b. worthy of offering blood over, e.g. ～故 *xìn'gù*, blameworthy offense.
2. schism, breach; hiatus.
   a. fault, slip, error; offense.
   b. feud, hostility.
3. sign, omen, portent.
4. excite, move to action or feeling.
5. rdup., move or progress ineluctably, passing ceaselessly.

頤　xìn　MC sinH　⊙ 囟 *xìn*.

xīng

惺　xīng　MC seng
1. (med.) sgl. or (bn.) ～鬆 or ～忪 *xīngsōng* (MC seng-sowng), awaken, come to one's senses, astute and aware; rdup., vigilant, astute, sharp-witted; quick-witted, intelligent.

星　xīng　MC seng

1. star; astral, sidereal, star-like; e.g. 〜漢 *xīng-hàn*, "the Han River in the stars, the starry Han," i.e. the Milky Way.
2. silver-specked, of hair partly gray.
3. one of the 28 lunar lodgings, comprised of stars in Hydra and Leo, in the southern quadrant (*chìniǎo* 赤鳥) of the sky.
    a. 〜紀 *xīngjì*, one of the 12 Jupiter stations, comprising the lunar lodgings *dou* 斗 and *niu* 牛.
4. (med.) an insignificant quantity of something.
5. (med.) ⊙ 惺 *xīng*, astute, quick-witted; awakened to.

猩　xīng　MC sraeng

1. rdup., orangutan.
2. weasel, stoat; ⊙ 鼪 *shēng*.
3. sgl. or in cmpd. 〜紅 *xīnghóng*, scarlet, carmine.

胜　xīng　MC seng

1. ⊙ 腥 *xīng*, raw meat; raw; putrid.
    shěng　MC sraengX
1. spare, lean, thin.

腥　·　xīng　MC seng

1. raw meat; raw, undressed.
    a. putrid, noisome, rank; reek, stench.
    b. grease of chicken or pork, chicken fat, pork fat, lard.

興　xīng　MC xing

1. to raise, lift up; exalt(ed); ascendant.
2. foster, support, promote; prosper.
3. evoke, excite, stimulate.
4. be active (opp. inert).
    xìng　MC xingH
1. exhilarated, elated; exaltation.
2. inspiration, mood.
    a. mettle, character, temper.
    b. inclination, particular interest.
3. evocative; esp. (lit.) traditional poetic trope in *Shijing* that begins a poem with an image drawn from the natural world, which is used as metaphor for human emotion or action portrayed afterward; e.g. 〜象 *xìngxiàng*, evocative imagery.

騂　xīng　MC sjeng

1. a roan horse.
    a. roan-colored, rufous.

xíng

刑　xíng　MC heng

1. punish by mutilation, corporal defiguring, "deform"; punish(ment); cf. 罰 *fá*, lighter punishment incl. fines.
    a. chastise physically; torture, cause to suffer.
2. mould; model; bring to proper form.
    a. correct formally; discipline by law.
3. ⊙ 型 *xíng*, mould; model; 形 *xíng*, form; 鉶 *xíng*, ritual cauldron.

型　xíng　MC heng

1. mould, of cast object; to mould; model.
2. shaped form of governmental, legal, or mental rule.

形　xíng　MC heng

1. outward form, appearance, shape.
    a. physical form of human being, often contrasted with spiritual essence.
    b. formal.
2. figure, configuration; structure, contour; outline.
3. to shape, configure, give form to.
    a. to outline, describe; show, reveal.
    b. 〜名 *xíngmíng*, "performance and name," evaluation of human behavior matching or contrasting what actually is with what is reputed.
4. to contrast, place against.
5. ⊙ 刑 *xíng* 1, punish(ment); 型 *xíng*, mould, model; 鉶 *xíng*, ritual cauldron.

滎　xíng　MC hweng

1. rivulet, streamlet, brook.
2. name of ancient marshland in central Henan, esp. place-name of district Xingyang 〜陽, often mispronounced as Yingyang.

硎　xíng　MC heng

1. whetstone.
2. to whet, hone; polish.
3. ⊙ 型 *xíng* mould, model.
    kēng　MC khaeng
1. ⊙ 坑 *kēng*, pit, fosse.

行   xíng   MC haeng

1. to march in order, as soldiers; walk forward; e.g. (Budd.) ～像 *xíngxiàng*, walking the Buddha's image in procession.
2. to move, proceed, act; perform(ance).
   a. actor, agent; e.g. 五～ *wǔxíng*, "the Five Agents."
   b. follower; e.g. (Budd.) ～人 *xíngrén*, ～者 *xíngzhe*, "follower [of Buddha]," Budd. monk.
3. to engage in; to conduct; to effect, put into practice, implement; e.g. (med.) ～散 *xíngsǎn*, stimulate or activate the effects of cold-food powder (*hanshisan* 寒食散) or five-mineral powder (*wushisan* 五石散) by walking.
4. pre-verbal indicator of future action, "is going to VB."
5. temporary, transient, e.g. ～宮 *xínggōng*, temporary residence of emperor when traveling away from capital; marker of provisional office, "acting as"—used between the nominal and substantive office-title when the former is higher (cf. 守 *shòu*).
6. to leave, depart from.
   a. leave one's home in order to marry (equiv. 嫁 *jià*).
7. (med.) "cursive script," calligraphic style freer than *kaishu* 楷書 but not as individualistic as *caoshu* 草書.

xìng   MC haengH

1. actions; conduct, behavior; custom(ary).
2. (Budd.) conditioned states, conditioned things, those things that arise out of causes and conditions and constantly change, trns. of Skt. *saṃskāra*.
   a. (Budd.) mental "formations" of habitual action.

háng   MC hang

1. walkway, road.
2. column, line, row, e.g. of soldiers, serried mountains, written text.
   a. order of clan relatives in one generation.

hàng   MC hangH

1. rdup., bold and unbending, steadfast and firm.

鉶   xíng   MC heng

1. ritual cauldron in shape of small tripod, for offerings of meat and vegetables.

陘   xíng   MC heng

1. mountain gorge, chasm, defile.

錫   xíng   MC zjeng

1. malt-sugar; dainty made from malt-sugar and glutinous rice; sweet rice-ball.
2. ⊙ 糖 *táng*, sugar.

xǐng

省   xǐng   MC sjengX

1. to scrutinize, examine closely; peruse; e.g. ～方 *xǐngfāng*, "examining in all directions," i.e. considering everything.
   a. to discern, realize that…; understand, be keenly aware of; e.g. ～得 *xǐngdé*, gain a realization that…
2. to reflect on, recall.
   a. introspect, engage in self-examination; e.g. 知～ *zhīxǐng*, reflective, self-examining; 不知～ *bùzhīxǐng*, unbalanced, non compos mentis.
3. visit relatives.
   a. ruler's visit to a vassal lord.
4. (med.) take in, accept; e.g. ～納 *xǐngnà*, take notice of, heed; accept, adopt.
5. (med.) ADV marker of past action.

shěng   MC srjaengX

1. reduce, diminish; spare, save; be sparing of, abrogate; revoke, cancel; dismantle.
2. spare of body, lean, slight; weakened, impaired.
3. governmental bureau.
4. taboo-substitute from late 1st-c. BCE for 禁 *jìn*, "forbidden precincts [of palace]" (to avoid given name of father of Han Yuandi's 元帝 [r. 48-32] Empress Wang); later commonly used for same.

醒   xǐng   MC sengX

1. to sober up; clear one's head, come to one's senses.
2. to wake up, awaken; open one's eyes to.

xìng

倖   xìng   MC heangX

1. ⊙ 幸 *xìng*, fortunate(ly), but with particular regard to human objects.
   a. (med.) ～門 *xìngmén*, benefit from position and influence.
2. ～願 *xìngyuàn*, "please!"

姓 xìng MC sjengH

1. from Han on, surname; patronymic family name.
2. descendant.

婞 xìng MC hengX

1. pertinacious, immovable; obstinate, stubborn.

幸 xìng MC heangX

1. good fortune; fortunate(ly), lucky.
   a. (med.) exactly (at the right moment); just so.
2. bring good fortune to, bestow fortune on.
   a. to grace with royal presence, referring to visit of emperor to a place or person; to favor with the fortune of imperial grace.
   b. favored by the ruler.
3. to hope for, desire as a favored outcome.
4. (med.) if fortune wills it that. . .
5. (med.) still, yet (Tang usage).

性 xìng MC sjengH

1. inborn; one's inborn nature, one's fundamental being.
2. native character, predisposition; one's endowment at birth.
   a. particular inherent quality; innate.
   b. inborn destiny.

悻 xìng MC heangX

1. rdup., angry, infuriated, peevish; impassioned.
2. (med.) ⊙ 婞, pertinacious.

杏 xìng MC haengX

1. common apricot (*Prunus armeniaca*), both tree and fruit.
   a. 〜葉 *xìngyè*, apricot leaf; (med.) also, ornament in this shape on horse's breast-strap.
   b. 〜仁 *xìngrén*, apricot kernel.
2. 銀〜 *yínxìng*, "silver apricot," ginkgo (*Ginkgo biloba*).
3. 巴旦〜 *bādànxìng*, almond (*Prunus amygdalus*), amygdaline.

漜 xìng MC hengX

1. (bn.) 〜溟 *xìngmǐng* (MC hengX-mengX) or 溟〜 *mǐngxìng*, broad and boundless, shoreless sweep; also, misted murk, obscure opacity, infinite obscurity.
2. to lead, bring to, conduce.

荇 xìng MC haengX

1. yellow floating heart, water-fringe (*Nymphoides peltatum*), a water plant with a long creeping stem that floats on the surface of the water, found in ponds and slow-moving waterways; ⊙ 莕 *xìng*.

莕 xìng MC haengX → 荇 *xìng*.

xiōng

兄 xiōng MC xjwaeng

1. elder brother; senior cousin.
   a. honorific address to friend or relative of the same generation: "you, my brother."

kuàng MC xjwangH
1. ⊙ 況 *kuàng* 2, augment; even more so.

兇 xiōng MC xjowng

1. dread(ful), ghastly, be terrified.
2. heinous, fiendish, flagitious.
   a. vicious, fell, truculent; murderous.
3. ⊙ 凶 *xiōng* 3, malignant; baleful.

凶 xiōng MC xjowng

1. inauspicious, unpropitious, ill-omened (ant. 吉 *jí*); e.g. 吉〜 *jíxiōng*, weal and woe.
2. death-related, lethal, mortal, deadly, mortiferous; e.g. 〜禮 *xiōnglǐ*, obsequies, funeral rites; 〜服 *xiōngfú*, mourning clothes.
3. malignant, fell, baleful.
   a. nefast, nefarious; malfeasance; malefic, maleficent.
4. dearth, want, scarcity; famine.
5. ⊙ 兇 *xiōng* 2, heinous; vicious.

匈 xiōng MC xjowng

1. ⊙ 胸 *xiōng*, chest, breast.
   a. core, center.
2. rdup., hue and cry, row and racket, blare and babble; uproar, commotion; also, scurry and scramble, unrest and agitation.
3. 〜奴 *xiōngnú*, an Inner Asian military confederation of nomadic tribes derived from different ethnic and linguistic groups, which threatened the northern border of China at various times during the Han dynasty and into the 4th century. N.B. No convincing argument holds for the several origins of the Xiongnu that have been attributed, including that which sees them as ancestors of the Huns.
4. ⊙ 兇 *xiōng* 2, heinous; vicious, truculent.

咰   xiōng   MC xjowng   ⊙ 詷 *xiōng*.

恟   xiōng   MC xjowng
1. frightened; discomposed, wrought-up.
2. rdup., ill at ease and unquiet, fretful and flustered.

洶   xiōng   MC xjowng
1. rdup. or (bn.) ～湧 *xiōngyǒng* (MC xjowng-ywngX), waves crashing and curling, bubble and boil, swell and billow.
    a. rdup., row and racket, cry and clamor.

胸   xiōng   MC xjowng
1. chest, breast, as seat of affections; inner mind.
    a. core, center.
    b. take to heart, hold close; feel deeply.
2. abreast of; in front of one, before one.

芎   xiōng   MC khjuwng
1. (bn.) ～藭 *xiōngqióng* (MC khjuwng-gjuwng), Sichuan lovage (*Ligusticum chuanxiong*).

詷   xiōng   MC xjowng   ⊙ 詾 *xiōng*.

詾   xiōng   MC xjowng
1. ⊙ 訩 2, rdup., hue and cry; tumult, uproar.
2. disruption, disturbance.
3. call into question, dispute; squabble, bicker; brawl.
    a. lodge a complaint.

xióng

熊   xióng   MC hjuwng
1. black bear (*Ursus torquatus*).
2. rdup., glowing glossily, shining sleekly.

雄   xióng   MC hjuwng
1. male of birds.
    a. cock(erel), gamecock; e.g. ～戟 *xióngjǐ*, cock-halberd, with spurs like those of a gamecock.
2. valiant, bold-spirited, gallant; dauntless, steadfast; manly, virile, robust; strong, overpowering; forceful, cocksure.
    a. hold sway over, rule the roost, intimidate; dominate, exercise control, preside over.
3. outstanding, salient, distinguished; egregious, apart from the crowd.

4. well-equipped; well-stocked; full, abundant.
5. ～黃 *xiónghuáng*, realgar, arsenic disulfide.
6. (med.) in Tang times, 2nd of 4 special categories designating selected prefectures (*zhou* 州) that, because of their importance were given special standing (in descending order of prestige: 輔 *fǔ* [buttressing], ～ *xióng* [dominant], 望 *wàng* [honored], 緊 *jǐn* [important]) outside the usual trilevel ranking (上, 中, 下) of prefectures.

xiòng

夐   xiòng   MC xjwiengH
1. distant, far off in space or time; e.g. ～古 *xiònggǔ*, far antiquity.
2. seek, search for; track down.

詗   xiòng   MC xjwiengH
1. make inquiries, ask about covertly; sound out; probe.

xiū

休   xiū   MC xjuw
1. rest, repose; respite; take a break.
    a. desist from, cease.
    b. (med.) retire from, resign; repudiate; divorce.
    c. (med.) be done for, finished with; dismiss(ed).
2. beneficent; blessing, benison.
    a. felicitous, favored, uplifted, fortunate, agreeable; e.g. ～悴 *xiūcuì*, uplifted and cast down, favor and failure.
3. of highest quality; sterling; first-rate.
4. (med.) GP imperative negative: "leave off . . ."; "don't . . ."

修   xiū   MC sjuw
1. refine, discipline, cultivate to perfection; put in best condition, put in order; tend (to); apply oneself to, devote oneself to; practice.
    a. improve(ment), ameliorate; adorn(ment), embellish(ment); e.g. ～奉 *xiūfèng*, adorn and refine.
    b. restore, reshape, redress; self-restoration; restorative, strengthen(ing); analeptic.
    c. burl, unknot (of textiles).
2. prepare; (re)formulate; put in order.
    a. be meticulous, take care with.

3. felicitate; felicitous; e.g. ～徵 *xiūzhēng*, felicitous manifestation, sign of cosmic approbation.
4. of highest quality; finest; excellent.
5. elongated, drawn out; tapering; e.g. ～竹
xiūzhú, tall, tapering bamboo; ～蛾 *xiū'é*, thin,
tapering eyebrows; ～齡 *xiūlíng*, long life,
extended years.
 a. pre-Han, length in opposition to breadth
(廣 *guǎng*); after mid-2nd c. BCE, in opposition to shortness (短 *duǎn*), because 長
cháng was avoided as taboo-word.
6. (med.) revise, edit; compile.
7. (med.) shape, fashion; build, erect.
8. (med.) perform, as ceremony; e.g. ～禊 *xiūxì*,
carry out the spring purification ritual.

咻　xiū　MC xjuw
1. hubbub, din; cry out, shout.

庥　xiū　MC xjuw
1. shade(d), covering.
 a. (med.) protect(ed), shelter(ed), guard(ed).
2. relax, take a respite from.

羞　xiū　MC sjuw
1. humble(d), modest(y); feel inferior, self-
conscious; abashed.
 a. (med.) timid, diffident, unsure; apolo-
getic.
2. delicacies, sweetmeats; savories, cates.
3. to offer, present, esp. food.

脩　xiū　MC sjuw
1. strips of dried meat, anciently offered from
student to master as payment for teaching.
 a. (med.) ceremonial offering of gifts to academic or religious master.
2. ⊙ 修 *xiū* 1-4.

貅　xiū　MC xjuw
1. (bn.) 貔～ *píxiū*, → 貔 *pí*.

飍　xiū　MC xjiw
1. fast as the wind; run swiftly, race; bolt, dash;
flit.

饈　xiū　MC sjuw
1. ⊙ 羞 *xiū* 2, delicacies, sweetmeats.

髤　xiū　MC xjuw
1. reddish-black, murrey-colored lacquer or
varnish.
 a. to lacquer, varnish.

鵂　xiū　MC xjuw
1. (bn.) ～鶹 *xiūliú* (MC xjuw-ljuw), nightjar,
nighthawk, goatsucker; also, pygmy owl.

xiǔ

朽　xiǔ　MC xjuwX
1. rotten wood; decay(ed); molder(ing); e.g.
三不～ *sān bùxiǔ*, the 3 things that do not decay:
establishing virtue (立德 *lì dé*), fine deeds (立功
lì gōng), and memorable words (立言 *lì yán*).
 a. decrepit; withered; infirm, enfeebled; aged.

滫　xiǔ　MC sjuwX
1. rinsewater that has been fouled by using it to
soak rice.
 a. stale or befouled water.

xiù

嗅　xiù　MC xjuwH　⊙ 齅 *xiù*.

宿　xiù　MC sjuwH　→ 宿 *sù*.

岫　xiù　MC zjuwH
1. hill-cleft, gap; chink, cave; notch of mountain
range.
 a. (med.) summit, peak; ragged outline of
mountain range.

琇　xiù　MC sjuwH
1. precious stone similar to jade, perhaps jasper.

秀　xiù　MC sjuwH
1. inflorescence of grain, grain coming into ear.
 a. ripen(ed), mature; accomplished, culminating; well-made.
 b. gracefully curved like feathery awn of
grain; exquisite; tasteful; charming.
2. flowering, be in full bloom, full-blown, flour-
ish(ing).
 a. burgeon; thrive, prosper.
3. eximious, salient; first-rate, excellent, "the
flower of…"

繡　xiù　MC sjuwH
1. multi-colored embroidery.
 a. embroider(ed), decorate(d), adorn(ed),
embellish(ed); ornate.

臭　xiù　MC xjuwH　→ 臭 *chòu*.

袖   xiù   MC zjuwH

1. sleeve, of clothing.
   a. ensleeve, place or hide in the sleeve.

褎   xiù   MC zjuwH   → 褎 *yòu*.

齅   xiù   MC xjuwH

1. to smell, sniff, nose, get a whiff of, inhale.

xū

吁   xū   MC xju

1. gasp, onom. of surprise, "Whew!" or dismay, "Oh no!".
2. to sigh, "Ahh...".

嘘   xū   MC xjo

1. onom. of exhaling serenely, in a satisfied and unhurried manner; a sigh of ease and contentment.
2. (med.) spit, expectorate.
3. ⊙ 歔 *xū*, breathe hard.

墟   xū   MC khjo

1. large mound, hill.
2. wasteland, barrens.
   a. abandoned area, desert(ed), neglect(ed); ruins.
3. graveyard, burial grounds, cemetery.
4. (med.) village, dorp, hamlet.
5. (med.) market-site, country fair.

戌   xū   MC swit

1. 11th of the 12 earthly branches, associated with dog as emblematic animal.
2. (bn.) ～削 *xūxuē* (MC swit-sjak), fittingly fashioned or tastefully tailored, of clothes; also, slim and spare, lean and lanky.

歔   xū   MC xjo

1. fnast, breathe hard or laboriously; exhale deeply; snort.
   a. (bn.) ～欷 *xūxī* (MC xjo-xj+j), break down in sobs, give way to tears, weep woefully; also, sigh sadly.

欻   xū   MC xjut

1. flicker upward; in a flash; sudden onset; all of a sudden; (bn.) ～吸 *xūxī* (MC xjut-xip), in a flash and a flicker, lickety-split.
   a. (med.) flaw, sudden heavy gust of wind, wind-shear.

盱   xū   MC xju

1. sgl. or rdup., look at wide-eyed; take it all in.
2. broad, wide; enlarge(d), expand.
3. saddened; afflicted by sorrow or disappointment.
4. cnidium (*Cnidium monnieri*), herbaceous flowering plant, an umbellifer similar to selinea (*miwu* 蘼蕪).

盇   xū   MC xwek

1. onom. of tearing meat from bones: "shyook."
   a. (med.) onom. of an arrow's flight or bird's skimming flight: "syoooh."
2. (med.) swiftly, rapidly; skimming quickly.

胥   xū   MC sjo

1. mutually, reciprocally.
   a. (al)together; completely.
   b. in all cases, every.
2. assist, come to the aid of.
   a. wait on, linger, tarry; attend to; see to; accompany.
3. survey, look over; inspect.
4. follow, conform with, adhere to.
5. treat distantly, be estranged from, set apart.
6. in a moment, quick as can be.
7. crab-pickle.
    xǔ   MC sjoX
1. subaltern official in local administration, usu. unranked.
2. village elder.

虚   xū   MC xjo

1. empty, unfilled, unoccupied, untenanted, void. Positive attribute in Dao. and *xuanxue* discourse, connoting formless but radical potentiality, e.g. 太～ *tàixū*, "Grand Void," reservoir of primal pneuma (*yuanqi* 元氣) associated with *yang* energy; (Budd.) the fundamental unreality and impermanence of all phenomena, often syn. 空 *kōng* 3.
   a. depleted, blighted, wasted; emptied, devoid of.
   b. death, as emptiness (ant. 生 *shēng*, life).
2. attenuate(d), stretched thin; of streams, shallow.
   a. insubstantial (ant. 實 *shí*); without definable content, plastic, changeable; immaterial.
   b. discontinuous; a weak point.
   c. imponderable, hard to grasp; subtle.
3. the air, the sky; space, as seemingly empty.
4. unreal, false; factitious, spurious.

5. to no avail, in vain; useless(ly), worthless; needless, pointless.

6. unassuming, dispassionate, self-effacing, humble; inconsequential, trifling.

7. "Barrens," one of the 28 lunar lodgings, comprised of β Aquarii and α Equulei, in the northern quadrant (*xuanwu* 玄武) of the sky.

xū　MC khjo

1. ⊙ 墟 *xū*, large mound, hill; wasteland, barrens, abandoned area, ruins.

訏　xū　MC xju

1. exaggerate, overstate; magnify; vaunt.
   a. mislead, deceive; cully.
2. sgl. or rdup., large(ly), vast(ly); grandiose.

諝　xū　MC sjo

1. intellect, aptitude; acumen; astute(ness).
   a. shrewd(ness), guile(ful); scheme, strategy.

需　xū　MC sju

1. wait for, await; stand by; anticipate; e.g. ～頭 *xūtóu*, empty space left at the front of an official petition, "awaiting" the ruler's written comment.
   a. hesitate, procrastinate, delay; tergiversate, shuffle; linger.
   b. "waiting," name of 5th hexagram of *Yijing*.
2. put a stop to; halt.
3. have need of, have occasion for; necessary; necessity, require(ment).

ruǎn　MC nywenX

1. ⊙ 軟 *ruǎn*, pliant, supple.

nuò　MC nwanH

1. weak, feeble; timid.

須　xū　MC sju

1. (ADV) need to VB, must needs VB, is necessary to VB, calls for VB-ing (cf. 必 *bì*, is certain to VB).
   a. require(d); want, demand, call for.
   b. necessary, needful.
2. wait for, stay for, attend on; attentive; expect(ant).
3. dilatory, slow, tardy; to retard, slow down, arrest the progress of.
4. sgl. or (bn.) ～臾 *xūyú* (MC sju-yu), shortly, presently, in a while, momentarily; bn. also, leisurely, at length; also, name of a *yinyang* 陰陽 divination method; 斯～ *sīxū* (MC sje-sju), in an instant.
5. turnip, field mustard (*Brassica rapa*).
6. barbel, slender tactile protrusion from the lips or jaw of certain fishes.

7. ⊙ 鬚 *xū*, beard, whiskers.

8. (Budd.) ～彌 *xūmí* (MC sju-mjie), abb. trsc. Skt. *sume*[*ru*], Mt. Sumeru, mythical axis mundi; ～菩提 *xūpútí* (MC sju-bu-dej), trsc. Skt. *subhūti*, Subhūti, name of a favored disciple of the Buddha; ～陀 *xūtuó* (MC sju-da), trsc. Skt. *sudhā*, ambrosia, nectar of the gods; ～陀洹 *xūtuóhuán* (MC sju-da-hwan), trsc. Skt. *srotāpanna*, "stream-winner," one who has entered the stream of the buddha-dharma and will eventually attain *nirvāṇa*; ～曼[那] *xūmànnà* (MC sju-mjonH-naH), trsc. Skt. *sumana*, great flowering jasmine.

項　xū　MC xjowk

1. rdup., disappointed and dejected; peeved and nettled
2. 顓～ *zhuānxū*, Zhuanxu, one of the 5 mythical god-kings (*di* 帝) of prehistory.

驉　xū　MC xjo

1. (bn.) 駏～ *jùxū*, → 駏 *jù*.

鬚　xū　MC sju

1. beard(ed), whiskers; hispid, bristly.
2. tendril, of vine; antenna, of animal; barbel, of fish.

xú

徐　xú　MC zjo

1. proceed calmly; sedate(ly), staid(ly), with dignity, deliberate(ly); unruffled.
   a. at one's ease, in relaxed fashion; leisurely.
2. a surname.

xǔ

煦　xǔ　MC xjuX

1. blow out, exhale; spit.
   a. blow or direct warm air on; rekindle, revive.
   b. protect; care for, comfort.
2. rdup., kind(ly), amiable; also (med.), cautious and careful.

姁　xǔ　MC xjuX

1. (bn.) ～媮 *xǔyú* (MC xjuX-yu), in fine fashion, in a handsome manner.

qú　MC gju

1. rdup., contentedly complacent; also, mild and moderate.

栩　xǔ　MC xjuX
1. rdup., glad and gay, happy and light-hearted; smug and satisfied.
2. the serrated oak (*Quercus serrata*), syn. 櫟 *lì*.

湑　xǔ　MC sjoX
1. to strain wine.
　　a. well-strained wine, clear and without sediment.
2. dew-like, dewy, moist like dew; refreshing as dew.
　　a. drip(ping).
3. sgl. or rdup., full and flourishing, in lavish profusion; rdup. also (med), fresh and favoring, clear and breezy, of the wind.
4. joyful, in high spirits.

糈　xǔ　MC sjoX
1. the finest, unmixed rice, suitable for use in sacrificial offerings.
2. grain, cereals; foodstuff.

絮　xǔ　MC sjuX
1. (med.) hobble the front feet of a horse or ox.
　　a. (med.) fetter, truss; hamper, hinder.

許　xǔ　MC xjoX
1. allow, permit, consent to; authorize; admit; e.g. 自～ *zìxǔ*, make allowances for oneself, speak or think highly of oneself.
　　a. acknowledge, approve of, endorse; admire, praise.
　　b. put one's trust in, agree with; promise, pledge.
2. bestow on, confer, consign; deliver, as a daughter in marriage.
　　a. devote or dedicate oneself to.
3. hope for; expect.
4. a place, often in conjunction with interr., e.g. 何～人 *héxǔ rén*, a person from who knows where.
　　a. (med.) mansion.
5. (med.) appraise, evaluate; calculate, forecast.
6. (med.) perhaps, probably.
　　a. (med.) be roughly equivalent to, approximate(ly), more or less; somewhat.
7. (med.) in this way, in this manner, like this.
　　a. (med.) interr., in what way? how?
8. (med.) GP, phrase-final particle expressing puzzlement or chagrin.

詡　xǔ　MC xjuX
1. indulge in a flight of fancy, exaggerate, overstate.
　　a. heighten, deck out, elaborate; garnish, trick out.
2. rdup., on good terms jointly, in mutual agreement; comfortable and content.

醑　xǔ　MC sjoX
1. (med.) choice wine.

xù

恤　xù　MC xwik
1. quiet(ness), sedate; peaceful, tranquil.

勖　xù　MC xjowk
1. put all one's effort into, do everything one can, go all out.
　　a. encourage, embolden; urge onward.

勗　xù　MC xjowk　⊙ 勖 *xù*.

卹　xù　MC swit
1. rub; brush, sweep.
2. ⊙ 恤 *xù*, to rue, have compassion for.

呴　xù　MC xjuH
1. breathe warmly upon.
　　a. spit; moisten.
2. (med.) soothing(ly); amiable.
　　hǒu　MC xuwX
1. roar or shriek of animal.
　　gòu　MC kuwH
1. cock's crow.

壻　xù　MC sejH
1. daughter's husband, son-in-law.
2. (med.) wife's term of address for husband, usu. 夫～ *fūxù*.

婿　xù　MC sejH　⊙ 壻 *xù*.

序　xù　MC zjoX
1. sequence, progress(ion), succession, e.g. sequence of the seasons.
　　a. order, arrangement; rank(ing), precedence.
　　b. put in order, arrange in sequence.
2. recount, narrate.

3. the foreword or afterword of a text; from early med. times on, always placed before the text, so > preface, prolegomenon.
    a. (med.) (lit.) a text written upon seeing someone off and presented to the departing person.
4. lateral (east-west) walls of a structure; lateral apartments, wings.
    a. antechamber.
5. anciently, a hamlet school where emphasis was traditionally said to be on learning the proper hierarchy (序) of old and young, a palestra; e.g. 庠～ *xiángxù*, district and hamlet schools, local lyceums and palestrae.

恤　xù　MC swit

1. to rue; heartache, woe(ful); have compassion for.
    a. care for; palliate, alleviate; relieve, mitigate.
    b. empathize with, be solicitous of.
2. charity; almsgiving.

慉　xù　MC xjuwk

1. be fond of, have a liking for; cherish.
2. ⊙ 蓄 *xù* 1, accumulate, store up.

敘　xù　MC zjoX

1. ⊙ 序 *xù* 1-3.

旭　xù　MC xjowk

1. the just risen sun, daystar; first sunlight of the day, aurora.
    a. crack of dawn, daybreak.
2. rdup., gleam(ing) and glow(ing), luciferous; also, (med.) self-satisfied, basking in one's own enjoyment.
3. (med.) sunlight, sun-glare; brilliance; shining, sheen.

昫　xù　MC xjuH

1. sgl. or rdup., warmth of the rising sun; become warm.
    a. (med.) warm(th); cordial(ity); gracious(-ness), kind(ness).

洫　xù　MC xwik

1. irrigation ditch, canal, trench.
2. moat, fosse, as barrier protecting city-wall.
3. sluice-gate, for regulating flow of water.
    a. to empty out, drain away.
4. deteriorate(d), destroy(ed).

    yì　MC yit

1. ⊙ 溢 *yì*, brim over; excessive; 鎰 *yì*, measure of weight, equiv. 24 兩 *liàng* ("ounces").

漵　xù　MC zjoX

1. (med.) riverside, strand.

煦　xù　MC xjuH　⊙ 昫 *xù*.

畜　xù　MC xjuwk　→ 畜 *chù*.

絮　xù　MC sjoH

1. silk floss; cotton wool.
    a. shaggy, flossy, fuzzy.
    b. to sleave: separate into filaments of silk; silk so separated.
2. catkins, floss-like aments esp. of willow or birch; also used as euph. for any white-colored flossy item, such as spiderwebs.
3. wadding, padding for clothing; to pad, stuff with wadding.

緒　xù　MC zjoX

1. clue, one end of a thread.
    a. starting point, beginning.
    b. remainder, oddment, something left over; linger(ing); e.g. ～言 *xùyán*, words left unfinished.
2. heartstrings; pang(s); e.g. 別～ *biéxù*, pangs of separation.
3. following one after another, succession, e.g. generations of a lineage; connected points in a joined sequence.
    a. hereditary possession, e.g. property, profession, title.
4. put in order; join up the links, make connections.

續　xù　MC zjowk

1. connect up with, tie together, join end to end; splice.
    a. continue, go on; carry forward, succeed; continuer, inheritor, successor.
    b. append(ix), supplement; follow(ing).
2. (Budd.) all the same, also; still.

蓄　xù　MC xjuwk

1. amass, accumulate; hoard, store up, stockpile; reserve, preserve.
    a. brood on or over (thoughts or animals); nurture, nurse, rear, raise, used esp. with regard to livestock (cf. 養 *yǎng*, usu. pertaining to humans).

2. wait for, abide.

3. (bn.) ～縮 *xùsuō* (MC xjuwk-srjuwk), shrink and shy away, draw back, pull away, cower and recoil.

蕒   xù   MC zjowk

1. water-plantain (*Alisma orientale*), hairless plant that grows in shallow water, flowers have three white or pale purple petals that open in the afternoon.

誶   xù   MC swit

1. induce or incite to action by force or threat; be so induced.

2. misadvise(d), misguide(d), misdirect(ed).

酗   xù   MC xjuH

1. indulge intemperately in wine, besotted, awash, crapulous.

    a. drunkenly out of control, raving, unthinking.

鱮   xù   MC zjoX

1. the silver carp, whitefish (*Hypophthalmich-thys molitrix*), syn. 鰱 *lián*.

xuān

亘   xuān   MC sjwen   → 亘 *gèn*.

儇   xuān   MC xjwien

1. astute, clever-witted, quick to catch on.

    a. spry, nimble.

2. crafty, wily, canny, shrewd.

3. frivolous, impertinent.

喧   xuān   MC xjwon

1. din, strident babble, stridulent; hubbub; e.g. ～鬧 *xuānnào*, babble and hubbub.

    a. shrieking, screaming; blaring.

宣   xuān   MC sjwen

1. spread, diffuse; circulate widely.

    a. widespread, extensive; comprehensive; e.g. ～遊 *xuānyóu*, travel widely.

    b. complete(ly), thorough(ly), explicit(ly); e.g. 不～ *bùxuān*, "I cannot express myself fully" (at end of personal letter).

2. exhibit publicly; proclaim, promulgate, esp. of ruler's orders; broadcast; manifest(o); e.g. ～室 *xuānshì*, proclamation hall, hall of state.

    a. (Budd.) to instruct, teach, preach.

3. seep away, drain off; disperse.

4. grizzled, graying, of hair.

5. (med.) epithet of respect, applied to Confucius: ～父 Xuanfu.

6. ancient measure of length, "cubit," equiv. 1.33 *chi* 尺 ("feet").

揎   xuān   MC sjwen

1. roll up, turn up.

暅   xuān   MC xjwon

1. gently warm, tepid; mild, genial; softly pleasant.

翾   xuān   MC xjwien

1. flit, dart(le); quiver.

    a. agile, light-footed; skip, jump.

2. flippant, flighty.

萱   xuān   MC xjwon

1. daylily (*Hemerocallis fulva*), syn. 忘憂 *wàngyōu*, plant that "allows one to forget one's sorrows."

諠   xuān   MC xjwon

1. ⊙ 喧 *xuān*, din, brawl; 諼 *xuān* 1, cheat, deceive; 2, forget.

諼   xuān   MC xjwon

1. to cheat, deceive, play false.

2. to forget.

3. ⊙ 萱 *xuān*, daylily, plant that "allows one to forget one's sorrows."

軒   xuān   MC xjon

1. a coach, esp. one used by grandees and above; e.g. ～冕 *xuānmiǎn*, lordly coach and coronet.

    a. fine coaches in general, esp. high-railed ones.

    b. a front-canted coach, lower in the rear.

2. railing, banister, balustrade, as of porch; e.g. 臨～ *línxuān*, railed platform in front of throne-hall whence the emperor temporarily holds sway.

    a. (med.) a privy, esp. the hand-rail.

3. window with wooden frame, casement.

    a. veranda or portico with casement windows.

4. (med.) lift up, raise(d), heighten(ed), e.g. 眉～ *méixuān*, raised eyebrows.

a. (med.) jump, rise up, bound.

b. (med.) high up, lofty, aloft; fly, soar(ing); rdup., light and airy; also, radiantly beaming.

xiàn　MC xjonH

1. meat cut in large slices (cf. 膾 *kuài*, in thin-minced slices; 胾 *zì*, large chunks).

xuán

懸　**xuán　MC hwen**

1. suspend, hang up; e.g. 〜鉤 *xuán'gōu*, suspended hook, also euph. for a waning moon; (Dao.)〜膺 *xuányīng*, "suspended in the breast," esoteric term for the trachea.

a. beetling, dangling, hanging; downward, headlong; precipitant; e.g. 〜河 *xuánhé*, a precipitant, headlong-rushing stream, descriptive of a waterfall, euph. for one with a ready flow of language.

b. without foundation, untied to reality; imaginary.

2. things you depend on or are tied to, e.g. 〜解 *xuánjiě*, "freeing of (loosening) the bonds," in complete conformity with what life offers.

3. be in suspense, preoccupied; anxious; "hung up on."

a. (med.) worry about, in various cmpds. e.g. 〜心 *xuánxīn*, 〜想 *xuánxiǎng*, 〜情 *xuánqíng*.

4. frame from which bells or lithophones are suspended.

a. (med.) musical tones, pitches; music in general.

5. (med.) far from, a long distance away, in space or time; e.g. (Budd.) 〜記 *xuánjì*, long-range prophecy.

a. (med.) isolated, off by oneself; e.g. 〜兵 *xuánbīng*, army that has gone far into enemy territory.

旋　**xuán　MC zjwen**

1. rotate, turn back on oneself, pivot; spin, whirl; twine, twirl; e.g. 〜胡 *xuánhú*, whirling fashion of dance brought into the Tang dynasty from Central Asia.

a. coil, whorl, like a tuft of hair.

b. 〜機 *xuánjī*, the 2 rotating ends of a loom's roller.

2. return, go back, turn back; circle round; e.g. 周〜 *zhōuxuán*, make a full circuit; 〜踵 *xuán-*

zhǒng, turn on one's heel; 不〜踵 *bùxuánzhǒng*, be unwavering, steadfast.

3. immediately, right away; soon after that, not long after.

a. (med.) temporarily, in short order, for the occasion.

b. (med.) 〜 A 〜 B, on the one hand A, on the other B.

4. (med.) frequent(ly); rdup., at a steadily measured pace, slowly but surely, bit by bit.

5. protrusion or bulging ring around the shank of a chime-bell.

6. urinate.

xuàn　MC zjwenH

1. 〜風 *xuànfēng*, whirlwind; tornado; vortex.

漩　**xuán　MC zjwen**

1. (med.) eddy(ing), vortex; whirling, whirlpool.

a. (bn.) 〜澴 *xuánhuán* (MC zjwen-hwaen), whirling and swirling, of water.

玄　**xuán　MC hwen**

1. the quality of permitting the passage of light but without making visible what is on the other side, translucent, semi-transparent, e.g. the sky as a medium through which light passes from beyond it (N.B. not "dark" as aphotic, cf. 冥 *míng* dark-cast, darkling).

2. not able to be fully known or described in detail, hinting at something beyond what is apparent > mysterious, mystery; abstruse, recondite, arcane, dark to the mind; inexplicable.

a. often used as syn. of 道 *dào*, the Way, "the mysterium"; e.g. 〜風 *xuánfēng*, a manner comporting with the mystery [of the Dao], exhibiting a vogue for the "mysterious"; 〜學 *xuánxúe*, "abstruse learning," "the learning of the mysterious," mode of thought and discourse developed in the 3rd century and remaining influential through the early 5th century, making much reference to the "3 texts of mystery" (*sānxuán* 三〜), i.e. *Yijing*, *Laozi*, *Zhuangzi*.

b. to deepen, darken; make mysterious.

3. as color, sloe or sloe-black (mainly an early usage).

4. dim, dun; darkling; murky, opaque.

a. associated with heaven, as "yellow" (*huang* 黃) is with earth, hence 〜黃 *xuán-huáng*, the realms of the dark and the yellow > heaven and earth.

b. common descriptor in Dao. esoteric terms, e.g. ～鄉 *xuánxiāng*, "murky parish," the kidneys; ～池 *xuánchí*, "murky pond," the bladder; ～元 *xuányuán*, "mysterious prime," state of the original undifferentiated *qi* 氣 of heaven and earth; also abb. form of ～元皇帝 *xuányuán huángdì*, "Illustrious Thearch of the Mysterious Prime," title of canonized Laozi, bestowed in 666.

c. syn. of black as symbolic color of north in *wuxing* correspondences; e.g. ～武 *xuánwǔ*, "dusky warrior," emblematic animal of the north usu. portrayed as snake wrapped round a tortoise; also, the northern quadrant of the sky.

5. ～枵 *xuánxiāo*, "Murky Hollow," one of the 12 Jupiter stations, incl. the lunar lodgings 女 *nǚ* ("Woman"), 虛 *xū* ("Barrens"), and 危 *wēi* ("Steep Roof").

璇   xuán   MC zjwen

1. jadestone, gemstone; descriptive of something finely decorated, e.g. (med.) ～閨 *xuánguī*, "jadestone boudoir," ornately accoutered women's quarters.

2. revolving or swiveling jade, jade-cog.

a. sgl. or in cmpd. 天～ *tiānxuán*, "Heaven's Jade-cog," 2nd star of the Big Dipper (β Ursae Majoris, = Merak).

b. ～機 *xuánjī*, "Jade-cog and Armil," the four stars of the bowl of the Dipper (α, β, γ, δ Ursae Majoris, = Dubhe, Merak, Phecda, Megrez); also, an ancient astronomical device, supposedly made at behest of the sage-king Shun 舜, reputedly the swiveling mechanism of an armillary sphere; also, "turning sphere," the constellations of heaven.

c. ～機圖 *xuánjītú*, "design of the turning sphere," said to be a multicolored brocade pattern of 840 graphs (29 horizontal columns by 29 vertical columns, with center spot blank) woven by Su Hui 蘇蕙 (fl. ca. 350) and sent to her husband Dou Tao 竇滔, comprising more than 200 poems when read in various patterns vertically, horizontally, diagonally, backwards, forwards, circularly, etc.

d. ～機玉衡 *xuánjī yùhéng*, "Jadestone Armil and Jade Transverse," the bowl and handle of the Dipper; also, reputedly the ancient armillary sphere and sighting tube; also > the dome of heaven.

璿   xuán   MC zjwen   ⊙ 璇 *xuán*.

xuǎn

烜   xuǎn   MC xjwonX

1. burning, flaming; dazzling, brilliant.

a. to singe; dry out, parch.

2. impressively manifest, brazen, of sight or sound; e.g. (bn.) ～爀 *xuǎnhè* (MC xjwonX-xaek), strepently sonorous, blazingly blaring.

huǐ   MC xjweX

1. blaze, fiery; heat of the sun.

選   xuǎn   MC sjwenX

1. select(ion), choose.

a. (med.) selection by recommendation and examination for a position in the bureaucracy.

b. (med.) (lit.) selection of literary compositions for inclusion in an anthology, e.g. *Wen xuan* 文～, "Selections of Refined Literature," compiled by Xiao Tong 蕭統 (501-531).

2. send away, dispatch.

xùn   MC swonH

1. ⊙ 巽 *xùn*, weak; yielding.

suàn   MC swanH

1. ⊙ 算 *suàn*, reckon, calculate.

shuā   MC srweat

1. unit of silver cash, weighing 8 ounces (*liang* 兩).

xuàn

泫   xuàn   MC hwenH

1. trickle; leak; to bead.

a. weep; flow, run.

b. glisten; reflect.

2. (bn.) ～沄 *xuànyún* (MC hwenH-hjunH), froth and foam.

炫   xuàn   MC hwenH

1. dazzling, resplendent; sparkling, scintillating.

a. (be)dazzle, daze; astonish.

b. highlight, accent; vaunt, flaunt, show off.

眩   xuàn   MC hwenH

1. eyesight dimmed, see vaguely as in a fog, blurred vision.

a. bedimmed, unclear; confused.

b. (bn.) ～湣 *xuànmiàn* (MC hwenH-menH), darken and bedim, bleared and blurred.

2. ～耀 *xuànyào*, dazzle and sparkle, shine brightly; also, show off, highlight, flaunt.

3. ⊙ 衒 *xuàn* 2, 炫 *xuàn*, (be)dazzle, delude.

huàn　MC hweanH

1. ⊙ 幻 *huàn*, illusory.

絢　xuàn　MC xwenH

1. beribboned, beautifully dressed.

   a. adorn, trim, embellish; enrich.

   b. exquisite, elegant.

2. (med.) measure-word for five ounces of silk.

衒　xuàn　MC hwenH

1. hawk wares along the road; offer for sale, peddle.

2. (be)dazzle; delude, beguile.

3. highlight, shed light on; show off, flaunt, vaunt; exhibit with flare.

袨　xuàn　MC hwenH

1. dark-colored ritual clothing.

2. (med.) splendid, resplendent, of clothing.

鉉　xuàn　MC hwenH

1. bent bar that one passes through the handles of a steaming cauldron, so it may be carried, usu. by two persons.

2. ⊙ 弦 *xián* 1, bowstring.

xuē

削　xuē　MC sjak

1. trimmer, curved double-edged knife used in ancient times to erase characters written on wood or bamboo strips, by paring them off.

   a. pare, skive, sheer; scrape away; trim; chisel.

   b. cut short, curtail; reduce, diminish.

   c. cut up, partition(ed), of land.

qiào　MC sjewH

1. ⊙ 鞘 *qiào*, sheath of sword.

薛　xuē　MC sjet

1. a species of artemisia, perhaps *Artemisia apiacea*, whose leaves may be woven together to make rain clothing.

2. (med.) ～延陀 *xuēyántuó*, Türkic tribe who were part of the Tang-time Tiele 特勒 confederation, one of the "nine clans" (九姓) of the Toquz Oghuz (N.B. not to be identified with the Syr Tardush).

3. a surname.

靴　xuē　MC xjwa　→ 鞾 *xuē*.

鞾　xuē　MC xjwa

1. (med.) boots, footgear covering up to shin or higher.

xué

學　xué　MC haewk

1. imitate, emulate, mimic; study, learn, esp. by imitation.

   a. copy, model oneself upon, perform in the manner of.

2. learned, knowledgeable; studious, well-schooled.

3. school of higher order in capital or important city; seminary, academy.

4. (Budd.) ～不～ *xuébùxué*, learners and those who have no more to learn; (Budd.) ～持者 *xuéchízhe*, those who study and retain [the scriptures] in their mind.

澩　xué　MC haewk

1. pool or small lake that is full in summer but dry in winter.

xiào　MC haewX

1. (bn.) ～獥 *xiàoqiāo* (MC haewX-khaew), hustle and bustle, tumultuous tangle, of a noisy throng; (bn.) ～灂 *xiàozhuó* (MC haewX-dzraewk), crashing and colliding, raging and roaring, of waves.

穴　xué　MC hwet

1. cave, cavern; rock-cut cavity; pit.

   a. enclosed, constricted area or view; e.g. ～見 *xuéjiàn*, tunnel vision, restricted view.

   b. coffin pit, gravesite, tomb.

2. lair, den; nest.

3. puncture, pierce; tunnel through, bore.

xuě

雪　xuě　MC sjwet

1. snow.

2. wipe clean as snow; purge dishonor snow-white.

   a. wipe away; e.g. ～泣 *xuěqì*, wipe away tears.

xuè

哎　xuè　MC xjwiet

1. a faint sound; wheeze, hiss.

沉 xuè MC xwet

1. ～寥 *xuèliáo*, empty infinity, measureless vastness, broad and everspreading (sky); also (med.), cold and alone, still and isolated.

血 xuè MC xwet

1. blood; sanguinary.
   a. blood-ties between relations, consanguinity.
2. tears cried so grievously that they are as blood.
3. blood-red in color.

衁 xuè MC xjwot

1. take wing, fly, take flight, soar off.

謔 xuè MC xjak

1. to joke, toy with, jest; raillery, badinage; quip.
   a. mirth, merriment, jollity.

xūn

勛 xūn MC xjun   → 勳 *xūn*.

勳 xūn MC xjun

1. meritorious deed, gest; exploit; accomplishment.
   a. merit(s); fine qualities.
2. guerdon, reward for merit.
   a. (med.) merit title, official title awarded as special honor, usu. graded coincident with one's regular rank.

塤 xūn MC xjwon   → 壎 *xūn*.

壎 xūn MC xjwon

1. vessel-flute, globular flute with six holes, made of fired clay; does not have the mouthpiece and internal duct that an ocarina does, rather the player blows against the rim of an apical hole.

曛 xūn MC xjun

1. twilight gloaming, crepuscular glimmer.
2. ⊙ 纁 *xūn*, color of twilight, pale orange.

熏 xūn MC xjun

1. fumes, smoke; haze, smog, (be)cloud.
   a. to cense, scent, aromatize; musk.
   b. (med.) ～陸(香) *xūnlùxiāng* (MC xjun-ljuwk), frankincense, trsc. of Skt. *kundu-ruka*, aromatic resin from the tree *Boswellia thurifera*.
   c. ～貍 *xūnlí*, "censing cat," the civet (*Viverridae*), so called because of the musk produced by its perineal glands.
2. to influence; touch; taint.
3. pleasantly warm; genial, warming.
4. broil.
5. ⊙ 曛 *xūn*, twilight gloaming.

纁 xūn MC xjun

1. pink, orange-pink, pale orange, color of twilight sky.
2. ⊙ 曛 *xūn*, twilight gloaming.

薰 xūn MC xjun

1. ⊙ 蕙 *huì*, sweet basil; also, melilot.
2. loosestrife (*Lysimachia foenum-graecum*), curry-scented perennial herb.
3. fragrant, sweet-smelling.
   a. (bn.) ～陸 *xūnlù* (MC xjun-ljuwk), trsc. Skt. *kunduruka*, Indian frankincense (*Boswellia serrata*).
4. censer, thurible; to cense; envelop in smoke; e.g. ～籠 *xūnlóng*, censing basket.
5. ⊙ 熏 *xūn*, all meanings.

xún

尋 xún MC zim

1. a measure of 8 ft. (*chi* 尺); armspan, measured from tip of middle finger of one outstretched arm to the other; e.g. ～步(間) *xúnbùjiān*, between a hop and a skip.
   a. cmpd. ～常 *xúncháng*, measure of an armspan plus a double-armspan; also (med.), commonplace, ordinary; habitual.
   b. rdup., unbounded; endless.
2. make use of, put to use, employ.
3. (med.) follow up, trace back; explore, search out, try to find; make one's way through or to; e.g. ～真 *xúnzhēn*, search for self-realization or spiritual perfection; ～思 *xúnsī*, think it through, ponder.
   a. (med.) trace the course of, move in the track of; e.g. ～橦 *xúntóng*, climb a pole; 相～ *xiāngxún*, follow one after another, without a break.
   b. (med.) seek out, look up, find (person).
4. (med.) sgl. or in various cmpds. (e.g. ～便 *xúnbiàn*, ～時 *xúnshí*, ～即 *xunjí*, ～則 *xúnzé*), immediately; soon after, ensuing; betimes; at last, finally.

5. (med.) rdup., Zoroastrian(ism).
6. a surname.

峋　xún　MC swin

1. (bn.) 嶙 ~ *línxún*, → 嶙 *lín*.

巡　xún　MC zwin

1. make a circuit of inspection, patrol; circum-scribe, make the rounds of.
   a. perambulate; circumabulate.
   b. exhibit along a planned route, parade.
2. everywhere, pervasive; all along the way.
   a. (med.) a round of wine poured for all the guests.
3. (bn.) 逡 ~ *qūnxún*, → 逡 *qūn*.

巡　xún　MC zwin　→ 巡 *xún*.

循　xún　MC zwin

1. follow the course of, run along with.
   a. follow after, conform to; accommodate.
   b. ⊙ 巡 *xún* 1, patrol; inspect.
   c. (med.) circle round, circumscribe.
2. everywhere, pervasive.
      xùn　MC zwinH
1. expose, reveal.
2. quick(ly), speed(ily).

恂　xún　MC swin

1. sgl. or rdup., guileless, unfeigning; simple and sincere; open-hearted and ingenuous.
2. unimpeded, unblocked.
3. fearful of, anxious over.
4. rdup., with respect and care; also (med.), with shame and regret; also (med.), in sequence, orderly, step-by-step.

旬　xún　MC zwin

1. a decade of days, three of which make up a month; the standard "week" in premodern times.
   a. (med.) a decade of years, sgl. or in cmpd.; e.g. ~ 年 *xúnnián*, ten years.
   b. (med.) a unit of ten, e.g. ~ 月 *xúnyuè*, ten months.
2. complete, full, a whole cycle; e.g. ~ 歲 *xún-suì*, a whole year, ~ 月 *xúnyuè*, a whole month.
3. (med.) time in general, as a whole unit.

洵　xún　MC swin

1. weep, cry, shed tears.
2. truly, in fact.
3. far away.

潯　xún　MC zim

1. riverside, riverbank.
   a. (med.) edge of, shore of; e.g. 天 ~ *tiānxún*, shore of the sky.
      yín　MC yim
1. (bn.) 浸 ~ *qīnyín* (MC tshim-yim), steeped and soaked, drenched and doused.

燖　xún　MC zim

1. parboil, heat quickly and briefly; scald.

紃　xún　MC zwin

1. cincture, cinch; cordon.
   a. braid; ribbon, strand; knitted silk-band.
2. guideline; restraint, rule; bound(ary).
3. ⊙ 循 *xún* 1, follow along.

詢　xún　MC swin

1. inquire into; seek an opinion, consult.
   a. investigate, interrogate.
2. truly, in fact.

馴　xún　MC zwin

1. tame(d), as of animals; domesticated, trained; brought to heel.
   a. docile; kind(ly), decent; well-bred.
2. attain to gradually.
      xùn　MC xjunH
1. ⊙ 訓 *xùn*, instruct, train.

鱘　xún　MC zim

1. beaked sturgeon, paddlefish (*Psephurus gladius*).

xùn

噀　xùn　MC swonH

1. (med.) sprinkle; splatter; spit.

巽　xùn　MC swonH

1. weak; yielding, compliant; gentle.
2. one of the 8 fundamental trigrams underlying the *Yijing*'s 64 hexagrams, made up of 1 broken line topped by 2 unbroken lines, betokening compliance, submissiveness, symbolic of the wind, also of southeast direction.
   a. "Compliance," name of 57th hexagram of the *Yijing*.

徇　xùn　MC zwinH

1. follow round on tour; pass in review; patrol.

2. seize for oneself, appropriate.
   a. spend oneself on.
3. quick(ly); quick-witted.
4. ⊙ 殉 *xùn*, follow to the death.

xún   MC zwin

1. ⊙ 巡 *xún*, make the rounds of; 循 *xún*, follow after, accommodate; 尋 *xún* 2, make use of.

殉   xùn   MC zwinH

1. follow to the death; die for an ideal, cause, or out of loyalty and devotion; sacrifice one's life.
   a. be buried sacrificially with one's lord, follow in death; later, bury a grave-figurine with a ruler.
2. (med.) track down, pursue; seek after.
3. ⊙ 徇 *xún*, follow round.

汛   xùn   MC sinH

1. sprinkle, asperge, cleanse with water.
2. flush away; cast off, discard, abandon.

訊   xùn   MC sinH

1. interrogate, ask after; examine into.
   a. call to account, investigate.
2. counsel, exhort; admonish.
   a. final section or coda of a poem in *fu* 賦 form, usu. with summarizing injunction.
3. (med.) report, announce.
   a. (med.) written communication, missive; information, news, tidings; report.

訓   xùn   MC xjunH

1. instruct, tutor; advise.
   a. model; set an example.
   b. caution, admonish.
2. train, discipline.
3. bring to an understanding of; explicate, gloss, elucidate.

迅   xùn   MC swinH

1. quick(ly), speed(ily); (make) haste; e.g. ～雷 *xùnléi*, sudden clap of thunder.

遜   xùn   MC swonH

1. flee from, escape.
2. retire, withdraw; abdicate, cede one's place.
   a. compliant, submissive; humble, self-effacing, modest(y).

餗   xùn   MC sinH

1. (Dao.) cmpd. ～飯 *xùnfàn*, black rice: rice steeped in the sap of *Xolisma ovalifolia*, then steam-dried till the kernels turn black; thought to have vivifying properties (in contrast to most grains, which were regarded as feeding the 3 corporeal worms that lead to physical corruption).

鷐   xùn   MC swinH

1. (bn.) ～鸃 *xùnyí* (MC swinH-ngje), the golden pheasant (*Chrysolophus pictus*).

Y

yā

丫   yā   MC 'ae

1. (med.) fork, crotch; ref. any Y-shaped object.
   a. (med.) ～頭 *yātóu*, young child with hair bound up in two tufts.

壓   yā   MC 'aep

1. press down on, force down; weigh down, compress.
   a. force, compel; oppress.
   b. close off; suppress; stifle, inhibit > place oneself above, override.
   c. suppress a malevolent influence; exorcise.
   d. bring under control, calm.
2. (med.) draw close to, approach closely; near to, close on.

3. one of the final steps in the process of making rice-wine, when the fermented mash is placed on a bamboo mat or screen in a trough and then pressed down with a board, causing the liquid to flow out.

押   yā   MC 'aep

1. (med.) sign and/or seal an official document.
2. (med.) control; direct, supervise, superintend.
3. (med.) hanger(s), as for curtains.
4. (med.) ⊙ 壓 *yā*, all meanings.

鴉   yā   MC 'ae

1. jackdaw, daw (*Corvus dauuricus*), a small crow.
2. crow-black in color.
   a. (med.) sometimes ref. to the yellow of the beak, e.g. ～黃 *yāhuáng*, "daw-yellow," yellow

cosmetic applied to woman's forehead, in proximity to the hair.

鴨　yā　MC 'aep

1. common duck; general term for waterfowl.
2. (med.) ～腳 yājiǎo, "duck-foot," a kind of mallow; later syn. with gingko; ～跖草 yāzhícǎo, "duck-pad plant," dayflower (*Commelina communis*), blooms for only one day.

yá

崖　yá　MC ngea

1. steeply banked land, embankment; bluff, scarp.
   a. high-banked shore.
2. margin, border; edge.
3. (med.) cmpd. ～公 yágōng, "the highly-placed lord," informal address of entertainers for the emperor.

涯　yá　MC ngea

1. water's edge, shore, riverbank, embankment.
2. boundary, margin; far edge, terminus; e.g. 天～ tiānyá, the edge of the sky, ends of the earth; 生～ shēngyá, the far shore of life, to the end of one's days.
3. be bounded, restricted, measured in one's actions.
4. gauge the limits of, measure, estimate.

牙　yá　MC ngae

1. canines and molars; teeth, in general (cf. 齒 chǐ, incisors).
   a. fang(ed), tusk(ed); prong(ed).
2. bite, bite off.
3. the prong or "fang" of a crossbow, behind which the bowstring is hooked.
4. (med.) serrated banner of an army leader > the general's headquarters.
   a. (med.) official headquarters of local government, later written 衙.
5. (med.) intermediary, middleman, in trade.
6. ⊙ 芽 yá, sprout(s).

睚　yá　MC ngeaH

1. open eyes wide; e.g. ～眥 yázì, stare angrily, glare at.
   a. have a grievance.

芽　yá　MC ngae

1. sprout, shoot; young growth.
   a. bud; burgeon.

衙　yá　MC ngae

1. forecourt or front hall of emperor's residence; by synecdoche, imperial palace.
2. (med.) public office of local government.
   a. (med.) to arrange in proper order, for audience with a magistrate.
   b. (med.) lay out in orderly fashion, e.g. a stand of trees.
      yú　MC ngjo
1. rdup., rushing and racing along, whirring and whirling.

yǎ

啞　yǎ　MC 'aeX

1. mumble, gibber, speak inarticulately; incoherent; rdup. or (bn.) 嘔～ ōuyǎ, gibber-jabber.
      yā　MC 'ae
1. rdup., onom. of a daw's or crow's cry, "ca-caw!"
      è　MC 'aek
1. rdup., onom. of laughter, "heh-heh."

庌　yǎ　MC ngaeX

1. covered gallery, loggia; veranda.
2. simply-built awninged shelter, as for travelers; stall, for horses.

雅　yǎ　MC ngaeX

1. in the most proper, correct manner (often glossed as 正 zhèng, correct, proper); to correct.
   a. courtly; decorous, in the best taste; elegant; noble.
   b. dignified; cultivated, refined; graceful, easy.
   c. sometimes associated phonetically (< OC *N-ˤGraʔ) with 夏 xià (OC gˤraʔ?), the earliest dynasty and, by metonymy, what is quintessentially "Chinese."
2. (lit.) collective name for odes in the 2nd and 3rd sections of *Shijing*, the Greater and Lesser Elegantiae, or Greater and Lesser Court Odes (大/小～).
3. ordinarily, normally.
4. (med.) extremely, especially.
5. (med.) a large beaker of wine.

yà

亞　yà　MC ʼaeH

1. next in order; secondary; junior.
2. inferior, second-rate.
3. (med.) be next to; equal to, well-matched.
4. ⊙ 婭 yà, term of address between sons-in-law.

圠　yà　MC ʼeat

1. (bn.) 块～ yǎngyà, → 块 yǎng.

婭　yà　MC ʼaeH

1. term of address between sons-in-law.

搎　yà　MC ʼeat

1. pull on, pull up; tug.
   a. lift up, raise.

猰　yà　MC ʼeat

1. (bn.) ～貐 yàyǔ (MC ʼeat-yuX), a fabulous dragon-headed man-devouring monster.

訝　yà　MC ngaeH

1. meet; receive.
2. astounded, amazed; dumbstruck.

軋　yà　MC ʼeat

1. roll over on, crush; grind against.
   a. overpower, overwhelm.
2. jostle, press against.
3. (med.) rdup., onom. of grinding, creaking, clattering, or rattling sounds, as of carts, looms, oars, etc.
4. (bn.) 块～ yǎngyà (MC ʼangX-ʼeat), → 块 yǎng.

迓　yà　MC ngaeH

1. to meet, come upon.
   a. welcome, receive.

yān

咽　yān　MC ʼen

1. gullet, throat, windpipe; e.g. ～帶 yāndài, throatband, of horse's bridle.

yàn　MC ʼenH

1. swallow; gulp.

yē　MC ʼet

1. choke down, choke back, muffle(d); catch in the throat, sob; gurgle, "glug," onom. of air or water escaping through narrow aperture.
   a. cram, fill up; gorge.

嫣　yān　MC ʼjen

1. full and beautiful; e.g. ～然 yānrán, with happy heart; ～紅 yānhóng, ravishingly red.

崦　yān　MC ʼjem

1. ～嵫 yānzī, name of mountain in the far west behind which the sun supposedly sets.
2. (med.) far peaks.
3. (med.) a piece of, patch of; portion, part.
4. (med.) simple dwelling in mountains, hermitage.

淹　yān　MC ʼjem

1. immerse(ed), submerge(d), sink.
   a. drench(ed), sodden; inundate(d), flood(ed).
2. sluggish, as slow-moving water; detain(ed), linger(ing), stall(ed).
   a. belated, time-marking.
3. (med.) full(y); thorough(ly); deep(ly); e.g. ～旬 yānxún, a full ten days; ～博 yānbó, comprehensively learned; ～通 yāntōng, thoroughly conversant with.
4. (med.) ⊙ 掩 yǎn, cover over.

湮　yān　MC ʼen

1. submerge, sink; bury; quench.
2. stop up, block.

烟　yān　MC ʼen

1. haze, steam(y); mist(y); brumous, smoky.
   a. smoke, as from homefire or hearth, or beacon fires.
   b. infiltrate; permeate; imbrue.
2. piled ashes, used in making ink.

yīn　MC ʼjin

1. (bn.) ～氳 yīnyūn (MC ʼjin-ʼjun), vaporous haze, unparted fog, as before heaven and earth were separated.

焉　yān　MC ʼjen

1. VB-phrase initial interrog. GP: how? where? wherein?; e.g. 其 子～往 qí zǐ yān wǎng, As for his sons, where will they go?; ～用戰 yān yòng zhàn, Wherein is there any use for battling?; cog. 安 ān 4, how? where? whence?

yān　MC hjen

1. VB-phrase final GP indicating any indirect or locative relation + OBJ-pronoun: in, at, from, to, on, in regard to + it (her, him, this, that, etc.); there, therein, thereto, thereon, therefrom; e.g. 見鬼～ jiàn guǐ yān, we saw a ghost there; 寡人傳國～ guǎrén chuán guó yān, I, the sol-

itary one, handed the state over to him; 欲求富貴～ *yù qiú fùguì yān*, They wish to seek riches and honor therefrom.

   a. VB-phrase final GP indicating comparative sense: than it, than this, than that; e.g. 亂莫大～ *luàn mò dà yān*, As for chaos, nothing is greater than this; 如是其美～者乎 *rúshì qí měi yān zhě hū*, Could there be anyone lovelier than this?

2. ADV suffix: "-ly", "-ful"; e.g. 少～ *shǎoyān*, shortly (later); 使天下欣欣～ *shǐ tiānxià xīnxīn yān*, He made the subcelestial realm joyful and delightful; cog. 然 *rán*, ADV suffix.

煙　yān　MC 'en
1. ⊙ 烟 *yān* 1, 2.

閹　yān　MC 'jem
1. castrate(d); eunuch; geld(ing).
   a. ～然 *yānrán*, cringingly, obsequiously.
2. shut off, close up.

yán

嚴　yán　MC ngjaem
1. exact(ing), severe, grave, austere; rigorous, earnest.
   a. impressive, imposing; honor(able), dignified.
   b. formidable, forbidding; inspiring respect and fear; harsh; pitiless.
   c. something to beware of, be careful of, e.g. ～更 *yán'gēng*, "beware the [night-]watch," i.e. curfew drum.
2. imperative; urgent.
3. (med.) set in order, neat(en), fit out, make ready, adjust, as e.g. makeup, a carriage, etc.
   a. (med.) order, instruct; dominate, control.
4. (Budd.) garland, adorn(ment); e.g. 華～ *huáyán*, flower garland, trns. of Skt. *avataṁsa*; ～淨 *yánjìng*, adorned and purified, wholly purified.

埏　yán　MC yen
1. limits, bounds, esp. of a large area; periphery; rim, border(land).
2. (med.) tomb-path, tomb-road, route leading from the territory of the living to that of the dead.
   shān　MC syen
1. malleable clay; mud.

妍　yán　MC ngen
1. alluring beauty, captivating in appearance.
   a. superficial charm, meretricious attraction; seductive; feminine artifice.

巖　yán　MC ngaem
1. cliff; ledge; rockface overlooking land below, beetling.
   a. steep, lofty; piled high.
   b. rugged, inaccessible; precarious; forbidding.
2. mountain cave, rocky hollow.

延　yán　MC yen
1. extend, lengthen; extensive.
   a. stretch out; expand.
   b. last long, perpetual.
2. lead on, lead in; invite; attract.
   a. welcome, receive.
3. (bn.) 祥～ *fányán*, → 袢 *fán*.

檐　yán　MC yem
1. eaves, of a roof.
   a. (med.) outhanging edge, e.g. rim of a hat, lip of a goblet.
   dàn　MC tamH
1. raise, hoist.
2. ⊙ 石 *dàn*, picul.

沿　yán　MC ywen
1. follow the course of a river, follow downstream; coast.
   a. go along with, comply with, follow after.
2. adopt, accept; assume; come into.

炎　yán　MC hjem
1. burningly hot, fiery; aflame, blazing.
   a. sweltering, sweltry.
   b. incalescent, lurid, aglow.
2. inflamed; fervent, fervid, ardent.

研　yán　MC ngen
1. grind, crush to powder; rub fine, corrade; scrub.
2. sift, separate fine from coarse.
   a. sift through, pore over; examine carefully; handle in a precise way; e.g. ～究 *yánjiū*, sift and probe.
   yàn　MC ngenX
1. ⊙ 硯 *yàn*, inkstone.

筵 yán MC yen

1. groundmat, undermat made of bamboo (cf. 席 *xí*, overmat; but by med. times the distinction is rarely made); sitting-mat.

    a. seat, in general.

2. by metonymy, a convivial occasion at which one is seated > party, entertainment, revel.

簷 yán MC yem

1. ⊙ 檐 *yán* 1, eaves of a roof.

綖 yán MC yen

1. rectangular-shaped headpiece with hanging fringe of pearls, worn by the ruler or highest dignitary in a state; functionally a crown.

2. ⊙ 延 *yán* 1, extend, stretch.

xiàn MC sjenH

1. ⊙ 綫 *xiàn*, thread.

蜒 yán MC yen

1. undulant, serpentine; e.g. (bn.) 蜿～ *wānyán* (MC ʼjwon-yen), sliding and slithering.

    a. (bn.) ～蚰 *yányóu* (MC yen-yuw), slug.

    b. ～蚰蠃 *yányóuluó*, snail; syn. 蝸 *wō*.

    c. (bn.) 蚰～ *yóuyán*, → 蚰 *yóu*.

    d. (bn.) 蜻～ *qīngyán*, → 蜻 *qīng*.

言 yán MC ngjon

1. speak, talk, utter; usu. unbidden words (cf. 語 *yǔ*, words prompted in response to another's). N.B. 言 does not take as direct or indirect OBJ a personal pronoun; its OBJ must be the thing spoken about.

2. speech, talk, utterance; language.

    a. a phrase or sentence.

    b. a word; a syllable; in poetry, a beat.

3. meaningless verbal prefix or suffix; in poetry, a rhythmic particle usually found in first or second position in a line of verse or immediately after caesura.

4. a theory, teaching, doctrine.

5. (med.) regard as, take as, consider to be; count as.

    a. (med.) act as, be, esp. in interr. words, e.g. 何～ *héyán*, why? 誰～ *shéiyán*, what for?

閻 yán MC yem

1. gate within a village.

    a. a village lane.

2. (Budd.) ～浮提 *yánfútí* (MC yem-bjuw-dej), trsc. of Skt. *Jambudvīpa* (rose-apple island), continent situated south of Mt. Sumeru; ～羅 *yánluó* (MC yem-la), trsc. (with final syllable elided) of Skt. *yamarā(ja)*, name of the god of the dead, regent of hell.

3. a surname.

顏 yán MC ngaen

1. forehead.

2. face, countenance, facial features; e.g. ～色 *yánsè*, features and complexion, facial expression.

3. (med.) color(ing), tint; e.g. ～色 *yánsè*, coloring and hue.

4. (med.) plaquette, inscribed placard above a gate or entrance.

5. a surname.

鹽 yán MC yem

1. salt; brine.

    a. ～花 *yánhuā*, crystallized salt; 印～ *yìnyán*, sigilliform salt, a coarsely crystallized salt, usu. in large cubes, produced by evaporation of highly concentrated brine.

    b. ～膚 or ～麩 *yánfū*, sumac (*Rhus chinensis*).

yàn MC yemH

1. to salt, cure, pickle.

2. to season; balance; moderate, temper, render pleasing, as e.g. music.

yǎn

偃 yǎn MC ʼjonX

1. lie supine; loll.

    a. decline, fall off; diminish.

    b. fall backwards; fall down.

    c. (med.) ～仰 *yǎnyǎng*, adapt to need or custom, lean high or low; also, pompous and presumptuous.

2. in a lower position physically, below the general surface, depress(ed).

3. be at ease; repose, rest; pause; bring to an end.

    a. cut down on, reduce; withdraw from, give way; put away.

    b. place to ease oneself, privy.

4. (bn.) ～蹇 *yǎnjiǎn* (MC ʼjonX-kjonX), bending and twisting, hunched and crouched; also, drained and done in, spent and played out; also, tall and towering, raised up and aloft; also, high and haughty.

5. ⊙ 鼴 *yǎn*: ～鼠 *yǎnshǔ*, Temminck's mole, Japanese mole (*Mogera wogura*).

儼　yǎn　MC ngjaemX
1. serious(ly), grave(ly), solemn(ly), stern.
     a. reverend; ceremonious(ly), worshipful(ly).
2. neatly laid out, precisely arranged.
3. as though, like unto, seeming(ly).

剡　yǎn　MC yemX
1. sharp(en); pointed, cusp(ed); acute, keen.
     a. rise up; raise(d) up; lift(ed).
2. cut off, shear; pare.
          shàn　MC dzyemX
1. name of a river in Zhejiang and its associated area.

匽　yǎn　MC ʼjonX
1. ⊙ 偃 yǎn 1, fall, topple; 3, cease, pause.
          yàn　MC ʼenH
1. roadside latrine.
     a. wastewater ditch.

噞　yǎn　MC ngjemX
1. gape-mouthed, as fish; gaping; e.g. (bn.) ～喁 yǎnyóng (MC ngjemX-ngjowng), gaping and gawping.
     a. taste, nibble.
2. teeth-bared; fierce, ferocious.

奄　yǎn　MC ʼjemX
1. cover; extend over; enclose.
2. wholly, totally; uniformly.
3. soon, anon.
     a. (med.) sudden(ly), abrupt(ly); e.g. ～忽 yǎnhū, all at once, all of a sudden, unforeseen; also, gone for good, defunct, deceased.
          yān　MC ʼjem
1. ⊙ 淹 yān 2, linger(ing), remain(ing), halt(ed); 閹 yān, castrate(d).
2. (med.) rdup., weak(ly), faint(ly).

巘　yǎn　MC ngjonX
1. stacked mountain formation, seemingly made up of a smaller hill atop a larger one (cf. 甗 yǎn, double-steamer for cooking).
     a. hilltop; precipice.

弇　yǎn　MC ʼjemX
1. cover; conceal, veil, hide.
     a. hidden; withdrawn, secluded.
     b. overcast, clouded over.
2. deep; ample.

3. narrow(ed), strait(ened); narrow road.
     a. narrow-necked container.
4. follow, take after; succeed to; adopt.

掩　yǎn　MC ʼjemX
1. hide from view, cover up; store away (more literal than 蔽 bì).
     a. obstruct; secrete.
     b. (med.) shadow, loom over.
2. (med.) close up, close off; shut off.
3. (med.) overwhelm, overpower; exceed, surpass.
4. complete(ly), full(ly).
5. make a surprise attack; attack from hiding.

㩔　yǎn　MC ʼjemX
1. trap, esp. by covering with a net; catch, seize; gather in.
2. cover over; bury; conceal, hide.
3. perpetuate; continue.
     a. conform to, accord with.
4. hard-pressed, in difficulty.
5. (med.) outdo, better; prevail over.

渰　yǎn　MC ʼjemX
1. billowing up, of clouds, mist, vapor, etc.
          yān　MC ʼjem
1. ⊙ 淹 yān 1, immerse(d), submerge(d).

演　yǎn　MC yenX
1. flow at length, course along.
     a. extend, spread on, stretch out.
     b. reach onward; prolong, continue.
2. rehearse; represent, act out; practice.
3. develop or elaborate from a set point, play out.
4. (Budd.) expound, explain; declare, preach; emit; manifest.

琰　yǎn　MC yemX
1. pointed jade tablet or baton.

甗　yǎn　MC ngjenX
1. double-steamer, double-boiler, made up of two stacked pots, the bottom one used for boiling and the top for cooking.

眼　yǎn　MC ngeanX
1. eye; eyeball.
     a. sight, vision.
     b. the present moment; e.g. ～下 yǎnxià, right now, before one's eyes.

2. small hole, opening.
3. (med.) measure-word for wells, springs, etc.

繵   yǎn   MC yenX
1. lengthen, extend; draw out; elaborate.

罨   yǎn   MC ʻjemX
1. (med.) net, with which to trap birds or small animals.
   a. (med.) drape over, cover with; enmesh.
2. (med.) 〜畫 yǎnhuà, "reticulated with paint," gaily or brightly colored.

萫   yǎn   MC ʻjemX   → 萫 ān.

蝘   yǎn   MC ʻjonX
1. crested cicada.
      yǎn   MC ʻenX
1. (bn.) 〜蜓 yǎndiàn (MC ʻenX-denX), gecko.

衍   yǎn   MC yenX
1. overflow; flood over.
   a. run on, spread outward.
2. copious; ample; abundant; generous.
   a. superfluous, overrunning; excessive, extra; unnecessary.
   b. words added to a text by a copyist.
3. declivity; lowland.
   a. marshland; pool.
4. mountain slope.
5. bamboo basket, hamper.
      yán   MC yen
1. (med.) bring in; introduce, present.
2. (Budd.) trsc. of Skt. *yāna*, vehicle; career.

魘   yǎn   MC ʻjiemX
1. (med.) nightmare.
   a. (med.) freak(ish), grotesque, monstrous; terrifying.
2. (med.) enchant(ment), bewitch(ing).

鰋   yǎn   MC ʻjonX
1. culter, sheatfish; syn. 鮎 nián.

鷃   yǎn   MC ʻjonX
1. alt. name for 鳳 fèng, "phoenix."

黬   yǎn   MC ʻeamX
1. blue-black; bruised-looking; esp. of darkly threatening clouds.

黤   yǎn   MC ʻomX
1. black; lightless.
   a. overcast; darkened.
   b. unenlightened; in the dark; ignorant.
2. ⊙ 奄 yǎn 3, suddenly, abruptly.

黶   yǎn   MC ʻjiemX
1. black spot on the skin, mole, nevus.
   a. black-colored; swart(hy).
   b. (bn.) 〜翳 yǎnyì (MC ʻjiemX-ʻejH), sombrously shaded.

鼴   yǎn   MC ʻjonX
1. sgl. or in cmpd. 〜鼠 yǎnshǔ, Temminck's mole, Japanese mole (*Mogera wogura*), large, generally solitary mole.

齴   yǎn   MC ngenX
1. prognathous; protuberant teeth, buck-toothed.

yàn

厭   yàn   MC ʻjiemH
1. surfeit(ed), sate(d), satiate(d); fed up with; (over)full, (over)satisfied.
   a. tired of; bored with, apathetic about.
2. disgusted with, displeased.
   a. loathe, despise; spurn; cast aside.
   b. (med.) 〜禱 yàndào, imprecate.
3. convince(d); completely accept.
4. have a nightmare; ⊙ 魘 yǎn.
      yān   MC ʻjiem
1. sgl. or rdup., satisfied, content(ed); tranquil; still and serene; rdup. also, darkly dim.
      yā   MC ʻjiep
1. ⊙ 壓 yā 1, press, suppress; force down.

唁   yàn   MC ngjenH
1. solace, comfort; commiserate, condole.

喭   yàn   MC ngjenH
1. surly, rude; coarse, unmannered.
2. (med.) solace, comfort; ⊙ 唁 yàn.
3. (med.) adage, dictum.

嚥   yàn   MC ʻenH
1. swallow down.
   a. swallow back; hold back; choke back.

堰　yàn　MC ʼjonH
1. (med.) dam, dike; weir; barrier to hold back water.
    a. (med.) dam up; obstruct.

嬿　yàn　MC ʼenH
1. lovely, beautiful, comely.
2. joyous, happy.
    a. ～私 *yànsī*, affection between man and woman, love, tenderness.

宴　yàn　MC ʼenH
1. repose(ful); at ease; sedate; calm, composed.
2. serve wine and meat to guests, fête, feast, banquet; party; revel, carouse.
3. ⊙ 淹 *yān* 2, linger(ing), late.

彥　yàn　MC ngjenH
1. an intellectual, a pundit; salient talent.
2. a surname.

晏　yàn　MC ʼaenH
1. cloudless, fair, clear.
    a. vivid; bright; vibrant.
2. ～如 *yànrú*, tranquil, peaceful, reposeful, contented.
3. rdup., mild and mellow, gentle and benign, soft and soothing; also, in great abundance, richly resplendent.
4. late; linger(ing); slow-paced.

灔　yàn　MC yemH
1. sgl. or rdup., shimmering sparks of light reflected on water; also, rolling and roiling, of waves.

焰　yàn　MC yemH
1. tongue of flame, flame-tip.
    a. candle-flame.
    b. sgl. or rdup., flicker, shimmer; glimmer; quaver; flash; ray of light.
2. parboil.

焱　yàn　MC yemH
1. flaming, blazing; (bn.) ～悠 *yànyōu* (MC yemH-yuw), like flickering flames, shimmering sparks.
    biāo　MC pjiew
1. shimmering, of light; also, tempest, whirlwind; ⊙ 飆 *biāo*.

㷍　yàn　MC yemX　⊙ 焰 *yàn*.

燕　yàn　MC ʼenH
1. the swallow, martin (*Hirundinidae*).
    a. ～烏 *yànwū*, collared crow (*Corvus torquatus*).
    b. ～麥 *yànmài*, "swallow's wheat," wild oats.
2. repose(ful), at ease.
3. serve wine and meat to guests; feast, banquet; revel, carouse.
4. be familiar with, close to; intimate.
    a. ～支 or ～脂 *yànzhī*, general term for cosmetic(s).
5. name of one of the 7 major states of the Warring States period, comprising areas in present-day northern Hebei and southern Liaoning.

燗　yàn　MC yemH
1. flame, burn(ing).
    xún　MC zjem
1. ⊙ 燖 *xún*, parboil; scald.

硯　yàn　MC ngenH
1. inkstone, inkslab.
2. grind; rub; ⊙ 研 *yán* 1.

艶　yàn　MC yemH　⊙ 豔 *yàn*.

諺　yàn　MC ngjenH
1. adage, dictum, proverb.
2. (med.) surly, rude; coarse; ⊙ 喭 *yàn* 1.
3. (med.) solace; ⊙ 唁 *yàn*.

讌　yàn　MC ʼenH
1. ⊙ 宴 *yàn* 2, feast, banquet; revel.
2. general chatter, chitchat; gay talk; bonhomie.
3. (Budd.) ⊙ 燕 *yàn* 2, repose(ful), at ease, e.g. ～室 *yànshì*, quiet room, retreat.

讞　yàn　MC ngjenH
1. pronounce a sentence or judgment.
    a. appeal for judgment, lodge a complaint.

豔　yàn　MC yemH
1. seductive allure, alluring; glamor(ous), voluptuous.
    a. ravishing, luscious, of erotic or sensual appeal.
2. gorgeous, sumptuous; splendrous; of highly-wrought literary or artistic design and ornamentation.

贗　yàn　MC ngaenH
1. (med.) artificial; false.

釅 yàn   MC ngjaemH
1. (med.) heady, strong, of wine, tea, seasoning, etc.
2. (med.) deep, rich, of colors.

雁 yàn   MC ngaenH
1. wildgoose, esp. white-chested wildgoose (*Anser albifrons*).
 a. ～喙 *yánhuì*, "goose-beak," prickly water-lily, syn. 茨 *cì*.
2. ⊙ 贗 *yàn*, artificial; false.

厭 yàn   MC ʼjiemH
1. eat one's fill; sated; overfull.
2. fed up with, tired of; disgusted with.

驗 yàn   MC ngjemH
1. prove, confirm(ation), verify; substantiate, corroborate.
 a. investigate the facts of, examine for proof.
2. results, effects; resolution.

鷃 yàn   MC ʼaenH   ⊙ 鷃 *yàn*, turnix.

鷃 yàn   MC ʼaenH
1. turnix; buttonquail, bustard-quail (*Turnicidae*).
 a. 尺～ *chǐyàn*, "meager quail," "mere quail," small turnix.

yāng

央 yāng   MC ʼjang
1. center; interior, inside; e.g. 中～ *zhōngyāng*, the exact center.
2. to end, finish, complete; e.g. 夜未～ *yè wèiyāng*, the night is not finished; 未～ *wèiyāng*, not yet run its course, yet to be ended; also, "The Night-is-Young," name of a royal palace.
3. (med.) implore, entreat.

殃 yāng   MC ʼjang
1. to die, by foul play or mishap, before one's allotted time; fall afoul.
2. mischance, miscarriage, misfortune; bad or broken fortune.
 a. calamity; harm; tragedy.
 b. (Budd.) deadly, e.g. ～罪 *yāngzuì*, deadly sin.

泱 yāng   MC ʼjang
1. rdup., swelling and surging, rolling and rising, of waves, clouds; grandly gusting, blowing and billowing, of wind; trailing and wavering, throbbing tremulously, lingering in the air, of music.

 yǎng MC ʼangX
1. (bn.) ～漭 *yǎngmǎng* (MC ʼangX-mangX), broad and boundless, far-stretching and endless; also, darkly lowering, heavily leaden, gloomy and grim; also, glimmering faintly, faintly spreading (light).
2. (bn.) ～灢 *yǎngnǎng* (MC ʼangX-nangX), trickling and trilling, running and rushing (water).

秧 yāng   MC ʼjang
1. (med.) seedling, sprout, esp. of rice.
 a. (med.) transplant seedlings.
 b. (med.) general term for the very young of plants, fish, etc.

鉠 yāng   MC ʼjang
1. rdup., jangle-jingle, ting-ting, of small bells.

鞅 yāng   MC ʼjangX
1. martingale, made of leather, consisting of a girth-strap that passes between a horse's forelegs and through a loop in the neckstrap and is fastened to the noseband. N.B. This is not a halter, which is 縻 *mí*.
 a. strap, cinch.
 b. harness.
2. rdup., dissatisfied, displeased; feel wronged; inequitable.
3. (bn.) ～掌 *yāngzhǎng* (MC ʼjangX-tsyangX), bothered and beleaguered, pester(ed) and pick(ed) at, provoked and piqued.
4. (bn.) ～常 *yāngcháng* (MC ʼjangX-dzyang), ample and abundant, more than one wants or needs.

鴦 yāng   MC ʼjang
1. (bn.) 鴛～ *yuānyāng*, mandarin-duck, → 鴛 *yuān*.
2. ～龜 *yāngguī*, small, long-tailed, snake-eating turtle.

yáng

佯 yáng MC yang
1. sgl. or rdup., simulate, feign; pretend; affect, take on the air of.
2. rdup., many and multiple, manifold and multifarious.

峣 yáng MC ngaewng
1. (bn.) 崆～ *kōngyáng*, → 崆 *kōng*.

徉 yáng MC yang
1. (bn.) 徜～ *chángyáng* (MC dzyang-yang), 彷～ *pángyáng* (MC bang-yang), shilly-shally, shift back and forth, havering and wavering.

揚 yáng MC yang
1. raise, lift, lift up (ant. 抑 *yì*, push down).
    a. cast into the air, raise aloft; stir up; swing up.
    b. winnow, fret; scatter; spread abroad; waft.
2. arouse; prompt; bring up; agitate.
3. display, flaunt; flourish; publish, proclaim.
    a. make manifest; stand out.
    b. exalt, praise; laud; recommend, extol.
    c. don, put on, as clothes.
4. forehead, incl. eyebrows.
    a. broad; open, patulous.
5. rdup., in high spirits, elated and excited; as pleased as can be.
6. battle-axe.
7. a surname.

暘 yáng MC yang
1. sunrise; the rising sun; e.g. ～谷 *yánggǔ*, Sunrise Vale, legendarily the valley whence the sun emerges each day.
2. clear light, bright light; sunlight.
    a. clear, cloudless, of sky.

楊 yáng MC yang
1. poplar (*Salix populus*), deciduous tree having light soft wood and flowers borne in catkins; 白～ *báiyáng*, "white poplar," aspen.
    a. ～柳 *yángliǔ*, willow (*Salix babylonica*), deciduous tree with pendulous branches and flowers arranged in catkins; ～花 *yánghuā*, willow down.
2. ～梅 *yángméi*, bayberry, wax myrtle, box myrtle (*Myrica rubra*), subropical medium-sized evergreen tree bearing sweet, crimson fruit.

3. ～桃 *yángtáo*, carambola, starfruit (*Averrhoa carambola*), subropical medium-sized deciduous tree bearing sour to mildly sweet, orange-yellow fruit; syn. 陽桃 *yángtáo*, 羊桃 *yángtáo*; also, gooseberry, kiwi (*Actinidia chinensis*), woody vine bearing brown, egg-shaped fruit with green, many-seeded flesh; syn. 獼猴桃 *míhóutáo*.
4. ～桐 *yángtóng*, nandina (*Nandina domestica*), evergreen flowering shrub, syn. 南天 *nántiān*.
5. a surname, notably that of ruling family of the Sui (589-618) dynasty.

洋 yáng MC yang
1. rdup., stretching on and on, immense and unending; also, rippling and purling; also, endlessly adrift; also, completely self-content, in ease and enjoyment; also, onom. of bells, yong-yong.
2. (bn.) 望～ *wàngyáng* (MC mjangH-yang), 汪～ *wāngyáng* (MC 'wang-yang), wide-eyed with wonder.
3. (med.) body of water whose other shore cannot be seen; sea; ocean.

煬 yáng MC yangH
1. bake; roast.
    a. to dry or warm by a fire.
2. burn, set fire to.
3. ardent, fervid; zealous.
    a. flagrant.

痒 yáng MC zjang
1. malady.
    a. wound, sore.
        yǎng MC yangX
1. ⊙ 癢 *yǎng*, itch, tingle, prickle.

瘍 yáng MC yang
1. carbuncle; ulcer; suppuration.
    a. fester; ulcerate.

羊 yáng MC yang
1. sheep, goat; ovine.
    a. ～裘 *yángqiú*, budge: fur made from lambskin with the wool dressed outwards.
    b. ～腸 *yángcháng*, "sheep-gut," twisting and tortuous, narrow and winding, many-curved, double-curved and backtracking, of road; also, gooseberry, kiwi (*Actinidia chinensis*).

2. 〜桃, *yángtáo*, "sheep's peach," gooseberry, kiwi (*Actinidia chinensis*); also, carambola, starfruit (*Averrhoa carambola*); → 楊 *yáng* 3.

3. 〜蹄 *yángtí*, "sheep's hooves," dock, dockweed (*Rumex japonicus*), herbaceous plant; 〜蹄甲 *yángtíjiǎ*, "sheep's toes," bauhinia, orchid tree (*Bauhinia purpurea, Bauhinia variegata*), syn. 荊 *jīng*.

4. 〜躑躅 *yángzhízhú*, "sheep's stagger," azalea (*Rhododendron molle*), syn. 杜鵑 *dùjuān*.

5. a surname; also, 〜舌 *yángshé*, a bisyllabic surname.

6. ⊙ 祥 *xiáng*, auspicious.

錫   yáng   MC yang

1. frontlet, metallic ornament bound to a horse's forehead; syn. 當盧 *dānglú*.

   a. the same on boss of a shield.

陽   yáng   MC yang

1. sunlight; sun-lit, hot-lit; solar(ity); e.g. 夕〜 *xīyáng*, evening sunlight, eventide; 〜臺 *yángtái*, sun-lit terrace; 〜燧 *yángsuì*, "solar kindler," concave bronze mirror also used as burning-glass.

   a. brilliance, light.

2. south side of a mountain, north side of a river, esp. in place-names.

3. warm(th); lively, full of life; seasons of spring and summer; e.g. 〜春 *yángchūn*, springtime as the season when light, warmth, life are renewed.

   a. revive, renew.

4. masculine principle (opp. 陰 *yīn*), associated with the sun, heaven, light, warmth, strength, hardness, height, mastery, potency, action, etc.

   a. unbroken lines in *Yijing* hexagrams.

   b. symbolic of the number 9 as the most fully *yang* of the nine fundamental numerals; e.g. 重〜 *chóngyáng*, "double ninth," the ninth day of the ninth month; 〜九 *yángjiǔ*, end of a cosmic cycle, owing to exhaustion of *yang* energy.

5. on the surface (as opposed to recessed), e.g. 〜文 *yángwén*, characters carved in relief.

   a. superficial; feign, simulate; ⊙ 佯 *yáng*.

6. taboo-substitute from late 4th-c. for 春 *chūn*, "spring," esp. in cmpd. 〜秋 *yángqiū*, springs and autumns (to avoid given name of Jin Jian-wendi's 晉簡文帝 [r. 371-373] mother).

7. 〜桃 *yángtáo*, carambola, starfruit (*Averrhoa carambola*), syn. 楊桃 *yángtáo*.

8. 〜馬 *yángmǎ*, corner-beam of a roof, syn. *jueliang* 角梁.

颺   yáng   MC yang

1. wind-tossed; buffeted.

   a. gently rocking, swaying, rolling.

2. ⊙ 揚 *yáng* 1, 3.

yǎng

仰   yǎng   MC ngjangX

1. look up, raise the head; upward; e.g. 〜俯 *yǎngfǔ*, upward and downward; look up and look down; a moment, the time it takes to look up and look down; 〜臥 *yǎngwò*, lie back and look upward; 〜止 *yǎngzhǐ*, gaze at astonished.

2. look up to, regard with respect or reverence.

   a. put one's confidence in; rely on; e.g. 〜給 *yǎngjǐ*, depend on for supplies.

3. (med.) eagerly anticipate or hope for, look forward to, as polite formality used in documents from a superior to an inferior.

块   yǎng   MC 'angX

1. dust(y); powder(ed); dull; faded.

   a. uneven; ragged.

2. (bn.) 〜軋 or 〜圠 *yǎngyà* (MC 'angX-'eat), everywhere and everyplace, far and wide, vast and boundless; of infinite variety, inexhaustible diversity.

懩   yǎng   MC yangX

1. (med.) ⊙ 癢 *yǎng* 1a, itching to do, eager to, keen to, avid.

柍   yǎng   MC 'jangX

1. black plum (*Prunus mume*), syn. 梅 *méi*.

2. space below the center of a roof.

癢   yǎng   MC yangX

1. itch; tingle; prickle.

   a. be "itching to" do X, on edge to, keen to.

養   yǎng   MC yangX

1. nurture; rear, raise, foster.

   a. nourish; tend, care for, look after; e.g. (Dao.) 〜氣 *yǎngqì*, nourishing the vital breath, methods involving breath control, meditation, dietary and sexual regimes, etc., conducing to the strengthening and maintenance of one's vital energy.

2. support by providing basic necessities; provide for.

    a. maintain, keep in good condition; sustain; preserve; watch over.

    b. fundamental resources, needs.

3. train; groom; educate in the proper way of carrying out one's responsibilities; cultivate.

4. nurse, treat so as to aid in recuperation.

5. master of food preparation and kitchen-work; cook.

6. ⊙ 癢 *yǎng*, itch; tickle.

yàng

快　yàng　MC ‘jangX

1. sgl. or rdup., despondent, dissatisfied; heart-struck; crestfallen.

    a. (bn.) ～悒 *yàngyì* (MC ‘jangX-‘ip), glum and dolorous, chagrined and thwarted.

恙　yàng　MC yangH

1. distress(ed), trouble(d); sad(dened); uneasy, tense.

    a. 無～ *wúyàng*, comfortable, without complaint, all right, either physically or mentally; conventional greeting or valedictory statement: "May you be well (or unharmed)."

樣　yàng　MC yangH

1. (med.) style, type; model, kind.

    a. (med.) measure-word, for one or more kind(s) of.

2. (med.) appearance, aspect; look of.

漾　yàng　MC yangH

1. bob, toss, on waves; undulating, rolling.

    a. jostle, rock; sway; drift.

2. extended, lengthy, of waterway.

瀁　yàng　MC yangH

1. (med.) sgl. or rdup., restive, uneasy; jittery, jumpy; unquiet, agitated.

    yǎng　MC yangX

1. (bn.) 瀇～ *wǎngyǎng* (MC ‘wangX-yangX), shoreless and immeasurable.

yāo

唖　yāo　MC ‘jiew

1. rdup., onom. of the stridulation of insects; shrilling, grating; heavy humming.

夭　yāo　MC ‘jew(X)

1. mortal frailty; die young, before one's time; ill-starred; sickly.

    a. curtail, cut short; break off; nip.

2. aberrant, irregular.

    a. calamitous, disastrous; devastating.

3. deflected from target, distorted; crooked, warped; deformed.

4. sgl. or rdup., lush growth, luxuriant, unhindered abundance; rdup. also, relaxed and unruffled.

    a. unrestrained, unchecked; e.g. (bn.) ～矯 *yāoqiǎo* (MC ‘jewX-kjewX), wanton wafture, unrestricted indulgence.

妖　yāo　MC ‘jew

1. bewitching, captivating, enchanting, irresistible, fetching, of extraordinary beauty; e.g. ～靡 *yāomí*, irresistibly exquisite; (bn.) ～冶 *yāoyě* (MC ‘jew-yaeX), winningly appealing; (bn.) ～嬈 *yāoráo* (MC ‘jew-nyew), comely and charming.

2. uncanny, unnatural; abnormal; prodigious.

    a. monster, monstrous; weird; freak(ish), grotesque.

幺　yāo　MC ‘ew

1. tiny, teeny; scant; slight.

    a. (bn.) ～麼 *yāomó* (MC ‘ew-ma), scant and slight.

殀　yāo　MC ‘jewX

1. mortal frailty; die young, before one's time; ill-starred; sickly.

    a. curtail, cut short; break off; nip.

祅　yāo　MC ‘jew

1. ⊙ 妖 2, uncanny, unnatural; preternatural; anomalous.

腰　yāo　MC ‘jiew

1. the waist; midriff, midsection.

    a. midpoint, centermost.

    b. ～機 *yāojī*, backstrap loom, with warp-threads stretched from post to belt worn around weaver's waist.

    c. (med.) ～鼓 *yāogǔ*, "cinched drum," small two-headed hand-drum, tapering from both ends to a narrow midpoint for holding; different from the larger drum called by same term in late imperial times.

2. informal term for the loins.

3. (med.) measure-word for belts, sashes.

葽   yāo   MC ʼjiew

1. sgl. or 〜草 *yāocǎo*, green foxtail, green bristlegrass (*Setaria viridis*), a wild grass with erect stem and a spikelike panicle; syn. 狗尾草 *gǒuwěicǎo*.

2. sgl. or (bn.) 〜繞 *yāorào* (MC ʼjiew-nyewH), Chinese senega (*Polygala tenuifolia*), herbaceous perennial with light-blue to purple flowers, root used medicinally; syn. 遠志 *yuǎnzhì*.

要   yāo   MC ʼjiew

1. the waist, ⊙ 腰 *yāo* 1.
  a. to cinch, belt, gird; bind, restrain.
  b. waistband, skirt-waist.
2. require, need; insist on, demand; e.g. 不〜 *bùyāo*, no need to.
  a. obtain; lay claim to; be deserving of.
  b. strive for; seek to gain; pursue.
3. compel(ling); threaten, intimidate.
  a. gain control of, dominate; direct.
4. meet midway; encounter; intercept, obstruct.
5. agree with; compact; comport with.
6. (med.) invite, solicit; attract; welcome.

   yào   MC ʼjiewH

1. crux, midpoint; crucial; core, nucleus, kernel, gist.
  a. what is necessary, requisite; essential; e.g. 〜妙 *yàomiào*, essential and subtle.
  b. (med.) strategic, important, esp. as classification of certain administrative districts.
2. (med.) sum up, summarize; generalize.
3. (med.) GP adverbial indicator of future or imminent action: "about to . . .," "soon will . . ." "is going to . . ."

邀   yāo   MC ʼjiew

1. meet on the way; intercept.
  a. block; impede and attack.
2. strive for; look for, seek; venture upon, endeavor to.
  a. solicit; angle for; undertake.
3. (med.) invite; request; welcome.
  a. (med.) appeal to do X; press to do X.

yáo

僥   yáo   MC ngew

1. (bn.) 僬〜 *jiāoyáo*, → 僬 *jiāo*.

   jiǎo   MC kewX

1. 〜倖 *jiǎoxìng*, gamble, trust to luck, hope for the best.

堯   yáo   MC ngew

1. name of legendary sage-king of high antiquity, whose reign was reputedly one of virtue and prosperity and who passed on the throne not to his son but to the worthiest man in the kingdom, Shun 舜; his clan was called the Taotang 陶唐, after the place-names of his first two fiefs.

2. sgl. or rdup., tall, lofty.

姚   yáo   MC yew

1. feateous, featly; graceful; (bn.) 〜冶 *yáoyě* (MC yew-yaeX), fine and featly, graceful and seemly; (bn.) 嫖〜 *piāoyáo*, → 嫖 *piāo*.

2. a surname, notably that of the ethnically Qiang 羌 ruling family of the Later Qin (後秦, 384-417) dynasty.

3. ⊙ 遙 *yáo*, distant, remote.

嶢   yáo   MC ngew

1. sgl. or rdup., tall, lofty; in various bns., e.g. 嶕〜 *jiāoyáo* (MC dzjew-ngew), 〜嶭 *yáoè* (MC ngew-ngat), etc., tall and towering.

徭   yáo   MC yew

1. corvée labor.

搖   yáo   MC yew

1. shake, sway; rock; joggle, jiggle; toss; unsteady.
  a. quiver, quaver, vibrate, tremble; quake; throb.
  b. waver, falter, stagger; swing.
2. stir, agitate; buffet, brandle; upset.
3. cast into the air, waft; send aloft, rise up, raise, lift; e.g. (med.) (bn.) 〜曳 *yáoyè* (MC yew-yejH), wafted aloft, drifting adangle; also, quivering tremulously; (bn.) 飄〜 *piāoyáo*, → 飄 *piāo*.
  a. untethered; cast off from norms; e.g. (med.) (bn.) 〜曳 *yáoyè* (MC yew-yejH), free and unfettered.

爻   yáo   MC haew

1. lines that form the hexagrams in the *Yijing*.
  a. the interpretations given to such individual lines.

瑤   yáo   MC yew

1. jadelike stone, perhaps chalcedony, occurring in many colors from translucent white to reddish-brown, blue, and green; depending on context, translate as "chalcedony," "carnelian," "agate," "blue-gem," "green-gem"; e.g. 〜池

yáochí, Chalcedony Pool, associated with Queen Mother of the West 西王母 and therefore with the color white.

   a. gemmy, richly ornamented; jadelike, precious; literally of physical items, also figuratively of valued writings, human beauty, majestic buildings, etc.

   b. lustrous, glossy, gleaming, esp. of white or shining objects.

絲　yáo　MC yew

1. abundant, lush, dense, of vegetation.
2. ⊙ 傜 *yáo*, corvée; 遙 *yáo*, far off; 謠 *yáo*, popular song; 搖 *yáo*, sway, shake.

   yóu　MC yuw

1. from, out of.

   zhòu　MC drjuwH

1. interpretation of hexagrams in the *Yijing*.

肴　yáo　MC haew

1. cates, delicacies; viands, esculent(s); provisions; e.g. 〜饌 *yáozhùan*, cates and dainties.
2. ⊙ 淆 *xiáo*, roil(ed); muddle(d), confuse(d); mingle(d).

謠　yáo　MC yew

1. folk saying or ditty circulated by children and considered prophetic; mantic song, portent.

   a. popular song, ballad.

2. song performed without instrumental accompaniment, a cappela.
3. sgl. or in cmpd. 〜言 *yáoyán*, rumor, hearsay, baseless gossip.

   a. cajole(ry), wheedle, persuade with empty compliments.

輶　yáo　MC yew

1. light one-horse carriage, cabriolet, often used for urgent tasks or missions.

   a. drive quickly, with unusual speed.

遙　yáo　MC yew

1. sgl. or rdup., distant, remote, in space or time; lengthy, stretching.
2. stray; meander, rove; wander; drift.

   a. (bn.) 逍〜 *xiāoyáo* (MC sjew-yew), directionless drifting, easy and effortless, footloose and fancy-free, free and easy.

銚　yáo　MC yew

1. large hoe; spadelike hoe, scuffle.

   diào　MC dewH

1. kettle with a handle and spout.

   tiáo　MC dew

1. long spear, lance.

飆　yáo　MC yew

1. floating on the air; (bn.) 〜颺 *yáoyáng* (MC yew-yang), 飄〜 *piāoyáo* (MC bjiew-yew), borne on the breeze, adrift on the wind, afloat and aflutter, drifting to and fro, lightly aloft.

餚　yáo　MC haew

1. ⊙ 肴 *yáo* 1, viands; delicacies.

鰩　yáo　MC yew

1. flying fish (*Exocoetidae*).

              yǎo

咬　yǎo　MC ngaewX

1. bite off, gnaw at; champ, masticate, crunch.

   a. eat away, wear away; corrode.

   jiāo　MC kaew

1. rdup., chaffering, chittering of birds.

杳　yǎo　MC 'ewX

1. sgl. or rdup., indistinct, obscure; vague, blurred.

   a. gloom(y), dismal; dark, dim; (bn.) 〜眇 *yǎomiǎo* (MC 'ewX-mjiewX), dark and dense; also, masked and mysterious.

   b. impenetrable, unfathomable.

2. receding into distance; far off; secluded.

   a. broad, wide; incommensurable.

3. dimness of far time.

溔　yǎo　MC yewX

1. (bn.) 灝〜 *hàoyáo*, → 灝 *hào*.

窅　yǎo　MC 'ewX

1. deep-set, sunken, of eyes.
2. hidden, veiled; inscrutable; inexplicable.

   a. dim; hard to bring into focus; e.g. 〜冥 *yǎomíng*, indistinct, inscrutable; recondite, mysterious; 〜然 *yǎorán*, deep into the distance; also, inscrutably; also, distractedly.

3. profound, penetrating; deep.

   a. removed from immediate presence, set afar; retired, secluded.

4. ⊙ 杳 *yǎo*, all meanings.

窅 yǎo MC 'ewX

1. (bn.) 〜窱 yǎotiǎo (MC 'ewX-thewX), dark and deep; also ⊙ 窈窕 yǎotiǎo, → 窈 yǎo; also (med.) supple suavity.

窈 yǎo MC 'ewX

1. set apart, removed; secluded.
2. (bn.) 〜窕 yǎotiǎo (MC 'ewX-dewX), of women, coy and comely, reticent and withdrawn, winsome but withdrawn, delicate and demure; but some indication that the term can instead imply seductive sensuality; also, covert depths, hidden recesses; also, quiet(ly) and private(ly).
3. rdup., obscure and indistinct, somber and subtle; calm and charming.

舀 yǎo MC yewX

1. ladle from one container to another.
2. bale out (liquid).

䠢 yǎo MC 'ewX

1. (bn.) 〜裊 yǎoniǎo (MC 'ewX-newX), "graceful galloper," fabulous horse having a gold snout and red body, able to run untiringly.

鷕 yǎo MC yewX

1. onom. for call of the wild pheasant.
    a. onom., general term for birdcalls.
        xiào MC hewX
1. wild pheasant.

齩 yǎo MC ngaewX

1. ⊙ 咬 yǎo 1, gnaw, champ.

yào

曜 yào MC yewH

1. general term for asterial light, radiance from a celestial body; starshine incl. that of the sun.
    a. coruscate, coruscant, coruscation; scintillant, scintillance; nitid(ity); flashing, sparkling, glittering; e.g. 七〜 qīyào, Seven Scintillances, Seven Planetoids, ref. to sun, moon, and 5 naked-eye planets; (med.) 〜靈 yàolíng, sparkling numen, i.e. the sun; (Dao.) 九〜生 jiǔyàoshēng, Vitality of Ninefold Scintillance, esoteric name for the sun used by Shangqing divinities.
    b. dazzle, blind with light.
2. reveal or show forth vividly.

燿 yào MC yewH

1. ⊙ 曜 yào.
        shuò MC syak
1. ⊙ 鑠 shuò, melt, (in)fuse.
        shào MC sraewH
1. thin and pointed, slenderly tapering.

突 yào MC 'ewH ⊙ 窔 yào.

窔 yào MC 'ewH

1. southeast corner of a house; e.g. 〜奥 yào'ào, southeast and southwest corners of house, euph. for secret places.
2. recesses, hidden depths.
    a. storeyed, extensive, sprawling, of buildings.

燿 yào MC yewH

1. shine forth, irradiate; sparkle; dazzle.
    a. give glory or honor to; glorious; resplendent.
2. ⊙ 曜 yào.

藥 yào MC yak

1. medicinal herb, simple; pharmaka.
    a. (med.) esp. herbs conducing to longevity.
2. physic, remedy, cure; potion, philtre; drug, medicine.
3. (med.) abb. of (bn.) 芍〜 or 勺〜 sháoyào (MC dzyak-yak), herbaceous peony (*Paeonia lactiflora*).
        lüè MC ljak
1. (bn.) 勺〜 or 芍〜 zhuólüè (MC tsyak-ljak), "peony blend," food additive consisting of a blend of peony-root, thoroughwort, cinnamon, and other items.

鷂 yào MC yewH

1. kestrel, sparrowhawk, windhover.

yē

噎 yē MC 'et

1. stuck in the throat.
    a. block(ed), wedge(d), jam(med); stoppage.

枒 yē MC yae

1. ⊙ 椰 yē, coconut.
        yā MC ngae
1. (bn.) 〜杈 yāchā (MC ngae-tsrhae) or 杈〜 chāyā, bifurcating branches, split and spread apart.

椰 yē MC yae

1. coconut, tree and fruit (*Cocos nucifera*).

yé

挪 yé MC yae ⊙挪 *yé*.

挪 yé MC yae

1. (bn.) ～揄 *yéyú* (MC yae-yu), tease and tweak, chaff and chide.

爺 yé MC yae

1. (med.) father; also, dad (informal).
2. (med.) uncle.

耶 yé MC yae

1. ⊙邪 *yá* (*xié*), sentence-final interr. GP equiv. to (and phonetic fusion of) *yě* 也 + *hū* 乎: is it that . . .?; phrase-final GP implying probable assent interrogatively: ". . . yes?; . . . mm?"; 爺 *yé*, (med.) father, dad.

鎁 yé MC yae

1. (bn.) 鏌～ *mòyé* (MC mak-yae), name of a legendary sword.

yě

也 yě MC yaeX

1. final GP in nominal (noun-predicate) sentences, indicating that one noun or noun phrase is equivalent to, or to be identified with, another; e.g. 此文王之勇 ～ *cǐ wénwáng zhī yǒng yě*, This is King Wen's valor; 此五者皆生之害 ～ *cǐ wǔzhě jiē shēngzhi hài yě*, These five things are in all cases the bane of life.

 a. having to do with, implying; e.g. 死生命 ～ *sǐshēng mìngyě*, Life and death are matters having to do with Fate; 有人天～有天亦天～ *yǒu rén tiān yě, yǒu tiān yì tiān yě*, That there are people has to do with heaven; that there is heaven also has to do with heaven.

 b. of a certain kind, belonging to a certain category; e.g. 秦虎狼之國也 *qín hǔlángzhiguó yě*, Qin is a vicious tiger-like, wolf-like state; 周公何人 ～ *zhōugōng hérén yě*, The Duke of Zhou was what kind of person?

 c. due to, because of, owing to; e.g. 失其民 ～ *shī qí mín yě*, because of losing [the alle-

giance of] his people; 是天下無人也 *shì tiānxià wú rén yě*, This was due to the subcelestial realm having no one else.

 d. marking a VB-phrase as a nominal predicate; e.g. 封之～ *fēng zhī yě*, It was [a case of] enfeoffing him; 是無義無命～ *shì wúyì wúmìng yě*, This is dismissive of propriety and dismissive of the decree.

2. (GP) marking sentence-initial noun-phrases as topics: "as for"; e.g. 其為人 ～ *qí wéirén yě*, as for his behaving as a person [is expected to behave]; 人性之不分於善不善～ *rénxìngzhi bùfēn yú shàn bùshàn yě*, as for human nature's not distinguishing between good and bad.

 a. (GP) marking sentence-initial noun-phrases as temporal: "when"; e.g. 孔子之仕於魯 ～ *kǒngzǐzhi shì yú lǔ yě*, when Confucius was holding office in the state of Lu; 昔桓公之霸～ *xī huángōngzhi bà yě*, in the past, when Duke Huan served as hegemon.

 b. (GP) marking proper names as topics: "as for"; e.g. 賜～何如 *cì yě hérú*, As for [me,] Ci, what am I like?; 根～慾 *chéng yě yù*, As for Cheng, he is avaricious.

3. final GP in verbal sentences marking continuative aspect, i.e., ongoing or enduring conditions or circumstances, including enduring opinions or judgments (particularly suited to negated VB-phrases as expressing unchanged, hence ongoing, conditions); e.g. 是不可忍～ *shì bùkě rěn yě*, This cannot be endured; 不知其仁～ *bùzhī qí rén yě*, I do not know if he is humane.

 a. ongoing, continuing > enduring > asserted to be true; e.g. 存危國美名～ *cún wéiguó měi míng yě*, sustaining an endangered state enhances one's reputation; 國君不可戮～ *guójūn bùkě lù yě*, The lord of a state cannot be murdered.

冶 yě MC yaeX

1. smelt; cast in a mould.
 a. smith, blacksmith.
 b. foundry.
2. ravishing, in appearance.
 a. flirtatious, coquettish.
 b. ～葛 *yěgé*, "attractive kudzu," heartbreak grass (*Gelsemium elegans*), a twining climber.
3. ⊙野 *yě*.

埜 yě MC yaeX ⊙野 *yě*.

壄 yě   MC yaeX   ⊙ 野 yě.

野 yě   MC yaeX
1. beyond the suburbs; countryside (often opp. 朝 cháo, court).
  a. open fields, open ground; moor, wilderness.
  b. wild; rustic, rural > uncultivated; unrestricted, unqualified, ungoverned, untenanted; e.g. ～情 yěqíng, untenanted or uncontrolled feelings.
2. celestial regions; e.g. 分～ fēnyě, "allotted countrysides," the astrological correlation between terrestrial regions and celestial counterparts, involving 12 classical provinces or territories, the 12 Jupiter stations, and 28 lunar lodgings; 九～ jiǔyě, 9 wilds, the ninefold heavens, corresponding to the classical 9 "isles" or provinces (zhou 州) of the Chinese land.
3. ～葛 yěgé, "wild kudzu," heartbreak grass (Gelsemium elegans), a twining climber.

yè

夜 yè   MC yaeH
1. night, nighttime (opp. 晝 zhòu, daytime).
  a. ～光 yèguāng, night-shining, noctilucent; ～來 yèlái, during the night; ～分 yèfēn, midnight.
2. evening, nightfall.
3. (Budd.) ～叉 yèchā (MC yaeH-tsrhae), trsc. of Skt. yakṣa, demon.

嶪 yè   MC ngjaep   ⊙ 嶫 yè.

嶫 yè   MC ngjaep
1. rdup. or (bn.) ～峨 yè'é (MC ngjaep-nga), jaggedly jutting, heaped high.

拽 yè   MC yet
1. ⊙ 拽 yè, drag, pull, tug.
2. straightening board.
3. ⊙ 枻 yì, gunwales; also, (row with) oars.

拽 yè   MC yet
1. drag, pull, tug; draw.
  a. trail behind.
2. wag; vibrate, resonate.
3. side-planks of a boat, gunwales.

掖 yè   MC yek
1. support under both arms; uphold, sustain, hold up; prop up.
  a. lead on, pull forward.
2. ⊙ 腋 yè, armpits.
3. sides, flank(ing); lateral; e.g. ～庭 yètíng, Annex Court, lateral apartments in imperial compound where palace women reside; 宮～ gōngyè, palace seraglio; 西～ xīyè, Western Annex, alt. Tang name for 中書省 zhōngshūshěng, imperial secretariat; ～省 yèshěng, "lateral bureaus," alt. Tang combined name for 中書省 zhōngshūshěng, imperial secretariat, and 門下省 ménxiàshěng, chancellery.

擪 yè   MC 'jiep
1. press down with finger(s); e.g. ～笛 yèdí, play (finger) the flute.
  a. smoothe; draw together.

撎 yè   MC 'jiep   ⊙ 擪 yè.

暍 yè   MC 'jot
1. insolation, heatstroke, sunstroke.
  a. intense heat, sultry, torrid.
2. change color, esp. fade in the sun.

曄 yè   MC hjep
1. sgl. or rdup., brightly shining; flashing, flaring, gleaming.
  a. brilliant; striking.
2. flourish(ing).

曳 yè   MC yejH
1. drag, pull, tug; draw.
  a. trail behind.
2. drape over (clothing).
3. fatigued, worn out, done in.
4. wag; vibrate, resonate.
5. leap, bound; exceed, go beyond.
6. (med.) rdup., continuous, successively connected, in unbroken order.
7. (med.) ～落河 yèluòhé (MC yejH-lak-ha), soldier(s), troop(s), trsc. of Turk. yürek(lig), brave, stout-hearted, doughty.

業 yè   MC ngjaep
1. patrimony, heritage, legacy, esp. inherited responsibility or hereditary trade.

a. activity to which one devotes oneself, occupation, profession, métier; endeavor.
b. training, teaching, instruction; learning, scholarship.
2. estate, property, possessions.
3. enterprise, undertaking; deed, action, behavior.
a. great achievement, meritorious deed.
4. sequence, order(ly).
a. continue on with, carry on.
5. rdup., strong and strapping, lusty and full of life; also, fearful and frightened, dreadful and disquieted.
6. (ADV) indicator of completed action: already, having done VB.
7. begin, start; create.
8. horizontal board of a bellstand or frame.
a. tablature, wooden board for writing.
9. (Budd.) trns. of Skt. *karma*, law of universal causality and retribution of deeds.
10. ⊙ 墅 *shù*, villa.

液　yè　MC yek
1. fluid, esp. heavy or dense fluid; secretion(s); sap; juice(s); liquor.
a. liquor with life-enhancing qualities, ichor; e.g. 太～池 *tàiyèchí*, Grand Ichor Pool, pleasure spot in imperial compound.
b. bodily fluids, humors.
2. melt together, fuse, meld.
3. imbrue, steep.
4. ⊙ 掖 *yè* 3, side, flank(ing), lateral.

燁　yè　MC hjep　⊙ 曄 *yè*.

腋　yè　MC yek
1. armpits, of humans; undertail to belly area of birds, underleg to belly area of quadrupeds.

葉　yè　MC yep
1. leaf, of a plant; petal.
a. come into leaf; grow.
2. period of time, such as a generation or dynastic segment, thought of by analogy with the cycle of plant life, comprising a time of growth followed by one of withering.
3. metaphor for something small and light, e.g. a small boat.
4. ～護 *yèhù* (MC yep-huH), yabghu, trsc. of Turk. *yabɣu*, Türkic title usu. held by second highest male member of ruling clan (the first being the kaghan), sometimes of significant independent power or influence.

謁　yè　MC ʻjot
1. make known, announce.
a. ～者 *yèzhe*, internuncio.
2. announce oneself, present oneself to a superior; present one's card and seek audience; e.g. 干～ *gānyè*, importune with a visit (in hope of self-advancement).
a. name-card, incl. name, ancestry, position, etc., presented when making a call.
3. pay respects to; make a pilgrimage to.

鍱　yè　MC yep
1. sheets or leaves of metal.
a. to plate with metal.

靨　yè　MC ʻjiep
1. sgl. or ～輔 *yèfǔ*, dimple.
a. beauty-mark, mouche.
2. make-up.

饁　yè　MC hjep
1. send food to field-workers; food so sent.
2. sgl. or ～獸 *yèshòu*, sacrificial offering of game taken in a hunt, to the spirits of the four directions.

鮺　yè　MC ʻjaep
1. salted fish.

yī

一　yī　MC ʻjit
1. numeral one; once; first; rdup., one after another, consecutive(ly).
a. single, singly; sole; unique; one and only; e.g. ～息 *yīxī*, in a single breath; also, one lifetime; ～時 *yīshí*, for a single moment, in an instant.
b. an iota, trifling bit, least particle; e.g. ～介 *yījiè*, merest trifle, insignificant person or item.
2. unity; monad.
a. unify, bring together, concentrate; e.g. (Budd.) ～心 *yīxīn*, concentrate the mind, contemplate.
b. alike, similar(ly), all the same; uniform(ly); e.g. ～等 *yīděng*, one and the same, of one kind.
3. whole(ness), wholely; total(ly), totality; e.g ～夜 *yīyè*, the whole night; ～切 *yīqiè*, each and every; also, for this discrete period of time; ～片月 *yīpiànyùe*, a swathe of moonlight.

4. preceding verb phrase: all at once, as soon as; ever since.

伊   yī   MC ʾjij

1. (GP) demonstrative pronoun: this, that.
2. (GP) pre-Han usage: indicator that following statement is contrary to what is expected; in contrast with others.
3. (med.) 3rd-person pronoun: (s)he, him, his.
4. phrase-initial exclamation, esp. in poetry: Ah!, Oh!
5. phrase-middle exclamation or rhythmic particle, in poetry.
6. (bn.) ～鬱 yīyù (MC ʾjij-jut), pent up with rage, vexed and exasperated; (bn.) ～邑 yīyì (MC ʾjij-ʾip), fuddled and fretful, grieved, despondent.
7. (bn.) ～威 yīwēi (MC ʾjij-ʾjw+j), wood-louse, syn. 鼠婦 shǔfù, 委黍 wěishǔ.
8. ～吾(盧) yīwú(lú), ～州 yīzhōu, Qāmul, oasis city near eastern end of the Tianshan 天山, modern Hami.

依   yī   MC ʾj+j

1. lean on, depend on, rely on; prop; fall back on; e.g. ～歸 yīguī, take refuge with, have confidence in, go to live with.
   a. incline toward, lean toward; favor, prefer.
   b. cling to; attach(ed) to.
2. follow with; conform with, comply with (ant. 違 wéi, go against, wayward).
   a. guided by; acquiesce to, consent to.
3. according to.
4. rdup., gentle and graceful, gently and easily; also, lush and full; also, linger(ing) on.
5. (bn.) ～稀 yīxī (MC ʾj+j-xj+j), slight and scanty, mere and meager; also, the merest seeming, as though it just might be; (bn.) ～約 yīyuē, might as well be.

噎   yī   MC ʾi

1. exclamatory particle expressing wonder or dissatisfaction.
      ài   MC ʾeajH
1. exhale, expel; blow.

壹   yī   MC ʾjit

1. concentrate solely on; single-minded.
2. bring into agreement, conformity.
   a. consistent, uniform(ity); all the same.
3. wholly, total(ity).

4. suprisingly, unexpectedly; actually.
5. truly, really.
6. ⊙ 一 yī.

揖   yī   MC ʾjip

1. bow, salute, lout, with hands joined at chest; e.g. 長～ chángyī, lout low or long.
2. cede, relinquish; decline.
      jí   MC tsip
1. ⊙ 輯 jí, collect, arrange.

椅   yī   MC ʾje

1. idesia (*Idesia polycarpa*), medium-sized tree producing small green fragrant flowers and edible red berries.
2. ～桐 yītóng, royal paulownia (*Paulownia imperialis*); ～楊 yīyáng, aspen (*Populus suaveolens*).
      yǐ   MC ʾjeX
1. (bn.) ～柅 yǐnǐ (MC ʾjeX-nrjeX), swinging and swaying, lithe and lissome, ⊙ 猗狔 yǐnǐ.
2. (late med.) chair.

漪   yī   MC ʾje

1. undulation, ripple(s) of water; purl(ing), curl(ing), ruffle.
   a. (bn.) 漣～ liányī, → 漣 lián.
2. riverbank, shore.

猗   yī   MC ʾje

1. onom. of sigh or gasp expressing admiration, approval; often combined with another exclamatory particle, e.g. (bn.) ～歟 yīyú (MC ʾje-yo), "ah yes!, o indeed!"
   a. in poetry, a line-final particle expressing satisfaction.
2. rdup., lush and luxuriant; also, lingering in the air, of music.
      yǐ   MC ʾjeX
1. (bn.) ～狔 yǐnǐ (MC ʾjeX-nrjeX), swinging and swaying, lithe and lissome.
2. ⊙ 倚 yǐ, lean on, rely on.
      ě   MC ʾaX
1. (bn.) ～儺 ěnuó (MC ʾaX-naX), same as ～狔 yǐnǐ, above.

繄   yī   MC ʾej

1. phrase-initial particle, similar to pre-classical copula 惟, "It is the case that . . ., Let it just be that . . ."
2. phrase-middle exclamatory particle, most often expressing disappointment: "alas."

衣　yī　MC ʼj+j

1. upper garment (opp. 裳 *cháng*, lower garment, skirt); jacket, tunic; robe; e.g. ～冠 *yīguān*, those who are robed and capped, i.e. officialdom; (Budd.) ～鉢 *yībō*, monk's robe and alms-bowl, esp. those of first 5 patriarchs of Chan sect, transmitted as sign of legitimate succession.

    a. by synecdoche, gen. term for clothes, clothing; vestment(s), raiment; garb, attire, apparel.

2. outer covering, such as the husk, rind, peel of grain or fruit, the plumage of a bird.

    a. moss, lichen.

    b. (med.) cmpd. ～架 *yījià*, "[skin-]cover and frame," bodily frame, physique.

    yì　MC ʼj+jH

1. to clothe, wear, don, put on; garb, outfit; cover, cloak.

褘　yī　MC ʼje　→褘 *huī*.

醫　yī　MC ʼi

1. medicine, medic(al).
2. physician, healer.

    a. heal, cure; return to health.

鷖　yī　MC ʼej

1. seagull, syn. 鷗 *ōu*.
2. Eurasian widgeon (*Anas penelope*).

    yì　MC ʼejH

1. alt. name for phoenix (鳳 *fèng*).

2. (bn.) ～彌 *yìmí* (MC ʼejH-mjie), new-born child, baby, nursling.

鷖　yī　MC ʼej

1. small facial mole.

    a. black-colored.

yí

儀　yí　MC ngje

1. demeanor, deportment; outer form, external appearance, esp. in ceremony; e.g. 來～ *láiyí*, arrival and proper display of a phoenix at court, being an auspicious sign of heavenly approval.

    a. embellishment, garniture; emblem(atic); e.g. 羽～ *yǔyí*, plumed ornaments > plumed exemplars > feathered form > noble appearance or conduct.

    b. regalia, formal dress and accoutrements.

2. ritual observances, ceremony, ceremonial; (religious) liturgy; correct behavior, suited to formal occasions; measured manners; e.g. ～禮 *yílǐ*, ceremony and ritual; (Dao.) 威～ *wēiyí*, awesome observances.

    a. procedures, procedural; prescribed usages; e.g. ～典 *yídiǎn*, procedural norms, ceremonial precepts.

3. norm, standard, criterion; principle; exemplar(y); e.g. 兩～ *liǎngyí*, 二～ *èryí*, the Two Principles, i.e. *yin* and *yang*, heaven and earth.

4. analogue, correlative; complementary object or person, match, mate.

    a. suited to, befit(ting).

5. present(s), gift(s).

6. instrument, apparatus, device, gauge, esp. for precise astronomical measurements.

    a. establishment of the calendar by measuring, esp. by instruments such as gnomon, sun-shadow, celestial sphere.

7. inclination, tendency; trend.

匜　yí　MC ye

1. water-jug, ewer, pitcher.

圯　yí　MC yi

1. Chu dialect word for bridge.

    a. embankment.

夷　yí　MC yij

1. non-Chinese people, esp. to the northeast; barbarian, alien; foreign(er).

    a. uncouth, crude.

2. flatland; level, even.

    a. leveled down, worn away; deteriorate(d), decline; e.g. (bn) ～靡 *yímí* (MC yij-mje), worn and eroded, collapsed and crumbled; 明～ *míngyí*, "fading of the light," name of hexagram 36 of *Yijing*.

3. level-headed, even-tempered; balance(d), equanimity; calm, unruffled; e.g. ～神 *yíshén* maintain a calm spirit.

    a. allay, put to rest; temper, moderate; smooth over, compose.

4. hoe, scuffle-hoe.

    a. eradicate; scrape away; destroy; exterminate.

5. wound(ed), harm(ed), injure(d).

6. faint; invisible; e.g. (bn.) 希～ *xīyí* (MC xj+j-yij), mysteriously inaudible and invisible.

7. sit with legs splayed, in careless posture; sprawl.

    a. disrespectful, uncaring; contemptuous, arrogant.

8. common, ordinary; banal, mediocre.
　a. of the same kind; same generation.
9. (bn.) ～猶 *yíyóu*, equivocate and avoid, faltering qualms.

姨　*yí*　MC yij
1. wife's sisters; e.g. ～兄弟 *yíxiōngdì*, husbands of wife's sisters, brothers-in-law.
2. mother's sisters, e.g. ～兄弟 *yíxiōngdì*, sons of maternal aunts, cousins.
3. (med.) term of address for concubine.

宜　*yí*　MC ngje
1. proper, suited to, (be)fit(ting); apt for; commensurate with, in line with, congruent, in keeping with.
2. proper to do, should, ought to.
3. likely, probably, liable to; e.g. ～若 *yíruò*, seems to be, most likely.

嶷　*yí*　MC ngi　→ 嶷 *nì*.

彝　*yí*　MC yij
1. general term for sacred vessels used for ritual libations in ancestral shrine.
2. customary moral law, universally recognized principle.
　a. eminently moral conduct.

怡　*yí*　MC yi
1. consonant, agreeable; congenial, amiable.
　a. content; in good spirits; pleased.

栘　*yí*　MC ye
1. serviceberry (*Amelanchier sinica*), producing pomes that are dark-blue when ripe.
2. ～楊 *yíyáng*, same as above; also, aspen (*Populus davidiana*); ～柳 *yíliǔ*, purple willow, purple osier (*Salix sinopurpurea*).

桋　*yí*　MC ye
1. wooden frame on which to hang clothes.
2. low table placed in front of a couch.

澄　*yí*　MC ngj+j
1. (bn.) 漼～ *cuīyí*, → 漼 *cuī*.

疑　*yí*　MC ngi
1. be uncertain about, have doubts.
　a. be suspicious of, distrust; suspect.
2. wonder whether…; wonder if one might…
　a. fancy that…; think it possible that…

3. seems to be, might be.
　a. similar to; e.g. A～B: A suggests B.
4. hesitate, vacillate; have qualms about.
　nǐ　MC ngiX
1. fix, set; determine.
2. ⊙ 擬 *nǐ* 3, imitate; mimic; copy, model; aim at.

痍　*yí*　MC yij
1. ⊙ 夷 5, wound(ed), harm(ed), injure(d).

移　*yí*　MC ye
1. move or shift from one place to another; transfer; convey.
　a. slue, slide over; drift over.
　b. remove, move aside, move out of the way.
2. circulate or dispatch a document.
　a. (lit.) a lit. genre, "dispatch," proclamation, usu. of official nature, meant to be circulated and to effect a change of opinion or behavior.
　b. (med.) claim, notify of having particular opinion or condition; e.g. ～病 *yíbìng*, claiming illness.
3. change, alter, modify; adjust.
4. transplant grain seedlings.

訑　*yí*　MC ye
1. surquidry, surquidrous, presumptuous(ness); rdup., proud and preening, smug and self-important.
　tuó　MC da
1. cheat, swindle; deceive.

詒　*yí*　MC yi
1. pass on, hand down, bequeath; present to; ⊙ 貽 *yí*.
　dài　MC dojX
1. trick, cheat; obtain by ruse; abuse.

貽　*yí*　MC yi
1. present to, bestow; give; dedicate to (esp. in poem titles).
2. pass on, hand down; bequeath.

跠　*yí*　MC yij
1. ⊙ 夷 7, sit with legs splayed, in careless posture; sprawl.

迻　*yí*　MC ye
1. move or shift a physical object from one place to another.

遺　**yí**　MC ywij

1. pretermit, leave undone; neglect, omit; e.g. ～事 *yíshì*, ignored matters, events not included in official histories.

　　a. set aside, reject, cast off.

2. lose, let slip; lapse(d).

　　a. let fall, drop, leave behind.

3. leave to one's heirs; bequeath; testamentary; e.g. ～詔 *yízhào*, testamentary edict of (deceased) emperor.

4. vestige, residuum; relic, reliquary.

　　a. deceased, passed on; e.g. ～象 *yíxiàng*, statue of the deceased.

5. suffer from incontinence.

　　wèi　MC ywijH

1. turn over to, deposit with; deliver to, present to.

　　a. send, convey.

酏　**yí**　MC ye

1. thin gruel, made from rice or millet.

2. rice-wine.

頤　**yí**　MC yi

1. chin, jaw; jowls.

2. foster, nurture; protect.

　　a. "nourishment," name of 27th hexagram of *Yijing*.

飴　**yí**　MC yi

1. maltose, malt sugar; sugar syrup; honey-cakes.

2. ⊙ 飼 *sì*, give food to, feed.

3. ⊙ 貽 *yí*, hand down, bequeath.

鯟　**yí**　MC yij

1. (med.) (bn.) 鼆～ *zhúyí*, → 鼆 *zhú*.

鵋　**yí**　MC ngje

1. (bn.) 鵔～ *jùnyí* (MC swinH-ngje), → 鵔 *jùn*.

yǐ

乙　**yǐ**　MC ʾit

1. 2nd of the 10 heavenly stems; used for "B" in a sequential order.

　　a. ～夜 *yǐyè*, 2nd of the 5 night-watches, approx. 9-11 p.m.

2. second-order, second-rate.

3. recurve(d), curve back on.

4. mark a text when reading, esp. to indicate a sentence break or to indicate where characters should be transposed.

5. intestines of fish.

6. ⊙ 鳦 *yǐ*, the swallow, martin.

以　**yǐ**　MC yiX

1. to use; typically occurring in secondary-VB phrases, i.e., in co-VB phrases, indicating "to take up and use as a means for some purpose or to some end," where the main-VB phrase indicates the purpose or end:

　　a. transitively, to use, take (up); e.g. ～兵二萬伐大荔 *yǐ bīng èrwàn fá Dàlì*, using 20,000 troops they mounted a strike on Dali; ～陽人地賜周君 *yǐ Yángrén dì cì Zhōujūn*, he took the area of Yangren and bestowed it on the lord of Zhou; 周人～殷人之棺槨葬長殤 *Zhōurén yǐ Yīnrén zhī guānguǒ zàng chángshāng*, The people of Zhou used the coffin-sets of the Yin to bury those who died in late adolescence. (This sense is often the equivalent of 2a below.)

　　b. intransitively, the grammatical SUBJ of the co-VB phrase being the patient of the "taking up and using": e.g. 禮～行之 *lǐ yǐ xíng zhī*, implement it using the rites; 巾～帨手 *jīnyǐ shuì shǒu*, use a kerchief to wipe off one's hands; 器～鍾之 *qìyǐ zhōng zhī*, gather them up using the instruments. (This sense is seen mostly in the attenuated forms of 3a-3e below.)

2. transitive uses where the VB-sense has become reduced or attenuated:

　　a. use as a tool, instrument, or means > with, by means of; e.g. 臣事君～忠 *chén shì jūn yǐ zhōng*, the vassal serves the lord with loyalty; 不～其道得之 *bùyǐ qí dào dé zhī*, one does not obtain it by means of his proper doctrine; 欲～力征經營天下 *yù yǐ lì zhēng jīngyíng tiānxià*, he wanted to undertake a corrective expedition to gain complete control of the subcelestial realm by force. (This sense is often the equivalent of 1a and can functionally be thought of as "instrumental.")

　　b. use as a basis, rationale, pretext, model or guideline > because of, according to; e.g. 君使臣～禮 *jūn shǐ chén yǐ lǐ*, the lord employs the vassal according to the rites; 使民～時 *shǐ mín yǐ shí*, employ the people according to the season; ～芻蕘之難，從者之病，將館子於都 *yǐ chúráo zhī nán, cóngzhě zhī bìng, jiāng guǎn zǐ yú dū*, Because of the problem with fodder and feed, and the illnesses of your followers, we will lodge you in the capital city; 〜是知其能 *yǐshì zhī qí néng*, By means of this (> thus) he knew their abilities.

c. in 〜 X 為 Y constructions: to make X into Y, take up X as Y, regard or consider X as Y; e.g. 〜國為姓 *yǐ guó wéi xìng*, to take the state (name) as a surname; 秦方〜天下為事 *qín fāng yǐ tiānxià wéi shì*, Qin now is regarding the whole subcelestial realm as its affair; 〜其地為郡 *yǐ qí dì wéi jùn*, they made his land into an administrative district.

d. after 何 *hé* "what": interr., by means of what > how; e.g. 何〜行之 *héyǐ xíng zhī*, how to put it into practice?; 何〜相救哉 *héyǐ xiāngjiù zāi*, how will they ever come to the aid of each other?

e. after the main VB-phrase in a transfer-VB construction, introducing the thing transferred; e.g. 授舜〜天下 *shòu Shùn yǐ tiānxià*, he handed the subcelestial realm over to Shun; 天子賀〜黼黻 *tiānzi hè yǐ fǔfú*, the Son of Heaven rewarded him with an ornately embroidered ritual garment; 教之〜仁政 *jiào zhī yǐ rén zhèng*, they instructed him in the ways of humane government; 必告之〜其制 *bì gào zhī yǐ qí zhì*, you must advise him of their institutions.

f. preceding the VB-phrase in a transfer-VB construction when the word or phrase for the thing transferred (i.e. the direct object of 〜) is deleted; e.g. 必〜告新令尹 *bì yǐ gào xīn lìngyǐn*, you must report it to the new commanding officer; 〜告於君 *yǐ gào yú jūn*, he reported it to the lord.

g. as an apocopated form of 所〜 *suǒyǐ* "that which is used (as a means for some purpose or to some end)": means, wherewithal; e.g. 不知命，無〜為君子也。不知禮，無〜立也。不知言，無〜知人也 *bù zhī mìng, wú yǐ wéi jūnzi yě; bù zhī lǐ, wú yǐ lì yě; bù zhī yán, wú yǐ zhī rén yě*, If you do not understand fate, then you lack the means to serve as a junior lord; if you do not understand the rites, then you lack the means to be established; if you do not understand language, then you lack the means to understand mankind.

3. intransitive uses where the verbal sense has become reduced or attenuated:

a. taking up and using as a reference point or starting point > from: e.g. 地震河南〜東四十九郡 *dìzhèn Hénán yǐ dōng sìshíjiǔ jùn*, the earthquake extended to 49 commander-ies east from Henan; 易水〜北未有所定也 *Yìshuǐ yǐ běi wèiyǒu suǒdìng yě*, there are not yet any settlements in the area from the Yi river north.

b. after 是 *shì* "this": in this way, by means of this > thus, hence; e.g. 是〜謂之文 *shì yǐ wèi zhī wén*, Thus we refer to him as "cultured"; 是〜久秦晉不相攻 *shì yǐ jiǔ Qín Jìn bùxiāng gōng*, In this way for a long time Qin and Jin did not attack each other.

c. in a VB-phrase 1 〜 VB-phrase 2 context: use VB-phrase 1 to achieve VB-phrase 2, by means of VB-phrase 1 to carry out VB-phrase 2; (given, in view of) VB-phrase 1, thereby VB-phrase 2 > in order to, as a means or basis for, thereby" e.g. 阻其山〜保魏之河內 *zǔ qí shān yǐ bǎo Wèi zhī Hénèi*, they blocked off their mountainous region in order to protect the Henei area of Wei; 欲請兵〜攻豐 *yù qǐng bīng yǐ gōng Fēng*, they were about to request troops in order to attack Feng; 能執干戈〜衛社稷 *néng zhí gān'gē yǐ wèi shèjì*, they are able to grasp staff and spear in order to protect the altars of soil and grain; 聰〜知遠，明〜察微 *cōng yǐ zhī yuǎn, míng yǐ chá wēi*, in view of his intelligence, he will understand remote matters; in view of his perspicacity, he will discern fine details.

d. when occurring alone: using (unspecified OBJ) for some purpose or to some end > thereby, in this way, by this means; e.g. 欲〜并天下 *yù yǐ bìng tiānxià*, he wished thereby to unite the subcelestial realm; 不敢〜治水 *bùgǎn yǐ zhì shuǐ*, he dared not in this way try to control the waters; 〜服事殷 *yǐ fú shì Yīn*, in this way he submitted and served the Yin.

e. in 〜為 Y constructions: to take (some X not stated) as Y, regard (some X not stated) as Y, to think or consider that, to make (some X not stated) into Y; e.g. 〜為秦國尉 *yǐ wéi Qín guó wèi*, he made him the state protector of Qin; 〜為楚地兵不足憂 *yǐ wéi Chǔ dì bīng bùzú yōu*, he thought that the troops of the Chu area were not worth being concerned about; 民〜為將拯己於水火之中也 *mín yǐ wéi jiāng zhěng jǐ yú shuǐ huǒ zhī zhōng yě*, the people thought that he would raise them up from amidst the water and fire.

f. after 可 *kě* "to be able," 足 *zú* "to be sufficient," 難 *nán* "to be difficult," and 易 *yì* "to be easy," makes the following VB-phrase active; e.g. 可〜終身行之 *kěyǐ zhōngshēn xíng zhī*, one can practice it to the end of one's days; 書足～記名姓而已 *shū zúyǐ jì míngxìng éryǐ*, writing is sufficient for nothing more than recording names.

伲　yǐ　MC yiX

1. dumfounded, nonplussed.
   a. stop in one's tracks, unable to advance; immobile, stuck.
2. ponder deeply, reflect on.

chì　MC trhiH

1. (bn.) ～儗 *chìyì* (MC trhiH-ngiH), stuck fast, inert and immobile, at a standstill; also, (med.) easy and relaxed, slow and measured.

倚　yǐ　MC 'jeX

1. incline toward, inclination, lean toward, e.g. ～盧 *yǐlú*, "lean-to hut," simple hut for mourning.
   a. lean on, rest on, rely on, depend on, e.g. ～傍 *yǐbàng*, pattern after, emulate, use as prop; ～伏 *yǐfú*, "leaning on and hiding under," mutual dependence of prosperity and calamity (< *Laozi* 58).
   b. self-reliant, self-confident; confident of.
   c. be partial or biased toward, favor.
   d. according to, in accord with.
2. draw near, bring close; be reconciled with.
3. pause temporarily; (bn.) 徙～ *xǐyǐ* (MC sjeX-'jeX), halting and hesitant, troubled and undecided.
4. (med.) chair, only from ca. 8th century but rare; item becomes common post-Tang and then written 椅.

巇　yǐ　MC ngjeX

1. rdup., steeply spiring, tall and towering.

巳　yǐ　MC yiX

1. stop, cease; finish, complete; e.g. 每一書～ *měi yīshū yǐ*, when each copying (of a text) was finished . . .; X～, *X yǐ*, (with) X being done, . . .; X 而～, *X éryǐ*, X and that's all, no more than X, merely X.
2. (ADV) already . . .; is now . . ., has now become . . .
   a. (ADV) not long (since), quite soon.
3. very (much), quite; e.g. ～甚 *yǐshèn*, greatly, exceedingly, to an extreme degree; completely.
4. ⊙ 以 *yǐ* 3a, in phrases such as ～東 *yǐdōng*, from the east, and eastward; ～上 *yǐshàng*, and above, from above, and more.

宸　yǐ　MC 'j+jX

1. space between door and window of audience hall.
   a. partition or standing screen, usu. placed on north side of hall behind the ruler.

旖　yǐ　MC 'jeX

1. (bn.) ～旎 *yǐnǐ* (MC 'jeX-nrjeX), gracefully fluttering, rippling with the wind; also, thickly spreading, of plants.

欘　yǐ　MC ngjeX

1. southern dialect word for mooring a boat on shore.
   a. (med.) tie, truss, lash.

矣　yǐ　MC hiX

1. sentential marker of perfective aspect, i.e., perfected, completed action unrelated to VB-tense: has, have, had + VB; cog. 已 *yǐ*; e.g. 西周弱～ *xīzhōu ruò yǐ*, Western Zhou has become debilitated; 功已成～ *gōng yǐ chéng yǐ*, success has already been achieved; 秦王老～ *qínwáng lǎo yǐ*, the king of Qin has become old; 故能得欲～ *gù néng déyù yǐ*, to be sure, you will have been able to gain your wish.
   a. sentential marker of hypothetical perfective aspect: would (have) + VB; e.g. 今秦攻周而得之，則眾必多傷～ *jīn qín gōng zhōu ér dé zhī, zé zhòng bì duōshāng yǐ*, If Qin attacks and then gains control over Zhou, large numbers of the populous would inevitably come to harm; 則兩國者必為天下笑～ *zé liǎngguózhe bì wéi tiānxià xiào yǐ*, then these two states would become the laughing-stock of the subcelestial realm.
2. perfected, completed action > change of state, new situation: now; e.g. 可謂能自知人～ *kě wèi néng zìzhī rén yǐ*, he can now be referred to as someone who understands himself; 敬聞命～ *jīngwén mìng yǐ*, I will now respectfully hear your advice; 吾不能守～ *wú bùnéng shǒu yǐ*, we are no longer able to protect it.
3. perfected > finished > sentence-final GP of rhetorical finality: surely, definitely, that's it!; e.g. 趙將亡～ *zhào jiāng wáng yǐ*, Zhao is certainly going to perish; 盡美～ *jìnměi yǐ*, it is perfectly splendid; 子慟～ *zǐ tòng yǐ*, you are surely grieved.

礒 yǐ MC ngjeX
1. (bn.) 碕～ *qǐyǐ*, → 碕 *qí* (*qí*).

艤 yǐ MC ngjeX ⊙ 檥 *yǐ*.

苡 yǐ MC yiX ⊙ 苢 *yǐ*.

苢 yǐ MC yiX
1. (bn.) 芣～ *fúyǐ*, →芣 *fú*; (bn.) 薏～ *yìyǐ*, → 薏 *yì*.

螘 yǐ MC ngjeX ⊙ 蟻 *yǐ*, ant.

蟻 yǐ MC ngjeX
1. ant; ant-like, formican; e.g. ～附 *yǐfù*, (like) a mass of ants.
   a. ant-colored, black.
2. lees floating atop wine.

轙 yǐ MC ngjeX
1. yoke-ring, ring attached to a carriage's yoke through which the reins pass.

迆 yǐ MC yeX ⊙ 迤 *yǐ*.

迤 yǐ MC yeX
1. move awry, off-center, in an oblique path; deviate.
   a. oblique, slanted; bent; canted.
2. (bn.) ～邐 *yǐlǐ* (MC yeX-ljeX) or 邐～ *lǐyǐ*, continuously twisting and turning, one after another; (bn.) ～靡 *yǐmǐ* (MC yeX-mjeX), continuously connected, unbroken, succeeding in series.

yí MC ye
1. (bn.) 逶～ *wēiyí* (MC 'jwe-ye), tortive and twisted, roundabout, meandering endlessly, proceeding persistently.

鳦 yǐ MC 'it
1. the swallow, martin; syn. 燕 *yàn*.

齮 yǐ MC ngjeX
1. bite; gnaw.
   a. eat through > damage, wound, impair, despoil.

yì

乂 yì MC ngjojH
1. put in order, bring order to; govern, regulate, rule.
   a. make secure, protect.

2. a person who stands out from the crowd, nonpareil.

亦 yì MC yek
1. occurring before a VB or VB-phrase, or before noun predicates in nominal sentences, refers reflexively to the topic or subject of the sentence, with a limiting sense, i.e. specifically in regard to that topic or subject: for his (her, its, their) part; e.g. 王～不好士 *wáng yì bùhào shì*, The king for his part is not fond of officials; 此～飛之至也 *cǐ yì fēi zhī zhì yě*, This for its part is the ultimate form of flying.
   a. for his (her, its, their part) > the one or the case in question > "in this (that) case"; e.g. 若其未有君～圖之 *ruò qí wèiyǒu jūn yì tú zhī* If by chance you do not yet have this, my lord in that case ought to plan for it.
   b. for his (her, its, their) part > the one in particular > the one also > "also", "too", "besides"; e.g. 此～聖人之過也 *cǐ yì shèngrén zhī guò yě*, This too is an error of the sage; 大言～然 *dàyán yì rán*, Great speech is also like that. (This sense can be difficult to distinguish from 1.)
   c. "also," "too" > used to emphasize an extreme case > "too", "still"; e.g. 雖桀紂～不能去民之好義 *suī jié zhòu yì bùnéng qù mín zhī hàoyì* Even Jie and Zhou, they too were unable to eradicate the people's preference for Propriety; 寡人雖死～無悔焉 *guǎrén suī sǐ yì wú huǐ yān* Even should I, the Solitary One, die, still I will have no remorse in regard to it.
2. occurring before a VB or VB-phrase, restricts the reference to the particular person, thing, or event in question (often reinforced by a suitable rhetorical sentence coda): this one > just, only; e.g. ～有仁義而已 *yì yǒu rényì éryǐ*, I have just Humaneness and Propriety [to offer] and that's all; ～不用于耕耳 *yì bùyòng yú gēng ěr*, They only did not apply [their efforts] to plowing, that's all.
3. used after the negative GP *bù* 不 and before a scalar predicate adjective, indicates that the quality or sense of the predicate adjective does not apply to the subject, yet does not allow for attributing the negative or opposite quality to the subject; in other words, allows for a neutral judgment; e.g. 不～大 *bùyìdà*, is not great (but is not necessarily small, cf. 不大 *bùdà*, is small); 不～

善乎 *bùyìshàn hū*, is it not good? (but not necessarily bad?, cf. 不善乎 *bùshàn hū*, is it bad?).

仡　yì　MC ngj+t

1. sgl. or rdup., brave and bold, strong and stalwart, hardy, unassailable.
2. (med.) fixedly staring.

佚　yì　MC yit

1. seclude(d), keep(ing) apart; exclude(d).
   a. scattered, lost over time, esp. of books.
2. reject(ed), cast aside, discard(ed); disregard, treat lightly.
3. mistake(n), in error, erroneous(ly).
4. unconventional, unaccepting of normal standards, ⊙ 逸 *yì*.
   a. (bn.) ～豫 *yìyù* (MC yit-yoH), lax and careless, nonchalant; also, speeding swiftly.
5. ⊙ 迭 *dié*, in turn, successively.

佾　yì　MC yit

1. a row of ritual dancers at ancestral sacrifices in Zhou times; tradition permitted eight rows of eight for rulers, six rows of six for nobles, four rows of four for grandees.

億　yì　MC 'ik

1. one hundred thousand; (Budd.) a lakh.
   a. an immeasurable number or amount, a myriad myriads.
2. conjecture, estimate; supposition.
3. put at rest; satisfy; allay.
   a. supply something lacking.
4. ⊙ 臆 *yì*, chest.
5. ～尼 *yìní* (MC 'ik-nrij), Agni, i.e. Argi, Budd. Skt. name for Qarashāhr 焉耆 (Yanqi), east of Kucha on the northern branch of the Silk Road.

刈　yì　MC ngjojH

1. to mow, cut down.
   a. math, crop that has been mowed.
2. sickle, scythe.

劓　yì　MC ngijH

1. cut off the nose, as punishment.

勩　yì　MC yejH

1. labors, toil; fatigue; drudge(ry).

嗌　yì　MC 'jiek

1. throat.

　　ài　MC 'eaH

1. choke; gasp out.
2. (med.) cloying to the taste.

囈　yì　MC ngjiejH

1. (bn.) 唵～ *ānyì*, → 唵 *ān*.

塲　yì　MC yek

1. boundaries of farming fields.
   a. frontier boundary.

奕　yì　MC yek

1. rdup., great and grand, imposing, richly replete; also, (med.) proudly aloof; also, (med.) flashing and shining, gleaming.
2. accumulated, layered; e.g. ～世 *yìshì*, ～葉 *yìyè*, successive ages.
   a. deployed in sequence.

屹　yì　MC ngj+t

1. sheer-standing, steep; abrupt; acclivitous.
   a. (bn.) ～崒 *yìzú* (MC ngj+t-dzwit), steep and sheer.
2. (med.) stonewalled, resolute; dauntless, unshakeable.

弈　yì　MC yek

1. to play the game of *wéiqí* 圍棋, "encirclement chess."
   a. (med.) ～棋 *yìqí*, general term for board games.
2. ⊙ 奕 *yì*.

弋　yì　MC yik

1. arrow attached to a string, for hunting, corded dart.
   a. shoot at with strung-arrow.
2. seize, capture; catch; take.
3. ⊙ 杙 *yì*, stake, short wooden post; 黓 *yì*, black.

役　yì　MC ywek

1. corvée labor, seasonal tax-service.
   a. forced labor.
2. military service, esp. at the borders; conscript.
   a. be on campaign; e.g. 征～ *zhēngyì*, go on military campaign.
3. do service as an official, esp. requiring one to go elsewhere; e.g. 行～ *xíngyì*, travel on official business or an official mission; also, travel in general.

4. provide service in a private capacity; servant.
   a. serf.
   b. adherent, disciple.
   c. thrall(dom), in thrall to.

悒　yì　MC ʻip

1. sgl. or rdup., chagrin(ed); discontent(ed); doleful, depressed.
   a. (bn.) 怏～ *yàngyì* (MC ʻjangH-ʻip), glum and dolorous, chagrined and thwarted.

意　yì　MC ʻejH

1. thought, idea; mentation; concept.
   a. (Budd.) ～根 *yìgēn*, mental faculty.
   b. meaning, significance; overtone.
2. intent(ion), purpose.
   a. attitude, mood, frame of mind, feeling; mind-set, way of thinking.
   b. expression of intent > demeanor, mien.
3. conjecture, estimate; anticipate; intuit.
   a. imagine that X is the case > supposedly, perhaps.
4. (med.) ⊙ 憶 *yì*, call to mind, remember; think over; e.g. ～況 *yìkuàng*, ponder, think on; considerations.

憶　yì　MC ʻik

1. think of, think on, think over, call to mind.
   a. recollect, recall; reminisce.
2. remember, keep in mind; commit to memory.

懌　yì　MC yek

1. joyful, cheerful; content; pleased with.

懿　yì　MC ʻijH

1. perfect(ion); excellent, admirable.
   a. praise, laud; admire.
2. deep; capacious.

抑　yì　MC ʻik

1. press down, push down, hold down; compress (more forceful than 按 *àn* and more often used in abstract sense; ant. 揚 *yáng*, lift up, raise).
   a. suppress, restrain; hold back, keep back.
   b. control; force.
   c. depress(ed); e.g. (bn.) ～鬱 *yìyù* (MC ʻik-ʼjut), oppressive dejection, depressed and despondent.
2. lower; bow the head.
   a. abase oneself; cede place.
3. withdraw, retire.

4. arrest, stop; curb; bring to a halt.
   a. forbid(ding).
5. lever, lever-arm, in a roof-bracket construction a pole placed obliquely with its lower end carrying the eaves while its upper end is balanced by a purlin; syn. 昂 *áng*.
6. (GP) indicating an alternative or a disjunction: or; e.g. 求之與～與之與 *qiú zhī yū yì yǔ zhī yū*, does he seek it or is it given to him?
7. onom. of approval or wonder: "Ah!"

挹　yì　MC ʻjip

1. strain liquid, draw off, draw from, broach, tap.
   a. decant.
2. draw toward oneself, bring over.
   a. take to one's own.
3. assess, deliberate.
4. (med.) ～怛 *yìdá* (MC ʻjip-tat), Hephthalites, a people of Iranian descent who established a kingdom in Transoxiana and Chinese Turkestan during last quarter of the 5th and first half of 6th-c.
5. ⊙ 抑 *yì* 1, press down.

yī　MC ʻjip

1. ⊙ 揖 *yī*, bow with hands clasped.

斁　yì　MC yek

1. tired of, weary of; enough of, full of.
   a. replete, filling; swelling; full-throated.

dù　MC tuH

1. ruin, destroy.

tú　MC du

1. to plaster, coat.

易　yì　MC yek

1. change; transform, metamorphose; alter.
   a. sgl. or cmpd. ～經, (*Classic of*) *Changes*, name of a canonical text.
2. exchange, interchange(ability); swap, trade.
3. ⊙ 場 *yì*, field-boundary; frontier; (de)limit.

yì　MC yeH

1. easy (ant. 難 *nán*, difficult).
   a. facilitate; mitigate, lighten.
2. consider inconsequential, regard lightly; disrespect.
3. be at ease, at peace; relieved.
   a. (Dao.) ～遷 *yìqiān*, "Easeful Remove," name of celestial paradise for women.
4. flat, of terrain.
5. well-tended, well-cultivated, of grain.
   a. lie fallow, in order to restore fertility; e.g. 再～ *zàiyì*, let a field lie fallow for 2 years.

瞖　yì　MC ʼejH
1. lowering sky; overclouded.

杙　yì　MC yik
1. stake, short wooden post; paling; peg.
2. drive in, peg, drive down.
3. awl.

枻　yì　MC yejH
1. rowing-sweep.
   a. rudder.
2. oar(s).
   a. ply the oars, row.
3. side-planks of a boat, gunwales, bulwarks.
4. by synecdoche, general term for a boat.
   　　xiè　MC sjet
1. straightening board, used in making bows.

栧　yì　MC yejH　⊙ 枻 *yì*.

殪　yì　MC ʼejH
1. kill with bow and arrow.
   a. perish(ed), dead, kill(ed).
2. collapse, fall, give way.

毅　yì　MC ngj+jH
1. resolute, decisive; staunch, steadfast.
2. ruthless, implacable; unrelenting.

泆　yì　MC yit
1. gush forth, inundate, flood.
2. reckless, unchecked; let loose.
   a. lax, dissolute.

浥　yì　MC ʼip
1. soak; moisten, wet, damp.
2. rdup., (med.) perfused with scent.
   　　yà　MC ʼeap
1. a low spot, depression; indentation.
2. (med.) flow down, drain.

溢　yì　MC yit
1. overflow, spill over, brim over.
2. superfluity; excess(ive); extravagance.
3. fill to the brim, overstuff(ed); override, place above.
   a. satisfied; satiate(d).
4. split apart, split open.
5. ⊙ 鎰 *yì*, measure of weight, double-pound.

潏　yì　MC yejH
1. (bn.) 溶～ *róngyì*, → 溶 *róng* 2.

熠　yì　MC yip
1. rdup., vividly bright; (bn.) ～燿 *yìyào* (MC yip-yewH), fitfully glinting; also, firefly, glow-worm.

燡　yì　MC yek
1. rdup., grandly aglow, blazingly brilliant.

異　yì　MC yiH
1. differ(ent), dissimilar; differentiate; ～端 *yìduān*, (from a) different angle, an opinion not normally accepted.
   a. other; the other of two.
2. unusual, uncommon; exceptional, extraordinary; of a different order than the norm.
   a. aberrant, erratic, peculiar; diverge(nt); bizarre; eccentric.

疫　yì　MC ywek
1. contagion, epidemic, pestilence.
   a. disease demon.

瘞　yì　MC ʼjejH
1. inter(ment), bury in the earth, inhumation.
   a. hide, bury away, conceal.
2. make ritual offering or sacrifice to.

益　yì　MC ʼjiek
1. increase, add to; augment; e.g. ～智子 *yìzhìzǐ*, "wisdom-augmenting seeds," black or bitter cardamom; also, nutmeg.
   a. more, even more X.
   b. gradually, progressively, increasingly.
   c. "increase," name of 42nd hexagram of *Yijing*.
2. advantage; benefit; e.g. 三～ *sānyì*, "three benefactors," i.e. bamboo, wood, stone.
3. plentiful, more than enough, abundant; well off.
4. ⊙ 溢 *yì*, overflow.

縊　yì　MC ʼjieH
1. hang by the neck.
   a. strangle with a cord.

繹　yì　MC yek
1. reel off or unwind raw silk from a cocoon.
   a. unravel, disentangle; find the clue.
   b. unscramble, unsnarl; unfold; separate; straighten out.
2. following a single thread > continuous(ly), unbroken.
3. state or present directly, item by item.

義　yì　MC ngjeH

1. what is right, right-principled, right-minded; proper, propriety; dutiful(ness), esp. of responsibilities and appropriate actions owed to one's acknowledged "we" group, as function of one's proper social relations and status; social obligations; socially conscious, responsible; devoted to the good of one's family, clan, and state; often paired with "humaneness" (仁 rén) as the 2 fundamental Ruist moral principles.

2. meaning, significance; proper understanding, sense; interpret(ation), purport; properly adapted, congruous.

3. appropriate(d); adoptive, adopted; e.g. ～子 yìzǐ, adoptive son, who has been "made one's own."

　　a. accept responsibility for other's welfare; charity; generosity; e.g. (Dao.) ～舍 yìshè, charity lodge, early Tianshi site for administering neighborhoods and providing lodging and food for travelers.

4. ⊙ 議 yì, opinion, judgment.

羿　yì　MC ngejH

1. name of mythological archer said to have shot down nine of ten suns that were roasting the earth.

翊　yì　MC yik

1. rdup., aloft and above, in flight aloft; also, languid and listless, creeping along; also, respectful and mannerly.

2. assist, aid; prop up, support.

3. ⊙ 翌 yì, next day, next year.

翌　yì　MC yik

1. the next day; next year.

2. ⊙ 翼 yì, wing.

翳　yì　MC 'ejH

1. hide from view, mask, screen; conceal.
　　a. shade; obscure.
　　b. hiding-place; blind, as for hunting.

2. feathered fan used by dancers.

3. feather-fringed canopy for a carriage.

4. shield, buckler, of a soldier.

5. (med.) line-initial particle in verse, onom. of emphasis: "O!"

翼　yì　MC yik

1. wings, of bird or insect.

　　a. enfold; screen, veil; shelter, safeguard.
　　b. pennate, alar.

2. come to the side of; join with; assist, aid; supplement.

3. flanks of an army.

4. one of the 28 lunar lodgings, comprised of 22 stars in Hydra and Crater, in the southern quadrant (chiniao 赤鳥) of the sky.

5. rdup., reverent and respectful; also, neat and even, well-matched; also, lush and luxuriant; also, placidly winging, easily advancing.

6. ⊙ 翌 yì, next day (year).

肄　yì　MC yijH

1. exercise, train, practice; rehearse.

2. take pains, labor at, toil; apply oneself to.

3. sucker, shoot, runner, of a tree.
　　a. offshoot, young growth; descendant.

4. examine, inspect.

臆　yì　MC 'ik

1. chest, breast.

2. what is in one's heart, thoughts.
　　a. conjecture, suppose; infer.

藙　yì　MC ngjiejH

1. ⊙ 藝 yì 3, to plant; 藝 yì 1, skill, art; 刈 yì, mow, cut down.

薏　yì　MC 'ik

1. hollow center of the lotus-stalk.

2. (bn.) ～苢 yìyǐ (MC 'ik-yiX), tear-grass, Job's tears (Coix lachyrma-jobi).

藝　yì　MC ngjiejH

1. skill(fullness), expertness; mastery; art, craft; e.g. ～術 yìshù, arts and crafts requiring technical mastery.

　　a. 六～ liùyì, Six Arts—ritual (禮 lǐ), music (樂 yuè), archery (射 shè), chariot driving (御 yù), calligraphy (書 shū), mathematics (數 shù)—in which a gentleman of pre-imperial times was supposed to be trained.
　　b. expert in particular art, artiste.

2. standard(s), norm(s); constant(s), canon(s); ～文 yìwén, texts of educational and moral importance, texts that make for proper training of a gentleman.

　　a. 六～ liùyì, Six Canons of Ruist education, Six Classics, i.e. Documents (書 shū), Odes (詩 shī), Changes (易 yì), Ritual (禮 lǐ), Music (樂 yuè), Annals (春秋 chūnqiū).

3. plant, sow; cultivate.
4. (de)limit, bound.

翳　yì　MC 'ejH

1. thick, dense plant growth.
    a. (bn.) ～薈 *yìhuì* (MC 'ejH-'wajH), ～蔚 *yìwèi* (MC 'ejH-'jw+jH), rich and rampant, rich and rank, thick and thronging.

蜴　yì　MC yek

1. (bn.) 蜥～ *xīyì*, → 蜥 *xī*.

裔　yì　MC yejH

1. hem of a garment.
2. edge, border of a state; frontier, marchland; e.g. ～民 *yìmín*, those banished to the frontier.
    a. peoples across the frontier, outlanders.
    b. distant lands.
3. those connected to one in later times; descendants, posterity.
4. rdup., walking daintily, advancing modestly; also, advancing steadily, marching forward; also, gracefully gliding, serenely soaring.

裛　yì　MC 'ip

1. protective wrapper or casing for scroll.
2. wrap, bind; envelop.
3. (med.) scent or perfuse clothes with fragrance or incense; rdup., imbue and infuse, waft and spread.
4. ⊙ 浥 *yì* 1, soak, moisten.

詣　yì　MC ngejH

1. go to a destination, arrive at a place.
    a. get directly to the point.
2. pay a visit to, make a call on.
3. (med.) purposeful(ness).

誼　yì　MC ngjeH

1. ⊙ 義 1-2 dutiful, right-principled, responsible; congruence, meaning, significance, purport; 議 *yì*, discuss, deliberate, critique.
2. (med.) friendship, amity; congenial, amicable.
    a. (med.) relations of sympathy or blood.

譯　yì　MC yek

1. interpret, translate; e.g. 九～ *jiǔyì*, "[through] nine interpreters," i.e. nearly unintelligible.
    a. explicate, elucidate.
2. (med.) glad, pleased; elated.

議　yì　MC ngjeH

1. discuss(ion), assess(ment); deliberate on, deliberation.
    a. (med.) right of deliberation regarding judicial sentence.
2. opinion, judgment; finding, determination; counsel(or).
    a. critique, evaluation.
3. (med.) prose literary genre, in which various opinions are considered and what is deemed the correct or appropriate (義 *yì*) judgment is reached.

貤　yì　MC yeH　⊙ 貤 *yì*.

貤　yì　MC yeH

1. piled, layered, heaped; amassed.
    a. repeated(ly), over and again.
2. extend, lengthen; stretch on, stretch out.
yí　MC ye
1. move, shift, change position; e.g. ～封 *yífēng*, transfer one's fief and title.

軼　yì　MC yit

1. overrun, overtake, outrace; rush by.
    a. outdo; surpass, exceed.
2. overflow, pour over.
3. invade, raid.
4. ⊙ 佚 *yì* 1-2, secluded, out of the way; scattered, lost.
    dié　MC det
1. to alternate, change places; successive(ly), ⊙ 迭 *dié*.
    zhé　MC drjet
1. ⊙ 轍 *zhé*, carriage tracks; follow in the tracks.

逸　yì　MC yit

1. flee, escape, evade.
    a. get free, get loose; unbridled; throw off the traces; e.g. ～轡 *yìpèi*, relax the reins; ～觀 *yìguān*, exceed or get beyond the purview of.
2. uninhibited, unconfined, free; unconventional; e.g. ～氣 *yìqì*, uninhibited inspiration.
    a. unattached, untroubled, free of responsibility, independent; displaced; e.g. ～民 *yìmín*, unrestricted folk, evasive folk, those who have withdrawn from society.
    b. of a different, higher order than the norm; beyond usual expectations; e.g. ～品 *yìpǐn*, in a special or exceptional class.

3. idle, unoccupied; lethargic; e.g. ～慢 *yìmàn*, indolence; ～盪 *yìdàng*, idle indulgence.

4. ◉ 軼 *yì* 1, outrun, outdo; 佚 *yì*, scattered, lost.

邑   yì   MC ʽip

1. borough, self-governing municipality.
   a. town, settlement.
2. in Zhou times, major city of a feudal state, capital; also, a small state.
3. fief, appanage.
4. (med.) a district, township, sometimes syn. 縣 *xiàn*.
5. ◉ 悒 *yì*, chagrin, discontent.

醳   yì   MC yek

1. spirits, liquor.
   a. rdup., clear and unclouded, of wine.
2. provide food and drink.
3. ◉ 釋 *shì*, release, deliver from.

鎰   yì   MC yit

1. measure of weight, equiv. 20 or 24 兩 *liǎng* ("ounces").
   a. (med.) in Tang times, equiv. .895 kilogram or 1.969 pounds, a "double-pound."

饐   yì   MC ʽijH

1. spoiled, tainted, turned, of food or drink.

   yē   MC ʽet

1. ◉ 噎 *yē*, stuck in the throat; choke; ◉ 咽 *yē* (*yān*), catch in the throat; sob.

驛   yì   MC yek

1. government post-station, relay-station.
   a. post-horses, post-carriages.

鶂   yì   MC ngek

1. rdup., "cackle-cackle," of goose.

鷁   yì   MC ngek

1. heron.
   a. "heron-prowed boat," a boat with a heron painted on its prow, to ward off water demons; often, general term for boats.

黓   yì   MC yik

1. black; nigrescent.

yīn

喑   yīn   MC ʽim

1. ◉ 瘖 *yīn*, go mute, dumb; speechless, taciturn.

   yìn   MC ʽimH

1. (bn.) ～噁 *yìnwù* (MC ʽimH-ʽuH), ～嗚 *yìnwū* (MC ʽimH-ʽu), rant and rave, fume and fulminate.

因   yīn   MC ʽjin

1. follow from, retain the nature of, in accordance with.
   a. rely on, adhere to; adopt; be founded on.
   b. adapt to.
2. following from X, because of X; thence, therefore; since.
   a. ensuing from, proceed(ing) from; owing to, on account of, by reason of.
   b. take the opportunity for, take the occasion for; based on.
3. criterion; standard or principle of judging or testing a statement, or for explaining a result or effect; basis on which something is decided or determined.
   a. cause; causality.
   b. (Budd.) principal causes or conditions, e.g. ～緣 *yīnyuán*, principal and subsidiary causes of karmic results, the principle of dependent origination (*pratītyasamutpāda*); also, general term for karma; ～果 *yīnguǒ*, cause and result, cause and effect, karma.
4. (med.) (bn.) ～循 or ～巡 *yīnxún* (MC ʽjin-zwin), casually, carelessly, as one wishes, at one's whim; idly and unhurried; also, linger and dally, stall and stay on.

堙   yīn   MC ʽjin

1. block up, dam up, esp. with earth or loam; mound up.
   a. fill a gap, stifle; a stopgap.
   b. bury, cover up; obliterate, efface.
2. raise earthworks, esp. for attack against a city.

姻   yīn   MC ʽjin

1. husband's father (cf. 婚 *hūn*, wife's father).
2. marriage; e.g. 婚～ *hūnyīn*, joining of wife's family with husband's > marriage.
   a. relations by marriage.

愔   yīn   MC ʽjim

1. rdup., quiet and gentle, mellow and mild, amiable and relaxed.
   a. (bn.) ～翳 *yīnyì* (MC ʽjim-ejH), quiet and composed, serenely placid.

慇　yīn　MC ʻj+n
1. (bn.) ～懃 or ～勤 yīnqín (MC ʻj+n-gj+n), ardently attentive, eagerly earnest, with care and courtesy, devoted and diligent, solicitous, sedulous, graciously gallant.
2. rdup., sad and sorrowful.

殷　yīn　MC ʻj+n
1. abundant, full.
　　a. opulent, opulence; prosper(ous).
2. just when, just at that time.
3. sgl. or rdup., sad, sorrowful, anxious, unquiet.
4. (bn.) ～勤 yīnqín (MC ʻj+n-gj+n), ardently eager, solicitous, ⊙ 慇懃 yīnqín, → 慇 yīn.
5. alt. name of Shang dynasty after its capital was moved to Yin.
　　yǐn　MC ʻj+nH
1. onom. of the roll of thunder; also, of the resonance of a large bell; also, loud lapping or churning of fountain.
　　yān　MC ʻean
1. reddish-purple, magenta, amaranth.

磤　yīn　MC ʻjin
1. (bn.) ～氳 yīnyūn (MC ʻjin-ʻjun), full and favoring pneuma, brumously fertile mingling of yin and yang, benign balm, favoring vapors, full and invigorating; also, thick-gathering mists, heavy haze, enveloping fog.

湮　yīn　MC ʻen
1. submerge(d), engulf(ed); drown(ed).
2. stop up, dam; clog; obstruct.

瘖　yīn　MC ʻim
1. lose one's voice, go mute; lacking the ability to speak; dumb.
　　a. taciturn, speechless; close-mouthed.

禋　yīn　MC ʻjin
1. sacrifice to Heaven using smoke or incense.
　　a. incense-rite > general term for sacrifice.

綑　yīn　MC ʻjin
1. (bn.) ～縕 yīnyūn, ⊙ 氤氳 yīnyūn, → 氤 yīn.
2. ⊙ 茵 yīn, seat-pad, cushion, pallet.

茵　yīn　MC ʻjin
1. carriage pad, seat-pad.
　　a. pallet, mattress, ticking; cushion.

2. (bn.) ～蔯 yīnchén (MC ʻjin-drin), capillary wormwood (Artemisia capillaris), small deciduous shrub, autumn-flowering.
3. (bn.) ～蒕 yīnyùn (MC ʻjin-ʻjun), equiv. 氤氳 yīnyūn, → 氤 yīn.

蔭　yīn　MC ʻim
1. shade(d); shadow(ed); screen(ed).
　　a. umbrous, umbrage.
2. (med.) arable, fit for cultivation.
　　yìn　MC ʻimH
1. afford shelter; to shade, protect; benefit.
　　a. (med.) in Sui and Tang times, a privilege extended to the offspring of certain high-ranking officials or nobility, allowing a descendant to enter officialdom directly though at a relatively low level.

闉　yīn　MC ʻjin
1. small protective wall outside the main wall of a city, curtain-wall; also, the gate in such a wall, sometimes raised above ground level.
　　a. general term for fortified wall.
2. sinuous, twisting, curved.
3. ⊙ 堙 yīn, block, mound up; earthworks.

陰　yīn　MC ʻim
1. shade(d), shadow(ed); cold-lit.
　　a. dark(ness), dim(ly).
2. north side of a mountain, south side of a river, esp. in place-names.
3. cold(ness); inactivity, declining strength, seasons of autumn and winter; e.g. ～氣 yīnqì, cool vapors and aura of autumn and winter; ～風 yīnfēng, cold wind, esp. north wind.
　　a. decline, weaken.
4. feminine principle (opp. 陽 yáng), associated with the moon, earth, darkness, cold, weakness, softness, hiddenness, latency, stillness, etc.
　　a. broken lines in Yijing hexagrams.
　　b. symbolic of the number 6 as the most fully yin of the nine fundamental numerals.
5. below the surface, secretive, out of sight; retract(ed); e.g. ～德 yīndé, actions helpful for others done without their knowledge; ～室 yīnshì, private room(s); ～通 yīntōng, secret communications.
　　a. suggest(ion), intimation; innuendo.
6. pertaining to the reproductive organs; e.g. ～痿 yīnwěi, impotence; ～蝕 yínshí, vaginal ulcers.

7. (Budd.) group, aggregate, trns. of Skt. *skandha*, as in the 5 *skandha* that make up a human being: form, perception, consciousness, action, knowledge; syn. 蘊 *yùn*.

yìn   MC 'imH

1. afford shelter, protect; benefit.
2. cover over; conceal, hide.

陻   yīn   MC 'jin

1. ⊙ 堙 *yīn* 1, block up, dam up.

音   yīn   MC 'im

1. sound.
2. tone, timbre, modulated musical sound; musical note; e.g. 知～ *zhīyīn*, one who appreciates the tone, a friend who understands what one means without explanations.
    a. by synecdoche, tune; music in general.
    b. 八～ *bāyīn*, 8 categories of materials from which musical instruments were made, i.e. metal, stone, earth (pottery), hide, silk, wood, gourd, bamboo.
3. voice, words.
    a. tone of voice; accent; nuance.
4. reputation, rumor.
    a. news, tidings, message, sgl. and in various cmpds, e.g. ～信 *yīnxìn*, ～訊 *yīnxùn*, 書～ *shūyīn*.

駰   yīn   MC 'jin

1. dapple-gray horse.

yín

吟   yín   MC ngim

1. chant, intone, esp. poetry; speak rhythmically.
    a. vibrato, produced on zither.
2. drone, hum, of insects; cry, call, song, of birds.
3. sigh, moan.
    a. (bn.) 呻～ *shēnyín* (MC syin-ngim), recite by rote; also, moan piteously, esp. from pain or illness.
4. stammer, stutter.
5. (lit.) name of a type of verse similar to a ballad, sometimes with connotation of being a local song.

jìn   MC gimH

1. ⊙ 噤 *jìn*, close the mouth, close-mouthed.

嚚   yín   MC ngin

1. fatuous; thickheaded; obstinate.
    a. untrustworthy, unreliable in speech, insincere; duplicitous, deceitful.

垠   yín   MC ngj+n

1. limit(s), bound(ary), margin, end; edge, borderline.
    a. outline, shape.
2. dike, raised border; riverbank, shore.
3. rift, fissure, ⊙ 圻 *qí* 3.

夤   yín   MC yin

1. (med.) (bn.) ～緣 *yínyuán* (MC yin-ywen), climbing and clambering; steadily scrabbling, advancing constantly, continuing ceaselessly; creeping close; also, following or tracing the outline of.
2. respectful, regardful.

寅   yín   MC yin

1. 3rd of the 12 earthly branches, associated with the tiger as emblematic animal.
    a. 3rd double-hour of the day, from approximately 3 a.m. to 5 a.m.
2. respectful, regardful.
3. (med.) (bn.) ～緣 *yínyuán* (MC yin-ywen), ⊙ 夤 *yín* 1.

崟   yín   MC ngim

1. lofty, tall; peak(ed).
    a. rdup., tall and towering, high and steep, most precipitous; also, salient and outstanding; also, thick and dense.

嶔   yín   MC ngim   ⊙ 崟 *yín*.

殥   yín   MC yin

1. far-flung, on the farther side of, far reaches; e.g. 八～ *bāyín*, the "eight beyonds," or "eight extremities," lands in all directions beyond the traditional Chinese borders.

淫   yín   MC yim

1. excessive, prodigal, unrestrained; unregulated; e.g. ～放 *yínfàng*, loose and unrestrained.

a. irregular, illegitimate, unsanctioned by authority; e.g. (med.) 〜祠 *yíncí*, irregular cults, cults offering blood sacrifices to local deities.

b. intemperate, immoderate, overly bold, irresponsible; wanton, depraved; spurcitious.

2. indulge to excess, vitiate by excess; debauch(ed).

　a. lust, licentious(ness); e.g. (Budd.) 〜怒癡 *yínnùchī*, lust, anger, and ignorance.

3. soak, saturate, imbrue.

猌　yín　MC ngin

1. rdup., bark and bay, yap and yowl; snap and snarl.

蟫　yín　MC yim

1. silverfish, fishmoth (*Thysanura*), small wingless insect that pestiferously eats through clothing and esp. paper.

xún　MC zim

1. rdup., follow closely, one behind another, tread in one's tracks; also, wriggling and writhing, worming one's way.

誾　yín　MC ngin

1. rdup., agreeable and respectful, affable and obliging; also, pungent and strong, of scent.

銀　yín　MC ngin

1. silver (metal).

　a. silver as medium of exchange.

2. silver-colored, silvery, argent; e.g. 〜河 *yínhé*, 〜漢 *yínhàn*, Silver River ("Silver He" or "Silver Han" in the night sky), i.e. the Milky Way; (med.) 〜青 *yínqīng*, argenticerulean, "with silver [seal] and blue [ribbon]," prefixed to some prestige titles in the Tang, one step lower than 金紫 *jīnzǐ*, auriporphyrian, "with golden [seal] and purple [ribbon]."

3. 〜杏 *yínxìng*, "silver apricot," i.e. gingko (*Gingko biloba*).

4. ⊙ 垠 *yín* 1, borderline, edge.

霪　yín　MC yim

1. persistent rain; deluge, downpour.

鷣　yín　MC yim

1. harrier (*Circus cyaneus*), a small kestrel.

齗　yín　MC ngj+n

1. ⊙ 齦 *yín*.

　a. rdup., bare one's teeth, show one's gums; snarl at.

齦　yín　MC ngj+n

1. gums, of teeth.

　a. jaw.

　b. (med.) basis, ground(s), foundation; principle.

2. redup., argue, "jaw at"; contend; also, banter and badinage, raillery.

kěn　MC khonX

1. (med.) gnaw, chew; bite.

yǐn

听　yǐn　MC ngj+nX

1. 〜然 *yǐnrán*, smiling(ly), with a grin.

尹　yǐn　MC ywinX

1. put in order; straighten, regulate; administer, govern.

　a. governor, title of a chief official, esp. the chief administrator of a capital metropolis.

2. 關〜 *guānyǐn*, Keeper of the Pass, reputed to have asked Laozi to write down his teachings (the *Daodejing* 道德經) before the latter left the corrupt Zhou empire through the northwest frontier.

引　yǐn　MC yinX

1. draw or pull a bow.

　a. stretch, extend; stretch out, draw out; e.g. 〜伸 *yǐnshēn*, "drawing out," technique used when spinning plant fibers or wool to get an equally twisted yarn in which the whole length has the same thickness; also, disciplined stretching exercises akin to *qigong*.

　b. pull along, drag with.

2. lead, conduct, guide.

　a. induce; attract(ive).

　b. draw forth, adduce; cite, quote.

3. bring to the front; call attention to, summon, recommend; promote.

　a. (med.) make clear, account for.

4. draw back; retreat, withdraw.

5. tune, refrain.

　a. (lit.) a "lay," style of verse modeled on or suggestive of a song; the term is usu. found at the end of the poem's title.

6. (med.) (lit.) a "lead-in," preface, introduction to a composition, prelude.

檼　yǐn　MC 'j+nX　⊙ 㡾 *yǐn*.

隱   yǐn   MC ʼj+nX

1. press-frame, board used for straightening crooked or warped wood.
    a. straighten, bring to standard; e.g. 〜括 or 〜栝 *yǐnkuò*, straighten and bind, give proper form to.
2. bevel-square, for determining angles.

蚓   yǐn   MC yinX

1. earthworm, mudworm.
    a. inch along.

螾   yǐn   MC yinX

1. ⊙ 蚓 *yǐn*, earthworm.
2. wriggle; inch along.

讔   yǐn   MC ʼj+nX

1. enigma(tic), riddle; conundrum, puzzle.

隱   yǐn   MC ʼj+nX

1. conceal(ment), hide away, keep under wraps; disguise, camouflage.
    a. place away from normal view, out of sight; ensconce, secrete; e.g. 〜曲 *yǐnqū*, remote and out of the way.
    b. secretly, covertly; in private.
    c. quiet(ly), without fuss; e.g. 〜定 *yǐndìng*, quiet certitude.
2. reticent, reticence; e.g. 〜約 *yǐnyuē*, taciturn yet telling; also, secluded and straitened.
    a. withdraw(n), seclude; reclusion, retire (-ment), out of the public eye, esp. avoid taking office; e.g. 〜淪 *yǐnlún*, "sunk in obscurity," reclusive.
    b. regard as taboo, avoid saying or doing.
3. obscure, dark(en); dull, make dull; veil(ed); indistinct; e.g. (med.) 〜化 *yǐnhuà*, "transform mysteriously (or, into darkness)," euph. for to die.
    a. enigma(tic), riddle; puzzle, conundrum.
    b. inexplicable, undefinable; arcane, recondite.
4. grieve, be pained at.
5. ornamental inlay on zither.
6. a surname.
    yìn   MC ʼj+nH
1. lean on, rest against; e.g. 〜几 *yìnjī*, low table or armrest to lean against while seated on floor.

靷   yǐn   MC yinX

1. leather strap connecting the yoke round a horse's neck to the axletree of a carriage.
2. leading rope tied to an ox's nose.

飲   yǐn   MC ʼimX

1. to drink, imbibe, quaff.
    a. drink, beverage, potable.
    b. swallow down, swallow back, stifle; e.g. 〜恨 *yǐnhèn*, stifle one's resentment, keep one's counsel.
    c. (med.) 〜流 *yǐnliú*, wine-bibber, tippler; 〜子 *yǐnzǐ*, decoction, for medical use.
2. rinse the mouth.
3. hide, conceal.
    yìn   MC ʼimH
1. give to drink.
2. permeate, soak into.

yìn

印   yìn   MC ʼjinH

1. to transfer a pattern from one surface to another, print; seal, imprint, stamp.
    a. brand for identification.
2. (med.) 〜度 *yìndù* (MC ʼjinH-duH), gen. term for India, trsc. of Iran. *hinduka* (< Skt. *sindhu*, name of Indus River) ref. to people who live beyond the Indus River.

廕   yìn   MC ʼimH   ⊙ 蔭 *yín*.

憖   yìn   MC nginH

1. wish to, prefer to, would rather.
    a. resign oneself to, agree to.
2. rdup., (med.) shocked and surprised; also, consider carefully, attentive to detail.
    xìn   MC xj+nH
1. (med.) smile with pleasure.

窨   yìn   MC ʼimH

1. underground chamber, which can be kept warm by fire.

胤   yìn   MC yinH

1. posterity, descendants, later generations of the same clan; heirs, successors.

yīng

嚶   yīng   MC ʼeang

1. sgl, rdup., or (bn.) 〜喔 *yīngwō* (MC ʼeang-ʼaewk), onom. birdcall, crying of birds, "wee-ang," "wee-ang wawk."
2. onom. of small bells attached to carriage or horse, "ying-ging."

嬰　yīng　MC ʾjieng

1. neck ornament, necklace; wear around the neck.

    a. encircle, wind around, enwrap; surround; be bound by.

2. suffer, sustain; encounter.

3. sgl. or ～兒 *yīng'ér*, newborn babe, infant.

應　yīng　MC ʾing

1. auxiliary VB of obligation: ought to, should > needful to, must.

    a. (med.) most likely, will; ADV indicating future probability verging on certitude.

2. (med.) soon; soon after; immediately; e.g. ～時 *yīngshí*, at once, at that moment; ～手 *yīngshǒu*, right away, ready at hand.

    yìng　MC ʾingH

1. respond to, reply, answer.

    a. riposte; criticism.

2. correspond(ing) to; worthy of; due to be; e.g. ～制 *yìngzhì*, (do X) in response to fiat, act in acknowledgment of imperial command; (med.) ～時 *yìngshí*, at the proper time; (med.) ～是 *yìngshì*, "corresponding to this" > it is evident that…; also, Tang colloquialism for "everything," all of X, whatever X (with this meaning, likewise ～有 *yìngyǒu*); (med.) ～未 *yìngwèi*, never, not heretofore.

    a. acknowledge, corroborate; fulfill; e.g. (Budd.) ～真 *yìngzhēn*, one who "acknowledges (or corresponds to) the true," early trns. of Skt. *arhat*, highest level of Hīnayāna attainment.

3. ⊙ 膺 *yìng* 1 (*yīng*), accept, receive, take to heart, esp. in formulas of transmission of omens, apocryphal writings, Daoist registers, etc.; in this context also understood as "worthy of."

攖　yīng　MC ʾjeng

1. come into contact with, confront; attack.

    a. ～龜 *yīngguī*, "attack-tortoise," snake-eating tortoise, ⊙ 蠳龜 *yīngguī*.

2. damage, harm.

3. throw into disorder, disturb, unsettle.

櫻　yīng　MC ʾeang

1. sgl. or (bn.) ～桃 *yīngtáo*, cherry, both tree and fruit (*Prunus pseudocerasus*), blooms white or light-pink flowers in early spring, fruits before summer.

瑛　yīng　MC ʾjaeng

1. luster of jade.

2. translucent jade.

瓔　yīng　MC ʾjieng

1. gemstone.

2. (bn.) ～珞 *yīngluò* (MC ʾjieng-lak), string of gemstones, necklace of precious stones, festoon of jewels.

罌　yīng　MC ʾeang　⊙ 罌 *yīng*.

纓　yīng　MC ʾjieng

1. strings, cords.

    a. hat-tie, capstrings.

    b. throat-band, neck-ornament.

2. harness-rope placed around a horse's neck.

3. decorative ribbon.

4. encircle, wrap, gird.

    a. tie together, bind.

    b. entangle, snarl.

罌　yīng　MC ʾeang

1. ewer, large-bodied and small-mouthed pitcher.

膺　yīng　MC ʾing

1. chest, breast.

    a. innermost thoughts.

    b. (med.) 玄～ *xuányīng*, "murky chest," or 懸～ *xuányīng*," suspended on the chest," Dao. esoteric name for the trachea.

2. breast-band, of horse.

    yìng　MC ʾingH

1. accept, receive, take to heart, incline oneself toward, embrace, esp. a heaven-sent sign, e.g. ～籙 *yìnglù*, receive the prophetic register; ～命 *yìngmìng*, embrace the mandate (of heaven).

2. stand against, withstand.

    a. strike, run against; confront.

英　yīng　MC ʾjaeng

1. bloom, blossom; ref. flowers before the fruit sets.

    a. blossoming without bearing seeds.

    b. used as final element in names of several stones; e.g. 紫石～ *zǐshíyīng*, "bloom of purple stone," amethyst; 雲～ *yúnyīng*, "cloud bloom," mica.

2. finest flower of, bloom of; the cream of; finest, best, peerless; e.g. ～特 *yīngtè*, a peerless original.

3. gallant; noble; e.g. ～風 *yīngfēng*, a noble air, gallant aura or style.
4. feathered ornament on a lance.

蔓   yīng   MC ʼjieng

1. (bn.) ～薁 *yīngyù* (MC ʼjieng-ʼjuwk), wild grapevine, small wild grape (*Vitis adstricta*), native to east China, used in wine-making.

蠳   yīng   MC ʼjieng

1. sgl. or ～龜 *yīngguī*, snake-eating tortoise.

霙   yīng   MC ʼjaeng

1. (med.) snowflake(s).
2. (med.) sleet.

鶯   yīng   MC ʼeang

1. sgl. or 黃～ *huángyīng*, oriole, esp. black-naped oriole (*Oriolus chinensis*), esp. associated with summer; syn. 黃鳥 *huángniǎo*, 黃鸝 *huánglí*, 倉庚 *cānggēng*.
   a. small songbirds in general.
2. bright plumage, patterned plumage.

鷹   yīng   MC ʼing

1. goshawk, accipiter (*Aquilidae*); e.g. ～揚 *yīngyáng*, "hawk-spiring," euph. for a man of outstanding ability who has "spread his wings"; also, for a brave general, used as epithet in some military titles.
   a. general term for raptors.
   b. metaphor for sharp or brisk wind, e.g. ～風 *yīngfēng*, "hawk-wind," i.e. autumn wind.

鸎   yīng   MC ʼeang   ⊙ 鶯 *yīng*.

鸚   yīng   MC ʼeang

1. (bn.) ～鵡 *yīngwǔ* (MC ʼeang-mjuX), parrot (*Psittacoidae*), assoc. with Central Asia and with both the metal and fire phases of *wuxing* correlations.

yíng

塋   yíng   MC yweng

1. tomb.
   a. entomb, inter.

嬴   yíng   MC yeng

1. full(ness), plenitude, ⊙ 盈 *yíng* 1.
   a. fecund, fertile; productive.
2. surplus, overfull, ⊙ 盈 *yíng* 2.
3. vanquish; gain control; (med.) excel, surpass.
4. be in charge of, take responsibiity for.
5. a surname.

楹   yíng   MC yeng

1. pillar, column, esp. in front of a hall > fore-column, forepillar.

瀛   yíng   MC yeng

1. large sea, ocean.
2. marsh, mere.
3. ～洲 Yingzhou, one of the three fabled isles of the immortals in the Eastern Sea.

瀯   yíng   MC yweng

1. (med.) rdup., whirling eddy, swirling whirl.
2. (bn.) 淳～ *tíngyíng*, → 淳 *tíng*.

熒   yíng   MC hweng

1. glimmer, flicker; sparkle.
2. shimmer; (be)dazzle; bewilder.
   a. (bn.) ～惑 *yínghuò* (MC hweng-hwok), dazzle and delude; also "Shimmering Deceiver," i.e. the planet Mars.
3. ⊙ 螢 *yíng*, firefly.

營   yíng   MC yweng

1. to lay out, plan, design; e.g. 世～ *shìyíng*, worldly designs.
   a. layout, plan; template, design, mock-up.
   b. erect a building, build.
2. to project; undertake, carry out; operations; e.g. ～田 *yíngtián*, work the fields.
   a. arrange(ment), dispose; survey, measure.
   b. found, establish; build.
3. encamp(ment), garrison.
   a. guard, keep watch over.
   b. follow through as engaged or commited to do; e.g. (Budd.) ～從 *yíngcóng*, followers.
4. hasten (to), move anxiously; agitated, urgent(ly); restless.
   a. rdup., convulsive fluttering, agitated flitting and fluster; also, buzz and hiss, of flies or flatterers; also, ceaselessly circling, go round and about.

5. region, zone, district, area.
6. alt. name of the lunar lodging "House," → 室 *shì* 6.

瑩　yíng　MC hjwaeng

1. luster of polished jade.
    a. crystal(line), hyaline.
2. polish(ed) to a high gloss.
3. set a bright stone in place, stud.
    a. bedeck; encrust; ornament.
4. make idea or statement clear; elucidate.

盈　yíng　MC yeng

1. plenitude, plenteous; full, abundant; replete; e.g. ～虛 *yíngxū*, fullness and emptiness, success and failure.
    a. fraught; wholly involving, full of.
2. full to excess, overfull, superabundant; surplus, overflow; e.g. ～逸 *yíngyì*, wanton, indulging.
    a. increase(d); enlarge(d); e.g. ～縮 *yíngsuō*, increase and decrease; measures of length; extent of a lifespan.
3. full to expectation or need; satisfactory; sufficient; complete(d); assure(d).
4. rdup., (med.) clear and limpid; also, beautiful and becoming.

籯　yíng　MC yeng

1. cylindrical bamboo container.

縈　yíng　MC 'jwieng

1. wind through, wind around; enlace, enwreath; entwine, loop, coil round; embrangle(d).
    a. (bn.) ～紆 *yíngyū* (MC 'jwieng-ju), twining and twisting, looping and wreathing.
2. bind to, constrain; tie up.

螢　yíng　MC hweng

1. firefly, glow-worm.
    a. glimmer; flash intermittenlty.

蠅　yíng　MC yeng

1. fruit fly.

贏　yíng　MC yeng

1. excess, exceed(ing); surplus.
2. receive; admit.
    a. acquire, obtain; gain control of.
3. be in charge of, take responsibility for.
4. (med.) triumph; vanquish.

迎　yíng　MC ngjaeng

1. receive, accept.
    a. welcome, usher in; greet.
2. acquiesce to, comply with.
    a. respond to, echo, fall in line with.
3. turn(ed) toward; e.g. (med.) ～先 *yíngxiān*, in advance, beforehand; also (Budd.) previous existence.

yǐng

嶸　yǐng　MC 'engX

1. (med.) (bn.) ～冥 *yǐngmíng* (MC 'engX-mengX), dark and dense.

影　yǐng　MC 'jaengX

1. shadow, produced by light (ant. 形 *xíng*, outward form).
    a. light-image, silhouette.
    b. ～響 *yǐngxiǎng*, shadow and echo > influence, affect; response, answer; also, (med.) in a moment, instantly; also, (med.) trace, sign; also, (med.) randomly, wilfully; also (med.) approximating vaguely, seemingly, obscurely.
2. image reflected in water or in a mirror.
3. (med.) likeness, replica; portrait.
    a. (med.) icon; image, statue; e.g. (Budd.) ～殿 *yǐngdiàn*, Image Hall, main hall featuring a statue or other icon of the Buddha.
4. fuzzy, vague, blur(ry).
    a. indirect; oblique; suggestive of.

渶　yǐng　MC 'wengX

1. (bn.) 濎～ *tìngyǐng*, → 濎 *tìng* (*dǐng*); (bn.) 淳～ *tíngyǐng*, → 淳 *tíng*.

癭　yǐng　MC 'jiengX

1. goiter.
2. tree goiter, burr, swelling or nodulation on trunk of tree.
    a. (med.) bulge-cup, cup made from the wood of a tree burr.

穎　yǐng　MC ywengX

1. awn of an ear of grain, beard on a glume of grass.
2. bristle-like, spiked, sharp, acute, acuminate(d), point(ed).
    a. well-defined, in fine detail.

b. sharp or acute in perception; discriminating.
c. salient in ability, outstanding.
3. ring on the end of a sword handle.

郢   **yǐng**   MC yengX
1. name of a capital (or series of capitals) of the ancient state of Chu 楚, location(s) disputed but traditionally thought to be near present-day Jiangling 江陵 in southern Hubei.

yìng

媵   **yìng**   MC yingH
1. servant who accompanies a bride to her new family.
  a. escort, accompany; companion.
2. concubine, paramour.

應   **yìng**   MC ʻingH   → 應 yīng.

映   **yìng**   MC ʻjaengH
1. (med.) glint; reflect(ion), refulgence.
  a. (med.) glare, dazzle.
2. (med.) put in the shade, cover over; shade, eclipse.

暎   **yìng**   MC ʻjaengH   ⊙ 映 yìng.

瀯   **yìng**   MC yweng   ⊙ 瀠 yìng.

瀠   **yìng**   MC ʻwengH
1. (med.) (bn.) ～瀯 yìngyíng (MC ʻwengH-yweng), gurge and circle, eddy and whirl.
2. (med.) (bn.) 汀～ tìngyìng → 汀 tìng (tīng).

硬   **yìng**   MC ngeangH
1. (med.) hard, rigid, stiff; inflexible, unyielding (ant. 軟 ruǎn, soft, flexible).
  a. (med.) intractable, obstinate.
2. (med.) firm, solid, sturdy; staunch.
3. (med.) forceful, powerful.

yōng

傭   **yōng**   MC yowng
1. hire one's labor out for payment, take wages for service; e.g. ～人 yōngrén, hired laborer.
  a. wages, pay.
2. ⊙ 庸 yōng 2, usual, ordinary.

chōng   MC trhjowng
1. even-handed, equitable, neutral; just.

墉   **yōng**   MC yowng
1. fortification; fortified, castellated.
2. screen-wall, dividing wall.

壅   **yōng**   MC ʻjowng
1. dam, dam up.
  a. obstruct, close off; block, barricade.
  b. ～沮 yōngjǔ, "blocked channel," conjunction of Saturn (earth) and Mercury (water).
2. bank up, embankment; berm, bed(ded); earthwork.

庸   **yōng**   MC yowng
1. use(ful), employ(ment), application; e.g. 中～ zhōngyōng, the application of the mean.
  a. contribute, contribution.
2. usual; norm(al), common(place); popular; e.g. ～夫 yōngfū or ～民 yōngmín, ordinary fellow; also, hired hand (see next); ～狗 yōnggǒu, common cur, pejorative epithet for someone of no consequence.
  a. unpretentious, undistinguished; inconsiderable; mediocre in quality; e.g. ～田 yōngtián, second-rate fields.
3. work for pay, hire(d).
  a. (med.) obligatory labor service, corvée.
4. interr., sgl. or cmpd. ～詎 yōngjù, how is it possible that…? can it be that…?
  a. (med.) ～非 yōngfēi, could it not be that…? obviously it must be…
5. ⊙ 壅 yōng, fortification; 鏞 yōng, large hanging bell; 雍 yōng, harmonious, concordant.

慵   **yōng**   MC dzyowng
1. (med.) indolent, slothful; sluggish, lethargic.

擁   **yōng**   MC ʻjowngX
1. close round; hold or take into one's arms; embrace, hug.
  a. hold or take into one's hand; possess, own.
2. bunch together; crowd around, press together; close round, surround.
  a. beset with, press upon.
3. protect, close ranks; guard, defend.
4. close up, cover, conceal.
5. close off, prevent, obstruct; delay.

癰　**yōng**　MC ʼjowng
1. abscess; malignant boil.

薤　**yōng**　MC ʼjowng
1. (med.) clump, cluster; tussock.
　　wèng　MC ʼjowngH
1. (med.) water spinach, swamp cabbage (*Ipomoea aquatica*).

邕　**yōng**　MC ʼjowng
1. ⊙ 雍 *yōng*, harmonious, concordant; 壅 *yōng*, dam, embankment.

鄘　**yōng**　MC yowng　⊙ 墉 *yōng*.

鏞　**yōng**　MC yowng
1. large clapperless bell, hung from a frame and struck with mallet in ritual ceremonies.
　　a. (med.) large bell of Budd. or Dao. monastery.

雍　**yōng**　MC ʼjowng
1. harmonious, concordant; affable; smooth; e.g. (bn.) ～容 *yōngróng* (MC ʼjowng-yowng), poised and polite, poised and composed, gentle and smooth, affably agreeable; 三～ *sānyōng*, 3 Harmonious Chambers, i.e. Hall of Light (Mingtang 明堂), Circular Moat (Biyong 辟雍), and Spirit Tower (Lingtai 靈臺), for ruler's special rituals.
2. name of music played when clearing away a ruler's sacrificial food and utensils.
3. ⊙ 壅 *yōng*, dam up, embankment; 擁 *yōng*, close round; 饔 *yōng*, cooked; 癰 *yōng*, abscess.

雝　**yōng**　MC ʼjowng
1. sgl. or rdup., melodious, harmonious, sweet-sounding; pleasantly agreeable.
2. (bn.) ～渠 *yōngqú* (MC ʼjowng-gjo), wagtail (*Motacillidae*); syn. 鶺鴒 *jílíng*.

饔　**yōng**　MC ʼjowng
1. cooked food, esp. meat.
2. a cook, chef.
3. morning meal, breakfast.

yóng

喁　**yóng**　MC ngjowng
1. gape-mouthed, gawp(ing); rdup., eagerly expectant.

2. sgl. or rdup., answer in agreement, be in tune with, jibe with; chime in compliantly; accompany.

顒　**yóng**　MC ngjowng
1. large in size; considerable.
2. stern, serious.
3. rdup. or ～然 *yóngrán*, eagerly expectant; also, meek, mild.

鱅　**yóng**　MC yowng
1. bighead carp, bleak (*Aristichthys nobilis*).

yǒng

俑　**yǒng**　MC yowngX
1. grave figurines, made of wood or pottery.
　　a. puppet, dummy.

勇　**yǒng**　MC yowngX
1. brave, courage(ous), valor(ous); doughty; intrepid; daring, fearless.

咏　**yǒng**　MC hjwaengH　⊙ 詠 *yǒng*.

永　**yǒng**　MC hjwaengH
1. long-extending in time or space.
2. long-lasting, enduring, continuing, persistent.
　　a. perennial; perpetual, eternal, endless, forever.
3. all the way through, throughout, from first to last, complete(ly).
4. far-reaching, far-extended; far distant; e.g. ～巷 *yǒngxiàng*, "far-removed precincts," forbidden quarters of palace ladies; also, out-of-the-way corners.
5. prolong, extend, stretch out.
6. ⊙ 詠 *yǒng*, declaim, chant.

泳　**yǒng**　MC hjwaengH
1. wade, enter the water; immerse oneself.
　　a. float; swim.

涌　**yǒng**　MC yowngX
1. gush forth, surge; bob.
　　a. froth, foam, spume.

湧　**yǒng**　MC yowngX　⊙ 涌 *yǒng*.

甬　**yǒng**　MC yowngX
1. shank or loop of a bell, which suspends it from a frame.

2. ～道 *yǒngdào*, road or passage with walls on either side, sometimes paved or covered; passageway, throughway; alley.

榮　*yǒng*　MC hjwaeng

1. enclose or encircle an area for sacrificial purposes.

    a. sacrifice to avert calamity; exorcistic sacrifice.

蛹　*yǒng*　MC yowngX

1. silkworm cocoon, chrysalis.

詠　*yǒng*　MC hjwaengH

1. declaim; chant; speak with measured rhythm and accent.

    a. recite, intone; prolong the sound of.

2. celebrate, portray in words, esp. in a topical or thematic poem; e.g. (lit.) ～物詩 *yǒngwùshī*, poems in celebration of things (plants, animals, objects, etc.).

踊　*yǒng*　MC yowngX

1. leap, bound; jump, hop.

    a. mount up, (a)rise; surge; emerge from.

    b. (med.) ～移 *yǒngyí*, restless, anxious, nervous, impatient, on edge, shifting from one foot to the other.

2. toeless shoes, worn by criminals whose toes have been cut off.

踴　*yǒng*　MC yowngX　⊙ 踊 *yǒng*.

yòng

用　*yòng*　MC yowngH

1. use, employ, make use of; apply, ply, wield, exert; avail oneself of, put to use; exploit.

    a. usage, practice, effect; function, functional aspects (cf. 體 *tǐ*, immanent substance); e.g. (Budd.) 作～ *zuòyòng*, create an effect, evince insight through practice.

    b. useful, practical, applicable.

2. use up, consume, run through.

3. by means of, on the basis of; because of (similar in this usage to 以 *yǐ* 2).

4. (med.) must, need to; needful, necessary.

yōu

優　*yōu*　MC ʼjuw

1. superior, superlative; more than needed; paramount; excellent (ant. 劣 *liè*, inferior; less than needed).

    a. copious, bountiful; superfluous; advantage(ous).

2. cordial, gracious, hospitable, treat preferentially; be indulgent, munificent.

3. comfortable; (bn.) ～遊 *yōuyóu* (MC ʼjuw-yuw) or ～柔 *yōuróu* (ʼjuw-nyuw), loose and leisurely, freely and liberally, relaxed and amiable; genial and generous; broadly forbearing; also, unhurried and easy; also, indecisive and uncertain.

4. entertain(er), play(er).

5. (Budd.) ～波塞 *yōubōsài* (MC ʼjuw-pa-sak), trsc. Skt. *upāsaka*, Buddhist layman.

呦　*yōu*　MC ʼjiw

1. rdup., onom. of the bleating or mewling of deer: "nyaaoo-nyaaoo"; (med.) also, onom. of weeping: "ngew-ngew."

幽　*yōu*　MC ʼjiw

1. shrouded, hidden; darkened, obscure; e.g. ～明 *yōumíng*, realms of light and dark, i.e. the living and the dead, formed and formless, day and night.

2. seclude(d), isolate(d), keep apart; celate, ensconce(d); quieten(ed); e.g. ～冥 *yōumíng*, secluded and dark, the unseen world, the netherworld.

    a. encell(ed), imprison(ed).

3. exceptional, especial; of a different, more exclusive or awe-inspiring character than normal; distinctly impressive.

    a. richly or subtly profound; mysteriously haunting, sublime though not showy; e.g. ～雅 *yōuyǎ*, subtly tasteful, aristocratically elegant, hauntingly fine.

4. deep-held, deep-seated; concentrated.

    a. inner, inward; private, secret; tacit.

悠　*yōu*　MC yuw

1. pensive, wistful; thoughtful; with heart cast afar; abstracted.

2. long drawn out, far off, in space or time.
3. relaxed, leisurely.
4. rdup., carrying many different meanings, depending on context, most with some sense of distance, dimness, uncertainty, or mystery, either in space or time; e.g. far-fading, dim-dwindling, far-stretched and unreachable, remote and far-reaching; faint and indefinable, elusive and evanescent, unclear and uncertain; feeling "strung out" > cares and confusions; helter-skelter, several and sundry, fluttering in confusion; in haste and hurry; loose and relaxed, placid and serene, detached and out of the way, carefree and disengaged; deserted and interminate; also (med.), ordinary and everyday, common; irrelevant, pointless, beyond concern.
5. (bn.) ～揚 *yōuyáng* (MC yuw-yang), rippling and waving, fluttering and flapping; lingering lightly, fading slowly, faintly throbbing.

憂　yōu　MC ʻjuw
1. anxious, concerned over; fretful; troubled by, burdened with care.
   a. persistent state of being worried; depressed by, sorry over.
2. mourn(ful), luctiferous, grief, esp. mourning for a parent; e.g. ～服 *yōufú*, be in mourning attire; ～闕 *yōuquē*, official post vacated because of mourning obligation; 丁～ *dīngyōu*, observe mourning.
3. afflicted, indisposed; ailment, affliction, indisposition.
4. (med.) care exceedingly for, sympathize with.

攸　yōu　MC yuw
1. sgl. or rdup., move swiftly, quickly; smoothly slipping by, rapidly rushing.
2. place, place where.
3. preverbal relative pronoun, similar to 所 *suǒ*, "that which; he who," etc.
4. ⊙ 悠 *yōu*, distant; pensive.

櫌　yōu　MC ʻjuw　⊙ 耰 *yōu*.

耰　yōu　MC ʻjuw
1. harrow, implement to break up clods of earth.
   a. to harrow, the action of said implement.

逌　yōu　MC yuw
1. ⊙ 攸 *yōu* 3, preverbal relative pronoun.
2. carefree, leisurely.

尤　yóu　MC yuw
1. ⊙ 由 *yóu* 1, deriving from, owing to.

麀　yōu　MC ʻjuw
1. hind, adult female deer.
   a. female of any quadruped.

yóu

尤　yóu　MC hjuw
1. fault, error; shortcoming.
   a. find fault, blame, take exception to; reproach.
2. exceptional, unusual; special, remarkable.
   a. an extreme case of, particularly, especially; even more, excessive; full well.

油　yóu　MC yuw
1. ～然 *yóurán*, boiling up, swelling, like fuming vapor or rising clouds; also, as easily or smoothly as can be.
2. rdup., slipping and sliding along, moving easily and naturally; also, glossy and glistening, shining wetly, with a sheen, sleek and shiny.
3. (med.) oil(y), greasy; sap.
   a. slick, unctuous; e.g. ～衣 *yóuyī*, "slicker," outer garment treated with tung-oil to repel rain.
   b. ～桐 *yóutóng*, tung-oil tree (*Vernicia fordii*), medium-sized deciduous tree from whose seeds an oil was pressed for use in lamps; ～菜 *yóucài*, bird-rape, celery cabbage (*Brassica campestris*); ～麻 *yóumá*, sesame (*Sesamum indicum*), syn. 胡麻 *húmá*.

浟　yóu　MC yuw
1. rdup., freely flowing, smoothly slipping by.
   dí　MC dek
1. rdup., contentious and querulous, disputatious, aggressive.

游　yóu　MC yuw
1. float, drift along water's surface; swim.
   a. skim the surface; superficial, impractical.
2. ⊙ 遊 *yóu*, all meanings.
3. slip-rings, attached to backs of inside horses of team-of-four, through which the off-reins (outside) were drawn to keep inner pair from bolting.

猶　yóu　MC yuw
1. similar to, approximately the same as; conjoining topics with noun predicates, introduces

a measure of approximation or inexactness to the identity implied by a nominal sentence; e.g. 人之於君〜子之於父母也 *rén zhī yú jūn yóu zǐ zhī yú fùmǔ yě*, a man's relation to his lord is similar to a son's relation to his parents; 今之樂〜古之樂也 *jīn zhī yuè yóu gǔ zhī yuè yě*, music of the modern day is approximately the same as music of the past.

2. as modifier to VB-phrases: still, yet; e.g. 麻子小，〜可見也 *mázi xiǎo yóu kějiàn yě*, sesame seeds are small, but still they can be seen; 足下〜不知也 *zúxià yóu bùzhī yě*, you still do not understand.

    a. sgl. or 〜尚 *yóushàng*, even still, even so.

3. (bn.) 〜豫 *yóuyù* (MC yuw-yoH), timid and timorous, wavering and havering, wary and cautious, hesitate and hold off, faltering qualms.

4. (med.) 〜子 *yóuzǐ*, "like a son," common term for nephew or for Budd. or Dao. disciple.

5. ⊙ 由 *yóu* 1, deriving from, by way of, following from; owing to, by means of; 猷 *yóu* 1, plan, scheme, design, draw up; 2, method, means, principle; 尤 *yóu* 1, (find) fault, error, blame.

    yáo   **MC yew**

1. ⊙ 搖 *yáo* 1, shake, sway, unsteady, quiver; 2, stir, agitate.

猷   yóu   MC yuw

1. plan, scheme, design; draw up, project.
2. method, means; principle.

由   yóu   MC yuw

1. deriving from, out of; by way of, following from.

    a. owing to, by means of, because; e.g. 何〜 *héyóu*, in what way . . .? owing to what . . .? on what account . . .?; 無〜 *wúyóu*, there is no possibility of.

    b. depending on, based on.

2. with regard to, pertaining to.

3. as time-word: from the beginning, starting from, all along; e.g. 〜來 *yóulái*, from the beginning till now, always.

4. make use of, avail oneself of.

5. rdup., calm(ly) and contented(ly), fully in control; also, hesitant and careful.

6. (Budd.) 〜延 *yóuyán* (MC yuw-yen), 〜旬 *yóuxún* (MC yuw-zwin), trsc. Skt. *yojana*, measurement of distance variously defined as equiv. from 5 to 8 miles, the distance an oxcart can travel in a day.

7. ⊙ 猶 *yóu* 1, like, similar to; 2, still, yet.

疣   yóu   MC hjuw

1. ⊙ 肬 *yóu*, wart, wen, excrescence.

繇   yóu   MC yuw   → 繇 *yáo*.

肬   yóu   MC hjuw

1. wart, wen.

    a. excrescence > metaphor for anything worthless or unnecessary.

茜   yóu   MC yuw

1. fritillary (*Fritillaria*, various species), used medicinally; syn. 蝱 *méng*.

蕕   yóu   MC yuw

1. bluebeard (*Caryopteris divaricata*), herbaceous plant 3 to 6 feet tall, with light-blue or white flowers that emit a foul odor when crushed.

蚰   yóu   MC yuw

1. (bn.) 〜蜒 *yóuyán* (MC yuw-yen), scutigera, spider-centipede (*Cermatiae*); syn. 蛉窮 *língqióng*.

蝣   yóu   MC yuw

1. (bn.) 蜉〜 *fúyóu* → 蜉 *fú*.

輶   yóu   MC yuw

1. light (therefore rapid) carriage, often used by imperial emissaries.

    a. light, airy; insubstantial.

遊   yóu   MC yuw

1. roam, rove, ramble; wander; gad about, jaunt, meander; e.g. 〜盤 *yóupán*, ramble round.

    a. peripatetic, unsettled; travel(er); e.g. 〜說 *yóushuì*, traveling persuader.

    b. saunter, promenade.

2. drift, sweep over; e.g. 〜目 *yóumù*, sweep one's eyes over, let one's view drift.

3. (go on) a pleasure outing to a particular destination, make a visit; excursion.

4. associate with; fellow traveler, companion, associate.

5. ruler's spring progress or visitation; e.g. 〜豫 *yóuyù*, ruler's spring and autumn progresses.

6. maneuver, ply; manipulate, handle freely; exploit.

7. let loose, set free; indulge, be at ease with; e.g. 〜言 *yóuyán*, playful or permissive talk, banter.

郵 yóu MC hjuw
1. courier station, for relaying official documents and letters, giving lodging and board for traveling officials, and providing horses and carriages for transportation.
    a. courier, messenger; to send a message by courier, in early times esp. on foot (cf. 置 zhì 3, by post-horse).
2. ⊙ 尤 yóu, all meanings.

鮋 yóu MC yuw → 鮋 chóu.

yǒu

卣 yǒu MC yuwX
1. ancient wine vessel used for sacrificial libations, usu. with handles, a cover, oval-shaped with square bottom.

友 yǒu MC hjuwX
1. friend, companion; ally.
    a. befriend; friendly; fraternal.

有 yǒu MC hjuwX
1. to have, be possessed of, provided with OBJ; own, hold (ant. 無 wú, be without, lack).
    a. 大〜 dàyǒu, "greater holdings," name of 14th hexagram of Yijing.
2. there is (an occasion for, instance of) OBJ; presence of OBJ.
3. what there is, what exists; actual(ity); something.
    a. determinate, having distinctive character (ant. 無 wú, indeterminate).
    b. (Budd.) trns. of Skt. bhāva, being, existence, affirmation.
4. when placed after a multiple of ten and before a single numeral: and, with, e.g. 三十〜六 sānshíyǒuliù, six and thirty.
5. (Budd.) 〜情 yǒuqíng, "with sentience," sentient being; 〜命 yǒumìng, "with a lifespan," living being; 〜底 yǒudǐ, finite; 〜為 yǒuwéi, constituted things.

牖 yǒu MC yuwX
1. window, esp. lattice window.
    a. lattice-figured.

呦 yǒu MC ʼjiwX
1. rdup., deep-sunken and deep-reaching.

羑 yǒu MC yuwX
1. ⊙ 誘 yòu, lead, induce.
2. 〜里 yǒulǐ, ancient site in northern Henan where the last king of the Shang dynasty was said to have incarcerated Wenwang 文王 of Zhou.

莠 yǒu MC yuwX
1. green foxtail, green bristlegrass, false millet (Setaria viridis), syn. 狗尾草 gǒuwěicǎo.
    a. coarse feed; fodder > ill-favored, noxious.

蚴 yǒu MC ʼjiwX
1. (bn.) 〜虯 yǒuqiú (MC ʼjiwX-gjiw), curling and coiling, sinuously snaking.

酉 yǒu MC yuwX
1. 10th of the 12 earthly branches, associated with the cock as emblematic animal.
    a. 10th double-hour of the day, from approximately 5 p.m. to 7 p.m.
2. mature wine; metaphor for what is oldest and best.

黝 yǒu MC ʼjiwX
1. sgl. or rdup., steel-gray; glossy black, vitreous, livid, swarthy.
2. (bn.) 〜糾 yǒujiū (MC ʼjiwX-kjiwX), conjoined and connected.

yòu

佑 yòu MC hjuwH
1. aid, assist(ance), second, support; succor.
    a. safekeeping, protect(ion).

侑 yòu MC hjuwH
1. urge to eat or drink, esp. with blandishments.
2. ⊙ 宥 yòu, indulgent, generous.

又 yòu MC hjuwH
1. ADV indicating repetition or continuation: again, also; once more; in addition, further(more); next.
    a. ADV indicating coincidence: and at the same time, simultaneously.

右 yòu MC hjuwH
1. right (hand, side, etc.).
    a. traditionally, the side of honor, to which priority is given.

b. the side where a warrior places himself in a war-chariot.

2. equivalent to west, deriving from the viewpoint of the ruler who sits facing south.

3. ⊙ 佑 *yòu*, aid, assist.

囿　yòu　MC hjuwH

1. wildlife enclosure, fenced animal preserve; pen(ned).

    a. enclosed garden or orchard, garth.

2. confine(d), circumscribe(d), of space or ideas.

宥　yòu　MC hjuwH

1. generous, indulge(nt), magnanimous; lenient, to pardon.

2. ⊙ 侑 *yòu*, urge to eat or drink; 右 *yòu*, right; 囿 *yòu*, circumscribed area; confine.

幼　yòu　MC ʼjiwH

1. young; immature.

    a. youth, childhood, young child, tyke; adolescence.

    yào　MC ʼjiewH

1. (bn.) 〜妙 or 〜眇 *yàomiào* (MC ʼjiewH-mjiewH), dulcet and delicate, faint and fine; also, beautiful and becoming.

柚　yòu　MC yuwH

1. pomelo, shaddock (*Citrus maxima*).

    zhú　MC drjuwk

1. cylinder on loom to which the warp-threads are attached.

狖　yòu　MC yuwH

1. long-tailed langur (*Colobidae*), prob. douc langur (*Pythagrix*) or snub-nose monkey (*Rhinopithecus*), now only in southeast Asia.

祐　yòu　MC hjuwH　⊙ 佑 *yòu*.

褎　yòu　MC yuwH

1. full long-sleeved dress, full ritual apparel.

2. grow, sprout, burgeon, of plants.

    a. (med.) 〜然 *yòurán*, outstandingly, prominently, pronouncedly.

    xiù　MC zjuwH

1. ⊙ 袖 *xiù*, sleeve of clothing; ensleeve.

誘　yòu　MC yuwX

1. lead, guide; direct.

2. coax, attract.

    a. lure, entice, tempt, seduce.

鼬　yòu　MC yuwH

1. weasel, stoat (*Mustelidae*), esp. used for hunting small animals; also called 黃〜 *huángyòu*, syn. 鼪 *shēng*.

2. (bn.) 髟〜 *biāoyòu*, → 髟 *biāo*.

yū

淤　yū　MC ʼjo

1. alluvial deposit, silt; sediment.

    a. silt up, block with mud or sand; clog, clot; e.g. 〜閼 *yūè* (MC ʼjo-ʼat), choked with silt.

    b. squelchy; smushy, squishy.

2. sandbar, sand-mound.

紆　yū　MC ʼju

1. crooked, bent; skewed.

    a. twisted, knotted, bound up, tied up, of thread, cords, or thoughts.

    b. (bn.) 〜餘 *yūyú* (MC ʼju-yo), crooks and quirks, twists and turns.

2. indirect; meandering; e.g. 〜徐 *yūxú*, unhurried.

迂　yū　MC ʼju

1. astray, off the track; deflect(ed), indirect.

    a. circuitous, roundabout; winding; anfractuous.

    b. turning, stretching on endlessly; e.g. 〜久 *yūjiǔ*, a long stretch of time, twists and turns of time.

2. far from fact; irrational; wild.

    a. ill-advised; inappropriate; e.g. 〜闊 *yūkuò*, off the mark, ill-adapted, impractical.

yú

予　yú　MC yo

1. 1st-person pronoun.

    yǔ　MC yoX

1. ⊙ 與 *yǔ* 1, give to; commend.

于　yú　MC hju

1. typically occurs after a VB or VB-phrase and before a noun or noun-phrase, indicating any indirect or locative relation: in, at, from, to, on, with regard to, vis-à-vis, etc.; e.g. 入〜幽谷 *rù yú yōugǔ*, entering into a dark valley; 君告〜天子 *jūn gào yú tiānzǐ*, The lord reported it to the Son of

Heaven; cog. *yú* 於 in, at, from, to, on, with regard to, etc. N.B. From the Warring States period on 于 *yú* and 於 *yú* are generally interchangeable, save for stylistic preferences; prior to the Warring States period they are not equivalent to each other.

a. preceding a time-word (and often after *zhì* 至): arriving at, up to, at [the time in question]; e.g. 而至～今 *érzhì yú jīn* , and still it continues up to the present; ～時以為蜀得其龍 *yú shí yǐwéi shǔ dé qí lóng*, by that time they figured that Shu had gotten its dragon; 二世三世至～萬世 *èrshì sānshì zhì yú wànshì*, for two generations, three generations, up to a myriad of generations.

b. after a VB or VB-phrase and before a noun or noun-phrase, indicating comparative sense: than; e.g. 多～前功 *duō yú qiángōng*, more than previous merit; 異～今人 *yì yú jīnrén*, more unusual than people of the present day.

2. pre-classical VB prefix of uncertain meaning, possibly an inchoative sense or rhetorical emphasis; e.g. 黃鳥～飛 *huángniǎo yú fēi*, The yellow birds are taking to flight; 之子～歸 *zhīzǐ yú guī*, That fellow is on his way home.

3. (bn.) ～闐 *yútián* (MC hju-den), Khotan, oasis city on the southern Silk Road in the Tarim Basin, the main source of nephrite imported to China.

4. arch-shaped rim or sound-bow of a chimebell's mouth.

余　yú　MC yo

1. 1st-person pronoun.

俞　yú　MC yu

1. affirmative reply: "yes! agreed; approved."
　　a. reply, respond.
2. rdup. or ～然 *yúrán*, contented, satisfied; at ease.

yù　MC yuX

1. ☉ 愈 *yù*, even more, additionally; 癒 *yù*, cure(d) of illness.

妤　yú　MC yo

1. (bn.) 婕～ *jiéyú*, official title of palace lady, → 婕 *jié*.

娛　yú　MC ngju

1. amuse(ment), divert, diversion, entertain(-ment); cheer(ed).

媮　yú　MC yu

1. happy, enjoy(ment), merriment; light-hearted.

tōu　MC thuw

1. ☉ 偷 *tōu* 1, negligent, nonchalant, perfunctory; contemn, disesteem; 2, stealth(y), cunning.

嵎　yú　MC ngju

1. mountain crook, fold, veer, bend, niche.
2. ～谷 *yúgǔ*, Yu Valley, according to mythology, place where the sun sets.

愉　yú　MC yu

1. pleasant, enjoy(able), please(d), amuse(d).

tōu　MC thuw

1. ☉ 偷 1, negligent(ly), nonchalant(ly), perfunctory; contemn, disesteem.

愚　yú　MC ngju

1. ignorant, witless, untaught, dull-witted.
　　a. humble self-reference: "I who am untutored, I in all humility."

揄　yú　MC yu

1. draw after, draw out, pull out.
2. (bn.) ～揚 *yúyáng* (MC yu-yang), hail and proclaim, praise and applaud, acclaim and extol.

於　yú　MC 'jo

1. (GP) typically occurs after a VB or VB-phrase and before a noun or noun-phrase, indicating any indirect or locative relation: in, at, from, to, on, with regard to, vis-à-vis, etc.; e.g. 王坐～堂上 *wáng zuò yú tángshàng*, The king was sitting in the hall; 千里之行始～足下 *qiānlǐzhī xíng shǐ yú zúxià*, A journey of a thousand *li* starts from under one's foot; 敏～事而慎～言 *mǐn yú shì ér shèn yú yán*, diligent vis-à-vis affairs and careful vis-à-vis speech; cog. *yú* 于 in, at, from, to, on, with regard to, etc. N.B. Fom the Warring States period on 于 *yú* and 於 *yú* are generally interchangeable, save for stylistic preferences; prior to the Warring States period 於 *yú* is rare, and the two are not equivalent to each other.

　　a. (GP) after a VB or VB-phrase and before a noun or noun-phrase, indicating comparative sense: than; e.g. 民少～今日 *mín shǎo yú jīnrì*, The citizens were fewer in number than [those of] the present day; 青～藍 *qīnq yú lán*, bluer than indigo.

2. (Budd.) (GP) in Budd. texts often simply a marker preceding the OBJ, with no translatable meaning.

　　　　wū　MC ʼu

1. old form of 烏 *wū* 1, crow, raven.

2. ⊙ 烏 *wū* 4, in ～乎, ～呼 *wūhū*, sigh of sadness: alas!

旟　yú　MC yo

1. falcon-banner, flag with falcons painted on it.
　　a. banderole.
2. curled, wavy hair.

杅　yú　MC hju

1. large bowl, tureen.
2. wash-basin, bathing tub.

楡　yú　MC yu

1. elm tree (*Ulmus pumila*); e.g. 桑～ *sāngyú*, mulberry and elm, among whose branches the westering rays of the setting sun linger > waning time, advancing age.

歟　yú　MC yo

1. ⊙ 與 *yú* (*yǔ*), sentence-final interrogative GP equiv. to (and phonetic fusion of) *yě* 也 and *hū* 乎.

渝　yú　MC yu

1. change, alter.
　　a. renounce, abandon.
2. overflow, flood.

漁　yú　MC ngjo

1. to fish, catch fish.
　　a. fisherman.
2. snatch, grab; take for oneself.

貐　yú　MC yu

1. (bn.) 猰～ *yàyú* (MC ʼeat-yu), → 猰 *yà*.

瑜　yú　MC yu

1. nephrite.
　　a. luster; gem-like quality.
2. (Budd.) ～伽 *yúqié* (MC yu-gja) or ～珈 *yújiā* (MC yu-kae), trsc. Skt. *yoga*.

璵　yú　MC yo

1. ～璠 *yúfán*, precious stone treasured in the ancient state of Lu 魯.
　　a. treasured item, jewel of great price, pride and joy.

畬　yú　MC yo

1. field left fallow for 2 or 3 years.

　　　　shē　MC syae

1. slash-and-burn cultivation, swidden, milpa.

盂　yú　MC hju

1. large bucket-like vessel with two handles and no cover, for sacrificial offerings of wine or food.
　　a. measure of capacity, a basin's-worth.
2. row of men who beat the bushes on a hunt.
3. (Budd.) ～蘭盆 *yúlánpén* (MC hju-lan-bwon), name of the "ghost festival" on the 15th day of the 7th month; etymology disputed but traditionally considered trsc. of Skt. *ullambana*, those "hanging upside-down" in hell for whom on this festival food offerings are made to secure their salvation.

禺　yú　MC ngju

1. plot of land, tract.
2. (med.) forenoon, late morning.

　　　　yù　MC ngjuH

1. kind of monkey, said to be born from a macaque but with variously described odd features.
　　a. monkeyish, simian; grotesque in appearance.

　　　　yóng　MC ngjowng

1. rdup., a striped fish.

窬　yú　MC yu

1. small door to the side of main gate.
2. opening, aperture; hole.
　　a. break through, force an opening, penetrate.
3. ⊙ 踰 *yú* 1, pass over, climb beyond.

竽　yú　MC hju

1. reed-organ, mouth-organ; larger and older version of the 笙 *shēng*, originally with 36 pipes, later 19, of different lengths bound around a wooden resonance chamber.

鸆　yú　MC yu

1. black ewe.
2. of good quality, fine.

腴　yú　MC yu

1. fat from the belly of animals.
　　a. grease; greasy, oily.
　　b. paste.

2. fertile, fruitful, fecund.
  a. having or productive of plenty, well provided; rich.
3. full- or rich-tasting savory.

臾 yú MC yu
1. (bn.) 須～ *xūyú* (MC sju-yu), shortly, presently, in a while, momentarily; also, leisurely, at length.

舁 yú MC yo
1. carry, lift up.
  a. transport, convey by lifting.
2. (med.) load, pack up.
3. (med.) palanquin, sedan-chair; convey by such.

萸 yú MC yu
1. (bn.) 茱萸 *zhūyú*, → 茱 *zhū*.

蕍 yú MC yu
1. full bloom of flowers.

虞 yú MC ngju
1. foresee, anticipate; expect(ation); have a prospect or chance of; estimate.
  a. prepare, take precautions.
2. be concerned about, think anxiously about, uneasy, apprehensive; troubles, worries; threats.
3. deceive, fool.
4. gamekeeper; fowler; forester.
  a. warden; custodian.
5. ⊙ 娱 *yú*, amuse, divert.
6. name of dynasty supposedly established by sage-king Shun 舜.

褕 yú MC yu
1. (bn.) ～翟 *yúdí* (MC yu-dek), empress's ceremonial robe embroided with pheasant design.
2. 襜～ *chānyú*, short informal and unlined jacket.
3. splendid, finely wrought (clothing).

覦 yú MC yu
1. desire beyond measure, crave, long for.

諛 yú MC yu
1. blandish(ment), gloze, flatter, beguile; play up to, esp. with words (cf. 諂 *chǎn*, fawning of all kinds).

踰 yú MC yu
1. pass over; climb past, climb beyond.
  a. go past, exceed, excel; over and above the norm; e.g. ～侈 *yúchǐ*, wasteful indulgence.
  b. pass to the other side.
2. (Budd.) ～旬 *yúxún* (MC yu-zwin), trsc. Skt. *yojana*, measure of distance, traditionally the distance an oxcart can cover in a day, variously defined as 5 to 8 miles.

yáo MC yew
1. ⊙ *yáo*, remote, distant.

輿 yú MC yo
1. chassis of a carriage, esp. the base of the carriage-box; cf. 軫 *zhěn*, the 4 horizontal boards of the carriage-box > chassis.
  a. by synecdoche, carriage, vehicle; conveyance.
  b. convey by carriage or cart.
2. metaphorically the earth, as carrier of people, also because thought of as square (complementary to 堪 *kān*, canopy of carriage, metaphorical of round heaven).
3. lift, raise up.
4. (med.) sedan-chair, litter, palanquin.
5. underling, subordinate, subaltern.
  a. lackey, menial; slave.
6. multitudinous, multitudes, esp. ref. to people.

逾 yú MC yu
1. ⊙ 踰 *yú*, pass over; go past, exceed.
2. even more, additionally.

釪 yú MC hju
1. (Budd.) alms bowl.

隃 yú MC yu
1. ⊙ 踰 *yú*, passs over; go past, exceed.

yáo MC yew
1. ⊙ 遙 *yáo*, remote, distant.

隅 yú MC ngju
1. niche, nook, hern, crook, corner.
  a. cove, bight.
2. to the side, to one side.
3. punctilious, scrupulous, covering all corners.

雩 yú MC hju
1. ritual sacrifice to bring rain.
  a. rain-altar, for preceding.

餘   yú   MC yo

1. more than enough, X to spare; surplus, excess; e.g. 有〜 *yǒuyú*, enough and to spare; 空〜 *kōngyú*, space to spare, extra margin for, leeway; 自〜 *zìyú*, spontaneous excess.
   a. suffuse, fill beyond what is necessary or normal.
2. remainder, left-over, balance, extra; remaining, remnant.
   a. lingering, surviving; carried on, often with lessening strength.
   b. the rest; the others; e.g. 〜人 *yúrén*, the other people (besides those already mentioned).
   c. (med.) in the aftermath, afterward; aftercomers, followers, descendants.
3. complement(ary); addition(al).

騟   yú   MC yu

1. bay horse.

魚   yú   MC ngjo

1. fish, generic term; piscine.
2. name of a small star in the constellation Tail (尾 *wěi*).

璵   yú   MC ngjowk

1. (bn.) 璵〜 *zhúyú*, → 璵 *zhú* (*zhuó*).

yǔ

傴   yǔ   MC ʾjuX

1. crookback, humpback, hunchback; bent, crippled.
2. bend or bow humbly, show respect.

圄   yǔ   MC ngjoX

1. prison.
   a. imprison, incarcerate.
2. defend, guard.

圉   yǔ   MC ngjoX

1. tend horses.
   a. one who tends horses, groom, stableman, ostler.
   b. stable.
2. border, frontier.
3. ⊙ 圄 *yǔ*, prison; 敔 *yǔ*, tiger-box.
   ### yù   MC ngjoH
1. ⊙ 禦 *yù*, resist, defend.

宇   yǔ   MC hjuX

1. eaves; roof.
   a. 〜宙 *yǔzhòu*, eaves and ridgepole, euph. for celestial or cosmic edifice; also, space and time, heaven and earth > universe, cosmos.
   b. firmament, celestial canopy; spatial extent; e.g. 〜內 *yǔnèi*, all points of space, all under the heavens, whole world.
2. area under the eaves; habitation, dwelling; grounds, precincts, domain.
   a. protect, shelter.
3. bearing, manner; attitude, tolerance.
4. 〜文 *yǔwén*, bisyllabic surname of Särbi (Xianbei 鮮卑) origin, notably that of the ruling family of the Northern Zhou (557-581) dynasty.

峿   yǔ   MC ngjoX

1. (bn.) 岨〜 *jǔyǔ*, → 岨 *jǔ* (*jū*).

嶼   yǔ   MC zjoX

1. small hilly island; islet, eyot.

庾   yǔ   MC yuX

1. stacks of grain in the fields, open-air granary.
   a. granary.
2. measure of capacity, equiv. 16 斗 (*dǒu*) pecks.
3. a surname.

敔   yǔ   MC ngjoX

1. tiger-box, tiger-scraper, ancient musical instrument made of wood, in shape of crouching tiger on a rectangular box, the tiger's back carrying three rows of nine serrations which are scraped with a split rod of bamboo to indicate the end of a piece of ritual music.

瘐   yǔ   MC yuX

1. die in prison from beating or from illness resulting from privation.

禹   yǔ   MC hjuX

1. name of mythological tamer of empire-wide flood and reputed founder of Xia 夏 dynasty.

窳   yǔ   MC yuX

1. depression in ground, from draining water.
2. deteriorate(d), worn down; defect(ive), flaw(ed).
   a. weak(ness), feeble(ness).

3. stagnant, torpid; lazy, slothful.
4. shoddy; cheap; of poor quality.

羽　yǔ　MC hjuX

1. plumes or feathers on wings; plumage.
    a. synecdoche for wing or for bird; also, gen. term for winged creatures.
2. fletchings, feathers attached near the base of arrow to aid stability in flight.
3. gen. term for outer adornment.
4. plumed fan or feathered article used in ritual dances.

yù　MC hjuH

1. name of one of the notes of the pentatonic scale, corresponding symbolically to water, winter, the color black, etc.

與　yǔ　MC yoX

1. give to, grant to, accord to, render unto; e.g. ～巵酒 yǔ zhī jiǔ, give him a flagon of wine.
    a. provide for; assist, give help to; e.g. 君～不勝者 jūn yǔ bùshèngzhe, milord aids the one that is not victorious.
2. connecting VB-phrases: accompanying > joined together with > in conjunction with, together with, with; e.g. 朝～下大夫言 cháo yǔ xiàdàfū yán at court, speaking with the lower-grade magnates; ～人恭而有禮 yǔ rén gōng ér yǒulǐ, with others he is respectful and shows proper ceremonial deference; 孔子～之坐 kǒngzi yǔ zhī zuò, Confucius sat together with him.
    a. conjoining nouns or noun-phrases: together with, both . . . and . . .; e.g. 穀～魚鱉不可勝食 gǔ yǔ yúbié bùkěshèng shí, both the grains together with the fishes and turtles will be more than can be completely consumed; 配義～道 péi yì yǔ dào, it accompanies both propriety and proper procedure.
    b. in comparisons: with, or; e.g. 吾～徐公孰美 wú yǔ xúgōng shú měi, who is more handsome, Lord Xu or me?; 吾子～子路孰賢 wúzǐ yǔ zǐlù shú xián, who is worthier, you, sir, or Zilu?
    c. ～其 yǔqí, in the frame ～其 yǔqí X, 寧 nìng Y: in comparison with X, Y is preferable; rather than X, better (to do) Y; e.g. 禮，～其奢也，寧儉 lǐ, yǔqí shē yě, nìng jiǎn, as for ceremonies, in comparison with being extravagant, it is preferable to be frugal; 喪，～其易也，寧戚 sāng, yǔqí yì yě, nìng qì, as for mourning rites, rather than being officious, better to be moved by compassion; → 其 qí 1d.

    d. X～Y: either X or Y; 見冕者～瞽者 jiàn miǎnzhe yǔ gǔzhe, when he saw either a formally capped person or a blind person; 殺人以梃～刃 shārén yǐ tǐng yǔ rèn, to kill someone using a cudgel or a blade.
    e. (Budd.) marks object of VB; e.g. 轉～法輪 zhuǎn yǔ fǎlún, turn the Wheel of the Law; 聞～斯經典 wén yǔ sī jīngdiǎn, give ear to this scripture; 陰蔽～日月 yīnbì yǔ rìyuè, shade and obscure the sun and moon.

yù　MC yoH

1. be associated with; join with, unite with; be near to, familiar with; e.g. 諸侯多～己 zhūhóu duō yǔ jǐ, most of the noble lords joined with him(self); 飛鳥相～還 fēiniǎo xiāngyǔ huán, the flying birds return with one another.
    a. accord with; approve of, allow, concede to; e.g. ～其進也 yǔ qí jìn yě, I approve of their approach to me.
2. participate in, take part with, join in, involve(d); e.g. 不～政事 bùyù zhèngshì, not take part in matters of government.

yú　MC yo

1. sentence-final interrogative GP equiv. to (and phonetic fusion of) yě 也 + hū 乎; e.g. 女弗能救～ rǔ fúnéng jiù yú, are you incapable of saving him from that?; 非惑～ fēi huò yú, is this not a case of delusion? 管仲非仁者～ guǎn zhòng fēi rénzhe yú, was Guan Zhong not a humane person?

語　yǔ　MC ngjoX

1. speak of, tell of, usu. prompted by another's words; converse, conversation, colloquy; anecdote. Unlike 言 yán, can take personal pronoun as direct or indirect OBJ.
2. speech, language.
3. adage, aphorism, saying.

yù　MC ngjoH

1. say to, tell to.

貐　yǔ　MC yuX

1. (bn.) 猰～ yàyǔ, → 猰 yá.

鋙　yǔ　MC ngjoX

1. (bn.) 鉏～ jǔyǔ, → 鉏 jù (chú).

雨　yǔ　MC hjuX

1. rain, rainfall.

yù　MC hjuH

1. to rain down, ref. not only to rain but also snow, sleet, tears, etc.
2. shower, moisten.

麌   yǔ   MC ngjuX
1. male musk-deer.
    a. (med.) river-deer.
2. rdup., herd and huddle together.

齬   yǔ   MC ngjoX
1. sgl. or bn. 鉏～ *jǔyǔ* (MC dzrjoX-ngjoX), irregularly fitting teeth, unmatched and uneven; jutting and jagged; also, discordant.

yù

喻   yù   MC yuH   ⊙ 諭 *yù*.

域   yù   MC hwik
1. territory; circumscribed area, limits, precincts; tract.
    a. state; region; dominion.
    b. outlying region, borderland; e.g. 西～ *xīyù*, Western Regions, i.e. Chinese Turkestan, Central Asia.
2. graveyard.

奧   yù   MC ʔjuwk   → 奧 *ào*.

嫗   yù   MC ʔjuH
1. old woman, granddam, matriarch.
    a. crone, hag, beldam.
2. (med.) married woman, wife.
        yǔ   MC ʔjuX
1. warm with the body; sit on eggs, brood; tend lovingly.

寓   yù   MC ngjuH
1. to lodge, reside.
2. relocate, transfer, move to temporary lodgings; take refuge in; sojourn(er).
3. impute; attribute or ascribe an intended meaning; e.g. ～言 *yùyán*, imputed words, allegory, parable.

或   yù   MC ʔjuwk
1. rdup., flourishing fully, lush and thriving; also, unusually accomplished, exquisitely elegant.

御   yù   MC ngjoH
1. drive a chariot; hold the carriage reins; steer, appulse; charioteer, driver.
    a. the one driving the carriage of state, ruler, autocrat, emperor; imperial; aurigal.

2. hold sway, preside over, often ref. emperor's presence at particular location.
    a. euph. for sexual intercourse of ruler or nobility.
3. direct, govern, control.
    a. set in motion, set to work; ply, wield.
4. attend on, serve; attendant, servitor, servant.
    a. put at superior's disposal, offer to, tender, extend.
5. ～史 *yùshǐ*, from Qin dynasty onward prefix designating various officials associated with the Censorate (～史台 *yùshǐtái*)
6. ⊙ 禦 *yù*, resist, defend.
        yà   MC ngaeH
1. ⊙ 迓 *yà*, meet, welcome.

愈   yù   MC yuX
1. ever more, increasingly, additionally; e.g. ～ X ～ Y, the more X, the more Y.
2. surpass, excel.
3. heal, cure, repair to health.

慾   yù   MC yowk
1. crave, covet(ous); desire, lust; avaricious.

昱   yù   MC yuwk
1. sgl. or rdup., illuminate(d), bright(en), burnish; shine, shed light on; glow(ing).

櫲   yù   MC yoH
1. ～樟 *yùzhāng*, camphor tree (*Cinnamomum camphora*).

欲   yù   MC yowk
1. want(s), desire(s); craving; desiderate.
    a. (Budd.) esp. sensual desires, sensual pleasure, passion.
2. hope for, strive for; "would that I might…"
    a. wish for, long for, fancy; prefer; be enthusiastic about, enthusiasm(s).
    b. (med.) (GP) marker of conditional clause: if, "were it that…"
3. fain to, willing, ready; on the verge of, close to doing X; tend to(ward), incline to(ward); shall, will.
    a. (med.) already, having just passed from the verge of completion to completion; > just now, just exactly.
4. (med.) seemingly, apparently; e.g. ～知 *yùzhī*, expect, infer, presume.

毓 yù　MC yuwk
1. nurture, raise.
2. develop, train; cultivate.
   a. yield of the land, produce.

浴 yù　MC yowk
1. wash the body, bathe, lave.
   a. ablution; purify.
2. swoop and soar, of birds.

澳 yù　MC 'juwk
1. back-water, back-bay; cove in a riverbank.
   a. curving raised riverbank.
   　　ào　MC 'awH
1. (med.) brush; scrub, wash.

煜 yù　MC yuwk
1. sgl. or rdup., burning brightly, flamboyant; blazing, flaming.
   a. sweltering, excessively hot and humid.

熨 yù　MC 'jut
1. sgl. or ～斗 yùdǒu, ironing pan; dipper-shaped flatiron filled with embers.

燠 yù　MC 'juwk
1. sultry, oppressively hot.
   a. (bn.) ～煜 yùyù (MC 'juwk-yuwk), sultry and sweltering.
   　　yù　MC 'juH
1. ～休 yùxiū, comfort, console, esp. the sick or ailing.

獄 yù　MC ngjowk
1. prison, e.g. (Budd.) 地～ dìyù, "earth-prison," hell-realm.
   a. imprison.
2. lawsuit, lodge a legal complaint.

玉 yù　MC ngjowk
1. jade; strictly, nephrite since jadeite was unknown in China until relatively late. Most Chinese "jade" through medieval times came from Khotan. Polished and shaped for all manner of sacred ritual objects as well as objects of utility and pleasure.
   a. having the beauty or luster of jade; e.g. ～容 yùróng, jade[-white] countenance.
   b. respectful epithet of items associated with the gods or the emperor; e.g. (Dao.) ～清 yùqīng, Jade Clarity, name of the highest of the 3 heavens of "Clarity"; ～牒 yùdié, jade tablets, inscribed and used by emperor in the *fengshan* 封禪 sacrifices; also, genealogical records of emperor; also, (Dao.) registers of divinities; (Dao.) ～女 yùnǚ, jade maidens, celestial subordinates who often serve as guardians of sacred scriptures or attendants of major female divinities.
2. as a color word, always indicates lustrous or pure white (N.B. never green); hence has symbolic *wuxing* associations with the west, metal, autumn, the moon, etc.; e.g. (med.) ～環 yùhuán, jade ring or ～輪 yùlún, jade wheel, both metaphorically ref. the moon.
3. gen. term for fine ornamental stone, such as marble.

癒 yù　MC yuX
1. heal, cure, return to health.
2. ⊙ 愈 yù 1, ever more; 2, surpass, excel.

砡 yù　MC ngjuwk
1. evenly placed or piled.

禦 yù　MC ngjoX
1. resist, forestall; repel, repulse.
2. defend, guard, safeguard; secure.
   a. prevent, block, withstand.
3. (med.) violence, force; cruelty.

籲 yù　MC yuH
1. implore, exhort, entreat, beseech.

絨 yù　MC hwik
1. seam of a garment.

繘 yù　MC ywit
1. well-rope, for drawing water with bucket.

罭 yù　MC hwik
1. fine-meshed net for catching small fish.

聿 yù　MC ywit
1. writing brush.
   a. tell of, tell about.
2. freely, unrestrained.
3. (GP) pre-classical particle, similar in usage to 惟 wéi, verily, indeed, let it be that...

育 yù　MC yuwk
1. nurture, raise, rear; nourish, foster.
   a. train, develop; educate.
2. produce, breed, engender.

芋   **yù**   MC hjuH
1. taro, dasheen (*Colocasia esculenta*).
　　hū   MC xu
1. ⊙ 幠 *hū* shelter; grand.

蕷   **yù**   MC yoH
1. (med.) (bn.) 薯～ *shǔyù*, → 薯 *shǔ*.

薁   **yù**   MC 'juwk
1. sgl. or (bn.) 蘡～ *yīngyù*, → 蘡 *yīng*.
2. sgl. or (bn.) ～棣 *yùdì* (MC 'juwk-dejH), dwarf cherry (*Prunus japonica*).

蜮   **yù**   MC hwik
1. sand-spitter; legendary invertebrate creature of the southern rivers, said to harm people by shooting sand at them; variously described but with no conclusive taxonomic identification; also called 射工 *shègōng*, shooting artist; 射影 *shèyǐng*, shadow-shooter; 水弩 *shuǐnǔ*, water-crossbow; 短狐 *duǎnhú*, short-bodied fox. In Tang times reputedly a companion of the 鸜鵒 *qúyù*, crested myna.

裕   **yù**   MC yuH
1. ample, abundant; opulent, bountiful.
　　a. enrich, enhance; give broader scope to; endow.
　　b. (med.) surplus, extra; syn. 餘 *yú*.
2. wide, diffuse; all-accepting; magnanimous.

諭   **yù**   MC yuH
1. instruct about; elucidate, expound; illustrate.
2. explain or suggest by means of analogy or parable; analogous.
　　a. (med.) resemble, simulate; e.g. ～若 *yùruò*, seem like, be similar to.
3. notify, notification, esp. from superior to subordinates; injunction.

譽   **yù**   MC yoH
1. acclaim, extol(ment), preconize, commend publicly.
　　a. reputation, public regard, acclaim; applause.

豫   **yù**   MC yoH
1. happiness, content(ment); comfort(able), ease; e.g. ～附 *yùfù*, contentedly acquiesce; 不～ *bùyù*, indisposed, ill at ease, out of sorts.
　　a. "Contentment," name of 16th hexagram of *Yijing*.

2. royal or imperial inspection tour, esp. ruler's autumn progress or visitation.
3. beforehand, in advance; preparatory.
　　a. prepare for, make ready, anticipate, prevene; take precautions.
　　b. (bn.) 猶～ *yóuyù*, → 猶 *yóu*.
4. ⊙ 與 *yù* (*yǔ*), participate, take part in.
5. ～章 *yùzhāng*, camphor tree (*Cinnamomum camphora*), also used metaphorically for men of talent; ～木 *yùmù*, silky spicebush (*Lindera sericea*).
6. large elephant (ancient usage).

遇   **yù**   MC ngjuH
1. come upon, happen upon, befall, meet unplanned.
　　a. happenstance, fortune; e.g. 不～ *bùyù* or 失～ *shīyù*, unmet by fortune, hapless.
2. treat, approach, handle.
3. get along with, fall in step with.
4. ⊙ *ǒu*, perchance, accidentally.

遹   **yù**   MC ywit
1. go awry, go to extremes; perverse.
　　a. deteriorate; vitiate.
2. follow; adhere to.

郁   **yù**   MC 'juwk
1. richly accomplished, culturally admirable; finely ornamented.
　　a. rdup., tasteful and finished, refined and elegant.
2. richly aromatic, redolent; pungent; ⊙ 鬱 *yù* 4.
3. ⊙ 燠 *yù*, sultry.

閾   **yù**   MC xwik
1. threshold, doorsill, groundsel.
　　a. by metonymy, doorway, entrance.
2. borderland, boundary between two states.

隩   **yù**   MC 'juwk
1. ⊙ 澳 *yù*, back-bay, cove; curving raised riverbank.
　　ào   MC 'awH
1. distant habitable land, far-removed territory; periphery.

預   **yù**   MC yoH
1. (med.) ⊙ 豫 3, beforehand, in advance; prepare, anticipate.

颰　yù　MC hwit

1. gale, tempest, blast of wind.

飫　yù　MC ʼjoH

1. private banquet; familial feast.
   a. to feast, fête.
2. satiate, surfeit, have one's fill of; e.g. (med.) ～聞 *yùwén*, oft-heard, widely rumored.

馭　yù　MC ngjoH

1. ◉ 御 *yù* 1, 3.

驈　yù　MC ywit

1. white-rumped black horse.

鬱　yù　MC ʼjut

1. densely growing, thickly massed; clustered, crushed together; esp. of vegetation or of clouds and mists.
   a. rdup., jungly and jumbled, densely and darkly forested; closely clustered, matted mesh, bunched and clumped; also, the mental equivalent of this state, → 2a.
2. heaviness of mind, mental stasis; gloom.
   a. rdup. or (bn.) ～悒 *yùyì* (MC ʼjut-ʼip), feeling stifled and smothered, grim and glum, dour and depressed, with thoughts bound and knotted.
3. projected or distended upward; swelling, thickening; looming; e.g. ～雲 *yùyún*, clouds massed and swelling; ～樑 *yùliáng*, extended or soaring roofbeams; (med.) (bn.) ～律 *yùlǜ* (MC ʼjut-lwit), thickly swollen; also, richly abundant.
   a. ref. the movement of steaming vapors; also, sparkling or twinkling of lights; also, effervescence of life in its nascent state.
4. richly odoriferous, redolent.
5. ～金 *yùjīn*, ～金香 *yùjīnxiāng*, wild turmeric (*Curcuma aromatica*), or turmeric, saffron, yellow ginger (*Curcuma longa*); syn. 姜黃 *jiānghuáng*.
6. (Dao.) ～儀 *yùyí*, "Steamy Exemplar," esoteric name of the sun, often paired with 結璘 *jiélín*, "Bundled Luster," esoteric name of the moon.

鬻　yù　MC yuwk

1. peddle, hawk; vend, sell.
2. ◉ 育 *yù*, nourish, raise.
   zhōu　MC tsyuwk
1. ◉ 粥 *zhōu*, congee, thin gruel.

魆　yù　MC hwik　◉ 螆 *yù*.

鱊　yù　MC ywit

1. whitebait, lampfish (*Stenobrachius leucopsarus*).

䬒　yù　MC ywit

1. fly swiftly, dart, hurtle.

鴥　yù　MC yowk

1. (bn.) 鸲～ or 鸜～ *qúyù*, →鸲 *qú* or 鸜 *qú*.

鷸　yù　MC ywit

1. snipe (*Gallinago gallinago*), long-billed wading bird; also ref. various other shorebirds of similar appearance incl. sandpiper, godwit, dowitcher (mostly Charadriformes).
2. swiftly winging.

鵒　yù　MC yoH

1. sgl. or ～斯 *yùsī*, Daurian jackdaw (*Corvus dauuricus*); sometimes Eurasian jackdaw (*Corvus monedula*), esp. if more westerly.

yuān

冤　yuān　MC ʼjwon

1. injustice, wrong.
2. resentful because wronged; rancor(ous); vindictive.
3. crook, bend; twist.

悁　yuān　MC ʼjwien

1. annoyed, unhappy; dissatisfied, displeased.

淵　yuān　MC ʼwen

1. vortex, gyre; whirlpool, maelstrom; e.g. 太～ *tàiyuān*, "Grand Vortex," reservoir of primal pneuma (*yuanqi* 元氣), associated with *yin* energy.
2. abyss, seemingly bottomless gulf.
   a. deep pool; deep water.
3. deep, profound; unplumbable, immeasurable.

瞘　yuān　MC ʼjwon

1. dull-eyed, blank-eyed; blind, unseeing.
2. a dried-up well; desiccated.

蜎　yuān　MC ʼjwien

1. rdup., creeping and crawling, advancing slowly.
2. crooked, curved, bent.
   xuān　MC xjwien
1. ◉ 翾 *xuān*, flit, dart(le).

鳶   **yuān**   **MC ywen**
1. black kite, glede (*Milvus migrans*), medium-sized bird of prey.

鴛   **yuān**   **MC ʼjwon**
1. (bn.) ～鴦 *yuānyāng* (MC ʼjwon-ʼjang), mandarin-duck, love-duck (*Aix galericulata*).
2. ⊙ 鵷 *yuān*.

鵷   **yuān**   **MC ʼjwon**
1. (bn.) ～雛 *yuānchú* (MC ʼjwon-dzrju), species of "phoenix," mentioned in *Zhuangzi*, most fastidious in its roosting places, food, and drink.

yuán

元   **yuán**   **MC ngjwon**
1. primary, primal, prime; basic, foundational; e.g. ～氣 *yuánqì*, primal pneuma, undifferentiated reservoir of energy before inauguration of the world; also, naturally existing *qi* that fills the world; (med.) 三～ *sānyuán*, 3 primary components of the world: heaven, earth, man; also, (Dao.) 3 executive realms of being: heaven, earth, water.
2. principal; paramount; premier.
   a. first in sequence or importance, foremost; e.g. ～年 *yuánnián*, "prime year," designation for first year of a reign-period; ～帥 *yuánshuài*, paramount commander, esp. of army on campaign; ～君 *yuánjūn*, "foremost lord," ruler of a state; also, honored early ancestor; also, (Dao.) "primal mistress," female divinites of immeasurable years; ～宵 *yuánxiāo*, "primal night," first full moon of the year.
   b. original, primordial, principiate; beginning; e.g. (Dao.) ～始天尊 *yuánshǐtiānzūn*, Celestial Worthy of Primordial Commencement, creator of the cosmos and producer of sacred scriptures and talismans.
   c. epochal, era, epoch, epoch-making, often used as second element in reign-titles, indicative of a new beginning; also, marker of |start of certain calendrical divisions, e.g. 三～ *sānyuán*, i.e. full-moon days of first (上～), seventh (中～), and tenth (下～) months.
3. (med.) basically, originally, actually.
4. N.B. used in Song and Qing dynasties as taboo-substitute for 玄 *xuán*, hence cause of

some interpretive confusion with regard to texts reprinted from earlier times.

原   **yuán**   **MC ngjwon**
1. source, of a stream, river, or other body of water; font, fount; ⊙ 源 *yuán*.
   a. origin(al), beginning, start; provenance; primary.
   b. trace to the source, proceed all the way back to the origin of.
2. highland, upland; plateau, tableland; terrace; level plain; campestral.
3. pardon, absolve, forgive; lenient, forbearing.
4. twice, a second time.

員   **yuán**   **MC hjwen**
1. functionary, member; personnel; one of an associated group; e.g. (med.) ～外郎 *yuánwàiláng*, "supernumerary esquire," assistant to the head of a government ministry.
2. ⊙ 圓 *yuán*, round, circle; perimeter, circumference.

   yún   **MC hjun**
1. ⊙ 云 *yún*, (GP) verbal prefix.

   yùn   **MC hjunH**
1. a surname.

園   **yuán**   **MC hjwon**
1. garden; enclosed area of trees, plants, flowers; bower.
   a. hortulan, of or relating to a garden.
   b. enclosure, park, to be visited by officials and nobility for recreation.
2. country residence, villa.
3. burial ground for rulers, their family, and favored officials.

圓   **yuán**   **MC hjwen**
1. round, circular; circle; e.g. ～光 *yuánguāng*, "round glow," the moon; also, (Budd.) the light that emanates from the crown of a buddha's or bodhisattva's head; (Dao.) ～珠 *yuánzhū*, "round pearl," esoteric name for sun.
   a. perimeter, circumference.
   b. (med.) ful(ly), wholly, complete(ly); perfect(ly); inclusive; e.g. (Budd.) ～寂 *yuánjì*, perfect tranquility, i.e. *nirvāṇa*, syn. 滅度 *mièdù*; (Budd.) ～教 *yuánjiào*, the inclusive doctrine, highest teachings of various sects.
2. by metonymy, heaven (opp. [square] earth).
3. draw a bow to its fullest (nearly forming a circle).

垣 yuán MC hjwon

1. enclosing wall; enclosure; fence; paling.
2. region of the night sky outlined by a long constellation, esp. the 3 constellations known as 紫微 *zǐwēi*, Purple Tenuity, 太微 *tàiwēi*, Grand Tenuity, and 天市 *tiānshì*, Heaven's Marketplace.
3. (med.) euph. for government office.

媛 yuán MC hjwon → 媛 *yuàn*.

援 yuán MC hjwon

1. pull up, pull on.
    a. take in hand, take by hand; draw toward one; e.g. ～筆 *yuánbǐ*, take up the writing-brush.
2. pull along, lead on, guide.
    a. cite, adduce.
    b. recommend; appoint.
3. resort to, draw on, have recourse to, bring to bear.
4. (med.) reap, as crops.
        yuàn MC hjwenH
1. aid, assist; succor

櫞 yuán MC ywen

1. (med.) sgl. or cmpd. 枸～ *gǒuyuán*, 香～ *xiāngyuán*, bitter citron (*Citrus medica*).

湲 yuán MC hjwen

1. (bn.) 潺～ *chányuán*, → 潺 *chán*.

源 yuán MC ngjwon

1. ⊙ 原 *yuán* 1, source of a stream, river, or other body of water; font, fount, spring.
    a. origin(al), beginning, start; provenance; primary; e.g. ～流 *yuánliú*, "source and flow," origin and development of.
    b. trace to the source, proceed all the way back to the origin of.
2. rdup., continuously connected; unbroken line.

爰 yuán MC hjwon

1. go [there], all the way to >
    a. (GP) to it, in it (similar → 焉 *yán*).
    b. phrase-initial: thereupon, then; e.g. ～因 *yuányīn*, "As it happens…"
    c. the whole extent of.
2. interr., "how…?"
3. rdup., surely and easily, cooly and carelessly.
4. change, alter; move.
5. ⊙ 猿 *yuán*, gibbon.
6. a surname.

猨 yuán MC hjwon ⊙ 猿 *yuán*.

猿 yuán MC hjwon

1. gibbon; tailless, long-armed lesser ape of the family *Hylobatidae*, various species and colors; most often ref. in lit. for their mournful, haunting cries which evoke feelings of loneliness and thoughts of home. N.B. not an "ape" or "monkey."

緣 yuán MC ywen

1. hem of a garment; edge, border.
    a. to hem, go along the edge of, follow the outline of; trace.
    b. climb, scale the edge of.
    c. cling to, adhere to.
2. have affinity with, esp. predestined affinity; relationship by means of earlier causes; current circumstances being the effect of previous connections.
    a. (Budd.) (pre)condition(ed); causal, causation; e.g. 因～ *yīnyuán*, primary and secondary conditions, causal affinity, karmic cause and effect; (Budd.) ～起 *yuánqǐ*, conditional arising, origin, dependent origination; (Budd.) 本～ *běnyuán*, "original affinities," ref. *avadāna* tales of Buddha's past lives; (Budd.) ～覺 *yuánjué*, enlightenment by [understanding] causation, those who understand causation, esp. ref. to pratyeka-buddhas.
3. (med.) rely on, be the result of, depend on; e.g. ～…故 *yuán…gù*, owing to…, for the reason that…, because of…; ～何 *yuánhé* or ～沒 *yuánmò*, for what reason, why?
4. (med.) occasion for, opportunity; leads to, occasions.

芫 yuán MC ngjwon

1. ～華 *yuánhuā*, Chinese daphne, lilac daphne (*Daphne genkwa*).
        yán MC ngjon
1. ～荽 *yánsuī*, coriander, Chinese parsley, cilantro (*Coriandrum sativum*).

螈 yuán MC ngjwon

1. ～蠶 *yuáncán*, 2nd emergence of silkworms in same year.
2. 蠑～ *róngyuán*, → 蠑 *róng*.

袁 yuán MC hjwon

1. long garment.
2. a surname.

轅   yuán   MC hjwon

1. straight thills, shafts between which an animal is harnessed to pull a vehicle (cf. 辀 zhōu, single curved shaft, used in pre-Qin times).
2. temporary resting-place of emperor while on a hunt or an outing; chariots originally arranged as protecting wall, with the thills of two vehicles placed face-to-face so they could be raised to allow passage in or out.
   a. because of preceding, used as ref. to entrance of military encampment.
3. (med.) outermost gate to the residence of a nobleman or high official; also, the gate to government offices overseeing military affairs.

騵   yuán   MC ngjwon

1. white-bellied bay horse.

鶰   yuán   MC hjwon

1. (bn.) ～鵾 yuánjū (MC hjwon-kjo), frigatebird (*Fregata minor*); also, adjutant stork (*Leptoptilus javanicus*); both somewhat rare and seen mainly in the south.

黿   yuán   MC ngjwon

1. larger soft-shelled turtle (*Pelochelys bibroni*) (cf. 鱉 biē, lesser soft-shelled turtle, trionyx).

yuǎn

遠   yuǎn   MC hjwonX

1. distant, far, long off, in space or time.
   a. regard as distant.
2. far-reaching, extend far or deeply in influence or effect.
3. separate(d) from, have or give rise to distance or difference between SUBJ and OBJ.
   a. estranged from; indifferent to.
4. ～志 yuǎnzhì, milkwort (*Polygala tenuifolia*), herb used medicinally, produces lavender to purple flowers; syn. 細草 xìcǎo.

yuàn

媛   yuàn   MC hjwenH

1. beautiful; attractive, appealing.
   yuán   MC hjwon
1. (bn.) 嬋～ chányuán, → 嬋 chán.

怨   yuàn   MC 'jwonH

1. complaint, grudge; reproach; discontent; resentment, bitterness; bitterness of spirit.
   a. repine, complain; plaint.
2. regard as enemy, hate, loathe.

愿   yuàn   MC ngjwonH

1. devoted to, diligent; attentive, careful, prudent.

掾   yuàn   MC ywenH

1. designation of low-level clerk or administrator; often gen. term for official colleagues, bureaucrats.

瑗   yuàn   MC hjwenH

1. narrow-banded jade disc with large opening.

苑   yuàn   MC 'jwonX

1. a preserve, esp. for animals; park, to be enjoyed on outings by ruler or nobles.
   a. collection of literary pieces, anthology, florilegium.
2. meadow, glade.
3. breeding place; incubator; matrix.

院   yuàn   MC hjwenH

1. walled courtyard.
   a. wall enclosing a courtyard; the buildings within it.
   b. apartment, as of palace lady.
2. compound, close; parvis; (Budd.) cloister.

願   yuàn   MC ngjwonH

1. wish for, hope for, desire.
   a. solicit, implore, ask for.
   b. prefer, opt for, favor; select.
2. marker of optative: "Would that I might . . .; Pray, let me . . ."
3. (Budd.) vow, pledge, esp. to fulfill certain religious aspirations.
4. admire, look up to.

yuē

曰   yuē   MC hjwot

1. introduces direct quotation, to say "X"; basically stands for quotation marks but usu. translated "X said (or says), '. . .'"
2. (med.) rarely introduces indirect quotation or summary, similar to 云 yún 2.

矱　yuē　MC ʼjwak
1. standard, convention; rule, law.

約　yuē　MC ʼjak
1. bind, tie together; gird; fasten.
   a. bond, agreement, pact, covenant; promise, pledge.
   b. comply with, agree > contain, gather.
2. restrain(t), reserve(d); moderate, temper(ate); conservative, convention(al).
   a. restrict(ed), straitened, constrict(ed).
   b. sparing, few, meager.
   c. abbreviate(d), condense(d); in brief, succinct(ly).
3. frets of stringed instrument.
4. (med.) roughly, generally; probably, likely.

yuè

刖　yuè　MC ngjwot
1. punish(ment) by amputating a foot.
2. (bn.) 臲～ *nièyuè*, → 臲 *niè*.

岳　yuè　MC ngaewk　⊙ 嶽 *yuè*.

嶽　yuè　MC ngaewk
1. high peak, alp; sacred peak, commanding mountain, marchmount, esp. ref. to 五～ *wǔyuè*, the "5 Marchmounts" that symbolically mark the 5 directional points of the empire: Mt. Tai 泰 (east), Mt. Hua 華 (west), Mt. Heng 衡 (south), Mt. Heng 恒 (north), Mt. Song 嵩 (center).
2. rdup., stand straight, awesome and uplifted, upright and erect.

悦　yuè　MC ywet
1. pleased, relaxed; happy, content.
   a. pleased with, take a liking to.

戉　yuè　MC hjwot　⊙ 鉞 *yuè*.

月　yuè　MC ngjwot
1. moon; lunar; e.g. ～華 *yuèhuá*, "lunar efflorescence," moonlight; also, lunar halo; also, realgar.
2. moonlight; e.g. ～波 *yuèbō*, wavering silvery moonlight; ～孤 *yuègū*, "orphan of moonlight," i.e. mercury, quicksilver.
3. month, span of days from one new moon through the day before the next, either 30 days

(大月) or 29 (小月); e.g. ～殺 *yuèshā*, "death-days of the month," 5th, 14th, 23rd, on which doing business, going on trips, etc., should be avoided.
   a. monthly; month after month.
4. descriptive of items shaped like the moon, either in its full or crescent shape; e.g. ～眉 *yuèméi*, "moon-brows," woman's thinly-arched eyebrows; ～面 *yuèmiàn*, moon-faced, round and white, esp. (med.) describing the Buddha.
5. ～氏 *yuèzhī* (MC ngjwot-tsye), name of pre-Han and Han Central Asian tribe(s) usu. identified as Tokharians, migrated from Gansu to Bactria in 2nd century BCE; in med. times used as ref. to Turks and Iranians who lived beyond the Pamirs.
6. ～貴 *yuèguì*, China rose (*Rosa chinensis*), syn. ～季花 *yuèjìhuā*.

樂　yuè　MC ngaewk
1. music, glee; usu. paired in Ruist texts with 禮 *lǐ*, ritual or ceremonial form, as the 2 basic activities of social coordination.
   a. musician, gleeman.
   b. instrument(s) for making music.
      lè　MC lak
1. merry, blithe; delighted; gleeful; (en)joy(ment); take pleasure in, delight in.
      yào　MC ngaewH
1. (med.) be fond of, enjoy, appreciate.
      luò　MC lak
1. (bn.) ～託 *luòtuō* (MC lak-thak), aimless and unrestrained, wild and unbridled.

樾　yuè　MC hjwot
1. shade of trees; umbrage; shaded passage between trees.

瀹　yuè　MC yak
1. soak, moisten.
2. drain off; leak out; tap.
   a. cleanse; purify.
3. cook in a soup.

爚　yuè　MC yak
1. firelight; blaze.
   a. rdup., flashing and flickering, blazingly bright.
   b. burn; ignite.
2. illumine, shine on, light up.
3. to blind, daze; baffle, perplex.

礿   yuè   MC yak

1. name of ancestral sacrifice offered by ruler, in spring (Xia and Shang dynasties) or summer (Zhou dynasty).

禴   yuè   MC yak   ⊙ 礿 *yuè*.

籥   yuè   MC yak

1. transverse flute of early times.
2. bellows, for increasing draft to a fire.
3. ⊙ 鑰 *yuè*, cotter, key.

粤   yuè   MC hjwot

1. (GP) pre-classical phrase-initial (rarely phrase-middle) particle lending tone of solemnity or circumspection to following statement: "Yea…, Verily…"; used later for archaizing effect.

葯   yuè   MC ʻjak

1. Chinese angelica (*Angelica dahurica*), perennial plant that grows along riverbanks and streams; roots and leaves highly fragrant; in lit. symbolic of high morality and integrity. N.B. Do not confuse with modern abbrev. form of 藥 *yào*.

越   yuè   MC hjwot

1. overrun, outrace; stride over, go past.
   a. exceed, go beyond.
   b. transcend(ent); supernal.
   c. high-pitched, penetrating, of sounds.
2. far off, distant; move away from; e.g. ～席 *yuèxí*, leave one's sitting-mat.
   a. unrealistic, impractical; e.g. ～次 *yuècì*, out of sequence, non-standard.
3. disperse, dissipate.
   a. spread far and wide.
   b. publish, proclaim.
4. fall off, drop down; decline.
5. (med.) more, further, more and more.
6. name of feudal state in pre-Qin times, largely the area of Zhejiang.
   a. gen. term for various peoples inhabiting the eastern and southeastern coastal lands and inward territories.
   b. ～南 *yuènán*, the lands "south of Yue," esp. area of modern Vietnam.

躍   yuè   MC yak

1. leap over, jump, vault, bound; canter.
   a. sgl. or rdup., exult, exilient; jubilate, be in high spirits; skip with joy; caper.

tì   MC thek

1. rdup., swiftly and speedily, racing rapidly.

軏   yuè   MC ngjwot

1. curved collar-bar of small carriage (cf. 輗 *ní*, for large carriage), bar-lock, attached at end of the thills for yoking horses or oxen.

鉞   yuè   MC hjwot

1. battleaxe, large axe with crescent-shaped blade that was attached to a long staff, used for beheadings and as object of authority wielded by honor guard of ruler, rarely in battle.
2. name of the star Propus (η Geminorum), in the lunar lodging "Well" (*jing* 井).

鑰   yuè   MC yak

1. (med.) cotter, key; lock.
2. (med.) decorative reinforcements of palace doors.

閲   yuè   MC ywet

1. right-hand gate-column of influential family, carrying half of parallel inscription regarding family's ancestral merits and rank (cf. 閥 *fá*, left-hand column).
2. scrutinize, inspect, examine, eye thoroughly and carefully; review.
   a. (med.) peruse a text, pore over, perlegate, perlection.
3. search, hunt for, comb through.
4. pass through, traverse; experience.
5. count up, add up, calculate, reckon.
   a. collect, gather in; gather together, unite.

鸑   yuè   MC ngaewk

1. (bn.) ～鷟 *yuèzhuó* (MC ngaewk-dzraewk), a kind of "simurgh."

龠   yuè   MC yak

1. ⊙ 籥 *yuè*, transverse flute of early times.
2. measure of capacity, amounting to 1200 grains of millet.

yūn

氲   yūn   MC ʻjun

1. (bn.) 氤～ *yīnyùn*, → 氤 *yīn*.

熅　yūn　MC ʼjun
1. flameless fire; embers, coals.
　　a. grill, broil.
2. (bn.) 烟～ *yīnyūn*, → 烟 *yīn* (*yān*).

萻　yūn　MC ʼjun
1. sacred lily (*Rohdea sinensis*), with evergreen leaves, flowers on a short dense spike; syn. 萬年青 *wànniánqīng*.
2. (bn.) 茵～ *yīnyūn*, 蒕～ *fényūn*, ⊙ 氤氲 *yīnyūn*, → 氲 *yīn*.

yún

云　yún　MC hjun
1. to say so; e.g. 再三～ *zàisān yún*, he said so three more times; cog. 曰 *yuē*, say.
2. introduces indirect quotation or summary, non-citation speech: say(s) that; e.g. 黃帝之書～至人居若死動若械 *huángdì zhī shū yún zhìrén jū ruò sǐ, dòng ruò xiè*, the Documents of Huangdi say that a perfected individual at rest is as if dead, in motion is as if a machine.
　　a. 云爾 *yún'ěr*, used to indicate substance of speculation, imagined or hypothetical speech: said (or thought) thus, said (or thought) like this > so one thought: 其心曰是何足與言仁義也～～ *qí xīn yuē shì hézú yǔ yán rényì yě yún'ěr*, in their hearts they were saying, "this person, how is he adequate to discuss Humaneness and Propriety with," so they were saying (thinking); 曰薄乎～～惡得無罪 *yuē bó hū yún'ěr, wùdé wúzùi* (Mencius) said, "It was indeed slight," so he was saying (thinking); but how can he be without fault?
3. clause- or sentence-final particle closing off a direct or indirect quotation or citation: so (it was) said 子曰汝安知魚樂 *zǐ yuē rǔ ān zhī yú lè yún*, You said [to me], "wherein do you know about the pleasures of a fish?" (so you said); 入～則入坐～則坐食～則食 *rù yún zé rù, zuò yún zé zuò, shí yún zé shí* if "enter" is said, then he enters; if "sit" is said, then he sits; if "eat" is said, then he eats.
4. as a reference to any kind of vocal expression: 事已敗矣乃重太息其～益乎 *shì yǐ bài yǐ, nǎi chóng tàixī qí yún yì hū* the matter has been completely defeated; as for your repeated great sighing, is that kind of vocal expression helpful?
5. reaching to the point, up to, come (round) to … (esp. in *Shijing*); e.g. 日之～夕 *rì zhī yún xī*, when day turns to evening.
　　a. ～何 *yúnhé*, reaching to what point; how much more …

匀　yún　MC ywin
1. (med.) well-proportioned; equally arranged, well-balanced; matched, symmetrical; orderly, even, uniform.

畇　yún　MC ywin
1. rdup., cleared and cultivated, of farming plots; aligned and evened up.

筠　yún　MC hwin
1. green culm or rind of bamboo.
　　a. synecdoche for bamboo.
2. (med.) bamboo flute.

紜　yún　MC hjun
1. rdup., in jumbled disorder, ravelled and tangled, helter-skelter, scrambled clutter.

耘　yún　MC hjun
1. to weed, hand-weeding; uproot.
　　a. eradicate, do away with; extirpate.

芸　yún　MC hjun
1. sgl. or ～香 *yúnxiāng*, rue, honey-bush (*Ruta graveolens*), used in cooking and medicinally but esp. as insectifuge for books.
2. sgl. or ～花 *yúnhuā*, lilac daphne (*Daphne genkwa*), evergreen shrub, produces long wands of lavender or white flowers, seeds poisonous.
3. rdup., manifold and plentiful.
4. sere or amber-yellow.
5. ⊙ 耘 *yún*, to weed.

薹　yún　MC hjun
1. (med.) ～薹 *yúntái*, bird-rape, celery cabbage (*Brassica campestris*), syn. 油菜 *yóucài*.

雲　yún　MC hjun
1. cloud; cloudy, billowy; e.g. 青～ *qīngyún*, clouds in the blue [sky]; ～漢 *yúnhàn*, "the Han River in the clouds," or ～津 *yúnjīn*, "the cloudy ford," i.e. the Milky Way.
　　a. by metonymy, the sky, heaven(s) > high status, official success.

2. first element in many compounds ref. to mica; e.g. ～母 *yúnmǔ*, "cloud-mother," gen. term for mica; ～珠 *yúnzhū*, "cloud-pearl," pinkish or yellow-gray mica, margarite; ～英 *yúnyīng*, "cloud-bloom," greenish or reddish-brown mica, phlogotite; ～膽 *yúndǎn*, "cloud-gall," dark mica, biotite (syn. ～涿 *yúnzhuó*, "cloud-drip").

3. ～木香 *yúnmùxiāng*, putchuk (*Saussurea lappa*, *S. costus*), originally brought from north India, fragrant root used in incense and perfume; syn. 廣木香 *guǎngmùxiāng*.

yǔn

允　yǔn　MC ywinX

1. pre-classical assenting ADV: verily, certes, it really did VB; later used for archaizing effect.
　　a. (med.) assent, give assent to; permit, allow; admit, consent.
2. with confidence, with trust; truly; indeed.
3. fair(ly), just(ly); apt(ly).

殞　yǔn　MC hwinX

1. languish, lapse, fail; fall away, die.
　　a. bring down, fell.
2. ⊙ 隕 *yǔn* 1, fall, descend; decline; let fall, neglect.

狁　yǔn　MC ywinX

1. (bn.) 玁～ *xiǎnyǔn*, →玁 *xiǎn* 2.

隕　yǔn　MC hwinX

1. fall, descend; decline.
　　a. let fall, neglect.
2. fail, languish, lapse; drop away, die.

yùn

孕　yùn　MC yingH

1. pregnant, with child, gravid.
　　a. embody, contain; fraught with; expectant.

慍　yùn　MC 'junH

1. nourish a grudge, feel resentment but not act on it, chafe at.
　　a. displeasure, pique; loathe; be averse to.

暈　yùn　MC hjunH

1. solar or lunar halo, nimbus, usu. with grayish-white haze and a faint band of prismatic colors around outside of ring.
　　a. hazy blur, misty smudge, cloudy film.
2. (med.) bedim, blur, veil.

熨　yùn　MC 'jut　→熨 *yù*.

縕　yùn　MC junH

1. tag-silk, floss-silk, waste silk; tag-hemp, waste hemp; tag-wool, flock-wool.
　　a. tangled, raveled; bunched.
2. conceal, contain.
　　a. ⊙ 蘊 *yùn* 4, place of mystery, secret cache.
3. ⊙ 茵 *yīn*, seat-pad, cushion, pallet.
　　yūn　MC 'jun
1. (bn.) 絪～ *yīnyūn*, ⊙ 氤氳 *yīnyūn*, → 氲 *yīn*.

蘊　yùn　MC 'junH

1. collect in a pile, heap up; accumulate, bundle; aggregate.
　　a. (Budd.) trns. of Skt. *skandha*, esp. 五～ *wǔyùn*, the 5 physical and mental constituents that make up a sentient being: form, perception, conception, volition, consciousness.
　　b. cluster; bouquet.
　　c. (med.) most, excessively, exceedingly.
2. store up, hoard, (p)reserve.
　　a. stored resources; inner capabilities; e.g. 意～ *yìyùn*, intimations, inner purport; ～藉 *yùnjí*, generous and large-hearted.
　　b. rdup., deep and profound, deep-seated and downright.
3. blocked; pent-up, suppressed; frustrated.
4. place of mystery, secret cache.

運　yùn　MC hjunH

1. turn round, revolve, circumvolve; rotate, gyre; e.g. ～褰 *yùnyì*, turning and twining; ～掌 *yùnzhǎng*, in a turn of the hand, easily.
　　a. cyclic movement of the universe; turn of fortune or destiny; phase; e.g. 四～ *sìyùn*, "fourfold cycle," i.e. the seasons; 五～ *wǔyùn*, "fivefold cycle," i.e. interaction of the 5 Phases.
2. transport, displace; move, convey.
　　a. advance; evolve; e.g. ～遇 *yùnyù*, advance toward, meet.
3. make use of, ply, wield; handle, manage.
4. measure of distance on north-south axis (cf. 廣 *guàng* [*guǎng*], east-west).

醞　yùn　MC ʼjunH

1. to ferment wine.
   a. (med.) by metonymy, wine.
2. ～藉 *yùnjí*, ⊙ 蘊藉 *yùnjí*, generous and large-hearted.

韞　yùn　MC ʼjunX

1. store away, (p)reserve, hoard; secrete; cache.

韻　yùn　MC hjunH

1. consonance, agreement, accord.
   a. rhyme; resonance.
   b. go together, appropriate(ness).
   c. abb. for ～母 *yùnmǔ*, final of a Chinese syllable; cf. 聲母 *shēngmǔ*, initial.
2. attitude; manner, demeanor.

餫　yùn　MC hjunH

1. transport food provisions.

Z

zā

匝　zā　MC tsop

1. go around, circle round.
   a. complete turning, circuit; fully round.

拶　zā　MC tsat

1. (med.) compel, coerce; force.

zá

囋　zá　MC dzat

1. babble, chatter, blather.
   a. (bn.) 嘈～ *cáozá*, → 嘈 *cáo*.

雜　zá　MC dzop

1. mixed, various, variegated, variety, eclectic; diverse, sundry, of all kinds.
   a. disparate, discrepant; assorted.
   b. disorganized, disarray; confused; alloyed, impure; distracted, scattered.
   c. (lit.) unsorted, unclassified, esp. of poems not belonging to a particular genre or subgenre.
   d. (bn.) ～錯 *zácuò* (MC dzop-tshak), merged and mingled; (bn.) ～襲 *záxí* (MC dzop-zip), meshed and melded; (bn.) ～遝 *zátà* (MC dzop-dop), teeming throng, mingled mass.

zāi

哉　zāi　MC tsoj

1. exclamatory sentence-final GP; e.g. 吾何以觀之～ *wú héyǐ guān zhī zāi*, how, indeed, should I observe it?!; 為仁由己而由人乎～ *wéirén yóujǐ ér yóurén hū zāi*, behaving in a humane way, does this really arise from oneself or from others?!; 彼惡敢當我～ *bǐ wū gǎndāng wǒ zāi*, how would he dare to confront me?! ；豈有他～ *qǐ yǒu tā zāi* could there really be any other?!
   a. exclamatory GP following a preposed VB or VB-phrase; e.g. 賢～回也 *xián zāi húi yě*, worthy indeed is Hui!; 善～問 *shànzāi wèn*, excellent ! to ask this question; 大～堯之為君 *dà zāi yáo zhī wéijūn*, Great indeed! was Yao's serving as a lord.

栽　zāi　MC tsoj

1. to plant; tend, husband.
2. young sprouts, new growth of plants; shoots, saplings.
   zài　MC dzojH
1. build a wall of rammed earth.

災　zāi　MC tsoj

1. natural disaster, catastrophe, visitation, esp. conflagration but also of wind, flood, earthquake, etc.
2. calamity; adversity; suffering; ruin(ation), damage.
   a. untoward; ill-fated, ill-starred.

zǎi

宰　zǎi　MC tsojX

1. majordomo of noble household, steward of fief or borough.
2. ～相 *zǎixiàng*, chief minister, grand councilor, one of several officials with primary or major responsibilities of advising ruler personally.

3. manage, govern; oversee; judge.
4. butcher and dismember sacrificial animal; mactate, mactatory.
   a. break up, partition, dis(sever).

zài

再   zài   MC tsojH
1. twice; a second time, again.
   a. second, in sequence.

在   zài   MC dzojX
1. be located at, situated; rest in; reside in, lie in; consist in, depend on.
   a. place at or on.
2. be present; exist, live.
3. (GP) locative particle, preceding place, time, extent, etc.: at, in, on.
   a. rdup., wherever; ～所 zàisuǒ, everywhere.

載   zài   MC tsojH
1. load a carriage, be laden with, take aboard.
   a. carry, esp. in vehicle; be conveyed in; transport, convey(ance); portage.
   b. fill up, pack.
2. set down, place, set out, as for sale or display.
3. begin, commence.
4. in verse, exclamatory pre-verbal particle: "ah!"
    zǎi   MC tsojX
1. indite, set down in writing; record.
2. a legal year, comprising period from any given month to its recurrence, incl. any intercalary month; also, more formal syn. of 年 nián, year, esp. as designating a particular year, e.g. XY 三～ sānzài, 3rd year of XY reign-era.

zān

簪   zān   MC tsom
1. hatpin; hairpin.
   a. insert, stick in; stab.
2. 玉～花 yùzānhuā, fragrant hosta, fragrant plantain lily (*Hosta plantaginea*), white-flowering.

zàn

暫   zàn   MC dzamH
1. for a while, temporarily; for a short time, briefly, short-term.
   a. temporize, hesitate; stall, delay.

2. suddenly, at once.
   a. just now.

瓚   zàn   MC dzanX
1. impure jade, consisting of jade and stone.
2. 2-handled jade ladle for ritual libations of millet-wine, with capacity of approx. 1 liter.

讚   zàn   MC tsanH   ⊙ 贊 *zàn* 2, 3.

贊   zàn   MC tsanH
1. assist, aid, second; e.g. (med.) ～府 zànfǔ, "assistant repositor," informal designation of Tang district adjuvant (*cheng* 丞).
   a. take part in, participate.
2. praise, acclaim, laud, appreciate, esteem.
   a. (lit.) verse genre: encomium, laud, often pertaining to persons or paintings.
3. sum up, appraise, evaluate.
   a. (lit.) prose genre: appraisal, summation, esp. in historical texts, often incorporating concluding verses and placed at end of chapter.
4. promote, advance; (re)commend.
5. proclaim, announce; e.g. ～禮 zànlǐ, ritual nuncio, official in early times who voiced the order of events during ritual performance; (Budd.) ～唄 zànbèi, recite scriptures.
6. (med.) ～普 zànpǔ (MC tsanH-phuX), trsc. Tib. *brtsan po*, title of Tibetan emperor.

蹔   zàn   MC dzamH   ⊙ 暫 *zàn*.

酇   zàn   MC tsanH
1. administrative unit in pre-imperial times, traditionally consisting of 100 households.

zāng

牂   zāng   MC tsang
1. ewe.
2. rdup., burgeon thickly.

臧   zāng   MC tsang
1. prized; advantageous, favorable.
   a. ～否 zāngpǐ, better and worse, gain and loss, prized and misprized; also, evaluate the qualities of someone.
2. pejorative term for slave, chattel; e.g. ～獲 zānghuò, "chattel and wenches," male and female slaves.
3. ⊙ 贓 *zāng*, plunder, spoils, contraband; larceny, embezzle(ment); bribe(ry).

cáng　MC dzang

1. ⊙ 藏 *cáng* 1, store up, hoard, reserve.

zàng　MC dzangH

1. ⊙ 藏 *zàng* (*cáng*), storehouse, depository, treasury.

臟　zāng　MC tsang

1. stolen goods, plunder, spoils, booty; contraband.
    a. larceny, embezzle(ment).
2. bribe(ry), buy off; suborn.
3. gross corruption.

zǎng

駔　zǎng　MC tsangX

1. stallion; steed.
2. middleman, broker, jobber, dealer, esp. for cattle transactions.

騣　zǎng　MC tsangX

1. (bn.) 骯～ *kǎngzǎng*, → 骯 *kǎng*; (bn.) 抗～ *kàngzǎng*, → 抗 *kàng*.

zàng

奘　zàng　MC dzangX

1. robust, doughty, virile.

臟　zàng　MC dzangH

1. viscera, inner organs; usu. thought of as organic systems, hence sometimes rendered "orbs"; e.g. 五～ *wǔzàng*, the 5 viscera or orbs, i.e. liver (*gan* 肝), heart (*xin* 心), spleen (*pi* 脾), lungs (*fei* 肺), loins (*shen* 腎).

葬　zàng　MC tsangH

1. bury, inter(ment); burial.

藏　zàng　MC dzangH　→ 藏 *cáng*.

zāo

糟　zāo　MC tsaw

1. lees, dregs, sediment left after fermentation of alcohol.
    a. grain-mash, residuum of filtering in process of making wine, which is spread on a board or shallow trough for pressing; e.g. ～牀 *zāochuáng*, mash-bed, the board or trough used in the pressing.

2. marinate or macerate in wine dregs.
3. euph. for something of inferior or worthless quality.

遭　zāo　MC tsaw

1. encounter, have happen to one, usu. unexpectedly, often unfavorably.
    a. experience, undergo.
2. measure-word for an occurrence: a time, a turn, a happening.

záo

鑿　záo　MC dzak

1. chisel, for woodworking.
    a. cut into, delve; chisel, bore; gouge a furrow, groove, or hole.
    b. force an interpretation, of idea or text, as if (over)straining to make a point.
2. brand, for gouging a tattoo on criminal's face or body.

zuò　MC dzawH

1. hole, puncture.
    a. mortise, cavity in a piece of wood prepared to receive a similarly shaped tenon.

MC tsak

1. finely cleaned, hulled, as of grain.
2. rdup., bright and vivid.
3. (med.) (bn.) ～落 *zuòluò* (MC tsak-lak), uneven; rough-hewn and ragged.

zǎo

早　zǎo　MC tsawX

1. morning.
2. early, ahead of time.
    a. anticipate; antedate.

棗　zǎo　MC tsawX

1. jujube, red date (*Zizyphus jujuba*), medium-sized tree or shrub with thorny branches, also its fruit which is a single-stoned drupe, wrinkled, and of dark-red or reddish-brown color.
    a. 楔～ *ruǎnzǎo*, date-plum, lilac persimmon (*Diospyrus lotus*), fruit yellow and juicy.

澡　zǎo　MC tsawX

1. wash the hands > wash, bathe; cleanse.
    a. purge, rid of impurities real or figurative.

璪 zǎo   MC tsawX

1. varicolored silk strings of small beaded jades, pearls, or other precious stones pendant from a ceremonial cap as decorative fringe.

繅 zǎo   MC tsawX

1. ⊙ 璪, hanging strings of small beads, as fringe on ceremonial headwear; 澡 *zǎo*, wash, bathe.

藻 zǎo   MC tsawX

1. pondweed, various aquatic plants similar to hornwort or mare's-tail (*Hippuris vulgaris*).
    a. 〜井 *zǎojǐng*, "pondweed well," caisson or sunken panel of ceiling, usu. figured.
2. wrack, tangled mass of seaweed or waterplants.
    a. literary ornamentation; ornate, intricate; eloquent.
    b. embellish, trim, adorn; polish, as of writing.

蚤 zǎo   MC tsawX

1. flea.
2. recessed spots or mortises of a wheel's felloe into which the spokes are fitted.
3. ⊙ 早 *zǎo*, morning; early.
    zhǎo   MC tsraewX
1. ⊙ 爪 *zhǎo*, claw, talon; nail, of fingers or toes.

zào

噪 zào   MC sawH

1. racketing clamor of birds, incessant buzzing of cicadas.
    a. din, commotion, brawl, uproar, of people.

慥 zào   MC tshawH

1. hurriedly, in a rush; rashly.
2. rdup., reliable and right-minded, honest and open.

燥 zào   MC sawX

1. dry(ness); dry out from heat.
2. warm(ed), heat(ed).
    a. provoke(d), agitate(d), burning to act; impetuous.

皂 zào   MC dzawX

1. acorn, oak-gall, which yields a black dye.
    a. ink-black, made from oak-gall; inky-black as color.
2. manger, fold, horse-stall.
    a. menial, lackey, esp. groom.

皂 zào   MC dzawX   ⊙ 皁 *zào*.

竈 zào   MC tsawH

1. stove; cooking-place, kitchen.
    a. alchemist's crucible, athanor.
    b. any man-made fire, incl. campfire.

簉 zào   MC tsrhjuwH

1. second(ary), assist(ant); subordinate, ancillary, not primary.
    a. sgl. or (med.) cmpd., 〜室 *zàoshì*, concubine.
2. (med.) located or situated in a series.
3. (med.) collect; converge.

譟 zào   MC sawH

1. din, clamor; commotion, brawl, uproar, turmoil, of people.

趮 zào   MC tsawH   ⊙ 躁 *zào*.

躁 zào   MC tsawH

1. restless, unsettled, unquiet; agitated (ant. 靜 *jìng*, still, quiet).
    a. irascible; impulsive, rash, impetuous; heated activity.
    b. disturb(ance), create turmoil.
2. (med.) quickly; urgently.

造 zào   MC tshawH

1. go to, aim for; reach, arrive at, attain; accomplish(ment); 〜詣 *zàoyì*, go to pay a call on, come to visit; also, attain a certain degree of expertise; 不〜 *bùzào*, unsuccessful, unattained, untoward.
2. (bn.) 〜次 *zàocì* (MC tshawH-tshijH), negligently, indifferently, perfunctory, as one will; hastily, summarily, impetuous and disorganized.
3. action of a woman moving to her husband's home in marriage.
    zào   MC dzawX
1. make, fashion, shape; fabricate; e.g. 〜化者 *zàohuàzhe*, Fashioner of Change, Shaper of Mutations, the selecting and synthesizing principle of Nature; 〜物者 *zàowùzhe*, Fashioner of Creatures; N.B. do not translate either of the preceding as "the Creator," since they signify nothing god-like and are not creation *ex nihilo*.
    a. construct, build; establish, found, institute.
    b. begin, commence.

zé

則　**zé**　MC **tsok**

1. standard, norm, precept; rule; example; usual, what is expected, assumed to be X.

　　a. according to norm; follow a law; make sure to . . .

　　b. conform to; imitate; e.g. ～天 *zétiān*, conformable to Heaven.

2. VB-phrase conjunction, occurs between two VB-phrases subordinating the former to the latter, specifically with the meaning "if VB-phrase 1, then VB-phrase 2"; cog. *nǎi* 乃 "only then," *ér* 而 "then"; e.g. 得之～存，失之～亡 *dé zhī zé cún, shī zhī zé wáng*, If we obtain it, then we survive; if we lose it, then we perish; 不用賢人～不行 *bùyòng xiánrén zé bùxíng*, If you do not take advantage of worthy people, then it will not work. N.B. The use of *zé* 則 typically refers to situations and expectations that reflect general patterns; that is, "if VB-phrase 1, then *as a general rule* (as usual, as expected, obviously) VB-phrase 2." It is not normally used to refer to specific "if . . ., then . . ." circumstances.

　　a. occurring after a noun or noun-phrase and before a VB-phrase, gives the noun or noun phrase a verbal "flavor" by raising it as the proposed topic of the sentence, "if it is noun-phrase that we are talking about, then . . .," "if it is noun-phrase that is at issue, then . . ." "given noun-phrase as the focus of our attention, then . . ."; e.g. 臣～可, 君～不可 *chén zé kě, jūn zé bùkě*, If it is a vassal that we are talking about, then it is okay; if it is a lord, then it is not okay; 國王～大夫必從 *guówáng zé dàfū bì cóng* If it is the king of the state, then the grand masters will inevitably follow.

　　b. following interr. or imperative phrase, indicates consequential intention: "therewith, so that . . ."; e.g. 何為～民服 *héwéi zé mín fú*, What to do with them, so that the commonfolk be submissive?; 民必教～可使矣 *mín bì jiào zé kěshǐ yǐ*, The commonfolk must be instructed and therewith may be made use of.

嘖　**zé**　MC **dzreak**

1. contest, dispute.

　　a. pother; outburst; outcry.

嘖　**zé**　MC **tsreak**

1. rdup., twittering and chirping of birds, creaking of insects; also, clucking and chirking in approbation.

幘　**zé**　MC **tsreak**

1. headkerchief, headwrap; turban; in early times worn by commonfolk, by mid-Han times worn by all classes.

擇　**zé**　MC **draek**

1. select, choose; separate out, prefer.

　　a. mark off, delineate; distinguish.

澤　**zé**　MC **draek**

1. low-lying and well-watered open terrain: marsh(y), marshland, mere; palustral.

　　a. ～蘭 *zélán*, marsh thoroughwort, syn. 山蘭 *shānlán*, wild eupatory or thoroughwort (*Eupatorium japonicum, Eupatorium fortunei*); also, bugleweed (*Lycopus lucidus*), a kind of flowering mint; ～漆 *zéqī*, "marsh lacquer," euphorbia, spurge (*Euphorbia helioscopa*), so named because of its lacquer-like sap; ～芹 *zéqín*, "marsh dropwort" (*Sium suave*), water parsnip.

2. dew-moistened, dewy; bedew.

　　a. imbue, moisten; saturate.

　　b. glossy; sheen, glisten(ing); polish.

3. enrich; fructify, as with life-enhancing moisture.

　　a. of writings, enhance, polish, embellish; make better, improve.

4. bounty, favor, beneficence, special kindliness granted by someone in superior position, esp. the ruler; almifluence.

5. saliva; sweat; bodily moisture.

　　a. underclothes, ⊙ 襗 *zé*.

6. open terrain (not under water) covered with grass, bushes, shrubs, trees, susceptible to occasional flooding: grassland, meadow, heath, moor.

　　a. ～虞 *zéyú*, "warden of the moor," short-eared owl (*Asio flammeus*).

笮　**zé**　MC **tsraek**

1. narrow, constrained; strait(ened).

　　a. in straitened or trying circumstances.

2. press, constrain.

　　a. a press, for squeezing juice, oil, wine, etc.

　　b. constrain(ed), press(ed), force(d).

3. bamboo quiver, for arrows.
4. bamboo lathwork under the tiles of a roof.

zuó   MC dzak
1. bamboo plaiting, cable made of twisted bamboo fibers.
2. ⊙ 鑿 *záo*, bore, drill.

簀   zé   MC tsreak
1. bamboo-plaited bed.
   a. bamboo-plaited sitting-mat.

舴   zé   MC traek
1. (med.) (bn.) ～艋 *zéměng* (MC traek-maengX), small boat, bark, skiff.

襗   zé   MC draek
1. underclothes.

賾   zé   MC tsreak
1. demand, exact; require; e.g. ～善 *zéshàn*, demand goodness (in friendship).
   a. procure, appropriate, wrest from.
2. call to account, insist on explanation.
3. dispraise, reprove; blame, criticize, censure.
   a. (med.) punish, penalize.
4. lay responsibility on; impose upon.

zhài   MC tsreaH
1. (med.) ⊙ 債 *zhài*, debt, be in debt to.

賾   zé   MC dzreak
1. recondite, abstruse; cryptic; mystery.

迮   zé   MC tsraek
1. press(ed), constrain(ed); force(d).
2. narrow, constrained.
3. block(ed), obstruct(ed).
4. hastily, in a hurry.

齰   zé   MC dzraek
1. bite, bite off; gnaw; e.g. ～舌 *zéshé*, bite one's tongue, be reticent; also, keep one's feelings inside.
   a. chew, munch.

zè

仄   zè   MC tsrik
1. slanting, oblique, loxotic.
   a. awry; irregular.
2. oblique or "deflected" tones of the spoken language, i.e., 上 *shǎng*, 去 *qù*, and 入 *rù* (as opp. to "level" tone 平 *píng*).

3. ～陋 *zèlòu*, petty, picayunish, of slight account.

昃   zè   MC tsrik
1. sun slanting westward; the afternoon hours.

zéi

賊   zéi   MC dzok
1. outlaw; bandit(ry), brigand(age); villain(y), esp. against ruler or state.
   a. thief, robber.
   b. (med.) used playfully: rascal, rogue.
2. despoil; injure, harm, maltreat; murder(er).
3. infringe on one's possessions or character.
4. (med.) violently, savagely.

zèn

譖   zèn   MC tsrimH
1. calumniate, slander, malign, accuse falsely; defame, vilify; insult, impugn.

zēng

增   zēng   MC tsong
1. increase, augment; add to.
   a. intensify; increment(al).

céng   MC dzong
1. ⊙ 層 *céng*, double(d); layer(ed), tier(ed).

憎   zēng   MC tsong
1. hate, loathe, despise, detest.

曾   zēng   MC tsong   → 曾 *céng*.

矰   zēng   MC tsong
1. leashed arrow, short arrow or dart with silk string attached for retrieval, used in shooting birds.

磳   zēng   MC tsong
1. (med.) (bn.) 碐～ *léngzēng*, → 碐 *léng*.

繒   zēng   MC dzing
1. tabby silk, plain-weave based on a unit of two warp ends and two weft picks in which each end passes over one and under one pick.
   a. gen. term for silk fabric, silk-stuff.
2. ⊙ 矰 *zēng*, leashed arrow.

罾　zēng　MC tsong

1. fishing-net.
   a. to catch fish with a net.

zèng

甑　zèng　MC tsingH

1. rice-steamer, pot with perforated bottom; also used for steaming mash in process of making wine.

贈　zèng　MC dzongH

1. present to, give to.
   a. bestow a posthumous title on.
2. chase away, esp. malevolent spirits.

zhā

㫲　zhā　MC traet

1. (bn.) 嘲～ zhāozhā, → 嘲 zhāo.

扎　zhā　MC tsreat

1. pull up or away, pull off.

攎　zhā　MC tsrae

1. take up, take in hand; grasp, seize.

楂　zhā　MC dzrae　→ 楂 chá.

樝　zhā　MC tsrae

1. Japanese quince, lesser quince (*Chaenomeles cathayensis*), small tree with thorny branches, yielding pink to white flowers and pear-shaped pomes which are yellow and smaller than the ordinary quince (*mugua* 木瓜).
2. sgl. or 山～ *shānzhā*, hawthorn, thornapple; haw(berry) (various species of *Crataegus*), fruits are small red pomes.

皻　zhā　MC tsrae　⊙ 皻 zhā.

皻　zhā　MC tsrae

1. (med.) red blisters on or prominent vascularity or blotching of the nose; brandy nose.

zhá

笧　zhá　MC treap

1. stab, prick; drive in; stitch.

札　zhá　MC tsreat

1. bundle of wooden tablets tied together, on which characters were written, primarily for official documents (cf. 冊 *cè*, same of bamboo tablets).
   a. (Dao.) register of life or death, in the keeping of certain divinities.
   b. (med.) transcribe, copy out.
2. letter, epistle, billet.
3. plates or leaves of armor.
4. contagion; die of contagion, epidemic.
5. rdup., onom. of the back-and-forth chucking of a shuttle when weaving on a loom.

閘　zhá　MC ʻaep

1. sluice-gate, water-gate, flood-gate; lock.

zhǎ

鮺　zhǎ　MC tsraeX

1. salted fish; fish-pickle.

zhà

乍　zhà　MC dzraeH

1. all at once; unexpectedly.
   a. (med.) just now; at first.
2. for the time being, temporarily.
   a. ADV of successive apposition, e.g. ～A～B, no sooner A than B.
3. (med.) auxiliary VB of preference: would rather (do X), better (do X).
4. (med.) just right, exactly.

吒　zhà　MC traeH

1. ⊙ 咤 *zhà* 1, rave at, curse, fulminate; reproach.

咋　zhà　MC dzraeH

1. ⊙ 乍 *zhà* 1, all at once; unexpectedly.
   zé　MC tsreak
1. bite; gnaw.
2. call out; shout.

咤　zhà　MC traeH

1. sgl. or in cmpd. 叱～ *chìzhà*, rave at, curse, fulminate; reproach.
2. onom. of eating noisily and with gusto, smacking the lips.
3. onom. of exclamatory admiration or sighing regret.

4. (med.) (bn.) ～沙 *zhàshā* (MC traeH-srae), open(ly), widespread.

chà   MC trhaeH

1. ⊙ 詫 *chà*, brag, vaunt, exaggerate.

褡   **zhà   MC dzraeH**

1. ancient festival at end of agricultural year, including collective sacrifice in thanksgiving to all divinities as well as eating and drinking on a grand scale.

蜡   **zhà   MC dzraeH**   ⊙ 褡 *zhà*.

詐   **zhà   MC tsraeH**

1. fraudulent, mendacious; duplicitous; disingenuous.

    a. cheat, deceive; pass off, defraud; treacherous.

    b. impose upon, take advantage of.

zhāi

摘   **zhāi   MC treak**

1. pick up by hand; pluck; gather up.

    a. extract from; select(ion).

2. pick at or out to hold accountable; reprove, reproach, criticize; blame.

    tì   MC thek

1. put in motion, activate, start; push off, as a boat.

2. vex, bother, disturb; agitate.

齋   **zhāi   MC tsreaj**

1. purify oneself before ritual ceremony, purge body and mind by various prescribed measures, e.g. bathing, fasting, meditation, etc.

    a. actions of ritual purification, such as abstinence and those named above.

    b. purge; refresh; clean out.

2. (Budd.) devotee's eating of vegetarian meal; offer of vegetarian food to a monk.

3. retreat, place of quiet withdrawal from the everyday world; study, studio, place for private reading, writing, and contemplation, often amidst a landscape garden.

4. (Dao.) various collective rituals particularly associated with Lingbao liturgy, incl. rites of repentance, for salvation of the dead, for relieving sickness, for protection of the emperor and welfare of the nation, etc.

zhái

宅   **zhái   MC draek**

1. residence, house, dwelling; accommodation; place to be at ease; cog. 託 *tuō*, take refuge in.

    a. reside at, dwell at.

    b. accommodate, contain comfortably.

2. place of official business, government site.

    a. occupy a public charge.

3. gravesite, burial place.

翟   **zhái   MC draek**   → 翟 *dí*.

zhǎi

窄   **zhǎi   MC tsraek**

1. narrow; contracted, straitened; squeezed; limited.

zhài

債   **zhài   MC tsreaH**

1. debt; be in debt to, for money or goods.

    a. ask for temporary use of with promise to repay; borrow.

2. money or goods themselves; also (med.), used metaphorically for something traded or given of worth, e.g. a poem.

寨   **zhài   MC dzraejH**

1. stockade, military camp; entrenchment, palisade; mountain stronghold.

瘵   **zhài   MC tsreajH**

1. congestion of the lungs.

    a. suffering, distress.

砦   **zhài   MC dzraejH**   ⊙ 寨 *zhài*.

zhān

占   **zhān   MC tsyem**

1. prognosticate, esp. by observing cracks produced from heated turtle-shell or by prescribed manipulation of yarrow stalks, prognostication; divine, divination; prefigure.

    a. unriddle omens, interpret signs; mantic; foresight; e.g. ～夢 *zhānmèng*, oneiromancy, interpret dreams; ～候 *zhānhòu*, prognosticate by means of atmospheric phenomena.

b. inspect carefully, look closely at; watch over; spy.

2. infer, deduce; conjecture, theorize.

3. (med.) first element in trsc. of the name Champa (kingdom of the Cham peoples, who were largely in control of central and of southern coastal Vietnam from the 2nd c.), e.g. 〜不勞 *zhānbùláo* (MC tsyem-pjuw-law) or 〜婆 *zhānpó* (MC tsyem-ba); sometimes stands for whole name, e.g. 〜稻 *zhāndào*, Champa rice.

zhàn　MC tsyemH

1. (med.) occupy, hold; take possession of, appropriate, take by force; usurp.

　　a. (med.) (bn.) 〜斷 *zhànduàn* (MC tsyemH-dwanH), control completely; also, enjoy alone, enjoy to the fullest.

2. (med.) take one's stand, stake out a position.

3. (med.) recount or instruct orally; e.g. 〜對 *zhànduì*, reply informally.

　　a. (med.) dictate, for someone else to record; read aloud.

4. report a particular number (as of a census or tax registry) to higher authority.

旃　zhān　MC tsyen

1. oriflamme, pure-red undecorated banner, indicative of authority.

　　a. exhibit, show forth, esp. one's power or influence.

2. ⊙ 氈 *zhān*, felt.

3. GP, contraction of 之焉 *zhī yān*, "OBJ in it, on it, toward it, etc."

4. (med.) (bn.) 〜檀 *zhāntán* (MC trjen-dan), trsc. of Skt. *candana*, sandal(wood).

旜　zhān　MC tsyen　⊙ 旃 *zhān*.

氈　zhān　MC tsyen

1. felt; items made of felt fabric, e.g. carpet, clothes, throws, blankets.

沾　zhān　MC trjem

1. moist(en), damp(en); soak, imbue with.

　　a. to steep.

2. pile with favors, provide benefits, bestowals; e.g. 〜洽 *zhānqià*, saturated with rain or dew; also, wholly bestowed with kindness; also, deeply steeped with learning; also, on the most deeply favorable terms.

3. rdup., boastful and blustering, smug and self-regarding.

瞻　zhān　MC tsyem

1. look upwards; gaze forward; e.g. 〜烏 *zhānwū*, look toward the raven (which roosts on the roof of the wealthy), hence seek favor or protection.

　　a. look up to, regard with respect; admire.

詹　zhān　MC tsyem

1. oversee(r), intend(ant); e.g. 〜事 *zhānshì*, intendant of affairs, chief executive of heir-apparent's establishment.

2. sgl. or rdup., garrulous, verbose, long-winded.

3. arrive at, reach to.

4. ⊙ 瞻 *zhān*, look upwards; regard; 蟾 *chán*, toad.

5. (med.) 〜糖香 *zhāntángxiāng*, a copal or elemi extracted from the kanari or Java almond tree (*Canarium commune*).

譫　zhān　MC tsyem

1. garrulous, verbose, prating, long-winded, ⊙ 詹 *zhān* 2.

2. delirious babble, prattle, blather, jabber.

邅　zhān　MC trjen

1. change course, change direction; veer away; detour.

　　a. circle round; e.g. 〜如 *zhānrú*, 〜回 *zhānhúi*, waver and skirt, dilly-dally, go round in circles.

2. (med.) (bn.) 〜迍 *zhānzhūn* (MC trjen-trwin) or 迍〜 *zhūnzhān*, perilous and precarious, arduous and hard-pressed, difficult and dangerous.

霑　zhān　MC trjem　⊙ 沾 *zhān* 1, 2.

饘　zhān　MC tsyen

1. thick congee or gruel, made of rice or millet (cf. 粥 *zhū*, thin congee).

鱣　zhān　MC trjen

1. the sturgeon (*Acipenser sinensis*); syn. 黃魚 *huángyú*.

shàn　MC dzyenX

1. the mud-eel (*Heterenchelyidae* or *Flutidae*).

鸇　zhān　MC tsyen

1. merlin, pigeon-hawk (*Falco columbarius*), a small falcon.

zhán

薝 **zhán**   MC tsyem

1. (bn.) 〜蔔 *zhánbó* (MC tsyem-bok), champak (*Magnolia champaca*), with strongly fragrant white or yellow flowers, trsc. Skt. *campaka*; syn. 黃蘭 *huánglán*.

zhǎn

展 **zhǎn**   MC trjenX

1. unfold, unroll; extend, spread out; open out, display.
   a. exhibit, show; express freely; reveal.
   b. prolong, lengthen, esp. time.
2. examine, scrutinize; turn over for inspection, look at from all sides.
3. be true, truly, sincere(ly).
4. 〜轉 *zhǎnzhuǎn*, toss and turn, as of restless sleep; turn over in one's mind; also, moving on without pause, from here to there; also, one after another, by turns, in turn.

嶄 **zhǎn**   MC dzreamX

1. sgl. or 〜然 *zhǎnrán*, eminent(ly), overtopping, elevated; prominent(ly), outstanding.

chán   MC dzraem

1. (bn.) 〜巖 *chányán* (MC dzraem-ngaem) cragged cliffs, craggy steeps, steeply scarped.
2. rdup., peaked and pinnacled.

斬 **zhǎn**   MC tsreamX

1. cut in two, bisect; cut off; cleave.
   a. as judicial punishment, cut in two at the waist; also, behead.
2. cut short, interrupt; put an end to.
3. mourning garment with unstitched lower border.
4. (med.) 〜新 *zhǎnxīn*, just now, only just, just a short time ago; also, brand-new, newfledged, fresh.

琖 **zhǎn**   MC tsreanX   ⊙ 盞 *zhǎn*.

盞 **zhǎn**   MC tsreanX

1. small or shallow wine-cup, cannikin.
   a. a paltry amount, jigger.
   b. measure-word for a number of wine-cups or (med.) a number of lamps.

蹍 **zhǎn**   MC trjenX

1. trample, stamp on, tread on.
   a. march onward.
2. (med.) 〜然 *zhǎnrán*, curled up, huddled.

輾 **zhǎn**   MC trjenX

1. 〜轉 *zhǎnzhuǎn*, ⊙ 展轉 *zhǎnzhuǎn*, → 展 *zhǎn* 4.

niǎn   MC nrjenX

1. (med.) crush, squash; compress; grind, roll over.
   a. (med.) roller, grinder.

醆 **zhǎn**   MC tsreanX

1. ⊙ 盞 *zhǎn*.
2. decanted wine.

颭 **zhǎn**   MC tsyemX

1. wind-tossed; wind-stirred, wind-whipped.

zhàn

戰 **zhàn**   MC tsyenH

1. battle, combat; fight with weapons; clash of arms; war.
   a. struggle, contend for; e.g. (med.) 〜勝 *zhànshèng*, contest the prize, i.e. sit for the civil-service exam.
2. tremble, shiver with fright (cog. 憚 *dàn*, quail at, shy away from); e.g. 〜汗 *zhànhàn*, sweat with trepidation.

暫 **zhàn**   → 暫 *zàn*.

棧 **zhàn**   MC dzraenH

1. sgl. or 〜道 *zhàndào*, edgeway, cliffway, railing, wooden walkway cantilevered out from the face of a cliff, esp. along the mountain route from the state of Qin 秦 to the state of Shu 蜀.
2. stall, shed, protective dwelling for livestock.
3. carriage box, made of bamboo or wooden laths, for conveying goods, provisions, soldiers, etc.
   a. barrow-cart, wagon, tumbrel.
4. a species of aloeswood.

湛 **zhàn**   MC dreamX

1. sgl. or rdup., thickly piled, deep; so deep as to be fathomless.

a. deeply placid, motionless, unstirring, still, tranquil.

2. let stand > set out, exhibit.

3. clear, crystal-clear, pellucid, limpid.

chén　MC drim

1. plunge into, immerse, sink.

    a. melt away, subside; blot out; die.

jiān　MC tsjem

1. soak(ing), steep(ed).

dān　MC tom

1. relish, revel, rejoice in; sunk, steeped, immersed in pleasure or enjoyment.

綻　zhàn　MC dreanH

1. unstitched; ripped apart, esp. at the seam.

    a. tear open, split; rupture, rend.

    b. burst open, break open.

2. mend, sew up, stitch.

蘸　zhàn　MC tsreamH

1. immerse in liquid, soak, macerate; marinade.

    a. brim over.

2. (med.) gen. term for dissolved matter, e.g. juice, powder, leavings, meltings.

輚　zhàn　MC dzraenH

1. caravan, carriage for reclining.

2. ⊙ 棧 zhàn 3a, barrow-cart, wagon, tumbrel.

轏　zhàn　MC dzreanX　⊙ 輚 zhàn.

顫　zhàn　MC tsyenH

1. head tremors.

    a. tremble, shudder, shiver, jitter.

shān　MC syen

1. able to distinguish odors, have a discerning nose.

驏　zhàn　MC dzraenX

1. unsaddled and unbridled horse.

    a. ride bareback.

zhāng

嫜　zhāng　MC tsyang

1. (med.) father-in-law.

張　zhāng　MC trjang

1. string a bow (ant. 弛 chí, unstring or loosen a bow).

    a. tune a zither or other stringed instrument; e.g. 高～ gāozhāng, tune to a high tone.

b. tense, taut, tightly strung; on edge, "uptight."

2. bend or draw a bow.

    a. stretch, extend; expand; dilate.

    b. magnify, amplify; exaggerate, inflate.

3. open out, spread out; gape; patulous, patulent; e.g. ～目 zhāngmù, open the eyes wide.

4. set out, arrange; set forth; e.g. ～飲 zhāngyǐn, set up [a tent] for a feast.

    a. dispose a net to trap birds or small game > entrap, draw in.

    b. bolster, prop; extend so as to provide support.

5. "Extension," one of the 28 lunar lodgings, comprised of υ, λ, φ, μ, χ, ν Hydrae in the southern quadrant (*chiniao* 赤鳥) of the sky.

6. measure-word for items with flat or relatively large surfaces.

7. a surname.

zhàng　MC trjangH

1. ⊙ 脹 zhàng, distend, swell, expand.

2. (med.) cover over; e.g. ～天 zhàngtiān, block out the sky.

彰　zhāng　MC tsyang

1. evident, manifest, clearly display(ed), show(n) in all distinctiveness; signal, call attention to.

2. decorate(d), beautifully designed; splendid; vivid, brilliant.

樟　zhāng　MC tsyang

1. 1. sgl. or in cmpd. 橡～ yùzhāng, camphor tree (*Cinnamomum camphora*).

獐　zhāng　MC tsyang　⊙ 麞 zhāng.

璋　zhāng　MC tsyang

1. jade demi-scepter, traditionally half of a *gui* 圭 divided vertically, used in ritual ceremonies (cog. 章 zhāng 1, distinctive item, emblem, insignia).

2. (em)blazon, render illustrious.

    a. announce, proclaim; display, exhibit.

章　zhāng　MC tsyang

1. embroidered pattern > distinctive mark, distinction, decoration, display; figure, figuring.

    a. design, (em)blazon; emblem(atic), insignia.

    b. woven article with colorfully ornamented pattern.

    c. distinctive item of authority, with special design, esp. a seal.

2. set forth, present to sight; evince, manifest, show forth; express(ive).

    a. make clear, illustrate; articulate.

    b. memorial, a composition forwarded to the ruler, usu. presenting advice or expressing gratitude; e.g. 上～ *shàngzhāng*, send up a petition to the throne; also, (Dao.) beseech the celestial officials for favor.

3. clearly and properly displayed, well-ordered.

    a. model, example for imitation > rule, regulation, standard.

4. a complete section of music, song, verse, or prose > stanza, strophe, paragraph.

    a. ～句 *zhāngjù*, chapter and verse, paragraph and line, esp. minutely detailed commentary on early or canonical texts.

    b. complete, consummate; coordinate.

5. Metonic cycle, equiv. 235 synodic months, i.e. 19 years incl. 7 intercalary months.

6. largest trees of a forest, the giants of the wood.

7. ～柳根 *zhāngliǔgēn*, pokeweed, pokebush, pokeberry (*Phytolacca acinosa*).

8. a surname.

粻   zhāng   MC trjang

1. provisions, provender.

蟑   zhāng   MC tsyang

1. (med.) ～蜋 *zhāngláng* (MC tsyang-lang), cockroach, esp. flying cockroach.

麞   zhāng   MC tsyang

1. roe-deer (*Moschus chinloo*).

    a. (med.) river-deer (*Hydropotes inermis*).

2. musk-deer (*Moschus moschiferus*), syn. 麝 *shè*.

zhǎng

掌   zhǎng   MC tsyangX

1. palm of the hand.

    a. paw or pad of an animal, hoof of a horse.

    b. strike with the hand, forehand, smack.

2. forehold, be preposited to; hold in hand, control, manage(r), in charge of.

    a. prefixed to official titles, with following OBJ designating activity or agency for which one is responsible.

3. ～參 *zhǎngshēn*, fragrant orchid (*Gymnodenia conopsea*), flowers varying from white and pink to pink-purple; syn. 手參 *shǒushēn*.

漲   zhǎng   MC trjangX

1. rising water, brimming.

    a. increase; mount, lift; advance.

2. replete, full(ness), copious, bountiful, plentiful.

    zhàng   MC trjangH

1. swell, dilate; distend, expand; engorge; fill out, puff up, billow, inflate; rise.

長   zhǎng   MC trjangX   → 長 *cháng*.

zhàng

丈   zhàng   MC drjangX

1. a measurement of length: 10 尺 *chǐ*, a ten-foot, a stave (cog. 杖 *zhàng*, staff, stave).

    a. to measure.

2. sgl. or in cmpd. ～人 *zhàngrén* or ～夫 *zhàngfū*, grown-up, adult male; also, an elder, venerable, esp. respectful term of address: (you) my elder; also, person of quality, doyen, dean; also, (med.) father-in-law.

仗   zhàng   MC drjangX

1. arms employed in warfare.

2. arms or insignia carried for ceremony, solemnity, or pageantry.

    a. honor-guard, soldiers detailed to enhance by their presence and appearance the dignity of the ruler; also, the ruler's personal guard unit.

3. hold to; brandish.

    a. rely on, lean on.

嶂   zhàng   MC tsyangH

1. hill-screen, mountain(s) set like a folding panel, barrier of peaks (cog. 障 *zhàng*, barrier, screen, partition).

帳   zhàng   MC trjangH

1. a fabric stretched (cog. 張 *zhāng*) to provide privacy or protection: drape, hanging; canopy, valance.

    a. the same but on a larger scale: tent, pavilion.

2. (med.) register of accounts, account-book.

杖   zhàng   MC drjangX

1. staff, stave, stock, walking-stick to lean on.

2. hold onto.

    a. rely on, lean on.

3. cudgel; bastinade; used in warfare or in administering judicial punishment; heavier punishment than 笞 *chī*.

4. (med.) drumstick, beater.

瘴 zhàng MC tsyangH

1. miasma, mephitis, pestilential vapors or exhalations, thought to rise from damp and putrid areas and to cause disease; esp. associated with the south.

脹 zhàng MC trjangH

1. bodily swelling, esp. of the stomach; distension; turgescent, tumescent; e.g. (med.) ～滿 *zhàngmǎn*, ascites, fluid build-up in peritoneal cavity.

   a. expand, dilate, blow up.

2. (med.) meatpuff, meatball.

障 zhàng MC tsyangH

1. barrier; interrupt(ion), separation.

   a. hinder, hindrance; prevent(ion); obstruct (-ion).

   b. (Budd.) karmic blockage from former life.

2. standing screen, panel, partition, often ornamental or painted.

   a. windbreak, of connected screens or extended silk curtains; e.g. 步～ *bùzhàng*, windbreak for walking.

3. frontier outpost at strategic point, fortification, barricade, redoubt.

4. ⊙ 瘴 *zhàng*, miasma.

zhāo

啁 zhāo MC traew

1. (bn.) ～哳 *zhāozhā* (MC traew-traet), onom. of chitter-chatter of birds; also, mestive murmur; also, shrill skirl of flute.

   zhōu MC trjuw
1. (bn.) ～噍 *zhōujiāo* or ～啾 *zhōujiū* (MC trjuw-tsjuw), wren, syn. 鵁鷯 *jiāoliáo*, onom. of its low cry, "tsew-tsyew"; also. onom. of other bird-calls; also, congruent concord of harmonious music.

抓 zhāo MC tsraew

1. scratch or scrape with nails or claws.

   a. touch lightly with the nails, tickle.

2. pick up with nails or claws; claw up, scrape up.

招 zhāo MC tsyew

1. call with a motion of the hand, summon, beckon.

   a. lead on, invite over, attract to; recruit, recommend; e.g. ～募 *zhāomù*, levy troops.

   b. provoke, incite, exhort to VB; bring about, effect; e.g. ～怨 *zhāoyuàn*, stir resentment.

2. target, mark, butt.

3. tie the legs of; shackle.

4. (med.) confess, acknowledge fault or crime; give public notice; ～認 *zhāorèn*, admit and acknowledge, take full responsibility for; ～念 *zhāoniàn*, extend thanks, express gratitude.

5. (bn.) ～搖 *zhāoyáo* (MC tsyew-yew), parade and make public, be open and overt, show off to all; also, "Brandishing Battler," name of the last star in the Northern Dipper's handle, Alkaid or Benetnash (ε Ursae Majoris), but sometimes identified as Nekkar (β Boötis) which is then considered as final extension of the Dipper's handle, in either case being symbolic of warfare.

6. (Budd.) ～提 *zhāotí* or ～提僧 *zhāotísēng* (MC tsyew-dej-song), trsc. of Skt. *caturdiśa*[*saṃgha*], "4-square," hence a term for rectangular monastic compound, sometimes interpreted as "4 quarters" because monasteries were supposed to belong to all the 4 quarters; official designation of monasteries after 424 in the Northern Wei; in Tang times usu. ref. a small sanctuary.

   qiáo MC gjiew
1. raise, bring forward.

   sháo MC dzyew
1. ⊙ 韶 *sháo*, name of the music traditionally identified with the sage-king Shun 舜.

2. (bn.) ～搖 *sháoyáo* (MC dzyew-yew), ⊙ 逍遙 *xiāoyáo*, wander free and easy.

昭 zhāo MC tsyew

1. radiant, shining, illuminant; splendid.

   a. bright; perceptive, percipient; astute.

2. shine on, illuminate, brighten; show, display, manifest.

   a. declare, proclaim.

3. ～穆 *zhāomù*, sequential order of ancestral tablets in family shrine, placed alternately to the left and right of the founder's tablet (facing south), those on the left designated *zhāo* being

the even-numbered successors (beginning with 2), those on the right designated *mu* being the odd-numbered successors.

朝   zhāo   MC trjew
1. morning, the time from after sunrise to the first meal; matinal; e.g. ～夕 *zhāoxī*, morning and evening; ～陽 *zhāoyáng*, morning sunlight.
2. by synecdoche, daytime, the whole day until nightfall.
   a. a particular day, indicating a specific occurrence or beginning of a certain period, e.g. 一～ *yīzhāo*, on a certain day, "once upon a time"; also, indicating an unplanned occurrence, "all at once one day."
   b. (med.) ～來 *zhāolái*, just now; a short while ago.

   cháo   MC drjew
1. court audience, imperial levee, gathering for audience with ruler and his discharge of public affairs, taking place in the first hours of the day; pay morning respects at court (cf. 夕 *xī*, pay evening respects, evening audience).
2. the court of a ruler; seat of government prestige, administration, and ceremony; e.g. ～野 *cháoyě*, court and countryside, the court and the rest of the state.
   a. administrative seat of a high-ranking local magistrate.
3. pay court, present oneself for imperial audience; e.g. ～宗 *cháozōng*, visits made by feudal lords to sovereign in spring and summer, respectively; also, proceed to where one owes allegiance or seeks refuge.
   a. "pay court" or treat with honor an individual whose rank, influence, or ability exceeds one's own; pay homage to.
4. gen. term for dynasty; succession of rulers from the same family or line.
5. be turned toward X, in the direction of X, facing X.

zhǎo

沼   zhǎo   MC tsyewX
1. pool, pond.

爪   zhǎo   MC tsraewX
1. claw, talon; e.g. ～牙 *zhǎoyá*, talons and teeth, euph. brave followers; also, henchmen, partisans; also, troublemaker, provocateur; 兵～ *bīngzhǎo*, "weapon-talon," first claw of a crane's foot.

2. fingernail, toenail.
   a. scratch, claw at; score, dig one's nails into.
3. plectrum, for use with stringed instruments, esp. *pipa* (lute).

zhào

兆   zhào   MC drjewX
1. divination by interpreting the cracks produced when heating dressed turtle-shells, cheloniomancy.
2. gen. term for divination; prophecy, mantic.
   a. sign, omen, portent(ous), manifestation.
3. begin(ning), origin(ate).
4. area reserved for specific purpose, esp. for sacrificial altar or as burial ground.
   a. 京～ *jīngzhào*, capital municipality.
5. sixth-order number, used imprecisely to designate an enormous amount: a million, a billion.
6. (Dao.) an individual person; one's own, my; also, you(r), yourself.

召   zhào   MC drjewH
1. call out to, call over.
   a. beckon; invite; lead on.

   shào   MC dzyewH
1. (lit.) ～南 *shàonán*, "Shaonan," 2nd of the first 2 groupings of *Shijing* odes (i.e. the "2 nan," the first being "Zhounan" 周南) in the "Guofeng" 國風 section of the anthology, Shao being the name of a fiefdom during the early Zhou.

旐   zhào   MC drjewX
1. banner ornamented with a serpent coiled round a tortoise (*xuanwu* 玄武, emblematic sign of the north), indicative of warfare.
2. funeral banner, placed at head of cortege taking deceased's coffin to the burial site.

棹   zhào   MC draewH
1. ⊙ 櫂 *zhào*, oar; row(er); boat.

   zhuō   MC draewk
1. large subtropical evergreen tree resembling the Chinese cedrela (*chun* 椿), possibly the neem-tree (*Azadirachta indica*).

櫂   zhào   MC draewH
1. long oar, scull, sweep.
   a. to row; rower; e.g. ～歌 *zhàogē*, rowing song; ～謳 *zhào'ōu*, barcarole.
   b. by synecdoche, gen. term for boat.

炤　zhào　MC tsyewH　⊙ 照 zhào.

照　zhào　MC tsyewH

1. shining, radiant, light-filled.
   a. beams or rays of light, esp. of sun or moon.
2. light up, illuminate; make visible, show forth.
3. reflect(ion), in mirror or water; look at one's reflection.
   a. (med.) image, portrait, likeness.
4. inspect, regard, look carefully at.
   a. perceive, be conscious of.

罩　zhào　MC taewH

1. fish-trap, made of bamboo.
   a. catch, trap.
2. cover; overtop.

肇　zhào　MC drjewX

1. commence(ment), institute, found; advent; often used in med. times for archaic flavor.
   a. begin(ning), introduce; instigate; e.g. ～跡 zhàojī, start making visible tracks, make one's first mark.
   b. activate, active; diligent.
2. form the design or plan of.
3. rectify, bring to standard.

詔　zhào　MC tsyewH

1. imperial order containing specific command or prohibition; proclamation, fiat.
2. declare, proclaim; order.
   a. instruct; admonish.
3. convene, call together.
   a. draft, conscript.
4. (med.) term for "king" in the local language of southwestern peoples during the Tang.

趙　zhào　MC drjewX

1. hasten, move quickly toward.
2. name of one of the 7 major states of the Warring States period, comprising parts of present-day northern Shanxi, western and southern Hebei.
3. a surname.

diào　MC dewX

1. cut into the ground, delve, with hoes or mattocks.

zhē

遮　zhē　MC tsyae

1. place obstacles before, obstruct; block, interpose; arrest, interrupt.
   a. make a distinction between, separate, e.g. 無～ wúzhē, without distinction, (Budd.) ref. to both monks and laymen.
2. (med.) cover, mask, block the view of; stop up.
   a. (med.) place in the shade, screen, trap; e.g. ～羅 zhēluó, trap and net.
   b. (med.) place in one's debt; e.g. ～囑 zhēzhǔ, entrust, enjoin, ask to do.
3. (med.) demonstrative pronoun: "this, these"; ⊙ 這 zhè.
   a. (med.) ～莫 zhēmò or ～不 zhēbù, even though, despite, no matter if…, who cares if…?

zhé

哲　zhé　MC trjet

1. wise, possessing discernment of what is true and proper; insightful.
   a. shrewd, cunning, crafty (when used in pejorative sense).

喆　zhé　MC trjet　⊙ 哲 zhé.

慴　zhé　MC tsyep

1. fear, dread, dismay.
   a. intimidate(d), fright(en).

折　zhé　MC tsyet

1. break with the hands; break off or apart; e.g. ～柳 zhéliǔ, break off a willow-branch (at parting).
   a. analyze, break up, dissect; e.g. ～字 zhézì, prognosticate from analyzing the graphic components of personal names, glyphomancy.
2. bend, twist; crook; bow.
   a. eddy, swirl (of water).
3. break down, fracture; overpower, smash; crush.
   a. humble, bring down, subdue; overthrow.
4. cut off > decide, determine; adjudicate; e.g. ～獄 zhéyù, settle a litigation; ～中 zhézhōng, take the middle course, compromise, mediate.

5. have one's destiny cut short, die, esp. prematurely or unexpectedly.

6. lose, deteriorate; forfeit, yield.

7. ⊙ 坼 *chè*, crack open, burst forth.

zhé   MC dzyet

1. MC pronunciation for intransitive VB forms of meanings above.

摺 **zhé   MC tsyep**

1. (med.) fold, crease, pleat.

lā   MC lop

1. pull out, wrench apart; break.

晢 **zhé   MC tsyet**   ⊙ 晰 *zhé*.

晰 **zhé   MC tsyet**

1. sgl. or rdup., brilliant, luminous, lustrous and lucent.

2. perspicacious, perceptive, discerning.

磔 **zhé   MC traek**

1. rend and lay open a sacrificial animal for ritual offering.

   a. judicial punishment of dismembering by being torn limb from limb by chariots pulling in different directions; also, splitting open the chest of a corpse, laying bare its organs to be scavenged.

2. split open, stretch open, split, crack.

3. bristle, stand up, as hair.

蜇 **zhé   MC trjet**

1. sting of a venomous insect or snake; syn. 螫 *shì*.

2. nettle, tease, prick; irritate, vex.

N.B. Do not confuse with modern abbrev. form of 蟄 *zhé*.

蟄 **zhé   MC drip**

1. hibernate, as insects and snakes in winter; dormant animals.

   a. hide away, not show one's head; reclusive.

2. rdup., thick and dense, clustering together, massed and merged.

讁 **zhé   MC dreak**

1. censure, blame; accuse, reproach.

2. punish, sentence; discipline; relegate to a less desirable place, position, or sphere of activity.

   a. degrade in office for a crime; ostracize, banish (not as extreme as 流 *liú*, exile); e.g. ～仙 *zhéxiān*, banished transcendent, sent

to live for a time in the mortal world for an offense; epithet associated with Li Bo 李白 (701-762?), thereafter euph. for official sent to the south as degradation for offense.

3. shortcoming, failing; error.

4. ominous change in appearance of heavenly phenomena.

讋 **zhé   MC tsyep**

1. fear, dread; cowardly.

   a. frighten(ed), scare(d); avoid, shirk.

   b. gather into; shrink into.

2. (med.) speak deceptively, mislead.

輒 **zhé   MC trjep**

1. (GP) ADV following SUBJ, indicating consistent occurrence: each time, in every instance, always.

   a. (GP) ADV following SUBJ, emphasizing agent of action: for X's part.

2. straightaway, immediately, then.

3. arbitrarily, wilfully, on one's own initiative.

4. (med.) ～不得 *zhébùdé*, ～莫 *zhémò*, emphatic prohibition: "better not, don't in any event."

5. paralysis of the foot.

   a. unmoving(ly), stuck in place; insensible, numb.

轍 **zhé   MC drjet**

1. carriage-tracks, wheel-tracks, wheel-ruts.

   a. euph. for examples of former worthies to be followed, precedents to be imitated.

2. track, route, road.

zhě

者 **zhě   MC tsyaeX**

1. VB or VB-phrase suffix that nominalizes VB with respect to its subject: that which, the one who (performs the action of VB); e.g. 鬥～皆自以為是而以他人為非 *dòuzhě jiē zì yǐwéi shì ér yǐ tārén wéi fēi*, Those who fight regard themselves in all cases as right and the other person as wrong; 知之～不如好之～ *zhīzhī zhě bùrú hàozhīzhě*, those who understand it do not compare with (are not as good as) those who are fond of it.

   a. when suffixed to a single VB, makes a noun indicating the practitioner of the action of the VB: one who, "-er"; e.g. 學～*xuézhě*, one who studies > student; 從～*cóngzhě*, one who follows > a follower; 卜～ *bǔzhě*, one who divines > diviner.

2. sentential topic marker for nouns and noun-phrases: as for; e.g. 西周～故天子之國也 *xīzhōu zhě gù tiānzǐ zhī guó yě*, As for the Western Zhou, it was assuredly the Son of Heaven's state; 死～人之所必不免也 *sǐ zhě rén zhī suǒ bì bùmiǎn yě*, As for death, it is something from which people inevitably will not escape.

a. sentential topic marker for VB-phrases: as for > when, if; e.g. 大臣太重～國危 *dàchén tàizhòngzhě guó wéi*, When the great vassals become too influential, the state will become imperiled; 地大～國多憂 *dì dà zhě guó duō-yōu*, If the territory is large, the state will have many concerns.

3. noun or noun-phrase suffix that generalizes a statement: in general, generally; e.g. 君～為主 *jūn zhě wéi zhǔ*, lords in general function as overseers; 人事～吾已盡知之矣 *rénshì zhě wú yǐ jìnzhī zhī yǐ*, As for human affairs in general, I have become completely familiar with them.

a. when suffixed to a noun that typically does not represent a class of things, but one thing only, the generalizing sense is to all aspects or all perspectives generally of the noun in question: in all respects, generally; e.g. 天子～與天地參 *tiānzǐ zhě yǔ tiāndì cān*, The Son of Heaven in all respects forms a trinity with heaven and earth; 天～百神之大君也 *tiān zhě bǎishén zhī dàjūn yě*, Heaven in all respects is the lord of the hundred spirits.

b. in combination with *fū* 夫: in general any instance of; e.g. 夫戰～萬乘之存亡也 *fū zhàn zhě wànshèng zhī cúnwáng yě*, As for any instance of a battle in general, it is a matter of the survival or demise of the myriad chariots.

c. with initial *fū* 夫, when suffixed to a noun that typically does not represent a class of things, but one thing only, the generalizing sense is to any aspect or any perspective on the noun in question: in any particular respect, generally; e.g. 夫明堂～王者之堂也 *fū míngtáng zhě wángzhě zhī táng yě*, In any particular respect, generally, the Hall of Light is a king's hall.

褶 zhě　MC dzyip　→ 褶 *dié*.

赭 zhě　MC tsyaeX

1. reddish-brown color, russet, sienna, rutile; dye originally from bark of → 柘 *zhè*-tree.

a. (Budd.) ～服 *zhěfú*, "russet-garbed," i.e. monks, in their reddish-brown robes.

2. hematite, mineral form of iron oxide; also, reddish ocher.

3. denude and leave no cover; strip, lay bare; remove surface covering.

4. (med.) ～時 *zhěshí* (MC tsyaeX-dzyi), trsc. of Chāch, name by which Tashkent was known in med. times.

zhè

柘 zhè　MC tsyaeH

1. silkworm-thorn, cudrania (*Cudrania tricus-pidata*), an evergreen tree the leaves of which were used in silkworm culture, the bark of which yielded a reddish-brown dye called → 赭 *zhě*, and the bark fibers of which were used in making paper.

2. ⊙ 蔗 *zhè*, sugarcane.

3. (med.) ～支 *zhèzhī* (MC tsyaeH-tsye), Chāch, i.e. Tashkent; syn. 石國 *shíguó* 赭時 *zhěshí*.

蔗 zhè　MC tsyaeH

1. sgl. or in cmpd. 甘～ *gānzhè* or 諸～ *zhūzhè*, sugarcane (*Saccharum officinarum*).

這 zhè　MC tsyaeH

1. (med.) demonstrative pronoun: "this, these"; ⊙ 遮 *zhe* 3; a usage arising only in the Tang.

2. (med.) as soon as, immediately after, when.

鷓 zhè　MC tsyaeH

1. (bn.) ～鴣 *zhègū* (MC tsyaeH-ku), chukar (*Alectoris chukar*), francolin (*Francolinus pintadeanus*), the name said to be onom. of its call.

a. (med.) 山～ *shānzhè*, blue magpie, red-billed blue magpie (*Urocissa erythrorhyncha*).

zhēn

偵 zhēn　MC trhjeng

1. scout out, reconnoiter; spy, search for.

斟 zhēn　MC tsyim

1. draw from a pot or jug; ladle out.

2. (bn.) ～酌 *zhēnzhuó* (MC tsyim-tsyak), pour from pot or jug into cup or bowl; also, deliberate, consider carefully, perpend, evaluate and weigh.

3. broth, stew.

a. season, blend, temper.

椹   zhēn   MC trim

1. ⊙ 砧 *zhēn* 1, fulling block; 2, chopping block.
2. block of wood serving as target, for arrows.

shèn   MC zyimX

1. (med.) mulberry fruit.
2. (med.) tree mushroom, perhaps the golden-oyster mushroom (*Pleurotus citrinopileatus*).

楨   zhēn   MC trjeng

1. glossy privet, tree privet, wax-tree privet, broad-leaf privet (*Ligustrum lucidum*), small evergreen tree with glossy leaves and white flowers.
2. the piles or posts that support the ends of a wall's framework in building; e.g. ～幹 *zhēn'gàn*, the piles at the extremities and those at the flanks; > euph. for sustain, support, bear up, brace, esp. in assistance to the ruler.
    a. cornerstone, fundament.
3. (med.) open out, like a screen; extend, unroll.

榛   zhēn   MC tsrin

1. hazelnut tree (*Corylus heterophylla*).
2. tangle(d); thicket, spinney; underbrush.
    a. clutter(ed).
3. sgl. or rdup., manifold, massed, rampant, profuse, proliferate, of vegetation.

珍   zhēn   MC trin

1. precious, esp. because of rarity (cf. 寶 *bǎo*, precious, treasured, because of value or importance).
    a. exquisite, fine, admirable.
2. rare, rarity; choice, select, nonpareil, of unusual quality or provenance.
3. prize, value, esteem, regard as special.
4. (med.) ～重 *zhēnzhòng*, somewhat formal expression of parting: "Fare thee well"; also, a parting wish: "Take good care!" also, expression of gratitude: "Many thanks; I'm deeply touched."
5. ～珠蓮 *zhēnzhūlián*, "fine-gem lotus," henbit deadnettle (*Lamium amplexicaule*), blooms in early spring, flowers pink to purple, syn. 寶蓋草 *bǎogàicǎo*; ～珠花 *zhēnzhūhuā*, "fine-gem flower," tiger lily (*Lilium lancifolium*); also, Chinese elderberry (*Sambucus chinensis*); ～珠梅 *zhēnzhūméi*, "fine-gem prunus," bridal wreath (*Spiraea blumei*), double-white flowers opening in mid-spring.

甄   zhēn   MC tsyin

1. potter's wheel.
    a. fashion from clay; turn, cast, mold.
2. form or shape by instruction and counsel; train, foster.
3. expose, reveal, make clear.
4. distinguish, differentiate, discriminate.
    a. select, choose; e.g. ～拔 *zhēnbá*, select out for advancement.
5. flanks of an army that has been divided in two; set out such a formation.
6. rdup., wafting and winging, of birds.

真   zhēn   MC tsyin

1. real, true < true to its own nature; natural, authentic, genuine.
    a. what really is supposed to be (cf. 實 *shí*, what actually is or happens to be).
    b. pure, perfect, of thoroughgoing genuineness; e.g. ～金 *zhēnjīn*, pure gold, finest gold.
    c. realize(d), perfect(ed), actualize or bring to completion one's inherent qualities; e.g. (Dao.) ～人 *zhēnrén*, Realized Persons, the Perfected, term found as early as the 6th chapter of *Zhuangzi* and used in various movements, but esp. influential in Shangqing Dao. to designate the highest class of divine beings whose home is in the Shangqing heaven and who are completely spiritualized.
    d. ideal, worthy to be imitated.
2. true < what is real and not illusory; e.g. (Budd.) ～人 *zhēnrén*, "one who embodies truth," trns. of Skt. *arhat*; ～諦 *zhēndì*, absolute truth; ～心 *zhēnxīn*, the true mind, trns. of Skt. *anākula*, calm and unperplexed; ～如 *zhēnrú*, true suchness, trns. of Skt. *bhūtatathatā*, unchanging absolute reality that transcends the duality of subject and object, as intuited through gnosis.
    a. consistent with fact or reality (ant. 假 *jiǎ*, false, simulated).
    b. accurate; truthful(ness); verity; e.g. ～率 *zhēnshuài*, straightforward and honest.
3. really, actually, truly, indeed.
4. (med.) ～臘 *zhēnlà* (MC tsyin-lap), Chinrap, trsc. of Viet. *Chân Lạp*, name for kingdom that occupied most of present-day Cambodia, Laos, and part of Vietnam till 802 when supplanted

by the Khmer empire; (Budd.) ～丹 *zhēndān*, name for China when spoken of by foreign figures in pre-Tang Budd. texts.

砧　zhēn　MC trim

1. fulling block, on which one beats cloth or padded garments with wooden mallet to shrink their size and increase their bulk and weight.
    a. to full clothes; onom. of the sound of the fulling mallet.
2. chopping block, esp. for beheading of criminals; butcher's block.
3. anvil.

碪　zhēn　MC trim

1. (med.) ⊙ 砧 *zhēn*.

禎　zhēn　MC trjeng

1. auspicious, favorable, propitious, betokening good fortune.

箴　zhēn　MC tsyim

1. sewing needle; also, acupuncture needle, a probe.
2. admonish, chide, counsel against.
    a. (lit.) admonition, a genre of prose that "probes" the effects of a particular action, warning against harmful or ill-considered behavior and exhorting to better conduct, usu. presented in a formal context or at court.

臻　zhēn　MC tsrin

1. arrive, reach; find the way to.
    a. take to the end, culminate; consummate.

蓁　zhēn　MC tsrin

1. sgl. or rdup., profuse proliferation of foliage, lush, luxuriant, leafy.
2. tangled thicket, underbrush; thorn-brake.

貞　zhēn　MC trjeng

1. determination of divination, e.g. 休～ *xiūzhēn*, favorable determination.
    a. the charge or question posited in turtle-shell divination, to be verified or not: "suppose *this* to be correct..."
2. steadfast, staunch, determined, firm of character; possessed of probity; constancy.
    a. respectable, honor(able).
    b. chaste, pure, loyal, esp. of widows who do not remarry.

3. sincere devotion to one's ruler.
4. upright, correct, orthodox.
5. the lower trigram of each of the 64 *Yijing* hexagrams (cf. 悔 *huǐ*, the upper trigrams).

針　zhēn　MC tsyim (med.)　⊙ 鍼 *zhēn*.

鍼　zhēn　MC tsyim

1. needle; acicular, aciculate; esp. for use in sewing or in medical treatments and acupuncture.
    a. acupuncture, by metonymy.
    b. (med.) needlework, sewing.
2. criticize or mock pointedly, needle; goad, sting; prick, nettle; provoke.

zhěn

抮　zhěn　MC tsyinX

1. turn, twist; change, alter.
    a. ～抱 *zhěnbào*, spiral round, wrapped up in; also, brood over, like birds hatching eggs.

枕　zhěn　MC tsyimX

1. pillow, usu. made of wood or ceramic.
2. ⊙ 軫 *zhěn* 1, crossboard at rear of carriage-box > chassis.
    zhèn　MC tsyimH
1. to pillow, lay one's head on; lie on.
2. abut, lean on; lie next to.
3. nudge, prod.

畛　zhěn　MC tsyinX

1. irrigation ditches between fields.
2. path between farm-plots.
    a. boundary, limit; demarcation.
3. pathway, footpath; road.
4. pray to, implore; propitiate.

疹　zhěn　MC tsyinX

1. rash, cutaneous eruption.
    chèn　MC trhimH
1. ⊙ 疢 *chèn*, fever.

稹　zhěn　MC tsyinX

1. packed together, closely set; consolidated, compressed; compact.

紾　zhěn　MC tsyinX

1. turn, twist, ⊙ 抮 *zhěn*,
2. unlined robe, ⊙ 袗 *zhěn*.

縝　zhěn　MC tsyinX
1. fine-textured, threadlike.
 a. exquisite; well-finished, delicate.
2. meticulous, scrupulous, particular; exact; searching.
3. thick, black hair, ⊙ 鬒 *zhěn*.

袗　zhěn　MC tsyinX
1. unlined gown.
 a. ～玄 *zhěnxuán*, clothing all of the same dark color, above and below; ～衣 *zhěnyī*, embroidered robe, of ruler.

診　zhěn　MC tsyinX
1. examine, esp. a patient; diagnose; e.g. ～脈 *zhěnmài*, taking the pulse, to determine medical condition.
 a. diagnosis; condition.
2. inquire into, investigate; interpret the meaning of.

軫　zhěn　MC tsyinX
1. horizontal crossboard at rear of carriage chassis; sometimes ref. to all 4 lower boards of carriage chassis. N.B. Does not ref. to the axletree.
 a. by synecdoche, the whole carriage box or chassis, syn. 輿 *yú*; by further synecdoche, the entire carriage.
2. square, square-shaped; rectangular < the square shape of the carriage box.
3. name of one of the 28 lunar lodgings, "Chassis," comprising β, δ, γ, ε Corvi arranged in a box-like outline, in the southern quadrant (*chiniao* 赤鳥) of the sky; also called 天車 *tiānchē*, "Heaven's Carriage."
4. tuning pegs of stringed instruments, syn. 軸 *zhóu* 3.
 a. by synecdoche, zither (*qin* 琴).
 b. turn, rotate, turn round.
5. pained, smarting; sorrowful; troubled.

鬒　zhěn　MC tsyinX
1. thick, black hair (on head).

zhèn

振　zhèn　MC tsyinH
1. shake, shock; agitate; vibrate, tremble; joggle, jounce; ～衣 *zhènyī*, shake out one's sleeves.
 a. excite to movement, start, rouse, incite, activate, bestir; exert oneself; e.g. ～古

zhèngǔ, beginning from the past, heretofore; ～藻 *zhènzǎo*, rouse one's elegance.
 b. wield, ply; e.g. ～羽 *zhènyǔ*, ply the wings.
 c. throw open, break out; e.g. ～廩 *zhènlǐn*, throw open the granary.
2. relieve, aid, assist; succor; restore to prior condition; ⊙ 賑 *zhèn* 2.
 a. reorganize, rearrange; return to order; sound retreat.
3. ⊙ 震 *zhèn* 2a, jolt, tremor.

揕　zhèn　MC trimH
1. stab, impale; pierce; plunge, thrust; strike at.

朕　zhèn　MC drimX
1. 1st-person pronoun in early times.
 a. after founding of Qin dynasty in 221 BCE, 1st-person plural pronoun for emperor, the "royal We": capitalize as "We, Our."
2. sign, indication, marking.
 a. portent, presage.

紖　zhèn　MC drinX
1. rope or cord by which one leads an ox by the nose.
 a. nose-rope for any animal.

賑　zhèn　MC tsyinH
1. richly endowed, well-stocked; opulent, affluent, prosperous.
 a. fertile, rich, of fields.
2. relieve, aid, assist, succor, restore to previous condition, esp. with goods or money.

酖　zhèn　MC drimH
1. poisoned wine.

鎮　zhèn　MC trinH
1. weigh down, press down; clamp down.
 a. quell, restrain, suppress, inhibit; control, settle.
 b. guard closely, protect, defend; guardian.
2. of the most weighty importance.
 a. stronghold, fastness, area of unusually difficult terrain or strong natural defenses; also, (med.) area of strategic significance, often provided with a garrison.
3. ～星 *zhènxīng*, "Quelling Star," Saturn, most distant of the 5 naked-eye planets, associated in *wuxing* correspondences with the earth, the color yellow, the center, etc.
4. (med.) enduringly, for a long time; regularly.

陣　zhèn　MC drinH

1. military formation, battle array, line of battle; deployment of troops.
   a. battleground, battlefield.
2. (med.) measure-word for occurrences or stages of experienced situations.
3. (med.) rdup., fitfully continuing, sporadic, intermittent.

震　zhèn　MC tsyinH

1. thunderclap, thunderbolt; thunderstruck.
2. earthquake, earth-shaking.
   a. jolt, tremor, quake; tremulous.
3. terrify, shock; awe.
   a. overwhelm, overpower with redoubtable majesty.
4. ⊙ 振 zhèn 1, 1a, shake, agitate; (a)rouse, bestir to do.
5. one of the 8 fundamental trigrams underlying the *Yijing*'s 64 hexagrams, made up of an unbroken line topped by 2 broken lines.
   a. "Arousing," name of 51st hexagram of the *Yijing*.

鴆　zhèn　MC drimH

1. serpent eagle, "poison bird" (*Spilornis cheela*), raptor that is a specialist reptile eater, thought traditionally to have poisonous wings that when dipped in wine would render it lethal; male was called 運日鳥 *yùnrìniǎo* and the female 陰諧鳥 *yīnxiéniǎo*.
   a. poisonous, to poison; e.g. ～酒 *zhènjiǔ*, poisoned wine; ～殺 *zhènshā*, to poison.

zhēng

崢　zhēng　MC dzreang

1. lofty, eminent; peaked.

zhēng　MC dzraeng

1. (bn.) ～嶸 *zhēngróng* (MC dzraeng-hjwaeng), craggy, precipitous masses of rock; loftily lifted; sheer steepness; high-piled; rocky heights; also, of time, adding up and accumulating, advance and accrue.

征　zhēng　MC tsyeng

1. journey, of some distance; travel afar; trek; e.g. ～鴻 *zhēnghóng*, far-going swan-goose; ～帆 *zhēngfán*, journeying sail.
2. punitive attack, advance against militarily, engage in or be on campaign, military expedition.
   a. chasten, compel submission; contest or fight for advantage.
3. impose or levy a requirement on, esp. a tax levy or corvée obligation; impost.
4. (bn.) ～營 *zhēngyíng* (MC tsyeng-yweng), discomposed, disconcerted, upset and unnerved, timidly.

徵　zhēng　MC tring

1. summon, call to participate in; e.g. ～士 *zhēngshì*, ～君 *zhēngjūn*, summoned gentleman, someone who has received an invitation to have audience at court and likely be appointed to a position but who declines the honor.
   a. recruit, levy, esp. troops or taxes.
   b. to exact, call for, require.
2. seek out, look for, ask after.
   a. look into, examine the situation; interrogate; test.
3. prove, verify; testify to, witness, confirm(ation); realization.
   a. approve, endorse.
   b. standard of approval, criterion.
4. manifestation, presentiment; omen, sign, foretoken.

zhǐ　MC triX

1. one of the notes of the pentatonic scale, with *wuxing* correspondences to fire, summer, the color red, etc.

伀　zhēng　MC tsyeng

1. (med.) ～忪 *zhēngzhōng* (MC tsyeng-tsyowng), dismayed in dread, in fright and fear.

烝　zhēng　MC tsying

1. to steam; rising of steam.
   a. feverish.
2. (pr)offer, present; hand up.
   a. ascend, rise; climb.
3. teeming, numerous; mass(ed), accumulated, like clouds of steam; e.g. ～民 *zhēngmín*, all the people, the multitudes.
4. having sexual relations with someone of parents' generation or of notably higher status, upward licentiousness.
5. winter sacrifice to the ancestors, in early times.
6. ⊙ 蒸 *zhēng* 1, kindling.

爭　zhēng　MC tsraeng

1. vie, contend for, fight over, dispute, contest; wrangle.

a. disputatious, quarrel(some), querulous; fractious.

b. (med.) differ, vary, contrast.

2. (med.) advise against, fight against, object, protest, remonstrate.

3. (med.) extremely, very much; vehemently.

4. (med.) interr. or exclamatory: "how? how X; so X."

癥   zhēng   MC tring

1. intestinal obstruction; occlusion.

箏   zhēng   MC tsreang

1. zither-like instrument described as having various number of strings from 12 (most often) or 13 to 25, with movable bridges, ancestral to the 琴 *qín* ("zither"); translate as "cither" to distinguish from the latter which is a 7-string zither without bridges, and from 瑟 *sè* ("zithern"), 25-string zither with bridges. N.B. Do not translate any of these as "lute," which is the *pipa* 琵琶, a quite different, round-bodied instrument held before one's chest.

蒸   zhēng   MC tsying

1. kindling, small twigs used as firewood; brushwood.

2. torch, brand, made from bundles of hemp- or bamboo-stalks.

3. rdup., pure and honest; also, filial devotion.

4. ⊙ 烝 *zhēng* 1, 2, 3, 4.

鉦   zhēng   MC tsyeng

1. narrow-shaped mallet-struck bell mounted on a long shank with its mouth upward, similar to the shorter-handled 鐃 *náo*, struck to signal a halt or retreat to army troops; also called 丁寧 *dīngníng*. N.B. Do not confuse this with 3, a very different instrument used for different purposes.

2. upper exterior part of a downward-facing chime-bell, on which it is struck.

3. gong, round like a cymbal, of various sizes, used in med. times in Budd. monasteries.

錚   zhēng   MC tsrheang

1. onom. of struck metal: "tching! tchong!"

騬   zhēng   MC dzraeng

1. (med.) (bn.) ～ 鬡 *zhēngníng* (MC dzraeng-nreang), ragged and shabby, scruffy and scraggly, esp. of animal fur; also, foul and hideous, repulsive, odious and obnoxious.

鯖   zhēng   MC tsyeng

1. chowder or fricasee of boiled fish and meat.

zhěng

拯   zhěng   MC tsyingX

1. save from drowning.

a. rescue, relieve; come to the aid of.

b. raise up, lift up.

整   zhěng   MC tsyengX

1. well arranged, orderly, well disposed, organized.

a. formal, punctilious; regular, even.

2. make adjustments, put in order; e.g. ～翰 *zhěnghàn*, preen the feathers.

a. correct, reorganize, rectify.

3. make whole, prepare completely.

a. whole number, with no remainder.

zhèng

政   zhèng   MC tsyengH

1. government, proper ordering of public and political affairs; regime, administration, seat of authority.

a. regulations, authority; law; standards, orders.

2. ⊙ 正 *zhèng* 1, 5.

zhēng   MC tsyeng

1. ⊙ 征 *zhēng* 2, punitive attack; 3, impost.

正   zhèng   MC tsyengH

1. correct, proper; conforming to standards, orthodox.

a. not inclined to one side, upright; just, impartial; exact.

b. normal, norm(ative); established, accepted.

2. rectify, correct, set right, regulate; organize; e.g. ～名 *zhèngmíng*, get the words right, a particular concern of Confucius to have words match the reality of what they are applied to.

3. govern(ment), proper ordering of public and political affairs, ⊙ 政 *zhèng*.

4. principal, most important among several, often contrasted with 副 *fù*, secondary, auxiliary, assistant.

5. exactly, precisely, rightly, just this way.

a. just, merely, only.

zhēng　MC tsyeng

1. ～月 *zhēngyuè*, first ("principal") month of the lunar year, on which the rest of the calendar depends. N.B. According to the Xia 夏 calendar, *zhengyue* was the 1st month (i.e. 1st month of spring); but according to Yin 殷 calendar, *zhengyue* was the 12th month (i.e. last month of winter), and according to Zhou 周 calendar, *zhengyue* was the 11th month (i.e. 2nd month of winter).
2. target zone, exact center of a target.
3. ⊙ 征 *zhēng* 3, impost.
4. (bn.) ～營 *zhēngyíng* (MC tsyeng-yweng), discomposed, disconcerted, upset and unnerved, timidly.

証　**zhèng**　MC tsyengH

1. admonish, advise against, ⊙ 證 *zhèng* 2. N.B. Do not confuse with modern simplified form for all meanings of 證.

諍　**zhèng**　MC tsreangH

1. remonstrate emphatically and directly, lay out one's opinions, admonish fearlessly.

zhēng　MC tsreang

1. ⊙ 爭 *zhēng* 1, vie, contend; quarrel, dispute.

證　**zhèng**　MC tsyingH

1. evidence, verification, proof, confirmation, authentication.
   a. ascertain, verify, confirm.
   b. attest to, witness.
2. admonish, advise against.

鄭　**zhèng**　MC drjengH

1. (bn.) ～重 *zhèngzhòng* (MC drjengH-drjowngH), repeatedly, frequently, again and again; also, (med.) earnestly and attentively, diligently, assiduously.
2. during Western Zhou a royal fiefdom near present-day Huaxian 華縣, Shaanxi; in Chunqiu times a small state centered on present-day Xinzheng 新鄭, Henan, absorbed by Han 韓 in Warring States period.
3. a surname.

zhī

之　**zhī**　MC tsyi

1. direct-OBJ pronoun (sometimes demonstrative): "her," "him," "it," "them," "this," "that," "these," "those"; e.g. 終身由～ *zhōngshēn yóu*

zhī, to follow it to the end of one's life; 无復言～ *wú fù yán zhī*, Don't speak anymore about this.
   a. demonstrative adjective: "this," "that," "these," "those"; e.g. ～二蟲又何知 *zhī èrchóng yòu hézhī*, These two bugs, what do they know?; ～狙 *zhī jū*, this monkey.
2. (GP) marker of noun-phrase modification; e.g. 廣莫～野 *guǎngmò zhī yě*, a broad and barren wilderness; 若垂天～雲 *ruò chuítiān zhī yún*, like clouds hanging down from the sky.
   a. (GP) possessive marker; 堯治天下～民 *yáo zhì tiānxiàzhī mín*, Yao brought order to the people of the subcelestial realm; 人～罪 *rénzhi zuì*, a person's crime.
   b. (GP) marker of sentential nominalization; 聖人～愛人 *shèngrénzhi àirén*, the sage person's showing care for others; 日月～自明 *rìyuèzhi zìmíng*, the sun and the moon's shining brightly on their own.
   c. (GP) marker of agency in object nominalizations; 楚人～所美 *chǔrénzhi suǒměi*, what is regarded as fine by the people of Chu; 人～所用 *rénzhi suǒyòng*, that which people take advantage of.
3. to go; e.g. 牛何～ *niú hé zhī*, Where is the ox going?; ～一邦 *zhī yībāng*, going to another state.

卮　**zhī**　MC tsye　⊙ 巵 *zhī*.

巵　**zhī**　MC tsye

1. flagon, stoup, covered tankard, sometimes said to have capacity of 4 "pints" (升 *shēng*), i.e. .4 斗 *dǒu*.
2. ⊙ 梔 *zhī*, gardenia.

支　**zhī**　MC tsye

1. branch, limb of tree, bough, rame.
   a. limb of person or animal.
2. support, sustain; hold up, prop up; take the part of.
   a. stand against, resist, stand off, hold off; endure, bear.
   b. (bn.) ～離 *zhīlí* (MC tsye-lje), "limb-limp," debilitated, mangled, crimpled and crooked; shorn of support.
3. branch off, separate, diverge, offshoot, e.g. branch of a river or a family.
   a. divergent, differing, unusual.
   b. (med.) distribute, arrange, dispose.
4. supply, provide with.
   a. (med.) handle a situation, cope with; e.g. ～吾 *zhīwú*, ～准 *zhīzhǔn*, deal with, make do.

5. abb. of 地～ *dìzhī*, ref. the 12 "earthly branches" used in counting and classifying.
6. (Budd.) ～提 *zhītí* (MC tsye-dej), trsc. of Skt. *caitya*, temple.
7. (Budd.) abb. ethnonym of monks with Indo-Scythian (Yuezhi 月～, → 月 *yuè*) ancestry.

枝   zhī   MC tsye
1. ⊙ 支 *zhī* 1-3.
2. (med.) measure-word: spray, sprig, of blossoms.

栀   zhī   MC tsye
1. gardenia, cape jasmine (*Gardenia jasminoides*), with shiny leaves and large white, fragrant summer-blooming flowers; the fruit was used to make a yellow dye.
   a. to dye yellow.

楂   zhī   MC tsye
1. base of a pillar or column.
   a. sustain, uphold, support.

汁   zhī   MC tsyip
1. juice; sap.
   a. sauce.

   ### xié   MC hep
1. ⊙ 叶 *xié*, i.e. 協 *xié*, concord, harmony.

知   zhī   MC trje
1. know, perceive with senses or mind, factual knowing.
   a. comprehend, understand.
2. recognize, acknowledge, be(come) acquainted with, ken.
   a. appreciate; rightly recognize and value true quality.
   b. be on terms of closeness with, befriend; e.g. (med.) ～聞 *zhīwén*, friendship, intimacy.
3. make known, reveal; notify.
4. have mastery over, control, manage, superintend, esp. in governmental contexts and certain official titles, the one "in the know," the one responsible for affairs.
5. (med.) presume, expect, look forward to, foresee, often in conjunction with interr.; e.g. 豈～ *qǐzhī*, 何～ *hézhī*, how could one (have) predict(ed)?; ～復何言 *zhīfù héyán*, ～復奈何 *zhīfù nàihé*, how can this be made better? can we expect something else?

   ### zhì   MC trjeH
1. ⊙ 智 *zhì*, knowledge, wisdom.

衹   zhī   MC tsyij
1. respect(ful), honor; e.g. (med.) ～承 *zhīchéng*, respectfully receive; also, wait upon respectfully; (med.) ～承人 *zhīchéngrén*, disciple, follower; (med.) ～備 *zhībèi*, ～當 *zhīdāng*, take care of, handle, see to.
2. only, merely, just; still, as before. N.B. Through the Tang this graph (or 衹 *zhǐ* or 秖 *zhǐ*) is usu. found for the meaning now associated with 只 *zhǐ* which was not commonly used with this meaning until after the Tang.

秖   zhī   MC tsye
1. merely, only, just; still, ⊙ 衹 *zhǐ* (→ 衹 *qí*).

稙   zhī   MC trik
1. grain that is planted early and ripens early.

織   zhī   MC tsyik
1. weave, make cloth.
   a. ～女 *zhīnǚ*, Weaving Maid, the star Vega (α Lyrae).
2. woven items.

肢   zhī   MC tsye
1. limb of person or animal, ⊙ 支 *zhī* 1a.

胝   zhī   MC trij
1. sgl. or (bn.) 胼～ *piánzhī* (MC ben-trij), callous on hands or feet.

脂   zhī   MC tsyij
1. fatty tissue of animals, lard, suet; tallow.
   a. of flesh, firm, firmly white, sleek.
2. grease, for lubrication (harder and less oily than 膏 *gāo*).
   a. spread grease on, smear > glossy, smooth.
3. gum or resin, of trees.
4. make-up, with grease as an ingredient; greasepaint.

芝   zhī   MC tsyi
1. mushroom, in general.
   a. an object shaped like a mushroom, e.g. a chariot canopy.
2. sgl. and in cmpd. 靈～ *língzhī*, "numinous mushroom" and 紫～ *zǐzhī*, "purple mushroom" (*Ganoderma lucidum, G. japonicum*), a type of polypore mushroom that grows on wood, especially rotting logs; particularly striking examples sometimes regarded as auspicious celestial

omens or as having qualities conducing to long life > an entheogenic plant, wondergrowth.

3. fragrant plant often equated with 白芷 *bái zhǐ*, Chinese angelica; in combination with 蘭 *lán* represents a person of high morality and integrity.

4. ～麻 *zhīmá*, sesame (*Sesamum indicum*) or sesame seeds.

藏　zhī　MC tsyik

1. fisalia, ground-cherry (*Physalis angulata*), producing yellow-orange fruit.

蜘　zhī　MC trje

1. (bn.) ～蛛 *zhīzhū* (MC trje-trju), gen. term for spider.

隻　zhī　MC tsyek

1. one bird.
　　a. a single one, individual.
　　b. one of a pair, only one.

2. measure-word, usu. for things occurring in pairs, almost always following "one" 一 *yī*; (med.) applied to other than paired objects.

鴟　zhī　MC tsye

1. (bn.) ～鵲 *zhīquè*, ostrich, first offered in tribute by Seleucid (Tiaozhi 條支) empire during reign of Han Wudi 漢武帝 (r. 141-87 BCE); also, sometimes jaybird, though that seems to be a later designation of a different, local bird.

罜　zhī　MC trje　⊙蜘 *zhī*.

zhí

值　zhí　MC driH

1. come straight up against, come upon, come face to face with; encounter; ⊙直 *zhí* 2.
　　a. oppose, conflict with; resist.

2. (med.) ⊙直 *zhí* 2a, on duty, in charge of; 3, worth X, have the value of X; 4, only, merely.

埴　zhí　MC dzyik

1. clay, esp. for making pottery.

執　zhí　MC tsyip

1. take up; grasp, seize, clutch; e.g. ～鞭 *zhíbiān*, hold the whip, as a coachman.
　　a. hold tightly to, clasp, hold on to; adhere to, be attached to; persevere; e.g. ～中 *zhízhōng*, keep to the balanced mean; ～別 *zhíbié*,

clasp in parting; (Budd.) ～著 *zhízhuō*, attachments (to worldly matters).

2. take charge of, be in control of; e.g. ～行 *zhíxíng*, carry out, execute; ～事 *zhíshì*, take care of matters > the official in charge; also, complimentary 2nd-person pronoun: you [to whom I defer].
　　a. set one's hand to, engage in.

3. draw close to, draw in to one.
　　a. closely-held friend, intimate; e.g. ～友 *zhíyǒu*, fast friend.

姪　zhí　MC drit

1. term used by woman to refer to children of her brothers: nephew, niece.
　　a. (med.) from 4th-century also used by men in this way.

2. (med.) self-depreciatory term used by young men when addressing elders: "I, your youngling."

拓　zhí　MC tsyek

1. ⊙摭 *zhí*, pick up, gather up.
　　　tuò　MC thak
1. lift up, raise.
　　a. offer to.
2. extend, enlarge; open up, develop.
　　　tà　MC thop
1. (med.) ⊙搨 *tà* 2, make a white-on-black rubbing of an inscription with ink and paper.

摭　zhí　MC tsyek

1. pick up, lay one's hand on; glean; retrieve, gather up.

植　zhí　MC dzyik

1. to plant in the ground (flowers, trees, vegetation).
　　a. growth of plants.
　　b. gen. term for plants.

2. implant, embed, set firmly in or on.
　　a. set up, organize, dispose.

3. perpendicular slat with which to latch a door or gate.

4. superintend military fortifications.

殖　zhí　MC dzyik

1. propagate, generate; breed, cultivate.
　　a. increase, batten.

2. plant in the ground.
　　a. implant, embed; set up.

3. engage in trade; seek to profit; e.g. 貨～ *huòzhí*, trade in goods; also, tradesman, merchant.

4. rdup., level and smooth, even and flat.

直 **zhí** MC drik
1. straight, not turning (ant. 曲 *qǔ*, curved); direct(ness); unswerving; right.
    a. upright, erect; set up; straighten.
    b. descriptive of staunch character: upright, upstanding, straightforward, unswerving, direct, candid, unreserved, forthright.
2. face to face with, meet head on, confront.
    a. on duty, take up duty for, accept responsibility, be in charge of; (med.) often prefixed to official titles indicating holder's primary appointment was elsewhere.
3. worth X, have the value of or be valuable for X.
4. only, merely, just this and nothing else.
    a. especially, in particular.
    b. ～到 *zhídào*, ～得 *zhídé*, cause, result in; ～令 *zhílìng*, ～饒 *zhíráo*, ～使 *zhíshǐ*, even so, even if; ～下 *zhíxià*, just now, exactly here; ～須 *zhíxū*, just have to, simply must.
5. but then, after all; on the contrary.

縶 **zhí** MC trip
1. tether, esp. a horse.
    a. tether-cord, binding rope.
2. hobble, bind front feet of horse; fetter, trammel; impede.
    a. tie up; constrain; shut up, enclose.

職 **zhí** MC tsyik
1. attend to, be responsible for.
2. responsibilities, duties, obligations, esp. of governmental office (cf. 官 *guān*, rank of office).
    a. essential matter, primary item or factor.
    b. what is due or owing to one, e.g. 得～ *dézhí*, obtain one's due, be satisfied.
3. offer as tribute; tribute items, incl. annual contributions to court from prefectures.
    zhì MC tsyiH
1. ⊙ 志 *zhì*, record; 幟 *zhì*, pennon; 識 *shì*, acquainted with.

跖 **zhí** MC tsyek
1. sole of the foot.
    a. ball of a bird's claw.
2. stamp, tramp; pad.

蹠 **zhí** MC tsyek
1. ⊙ 跖 *zhí*.
2. go to, arrive at.

躑 **zhí** MC drjek
1. (bn.) ～躅 *zhízhú* (MC drjek-drjowk), wary and wavering, weak-kneed and faltering, tarrying and marking time; also, at a slow but certain pace, in a measured rhythm; also, abb. of 羊～躅 *yángzhízhú*, "sheep's-stagger," Chinese azalea (*Rhododendron molle*).

疐 **zhí** MC trip
1. ⊙ 縶 *zhí*, except 2a.

zhǐ

只 **zhǐ** MC tsyeX
1. phrase-middle or phrase-final rhythmic particle in early verse.
2. N.B. this graph is not often found with the meaning "only, merely; still" until after the Tang; before that the word is usu. written 祇 *zhǐ* (→ 祇 *qí*), 祗 *zhī*, or 祇 *zhī*.

咫 **zhǐ** MC tsyeX
1. pre-Han unit of length measurement equaling 8 "inches" (*cun* 寸).
    a. (bn.) ～尺 *zhǐchǐ* (MC tsyeX-tsyhek), as close as can be, within a foot's length, cheek by jowl; also, as slight as can be, hardly noticeable, just a smitch and a smidgen; a brief span.

址 **zhǐ** MC tsyiX
1. basis, base, ground, foundation; site.

徴 **zhǐ** MC triX → 徴 *zhēng*.

抵 **zhǐ** MC tsyeX
1. strike, smite, smack; e.g. ～掌 *zhǐzhǎng*, clap the hands.
2. throw, cast, hurl, pitch.

指 **zhǐ** MC tsyijX
1. finger, digit.
    a. toe.
2. point, gesture; indicate, point out; guide to; e.g. ～掌 *zhǐzhǎng*, point to the palm of the hand, euph. for something very easy to do; ～顧 *zhǎnggù*, in a twitch and a blink, speedily.

a. bend, bend one's way, incline toward.

b. advert to, allude to.

c. turn up; erect.

3. take under one's own guidance, exercise responsibility for.

4. purport, aim; meaning, significance; ⊙ 旨 zhǐ 1.

旨　zhǐ　MC tsyijX

1. purport, aim; meaning, significance.

a. aim at, intend.

b. opinion, slant, viewpoint.

2. (med.) directive, imperial rescript.

3. fine-tasting; delightful; excellent.

枳　zhǐ　MC tsyeX

1. trifoliate orange (*Poncirus trifoliata, Citrus trifoliata*), mainly a decorative tree, with spiny branches and large white flowers, fruit too bitter to eat fresh.

2. ～枸 zhǐjǔ, ～椇 zhǐjǔ, honey-tree, oriental raisin-tree (*Hovenia dulcis, H. acerba*), medium to tall summer-flowering tree, fruit-stalks (rachis) and drupes edible and used medicinally.

止　zhǐ　MC tsyiX

1. stop one's movement or activity, arrest oneself from; cease, cessation; halt, stop, end; ～足 zhǐzú, cessation and contentment, cease in fulfillment, stop when one has enough.

a. refrain (from), give up, keep from doing; prevent; abolish, abrogate.

2. come to the end of, reach the end, conclude, reach the limit, delimit.

3. come to a stop in, be fixed in, remain in; fixed in place.

a. rest, repose, settle in.

b. (Budd.) trns. Skt. *śamatha*, the calmness or serenity produced by cessation of mentation through concentrated meditation, leading to *vipaśyanā* or "insight" (→ 觀 *guàn* 3 [*guān*]).

4. customary bearing, deportment.

5. only, merely, just, ⊙ 只 zhǐ.

6. phrase-ending rhythmic particle, in *Shijing* verse.

7. a foot, appendage.

沚　zhǐ　MC tsyiX

1. ait, eyot, small river-isle.

祇　zhǐ　MC tsyeX　→ 祇 qí.

祉　zhǐ　MC trhiX

1. good fortune, blessings, felicity; prosperity; godsend.

a. happiness, elation.

紙　zhǐ　MC tsyeX

1. paper, material on which texts were written; up to mid-Han ref. to silk rolls for writing, afterward increasingly just to "paper" made, with advancing skill and variety, from disintegrated fibers (of tree bark, hemp, rags, etc.) upon a flat mold.

芷　zhǐ　MC tsyiX

1. sgl. or 白～ *báizhǐ*, Chinese angelica (*Angelica dahurica*), perennial plant that grows along riverbanks and streams; roots and leaves highly fragrant; in lit. symbolic of high morality and integrity, syn. 芳香 *fāngxiāng*, 蕭 *xiāo*.

茞　zhǐ　MC tsyiX

1. ⊙ 芷 zhǐ angelica.

趾　zhǐ　MC tsyiX

1. foot; toe.

2. foot-track, footprint; trace.

3. basis, foundation, ground; foot of a mountain.

4. 交～ *jiāozhǐ*, Tonkin, northern part of Vietnam, incl. Red River delta.

軹　zhǐ　MC tsyeX

1. wheel-hub of a carriage, with opening in which to fit the linchpin.

a. by metonymy, linchpin.

2. stave-side, rack, of a carriage box.

3. ⊙ 只 zhǐ 1, rhythmic particle in verse.

阯　zhǐ　MC tsyiX

1. basis or foundation, e.g. foot of a mountain, base of a wall.

2. ⊙ 趾 zhǐ, in 交～ *jiāozhǐ*, Tonkin.

黹　zhǐ　MC trijX

1. embroider(y), fine needlework on clothing.

a. (med.) euph. for finely crafted writing.

zhì

乿　zhì　MC driH

1. ancient-script form of → 治 *zhì*.

制   zhì   MC tsyejH

1. cut to measure, as in tailoring.
    a. work from a pattern or plan, make to fit.
2. complete a design; fabricate, make; give definition to.
    a. craft, compose (writing).
3. arrange(ment), control; regulate, regulation, institution, standard of expectation.
    a. make conform; restrain(t), constrain(t) > interdict(ion), prohibit(ion).
    b. subdue, exercise authority over; e.g. ～於 X, *zhì yú X*, at the mercy of X; (Dao.) ～神 *zhìshén*, invoke a spirit (whom one has control over).
4. imperial announcement, fiat.
5. early measure of length equal to 1 *zhang* 丈 and 8 *chi* 尺.

寘   zhì   MC tsyeH

1. set in place, fix; arrange, install (physical objects only, cf. 置 *zhì*).
    a. set aside, reject; abandon.

峙   zhì   MC driX

1. mountain spur; stand aloft, upthrust; sheer.
    a. stand, stand erect.
    b. stand against (one another).
2. pile up, lay up, store away.

袠   zhì   MC drit

1. protective box, bin, case, or wrap for scroll(s).
    a. measure-word for book.
    b. protective wrap for sword.
2. (med.) bundle of writings.
3. (med.) put in proper order or sequence, arrange, esp. several scrolls of a single text.

幟   zhì   MC tsyhiH

1. pennon, banner, standard.
    a. to signal, give a sign, wave; betoken.

庤   zhì   MC driX

1. lay in stock; reserve.

豷   zhì   MC drjejH

1. wild boar; swine.

志   zhì   MC tsyiH

1. what is in, or on, one's mind; intent(ion), resolve; will; the dictates of one's heart.
    a. goal, aim, aspiration; be intent on, resolve to; e.g. ～士 *zhìshì*, person of great ambition.
    b. be attentive to; attention.
2. remember, keep in mind; memory.
3. record in writing; set down, note down.
    a. tractate, monograph, treatise, study; e.g. 藝文～ *yìwénzhì*, bibliographic monograph (in dynastic histories).
4. ⊙ 幟 *zhì*, banner, standard, streamer.

忮   zhì   MC tsyeH

1. object to, be hostile to, averse to.
2. refractory, intractable, contrary.

摯   zhì   MC tsyijH

1. grab onto, catch; seize, clutch; hold in hand.
2. earnest, zealous, intent.
3. ⊙ 贄 *zhì*, ceremonial present handed over to superior; 鷙 *zhì*, raptor; vicious, merciless; 至 *zhì*, arrive, come to; extreme point, highest degree.

擲   zhì   MC drjek

1. throw away, pitch, cast, fling, hurl.
2. wrench upward, spring up.

擿   zhì   MC drjek

1. scratch, rub; irritate, annoy.
    a. woman's hairpin, hair ornament; leg of a hairpin.
2. ⊙ 擲 *zhì*, throw, fling, pitch.
      tì   MC thek
1. pick at, pick out; provoke.
    a. pick open, pry open; reveal.
2. pick out to do, employ, commission.
      zhāi   MC treak
1. ⊙ 摘 *zhāi* 1, pick by hand, pluck; 2, select, extract.

智   zhì   MC trjeH

1. wisdom, knowledge; cognition, intelligence; sentience.
    a. insight; gnosis.
    b. (Budd.) trns. of Skt. *jñāna*, knowledge or cognition of an object inseparable from the total experience of reality.

桎   zhì   MC tsyit

1. shackles, fetters.
2. bind round, enchain; constrain.

櫍　zhì　MC tsyit

1. executioner's block, made of wood (cf. 鑕 *zhì*, iron block).

櫛　zhì　MC tsrit

1. gen. term for combs.
   a. comb the hair.
2. (med.) rdup., close-set, like the teeth of a comb; squeezed tight, packed together.
3. (med.) weed out, screen, eliminate.

治　zhì　MC driH

1. set things in their proper channels; put in good order, set or bring to order, set right.
   a. govern, direct (state policy); heal, cure (sickness); dress (stones, gems); work up (studies); solve (difficulties); organize (plans).
   b. pay attention to, focus on for a particular goal.
2. in good order, well-governed, well-managed, rendered stable and untroublesome.
   a. properly handled, neatly done.
   b. set right, keep in line; discipline, train.
3. seat of government.
4. (Dao.) parish, one of the 24 (later 28) administrative centers in Sichuan and southern Shaanxi combining governmental and religious functions of original Tianshi organization.
5. ⊙ 始 *shǐ* 2, just now; now it is that . . .

滯　zhì　MC drjejH

1. clog, block up, choke off; stuck; stagnate.
   a. obstruct, interrupt; bring to a halt.
   b. obstinate, stuck in place; immovable; detain(ed), linger(ing).
2. trickled away > left out, left behind; omit(ted).
   a. discarded, cast away.

炙　zhì　MC tsyek

1. spit-roast, roast on a skewer; broil; barbecue.
2. roasted meat.

狾　zhì　MC tsyejH

1. rabid dog.
   a. rabid, furious, wild, out of control, mad, (en)rage(d).

畤　zhì　MC driX

1. ritual area where emperors in Qin and Han times performed sacrifices to heaven, to earth, and to the legendary five first sovereigns.
2. ⊙ 沚 *zhǐ*, ait, eyot.

疐　zhì　MC trijH

1. slip, trip; stumble.

痔　zhì　MC driX

1. piles, hemorrhoids.

痣　zhì　MC tsyiH

1. mole, on skin.
   a. freckle.

瘈　zhì　→ 瘈 *chì*.

秩　zhì　MC drit

1. official rank and grade according to hierarchy.
   a. regular order, sequence; succession.
2. regular procedure or duties, routine activities; regimen.
3. official stipend, salary, usu. a certain allotment of grain or other provisions.
4. (med.) a cycle of 10 years, decade.

稚　zhì　MC drijH

1. sprout, tender shoot of unripe grain.
   a. late-planted and late-ripening grain.
   b. immature, unripe.
2. youngster, stripling, slip of a lad (or girl).

穉　zhì　MC drijH　⊙ 稚 *zhì*.

窒　zhì　MC trit

1. block up, fill up; obstruct(ion), stop(page).
   a. restrain, curb; prevent; foreclose.
   b. various kinds of nasal blockage.
   c. blockhead(ed), obtuse.
2. alt. name for the 7th month of the year.
      dié　MC tet
1. ～皇 *diéhuáng*, pylons before a tomb complex; also, underground corridor leading to tomb.

紩　zhì　MC drit

1. sew, stitch.
   a. mend.

置　zhì　MC triH

1. place, set in a certain place, dispose, arrange, lay down; placement, disposition; e.g. ～酒 *zhìjiǔ*, set out wine; ～頓 *zhìdùn*, "dispose the gests," arrange the emperor's overnight stops when on travel.
   a. install, set up, establish (abstract objects as well as physical ones; cf. 真 *zhì*).

b. posit (opinion), organize (words); hand down, decide (punishment); put down cash for, buy.

2. set aside, set apart; release, dismiss; exempt, pardon, put aside.

3. post-station, relay station; post horse; courier.

至   zhì   MC tsyijH

1. arrive at, reach; attain to, get all the way to (through med. times often an intransitive VB without stated OBJ; cf. 到 *dào*).

    a. when it comes to, with regard to (abstract destination or idea).

2. to the farthest degree, far-reaching; extreme; fraught with.

    a. utmost, utter(ly), ultimate; culminate; perfect, accomplish(ed); complete(ly).

3. advent, esp. 夏～ *xiàzhì*, advent of summer, and 冬～ *dōngzhì*, advent of winter, i.e. summer and winter solstice.

致   zhì   MC trijH

1. causative mode of 至 *zhì*: cause to arrive at, bring about, bring to; effect, result in; provoke.

    a. effects, efficacy, manage to do, succeed in; ends, results.

2. cause to be brought or to come; attract, summon.

    a. bring, deliver; convey, take there; provide.

    b. present, send; offer, give up to.

3. ⊙ 至 *zhì* 1, arrive at, reach; come to; 2, utmost, farthest degree; completely.

4. quality that attracts; interest, appeal.

5. in detail, all the way to finest or most extreme points.

蛭   zhì   MC tsyit

1. leech (*Hirudineae*).

袟   zhì   MC drit   ⊙ 帙 *zhì*.

裘   zhì   MC drit   ⊙ 帙 *zhì*.

製   zhì   MC tsyejH

1. ⊙ 制 *zhì* 1, cut to measure, tailor; 2, fabricate, make; compose.

2. completed composition, writing.

3. demeanor, deportment.

觶   zhì   MC tsyeH

1. ancient wide-shouldered covered beaker, for offerings of wine.

誌   zhì   MC tsyiH

1. (med.) record in writing, set down, note down; ⊙ 志 *zhì* 3.

    a. document, writing, report.

    b. record of events, commemorative record; e.g. 墓～詺 *mùzhìmíng*, commemorative grave inscription.

2. (med.) remember, keep in mind; ⊙ 志 *zhì* 2.

    a. mark, leave a mark, sign; notation.

3. ⊙ 痣 *zhì*, marks on one's body, moles, freckles.

豸   zhì   MC drjeX

1. wug, slinker, fabulous creature that glides like a cat but without feet.

2. (bn.) 獬～ *xièzhì*, → 獬 *xiè*, fabulous animal with ability to decide between disputants.

    a. determine, settle, decide; e.g. ～冠 *zhìguān*, cap worn by judges.

質   zhì   MC tsyit

1. substance, basic stuff; natural constituent(s) or quality.

    a. natural, genuine, unchanged from basic state, plain, austere; unaffected, artless, unadorned (ant. 文 *wén* 2, 3, surface ornament, refinement, elaboration).

2. ground, base, fundament(al), rudiment(ary); background to what appears most visible; e.g. ～本 *zhìběn*, capital, resources.

3. confront(ation) before a judge, offer or demand proof.

    a. interrogate; adjudge, call to account.

4. target, butt; aim, goal; object(ive).

    a. necessary complement, counterpart.

5. executioner's block, ⊙ 櫍 *zhì*.

zhì   MC trijH

1. pledge, gage, collateral, security, given in earnest of payment of debt or fulfillment of obligation.

    a. hostage, usu. ruler's son sent to live at court of another state to guarantee favorable relations.

    b. material on which contract was written.

贄   zhì   MC tsyijH

1. ceremonial gift offered on first visit to respected elder or superior.

    a. gift presented upon visiting someone.

zhí   MC trip

1. ～然 *zhírán*, staunchly, immovably, motionless, at a standstill.

跱　zhì　MC driX　⊙峙 *zhì*.

躓　zhì　MC trijH
1. stumble; trip.
    a. encounter a stumbling block, run into difficulties; setback; besetting.
2. (med.) crabbed, forced, laborious, overdone, of literary style.
3. (med.) exhausted, weary, overworked.

輊　zhì　MC trijH
1. front-laden wagon.
    a. weighed down.

迣　zhì　MC tsyejH
1. block, impede; barricade.
2. leap over, jump; go across.

銍　zhì　MC trit
1. sickle, reaping-hook.
    a. cut grain with sickle; collect the crop.

鑕　zhì　MC tsyit
1. executioner's block, made of iron.
    a. punishment or sentence of decapitation.

陟　zhì　MC trik
1. ascend, move higher; scale, climb.
    a. euph. for death of ruler: surmount the mundane world.
2. advance along a route, progress.
    a. promote(d) in office.
    b. reward, recompense.

雉　zhì　MC drijX
1. ring-necked pheasant (*Phasianus colchicus*).
2. section measurement of a wall, being 3 *zhang* 丈 long and 1 *zhang* 丈 high.
3. second-best throw in the game of *chaupar* (best is *lu* 盧).

鮆　zhì　MC tsyejH
1. sardines (*Sardinella zunasi*).

騭　zhì　MC tsyit
1. stallion.
2. settle, stabilize.
3. climb, ascend.

鷙　zhì　MC tsyijH
1. raptor, bird of prey.
2. ferocious, vicious; merciless.

zhōng

中　zhōng　MC trjuwng
1. in, inner, innermost, inside; among; e.g. 〜國 *zhōngguó*, the Inner States, homeland of Chinese civilization in the central plains and course of the Yellow River, traditionally contrasted with states to the north and west and those along and south of the Yangzi River (N.B. Do not translate as "China"); 〜腸 *zhōngcháng*, one's "deepest innards," i.e. inmost feelings.
    a. center, central, middle; e.g. 〜央 *zhōngyāng*, the exact center; 〜臟 *zhōngzàng*, middlemost of the 5 viscera, i.e. gall bladder, associated with earth, yellow, the center, etc.; 〜池 *zhōngchí*, (Dao.) "central pond," esoteric name for gall bladder.
    b. in the midst of; halfway; e.g. 〜道 *zhōngdào*, in mid-path, mid-course; 〜流 *zhōngliú*, in mid-current, midstream; 〜午 *zhōngwǔ*, mid-day.
    c. inner grounds of palace compound, recesses, penetralia (ant. 外 *wài*, outside the court); e.g. 〜書省 *zhōngshūshěng*, "Bureau of Documents of the Inner Court," i.e. imperial secretariat; 〜詔 *zhōngzhào*, pronouncement from the innermost court, imperial fiat.
2. intermediate; neither highest nor lowest; of middling quality, ability, or intelligence; e.g. (med.) 〜隱 *zhōngyǐn*, middling recluse, one who displays an inconspicuous balance in his affairs and actions; (Budd.) 〜劫 *zhōngjié*, intermediate kalpa, period between major kalpas.

    zhòng　MC trjuwngH
1. hit the target, be on mark; 〜的 *zhòngdì*, hit the target, attain one's goal.
    a. be in the midst of; strike true, hit home; harm; be struck, hit with, suffer; e.g. 〜惡 *zhòng'è*, heart attack; 〜壞 *zhònghuài*, destroy; (med.) 〜酒 *zhòngjiǔ*, be dead drunk; (med.) 〜間 *zhòngjiān*, in the interval of time specified: in the past; recently; afterward.
2. strike the right balance; be plumb on, "right on"; accord with, match with; correspond; fitting, suitable.
3. a celestial body being at the meridian.

妐　zhōng　MC tsyowng
1. husband's father.
    a. 女〜 *nǚzhōng*, husband's younger sister.

忠   zhōng   MC trjuwng
1. wholehearted(ness), put all one's heart and effort into something; do one's best without self-delusion.
   a. dedicated, devoted to a goal, principle, or person; loyal to one's ruler; allegiance.

籦   zhōng   MC tsyowng
1. (bn.) 〜籠 zhōnglóng (MC tsyowng-ljowng), rare kind of bamboo reputedly from the Kunlun mountains 崑崙山 and good for making into flutes or pitch-pipes.

終   zhōng   MC tsyuwng
1. end, finish, conclude (ant. 始 shǐ, begin).
   a. come to the end of life; death, demise.
2. all the way to the end, through to the finish; all of, the whole, complete(ly); e.g. 〜夜 zhōngyè, the whole night; 〜古 zhōnggǔ, through all the ages, all time past; also, to the end of time.
3. in the end, finally, after all, in conclusion.
   a. (med.) sgl. or 〜然 zhōngrán, even if, although; if finally.
4. first half of archaic phrase of grammatical symmetry: 〜A且B, both A and B.

螽   zhōng   MC tsyuwng
1. sgl. or (bn.) 〜斯 zhōngsī (MC tsyuwng-sje), locust; also, used as simile in wishes of abundant progeny.
   a. 即〜 jízhōng, long-horned grasshopper.

衷   zhōng   MC trjuwng
1. undergarb, worn nearest the skin.
   a. wear under one's clothing; keep hidden.
2. inner person, inner self, inmost feelings.
3. ⊙ 中zhōng 1, inside, inner; 2, central, middle.
   zhòng   MC trjuwngH
1. ⊙ 中 zhòng 2, strike the right balance, be plumb on, accord with.

鍾   zhōng   MC tsyowng
1. wine vessel, stoup, fat-bellied with round bottom and top, lidded, similar to small jug.
2. measure of capacity, equal to 6 hu 斛 and 4 dou 斗 (i.e. 64 dou); e.g. 十萬〜 shíwànzhōng, salary of a high minister (qing 卿) in Mencius's time.
3. concentrate, accumulate, aggregate, consolidate.
   a. fully endow(ed), bestow(ed), grant(ed).

4. ⊙ 鐘 zhōng, bell.

鐘   zhōng   MC tsyowng
1. bell, in early times usu. ref. to sets of differently tuned bells of various sizes, clapperless and struck with a mallet to produce resonant tone, used traditionally as part of ensembles including stringed instruments, wind instruments, and drums, in ritual ceremonies and on formal occasions; e.g. 〜鼎 zhōngdǐng, bell and tripod, important items used in state sacrifices > by metonymy, affairs of state.
   a. (med.) ref. to single large bells, esp. of Budd. monasteries; also, large bell struck to signal evening closing of city gates.
2. concentrate; amass, collect.
3. ⊙ 鍾 zhōng 1, wine-vessel, stoup; 2, measure of capacity.

zhǒng

冢   zhǒng   MC trjowngX
1. barrow, hummock.
   a. mounded tomb; sepulchre, burial vault.
2. hereditary; eldest son of principal wife; e.g. 〜君 zhǒngjūn, hereditary ruler; 〜嗣 zhǒngsì, hereditary descendant.
3. crest of a mountain, peak.
   a. foremost, chief.

塚   zhǒng   MC trjowngX
1. (med.) ⊙ 冢 zhǒng 1, tomb, barrow; sepulchre.

尰   zhǒng   MC dzyowng
1. swelling of feet or legs; gout.

種   zhǒng   MC tsyowngX
1. sgl. or cmpd. 〜子 zhǒngzǐ, seed, of plant.
   a. germ of something that will propagate a new development; e.g. (Dao.) 〜民 zhǒngmín, "seed people," the elect who, following the Way of the Celestial Masters (Tianshi dao 天師道), will survive the apocalypse and see the era of Great Peace (taiping 太平).
2. kind, sort, category; class, species; rdup., all kinds, sundry sorts, manifold, various.
   a. clan, race, tribe.
3. (Budd.) offspring, descendant; secondary; e.g. 〜好 zhǒnghǎo, minor or secondary characteristics (physical signs of a buddha).

zhòng　MC tsyowngH
1. to sow, to seed, plant.
　　a. nurture, foster.

腫　zhǒng　MC tsyowngX
1. gen. term for dropsies with swelling.
　　a. swollen; tumorous.

踵　zhǒng　MC tsyowngX
1. heel, of foot or shoe.
2. plod, trudge.
3. tread on the heels of, follow after; e.g. ～武 *zhǒngwǔ*, walk in the tracks of > imitate, follow the lessons or example of.
　　a. continue, perpetuate; inherit, assume.
4. go to, arrive at.

zhòng

仲　zhòng　MC drjuwngH
1. 2nd in seniority of a sequence of 3 or 4 brothers (1=伯 *bó*, 3=叔 *shū*, 4=季 *jì*).
　　a. intermediate, second in sequence of three; e.g. ～秋 *zhòngqiū*, 2nd month of autumn, 8th month of the year.
2. first element in many given names, bynames, or epithets; e.g. ～尼 *zhòngní*, byname of Confucius; ～父 *zhòngfù*, "Zhong the father," honorific name given by Duke Huan of Qi 齊桓公 to his chief counselor Guan Zhong 管仲, afterward used by rulers to ref. to respected counselors; also, honorific term for Confucius.

眾　zhòng　MC tsyuwngH
1. multitude, throng; manifold, numerous legion; throng(ing); sundry, diverse; e.g. ～族 *zhòngzú*, sundry kinds of creatures; ～諸 *zhòngzhū*, prolix and profuse, esp. of human speech or animal sounds.
　　a. the crowd, common run, mass of; average, normal; e.g. ～人 *zhòngrén*, all the people, everybody; ～庶 *zhòngshù*, common folk, commoners; ～鼎 *zhòngdǐng*, normal, everyday tripod (i.e. not used for ritual occasions); (Budd.) ～生 *zhòngshēng*, sentient beings, early trns. of Skt. *sattva*, later usu. 情物 *qíngwù*.
2. in everyone's presence, public(ly).

種　zhòng　MC tsyowngH　→ 種 *zhǒng*.

重　zhòng　MC drjowngX
1. heavy, weight(y), substantial (ant. 輕 *qīng*, light).
　　a. weighty, significant, momentous.
　　b. grave, sad; troublesome, something that weighs on one.
2. give weight to, stress, emphasize; esteem, consider important; favor, honor; respect.
　　a. emphatically, with extra stress, in a manner more than usual, very much.

　　chóng　MC drjowng
1. repeat(ed), double(d); add(ed); e.g. ～陽 *chóngyáng*, doubled *yang*, esp. ref. 9th day of 9th month.
　　a. layer(ed), tier(ed), fold(ed), as of mountain ranges, mountain heights, multi-storeyed buildings, walls surrounding palaces, etc.
　　b. (med.) again, once more, additionally.

zhōu

侜　zhōu　MC trjuw
1. sgl. or (bn.) ～張 *zhōuzhāng* (MC trjuw-trjang), cheat, deceive, defraud; also, presume on, impose on, finagle.

周　zhōu　MC tsyuw
1. dense, thick, close; near, intimate; e.g. ～親 *zhōuqín*, close relatives.
2. conform to, adapt to, suitable for.
3. encircle, surround; e.g. ～匝 *zhōuzā*, circling round.
　　a. engird, wear at the waist.
4. encompass, pervade; pervasive, thorough; all-embracing; e.g. ～道 *zhōudào*, ～行 *zhōuxíng*, all-encompassing path, perfect path; also, moral and political way of the Western Zhou (1046-771 BCE) dynasty; ～澤 *zhōuzé*, thoroughgoing graciousness
　　a. make a circuit of, complete a cycle; cyclic; revolve around a path, like sun and moon; all the way around; whole, complete(ly); e.g. 遊 *zhōuyóu*, ～流 *zhōuliú*, make a full circuit; 不～ *bùzhōu*, name of mountain in far northwest reputedly battered in anger by legendary malefactor Chiyou 蚩尤 and so made "incomplete," causing earth to slant to the southeast; also, old designation of northwest wind.

5. give aid, assist; relieve; e.g. ～急 *zhōují*, assist those in difficulty; (med.) ～匝 *zhōuzā*, solicitous, attentive, assiduous.
6. bend, turn; e.g. 道～ *dàozhōu*, bend in the road.
7. name of several dynasties: 1046-256 BCE; 557-581, Northern Zhou; 690-705, Empress Wu interregnum.

州   zhōu   MC tsyuw
1. isle, land area surrounded by water.
2. administrative unit.
   a. original 9 "isles" or provinces that emerged after the sage-king Yu 禹 drained the empire-wide flood.
   b. prefecture, coordinating several *xian* 縣 "districts" or "counties"; through 3rd century a unit larger than a *jun* 郡 "commandery"; in Sui-Tang times alt. designation for "commandery"; chief administrative officer a *cishi* 刺史.

洲   zhōu   MC tsyuw
1. isle, islet, ⊙ 州 *zhōu* 1.

粥   zhōu   MC tsyuwk
1. congee, thin gruel (more watery than 糜 *mí*).
   yù   MC yuwk
1. ⊙ 鬻 *yù*, peddle, hawk.

舟   zhōu   MC tsyuw
1. boat, usu. inland water-going vessel (cf. 船 *chuán*, usu. larger, graph in common use only from 3rd century BCE and Han dynasty); ～子 *zhōuzǐ*, boatman; ～航 *zhōuháng*, floating bridge made of boats lashed together.
   a. go or travel by boat; transport by boat, to ship.
2. boat-shaped saucer, used in sacrificial ceremonies.
3. ⊙ 周 *zhōu* 3, wear at the waist, engird; encircle; 6, dynastic name, esp. Western Zhou (1046-771 BCE).

譸   zhōu   MC trjuw
1. (bn.) ～張 *zhōuzhāng* (MC trjuw-trjang), ⊙ 侜張 *zhōuzhāng*, cheat, deceive, defraud.
2. ⊙ 籌 *chóu*, count, calculate; conjecture, approximate.

賙   zhōu   MC tsyuw
1. help out, assist; relieve (the needy); donate goods or provisions.

輈   zhōu   MC trjuw
1. single curved shaft by which an animal was hitched to carriage and yoke, used in pre-Qin times but largely abandoned afterward (cf. 轅 *yuán*, pair of straight shafts between which a carriage animal was hitched).
2. (bn.) ～張 *zhōuzhāng* (MC trjuw-trjang), surly and disagreeable, terse and irascible; also, panic-stricken, stunned and aghast.

週   zhōu   MC tsyuw
1. encircle, surround; encompass; pervasive.
   a. make a full circuit of, complete a cycle of time or distance; go all the way around.

鬻   zhōu   MC tsyuwk   ⊙ 粥 *zhōu*.

鵃   zhōu   MC trjuw
1. (bn.) 鶻～ *gǔzhōu*, → 鶻 *gǔ* (*hú*).

zhóu

妯   zhóu   MC drjuw   → 妯 *chōu*.

軸   zhóu   MC drjuwk
1. axle, axletree.
   a. by synecdoche, carriage.
2. spindle, for weaving; also, spindle-stick, spindle-shaft.
3. tuning-peg of stringed instrument, syn. 軫 *zhěn* 4.
4. roller(s) attached to end(s) of scroll.
   a. by synecdoche, scroll.
   b. roll up.

zhǒu

帚   zhǒu   MC tsyuwX
1. broom; besom (made of twigs).

疛   zhǒu   MC trjuwX
1. intestinal pain; cramps.

肘　zhǒu　MC trjuwX

1. elbow; e.g. ～後 *zhǒuhòu*, behind the elbow, i.e. in one's sleeve.
   a. to elbow, push aside.

zhòu

呪　zhòu　MC tsyuwH

1. incantation, ritualized performance of oral prayers or spells to attain a desired goal; conjure.
   a. supplicate, adjure.
   b. imprecation, malediction; curse.
2. (Budd.) trns. of Skt. *dhāraṇī*, charm, spell, allowing a bodhisattva to retain in memory all that he has learned or will ever learn, also a device for protecting sutras as well as those who promote and disseminate them from malign powers; untranslatable and to be recited in Sanskrit.

咒　zhòu　MC tsyuwH　→ 呪 *zhòu*.

咮　zhòu　MC trjuwH　⊙ 噣 *zhòu*.

噣　zhòu　MC trjuwH

1. beak of a bird.
2. alt. name for 柳 *liǔ*, Willow, one of the 28 lunar lodgings, made up of 8 stars in Hydra, in the southern quadrant (*chìniǎo* 赤鳥) of the sky.

宙　zhòu　MC drjuwH

1. ridgepole, central beam; structural mainstay.
   a. 宇～ *yǔzhòu*, eaves and ridgepole, euph. for celestial or cosmic edifice; also space and time, heaven and earth > universe, cosmos.
2. gen. term for time; all time.

晝　zhòu　MC trjuwH

1. daytime (ant. 夜 *yè*, nighttime).
   a. cmpd. ～日 *zhòurì*, the entire day; also, the sun.

甃　zhòu　MC tsrjuwH

1. riprap, revetment, ornamental facing of masonry, esp. for wells, also embankments and walls.
   a. by metonymy, well.
   b. brickwork.
2. revet with brickwork.
   a. embellish(ment), ornament, adorn(ment), spruce up, deck.

   b. (med.) inlay, set decorative pieces of precious or semi-precious stone into a surface.
3. (med.) flagstone.

皺　zhòu　MC tsrjuwH

1. (med.) lined, creased, wrinkled, esp. of skin.

籀　zhòu　MC drjuwH

1. large seal-script, invention attributed to the Historian Zhou 史籀 (?827-782 BCE); later modified as standard script (～文 *zhòuwén*) of the Qin dynasty.
2. explicate a text and recite it aloud.
3. take to oneself, take for oneself.

紂　zhòu　MC drjuwX

1. posthumous name of despicably cruel last king of Shang dynasty.
2. leather strap tied from horse's rump to carriage shafts.

縐　zhòu　MC tsrjuwH

1. fine-woven bast linen.
2. crinkled, wreathed, creased, wrinkled.

繇　zhòu　MC drjuwH　→ 繇 *yáo*.

冑　zhòu　MC drjuwH

1. battle helmet, helm; headpiece.
2. descendants, posterity.
   a. inheritance, legacy; birthright.

酎　zhòu　MC drjuwH

1. wine that has been fermented in 3 successive batches of cooked grain in the same medium, hence having high alcohol content; strong drink, fortified wine.

驟　zhòu　MC dzrjuwH

1. tantivy, full gallop, speed along, bound.
   a. headstrong; dart off, spring; bolt.
2. quick onset > compelling, imperative.
3. frequent(ly), recurrent(ly).

zhū

侏　zhū　MC tsyu

1. dwarf(ish), midget.
   a. (bn.) ～儒 *zhūrú* (MC tsyu-nyu), runty-stunted, diminutively dwarfish; also, (med.) short beams, stubby rafters.

朱   zhū   MC tsyu

1. the color vermilion, bright vivid red of high luster; vermeil; dye produced from cinnabar; e.g. ～門 *zhūmén*, vermilion gates, euph. for mansions of the nobility or the powerful, because gateways of nobility were anciently granted privilege of being painted this color; ～丹 *zhūdān*, "vermilion cinnabar," cosmic germ-essence of the south, because of red's association in *wuxing* correspondences with fire, south, summer, etc.

   a. metonymy for items colored vermilion, such as rouge makeup.
2. cinnabar, mercuric sulfide.

   a. ～粉 *zhūfěn*, minium, red lead, lead tetroxide, used as rouge for women's makeup.
3. ☉ 侏 *zhū*, in (bn.) ～儒 *zhūrú*, → 侏 *zhū* 1a.
4. (med.) ～俱波 *zhūjùbō* (MC tsyu-kju-pa), Yarkand, oasis kingdom on the southern track of the Silk Road.
5. a surname.

株   zhū   MC trju

1. tree trunk.
2. measure-word for trees.

   a. gen. term for plants and trees.
3. (med.) involve, implicate in legal case.

瀦   zhū   MC trjo

1. reservoir, basin; water stored in a natural or artificial lake.

   a. collect, gather, accumulate.

珠   zhū   MC tsyu

1. pearl.

   a. bead-cut gem of other precious or semi-precious stones.

   b. orb, spherule; pearl-shaped item, esp. decorative, or euph. imparting overtone of elegance or charm; e.g. 火～ *huǒzhū*, "fire orb," rump ornament for horse; also, (med.) brilliant round crystal; also, (med.) large spherical ornament placed atop certain tall structures during reign of Empress Wu (690–705); 露～ *lùzhū*, beads of dew; ～淚 *zhūlèi*, beaded tears.
2. euph. for writings or conversation of unusual brilliance; e.g. (lit.) 連～ *liánzhū*, "linked pearls," admonitory sayings or epigrams usu. in series, often meant for ruler or ministers, later expanded to other topics.

茱   zhū   MC dzyu

1. (bn.) ～萸 *zhūyú* (MC dzyu-yu), prickly-ash (*Zanthoxylum ailanthoides*), pungently fragrant tree whose fruit was used in making hot pepper and whose small pale-yellow flowers were gathered esp. on *chongyang* 重陽 (9/9) day to attach to household doorway as protective against malignant spirits; sometimes ref. euodia or evodia (*Tetradium ruticarpum*), aromatic deciduous small tree or large shrub that produces clusters of red rounded seed pods.

蛛   zhū   MC trju

1. (bn.) 蜘～ *zhīzhū*, → 蜘 *zhī*.

誅   zhū   MC trju

1. denounce, censure; declaim against, berate.

   a. assail, attack (either verbally or physically).

   b. punish, inflict a penalty on; handle roughly.
2. do to death, slay, execute.

   a. extirpate, eradicate; remove forcibly; clear away.
3. demand from, exact; impose.

諸   zhū   MC tsyo

1. attributive GP indicating membership in a class: one of, some of, the class of; e.g. 王之～臣皆足以供之 *wáng zhī zhū chén jiē zúyǐ gōng zhī*, those of the king's vassals are in all cases sufficient to provide it; ～侯朝於天子 *zhūhóu cháo yú tiānzǐ*, the assembly of noble lords pays court respects to the Son of Heaven.

   a. the several, the many, various, sundry, all of; e.g. ～生 *zhūshēng*, all living beings; ～書 *zhūshū*, the various documents; ～侯 *zhūhóu*, all the feudal lords, the sundry vassal lords.

   b. (med.) in all cases of; esp. in introducing legal statutes or decisions.
2. phonetic fusion of *zhī* 之 + *yū* 於: it/him/her/them (as direct-OBJ pronoun) in relation to; e.g. 吾亦欲無加～人 *wú yì yù wú jiā zhū rén*, I for my part prefer not to impose it on others; 吾聞～夫子 *wú wén zhū fūzǐ*, I heard about it from Confucius; 求～己 *qiú zhū jǐ*, to seek for it within oneself.

   a. phonetic fusion of *zhī* 之 + *hū* 乎 : it/him/her/them (as direct-OBJ pronoun) in an interr. sentence; e.g. 不識有～ *bù shì yǒu zhū*, I don't know, was there such a thing?; 毀～ *huǐ zhū*, shall I destroy it? 使楚人傳～ *shǐ chǔrén fù zhū*, will he send a person from Chu to tutor him?

3. first element in the 2-syllable surname ～葛 *zhūgé*, Zhuge.

豬　zhū　MC trjo

1. pig, hog.

    a. ～貛 *zhūhuān*, Asian badger (*Meles leucurus, Meles amurensis*); syn. 猯 *tuān*.

2. ～苓 *zhūlíng*, "hog fungus," umbrella polypore (*Polyporus umbellatus*), large edible mushroom growing from roots and trunks of deciduous trees, esp. oaks; ～櫟 *zhūlì*, whitebark stone-oak (*Lithocarpus dealbatus*).

銖　zhū　MC dzyu

1. unit of weight, a scruple, equiv. about .6 gram or 100 grains of millet; 6 *zhu* equiv. 1 *zi* 錙; 24 *zhu* equiv. 1 *liang* 兩, "ounce."

    a. 五～ *wǔzhū*, 5-zhu coin, introduced in 118 BCE as standard unit of currency, replacing the *banliang* 半兩; in 621 was replaced as standard by the *qian* 錢.

2. flimsy, fine, slight, minim; infinitesimal.

3. blunt, dull, as of weapons.

黿　zhū　MC trju　⊙ 蛛 *zhū*.

zhú

斸　zhú　MC trjowk

1. large hoe.

    a. delve, dig up, turn over ground, excavate.

朮　zhú　MC drwit

1. atractylis, hill-thistle (*Atractylodes macrocephala*), small perennial flowering plant, root used in various medicinal compounds, esp. favored in Dao. circles as conducing to longevity; syn. 白～ *báizhú*, 山精 *shānjīng*. Do not confuse with modern simplified form of 術 *shù*.

术　zhú　MC drwit　→ 朮 *zhú*.

柚　zhú　MC drjuwk　→ 柚 *yòu*.

燭　zhú　MC tsyowk

1. torch, flambeau.

    a. (med.) candle, made of wax.

2. light up an area, shed light all around.

    a. shed light on a question, understand clearly.

瘃　zhú　MC trjowk

1. chilblain.

竹　zhú　MC trjuwk

1. bamboo, all species.

2. musical instruments made from bamboo, esp. wind instruments, flutes, pipes, etc.; e.g. 弦～ *xiánzhú*, strings and bamboo, i.e. stringed instruments and wind instruments.

3. bamboo strips on which writing was done in early times; e.g. ～簡 *zhújiǎn*, bamboo slips for writing; ～帛 *zhúbó*, bamboo and silk, media for writing.

竺　zhú　MC trjuwk

1. (med.) abb. form of 天～ *tiānzhú* (MC xen-trjuwk, 天 here being read as 祆 *xiān*), one of the gen. terms for India, others being 身毒 *yuāndú* (MC ywen-dowk), 賢豆 *xiándòu* (MC hen-duwH), and 印度 *yìndù* (MC 'jinH-duH), all trsc. of Iran. *hinduka* (< Skt. *sindhu*, name of Indus River) ref. to people who live beyond the Indus River.

    a. abb. choronym for Indic peoples, esp. Budd. monks, in China.

2. ref. to the Buddha; descriptor for Buddhist-related terms.

    dù　MC towk

1. ⊙ 篤 *dù*, dedicated, devoted; genuine.

筑　zhú　MC drjuwk

1. bamboo zither, 5-stringed zither played with bamboo plectrum.

舳　zhú　MC drjuwk

1. stern of a boat, where rudder is placed; e.g. ～艫 *zhúlú*, stern to stem, ships in tight convoy.

    a. by synecdoche, boat.

蠋　zhú　MC tsyowk

1. immature caterpillar.

躅　zhú　MC drjowk

1. footprint.

    a. trace, track.

2. (bn.) 躑～ *zhízhú*, → 躑 *zhí*; (bn.) 跼～ *júzhú*, → 跼 *jú* 1a.

逐 **zhú** **MC drjuwk**

1. chase after, pursue (originally animals; by Han times, people also; cf. 追 *zhuī*).
   a. follow, go behind, go after.
   b. go in order, in succession.
   c. (med.) go along with, accompany, as in music.
2. seek after, pursue to obtain, chase down, run down.
3. compete, jockey for position.
4. drive away, chase away; expel.

鱁 **zhú** **MC drjuwk**

1. (med.) (bn.) ～鮧 *zhúyí* (MC drjuwk-yij), fish-maw sauce or soup, fish stock.

zhǔ

主 **zhǔ** **MC tsyuX**

1. the one in a dominant, principal, or presiding position.
   a. ruler of a state, lord, usu. of part (at least notionally) of larger kingdom; chief of an alliance.
   b. gen. term for high official or dignitary.
   c. master, host.
   d. (Budd.) (Dao.) abbot.
   e. (med.) proposer of topic at a session of "pure conversation" (*qingtan* 清談).
2. rule; control, dominate, preside; be in charge, have mastery over.
3. sgl. or cmpd. 公～ *gōngzhǔ*, princess, daughter of emperor.
4. of most importance, dominant; regard as most important; the main point.
5. tablet on which is inscribed the name of deceased ancestor, in ancestral shrine.

囑 **zhǔ** **MC tsyowk**

1. entrust with, enjoin, charge with carrying out request.

屬 **zhǔ** **MC tsyowk**

1. attach(ed), attach to; link up, connect; e.g. ～文 *zhǔwén*, put words together, compose literature.
   a. follow along, trail along; e.g. ～和 *zhǔhé*, sing in harmony; also, write a matching poem to answer one composed by someone else.
   b. (med.) clash together, sharpen (teeth).
2. entrust to, consign, turn over to, give up to.
   a. enjoin; adjure.
3. gather, assemble, collect; comprise, compound.
4. ⊙ 矚 *zhǔ*, stare at, fix one's gaze on.
5. proper for, meet for; oblige, suitably matching, just right.
   a. just now; e.g. ～者 *zhǔzhě*, quite recently, recent past.
6. pour into; be absorbed in.

shǔ **MC dzyowk**

1. subjoin(ed), subordinate to, dependent on; in the employ of; belong to.
   a. subordinate, subaltern; client, dependent; lesser member of family.
2. pertain(ing) to; due to, owing to; depending on.
   a. correlate.
3. category, class; kind, type; variety; e.g. 吾～ *wúshǔ*, people of our sort.

拄 **zhǔ** **MC trjuX**

1. support, sustain, prop up.
2. ridicule, mock; scoff at; taunt.

渚 **zhǔ** **MC tsyoX**

1. islet, holm.
   a. sandbar, sandspit, shoal.
2. shoreline, strand, beach.
3. streambed.

煮 **zhǔ** **MC tsyoX**

1. boil; cook with water.
   a. decoct.
2. to blanch, in cooking.

矚 **zhǔ** **MC tsyowk**

1. stare at, fix one's gaze on; scrutinize.

褚 **zhǔ** **MC trjoX**

1. sack, bag; satchel.
   a. store away, put away safely.
2. decorate clothing with damask embroidery.
   a. clothing so decorated.
3. red-colored shroud draped over a coffin.

zhě **MC tsyaeX**

1. form of address to ordinary soldier: "trooper," or "brownie" from russet color (赭 *zhě*) of garb.

chǔ **MC trhjoX**

1. a surname.

陼 **zhǔ** **MC tsyoX** ⊙ 渚 *zhǔ*.

麈　zhǔ　MC tsyuX

1. sambar (*Rusa unicolor*), large deer, the male having large 3-tined antlers.

   a. (med.) ～尾 *zhǔwěi*, sambar-tail [chowry], fly-whisk used as elegant accessory by gentlemen of the Six Dynasties period, esp. those engaged in "pure conversation" (*qingtan* 清談).

麞　zhǔ　MC tsyoX　⊙ 煮 *zhǔ*.

zhù

佇　zhù　MC drjoX

1. stand for a long time; stand waiting.

   a. (a)wait, wait for; anticipate, expect(ant).

住　zhù　MC trjuH

1. stay behind, remain.

   a. stay the night.

2. pause, halt; stop, cease.

   a. (Budd.) trns. Skt. *bhumi*, stage (of progress).

3. hold down, keep in place; e.g. ～後 *zhùhòu*, "rear-stay cap," with the rear stay made of iron, worn by judicial officers and imperial secretary.

   MC drjuH

1. (med.) stay at, reside; dwell at; e.g. (Budd.) ～忍 *zhùrěn*, dwell in forbearance.

2. (med.) be attached to, adhere to; e.g. (Budd.) ～持 *zhùchí*, adhere to the buddhadharma.

助　zhù　MC dzrjoH

1. help, lend a hand; assist.

2. (med.) send regards to; congratulate.

宁　zhù　MC drjoX

1. area in palace hall between the doorway and the standing screen.

杼　zhù　MC drjoX

1. shuttle, of a loom.

2. sharpen; slice thin.

   shù　MC zyoX

1. sawtooth oak (*Quercus acutissima*).

2. abb. form of 楙 *mào*, quince.

3. ⊙ 抒 *shū* 1, open out, divulge; 2, clear away foulness.

柱　zhù　MC drjuX

1. pillar, post, column of a building.

   a. gen. term for weight-bearing supporting element; strut.

2. wooden bridges ("posts") of a *se* 瑟, zithern.

   a. tuning pegs or frets of a *pipa* 琵琶, lute.

3. "stops," pressure of finger(s) on strings of stringed instrument, thus changing pitch; e.g. 促～ *cùzhù*, tighten the stops, producing higher pitch or rapid tempo; also, ref. to tightening the strings to change key.

   zhǔ　MC trjuX

1. support, sustain, bear up; take the weight of.

柷　zhù　MC tsyuwk

1. box-rattle, churn-box, in which is an attached stick that, when used to strike the inner sides of the box, signals the onset of a musical performance.

注　zhù　MC tsyuH

1. pour out, gush; sluice; flow into; drench; e.g. ～射 *zhùshè*, come down in torrents, gush forth.

   a. drip(pings); infuse, infusion; e.g. (med.) ～子 *zhùzǐ*, pipette, used for ladling wine.

2. possession of one's soul by the revenant of a deceased peson; inflict harm (cog. 疰 *zhù*, infectious disease); (Dao.) miasmas, baleful influences or noxious emanations of various sorts, incl. putrescent organic matter, inauspicious astrological conjunctions, exhalations of stale *qi*, etc.

3. gather together; focus, concentrate; e.g. ～目 *zhùmù*, focus one's gaze on; ～心 *zhùxīn*, concentrate one's attention on.

4. attach to, place on or with; arrange; e.g. ～錯 or ～措 *zhùcuò*, take care of, dispose, put in proper place.

5. annotate, comment(ary) on a text; e.g. ～疏 *zhùshū*, commentary and subcommentary.

6. record, set down in writing.

   a. (med.) in Tang times, to register the assignments of officials either newly appointed or whose offices have been changed.

炷　zhù　MC tsyuH

1. (med.) wick of a lamp.

   a. (med.) burning-stick, such as incense or moxa.

2. (med.) burn, (in)flame; light up.

疰　zhù　MC tsyuH

1. gradually presenting to chronic illness, often contagious; e.g. ～忤 *zhùwǔ*, intractable posses-

sion, incl. consumption, grand mal epilepsy, psychosis.

    a. spread of infectious disease from one person to another.

貯   zhù   MC drjoX

1. gaze far off, look into the distance.

祝   zhù   MC tsyuwk

1. person in charge of invoking the spirits during ancient sacrificial rites; cantor, invoker.
    a. invoke, supplicate, pray; invocation, supplication, prayer.
2. (Dao.) incant(ation), incantatory forumula, usu. directed to particular god(s); (en)chant.
3. break off, cut off, sever.
    zhòu   MC tsyuwH
1. ⊙ 呪 *zhòu* 1b, imprecation, malediction; curse.

竚   zhù   MC drjoX   ⊙ 佇 *zhù*.

筯   zhù   MC drjoH

1. chopsticks, ⊙ 箸 *zhù* 1.

箸   zhù   MC drjoH

1. chopsticks.
2. ⊙ 著 *zhù* 1, bring forth, make evident; 著 *zhuó* (*zhù*) 1, attach.

築   zhù   MC trjuwk

1. pestle for pounding earth, earth-ram.
    a. build of rammed earth; rammed-earth walls.
2. pound, beat; batter.
3. build, construct; make.

紵   zhù   MC drjoX

1. ramie, ⊙ 苧 *zhù*.
2. ramie cloth; bark-cloth.
    a. ～絲 *zhùsī*, gen. term for satins.

紸   zhù   MC tsyuH

1. ～纊 *zhùkuàng*, place a silk thread under the nose of someone newly deceased, to verify no longer breathing.

羜   zhù   MC drjoX

1. lamb; kid.

翥   zhù   MC tsyoH

1. take flight freely, lift away lightly.

芋   zhù   MC drjoX

1. chufa sedge (*Cyperus esculentus*), or nutgrass (*Cyperus rotundus*).
    shù   MC zyoX
1. ⊙ 杼 *shù* (*zhù*), sawtooth oak.

苧   zhù   MC drjoX

1. ramie (*Boehmeria nivea*), herbaceous perennial in the nettle family, the bark of its stalks producing a bast fiber.
2. ⊙ 茅 *máo*, floss-grass, cogon (*Imperata cylindrica*), esp. used for thatching.

著   zhù   MC trjoH

1. make visible or evident, divulge; bring forth, bring out; bring into focus; e.g. ～聞 *zhùwén*, evidently known.
    a. distinguished for or by; apparent; distinctive, conspicuous; e.g. ～姓 *zhùxìng*, distinguished clans.
2. put forth in writing, indite; compose; compile.
    a. register, enroll, record; e.g. ～錄 *zhùlù*, inscribe in the record, as for tax purposes; also, list as a catalogue.
    zhù   MC drjoX
1. ⊙ 宁 *zhù*, space between doorway and standing screen; 佇 *zhù*, stand waiting.
    zhuó   MC trjak
1. attach or add one thing to another; affix, adhere to; ～實 *zhuóshí*, intent on practicality or results; (Budd.) 無所～ *wúsuǒzhuó*, free of attachments; (Budd.) 貪～ *tánzhuó*, graspingness, clinging; 銘～ *míngzhuó*, imprint or engrave on one's mind.
    a. those attached to a particular place, locals, natives.
2. (med.) put on; wear; e.g. ～花 *zhuóhuā*, put on blossoms, bloom; ～物 *zhuówù*, put something on (to wear), the item one wears > Jpns. *kimono*; ～衣 *zhuóyī*, don clothing; also, a clothing mirror.
3. (med.) make use of, ply; e.g. ～手 *zhuóshǒu*, set one's hand to, apply oneself to; ～便 *zhuóbiàn*, do what's easiest or most fitting.
4. (med.) to line, in needlework.
    zháo   MC drjak
1. (med.) be afire, aflame; inflame.
2. (med.) encounter, come upon; experience, undergo.
3. (med.) (GP) post-VB indicating action of VB has attained its goal or is fulfilled.

蛀　zhù　MC tsyuH

1. (med.) cerambycid larvae, larvae of wood-boring longhorn beetles.
2. (med.) worm-eaten, insect-gnawed, eaten away; decay, rot(ten).
　　a. (med.) infected, contagious.

註　zhù　MC trjuH

1. ⊙ 注 zhù 4, annotate, commen(tary); 5, record in writing.

貯　zhù　MC trjoX

1. accumulate, store up.
　　a. put in a safe place, reserve; hoard.
2. ⊙ 佇 zhù, await.

鑄　zhù　MC tsyuH

1. cast metal, esp. bronze; cast in a mould; melt down and reform, forge.
　　a. mould, fashion, form, shape, create.

騹　zhù　MC tsyuH

1. horse with a white left leg.

駐　zhù　MC trjuH

1. pause, halt, check, restrain, arrest temporarily, esp. horse or carriage.
　　a. way-station, post-halt.
2. garrison; defend, guard; be stationed at.

zhuā

撾　zhuā　MC trwae

1. strike, smite; flog.
　　a. beat, as drums.

檛　zhuā　MC trwae

1. horsewhip.
　　a. flog with a whip.
2. strike, smite; beat.

髽　zhuā　MC tsrwae

1. woman's topknot tied with hemp strands, esp. during mourning.
2. (med.) woman's hairstyle of two topknots, one on either side of the head.

zhuān

嫥　zhuān　MC tsywen

1. (bn.) ～捖 zhuānwán (MC tsywen-hwan), combine and complement, bring into harmony, blend and temper.

專　zhuān　MC tsywen

1. exclusive(ly), specialize(d); sole(ly).
　　a. have sole charge of, control solely, monopolize; occupy unique position.
　　b. pay sole attention to, wholly concentrated on; conscientious(ly); rely exclusively on.
2. entirely, all of, without exception.
3. focus; condense, shrink down, compact.
4. spool of thread, yarn, silk.

甎　zhuān　MC tsywen　⊙ 磚 zhuān.

磚　zhuān　MC tsywen

1. (med.) brick; brickwork; cover with brick; syn. 甓 pì.

顓　zhuān　MC tsywen

1. untaught, ignorant; benighted; slow to understand.
2. decent, worthy; honest.
3. ⊙ 專 zhuān, exclusive(ly); control solely; without exception.
4. ～頊 zhuānxū, Zhuanxu, one of the 5 mythical god-kings (dì 帝) of prehistory.

zhuǎn

轉　zhuǎn　MC trjwenX

1. turn off course, turn to a different direction.
　　a. turn away; diverge; deflect(ion).
　　b. turn over, roll over; e.g. 展～ or 輾～ zhǎnzhuǎn, toss and turn, as of restless sleep; also, turn over in one's mind; also, without pause, from here to there; also, by turns; (Budd.)～輪王 zhuǎnlúnwáng, wheel-turning king, trns. Skt. cakravartin, enlightened universal ruler in whose realm the wheel of the buddhadharma turns freely.
2. change, alter; shift; transpose.
　　a. transfer, relocate; reassign, esp. official position.

b. transport, convey by wagon; relay; e.g. ～輸 *zhuǎnshū*, convey goods or provisions.
c. (Dao.) successive rounds of refinement in the process of compounding an elixir of immortality, e.g. 九～丹 *jiǔzhuǎndān*, nine-times transmuted (or cycling) cinnabar.
d. (med.) move from one SUBJ to another; e.g. ～相 *zhuǎnxiāng*, one in relation to the other, each other, one another.
e. (med.) on the contrary, to the contrary.
3. roll along, proceed easily and without obstructions; e.g. ～圓 *zhuǎnyuán*, follow along the circle, or ～規 *zhuǎnguī*, follow along the circle-compass, both meaning to be right on track.
4. follow the modulations of, rhythmically accompany as in music or song.
5. (med.) speak aloud, recite (< Turk. *tin-*, breathe a word, speak); e.g. ～說 *zhuǎnshuō*, tell; ～讀 *zhuǎndú*, read aloud; (Budd.) ～經 *zhuǎnjīng*, intone or recite a sutra, esp. "in rotation" by several monks or groups.
6. (med.) increasingly, even more, further, in a greater degree; syn. 益 *yì* 1, 越 *yuè* 5.
   a. (med.) rdup., gradually, little by little.
7. (med.) prefixed to official title indicates the following is a merit title (*xun* 勳), merit rank.
   zhuàn   MC trjwenH
1. turn round a fixed point, rotate, revolve, pivot.

zhuàn

傳   **zhuàn   MC drjwenH**   → 傳 *chuán*.

僝   **zhuàn   MC dzrjwenH**
1. provide(d), make ready; possessed of.
2. reveal, make seen, be manifest.

囀   **zhuàn   MC trjwenH**
1. modulations of sound, such as rippling or quavering of a flute, twittering or trilling of birds, purling or murmuring of a stream.

撰   **zhuàn   MC dzrwaenX**
1. take in hand.
   a. make by hand, manufacture.
2. compose, write; compile, edit.
3. provide, furnish; prepare.
4. calculations or enumerations that accord with and represent Heaven and Earth in the *Yijing*.

篆   **zhuàn   MC drjwenX**
1. ancient style of writing; esp. seal script.
   a. by metonymy, seal.
2. inscribe or incise characters on stone.
3. ridged bands on the face of a bell-chime.

篹   **zhuàn   MC dzrjwenH**
1. ⊙ 饌 *zhuàn* 1, food; eat and drink; 撰 *zhuàn* 2, compose, write; compile.

譔   **zhuàn   MC dzrjwenX**
1. ⊙ 撰 *zhuàn* 2, compose, write; compile; 3, provide, furnish, prepare.
2. (med.) eulogize, speak highly of.

賺   **zhuàn   MC dreamH**
1. (med.) dupe, trick, deceive.

饌   **zhuàn   MC dzrjwenH**
1. set out, prepare, or provide food.
2. food, esp. fine food.
   a. eat and drink.
   xuǎn   MC sjwenX
1. old unit of cash, equiv. 6 ounces (*liang* 兩).

zhuāng

妝   **zhuāng   MC tsrjang**
1. woman's adornment, esp. face and hair; makeup, gen. term or ref. individually to rouge, powder, mascara, hair ornaments, etc.
   a. apply cosmetics or make-up to make oneself appealing; deck oneself; dress up; adorn, titivate.
2. boudoir, place for applying makeup.

樁   **zhuāng   MC traewng**
1. (med.) post embedded in ground, stake, pile.

粧   **zhuāng   MC tsrjang**   ⊙ 妝 *zhuāng*.

莊   **zhuāng   MC tsrjang**
1. serious; formal; impressive, imposing; dignified.
   a. spacious, generously arranged.
2. finely dressed, adorn(ed); e.g. ～嚴 *zhuāngyán*, dress formally; decorate, ornament (persons, buildings, grounds, in splendid or august manner; a brave show; (Budd.) adorn(ed) and garland(ed), applied as VB or adjective to various items, incl. statues, monasteries, buddha-realms, the result of merit transferred from ritual offerings.

3. avenue, meeting of 6 or several roads.

4. (med.) farmstead, toft, house and its arable land and/or outbuildings; estate, manor, compound, curtilage; e.g. 〜客 *zhuāngkè*, tenant farmer; 〜宅 *zhuāngzhái*, landed estate; 〜田 *zhuāngtián*, toft and croft.

裝　zhuāng　MC tsrjang

1. outfit for a journey; prepare by putting items in proper place.

    a. pack up, stow (away), load, put away.

2. adorn(ment), makeup; ornament, bedeck; dress up, outfit.

    a. coat(ing), encrusted; guise, costume; garb, attire, outfit.

    b. feign, pretend, put-on.

zhuàng

壯　zhuàng　MC tsrjangH

1. hale, in the prime of health; robust, sturdy, stout, strong; vigorous, virile, manly; lusty, doughty.

    a. brave; mighty; grand, heroic; magnificent.

    b. (med.) burly; portly, plump.

2. in the prime of life, traditionally 30 years of age.

    a. in one's young manhood, late teens and early twenties.

3. self-confidence, *savoir-faire*, e.g. 無〜 *wúzhuàng*, unmannerly.

4. measure-word for a burning of moxa cone as medical treatment.

5. 大〜 *dàzhuàng*, "great strength," name of 34th hexagram of the *Yijing*.

戇　zhuàng　MC traewngH

1. honest but simple; straightforwardly dull-witted; gauche, tactless.

撞　zhuàng　MC draewngH

1. strike against; bump against, dash against; join in contact, collide.

    a. jolt, jostle.

    b. strike a bell with mallet.

狀　zhuàng　MC dzrjangH

1. physical aspect, appearance, shape; representation of.

2. condition, circumstances, situation; e.g. 無〜 *wúzhuàng*, without success, without accomplishment; also, lacking proper appearance or demeanor > humble self-reference, "I the unsuitable one"; also, without fact or reliability, without justification.

3. attest(ation), description, describe, representation, esp. of situation reported to the throne or superiors; e.g. (med.) 〜元 *zhuàngyuán*, "first on the avouchment," i.e. candidate who placed first in the *jinshi* 進士 exam and whose name headed the official announcement of successful graduates.

    a. (med.) (lit.) sgl. or cmpd. 行〜 *xíngzhuàng*, account of conduct, first record of a deceased compiled in the process of potential inclusion of a biography in official history or granting of posthumous title, usu. prepared by someone with personal knowledge of the deceased, such as sons, junior relatives, disciples, official associates.

zhuī

追　zhuī　MC trwij

1. pursue, chase (originally enemy army, soon also incl. individuals and abstractions; cf. 逐 *zhú*).

    a. follow after, go in the tracks of.

    b. escort, accompany; e.g. 〜胥 *zhuīxū*, escort and suite.

2. seek after, run after, try to obtain.

3. follow back to the beginning.

    a. recollect, recall, catch the remembrance of; 〜念 *zhuīniàn*, think back to.

    b. retroactive, retrospective > posthumous; e.g. 敕〜 *chìzhuī*, retroactive decree; 〜加 *zhuījiā*, posthumous corollary, action taken posthumously either to bestow or expunge honors and titles.

4. remedy, correct; repair or supplement afterward.

    duī　MC twoj

1. carve, engrave.

錐　zhuī　MC tsywij

1. awl, bodkin, gimlet, implement for making holes.

    a. pointed; acute; puncture(d).

騅　zhuī　MC tsywij

1. horse of mixed black and white color, dappled, skewbald.

zhuì

墜 **zhuì** MC drwijH
1. fall, drop, drop off, shed.
   a. fall down, tumble; fall in, collapse; inward declivity; e.g. ～谷 *zhuìgǔ*, precipitous valley, box canyon; impasse, dead-end.
   b. hang down, dangle; e.g. ～子 *zhuìzǐ*, pendant, earring; toggle, by which a hanging item is secured.
   c. fall short of, fail in, give up on; subside; lose.

惴 **zhuì** MC tsyweH
1. sgl. or rdup., anxious, fearful, fretful, frightened.
   chuǎn MC tsyhwenX
1. (bn.) ～叞 *chuǎnruǎn* (MC tsyhwenX-nywenX), creep and crawl, esp. insects.

槌 **zhuì** MC drjweH → 槌 *chuí*.

畷 **zhuì** MC trjwejH
1. paths along irrigation ditches between farm fields.
2. ⊙ 綴 *zhuì* 2, connect, tie together.

硾 **zhuì** MC drjweH
1. weigh down an object to make it fall or sink more quickly.

綴 **zhuì** MC trjwejH
1. stitch or sew together.
   a. (med.) euph. for composing lit. text.
2. connect, bind up, tie up; fasten together.
3. embellish, ornament; embroider.
   a. tessellate(d), mosaic.
   chuò MC trjwet
1. ⊙ 輟 *chuò*, halt, bring to a stop; put an end to.

縋 **zhuì** MC drjweH
1. let down or raise by means of rope or cord.
   a. cord for lowering or raising.

腄 **zhuì** MC drjweH
1. swelling of the feet, gout(y).
   a. heavy-footed, lumbering; clumsy; club-footed.

贅 **zhuì** MC tsywejH
1. give as pledge of security, collateral; debenture.

2. attach oneself or cling to for one's own benefit; freeload, parasite, esp. husband who lives in household of his wife's family.
   a. ⊙ 綴 *zhuì* 2, connect, bind together.
3. excrescence, tumor, wen.
   a. superfluous, supernumerary, excessive; unnecessary, extraneous, inessential; tautological, irrelevant.

醊 **zhuì** MC trjwejH
1. make a libation in ritual sacrifice.
2. sacrifice on successive occasions, continuously.

錣 **zhuì** MC trjwejH
1. sharp goad on the tip of a horsewhip.
2. sticks or chips for counting.

zhūn

屯 **zhūn** MC trwin
1. difficulty, throes; struggle; troubles.
   a. "Throes," name of 3rd hexagram of the *Yijing*.
   b. (med.) (bn.) ～邅 *zhūnzhān*, ⊙ 迍邅 *zhūnzhān*, → 迍 *zhūn*.
   c. rdup., ⊙ 肫 *zhūn* 2.
2. reach the full extent of.
   tún MC dwon
1. gather, mass, collect, assemble.
   a. show or lay forth in abundance.
2. defend, guard; e.g. ～田 *túntián*, military colony, with troops bringing land under cultivation or supervising others to do so, usu. established in troublesome areas that the state wants to incorporate and not simply garrison.
3. slope or bank of a hill.

窀 **zhūn** MC trwin
1. cmpd. ～穸 *zhūnxī* (MC trwin-zjek), unfathomable night > inter, inhume, entomb; also, tomb-pit, grave.

肫 **zhūn** MC tsywin
1. gizzard of fowls.
2. rdup., intense and ardent, sincere and persevering.
   chún MC dzywin
1. morsels of remaining meat from animals presented as sacrificial offerings.
2. ⊙ 純 *chún* 4, completely, entirely, all of.

tún　MC dwon

1. ⊙ 豚 *tún*, pigling, shoat.

訰　zhūn　MC tsywin

1. rdup., assiduous repetition, tireless attention, esp. for instruction, inculcation, guidance; also, earnest and sincere; also, blunt and dull-witted, listless.
2. assist, esp. in governing.

迍　zhūn　MC trwin

1. (med.) (bn.) ～邅 *zhūnzhān* (MC trwin-trjen) or 邅～ *zhānzhūn*, perilous and precarious, arduous and hard-pressed, difficult and dangerous.

zhǔn

准　zhǔn　MC tsywinX　⊙ 準 *zhǔn*.

準　zhǔn　MC tsywinX

1. water-level; instrument to measure water-level.
   a. measure, gauge; plumb; weigh (both physical objects and abstractions); e.g. ～擬 *zhǔnní*, anicipate, consider in advance; plan; expect.
2. norm, standard; proper level; model; e.g. ～的 *zhǔndì*, target, goal; benchmark.
   a. accurate, correctly measured; just, proper, appropriate; on the mark.
3. equate, equalize; make level or uniform; adjust to standard.
4. the nose; e.g. 隆～ *lóngzhǔn*, arched nose.
5. (med.) stringed instrument used to determine pitch of bells.

zhuō

倬　zhuō　MC traewk

1. grand and outstanding; magnificent.

卓　zhuō　MC traewk

1. stand tall or sheer; high-looming.
   a. outstanding, salient; prominent; above the crowd; excellent (med.) (bn.) ～犖 *zhuōluò* (MC traewk-laewk), same as preceding.
2. distant, far extended.

拙　zhuō　MC tsywet

1. awkward, clumsy; inept, maladroit; gauche.
   a. (med.) humble self-reference.

捉　zhuō　MC tsraewk

1. fold the hand around; grasp, hold on to, clasp.
   a. catch, seize; take control of; take advantage of.
   b. (med.) capture, arrest, apprehend.

梲　zhuō　MC tsywet　→ 梲 *tuō*.

涿　zhuō　MC traewk

1. runoff from eaves of a roof; trickle, drip.
2. sexual organs, private parts; vulva; penis.

zhuó　MC traewk

1. (med.) (bn.) ～鹿 *zhuólù* (MC traewk-luwk), judicial punishment of a mark carved onto one's forehead.

焯　zhuō　MC tsyak

1. shine; bright(ness); burn with light.
2. burn with heat, scorch.

zhuó

啄　zhuó　MC traewk

1. peck at, as a bird with food.
   a. chew, gnaw.
2. tap at, rap; knock.

zhòu　MC tsyuwH

1. beak of a bird.

擢　zhuó　MC draewk

1. pick up, draw toward one; pull up or out.
   a. gather up, seize; carry off; e.g. ～身 *zhuóshēn*, "gathering up one's body," i.e. with body erect.
2. select, choose; cull; promote or raise in office.
   a. take out, set aside; eliminate.
3. burgeoning of plants.

斫　zhuó　MC tsyak

1. cut in two, cleave; lop off; sever.
   a. strike, smite; fell, bring down.

斱　zhuó　MC tsrjak

1. chop, cut; sever.
   a. strike, smite.

斮　zhuó　MC traewk

1. chop, hew.
2. carve away, pare; trim, prune; slice off.
   a. sculpt; engrave.
   b. knife or other implement for carving.

斲 zhuó   MC traewk   ⊙ 斲 *zhuó*.

柭 zhuó   MC traewk
1. strike, esp. with a club; beat on, batter; hit, pound.
    a. assail, attack.
2. mutilate, maim.
    a. judicial punishment of castration; eunuch.
3. attack verbally; impugn; calumniate, denounce; abuse.

汋 zhuó   MC dzyak
1. of water, gush, sluice, run out.
2. ⊙ 酌 *zhuó*, pour a drink; shenk.
    chuò   MC tsyhak
1. (bn.) ～約 *chuòyuē* or 綽約 *chuòyuē* (MC tsyhak-'jak), tender and listless, relaxed and restrained.

濁 zhuó   MC draewk
1. muddied or disturbed by alien matter, turbid, lutulent; unclear, murky; impure.
    a. (med.) phonetically, ref. to low register phonemes, esp. voiced aspirates (cf. 清 *qīng*, plain voiceless); deep and thick.
2. muddled, blurred; confused.
    a. corrupt, debased, defiled; reprobate; turgid.
3. the lower 6 notes of the 12-tone gamut of pitches.

濯 zhuó   MC draewk
1. wash, rinse; soak; clean(se), purify; ～纓 *zhuóyīng*, wash the capstrings, euph. for leaving the corrupt world behind.
    a. poach, in water or broth.
2. rdup., sleek and shining, lustrous and lambent, sleek and spruce; also, stark and sheer, nakedly bald.

瀺 zhuó   MC dzraewk
1. (bn.) 瀺～ *chánzhuó* (MC dzream-dzraewk), plash and splash, of rushing waters; rdup., dumdrum, pash-dash, of falling rain; (bn.) 㴢～ *xiàozhuó* (MC haewX-dzraewk), crashing and colliding, raging and roaring, of waves.
    jiào   MC tsjewH
1. glistening lacquer of carriage shafts.

灼 zhuó   MC tsyak
1. burn; scorch; roast.
2. sgl. or rdup., evident, brilliant, aglow, vivid and vibrant, brightly blazing, plain and patent.
    a. (med.) ～然 *zhuórán*, obviously, evidently, clearly; certainly.

琢 zhuó   MC traewk
1. polish, esp. precious stone; figuratively, polish one's character
    a. grind, abrade, rub between hard surfaces; e.g. ～齒 *zhuóchǐ*, grind the teeth; ～釘 *zhuódīng*, rubbing spikes, boy's game similar to mumblety-peg > euph. for someone 8 or 9 years old.

繳 zhuó   MC tsyak
1. string or cord attached to arrow, for retrieval; corded arrow, leashed dart.
    jiǎo   MC kewX
1. sgl. or cmpd. ～繞 *jiǎorǎo*, wind round, bind up, bind together; complicate(d), complications.
2. (med.) hand over, give over.

茁 zhuó   MC tsrjwet
1. first noticeable growth of plants; push up, sprout.
    a. grow, increase; burgeon.

諑 zhuó   MC traewk
1. defame, traduce, slander, speak ill of.

酌 zhuó   MC tsyak
1. pour into a cup, ladle, esp. wine; shenk.
    a. imbibe, drink; draw from.
    b. wine-cup.
2. ponder, (re)consider, deliberate; e.g. ～中 *zhuózhōng*, ponder the best course between alternatives; ～量 *zhuóliàng*, evaluate, appraise.
    a. select, opt for.
3. (med.) ～然 *zhuórán*, obviously, clearly, evidently; certainly; ⊙ 灼然 *zhuórán*.

鷟 zhuó   MC dzraewk
1. sgl. or (bn.), 鸑～ *yuèzhuó*, a kind of "simurgh," → 鸑 *yuè*.

鸀 zhuó   MC draewk
1. yellow-billed chough, alpine chough (*Pyrrhocorax graculus*); red-billed chough (*Pyrrhocorax pyrrhocorax*).

zhú　MC tsyowk

1. (bn.) 〜鵒 *zhúyù* (MC tsyowk-ngjowk), crested myna (*Acridotheres cristatellus*).

zī

咨　**zī**　MC tsij

1. consult or seek an opinion about, inquire into, query; share an opinion with; e.g. 〜議 *zīyì*, consult and deliberate.
   a. form an opinion of, plan.
   b. (med.) report, relate, give account of; e.g. 〜白 *zībái* or 〜說 *zīshuō*, make the facts plain.
2. onom. of weariness, discouragement, heartache: ah me!; (bn.) 〜嗟 *zījiē* (MC tsij-tsjae), oh no!, ah alas!

姿　**zī**　MC tsij

1. physical bearing, attitude, demeanor, manner; posture; figure.
   a. appearance, looks; features; presence.
2. ⊙ 資 *zī* 2, natural faculties; assets.

孜　**zī**　MC tsi

1. rdup., assiduous and alert, determined and tireless; indefatigable, persevering.

孳　**zī**　MC tsi

1. propagate, breed; produce.
   a. multiply; increase; proliferate.
2. rdup., ceaselessly assiduous, fervently indefatigable, ⊙ 孜孜 *zīzī*.

孳　**zī**　MC tsi　⊙ 孳 *zī*.

嵫　**zī**　MC tsi

1. (bn.) 〜釐 *zīlí* (MC tsi-li), peaked and pinnacled, crested and cusped.
2. 崦〜 *yānzī*, → 崦 *yān* 1.

楢　**zī**　MC tsri　⊙ 葘 *zì* (*zī*).

滋　**zī**　MC tsi

1. propagate, produce; fecund(ity), uberty, feracity.
   a. multiply; increase.
   b. (med.) even more, all the more; the more X.
2. plant, cultivate; grow, thrive, proliferate.

3. juice, sap, fluid.
   a. succulent, juicy; rich in flavor.

兹　**zī**　MC tsi　⊙ 茲 *zī*.

粢　**zī**　MC tsij

1. broomcorn millet, proso millet (*Panicum miliaceum*), used in ritual sacrifices.
   a. gen. term for grains.

cí　MC dzij

1. (med.) rice-cakes.

緇　**zī**　MC tsri

1. gray-black; ebon; somber-hued.
   a. (med.) the ebon-robed, i.e. Budd. monks; by metonymy, Buddhism (religion of the ebon-robed).

茲　**zī**　MC tsi

1. "near" demonstrative pronoun: this, these, this place > here (somewhat archaic and less common than 此 *cǐ*); e.g. 今〜未能 *jīn zī wèi néng*, at present this is not yet able to be done; 文不在〜乎 *wén bùzài zī hū*, is not "culture" located here?
   a. at this time, now.
   b. in this way, like this.
2. increasingly, more and more.
3. year, esp. in cmpds. 今〜 *jīnzī*, this year; 來〜 *láizī*, the coming year, next year.
4. reed mat, for sitting.
5. ⊙ 滋 *zī* 1, propagate, fecund(ity); multiply, increase; 2, thrive, proliferate.

cí　MC dzi

1. (bn.) 龜〜 *qiūcí* (MC khjuw-dzi), Kucha, oasis city on the northern Silk Road in the Tarim Basin, esp. important in Tang times for popularity of its music and musical instruments brought to China.

葘　**zī**　MC tsri

1. cultivate fallow land.
   a. land that has been cultivated for no more than a year.
   b. field cleared by slash and burn.
2. thick or dense vegetation.

zì　MC tsriH

1. standing but rotten tree; something that looks fine but is inwardly wasted.

zāi　MC tsoj

1. ⊙ 災 *zāi* 2, calamity, disaster, ruin.

觜 zī MC tsje

1. feathered crest of owl.
2. (bn.) ～蠵 zīxī (MC tsje-hwej), loggerhead turtle (*Caretta caretta*), ⊙ 蠵蠵 zuīxī (MC tsjwe-hwej); also, name of one of the 12 Jupiter stations; also, sgl. or (bn.), name of one of the 28 lunar lodgings, made up of 3 stars in Orion, in the western quadrant (*baihu* 白虎) of the sky.

    zuǐ   MC tsjweX

1. beak of a bird.
    a. beak-shaped.
    b. (med.) peck at.

諮 zī MC tsij

1. ⊙ 咨 zī 1, consult, inquire; share an opinion with.

貲 zī MC tsje

1. cash or goods used to commute judicial punishment.
    a. (med.) cash or goods used to substitute for tax requirement.
2. calculate, reckon; estimate, evaluate.
    a. value, valuation; cost.
3. ⊙ 資 zī, resources; aid.

資 zī MC tsij

1. resource(s); property, wealth; capital, material at one's disposal, whether earnings or outlay; e.g. (med.) ～從 zīcóng, "property that follows one," i.e. dowry.
2. natural endowments, inner resources one is born with; competence; intelligence, character, personal faculties.
    a. qualifications; assets.
3. supply, purvey(or); provide as a resource; aid, contribute to the success of with either material or moral support; sustain, fortify; imbue(d) with.
4. rely, depend on; count on for assistance.
5. conserve, set aside, reserve for future use.
    a. be provided with, possess; supplied with in advance.
6. ⊙ 咨 zī, inquire into, examine; consult; 齎 jī, deliver, give to.

趑 zī MC tshij

1. (bn.) ～趄 zījū (MC tshij-tsjo), stir about, shift and stumble; hover and hang back, be put off; also, harsh and high-handed, insolent and overweening.

趦 zī MC tshij (med.)   ⊙ 趑 zī.

輜 zī MC tsri

1. covered carriage in which one may sit or lie.
2. baggage wagon, esp. for military equipment.

錙 zī MC tsri

1. ancient unit of weight, equiv. 6 zhu 銖 or 600 grains of millet; 4 zī (24 zhu) equiv. 1 liang 兩, "ounce."
    a. small bit, minimal portion; e.g. ～銖 zīzhū, the least amount, to the smallest measure, insignificant, inconsequential.
2. ～基 zījī, large hoe.

頿 zī MC tsje

1. moustache.
2. whiskers of a horse.

髭 zī MC tsje   ⊙ 頿 zī.

鯔 zī MC tsri

1. gray, flathead, or striped mullet (*Mugil cephalus*).

鼒 zī MC tsi

1. small-mouthed tripod.

zǐ

仔 zǐ MC tsiX

1. bear responsibility; e.g. ～扁 zǐbiǎn, take a burden on one's shoulders.
    a. (med.) ～細 zǐxì, "take up the details," i.e. careful, meticulous, painstaking; also, clearly, distinctly.

姉 zǐ MC tsijX   ⊙ 姊 zǐ.

姊 zǐ MC tsijX

1. elder sister.

子 zǐ MC tsiX

1. offspring, progeny, child; treat as one's child, with paternal care.
    a. (med.) most often ref. to son(s).
    b. follower, student, pupil, cadet; e.g. ～弟 zǐdì, "sons and younger brothers" > young fellows, younger generation, young bloods, demoiselle; disciples, acolytes; (med.) apprentices, esp. entertainers.

2. person, man, woman.

   a. honorific designation of man, woman, teacher, master; often suffixed to surname or epithet.

   b. bibliographic classification of works usu. philosophical, technical, or religious.

3. 4th of the 5 ranks of nobility, usu. translated "viscount."

4. 2nd-person pronoun: you(r); originally honorific, by med. times neutral.

5. the young of animals.

   a. eggs of birds, fishes, insects.

6. of plants, seed, grain, pip, kernel; offshoot.

   a. something small and solid, e.g. counter, bead, pebble.

7. spot(ted), blotch(ed).

8. 1st of the 12 earthly branches, associated with the rat as emblematic animal.

   a. 1st double-hour of the day, from approximately 11 p.m. to 1 a.m.

9. enclitic suffix, often designating person, e.g. 舟～ *zhōuzi*, boatman; also, often suggestive of youth or smallness: -kin, -ling, -let.

10. interest on money; cf. *mu* 母, principal.

梓　*zǐ*　MC tsiX

1. catalpa tree (*Catalpa ovata*), esp. associated with the mulberry tree as symbolic of home and hearth, e.g. 桑～ *sāngzǐ*, mulberry and catalpa, i.e. one's homeplace, hometown, also ～里 *zǐlǐ*, "catalpa hamlet"; its wood prized for making various items, esp. coffins, e.g. ～宮 *zǐgōng*, "catalpa dwelling," coffin of an emperor or empress; in late summer sets creamy-white foxglove-like flowers tinged with yellow (cf. 楸 *qiū*, another species [*Catalpa bungei*]).

2. woodworker, joiner; sgl. or cmpd. ～匠 *zǐjiàng*

滓　*zǐ*　MC tsriX

1. dregs, lees, sediment, material that settles to the bottom of a liquid.

   a. undesirable, impure; contaminate(d), sullied; tainted, foul.

秭　*zǐ*　MC tsijX

1. ancient unit of agricultural measurement, 200 sheaves of grain.

2. extraordinarily high number: million, billion.

筸　*zǐ*　MC tsriX

1. mat-frame for bed, made of plaited bamboo.

   a. by synecdoche, bed.

紫　*zǐ*　MC tsjeX

1. purple, incl. colors from lavender to violet; the intermediate or secondary color between blue and red, usu. a dark reddish-blue; dye traditionally produced from root of gromwell (*Lithospermum arvense*, ～草 *zǐcǎo*, "purple plant"), in med. times also from heartwood juice of sapanwood (*Caesalpina sappan*, 蘇枋目 *sūfāngmù*).

   a. associated emblematically with the monarch and his possessions; e.g. ～禁 *zǐjìn* or ～宸 *zǐchén*, the purple adyta, restricted area of imperial palace, private apartments; ～衣 *zǐyī*, purple robes, attire of emperor; in Tang times also the color of robes of those in the highest 3 (of 9) bureaucratic grades.

   b. (Dao.) associated emblematically with the depths of heaven, astral divinities, celestial phenomena, spectral visitations, cosmic totality and wholeness; e.g. ～虛 *zǐxū*, purple void, ～冥 *zǐmíng*, purple gulf, ～宙 *zǐzhòu*, purple firmament, all ref. to heaven; ～煙 *zǐyān*, purple haze, ～霞 *zǐxiá*, purple auroras, both ref. mystical mists; ～曜明 *zǐyàomíng*, light of purple scintillance, esoteric name for sun; ～清 *zǐqīng*, Purple Clarity, alt. name for heaven of Jade Clarity (玉清), highest of Dao. heavens; ～雲 *zǐyún*, purple clouds, auspicious signal of heaven's support or protection; ～河 *zǐhé*, Purple River, i.e. river in the deep sky, Milky Way.

2. ～微 *zǐwēi*, Purple Tenuity, name of constellation of 15 stars arranged like a protective screen around Northern Dipper and Polestar (eastern screen having 8 stars, western 7), comprising stars in Draco, Cepheus, and Camelopardus; seat of heaven's god-king, symbolic seat of earthly emperor, also ref. to emperor's earthly compound; (Dao.) name of important Shangqing goddess.

3. ～塞 *zǐsài*, Purple Fortress, i.e. the Great Wall, because the earth Qin built it with was said to be purple.

4. used in various plant or mineral names; e.g. ～石英 *zǐshíyīng*, bloom of purple stone, i.e. amethyst; ～檀 *zǐtán*, purple rosewood, i.e. sanderswood (*Pterocarpus santalinus*); ～藤 *zǐténg*, purple liana, i.e. wisteria (*Wisteria chinensis*); ～菫 *zǐjǐn*, purple dock, i.e. corydalis (*Corydalis edulis*); ～菜 *zǐcài*, purple laver (*Porphyra coccinea*); ～微, ～薇 *zǐwēi*, crepe-myrtle (*Lagerstroemia indica*).

籽　zǐ　MC tsiX

1. bank up earth around plants with a hoe.

胏　zǐ　MC tsriX

1. dried meat still with its bones.

芓　zǐ　MC tsiX

1. bank up earth around plants, ⊙ 籽 *zǐ*.

zì　MC dziH

1. female hemp plant (*Cannabis sativa*).

茈　zǐ　MC tsjeX

1. sgl. or ～草 *zǐcǎo*, gromwell (*Lithospermum arvense*), white-flowering plant from whose root a purple dye is made; syn. 藐 *mào* (*miǎo*).

cí　MC dzje

1. 凫～ *fúcí*, water-chestnut (*Eleocharis dulcis, Eleocharis tuberosa*), sedge whose corms (not actually nuts) are eaten.

cǐ　MC tshjeX

1. (bn.) ～厜 *cǐzhì* (MC tshjeX-dryeX), uneven, high and low, higgledy-piggledy.

chái　MC dzrea

1. (med.) ～胡 *cháihú*, thorowax (*Bupleurum chinense*), yellow-flowering herb whose root was used medicinally, syn. 柴胡 *cháihú*.

訾　zǐ　MC tsjeX

1. vilify, denigrate, malign; badmouth; reproach.
    a. detest, despise, be disgusted with.

zī　MC tsij

1. ⊙ 資 *zī* 1, resources; 咨 *zī* 2, onom. sigh; 恣 *zì*, indulge.

cī　MC dzje

1. ⊙ 疵 *cī*, defect(ive), blemish; wound.

zì

倳　zì　MC tsriH

1. stab with knife or sword, impale.
    a. insert, plant.
2. pick, hoe.

剚　zì　MC tsriH　⊙ 倳 *zì*.

字　zì　MC dziH

1. procreate, engender.
    a. foster; care for, love.
2. secondary or polite name taken by male upon reaching marriageable, procreating age;

byname, cognomen, used by non-family members; the byname often had a semantic similarity with the *míng* 名, personal name given at birth.
    a. betroth a daughter; e.g. 待～ *dàizì*, awaiting [someone with] a byname, i.e. yet to be married.
3. a graph consisting of 2 or more components, compound or diagrammatic character; cf. *wén* 文, graph consisting of a single component.

恣　zì　MC tsijH

1. indulge, give license to; as one will, at one's whim, however one wishes.
    a. self-indulgent, lose oneself in; dissolute.
    b. (bn.) ～睢 *zìsuī* (MC tsijH-swij), forgetful and free, freewheeling, catch-as-catch-can; also, unrestrained appetite, fit of frenzy, carried away with, uncontrolled.
2. give way to, allow, concede.

漬　zì　MC dzjeH

1. macerate, steep; saturate(d), imbue.
2. dye; stain.
    a. infect(ion).

牸　zì　MC dziH

1. female ox, cow; milch cow.
    a. gen. term for female of domestic animals.

眥　zì　MC dzjeH

1. eye socket; corner of the eye.
2. look askance at; look with cut vision, incensed.

眦　zì　MC dzjeH　⊙ 眥 *zì*.

胔　zì　MC dzjeH

1. rotting corpse.

jí　MC dzjek

1. ⊙ 瘠 *jí*, emaciated, gaunt.

裁　zì　MC tsriH

1. meat cut in large chunks, gobbets (cf. 軒 *xiàn*, in large slices; 膾 *kuài*, in thin slices).

自　zì　MC dzijH

1. reflexive pronoun, always occuring immediately before VB and ref. to SUBJ as agent of VB (cf. 己 *jǐ*, which may occur as SUBJ or OBJ of VB or attributive to noun): for oneself, of oneself, personally; e.g. ～在 *zìzài*, self-abiding, self-possessed, calm, poised; ～省 *zìxǐng*, exam-

ine oneself; 君子〜強不息 *jūnzǐ zìqiáng bùxī*, the noble man never rests in strengthening himself; 于是河伯欣然〜喜 *yúshì hébó xīnrán zìxǐ*, at this the Count of the River was exuberantly pleased with himself.

   a. 〜然 *zìrán*, what is so-of-itself, what is as it is, self-determined, *natura naturans*, what is the way it is simply because it is so; although often translated as "Nature," that rendering is misleading (esp. in common connotation of "Mother Nature") and does not do justice to the concept; better to retain the complete denotation; cf. (Budd.) 真如 *zhēnrú*, → 真 *zhēn*.

2. instinctively, naturally, freely, spontaneously; as a matter of course, automatically; of one's own accord, voluntarily; indifferently.

3. from; e.g. 有朋〜遠方來 *yǒu péng zì yuǎnfāng lái*, there being a friend who has come from a far place; 〜此之時 *zì cǐzhī shí*, from this time forth.

   a. owing to, deriving from; e.g. 侯〜我得之〜我損之 *hóu zì wǒ dé zhī, zì wǒ sǔn zhī*, as to the title of marquess, it is owing to myself that I have obtained it and owing to myself that I shall relinquish it.

4. prefixed to negative as conditional marker: except for, unless; e.g. 〜非亭午夜分，不見曦月 *zìfēi tíngwǔ yèfēn bùjiàn xīyuè*, unless it is noontime or midnight, one will not see blazing sun or moonlight; 〜非聖人，外寧必有內憂 *zìfēi shèngrén wàiníng bì yǒu nèiyōu*, except under a sage ruler, when there is peace outside the state, there is sure to be anxiety at home.

zōng

宗 zōng　MC tsowng

1. ancestors, forebears; esp. founding ancestor of a clan.

   a. sept or kin-group with same ancestor; lineage.

   b. ancestral temple.

2. venerate(d), revere(nd), honor(ed); pay homage to; e.g. (med.) 〜奉 *zōngfèng*, 〜仰 *zōngyǎng*, 〜重 *zōngzhòng*, pay respects to, treat with reverence.

3. prototype, exemplar; ideal.

   a. necessary, essential; fundamental.

   b. cynosure; summative, summation.

4. visit made by feudal lords to sovereign in summer; e.g. 朝〜 *cháozōng*, spring and summer visits of feudal lords to sovereign; also, proceed to where one owes allegiance or seeks refuge.

5. (Budd.) sect, school, usu. emphasizing particular sutras or set of practices.

嵕 zōng　MC tsuwng

1. massif, group of connected mountains.

   a. mountain with several peaks.

棕 zōng　MC tsuwng

1. sgl. or 〜櫚 *zōnglǘ*, windmill palm, coir palm (*Trachycarpus fortunei*).

   a. 〜竹 *zōngzhú*, broadleaf lady palm, bamboo palm (*Rhapis excelsa*).

2. brown-colored.

椶 zōng　MC tsuwng　⊙ 棕 *zōng*.

綜 zōng　MC tsowngH　→ 綜 *zòng*.

豵 zōng　MC tsuwng

1. piglet or farrow less than 1 year old, a suckling.

   a. gen. term for infants of 4-footed animals, whelp.

2. litter of 3 pigs.

踪 zōng　MC tsjowng

1. (med.) ⊙ 蹤 *zōng*.

蹤 zōng　MC tsjowng

1. footprint, tracks, imprint; of animal, spoor.

   a. scar; vestige, remaining mark.

2. follow in the track of; track, trace; imitate, follow suit.

騣 zōng　MC tsuwng

1. (med.) ⊙ 騌 *zōng*.

騌 zōng　MC tsuwng

1. horse's mane; pig's bristles.

   a. shaggy; bristly.

鬃 zōng　MC dzowng

1. (med.) tall chignon.

2. (med.) ⊙ 騌 *zōng*, horse's mane, pig's bristles.

鯼 zōng　MC tsuwng

1. the croaker fish (*Sciaenidae*).

zǒng

傯 　zǒng 　MC tsuwngX
1. (bn.) 倥〜 *kǒngzǒng*, → 倥 *kǒng* 2.

總 　zǒng 　MC tsuwngX
1. bring together, bind together; tie up, knot up.
   a. gather up, pull together; e.g. 〜轡 *zǒngpèi*, gather the reins, rein in.
2. assemble, collect; consolidate; compile; e.g. (Budd.) 〜持 *zǒngchí*, collect and hold in mind, trns. Skt. *dhāraṇī*, bear in mind, remember > magic spell, mystical formula.
3. control, manage, direct; command.
4. (med.) altogether, completely, wholly; extensive(ly), comprehensive(ly).
   a. (med.) after all.

zòng

瘲 　zòng 　MC tsjowngH
1. (bn.) 瘛〜 *chìzòng*, → 瘛 *chì*.

糉 　zòng 　MC tsuwngH
1. (med.) ⊙ 糭 *zòng*.

糭 　zòng 　MC tsuwngH
1. (med.) rice dumpling wrapped in reeds or bamboo leaves.

綜 　zòng 　MC tsowngH
1. heddle-shaft, one of a set of vertical cords in a loom that form the main part of harness that guides warp threads, esp. the loop of thread through which warp-thread is passed.
　　zōng 　MC tsowng
1. bring together, group, assemble.
   a. summation; in book titles: summa, omnibus.
2. arrange, put in order.

縱 　zòng 　MC tsjowngH
1. give rein to, unleash, unbridle; release(d), loosen, let loose, free to do X.
   a. set aside constraints, abandoned; reckless, heedless.
2. leaving aside X, allowing for X, even if X.
　　zōng 　MC tsjowng
1. perpendicular, longitudinal, vertical, north-south direction; ant. 橫 *héng*; e.g. 〜橫 *zōnghéng*, this way and that, across and athwart; also,

sophistical eloquence in political matters and those who practice it, persuaders who can argue one way or another; also, 2 alliances during the late Warring States period, *zōng* being that of 6 states against Qin 秦, *héng* being that of 6 eastern states allied with Qin.
2. rise up, straighten to full height.
3. ⊙ 蹤 *zōng*, footprint; follow after.
　　zǒng 　MC tsuwngX
1. rdup., hasty and hurried, over and done with; also, assembled en masse.

zōu

揿 　zōu 　MC tsuw
1. make the rounds sounding the night-watches.

椒 　zōu 　MC tsuw
1. brushwood; kindling; shavings, tinder.
2. hemp stalk.
　　sǒu 　MC suwX
1. ⊙ 藪 *sǒu*, fen; underbrush.

緅 　zōu 　MC tsuw
1. magenta-colored silk.

菆 　zōu 　MC tsrjuw
1. hemp stalk.
   a. gen. term for plant stalks, stems.
2. finely fashioned arrow.

諏 　zōu 　MC tsju
1. inquire about, seek counsel or advice.
   a. deliberate, discuss, offer opinion.
2. choose, select, esp. by divination.

陬 　zōu 　MC tsuw
1. corner, angle; hern, hirn, nook.
   a. out-of-the-way place, alcove, retreat.
2. foot of a mountain.
3. bank of a river or lake, strand.
4. old term for 1st month of the year.

騶 　zōu 　MC tsrjuw
1. stableman, ostler; coachman.
2. outrider, mounted escort.
3. ⊙ 菆 *zōu* 2, finely fashioned arrow.
　　zhòu 　MC dzrjuwH
1. ⊙ 驟 *zhòu*, tantivy, full gallop.
　　qū 　MC tsrhju
1. ⊙ 趨 *qū*, hasten, run quickly.

鯫　zōu　MC tsuw
1. small fish, small fry.
2. ninny, nitwit, half-wit.

齺　zōu　MC tsrjuw
1. (bn.) ～齵 zōu'óu (MC tsrjuw-nguw), crooked teeth; mismatched, misaligned.
　　chuò　MC tsrhaewk
1. (bn.) 握～ wòchuò, → 握 wò.

齱　zōu　MC tsrjuw
1. closely fitting teeth.
　　a. be in close alignment, in perfect accord.

zǒu

走　zǒu　MC tsuwX
1. run; flee, run from, run away; clear out.
　　a. (med.) run off; spread, extend.
2. gressible, of beasts.
　　a. humble self-reference: "I, a mere lackey [who am no better than a beast]."
3. amble, ambulatory; movable.
4. (med.) errant, off the path; e.g. ～作 zǒuzuò, differ(ent) from what is expected.
　　MC tsuwH
1. hasten to, run toward.
　　a. look after; e.g. ～使 zǒushǐ, do a service for, wait upon.

zòu

奏　zòu　MC tsuwH
1. propose, lay before; advance, put forward, address; present, tender.
　　a. (lit.) proposal, formal policy statement submitted to the ruler.
2. perform, esp. music.
　　a. rhythm, beat, in music; e.g. 節～ jiézòu, measured beat or cadence.
3. present and carry through in finished form, accomplish.

zū

租　zū　MC tsu
1. land tax, payable in grain; e.g. (med.) ～庸 zūyōng, grain tax and corvée.
　　a. by metonymy, taxes of any kind.
2. rent, let out.
3. gather, collect; hoard.

菹　zū　MC tsrjo
1. pickle(d) vegetables, preserved in solution of brine or vinegar.
2. sgl. or cmpd. ～醢 zūhǎi, mince(d) and pickled meat.
　　a. torture, or judicial punishment of heinous crimes such as patricide, in which the corpse is cut into small pieces.
3. decayed or withered plants.
　　jù　MC kju
1. bog or fen overgrown with aquatic plants.

zú

卒　zú　MC tswot
1. foot-soldiers, common soldiers; troops.
　　a. unit of 100 soldiers, a company; centurions.
2. minor official, serviceman, underling; runner, lictor.
　　zú　MC tswit
1. pass away, meet one's end, die; in Zhou times esp. used for grandees (dafu 大夫).
　　a. conclude, conclusion; terminate; outcome; bring to an end, accomplish, complete.
2. in the end, finally.
　　cù　MC tshwot
1. brusque, abrupt; hurried, sudden, ⊙ 猝 cù; (bn.) 倉～ cāngcù, → 倉 cāng.

崒　zú　MC dzwit
1. jut up; (bn.) ～兀 zúwù (MC dzwit-ngwot), rearing ruggedly, precipitously poised.
　　cuì　MC dzwijH
1. ⊙ 萃 cuì, concentrate(d), bunch up.

族　zú　MC dzuwk
1. kin-group, sept, families tracing descent from common agnatic ancestor.
　　a. when preceding kinship term, ref. to sib-relative from 4th collateral line or beyond.
2. class, kind, category, grouping; e.g. 羽～ yǔzú, feathered kind, i.e. birds.
　　a. most > usual, average, e.g. ～庖 zúpáo, most cooks, i.e. the usual kind of cook.
3. extirpate a kin-group, as punishment for unforgivable crime, usu. incl. all in the criminal's generation as well as that of his parents and children.
4. group together, gather, as of clouds.
5. (med.) intricate, involved.

zòu　MC tsuwH

1. ⊙ 奏 *zòu* 3, rhythm, beat, in music.

足　**zú**　MC tsjowk

1. foot; pedestrian; by synecdoche, the lower leg.
   a. foot of made objects such as cauldrons, furniture, or of natural objects such as mountains.
2. footfall; patter(ing); e.g. 雨～ *yǔzú*, pattering of rain.
3. sufficient, adequate; enough.
   a. content(ment), satisfied with.
   b. fill up; complete; suffice.
   c. plenty of, more than enough; add to, supplement.
4. be worth X, amount to X, commensurate with.
5. (med.) allow(able), permit.
6. ～下 *zúxià*, "you below whose foot I am," respectful address to superior; (med.) honorific address to an equal, esp. in letters.

踤　**zú**　MC dzwit

1. bump, butt; crash, collide.

cuì　MC dzwijH

1. ⊙ 萃 *cuì*, concentrate(d), bunch(ed).

鏃　**zú**　MC tsuwk

1. arrowhead.
   a. sharp(ly), pointed(ly).
2. (med.) rdup., avant-garde, out in front, best and brightest.

zǔ

俎　**zǔ**　MC tsrjoX

1. meat-tray for offerings of meat at ritual sacrifice.
   a. morsels, tidbits; samplings; rasher.
2. butcher block, chopping block.

祖　**zǔ**　MC tsuX

1. paternal grandfather.
2. forefather, progenitor, patriarch, esp. of clan, dynasty, teaching.
   a. ancestral temple.
3. found, begin; inaugurate, initiate.
4. follow the example of, carry on in reverence for; venerate.
5. sacrifice before setting out on a journey; e.g. ～道 *zǔdào*, setting-out sacrifice to the spirit of the roads; ～度 *zǔdù*, setting-out sacrifice for safe passage.
   a. (med.) farewell or seeing-off party.

組　**zǔ**　MC tsuX

1. weave, bind together.
   a. connect with, link up; attach to.
2. woven silk cord or band, sash.
   a. silk cord from which hangs a seal of office symbolic of authority, seal-cord > by metonymy, an official.
3. organization, group.
   a. section of a larger group; squad.

蒩　**zǔ**　MC tsuX　⊙ 葅 *zǔ*.

葅　**zǔ**　MC tsuX

1. heartleaf, fishwort (*Houttuynia cordata*), perennial herb used medicinally; syn. 蕺菜 *jícài*, 魚腥草 *yúxīngcǎo*.

詛　**zǔ**　MC tsrjoX

1. imprecate, call down a curse; malediction.
   a. swear an oath, accompanied by imprecations against any who break it.

阻　**zǔ**　MC tsrjoX

1. impasse; place of obstruction; cul-de-sac, dead-end.
   a. obstruct, block; impede; fend off; bring to a standstill.
2. predicament; dilemma.
   a. be faced with hopeless situation, suffer from; trials, suffering.
3. put one's last hope on, rely on as last resort; trust to completely.

zuān

劗　**zuān**　MC tswan

1. trim, pare; cut, shear.

zuǎn

纂　**zuǎn**　MC tswanX

1. of documents, collect, assemble, compile, edit; e.g. ～修 *zuǎnxiū*, sort and tend, organize and arrange.
2. ⊙ 纘 *zuǎn*, continue, succeed to.
3. extra-fine needlework.

纘　zuǎn　MC tswanX

1. continue, succeed to, inherit; follow in the line of.
2. ⊙ 纂 zuǎn, collect, compile; edit.

zuàn

鑽　zuàn　MC tswanH

1. auger, bore, gimlet; drill.
2. judicial punishment in which the knee-cap is pierced.

　　　zuān　MC tswan

1. pierce, perforate; bore, drill.
2. study intensively, bore into a subject or question, go deeply into.
3. start a fire by kindling wood with a hand drill or bow drill; e.g. ～燧 zuǎnsuì, kindling by drill.

　　　cuán　MC dzwan

1. ⊙ 攢 cuán, gather, concentrate, clump.

zuī

蟕　zuī　MC tsjwe

1. (bn.) ～蠵 zuīxī (MC tsjwe-hwej), loggerhead turtle (*Caretta caretta*), ⊙ 觜蠵 zīxī (MC tsi-hwej); also, name of one of the 12 Jupiter stations; also, name of one of the 28 lunar lodgings, made up of 3 stars in Orion, in the western quadrant (*baihu* 白虎) of the sky.

zuǐ

嘴　zuǐ　MC tsjweX

1. (med.) ⊙ 觜 zuǐ (zī), beak; peck at.

觜　zuǐ　MC tsjweX　→ 觜 zī.

zuì

晬　zuì　MC tswojH

1. (med.) completion of a designated time period; e.g. ～時 zuìshí, a round of all the hours, full day; sgl. or cmpd. ～日 zuìrì, first anniversary of birth.

最　zuì　MC tswajH

1. indicator of superlative: most X of all; e.g. ～高 zuìgāo, all-highest, most high; (Budd.) ～勝 zuìshèng, most victorious > best, most excellent, ref. to a buddha.

a. commend(able), commendatory, in assessment of official or military matters (cf. 殿 diàn, of lesser or unsatisfactory grade).
2. pull together; gathered in; cache, hoard.
3. total up; accounting for everything, all things considered.
4. (med.) of time: just now, exactly then, at that moment.

罪　zuì　MC dzwojX

1. wrongful conduct; crime, offense, malefaction; if small, pecadillo.
2. blame, hold accountable, find or lay fault, accuse; convict.
   a. guilt(y), culpable, blamable, at fault, peccant; convicted; e.g. 得～ dézuì, incur blame.
3. punish(ment), chastise(ment); e.g. 待～ dàizuì, awaiting sentence.

蕞　zuì　MC dzwajH

1. (bn.) ～爾 zuì'ěr (MC dzwajH-nyeX), inconsequential, negligible, of no account.

　　　zhuó　MC tsrjwet

1. concentrate(d), group(ed) together.

　　　jué　MC tsjwet

1. ⊙ 蕝 jué, ancient practice for court ceremonies of erecting fascicles of floss-grass to mark where particular people should stand in order of precedence.

醉　zuì　MC tswijH

1. drunk, intoxicated, drink one's fill, in one's cups, inebriated.
   a. drunk on, awash in, fuddle(d), exhilarated by, delirious about.

zūn

尊　zūn　MC tswon

1. covered wine-vessel, originally used in sacrificial ceremonies.
   a. goblet, wine-cup.
2. honor(ed), venerate(d), venerable, respect(ed); e.g. ～重 zūnzhòng, show great respect to.
   a. often used in honorific terms; e.g. (med.) ～上 zūnshàng, honored forebears, honorific term for parents of someone not related to speaker; (med.) ～府 zūnfǔ, honorific term for father of someone not related to speaker; ～堂 zūntáng, honorific term for mother of someone not related to speaker.

b. honorific; e.g. ～號 *zūnhào*, honorific title (of sovereign).

c. used in med. religious titles; e.g. (Budd.) 天～ *tiānzūn*, trns. Skt. *bhagavat*, "most honored among devas" > Heaven-Honored One, epithet of a buddha; also (Dao.) borrowed by Lingbao Dao. for title of exalted deity 元始 天～ *yuánshǐtiānzūn*, Celestial Honored One (usu. rendered Celestial Worthy) of Primordial Beginning; (Budd.) 世～ *shìzūn*, World-Honored One, epithet to replace 天～ *tiānzūn* after latter adopted by Dao.

3. supreme, pre-eminent; e.g. ～子 *zūnzǐ*, eldest son; (Budd.) ～法 *zūnfǎ*, the pre-eminent Dharma; (Budd.) ～覺 *zūnjué*, supreme enlightenment.

4. (med.) measure-word for items of special worth, such as gifts.

樽   zūn   MC tswon

1. ⊙ 尊 *zūn* 1a, wine goblet.

zǔn   MC tswonX

1. ⊙ 撙 *zǔn*, restrain, curb.

鐏   zūn   MC tswon   ⊙ 樽 *zūn*.

遵   zūn   MC tswin

1. follow, as a road; follow along.

2. honor, obey; be in accord with, abide by.

鐏   zūn   MC tswon

1. pointed ferrule at the butt-end of long-handled weapons, for protection and to allow it to be stood upright in the earth.

2. (med.) ⊙ 尊 *zūn* 1a, wine-goblet.

鱒   zūn   MC dzwonX

1. barbel chub (*Squaliobarbus curriculus*).

zǔn

噂   zǔn   MC tswonX

1. rdup. and cmpd. ～沓 *zǔntà*, confused chatter, jumbled babble, cross-talk.

撙   zǔn   MC tswonX

1. restrain, curb; hold back.

a. limit, regulate; temper, moderate.

蕆   zǔn   MC tswonX

1. (bn.) 苯～ *běnzǔn*, → 苯 *běn*.

zuó

岝   zuó   MC dzak

1. (bn.) ～崿 *zuó'è* (MC dzak-ngak), rugged and steep, perilously peaked.

捽   zuó   MC dzwot

1. lay hold of, grasp in the hand; hold fast, clutch; seize.

a. catch, capture.

2. pull up, pull out; tug at; lift up; e.g. (med.) ～兀 *zuówù*, with head held high; fixed and steadfast.

3. come to grips with, confront; pull up against, meet face-to-face; encounter.

昨   zuó   MC dzak

1. yesterday.

a. yestertime, yesteryear.

b. recently, lately.

筰   zuó   MC dzak

1. (med.) cord made of bamboo slats.

2. press together, squeeze.

zuǒ

佐   zuǒ   MC tsaX

1. assist(ant), aid(e), second.

a. uphold, support, back; guarantee, verify.

左   zuǒ   MC tsaX

1. left side, ant. 右 *yòu*, right side. The relative values of left and right depended on context. Anciently, the master stood on the left side of the chariot. For the ruler, who ceremonially faced south, left was east, direction of the rising sun and more auspicious than west. In office titles prefaced with "left" and "right," the occupant of the "left" appointment usu. took precedence. But left was often the inferior side, → 3 below.

2. cmpd., ～右 *zuǒyòu*, left and right, to the left and right, esp. those to the left and right of the ruler, close advisers, attendants and acolytes; also, all around; also, when used with number, approximately; also, aid and assist, be at one's elbow; also, control, command; also, indirect term (hence honorific) for addressee of a letter.

3. gauche, improper, unfitting; heterodox; deviant, sinister; e.g. ～衽 *zuǒrèn*, leftward-fastening lappet, worn by foreigners (Chinese lappets fastened rightward) > by metonymy, those who are uncouth, barbaric.

a. inferior, place in inferior position, esp. demote an official in rank; e.g. ～遷 *zuǒqiān*, demoted and transferred [to a lesser position].
4. ⊙佐 *zuǒ*, assist; guarantee.

zuò

作　zuò　MC tsak
1. rise, stand up, get up; raise up.
   a. rise in excitement, be aroused to act.
2. arise, begin, commence, start from.
3. devise, create, make.
   a. compose, esp. written text.
   b. organize, put in order.
4. undertake, take on; assume the role of, act as; act, do.
   a. undertaking, action; accomplish(ment).
5. regard as, look on as, take for.

做　zuò　MC tsaH
1. (med.) ⊙作 *zuò* 3, create, make; 4, undertake, act, do.

坐　zuò　MC dzwaX
1. sit; most often without chair, usu. means to kneel with hams on back of heels, "Japanese-style" (cf. 跪 *guì*, kneel with torso held upright).
   a. be seated, take a seat; find one's place, be situated.
   b. sit at ease, settle; abide, repose; ～食 *zuòshí*, eat without a care; (Dao.) ～忘 *zuòwàng*, sit in forgetfulness, oblivious of distinctions between subject and object; (Budd.) ～禪 *zuòchán*, sit in still meditation.
   c. session, hold a session of.
2. stick to, hold fast to; be entrenched in.
   a. sit by, mount guard, protect.
   zuò　MC dzwaH
1. seat; position, site.
   a. base; plinth, pedestal.
   b. throne, seat of authority and status, for ruler, host, chief member of community; e.g. (Budd.) 上～ *shàngzuò*, the high seat(ed one), chief bonze or dean of a monastery, trns. Skt. *sthavira*, most venerable.
   c. bureaucratic position occupied by an official.
2. be incriminated in wrongdoing; convict(ed) of a crime.
   a. implicate(d), involve(d) in a usu. wrongful act.

b. (med.) also, indicating neutral involvement: because, owing to; e.g. ～自 *zuòzì*, because of, for the reason that.
3. in all naturalness (cf. dzwaX, 1b above); also (med.), to no purpose, in vain.
   a. (med.), for the time being; just on the verge of, right now.
   b. just now, suddenly.
   c. (med.) ～來 *zuòlái*, not of one's own doing; also, immediately, forthwith.
4. (med.) ～令 *zuòlìng*, ～使 *zuòshǐ*, bring about, cause (to).

座　zuò　MC dzwaH
1. (med.) ⊙坐 *zuò* 1b, seat, throne.

怍　zuò　MC dzak
1. abashed, ashamed.
   a. discomforted, disconcerted; out of countenance, shamefaced.

柞　zuò　MC tsak
1. sgl. or ～樹 *zuòshù*, ～櫟 *zuòlì*, sawtooth oak (*Quercus acutissima*).
   a. oaken, quernal.
2. sgl. or ～木 *zuòmù*, brush-holly, logwood (*Xylosma japonicum*), spiny evergreen shrub.
   zé　MC tsraek
1. chop or fell trees.
2. narrow; slender, spare, spindly.

硸　zuò　MC dzak
1. (bn.) ～硌 *zuòluò* (MC dzak-lak), crookedly cragged, jaggedly jutting.
   zhà　MC dzraeH
1. hack, hew; rend.

祚　zuò　MC dzuH
1. celestial favor, heaven-bestowed fortune.
   a. benediction, blessing; confirmation.
   b. continuous lineage, succession, legacy, as guaranteed by heaven; destiny.
2. ⊙阼 *zuò* 1a, royal throne.

齚　zuò　MC tsak
1. pound grain to remove the husk.
   a. polished rice.

胙　zuò　MC dzuH
1. sacrificial meat, offered for good fortune.
   a. the same, divided and distributed to participants after the sacrifice > bestow, recompense.
   b. good fortune.

酢   **zuò**   **MC dzak**

1. guest's return toast to host, following latter's to him (*chou* 酬).

   a. reciprocate, requite, repay.

2. offer libation in sacrifice to spirits.

   cù   **MC tshuH**

1. ⊙ 醋 *cù*, vinegar (of which 酢 was original form).

鑿   **zuò**   **MC dzawH**   → 鑿 *záo*.

阼   **zuò**   **MC dzuH**

1. east-side steps of a great hall, used by the lord of the house.

   a. by metonymy, the royal throne, because ruler mounts to the throne hall or the hall of sacrifice by east-side steps.

2. ⊙ 祚 *zuò* 1b, dynastic or lineage destiny.

Appendix 1
干支表 The Sexagesimal Cycle

1 甲子 jiǎzǐ	2 乙丑 yǐchǒu	3 丙寅 bǐngyín	4 丁卯 dīngmǎo	5 戊辰 wùchén	6 己巳 jǐsì	7 庚午 gēngwǔ	8 辛未 xīnwèi	9 壬申 rénshēn	10 癸酉 guǐyǒu
11 甲戌 jiǎxū	12 乙亥 yǐhài	13 丙子 bǐngzǐ	14 丁丑 dīngchǒu	15 戊寅 wùyín	16 己卯 jǐmǎo	17 庚辰 gēngchén	18 辛巳 xīnsì	19 壬午 rénwǔ	20 癸未 guǐwèi
21 甲申 jiǎshēn	22 乙酉 yǐyǒu	23 丙戌 bǐngxū	24 丁亥 dīnghài	25 戊子 wùzǐ	26 己丑 jǐchǒu	27 庚寅 gēngyín	28 辛卯 xīnmǎo	29 壬辰 rénchén	30 癸巳 guǐsì
31 甲午 jiǎwǔ	32 乙未 yǐwèi	33 丙申 bǐngshēn	34 丁酉 dīngyǒu	35 戊戌 wùxū	36 己亥 jǐhài	37 庚子 gēngzǐ	38 辛丑 xīnchǒu	39 壬寅 rényín	40 癸卯 guǐmǎo
41 甲辰 jiǎchén	42 乙巳 yǐsì	43 丙午 bǐngwǔ	44 丁未 dīngwèi	45 戊申 wùshēn	46 己酉 jǐyǒu	47 庚戌 gēngxū	48 辛亥 xīnhài	49 壬子 rénzǐ	50 癸丑 guǐchǒu
51 甲寅 jiǎyín	52 乙卯 yǐmǎo	53 丙辰 bǐngchén	54 丁巳 dīngsì	55 戊午 wùwǔ	56 己未 jǐwèi	57 庚申 gēngshēn	58 辛酉 xīnyǒu	59 壬戌 rénxū	60 癸亥 guǐhài

Appendix 2

天干 Heavenly Stems

甲	乙	丙	丁	戊	己	庚	辛	壬	癸
jiǎ	*yǐ*	*bǐng*	*dīng*	*wù*	*jǐ*	*gēng*	*xīn*	*rén*	*guǐ*
(A	(B	(C	(D	(E	(F	(G	(H	(I	(J

木東青春青龍角肝		火南赤夏赤鳥徵心		土中黃季夏宮脾		金西白秋白虎商肺		水北黑冬玄武羽腎	
Jupiter		Mars		Saturn		Venus		Mercury	

地支 Earthly Branches

子	丑	寅	卯	辰	巳	午	未	申	酉	戌	亥
zǐ	*chǒu*	*yín*	*mǎo*	*chén*	*sì*	*wǔ*	*wèi*	*shēn*	*yǒu*	*xū*	*hài*
A)	B)	C)	D)	E)	F)	G)	H)	I)	J)	K)	L)
23	01	03	05	07	09	11	13	15	17	19	21
rat/ murine	ox/ bovine	tiger/ tigrine	hare/ leporine	dragon/ draconian	serpent/ ophidian	horse/ equine	sheep/ ovine	monkey/ simian	cock/ gallorine	dog/ canine	boar/ verrine

Appendix 3
The *Yijing* Trigrams and Hexagrams

Trigrams							
1	2	3	4	5	6	7	8
乾	坤	震	坎	艮	巽	離	兌
Qian	Kun	Zhen	Kan	Gen	Sun	Li	Dui
Hexagrams							
1	2	3	4	5	6	7	8
乾	坤	屯	蒙	需	訟	師	比
Qian	Kun	Zhun	Meng	Xu	Song	Shi	Bi
9	10	11	12	13	14	15	16
小畜	履	泰	否	同人	大有	謙	豫
Xiaoxu	Lü	Tai	Pi	Tongren	Dayou	Qian	Yu
17	18	19	20	21	22	23	24
隨	蠱	臨	觀	噬嗑	賁	剝	復
Sui	Gu	Lin	Guan	Shihe	Bi	Bo	Fu
25	26	27	28	29	30	31	32
无妄	大畜	頤	大過	坎	離	咸	恆
Wuwang	Daxu	Yi	Daguo	Kan	Li	Xian	Heng
33	34	35	36	37	38	39	40
遯	大壯	晉	明夷	家人	睽	蹇	解
Dun	Dazhuang	Jin	Mingyi	Jiaren	Kui	Jian	Xie
41	42	43	44	45	46	47	48
損	益	夬	姤	萃	升	困	井
Sun	Yi	Guai	Gou	Cui	Sheng	Kun	Jing
49	50	51	52	53	54	55	56
革	鼎	震	艮	漸	歸妹	豐	旅
Ge	Ding	Zhen	Gen	Jian	Guimei	Feng	Lü
57	58	59	60	61	62	63	64
巽	兌	渙	節	中孚	小過	既濟	未濟
Sun	Dui	Huan	Jie	Zhongfu	Xiaoguo	Jiji	Weiji

Appendix 4
The Lunar Lodgings (宿 *xiu*) and
Jupiter Stations (次 *ci*)

SKY SECTOR	LUNAR LODGING	LOCATION	JUPITER STATION
青龍 *qinglong*	角 *jiao* Horn	α, ξ Virginis	壽星 *Shouxing*
	亢 *kang* Gullet	ι, κ, λ, μ Virginis	
	氐 *di* Base	α, β, γ, ι Librae	大火 *Dahuo*
	房 *fang* Chamber	β, δ, π, ρ Scorpii	
	心 *xin* Heart	α (Antares), σ, τ Scorpii	
	尾 *wei* Tail	ε, μ 2, μ 1, η, θ, ι, κ, λ, υ Scorpii	析木 *Ximu*
	箕 *ji* Winnowing Basket	γ, δ, ε, η Sagittarii	
玄武 *xuanwu*	斗 *dou* Dipper (South)	μ, λ, φ, σ, τ, ζ Sagittarii	星記 *Xingji*
	牛 *niu* Ox	α², β, ξ, o, π, ρ Capricorni	
	女 *nü* Maiden	ε², μ, 3, 4 Aquarii	玄枵 *Xuanxiao*
	虛 *xu* Barrens	β Aquarii and α Equulei	
	危 *wei* Steep Roof	α Aquarii and θ, ε Pegasi	
	室 *shi* House	α, β Pegasi	娵訾 *Zixi*
	壁 *bi* Wall	γ Pegasi, α Andromedae	
白虎 *baihu*	奎 *kui* Strider	9 stars in Andromeda and 7 in Pisces	降婁 *Jianglou*
	婁 *lou* Harvester	α, β, γ Arietis	

SKY SECTOR	LUNAR LODGING	LOCATION	JUPITER STATION
	胃 *wei* Granary	35, 39, 41 Arietis	
	昴 *mao* Mane (Concluder)	16, 17, 19, 20, 23, η, 28 Tauri (Pleiades)	大梁 *Daliang*
	畢 *bi* Net	ε, δ¹, δ², γ, α, ϑ¹, 71, λ Tauri (Hyades)	
	觜(蠵) *zi(xi)* Loggerhead Turtle	λ, φ¹, φ² Orionis	
	參 *shen* Triaster (Ginseng?)	ζ, ε, δ, α, γ, κ, β Orionis	實沉 *Shichen*
赤鳥 *chiniao*	井 *jing* Well	λ, ζ, δ, ε, ξ, γ, ν, μ Geminii	
	鬼 *gui* Revenant	γ, δ, η, θ Cancri	鶉首 *Chunshou*
	柳 *liu* Willow	δ, ε, ζ, η, θ, ρ, σ, ω Hydrae	
	星 *xing* Star	α, τ¹, τ², ι, 27, and 2 others in Hydra	鶉火 *Chunhuo*
	張 *zhang* Extension	υ, λ, φ, μ, χ, ν Hydrae	
	翼 *yi* Wing	22 stars in Hydra and Crater	
	軫 *zhen* Chassis	β, δ, γ, ε Corvi	鶉尾 *Chunwei*

Appendix 5
Reign Titles (*nianhao* 年號), Han through Tang

Lefthand column is Western year in which a particular reign-title was adopted. Ruler's accession date (in parenthesis) follows name. Note that sometimes a ruler's first new reign-title was not adopted until months after his actual accession or in the following year; e.g. Tang Taizong's reign actually began in 626, not 627 when for the first time he proclaimed a new reign-title. Column following a reign-title gives the Chinese month and day of that reign-title's adoption; righthand column gives corresponding Western month and day. Note also that when a Chinese 11th or 12th lunar month is equated with a January or February date in a Western year (e.g. inauguration of Zhongping era on 16 February, 185, in the 12th month of Chinese year), it signifies the 11th or 12th month of the Chinese year which would mostly correlate with the preceding Western year.

Han Dynasty 漢 (206 BCE-220 CE)

Western Han 西漢 (206 BCE-25 CE)

BCE

141	Wudi 武帝 (9 Mr, 141)	Jianyuan 建元	x.1*	Nv 4
135		Yuanguang 元光	x.1*	Ot 29
129		Yuanshuo 元朔	x.1 *	Nv 21
121		Yuanshou 元狩	x.1*	Nv 22
117		Yuanding 元鼎	x.1*	Nv 8
111		Yuanfeng 元封	x.1*	Nv 3
105		Taichu 太初	x.1*	Nv 26
100		Tianhan 天漢	i.1	Fb 8
96		Taishi 太始	i.1	Fb 23
92		Zhenghe 征和	i.1	Fb 9
88		Houyuan 後元	i.1	Ja 26
(*Qin calendar i.1)				
86	Zhaodi 昭帝 (30 Mr, 87)	Shiyuan 始元	i.1	Fb 3
80		Yuanfeng 元鳳	viii.1	Sp 21
74		Yuanping 元平	i.1	Fb 21
73	Xuandi 宣帝 (10 Sp, 74)	Benshi 本始	i.1	Fb 10
69		Dijie 地節	i.1	Ja 27
65		Yuankang 元康	i.1	Fb 11
61		Shenjue 神爵	iii.1	Mr 28
57		Wufeng 五鳳	i.1	Fb 13
53		Ganlu 甘露	i.1	Ja 30
49		Huanglong 黃龍	i.1	Fb 15
48	Yuandi 元帝 (29 Ja, 48)	Chuyuan 初元	i.1	Fb 3
43		Yongguang 永光	i.1	Fb 8
38		Jianzhao 建昭	i.1	Fb 13
33		Jingning 竟寧	i.1	Fb 18
32	Chengdi 成帝 (4 Ag, 33)	Jianshi 建始	i.1	Fb 6
28		Heping 河平	iii.1	Ap 22
24		Yangshuo 陽朔	i.1	Fb 8
20		Hongjia 鴻嘉	i.1	Fb 23

16		Yongshi 永始	i.1	Fb 9
12		Yuanyan 元延	i.1	Ja 26
8		Suihe 綏和	i.1	Fb 11
6	Aidi 哀帝 (7 My, 7)	Jianping 建平	i.1	Fb 19
2		Yuanshou 元壽	i.1	Fb 5

CE

1	Pingdi 平帝 (17 Ot, 1)	Yuanshi 元始	i.1	Fb 12
6	Wang Mang 王莽 regency 　　　Ruzi Ying 孺子嬰 (17 Ap, 6)	Jushe 居攝	i.1	Fb 17
8		Chushi 初始	xi.1	De 17

Xin 新 interregnum (9-25)

9	Wang Mang 王莽 (10 Ja, 9)	Shijianguo 始建國	xii.1*	Ja 15
14		Tianfeng 天鳳	xii.1*	Ja 20
20		Dihuang 地皇	xii.1*	Ja 14
(*Yin calendar i.1)				
23	Huaiyangwang 淮陽王 (10 Fb, 23)	Gengshi 更始	i.1*	Fb 10
(*Yin calendar ii.1)				

Eastern Han 東漢 (25-220)

25	Guangwudi 光武帝 (5 Ag, 25)	Jianwu 建武	vi.22	Ag 5
56		Jianwu zhongyuan 　建武中元	iv.11	My 14
58	Mingdi 明帝 (29 Mr, 57)	Yongping 永平	i.1	Fb 13
76	Zhangdi 章帝 (5 Sp, 75)	Jianchu 建初	i.1	Fb 24
84		Yuanhe 元和	viii.20	Ot. 8
87		Zhanghe 章和	vii.27	Sp 12
89	Hedi 和帝 (9 Ap, 88)	Yongyuan 永元	i.1	Ja 30
105		Yuanxing 元興	iv.27	My 28
106	Shangdi 殤帝 (13 Fb, 106)	Yanping 延平	i.1	Fb 21
107	Andi 安帝 (23 Sp, 106)	Yongchu 永初	i.1	Fb 10
114		Yuanchu 元初	i.2	Fb 24
120		Yongning 永寧	iv.11	My 25
121		Jianguang 建光	vii.1	Ag 1
122		Yanguang 延光	iii.2	Ap 25
126	Shundi 順帝 (16 De, 125)	Yongjian 永建	i.1	Fb 10
132		Yangjia 陽嘉	iii.13	Ap16
136		Yonghe 永和	i.15	Mr 5
142		Han'an 漢安	i.14	Fb 26
144		Jiankang 建康	iv.15	Je 3

145	Chongdi 沖帝 (20 Sp, 144)	Yongjia 永嘉	i.1	Fb 10
146	Zhidi 質帝 (6 Mr, 145)	Benchu 本初	i.1	Ja 30
147	Huandi 桓帝 (1 Ag, 146)	Jianhe 建和	i.1	Fb 18
150		Heping 和平	i.1	Fb 15
151		Yuanjia 元嘉	i.16	Fb 19
153		Yongxing 永興	iv.22	Je 1
155		Yongshou 永壽	i.14	Mr 5
158		Yanxi 延熹	vi.4	Jl 17
167		Yongkang 永康	vi.8	Jl 12
168	Lingdi 靈帝 (17 Fb, 168)	Jianning 建寧	i.21	Fb 17
172		Xiping 熹平	v.16	Je 24
178		Guanghe 光和	iii.21	Ap 26
185		Zhongping 中平	xii.29	Fb 16
190	Xiandi 獻帝 (28 Sp, 189)	Chuping 初平	i.1	Fb 23
194		Xingping 興平	i.13	Fb 21
196		Jian'an 建安	i.7	Fb 23
220		Yankang 延康	iii.1	Ap 21

Three Kingdoms 三國 (220–280)

Wei 魏 (220-265)

220	Wendi 文帝 (11 De, 220)	Huangchu 黃初	x.29	De 11
227	Mingdi 明帝 (29 Je, 226)	Taihe 太和	i.1	Fb 4
233		Qinglong 青龍	ii. 6	Mr 4
237		Jingchu 景初	iii.1	Ap 13
240	Qiwang 齊王 (22 Ja, 239)	Zhengshi 正始	i.1	Fb 10
249		Jiaping 嘉平	iv.8	My 7
254	Gaoguixianggong 高貴鄉公 (2 Nv, 254)	Zhengyuan 正元	x.5	Nv 2
256		Ganlu 甘露	vi.1	Jl 10
260	Yuandi 元帝 (27 Je, 260)	Jingyuan 景元	vi.2	Je 27
264		Xianxi 鹹熙	v.15	Je 26

Shu 蜀 (221-263)

221	Zhaoliedi 昭烈帝 (15 My, 221)	Zhangwu 章武	iv.6	My 15
223	Houzhu 後主 (16? Je, 223)	Jianxing 建興	v.1?	Je 16?
238		Yanxing 延熙	i.1	Fb 2
258		Jingyao 景耀	i.1	Fb 21
263		Yanxing 炎興	viii.1	Sp 21

Wu 吳 (222-280)

222		Huangwu 黃武	x.1	Nv 22
229	Dadi 大帝 (23 My, 229)*	Huanglong 黃龍	iv.13	My 23
232		Jiahe 嘉禾	i.1	Fb 9
238		Chiwu 赤烏	viii.1	Ag 28

| 251 | | Taiyuan 太元 | v.1 | Je 6 |
| 252 | | Shenfeng 神鳳 | ii.1 | Fb 27 |

(*Although the sovereign of Wu declared an initial reign-title in 222, he did not declare himself emperor until 229 when he adopted a new reign-title.)

252	Guijiwang 會稽王 (26? Ap, 252)	Jianxing 建興	iv.1?	Ap 26?
254		Wufeng 五鳳	i. 1	Fb 5
256		Taiping 太平	x.6	Nv 10
258	Jingdi 景帝 (30 Nv, 258)	Yong'an 永安	x.18	Nv 30
264	Wuchenghou 烏程侯 (3? Sp, 264)	Yuanxing 元興	vii.25	Sp 3?
265		Ganlu 甘露	iv.1	My 3
266		Baoding 寶鼎	viii.1	Sp 17
269		Jianheng 建衡	x.1	Nv 11
272		Fenghuang 鳳皇	i.1	Fb 16
275		Tiance 天冊	i.1	Fb 13
276		Tianxi 天璽	vii.1	Jl 28
277		Tianji 天紀	i.1	Fb 20

Jin Dynasty 晉 (265–420)

Western Jin 西晉 (265–317)

266	Wudi 武帝 (8 Fb, 266)	Taishi 泰始	xii.17	Fb 8
275		Xianning 鹹寧	i.1	Fb 13
280		Taikang 太康	iv.29	Je 13
290		Taixi 太熙	i.1	Ja 28
290	Huidi 惠帝 (16 My, 290)	Yongxi 永熙	iv.29	My 16
291		Yongping 永平	i.1	Fb 16
291		Yuankang 元康	iii.9	Ap 24
300		Yongkang 永康	i.1	Fb 7
301		Yongning 永寧	iv.9	Je 1
303		Tai'an 太安	xii.25	Ja 29
304		Yong'an 永安	i.1	Fb 22
304		Jianwu 建武	vii.25	Sp 10
304		Yong'an 永安	xi.12	De 25
305		Yongxing 永興	xii.24	Fb 4
306		Guangxi 光熙	vi.16	Jl 13
307	Huaidi 懷帝 (11 Ja, 307)	Yongjia 永嘉	i.2	Fb 20
313	Mindi 湣帝 (7 Je, 313)	Jianxing 建興	iv.27	Je 7

Eastern Jin 東晉 (317-420)

317		Jianwu 建武	iii.9	Ap 6
318	Yuandi 元帝 (26 Ap, 318)*	Taixing 太興	iii.10	Ap 26
322		Yongchang 永昌	i.1	Fb 3

(*Yuandi declared an initial reign-title on 6 Ap 317, as King of Jin; he declared himself emperor, with a new reign-title on 26 Ap 318.)

| 323 | Mingdi 明帝 (4 Ja, 323) | Taining 太寧 | iii.1 | Ap 22 |

326	Chengdi 成帝 (19 Ot, 325)	Xianhe 鹹和	ii.27	Ap 15
335		Xiankang 鹹康	i.1	Fb 10
343	Kangdi 康帝 (27 Jl, 342)	Jianyuan 建元	i.1	Fb 11
345	Mudi 穆帝 (18 Nv, 344)	Yonghe 永和	i.1	Fb 18
357		Shengping 升平	i.1	Fb 6
362	Aidi 哀帝 (13 Jl, 361)	Longhe 隆和	i.20	Mr 2
363		Xingning 興寧	ii.3?	Mr 4?
366	Haixigong 海西公 (31 Mr, 365)	Taihe 太和	i.1	Ja 28
372	Jianwendi 簡文帝 (6 Ja, 372)	Xian'an 鹹安	xi.15	Ja 6
373	Xiaowudi 孝武帝 (12 Sp, 372)	Ningkang 寧康	i.1	Fb 9
376		Taiyuan 太元	i.3	Fb 9
397	Andi 安帝 (7 Nv, 396)	Long'an 隆安	i.1	Fb 13
402		Yuanxing 元興	i.1	Fb 18
405		Yixi 義熙	i.16	Mr 2
419	Gongdi 恭帝 (28 Ja, 419)	Yuanxi 元熙	i.1	Fb 11

Southern and Northern Dynasties 南北朝

Southern Dynasties
Song 宋 (420–479)

420	Wudi 武帝 (10 Jl, 420)	Yongchu 永初	vi.14	Jl 10
423	Shaodi 少帝 (26 Je, 422)	Jingping 景平	i.1	Ja 28
424	Wendi 文帝 (17 Sp, 424)	Yuanjia 元嘉	viii.9	Sp 17
454	Xiaowudi 孝武帝 (20 My, 453)	Xiaojian 孝建	i.1	Fb 14
457		Daming 大明	i.1	Fb 10
465	Qianfeidi 前廢帝 (12 Jl, 464)	Yongguang 永光	i.1	Fb 12
465		Jinghe 景和	viii.13	Sp 18
466	Mingdi 明帝 (9 Ja, 466)	Taishi 泰始	xii.7	Ja 9
472		Taiyu 泰豫	i.1	Ja 26
473	Houfeidi 後廢帝 (11 My, 472)	Yuanhui 元徽	i.1	Fb 13
477	Shundi 順帝 (5 Ag, 477)	Shengming 升明	vii.11	Ag 5

Qi 齊 (479–502)

479	Gaodi 高帝 (29 My, 479)	Jianyuan 建元	iv.23	My 29
483	Wudi 武帝 (11 Ap, 482)	Yongming 永明	i.2	Ja 25
494	Yulinwang 鬱林王 (27 Ag, 493)	Longchang 隆昌	i.1	Ja 23

494	Hailingwang 海陵王 (10 Sp, 494)	Yanxing 延興	vii.25	Sp 10
494	Mingdi 明帝 (5 De, 494)	Jianwu 建武	x.22	De 5
498		Yongtai 永泰	iv.3	My 9
499	Donghunhou 東昏侯 (1 Sp, 498)	Yongyuan 永元	i.1	Ja 28
501	Hedi 和帝 (14 Ap, 501)	Zhongxing 中興	iii.11	Ap 14

Liang 梁 (502–557)

502	Wudi 武帝 (19? Je, 502)	Tianjian 天監	iv.29	Je 19?
520		Putong 普通	i.1	Fb 4
527		Datong 大通	iii.11	Ap 27
529		Zhongdatong 中大通	x.1	Nv 17
535		Datong 大同	i.1	Fb 18
545		Zhongdatong 中大同	iv.14	My 29
547		Taiqing 太清	iv.21	My 25
550	Jianwendi 簡文帝 (7 Jl, 549)	Dabao 大寶	i.1	Fb 2
552	Yuandi 元帝 (13 De, 552)	Chengsheng 承聖	xi.12	De 13
555	Jingdi 敬帝 (1 Nv, 555)	Shaotai 紹泰	x.2	Nv 1
556		Taiping 太平	ix.1	Ot 19

Chen 陳 (557–589)

557	Wudi 武帝 (16 Nv, 557)	Yongding 永定	x.10	Nv 16
560	Wendi 文帝 (17 Ag, 559)	Tianjia 天嘉	i.1	Fb 12
566		Tiankang 天康	ii.29	Ap 4
567	Feidi 廢帝 (31 My, 566)	Guangda 光大	i.3	Ja 28
569	Xuandi 宣帝 (5 Fb, 569)	Tianjian 太建	i.4	Fb 5
583	Houzhu 後主 (20 Fb, 582)	Zhide 至德	i.3	Ja 31
587		Zhenming 禎明	i.3	Fb 15

Northern Dynasties
Northern Wei 北魏 (386–534)

386	Daowudi 道武帝 (20 Fb, 386)	Dengguo 登國	i.6	Fb 20
396		Huangshi 皇始	vii.1	Ag 20
399		Tianxing 天興	xii.2	Ja 24
404		Tianci 天賜	x.28	De 15
409	Mingyuandi 明元帝 (10 Nv, 409)	Yongxing 永興	x.17	Nv 10
414		Shenrui 神瑞	i.1	Fb 6
416		Taichang 泰常	iv.5	My 17
424	Taiwudi 太武帝 (27 De, 423)	Shiguang 始光	i.1	Fb 16
428		Shenjia 神麚	ii.1	Mr 2
432		Yanhe 延和	i.1	Fb 17
435		Taiyan 太延	i.26	Mr 11

440		Taipingzhenjun 太平真君	vi.21	Ag 4
451		Zhengping 正平	vi.9	Jl 23
452	Nan'anwang 南安王 (9 Ap, 452)	Yongping 永平	ii.5	Mr 9
452	Wenchengdi 文成帝 (31 Ot, 452)	Xing'an 興安	x.3	Ot 31
454		Xingguang 興光	vii.6	Ot 15
455		Tai'an 太安	vi.2	Jl 2
460		Heping 和平	i.1	Fb 8
466	Xianwendi 獻文帝 (21 Je, 465)	Tian'an 天安	i.1	Fb 1
467		Huangxing 皇興	viii.29	Ot 13
471	Xiaowendi 孝文帝 (20 Sp, 471)	Yanxing 延興	viii.20	Sp 20
476		Chengming 承明	vi.14	Jl 21
477		Taihe 太和	i.1	Ja 30
500	Xuanwudi 宣武帝 (7 My, 499)	Jingming 景明	i.5	Fb 19
504		Zhengshi 正始	i.19	Fb 19
508		Yongping 永平	viii.16	Sp 26
512		Yanchang 延昌	iv.25	My 26
516	Xiaomingdi 孝明帝 (12 Fb, 515)	Xiping 熙平	i.1	Fb 18
518		Shengui 神龜	ii.23	Mr 20
520		Zhengguang 正光	vii.19	Ag 18
525		Xiaochang 孝昌	vi.10	Jl 15
528		Wutai 武泰	i.8	Fb 13
528	Xiaozhuangdi 孝莊帝 (18 My, 528)	Jianyi 建義	iv.14	My 18
528		Yong'an 永安	ix.21	Ot 19
530	Changguangwang 長廣王 (5 De, 530)	Jianming 建明	x.30	De 5
531	Jiemindi 節閔帝 (1 Ap, 531)	Putai 普泰	ii.29	Ap 1
531	Andingwang 安定王 (31 Ot, 531)	Zhongxing 中興	x.6	Ot 31
532	Xiaowudi 孝武帝 (13 Je, 532)	Taichang 太昌	iv.25	Je 13
534		Yongxing 永興	xii.28	Fb 7
534		Yongxi 永熙	quickly after preceding	

Eastern Wei 東魏 (534–550)

534	Xiaojingdi 孝靜帝 (8 Nv, 534)	Tianping 天平	x.17	Nv 8
538		Yuanxiang 元象	i.7	Fb 21
539		Xinghe 興和	xi.14	De 9
543		Wuding 武定	i.1	Ja 21

Western Wei 西魏 (535–556)

535	Wendi 文帝 (18 Fb, 535)	Datong 大統	i.1	Fb 18
552	Feidi 廢帝 (28 Mr, 551)	Qianming 乾明?	i.1?	Fb 11?

554	Gongdi 恭帝 (3? Mr, 554)	no reign title		

Northern Qi 北齊 (550–577)

550	Wenxuandi 文宣帝 (9 Je, 550)	Tianbao 天保	v.10	Je 9
560	Feidi 廢帝 (4 De, 559)	Qianming 乾明	i.1	Fb 12
560	Xiaozhaodi 孝昭帝 (8 Sp, 560)	Huangjian 皇建	viii.3	Sp 8
561	Wuchengdi 武成帝 (3 De, 561)	Taining 太寧	xi.11	De 3
562		Heqing 河清	iv.6	My 24
565	Houzhu 後主 (8 Je, 565)	Tiantong 天統	iv.24	Je 8
570		Wuping 武平	i.1	Ja 22
577		Longhua 隆化	xii.13	Ja 17
577	Youzhu 幼主 (18 Ja, 577)	Chengguang 承光	xii.14	Ja 18

Northern Zhou 北周 (557–581)

557	Xiaomindi 孝閔帝 (15 Fb, 557)	no reign title		
559	Mingdi 明帝 (5 Nv, 557)	Wucheng 武成	viii.15	Ot 1
561	Wudi 武帝 (31 My, 560)	Baoding 保定	i.1	Fb 1
566		Tianhe 天和	i.6	Fb 10
572		Jiande 建德	iii.14	Ap 12
578		Xuanzheng 宣政	iii.25	Ap 17
579	Xuandi 宣帝 (22 Je, 578)	Dacheng 大成	i.1	Fb 12
579	Jingdi 靜帝 (1 Ap, 579)	Daxiang 大象	ii.20	Ap 1
581		Dading 大定	i.1	Ja 21

Sui Dynasty 隋 (581–618)

581	Wendi 文帝 (4 Mr, 581)	Kaihuang 開皇	ii.20	Mr 4
601		Renshou 仁壽	i.1	Fb 8
605	Yangdi 煬帝 (21 Ag, 604)	Daye 大業	i.1	Ja 25
617	Gongdi 恭帝 (18 De, 617)	Yining 義寧	xi.15	De 18

Tang Dynasty 唐 (618–907)

618	Gaozu 高祖 (18 Je, 618)	Wude 武德	v.20	Je 18
627	Taizong 太宗 (4 Sp, 626)	Zhenguan 貞觀	i.1	Ja 23
650	Gaozong 高宗 (15 Jl, 649)	Yonghui 永徽	i.1	Fb 7
656		Xianqing 顯慶	i.7	Fb 7

661		Longshuo 龍朔	ii.30	Ap 4
664		Linde 麟德	i.1	Fb 2
666		Qianfeng 乾封	i.5	Fb 14
668		Zongzhang 總章	iii.6	Ap 22
670		Xianheng 咸亨	iii.1	Mr 27
674		Shangyuan 上元	viii.15	Sp 20
676		Yifeng 儀鳳	xi.8	De 18
679		Tiaolu 調露	vi.3	Jl 15
680		Yonglong 永隆	ix.23	Sp 22
681		Kaiyao 開耀	ix.30	Nv 15
682		Yongchun 永淳	ii.19	Ap 2
683		Hongdao 弘道	xii.4	De 27
684	Zhongzong 中宗 (3 Ja, 684)	Sisheng 嗣聖	i.1	Ja 23
684	Ruizong 睿宗 (27 Fb, 684)	Wenming 文明	ii.6	Fb 27
684		Guangzhai 光宅	ix.6	Ot 19
685		Chuigong 垂供	i.1	Fb 9
689		Yongchang 永昌	i.1	Fb 27
689		Zaichu 載初	i.1*	De 18

Zhou 周 interregnum (690-705)

690	Wu Zetian 武則天 (16 Ot)	Tianshou 天授	ix.9*	Ot 16
692		Ruyi 如意	iv.1*	Ap 22
692		Changshou 長壽	ix.9*	Ot 23
694		Yanzai 延載	v.11*	Je 9
694		Zhengsheng 證聖	i.1*	Nv 23
695		Tiance wansui 天冊萬歲	ix.9*	Ot 22
696		Wansui dengfeng 萬歲登封	*la*.20*	Ja 20
696		Wansui tongtian 萬歲通天	iii.16*	Ap 22
697		Shengong 神功	ix.9*	Sp 28
697		Shengli 聖曆	i.1*	De 20
700		Jiushi 久視	v.5*	My 27
701		Dazu 大足	i.3	Fb 15
701		Chang'an 長安	x.22	Nv 26

(* From Zaichu through Jiushi, old Zhou calendar employed, with usual 11th month designated as *zhengyue* 正月 and 12th month as *layue* 臘月.)

Restored Tang

705	Zhongzong 中宗 (23 Fb, 705)	Shenlong 神龍	i.1	Ja 30
707		Jinglong 景龍	ix.5	Ot 5
710	Shaodi 少帝 (5 Jl, 710)	Tanglong 唐隆	vi.4	Jl 5
710	Ruizong 睿宗 (25 Jl, 710)	Jingyun 景雲	vii.20	Ag 19
712		Taiji 太極	i.15	Mr 1
712		Yanhe 延和	v.13	Je 21
712	Xuanzong 玄宗 (8 Sp, 712)	Xiantian 先天	viii.7	Sp 12
713		Kaiyuan 開元	xii.1	De 22
742		Tianbao 天寶	i.1	Fb 10

756	Suzong 肅宗 (12 Ag, 756)	Zhide 至德	viii.12	Ag 12
758		Qianyuan 乾元	ii.5	Mr 18
760		Shangyuan 上元	iv.19	Je 7
762		Baoying 寶應	iv.15	My 13
763	Daizong 代宗 (18 My, 762)	Guangde 廣德	vii.11	Ag 24
765		Yongtai 永泰	i.1	Ja 26
766		Dali 大曆	xi.12	De 18
780	Dezong 德宗 (12 Je, 779)	Jianzhong 建中	i.1	Fb 11
784		Xingyuan 興元	i.1	Ja 27
785		Zhenyuan 貞元	i.1	Fb 14
805	Shunzong 順宗 (28 Fb, 805)	Yongzhen 永貞	viii.5	Sp 1
806	Xianzong 憲宗 (5 Sp, 805)	Yuanhe 元和	i.2	Ja 25
821	Muzong 穆宗 (20 Fb, 820)	Changqing 長慶	i.4	Fb 9
825	Jingzong 敬宗 (29 Fb, 824)	Baoli 寶曆	i.7	Ja 29
827	Wenzong 文宗 (13 Ja, 827)	Taihe 太和	ii.13	Mr 14
837		Kaicheng 開成	i.1	Ja 22
841	Wuzong 武宗 (20 Fb, 840)	Huichang 會昌	i.9	Fb 4
847	Xuanzong 宣宗 (25 Ap, 846)	Dazhong 大中	i.17	Fb 6
860	Yizong 懿宗 (13 Sp, 859)	Xiantong 咸通	xi.12	De 17
874	Xizong 僖宗 (15 Ag, 873)	Qianfu 乾符	xi.5	De 17
880		Guangming 廣明	i.1	Fb 14
881		Zhonghe 中和	vii.11	Ag 9
885		Guangqi 光啟	iii.14	Ap 2
888		Wende 文德	ii.22	Ap 7
889	Zhaozong 昭宗 (22 Ap, 888)	Longji 隆紀	i.1	Fb 4
890		Dashun 大順	i.1	Ja 25
892		Jingfu 景福	i.21	Fb 22
894		Qianning 乾寧	i.1	Fb 10
898		Guanghua 光化	viii.27	Sp 16
901		Tianfu 天復	iv.25	My 16
904		Tianyou 天佑	iv.11	My 28
904	Aidi 哀帝 (26 Ot, 904)			
907		end of Tang	iv.22	Je 5

Index of Entries by Radical and Number of Added Strokes

Every character included in the dictionary is listed in the index. First-level sorting is by a character's "radical" in the standard sequence of 214 Kangxi "radicals" or significs, then by residual stroke-count. Within a grouping of the same radical and identical stroke-count, arrangement is according to pinyin.

678   Radical 9   人（亻, 八）

Index of entries by radical and number of added strokes

Index of entries by radical and number of added strokes

Index of entries by radical and number of added strokes

Index of entries by radical and number of added strokes

Index of entries by radical and number of added strokes

Index of entries by radical and number of added strokes

Index of entries by radical and number of added strokes

Index of entries by radical and number of added strokes

Index of entries by radical and number of added strokes

Index of entries by radical and number of added strokes

Index of entries by radical and number of added strokes

Index of entries by radical and number of added strokes

Index of entries by radical and number of added strokes

Index of entries by radical and number of added strokes

Index of entries by radical and number of added strokes

Index of entries by radical and number of added strokes

Index of entries by radical and number of added strokes

Index of entries by radical and number of added strokes

Index of entries by radical and number of added strokes

Index of entries by radical and number of added strokes

Index of entries by radical and number of added strokes

Index of entries by radical and number of added strokes

Index of entries by radical and number of added strokes

Index of entries by radical and number of added strokes

Index of entries by radical and number of added strokes

Index of entries by radical and number of added strokes

Index of entries by radical and number of added strokes

Index of entries by radical and number of added strokes

Index of entries by radical and number of added strokes

Index of entries by radical and number of added strokes

Index of entries by radical and number of added strokes

Index of entries by radical and number of added strokes

Index of entries by radical and number of added strokes

Index of entries by radical and number of added strokes

Index of entries by radical and number of added strokes

Index of entries by radical and number of added strokes

Index of entries by radical and number of added strokes

Index of entries by radical and number of added strokes

Index of entries by radical and number of added strokes

Index of entries by radical and number of added strokes

The 214 Kangxi Radicals

Stroke						
1	1 一	2 丨	3 丶	4 丿	5 乙 乚	6 亅
2	7 二	8 亠	9 人 亻	10 儿	11 入	12 八
	13 冂	14 冖	15 冫	16 几	17 凵	18 刀 刂
	19 力	20 勹	21 匕	22 匚	23 匸	24 十
	25 卜	26 卩	27 厂	28 厶	29 又	
3	30 口	31 囗	32 土	33 士	34 夂	35 夊
	36 夕	37 大	38 女	39 子	40 宀	41 寸
	42 小 ⺌	43 尢	44 尸	45 屮	46 山	47 川 巛
	48 工	49 己 已 巳	50 巾	51 干	52 幺	53 广
	54 廴	55 廾	56 弋	57 弓	58 彐 彑	59 彡
	60 彳					
4	61 心 忄	62 戈	63 戶 戸	64 手 扌	65 支	66 攴 攵
	67 文	68 斗	69 斤	70 方	71 无 旡	72 日
	73 曰	74 月	75 木	76 欠	77 止	78 歹 歺
	79 殳	80 毋 母	81 比	82 毛	83 氏	84 气
	85 水 氵	86 火 灬	87 爪 爫	88 父	89 爻	90 爿
	91 片	92 牙	93 牛 牜	94 犬 犭		
5	95 玄	96 玉 王	97 瓜	98 瓦	99 甘	100 生
	101 用	102 田	103 疋	104 疒	105 癶	106 白
	107 皮	108 皿	109 目	110 矛	111 矢	112 石
	113 示 礻	114 禸	115 禾	116 穴	117 立	
6	118 竹	119 米	120 糸	121 缶	122 网 罒	123 羊
	124 羽	125 老 耂	126 而	127 耒	128 耳	129 聿
	130 肉 月	131 臣	132 自	133 至	134 臼	135 舌
	136 舛	137 舟	138 艮	139 色	140 艸 艹	141 虍
	142 虫	143 血	144 行	145 衣 衤	146 襾 西	
7	147 見	148 角	149 言	150 谷	151 豆	152 豕
	153 豸	154 貝	155 赤	156 走	157 足 ⻊	
	158 身	159 車	160 辛	161 辰	162 辵 辶	163 邑 阝
	164 酉	165 釆	166 里			
8	167 金 釒	168 長 镸	169 門	170 阜 阝	171 隶	172 隹
	173 雨 ⻗	174 青 靑	175 非			
9	176 面	177 革	178 韋	179 韭	180 音	181 頁
	182 風	183 飛	184 食 飠	185 首	186 香	
10	187 馬	188 骨	189 高 髙	190 髟	191 鬥	192 鬯
	193 鬲	194 鬼				
11	195 魚	196 鳥	197 鹵	198 鹿	199 麥	200 麻
12	201 黃	202 黍	203 黑	204 黹		
13	205 黽	206 鼎	207 鼓	208 鼠		
14	209 鼻	210 齊				
15	211 齒					
16	212 龍					
17	213 龜	214 龠				

The radicals are classified by number of strokes (from 1 to 17 strokes)
The main alternative written forms are given for each radical

Christian Olaf Christiansen ·
Mélanie Lindbjerg Machado-Guichon ·
Sofía Mercader · Oliver Bugge Hunt ·
Priyanka Jha
Editors

Talking About Global Inequality

Personal Experiences and Historical Perspectives

Editors
Christian Olaf Christiansen
Department of Philosophy
and History of Ideas
Aarhus University
Aarhus, Denmark

Sofía Mercader
Department of Philosophy
and History of Ideas
Aarhus University
Aarhus, Denmark

Priyanka Jha
Department of Political Science
Banaras Hindu University
Varanasi, Uttar Pradesh, India

Mélanie Lindbjerg Machado-Guichon
Department of Philosophy
and History of Ideas
Aarhus University
Aarhus, Denmark

Oliver Bugge Hunt
Department of Food and Resource
Economics
University of Copenhagen
Frederiksberg, Denmark

ISBN 978-3-031-08041-8   ISBN 978-3-031-08042-5   (eBook)
https://doi.org/10.1007/978-3-031-08042-5

Cover illustration: Logo designer: Kasper Jacek

This Palgrave Macmillan imprint is published by the registered company Springer Nature
Switzerland AG
The registered company address is: Gewerbestrasse 11, 6330 Cham, Switzerland

PREFACE

The book you now hold in your hands is the result of a long and rewarding journey. In September 2019, we started working on our research project, '*An Intellectual History of Global Inequality, 1960–2015*', based at Aarhus University in Denmark. The project would investigate the historical relationships between peoples' location in the world and how they have thought about global inequality. Global inequality is of obvious, key concern today. It is therefore hugely important to learn what people in the past thought about it. Excited about studying the thinking on global inequality in the past, we were equally enthusiastic about doing a *different* kind of intellectual history. This time around it was going to be one which, for once, was truly more concerned with the history of thought in the 'Global South' than in the 'North'.

Yet, as we set out to uncover the myriad intellectual genealogies of global inequality, the unlikely entanglements, and surprising migrations of ideas across countries and continents, a new idea emerged. What if we did not just listen to the voices of the past, but also to those of the present? Wouldn't it be exciting to learn how intellectuals and scholars from around the whole globe think about global inequality, *today*? What if we posed these people the same five questions on global inequality, giving them time to carefully think through their answers, and write them down?

These were the questions and the original idea which shaped this book. The very first person to answer our five key questions on global inequality was Simon Reid-Henry, Professor of Historical and Political Geography at Queen Mary University of London, and author of *The Political Origins of Inequality*. If we had any doubts about our idea, our interview with Simon—an oral interview still available as a podcast on the research project's website (http://global-inequality.com)—erased all doubts about its viability. It was fascinating to hear Simon's story and his reflections on Britain as a class society, on doing research in Cuba, and much more. It left us eager to learn more.

And so our journey continued. A journey and a team effort, with shifting commitments and involvements along the way, as it needs to be. If this book is the product of an idea, then, it is also the product of many people's thinking, work, openness, and kindness. During this journey, we have accumulated quite a few debts. We would like to thank all our contributors for their wonderful contributions and their patience, our editors at Palgrave for helpful comments and advice, and the anonymous reviewers for their critical support. We would also like to thank speakers of our monthly research seminars, Frederik Møller Rosendal for his valuable help and work as student assistant, and our intellectual history colleagues at Aarhus University. We want to thank Independent Research Fund Denmark for supporting our research.[1] Last, but not least, allow us to thank all of those people who voiced their concerns about inequalities—past *and* present.

Aarhus, Denmark	Christian Olaf Christiansen
Aarhus, Denmark	Mélanie Lindbjerg Machado-Guichon
Aarhus, Denmark	Sofía Mercader
Frederiksberg, Denmark	Oliver Bugge Hunt
Varanasi, India	Priyanka Jha

[1] Independent Research Fund Denmark, Sapere Aude Research Leader Grant, case number 8047-00068B.